Fodor's

AUSTRALIA

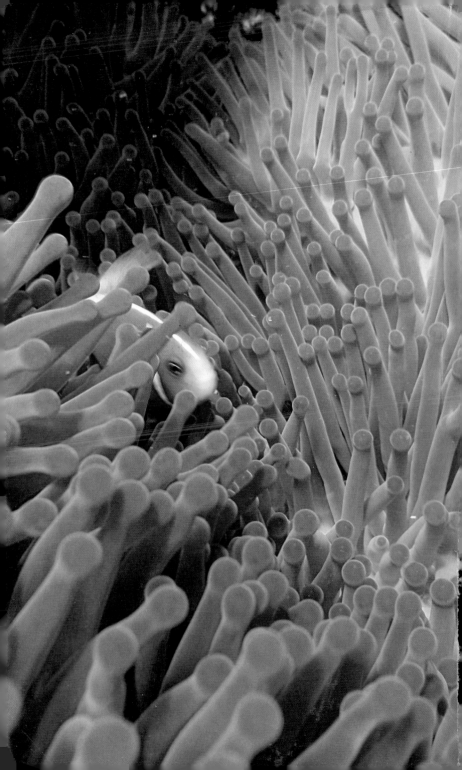

WELCOME TO AUSTRALIA

A vast island continent, Australia teems with natural and cultural treasures. Relax on gorgeous beaches along the sprawling coastline, or plunge below the water in Queensland to explore the Great Barrier Reef. Nature enthusiasts revel in exciting adventures in the interior, from trekking around majestic Uluru to spotting wildlife in tropical rain forests. But there's more to life down under than outdoor activities. Cosmopolitan cities like Sydney and Melbourne entice with thriving dining and arts scenes, while world-class vineyards abound.

TOP REASONS TO GO

★ **Cool Cities:** Vibrant Sydney, artsy Melbourne, laidback Brisbane, far-flung Perth.

★ **Beaches:** From Bondi to the Gold Coast, stylish strands cater to all tastes.

★ **Food and Wine:** Mod Oz cuisine, top-notch whites and reds, and, of course, the barbie.

★ **Untamed Nature:** Adventures await in the Great Barrier Reef, the Outback, and Tasmania.

★ **Aboriginal Culture:** A rich heritage of music, art, and stories continues to thrive.

★ **Unique Wildlife:** From kangaroos to koalas, the wildlife here is sure to delight.

Fodor's AUSTRALIA

Publisher: Amanda D'Acierno, *Senior Vice President*

Editorial: Arabella Bowen, *Editor in Chief*; Linda Cabasin, *Editorial Director*

Design: Fabrizio La Rocca, *Vice President, Creative Director*; Tina Malaney, *Associate Art Director*; Chie Ushio, *Senior Designer*; Ann McBride, *Production Designer*

Photography: Melanie Marin, *Associate Director of Photography*; Jessica Parkhill and Jennifer Romains, *Researchers*

Maps: Rebecca Baer, *Senior Map Editor*; David Lindroth, Mark Stroud (Moon Street Cartography) *Cartographers*

Production: Linda Schmidt, *Managing Editor*; Evangelos Vasilakis, *Associate Managing Editor*; Angela L. McLean, *Senior Production Manager*

Sales: Jacqueline Lebow, *Sales Director*

Marketing & Publicity: Heather Dalton, *Marketing Director*; Katherine Punia, *Senior Publicist*

Business & Operations: Susan Livingston, *Vice President, Strategic Business Planning*; Sue Daulton, *Vice President, Operations*

Fodors.com: Megan Bell, *Executive Director, Revenue & Business Development*; Yasmin Marinaro, *Senior Director, Marketing & Partnerships*

Copyright © 2014 by Fodor's Travel, a division of Random House LLC

Writers: Lee Atkinson, Fleur Bainger, Tim Baker, Chris Canty, Tess Curran, Caroline Gladstone, Tim Richards, Russell Ward, Merran White

Editor: Luke Epplin

Editorial Contributors: Margaret Kelly, Andrew Collins, Alexis Kelly

Production Editor: Elyse Rozelle

22nd Edition

ISBN 978-0-8041-4218-2

ISSN 1095-2675

All details in this book are based on information supplied to us at press time. Always confirm information when it matters, especially if you're making a detour to visit a specific place. Fodor's expressly disclaims any liability, loss, or risk, personal or otherwise, that is incurred as a consequence of the use of any of the contents of this book.

SPECIAL SALES

This book is available at special discounts for bulk purchases for sales promotions or premiums. For more information, e-mail specialmarkets@randomhouse.com

PRINTED IN COLOMBIA

10 9 8 7 6 5 4 3 2 1

CONTENTS

1 EXPERIENCE AUSTRALIA. 9
What's Where 10
Australia Planner 12
Australia World Heritage Sites 14
If You Like 18
Quintessential Australia 20
Australia Today 22
Beachgoing in Australia 23
Great Itineraries. 24
When to Go 42

2 SYDNEY 43
Welcome to Sydney 44
Top Sydney Sights. 46
Exploring 54
Beaches. 93
Sports and the Outdoors 98
Where to Eat. 103
Best Bets for Sydney Dining 104
Where to Stay 124
Nightlife and the Arts 128
Shopping 135

3 NEW SOUTH WALES 141
Welcome to New South Wales. . . .142
The Blue Mountains 146
The Hunter Valley Wine Region . . .166
The North Coast. 172
Canberra and the A.C.T. 192

4 MELBOURNE. 211
Welcome to Melbourne 212
Exploring 218
Beaches. 231
Sports and the Outdoors 232
Where to Eat. 235
Best Bets for Melbourne Dining . . .236
Where to Stay 245
Nightlife and the Arts 248
Shopping 253

5 VICTORIA 257
Welcome to Victoria 258
Side Trips from Melbourne 262
Great Ocean Road 293
The Gold Country 305

Fodor's Features

Aboriginal Art: Past And Present. 32
Modern Australia Cuisine 110
Hiking The Blue Mountains 151
Wines Of Australia 278
Following The Convict Trail 337
Diving The Reef 512

The Grampians 312
Murray River Region 317

6 TASMANIA 327
Welcome to Tasmania 328
Hobart. 333
Side Trips from Hobart. 349
Freycinet National Park and
East-Coast Resorts 354
The Northwest. 361

7 BRISBANE AND ITS BEACHES 367
Welcome to Brisbane and
Its Beaches. 368
Sunshine Coast's Top Beaches 370
Coastal and Wilderness Walks. . . .372
Brisbane 377
Winery Tours from Brisbane:
Southern Downs 394
The Gold Coast 397
The Sunshine Coast 411
Sunshine Coast Hinterland 420
Mackay–Capricorn Islands. 428
Fraser Island. 435

8 THE GREAT BARRIER REEF . . .441
  Welcome to Great Barrier Reef . . .442
  Sailing the Whitsunday Islands . . .444
  Outdoor Adventures in Daintree. . .446
  Cairns 451
  North of Cairns 467
  The Whitsunday Islands
  and Airlie Beach 489
  North Coast Islands 511
  Townsville and Magnetic Island . . .526

9 ADELAIDE AND
  SOUTH AUSTRALIA 537
  Welcome to Adelaide and
  South Australia 538
  Adelaide 543
  The Barossa Wine Region. 567
  The Clare Valley. 577
  Fleurieu Peninsula 580
  Kangaroo Island. 587
  The Outback 595

10 THE OUTBACK. 601
  Welcome to The Outback 602
  Aboriginal Culture. 604
  Red Centre 610
  The Top End 630
  The Kimberley 648

11 PERTH AND WESTERN
  AUSTRALIA. 663
  Welcome to Perth and
  Western Australia. 664
  Perth. 669
  Fremantle. 694
  Rottnest Island 704
  The South West Wine Region 709

  TRAVEL SMART AUSTRALIA. . .727
  INDEX. 746
  ABOUT OUR WRITERS. 760

MAPS

Sydney Harbour 58
The Rocks and
Sydney Harbour Bridge 62
Domain and Macquarie Street 70
The Opera House and
Royal Botanic Gardens. 74
Darling Harbour. 78
Sydney City Center 82
Inner City and the Eastern Suburbs. . 86
Greater Sydney 89
Sydney Beaches. 95

Where to Eat and Stay
in Sydney 106–107
Where to Eat and Stay in Bondi
Beach & the Eastern Suburbs 125
The Blue Mountains 147
Hunter Valley Wine Region 165
The North Coast. 173
Canberra 196
Wine Touring Around Canberra . . . 200
Where to Eat and Stay
in Canberra. 206
Melbourne City Center. 220
Melbourne Suburbs. 228
Where to Eat and Stay
in Melbourne City Center 238
Where to Stay and Eat
in the Melbourne Suburbs 243
Side Trips from Melbourne 264
Mornington Peninsula Wineries . . . 276
Great Ocean Road and
the Gold Country 298
Grampians National Park 313
Murray River Region 318
Downtown Hobart 334
Side Trips from Hobart. 350
The Northwest. 362
Brisbane 378
Where to Eat and Stay in Brisbane. . 388
The Gold Coast 399
The Sunshine Coast and
Sunshine Coast Hinterland. 421
Mackay-Capricorn Islands. 429
Fraser Island 437
Cairns 455
Where to Eat and Stay in Cairns. . . 464
North of Cairns 471
The Whitsunday Islands
and Airlie Beach 491
North Coast Islands, Townsville,
and Magnetic Island 524
Adelaide 546
Where to Eat and Stay in Adelaide. . 554
The Barossa Wine Region. 570
Fleurieu Peninsula and
Kangaroo island. 581
The Red Centre 611
Alice Springs. 616
The Top End and the Kimberley . . . 632
Darwin 634
Perth. 670
Where to Eat and Stay in Perth . . . 684
The South West Wine Region 710

ABOUT
THIS GUIDE

Fodor's Recommendations
Everything in this guide is worth doing—
we don't cover what isn't—but exceptional sights, hotels, and restaurants are
recognized with additional accolades.
Fodor's Choice ★ indicates our top recommendations; and **Best Bets** call attention to
notable hotels and restaurants in various
categories. Care to nominate a new place?
Visit Fodors.com/contact-us.

Trip Costs
We list prices wherever possible to help
you budget well. Hotel and restaurant
price categories from **$** to **$$$$** are noted
alongside each recommendation. For
hotels, we include the lowest cost of a
standard double room in high season.
For restaurants, we cite the average price
of a main course at dinner or, if dinner
isn't served, at lunch. For attractions,
we always list adult admission fees; dis-
counts are usually available for children,
students, and senior citizens.

Hotels
Our local writers vet every hotel to recom-
mend the best overnights in each price cat-
egory, from budget to expensive. Unless
otherwise specified, you can expect pri-
vate bath, phone, and TV in your room.
For expanded hotel reviews, facilities, and
deals visit Fodors.com.

Restaurants
Unless we state otherwise, restaurants are
open for lunch and dinner daily. We men-
tion dress code only when there's a specific
requirement and reservations only when
they're essential or not accepted. To make
restaurant reservations, visit Fodors.com.

Credit Cards
The hotels and restaurants in this guide
typically accept credit cards. If not, we'll
say so.

Top Picks
★ Fodor's Choice

Listings
- ✉ Address
- ✉ Branch address
- ☎ Telephone
- 🖷 Fax
- ⊕ Website
- ✉ E-mail
- ✉ Admission fee
- ⊙ Open/closed times
- Ⓜ Subway
- ✛ Directions or Map coordinates

Hotels & Restaurants
- 🏨 Hotel
- ↳ Number of rooms
- 🍽 Meal plans
- ✗ Restaurant
- ✍ Reservations
- 👔 Dress code
- ▭ No credit cards
- ⑀ Price

Other
- ⇨ See also
- ☞ Take note
- ⛳ Golf facilities

EXPERIENCE
AUSTRALIA

WHAT'S WHERE

Numbers refer to chapters.

2 Sydney. One of the most naturally beautiful cities in the world, Sydney blends beachside cool with corporate capitalism and Victorian-era colonial architecture. Arts, tourism, and business thrive around Sydney Harbour.

3 New South Wales. Southeastern Australia displays most of the continent's rural and coastal variations: historic towns, mountains, dramatic beaches, and world-class vineyards. The nation's spacious capital showcases myriad Australian national monuments.

4 Melbourne. Melbourne is Australia's most European city and a cultural melting pot and you can see that in its fantastic food scene.

5 Victoria. Rugged coastline, fairy penguins, wineries, historic towns, and national parks are reason enough to explore the Victorian countryside.

6 Tasmania. From Freycinet Peninsula to wild South West National Park, Tasmania's natural beauty testifies to Australia's topographic diversity. Don't miss the relics of the island's volatile days as a penal colony.

7 Brisbane and Its Beaches. Name your pleasure and you'll find it in Queensland: mini-Miamis, nearly deserted beaches, and lush rain forests, great restaurants, and easy access to family-friendly parks.

8 The Great Barrier Reef. Queensland's crown jewel is the 2,600-km-long (1,616-mile-long) Great Barrier Reef. More than 3,000 individual reefs and 900 islands make up this vast aquatic universe.

9 Adelaide and South Australia. Well-planned and picturesque Adelaide has many charms, including its famous biennial festival of the arts. Be sure to take a tour of the renowned wine country, and then unwind on a Murray River cruise.

10 The Outback. This region stuns with its diversity. In the country's vast, central desert region are Uluru and Kata Tjuta, monoliths of deep significance to the local Aboriginal people. Darwin is the gateway to World Heritage wetlands, monster cattle ranches, and rock art.

11 Perth and Western Australia. This vast region is a remote, awe-inspiring place and the producer of much of Australia's mineral wealth. It includes the country's sunniest capital, Perth, and top-notch wine valleys.

AUSTRALIA PLANNER

Visitor Information

Tourism Australia's website is one of the best places to start planning your trip. As well as general information, they have package deals and searchable listings for U.S. travel agents who specialize in Australia.

Tourism Australia ⊕ www.australia.com.

Each Australian state has its own tourism website where you can find state-specific maps, thematically organized listings, travel information, and links to accommodation and transport. Some have free state travel guides that they'll send to you. In general, they handle queries online.

Australian Capital Tourism ⊕ www.visitcanberra.com.au.

South Australian Tourism Commission ⊕ www.southaustralia.com.

Tourism New South Wales ⊕ www.visitnsw.com.

Tourism Northern Territory ⊕ www.travelnt.com.

Tourism Queensland ⊕ www.queenslandholidays.com.au.

Tourism Tasmania ⊕ www.discovertasmania.com.

Tourism Western Australia ⊕ www.westernaustralia.com.

Tourism Melbourne and Victoria ⊕ www.visitvictoria.com.

Safety

Given Australia's relaxed lifestyle, it's easy to be seduced into believing that crime is nonexistent. While Australia has its share of poverty, drugs, and crime, rates aren't high by world standards. Just be wary and you should have no problems. Wearing jewelry in public isn't a risk, and using ATMs in daylight hours is usually fine. Theft—especially pickpocketing—is a problem only in major tourist areas such as Sydney's Bondi or Queensland's Gold Coast. Try to avoid leaving valuables on the beach when you go for a swim or in your car when you park.

Traveling in Australia is generally safe for women, provided you take a few common-sense precautions. Avoid isolated areas such as empty beaches and quiet streets at night. Single women usually receive attention entering pubs or clubs alone, but a few firm, polite words are normally enough to put a stop to it, if it's unwanted.

Emergencies

Australian emergency services are extremely efficient. Local people usually help each other unquestioningly, too. For theft, wallet loss, small road accidents, and minor emergencies, contact the nearest police station. In a medical or dental emergency, ask your hotel staff for information on and directions to the nearest hospital or clinic; taxi drivers should also know how to find one.

Pack a basic first-aid kit, especially if you're venturing into more remote areas. If you'll be carrying any medication, bring your doctor's contact information and prescription authorizations. Most Australian pharmacies only fill prescriptions from Australian doctors, so bring enough medication for your trip.

Pharmacies usually open between 9 and 5, but most towns have a 24-hour pharmacy system so that one pharmacy is always open. In an emergency, the local police station can tell you which pharmacy is open, as can hospitals.

Eating Out

These days fusion food is what's putting Australia on the foodie map—indeed, many claim that the very term was invented Down Under. The huge Asian communities in cities like Sydney and Melbourne have brought their traditional condiments and cooking styles to bear on local staples: the resulting combinations are what many of the country's most famous eateries specialize in.

Bush tucker, or indigenous Australian food, was once something you came across only on bushwalking expeditions in the Outback. Suddenly it's become fashionable, and uniquely Australian ingredients like lemon myrtle, wattle seed, and rosella (not to mention kangaroo meat) are appearing on fancy restaurant menus all over the country. Food is an international language, but your English may fail you in Australian restaurants. "Entrée" means appetizer, and "main courses" are what American entrées go by. The term "silver service" indicates upscale dining. French fries are called "hot chips," chickens are "chooks," sausages are known as "snags," and if you want ketchup, ask for "tomato sauce."

Wines, Beer, and Spirits

Beer and wine are an important part of Australian life. Australia is the world's 10th-largest wine producer, and Australian wine is gaining considerable respect worldwide. Australia's most famous wine-producing areas are the Hunter Valley in New South Wales, the Barossa Valley in South Australia, and Western Australia's Margaret River region. Although there are no native grape varietals in Australia, Shiraz (also known as Syrah) is a local specialty. Cabernet Sauvignon and Pinot Noir are common reds; popular whites include Chardonnay, Sauvignon Blanc, and Pinot Grigio. Australia produces a wide range of beers. As well as big national brands like Fosters, each state has its own brew: Victoria Bitter in Victoria and XXXX (called four-ex) in Queensland, for example.

If you're invited to an Australian's home, it's common—indeed, expected—practice to take a bottle of wine at dinnertime or a case of beer for a barbecue. When drinking at pubs, Australians always drink in rounds, British-style.

Accommodations

Australia's state capitals run the gamut of lodging options. But that's doesn't mean *all* the interesting accommodation is in town. Family-run bed-and-breakfasts, farm-stays, country hotels, and even small-town pubs are some of the alternatives Australia has to offer. Sleeping Down Under is generally cheaper than in North America, and money-saving accommodation is particularly varied—be it a serviced apartment, a well-appointed caravan, or a bed at a backpackers' dorm.

For more detailed information on accommodations, see the Travel Smart chapter at the end of the Guide.

Tipping

Australians don't expect tips, and hotels and restaurants rarely add service charges. That said, a small tip for good service is common practice and appreciated. Room service and housemaids are only tipped for special services. Taxi drivers don't expect a tip, but leaving small change will win you a smile. Guides, tour-bus drivers, and chauffeurs don't expect tips either, though they're grateful if someone in the group takes up a collection for them. No tipping is necessary—indeed, it would cause confusion—in hair salons or for theater ushers.

AUSTRALIA
WORLD HERITAGE SITES

Australia has more cultural and natural treasures than is fair to many other countries. It also, fortunately, has the wealth and resolve to protect them as best it can. Eighteen sites across the country, including two offshore territories in sub-Antarctic waters, have been World Heritage listed.

Tasmanian Wilderness

(A) Harsh glacial action over millions of years has put the wild in the Tasmanian Wilderness. Remote and subject to extreme weather, this vast World Heritage area—it covers a fifth of Australia's island state—protects one of the few expanses of temperate rain forest on Earth. Here, too, are stunning landforms fashioned by complex geology, diverse habitats for flora and fauna found nowhere else, and evidence of tens of thousands of years of Aboriginal occupation. Angling, whitewater rafting, and hiking national park walking trails, most of which are suited

only to experienced hikers, are some favorite activities in the Tasmanian Wilderness World Heritage Area.

Fraser Island

(B) Remnant rain forest, shifting sand dunes, and half of the world's perched lakes (lakes that are isolated above the groundwater table by rock or organic material) contributed to Fraser Island's World Heritage listing in 1992. The largest sand island on Earth, Fraser lies just off Queensland's coast, about 200 km (124 miles) north of Brisbane. This exquisite island is both ecologically precious and extremely popular for soft-adventure holidays—a sometimes problematic combination. Fraser's dingo population is one of Australia's purest, but be aware that visitors have had fatal interactions with these wild dogs. Humpback whales frequent Fraser's west-coast waters June to November, and the spring tailor fish run lures anglers to the island's wilder ocean

shore. Four-wheel-drives barrel along the 122-km (76-mile) ocean beach, which is Fraser Island's unofficial main highway.

Sydney Opera House

(C) One of Australia's recent World Heritage properties is the country's most recognizable building. A realization of visionary design and 20th-century technological innovation, the Sydney Opera House was listed in 2007 as a masterpiece of human creative genius. It is also a structure of extraordinary beauty. Danish architect Jorn Utzon's interlocking vaulted "shells" appear to hover like wind-filled sails on their Sydney Harbour promontory. Floodlighting at night increases the sense of movement.

Awarded the project in 1957 by an international jury, Jorn Utzon never saw his creation finished. Utzon resigned and left Australia in 1966, amid funding controversies and political change, and his architectural sculpture was completed by others. Familiar to people around the world, the Sydney Opera House is a world-class performing arts venue.

Greater Blue Mountains Area

(D) Sunlight refracting off a mist of eucalyptus oil gives the Blue Mountains, west of Sydney, their distinctive hue. The variety of eucalypts (commonly called gum trees) across this mountain range's varied habitats was integral to its World Heritage listing. The 1.03 million hectares of sandstone country encompasses the Blue Mountains National Park. Ninety-one varieties of eucalypts grow here. So, too, do significant numbers of rare species and "living fossils" such as the Wollemi pine, which was discovered in 1994.

Great Barrier Reef

(E) While its name suggests otherwise, Australia's most famous World Heritage site is not a single reef. The 2,600-km-long (1,616-mile-long) Great Barrier Reef is actually the world's largest collection of

reefs. This fragile natural wonder contains 400 types of coral and 1,500 fish species of every size and almost every conceivable color combination. The giant clam, with its voluptuous purple, green, or blue mantle (algae dictate the color) is one of the 4,000 mollusks the reef supports.

Uluru-Kata Tjuta National Park

(F) What you see projecting from the sandy plains of Australia's Red Centre is just the tip, but this majestic monolith still packs a physical and spiritual punch well above its weight. Uluru (also called Ayers Rock) and Kata Tjuta, the seemingly sculpted rock domes clustered 55 km (34 miles) to the west, are deeply significant to the park's traditional owners, the Anangu Aboriginal people.

The Anangu ask visitors not to climb Uluru. Some controversy continues, however, about whether this is because the climb is the traditional route of the ancestral Mala men or because the

Anangu think the ascent is just too dangerous. At least 35 people have died on the steep, exposed climb. Independent walks, ranger-guided walks, and Anangu-guided walks (fees apply) offer fascinating cultural perspectives of Uluru and Kata Tjuta from the ground.

Wet Tropics of Queensland

(G) Verdant and ancient, the Wet Tropics of Queensland are the hothouse of Australian flora and fauna. Three thousand plant species, hundreds of mammal types, and over half the country's recorded birds inhabit the tangled rain forests north, south, and west of Cairns, on Australia's far northeastern coast. The remarkable tree kangaroo and the green possum are found only in this World Heritage area. Reptile residents of the Wet Tropics vary in size from inches-long geckos to 7-meter-long (23-foot-long) amethystine pythons. A shorter but considerably

meaner local is the estuarine crocodile, or salty as it is commonly called.

Purnululu National Park

(H) Geological history is written large across this World Heritage site in Australia's northwest Kimberley region. Twenty million years of erosion and weathering have deeply dissected the Bungle Bungle Range into banded, beehive-shape sandstone towers. Other examples of cone karst in sandstone, as this remarkable phenomenon is called, are found around the world. None of these sites rival Purnululu for the diversity, size, and grandeur of formations.

Purnululu means sandstone in the Kija Aboriginal language, and spectacularly sculpted sandstone is the highlight of the park. Hard-edged gorges softened by fan palms separate the orange-and-black striped towers, however. Wild budgerigars are among the 100-plus bird species in the park. Wallabies, too, are sometimes spotted among the rocks.

Kakadu National Park

(I) X-ray paintings of barramundi, long-necked turtles, and other animals festoon the main gallery at Ubirr Rock in Kakadu National Park. This menu-in-ocher is one of more than 5,000 art sites in the park that collectively date back 20,000 years. Archaeologists have put human habitation at twice that long. Ongoing and uninterrupted connection with Top End Aboriginal peoples was a key factor in Kakadu's World Heritage listing. So were the park's diverse habitats. Estuarine crocodiles prowl the Alligator River. Red-billed jabiru, Australia's only stork, stroll the flood plains. Waterfalls cannon off the Arnhem Land escarpment. Nowhere else in Australia are cultural and ecological significance so richly intertwined.

IF YOU LIKE

Beautiful Beaches

Whether you want to bake in the sun, see and be seen, or try body- or board-surfing in the white-capped waves, Australia has an abundance of beautiful beaches. Miles and miles of pristine sand line the coastline, so you can choose to join the crowd or sunbathe in blissful solitude.

■ **Bondi Beach.** On the edge of the Tasman Sea, Bondi Beach is the most famous perhaps in all of Australia. You can take a surfing lesson here or just immerse yourself in the delights of suburban sand and water. Don't miss the Coast Walk from Bondi to Bronte Beach—it's a breathtaking 2½-km (1½-mile) path that will take you along dramatic coastal cliffs to a string of eastern beaches. The walking track continues beyond Bronte Beach to Waverley Cemetery, where many famous Australians are buried in cliff-top splendor.

■ **Queensland's Gold Coast and Islands.** Warm, moderate surf washes the 70-km (43-mile) stretch of Gold Coast beaches, which are perfect for board riding, swimming, or just collecting shells at sunset. Beach bums, however, know to head north to the Great Barrier Reef islands for less crowded, tropical stretches of sand.

■ **West Coast.** Fringing the Indian Ocean between Perth and South Fremantle are 19 wide beaches with good breaks, but head down to the south coast for a dip in the crystal clear waters of the deserted, sandy white beaches around Margaret River.

■ **Whitehaven.** The Whitsunday Islands are home to arguably Australia's most beautiful beach. The near-deserted arc of Whitehaven Beach has some of the whitest and most powdery sand on Earth.

Wine

Australian wines are among the best in the world, a judgment that international wine shows consistently reinforce. Australians are very proud of their wine. You'll be hard-pressed to find anything but Australian wines on the menus at most places, so take this opportunity to expand your palate beyond the export brands you may have tried at home, like Rosemount, Jacob's Creek, and Penfolds.

■ **Hunter Valley.** The largest grape-growing area in New South Wales, Hunter Valley has more than 120 wineries and a reputation for producing excellent wines. Expect some amazing Semillons and Cabernets.

■ **Margaret River.** In Western Australia the Margaret River region produces just 1% of the country's total wine output. Yet 25% of Australia's premium and ultra-premium wines come from this small area. Margaret River's Bordeaux-like climate helps producers grow excellent Cabernet-Merlot blends, since these grapes originally came from that region.

■ **South Australia.** The Barossa Valley, about an hour's drive northeast of Adelaide, produces some of Australia's most famous Syrah (or Shiraz, as they call it Down Under). You might recognize the Penfolds label, as makers of the renowned Grange Shiraz blend. In the nearby Clare Valley, German immigrants planted Riesling many decades ago and the grape has met with great success there.

■ **Yarra Valley.** More than 70 wineries fill the floor of the Yarra Valley, where Pinot Noir thrives.

Incredible Wildlife

Australia's diverse habitats are home to countless strange and amazing creatures.

■ **Birds.** Australia has many wild and wonderful creatures of the non-marsupial variety. The waterholes at Kakadu National Park in the Northern Territory attract more than 280 species of birds, including the stately jabiru, Australia's only stork, and the fluorescent rainbow bee-eater, as well as crocodiles, the ubiquitous creatures of Australia's Top End. The much friendlier and cuter fairy penguins draw nighttime crowds at **Philip Island** in Victoria.

■ **Camels.** Don't be surprised if you catch the eye of a camel wandering the desert of the Red Centre. These are descendants of dromedaries shipped in during the 19th century for use on exploratory expeditions and Outback construction projects and for desert transport.

■ **Creatures of the Deep.** The Great Barrier Reef gets plenty of attention for underwater wildlife, but Western Australia has two phenomenal spots of its own. The dolphins at Shark Bay in Monkey Mia, Western Australia, can be hand-fed. Ningaloo Reef, off the Exmouth Peninsula, is home to humpback whales and whale sharks.

■ **Koalas and Kangaroos.** No trip to Australia would be complete without an encounter with Australia's iconic animals: kangaroos and koalas. The Lone Pine Koala Sanctuary in Brisbane is one of many wildlife parks around Australia that let you take a picture with a cuddly koala or hand-feed a mob of kangaroos.

Water Sports

With 36,735 km (22,776 miles) of coast bordering two oceans and four seas, Australians spend a good deal of their time in and on the water. Opportunities abound for scuba diving, snorkeling, surfing, waterskiing, windsurfing, sailing, and just mucking about in the waves. Prime diving seasons are September–December and mid-March–May.

■ **Diving.** Avid divers will want to visit the resort islands of the Great Barrier Reef, which provide upscale accommodation and access to some of the country's top diving spots. Cod Hole, off the Lizard Island reef, in far north Queensland, ranks highly among them. You can do a one-day introductory or resort dive, and four-day open-water dive certification courses, or if fins and oxygen tanks aren't your speed, opt for snorkeling off the island beaches. Diving expeditions are a specialty of the Cairns area, with carriers like Quicksilver and Tusa Dive running day trips to the reef for diving and snorkeling.

■ **Sailing.** Sailors love the Whitsunday Islands off the mid-north Queensland coast. Almost all the 74 islands in this group are national parks, and only 7 have resorts on them, making this an ideal spot to drop anchor and moor for a few days, or to try a vacation on a live-aboard boat or yacht. You can also experience the swashbuckling romance of olden-day sailing on multiday tall-ship cruises.

QUINTESSENTIAL AUSTRALIA

Go Bush

When Aussies refer to the bush, they can mean either a scrubby patch of ground a few kilometers outside the city or the vast, sprawling desert Outback. In most cases it's a way to describe getting out of the daily routine of the city and getting in touch with the natural landscape of this incredibly diverse country.

With 80% of its population living on eastern shores, and with all of its major cities (except Canberra) on or near the coast, most of Australia's wild, wonderful interior is virtually empty. Whether you find yourself watching the sun rise (or set) over Uluru, taking a camel trek through the Kimberley, or sleeping under the stars in a swag (traditional Australian camping kit), there are countless ways to go bush and see Australia's most natural, rural, and stunning sights.

Aussie! Aussie! Aussie! Oi! Oi! Oi!

From world-class sporting events like the Australian Open tennis to national obsessions like the Australian Football League Grand Final, Aussies love their sports. The calendar is chock-full of sporting events that give Aussies good reason to drink a cold beer and gather with mates to barrack for (cheer on) their favorite team.

Aussie Rules Football (or footy) is a popular, fast-paced, and rough-and-tumble sport that's played without padding and uses what looks like an American football through four 25-minute quarters. Rugby League Football is a 13-a-side game that is played internationally. Cricket test matches are the sport of summer, though much less happens during these games than in footy matches. Spectators get to soak up the sun and drink a lot of beer while watching the Australians duel international teams in matches that can go for one to five days.

Aussies refer to authentic or genuine things as *fair dinkum*. The folks Down Under are a fun-loving bunch, so don't be shy. Here are a few ways to experience Australia like the locals do.

Swimming Between the Flags

Australians love their beaches as much as they love their barbies, so put on your bathers or your cossie (slang for bathing costume) and slather on good sunblock—the damage to the ozone layer above Australia is very severe.

Many Australian beaches are patrolled by volunteer members of the Surf Lifesaving Association (SLSA), who post red and yellow flags to demarcate the safest areas to swim on any beach. The SLSA was formed in 1907, and its tan, buff lifesavers make the *Baywatch* team look like amateurs—it's rumored that no one has ever drowned while swimming in the areas that they patrol. Of course, these hunky heroes can't be everywhere all the time, so use caution when swimming on those picturesque deserted beaches you're bound to come across in your travels. The undertow or rip can be strong and dangerous.

The Barbie

Paul Hogan, aka Crocodile Dundee, showed the world laid-back Australian hospitality by inviting visitors to say "G'day," then throw another shrimp on the barbie, or barbecue. But it's unlikely you'll find shrimp on a barbie in Australia. What you will find is Aussies cooking up steak, sausages (often called snags), beef, chicken, and lamb on gas grills all over the country.

Barbies are so ubiquitous in Australia that almost every public park or beach will have a barbecue area set up for people to come and grill at will. The tools required for "having a barbie" the traditional Aussie way are newspaper and butter. The newspaper helps wipe the barbie clean from the previous grilling, and butter greases it back up again before putting the meat on. Sometimes an onion instead of a newspaper is used to clean off the grill—a slightly more hygienic system.

AUSTRALIA TODAY

Government

Australia is a constitutional monarchy, and the Queen of England is still officially Australia's Queen as well. Her only role under the constitution, however, is to appoint her representative in Australia, the Governor General, which she does on advice from Australia's Prime Minister. In 1975 the then Governor General caused a political crisis when he sacked the Prime Minister and his government and installed the Opposition minority as caretaker until new elections could be held. Today the Governor General still retains that power, but his or her duties are primarily ceremonial. Australia's government is elected for three-year terms, with no limit on how many terms a Prime Minister can serve. Voting is compulsory for all citizens 18 years and older, and failure to vote can result in a fine.

Economy

Australia is a major exporter of wheat and wool, iron-ore and gold, liquefied natural gas and coal, particularly to countries such as China and India. The major industries are mining, industrial and transport equipment, food processing, chemicals, and steel manufacturing. The services sector dominates the domestic economy.

Abundant natural assets and massive government spending initially softened the short-term impact of the global financial crisis that started in 2008. As of this writing, demand for Australia's commodities from China and India has dipped, and mining also has slowed. These developments have led to a slowdown in the country's overall economic growth.

Tourism

On- and offshore wonders, unique wildlife, beach culture, indigenous history, and multicultural cuisines help maintain Australia's multibillion-dollar tourism industry. The major challenges are keeping Australia on travelers' radars as other countries gain popularity, and protecting the most fragile attractions. Climate change has already affected the Great Barrier Reef, a World Heritage site on most visitors' must-see lists, and programs are in place to try to minimize the impact of rising sea temperatures. Contentious logging of old-growth forests for pulp, particularly in Tasmania, continues, and the opening of new mines rarely fits comfortably with conservation and cultural issues.

Religion

Australia's first settlers were predominantly English, Irish, and Scottish Christians. Two centuries later, almost two-thirds of Australians call themselves Christians (64%), with Buddhism a distant second (2.5%), and Islam third (2.2%); however, more than one-fifth of the population (22.9%) ticked "no religion" on the 2011 census. Active church worship has declined over recent decades, and many religious orders struggle to attract members.

Literature

Life Down Under has bred contemporary writers who speak with distinctly Australian voices. Tim Winton's book *Breath* brilliantly evokes the power of surfing and the angst of adolescence. Look out for Kate Grenville, Richard Flanagan, Peter Carey, Bryce Courtenay, and Geraldine Brooks, among others. Morris Gleitzman and Paul Jennings write (mostly) laugh-out-loud books for children and the young at heart.

BEACHGOING IN AUSTRALIA

With more than 85% of Australians living less than one hour from the coastline, the beach has always held a special place in Australia's national identity. The country boasts some of the finest beaches on the planet, and they're places where Australians and tourists alike come to relax, sunbath, and swim.

The coastline stretches for almost 37,000 km (22,940 miles) and encompasses more than 11,000 beaches. While many of these beaches are deserted, others closer to the major cities and towns are often treated as extensions of the typical Australian family's house or backyard.

Aussie Beach Culture

Going to the beach is a way of life for most Australians, as routine as grilling on the barbie or enjoying a cold beer with mates. It's an integral part of the Aussie lifestyle and a place where people spend their weekends and annual holiday celebrations such as Christmas, New Year's Eve, and Australia Day.

Australians look after their beaches, which are generally clean and pollution-free, and almost always of a high quality. Some people go to the beach for the sun and the surf; others choose to fish, sail, snorkel, or scuba dive. Whatever the reason, the beach unites Australians from all walks of life on a regular basis.

The Top Beaches

With so many top-notch beaches across the country, Australians are spoiled for choice. In Sydney, Bondi Beach is arguably Australia's most iconic strand, only minutes' driving distance from the city. It attracts more than 40,000 people on Christmas Day alone. Bells Beach in Victoria is well known for its annual surfing festival; it lures in world-famous surfers and international travelers alike.

The border between northern New South Wales and southern Queensland is where beaches at Byron Bay, Burleigh Head, and the Gold Coast and Surfers Paradise come together. Farther afield, the Whitsunday Islands consist of dazzling white sands and warm azure waters. These islands are home to many of Australia's ultimate beach retreats. In Western Australia, Perth's Cottesloe Beach is the region's most popular strand to visit.

Beach Safety in Australia

Although Australia has some of the most beautiful beaches in the world, it's necessary to take certain precautions when visiting. At any given beach, you might find large waves, rip currents, and shifting sandbars in the water, along with harsh UV rays on land.

It's common practice to never stray from an unpatrolled beach in Australia unless you're an experienced swimmer. Thousands of trained volunteer surf lifesavers don their red swimsuits and red-and-yellow swim caps every summer to keep the most popular swimming and surfing beaches around Australia safe.

Pay close attention to the flags raised on beaches, and only swim in areas patrolled by lifeguards. If you get caught in a rip, the standard advice is never to swim against it, as you rapidly become exhausted. Instead, try to relax and float parallel to the shore. Always bring plenty of suntan lotion and water to the beach, and protect your eyes with good-quality sunglasses.

GREAT ITINERARIES

THE GOLDEN TRIANGLE: SYDNEY, THE GREAT BARRIER REEF, ULURU

This classic 10-day journey takes in three of Australia's most famous areas, including the Blue Mountains, the Great Barrier Reef, and Uluru.

Day 1–2: Exploring Sydney

On your first day in Australia's largest city, visit the world-renowned Opera House, stopping for lunch at the Opera Bar with its sweeping views of the cityscape and Harbour Bridge. In the afternoon, take a guided walking tour through the historic Rocks area beyond Circular Quay, stopping at the Spirit Gallery to browse through an impressive array of Aboriginal arts and crafts. After some much-needed rest, start the second day with a harbor cruise. You can enjoy the best vantage points for seeing this spectacular city and its magnificent waterfront setting. In the afternoon, trek over to Sydney Harbour Bridge, where a trek up the stairs of the South East Pylon rewards you with an unbeatable harbor panorama.

Day 3: Day-Trip to the Blue Mountains

Leave Sydney in the morning on a day trip to the Blue Mountains, approximately one hour away by car or bus. Head for Katoomba at the peak of the Blue Mountains National Park, where the Three Sisters await, an unusual rock formation representing three sisters who were turned to stone according to Aboriginal legend. Head to neighboring Scenic World and choose the scenic skyway, walkway, railway, or cableway to experience the majesty of the Jamison Valley. On your way back, make a small detour in the pretty garden village of Leura, with its many fine coffee shops, restaurants, and galleries.

Day 4: Wine Tour of the Hunter Valley

Take an organized day trip to the Hunter Valley Wine Region, 150 km (93 miles) north of Sydney, and spend the day experiencing a selection of more than 150 wineries and cellar doors. Discover the region's finest Shiraz or Chardonnay and taste some of the freshest produce and best cheeses that Australia has to offer. After a day spent tasting the area's wines, take a well-earned break at the Bluetongue Brewery in Pokolbin where you can shift to beer tastings.

Day 5: Flight to Cairns

Fly to Cairns, a tropical city nestled in North Queensland and the gateway to the Great Barrier Reef. Relax after your three-hour flight from Sydney with a visit to the Cairns Tropical Zoo to cuddle a koala.

Day 6: Kuranda Village and Tjapukai Aboriginal Cultural Park

Take a full-day tour of nearby Kuranda village and the surrounding rain forest. Experience one of Australia's most scenic rail journeys, the Skyrail, for a bird's-eye view over the forest. After lunch, head to the Tjapukai Aboriginal Cultural Park to watch Aboriginal dances and listen to music and informational talks—perhaps even try your hand at throwing a boomerang or playing the didgeridoo!

Day 7: Cruise to the Great Barrier Reef

Book a full-day cruise from Cairns to the Great Barrier Reef and get up close and personal with the abundant sea life of the world's largest coral reef system. With some of the best snorkeling and diving on the planet, nothing beats getting in the water and swimming with groupers, clown fish, and rays. Then revel in the fact you're experiencing one of the seven wonders of the natural world firsthand.

INDIAN OCEAN

Gulf of Carpentaria

Coral Sea

NORTHERN TERRITORY

Great Barrier Reef

Cairns

QUEENSLAND

Uluru (Ayers Rock)

SOUTH AUSTRALIA

WESTERN AUSTRALIA

NEW SOUTH WALES

Hunter Valley

Blue Mountains

Sydney

SOUTHERN OCEAN

VICTORIA

TASMANIA

Day 8–9: Two Days in Uluru

Take an early morning flight to Sydney and then catch a connecting flight to the physical and spiritual heart of Australia: World Heritage–listed Uluru, the iconic symbol of the Australian Outback. Once you arrive and check in at Ayers Rock Resort, book a seat at the Sounds of Silence Dinner, where you can feast on a barbecue buffet of kangaroo, crocodile, and barramundi and marvel at the immense desert sky.

Wake up early the next morning to catch the majestic sunrise over Uluru (Ayers Rock). See the magnificence of Uluru as its surface changes color with the rising sun, from pink to blood red to mauve throughout the day. Afterward, walk around Uluru's base with a guide and learn about how this sacred site was created by spirit ancestors in the Dreamtime. In the afternoon, sign up for a tour of Kata Tjuta (the Olgas), the nearby rock domes over which you can watch the sunset.

Day 10: Back to Sydney

Once you return to Sydney, take the short ferry ride to Taronga Zoo and stroll around the zoo's harborside location, spying kangaroos, koalas, and other animal natives. If you have time, a short bus or train ride to the world famous Bondi

NUTS AND BOLTS

■ If driving around Sydney, avoid traveling at peak times. Either leave early or head off later, once the commuter traffic has died down.

■ Cairns has a wide range of hotels and resorts to suit any budget—a romantic getaway, weekend escape, or family vacation. It's worth booking ahead and finding somewhere central to the city.

■ When visiting the Great Barrier Reef for a dive or snorkel experience, the best time of year is in the winter months when marine stingers aren't present in the water and there is less need for a protective wet suit.

Beach is in order for a taste of Sydney's much heralded beach life. Spend early evening at the Bondi Icebergs club, where you can enjoy a glass of Australian wine while gazing out over the south end of the beach.

GREAT ITINERARIES

THE SOUTHERN EXPERIENCE: MELBOURNE, TASMANIA, KANGAROO ISLAND

Taking in the best of the south of the country, this 11-day trip combines Australia's second city, Melbourne, and the surrounding region with the great Tasmanian outdoors and South Australia's Kangaroo Island.

Day 1: Melbourne

Start off in Australia's cultural capital, Melbourne, with its world-class shopping and thriving arts scene. No visit to Melbourne is complete without a freshly made espresso. Some of the best are on Degraves Street, directly off Flinders. Sit down at one of the RMB Café Bar's outdoor tables and enjoy delicious eggs Benedict with your coffee. Jump on the free city circle tram to get an overview of the city. It offers good hop-on, hop-off transportation for visitors and locals alike.

Day 2: Yarra Valley Wine Region

Leave the sights and sounds of Melbourne for a day of wine tasting at the Yarra Valley. It's within easy driving distance of the city, but your best bet is to go with a winery tour. These generally include visits to four or five wineries and lunch.

Day 3: Melbourne and Phillip Island

Explore the farther reaches of the city by visiting suburbs such as Richmond, St Kilda, Fitzroy, or Prahran. All offer great café strips with a more laid-back feel than in downtown Melbourne. Take an evening tour to nearby Phillip Island to see the Little Penguin Parade, when the world's smallest penguins come ashore after a day's fishing.

Day 4: Hobart

Fly direct from Melbourne to Hobart (one-hour flight) to explore Tasmania, Australia's natural state. In the harbor capital, sate your Tasmanian appetite with a mix of history and contemporary art and culture. Start at Salamanca Place on the harbor-front and browse the galleries, art studios, cafés, and restaurants lining the quaint waterfront in original 19th-century warehouses. Then make your way up the hill to Battery Point and wander streets where grand colonial houses face out over the Derwent River. If time permits, the Museum of Old and New Art (MONA) is a must-see for art lovers and visitors alike, and is only a 15-minute drive from the center of Hobart.

Day 5: Port Arthur

Hire a car and make the 90-minute drive to Port Arthur on the Tasman Peninsula or join the cruise from Hobart to Port Arthur aboard the MV Marana, which takes approximately 2½ hours. Experience Australia's most intact convict site with more than 30 buildings, ruins, and restored homes. Hop on board a short cruise to the Isle of the Dead to join a guided tour of the settlement's island burial ground and learn about the lives of the people who lived in Port Arthur. On your return to Hobart, grab at bite to eat at Salamanca Place and enjoy some art, craft, music, and theater at the Salamanca Arts Centre.

Day 6: Bruny Island

Opt for a day-tour to Bruny Island, just south of Hobart. Enjoy morning tea on the island at Adventure Bay followed by a three-hour wilderness cruise along the spectacular coastline of the South Bruny National Park. You'll likely see seals, whales, albatross, and various birds of

prey. After lunch, relax with a walk on the beach before heading back to Hobart.

Day 8: Back to Melbourne

Fly back to Melbourne in the morning, and then it's time for shopping. A great place to start is at the Queen Victoria Market on Elizabeth Street, a shopping institution that showcases a wide range of quality seafood, clothing, jewelry, new-age products, and souvenirs. If you're feeling shopped out, take a trip to the Eureka Skydeck 88 for impressive and expansive views of the city from the Southern Hemisphere's highest viewing platform.

Day 9: The Dandenong Ranges

You've tried the Yarra Valley region but haven't yet explored the Dandenong Ranges, a tranquil place of towering forests and intriguing villages. You can hike through the Dandenong Ranges National Park and enjoy incredible views of Melbourne's skyline from the Sky-high, perched on top of Mt. Dandenong. Afterward, explore your creative interests among the shops and galleries of nearby Olinda, Belgrave, and Sassafras.

Days 10–11: Kangaroo Island

Visiting the southern tip of Australia wouldn't be complete without a trip to Kangaroo Island, Australia's third-largest island. The island is a pristine wilderness located southwest of Adelaide and home to some of the largest untouched populations of native Australian animals. From Melbourne, choose the Coastal Explorer or Country Lovers Way (let TravelLink.com.au guide you through Victoria and South Australia) or take the short flight to Adelaide from Melbourne and then a further flight or ferry ride across to the Island.

If adventure is your thing, Kangaroo Helicopters offers a Heli Experience and Scenic Flight or, for wildlife enthusiasts, options include guided tours within the Seal Bay or Kelly Hill Conservation Parks. Fly via Adelaide back to Melbourne or on to the next stage of your journey.

GREAT ITINERARIES

ROAD TRIP: FROM SYDNEY TO BRISBANE

Drive along one of the most glorious and seductive stretches of land in northern New South Wales. It's a big trip—1,100 km (687 miles)—so allow a minimum of seven days if you decide to drive the entire route.

Day 1: 175 km (109 miles)

Frame the Harbour Bridge in your rear-vision mirror and head north out of Sydney. Take the Sydney–Newcastle (F3) Freeway about 75 km (47 miles) north to the Peats Ridge Road exit, and wind through the forested hills to Wollombi, a delightful town founded in 1820. Browse the antiques shops, sandstone court-house, and museum. Next, head north-east to Cessnock and Pokolbin, the hub of the Lower Hunter, and spend the day tasting—and buying—fine wines and artisanal cheeses. Know that Australia has a zero tolerance policy for driving and drinking. Be sure to choose a designated driver or, better yet, take one of our recommended wine-tasting tours.

Day 2: 271 km (168 miles)

Get up with the birds and drive east via Cessnock to the Pacific Highway. Turn north for the long drive to Port Macquarie, Australia's third-oldest settlement. Have a well-earned lunch break in the café at Sea Acres Rainforest Centre and then stroll the elevated boardwalk—or take a guided tour—through centuries-old cabbage tree palms. Now it's into Port Macquarie for a lazy afternoon on a beach, but which of the 13 regional beaches do you laze on?

Day 3: 260 km (162½ miles)

Visit Port Macquarie's Koala Hospital for feeding time (8 am). Then resume driving up the Pacific Highway. Leave the highway 140 km (88 miles) north at the exit to Bellingen, one of the prettiest towns on the New South Wales north coast. It's a nice place to stop for lunch and a quick peek into a few galleries. Continue inland up onto the Dorrigo Plateau. Dorrigo National Park is one of about 50 reserves and parks within the World Heritage–listed Gondwana Rainforests of Australia. Stopping into the Dorrigo Rainforest Centre to learn about the area is gratifying, as is the forest canopy Skywalk. Back in your car, drive on to Dorrigo town and turn right onto the winding, partly unsealed, but scenic road to Corumba and Coffs Harbour. Now you've earned a two-night stay in Coffs.

Day 4: No driving

Scuba-dive on the Solitary Isles? White-water raft the Nymboida River? Or kick back on a beach? However you spend your day, don't miss an evening stroll to Muttonbird Island from Coffs Harbour marina. From September to April you can watch muttonbirds (or shearwaters) returning to their burrows. When the whales are about, it's also a good humpback viewing spot.

Day 5: 247 km (154 miles)

North again, past Coffs Harbour's landmark Big Banana and up the coast to Byron Bay.

There is just too much to do in Byron: kayak with dolphins; dive with gray nurse sharks; go beachcombing and swimming; tread the Cape Byron Walking Track; or tour the lighthouse atop Cape Byron, which is mainland Australia's easternmost point. It's best to decide over lunch

Brisbane ✪

QUEENSLAND

GOLD COAST

Mt. Warning ◆   ○ Murwillumbah

Byron Bay ○

SOLITARY ISLANDS

Dorrigo ○   ○ Coffs Harbour
Dorrigo National Park ◆ ○
Bellingen

Port Macquarie ○
◆ Sea Acres Rainforest Centre

NEW SOUTH
WALES

Pokolbin ○
Wollombi ○   ○ Cessnock

Sydney ✪

at open-air Byron Bay Beach Café, a local
legend. When the sun sets, wash off the
salt and head out for some great seafood
and then overnight in Byron Bay—there's
everything from hostels to high-end villas.

Day 6: 53 km (33 miles)

Catch up on the Byron Bay you missed
yesterday before driving north to Murwillumbah and its remarkable natural
landmark. Mt. Warning is the 3,800-foot
magma chamber of an extinct shield volcano. From the top, on a clear day, there
is a 360-degree view of one of the world's
largest calderas, with mountainous rims on
three sides and the Tweed River running
through its eroded east rim. Climb this
mountain (four hours return), then reward
yourself with a night at Crystal Creek
Rainforest Retreat (bookings essential).

Day 7: 50 km (31 miles)

Relaxed and reinvigorated, it's over the
New South Wales border to Queensland
and Australia's most developed stretch
of coastline. With Brisbane just 90 minutes' drive farther north, you can spend
as much or as little time as you want on
the Gold Coast. Visit theme parks; toss
dice at the casino; ride waves in gorgeous
sunshine. Don't miss feeding the lorikeets
at Currumbin Wildlife Sanctuary before
Brisbane beckons.

TIPS AND LOGISTICS

■ Unleaded petrol, diesel, and LPG are
available at gas stations along most of this
route.

■ Motel rooms are easy to find, except
during school holidays and long weekends.
To avoid driving around after a day at the
wheel, book ahead. The staff at your previous night's accommodation should be able
to help you arrange the next night.

■ If hiring a car for the trip, check that it
contains a street directory. Pick up a good
road map or touring atlas heading out of
Sydney.

■ Mobile speed radars are used throughout
Australia, and fines are high. Stick to the
speed limits.

GREAT ITINERARIES

ROAD TRIP: GREAT OCEAN ROAD

Arguably one of the country's most spectacular drives, the iconic Great Ocean Road hugs the windswept, rugged coastline just west of Melbourne. Allow six days for this 900-km (562-mile) road trip and be prepared to enjoy some of Victoria's best.

Day 1: 187 km (117 miles)

Having escaped Melbourne, drive down the Princes Freeway for about 75 km (47 miles) to the Torquay/Great Ocean Road turnoff. A quarter hour more at the wheel brings you to Torquay, Australia's premier surfing and windsurfing resort town. On your way out of town, detour to Bell's Beach, the setting for Australia's principal surfing competition each Easter. The renowned Great Ocean Road officially starts 30 km (19 miles) beyond Bell's Beach, but the dramatic splendor of Victoria's southwest coast reveals itself sooner. Stop in Lorne, at the foot of the lush Otway Ranges, for lunch. Once you're back on the road, slow down and enjoy it. The winding Great Ocean Road is narrow; don't pass unless you can see far ahead, and don't pull onto the shoulder to admire the view! There are designated pull-over areas where you can safely enjoy the vista.

Drive the 45 km (28 miles) to Apollo Bay for dinner and the night.

Day 2: 234 km (146 miles)

The 91-km (57-mile) Great Ocean Walk starts just west of Apollo Bay in Marengo. Here the Great Ocean Road heads inland. Stay on the main road to Lavers Hill; then detour about 17 km (11 miles) east to the Otway Fly. This 1,969-foot-long elevated treetop walk takes you up into the rain-forest canopy for a bird's-eye view of giant myrtle beech, blackwood, and mighty mountain ash. Backtrack to Lavers Hill and the Great Ocean Road. The road's most famous landmarks lie along a 32-km (20-mile) stretch of coast within Port Campbell National Park. First stop is the Twelve Apostles—there are now only seven of these offshore limestone stacks, but who's counting? Take a helicopter flight for a jaw-dropping view of the eroded and indented coast. Next stop is Loch Ard Gorge, named after the iron-hulled clipper that hit a reef and sank here in 1878. Loch Ard is a natural gallery of sea sculpture, where you could wander for hours on a sunny day. Don't stay in your car if the sun doesn't show, though. Only when a howling wind is roughing up the Southern Ocean will you fully appreciate why this is called the Shipwreck Coast. Leaving the Great Ocean Road now, drive to the maritime village of Port Fairy for the night. In whale season (June–November), divert to Logan's Beach, in Warrnambool, where southern right cows and calves often loll just off the beach.

Day 3: 146 km (91 miles)

Take a leisurely post-breakfast promenade around Port Fairy, Victoria's second-oldest town and widely considered to be its prettiest. Then backtrack 7 km (4½ miles) to the Penshurst/Dunkeld Road and drive 74 km (46 miles) north to Dunkeld, on the edge of the Grampians National Park. Stop for lunch before undertaking the 60-km (37-mile) drive to Halls Gap, the main accommodation base. Be sure to slow down and enjoy one of the most picturesque drives in the Grampians; pull in at the Brambuk Cultural Centre, just

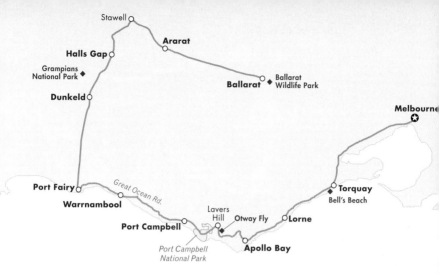

before Halls Gap, and learn about the park's rich Aboriginal history.

Check into your Halls Gap accommodation for two nights.

Day 4: No driving

Spend a day exploring on foot. Walks of varied grades showcase the Grampians' extraordinary geology; don't miss the Pinnacle Walk, just out of Halls Gap, the valley and ranges view from Chatauqua Peak, and Hollow Mountain in the park's north.

Day 5: 140 km (88 miles)

Drive out of Halls Gap to Ararat, on the Western Highway, and follow the highway east to the famous gold town of Ballarat. Spend the rest of the morning among the gold-rush-era Victorian architecture on Sturt and Lydiard streets. Visit the Ballarat Fine Art Gallery, if only to see the tattered remains of the Southern Cross flag that the rebels flew during the 1854 Eureka uprising over mine license fees. Spend the afternoon at Sovereign Hill, where you can pan for gold, ride a horse-drawn stagecoach through dusty streets, and stick your teeth together with old-fashioned candy.

Day 6: 111 km (69 miles)

Have close and not-so-close encounters with saltwater crocodiles, snakes, wombats, kangaroos, and other Australian fauna at Ballarat Wildlife Park. After that, continue your journey or head back to Melbourne.

ABORIGIN
PAST

Today's Australian Aboriginals are guardians of the world's oldest living culture. Most experts agree that it was about 50,000 years ago (possibly as many as 80,000) when the continent's first inhabitants migrated south across a landmass that once connected Australia to Indonesia and Malaysia. These first Australians brought with them a wealth of stories, songs, tribal customs, and ceremonies—many of which are still practiced today.

By Sarah Gold

AL ART, AND PRESENT

All Aboriginal ideology is based upon the creation period known as The Dreaming. During this primordial time, totemic ancestors (who were associated with particular animals, plants, and natural phenomena) lived on and journeyed across the earth. The legends of these ancestors—what they did, where they traveled, who they fought and loved— are considered sacred, and have been passed down among Aboriginal tribes for thousands of years. Though these stories are largely shared in secret rituals, they have also been documented through the creation of unique, highly symbolic artworks.

This is why Aboriginal art, despite traditional beginnings as rock carvings and ochre paintings on bark, now hang in some of the world's finest museums. These works aren't just beautiful; they're also profound cultural artifacts—and a window into humanity's oldest surviving civilizaion.

(top right) Nourlangie Rock, Kakadu;
(top left) Art by Emily Kame Kngwarreye;
(bottom left) Work from Papunya Tula;
(bottom right) Maningrida Art and Culture, Darwin

EARLY ABORIGINAL ART

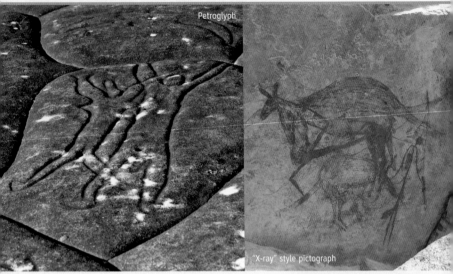

Petroglyph

"X-ray" style pictograph

While dot paintings are the most widely recognized Aboriginal artworks today, they're only the latest incarnation of a creative legacy that stretches back thousands of years. The achievements of Australia's earliest artists can still be seen—etched right onto the sacred landscapes that inspired them.

PETROGLYPHS

The earliest Aboriginal artworks were petroglyphs—engravings carved into flat rock surfaces or faces of cliffs (most likely using pointed stones or shards of shell). Some surviving etchings show lines and circles similar to those in modern-day paintings; others depict animals, fish, birds, and human or spirit figures. The oldest known engravings on the continent, at Pilbara in Western Australia and Olary in South Australia, are estimated to be 40,000 years old. Perhaps the most visited, though, are those in Ku-rin-gai Chase National Park, less than an hour's drive north of Sydney.

PROTECTING ROCK-ART SITES

Given the centuries of weathering they've endured, it's remarkable that so many ancient rock art sites remain intact. In many places, the longevity of the artworks can be attributed to local Aboriginal tribes, who consider it a sacred responsibility to preserve and repaint fading images. Help preservation efforts by staying on marked paths, not touching the artwork, and taking a tour of the site with an indigenous guide.

Freehand pictograph

Stencil painting

PICTOGRAPHS

Other early Aboriginal artists chose to paint images rather than etch them. Using ochres and mineral pigments, and employing sticks, feathers, and their own fingers as brushes, these ancient painters chose sheltered spots—like the insides of caves and canyons—for their mural-like images. Protection from the elements allowed many of these ancient rock paintings to survive; today they're still found all over Australia.

REGIONAL STYLES

The styles of painting varied by region. In the Northern Territory, in Arnhem Land and what is now Kakadu National Park, early Aboriginals painted "X-ray" portraits of humans and animals with their skeletons and internal organs clearly displayed. The Kimberley and Burrup Peninsula in Western Australia are rich repositories of elegant freehand paintings portraying human, animal, and ancestral Dreaming figures. And Queensland, especially the area that is now Carnarvon National Park, is known for its stencil paintings, in which the artists sprayed paint from their mouths.

EARTH TONES (LITERALLY)

Early Aboriginal artists used the earth to make pigments. Red, yellow, and brown were made from mineral-rich clays. Black was created with charcoal or charred tree bark; white from crushed gypsum rock; and grey from ashes left over from cooking fires. Modern artists may mix their pigments with oil or acrylic, but the traditional palette remains the same.

DECIPHERING "DOT PAINTINGS"

An artist uses a small, straight stick dipped in paint to create a dot painting. Ancient symbols and intricate dot motifs combine to create powerful works of art.

To a visitor wandering through a gallery, Aboriginal artwork can seem deceptively simple. Many traditional paintings feature basic designs—wavy lines, concentric circles—comprised of myriad tiny dots. They look as though they were created with the end of a paint-covered stick (and indeed, most were).

But the swirling motifs in these "dot paintings" aren't just abstractions—they're visual representations of ancestral legends.

According to Aboriginal beliefs, as the ancestors lived their lives during the Dreaming, they also gave shape to the landscape. In each spot where the ancestor shot an arrow, danced, or gave birth, an enduring mark was left on the topography: a hill, a ravine, a rock spire. As they conjured these geographical features, they sang out their names—composing singing maps of the territory they covered. Each is known as a "songline," and they criss-cross the entire continent.

Now thousands of years old, these songs are still memorized and sung by many of today's Aboriginal peoples. Songlines are the basis of all indigenous traditions and tribal laws; learning and teaching the songs are considered sacred—and very secret—duties. Over many centuries, however, artists have revealed parts of the songlines through the symbology of dot paintings.

The symbols may seem cryptic, but many are recurring and give clues to the ancestral stories they depict. Shapes punctuating dot paintings usually correspond to landmarks: bodies of water, rock formations, campsites, or resting places. The lines that surround the shapes and connect them represent the tracks of the ancestors as they moved from place to place. Each dot painting is, in effect, a sacred walking map that plots an ancestor's journey.

COMMON SYMBOLS IN ABORIGINAL ART

woman

emu tracks

four women
sitting around
a campfire

ants, fruits,
flowers, or eggs

well or
main campsite

water, fire,
smoke, lightning,
or bushfire

holes, clouds,
or nests

Honey ant

Coolamon
(wooden dish)

kangaroo
tracks

star

meeting place

traveling paths
or heavy rain

running water
connecting
two waterholes

man

Witchetty grub

possum tracks

boomerang

snake

spear

cloud, rainbow,
sandhill, or cliff

people sitting

THE DAWNING OF ABORIGINAL ART APPRECIATION

(left) Contemporary painting done in earth tones by a member of the Papunya Tula Artists collective; (top right) artwork from the Warlukurlangu Artists Aboriginal Corporation; (bottom right) Papunya Tula artwork.

IN THE BEGINNING . . .

It took a long time for Aboriginal art to gain the recognition it enjoys today. Australia's first European colonists, who began arriving in the late 18th century, saw the complex indigenous cultures it encountered as primitive, and believed that, as "nomads," Aboriginals had no claim to the land. Consequently, expansion into tribal lands went unchecked; during the 19th and early 20th centuries, most Aboriginals were forced onto white-owned cattle stations and missionary outposts.

Aboriginal land rights weren't formally acknowledged until 1976, when the first legislation was passed granting claim of title to natives with "traditional association" to the land. This watershed decision (called the Aboriginal Land Rights Act) allowed for the establishment of tribal land councils, which—in partnership with the Australian government—today manage many of the country's national parks and sacred ancient sites.

BREAKING GROUND

The growing awareness of Aboriginal heritage brought with it an increased interest in indigenous art. Before the 1970s, there had been only one celebrated Aboriginal artist in Australia—Albert Namatjira, who grew up on a Lutheran mission in Hermannsburg (in what is now the Northern Territory). In the 1930s, Namatjira studied under a white Australian artist and learned to paint sophisticated watercolor landscapes. Though these had almost nothing in common with traditional indigenous artworks, they won Namatjira enormous fame (by the 1950s, he was listed in *Who's Who*)

Curators often provide relevant historical context.

which reinforced an idea that was already burgeoning in the country: that Aboriginal creativity should receive the same attention and scholarship as non-Aboriginal forms of art.

ABORIGINAL ART CENTERS

Perhaps the single most significant event in modern Aboriginal art history occurred in 1973, with the formation of the Aboriginal Arts Board. The advent of this agency, as part of the government-funded Australia Council for the Arts, heralded a new level of respect for indigenous art. Its aim was to establish a standardized support system for Aboriginal artists through grant money.

But early board members (who came from both European and Aboriginal backgrounds) found this to be another challenge. Aboriginal artists were scattered all over the continent, many of them in isolated, far-flung camps surrounded by vast desert or impenetrable rainforests. How was the organization to find these artists, decide which of them deserved funds, and then dispense those funds in an organized way?

The solution was to set up art centers at specific Aboriginal communities around

Renouned artist David Malangi, Central Arnhem Land

the country—helmed by art-industry specialists who could both cultivate connections with local artists and manage their nuts-and-bolts requirements (like arranging for deliveries of art supplies, and for transport of finished artworks to exhibitors and buyers).

The plan worked, and is still working. There are some 50 Aboriginal art centers in Australia today (most in the Northern Territory and Western Australia), and they collectively represent more than a thousand artists. These centers are the conduit by which most modern Aboriginal works get to art dealers—and then on to galleries, museums, auction houses, and private collectors.

PAPUNYA TULA

Brenda Nungarrayi Lynch, well-known Western Desert artist

The founding members of the Aboriginal Arts Board were inspired by the example of a particular Northern Territory desert settlement, Papunya Tula. Here, with the help of a white Australian art teacher, residents had begun to create and then sell "Dreaming paintings" (what are known today as dot paintings) to nearby galleries. By 1972, the community had established its own thriving and successful art collective, Papunya Tula Artists.

Today Papunya Tula Artists (which has never been government-subsidized) is the most famous Aboriginal art center in the country. The highly acclaimed dot paintings of its artists have hung in New York's Metropolitan Museum of Art and Paris's Musée du Quai Branly; their annual dollar sales are in the millions.

ABORIGINAL ART TODAY

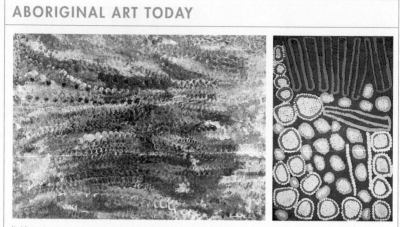

(left) Art by Emily Kame Kngwarreye, Utopia Central Australia; (right) Papunya Tula

Over the past 30 years, the art world's regard for Aboriginal works has sky-rocketed—not just in Australia, but all over the world. Ancient etchings and modern dot paintings now hang in museums from London's British to the Chicago Art Institute; gallerists and art dealers vie to represent rising Aboriginal art stars; and many artists who got their start at art centers in the 1980s (such as Dorothy Napangardi, Michael Nelson Tjakamarra, and Paddy Stewart Tjapaljarri) are near-celebrities today. A few of these pioneers of the modern Aboriginal art movement (like Rover Thomas and David Malangi) were in their seventies and eighties by the time their canvases began decorating exhibit halls and commanding six-figure auction bids.

Some of Australia's most celebrated Aboriginal artists, though, never got to see just how popular their work became. Clifford "Possum" Tjapaltjarri, for example, whose painting *Warlugulong* sold at a Sotheby's auction in 2007 for $2.4 million—the highest price ever paid for a piece of Aboriginal art—died five years beforehand. And Emily Kame Kngwarreye died in 1996, a dozen years before the National Museum of Australia mounted a huge solo exhibition of her work.

The new generation of Aboriginal artists faces its own set of obstacles. The appetite among art dealers for a steady supply of works to sell has led some of them to cut exploitative deals directly with artists (rather than working through the relative safety net of art centers). Other opportunists have mass-produced paintings and then sold them as "authentic"—thus tainting the integrity of the real Aboriginal art market.

But even these problems, unsavory though they are, can be seen from a certain angle as signs of positive change. It was only decades ago, after all, that the phrase "Aboriginal artist" seemed oxymoronic for many Australians. Today, those "primitive" assemblages of lines, circles, and dots account for almost 75 percent of the country's art sales. They have, in effect, helped put Australia on the map.

Today, symbols might be just half the story: colors can range from calm and subdued to bright and vibrant.

TIPS FOR WHERE AND HOW TO BUY ART

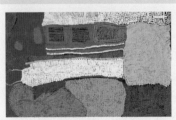

The most easily accessible sources for buying Aboriginal art are galleries. When considering a purchase, ascertain the art's authenticity and ethicality. The Australian Indigenous Art Trade Association recommends asking:

■ Is the artwork documented with a certificate of authenticity from a reputable source, or by photos of the artist with the art?

■ How did the artwork get to the gallery? Is the artist represented by a recognized art center, cooperative, or respected dealer?

■ Is it clear that the artist was treated fairly and paid a fair price for putting the artwork on the market?

MUSEUM AND GALLERY COLLECTIONS

Australia has hundreds of galleries and museums at least partially devoted to Aboriginal artworks. Here are some of the best:

PERMANENT COLLECTIONS

The Australian Museum, Sydney
australianmuseum.net.au

The National Gallery of Australia, Canberra
nga.gov.au

Queensland Art Gallery, Brisbane
www.qagoma.qld.gov.au

National Gallery of Victoria, Melbourne
www.ngv.vic.gov.au

ROTATING EXHIBITIONS

Aboriginal Fine Arts Gallery, Darwin
www.aaia.com.au

Gallery Gabrielle Pizzi, Melbourne
www.gabriellepizzi.com.au

WHEN TO GO

Australia is in the southern hemisphere, so the seasons are reversed. It's winter Down Under during the American summer.

The ideal time to visit the north, particularly the Northern Territory's Kakadu National Park, is early in the dry season (around May). Birdlife remains profuse on the drying floodplains, and waterfalls are still spectacular and accessible. The Dry (April–October) is also a good time to visit northern Queensland's beaches and rain forests. You can swim off the coast without fear of dangerous stinging box jellyfish, which infest ocean waters between November and March. In rain forests, heat and humidity are lower than later in the year, and crocodile viewing is at its prime.

During school holidays, Australians take to the roads in droves. The busiest period is mid-December to the end of January, which is the equivalent of the U.S. and British summer break.

Climate

Australia's climate is temperate in southern states, such as Victoria and Tasmania, particularly in coastal areas, and tropical in Australia's far north. The Australian summer north of the Tropic of Capricorn is a steam bath. From September through November (the Australian spring), or from February through April (late summer–autumn), southern regions are generally sunny and warm, with only occasional rain in Sydney, Melbourne, and Adelaide. Perth and the south of Western Australia are at their finest in springtime, when wildflowers blanket the land.

Here are the average daily maximum and minimum temperatures for some major Australian cities.

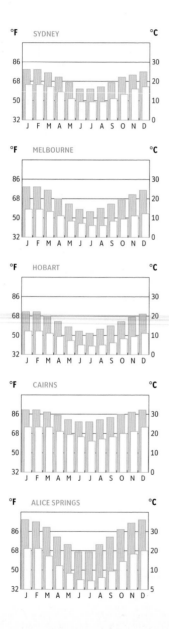

SYDNEY

2

Visit Fodors.com for advice, updates, and bookings

WELCOME TO SYDNEY

TOP REASONS TO GO

★ **A Harbor Sail:** Take a ferry, sail a yacht, or paddle a kayak, but make sure you get out into Sydney Harbour. It's a glorious sight. Check out the Sydney Harbour section for tours of the harbor by boat.

★ **Exquisite Dining:** Sydney restaurants are among the finest eateries in the world. The harbor shines with gems like Aria and Quay, and mouthwatering smells waft through the air in the trendy food burbs of Surry Hills and Darlinghurst.

★ **Glorious Beaches:** Sydneysiders are besotted by the beach, and you'll be, too. With 40 to choose from, including world-famous Bondi, you can watch surfers ride the waves or paddle around the calmer waters of a sheltered harbor beach.

★ **National Parks and Wildlife:** Sydney's untamed beauty is close at hand. See native birds and colorful wildflowers just a few miles from the city; you may even spot a kangaroo in the Royal National Park.

1 Sydney Harbour. This spectacular waterway has a 240-km (149-mile) shoreline of bays, headlands, and quiet beaches. It's the city's jewel.

2 The Rocks. Sydney's oldest area, The Rocks, is full of restored 19th-century warehouses and pubs with great views of the famous bridge.

3 Domain and Macquarie Street. This stately quarter of town contains Parliament House, formal gardens, and the Domain, where rallies and concerts are staged.

4 The Opera House and the Royal Botanic Gardens. The white "sails" of the Opera House dominate the harbor; the neighboring Royal Botanic Gardens are an oasis on the harbor's edge.

5 Darling Harbour. Occupying a former goods yard on the city's western edge, Darling Harbour now houses museums, the aquarium, restaurants, and hotels.

6 Sydney City Center. Dominated by 880-foot Sydney Tower, the city center is packed with historic and modern shopping arcades.

2

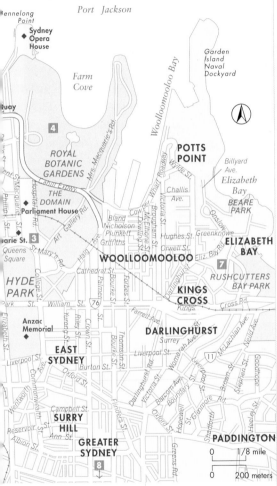

Port Jackson

Bennelong Point

Sydney Opera House

Farm Cove

Quay

4

ROYAL BOTANIC GARDENS

THE DOMAIN

Parliament House

Marie St. 3

Queens Square

HYDE PARK

Anzac Memorial

EAST SYDNEY

SURRY HILL

GREATER SYDNEY

8

Woolloomooloo Bay

Garden Island Naval Dockyard

POTTS POINT

Billyard Ave.

Elizabeth Bay

BEARE PARK

Greenknowe

ELIZABETH BAY

7

WOOLLOOMOOLOO

RUSHCUTTERS BAY PARK

KINGS CROSS

DARLINGHURST

Surrey

PADDINGTON

0   1/8 mile

0   200 meters

GETTING ORIENTED

Sydney is built around its huge harbor. The city center and main attractions are on the south shore. Harbour Bridge connects The Rocks on the south side with Milsons Point on the north side. Greater Sydney is vast, some 80 km (50 miles) from north to south and 70 km (43 miles) from east to west; however, the city center is relatively small. From the Opera House and Circular Quay the city stretches south for about 3 km (2 miles), and east to west for about 2 km (1 mile). It's relatively flat, making it easy to walk around. Beyond the harbor, the city center is essentially a business and shopping precinct, with colonial and modern buildings. The restaurant and nightlife suburbs of Kings Cross, Darlinghurst, and Surry Hill flank the city's eastern and southern edges.

7 Inner Sydney and the Eastern Suburbs. A few miles east of the city you'll find palatial harborside homes, beaches, and café-culture, bohemian-chic enclaves.

8 Greater Sydney. National parks, beautiful beaches, and relics of Sydney's colonial past can all be explored within an hour of the city center.

TOP SYDNEY SIGHTS

Ringed with world-class beaches and some of the most spectacular nature on the continent, Sydney is the continent's cosmopolitan hub, and home to two renowned architectural icons—the Opera House and the Harbour Bridge.

No one ever tires of Sydney's magnificent nature and its two landmark structures. The Sydney Opera House is both awe inspiring and utterly welcoming. Its stunning "sail" design was the brainchild of Danish architect Joern Utzon, who won an international design competition from 233 submissions. Sydney Harbour Bridge is equally loved, especially when the city comes out to see the fireworks explode over it for New Year's Eve celebrations. Opened in 1932, it can be experienced by car or train, but we recommend taking it slower and walking across it. Adventure seekers can even climb up and over the arch to the top. Sydney Harbour's shoreline is dotted with large swaths of national park perfect for hiking and picnics. On the north side of the harbor is Taronga Zoo, the ultimate zoo with a view.

NEED A BREAK

The historic Harbour View Hotel is the place to sit with a drink and watch the folks in their special jumpsuits begin their climb up the Sydney Harbour Bridge. The pub is so close to the bridge that you feel you could reach out and touch it! The bar menu includes snacks of salt-and-pepper calamari and chicken schnitzel ($); the more upscale restaurant menu features sizzling steaks, slow-cooked lamb shanks, and decadent desserts ($). It's near the south pylon of the bridge, at 18 Lower Fort Street and Cumberland Street (☎ 02/9254–4111 ⊕ www. harbourview.com.au).

FODOR'S CHOICE SIGHTS

2

SYDNEY HARBOUR BRIDGE

Despite its nickname "the coat hanger," the bridge has a fond place in all Sydneysiders' hearts. Its opening on March 19, 1932 (during the height of the Great Depression), lifted the spirits of citizens and provided some very unexpected theater. As NSW Premier Jack Lang waited to cut the ribbon, Captain Francis de Groot, a member of the paramilitary New Guard, galloped up on his horse, drew his sword, and slashed the ribbon first.

SYDNEY HARBOUR NATIONAL PARK

This national park is a collection of separate areas of native bush land flanking both sides of the harbor and dotted with walking tracks. Miles of paths wind through the bush and up and down rocky outcrops and headlands. One of the best walks is the 9½-km (6-mile) Manly Scenic Walkway, which travels from Manly Beach to the Spit Bridge via pockets of rain forest, several little beaches, ancient Aboriginal sites, and the historic Grotto Point Lighthouse.

SYDNEY OPERA HOUSE

Sydney's most famous landmark, listed as a World Heritage site in 2007, had such a long and troubled construction phase that it's almost a miracle it was ever completed. Architect Joern Utzon's concepts were dazzling, and so far ahead of their time that the soaring "sails" that formed the walls and roof could not be built by existing technology.

TARONGA ZOO

Sydney's major wildlife sanctuary occupies one of the most prized positions on the north shore of Sydney Harbour. Daily shows, such as the seal and the birds of prey show, are included in the admission price of A$44. A Zoo Pass, using Sydney Ferries, is an excellent deal at A$52.

TIMING

THE HARBOR

Sydney Harbour and its many sites are best visited in spring (September–November) and autumn (March–May). Summers can be hot and sticky and crowded with kids on school break. Winters (June–August) can be mild, and you may even find some lunch bargains at nice restaurants. Midweek visits are always recommended.

THE OPERA HOUSE AND BRIDGE

A guided Opera House tour takes one hour, while the backstage tour, complete with a full breakfast, takes two hours. If you're exploring sans guided tour, allot about 30 minutes to walk around the outside of the building and into some of the interior areas. The two sites are about 1 km (½ mile) apart, which is a leisurely 30- to 45-minute stroll. It takes three hours to do the Bridge Climb tour and around 30 to 45 minutes if you do your own walk across the Harbour Bridge from the south to the north side.

Updated
by Caroline
Gladstone

Sydney belongs to the exclusive club of cities that generate excitement. At the end of a marathon flight there's renewed vitality in the cabin as the plane circles the city, where thousands of yachts are suspended on the dark water and the sails of the Opera House glisten in the distance. Blessed with dazzling beaches and a sunny climate, Sydney is among the most beautiful cities on the planet.

With 4.6 million people, Sydney is the biggest and most cosmopolitan city in Australia. A wave of immigration from the 1950s has seen the Anglo-Irish immigrants who made up the city's original population joined by Italians, Greeks, Turks, Lebanese, Chinese, Vietnamese, Thais, and Indonesians. This intermingling has created a cultural vibrancy and energy—and a culinary repertoire—that was missing only a generation ago.

Sydneysiders embrace their harbor with a passion. Indented with numerous bays and beaches, Sydney Harbour is the presiding icon for the city, and urban Australia. Captain Arthur Phillip, commander of the 11-ship First Fleet, wrote in his diary when he first set eyes on the harbor on January 26, 1788: "We had the satisfaction of finding the finest harbor in the world."

Although a visit to Sydney is an essential part of an Australian experience, the city is no more representative of Australia than Los Angeles is of the United States. Sydney has joined the ranks of the great cities whose characters are essentially international. What Sydney offers is style, sophistication, and great looks—an exhilarating prelude to the continent at its back door.

PLANNING

WHEN TO GO

The best times to visit Sydney are in late spring and early fall (autumn). The spring months of October and November are pleasantly warm, although the ocean is slightly cool for swimming. The summer months of December through February are typically hot and humid, February being the most humid. In the early-autumn months of March and April weather is typically stable and comfortable, outdoor city life is still in full swing, and the ocean is at its warmest. Even the coolest winter months of July and August typically stay mild and sunny, with average daily maximum temperatures in the low 60s.

GETTING HERE AND AROUND

AIR TRAVEL

Sydney's main airport is Kingsford–Smith International, 8 km (5 miles) south of the city. Kingsford–Smith's international (T1) and domestic terminals (T2 and T3) are 3 km (2 miles) apart. To get from one to the other, take a taxi for about A$12, use the Airport Shuttle Bus (called the TBus) for A$5.50 (it takes 10 minutes), or take the Airport Link train, A$5, which takes 2 minutes. Destination New South Wales has two information counters in the arrival level of the international terminal. One provides free maps and brochures and handles general inquiries. The other books accommodations and tours, and sells travel insurance. Both counters are open daily from approximately 6 am to 11 pm. You can convert your money to Australian currency at the Travelex offices in both the arrival and departure areas.

AIRPORT TRANSFERS Airport Link rail travels to the city center in 15 minutes. A one-way fare is A$16.70. Taxis are available outside the terminal buildings. Fares are about A$45 to A$55 to city and Kings Cross hotels. There are a couple of shuttle-bus services from the airport that drop passenger at hotels in the city center, Kings Cross, and Darling Harbour for around A$15 to A$17 one-way and A$28 return. ■TIP→ Passengers with only a little luggage can save money by taking the state government run bus No. 400, to Bondi Junction. The fare is a mere A$5 for the hour-long bus ride, and is ideal for those staying at nearby Bondi Beach.

BUS TRAVEL

Bus travel in Sydney is slow due to congested streets and the undulating terrain. Fares are calculated in sections; the minimum section fare (A$2.20) applies to trips in the inner-city area, such as between Circular Quay and Kings Cross, or from Bondi Junction railway station to Bondi Beach. Bus information can be found at ⊕ *www.sydneybuses.info*.

CAR TRAVEL

With the assistance of a good road map you shouldn't have too many problems driving in and out of Sydney, thanks to the decent freeway system. However, driving a car around Sydney is not recommended because of congestion and lack of parking space. If you decide to drive a rental car, it will cost between A$75 and A$85 per day. Local operator Bayswater Car Rental has cars from as little as A$27 per day (on a seven-day rental plan) for a one-year-old vehicle. Camper-vans that sleep two people can be hired from operator Jucy Rentals for A$75 a day and A$130 in the January peak season.

TAXI TRAVEL

Taxis charge A$2.14 per km (½ mile), plus a flag fall (hiring charge) of A$3.50. Extra charges apply to baggage weighing more than 55 pounds, telephone bookings, and Harbour Bridge and tunnel tolls. Fares are

20% higher between 10 pm and 6 am, when the numeral "2" will be displayed in the tariff indicator on the meter.

TRAM AND TRAIN TRAVEL

The Sydney Light Rail is an efficient link between Central Station, Darling Harbour, the Star City casino/entertainment complex, Sydney fish markets, and two inner western suburbs. The modern trams operate at 10- to 30-minute intervals 24 hours a day. One-way tickets are A$3.50; the A$9 Day Pass is good value. The main terminal for long-distance, intercity, and Sydney suburban trains is Central Station. There are a number of good-value train passes including the Backtracker Pass, which at A$232 (for 14 days) allows unlimited travel between Sydney and Melbourne (and back to Brisbane), a trip to the Blue Mountains, and one day's unlimited travel on Sydney buses, trains, and ferries. Sydney's suburban train network, City Rail, links the city with dozens of suburbs as well as Blue Mountains and South Coast towns. Tickets start from A$3.60 one-way and are sold at all City Rail stations. Off-peak day return tickets are the best option.

DISCOUNTS AND DEALS

For the price of admission to two or three main attractions, the **See Sydney Attractions Pass** (☎ *1300/366476* ⊕ *www.seesydneycard.com*) gets you into 40 Sydney sights and attractions—including the Opera House, Sydney Aquarium, and Koala Park Sanctuary. Several different cards are available, including two-, three-, and seven-day versions. Some cards can even include public transportation. Prices start at A$155 for a two-day adult card without transportation. Cards are available from the Sydney Visitor Centre at The Rocks.

NSW Transport operates all of the Sydney trains, buses, and ferries. They offer the **MyZone tickets** (☎ *13–1500* ⊕ *www.131500.com.au*), which include MyBus, MyTrain, MyFerry, and MyMulti tickets. The latter provides unlimited travel on the Light Rail, and on buses, trains, and ferries (the latter only with a MyMulti2 or MyMulti3 ticket, which covers Zones 2 and 3) for a day, a week, a month, and longer. A daily ticket is A$22; a weekly is A$44 for Zone 1. The AirportLink rail service and sightseeing buses are not included in the price. MyMulti tickets can be bought at various kiosks and newsstands in the city (and suburbs) and at railway stations.

RESTAURANTS

Sydney is blessed with excellent dining. Its 4,000+ restaurants range from ultrahip and expensive celebrity chef venues overlooking the harbor to uber-cool eateries in the fringe suburbs of Darlinghurst and Surry Hills to neighborhood Italian and Asian joints loved by locals. *Prices in the reviews are the average cost of a main course at dinner or, if dinner isn't served, at lunch.*

HOTELS

Sydney hotels range from the international five-star properties with stunning views over Sydney Harbour to boutique hotels in heritage buildings and historic pubs in The Rocks. Harborside hotels are modern and large with executive levels, pools, and day spas. Smaller hotels and apartment hotels are located on the city fringes, in Surry Hills,

GREAT ITINERARIES

You really need three days in Sydney to see the essential city center, while six days would give you time to explore the beaches and inner suburbs. A stay of 10 days would allow trips outside the city and give you time to explore a few of Sydney's lesser-known delights.

IF YOU HAVE 3 DAYS

Start with an afternoon Harbour Express Cruise for some of the best views of the city. Follow with a tour of The Rocks, the nation's birthplace, and take a sunset walk up onto the **Sydney Harbour Bridge.** The following day, take a Sydney Explorer tour to the famous **Sydney Opera House** and relax in the afternoon in the **Royal Botanic Gardens and Domain park.** On the third day, explore the city center, with another spectacular panorama from the **Sydney Tower.** Include a walk

around Macquarie Street, a living reminder of Sydney's colonial history, and the contrasting experience of futuristic Darling Harbour, with its museums, aquarium, and cafés.

IF YOU HAVE 6 DAYS

Follow the three-day itinerary *above*, then visit Kings Cross, Darlinghurst, and Paddington on the fourth day. You could continue to **Bondi,** Australia's most famous beach. The next day, catch the ferry to **Manly** to visit its beach and the historic Quarantine Station. From here, take an afternoon bus tour to the northern beaches, or return to the city to shop or visit museums and galleries. Options for the last day include a trip to a wildlife or national park, **Taronga Zoo,** or the **Sydney Olympic Park** west of the city.

Darlinghurst, and Kings Cross/Potts Point, with easy access to the city center and harbor. *Prices in the reviews are the lowest cost of a standard double room in high season. For expanded reviews, facilities, and current deals, visit Fodors.com.*

TOURS

SIGHTSEEING TOURS

City Sightseeing Sydney. This fleet of brightly colored double-decker buses (with open tops) operate have two routes: the Sydney route has 25 stops, and the Bondi and Bays has 10 stops. Both trips take 90 minutes. Sydney trips depart Circular Quay at 8:30 am daily (last bus departs at 7:30 pm), the Bondi bus departs Eddy Avenue, Central Station at 9 am daily (last bus at 7:30 pm). ■TIP→ These days the operators are adding the Bondi and Bays trip at no extra charge—meaning the two trips will cost A$40 if taken in a 24-hour period, and A$60 if taken over a 48-hour period. ☎ 02/9567–8400 ⊕ *www.theaustralianexplorer.com.au.*

Mount 'n Beach Safaris. This company operates tours to the Blue Mountains and minicoach tours around Sydney, including the northern beaches and to NSW's North and South Coast areas. The Blue Mountains 4WD Canyon and Wildlife Discovery (A$246), the company's most popular tour, provides opportunity to see koalas and kangaroos; have morning tea in the bush; see the highlights of the Blue Mountains;

and have lunch at an historic hotel in the area. ☎ *02/9439–3010* ⊕ *www.mountnbeachsafaris.com.au.*

Oz Jet Boating. These bright red boats are the most distinctive of the jet boats operating on Sydney Harbour. The bow is painted with huge white teeth to resemble a shark. The 30-minute rides, at 75 kph (47 mph), zip past the Opera House, Harbour Bridge, and Clark and Shark islands, and perform 270-degree spins. Despite passengers being issued hooded raincoats, they always get wet. At least two trips run every day (at noon and 3) and more on the weekends and summertime. Rides are A$75, and occasional discounts (for Internet bookings) are offered in the winter and spring. ☎ *02/9808–3700* ⊕ *www.jetboating.com.*

SPECIAL-INTEREST TOURS

Aboriginal Heritage Tour. This tour (A$36.50) takes you through the Royal Botanic Gardens' display of plants that were growing before Europeans arrived on Sydney's shores in 1788. It operates Friday at 10 am (1½ hours duration) and is led by an Aboriginal guide who explains the plants and their uses. ☎ *02/9231–8134, 02/9231–8111* ⊕ *www. rbgsyd.nsw.gov.au.*

Bass and Flinders Cruises. You can go whale-watching from Sydney Harbour with Bass and Flinders Cruise. Boats leave from mid-May to early December, venturing a few miles outside Sydney Heads. The two-hour cruise (A$60) aboard fast boat *Totally Wild* takes just 27 passengers; the half-day photo safari cruise (A$199) is limited to 20 keen amateur photographers. ☎ *02/9583–1199* ⊕ *www.whalewatchingsydney.net.*

Bonza Bikes. Bonza Bikes lets you see the best Sydney sights without having to worry about heavy traffic. The half-day Classic Sydney Tour cruises past the Opera House, winds around the harbor, and cycles through the Royal Botanic Gardens. Trips start from A$119 for a half day (bike and helmet included). ☎ *02/9247–8800* ⊕ *www. bonzabiketours.com.*

BridgeClimb. This unique tour affords the ultimate view of the harbor and city center from Sydney Harbour Bridge. The popular tours take 3½ hours and cost A$198 per person (night climb); the day climb is A$235 and the dawn climb (with limited numbers) is A$308. Another option is the Discovery Climb, which takes climbers within the bridge's structure on their way to the top. Prices are higher during the peak season December 25–January 14. Tours depart from 5 Cumberland Street in The Rocks. ☎ *02/8274–7777* ⊕ *www.bridgeclimb.com.*

Easyrider Motorbike Tours. These exciting, chauffeur-driven (you ride as a passenger) Harley-Davidson tours take you to the city's landmarks, beaches, and rural areas. A 15-minute ride is A$35, a two-hour tour is A$190 per person; a six-hour trip taking in the Blue Mountains' best views is A$350, while an eight-hour trip to the South Coast and the lovely town of Berry starts at A$410. ☎ *1300/882065* ⊕ *www. easyrider.com.au.*

Sydney Pub Tours. This tour lets visitors drink in Sydney's history at five historic pubs in The Rocks, and dine on some unusual pizzas during a 3½-hour jaunt. Operated by history-lover Gary West—a man who relishes handcrafted beers—the walking tour sets off from the Mercantile

2

Hotel at 6 pm. It is designed for those who want to learn more about The Rocks' fascinating history (rather than party types). Gary regales folks with tales of 19th-century rum smuggling and the quirky characteristics of each watering hole. There's a visit to one of the cellars, which is normally off-limits to the public. Adventurous diners might like to order the kangaroo or even crocodile pizza at the Australian Heritage Hotel. Non-beer drinkers are offered wine or a soft drink at each pub. ⊠ *Mercantile Hotel, 25 George St., The Rocks* ☎ *0419/669832 Gary's mobile* ⊕ *www.sydneypubtours.com* ✉ *A$125* ☼ *Tours depart weekdays 6 pm.*

Sydney Seaplanes. A flight on Sydney Seaplanes is a wonderful way to see Sydney's sights and soar over beaches. Short flights taking in the harbor, Bondi Beach, and Manly cost from A$200 per person. The seaplanes take off from Rose Bay. ☎ *02/9388–1978, 1300/732752* ⊕ *www. seaplanes.com.au.*

SYDNEY BY BOAT

Aboriginal Culture Cruise. Former Sydney tugboat the *Mari Nawi* is owned by the Tribal Warrior Association, an organization committed to empowering disadvantaged Aboriginal people. They operate cultural cruises year-round, showing passengers the sights and telling stories associated with tribes including the Eora, Cadigal, and Wangal who inhabited areas around Sydney Harbour. After departing from Circular Quay, the cruises head to Clark Island for a traditional welcoming ceremony and dance performance. Back on board, passengers are shown cultural landmarks, fishing spots, and ancient rock carvings. The two-hour cruises cost A$60 per person and depart Wednesday to Sunday April–September at 1 pm and October–March at 3 pm. ⊠ *Eastern Pontoon, Circular Quay, Sydney Harbour* ☎ *02/9699–3451* ⊕ *www. tribalwarrior.org.*

Aussie Water Taxis. A fun, fast, but somewhat expensive way to get around is by water taxi. (Circular Quay to Manly, for example, costs A$160 for four people, and A$10 for each extra person.) One company, Aussie Water Taxis, runs a taxi shuttle between Darling Harbour and the Opera House for A$15 one-way, A$25 return. Mini-tours of the harbor in these little yellow taxi boats begin at A$35 per person for 45 minutes. ☎ *02/9211–7730* ⊕ *www.aussiewatertaxis.com.*

Captain Cook Cruises. This company runs a number of good tours, but the best introduction to Sydney Harbour is Captain Cook's two-hour Coffee Cruise (A$39), which follows the southern shore to Watsons Bay, crosses to the north shore to explore Middle Harbour, and returns to Circular Quay. Other options include breakfast, lunch, and dinner cruises, and the popular Hop-on-Hop-Off "ferry service"; the latter can be bought as a 24-hour (A$39) or three-day pass (A$99) and includes eight stops around the harbor. ☎ *02/9206–1111* ⊕ *www.captaincook. com.au/sydney.*

Manly Ferry. There is no finer introduction to the city than a trip aboard one of the commuter ferries that ply Sydney Harbour. The hub of the ferry system is Circular Quay, and ferries dock at the almost 30 wharves around the harbor between about 6 am and 11:30 pm. One of the most popular sightseeing trips is the Manly Ferry, a 30-minute journey from Circular Quay that provides glimpses of harborside mansions and the sandstone cliffs and bushland along the north shore. The one-way Manly Ferry fare is A$7.20, and the Manly Fast Ferry, operated by a private company (⊕ *www.manlyfastferry.com.au*), costs A$9, although cheaper if a SmartCard is purchased. ☎ *13–1500* ⊕ *www.sydneyferries. info.*

WALKING TOURS

Ghost Tours. The Rocks' dark alleyways can be scary, and The Rocks Ghost Tours make sure people are suitably spooked, as the guides, dressed in long black cloaks and carrying lanterns, regale them with stories of the murders and other nasty goings-on in the early days of the colony. Tours depart nightly at 6:45 (April–September) and 7:45 (October–March) from Cadman's Cottage; A$42. ☎ *02/9247–7910* ⊕ *www.ghosttours.com.au.*

Rocks Walking Tours. The Rocks Walking Tours introduce you to Sydney's first European settlement, with an emphasis on the buildings and personalities of the convict period. The 1½-hour tour costs A$25. Tours leave daily at 10:30 and 1:30. ⊠ *Clocktower Sq., Argyle and Harrington Sts., Shop 4a, The Rocks* ☎ *02/9247–6678* ⊕ *www.rockswalkingtours. com.au.*

VISITOR INFORMATION

There are information kiosks at locations throughout the city, including Circular Quay (Alfred and Pitt streets), Martin Place (at Elizabeth Street), and Town Hall (at George and Bathurst streets). The Sydney Harbour Foreshore Authority, which manages The Rocks, Darling Harbour, and other harbor precincts, also has an informative website.

The Sydney Visitor Centre is the major source of information for Sydney and New South Wales. There are two locations: The Rocks and Darling Harbour.

Contacts Sydney Harbour Foreshore Authority. This government website provides information on the historic sites and new development projects at Circular Quay, Darling Harbour, and The Rocks. ☎ *02/9240–8500* ⊕ *www.shfa. nsw.gov.au.***Sydney Visitor Centre** ⊠ *Level 2, The Rocks Centre, Argyle and Playfair Sts., The Rocks* ☎ *02/9240–8788, 1800/067676* ⊕ *www.therocks.com* ⊠ *33 Wheat Rd., near IMAX Theatre, at Palm Grove between Cockle Bay Wharf and Harbourside, Darling Harbour* ☎ *02/9211–4288, 1800/067676* ⊕ *www. darlingharbour.com.*

EXPLORING

Sydney is a giant, stretching nearly 80 km (50 miles) from top to bottom and about 70 km (43 miles) across. The harbor divides the city into northern and southern halves, with most of the headline attractions on the south shore. Most travelers spend their time on the harbor's south side, within an area bounded by Chinatown in the south, Harbour Bridge in the north, Darling Harbour to the west, and the beaches and coastline to the east. North of Harbour Bridge lie the important commercial center of North Sydney and leafy but somewhat bland suburbs.

Ocean beaches, Taronga Zoo, Ku-ring-gai Chase National Park, and great shopping in the village of Mosman are the most likely reasons to venture north of the harbor.

Within a few hours' drive of Sydney are the World Heritage–listed Blue Mountains and the renowned Hunter Valley vineyards. Although both these spots are worthy of an overnight stay, they're also close enough to visit on day trips from the city.

SYDNEY HARBOUR

On a bright sunny day there's no more magical sight than glistening Sydney Harbour. The white sails of the Opera House are matched by the dozens of sailing boats skimming across the blue expanse. It's both a hive of activity and blissfully peaceful: It's easy to get away from the bustle in one of this area's many remote little corners. Explore by taking a ferry, walking across the bridge, or hiking around its native bushland edges. But whatever you do, get up close and enjoy the view.

GETTING HERE AND AROUND

Sydney is well served by public transport. Buses travel from a base in Circular Quay through the city center to the inner suburbs of Kings Cross, Darlinghurst, and Surry Hills and to the eastern suburb beaches. Trains travel from Central Station through the city on a circle line (calling at Circular Quay and Town Hall), out to Bondi Junction, over the bridge to the north shore and out to the west. Ferries leave Circular Quay for Manly, Balmain, Darling Harbour, and other suburbs, while the free 555 shuttle bus does a circuit through the city, calling at the main sights.

TOP ATTRACTIONS

Farm Cove. The original convict-settlers established their first gardens on this bay's shores, now home to the **Royal Botanic Gardens.** The enterprise was not a success: the soil was too sandy for agriculture, and most of the crops fell victim to pests, marauding animals, and hungry convicts. The long seawall was constructed from the 1840s onward to enclose the previously swampy foreshore. ⊕ *Enter the Botanic Gardens through gates near the Opera House and in Macquarie St. From the Opera House, turn right and walk along the harbor foreshore (the seawall will be on your left, the Botanic Gardens on your right). To enter the Macquarie St. gates, take a train to Martin Place railway station, exit the station, turn left, and walk a few hundred yards down Macquarie St.*

Fort Denison. For a brief time in the early days of the colony, convicts who committed petty offenses were kept on this harbor island, where they existed on such a meager diet that the island was named Pinchgut. Fortification of the island began in 1841, but was abandoned when cash ran out. It was finally completed in 1857, when fears of Russian expansion in the Pacific spurred the government on. Today the firing of the fort's cannon doesn't signal imminent invasion, but merely the hour—one o'clock. New South Wales National Parks and Wildlife Service runs half-hour tours at Fort Denison. Purchase tickets from either the NSW National Parks office (☎ *1300/072757*) or at Captain Cook Cruises' booth at Jetty 6, Circular Quay; the ferries depart for the island

"Hands-down, these giraffes have the best view." —photo by Carly Miller, Fodors.com member.

from 10:30 am to 4 pm daily from Jetty 6. Those arriving on the island by water taxi or other boat transport have the option to buy tour-only tickets, on a stand-by basis, for A$15.50. The island also has a restaurant, open daily from 10:30 to 3:30 (☎ 02/9358–1999) ✉ *Circular Quay, Alfred St., Jetty 6, Sydney Harbour* ☎ *1300/072757* ⊕ *www.nationalparks.nsw.gov.au; www.fortdenison.com.au* 💳 *A$37.50, including ferry ride* ⊗ *Tours run daily at 12:15 and 2:30, additional tours Wed.–Sun. at 10:45.*

Quarantine Station. From the 1830s onward, ship passengers who arrived with contagious diseases were isolated on this outpost in the shadow of North Head until pronounced free of illness. You can access the station as part of a guided tour, and now stay overnight in the four-star hotel and cottage accommodation known as Q Station; there are also two waterfront restaurants. There are day tours and five different evening ghost tours (the station reputedly has its fair share of specters) that depart from the visitor center at the Quarantine Station, and a "ghostly sleepover" for those who want to spent the night in reputedly haunted rooms. Tours are led by rangers from NSW National Parks and involve a fair bit of walking, so good shoes are a must. Reservations are essential. ■ TIP→ Visitors can also visit the site without taking a tour, however, if you want to dine, you must make prior restaurant reservations. ✉ *North Head, North Head Scenic Dr., Manly* ⚓ *Take the ferry to Manly from Circular Quay, then Bus 135 to site. Or catch Q Station's complimentary bus shuttle near the taxi rank in Belgrave St. opposite Manly Wharf* ☎ *02/9466–1500, 02/9466–1551 tour bookings* ⊕ *www.qstation.com.au* 💳 *Day tour A$35, ghost tours A$49–A$55;*

Quarantine Story A$35 ⊘ The visitor center and museum open daily at 10 am; the Quarantine Story tour weekends at 2 pm; adult ghost tours Wed., Thurs., and weekends 8 pm; family ghost tour Fri. at 6 pm.

Fodor'sChoice
★

Sydney Harbour National Park. This massive park is made up of 958 acres of separate foreshores and islands, most of them on the north side of the harbor. To see the best areas, put on your walking shoes and head out on the many well-marked trails. The Hermitage Foreshore Walk skirts through bushland around Vaucluse's Nielsen Park. On the north side of the harbor, Bradleys Head and Chowder Head Walk is a 5-km (3-mile) stroll that starts from Taronga Zoo Wharf. The most inspiring trail is the 9½-km (6-mile) Manly Scenic Walkway, which joins the Spit Bridge with Manly by meandering along sandstone headlands, small beaches, and pockets of rain forest, and past Aboriginal sites and the historic Grotto Point Lighthouse. You can take day tours of two harbor islands, Fort Denison and Goat Island, which have interesting colonial history and buildings. Call The New South Wales National Parks and Wildlife Service for tickets. You can also visit Shark Island (off Rose Bay) on a cruise with Captain Cook Cruises (A$20) departing daily from Jetty 6 at Circular Quay. The other two islands in the harbor park—Rodd and Clark—are recreational reserves that can be visited with permission from the NSW Parks and Wildlife and payment of a landing fee of A$7. Visitors are allowed on these islands in small groups only, between 9 am and sunset or until 8 pm in summer. As there is no public transport, access is via private vessel, or water taxi. Water taxi fares cost around A$70 to A$120 for six passengers one-way. ■TIP➔ The landing fee is included when you book a tour or a Captain Cook Cruises ferry tour. ⊠ *Jetty 6, Alfred St., The Rocks* ☎ *1300/072757.*

FAMILY
Fodor'sChoice
★

Taronga Zoo. Sydney's zoo, in a natural bush area on the harbor's north shore, houses an extensive collection of Australian fauna, including everybody's favorite marsupial, the koala. The zoo has taken great care to create spacious enclosures that simulate natural habitats. The hillside setting is steep in parts, and a complete tour can be tiring, but you can use the map distributed free at the entrance gate to plan a leisurely route. The views of the harbor are stunning. Use of children's strollers (the basic model) is free. The best way to get here from the city is by ferry from Circular Quay or Darling Harbour. From Taronga Wharf a bus or the cable car will take you up the hill to the main entrance. The ZooPass, a combined ferry-zoo ticket (A$52) is available at Circular Quay. You can also stay overnight at the zoo in what's billed as the "wildest slumber party in town." The "Roar and Snore" program includes a night tour, two behind-the-scenes tours, drinks, dinner, breakfast, and luxury tent accommodation at A$261 per adult on weeknights and A$290 per adult on Friday and Saturday. Other special programs include being a "Keeper for a Day." ⊠ *Bradleys Head Rd., Mosman* ☎ *02/9969–2777* ⊕ *www.taronga.org.au* ⊠ *A$44* ⊘ *Sept.–Apr., daily 9–5; May–Aug., daily 9–4:30.*

NEED A
BREAK?

Nielsen Park Kiosk & Restaurant. Hikers completing the Hermitage Foreshore Walk can pull up a chair at the lovely Nielsen Park Kiosk & Restaurant to soak in fabulous harbor views, and watch the sailing

Farm Cove **2**
Fort Denison ... **12**
Garden Island ...**3**
Kirribilli **13**
Middle
Harbour **9**
Middle Head ... **10**
Quarantine
Station **7**
Rose Bay **4**
Sydney Cove **1**
Sydney Harbour
National Park **8**
Taronga Zoo ... **11**
Vaucluse **5**
Watsons Bay **6**

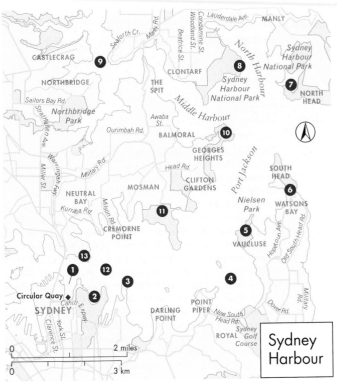

Sydney
Harbour

boats. Both kiosk and restaurant are open daily; the former serves casual takeaway snacks such as fish-and-chips, sandwiches, coffee, and pastries (which can be eaten at the kiosk's outside tables or in the park). The adjacent upscale restaurant is opened for breakfast and lunch and specializes in seafood—Atlantic salmon with coconut broth or seafood chowder may grace the seasonal menu. A new casual dining option at Nielsen Park is Twilight Fish and Chips (Friday to Sunday from 5 pm) at the park's Surf Club venue, a small wooden building with balcony right on the beach. Take the 325 bus from Circular Quay (which will be signposted to Watsons Bay) and tell the driver where you want to get off. ⊠ *Greycliffe Ave., Vaucluse* ☎ *02/9337-7333* ⊕ *www.nielsenpark.com.au* ⊘ *No dinner.*

Vaucluse. The palatial homes in this glamorous harbor suburb provide a glimpse of Sydney's high society. The small beaches at Nielsen Park and Parsley Bay are safe for swimming and provide wonderful views. Both beaches are packed with families in summer. ⊠ *Vaucluse.*

Vaucluse House. The suburb takes its name from the 1803 Vaucluse House, one of Sydney's most illustrious remaining historic mansions. The 15-room Gothic Revival house and its lush gardens, managed by Sydney Living Museums (previously called Historic Houses Trust), are

open to the public. The tearooms, built in the style of an Edwardian conservatory, are popular spots for lunch and afternoon tea on
weekends. Events are regularly held at the "House" including vintage Sundays (where visitors can picnic in the grounds and dress up
in costumes from various eras, such as Victorian and Edwardian) and
Christmas-carol singing. ⊠ *Wentworth Rd., Vaucluse* ✛ *Take Bus 325
from Circular Quay bus stand* ☎ *02/9388–7922* ⊕ *www.hht.nsw.gov.
au* ☜ *A$8* ◷ *Feb.–late Dec., Fri.–Sun. 11–4; Jan. and NSW school
holidays, daily 11–4.*

WORTH NOTING

Garden Island. Although it's still known as an "island," this promontory
was connected with the mainland in 1942. During the 1941–45 War
of the Pacific (WWII and a number of preceding conflicts), Australia's
largest naval base and dockyard was a frontline port for Allied ships.
Part of the naval base is now open to the public. Access, seven days a
week, to the site is via ferry from Circular Quay (take the Watsons Bay
ferry). Visitors can view the museum (A$5) and picnic on the hill. The
Naval Historical Society runs tours to the "secure" section of Garden
Island and these must be booked well in advance. The 90-minute tours
(A$15) run every Thursday and include morning tea and a video. Book-
ings are made by calling the society or through the website. ⊠ *Garden
Island* ✛ *Take the ferry from Circular Quay to Watsons Bay and ask
to be let off at Garden Island. No buses go directly to Garden Island.
To walk, catch the train from Central or Town Hall to Kings Cross station, then walk down either Macleay or Victoria Sts. toward the harbor
(or north). At the end of Victoria Street is a flight of stone steps that
leads down to Woolloomooloo, near Garden Island* ☎ *02/9359–2372*
⊕ *www.navyhistory.org.au.*

Kirribilli. Residences in this attractive suburb opposite the city and Opera
House have million-dollar views—and prices to match. Two of Sydney's most important mansions stand here. The more modest of the
two is **Kirribilli House,** the official Sydney home of the prime minister,
which along with Admiralty House is open to the public once a year.
⊠ *Kirribilli.*

Admiralty House. Next door and far more prominent is Admiralty
House—the Sydney residence of the governor-general, the Queen's representative in Australia. This impressive residence is occasionally open
for inspection. Both houses can be viewed (from the water) during harbor cruises. ⊠ *Kirribilli Ave., Kirribilli* ✛ *Both Kirribilli and Admiralty
House are at the harbor end of Kirribilli Ave.; to get there you can take
a ferry from Circular Quay to either Kirribilli Wharf or Milson's Point
Wharf, or take the train from Town Hall to Milson's Point Station.
The No. 267 bus does a loop from McMahon's Point to North Sydney
via Kirribilli. There is no public access to either of these grand houses.*

Middle Harbour. Except for the yachts moored in the sandy coves, the
upper reaches of Middle Harbour are almost exactly as they were when
the first Europeans set eyes on Port Jackson more than 200 years ago.
Tucked away in idyllic bushland are tranquil suburbs just a short drive
from the city. ⊠ *Middle Harbour* ✛ *The focal point of Middle Harbour*

The boardwalk around Sydney Cove on a typical sunny day

is Spit Bridge. To get there, take a train from either the Central or Town Hall station to Milson's Point then take Bus 229 to Spit Bridge. From Spit Bridge you can walk to Manly and view most of beautiful Middle Harbour.

Middle Head. Despite its benign appearance today, Sydney Harbour once bristled with armaments. In the mid-19th century, faced with expansionist European powers hungry for new colonies, the authorities erected artillery positions on the headlands to guard harbor approaches. One of Sydney's newest open spaces, Headland Park, has opened on a former military base. A walking track winds past fortifications, tunnels, and heritage buildings, several of which are now used as cafés, including the Tea Room Gunners' Barracks. The Sydney Harbour Federation Trust runs guided tours of the park on the first Sunday of the month at 10:30 am. ⌂ *1200 Middle Head Rd., Mosman ✢ Several buses travel from central Sydney to Mosman, Balmoral, and Chowder Bay, which are all suburbs within the Middle Head area and close to Headland Park. They include Buses 244, 245, 246, and 247* ☎ *02/8969–2100 Harbour Trust* ⊕ *www.harbourtrust.gov.au* ✉ *Free; A$8 for guided tour.*

NEED A BREAK?

Tea Room Gunners Barracks. Housed in a beautiful sandstone building that served a number of military purposes for over 130 years, the Tea Room Gunners Barracks offers breathtaking views of the harbor and the surrounding gardens and bushland. Their traditional afternoon tea (A$40; A$44 on weekends) is a great way to relax after exploring the armaments of Middle Head. ⌂ *202 Suakin Dr., Mosman* ☎ *02/8962–5900* ⊕ *www. thetearoom.com.au.*

Rose Bay. This large bay, the biggest of Sydney Harbour's 66 bays, was once a base for the Qantas flying boats that provided the only passenger air service between Australia and America and Europe. The last flying boat departed from Rose Bay in the 1960s, but the "airstrip" is still used by floatplanes on scenic flights connecting Sydney with the Hawkesbury River and the central coast. It's a popular place for joggers, who pound the pavement of New South Head Road, which runs along the bay. ⊠ *New South Head Rd., Rose Bay ⚓ Take Bus 325 from Circular Quay, or take the ferry to Watsons Bay (it stops at Rose Bay).*

Sydney Cove. Bennelong Point and the Sydney Opera House to the east and Circular Quay West and The Rocks to the west enclose this cove, which was named after Lord Sydney, the British home secretary at the time the colony was founded. The settlement itself was to be known as New Albion, but the name never caught on. Instead, the city took its name from this tiny bay. ⊠ *Sydney Cove ⚓ Take the train from Central or Town Hall to Circular Quay railway station; or take any number of buses to Circular Quay from all over Sydney. Ferries travel to Circular Quay from many different parts of Sydney, including the north side of the harbor, Rose Bay, Balmain, and Parramatta. Circular Quay is right in the middle of Sydney Cove.*

Watsons Bay. Established as a military base and fishing settlement in the colony's early years, Watsons Bay is a charming suburb, with a popular waterfront pub, that has held on to its village ambience despite the exorbitant prices paid for tiny cottages here. Unlike Watsons Bay's tranquil harbor side, the side that faces the ocean is dramatic and tortured, with the raging sea dashing against the sheer, 200-foot sandstone cliffs of The Gap. ⊠ *Military Rd., Watsons Bay.*

Macquarie Lighthouse. When the sun shines, the 15-minute cliff-top stroll along South Head Walkway between The Gap and the Macquarie Lighthouse affords some of Sydney's most inspiring views. Convict-architect Francis Greenway (jailed for forgery) designed the original lighthouse here, Australia's first, in 1818. Visitors climb the 100 stairs to the top of the lighthouse on guided tours (20 minutes duration; A$5) that are run every two months by the Sydney Harbour Federation Trust. Call or check the website for dates and bookings. ⊠ *Old South Head Rd., Vaucluse ⚓ To reach Watsons Bay either take the ferry from Circular Quay or Buses 324 or 325 from Circular Quay. Bus 324 goes past the lighthouse* ☎ *02/8969–2100* ⊕ *www.harbourtrust.gov.au.*

THE ROCKS

The Rocks is the birthplace not just of Sydney, but of modern Australia. Here the 11 ships of the First Fleet, the first of England's 800-plus ships carrying convicts to the penal colony, dropped anchor in 1788. This stubby peninsula enclosing the western side of Sydney Cove became known simply as The Rocks.

Most of the architecture here dates from the Victorian era, by which time Sydney had become a thriving port. Warehouses lining the waterfront were backed by a row of tradesmen's shops, banks, and taverns, and above them, ascending Observatory Hill, rose a tangled mass of

Argyle Cut .. **10**

Argyle Place **12**

Campbell's Cove **4**

Customs House **16**

Dawes Point Park **2**

Holy Trinity Garrison Church **11**

Lower Fort Street **3**

Museum of Contemporary Art **7**

Nurses Walk . **8**

Observatory Hill **13**

Overseas Passenger Terminal **6**

Suez Canal ... **9**

Sydney Harbour Bridge **1**

Sydney Observatory . **14**

Sydney Visitor Centre at the Rocks **15**

Upper George Street **5**

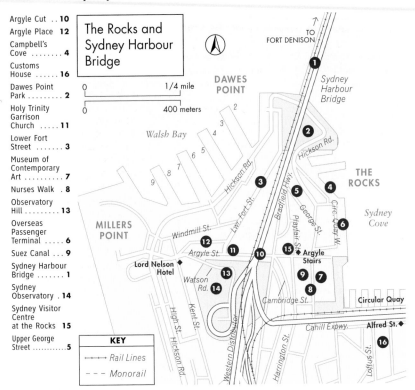

alleyways lined with the cottages of seamen and wharf laborers. By the late 1800s The Rocks was a rough and squalid area. Conditions were so bad that as late as 1900 the black plague swept through The Rocks, prompting the government to offer a bounty for dead rats in an effort to exterminate their disease-carrying fleas.

Today The Rocks is hardly the run-down area it once was. Since the 1970s it's been transformed into a hot spot of cafés, restaurants, and quaint boutiques, and it's one of the city's most popular destinations. And because it's Sydney's most historic area, the old architecture has been beautifully maintained.

GETTING HERE AND AROUND

You can take the train or any number of buses to Circular Quay and then walk to The Rocks. From Bondi and Paddington, take the 380, 382, or 333 bus to Circular Quay via Elizabeth Street. From Clovelly, take the 339 bus all the way to The Rocks, via Central Station. The 431, 432, and 433 buses travel the inner western suburbs and terminate in The Rocks. Once there, the best way to get around is on foot—there are quite a few sandstone steps and narrow alleyways to navigate, and your feet are your best friends.

EXPLORING THE ROCKS ON FOOT

Begin at Circular Quay, the lively waterfront ferry terminal, and walk west toward Harbour Bridge, passing the Museum of Contemporary Art, and climb the few stairs into George Street. Pass the historic Fortune of War pub, then as you round the corner head down the sandstone stairs on the right to **Campbell's Cove** and its warehouses. The waterfront restaurants and cafés are pleasant spots for a drink or meal. Continue along Hickson Road toward the Sydney Harbour Bridge until you are directly beneath the bridge's massive girders. Walk under the bridge to **Dawes Point Park** for excellent views of the harbor, including the Opera House and the small island of Fort Denison. Now turn your back on the bridge and walk south and west, via Lower Fort Street. Explore Argyle Place and continue walking south, past the **Sydney Observatory**. While you're in the neighborhood, be sure to pick up brochures and city information at the **Sydney Visitor Centre at The Rocks**, on the corner of Argyle and Playfair streets. Turn right at **Nurses Walk**, another of the area's historic and atmospheric backstreets, then left into Surgeons Court, and left again onto George Street. On the left is the handsome sandstone facade of the former Rocks Police Station, now a crafts gallery. From this point, Circular Quay is only a short walk away.

TOP ATTRACTIONS

Argyle Cut. Argyle Street, which links Argyle Place and George Street, is dominated by the Argyle Cut and its massive walls. In the days before the Cut (tunnel) was made, the sandstone ridge here was a major barrier to traffic crossing between Circular Quay and Millers Point. In 1843 convict work gangs hacked at the sandstone with hand tools for 2½ years before the project was abandoned due to lack of progress. Work restarted in 1857, when drills, explosives, and paid labor completed the job. On the lower side of the Cut an archway leads to the **Argyle Stairs,** which begin the climb from Argyle Street up to the Sydney Harbour Bridge walkway. There's a spectacular view from the South East Pylon. ⊠ *Argyle Pl., Millers Point.*

Campbell's Cove. Robert Campbell was a Scottish merchant who is sometimes referred to as the "father of Australian commerce." Campbell broke the stranglehold that the British East India Company exercised over seal and whale products, which were New South Wales's only exports in those early days. The cove's atmospheric sandstone **Campbell's Storehouse**, built from 1838 onward, now houses waterside restaurants. The pulleys that were used to hoist cargoes still hang on the upper level of the warehouses. The cove is also the mooring for Sydney's fully operational tall ships which conduct theme cruises around the harbor. ⊠ *Campbell's Storehouse, 7–27 Circular Quay W, The Rocks.*

Holy Trinity Garrison Church. Every morning, redcoats would march to this 1840 Argyle Place church from Dawes Point Battery (now Dawes Point Park), and it became commonly known as the Garrison Church. As the regimental plaques and colors around the walls testify, the church still retains a close military association. Sunday services are held at 9:30 am and 7 pm. ⊠ *Argyle Pl., Argyle and Lower Fort Sts., The Rocks* ☎ 02/9247–1268 ☉ *Daily 9–5.*

Fodor's Choice ★ **Sydney Harbour Bridge.** There are several ways to experience the bridge and its spectacular views. Two options are listed below. The third option is to walk to the midpoint of the bridge to take in the views free of charge, but be sure to take the eastern footpath, which overlooks the Sydney Opera House. Access is via the stairs on Cumberland Street (near the BridgeClimb meeting point) and close to the Shangri-La Hotel. ⊠ *Cumberland St., The Rocks.*

WORD OF MOUTH

"Sydney is special and worth your time. If you are adventurous, take the BridgeClimb on Sydney Harbour Bridge. Try to take a side trip to either the Hunter Valley wine area or the Blue Mountains."

—lcls

South East Pylon. To reach this city-side pylon of the Sydney Harbour Bridge, walk along the bridge's pedestrian pathway. Access is from stairs on Cumberland Street, The Rocks (near BridgeClimb). This structure houses a display on the bridge's construction, and you can climb the 200 steps to the lookout and its unbeatable harbor panorama. ⊠ *Cumberland St., The Rocks* ☎ 02/9240–1100 ⊕ *www.pylonlookout.com.au* ☞ A$11 ☉ *Daily 10–5.*

BridgeClimb tour. Another (more expensive) option—not for those afraid of heights—is the BridgeClimb tour, which takes you on a guided walking tour to the very top of Harbour Bridge, 439 feet above sea level. The cost is A$198 per person for a night climb midweek and A$235 for a day climb, with slightly higher prices on weekends. ⊠ *Sydney Harbour Bridge, The Rocks* ☎ 02/8274–7777 ⊕ *www.bridgeclimb.com.*

NEED A BREAK? **Lord Nelson Brewery Hotel.** While in the west end of Argyle Place, consider the liquid temptations of the Lord Nelson, which with at least one other contender claims to be Sydney's oldest hotel. (It has been licensed to serve alcohol since 1841.) The sandstone pub has its own brewery on the premises. One of its specialties is Quayle Ale, named after the former U.S. vice president, who "sank a schooner" (drank a beer) here during his 1989 visit to Australia, or try Nelson's Blood (for those who like Irish stouts). ⊠ *19 Kent St., at Argyle St., Millers Point* ☎ 02/9251–4044 ⊕ *www.lordnelsonbrewery.com.*

WORTH NOTING

Argyle Place. With all the traditional requirements of an English green—a pub at one end, a church at the other, and grass in between—this charming enclave in the suburb of Millers Point is unusual for Sydney. Argyle Place is lined with 19th-century houses and cottages on its northern side and overlooked by Observatory Hill to the south. ⊠ *Argyle Pl., Millers Point.*

Customs House. The last surviving example of the elegant sandstone buildings that once ringed Circular Quay, this former customs house now features an amazing model of Sydney under a glass floor. You can walk over the city's skyscrapers, all of which are illuminated by meters of fiber-optic lights. Recently renovated and with a new ground floor bar, Customs House has an excellent two-level library and plenty of art galleries. The rooftop Café Sydney, the standout in the clutch of restaurants and cafés in this late-19th-century structure, overlooks Sydney Cove. The building stands close to the site where the British flag was first raised on the shores of Sydney Cove in 1788. ⊠ *Customs House Sq., 31 Alfred St., Circular Quay* ☎ *02/9242–8551* ⊕ *www. sydneycustomshouse.com.au.*

Dawes Point Park. The wonderful views of the harbor (and since the 1930s, the Harbour Bridge) have made this park and its location noteworthy for centuries. Named for William Dawes, a First Fleet marine officer and astronomer who established the colony's first basic observatory nearby in 1788, this park was also once the site of a fortification known as Dawes Battery. The cannons on the hillside pointing toward the Opera House came from the ships of the First Fleet. ⊠ *Hickson Rd., The Rocks.*

Lower Fort Street. At one time the handsome Georgian houses along this street, originally a rough track leading from the Dawes Point Battery to Observatory Hill, were among the best addresses in Sydney. Elaborate wrought-iron lacework still graces many of the facades. ⊠ *Lower Fort St., The Rocks.*

Museum of Contemporary Art. This ponderous art deco building houses one of Australia's most important collections of modern art, as well as two significant collections of Aboriginal art and continually changing temporary exhibits. The museum almost doubled in size with the 2012 addition of a five-story wing, which now houses galleries and a sculpture garden. Free tours, talks, and hands-on art workshops are conducted regularly. ⊠ *140 George St., The Rocks* ☎ *02/9245–2400* ⊕ *www.mca.com.au* ⊴ *Free* ☉ *Daily 10–5.*

Nurses Walk. Cutting across the site of the colony's first hospital, Nurses Walk acquired its name at a time when "Sydney" and "sickness" were synonymous. Many of the 736 convicts who survived the voyage from Portsmouth, England, aboard the First Fleet's 11 ships arrived suffering from dysentery, smallpox, scurvy, and typhoid. A few days after he landed at Sydney Cove, Governor Phillip established a tent hospital to care for the worst cases. ⊠ *Between Harrington and George Sts., The Rocks* ⊕ *www.therocks.com.*

Observatory Hill. The city's highest point, at 145 feet, was known originally as Windmill Hill, since the colony's first windmill occupied this breezy spot. Its purpose was to grind grain for flour, but soon after it was built the canvas sails were stolen, the machinery was damaged in a storm, and the foundations cracked. The signal station at the top of the hill was built in 1848. This later became an astronomical observatory. This is a great place for a picnic with a view. ⊠ *Upper Fort St., The Rocks.*

Overseas Passenger Terminal. Busy Circular Quay West is dominated by this multilevel steel-and-glass port terminal, which is often used by visiting cruise ships. There are several excellent waterfront restaurants

in the terminal, all with magnificent harbor views. Even if you're not dining in the terminal, it's worth taking the escalator to the upper deck for a good view of the harbor and Opera House. ⊠ *Circular Quay W, The Rocks* ⊕ *www.therocks.com.*

Suez Canal. So narrow that two people can't walk abreast, this alley acquired its name before drains were installed, when rainwater would pour down its funnel-like passageway and gush across George Street. Lanes such as this were once the haunt of the notorious late-19th-century Rocks gangs, when robbery was rife in the area. ⊠ *Harrington and George Sts., The Rocks* ⊕ *www.therocks.com.*

Sydney Observatory. Originally a signaling station for communicating with ships anchored in the harbor, this handsome building on top of Observatory Hill is now an astronomy museum. During evening observatory shows you can tour the building, watch videos, and get a close-up view of the universe through a 16-inch mirror telescope. A new digital Sydney Planetarium opened at the site in mid-2013 that showcases the virtual night sky to just 20 visitors at a time in a small theater. Reservations are required for the evening shows only. ⊠ *Watson Rd., Millers Point* ☎ *02/9921–3485* ⊕ *www.sydneyobservatory.com. au* 🖃 *Museum free, daytime show A$8, evening show A$18; Sydney Planetarium A$10* ☉ *Daily 10–5; planetarium show weekends 2:30 pm, weekdays 1 and 4 pm.*

Sydney Visitor Centre at the Rocks. Known as The Rocks Centre, this ultra-modern space is packed with free maps and brochures, and the friendly staff dispenses valuable information and will book tours, hotel rooms, and bus travel. It's near the popular Löwenbräu Keller, where many tourists gather for a beer. ⊠ *The Rocks Centre, Argyle and Playfair Sts., The Rocks* ☎ *02/9240–8788, 1800/067676* ⊕ *www.therocks.com* ☉ *Daily 9:30–5:30.*

Upper George Street. The restored warehouses and Victorian terrace houses that line this part of George Street make this a charming section of the Rocks. The covered **Rocks Market** takes place here on weekends. ⊠ *George St., The Rocks.*

DOMAIN AND MACQUARIE STREET

Some of Sydney's most notable Victorian-era public buildings, as well as one of its finest parks, can be found in this area. In contrast to the simple, utilitarian stone convict cottages of The Rocks, these buildings were constructed at a time when Sydney was experiencing a long period of prosperity thanks to the gold rushes of the mid-19th century and an agricultural boom. The sandstone just below the surface of many coastal areas proved an ideal building material—easily honed into the ornamentation so fashionable during the Victorian era. Macquarie Street is Sydney's most elegant boulevard. It was shaped by Governor Macquarie, who planned the transformation of the cart track leading to Sydney Cove into a stylish street of dwellings and government buildings. An occasional modern high-rise breaks up the streetscape, but many of the 19th-century architectural delights here escaped demolition.

CLOSE UP

Building Sydney

Descended from Scottish clan chieftains, Governor Lachlan Macquarie was an accomplished soldier and a man of vision. Macquarie, who was in office from 1810 to 1821, was the first governor to foresee a role for New South Wales as a free society rather than an open prison. He laid the foundations for that society by establishing a plan for the city, constructing significant public buildings, and advocating that reformed convicts be readmitted to society.

Macquarie's policies of equality may seem perfectly reasonable today, but in the early 19th century they marked him as a radical. When his vision of a free society threatened to blur distinctions between soldiers, settlers, and convicts, Macquarie was forced to resign. He was later buried on his Scottish estate, his gravestone inscribed with the words "the Father of Australia."

Macquarie's grand plans for the construction of Sydney might have come to nothing had it not been for Francis Greenway. Trained as an architect in England, where he was convicted of forgery and sentenced to 14 years in New South Wales, Greenway received a ticket of prison leave from Macquarie in 1814 and set to work transforming Sydney. Over the next few years he designed lighthouses, hospitals, convict barracks, and many other government buildings, several of which remain to bear witness to his simple but elegant eye. Greenway was eventually even depicted on one side of the old A$10 notes, which went out of circulation early in the 1990s. Only in Australia, perhaps, would a convicted forger occupy pride of place on the currency.

GETTING HERE AND AROUND

The area is served by two train stations—Martin Place and St. James—but they are not on the same line. You can catch train trains to both stations from Central and Town Hall. St. James is right next to Hyde Park, and Martin Place has an exit on Macquarie Street. From Macquarie Street it's a short walk to the Domain via the passageway that cuts through Sydney Hospital. A number of buses (including the 380/382 and 333 from Bondi Beach and 555 free shuttle) travel along Elizabeth Street.

TOP ATTRACTIONS

Art Gallery of New South Wales. Apart from Canberra's National Gallery, this is the best place to explore the evolution of European-influenced Australian art, as well as the distinctly different concepts that underlie Aboriginal art. All the major Australian artists of the last two centuries are represented in this impressive collection. The entrance level, where large windows frame spectacular views of the harbor, exhibits 20th-century art. Below, in the gallery's major extensions, the Yiribana Gallery displays one of the nation's most comprehensive collections of Aboriginal and Torres Strait Islander art. There are monthly free audio tours and free talks. ■ TIP➔ The gallery is open until 9 pm on Wednesday. ⊠ Art Gallery Rd., The Domain ☎ 02/9225–1700 ⊕ www.artgallery.nsw.gov.au ⌧ Free; fee for special exhibits ⊙ Daily 10–5.

Art Gallery of
New South
Wales 4

Garden Palace
Gates 7

Hyde Park
Barracks 1

Museum of
Sydney 8

St. James'
Church 2

State Library
of New South
Wales 6

State Parliament
House 5

Sydney
Hospital 3

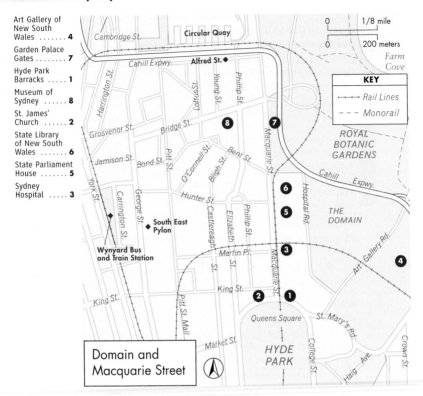

Domain and
Macquarie Street

Hyde Park Barracks. Before Governor Macquarie arrived, convicts were left to roam freely at night. Macquarie was determined to establish law and order, and in 1819 he commissioned convict-architect Francis Greenway to design this restrained, classically Georgian-style building. Today the Barracks houses compelling exhibits that explore behind the scenes of the prison. For example, a surprising number of relics from this period were preserved by rats, which carried away scraps of clothing and other artifacts for their nests beneath the floorboards. A room on the top floor is strung with hammocks, exactly as it was when the building housed convicts. The barracks are part of the Sydney Living Museums collection of 12 historic buildings. ⊠ *Queens Sq., Macquarie St., The Domain* ☎ *02/8239–2311* ⊕ *www.sydneylivingmuseums.com. au* 🎫 *A$10* ⌚ *Daily 9:30–5.*

Museum of Sydney. This museum built on the site of the original Government House documents Sydney's early period of European colonization. Aboriginal culture, convict society, and the gradual transformation of the settlement at Sydney Cove are woven into an evocative portrayal of life in the country's early days. A glass floor in the lobby reveals the foundations of the original structure. One of the most intriguing exhibits, however, is outside: the striking *Edge of the Trees* sculpture, the first collaborative public artwork in Sydney between an

Aboriginal and a European artist. ⊠ *Bridge and Phillip Sts., The Domain* ☎ *02/9251–5988* ⊕ *www. sydneylivingmuseums.com.au* ✉ *A$10* ⊙ *Daily 9:30–5.*

WORTH NOTING

Garden Palace Gates. These gates are all that remain of the Garden Palace, a massive glass pavilion that was erected for the Sydney International Exhibition of 1879 and destroyed by fire three years later. On the arch above the gates is a depiction of the Garden Palace's dome. Stone pillars on either side of the gates are engraved with Australian wildflowers. ⊠ *Macquarie St. between Bridge and Bent Sts., The Domain.*

ART AND ANGST

If you like a bit of controversy with your culture, head to the Art Gallery of New South Wales to view the finalists in the annual **Archibald Prize** (⊕ *www. thearchibaldprize.com.au*). Each year since 1921, the competition has attracted plenty of drama as everyone debates the merits of the winners. Prizes are announced in early March, and the exhibition hangs until mid-May.

NEED A BREAK?

Hyde Park Barracks Café. On a sunny day the courtyard tables of the Hyde Park Barracks Café provide one of the city's finest places to enjoy an outdoor lunch or morning or afternoon tea. The café and indoor restaurant serve light fare, full meals, and delicious desserts such as the Belgian milk chocolate and Grand Marnier ganache tart pudding with espresso gelato. There's also an extensive Australian wine list. ⊠ *Queens Sq., Macquarie St., The Domain* ☎ *02/9222–1815* ⊕ *www.hydeparkbarrackscafe.com.au* ⊙ *No dinner.*

St. James' Church. Begun in 1819, the colonial Georgian–style St. James' is the oldest surviving church in the City of Sydney, and another fine Francis Greenway design. Now lost among the skyscrapers, the church's tall spire once served as a landmark for ships entering the harbor. Plaques commemorating Australian explorers and administrators cover the interior walls. Free guided tours are given weekdays at 2:30 pm. Lunchtime concerts are presented every Wednesday from late February to late December. ⊠ *Queens Sq., 173 King St., Hyde Park* ☎ *02/9232– 3022* ⊕ *www.sjks.org.au* ⊙ *Weekdays 9–5, Sat. 9–3.*

State Library of New South Wales. This large complex is based around the Mitchell and Dixson libraries, which make up the world's largest collection of Australiana. Enter the foyer through the classical portico to see one of the earliest maps of Australia, a copy in marble mosaic of a map made by Abel Tasman, the Dutch navigator, in the mid-17th century. Through the glass doors lies the vast Mitchell Library reading room, but you need a reader's ticket (establishing that you are pursuing legitimate research) to enter. You can, however, take a free escorted history and heritage tour weekdays at 10:30 am. The library continuously runs free exhibitions, and the opulent Shakespeare Room is open to the public Tuesday 10–4. Inquire at the reception desk of the general reference library on Macquarie Street. ⊠ *Macquarie St. between the Royal*

Sydney has enough museums and art galleries to appeal to just about every taste.

Botanic Gardens and Parliament House, Domain ☎ 02/9273–1414, 02/9273–1768 ⊕ www.sl.nsw.gov.au ⊘ Mon.–Thurs. 9–8, Fri. 9–5, weekends 10–5 (Mitchell Library closed Sun.).

State Parliament House. The simple facade and shady verandas of this Greenway-designed 1816 building, formerly the Rum Hospital, typify Australian colonial architecture. From 1829, two rooms of the old hospital were used for meetings of the executive and legislative councils, which had been set up to advise the governor. These advisory bodies grew in power until New South Wales became self-governing in the 1840s, at which time Parliament occupied the entire building. The Legislative Council Chamber—the upper house of the parliament, identifiable by its red color scheme—is a prefabricated cast-iron structure that was originally intended to be a church on the goldfields of Victoria.

State Parliament generally sits between mid-February and late May, and again between mid-September and late November. You can visit the public gallery and watch the local version of the Westminster system of democracy in action. When parliament is not sitting, you can take a free escorted tour (they are conducted on the first Thursday of the month at 1 pm) or walk around at your leisure and view the large collection of portraits and paintings. You must reserve ahead for tours and to sit in the public gallery. ⊠ 6 Macquarie St., Domain ☎ 02/9230–2111 ⊕ www.parliament.nsw.gov.au ⊘ Weekdays 9–5; hrs. vary when Parliament is in session—call ahead.

Sydney Hospital. Completed in 1894 to replace the main Rum Hospital building which stood on the site since 1811, this institution offered an infinitely better medical option. By all accounts, admission to the Rum

Hospital was only slightly preferable to death itself. Convict nurses stole patients' food, and abler patients stole from the weaker. The kitchen sometimes doubled as a mortuary, and the table was occasionally used for operations. In front of the hospital is a bronze figure of a boar. This is *Il Porcellino,* a copy of a statue that stands in Florence, Italy. According to the inscription, if you make a donation in the coin box and rub the boar's nose, "you will be endowed with good luck." Sydney citizens seem to be a superstitious bunch, because the boar's nose is very shiny indeed. ✉ *8 Macquarie St., Domain* ☎ *02/9382–7111.*

THE OPERA HOUSE AND THE ROYAL BOTANIC GARDENS

Bordering Sydney Cove, Farm Cove, and Woolloomooloo Bay, this section of Sydney includes the iconic Sydney Opera House, as well as extensive and delightful harborside gardens and parks.

The colony's first farm was established here in 1788, and the botanical gardens were laid out in 1816. The most dramatic change to the area occurred in 1959, however, when ground was broken on the site for the Sydney Opera House at Bennelong Point. This promontory was originally a small island, then the site of 1819 Fort Macquarie, later a tram depot, and finally the Opera House, one of the world's most striking modern buildings. The area's evolution is an eloquent metaphor for Sydney's own transformation.

GETTING HERE AND AROUND

The best way to get to the Opera House is to take one of the many ferries, buses, or trains that go to Circular Quay and then walk the pedestrian concourse. Some buses travel down Macquarie Street to the Opera House, which involves a slightly shorter walk. To get to the Royal Botanic Gardens, take the CityRail suburban train from the Town Hall, Central, or Bondi Junction stations to Martin Place station, exit on the Macquarie Street side, and walk a few hundred yards.

TOP ATTRACTIONS

Fodor's Choice ★ **Royal Botanic Gardens.** More than 80 acres of sweeping green lawns, groves of indigenous and exotic trees, duck ponds, greenhouses, and some 45,124 types of plants—many of them in bloom—grace these gardens. The elegant property, which attracts strollers and botany enthusiasts from all over the country, is a far cry today from what it once was: a failed attempt by convicts of the First Fleet to establish a farm. Though their early attempts at agriculture were disastrous, the efforts of these first settlers are acknowledged in the Pioneer Garden, a sunken garden built in their memory.

Among the many other feature gardens on the property are the Palm Grove—home to some of the oldest trees in Sydney, the Begonia Garden, and the Rare and Threatened Plants Garden. Not to be missed is a cutting from the famous Wollemi Pine, a plant thought to be extinct until it was discovered in a secluded gully in the Wollemi National Park in the Blue Mountains in 1994. Plants throughout the gardens have various blooming cycles, so no matter what time of year you visit, there are sure to be plenty of flowers. The gardens include striking sculptures and hundreds of species of birds. There are spectacular views over the

Andrew (Boy)
Charlton Pool **3**

Mrs. Macquarie's
Chair **5**

Mrs. Macquarie'
Point **4**

Royal Botanic
Gardens **2**

Sydney
Opera House **1**

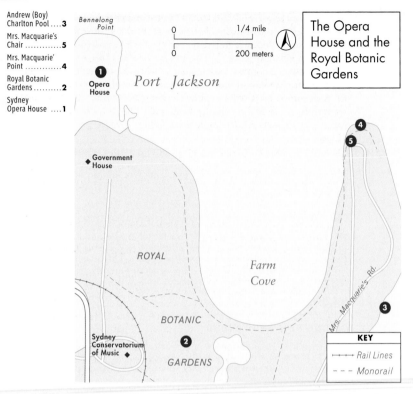

The Opera House and the Royal Botanic Gardens

harbor and the Opera House from the garden's seawall and two lovely restaurants are open for lunch and snacks. ■ TIP➜ For those who don't want to walk, the ChooChoo Express toy-like train offers a 25-minute ride through the gardens, making four stops (A$10).

Completed in 1843, the Government House, in a Gothic Revival building in the Royal Botanic Gardens, served as the residence of the Governor of New South Wales—who represents the British crown in local matters—until the government handed it back to the public in 1996. Prominent English architect Edward Blore designed the two-story building without ever having set foot in Australia. The sandstone house's restored stenciled ceilings are its most impressive feature. Paintings hanging on the walls bear the signatures of some of Australia's best-known artists. You are free to wander on your own around Government House's gardens, which lie within the Royal Botanic Gardens, but you must join a guided tour to see the house's interior. Tours leave from the visitor center, near the Art Gallery of New South Wales. There are also maps available for a variety of themed, self-guided walks. ⊠ *Mrs. Macquaries Rd., The Domain* ☎ *02/9231–8111* ⊕ *www.rbgsyd.nsw. gov.au; www.choochoo.com.au* ✉ *Free* ⊙ *Royal Botanic Gardens daily 7–dusk; tours at 10:30 am and 1 pm.*

Fodor's Choice   **Sydney Opera House.** Sydney's most famous landmark (listed as a World
★   Heritage site in 2007) had such a long and troubled construction phase
that it's almost a miracle that the building was ever completed. In 1954
the state premier appointed a committee to advise the government on
the building of an opera house. The site chosen was Bennelong Point
(named after an early Aboriginal inhabitant), which was, until that
time, occupied by a tram depot. The premier's committee launched
a competition to find a suitable plan, and a total of 233 submissions
came in from architects the world over. One of them was a young Dane
named Joern Utzon.

His plan was brilliant, but it had all the markings of a monumental
disaster. The structure was so narrow that stages would have minuscule
wings, and the soaring "sails" that formed the walls and roof could not
be built by existing technology.

Nonetheless, Utzon's dazzling, dramatic concept caught the judges'
imagination, and construction of the giant podium began in 1959. From
the start, the contractors faced a cost blowout; the building that was
projected to cost A$7 million and take 4 years to erect would eventually
require A$102 million and 15 years. Construction was financed by an
intriguing scheme. Realizing that citizens might be hostile to the use of
public funds for the controversial project, the state government raised
the money through the Opera House Lottery. For almost a decade, Australians lined up to buy tickets, and the Opera House was built without
depriving the state's hospitals or schools of a single cent.

Initially it was thought that the concrete exterior of the building would
have to be cast in place, which would have meant building an enormous
birdcage of scaffolding at even greater expense. Then, as he was peeling
an orange one day, Utzon had a flash of inspiration. Why not construct
the shells from segments of a single sphere? The concrete ribs forming
the skeleton of the building could be prefabricated in just a few molds,
hoisted into position, and joined together. These ribs are clearly visible
inside the Opera House, especially in the foyers and staircases of the
Concert Hall.

In 1966 Utzon resigned as Opera House architect and left Australia,
reportedly embittered by his dealings with unions and the government.
He never returned to see his masterpiece, although he had been invited
on several occasions.

A team of young Australian architects carried on, completing the exterior one year later. Until that time, however, nobody had given much
thought to the *interior*. The shells created awkward interior spaces, and
conventional performance areas were simply not feasible. It's a tribute
to the architectural team's ingenuity that the exterior of the building is
matched by the aesthetically pleasing and acoustically sound theaters
inside. Joern Utzon died in Denmark on November 29, 2008, aged
90. Then Prime Minister Kevin Rudd paid tribute to Utzon's genius
in speeches, while the lights of the Opera House sails were dimmed
and flags on the Harbour Bridge were flown at half-mast as a mark
of respect.

"The Opera House as seen from The Rocks side of Circular Quay" —photo by Gary Ott, Fodors.com member

Sydney Opera House showcases all the performing arts in its five theaters, one of which is devoted to opera. The Australian Ballet, the Sydney Dance Company, and the Australian Opera Company also call the Opera House home. The complex includes two stages for theater, two smaller performance venues—the Playhouse and the Studio—and the 2,700-seat Concert Hall, where the Sydney Symphony Orchestra and the Australian Chamber Orchestra perform. The box office is open Monday to Saturday 9–8:30.

Guided tours include the one-hour Essential Tour, departing daily from the lower forecourt level between 9 and 5; the two-hour backstage tour departing daily at 7 am; and the Tour & Tasting Plate, which is the Essential Tour followed by a three-tier plate of goodies such as Wagyu burgers and fresh seafood from Opera Kitchen restaurant. All tours include discount show tickets. Call in advance for bookings (☎ 02–9250–7250). Visitors are free to walk around inside the building throughout the day and night. ✉ 2 Macquarie St., Circular Quay ☎ 02/9250–7111 ⊕ www.soh.nsw.gov.au ✈ General tour A$35, backstage tour A$155; Tour & Tasting plate A$70.

WORTH NOTING

FAMILY **Andrew (Boy) Charlton Pool.** This heated saltwater eight-lane swimming pool overlooking the navy ships tied up at Garden Island has become a local favorite. Complementing its stunning location is a radical design in glass and steel. The pool also has a chic terrace café above Woolloomooloo Bay. It's open from September 1 until April 30. ✉ 1C Mrs. Macquarie's Rd., The Domain ☎ 02/9358–6686 ⊕ www.abcpool.org ✈ A$6 ⊗ 6 am–7 pm (until 8 pm Oct.–late Mar.).

2

Mrs. Macquarie's Chair. During the early 1800s, Elizabeth Macquarie often sat on the point in the Domain at the east side of Farm Cove, at the rock where a seat has been hewn in her name. The views across the harbor are sensational. ⊠ *Mrs. Macquaries Rd., Royal Botanic Gardens.*

NEED A BREAK?

Botanic Gardens Restaurant. Botanic Gardens Restaurant is a lovely place to have lunch during the week or brunch on the weekend. Wide verandas provide tranquil views over the gardens, and the sound of birdsong fills the air. The menu changes seasonally and may include starters such as grilled quail with roast quince, and main dishes of fettuccine with pine forest mushrooms and macadamia nuts. The downstairs café serves lighter more casual fare and is open daily from 8:30 am to 4 (and later in summer). The restaurant is open for lunch from noon weekdays and brunch on the weekends from 9:30, where decadent eggs Benedict is best accompanied by a glass of bubbly. ■ TIP → The restaurant is within the Royal Botanic Gardens; it can be accessed from either the Palace Gate on Macquarie Street or from Lion Gate on Mrs. Macquarie's Road. ⊠ *Royal Botanic Gardens, Mrs. Macquarie's Rd., Royal Botanic Gardens* ☎ *02/9241–2419* ⊕ *www.rbgsyd.nsw.gov.au.*

Mrs. Macquarie's Point. The inspiring views from this point, to the east of Bennelong Point (site of the Opera House), combine with the shady lawns to make this a popular place for picnics. The views are best at dusk, when the setting sun silhouettes the Opera House and the Harbour Bridge. ⊠ *Mrs. Macquaries Rd., Royal Botanic Gardens.*

DARLING HARBOUR

Until the mid-1980s this horseshoe-shape bay on the city center's western edge was a wasteland of disused docks and railway yards. Then, in an explosive burst of activity the whole area was redeveloped and opened in time for Australia's bicentenary in 1988. Now there's plenty to take in at the Darling Harbour complex: the National Maritime Museum, SEA LIFE Sydney Aquarium, WILD LIFE Sydney Zoo, and the gleaming Exhibition Centre, whose masts and spars recall the square-riggers that once berthed here. At the harbor's center is a large park shaded by palm trees. Waterways and fountains lace the complex together.

GETTING HERE AND AROUND

Take the train to either Town Hall or Central Station. From Town Hall it's a short walk down Druitt Street; from Central you walk through Haymarket and Chinatown, passing by the Sydney Entertainment Centre. The Light Rail tram (A$3.50 one-way; day pass A$9) connects Central Station with Darling Harbour and The Star casino a little farther to the west.

TOP ATTRACTIONS

FAMILY **Australian National Maritime Museum.** The six galleries of this soaring, futuristic building tell the story of Australia and the sea. In addition to figureheads, model ships, and brassy nautical hardware, there are

Australian
National
Maritime
Museum **1**

Chinatown **10**

Chinese Garden of
Friendship **9**

Cockle Bay
Wharf **6**

LG IMAX
Theatre **7**

Madame Tussauds
Sydney **5**

Powerhouse
Museum **8**

Pyrmont
Bridge **2**

SEA LIFE Sydney
Aquarium **4**

WILD LIFE Sydney
World **3**

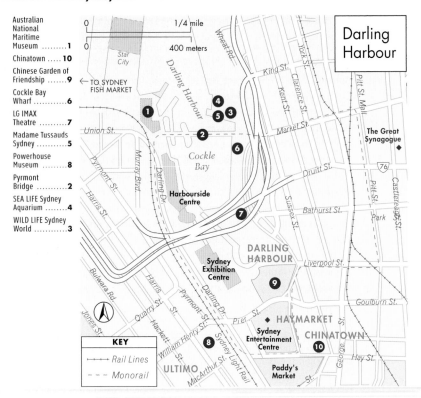

antique racing yachts and the jet-powered *Spirit of Australia,* current
holder of the world water speed record, set in 1978. The USA Gallery displays objects from such major U.S. collections as the Smithsonian Institution, and was dedicated by President George Bush Sr. on
New Year's Day 1992. An outdoor section showcases numerous vessels
moored at the museum's wharves, including the HMAS *Vampire,* a
retired Royal Australian Navy destroyer, and the historic tall ship the
James Craig. You can also climb to the top of the 1874 Bowling Green
lighthouse for free. ⊠ *Wharf 7, Maritime Heritage Centre, 2 Murray
St., Darling Harbour* ☎ *02/9298–3777* ⊕ *www.anmm.gov.au* 🖅 *Free*
☉ *Daily 9:30–5 (until 6 in Jan.).*

Madame Tussauds Sydney. Hugh Jackman as Wolverine, songstress Kylie
Minogue, and Olympic champion Cathy Freeman are among the con-
tingent of Australian wax figures at the new Madame Tussauds Sydney, the only version of the well-known museum in Australia. Located
between SEA LIFE Sydney Aquarium and WILD LIFE Sydney Zoo at
Darling Harbour, the museum has nine interactive themed areas where
patrons can, for example, jump on a surfboard with world champion
female surfer Layne Beachley or sing in the band with legendary Aussie rocker Jimmy Barnes. The 70 figures are grouped in themes such as
world leaders, cultural icons, and music and film stars. ▓ TIP➔ Save

more than A$12 on the "walk-up" price by buying single-entry tickets or combination tickets (which include any of four other attractions) online. ✉ *Aquarium Wharf near Wheat St., Darling Harbour* ☎ *02/8251–7800* ⊕ *www.madametussauds.com/sydney* 🎫 *A$38* ☉ *Daily 9–8.*

FAMILY
Fodor'sChoice
★

SEA LIFE Sydney Aquarium. Bay of Rays and Shark Valley are among 14 new themed areas at the revamped SEA LIFE Sydney Aquarium at Darling Harbour. Home to some 13,000 creatures, the huge aquarium also has two of only five dugongs (large, rare marine mammal [similar to a manatee] mainly found off the coast of northern Australia) that are on display anywhere in the world. The Sydney Harbour exhibit shows you what's underneath Sydney's huge expanse of water, while the new open coral tank is dazzlingly colorful. Fish and mammal feedings take place throughout the day, along with talks on some of these amazing creatures. A behind-the-scenes tour is good value at A$25 over the admission price. The aquarium is part of the Merlin Entertainments group and good combination ticket deals are available for the company's other attractions that include WILD LIFE Sydney Zoo, the new Madame Tussauds (both located next door to the Aquarium), and the Sydney Tower Eye (A$63). ■ TIP➜ Buy tickets online to save around A$14 on single-entry and various combo deals. ✉ *Aquarium pier, 1–5 Wheat Rd., Darling Harbour* ☎ *02/8251–7800* ⊕ *www.sydneyaquarium.com. au* 🎫 *A$38* ☉ *Daily 9–8.*

WORTH NOTING

Chinatown. Bounded by the Entertainment Centre, George Street, Goulburn Street, and Paddy's Market, Chinatown takes your senses on a galloping tour of the Orient. Within this compact grid are aromatic restaurants, traditional apothecaries, Chinese grocers, clothing boutiques, and shops selling Asian-made electronics. The best way to get a sense of the area is to take a stroll along Dixon Street, now a pedestrian mall with a Chinese Lion Gate at either end. Sydney's Chinese community was first established here in the 1800s, in the aftermath of the gold rush that originally drew many Chinese immigrants to Australia. For the next few years the area will be getting a major face-lift that will include new lighting, artwork, and more pedestrian walkways. Most Sydneysiders come here regularly to dine, especially on weekends for dim sum (called *yum cha*). ✉ *Dixon St., Haymarket.*

Chinese Garden of Friendship. Chinese prospectors came to the Australian goldfields as far back as the 1850s, and the nation's long and enduring links with China are symbolized by the Chinese Garden of Friendship, the largest garden of its kind outside China. Designed by Chinese landscape architects, the garden includes bridges, lakes, waterfalls, sculptures, and Cantonese-style pavilions—the perfect place for a refreshing cup of tea from the café. ✉ *38 Harbour St., Darling Harbour* ☎ *02/9240–8888* ⊕ *www.darlingharbour.com* 🎫 *A$6* ☉ *Daily 9:30–5.*

Cockle Bay Wharf. Fueling Sydney's addiction to fine food, most of this sprawling waterfront complex, on the city side of Darling Harbour, is dedicated to gastronomy. This is also the site of Sydney's biggest nightclub, Home. If you have a boat you can dock at the marina—and avoid the hassle of parking a car in one of the city's most congested

centers. ⊠ *201 Sussex St., Darling Harbour* ☎ *02/9269–9800* ⊕ *www.
cocklebaywharf.com.*

**NEED A
BREAK?**

Blackbird Café. Blackbird Café is great place to take a break while exploring Darling Harbour. The weekday lunch special of A$19.90 and bever-
age is a good deal, while happy hour (3–6 pm) has beers and cocktails at
affordable prices. There are great views from the balcony, so try and nab a
table there. The à la carte menu includes starters of haloumi and vegetable
stack or grilled prawns and crab, and there's a wide range of pizza, pasta,
burgers, and grills. ⊠ *Balcony level, Cockle Bay Wharf, 201 Sussex St.,
Darling Harbour* ☎ *02/9283-7385* ⊕ *www.blackbirdcafe.com.au.*

FAMILY **LG IMAX Theatre.** Both in size and impact, this eight-story-tall movie
screen is overwhelming. One-hour presentations take you on aston-
ishing, wide-angle voyages of discovery under the oceans and to the
summit of the world's highest mountains. ⊠ *Southern Promenade, 31
Wheat Rd., Darling Harbour* ☎ *02/9281–3300* ⊕ *www.imax.com.au*
⊠ *A$21.50–A$31.50* ⊙ *Daily 10–10.*

FAMILY **Powerhouse Museum.** Learning the principles of science is a painless process with this museum's stimulating, interactive displays ideal for all
ages. Exhibits in the former 1890s electricity station that once powered Sydney's trams include a whole floor of working steam engines,
space modules, airplanes suspended from the ceiling, state-of-the-art
computer gadgetry, and a 1930s art deco–style movie-theater auditorium. The museum also stages many excellent exhibitions that are
not science-based such as "The Beatles in Australia" show, which
documents the group's 1964 tour. ⊠ *500 Harris St., Ultimo, Darling
Harbour* ☎ *02/9217–0111* ⊕ *www.powerhousemuseum.com* ⊠ *A$12*
⊙ *Daily 10–5.*

Pyrmont Bridge. Dating from 1902, this is the world's oldest electrically
operated swing-span bridge. The structure once carried motor traffic,
but it's now a walkway that links Darling Harbour's western side with
Cockle Bay on the east. The center span still swings open to allow tall-
masted ships into Cockle Bay, which sits at the bottom of the horseshoe-
shaped shore. ⊠ *Darling Harbour.*

**OFF THE
BEATEN
PATH**

Sydney Fish Market. Second in size only to Tokyo's giant Tsukiji fish market, Sydney's is a showcase for the riches of Australia's seas. An easy
10-minute walk from Darling Harbour (and with its own stop on the
Metro Light Rail network), the market is a great place to sample sushi,
oysters, octopus, spicy Thai and Chinese fish dishes, and fish-and-chips
at the waterfront cafés overlooking the fishing fleet. Behind the scenes
guided tours, including the auction, begin at 6:40 am and run until 8:30
am on Monday, Thursday, and Friday ($A25). They also offer cooking
classes. Call ahead for advance reservations or book on the website.
⊠ *Pyrmont Bridge Rd. at Bank St., Pyrmont West* ☎ *02/9004–1100*
⊕ *www.sydneyfishmarket.com.au* ⊙ *Daily 7 am–4 pm.*

FAMILY **WILD LIFE Sydney Zoo.** This recently renamed Sydney attraction brings
thousands of Australian animals right to the heart of Sydney. Kangaroos, koalas, and dozens of other species come together under the one

The Maritime Museum at Darling Harbour

huge roof—in nine separate habitats—next door to the SEA LIFE Sydney Aquarium and the new Madame Tussauds. All three attractions are run by the same operator, Merlin Entertainments, and all are able to be visited on one combination ticket. In Devil's Den you'll see the famed Tasmanian devils; in Wallaby Cliffs there are yellow-footed wallabies and hairy-nosed wombats, while you can walk among the eastern gray kangaroos and agile wallabies with their joeys and the spiky echidnas in Kangaroo Walkabout. Watch out for Rex, the 5-meter (16.4-foot) saltwater crocodile in the Kadadu Gorge habitat. A popular spot is Gum Tree Alley where you'll meet koalas, while the endangered (and very cute) Greater Bilby is in the Nightfall nocturnal zone. Those who really want to get up close to the critters should book the Breakfast with the Koalas tour (A$55) that takes place on weekend mornings at 7:30 am. It includes zoo entry, private guided tour, hot breakfast on the rooftop surrounded by the furry creatures, and a chance to pose for photographs. ■TIP➔ The best deals for stand-alone tickets or combination tickets with other Merlin Entertainment attractions are online. There are savings of around A$12 for a single ticket, while the current combo ticket is just A$63. ⊠ *Aquarium Pier, Wheat Rd., Darling Harbour* ☎ *02/9333–9288* ⊕ *www.sydneywildlifeworld.com.au* ✉ *A$38* ☼ *Apr.–Sept., daily 9–5; Oct.–Mar., daily 9–8.*

SYDNEY CITY CENTER

Shopping is the main reason to visit Sydney's city center, but there are several buildings and other places of interest among the office blocks, department stores, and shopping centers.

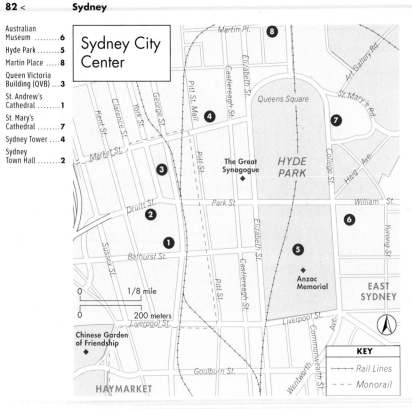

Australian
Museum 6

Hyde Park 5

Martin Place 8

Queen Victoria
Building (QVB) ...3

St. Andrew's
Cathedral 1

St. Mary's
Cathedral 7

Sydney Tower 4

Sydney
Town Hall 2

Sydney City Center

Martin Pl. ⑧

Queens Square

Pitt St. Mall ④

⑦

The Great
Synagogue ♦

⑦

**HYDE
PARK**

Market St.

③

②

①

⑥

Bathurst St.

⑤

Anzac
Memorial

**EAST
SYDNEY**

0 ⊢——⊣ 1/8 mile

0 ⊢——⊣ 200 meters

Chinese Garden
of Friendship ♦

HAYMARKET

KEY	
├──┤	*Rail Lines*
– – –	*Monorail*

GETTING HERE AND AROUND

Buses from the eastern suburbs run along Elizabeth Street on the western side of Hyde Park; buses from the inner western suburbs such as Balmain travel to and from the Queen Victoria Building. The main train stations are Town Hall and Martin Place, while Hyde Park is served by both St. James and Museum Station on the City Circle rail line. The free shuttle bus (No. 555) completes a circuit around the city center, stopping at the main attractions.

TOP ATTRACTIONS

FAMILY **Australian Museum.** The strength of this natural-history museum, a well-respected academic institution, is its collection of plants, animals, geological specimens, and cultural artifacts from the Asia-Pacific region. Particularly notable are the collections of artifacts from Papua New Guinea and from Australia's Aboriginal peoples. One of the most popular exhibits is "Dinosaurs" on Level 2, containing 10 complete skeletons, 8 life-size models and interactive displays, while "Surviving Australia" (about Australian animals) and "Indigenous Australia" are the most popular with overseas visitors. There are behind-the-scene tours (A$88), an excellent shop, and a lively café. ⊠ *6 College St., near William St., Hyde Park* ☎ *02/9320–6000, 02/9320–6009* ⊕ *www.*

2

australianmuseum.net.au ✉ *A$12* ◎ *Daily 9:30–5; free guided tours daily 11 and 2.*

Hyde Park. Declared public land by Governor Phillip in 1792 and used for the colony's earliest cricket matches and horse races, this area was turned into a park in 1810. The gardens are formal, with fountains, statuary, and tree-lined walks, and its tranquil lawns are popular with office workers at lunchtime. The park has two sections, with Park Street (a traffic street) dividing the two halves. Several events, such as the Night Noodle Markets (open-air Asian food markets) in October, are held in the park. ⊠ *Elizabeth, College, and Park Sts., Hyde Park* ⊕ *www.cityofsydney.nsw.gov.au.*

Anzac Memorial. In the southern section of Hyde Park (near Liverpool Street) stands the 1934 art deco Anzac Memorial, a tribute to the Australians who died in military service during World War I, when the acronym ANZAC (Australian and New Zealand Army Corps) was coined. The 120,000 gold stars inside the dome represent each man and woman of New South Wales who served. The lower level exhibits war-related photographs, and a beautiful, poignant sculpture of an ANZAC soldier and shield. ⊠ *Hyde Park* ☎ *02/9267–7668* ◎ *Daily 9–5.*

Fodor'sChoice
★

Sydney Tower. Short of taking a scenic flight, a visit to the top of this 309-meter (1,000-foot) golden-turret-topped spike is the best way to see Sydney's spectacular layout. This is the city's tallest building, and the views from its indoor observation deck encompass the entire Sydney metropolitan area. You can often see as far as the Blue Mountains, more than 80 km (50 miles) away. You can view it all from the Sydney Tower Eye Observation Deck 820 feet above the city streets, or for an adrenaline kick don a safety harness and do the Sky Walk, a guided walk around the outside of the golden turret some 880 feet above the city. Walkers are attached to the tower's superstructure by harness lines. A combination ticket for Sky Walk, the Eye Observation Deck (which includes a 4-D cinema), and three other Sydney attractions—including SEA LIFE Sydney Aquarium—is a great deal at A$99 when purchased online. ■ TIP➜ The building houses two restaurants in the turret. ⊠ *100 Market St., between Pitt and Castlereagh Sts., City Center* ☎ *02/9333–9222* ⊕ *www.sydneytowereye.com.au* ✉ *Eye Observation deck A$26, with Sky Walk A$69; cheaper tickets available on line* ◎ *Sydney Tower daily 9 am–10:30 pm; Sky Walk daily 9:30 am–8:45 pm.*

WORTH NOTING

NEED A
BREAK?

Marble Bar. Stop in at the Marble Bar to experience a masterpiece of Victorian extravagance. The 1890 bar was formerly in another building that was constructed on the profits of the horse-racing track, thus establishing the link between gambling and majestic public architecture that has its modern-day parallel in the Sydney Opera House. Threatened with demolition in the 1970s, the whole bar was moved—marble arches, color-glass ceiling, elaborately carved woodwork, paintings of voluptuous nudes, and all—to its present site in the basement of the Hilton Sydney Hotel. There is

The fountain in Hyde Park with the Australian Museum in the background

live music at night from Thursday to Saturday. ⊠ *Hilton Sydney, 488 George St., City Center* ☎ *02/9265-6026* ⊕ *www.marblebarsydney.com.au.*

Martin Place. Sydney's largest pedestrian precinct, flanked by banks, offices, and shopping centers, is the hub of the central business district. There are some grand buildings here—including the beautifully refurbished Commonwealth Bank and the 1870s Venetian Renaissance–style General Post Office building with its 230-foot clock tower (now a Westin hotel). Toward the George Street end of the plaza the simple 1929 cenotaph war memorial commemorates Australians who died in World War I. ⊠ *Between Macquarie and George Sts., City Center* ⊕ *www. sydneyofcity.nsw.gov.au.*

Queen Victoria Building (QVB). Originally the city's produce market, this huge 1898 sandstone structure was handsomely restored with sweeping staircases, enormous stained-glass windows, and the 1-ton Royal Clock, which hangs from the glass roof. The clock chimes the hour from 9 am to 9 pm with four tableaux: the second shows Queen Elizabeth I knighting Sir Frances Drake; the last ends with an executioner chopping off King Charles I's head. The complex includes more than 200 boutiques and restaurants including the lovely Tea Room on level 3. Boutiques on the upper floors are generally more upscale. ⊠ *455 George St., City Center* ☎ *02/9264-9209* ⊕ *www.qvb.com.au* ☉ *Fri.–Wed. 8 am–6 pm, Thurs. 8 am–9 pm.*

St. Andrew's Cathedral. The foundation stone for Sydney's Gothic Revival Anglican cathedral—the country's oldest—was laid in 1819, although the original architect, Francis Greenway, fell from grace soon after work began. Edmund Blacket, Sydney's most illustrious church architect, was responsible for its final design and completion—a whopping 50 years later in 1868. Notable features of the sandstone construction include ornamental windows depicting Jesus's life and a great east window with images relating to St. Andrew. ⊠ *George and Bathurst Sts., next to Town Hall, City Center* ☎ *02/9265–1661* ⊕ *www.sydneycathedral. com* ⊙ *Mon.–Sat. 10–4, Sun. for services only 8:30 am, 10:30 am; Wed. healing service 6 pm; tours by arrangement.*

St. Mary's Cathedral. The first St. Mary's was built here in 1821, but fire destroyed the chapel. Work on the present cathedral began in 1868. The spires weren't added until 2000, however. St. Mary's has some particularly fine stained-glass windows and a terrazzo floor in the crypt, where exhibitions are often held. The cathedral's large rose window was imported from England.

At the front of the cathedral stand statues of Cardinal Moran and Archbishop Kelly, two Irishmen who were prominent in Australia's Roman Catholic Church. Due to the high proportion of Irish men and women in the convict population, the Roman Catholic Church was often the voice of the oppressed in 19th-century Sydney, where anti-Catholic feeling ran high among the Protestant rulers. Call to check ahead for tours. Separate tours take in the cathedral, the crypt, and the bell tower. ⊠ *College and Cathedral Sts., Hyde Park* ☎ *02/9220–0400* ☎ *Tours free* ⊙ *Weekdays 6:30 am–6:30 pm, Sat. 8–7:30, Sun. 6:30 am–7:30 pm; tours operate at various times.*

Sydney Town Hall. Sydney's most ornate Victorian building—an elaborate sandstone structure—underwent a A$60 million upgrade in 2009 to spruce up its grand interior spaces, especially the vestibule and large Centennial Hall. A centerpiece of the building is the massive 8,000-pipe Grand Organ, one of the world's most powerful, which is used for lunchtime concerts. Tours, conducted by the "Friends of Town Hall" for A$5, can be booked through the website. Mingle with locals on the marble steps of the front entrance. ⊠ *483 George St., City Center* ☎ *02/9265–9198 general inquiries* ⊕ *www.cityofsydney.nsw.gov. au* ☎ *Free* ⊙ *Weekdays 8–6.*

INNER CITY AND THE EASTERN SUBURBS

Sydney's inner city and eastern suburbs are truly the people's domain. They are the hip zones of Sydney featuring the foodie precincts as well as some of the most expensive real estate, great shopping, and the most accessible beaches. Architecture ranges from the mansions of the colonial aristocracy and the humble laborers' cottages of the same period to the modernized terrace houses of Paddington, one of Sydney's most charming and most desirable suburbs. A good way to explore the area is to take the Bondi & Bays Explorer bus that stops at 10 sites including Bondi Beach, Double Bay, Paddington, and Rose Bay.

GETTING HERE AND AROUND

The inner city and eastern suburbs are well served by buses, although the journey out to the eastern suburbs beaches can be quite long in peak hour. Most depart from Circular Quay (Alfred Street). Travel to

Centennial
Park **5**

Elizabeth Bay **2**

Elizabeth Bay
House **1**

Paddington **6**

Sydney Jewish
Museum **3**

Victoria
Barracks **4**

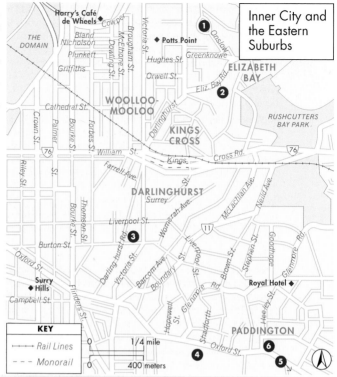

Paddington and Bondi is on Nos. 380, 333, and 382; and to Watsons
Bay and Vaucluse (via Double Bay and Rose Bay) on Nos. 323, 324,
and 325. Buses 380, 382, and 333 travel along Oxford Street, the main
artery of the alternative (and gay) neighborhood of Darlinghurst. It
is quicker to take the train to Edgecliff or Bondi Junction stations to
connect with buses traveling to many of the eastern suburbs including Coogee and Clovelly. A ferry operates between Circular Quay and
Watsons Bay, calling at Garden Island, Darling Point, Double Bay, and
Rose Bay. It is an easy walk to Darlinghurst and Surry Hills from the
city center, while Kings Cross has its own train station, just one stop
from the city center.

TOP ATTRACTIONS

Elizabeth Bay. Much of this densely populated but still-charming harborside suburb was originally part of the extensive Elizabeth Bay House
grounds. Wrought-iron balconies and French doors on some of the
older apartment blocks give the area a Mediterranean flavor. During
the 1920s and 1930s this was a fashionably bohemian quarter, and
it remains a favorite among artists and writers. ⊠ *Elizabeth Bay Rd.,
Elizabeth Bay.*

Elizabeth Bay House. This 1835–39 mansion was regarded in its heyday as the "finest house in the colony." It retains little of its original

furniture, although the rooms have been restored in Georgian style. The most striking feature is an oval-shaped salon with a winding staircase, naturally lighted by glass panels in the domed roof. The view from the front-facing windows across Elizabeth Bay is stunning. A variety of soirees and talks are held in the house throughout the year. ✉ *7 Onslow Ave., Elizabeth Bay* ☎ *02/9356–3022* ⊕ *www.hht.net.au* 💵 *A$8* ⊙ *Fri.– Sun. 11–4.*

Sydney Jewish Museum. Artifacts, interactive displays, and audiovisual displays chronicle the history of Australian Jews and commemorate the 6 million killed in the Holocaust. Exhibits are brilliantly arranged on eight levels, which lead upward in chronological order, from the handful of Jews who arrived with the First Fleet in 1788 to the 30,000 concentration-camp survivors who came after World War II—one of the largest populations of Holocaust survivors to be found anywhere. A 40-minute guided tour starts at noon on Monday, Wednesday, Friday, and Sunday. ✉ *148 Darlinghurst Rd., Darlinghurst* ☎ *02/9360–7999* ⊕ *www.sydneyjewishmuseum.com.au* 💵 *A$10* ⊙ *Sun.–Thurs. 10–4, Fri. 10–2.*

WORTH NOTING

Centennial Park. More than 500 acres of palm-lined avenues, groves of Moreton Bay figs, paperbark tree–fringed lakes, and cycling and horse-riding tracks make this a popular park and Sydney's favorite workout circuit. In the early 1800s the marshy land at the lower end provided Sydney with its fresh water. The park was proclaimed in 1888, the centenary of Australia's founding as a colony. The Centennial Park Café is often crowded on weekends, but a mobile canteen between the lakes in the middle of the park serves snacks and espresso. Bikes and blades can be rented from the nearby Clovelly Road outlets, on the eastern side of the park. The Moonlight Cinema screens movies during the summer months. ✉ *Oxford St. at Centennial Ave., Centennial Park* ☎ *02/9339– 6600* ⊕ *www.centennialparklands.com.au* ⊙ *Daily dawn–dusk.*

OFF THE
BEATEN
PATH

Harry's Café de Wheels. The attraction of this all-day dockyard food stall is not so much the delectable meat pies and coffee served as the clientele. Famous opera singers, actors, and international rock stars have been spotted here rubbing shoulders with shift workers and taxi drivers. This "pie cart" has been a Sydney institution since 1945, when the late Harry "Tiger" Edwards set up his van to serve sailors from the nearby Garden Island base. Drop in any time from 8:30 am (9 am on weekends) until the wee hours for a Tiger Pie, made with mushy peas, mashed potatoes, and gravy. Harry's now has nine other locations in Sydney. ✉ *1 Cowper Wharf Rd., Woolloomooloo* ☎ *02/9357–3074* ⊕ *www.harryscafedewheels.com.au.*

Paddington. Most of this suburb's elegant two-story terrace houses were built during the 1880s, when the colony experienced a long period of economic growth following the gold rushes that began in the 1860s. The balconies are trimmed with decorative wrought iron, sometimes known as Paddington lace, which initially came from England and later from Australian foundries. Rebuilt and repainted, the now-stylish Paddington terrace houses give the area its characteristic village-like charm.

The Oxford Street shopping strip is full of upscale and funky boutiques, cafés, and several good pubs. ⊠ *Oxford St. between Boundary and Queen Sts., Paddington.*

Royal Hotel. The Royal Hotel is an enjoyable Victorian pub with leather couches and stained-glass windows. It's a good place to stop for something cool to drink. The top floor has a balcony restaurant that's popular on sunny afternoons. ⊠ *237 Glenmore Rd., Paddington* ☎ *02/9331–2604.*

Victoria Barracks. If you're curious about the Australian military, you'll enjoy the free tours of this Regency-style barracks (built from 1841), which take place every Thursday at 10 am sharp. The tour includes entry to the Army Museum of New South Wales, which has exhibits covering Australia's military history from the days of the Rum Corps to the Malayan conflict of the 1950s. ⊠ *Oxford St. at Oatley Rd., Paddington* ☎ *02/8335–5330* ⊕ *www.armymuseumnsw.com.au* ⌨ *Tours free, museum only A$2* ☉ *Museum Thurs. 10–1, Sun. 10–4.*

GREATER SYDNEY

The Greater Sydney area has numerous attractions that can be easily reached by public transport. These include historic townships, the Sydney 2000 Olympics site, national parks where you can experience the Australian bush, and wildlife and theme parks that appeal to children.

Other points of interest are the north-side beaches, particularly Manly, and the historic city of Parramatta, founded in 1788 and 26 km (16 miles) to the west; and the magnificent Hawkesbury River, which winds its way around the city's western and northern regions. The waterside suburb of Balmain has pubs and restaurants, an atmospheric Saturday flea market, and backstreets full of character.

GETTING HERE AND AROUND

Trains travel from Central Station to Parramatta daily, and directly to Sydney Olympic Park on weekdays. To reach Olympic Park on weekends, take the train to Lidcombe and then change trains for the short ride to Olympic Park station. The RiverCat ferry travels from Circular Quay to Parramatta, calling at Sydney Olympic Park on the way. Trains depart from Central Station for the Hawkesbury River (alight at Hawkesbury River station in the town of Brooklyn). They also travel to the Royal National Park (alight at Engadine or Heathcote stations, or Loftus, where a tram travels from the station to the park on Sundays only).

TIMING

Each of the sights here could easily fill the better part of a day. If you're short on time, try a tour company that combines visits within a particular area—for example, a day trip west to the Olympic Games site, Featherdale Wildlife Park, and the Blue Mountains.

TOP ATTRACTIONS

FAMILY **Featherdale Wildlife Park.** This is the place to see kangaroos, dingoes, wallabies, and echidnas (and even feed some of them) in native bush settings 40 km (25 miles) west of Sydney. You can have your picture

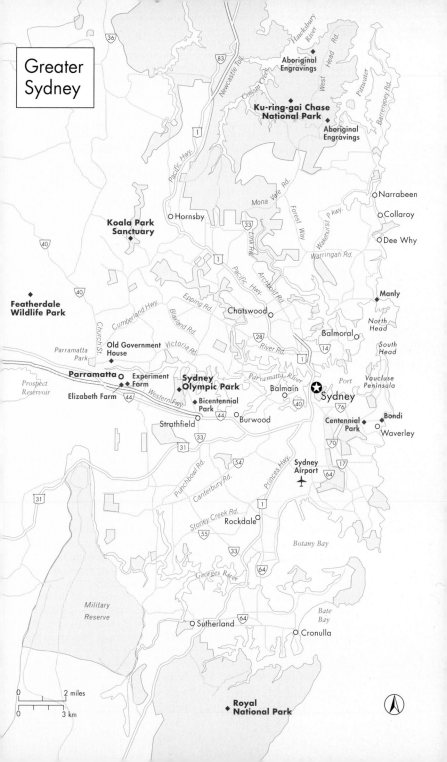

Greater Sydney

Aboriginal Engravings

Ku-ring-gai Chase National Park

Aboriginal Engravings

Narrabeen

Collaroy

Dee Why

○ Hornsby

Koala Park Sanctuary

Manly

North Head

Featherdale Wildlife Park

Chatswood

Balmoral

South Head

Parramatta Park

Old Government House

Sydney Olympic Park

Parramatta

Experiment Farm

Balmain

★ **Sydney**

Vaucluse Peninsula

Prospect Reservoir

Elizabeth Farm

Bicentennial Park

Centennial Park

Bondi

Waverley

Strathfield

Burwood

Sydney Airport

Rockdale

Botany Bay

Military Reserve

Bate Bay

○ Sutherland

○ Cronulla

0   2 miles
0   3 km

Royal National Park

taken with a koala for free. The daily crocodile feeding sessions are very popular. Take the train to Blacktown station and then board the 725 bus for the park. ■ TIP→ **The park is on the way to the Blue Mountains.** ✉ *217 Kildare Rd., Doonside* ☎ *02/9622–1644* ⊕ *www.featherdale. com.au* 🖃 *A$28* ⊘ *Daily 9–5.*

Parramatta. This bustling satellite city 26 km (16 miles) west of Sydney is one of Australia's most historic precincts. Its origins as a European settlement are purely agrarian. The sandy, rocky soil around Sydney Cove was too poor to feed the fledgling colony, so Governor Phillip looked to the banks of the Parramatta River for the rich alluvial soil they needed. In 1789, just a year after the first convicts-cum-settlers arrived, Phillip established Rosehill, an area set aside for agriculture. The community developed as its agricultural successes grew, and several important buildings survive as outstanding examples of the period. The two-hour self-guided Harris Park Heritage Walk, which departs from the River-Cat Ferry Terminal, connects the key historic sites and buildings. The ferry departs at frequent intervals from Sydney's Circular Quay, and is a relaxing, scenic alternative to the drive or train ride from the city. A free shuttle bus travels in a loop around Parramatta. ■ TIP→ **A good place to start discovering Parramatta is the Heritage Centre at 346A Church Street.** ✉ *Parramatta* ⊕ *www.discoverparramatta.com* ⊘ *Daily 9–5.*

Elizabeth Farm. The oldest European building in Australia, Elizabeth Farm was built by John and Elizabeth Macarthur in 1793. With its simple but elegant lines and long, shady verandas, the house became a template for Australian farmhouses that survives to the present day. It was here, too, that the merino sheep industry began, since the Macarthurs were the first to introduce the tough Spanish breed to Australia. Although John Macarthur has traditionally been credited as the father of Australia's wool industry, it was Elizabeth who largely ran the farm while her husband pursued his official and more-lucrative unofficial duties as an officer in the colony's Rum Corps. Inside are personal objects of the Macarthur family, as well as a re-creation of their furnishings. Free tours are at 11, noon, 1, and 2 each day. ✉ *70 Alice St., Rosehill* ☎ *02/9635–9488* ⊕ *www.hht.net.au/museums* 🖃 *A$8* ⊘ *Weekends 10:30–3.*

Experiment Farm. The site of the first private land grant in Australia, Experiment Farm was settled in 1789 by James Ruse, a former convict who was given 1½ acres by Governor Phillip on condition that he become self-sufficient—a vital experiment if the colony was to survive. Luckily for Phillip, his gamble paid off. The bungalow, with its wide verandas, was built by colonial surgeon John Harris in the 1830s; it contains a fine collection of Australian colonial furniture, and the cellar now houses an exhibition on the life and work of James Ruse. The surrounding ornamental garden is most beautiful in early summer, when the floral perfumes are strongest. ✉ *9 Ruse St., Harris Park* ☎ *02/9635–5655* ⊕ *www.nationaltrust.org* 🖃 *A$7; A$13 combined ticket with Old Government House* ⊘ *Wed.–Sun. 10:30–3:30, last guided tour at 3.*

Old Government House. On the bank of the Parramatta River, Old Government House (which was the country resident of Sydney's 10

A bird's-eye view of the boats in Parramatta River

early governors) is Australia's oldest surviving public building, and a notable work from the Georgian period. Built by governors John Hunter and Lachlan Macquarie, the building has been faithfully restored in keeping with its origins, and contains the nation's most significant collection of early Australian furniture. In the 260-acre parkland surrounding the house are Governor Brisbane's bathhouse and observatory and the Government House Dairy. ⊠ *Inside Parramatta Park, Parramatta* ☎ *02/9635–8149* ⊕ *www.nsw.nationaltrust.org.au* ◺ *A\$9; A\$13 combined ticket with Experiment Farm* ◷ *Tues.–Sun. 10–4, last guided tour at 3:30.*

NEED A BREAK? **Parramatta Park Cafe.** After visiting Old Government House, amble down to the bank of the river and pull up a seat in this shady spot, which was the park's former visitors' center. It's open for all-day breakfast, brunch, and lunch daily with a menu of gourmet burgers, soup, pastas, and sweet treats. ⊠ *Parramatta Park, Byrnes Ave., Parramatta* ☎ *02/9630–0144.*

Royal National Park. Established in 1879 on the coast south of Sydney, the Royal has the distinction of being the first national park in Australia and the second in the world, after Yellowstone National Park in the United States. Several walking tracks traverse the grounds, most of them requiring little or no hiking experience. The Lady Carrington Walk, a 10-km (6-mile) trek, is a self-guided tour that crosses 15 creeks and passes several historic sites. Other tracks take you along the coast past beautiful wildflower displays and through patches of rain forest. You can canoe the Port Hacking River upstream from the Audley Causeway; rentals are available at the Audley boat shed on the river.

The Illawarra train line, from Central Station, stops at Loftus, Engadine, Heathcote, Waterfall, and Otford stations, where most of the park's walking tracks begin. There are three campsites in the park. ⊠ *Royal National Park* ✛ *Royal National Park Visitor Centre, 35 km (22 miles) south of Sydney via Princes Hwy. to Farnell Ave., south of Loftus, or McKell Ave. at Waterfall* ☎ *02/9542–0648 Royal National park, 02/9542–0666 National Parks and Wildlife Service district office, 02/9542–0683 campsite reservations* ⊕ *www.nationalparks.nsw.gov.au* 🖃 *A$11 per vehicle per day, overnight camping A$10–A$28; booking required* ⊗ *Daily 7 am–8:30 pm.*

WORTH NOTING

FAMILY **Koala Park Sanctuary.** At this private park in Sydney's northern outskirts you can feed a kangaroo or cuddle a koala. (Koala presentations are daily at 10:20, 11:45, 2, and 3.) The sanctuary also has dingoes, wombats, emus, and wallaroos. There are sheep-shearing and boomerang-throwing demonstrations. ⊠ *84 Castle Hill Rd., West Pennant Hills* ☎ *02/9484–3141* ⊕ *www.koalaparksanctuary.com.au* 🖃 *A$26* ⊗ *Daily 9–5.*

Ku-ring-gai Chase National Park. Nature hikes here lead past rock engravings and paintings by the Guringai Aboriginal tribe, the area's original inhabitants for whom the park is named. Created in the 1890s, the park mixes large stands of eucalyptus trees with moist, rain-forest-filled gullies where swamp wallabies, possums, goannas, and other creatures roam. The delightful trails are mostly easy or moderate, including the compelling 3-km (2-mile) Garigal Aboriginal Heritage Walk at West Head, which takes in ancient rock-art sites. From Mt. Ku-ring-gai train station you can walk the 3-km (2-mile) Ku-ring-gai Track to Appletree Bay, while the 30-minute, wheelchair-accessible Discovery Trail is an excellent introduction to the region's flora and fauna. Leaflets on all of the walks are available at the park's entry stations and from the Wildlife Shop at Bobbin Head.

The park is 24 km (15 miles) north of Sydney. Railway stations at Mt. Ku-ring-gai, Berowra, and Cowan, close to the park's western border, provide access to walking trails. On Sunday, for example, you can walk from Mt. Ku-ring-gai station to Appletree Bay and then to Bobbin Head, where a bus can take you to the Turramurra railway station. By car, take the Pacific Highway to Pymble. Then turn into Bobbin Head Road or continue on the highway to Mt. Colah and turn off into the park on Ku-ring-gai Chase Road. You can also follow the Pacific Highway to Pymble and then drive along the Mona Vale Road to Terry Hills and take the West Head turnoff.

For more information on the park, contact the Sydney North Region Information Centre, which is located in the historic Bobbin Inn. ⊠ *Ku-ring-gai Chase National Park, Bobbin Head Rd., Mount Colah* ☎ *02/9472–8949* ⊕ *www.nationalparks.nsw.gov.au.*

Sydney Olympic Park. The center of the 2000 Olympic and Paralympic Games lies 14 km (8½ miles) west of the city center. Sprawling across 1,900 acres on the shores of Homebush Bay, the site is a series of majestic stadiums, arenas, and accommodation complexes. Among the park's sports facilities are an aquatic center, archery range, tennis center, and the centerpiece: the 85,000-seat ANZ Olympic Stadium. Since the conclusion of the 2000 Games it has been used for major sporting events like the 2003 Rugby World Cup and concerts for international acts including The Rolling Stone. The Explore interactive stadium tour, costing A$28.50 per person, takes you behind the scenes to sit in the media room and have your photo taken on the winners' dais. The new Gantry Tour (A$49) also includes a trip to the gantry (where the sound equipment and spotlights are kept, 140 feet above the stadium).

RUN FOR YOUR LIFE

Pack your jogging shoes for the biggest footrace in the country. **City to Surf** (⊕ *city2surf.com. au*) attracts more than 50,000 people each August—some taking it very seriously, others donning a gorilla suit or fairy outfit. The race starts at Hyde Park and winds through the eastern suburbs 14 km (9 miles) to Bondi Beach, via the notorious "Heartbreak Hill" at Rose Bay. For some reason, it never rains on the second Sunday in August.

Don't miss the adjacent Bicentennial Park, made up of 247 acres of swamps, lakes, and parks dotted with picnic grounds and bike trials. The area, a former quarry, was developed to commemorate Australia's Bicentennial celebrations in 1988. There's a visitor center outlining the history of the park, as well as a café (Lillies on the Park). The most scenic and relaxing way to get to Sydney Olympic Park is to take the RiverCat from Circular Quay to Homebush Bay. You can also take a train from Central Station, Sydney, to Olympic Park. ⊠ *1 Herb Elliot Ave., Homebush Bay* ☎ *02/9714–7888, 02/8765–2300* ⊕ *www. sydneyolympicpark.com.au; www.anzstadium.com.au* ☉ *Daily during daylight hrs.*

BEACHES

Sydney is paradise for beach lovers. Within the metropolitan area there are more than 30 ocean beaches, all with golden sand and rolling surf, as well as several more around the harbor with calmer water for safe swimming. If your hotel is on the harbor's south side, the logical choice for a day at the beach is one of the southern ocean beaches between Bondi and Coogee. On the north side of the harbor, Manly is easily accessible by ferry, but beaches farther north involve a longer trip by car or public transportation.

Lifeguards are on duty at most of Sydney's ocean beaches during summer months, and flags indicate whether a beach is being patrolled. "Swim between the flags" is an adage that is drummed into every Australian child, with very good reason: the undertow can be very dangerous. If you get into difficulty, don't fight the current. Breathe evenly, stay calm, and raise one arm above your head to signal the lifeguards.

Although there's no shortage of sharks inside and outside the harbor, the risk of attack is very low. These species are not typically aggressive toward humans, and shark nets protect many Sydney beaches. A more common hazard is jellyfish, known locally as bluebottles, which inflict a painful sting—with a remote risk of more serious complications (including severe allergic reactions). The staff at most beaches will supply a spray-on remedy to help relieve the pain, which generally lasts about 24 hours. Many beaches will post warning signs when bluebottles are present, but you can also determine the situation yourself by looking for the telltale bright-blue, bubble-like jellies washed up along the waterline.

Topless sunbathing is common at many Sydney beaches, but full nudity is permitted only at a couple of locations, including Lady Jane Beach, close to Watsons Bay on the south side of the harbor.

Details of how to reach the beaches by bus, train, or ferry are provided below.

INSIDE THE HARBOR

Balmoral Beach. This 800-yard-long, rarely crowded beach—among the best of the inner-harbor beaches—is in one of Sydney's most exclusive northern suburbs. There's no surf, but it's a great place to learn to windsurf (sailboard rentals are available). The Esplanade, which runs along the beachfront, has a handful of upscale restaurants, as well as several snack bars and cafés that serve award-winning fish-and-chips. In summer you can catch performances of Bard on the Beach. You could easily combine a trip to Balmoral with a visit to Taronga Zoo. To reach Balmoral, take the ferry from Circular Quay to Taronga Zoo and then board Bus 238. Or take Bus 247 from the city (near Wynyard Station) to Mosman and then walk down Raglan Street hill to the Esplanade, the main street running along Balmoral Beach. **Amenities:** food and drink; showers; toilets. **Best for:** swimming; walking; windsurfing. ⊠ *Raglan St., Balmoral.*

Camp Cove. Just inside South Head, this crescent beach is where Sydney's fashionable people come to watch and be seen. The gentle slope and calm water make it a safe playground for children. A shop at the northern end of the beach sells salad rolls and fresh fruit juices. The grassy hill at the southern end of the beach has a plaque to commemorate the spot where Captain Arthur Phillip, the commander of the First Fleet, first set foot inside Port Jackson. Parking is limited; arrive by car after 10 on weekends, and keep in mind it's a long walk to the beach. Dive company Abyss (☎ *02/9588–9662*) operates an easy dive off the beach here. Take Bus 324 or 325 from Circular Quay to Watsons Bay and walk along Cliff Street. **Amenities:** food and drink; toilets. **Best for:** solitude; swimming; sunset. ⊠ *Cliff St., Watsons Bay.*

Lady Jane. Officially called Lady Bay, Lady Jane is the most accessible of the nude beaches around Sydney. It's also a popular part of Sydney's gay scene. Only a couple of hundred yards long and backed by a stone wall, the beach has safe swimming with no surf. From Camp Cove, follow the path north and then descend the short, steep ladder leading down the cliff face to the beach. Take Bus 234 or 25 from Circular Quay to Watsons Bay. From there walk along Cliff Street toward Camp

Balmoral **4**
Bondi **8**
Bronte **10**
Camp Cove **6**
Clovelly **11**
Coogee **12**
Dee Why–
Long Reef **2**
Lady Jane **5**
Manly **3**
Nielsen Park **7**
Palm Beach **1**
Tamarama **9**

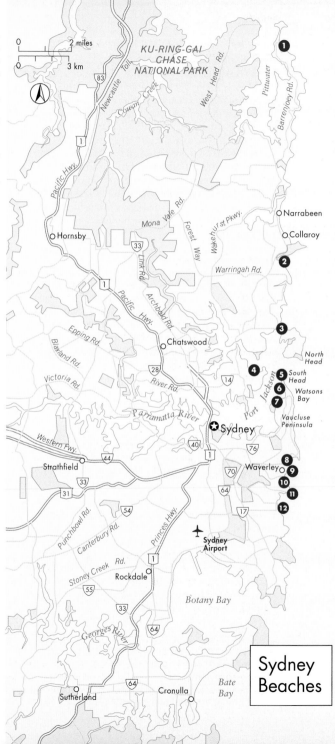

Sydney
Beaches

Cove. **Amenities:** toilets. **Best for:** solitude; nudists; swimming. ⊠ *Cliff St., Watsons Bay.*

Nielsen Park. By Sydney standards, this beach at the end of the Vaucluse Peninsula is small, but behind the sand is a large, shady park that's ideal for picnics. The headlands at either end of the beach are especially popular for their magnificent views across the harbor. The beach is protected by a semicircular net, so don't be deterred by the beach's correct name, Shark Beach. The casual café is open daily and sells drinks, snacks, and meals; there is also a more upscale restaurant open for lunch daily. Parking is often difficult on weekends. Historic Greycliffe House—built in 1840 and now used as National Park offices—is in the park, while the more elaborate and stately Vaucluse House is a 10-minute walk away. Take Bus 325 from Circular Quay. **Amenities:** food and drink; toilets; showers. **Best for:** solitude; swimming; walking. ⊠ *Greycliffe Ave. off Vaucluse Rd., Vaucluse.*

SOUTH OF THE HARBOR

Fodor'sChoice **Bondi Beach.** Wide, wonderful Bondi (pronounced *bon*-dye) is the most
★   famous and most crowded of all Sydney beaches. It has something for just about everyone, and the droves that flock here on a sunny day give it a bustling, carnival atmosphere unmatched by any other Sydney beach. Facilities include toilets, open-air showers for rinsing sandy feet and salty bodies, and a kiosk on the beach that rents out sun lounges, beach umbrellas, and even swimsuits. A café and restaurant are located in the historic Bondi Pavillion, while cafés, ice-cream outlets, restaurants, and boutiques line Campbell Parade, which runs behind the beach. Families tend to prefer the calmer waters of the northern end of the beach. Surfing is popular at the south end, where a path winds along the sea-sculpted cliffs to Tamarama and Bronte beaches. Take Bus 380, 382, or 333 all the way from Circular Quay, or take the train from the city to Bondi Junction and then board Bus 380, 381, 382, or 333. **Amenities:** food and drink; lifeguards; showers; toilets; water sports; parking (fee). **Best for:** partiers; sunrise; surfing; walking; swimming. ⊠ *Campbell Parade, Bondi Beach.*

Bronte. If you want an ocean beach that's close to the city, has both sand and grassy areas, and offers a terrific setting, this one is hard to beat. A wooded park of palm trees and Norfolk Island pines surrounds Bronte. The park includes a playground and sheltered picnic tables, and excellent cafés are in the immediate area. The breakers can be fierce, but swimming is safe in the sea pool at the southern end of the beach. Take Bus 378 from Central Station, or take the train from the city to Bondi Junction and then board Bus 378. Bus 362 runs between Bondi and Coogee beaches, stopping at Bronte Beach and Tamarama on the weekends only. **Amenities:** food and drink; showers; toilets; lifeguard. **Best for:** surfing; sunrise; walking. ⊠ *Bronte Rd., Bronte.*

Clovelly. Even on the roughest day it's safe to swim at the end of this long, keyhole-shaped inlet, which makes it a popular family beach. There are toilet facilities but no snack bars or shops in the immediate area. This is also a popular snorkeling spot that usually teems with tropical fish.

Sydneysiders have more than 30 beaches to choose from.

Take Bus 339 from Argyle Street, Millers Point (the Rocks), or Wynyard bus station; Bus 341 from Central Station; or a train from the city to Bondi Junction, then board Bus 329. **Amenities:** food and drink; toilets; showers; lifeguards; parking (fee). **Best for:** sunrise; snorkeling; swimming. ⊠ *Clovelly Rd., Clovelly.*

FAMILY **Coogee.** A reef protects this lively beach (pronounced *kuh*-jee), creating calmer swimming conditions than those found at its neighbors. A grassy headland overlooking the beach has an excellent children's playground. Cafés in the shopping precinct at the back of the beach sell ice cream, pizza, and the ingredients for picnics. Take Bus 373 and 374 from Circular Quay or Bus 372 from Central Station. **Amenities:** food and drink; showers; toilets; lifeguards; parking (fee). **Best for:** swimming; walking; sunrise. ⊠ *Coogee Bay Rd. and Arden St., Coogee.*

Tamarama. This small, fashionable beach—aka "Glam-a-rama"—is one of Sydney's prettiest, but the rocky headlands that squeeze close to the sand on either side make it less than ideal for swimming. The sea is often hazardous here, and surfing is prohibited. A café in the small park behind the beach sells sandwiches, fresh juices, and fruit whips. Take the train from the city to Bondi Junction and then board Bus 360 or 361, or walk for 10 minutes along the cliff path from the south end of Bondi Beach. **Amenities:** food and drink; toilets; showers; lifeguard. **Best for:** sunrise; surfing. ⊠ *Tamarama Marine Dr., Tamarama.*

NORTH OF THE HARBOR

Dee Why–Long Reef. Separated from Dee Why by a narrow channel, Long Reef Beach is remoter and much quieter than its southern neighbor. However, Dee Why has better surfing conditions, a big sea pool, and several good restaurants. To get here, take Bus 136 from Manly. **Amenities:** food and drink; toilets; showers; lifeguard; parking (fee). **Best for:** swimming; walking. ⊠ *The Strand, Dee Why.*

Fodor's Choice ★ **Manly Beach.** The Bondi Beach of the north shore, Manly caters to everyone except those who want to get away from it all. On sunny days Sydneysiders, school groups, and travelers from around the world crowd the 2-km-long (1-mile-long) sweep of white sand and take to the waves to swim and ride boards. The beach is well equipped with changing and toilet facilities and lockers. The promenade that runs between the Norfolk Island pines is great for people-watching and rollerblading. Cafés, souvenir shops, and ice-cream parlors line the nearby shopping area, the Corso. Manly also has several non-beach attractions, including Oceanworld, an aquarium about 200 yards from the ferry wharf. The ferry ride from the city makes a day at Manly feel more like a holiday than just an excursion to the beach. Take a ferry or the Manly Fast Ferry from Circular Quay. From the dock at Manly the beach is a 10-minute walk. The visitor center is located on the Forecourt of Manly Wharf. The Novotel Sydney Pacific Hotel and the Sebel Manly Beach Hotel are two upscale properties located on the beachfront. **Amenities:** food and drink; showers; toilets; lifeguards; parking (fee). **Best for:** sunrise; swimming; surfing; walking. ⊠ *Steyne St., Manly* ⊕ *www.manlyaustralia.com.au* ☺ *Manly Visitor and Information Centre weekdays 9–5, weekends 10–4.*

Palm Beach. The golden sands of Palm Beach glitter as much as the bejeweled residents of the stylish nearby village. The beach is on one side of the peninsula separating the large inlet of Pittwater from the Pacific Ocean. Bathers can easily cross from the ocean side to Pittwater's calm waters. You can take a circular ferry trip around this waterway from the wharf on the Pittwater side. The view from the lighthouse at the northern end of the beach is well worth the walk. Shops and cafés sell light snacks and meals. North Palm Beach is only patrolled by lifeguards in summer (December to February). Take Bus 190 and L90 from Wynyard bus station. **Amenities:** food and drink; showers; toilets; lifeguards. **Best for:** swimming; surfing. ⊠ *Ocean Rd., Palm Beach.*

SPORTS AND THE OUTDOORS

Given its climate and its taste for the great outdoors, it's no surprise that Sydney is addicted to sports. In the cooler months rugby league dominates the sporting scene, although these days the Sydney Swans, the city's flag bearer in the national Australian Rules Football (AFL) competition, attract far bigger crowds. In summer cricket is the major spectator sport, and nothing arouses more passion than international test cricket games—especially when Australia plays against England, the traditional enemy. Sydney is well equipped with athletic facilities,

CLOSE UP

Surf Lifesaving Clubs

2

In 2007 the Australian Surf Lifesaving Association celebrated its 100-year anniversary. The world's first Surf Lifesaving club was formed at Bondi Beach on February 21, 1907. Other clubs formed in quick secession, and today there are more than 300 clubs in Australia, with 38 in Sydney and 129 in New South Wales.

In the last century more than 500,000 swimmers have been rescued from patrolled beaches around the country, and more than 1 million swimmers have received first aid.

Lifesavers are Australian icons; volunteers undertake their five-hour beach patrols on a rostered basis during the summer season from September to April. In addition to the thousands of volunteers across Australia, there are also permanent, paid lifeguards who are employed by the local councils and are on duty year-round.

Lifesavers arrive at the beach bright and early, check the beach conditions, erect the red and yellow flags to indicate the safe swimming areas, and keep an eye on swimmers throughout their patrol. It's easy to spot a surf lifesaver—he or she wears the bright red-and-yellow cap and matching red-and-yellow uniform.

Bondi Beach lifesavers are the busiest in Australia. Each year about 2.5 million people come for a swim: some 2,500 rescues take place in an average year. The worst day in Bondi's history was February 6, 1938, known as Black Sunday. Lifesavers plucked 300 people from the huge surf. Five lives were lost.

It's not all work for Surf Lifesaving clubs. They hold competitions and surf carnivals throughout the summer months at numerous beaches. Events include surf swims, crew boat races (man-powered by oarsmen), surf ski races, and the macho-named "iron man" races where men (and women in separate events) perform all manner of endurance tests. Surf Lifesaving clubs opened their doors to women and children several decades ago.

---

from golf courses to tennis courts, and water sports come naturally on one of the world's greatest harbors.

Ticketek Phone Box Office. Ticketek Phone Box Office is the place to buy tickets for major sports events. ☎ *13–2849* ⊕ *www.premier.ticketek. com.au.*

AUSTRALIAN RULES FOOTBALL

Sydney Cricket Ground. A fast, demanding game in which the ball can be kicked or punched between teams of 22 players, Australian Rules Football has won a major audience in Sydney, even though the city has only one professional team—the Sydney Swans—compared to the dozen that play in Melbourne—the home of the sport. Sydney Cricket Ground hosts games April to September. ⊠ *Centennial Park, Moore Park Rd., Paddington* ☎ *02/9360–6601* ⊕ *www.sydneycricketground.com.au.*

BICYCLING

Sydney's favorite cycling track is Centennial Park's Grand Parade, a 3¾-km (2¼-mile) cycle circuit around the perimeter of this grand, gracious eastern suburbs park.

Centennial Park Cycles. Centennial Park Cycles rents bicycles for around A$20 per hour, A$70 per day. There is an additional location inside Centennial Park on Grand Drive. ⊠ *50 Clovelly Rd., Randwick* ☎ *02/9398–5027* ⊕ *www.cyclehire.com.au.*

Clarence Street Cyclery. This is a major store for all your cycling needs. Plus, you can rent hybrid bikes (an all-round leisure bike) for A$29 for half day and A$49 full day and road bikes for A$99 (half) and A$149 (full). ⊠ *104 Clarence St., City Center* ☎ *02/9295–0000* ⊕ *www.cyclery.com.au.*

BOATING AND SAILING

EastSail. EastSail rents bareboat sailing and motored yachts from about A$655 per half day (four hours); a manned yacht costs around A$915 for four hours and includes nine sailor and the skipper. It also conducts sailing schools. ⊠ *D'Albora Marine, New Beach Rd., Rushcutters Bay, eastern suburbs* ☎ *02/9327–1166* ⊕ *www.eastsail.com.au.*

Northside Sailing School. This company at Middle Harbour teaches dinghy sailing to individuals and children's groups. You can learn the ropes in a two-hour, one-on-one private lesson from A$110. ⊠ *The Spit, 77 Parriwi Rd., Mosman* ☎ *02/9969–3972* ⊕ *www.northsidesailing.com.au.*

Sydney Harbour Kayaks. Sydney Harbour Kayaks rents one- and two-person kayaks. The location beside Spit Bridge offers calm water for novices, as well as several beaches and idyllic coves. Prices per hour start from A$20 for a one-person kayak and A$40 for a double. Guided four-hour tours depart every Saturday and Sunday at 8:30 am ($A99 per person). Novices can take part in three-hour free lessons (A$50 for kayak hire). ⊠ *81 Parriwi Rd., Mosman* ☎ *02/9969–4590* ⊕ *www.sydneyharbourkayaks.com.au.*

CRICKET

Cricket is Sydney's summer sport, and it's often played in parks throughout the nation. For Australians the pinnacle of excitement is the Ashes, when the national cricket team takes the field against England. It happens every other summer, and the two nations take turns hosting the event. Cricket season runs from October through March.

Sydney Cricket Ground. International test series games are played at the Sydney Cricket Ground. ⊠ *Centennial Park, Moore Park Rd., Paddington* ☎ *02/9360–6601* ⊕ *www.sydneycricketground.com.au.*

HIKING

Fine walking trails can be found in the national parks in and around Sydney, especially in **Royal National Park** and **Ku-ring-gai Chase National Park** (32 km [20 miles] south and 25 km [15 miles] north of the city center, respectively) and **Sydney Harbour National Park,** which hugs the harbor shores. The **Bondi-to-Bronte Coast Walk** is a lovely 3½-km (2-mile) cliff walk, popular with just about everyone in the eastern suburbs.

Surf school at Bondi Beach

Signage explains the flora and Aboriginal history, and the area is the venue for the hugely popular Sculpture by the Sea outdoor art display (held every October and November). The **Federation Cliff Walk** from Dover Heights (north of Bondi Beach) to Vaucluse, and on to Watsons Bay, winds past some of Sydney's most exclusive suburbs. At Diamond Bay you can soak in great views of the 20-million-year-old sandstone cliffs from the steps and boardwalks.

RUGBY LEAGUE

Sydney Football Stadium. Known locally as football (or footy), rugby league is Sydney's winter addiction. This is a fast, gutsy, physical game that bears some similarities to North American football, although the action is more constant and the ball cannot be passed forward. The season falls between March and September. Sydney Football Stadium (now known by its corporate sponsorship name of Allianz Stadium) is the home ground of the Sydney Roosters. Other games are played at ANZ Stadium (Sydney Olympic Park) and stadiums throughout the suburbs. ⊠ *Centennial Park, Moore Park Rd., Paddington* ☎ *02/9360–6601* ⊕ *www.sydneycricketground.com.au.*

SCUBA DIVING

Dive Centre Manly. Located at the popular northern Sydney beach, Dive Centre Manly runs all-inclusive shore dives each day, which let you see weedy sea dragons and other sea creatures. PADI certification courses are also available. The cost for a shore dive is A$95 and A$125 for two dives. ⊠ *10 Belgrave St., Manly* ☎ *02/9977–4355* ⊕ *www.divesydney.com.*

Pro Dive. This PADI operator conducts courses and shore- or boat-diving excursions around the harbor and city beaches. Some of the best dive spots—with coral, rock walls, and lots of colorful fish—are close to the eastern suburb beaches of Clovelly and Coogee. The company also has a center in Manly. A four-hour boat dive with a guide costs around A$199, including rental equipment; a four-dive learn-to-dive course is A$399. ⊠ *27 Alfreda St., Coogee* ☎ *1800/820820* ⊕ *www.prodive.com.au.*

SURFING

All Sydney surfers have their favorite breaks, but you can usually count on good waves on at least one of the city's ocean beaches.

Lets Go Surfing. This is a complete surfing resource for anyone who wants to hang five with confidence. Lessons are available for all ages and you can rent or buy boards and wet suits. The two-hour beginner surfer lesson, in a small group, is A$99. ⊠ *128 Ramsgate Ave., North Bondi* ☎ *02/9365–1800* ⊕ *www.letsgosurfing.com.au.*

Manly Surf School. This company conducts courses for adults and children, and provides all equipment, including wet suits. Adults can join a two-hour group lesson (four per day) for A$70. Private instruction costs A$90 per hour. Stand-up paddling (on a board) lessons are also conducted for the same price, and are held on the calm waters of Balmoral and Narrabeen lakes. ⊠ *North Steyne Surf Club, North Steyne, Manly Beach, Manly* ☎ *02/9977–6977* ⊕ *www.manlysurfschool.com.*

Rip Curl. This store has a huge variety of boards and surfing supplies, including cool clothes. It's right at Bondi Beach. ⊠ *82 Campbell Parade, Bondi Beach* ☎ *02/9130–2660* ⊕ *www.ripcurl.com.au.*

Surfection Bondi Beach. Here is every surfer's idea of retail heaven: surfboards and cool clothing all housed in one huge sparkling store. ⊠ *31 Hall St., Bondi Beach* ☎ *02/9130–1051.*

Swellnet. This website has surf reports and weather details. ⊕ *www.swellnet.com.au.*

SWIMMING

Sydney has many heated Olympic-size swimming pools, some of which go beyond the basic requirements of a workout. Many Aussies, however, prefer to do their "laps" in ocean pools at Bondi and Manly.

Andrew (Boy) Charlton Pool. Andrew (Boy) Charlton Pool isn't just any heated Olympic-size saltwater pool. Its stunning outdoor location overlooking the ships at Garden Island, its radical glass-and-steel design, and its chic terrace café above Woolloomooloo Bay make it an attraction in itself. Admission is A$6, and it's open September–April, daily 6 am–7 pm. ⊠ *Mrs. Macquarie's Rd., The Domain* ☎ *02/9358–6686* ⊕ *www.abcpool.org.*

Cook and Phillip Park Aquatic and Fitness Centre. This fitness center includes wave, hydrotherapy, children's, and Olympic-size pools in a stunning high-tech complex on the eastern edge of the city center near St. Mary's Cathedral. Admission is A$6.80 to swim and A$18.60 for the gym, which includes pool entry. It's open weekdays 6 am–10 pm, and weekends 7 am–8 pm. ⊠ *College St., City Center* ☎ *02/9326–0444* ⊕ *www.cookandphillip.org.au.*

TENNIS

Cooper Park Tennis Centre. This complex includes eight synthetic-grass courts and a café in a park surrounded by native bushland, about 5 km (3 miles) east of the city. Court fees are A$25 per hour from 6 am to 5 pm on weekdays, and A$30 per hour from 5 pm to 10 pm (weekdays) and on weekends: Saturday 6 am to 7 pm, Sunday 6 am to 8 pm. ⊠ *Cooper Park, 1 Bunna Pl., off Suttie Rd., Woollahra* ☎ *02/9389–3100* ⊕ *www.cptennis.com.au.*

Parklands Sports Centre. Parklands Sports Centre has 11 courts in a shady park approximately 2½ km (1½ miles) from the city center. The weekday cost is A$20 per hour 9–5 and A$28 per hour 5–10 pm (Monday–Thursday) and until 7pm on Friday; it's A$28 per hour 8 am–6 pm on weekends. Many buses travel past the site including the 394, 396 and 397 from Circular Quay. ⊠ *Lang Rd. at Anzac Parade, Moore Park, Centennial Park* ☎ *02/9662–7033* ⊕ *www.parklandssports.com.au.*

WINDSURFING

Balmoral Windsurfing, Sailing, and Kayak School. This school runs classes from its base at this north-side harbor beach. Private windsurfing lessons are A$130 per hour, sailing from A$295 for four hours of lessons over a two-day period. Stand-up paddleboards and kayaks can be rented out for A$30 and A$25 per hour respectively. ⊠ *The Esplanade, Balmoral Beach* ☎ *02/9960–5344* ⊕ *www.sailboard.net.au.*

Rose Bay Aquatic Hire. Rose Bay Aquatic Hire has joined forces with kayak operator Oz Paddle. They now rent motorboats, kayaks, and stand-up paddleboards. Motorboats are A$100 for the first two hours; kayaks are A$20 an hour, as are paddleboards. Whatever mode of transport chosen, an hour or two on Sydney's beautiful harbor is time well spent. ⊠ *1 Vickery Ave., Rose Bay* ☎ *04/1623–9543, 04/1612–3339* ⊕ *www.rosebayaquatichire.com.*

WHERE TO EAT

Sydney's dining scene is as sunny and cosmopolitan as the city itself, and there are diverse and exotic culinary adventures to suit every appetite. Mod Oz (modern-Australian) cooking flourishes, fueled by local produce and guided by Mediterranean and Asian techniques. Look for such innovations as tuna tartare with flying-fish roe and wasabi; emu prosciutto; five-spice duck; shiitake mushroom pie; and sweet turmeric barramundi curry. A meal at Tetsuya's or Rockpool constitutes a crash course in this dazzling culinary language. A visit to the city's fish markets at Pyrmont, five minutes from the city center, will also tell you much about Sydney's diet. Look for rudderfish, barramundi, blue-eye, kingfish, John Dory, ocean perch, and parrot fish, as well as Yamba prawns, Balmain and Moreton Bay bugs (shovel-nose lobsters), sweet Sydney rock oysters, mud crab, spanner crab, yabbies (small freshwater crayfish), and marrons (freshwater lobsters).

BEST BETS FOR SYDNEY DINING

Fodor's Choice ★

bills, $, p. 119
Billy Kwong, $, p. 121
Buon Ricardo, $$$, p. 120
Icebergs Dining Room and Bar, $$, p. 123
Red Lantern on Crown, $, p. 122
Rockpool, $$$$, p. 118
Tetsuya's, $$$$, p. 118

Best by Cuisine

CHINESE

BBQ King, $, p. 108
Billy Kwong, $, p. 121
Golden Century, $, p. 109
Spice Temple, $$, p. 118

FRENCH

Bistro Moncur, $$, p. 120
Galileo, $$, p. 105
Marque, $$$$, p. 122
Mere Catherine, $$, p. 119

ITALIAN

Buon Ricardo, $$$, p. 120
Icebergs Dining Room and Bar, $$, p. 123

MALAYSIAN

The Malaya, $, p. 109

MODERN AUSTRALIAN

Altitude, $$, p. 105
The Deck, $, p. 105
Est, $$$$, p. 109
Oxford Social, $, p. 119
Quay, $$$$, p. 108
Rockpool, $$$$, p. 118
Swell, $$, p. 124
Tetsuya's, $$$$, p. 118

SEAFOOD

The Bucket List, $, p. 122
Catalina Restaurant, $$$$, p. 123

There are many expensive and indulgent restaurants in the city center, but the real dining scene is in the inner city, eastern suburbs, and inner-western suburbs of Leichhardt and Balmain. Neighborhoods like Surry Hills, Darlinghurst, Paddington, and beachside suburb Bondi are dining destinations in themselves. Plus, you're more likely to find a restaurant that will serve on a Sunday night in one of these places than in the central business district (the city center)—which can become a bit of a ghost town after offices close during the week. Circular Quay and The Rocks are always lively, and the Overseas Passenger Terminal (on the opposite side of the harbor from the Opera House) has several top-notch restaurants with stellar views.

Prices in the reviews are the average cost of a main course at dinner or, if dinner is not served, at lunch. Use the coordinate (✛ 1:B2) at the end of each listing to locate a site on the corresponding map.

SYDNEY HARBOUR

$$$
AUSTRALIAN

✕ **Bathers' Pavilion.** Balmoral Beach is blessed. Not only does it have an inviting sandy beach and great water views, but it also has one of the best eating strips north of the Harbour Bridge. Queen of the strip is Bathers' Pavilion, which includes a restaurant, café, and lavish private dining room. Serge Dansereau cooks with one hand on the seasons and the other on the best local ingredients at the acclaimed restaurant, but for a casual breakfast, lunch, afternoon tea, or dinner it's hard to beat the café ($). There's a choice of salad, wood-fired pizzas, and seafood dishes such as seared ocean trout fingers with fennel, orange segments, and white beans for around A$27.50. Breakfast dishes are a little on the expensive side with most around A$23. No reservations taken for the café. $ *Average main: A$48* ✉ *4 The Esplanade, Balmoral* ☎ *02/9969–5050* ⊕ *www.batherspavilion.com.au* ⬔ *Reservations essential* ✛ *2:C1.*

$ ✕ **The Deck.** If you've wanted to know just what's inside that giant face
MODERN on the north side of the harbor under the bridge, well this is your
AUSTRALIAN chance. The Deck is located in a swanky refurbished space just as you step through the giant mouth of Luna Park, Sydney's long-established fun park. The stunning view, however, across the harbor with the Opera House right in your sights, is the real draw. The restaurant and cocktail bar are above a live venue that cranks up on the weekend, so expect a fun night out rather than a quiet tête-à-tête. You may have the place to yourself at a midweek lunch. There's a selection of seafood and non-seafood tasting plates to share, while wonderful classics such as paella and bouillabaisse are on the menu. Sweet treats include orange and cardamam crème brûlée with brandied kumquats. $ *Average main: A$30* ✉ *Luna Park, 1 Olympic Dr., Milsons Point* ☎ *02/9033–7670* ⊕ *www.thedecksydney.com.au* ⊗ *Closed Mon. and Tues. No dinner Sun.* ✛ *2:A2.*

THE ROCKS

$$ ✕ **Altitude.** The lure of this decadent restaurant, perched high above
MODERN Sydney Harbour on the 36th floor of the luxurious Shangri-La Hotel,
AUSTRALIAN is the view through the floor-to-ceiling windows, but the food is equally impressive. Chef Steve Krasicki presents an enticing menu of Mod Oz dishes with a definite European influence. Seafood lovers will find ample selection among such dishes as ceviche of pink snapper and the sword-fish with corn, coconut, and curry. For a special occasion, gather a dozen friends to dine in the opulent, egg-shaped private dining room, or indulge in the seven-course degustation (A$150; A$215 with match-ing wines). On weekends the adjoining bar can be a little noisy as the night wears on, so it might be a good idea to beat it early or join in the fun. $ *Average main: A$45* ✉ *Shangri-La Hotel, 176 Cumberland St., The Rocks* ☎ *02/9250–6123* ⊕ *www.36levelsabove.com* ⬔ *Reserva-tions essential* ⊗ *Closed Sun. No lunch Mon.–Sat.* ✛ *1:B2.*

$$$$ ✕ **Aria.** With windows overlooking the Opera House and Harbour
AUSTRALIAN Bridge, Aria could easily rest on the laurels of its location. Instead, chef Matthew Moran creates a menu of extraordinary dishes that may be your best meal in the antipodes—and a steep bill to show for it. Make a reservation before you even get on the plane and look forward to the Peking Duck consommé with duck dumplings, shaved abalone, and mushrooms. Whether you dine à la carte, sample the seasonal tasting menu (A$120 for four courses; A$170 with matching wines), or order the pretheater menu, don't skip taking a look at the dessert list—the banana-and-chocolate-chip soufflé with a dulce de leche ice cream is well worth the 20-minute wait. $ *Average main: A$56* ✉ *1 Macqua-rie St., East Circular Quay* ☎ *02/9252–2555* ⊕ *www.ariarestaurant. com* ⬔ *Reservations essential* 🎩 *Jacket required* ⊗ *No lunch weekends* ✛ *1:C1.*

$$ ✕ **Galileo.** This gracious, salon-style restaurant within the newly named
FRENCH Langham Hotel at The Rocks will have you thinking you've been

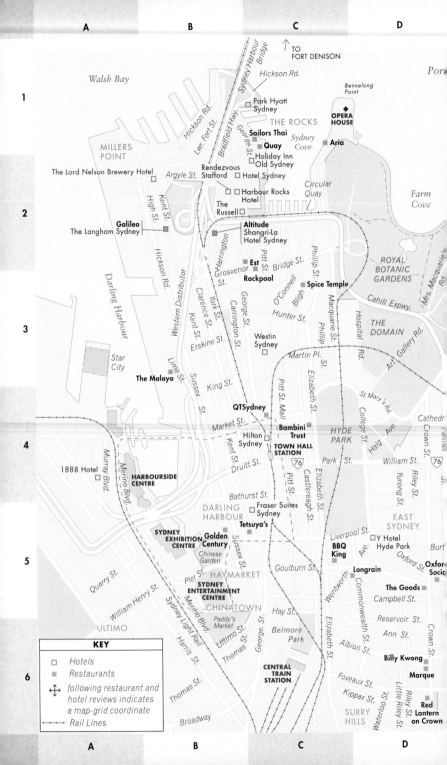

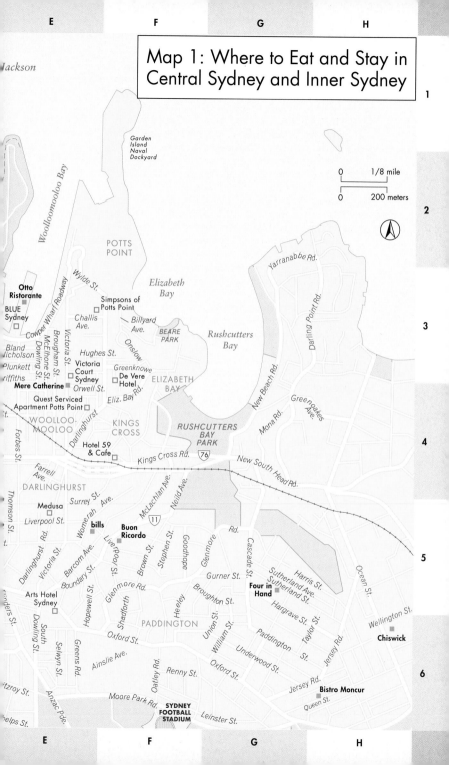

E F G H

1

Map 1: Where to Eat and Stay in Central Sydney and Inner Sydney

Jackson

Garden
Island
Naval
Dockyard

0   1/8 mile

0   200 meters

2

POTTS
POINT

Woolloomooloo Bay

Yarranabbe Rd.

Wylde St.

Otto
Ristorante

BLUE
Sydney

Cowper Wharf Roadway

Elizabeth
Bay

Simpsons of
Potts Point

Challis
Ave.

Billyard
Ave.

BEARE
PARK

Rushcutters
Bay

Darling Point Rd.

3

Bland
Nicholson

Plunkett

riffiths

Victoria St.

Brougham St.

McElhone St.

Dowling St.

Hughes St.

Victoria
Court
Sydney

Greenknowe
Ave.

De Vere
Hotel

Onslow

ELIZABETH
BAY

New Beach Rd.

Greenoaks
Ave.

Mere Catherine

Orwell St.

Eliz. Bay Rd.

ELIZABETH
BAY

Mona Rd.

Quest Serviced
Apartment Potts Point

WOOLLOO-
MOOLOO

Darlinghurst

KINGS
CROSS

RUSHCUTTERS
BAY
PARK

4

Forbes St.

Hotel 59
& Cafe

Kings Cross Rd.

76

New South Head Rd.

Farrell
Ave.

DARLINGHURST

Surrey St.

Womerah Ave.

McLachlan Ave.

Neild Ave.

Thomson St.

Medusa

Liverpool St.

bills

Buon
Ricordo

11

Goodhope

Rd.

Cascade St.

Sutherland Ave.

Harris St.

Ocean St.

5

Darlinghurst Rd.

Victoria St.

Barcom Ave.

Boundary St.

Liverpool St.

Brown St.

Stephen St.

Gurner St.

Glenmore

Broughton St.

Sutherland
St.

Four in
Hand

Hargrave St.

St.

Taylor St.

Jersey Rd.

Wellington St.

Chiswick

Arts Hotel
Sydney

Hopewell St.

Glenmore Rd.

Shadforth

Heeley

Union St.

William St.

Paddington
St.

PADDINGTON

Oxford St.

Oxford St.

Underwood St.

6

inders St.

Greens Rd.

Selwyn St.

South Dowling St.

Ainslie Ave.

Oatley Rd.

Renny St.

Jersey Rd.

Bistro Moncur

tzroy St.

Phelps St.

Anzac Pde.

Moore Park Rd.

SYDNEY
FOOTBALL
STADIUM

Leinster St.

Queen St.

E F G H

transported to Paris, as will the French menu reinvigorated by executive chef Anthony Craven. After years abroad working in Le Meridien Dubai and most recently the Peninsula Hotel, Manila, Craven returned to hometown Sydney and The Langham in mid-2013. His à la carte selections include Chatham Island Blue Cod with tomato and basil foam and olive tapenade, and the Galileo favorite, chocolate soufflé and lychee oolong milk ice cream which uses produce from the famous French chocolatier, Valrhona. There are several degustation menus to choose including the eight-course decadent banquet (A$120; add A$80 for matching wines). [$] *Average main: A$40* ✉ *89–113 Kent St., The Rocks* ☎ *02/8248–5252* ⏲ *No lunch* ✥ *1:B2.*

$$$$ MODERN AUSTRALIAN 🍴 **Quay.** In his take on Mod Oz cuisine, chef Peter Gilmore masterfully crafts a four-course à la carte menu including such dishes as mud crab congee with Chinese-inspired split rice porridge; quail breasts with eschallots and truffle-infused milk custard; and slow-cooked suckling pig ($175). Desserts are sublime—Gilmore's "snow egg," which changes with the seasons and can include white nectarine, apple, and jackfruit, had fans lining up to try it just hours after it stole the show on Australia's Masterchef. Glass walls afford wonderful views of the bridge and Opera House. [$] *Average main: A$175* ✉ *Upper Level, Overseas Passenger Terminal, West Circular Quay, The Rocks* ☎ *02/9251–5600* 🌐 *www.quay.com.au* ✍ *Reservations essential* ⏲ *No lunch Sat.–Mon.* ✥ *1:C1.*

$ THAI 🍴 **Sailors Thai.** Aussies love their Thai food and this stylish restaurant has been delivering some of the best in the city for 18 years. In a charming mid-19th-century sandstone building in The Rocks, there's a dining room on the lower level and a casual canteen, where you dine at a long shared table, on the top. Start with the shredded chicken wrapped in organic egg nets with creamy coconut sauce and then move on to the slow-cooked Massama curry of Tasmanian Cape Grim beef ribs. Everything on the five-course tasting menu (A$65) is delicious, or choose one of the small plates, such as the soft-shell crab spiced with garlic lime and fish sauce, from the à la carte menu. Finish your meal off with deep-fried coconut ice cream and tamarind caramel sauce. [$] *Average main: A$35* ✉ *Lower level, 106 George St., The Rocks* ☎ *02/9251–2466* 🌐 *www.sailorsthai.com.au* ✥ *1:C1.*

DARLING HARBOUR

$ CHINESE 🍴 **BBQ King.** You can find better basic Chinese food elsewhere in town, but for duck and pork, barbecue-loving Sydneysiders know that this is the place to come. The poultry hanging in the window are the only decor at this small Chinatown staple, where the food is so fresh you can almost hear it clucking—make sure you sample the duck pancakes. Barbecued pork is the other featured dish, and the suckling pig is especially delicious. It's open from 11 am until late at night, when the average customers are large groups of mates sprawled at the Formica tables feeding their drunken munchies, or Chinatown chefs kicking back after a day in the kitchen. The service can be a little brusque, but it's all part of the low-budget charm. [$] *Average main: A$29* ✉ *18–20 Goulburn St., Haymarket* ☎ *02/9267–2586* ✥ *1:C5.*

2

$ ✕ **Golden Century.** For two hours—or as long as it takes for you to con-
CHINESE sume delicately steamed prawns, luscious mud crab with ginger and
shallots, and *pipis* (triangular clams) with black-bean sauce—you might
as well be in Hong Kong. This place is heaven for seafood lovers, with
wall-to-wall fish tanks filled with crab, lobster, abalone, and schools of
barramundi, parrot fish, and coral trout. You won't have to ask if the
food is fresh: most of it is swimming around you as you eat. Come for
the big-ticket seafood or a simple meal of deep-fried duck. Supper is
served until 4 am so it's popular with late-night revelers. It's not the prettiest of places and service can be hit and miss, but it has a legion of fans.
■ TIP→ Make a reservation for early in the evening, otherwise you'll
encounter a long queue. $ *Average main: A$35* ✉ *393–399 Sussex St.,
Haymarket* ☎ *02/9212–3901* ⊕ *www.goldencentury.com.au* ✛ *1:B5.*

$ ✕ **The Malaya.** The cocktails (all A$17.50) are legendary, the view is cap-
MALAYSIAN tivating, and the food, a traditional Chinese/Malay fusion, is extraordinary. After 50 years in the business (first opened in 1963), in different
venues around Sydney, this modern Asian restaurant still does a roaring trade. Signature dishes include beef Rendang (Indonesian-style beef
curry), and the spanner crab *san choy bow*, a fabulous twist on a classic
dish. Szechuan eggplant that's so good it may just be the food of the
gods. Try one of the four set menus (for a minimum of three people and
A$48 per person) for a true feast on the extensive menu's flavor com-
binations. $ *Average main: A$30* ✉ *39 Lime St., King Street Wharf,
Darling Harbour* ☎ *02/9279–1170* ⊕ *www.themalaya.com.au* ☽ *No
lunch Sun.* ✛ *1:B3.*

SYDNEY CITY CENTER

$$ ✕ **Bambini Trust.** It's hidden behind huge black doors in one of the city's
ITALIAN historic sandstone buildings, but once you're inside you'd swear you
were in Paris. Dark-wood paneling, black-and-white photographs, and
mirrors bearing the day's specials in flowing script lend a bistro feel.
The fare is predominately Italian with a sprinkling of French fare and
Mod Oz dishes. Being in the heart of the city, it's also popular at break-
fast where the delicious crab omelet makes an exotic start to the work
day. At dinner you can't go wrong with the popular cracked pepper
spaghettini with a sauté of Yamba prawns, chili, and garlic. A pre- or
postmeal drink in the marble-lined, chandelier-adorned Bambini Wine
Room is a must. $ *Average main: A$36* ✉ *185 Elizabeth St., City Cen-
ter* ☎ *02/9283–7098* ⊕ *bambinitrust.com.au* ☽ *Closed Sun.* ✛ *1:C4.*

$$$$ ✕ **Est.** This elegant, pillared dining room is the perfect setting for show-
MODERN ing off chef Peter Doyle's modern, light touch with Mod Oz cuisine.
AUSTRALIAN Anything Doyle cooks with scallops is divine as is his salad of span-
ner crab, cauliflower, white radicchio, and nasturtiums. Seafood lovers
will relish the Murray cod with shaved abalone, or they can opt for
the tantalizing caramelized pork belly teamed with a bug tail (that's
a small crayfish). Finish off with a dessert of intriguing tastes—Earl
Grey ice cream with blood orange citrus curd donuts and blood orange
sorbet. The seven-course tasting menu (A$175) is a heavenly expe-
rience. There's also a four-course chef's menu (A$150) and various
two-, three-, and four-course lunch options, but no à la carte menu.

Continued on page 118

Australia's
Modern
Cuisine

It may be referred to as the land down under, but the culinary movement that's sweeping Australia means this country has come out on top. Modern Australian cuisine has transformed the land of Vegemite sandwiches and shrimp-on-the-barbie into a culinary Promised Land with local flavors, organic produce, and bountiful seafood, fashioned by chefs who remain unburdened by restrictive traditions.

Australia is fast proving to be one of the most exciting destinations in the world for food lovers. With its stunning natural bounty, multicultural inspirations, and young culinary innovators, it ticks off all the requisite foodie boxes.

In Sydney, chefs are dishing up new twists on various traditions, creating a Modern Australian (Mod Oz) cuisine with its own compelling style. Traditional bush tucker, for example, has been transformed from a means of survival into a gourmet experience. Spicy Asian flavors have been borrowed from the country's neighbors to the north, and homage has been paid to the precision and customs brought by Australia's early European settlers.

The diversity of the modern Australian culinary movement also means that it is more than just flavors: it's an experience. And one that can be obtained from the award-winning luxury restaurant down to the small Thai-style canteens, pubs, and outdoor cafés.

While purists might argue that Mod Oz cuisine is little more than a plagiarism of flavors and cultures, others will acknowledge it as unadulterated fare with a fascinating history of its very own. Either way, it still offers a dining experience that's unique from anywhere else in the world.

MENU DECODER

Barbie: barbeque | Snags: sausages | Chook: chicken | Vegemite: salty yeast spread | Lamington: small chocolate sponge cake with coconut | Pavlova: meringue dessert topped with cream and fruit | Floater: meat pie with mushy peas and gravy | Damper: simple bread cooked on a campfire | Sanga: sandwich | Cuppa: cup of tea | Tucker: food | Chips: French fries | Tomato sauce: ketchup | Muddy: mud crab | Prawn: shrimp

Seared tuna with avocado, cilantro, and black sesame seeds, topped with caviar

BUSH TUCKER

Bush Tucker food; Tropical rainforest fruits on paper bark

BACK THEN

Native Australian plants and animals have played a vital role in the diets of the Aboriginal people for more than 50,000 years. Generally referred to as bush tucker, these native fruits, nuts, seeds, vegetables, meats, and fish are harvested around the country—from arid deserts to coastal areas and tropical rainforests.

Once little more than a means of survival, today they're touted as gourmet ingredients. And you certainly don't need to go "walkabout" to find them.

RIGHT NOW

Bush tucker has undergone much transformation over the decades, experiencing a renaissance in recent years. Heavily influenced by multicultural cooking techniques, game meats such as emu and wallaby have been elevated from bush-stew ingredients to perfectly seared cuts of meat garnished with seasonal herbs and vegetables. Kangaroo is making its way into stir-fries and curries,

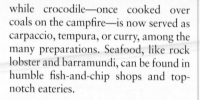

while crocodile—once cooked over coals on the campfire—is now served as carpaccio, tempura, or curry, among the many preparations. Seafood, like rock lobster and barramundi, can be found in humble fish-and-chip shops and top-notch eateries.

Of course, bush tucker isn't just about the protein. Native spices, wild fruits, and indigenous nuts have found favor in countless culinary applications. Lemon myrtle leaves lend a lemony flavor to baked goods and savory dishes. Alpine pepper, a crushed herb, gives foods a fiery zing. Quandong is a wild plum-like fruit with subtle apricot flavor. It once was dried as a portable energy source but now is made into jams and pie fillings. Kakadu plums are made into "super" juices with enormous vitamin C content. Bush tomatoes also have become popular in jams and sauces, and are available in supermarkets. Native nuts include the bunya nut, which is chestnut-like with pine notes, the shells of which are

Witchetty grub

Tandoori kangaroo

INDIGENOUS MEATS

CAMEL: With some one million camels in Australia, camel is fast being served up on many menus, though most are in the Northern Territory. The meat is often compared to mutton and has a similar taste and texture to beef.

CROCODILE: This meat may be fish-like in texture and appearance, but it tastes similar to chicken. The most popular cut is the tail, however legs and meat from the body are also consumed. Crocodile is growing in popularity because of its delicate flavor and versatility. It is often fried and grilled, but may be served raw in carpaccio or sushi rolls.

EMU: Although it's fowl, emu meat is similar in texture and flavor to beef with a light flavor and slight gamey tones on the palate. The meat is high in iron and very low in fat and cholesterol. Typical cuts include rump, strip loin, and oyster filet. It may be served pan-seared or lightly grilled.

KANGAROO: A dark red meat, it is extremely lean with only about 2% fat. The filet or rump is best eaten rare to medium rare, and is typically seared, barbecued, or stir-fried. Young kangaroo meat tastes like beef, while aged cuts take on a gamier flavor.

WALLABY: A cousin to the kangaroo, this meat has a somewhat milder flavor. It is a rich burgundy color and is best prepared with simple, delicate cooking styles, such as barbecuing or pan frying.

WITCHETTY GRUB: The larvae of ghost moths, these grubs are eaten raw or barbecued. People describe the taste as similar to egg, with the texture of a prawn.

used for smoking meat. Macadamia nuts, meanwhile, are among the country's biggest exports.

WHERE TO FIND IT

Despite the presence of numerous bush ingredients in Sydney restaurants, the modern bush tucker dining experience is more prominent in the northern parts of the country. You are most likely to find dishes such as kangaroo, and occasionally crocodile, on the menu of restaurants in the city's main tourist precincts of The Rocks and Circular Quay.

In Queensland and the Northern Territory, you'll find full degustation menus combining local meats and seafood with native herbs, spices, and berries. Some even offer tasting tours of their kitchen gardens where you can sample popular flavors like lemon myrtle, tarragon, and hibiscus flower straight from the bush.

Simple meal of grilled camel with vegetables

2

IN FOCUS AUSTRALIA'S MODERN CUISINE

UPDATED EUROPEAN FARE

Seafood Salad

BACK THEN

Although the foundation of Mod Oz cuisine stems from the arrival of early British settlers, the food scene has certainly steamed ahead since the days of boiled beef and damper.

The real progression of modern Australian food came after World War II, when European immigrants brought a new wave of cooking to the country. It was the French and Italians who really opened the eyes of Australians with their distinguished flavors, commitment to freshness, and masterful culinary techniques. They also laid the foundations for some of the finest vineyards and cheese makers in the country.

RIGHT NOW

Though small, there are still degrees of British influence in modern Australian cooking, albeit slightly updated. The quintessential English meat pie is now filled with ingredients such as Murray cod, lamb, bush tomato, and kangaroo. Traditional Sunday roasts and

fish-and-chips spring up in pubs and cafes, but often with a twist. And tea is still a staple on the breakfast table with a true Aussie favorite, Vegemite on toast.

Poaching, roasting, and braising are now popular methods to cook everything from reef fish and yabbies to lamb, suckling pig, and rabbit. Omelettes, cassoulets, and soufflés as well as pasta, risotto, and gnocchi are very well suited to the country's prize-winning meats, vegetables, and seafood. And the rigorous use of garlic, saffron, basil, and tarragon is common in many kitchens.

Greeks, Germans, and Spaniards have also greatly influenced dining, with tapas bars, tavernas, and schnitzel houses well represented throughout the country. Middle Eastern and North African flavors are also beginning to leave their marks.

Even casual pubs are updating dishes to reflect ethnic influences and local products. It's not unusual to see items like

Aussie meat pie

AUSTRALIA'S NATURAL BOUNTY

CHEESE FRUIT: Grown in tropical areas, this fruit high in vitamin C has long been used for medicinal purposes. It's eaten while still green since it has a distinct rotting cheese smell when ripe. Leaves can also be eaten raw or cooked.

ILLAWARRA PLUMS: Usually used in jams and chutneys or as a rich sauce to accompany kangaroo, venison, or emu. High in antioxidants, they have a subtle plum flavor with a hint of pine.

LEMON MYRTLE: A native tree with a citrus fragrance and flavor. Leaves can be used fresh or dried and ground in sweet and savory styles of cooking.

MACADAMIA NUTS: Known as Kindal Kindal by native Australians, the macadamia is a round white nut with a hard brown shell and creamy flavor.

MUNTRIES: Small berry-like fruit that have a distinct apple flavor. Also known as emu apples, they can be eaten fresh in salads or added to desserts.

PAPER BARK: Papery leaves from the Mellaluca tree, used to cook meat and seafood.

QUANDONG: A bright red fruit similar to a native peach. It's commonly used to make jams and sauces.

WARRIGAL GREENS: A herb-like vegetable with a flavor similar to spinach. They must be well cooked to eliminate their toxic oxalate content.

WATTLESEED: Also known as acacia seeds. They have a nutty to coffee-like flavor and are very high in protein. Often ground down and used in baking.

spicy chorizo pizza and Peking Duck pizza on their menus.

Another hallmark of Mod Oz cuisine—and one that parallels America's current culinary trends—is its fascination with seasonal vegetables and organic meats. Specialist farms raising free-range poultry and livestock have become extremely popular with many restaurants throughout the country. Menus often cite an ingredient's producer, i.e. "Blackmore's wagyu bresaola," and also note whether ingredients are "pasture-raised" or "locally grown."

The "paddock to plate" philosophy is getting more attention from top restaurateurs. This means a restaurant aims to source its produce from farmers and producers within their community, ensuring transport miles stay low while food is fresh and region-specific. Some establishments go a step further by growing and harvesting produce on-site in their own kitchen gardens.

Meringue topped with fresh fruit

ASIAN FUSION

Thai-style kangaroo curry

BACK THEN

Much has changed in the way of Asian food in Australia. Sixty years ago sushi didn't exist in the vocabulary, now there are Japanese restaurants on almost every street.

The Gold Rush of the mid-19th century brought an influx of Chinese immigrants to Australia, prompting Asian cuisine's humble beginnings here. Thai, Vietnamese, Indian, Malaysian, and Japanese migrants followed in various waves in the 20th century. Before long, a cuisine that had started out in family-run restaurants in the outer suburbs of Sydney had become a burgeoning new trend. And by the late 1990s the children of the first wave of immigrants had formed the new guard.

RIGHT NOW

Traditional Chinese, Thai, and Japanese restaurants are very popular in Australia. But Asian fusion restaurants are leading the charge in creating Australia-specific taste innovations. Asian fusion cuisine combines the traditional flavors of Thai, Chinese, Japanese, and Vietnamese cooking, using local Australian ingredients and Western culinary techniques. Chic contemporary interiors, often with long communal tables and shared dishes, are the latest trend. Robust herbs such as mint and coriander, fiery chili, zesty black vinegar, ginger, and pickled vegetables are core ingredients, often wok-fried with fresh Australian ingredients such as Barossa Valley chicken, Thirlmere duck, or Bangalow pork.

Leading the charge is world-renowned, Sydney-based chef Tetsuya Wakuda. His signature dish, a confit of Petuna Tasmanian Ocean Trout with konbu, apple, daikon, and wasabi is a prime example of Asian fusion, uniquely blending French techniques with his Japanese heritage and excellent Australian products.

Yet, smaller modern canteen-style eateries are also serving up contemporary Asian fare that pro-

Red chile peppers

Rock lobsters

LOCAL FISH AND SEAFOOD

ABALONE: A large sea snail with an edible muscular foot. It has a firm, rubbery texture with a very delicate flavor and can retail for about $100 per kilogram. Abalone are often seared or fried.

BALMAIN OR MORETON BAY BUGS: A smaller relative of the rock lobster with a short tail, flat head, and bug-like eyes. They have a sweet taste and a medium texture. A favorite served cold in salads and seafood platters, or split down the middle and grilled.

BARRAMUNDI: A member of the perch family, it's a highly versatile fish with a medium to firm flesh and white to light pink tones. Native to Australia, it lives in both fresh and salt waters and is farmed as well as caught in the wild.

ROCK LOBSTERS: A spiny lobster with long antennae and no claws. The four main types—eastern, southern, western, and tropical—each offer slightly different flavours and textures. The tropical are excellent as sashimi, while the eastern, southern and western lend themselves to baking and barbecue.

SYDNEY ROCK OYSTERS: Despite their name, these bivalves are commonly found throughout the east coast. They're prized for their distinct rich and creamy flavor, and are smaller in size than Pacific oysters. Try eating them raw with a squirt of lemon.

YABBIES: A fresh-water crayfish with firm white flesh and a sweeter taste than rock lobster. Small in size, they can be tricky to eat but are worth the effort. They're often cooked simply in a pot of salted, boiling water.

vides excellent quality at a fraction of the price. It's in these bustling restaurants that flavors and dishes such as shucked oyster with chili and galangal vinaigrette, roasted duck in coconut curry, wagyu-beef hotpot, soft-shell crab with chili jam, and green curry of barramundi bounce off their plates.

While the majority of Asian fusion food in Australia relies heavily on light cooking styles and fresh ingredients, clay pot cooking as well as heavier-style Malaysian and Indian curries, such as rendang and vindaloo made with local lamb and beef, are also becoming popular.

Asian influences have also made their mark on traditional seafood restaurants, where ginger, lime, coriander, and chili add extra zing to alfresco menus. Exquisite dishes include Japanese-inspired butter-grilled scallops, steamed mussels in Thai-style coconut broth, or ocean trout grilled with garlic, soy, and chili.

Salad of yabby tails

$ *Average main: A$150* ⊠ *Establishment Hotel, 252 George St., City Center* ☎ *02/9240–3000* ⊕ *www.merivale.com.au/est* ⚛ *Reservations essential* ⊙ *Closed Sun. No lunch Sat.* ✛ *1:C2.*

$$$$
MODERN
AUSTRALIAN
Fodor's Choice
★

✕ **Rockpool.** A meal at Rockpool is a crash course in what Mod Oz cooking is all about, conducted in a glamorous, long dining room with a catwalk-like ramp. After 24 years at the iconic Rocks location, the much-acclaimed restaurant has moved to new premises in the city center. Chefs Neil Perry and Phil Wood weave Thai, Chinese, Mediterranean, and Middle Eastern influences into their repertoire with effortless flair and originality. The seasonal four-course menu (A$155) constantly dazzles and may feature mud crab with stir-fried milk and Jerusalem artichoke or snapper with sour orange curry, cashew, and coconut. Don't miss the date tart for dessert, or hang on for 20 minutes as they prepare the passion-fruit soufflé with passion-fruit ice cream. Other dinner options are two courses (A$100) and three courses (A$135) for the same menu, while a six-course tasting menu is A$180. The Classic Lunch Menu, of three set courses, is popular at A$65. $ *Average main: A$145* ⊠ *11 Bridge St., City Center* ☎ *02/9252–1888* ⊕ *www.rockpool.com* ⚛ *Reservations essential* 🎩 *Jacket required* ⊙ *No lunch Sat.–Thurs. Closed Sun.* ✛ *1:B2.*

$$
CHINESE

✕ **Spice Temple.** The culinary focus of chic basement eatery—another of the restaurants owned by Neil Perry of Rockpool fame—is regional China. There are dishes from far-flung Yunnan, Hunan, and Sichuan provinces, and as the names suggests, they all have a kick. The food is meant to be shared, so pass around the ginger shallot crab, the pork belly, or the extra spicy hot and numbing crispy duck. ∎TIP➜ **The hottest dishes are marked in red on the menu.** It's a busy, trendy eatery (down a somewhat steep flight of stairs), so if you have to wait at the bar for a table, grab a cocktail and a spicy pork bun and take in the opium den ambience. Cocktails are named after the Chinese Zodiac; if you're born in the Year of the Dragon you might like to sip on a refreshing mix of lemongrass and rose soda, citrus, and Tanqueray gin. $ *Average main: A$38* ⊠ *10 Bligh St., City Center* ☎ *02/8078–1888* ⊕ *www.spicetemple.com.au* ⊙ *Closed Sun. No lunch Sat.* ✛ *1:C3.*

$$$$
MODERN
AUSTRALIAN
Fodor's Choice
★

✕ **Tetsuya's.** It's worth getting on the waiting list—there's *always* a waiting list—to sample the unique blend of Western and Japanese-French flavors crafted by Sydney's most applauded chef, Tetsuya Wakuda. The serene, expansive dining room's unobtrusive Japanese aesthetic leaves the food as the true highlight. Confit of ocean trout served with unpasteurized ocean-trout roe is a signature item on the set 11-course degustation menu (A$220 and A$97 extra for matching wines), while other dishes may include New Zealand Scampi with chicken liver parfait, or roasted breast of quail with quail leg rillettes. The menu changes often but never fails to dazzle. Views of a Japanese garden—complete with bonsai and a waterfall—make this place feel miles from the city center. It's open for dinner from Tuesday to Saturday, and lunch on Saturday only. $ *Average main: A$210* ⊠ *529 Kent St., City Center* ☎ *02/9267–2900* ⊕ *www.tetsuyas.com* ⚛ *Reservations essential* ⊙ *Closed Sun. and Mon. No lunch Tues.–Fri.* ✛ *1:B5.*

INNER SYDNEY AND THE EASTERN SUBURBS

DARLINGHURST

$
CAFÉ
Fodor's Choice
★

✕ **bills.** Named after celebrity chef and cookbook author Bill Granger, this sunny corner café is so addictive it should come with a health warning. It's a favorite hangout of everyone from local nurses to semi-disguised rock stars, and you never know who you might be sitting next to at the newspaper-strewn communal table. If you're not interested in the creaminess of what must be Sydney's best scrambled eggs, try the ricotta hotcakes with fresh banana and honeycomb butter or the corn fritters. The coconut-poached chicken sandwich with cucumber and lime mayonnaise makes an ideal lunch. Dinner selections, at the Surry Hills location, are similarly gourmet comfort food. $ *Average main: A$25* ⊠ *433 Liverpool St., Darlinghurst* ☎ *02/9360–9631* ⊕ *www.bills. com.au* ☽ *No dinner* ✢ *1:E5.*

$
CAFÉ

✕ **The Goods.** Griddle pan dishes are the draw at this friendly, and slightly noisy, organic café and food store on the city fringe. Served in cast iron skillets and topped with two baked eggs, the griddle choices include creamed corn with chorizo or their own home-cured smoky bacon. Cakes and baked goods are made on the premises; diners return time and time again for the coconut cake to savor with a great cup of tea or coffee. It's a perfect break after shopping in nearby trendy Darlinghurst. Much of the produce on the shelves are ingredients used in the meals, and the tea and coffee are grown on organic or biodynamic farms. Here's a place you can happily (and healthily!) browse. $ *Average main: A$14* ⊠ *253 Crown St., Darlinghurst* ☎ *02/9357–6690* ☽ *No dinner* ✢ *1:D5.*

$
MODERN
AUSTRALIAN

✕ **Oxford Social.** Good food and welcoming hosts pull in the crowds at this 60-seat eatery on the busy Oxford Street strip not usually know for its fine cuisine. Housed in restored early 20th-century building, Oxford Social has a straight-forward à la carte menu—main meal choices are simply deemed chicken breast, beef fillet, duck breast, and John Dory (a fish). Try to resist grazing on the mixed house nuts roasted in brown sugar soy and mild chili at the bar before tucking into the signature starter of arancini balls—two filled with spinach and Gorgonzola and two with pumpkin, Parmesan, and chili (A$15). The set menu for a group of eight or more diners (an affordable A$60) has a filling five portions of starters (including prawns in garlic Pernod cream) and choice of one main dish. With A$10 happy hour cocktails and lobster specials on Tuesday nights, it's not hard to be sociable here. $ *Average main: A$28* ⊠ *135 Oxford St., Darlinghurst* ☎ *02/9331–0557* ⊕ *www.oxfordsocial. com.au* ✢ *1:D5.*

KINGS CROSS AND POTTS POINT

$$
FRENCH

✕ **Mere Catherine.** You won't find the number of this little hole-in-the-wall restaurant in any trendy young thing's speed dial, but it is beloved by legions of fans who rejoiced when it reopened a couple of years ago. The decor is retro 1970s, and the dishes are classic French—onion soup, pâté, escargots, duck a l'orange, tarragon chicken, wonderful chateaubriand, and crème caramel for dessert. It only seats 18 in a tiny space that is akin to dining in some French family's home. The windows have lace curtains, the tables are candlelit, so come with someone you love and soak in the romantic atmosphere to the strains of Edith Piaf in the background. [$] *Average main: A$39* ✉ *166 Victoria St., Potts Point* ☎ *02/9358–2000* 💳 *No credit cards* ⏲ *No lunch Sun. and Mon.* ✣ *1:E4.*

WOOLLOOMOOLOO

$$ ITALIAN

🍴 **Otto Ristorante.** Few restaurants have the magnetic pull of Otto, a place where radio shock jocks sit side by side with fashion-magazine editors and confirmed foodies. Yes, it's a scene, but fortunately one with good Italian food prepared by chef Richard Ptacnik. The homemade pastas are menu standouts; try the strozzapreti pasta with prawns or the saffron fettuccine with rabbit ragout. The fennel-crusted swordfish, potato confit with heirloom carrots and pencil leek is also delicious. The selection of Italian wines is expensive but rarely matched this far from Milan. [$] *Average main: A$44* ✉ *Wharf at Woolloomooloo, Area 8, 6 Cowper Wharf Rd., Inner City and Eastern Suburbs* ☎ *02/9368–7488* 🌐 *www.ottoristorante.com.au* ✍ *Reservations essential* ✣ *1:E3.*

PADDINGTON

$$$ ITALIAN Fodor's Choice ★

🍴 **Buon Ricordo.** Walking into this happy, bubbly place is like turning up at a private party in the backstreets of Naples. Host, chef, and surrogate uncle Armando Percuoco invests classic Neapolitan and Tuscan techniques with inventive personal touches to produce such dishes as warmed figs with Gorgonzola and prosciutto, truffled egg pasta, and scampi with saffron sauce and black-ink risotto. The snapper fillet on a bed of zucchini flowers, mint, and zucchini is heaven for seafood lovers. Everything comes with Italian-style touches that you can see, feel, smell, and taste. Leaving the restaurant feels like leaving home, especially if you've partaken of the wonderful six-course degustation menu (A$135). [$] *Average main: A$48* ✉ *108 Boundary St., Paddington* ☎ *02/9360–6729* 🌐 *www.buonricordo.com.au* ✍ *Reservations essential* ⏲ *Closed Sun. and Mon. No lunch Tues.–Thurs.* ✣ *1:F5.*

$$ AUSTRALIAN

🍴 **Four in Hand.** At this cute, popular little pub in Paddington, chef Colin Fassnidge (an Irishman who emerged as the most controversial guest judge on Australian TV cooking show "My Kitchen Rules") has been wowing patrons for years with his shared dish for two of slow-braised lamb shoulder with kipfler potatoes, baby carrots, and salsa verde. His whole suckling pig is also a popular Sunday long-lunch treat. Starters and mains change monthly, and the restaurant's popularity has seen it open for lunch and dinner six days a week. [$] *Average main: A$39* ✉ *105 Sutherland St., Paddington* ☎ *02/9362–1999* ⏲ *Closed Mon.* ✣ *1:G5.*

WOOLLAHRA

$$ FRENCH

🍴 **Bistro Moncur.** Archetypically loud and proud, this bistro in the Woollahra Hotel spills over with happy-go-lucky patrons—mostly locals from around the leafy suburb of Woollahra—who have been coming back for more than 18 years now. The best dishes are inspired takes on Parisian fare, like the grilled Sirloin Café de Paris, French onion soufflé gratin, and port sausages with potato puree and lyonnaise onions. New head chef Sam Kane took over the reins in 2012 from Chef Damien Pignolet who established the eatery back in 1993.

Kane continues to focus on fresh, high-quality ingredients and has kept the much-loved Pignolet dish, twice-cooked soufflé, on the menu. The casual café and bar, Moncur Terrace, offers mains such as Wagyu beef burgers (A$23.90) and gourmet pizzas (A$24.50). $ *Average main: A$41* ⌂ *Woollahra Hotel, 116 Queen St., Woollahra* ☎ *02/9327–9713* ⊗ *No lunch Mon.* ✛ *1:H6.*

$$

MODERN
AUSTRALIAN

✕ **Chiswick.** Few central Sydney restaurants have access to their own homegrown produce, but here in trendy and leafy Woollahra—just a few kilometers east of the city—is an all-white and refreshingly bright restaurant surrounded by formal gardens and a large kitchen garden. Chiswick is all about stylish casual dining using the freshest of produce; since its opening in late 2012, it has become one of the hottest tickets in town. There are small plates for sharing, such as the char-grilled scallops; large plates for sharing with a group of four (try the lamb from Matt Moran's own farm); and main courses such as wood-fired pork chops with celeriac, apple, and house mustard. Folks rave about the bombe Alaska desserts, while small sweet treats—like the individual mulberry-and-crème-fraîche cannoli—are a snip at A$4 each. $ *Average main: A$34* ⌂ *65 Ocean St., Woollahra* ☎ *02/8388–8688* ⊕ *www. chiswickrestaurant.com.au* ✛ *1:H6.*

SURRY HILLS

$

CHINESE
Fodor'sChoice
★

✕ **Billy Kwong.** Locals rub shoulders while eating no-fuss Chinese food at TV chef Kylie Kwong's trendy drop-in restaurant. Kwong prepares the kind of food her family cooks, with Grandma providing not just the inspiration but also the recipes. The prawn wontons with brown rice vinegar are always popular, but the standout dish is the poached chicken with a dressing of tamari, chili, and coriander. If you have a big appetite, indulge in a variety of dishes with Kylie's banquet (A$95). A table for six to eight can be booked for 6 or 8:30 pm, otherwise it's turn up and wait with the other keen diners. When not behind the stove at Surry Hills, Kylie can be seen cooking at Eveleigh Farmers' Markets, held every Saturday near the inner-city suburb of Redfern (⊕ *www. eveleighmarket.com.au*). $ *Average main: A$34* ⌂ *3/355 Crown St., Surry Hills* ☎ *02/9332–3300* ⊗ *No lunch* ✛ *1:D6.*

$$

THAI

✕ **Longrain.** Fans of this popular Thai restaurant are loving its new look. The Bunker Bar, serving cocktails and snacks, has moved to a new basement level, leaving more room upstairs for new separate tables for six (groups of six must book to secure one), along with the traditional communal table. The generous-size mains are meant to be shared. Begin with a simple starter of either betel nut leaf with prawn-toasted coconut or a freshly shucked oyster with red chili and coriander. Mains include the stir-fried pork belly with chili and ginger, while eggnets—lacy omelets filled with prawns, pork, peanuts, and bean sprouts—are also a popular choice. Longrain's cocktails are legendary for their lethalness; try the ping pong, a luscious mix of passion fruit, lychee, and vodka. ■TIP➔ **Sign up for one of the monthly cocktail classes to learn the barman's secrets.** The Shortgrain casual venue has moved across the road to 8–10 Hunt Street, opposite the Hollywood Hotel (a pub). $ *Average main: A$38* ⌂ *85 Commonwealth St., Surry Hills* ☎ *92/9280–2888* ⊕ *www.longrain.com* ⊜ *Reservations not accepted* ✛ *1:C5.*

$$$$ ✕ **Marque.** Chef Mark Best insists on exemplary service and great food
FRENCH   at this elegant Surry Hills restaurant. Few chefs approach French flavors with such passion and dedication (and stints alongside three-star
demigods Alain Passard in Paris and Raymond Blanc in England haven't
done any harm either). Best's creative fare (which has been called "too
adventurous" by some diners) includes blue swimmer crab with almond
jelly, almond gazpacho and sweet corn, and roasted Muscovy duck with
carrots, kimchi pear, and nori. The night course-degustation (A$160;
A$85 extra for matching wines) will transport you to foodie heaven.
The best deal in town, though, is the Friday-only set-menu three-course
lunch for A$45. There are no individual à la carte prices and a minimum
of three courses. Ⓢ *Average main: A$160* ✉ *355 Crown St., Surry Hills*
☎ *02/9332–2225* 🍴 *Reservations essential* ◯ *Closed Sun. No lunch
Sat.–Thurs.* ✛ *1:D6.*

$ ✕ **Red Lantern on Crown.** Owned by Vietnamese TV chef Luke Nguyen,
VIETNAMESE   this little restaurant with bright red walls and lanterns is popular with
Fodor'sChoice   his legions of TV fans. Diners should always start with the country's
★   great export, rice paper rolls. Here you can have them filled with roast
duck, enoki mushrooms and herbs, or prawns and pork. A recommended main is the ultra tasty *go chien don*—crispy skinned chicken
slowly poached in master stock with ginger, shallot, and oyster sauce.
An unusual but yummy dessert is the black sesame-seed dumplings with
black sesame seed ice cream. For the full range of flavors, there's a tasting menu of nine dishes for A$65 per person (desserts an extra A$10).
Ⓢ *Average main: A$34* ✉ *545 Crown St., Surry Hills* ☎ *02/9698–4355*
⊕ *www.redlantern.com.au* ◯ *Closed Mon. No lunch weekends.* ✛ *1:D6.*

BONDI BEACH

$$ ✕ **Brown Sugar.** You have to seek out this Bondi Beach restaurant, as
MODERN   it's situated a few hundred meters back from the beach. You'll quickly
AUSTRALIAN   find out, however, why locals love this place, which serves organic, sea-
sonal, handcrafted food. This daytime café and evening bistro is small,
hip, and always buzzing. Weekend breakfasts and brunch/lunches are
popular especially if you like Moroccan eggs (slow-cooked with English
spinach, chorizo, spiced peppers, and tomatoes) and sweet treats such
as mouthwatering buttermilk pancakes. It's a popular place for dinner,
too, so book ahead. Main course favorites include fish pie with leek and
truffle oil, while the hazelnut chocolate fondant with honey-malt ice
cream has to be experienced. Ⓢ *Average main: A$34* ✉ *106 Curlewis
St., Bondi Beach* ☎ *02/9130–1566* ⊕ *www.brownsugarbondi.com.au*
◯ *Closed Mon. No breakfast or lunch Tues.–Thurs.* ✛ *2:D3.*

$ ✕ **The Bucket List.** In the famous buttercup-yellow Bondi Pavillon, this
SEAFOOD   beachfront restaurant has broad appeal—there are gatherings of fami-
FAMILY   lies having brunch; lunchers enjoying the spectacular views; twenty-
somethings in for an early evening cocktail at the swanky bar; and
couples tucking into seafood under the stars. The grilled haloumi with
shaved zucchini and the grilled chorizo with lemon are there to be
shared; larger dishes include fish-and-chips, John Dory fish burger with
fries, slipper lobster spaghetti with cherry tomatoes, spinach, chili, and
lemon, and there's a hearty steak or two. And, yes, the cutlery comes
in colorful little buckets and the beachy decor includes surfboards and

funky fish artwork. [$] *Average main: A$23* ✉ *Shop 1, Bondi Pavilion, Queen Elizabeth Dr., Bondi Beach* ☎ *02/9365–4122* 🌐 *www.thebucketlistbondi.com* ✥ *2:D3.*

$$$$ SEAFOOD 🍴 **Catalina Restaurant.** This harbor-front restaurant occupies the site of the old "airport," and has ringside views of the harbor and Shark Island. Patrons can watch modern seaplanes take off and land just meters away while dining on fine seafood. Perched on piers over the water, with a distinctive white profile, Catalina has been one of Sydney's standout fine-dining establishments since it opened in 1994. A unique concept for Sydney, the restaurant kitchen is open from midday to midnight (except on Sunday), allowing diners to turn up at any time; patrons can also pop in for a drink and graze on a casual bar menu. Seafood lovers will relish the oysters, sushi, and sashimi created by the sushi master chef, while the signature dish of roasted suckling pig with braised red cabbage and raisins (A$110) is sensational. The views from the floor-to-ceiling windows, the open deck, and the cozy fire in winter make this a restaurant for all seasons. [$] *Average main: A$46* ✉ *Lyne Park, New South Head Rd., Rose Bay* ☎ *02/9371–0555* 🌐 *www.catalinarosebay.com.au* ⏲ *No dinner Sun.* ✥ *2:C2.*

$$ ITALIAN Fodor's Choice ★ 🍴 **Icebergs Dining Room and Bar.** The fashionable and famous (including celebrities like Mick Jagger) just adore perching like seagulls over the swimming pool at the south end of Australia's most famous beach. After 11 years it is still one of the must-visit restaurants in Sydney, for both the sensational view and the exquisite food. Take a seat on a low-back suede chair, check your reflection in the frosted glass, and prepare to indulge in sophisticated Mediterranean creations like buffalo mozzarella air-freighted from Campania, wood-fried artichoke hearts, aged Sicilian salted anchovies, and ligurian olives served with bruschetta and an array of fresh seafood pasta dishes. If you're a hearty party of eight, tuck into the whole roasted suckling pig on bay leaves with grilled peppers (with 48 hours' notice). Those who just want to drink in the view, and a cocktail or two, can enjoy delicious morsels—such as oysters and mini-ciabattas—in the bar. [$] *Average main: A$44* ✉ *1 Notts Ave., Bondi Beach* ☎ *02/9365–9000* ✍ *Reservations essential* ⏲ *Closed Mon.* ✥ *2:D3.*

$$ AUSTRALIAN 🍴 **Sean's Panaroma.** North Bondi Beach wouldn't be the same without Sean's Panaroma, perched on a slight rise a stone's throw from the famous beach. It's been there since the mid-1990s and owner Sean Moran now graces his table with fresh produce grown on his farm in the Blue Mountains, aptly named "Farm Panaroma." Dishes change regularly and are only featured on a blackboard: they may include backed snapper with red capsicum (bell pepper), olives, eggplant, and tomato, or ravioli of zucchini, mozzarella, and lemons. There are many fans in Sydney, but also a few that say the service is hit-and-miss (if not a bit arrogant), so be warned. A good way to while away a lazy day is the five-course degustation for A$110 and A$160 with wine. [$] *Average main: A$45* ✉ *270 Campbell Parade, Bondi Beach* ☎ *02/9365–4924* 🌐 *www.seanspanaroma.com.au* ⏲ *Closed Mon.–Tues. No dinner Sun. No lunch Wed.–Fri.* ✥ *2:D2.*

$ ╳ **Swell.** When you finish the famous Bondi-to-Bronte coastal cliff walk,
MODERN this is a great place for a meal. By day it's a casual café, but at night it
AUSTRALIAN becomes more formal, thanks to white linen tablecloths and tea lights.
The crispy soft shell crab with green mango salad makes a great light
lunch. When the sun goes down, listen to the surf and order a cocktail,
or a glass of one of the many New South Wales wines, as you pon-
der seasonal menu delights such as Alaskan king crab with tortellini
sweet corn, Avruga caviar, and crispy pancetta. If you'd prefer to sup
in nearby Bronte park, the new adjacent Bronte Cucina serves casual
dine-in or dine-out meals (such as homemade gnocchi with Gorgonzola
sauce) from 5 to 10 pm. ■ TIP→ Swell is open daily for breakfast, lunch,
and dinner in the summer months (December to February). $ *Aver-
age main: A$34 ⊠ 465 Bronte Rd., Bronte ☎ 02/9386–5001 ⊕ www.
swellrestaurant.com.au ☯ Swell: no dinner outside of summer months.
Bronte Cucina: closed Tues.* ⊹ 2:D3.

WHERE TO STAY

From grand hotels with white-glove service to tucked-away bed-and-
breakfasts, there's lodging to fit all styles and budgets in Sydney. The
best addresses in town are undoubtedly in The Rocks, where the tranquil setting and harbor views are right near major cultural attractions, restaurants, shops, and galleries. The area around Kings Cross is
another hotel district, with a good collection of boutique properties as
well as a backpacker magnet. Keep in mind, however, that this is also
the city's major nightlife district, and the scene can get pretty raucous
after sunset.

*Prices in the reviews are the lowest cost of a standard double room in
high season. Use the coordinate (⊹ 1:B2) at the end of each listing to
locate a site on the corresponding map. For expanded hotel reviews,
facilities, and current deals, visit Fodors.com.*

THE ROCKS

$$ 🛏 **Harbour Rocks Hotel.** Formerly a wool-storage facility, this four-
HOTEL story hotel was treated to a total redesign and refurbish following its
rebranding as an Accor McGallery property, which is a select portfo-
lio of distinctive hotels in Australia. **Pros:** great location near harbor;
ultra-stylish refurbishment; unique courtyard in the city. **Cons:** heritage
rooms could be larger; Wi-Fi is an additional charge. $ *Rooms from:
A$269 ⊠ 34 Harrington St., The Rocks ☎ 02/8220–9998 ⊕ www.
harbourrocks.com.au ⤳ 57 rooms, 2 suites* ⍟ *Breakfast* ⊹ 1:B2.

$$ 🛏 **Holiday Inn Old Sydney.** Even though it's been around for a few
HOTEL decades, this hotel with its low-key facade is still a bit of a secret. **Pros:**
fantastic location near harbor; good value; top-story pool. **Cons:** still
has a dated look; street-facing rooms very noisy. $ *Rooms from: A$300
⊠ 55 George St., The Rocks ☎ 1800/669562 ⊕ www.holidayinn.com
⤳ 174 rooms* ⍟ *No meals* ⊹ 1:C2.

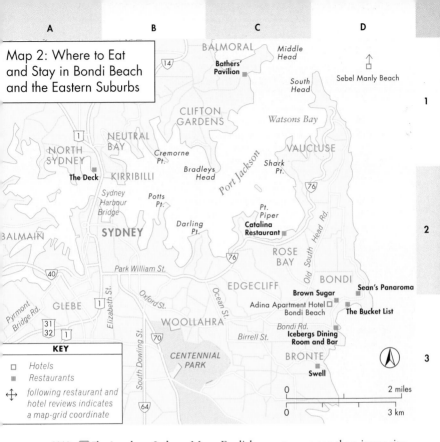

Map 2: Where to Eat and Stay in Bondi Beach and the Eastern Suburbs

KEY

☐ Hotels
■ Restaurants
✣ following restaurant and hotel reviews indicates a map-grid coordinate

$$$$ **The Langham Sydney.** More English country manor than inner-city
HOTEL hotel, this gorgeous property feels like a decadent, luxurious sanctu-
Fodor'sChoice ary. **Pros:** sumptuous; good location; excellent in-house restaurant;
★ afternoon teas. **Cons:** lack of views; Wi-Fi is extra for non–loyalty
member guests. $ *Rooms from: A$630 ⊠ 89–113 Kent St., The Rocks*
☎ *02/9256–2222* ⊕ *www.sydney.langhamhotels.com.au* ⬅ *79 rooms,
21 suites* ❘○❘ *Breakfast* ✣ *1:B2.*

$ **Lord Nelson Brewery Hotel.** If your idea of heaven is sleeping above
B&B/INN a pub that brews its own boutique beers (or ales, as they're rightly
called) then this is the place. **Pros:** great location near harbor; fun pub;
cheap rates. **Cons:** may be noisy on weekend nights; expensive Wi-Fi.
$ *Rooms from: A$180 ⊠ 19 Kent St., The Rocks* ☎ *02/9251–4044*
⊕ *www.lordnelsonbrewery.com* ⬅ *9 rooms* ❘○❘ *Breakfast* ✣ *1:B2.*

$$$$ **Park Hyatt Sydney.** A multimillion-dollar total rebuild, which included
HOTEL the addition of an entire top floor, has seen the iconic Park Hyatt Sydney
Fodor'sChoice reemerge as Sydney's best address. **Pros:** fantastic location; gorgeous
★ views. **Cons:** expensive. $ *Rooms from: A$960 ⊠ 7 Hickson Rd., The
Rocks* ☎ *02/9241–1234* ⊕ *www.sydney.park.hyatt.com* ⬅ *144 rooms,
11 suites* ❘○❘ *No meals* ✣ *1:C1.*

$$ **Rendezvous Stafford Hotel Sydney.** Situated in the heart of the historic
HOTEL Rocks precinct, the lodging has a boutique-hotel style. **Pros:** boutique

feel; great location; in-house movies; free Internet during certain hours; good breakfast/Internet package. **Cons:** simply appointed rooms; tired-looking decor. $ *Rooms from: A$260* ⊠ *75 Harrington St., The Rocks* ☎ *02/9251–6711* ⊕ *www.rendezvoushotels.com/sydney* ↗ *61 apartments, 7 terrace houses* ¶◎¶ *No meals* ✛ *1:B2.*

$$ **The Russell.** For charm, character, and central location, it's hard to
HOTEL   beat this ornate Victorian hotel. **Pros:** location; personal service; warm decor; includes breakfast. **Cons:** not all rooms have en suite bathrooms; near a pub and busy area, so can be noisy. $ *Rooms from: A$269* ⊠ *143A George St., The Rocks* ☎ *02/9241–3543* ⊕ *www.therussell. com.au* ↗ *30 rooms, 20 with en suites* ¶◎¶ *Breakfast* ✛ *1:B2.*

$$$$ **Shangri-La Hotel Sydney.** Towering above Walsh Bay from its prime
HOTEL   position alongside the Sydney Harbour Bridge, this sleek hotel is *the*
Fodor's Choice   place for a room with a bird's-eye view. **Pros:** breathtaking views; sooth-
★   ing decor; great in-house restaurant. **Cons:** impersonal and busy feel at times. $ *Rooms from: A$460* ⊠ *176 Cumberland St., The Rocks* ☎ *02/9250–6000* ⊕ *www.shangri-la.com* ↗ *523 rooms, 40 suites* ¶◎¶ *No meals* ✛ *1:B2.*

DARLING HARBOUR

$$$$ **1888 Hotel.** This former wool warehouse has been turned into one
HOTEL   of Sydney's most cutting-edge designer hotels. **Pros:** great design; free Wi-Fi. **Cons:** small rooms. $ *Rooms from: A$337* ⊠ *18 Murray St., Darling Harbour* ☎ *02/8586–1888* ⊕ *www.1888Hotel.com.au* ↗ *88 room, 2 suites* ¶◎¶ *No meals* ✛ *1:A4.*

SYDNEY CITY CENTER

$$$$ **Fraser Suites Sydney.** This serviced-apartment hotel is one of Sydney's
HOTEL   swankiest places to stay. **Pros:** cutting-edge design; well priced for lon-ger stays; free Wi-Fi throughout. **Cons:** minimalist design may not be everyone's taste. $ *Rooms from: A$650* ⊠ *488 Kent St., City Center* ☎ *02/8823–8888* ⊕ *www.sydney.frasershospitality.com* ↗ *55 room, 146 suites* ¶◎¶ *No meals* ✛ *1:C5.*

$$$ **Hilton Sydney.** At this landmark hotel in downtown Sydney you enter
HOTEL   a spacious, light-filled lobby displaying a stunning four-story sculpture. **Pros:** excellent service; lavishly appointed rooms; hip bar. **Cons:** imper-sonal, at-times busy feel; extra charge for Wi-Fi. $ *Rooms from: A$420* ⊠ *488 George St., City Center* ☎ *02/9266–2000* ⊕ *www.hiltonsydney. com.au* ↗ *550 rooms, 27 suites* ¶◎¶ *No meals* ✛ *1:C4.*

$$ **QT Sydney.** This hotel is the answer for those seeking color and quirki-
HOTEL   ness, teamed with style and super-efficient service. **Pros:** great location; catchy design; stylish bars; historic restoration. **Cons:** funkiness may not be to all tastes; super-soft beds. $ *Rooms from: A$370* ⊠ *49 Market St., at George St., City Center* ☎ *02/8262–2000* ⊕ *www.qtsydney.com. au* ↗ *200 rooms* ¶◎¶ *No meals* ✛ *1:C4.*

$$$ **Westin Sydney.** The Westin hotel chain is renowned for its heavenly
HOTEL   beds—in Sydney it offers heavenly service, too. **Pros:** in-room entertain-ment systems; great service; free Wi-Fi in public areas. **Cons:** slightly corporate feel; Wi-Fi extra for multiple devices. $ *Rooms from: A$370*

✉ 1 Martin Pl., City Center ☎ 02/8223–1111 🌐 www.westin.com/sydney 🛏 400 rooms, 16 suites 🍴 No meals ⊕ 1:C3.

$ HOTEL 🏨 **Y Hotel Hyde Park.** Comfortable and affordable lodgings in a prime city location means that rooms here are often booked months in advance. **Pros:** great value; excellent location. **Cons:** have to book far ahead of time. [$] *Rooms from: A$180* ✉ *5–11 Wentworth Ave., near Hyde Park at Oxford St., City Center* ☎ *1800/994994* 🌐 *www.yhotel.com.au* 🛏 *11 dorm rooms with shared baths, 6 studios, 104 rooms* 🍴 *Breakfast* ⊕ *1:D5.*

2

INNER SYDNEY AND THE EASTERN SUBURBS

PADDINGTON

$ HOTEL 🏨 **Arts Hotel Sydney.** On a quiet stretch in the trendy shopping precinct of Paddington, this small, friendly, family-run hotel has simple accommodations at an outstanding price. **Pros:** great value; personal service; warm feel. **Cons:** simply appointed rooms. [$] *Rooms from: A$175* ✉ *21 Oxford St., Paddington* ☎ *02/9361–0211* 🌐 *www.artshotel.com.au* 🛏 *64 rooms* 🍴 *No meals* ⊕ *1:E6.*

DARLINGHURST

$$$ HOTEL 🏨 **Medusa.** If you're tired of the standard travelers' rooms, this renovated Victorian terrace house may be just the tonic. **Pros:** good location; flashy decor; warm service; kitchenettes in every room; entry to off-site pool and gym; pet-friendly. **Cons:** urban location may get noisy. [$] *Rooms from: A$310* ✉ *267 Darlinghurst Rd., Darlinghurst* ☎ *02/9331–1000* 🌐 *www.medusa.com.au* 🛏 *18 rooms* 🍴 *No meals* ⊕ *1:E5.*

KINGS CROSS

$ B&B/INN 🏨 **Hotel 59 & Cafe.** In its character as well as its dimensions, this friendly B&B on a quiet part of a bar- and club-lined street is reminiscent of a European *pensione.* **Pros:** comfortable rooms, recently repainted; free Wi-Fi; free cooked breakfast. **Cons:** simply appointed; half hour to the city center. [$] *Rooms from: A$130* ✉ *59 Bayswater Rd., Kings Cross* ☎ *02/9360–5900* 🌐 *www.hotel59.com.au* 🛏 *9 rooms* 🍴 *Breakfast* ⊕ *1:F4.*

POTTS POINT

$ HOTEL 🏨 **De Vere Hotel.** "Simply comfortable and affordable" is the slogan at this 1920s-style hotel at the leafy end of Potts Point, and it's hard to disagree on either count. **Pros:** good value; spacious rooms; friendly staff. **Cons:** breakfast, although available on-site, is no longer included in rate. [$] *Rooms from: A$119* ✉ *44–46 Macleay St., Potts Point* ☎ *02/9358–1211* 🌐 *www.devere.com.au* 🛏 *117 rooms, 1 suite* 🍴 *No meals* ⊕ *1:F3.*

$ HOTEL 🏨 **Quest Serviced Apartments Potts Point.** This stylish, early 1920s–style boutique hotel is tucked down a lane in hip Potts Point on the eastern fringe of the city, an ideal base for exploring the eastern suburbs. **Pros:** funky rooms, some with amazing views; good location; free Wi-Fi. **Cons:** neighboring parts of Kings Cross can be seedy and noisy. [$] *Rooms from: A$189* ✉ *15 Springfield Ave., Potts Point*

☎ *2/8988–6999* ⊕ *www.questapartments.com.au* ➣*69 rooms* ¶◎¶ *No meals* ✛ *1:E4.*

$$ 🏨 **Simpsons of Potts Point.** This luxurious boutique hotel is the gem of

HOTEL inner Sydney. **Pros:** friendly, elegant, and cozy; free Wi-Fi and use of

Fodor'sChoice computers; limited free parking; 20-minute walk to city center. **Cons:**

★ no elevator. $ *Rooms from: A\$235* ✉ *8 Challis Ave., Potts Point* ☎ *02/9356–2199* ⊕ *www.simpsonshotel.com.au* ➣*12 rooms* ¶◎¶ *Breakfast* ✛ *1:E3.*

$ 🏨 **Victoria Court Sydney.** A small, smart hotel on a Potts Point street lined

B&B/INN with budget accommodations, the Victoria Court is appealing for more than just its reasonable rates. **Pros:** heritage feel; comfortable rooms. **Cons:** simple amenities; Wi-Fi is extra. $ *Rooms from: A\$165* ✉ *122 Victoria St., Potts Point* ☎ *02/9357–3200* ⊕ *www.victoriacourt.com. au* ➣*25 rooms* ¶◎¶ *Breakfast* ✛ *1:E3.*

WOOLLOOMOOLOO

$$ 🏨 **BLUE Sydney.** This ultrahip hotel, part of the prestigious Taj Hotel

HOTEL group of India, occupies a former warehouse. **Pros:** DVDs and iPod docking stations in all rooms; trendy bar; trendier location. **Cons:** Wi-Fi is extra. $ *Rooms from: A\$280* ✉ *Wharf at Woolloomooloo, 6 Cowper Wharf Rd., Woolloomooloo* ☎ *02/9331–9000* ⊕ *www.tajhotels.com/ sydney* ➣*100 rooms, 36 suites* ¶◎¶ *No meals* ✛ *1:E3.*

BONDI BEACH

$$$ 🏨 **Adina Apartment Hotel Bondi Beach.** This hotel apartment complex is

HOTEL just a few hundred meters from Bondi Beach and includes more than a dozen restaurants, bars, and stores. **Pros:** great location; spacious apartments; part of a new trendy complex. **Cons:** fee for room Wi-Fi and parking. $ *Rooms from: A\$349* ✉ *69–73 Hall St., Bondi Beach* ☎ *02/9300–4800* ⊕ *www.adinahotels.com.au* ➣*56 apartments, 55 rooms* ¶◎¶ *No meals* ✛ *2:D3.*

GREATER SYDNEY

MANLY

$$$ 🏨 **Sebel Manly Beach.** Right on the beachfront of beautiful Manly, this

HOTEL boutique hotel is a mixture of studios and one- and two-bedroom suites, all with private balconies; the more-spacious accommodations have hot tubs, kitchenettes, and high-tech goodies. **Pros:** beachside locale; well-appointed rooms. **Cons:** busy place; expect crowds in summer; expensive Wi-Fi. $ *Rooms from: A\$330* ✉ *8–13 S. Steyne, Manly* ☎ *02/9977–8866* ⊕ *www.accorhotels.com* ➣*83 rooms* ¶◎¶ *No meals* ✛ *2:D1.*

NIGHTLIFE AND THE ARTS

THE ARTS

Although Sydney's contemporary theater pays tribute to the giants of drama, it's also driven by distinctly Australian themes: multiculturalism, relating to the troubled relations between Aboriginal and white Australia, and the search for national identity, characterized by the famous Australian irreverence. Dance, music, and the visual arts are celebrated with equal enthusiasm. At their best, Sydney's artists and performers bring a new slant to the arts, one that reflects the unique qualities of their homeland and the city itself. Standouts on the Sydney arts scene include the Sydney Dance Company, the Museum of Contemporary Art, the Sydney Opera House, and Belvoir Street Theatre. The most comprehensive listing of upcoming events is in the "Metro" section of the *Sydney Morning Herald,* published on Friday. On other days, browse through the entertainment section of the paper.

Ticketek Phone Box Office. This major ticket reservations agency covers most shows and performances. ☏ *13–2849* ⊕ *premier.ticketek.com.au.*

> **A SEA OF TALENT**
>
> **Sculpture by the Sea.** A steel whale's tail sticking out of the ocean and retro kettles cunningly disguised as penguins strapped to a huge rock being lashed by waves are some of the imaginative artworks that have wowed visitors to the annual show called Sculpture by the Sea. Since 1996, artists have positioned their sculptures on rocky outcrops and hilltops along the much-trodden Bondi-to-Bronte Coastal Walk. This free exhibition, which runs for two weeks beginning in late October or early November, attracts thousands of visitors. ⊠ *Bondi-to-Bronte Coastal Walk, Bondi Beach* ⊕ *www.sculpturebythesea.com.*

BALLET, OPERA, AND CLASSICAL MUSIC

Fodor's Choice ★ **Sydney Opera House.** This venue showcases all the performing arts in its five theaters, one of which is devoted to opera. The Australian Ballet, the Sydney Dance Company, and the Australian Opera Company also call the Opera House home. The complex includes two stages for theater and the 2,700-seat Concert Hall, where the Sydney Symphony Orchestra and the Australian Chamber Orchestra perform. The box office is open Monday to Saturday 9–8:30. ⊠ *Bennelong Point, Circular Quay* ☏ *02/9250–7777* ⊕ *www.sydneyoperahouse.com.*

DANCE

Bangarra Dance Theatre. An acclaimed Aboriginal dance company, Bangarra Dance Theatre celebrated its 24th anniversary in 2014. The company stages dramatic productions based on contemporary Aboriginal social themes. The performances are described as a fusion of contemporary dance and storytelling; some will have you transfixed by the sheer energy, lighting, and special effects. ⊠ *Pier 4, 15 Hickson Rd., The Rocks* ☏ *02/9251–5333* ⊕ *www.bangarra.com.au.*

Sydney Dance Company. Sydney Dance Company is an innovative contemporary dance troupe with an international reputation. Spanish choreographer Rafael Bonachela is the artistic director. The company performs in Sydney at the Wharf Theatre, the Sydney Opera House, and the new Sydney Theatre. ⊠ *The Wharf, Pier 4, Hickson Rd., The Rocks* ☏ *02/9221–4811* ⊕ *www.sydneydance.com.au.*

THEATER

Belvoir Street Theatre. This theater has two stages that host innovative and challenging political and social drama. The smaller downstairs space is the home of "B Sharp," which showcases a lineup of brave new Australian drama. The theater is a 10-minute walk from Central Station. ⊠ *25 Belvoir St., Surry Hills* ☎ *02/9699–3444* ⊕ *www.belvoir.com.au.*

Capitol Theatre. This century-old city landmark was refurbished with such modern refinements as fiber-optic ceiling lights that twinkle in time to the music. The 2,000-seat theater specializes in Broadway blockbusters, such as the *Lion King* and *Mary Poppins*, and also hosts pop and rock concerts. ⊠ *13 Campbell St., Haymarket* ☎ *02/9320–5000* ⊕ *www.capitoltheatre.com.au.*

State Theatre. This is the grande dame of Sydney theaters. It operates as a cinema in June each year, when it hosts the two-week-long Sydney Film Festival; at other times this beautiful space hosts local and international performers. Built in 1929 and restored to its full-blown opulence, the theater has a vaulted ceiling, mosaic floors, marble columns and statues, and brass and bronze doors. A highlight of the magnificent theater is the 20,000-piece chandelier that is supposedly the world's second largest, which actor Robin Williams once likened to "one of Imelda Marcos's earrings." ⊠ *49 Market St., City Center* ☎ *02/9373–6655* ⊕ *www. statetheatre.com.au.*

SWB Stables Theatre. SWB Stables Theatre is a small 120-seat venue and home of the Griffin Theatre Company, which specializes in new Australian writing. ⊠ *10 Nimrod St., Kings Cross* ☎ *02/8019–0292* ⊕ *www. griffintheatre.com.au.*

Sydney Lyric. At the newly relaunched Star casino and entertainment complex, Sydney Lyric is one of the city's most spectacular performing-arts venues. Despite its size, there's no better place to watch big-budget musicals. Every seat in the lavishly spacious, 2,000-seat theater is a good one. ⊠ *20–80 Pyrmont St., Pyrmont, Darling Harbour* ☎ *02/9777–9000* ⊕ *www.star.com.au.*

Wharf Theatre. On a redeveloped wharf in the shadow of Harbour Bridge, Wharf Theatre is the headquarters of the Sydney Theatre Company (STC), one of Australia's most original and highly regarded performance groups: Cate Blanchett and husband Andrew Upton are the artistic directors. Contemporary British and American plays and the latest offerings from leading Australian playwrights such as David Williamson and Nick Enright are the main attractions. The company also performs at the Sydney Opera House and at the new Sydney Theatre just a few doors away, located opposite Pier 6/7 at No. 22 Hickson Road. ⊠ *Pier 4, Hickson Rd., The Rocks* ☎ *02/9250–1777* ⊕ *sydney-theatre.com.au.*

NIGHTLIFE

The *Sydney Morning Herald*'s daily entertainment section is the most informative guide to the city's pubs and clubs. For club-scene coverage—who's been seen where and what they were wearing—pick up a

Inside Sydney's renowned Opera House

free copy of *The Music* magazine (⊕ *www.themusic.com.au*) available at just about any Oxford Street café or pub. The CitySearch (⊕ *www.sydney.citysearch.com.au*) and Ever Guide (⊕ *www.everguide.com.au*) are other good online sources of entertainment information.

All bars and clubs listed here are open daily unless noted. Entry is free unless we list a cover charge.

SYDNEY HARBOUR

BARS AND DANCE CLUBS

The Oaks. For a northern Sydney landmark, The Oaks encapsulates the very best of the modern pub. The immensely popular watering hole is big and boisterous, with a beer garden, a restaurant, and several bars offering varying levels of sophistication. It's packed on Friday and Saturday nights. ⊠ *118 Military Rd., Neutral Bay* ☎ *02/9953–5515.*

THE ROCKS

BARS AND DANCE CLUBS

Blu Bar on 36. Blu Bar on 36 has a stellar view! Situated on the 36th floor of the Shangri-La Hotel, this is a sophisticated place to relax after work or enjoy a late-night drink while taking in the sweeping views of Sydney Harbour and the Opera House. Get here early (just after 5 pm) for a ringside seat. ⊠ *Shangri-La Hotel, 176 Cumberland St., The Rocks* ☎ *02/9250–6000.*

Opera Bar. Perched beneath the concourse of the Opera House and at eye level with Sydney Harbour, Opera Bar has the best location in all of Sydney. Cozy up for a drink in the enclosed bar area or grab a waterside umbrella table and take in the glimmering skyline. Live music plays under the stars nightly from either 5:30 or 8 pm on weeknights, and from 2 pm on weekends. The bar has a full menu, though the attraction here is the scenery, not the cuisine. ⊠ *Sydney Opera House, Circular Quay* ☎ *02/9247–1666.*

JAZZ CLUBS

The Basement. A Sydney legend, The Basement is the premier venue for top local and international jazz, rock, and blues musicians. Lunch is available weekdays, dinner Monday–Saturday. Performances begin around A$35 (standing room), while dinner and show packags are from A$75. ⊠ *29 Reiby Pl., near Macquarie Pl., Circular Quay* ☎ *02/9251–2797* ⊕ *www.thebasement.com.au.*

PUBS WITH MUSIC

Mercantile Hotel. In the shadow of Harbour Bridge, Mercantile Hotel is Irish and very proud of it. Fiddles, drums, and pipes rise above the clamor in the bar, and lilting accents rejoice in song seven nights a week and on weekends from 3 pm. ⊠ *25 George St., The Rocks* ☎ *02/9247–3570.*

DARLING HARBOUR

BARS AND DANCE CLUBS

Bungalow 8. With its primo waterside location at the northern end of King Street Wharf, and famous mussels from its open kitchen, Bungalow 8 invites a night of posing and partying. This is the place to be seen bobbing your head to the spinning of several ultra-cool resident DJs. Tuesday is especially packed for the all-you-can-eat mussel extravaganza. ⊠ *King Street Wharf, 3 Lime St., Darling Harbour* ☎ *02/9299–4660* ⊕ *www.bungalow8sydney.com.*

Marquee—The Star Sydney. Nightclubbers are heading to Marquee—on the top level of the relaunched casino and entertainment complex, The Star Sydney—to dance the night away. The huge nightclub heaves with 1,500 twentysomethings who take to the dance floors in the Main Room and the smaller Boom Box, or chill out in the opulent Library bar. R&B artists and local and international DJs perform on weekends, with tickets from A$25. When it's time to cool down, there are great outdoor balconies overlooking the city and Darling Harbour. ⊠ *80 Pyrmont St., Darling Harbour* ☎ *02/9657–7737* ⊕ *www.marqueesydney.com.*

SYDNEY CITY CENTER

BARS AND DANCE CLUBS

The Arthouse Hotel. A former School of the Arts building, The Arthouse Hotel has been renovated into a modern, Belle Époque–style hot spot, with four bars and a restaurant spread over three cavernous floors. Art is the focus here, whether it's visual—life-drawing classes are given on Monday, a burlesque drawing class biweekly on Tuesday—aural, or comestible, and there is a full-time curator dedicated to programming events and installing exhibitions. ⊠ *275 Pitt St., City Center* ☎ *02/9284–1200* ⊕ *www.arthousehotel.com.au.*

Bambini Wine Room. Bambini Wine Room is a sparkling little jewel box encased in marble-clad walls and topped with lovely chandeliers. You can sip cocktails (A$17) and any number of fine wines late into the night and feast on affordable bar snacks. ⊠ *185 Elizabeth St., City Center* ☎ *02/9283–7098.*

Hemmesphere. One of a string of swanky venues in the area, Hemmesphere is still drawing a hip crowd 12 years after it first opened. Named for Justin Hemmes, son of iconic 1970s fashion designers Jon and Merivale Hemmes, this is where Sydney's hippest pay homage to cocktail culture from low, leather divans. The mood is elegant and sleek, and so are the well-dressed guests, who often include whichever glitterati happen to be in town. It's on the fourth level of the Establishment Hotel complex and draws those seeking an escape from the rowdy action downstairs. ⊠ *Level 4, 252 George St., City Center* ☎ *02/9240–3104* ⊙ *Closed Sun.*

Ivy. This mutlilevel complex of bars, pubs, and eateries is in an ultra-hip George Street complex. Cocktails are great, but expensive, and the crowd varies depending on night. If you don't fancy this bar, then there's the decadent Pool bar on the top floor, where if you get there early you can recline in your own cabana overlooking the swimming pool. Also on-site are the Den (a lavish bar with chaise lounge furniture, chandeliers, and cigar menu), the casual Royal George pub, and the Ash Street Cellar bistro. Add to all these watering-hole options A$12 jugs of beer, music most nights, and all-you-can-eat promos (at around A$20). ⊠ *330 George St., City Center* ☎ *02/9240–3000.*

Lobo Plantation. This Cuban-themed bar is a hit in Sydney. Patrons love the palm trees, the cane furniture, and the wall lined with Cuban bank notes. Cocktails (from around A$17) have a 1950s theme so you could try an Esther Williams, a Nuclear Daiquiri, or a Message in a Bottle that comes with its own miniature bottle. The affordable bar menu, which runs from tamales to black bean stew and pork crackling, helps soak up the alcohol. ⊠ *209 Clarence St., City Center* ☎ *02/9279–4335* ⊕ *www.thelobo.com.au* ⊙ *Closed Sun.*

O Bar and Dining. This is the place to come at sunset for the view, tapas, and cocktails—and the '70s kitsch of a revolving restaurant. Located on level 47 of the Australia Square building, O Bar has floor-to-ceiling windows, so no matter which seat you have, the view is great, and constantly changing. It's perfect for a predinner drink, or dinner, too. It's open daily from 5 pm and Friday lunch. ⊠ *Australia Sq., Level 47, 264 George St., City Center* ☎ *02/9247–7777* ⊕ *obardining.com.au.*

INNER SYDNEY AND THE EASTERN SUBURBS
BARS AND DANCE CLUBS
Beach Road Hotel. This Bondi institution is famous for its Sunday Sessions, when locals come to enjoy a barbecue, drink, and dance in the outdoor courtyard. There's music every night in summer time (except Monday), good affordable food, and A$15 chicken fajitas and a Corona (a Mexican beer) on Thursday nights. ⊠ *71 Beach Rd., Bondi Beach* ☎ *02/9130–7247* ⊕ *www.beachroadbondi.com.au.*

Eau de Vie. You might have to seek them out but speakeasy-style bars are the new thing in Sydney. Eau de Vie, at the rear of the trendy Kirkton Hotel in Darlinghurst, perfectly fits the bill, especially with its cocktail menu. It's designed with the decades in mind, with drinks that fit into themes such as "1920s—The Train from Paris to Milan" and "1930s—The Boat to Cuba and Caribbean." On board the Paris locomotive you can try the Absinthe Frappe (A$19), a mix of La Fee Absinthe, maraschino liqueur, and honey and lemon squeezed over fresh ice. Drinks are a little pricey, but the bar staff and the patrons are friendly and the jazz-infused music takes the pain out of the bill. There's a bar snack menu, too. ⊠ *229 Darlinghurst Rd., Darlinghurst* ☎ *0422/263–226* ⊕ *www.eaudevie. com.au.*

Hugo's Lounge. This is the place that transformed Kings Cross from a seedy crossroads of sex shops and smut to a must-be-seen-here destination for Sydney's beautiful people. Red lamps are a nod to the neighborhood's skin trade, but the deep couches, opulent ottomans, and decadent cocktail menu are purely upmarket. Three cocktail bars, a terrace on which to mix and mingle, and DJs every night, means there's something for every taste. The downstairs pizza bar is part of the Hugo's stable of eateries. ⊠ *Level 1, 33 Bayswater Rd., Kings Cross* ☎ *02/9357–4411* ⊗ *Closed Mon.–Wed.*

> ## HAVE A GAY OLD TIME
>
> If you're in Sydney in late February and early March, you'll think the whole city has gone gay. The Sydney Gay and Lesbian Mardi Gras parade, which celebrated its 36th anniversary in 2014, is one of Australia's major events. Dozens of floats covered with buff dancers make their way from College Street, near St. Mary's Cathedral, up Oxford Street to Taylor's Square. Thousands of spectators watch this amazing party parade.

COMEDY CLUBS

Sydney's Comedy Store. The city's oldest comedy club is in a plush 300-seat theater in the Entertainment Quarter, which most people still refer to as Fox Studios (its former name). The difficult-to-find theater is at the rear of the complex, close to the parking lot. Shows are Tuesday–Saturday at 8:30 pm, and admission runs A$20 to A$30. ⊠ *Entertainment Quarter, Bent St. off Driver Ave., Centennial Park* ☎ *02/9357–1419* ⊕ *www.comedystore.com.au.*

GAY AND LESBIAN BARS AND CLUBS

Most of the city's gay and lesbian venues are along Oxford Street, in Darlinghurst. The free *Sydney Star Observer,* available along Oxford Street, has a roundup of Sydney's gay and lesbian goings-on, or check the magazine's website (⊕ *www.starobserver.com.au*). A monthly free magazine, *Lesbians on the Loose* (⊕ *www.lotl.com*), lists events for women, and the free *SX* online magazine (⊕ *www.gaynewsnetwork. com.au*) lists bars and events.

ARQ. Sydney's biggest, best-looking, and funkiest gay nightclub, ARQ attracts a clean-cut crowd who like to whip off their shirts as soon as they hear the beat. (Some women head here, too.) There are multiple dance floors, a bar, and plenty of chrome and sparkly lighting. It's open from 9 pm until whenever Thursday through Sunday; a Thursday-night drag contest is free, while shows have a cover charge ranging from A$15 to A$25 (and sometimes a little more) depending on where you arrive. ⊠ *16 Flinders St., Darlinghurst* ☎ *02/9380–8700* ⊕ *www. arqsydney.com.au.*

The Midnight Shift. The Midnight Shift is Sydney's hard-core party zone, a living legend on the gay scene for its longevity and its take-no-prisoners approach. If anything, the upstairs nightclub, with drag acts and shows every night of the week and DJs every other night, is a little quieter than the ground-floor bars, where most of the leather-loving men go to shoot pool. Opening hours are weekdays from 4 pm until late; weekends from 2 pm. ⊠ *85 Oxford St., Darlinghurst* ☎ *02/9360–4463.*

JAZZ CLUBS

The Vanguard. The Vanguard is Sydney's answer to a New Orleans jazz joint, and purposely built by its music-loving owners to mimic the U.S. model. Australian and international jazz, blues, and roots performers love this intimate venue with its 1920s decor and friendly vibe. Ticket prices range from around A$30 (some performances are free); it's advised to book a dinner and show package to get the best seats in the house. ⊠ *42 King St., Newtown* ☎ *02/9550–3666.*

PUBS WITH MUSIC

Harold Park Hotel. This is a great comedy venue that also serves up excellent jazz, pop, rock, and blues performances, often featuring artists playing in Australia's top world music and blues festivals when they are in town. Often the performances are free. Comedy nights (around A$10 to A$15 for a performance) are held on Tuesday at 8 pm; international comedy stars have been known to drop into the pub when they're in town (and do a spot of stand-up). ⊠ *70A Ross St., Glebe* ☎ *02/9660–4745.*

Unity Hall Hotel. This quaint pub in the left-of-center suburb of Balmain declares itself the "spiritual home of jazz and live music for the past 40 years." Its resident jazz band has been playing there since 1972 and you can hear them for free each Sunday at 4 pm. A variety of live music including pop, rock, swing, and blues is also on the bill. Music cranks up on Friday and Saturday nights from 9 pm. The pub attracts a friendly, unpretentious crowd and supports up-and-coming bands. ⊠ *292 Darling St., Balmain* ☎ *02/9810–1331* ⊕ *www.unityhallhotel. com.au.*

SHOPPING

Sydney's shops vary from those with international cachet to Aboriginal art galleries, opal shops, craft bazaars, and weekend flea markets. If you're interested in buying genuine Australian products, look carefully at the labels. Stuffed koalas and didgeridoos made anywhere but in Australia are a standing joke.

Aboriginal art includes historically functional items, such as boomerangs, wooden bowls, and spears, as well as paintings and ceremonial implements that testify to a rich culture of legends and dreams. Although much of this artwork remains strongly traditional in essence, the tools and colors used in Western art have fired the imaginations of many Aboriginal artists. Works on canvas are now more common than works on bark. Much of the best work of Arnhem Land and the Central

Desert Region (close to Darwin and Alice Springs, respectively) finds its way into Sydney galleries.

Australia has a virtual monopoly on the world's supply of opals. The least expensive of these fiery gemstones are triplets, which consist of a thin shaving of opal mounted on a plastic base and covered by a plastic, glass, or quartz crown. Doublets are a slice of mounted opal without the capping. The most expensive stones are solid opals, which cost anywhere from a few hundred dollars to a few thousand. You can pick up opals at souvenir shops all over the city, but if you want a valuable stone you should visit a specialist. Sydney is also a good hunting ground for other jewelry, from the quirky to the gloriously expensive.

THE ROCKS

JEWELRY AND ACCESSORIES

Hathi Jewellery. Here you'll find a beautiful collection of handmade jewelry including earrings, necklaces, and bracelets. Most pieces are one of a kind. ⊠ *19 Playfair St., The Rocks* ☎ *02/9252–4328* ⊕ *www. hathijewellery.com.au.*

MARKETS

The Rocks Market. This sprawling covered bazaar transforms the upper end of George Street into a multicultural collage of music, food, arts, crafts, and entertainment. Open weekends 10–5. Be sure to check out the new Rocks Foodies Market with delicious fare, on Fridays 10–4. ⊠ *Upper George St. near Argyle St., The Rocks* ⊕ *www.therocks.com/ sydney-Shopping-The_Rocks_Markets.htm.*

DARLING HARBOUR

MARKETS

Paddy's Market. Paddy's Market is a huge fresh produce and flea market held under the Market City complex near the Sydney Entertainment Centre in the Chinatown precinct. There has been a market on this site since 1834, and much of the historic exterior remains. The Metro Light Rail stops at the door. ⊠ *9–13 Hay St., Haymarket* ⊕ *www. paddysmarkets.com.au* ⊗ *Wed.–Sun. 9–5.*

SYDNEY CITY CENTER

BOOKS

Ariel Booksellers. This is a large, bright browser's delight, and the place to go for literature, pop culture, avant garde, and art books. There is another location at 103 George Street in The Rocks. Both branches are open daily 9 am–10:30 pm. ⊠ *42 Oxford St., Paddington* ☎ *02/9332– 4581* ⊕ *www.arielbooks.com.au.*

Dymocks. This big, bustling bookstore is packed to its gallery-level coffee shop and is the place to go for all literary needs. ⊠ *424 George St., City Center* ☎ *02/9235–0155* ⊕ *www.dymocks.com.au* ⊗ *Mon.–Wed. and Fri. 9–6, Thurs. 9–8, Sat. 9:30–5:30, Sun. 10:30–5.*

CLOTHING

Country Road. The fashion here stands somewhere between Ralph Lauren and Timberland, with an all-Australian assembly of classic, countrified his 'n' hers, plus an ever-expanding variety of soft furnishings in cotton and linen for the rustic retreat. ⊠ *142–144 Pitt St., City Center* ☎ *02/9394–1818* ⊕ *www.countryroad.com.au.*

Marcs. The clothing here is located somewhere close to Diesel-land in the fashion spectrum, with a variety of clothing, footwear, and accessories for the fashion-conscious. Serious shoppers should look for the Marcs Made in Italy sub-label for that extra touch of class. ⊠ *Queen Victoria Building, 455 George St., Shop 1, City Center* ☎ *02/9267–0823* ⊕ *www.marcs.com.au.*

Mountain Designs. In the middle of Sydney's "Rugged Row" of outdoor specialists, this store sells camping and climbing gear and dispenses the advice necessary to keep you alive and well in the wilderness. ⊠ *499 Kent St., City Center* ☎ *02/9267–3822* ⊕ *www.mountaindesigns.com.au.*

Paddy Pallin. This should be the first stop for serious bush adventurers heading for wild Australia and beyond. Maps, books, and mounds of gear are tailored especially for the Australian outdoors. ⊠ *507 Kent St., City Center* ☎ *02/9264–2685* ⊕ *www.paddypallin.com.au.*

R. M. Williams. This is the place to go for riding boots, Akubra hats, Drizabone riding coats, and moleskin trousers—the type of clothes worn by Hugh Jackman and Nicole Kidman in the movie *Australia.* ⊠ *389 George St., City Center* ☎ *02/9262–2228* ⊕ *www.rmwilliams.com.au.*

DEPARTMENT STORES AND SHOPPING CENTERS

David Jones. The city's largest department store maintains a reputation for excellent service and high-quality goods. Clothing by many of Australia's finest designers is on display here, and the store also sells its own fashion label at reasonable prices. The women's store is at the corner of Elizabeth and Market streets; the men's store (which also has a great food hall in its basement) is at the corner of Castlereagh and Market streets. ⊠ *Women's store, Elizabeth and Market Sts., City Center* ☎ *02/9266–5544* ⊕ *www.davidjones.com.au.*

Pitt Street Mall. The heart of Sydney's shopping area includes the Mid-City Centre, the newly redeveloped and huge Westfield Sydney Shopping Centre, Skygarden, Myer, and the charming and historic Strand Arcade—five multilevel shopping plazas crammed with more than 500 shops, from mainstream clothing stores to designer boutiques. ■ TIP➔ Just a short walk away is the iconic David Jones store on Elizabeth St. ⊠ *Between King and Market Sts., City Center.*

Queen Victoria Building. This is a splendid Victorian-era building with more than 200 boutiques, cafés, and antiques shops. The building is open 24 hours, so you can window-shop even after the stores have closed. ⊠ *George, York, Market, and Druitt Sts., City Center* ☎ *02/9264–9209* ⊕ *www.qvb.com.au.*

JEWELRY AND ACCESSORIES

Dinosaur Designs. This fun store sells luminous bowls, plates, and vases, as well as fanciful jewelry crafted from resin and Perspex in eye-popping colors. There's another location at 339 Oxford Street in Paddington. ⊠ *Shop 77, Strand Arcade, George St., City Center* ☎ *02/9223–2953* ⊕ *www.dinosaurdesigns.com.au.*

The National Opal Collection. The National Opal Collection is the only Sydney opal retailer with total ownership of its entire production process—mines, workshops, and showroom—making prices very competitive. In the Pitt Street showroom, you can prearrange to see artisans at work cutting and polishing the stones or visit the on-site museum and learn about the process of opal development and opalized fossils. Hours are weekdays 9–6 and weekends 10–4. ⊠ *60 Pitt St., City Center* ☎ *02/9247–6344* ⊕ *www.gemtec.com.au.*

Paspaley Pearls. The jewelers here order their exquisite material from pearl farms near the remote Western Australia town of Broome. Prices start high and head for the stratosphere, but if you're serious about a high-quality pearl, this gallery requires a visit. ⊠ *Paspaley Bldg., 2 Martin Pl., City Center* ☎ *02/9232–7633, 1300/888080* ⊕ *www. paspaleypearls.com.*

Percy Marks Fine Gems. Here you'll find an outstanding collection of high-quality Australian gemstones, including dazzling black opals, pink diamonds, and pearls from Broome. ⊠ *62–70 Elizabeth St., City Center* ☎ *02/9233–1355* ⊕ *www.percymarks.com.au.*

Rox Gems and Jewellery. Come here for serious one-off designs at the cutting edge of lapidary chic. ⊠ *Shop 31, Strand Arcade, George St., City Center* ☎ *02/9232–7828* ⊕ *www.rox.com.au.*

MUSIC

Birdland Records. This institution for music lovers has an especially strong selection of jazz, blues, African, and Latin American music, as well as an authoritative staff ready to lend some assistance. ⊠ *Level 4, Dymocks Bldg., 428 George St., City Center* ☎ *02/9231–1188* ⊕ *www. birdland.com.au.*

INNER SYDNEY AND THE EASTERN SUBURBS

ART AND CRAFT GALLERIES

Cooee Aboriginal Art. This gallery, open Tuesday–Saturday 10–5, exhibits and sells high-end Aboriginal paintings, sculptures, and limited-edition prints. It's a five-minute walk from Bondi Beach. ⊠ *31 Lamrock Ave., Bondi Beach* ☎ *02/9300–9233* ⊕ *www.cooeeart.com.au.*

BOOKS

Gertrude & Alice Café Bookshop. Need something to read on Bondi Beach? Take a stroll to Gertrude & Alice Café Bookshop, named in honor of lovers Gertrude Stein and Alice B. Toklas. Always buzzing with people, it's a great place to sip coffee or chai lattes, or have lunch while perusing the mostly secondhand books. ⊠ *46 Hall St., Bondi Beach* ☎ *02/9130– 5155* ☉ *Daily 7:30 am–9:30 pm.*

Aboriginal paintings are visual representations of ancestral stories from "The Dreaming."

CLOTHING

Belinda. This is where Sydney's female fashionistas go when there's a dress-up occasion looming. From her namesake store that scores high marks for innovation and imagination, former model Belinda Seper sells nothing but the very latest designs off the catwalks. ⊠ *8 and 14 Transvaal Ave., Double Bay* ☎ *02/9328–6288, 02/9327–8199* ⊕ *www. belinda.com.au.*

Collette Dinnigan. One of the hottest names on Australia's fashion scene, Collette has dressed Nicole Kidman, Cate Blanchett, and Sandra Bullock. Her Paddington boutique is packed with sensual, floating, negligee-inspired fashions crafted from silks, chiffons, and lace in soft pastel colors accented with hand-beading and embroidery. Her clothes are also available at the David Jones women's store in the city center. ⊠ *104 Queen St., Woollahra* ☎ *02/9360–6691* ⊕ *www.collettedinnigan.com. au.*

Scanlan & Theodore. This is the Sydney outlet for one of Melbourne's most distinguished fashion houses. Designs take their cues from Europe, with superbly tailored women's knitwear, suits, and stylishly glamorous evening wear. ⊠ *122 Oxford St., at Glenmore Rd., Paddington* ☎ *02/9380–9388* ⊕ *www.scanontheodore.com.au.*

DEPARTMENT STORES AND SHOPPING CENTERS

Oxford Street. Paddington's main artery, from South Dowling Street east to Queen Street, Woollahra, is dressed to thrill. Lined with boutiques, home-furnishings stores, and cafés, it's a perfect venue for watching the never-ending fashion parade. Take Bus No. 380, 382 and 333 from Circular Quay. ⊠ *Oxford St., Paddington.*

MARKETS

Fodor's Choice   **Paddington Markets.** Paddington Markets (sometimes called Paddington
★   Bazaar) is a busy churchyard market with about 200 stalls crammed
with clothing, plants, crafts, jewelry, and souvenirs. Distinctly New
Age and highly fashion conscious, the market is an outlet for a handful
of avant-garde clothing designers. ⊠ *Paddington Uniting Church, 395
Oxford St., Paddington* ☎ *02/9331–2923* ⊕ *www.paddingtonmarkets.
com.au* ☉ *Sat. 10–4.*

GREATER SYDNEY

ART AND CRAFT GALLERIES

Kate Owen Gallery + Studio. This gallery showcases quality indigenous
art over three levels in Rozelle, a suburb about 15 minutes west of the
city center. Take the M50 or M52 bus from the bus station behind the
Queen Victoria Building; alight at the corner of Victoria Road and Darling Street. ⊠ *680 Darling St., at Victoria Rd., Rozelle* ☎ *02/9555–5283*
⊕ *www.kateowengallery.com.*

DEPARTMENT STORES AND SHOPPING CENTERS

Birkenhead Point. A factory outlet with more than 100 clothing, shoe,
and housewares stores on the western shores of Iron Cove about 7
km (4 miles) west of Sydney, Birkenhead Point is a great place to shop
for discounted labels including Alannah Hill, Witchery, Bendon (Elle
Macpherson's lingerie range), Rip Curl, and David Jones warehouse.
Take Bus 504, 506, 518 or the M52 (a new red metro bus) from Druitt
Street near Town Hall station and also Circular Quay. Water taxis
depart from the site for Circular Quay and Darling Harbour. ⊠ *Roseby
St., near the Iron Cove Bridge, Drummoyne* ☎ *02/9182–8800* ⊕ *www.
birkenheadpoint.com.au.*

MARKETS

Balmain Market. In a leafy churchyard less than 5 km (3 miles) from
the city, Balmain Market has a rustic quality that makes it a refreshing
change from city-center shopping. Crafts, handmade furniture, plants,
bread, toys, tarot readings, and massages are among the offerings at the
140-odd stalls. Inside the church hall you can buy international snacks.
Every Saturday 8:30–4. Take Bus No. 442 from the Queen Victoria
Building in York Street. ⊠ *St. Andrew's Church, Darling St., Greater
Sydney* ☎ *9555–1791* ⊕ *www.balmainmarket.com.au.*

NEW SOUTH WALES

with Canberra and the A.C.T.

WELCOME TO NEW SOUTH WALES

TOP REASONS TO GO

★ **Getting in Touch with Nature:** Exotic birds are prolific in the Blue Mountains and North Coast regions, and Canberra isn't known as the "Bush Capital" for nothing.

★ **The Great Australian Bite:** Fine restaurants abound in the Hunter Valley, as well as in the North Coast towns of Coffs Harbour and Byron Bay. Seafood can be excellent, and don't miss fish-and-chips on the beach.

★ **Outdoor Adventure:** The region's mountains and national parks offer opportunities for walks and hikes, horseback riding, rappelling, canyoning, and rock climbing. Outdoorsy folks will enjoy Canberra's wide-open spaces and cycling or walking around the city's Lake Burley Griffin.

★ **World-Class Wineries:** The Hunter Valley has an international reputation for producing excellent Chardonnay, Shiraz, and a dry Semillon.

1 The Blue Mountains. Sydneysiders flock to this UNESCO-protected wilderness region with its majestic mountain peaks and deep green valleys sprinkled with charming country guesthouses. The famous sandstone rock formations known as the Three Sisters are the area's best-known attraction.

2 Hunter Valley Wine Region. This is one of the oldest and best-known wine regions in Australia, with vineyards dating back to the 1830s. Oenophiles shouldn't miss a trip to this thriving and perennially busy destination. We also like the food, historic towns, and tranquil countryside.

3 The North Coast. This region has some of the most glorious and seductive stretches of beach in Australia—and that's saying something when you consider the competition. The almost continuous line of beaches is interspersed with lively towns and harbors, with the Great Dividing Range rising to the west.

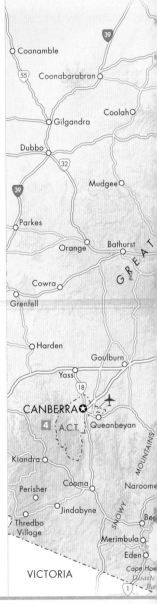

GETTING ORIENTED

New South Wales, with the country's capital city Canberra and the A.C.T. carved out in an area half the size of Rhode Island, covers the southeast corner of the country. Despite this being Australia's most populous state, the rich variety of landscapes is its biggest selling point. The Blue Mountains, a World Heritage site, lie approximately 100 km (60 miles) to the west of Sydney; the Hunter Valley is about 160 km (100 miles) or two hours north of Sydney. The North Coast is exactly where its name suggests, while Lord Howe Island is offshore, 700 km (435 miles) northeast of Sydney. Canberra is 288 km (180 miles) southwest of Sydney.

3

4 Canberra and the A.C.T. The nation's capital and its environs may be quiet and a little too well-mannered for some, but its museums and galleries are the best in the country, and its diverse range of parks and gardens is a major draw.

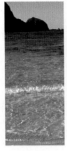

Updated by Caroline Gladstone

For many travelers Sydney is New South Wales, and they look to the other, less-populous states for Australia's famous wilderness experiences. However, New South Wales contains many of Australia's natural wonders. High on the list are the subtropical rain forests of the North Coast, lush river valleys, warm seas, golden beaches, the World Heritage areas of Lord Howe Island, and some of Australia's finest vineyards. Many travelers overlook Canberra, but history buffs and art aficionados love its selection of galleries and museums, which rank among the nation's finest.

Today, with approximately 7.3 million people, New South Wales is Australia's most populous state—it's home to about one-third of the nation's population. Although it's crowded by Australian standards, keep in mind that New South Wales is larger than every U.S. state except Alaska. In the state's east, a coastal plain reaching north to Queensland varies in width from less than a mile to almost 160 km (100 miles). This plain is bordered on the west by a chain of low mountains known as the Great Dividing Range, which tops off at about 7,300 feet in the Snowy Mountains in the state's far south. On this range's western slopes is a belt of pasture and farmland. Beyond that are the western plains and Outback, an arid, sparsely populated region that takes up two-thirds of the state.

PLANNING

WHEN TO GO

For visitors from the northern hemisphere the Australian summer (approximately December–February) has great pull. The best times to visit the Hunter Valley are during the February–March grape harvest season and the June Hunter Food and Wine Festival. Spring and autumn are also ideal times to visit Canberra; from March to May, autumn leaves paint the city with amber hues. The spring flower celebration, Floriade, lasts from mid-September to mid-October. The North Coast resort region is often booked solid between Christmas and the first half of January, but autumn and spring are good times to visit.

GETTING HERE AND AROUND

AIR TRAVEL

New South Wales is peppered with airports, so flying is the easiest way to get around if you're traveling long distances. You can score the best fares during the quieter seasons. From Sydney, REX (Regional Express) Airlines services Ballina and Lismore (both about thirty minutes from Byron Bay). Qantas flies into Canberra, Port Macquarie, and Coffs Harbour, while Virgin Australia (formerly Virgin Blue) flies into Canberra, Port Macquarie, Ballina, and Coffs Harbour.

Airline Contacts Qantas Airways ☎ *13–1313* ⊕ *www.qantas.com.au.*
REX Airlines ☎ *13–1713* ⊕ *www.regionalexpress.com.au.* **Virgin Australia**
☎ *13–6789* ⊕ *www.virginaustralia.com.*

CAR RENTAL

Hiring your own car is the most convenient way of getting around the region. The scenic Blue Mountains and Hunter Valley routes and attractions are outside the towns, so having your own set of wheels is helpful. When visiting the wine country, be aware that Australia has very strict rules against drunk driving. Most towns have major car-rental companies. You can pick up a car at one point and drop off at another for an extra fee.

TRAIN TRAVEL

As in the States, most people drive here, so train services aren't brilliant and can often cost more than other options. It is possible to travel by train to the Blue Mountains with the Sydney Trains (aka CityRail) commuter network. NSW TrainLink (aka CountryLink) connects Sydney to towns in the Hunter Valley and along the North Coast. Canberra is not conveniently reached by train; it's quicker to drive, fly, or catch a bus.

Train Information Sydney Trains ☎ *13–1500* ⊕ *www.sydneytrains.info.* **NSW TrainLink** ☎ *13–2232, 02/4907–7501* ⊕ *www.nswtrainlink.info.*

RESTAURANTS

Dining varies dramatically throughout New South Wales, from superb city-standard restaurants to average country-town fare. As popular weekend retreats for Sydneysiders, the Blue Mountains have a number of fine restaurants and cozy tearooms that are perfect for light meals. In the Hunter Valley several excellent restaurants show off the region's fine wines. Unsurprisingly, seafood dominates on the North Coast, and again, thanks to holidaying Sydneysiders with high standards, you should be able to tuck into some memorable meals. *Prices in the reviews are the average cost of a main course at dinner or, if dinner is not served, at lunch.*

HOTELS

Accommodations include everything from run-of-the-mill motels and remote wilderness lodges to historic, cliff-perched properties and expansive seaside resorts. Rates are often much lower on weekdays,

GREAT ITINERARIES

It's wise to decide in advance whether you'd like to cover a lot of ground quickly or choose one or two places to linger a while. If you have less than four days, stick close to Sydney. The most compelling choice is the Blue Mountains, followed by the Hunter Valley. In a busy four- to seven-day period you could visit the Blue Mountains plus the Hunter Valley.

IF YOU HAVE 4 DAYS

Start with a visit to the **Blue Mountains.** You could arrange a round-trip itinerary from Sydney in a fairly hectic day or, preferably, spend a night in **Katoomba, Blackheath,** or **Leura** and make it a two-day excursion. Return to Sydney, and then head north to the **Hunter Valley.** A two-day/one-night driving visit here allows you enough time to see the main sights and spend time touring the wineries before traveling back to Sydney on the second day. An alternative would be a quick visit to the Blue Mountains, then two days in Canberra to see the city's excellent museums and galleries.

particularly in the Blue Mountains and the Hunter Valley, as traffic from Sydney is heavier on weekends. The North Coast is popular during school holidays, so book as far ahead as possible. Hotels in Canberra, with one or two notable exceptions, don't have the character that other places do. But there are plenty of upscale chain hotel options and self-catering apartments. *Prices in the reviews are the lowest cost of a standard double room in high season. For expanded hotel reviews, facilities, and current deals, visit Fodors.com.*

THE BLUE MOUNTAINS

Sydneysiders have been doubly blessed by nature. Not only do they have a magnificent coastline right at their front door, but a 90-minute drive west puts them in the midst of one of the most spectacular wilderness areas in Australia—World Heritage Blue Mountains National Park. This rippling sea of hills is covered by tall eucalyptus trees and dissected by deep river valleys—the area is perfect terrain for hiking and adventure activities.

Standing 3,500-plus feet high, these "mountains" were once the bed of an ancient sea. Gradually the sedimentary rock was uplifted until it formed a high plateau, which was etched by aeons of wind and water into the wonderland of cliffs, caves, and canyons that exists today. Now the richly forested hills, crisp mountain air, cool-climate gardens, vast sandstone chasms, and little towns of timber and stone are supreme examples of Australia's diversity. The mountains' distinctive blue coloring is caused by the evaporation of oil from the dense eucalyptus forests. This disperses light in the blue colors of the spectrum, a phenomenon known as Rayleigh Scattering.

Visitor Information Blue Mountains Visitor Centre–Glenbrook ✉ *Great Western Hwy., Glenbrook* ☏ *1300/653408.* **Blue Mountains**

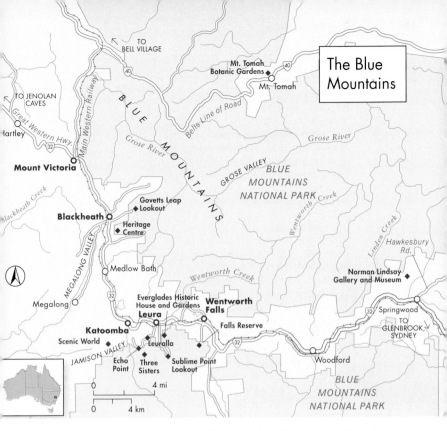

TO
BELL VILLAGE

Mt. Tomah
Botanic Gardens
Mt. Tomah

The Blue
Mountains

TO JENOLAN
CAVES

Bells Line of Road

Great Western Hwy.

Grose River

Hartley

Grose River

BLUE
MOUNTAINS

Main Western Railway

Mount Victoria

GROSE VALLEY

MOUNTAINS
NATIONAL PARK

Creek

Blackheath Creek

Govetts Leap
Lookout

Blackheath

Heritage
Centre

MEGALONG VALLEY

Wentworth Creek

Medlow Bath

Wentworth Creek

Linden Creek

Hawkesbury
Rd.

Norman Lindsay
Gallery and Museum

Megalong

Everglades Historic
House and Gardens

Leura

Wentworth
Falls

Springwood

TO
GLENBROOK,
SYDNEY

Falls Reserve

Katoomba

Scenic World

Leuralla

JAMISON VALLEY

Echo
Point

Three
Sisters

Sublime Point
Lookout

Woodford

BLUE
MOUNTAINS
NATIONAL PARK

0   4 mi

0   4 km

Visitor Centre–Katoomba ⊠ *Echo Point Rd. and Panorama Dr., Katoomba*
☎ *1300/653408* ⊕ *www.visitbluemountains.com.au.*

WENTWORTH FALLS

95 km (59 miles) west of Sydney.

This attractive township is home to the Blue Mountains' most stunning natural waterfalls and bush walking trails. The Falls themselves straddle the highway, but most points of interest and views of the Jamison Valley and Blue Mountains National Park are a short way south.

GETTING HERE AND AROUND

From Sydney, head west onto Parramatta Road, then take the M4, following signs to the Blue Mountains. You'll pay a toll at the end of the motorway. It's also easy to catch a train to Wentworth Falls; the journey from Sydney Central Station takes 1¾ hours, with trains leaving roughly every hour. The Blue Mountains Bus Company (☎ *02/4751–1077* ⊕ *www.bmbc.com.au*) connects towns within the region with routes 685 and 695, connecting Wentworth Falls to Leura and Katoomba.

EXPLORING

EN ROUTE

Norman Lindsay Gallery and Museum. If driving from Sydney, be sure to stop at the National Trust–listed Norman Lindsay Gallery and Museum, dedicated to the Australian artist and writer. Considered one of the cultural highlights of the Blue Mountains, Lindsay lived in this house during the latter part of his life until he died in 1969. Lindsay is best known for his paintings, etchings, and drawings (many of voluptuous nudes), but he also built model boats, sculpted, and wrote poetry and children's books, among which *The Magic Pudding* has become an Australian classic. The delightful landscaped gardens contain several of Lindsay's sculptures, and you can also take a short but scenic bushwalk beyond the garden or take refreshments in the café. Daily tours of Lindsay's studios run from 10:30 am to 2:30 pm and are included in the price, while dedicated art fans can stay in the cottage on the grounds for A$150 a night midweek or A$200 a night Friday, Saturday, and Sunday. ⊠ *14 Norman Lindsay Crescent, Faulconbridge* ☎ *02/4751–1067* ⊕ *www.normanlindsay.com.au* ☒ *A$12* ⊙ *Daily 10–4.*

> ## BLOOMIN' BEAUTIFUL
>
> **Leura Garden Festival.** When spring is in the air in the mountains, one of the most beautiful places to be is Leura. Dozens of cherry blossoms line the main street, and private gardens are open for viewing. The gardens are adorned with the work of local artists keen to win the annual art prize. A village fair caps off the celebrations. One ticket (A$20) buys entrance to all the gardens on show. ☎ *0431/095279* ⊕ *www.leuragardensfestival.com.au.*

SPORTS AND THE OUTDOORS

HIKING

Falls Reserve. From a lookout in Falls Reserve, south of the town of Wentworth Falls, you can take in magnificent views both out across the Jamison Valley to the Kings Tableland and of the 935-foot-high **Wentworth Falls** themselves. To find the best view of the falls, follow the trail that crosses the stream and zigzags down the sheer cliff face, signposted "national pass". If you continue, the trail cuts back across the base of the falls and along a narrow ledge to the delightful Valley of the Waters, where it ascends to the top of the cliffs, emerging at the Conservation Hut. The complete circuit takes at least three hours and is a moderately difficult walk. ⊠ *End of Falls Rd.*

WHERE TO EAT

$$
MODERN
AUSTRALIAN

✕ **Conservation Hut.** From its prime spot in Blue Mountains National Park, on a cliff overlooking the Jamison Valley, this spacious, mud-brick bistro serves simple, savory fare. Lovely breakfast dishes include herbed mushrooms with a poached egg and roast tomatoes on toast. For lunch and dinner (the latter served only on Friday and Saturday nights in summer; two-courses A$45 and three-courses A$60), dig into hearty soups, beef pies, or seared ocean trout with chervil and potato rösti. Be sure to save room for the dessert cakes. An open balcony is a delight on warm days, and a fire blazes in the cooler months. A hiking trail from the bistro leads down into the Valley of the Waters, one of the splendors of the mountains. It's a wonderful pre- or post-meal walk. $ *Average main: A$25* ⊠ *88 Fletcher St.* ☎ *02/4757–3827* ⊕ *www.conservationhut.com. au* ☼ *No dinner (except Fri. and Sat. in summer).*

$$ × **Mash Cafe.** In Glenbrook, one of the first Blue Mountains towns
MODERN you'll reach coming from Sydney, this is a great place for breakfast or
AUSTRALIAN a relaxing lunch before continuing toward Wentworth Falls, about a
30-minute drive farther west. Dinner, served only Thursday through
Saturday, features such warming dishes as slow-braised lamb shoulder,
poached free-range chicken, and roast duck with potato rösti. Mash
buys only fair-trade tea, coffee, and chocolate and uses many organi-
cally grown ingredients. $ *Average main: A$10* ⊠ *19 Ross St., Glenbrook* ☎ *02/4739–5908* ☼ *Closed Mon. and Tues. No dinner Wed.
and Sun.*

LEURA

5 km (3 miles) west of Wentworth Falls.

Leura, the prettiest and chicest of the mountain towns, is bordered by
bush and lined with excellent cafés, restaurants, and gift shops. From
the south end of the main street (the Mall), the road continues past
superb local gardens as it winds down to the massive cliffs overlooking the Jamison Valley. The dazzling 19-km (12-mile) journey along
Cliff Drive skirts the rim of the valley—often only yards from the cliff
edge—providing truly spectacular Blue Mountains views.

GETTING HERE AND AROUND

The train station at Leura is one stop beyond Wentworth Falls, and the
station is walking distance from all the town's shops and galleries. By
car, Leura is a few kilometers west of Wentworth Falls on the Great
Western Highway. Alternatively, catch a Blue Mountains Bus Company
bus—Routes 685 and 695 connect the town with Wentworth Falls and
Katoomba.

EXPLORING

Everglades Historic House and Gardens. Everglades Gardens, a National
Trust–listed, cool-climate arboretum and nature reserve established in
the 1930s, is one of the best public gardens in the Blue Mountains
region. This former home of a Belgian industrialist is surrounded by
5 hectares (13 acres) of native bushland and exotic flora, a rhododendron garden, an alpine plant area, and formal European-style terraces.
The views of the Jamison Valley are magnificent. ⊠ *37 Everglades Ave.*
☎ *02/4784–1938* ⊕ *www.evergladesgardens.com.au* ⊠ *A$10* ☼ *Oct.–
Mar., daily 10–5; Apr.–Sept., daily 10–4.*

Leuralla. This imposing 1911 mansion still belongs to the family of Dr.
H. V. ("Doc") Evatt (1894–1965), the first president of the General
Assembly of the United Nations and later the leader of the Australian Labor Party. A 19th-century Australian art collection and a small
museum dedicated to Dr. Evatt are inside the home. Baby boomers and
their children (and grandchildren) will love the collection in the New
South Wales Toy and Railway Museum, which is both inside the house
and in the gardens. The museum is comprised of an extensive collection of railway memorabilia, antique curios from yesteryear (including

lots of dolls depicting the Alice in Wonderland scenes), and exhibitions on iconic dolls like Barbie. Directly across the street from the mansion are the Leuralla Public Gardens (entry A$2), with spectacular views of the Jamison Valley. ✉ *36 Olympian Parade* ☎ *02/4784–1169* 🌐 *www.toyandrailwaymuseum.com.au* 🎟 *A$14* 🕒 *Daily 10–5.*

Sublime Point Lookout. This viewpoint just outside Leura lives up to its name with a great view of the Jamison Valley and the generally spectacular Blue Mountains scenery. It's a quiet vantage point that provides a different perspective from that of the famous **Three Sisters** lookout at nearby Katoomba. ✉ *Sublime Point Rd.*

WHERE TO EAT AND STAY

$$ AUSTRALIAN Fodor's Choice ★ 🍴 **Silk's Brasserie.** Thanks to its Sydney-standard food, wine, and service, Silk's still rates as one of the finest Blue Mountains restaurants after more than 20 years. The menu here changes seasonally, but popular dishes include the pan-seared scallops with tomato confit, asparagus, pancetta, and a chicory-watercress salad with honey-mustard-seed dressing, and the main course of corn-fed chicken on bok choy with shiitake mushrooms, soy-ginger broth, and wild-wasabi mayonnaise. A favorite dessert is the warm bittersweet chocolate fondant with vanilla-bean Chantilly cream and black cherries. The restaurant is housed in a Federation-era building, and in colder months a log fire warms the century-old simple but elegant interior, where yellow ocher walls reach from black-and-white checkerboard floor to sky-high ceiling. [$] *Average main: A$36* ✉ *128 The Mall* ☎ *02/4784–2534* 🌐 *www.silksleura.com.*

$$$ B&B/INN 🏨 **Bygone Beautys Cottages.** These five country cottages, scattered around Wentworth Falls and in the nearby village of Bullaburra, provide self-contained accommodations for couples, families, and small groups. **Pros:** antiques collectors will love the decor and the connected tearoom (at Leura); very romantic surrounds. **Cons:** if olde worlde leaves you cold, this isn't the place for you; bathrooms can be chilly in winter. [$] *Rooms from: A$220* ✉ *Grose and Megalong Sts.* ☎ *02/4784–3117* 🌐 *www.bygonebeautys.com.au* 🛏 *5 cottages* 🍽 *Breakfast.*

SHOPPING

Josophan's. This gorgeous chocolate boutique in Leura's main shopping street has fast become *the* place to stop for luscious handmade chocolates and drinking chocolate. You can also take part in classes (how does making chocolate truffles sound?) and take away lovely gift boxes of sweets. For a light snack and yummy chocolate desserts, walk across the road to Cafe Madeline (at 187a The Mall), which is also owned by Josophan's proprietor and chocolatier Jodie Van der Velden. ✉ *132 The Mall* ☎ *02/4784–2031.*

KATOOMBA

2 km (1 mile) west of Leura.

The largest and busiest town in the Blue Mountains, Katoomba developed in the early 1840s as a coal-mining settlement, turning its attention to tourism later in the 19th century. The town center on Katoomba

Continued on page 159

HIKING THE BLUE MOUNTAINS

Kanangra Falls

Head west of Sydney along the M4, or simply hop a bus or train, and within an hour you'll be on a gradual climb along a traditional Aboriginal pathway into the heart of the Blue Mountains—a sandstone plateau formed 150 million years ago that tops out at 3,600 feet. Dramatic valleys, canyons, and cliff faces to the north and south of the main road have been carved by wind and water over millennia. And the blue? That's light refracting off the fine oil mist from the world's most ecologically diverse tract of eucalypt forest.

(top) Looking out over the Jamison Valley.

A WORLD HERITAGE WONDERLAND

Part of the Greater Blue Mountains World Heritage Area, Blue Mountains National Park encompasses 2,678 sq km (1,034 sq ft) of prime hiking country. Most tracks skirt the cliff edges or run along the bottom of the canyons; paths that connect the two levels are often at points along the cliff that offer breathtaking panoramas of the Jamison, Megalong, or Grose Valleys.

While the geological landscape is worth the trip alone, the flora and fauna are some of the country's most unique. Within just a few square miles, the world's widest variety of eucalypts in one contiguous forest have evolved to thrive in everything from open scrub plains to dense valley rainforests. The Wollami pine, a tree that grew alongside dinosaurs, can only be found in a few small areas here. Then there are the rare or threatened creatures like the Blue Mountains water skink, the yellow-bellied glider, and the long-nosed potoroo. It seems only fitting that both Charles Darwin and John Muir visited here. In 1932 it became one of the first formally protected tracts of land in Australia.

Towns dot the main highway through the Blue Mountains, but Katoomba is the unofficial capital, fully outfitted with resources for visitors and the starting point for some of the most iconic walks. Less-bustling Blackheath, minutes up the road from Katoomba, has our favorite eco-lodges and is closest to the best walks of the Grose Valley. You can get a feel for the region on a day trip from Sydney, but if your schedule permits, stay a night (or three) to fit in a few different hikes.

HIKING LITE: THREE WAYS TO SEE THE JAMISON VALLEY WITHOUT BREAKING A SWEAT

Scenic Skyway

SCENIC CABLEWAY

Less crowded than the Scenic Railway, the world's steepest cable car feels gentle in comparison. The enclosed gondola glides between the valley floor and the cliff rim with views of the Three Sisters.

SCENIC SKYWAY

This Swiss-style, glass-bottom cable car takes you on a 720 m (1/2 mi) long journey 270 m (886 ft) above the gorge for great 360 degree views across the Jamison Valley, the Katoomba Falls, and the famous Three Sisters.

KATOOMBA SCENIC RAILWAY

An incline of 52 degrees makes this former coal-haul railway the world's steepest. Grab a seat in the front. Be prepared for lines at peak visiting times. The railway runs every 10 minutes until 4:50 pm.

Claustral Canyon

BLUE MOUNTAIN TRAIL OVERVIEW

Lookout at Echo Point

KATOOMBA-ECHO POINT	TRAIL TIPS	HIGHLIGHTS
ECHO POINT TO SCENIC RAILWAY: This may not be a long walk, but thanks to the 900 steps of the Giant Staircase, don't underestimate it.	This route is very popular, especially on weekends, so set off early. Be aware that the last railway and cable car up leave at 4:50 pm. If you miss them, you'll have to walk.	• Expansive views across the Jamison Valley and beautiful forest vistas. • Brings you right up against the Three Sisters. • Scenic Railway boarding area is at the end of the trail, so you don't have to walk back up.
PRINCE HENRY CLIFF WALK: Start at the Leura Cascades picnic area and head up the mountain to Echo Point. This is a tough hike and not for the faint of heart.	Olympian Rock and Elysian Rock are perfect spots to picnic.	• Thanks to the level of difficulty, you'll be able to escape the crowds at Katoomba. • Spot lyre birds, kookaburras, and glossy black cockatoos.
BLACKHEATH	TRAIL TIPS	HIGHLIGHTS
GRAND CANYON WALK: Possible for anyone who's reasonably fit (though there are some steps) and well worth the effort.	A great choice for hot days: the canyon's cool temperatures will come as welcome relief.	• A winding path through lush vegetation and around plummeting waterfalls. • Spectacular views of gorges, forest, and cliff lines at Evans lookout.
PERRY'S LOOKDOWN TO BLUE GUM FOREST: This track starts at Perry's Lookdown parking lot, 9 km (5.5 mi) northeast of Blackheath, and takes you down a steep track into the lovely Blue Gum Forest.	Stop by the Heritage Centre in nearby Blackheath for excellent information on historic sites and hiking trips.	• Experience for yourself why the ecologically unique Blue Gum Forest attracted conservationists' attention in Australia. • You might spot possums, gliders, bandicoots, brown antechinuses, and swamp wallabies.
GLENBROOK	TRAIL TIPS	HIGHLIGHTS
RED HANDS CAVE TRACK: This moderately difficult circuit walk goes up the Red Hands Creek Valley along a creek and through the rainforest.	It's best to park at the Visitors Centre on Bruce Road and then walk for 10 minutes following the signs to the Glenbrook causeway, as there is no easy parking at the causeway itself.	• Bring your binoculars, because there are many birdwatching opportunities. • See the Blue Mountains' most sacred Aboriginal site, Red Hands Cave. The cave is named after the displays of Aboriginal hand stencils on its walls.

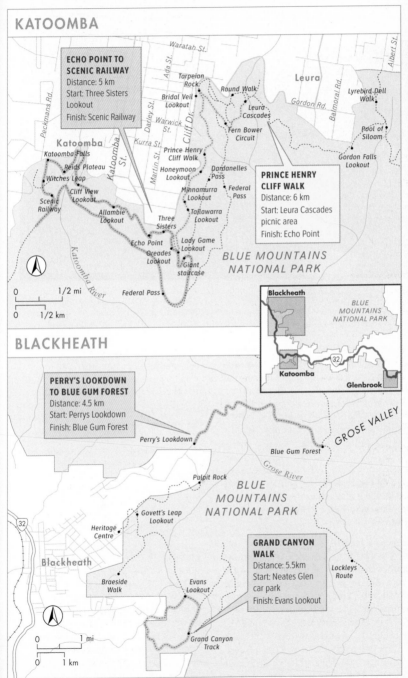

3

IN FOCUS HIKING THE BLUE MOUNTAINS

KATOOMBA

Waratah St.

Ada St.

Warwick St.

Cliff Dr.

Peckmans Rd.

ECHO POINT TO SCENIC RAILWAY
Distance: 5 km
Start: Three Sisters Lookout
Finish: Scenic Railway

Tarpeian Rock
Bridal Veil Lookout
Round Walk
Leura
Gordon Rd.
Lyrebird Dell Walk
Balmoral Rd.
Albert St.

Leura Cascades

Fern Bower Circuit

Katoomba St.

Katoomba

Katoomba Falls
Reids Plateau
Witches Leap
Cliff View Lookout
Scenic Railway
Allambie Lookout

Prince Henry Cliff Walk
Honeymoon Lookout
Dardanelles Pass
Minnamurra Lookout
Federal Pass
Tallawarra Lookout

Pool of Siloam

Gordon Falls Lookout

PRINCE HENRY CLIFF WALK
Distance: 6 km
Start: Leura Cascades picnic area
Finish: Echo Point

Three Sisters
Echo Point
Oreades Lookout
Lady Game Lookout
Giant staircase

BLUE MOUNTAINS NATIONAL PARK

Katoomba River

Martin St.
Kurra St.
Dalley St.

0   1/2 mi
0   1/2 km

Federal Pass

BLACKHEATH

PERRY'S LOOKDOWN TO BLUE GUM FOREST
Distance: 4.5 km
Start: Perrys Lookdown
Finish: Blue Gum Forest

Perry's Lookdown

GROSE VALLEY

Blue Gum Forest

Grose River

BLUE MOUNTAINS NATIONAL PARK

Pulpit Rock

32

Govett's Leap Lookout

Heritage Centre

Blackheath

Braeside Walk

Evans Lookout

GRAND CANYON WALK
Distance: 5.5km
Start: Neates Glen car park
Finish: Evans Lookout

Lockleys Route

Grand Canyon Track

0   1 mi
0   1 km

Inset map:

Blackheath
BLUE MOUNTAINS NATIONAL PARK
Katoomba
32
Glenbrook

KATOOMBA

View of Three Sisters from Echo Point lookout

ECHO POINT TO SCENIC RAILWAY

In the 1930s, the **Giant Staircase** was hewn out of the cliff by teams of park rangers. The top of the steps are near **Three Sisters Lookout** and the walk down is very steep and narrow in places. It's difficult going but the views make it all worthwhile. Look out for the encouraging half way sign. At the bottom, keep your eyes peeled for echidnas, brush-tailed and ring-tail possums, bandicoots, quolls, and grey-headed flying foxes. If you're keen for more exertion once you've reached the Railway, take the **Furber Steps**. It's a challenging but rewarding track that offers great views of **Katoomba Falls** and **Mt. Solitary** across the valley.

PRINCE HENRY CLIFF WALK

If you prefer to hike in the mountains rather than along the forest floor, you'll enjoy this section of the Cliff Walk with its superb vistas across the valley. From the picnic area, the trail descends beside Leura Cascades creek towards **Bridal Veil lookout**. Be sure to slow down and take in the great views over the **Leura Forest**. Continue on Prince Henry Drive; at **Tarpeian Rock** you can see Mt. Solitary.

Keep going uphill towards Olympian Rock and Elysian Rock. From here, follow the cliff line to **Millamurra** and **Tallawarra Lookouts**. The last part of the climb to the **Three Sisters** is perhaps the most challenging but also the most rewarding. Take a few minutes and savor the sweeping views of the valley.

QUICK BITES/SUPERMARKETS FOR PICNIC GOODIES

You can stock up at either Coles or ALDI supermarkets in Katoomba or Woolworths supermarket in Leura. Scenic World has two restaurants. For gourmet treats visit Carrington Cellars at the rear of the Carrington Hotel, or stop at Brown's Siding Store & Café at Medlow Bath for breakfast, lunch, and goodies.

STAY HERE IF:

On weekends tour buses descend on the town, but once they've headed back to Sydney, the place isn't over-run with vistors. Katoomba has a very relaxed feel helped in no small part by a small hippy community. It also has plenty of nice old pubs and cafés, cute vintage shops, and rural versions of big department stores.

BLACKHEATH

Mount Hay, Grose Valley

GRAND CANYON WALK

From the parking lot, 4.5 km (2.8 mi) from Blackheath, follow the Grand Canyon track signs as the path zig-zags down the hillside and the vegetation becomes more like a rainforest. The trail takes you down into the canyon and over a creek. It winds past a few overhanging rocks, then starts a steep decline towards a sandy overhang called the **Rotunda**. After a break here, follow the signs to **Evans Lookout**, which will lead you through a tunnel and past two waterfalls. You eventually reach the 10-meter-tall (33 ft) **Beauchamp Falls** in the center of the creek. From here head up through a gap in the cliffs, weaving through boulders, again following signs to Evans Lookout. From Evans Lookout, you can do a 6.5 km (4 mi) Cliffside walk to **Pulpit Rock** along the Cliff Top Track.

PERRYS LOOKDOWN TO BLUE GUM FOREST

From the parking lot, follow the signs pointing out the trail down the hill to **Perrys Lookdown**. You'll have fine views over the **Grose Valley** with its sheer sandstone cliffs with the Blue Gum Forest below. Next, head down the hill and do a quick detour to **Docker's Lookout** with its view of Mt. Banks to the north. Head back following the Perrys Lookdown–Blue Gum Forest walk signs. The descent to **Blue Gum Forest** will take about 90 minutes. Once you've explored the forest floor and its dense canopy, head back up the steep track to Perrys Lookout.

QUICK BITES/SUPERMARKETS FOR PICNIC GOODIES

Blackheath has something of a gourmet reputation. A particular highlight is **Ashcrafts** (18 Govetts Leap Rd.). There's also a small IGA supermarket.

STAY HERE IF:

Blackheath is smaller and less-visited than Katoomba, but the old weatherboard houses give it a similar feel. There's also enough quirky shops and quaint cafes and restaurants to keep it entertaining. Several Sydney restaurateurs relocated here, so there's a breadth of excellent dining venues.

GLENBROOK

Glenbrook Gorge

An echidna

Kookaburras

RED HANDS CAVE TRACK

Red Hands Cave has some well preserved Aboriginal hand stencillings. The stencils are behind Plexiglas (called Perspex here) to protect them from graffiti. There are a few good placards explaining the history and describing the artifacts found in the area. The walk starts on the southern side of the causeway, and after about 2 km (1.2 mi) of gentle steps down the gully, the well-defined track forks: take the right-hand path just after a large rocky outcrop near the edge of a gully. ▮TIP➜ Take care near the edge, there's a significant dropoff. Up the hill near **Camp Fire Creek**, keep an eye out for axe grinding grooves (oval-shaped indentations in sandstone outcrops that Aboriginal peoples used to shape and sharpen stone axes). The trail passes through several types of forest, including dry eucalypt forest, so there's a good variety of birds in the area. Watch for echidnas in the open forest and chestnut-rumped heathwrens and rock warblers in the sandstone area near the Red Hands Cave.

> **RED HANDS
> CAVE TRACK**
> Length: 6 km
> Start: Glenbrook
> Visitor Centre
> Finish: Red
> Hands Cave

Great Western Hwy

Glenbrook

32

Lapstone

Blue Pool
Track

Red Hands
Cave

Fire Creek

Car Park

Camp

Euroka-Nepean
River Track

Nepean River

The Oaks Trail

Euroka

BLUE
MOUNTAINS
NATIONAL PARK

QUICK BITES/SUPERMARKETS FOR PICNIC GOODIES

Glenbrook doesn't have the same variety of food and lodging options as Katoomba and Blackheath, but there's a small supermarket on Park Street. Ross Street has a few nice cafes; check out **Mash Café's** delicious breakfasts.

Street has shops, restaurants, and cafés, but the marvels at the lower end of town are an even greater draw.

GETTING HERE AND AROUND

Katoomba is just a few minutes' drive from Leura on the Great Western Highway. A train station connects the town with the rest of the region, as does the Blue Mountains Bus Company. A good deal is the Blue Mountains Explorer Link ticket (⊕ *www.sydneytrains.info/ tickets/which/explorerlink*), which can be purchased at Sydney railway stations. The A$49.60 pass combines a same-day return train ticket from Sydney to Katoomba and a day's access to the red double-decker Explorer buses that travel around Katoomba and Leura stopping at 29 stops (⊕ *www.explorerbus.com.au*). A three-day version of the pass costs A$71.60.

Another economical sightseeing option is the Blue Mountains Trolley bus (⊕ *www.trolleytours.com.au*), which provides a similar hop-on, hop-off tour, visiting 29 stops, in a vehicle that resembles a San Francisco streetcar. The cost is A$25, and tickets are available at the Trolley Shoppe near Katoomba railway station.

TOURS

Blue Mountains Adventure Company. The well-established Blue Mountains Adventure Company (which operates in partnership with Wild at Heart Safaris) runs abseiling, rock-climbing, canyoning, bushwalking, and mountain-biking trips. A full-day abseiling or bushwalking adventure costs A$195, and both include lunch, snacks, and all equipment needed. There are both introductory and intermediate levels of canyoning from A$220; you'll visit such places as Empress Falls or Serendipity Canyon. ✉ *84A Bathurst Rd.* ☎ *02/4782–1271* ⊕ *www.bmac.com.au.*

Blue Mountains Explorer Bus. This company operates the signature red buses coming out of Katoomba and running at regular intervals throughout the region, stopping at 29 sites. Different pass types are available that are tailored from everything from single rides to week-long passes. ✉ *283 Main St.* ☎ *1300/300915* ⊕ *www.explorerbus.com. au* 💷 *A$38.*

High n Wild. This outfitter conducts rappelling, canyoning, rock-climbing, and mountain-biking tours throughout the year. Half-day rappelling trips cost A$125; one-day trips are A$165; combination rappelling and canyoning tours cost A$185. The company's office is based at the YHA youth hostel, a short walk from the station. ✉ *207 Katoomba St.* ☎ *02/4782–6224* ⊕ *www.high-n-wild.com.au.*

Trolley Tours. These purple hop-on, hop-off trolleys operate on a convenient circuit throughout Katoomba and Leura, stopping at the major points of interest. ✉ *Main St.* ☎ *1800/801577* ⊕ *www.trolleytours.com. au* 💷 *A$25.*

ESSENTIALS

Visitor Information Blue Mountains Visitor Information Centre ✉ *Echo Point Rd.* ☎ *1300/653408* ⊕ *www.visitbluemountains.com.au.*

EXPLORING

Fodor'sChoice **Echo Point.** Overlooking the densely forested Jamison Valley and three
★ soaring sandstone pillars, this lofty promontory has the best views
around Katoomba. The formations—called the Three Sisters—take
their name from an Aboriginal legend that relates how a trio of siblings
was turned to stone by their witch-doctor father to save them from the
clutches of a mythical monster. The area was once a seabed that rose
over a long period and subsequently eroded, leaving behind tall formations of sedimentary rock. From Echo Point—where the visitor center
is located—you can clearly see the horizontal sandstone bedding in the
landscape. There is a wide viewing area as well as the start of walks
that take you closer to the Sisters. At night the Sisters are illuminated
by floodlights. There are cafés and a visitor information center near the
site. ⊠ *Echo Point Rd. off Katoomba St.* ⊕ *www.visitbluemountains.
com.au.*

FAMILY **Scenic World.** Thrill-seekers have more to enjoy since the 2013 reopening of the Scenic Railway, whose trains descend 1,000 feet down the
mountainside—they now have new seats that allow passengers to adjust
the incline angle from 52 to a hair-raising 64 degrees. The railway is one
of three attractions at Scenic World, which has carried more than 25
million passengers to the valley floor since it opened in 1945. Once at
the base, visitors can hike on easy trails through the rain forest or make
the 20-minute hike to Cableway, a huge cable car that whisks passengers back up the mountain. You can also hike back up, but it's a steep,
strenuous climb. The third attractions is Scenic Skyway, a glass-enclosed
and -floored cabin that travels from on one cliff to another, some 920
feet above the ravines below. The A$35 day pass provides unlimited
rides on all three attractions. ⊠ *Cliff Dr. at Violet St.* ☎ *02/4780–0200*
⊕ *www.scenicworld.com.au* ⊗ *Daily 9–5.*

SPORTS AND THE OUTDOORS

A good hiking brochure can be picked up at Blue Mountains Visitor
Centre at Echo Point, which lists walks varying in length from ½ hour
to three days.

ECO TOURS

Tread Lightly Eco Tours. This eco-minded company operates small-group
tours of Blue Mountains National Park and guided day and night walks
as well as four-wheel-drive tours and breakfast trips to view wildlife.
Half- and full-day walking tours take in such areas as Fern Bower,
Blue Gum Forest, and the Ruin Castle, starting at A$145 per person
with lunch. ⊠ *100 Great Western Hwy., Medlow Bath* ☎ *0414/976752*
⊕ *www.treadlightly.com.au.*

HIKING

Blue Mountains Guides. Single-day, overnight, and three-day walks are
offered through this guiding company. The half-day Grand Canyon
Walk near Blackheath (A$140) is a great way to experience the rain
forest if time is short, while the three-day iconic "Six Foot Track"
between Katoomba and Jenolan Caves includes one night of camping and another in a cabin, plus a cave tour on the last day (A$750).

Four-wheel-drive trips are also available. ✉ *2/187 Katoomba St.* ☎ *02/4782–6307* 🌐 *www.bluemountainsguides.com.au.*

Blue Mountains Walkabout. Experience the Blue Mountains from an Aboriginal perspective on this outfitter's challenging one-day walks, which follow a traditional walkabout song line. Indigenous guides take you on a 7-km (4½-mile) off-track walk through rain forests while giving some background on Aboriginal culture. You'll also taste bush tucker. The walk involves some scrambling, so you need to be fit. The tours departs from Faulconbridge Railway Station (near Springwood, in the lower Blue Mountains), about a 30-minute drive east of Katoomba. ✉ *Springwood* ☎ *0408/433822* 🌐 *www.bluemountainswalkabout.com* 🎟 *A$95.*

WHERE TO EAT

$ CAFÉ ✕ **Paragon Cafe.** With its chandeliers, gleaming cappuccino machine, and bas-relief figures above the booths, this wood-paneled 1916 art-deco café was a favorite Blue Mountains eatery in its heyday. Today visitors come more for the 52 varieties of homemade chocolates and the Devonshire Teas (a spread of scones, jam, cream, and a pot of tea). Owner Robyn Parker, who took over in 2011, is gradually restoring the café to its original glory—she's reopened the elegant cocktail bar at the rear of the building and stages a variety of events during the year, including Regency dances, 1920s tango nights, and screenings of classic movies. [$] *Average main: A$15* ✉ *65 Katoomba St.* ☎ *02/4782–2928* ⏲ *No dinner Sun.–Thurs.*

WHERE TO STAY

$$$ HOTEL 🏨 **The Carrington.** Established in 1880, this is one of the grande dames of the Blue Mountains, a Victorian-era relic that, in its heyday, was considered one of the four great hotels of the British Empire. **Pros:** drinks on their veranda are a pleasant way to end the day; breakfast included; free Wi-Fi in rooms. **Cons:** the newer rooms lack character. [$] *Rooms from: A$250* ✉ *15–47 Katoomba St.* ☎ *02/4782–1111* 🌐 *www.thecarrington.com.au* 🛏 *59 rooms, 49 with bath; 6 suites; 1 apartment* 🍴 *Multiple meal plans.*

$$$$ HOTEL 🏨 **Echoes Boutique Hotel & Restaurant.** Perched on the edge of the Jamison Valley, this stylish boutique hotel has one of the best views in the Blue Mountains. **Pros:** spectacular views from the terrace; slick and funky accommodation. **Cons:** a little pricey. [$] *Rooms from: A$500* ✉ *3 Lilianfels Ave.* ☎ *02/4782–1966* 🌐 *www.echoeshotel.com.au* 🛏 *14 suites* 🍴 *Breakfast.*

$$$$ HOTEL 🏨 **Lilianfels Blue Mountains Resort & Spa.** Teetering close to the brink of Echo Point, this glamorous boutique hotel adds a keen sense of manor-house style to the standard Blue Mountains guesthouse experience. **Pros:** luxurious and restful bathrooms; staff give friendly five-star service; lovely drawing room with views. **Cons:** 19th-century style is not for everyone; restaurant is very expensive. [$] *Rooms from: A$450* ✉ *Lilianfels Ave. at Panorama Dr.* ☎ *02/4780–1200* 🌐 *www.lilianfels.com.au* ✍ *Reservations essential* 🛏 *81 rooms, 4 suites* 🍴 *Breakfast.*

$$ B&B/INN Fodor's Choice ★ **Lurline House.** This historic little B&B is arguably the town's best. **Pros:** rooms have four-poster beds; warm and welcoming. **Cons:** younger trendsetters might find the place not to their taste. [$] *Rooms from: A$170* ✉ *122 Lurline St.* ☎ *02/4782–4609* 🌐 *www.lurlinehouse.com.au* 🛏 *7 rooms, 1 cottage* 🍴 *Breakfast.*

$$$ B&B/INN Fodor's Choice ★ **Melba House.** If Dame Nellie, Dame Joan, and Dame Edna are new to you, you'll certainly be well acquainted with the ladies after a stay in beautiful Melba House. **Pros:** genial host; located minutes away from great walking trails. **Cons:** no year-round dining area (except in summer when the veranda is an option, breakfast is served in rooms). [$] *Rooms from: A$230* ✉ *98 Waratah St.* ☎ *02/4782–4141* 🌐 *www.melbahouse.com* 🛏 *3 suites* 🍴 *Breakfast.*

$$ HOTEL **Mountain Heritage Hotel & Spa.** This hotel overlooking the Jamison Valley is steeped in history: it served as a "coffee palace" during the temperance movement, a rest-and-relaxation establishment for the British navy during World War II, and a religious retreat in the 1970s. **Pros:** friendly service; manicured gardens; public areas are charming with great valley views. **Cons:** furniture is a little dated. [$] *Rooms from: A$180* ✉ *Apex and Lovel Sts.* ☎ *02/4782–2155* 🌐 *www.mountainheritage.com.au* 🛏 *37 rooms, 4 suites* 🍴 *No meals.*

BLACKHEATH

12 km (7½ miles) north of Katoomba.

Magnificent easterly views over the Grose Valley—which has outstanding hiking trails—delightful gardens, good restaurants, and antiques shops head the list of reasons to visit the village of Blackheath, at the 3,495-foot summit of the Blue Mountains.

GETTING HERE AND AROUND

Blackheath is an easy drive north from Katoomba, traveling on the Great Western Highway, passing Medlow Bath on the way. There's also a train station on the Blue Mountains line, and the town is also serviced by Blue Mountains Bus Company on Route 698 between Katoomba and Mount Victoria.

ESSENTIALS

Visitor Information Heritage Centre ✉ *End of Govett's Leap Rd.* ☎ *02/4787–8877* 🌐 *www.nationalparks.nsw.gov.au* 🕘 *Daily 9–4:30.*

EXPLORING

Fodor's Choice ★ **Govetts Leap Lookout.** Blackheath's most famous view is from the Govetts Leap Lookout, with its striking panorama of the Grose Valley and Bridal Veil Falls. Govett was a surveyor who mapped this region extensively in the 1830s. This lookout is the start or finish of several excellent bushwalks. Brochures are available at the Heritage Centre. ✉ *End of Govett's Leap Rd.*

SPORTS AND THE OUTDOORS

HIKING

Auswalk. This environmentally conscious company, which also offers walks in other parts of Australia, has three-, five-, and seven-day self-guided or guided hiking tours through the region, staying at historic inns along the way, with all meals and admission to some local attractions included. The seven-day walk is A$1,545 per person (double-occupancy). The owners advise that you be in reasonable shape before you start. ☎ *03/5356–4971* 🌐 *www.auswalk.com.au.*

HORSEBACK RIDING

Megalong Australian Heritage Centre. This rural farm in a deep mountain valley off the Great Western Highway is the place to saddle up, hit a walking trail, or cycle on mountain trails. Both adults and children can go horseback riding around the farm's 2,000 acres, with prices ranging from A$50 for an hour's wilderness ride to A$95 for the most popular two-hour ride; a one-hour ride with picnic lunch is A$195 for two people. One-hour interpretative bushwalk and mountain-bike rentals are each A$50 for an hour, with longer rentals and walks available. You can also camp overnight on the property, with all equipment supplied. ✉ *993 Megalong Rd., Megalong Valley* ✢ *15 km (9 miles) south of Blackheath* ☎ *02/4787–8188* 🌐 *www.megalongcc.com.au* ⏲ *Daily 9–5.*

WHERE TO EAT AND STAY

$$$$ MODERN AUSTRALIAN 🍴 **Ashcrofts.** Nestled amid the antiques and vintage shops of Blackheath village, this acclaimed restaurant looks a little like a Parisian bistro, although the black-and-white photographs on the wall are of prominent Australians. Sydneysiders and locals turn up for Sunday lunch or dinner to feast on the two-course (A$78) or three-course (A$90) menus. You might start with a spring salad of honey-baked beetroot, house-made labneh, candied walnuts with tea-soaked muscats, and hibiscus vinaigrette, or the Egyptian-spice quail on Cape Malay carrot rémoulade with sticky-eggplant jam. Mains include fish pie with wild sea scallops, tiger prawns, and fennel-infused snapper velouté, and slow-roasted crispy-skin duck with Persian aromatics and citrus flavors. If you like the food and enjoy a good laugh, pick up a copy of co-owner Mary-Jane Craig's book, *Consummate,* which combines recipes with humor and quirky observations. [$] *Average main: A$78* ✉ *18 Govetts Leap Rd.* ☎ *02/4787–8297* 🌐 *www.ashcrofts.com* ⏲ *Closed Mon. and Tues. No lunch Wed.–Sat.*

$$$ B&B/INN 🏨 **Jemby Rinjah Eco Lodge.** Designed for urbanites seeking a wilderness experience, these rustic, self-contained wooden cabins and lodges are set deep in the bush. **Pros:** cabins and lodges are private and tranquil; hearty and healthy mountain fare is served at the restaurant. **Cons:** some might find the eco-toilet disconcerting; the lodges can be booked out by groups. [$] *Rooms from: A$250* ✉ *336 Evans Lookout Rd.* ☎ *02/4787–7622* 🌐 *www.jembyrinjahlodge.com.au* 🛏 *10 cabins, 3 lodges* 🍽 *No meals.*

MOUNT VICTORIA

7 km (4½ miles) northwest of Blackheath.

The settlement of Mount Victoria is the highest point in the Blue Mountains, and there's a Rip Van Winkle air about it—drowsy and only just awake in an unfamiliar world. A walk around the village reveals many atmospheric houses, stores, a charming old post office, and a stately old hotel with the patina of time spelled out in the fading paint of these buildings. Mount Victoria is at the far side of the mountains at the western limit of this region, and the village serves as a good jumping-off point for a couple of out-of-the-way attractions. Unfortunately, one of the big draws here, the Zig Zag Railway, was badly damaged in a fire in October 2013; the owners have announced plans to reopen sometime in 2014, but details haven't been confirmed as of this writing.

GETTING HERE AND AROUND
Mount Victoria is an easy drive north of Blackheath on the Great Western Highway, and it's also on the main Blue Mountains railway line linking Sydney with Lithgow. The 698V bus route connects the village with Katoomba, but only on weekdays.

EXPLORING
Hotel Imperial. The pink circa-1878 Hotel Imperial was one of several historic Blue Mountains inns built a few years after the railway line was opened from Sydney. It's worth popping in for a drink to have a look at the fading grand old lady. The hotel accommodations, which had received mixed reviews in the past, have been steadily improving since new owners took over in 2013. ⊠ *1 Station St.* ☎ *02/4787–1878* ⊕ *www.hotelimperial.com.au.*

Jenolan Caves. Stalactites, stalagmites, columns, and lacelike rock on multiple levels fill the fascinating Jenolan Caves, a labyrinth of vast limestone caverns sculpted by underground rivers. There are as many as 320 caves in the Jenolan area. Two caves (Nettles Cave and Devil's Coachhouse) near the surface can be explored on your own, but a guide is required to reach the most intriguing formations. Standard tours lead through the most popular caves—many say that Orient Cave is the most spectacular, while the more rigorous adventure tours last up to seven hours. The one- to two-hour walks depart every 15 to 30 minutes, on weekends less frequently. Prices range from A$30 for a standard tour to A$80 for the adventurous two-hour "plug hole" tour where you squeeze through ancient passageways—it includes a bit of rappelling. Concerts and murder mystery nights are also held in this spooky environment. Cave House, on the same site, is a nostalgic retreat and has been providing lodging since 1887. To get here, follow the Great Western Highway north out of Mount Victoria, then after Hartley, turn southwest toward Hampton. ⊠ *Jenolan Caves Rd., 59 km (37 miles) from Mount Victoria, Jenolan Caves* ☎ *1300/763311* ⊕ *www. jenolancaves.org.au* ☉ *Daily 9:30–5:30.*

Trains, Planes and Automobiles. Children and adults will enjoy a browse around this store that bills itself as the best antique toyshop in the world. ⊠ *86–88 Great Western Hwy.* ☎ *02/4787–1590* ⊕ *www. antiquetoys.com.au.*

WHERE TO EAT
$$
AUSTRALIAN
✕ **Apple Bar.** Bilpin is the apple capital of New South Wales and this friendly little roadside restaurant is set among the orchards. Wood-fired pizzas are a popular choice here, while the ever-changing specials blackboard may feature wood-grilled locally raised Black Angus beef eye fillet steak and the wood-grilled pork shoulder with caramelized applies (local, of course). This is a great place for a casual counter-style lunch

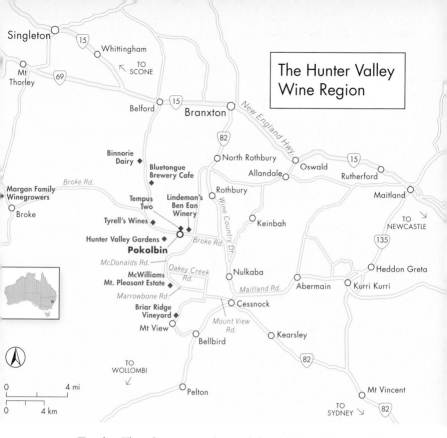

The Hunter Valley
Wine Region

Singleton
15
Whittingham
TO
SCONE
Mt
Thorley
69
Belford
15
Branxton
New England Hwy
82
Binnorie
Dairy
North Rothbury
Oswald
15
Bluetongue
Brewery Cafe
Allandale
Rutherford
Broke Rd.
Rothbury
Maitland
Margan Family
Winegrowers
Tempus
Two
Lindeman's
Ben Ean
Winery
Wine Country Dr.
Broke
Tyrell's Wines
Keinbah
TO
NEWCASTLE
Hunter Valley Gardens
Pokolbin
Broke Rd.
135
McDonalds Rd.
Oakey Creek
Rd.
Nulkaba
Heddon Greta
McWilliams
Mt. Pleasant Estate
Maitland Rd.
Abermain
Kurri Kurri
Marrowbone Rd.
Briar Ridge
Vineyard
Cessnock
Mt View
Mount View
Rd.
Kearsley
Bellbird
TO
WOLLOMBI
82
0   4 mi
0   4 km
Pelton
Mt Vincent
TO
SYDNEY
82

(Tuesday–Thursday) or a more upscale lunch Friday–Monday. Dinner is also served Friday–Sunday, so there are many eating options before or after touring the Mount Tomah Botanic Garden, which is about 10 km (6 miles) west—closer to Mount Victoria—on the same road. $ *Average main: A$29* ⊠ *2488 Bells Line of Rd., Bilpin* ☎ *02/4567-0335* ⊕ *www. applebar.com.au* ☉ *No dinner Mon.–Thurs.*

Mount Tomah Botanic Garden. This is the cool-climate branch of Sydney's Royal Botanic Gardens (30 km [19 miles] northeast of Mount Victoria). The garden is 3,280 feet above sea level, and is a spectacular setting for native and imported plants. You'll find beautiful rhododendrons and European deciduous trees, as well as plants that evolved in isolation for millions of years in the Gondwana Forest. The famous Wollemi Pine (once thought to be extinct) is also here. There are picnic grounds, a café with views of the ranges, and a daily guided tour at 11:30 am. Admission is free. ⊠ *Bells Line of Rd., Mount Tomah* ☎ *02/4567-2154* ⊕ *www.mounttomahbotanicgarden.com.au* ☉ *Weekdays 9–5, weekends 9:30–5.*

OFF THE
BEATEN
PATH

THE HUNTER VALLEY WINE REGION

To almost everyone in Sydney, the Hunter Valley conjures up visions of one thing: wine. The Hunter is the largest grape-growing area in the state, with more than 120 wineries producing excellent varieties. The Hunter is divided into seven subregions, each with its own unique character. The hub is the Pokolbin/Rothbury region, where many of the large operations are found, along with several boutique wineries.

The Hunter Valley covers an area of almost 25,103 square km (9,692 square miles), stretching from the town of Gosford north of Sydney to 177 km (110 miles) farther north along the coast, and almost 300 km (186 miles) inland. The meandering waterway that gives this valley its name is also one of the most extensive river systems in the state.

POKOLBIN AND ENVIRONS

163 km (100 miles) north of Sydney.

The Lower Hunter wine-growing region is centered on the village of Pokolbin, where there are antiques shops, good cafés, and dozens of wineries. In peak season, wineries are very busy with tour groups, so if you can visit midweek or off-season, all the better.

GETTING HERE AND AROUND

A car is the best way to visit the wineries and off-the-beaten-path attractions unless you are on a guided tour. Leave Sydney via the Harbour Bridge or Harbour Tunnel and get onto the Pacific Highway (keep following the signs for Newcastle). Just before Hornsby the road joins the Sydney–Newcastle Freeway, known as the F3. Take the exit from the freeway signposted "Hunter Valley vineyards via Cessnock." From Cessnock, the route to the vineyards is clearly marked. Allow 2½ hours for the journey.

TOURS

Any tour of the area's vineyards should begin at Pokolbin's **Hunter Valley Wine Country Visitors Information Centre,** which has free maps of the vineyards, brochures, and a handy visitor's guide.

From Sydney, AAT Kings operates a daylong wine-tasting bus tour of the Hunter Valley and another to Hunter Valley Gardens. Buses collect passengers from city hotels from 7 am with the final pickup from The Star casino (the new name for Star City casino complex). Tours cost from A$165, including lunch and wine tasting.

To avoid driving after sampling too many wines, hop aboard one of the Wine Rover buses, which will pick you up from Pokolbin or Cessnock. These minibuses travel between restaurants and about a dozen wineries, allowing you to hop on and off during the day. A day pass with unlimited stops is A$55.

Local operator Heidi's Hunter Valley operates personalized day tours to the wineries and restaurants in a sleek four-wheel-drive vehicle. Heidi Duckworth, who worked for the Hunter Valley Wine Tourism organization for 12 years, knows all the best places in the valley.

One of the hundreds of vineyards that dot the Hunter Valley

ESSENTIALS

Bus Contacts AAT Kings ☎ *1300/228546* ⊕ *www.aatkings.com.au.* **Heidi's Hunter Valley** ☎ *0408/623136* ⊕ *www.heidishuntervalley.com.au.* **Rover Coaches** ☎ *02/4990–1699, 0427/001100* ⊕ *www.rovercoaches.com.au.*

Visitor Information Hunter Valley Wine Country Visitors Information Centre ✉ *455 Wine Country Dr.* ☎ *02/4990–0900* ⊕ *www.winecountry.com. au.***Maitland Hunter Valley Visitor Information Centre** ✉ *New England Hwy. at High St., Maitland* ☎ *02/4931–2800* ⊕ *www maitlandhuntervalley. com.au* ⊙ *Daily 9–5.*

EXPLORING

Binnorie Dairy. Drop by this cheese maker at Tuscany Wine Estate to sample and buy Simon Gough's irresistible, handcrafted soft cow and goat cheeses made from locally sourced milk. You'd be hard-pressed to find a tastier marinated feta outside Greece—or even in it. ✉ *Hermitage Rd. at Mistletoe La.* ☎ *02/4998–6660* ⊕ *www.binnorie.com.au* ⊙ *Tues.–Sat. 10–5, Sun. 10–4.*

Bluetongue Brewery Cafe. Bluetongue beers have become so popular since this boutique brewery opened in the Hunter Valley in 2002 that the owners decided to move the brewery out of the valley to a large purpose-built facility in the Central Coast town of Warnervale, about 65 km (40 miles) away. However, the Bluetongue Brewery Cafe, in the old brewery space at Hunter Valley Resort, serves the brewer's acclaimed "three-hop" beers: premium lager, premium light lager, and pilsner, along with its alcoholic ginger beer. You can order a chef's beer tasting "paddle" with several small glasses for A$15. You can enjoy fish-and-chips, meatballs, pizzas, and other light fare, and there's live music most days. Bluetongue is part of a large complex that includes the resort, a wine school, the San Martino restaurant, and a wine-tasting cellar. ⊠ *Hermitage Rd.* ☎ *02/4998–7777* ⊕ *www.hunterresort.com. au* ⊗ *Daily noon–5.*

FAMILY   **Hunter Valley Gardens.** Garden lovers and those who admire beauty in general should flock to the Hunter Valley Gardens, in the heart of the Pokolbin wine-growing district. The 12 separate gardens occupy 50 acres and include European formal gardens, a Chinese Moongate garden, and a delightful children's storybook garden featuring characters such as the Mad Hatter and Jack and Jill. The gardens have a dazzling Christmas lights display each year; the park is open at night during the holiday season from 6 to 10. The adjacent complex houses restaurants, a popular pub, a hotel, a cute wedding chapel, the underground **Hunter Cellars,** and a selection of boutiques selling gifts as well as wonderful chocolates and fudge. ⊠ *Broke and McDonalds Rds.* ☎ *02/4998–4000* ⊕ *www.hvg.com.au* ⊡ *A$26* ⊗ *Daily 9–5.*

EXPLORING THE WINERIES

Briar Ridge Vineyard. In a delightful rural corner of the Mount View region, this is one of the Hunter Valley's most prestigious small wineries. It produces a limited selection of sought-after reds, whites, and sparkling wines. The Semillon, Chardonnay, Shiraz, and intense Cabernet Sauvignon are highly recommended. The vineyard is on the southern periphery of the Lower Hunter vineyards, about a five-minute drive from Pokolbin. Drop in for a daily tasting and for lunch from Wednesday to Sunday. If you want to extend your stay, they have B&B accommodation suitable for up to six people. ⊠ *593 Mount View Rd., Mount View* ☎ *02/4990–3670* ⊕ *www.briarridge.com.au* ⊗ *Daily 10–5.*

Lindeman's Ben Ean Winery. This has been one of the largest and most prestigious winemakers in the country since the early 1900s. In addition to its Hunter Valley vineyards, the company owns property in South Australia and Victoria, and numerous outstanding wines from these vineyards can be sampled in the tasting room. Try the Shiraz, Semillon, or Chardonnay. The winery has its own museum, displaying vintage wine-making equipment, the 1843 Harvest Cafe, and two picnic areas, one near the parking lot and the other next to the willow trees around the dam. ⊠ *McDonalds Rd. just south of DeBeyers Rd.* ☎ *02/4998–7684* ⊕ *www.lindemans.com.au* ⊗ *Daily 10–5.*

Margan Family Winegrowers. A leading light in the new wave of Hunter winemakers, Margan Family Winegrowers produces some of the valley's best small-volume wines. Try their full-bodied Verdelho, Rosé-style Saignée Shiraz, and Certain Views Cabernet Sauvignon. A riper-than-most Semillon is the flagship, and the 2004 Decanter World Wine Awards rated Margan's botrytis Semillon the world's best sweet wine at its price point (around A$20)—it's delicious. The ultramodern rammed-earth-design cellar door and restaurant is in the tiny village of Broke, 20 km (12 miles) from Pokolbin. Many items on the fine-dining Margan restaurant lunch menu are sourced from the chef's vegetable-and-herb garden on-site, along with fresh eggs. Tasting plates are a great way to sample many of the dishes on offer such as panetta-wrapped quail. ✉ *1238 Milbrodale Rd., Broke* ☎ *02/6579–1372* ⊕ *www.margan.com. au* ⊙ *Daily 10–5.*

Fodor's Choice **McWilliams Mount Pleasant Estate.** At this estate, part of Australia's biggest ★ family-owned wine company, chief winemaker Jim Chatto (only the fourth since the winery was founded in 1921) continues the tradition of producing classic Hunter wines. The flagship Maurice O'Shea Shiraz and Chardonnay, and the celebrated Elizabeth Semillon, are among the wines that can be sampled in the huge cellar door. You can also enjoy a tasting plate of seasonal delicacies on the terrace of Elizabeth's Café, best savored with three vintages of Elizabeth Semillon and one of premium Lovedale Semillon. Guided winery tours run daily at 11 am. ✉ *401 Marrowbone Rd.* ☎ *02/4998–7505* ⊕ *www.mcwilliams.com.au* ✎ *Tours A$5, tastings free* ⊙ *Daily 10–4:30.*

Tempus Two. You can't miss this ultramodern facility in the heart of Pokolbin. This futuristic winery is a joint venture between two leading Hunter Valley families: the Roches (owners of Hunter Valley Gardens) and the McGuigans, who have made wine for four generations. The winery is best known for its Pinot Gris; however, you can sample a wide variety, including Semillon, Sauvignon Blanc, Chardonnay, and Shiraz in the stylish tasting room. There's also a Goldfish Wine Bar and Oishii, an on-site fine-dining Japanese-Thai restaurant. If you can, stop in at the winery's branch of the Hunter Valley Smelly Cheese Shop. In the summer the winery hosts major concerts in its 10,000-seat amphitheatre—past performers have included Elton John, Rod Stewart, and the Beach Boys. ✉ *Broke and McDonalds Rds.* ☎ *02/4993–3999* ⊕ *www. tempustwo.com.au* ⊙ *Daily 9–5.*

Tyrrell's Wines. Founded in 1858, Tyrrell's Wines is the Hunter Valley's oldest family-owned vineyard. This venerable establishment crafts a wide selection of wines, and was the first to produce Chardonnay commercially in Australia. Its famous Vat 47 Chardonnay is still a winner. Enjoy the experience of sampling fine wines in the rustic tasting room, or take a picnic lunch to a site overlooking the valley. Guided tours (A$5) are given daily at 1:30. ✉ *Broke Rd., 2½ km (1½ miles) west of McDonalds Rd.* ☎ *02/4993–7000* ⊕ *www.tyrrells.com.au* ⊙ *Mon.–Sat. 9–5, Sun. 10–4.*

SPORTS AND THE OUTDOORS
BICYCLING
Hunter Valley Cycling. Your bike, helmet, and a map of the area will be delivered to your hotel door by owner Mark or one of his friendly staff. Half-day rentals are A$25, and full-day costs A$35. ☎ *0418/281480* ⊕ *www.huntervalleycycling.com.au.*

HELICOPTER TOURS
Slattery Helicopter Charter. Soaring over a patchwork of wineries and the dramatic Brokenback Range is a thrilling experience—and can be a relatively inexpensive one (as helicopter rides go) when three people share a chopper for a 15-minute ride (A$250 for three people). A great experience is the winery tour and three-course-lunch flight with the helicopter picking you up at and delivering you back to your

Many of the wineries also have excellent restaurants.

Hunter Valley accommodation (A$330 per person; minimum two people). ✉ *230 Old Maitland Rd., Hexham* ☎ *0408/649696* ⊕ *www. slatteryhelicoptercharter.com.au.*

HORSEBACK RIDING

Hunter Valley Horse Riding and Adventures. These friendly folks welcome equestrians of all levels and ages, and have a nice selection of guided rides around the valley. A one-hour ride costs A$55. A favorite is the sunset ride, when your most likely to see wildlife. ✉ *288 Talga Rd., Rothbury* ☎ *02/4930–7111* ⊕ *www.huntervalleyhorseriding.com.au.*

HOT-AIR BALLOONING

Balloon Aloft Hunter Valley. Drifting above the valley while the vines are still wet with dew is an unforgettable way to see the Hunter Valley. The award-winning Balloon Aloft has been operating since the late '70s and runs hour-long, sunrise flights with champagne and breakfast from A$289. ☎ *02/4991–1955, 1300/723279* ⊕ *www.balloonaloft.com.*

WHERE TO EAT

$$$
FRENCH
Fodor'sChoice
★

✕ **Bistro Molines.** Local French-born celebrity chef Robert Molines, who used to run Roberts Restaurant, has a restaurant on the grounds of the lovely Tallavera vineyard, which might just have one of the best views in the valley. Make sure you nab a table on or near the veranda. Food isn't overly complicated or styled, which fits nicely with the relaxed (but professional) service. The twice-roasted Hunter duckling on braised cabbage is delicious, while seafood fans will love the fillet of Red Emperor with Hervey Bay scallops. Those who want a nap after a long lunch, or don't want to drive home, might want to book into the two-bedroom cottage (operated by Robert and his wife Sally) that's just a stroll from the restaurant. *Average main: A$40* *Tallavera Grove, 749 Mount View Rd., Mount View* *02/4990–9553* *www.bistromolines.com.au* *Closed Tues. and Wed. No lunch Mon. and Thurs.*

$$ MODERN AUSTRALIAN **Cafe Enzo.** This breakfast and lunch café is at Peppers Creek Village, a charming little shopping and dining enclave in Pokolbin with a village green atmosphere. Housed in a sandstone building, with a lovely attached sun-drenched courtyard overlooking a fountain, this is a great spot for a hearty lunch after a visit to neighboring David Hooks winery and the clothing and antiques shops. Meals are substantial and may include handmade linguine with tiger prawns and fresh chili or zucchini and corn fritters with beetroot-cured Atlantic salmon. It's a popular place in the warmer months. *Average main: A$28* *Peppers Creek Village, Broke and Ekerts Rds.* *02/4998–7233* *www.enzohuntervalley.com.au* *No dinner.*

$$ ASIAN FUSION **Leaves & Fishes.** A rustic boathouse-style café with a deck that projects over a fish-stocked dam and a lovely garden, this is the place to savor delicious seafood with an Asian twist, and share antipasto dishes. Fish comes straight from farm to plate, and wines are from local vineyards. You could start with the mussels and prawn hot pot with chorizo or go straight to the hearty seafood chowder. Those who are not fans of seafood can tuck into the crispy skin duck with steamed asparagus and confit of potato. Desserts from the specials board might include mango and coconut pudding with fresh papaya. Reservations are recommended, especially on weekends. There is also boathouse-style accommodation on the property, ideal for couples. *Average main: A$35* *737 Lovedale Rd., Lovedale* *02/4930–7400* *www.leavesandfishes.com.au* *Closed Mon. and Tues. No dinner Wed., Thurs., and Sun.*

$$$ MODERN AUSTRALIAN **Roberts Restaurant.** This restaurant in grapevine-covered, 1876-built Pepper Tree Cottage wins the ambience award hands down. Although chef Robert Molines departed a few years ago to start his own restaurant, Roberts had such a loyal following that the name stayed with the cute cottage. The seasonal Mod Oz menu draws inspiration from regional recipes of France and Italy and applies it to local game, seafood, beef, and lamb. A good choice is the chef specialty duck breast roulade with ham or the blue-eye trevalla served with Thai green curry and mussels. The cozy fireside lounge is perfect for enjoying after-dinner liqueurs, or another wine from the extensive wine list, many of which come from nearby Tower Estate, which owns the restaurant. *Average main: A$42* *64 Halls Rd.* *02/4998–7330* *www.robertsrestaurant.com.*

WHERE TO STAY

For expanded hotel reviews, visit Fodors.com.

$$ B&B/INN **Carriages Country House.** On 36 acres at the end of a quiet country lane, this rustic-looking but winsome guesthouse, set on a small vineyard, is all about privacy. **Pros:** romantic in winter with roaring fireplaces in some rooms; lovely verandas overlooking the grounds **Cons:** no children allowed; wedding groups sometimes book out most of the place. *Rooms from: A$250* *102 Halls Rd.* *02/4998–7591* *www.thecarriages.com.au* *10 suites* *Breakfast.*

$$$$ B&B/INN Fodor's Choice ★ **Cedars Mount View.** This property nestled in the hills above the valley might tempt you to forget about wine tasting for a few days. **Pros:** private and luxurious; the bathrooms have decadent sunken whirlpool baths. **Cons:** the location may be a bit too remote for some. [$] *Rooms from: A$450* ✉ *60 Mitchells Rd., Mount View* ☎ *02/4959–3072* 🌐 *www.cedars.com.au* 🛏 *4 villas, 1 cottage* 🍴 *Breakfast.*

$$$ B&B/INN **The Cooperage Bed and Breakfast.** This lovely B&B is in the heart of Kelman Vineyards Estate, a working vineyard with a cellar door just a stone's throw from the rooms. **Pros:** big comfy beds; guesthouse rooms have private decks; free Wi-Fi. **Cons:** not suitable for children under 10; can be booked out months ahead. [$] *Rooms from: A$278* ✉ *41 Kelman Vineyards, off Oakey Creek Rd.* ☎ *02/4990–1232* 🌐 *www.huntervalleycooperage.com* 🛏 *5 rooms* 🍴 *Breakfast.*

$$$$ B&B/INN **Peppers Convent.** This former convent, built in 1909 and transported 605 km (375 miles) from its original home in western New South Wales, is ideal for those who love traditional guesthouses. **Pros:** romantic and secluded; balconies are a superb place to watch the sunset. **Cons:** standard rooms are on the small side; a bit noisy. [$] *Rooms from: A$345* ✉ *88 Halls Rd.* ☎ *02/4998–4999* 🌐 *www.peppers.com.au* 🛏 *17 rooms* 🍴 *Breakfast.*

$$$$ B&B/INN **Tower Lodge.** This imposing lodge, a cross between a castle and a Tuscan villa, is the place for an indulgent getaway. **Pros:** lovely courtyard; impressive rooms. **Cons:** expensive. [$] *Rooms from: A$720* ✉ *6 Halls Rd.* ☎ *02/4998–7022* 🌐 *www.towerestate.com* 🛏 *12 rooms* 🍴 *Breakfast.*

THE NORTH COAST

The North Coast is one of the most glorious and seductive stretches of terrain in Australia, stretching almost 680 km (422 miles) from Newcastle up to the Queensland border. An almost continuous line of beaches defines the coast, with the Great Dividing Range rising to the west the farther you travel north. These natural borders frame a succession of rolling green pasturelands, mossy rain forests, towns dotted by red-roof houses, and waterfalls that tumble in glistening arcs from the escarpment.

A journey along the coast leads through several rich agricultural districts, beginning with grazing country in the south and moving into plantations of bananas, sugarcane, mangoes, avocados, and macadamia nuts. Dorrigo National Park, outside Bellingen, and Muttonbird Island, in Coffs Harbour, are two parks good for getting your feet on some native soil and for seeing unusual birdlife.

NEWCASTLE

160 km (100 miles) north of Sydney

Once known as the Steel City, today Newcastle is one of Australia's hippest cities. It's flanked by the Pacific Ocean and six beaches on its eastern side and a harbor on its west side. Gentrification began when the steel mills closed in 1999. Nowadays the old wharves and warehouses

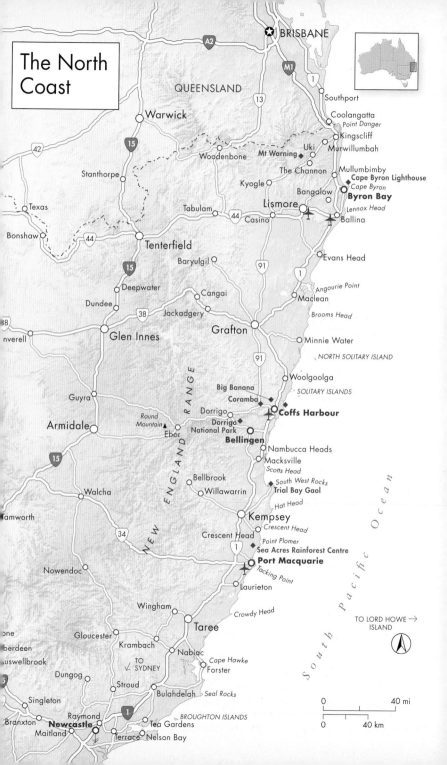

The North Coast

QUEENSLAND

BRISBANE

A2
M1
13

Southport
Coolangatta
Point Danger
Kingscliff
Murwillumbah
Mullumbimby
Cape Byron Lighthouse
Cape Byron
Byron Bay
Lennox Head
Ballina
Evans Head

Warwick
Woodenbone
Mt Warning
Uki
The Channon
Kyogle
Bangalow
Lismore
Casino

Stanthorpe

42
15

Texas
Tabulam
44

Bonshaw
44
Tenterfield
Baryulgil
91

Deepwater
Cangai
Angourie Point
Maclean
Brooms Head

Dundee
38
Jackadgery
Grafton

15
Glen Innes
91

nverell
Minnie Water
NORTH SOLITARY ISLAND

Guyra
Woolgoolga
SOLITARY ISLANDS

Big Banana
Coramba
Coffs Harbour

Armidale
Round Mountain
Ebor
Dorrigo
Dorrigo National Park
Bellingen

N
E
W

E
N
G
L
A
N
D

R
A
N
G
E

Nambucca Heads
Macksville
Scotts Head
South West Rocks
Trial Bay Gaol
Hat Head

Bellbrook
Willawarrin

Kempsey
Crescent Head
Crescent Head
Point Plomer
Sea Acres Rainforest Centre
Port Macquarie
Tacking Point

Walcha
34

Tamworth

Nowendoc
Laurieton
Crowdy Head

Wingham
Taree

one
berdeen
uswellbrook

Gloucester
Krambach
Nabiac
Cape Hawke
Forster

TO SYDNEY

Dungog
Stroud
Bulahdelah
Seal Rocks

Singleton
BROUGHTON ISLANDS

Branxton
3
1
Raymond
Newcastle
Maitland
Terrace
Tea Gardens
Nelson Bay

South Pacific Ocean

TO LORD HOWE →
ISLAND

0   40 mi

0   40 km

form part of the lively Honeysuckle precinct, which buzzes with hotels, cafés, and restaurants.

GETTING HERE AND AROUND

This city of about 500,000 is easy to navigate, as the harbor area and city center are just 3 km (2 miles) from the beaches, and buses run between them. Hunter Street—the main artery—and the railway line from Sydney both run parallel to the harbor, and it's only a five-minute walk from harbor to downtown. Trains stop at two stations in the city center, and buses travel from Hunter Street to Darby Street, the main shopping and dining area.

EXPLORING

Fort Scratchley. This was one of several forts built on headlands along Australia's shore in the mid- to late 19th century to defend the colony against a possible Russian attack. Built in 1882, its guns had never been fired in anger until June 8, 1942, when the fort returned fire from Japanese submarines in a little-known World War II confrontation called "the shelling of Newcastle"—the city sustained 34 shells but neither damage nor loss of life. The fort, situated on Flagstaff Hill in Newcastle's east end (not far from the railway station), was occupied by the Australian Army until 1972, after which it became a historic site. Although admission is free, a tour of the fort's tunnels is A$12, and a tunnel and fort tour is A$15. Tours run from 10:30, with the last one at 2:30. ⊠ *Nobby's Rd., New Castle, New South Wales* ⊕ *www. fortscratchey.org.au* ⊘ *Wed.–Mon. 10–4.*

Merewether Baths. The largest ocean baths (swimming pools) in the southern hemisphere, Merewether Baths are a Newcastle icon perfect for swimming and splashing all year round. Opened in 1935 at one of the city's six fabulous beaches, they comprise two pools, with one suitable for children. Complete with barbecues and picnic tables, the baths are the ideal place for a family outing. ■TIP→ **The baths are patrolled by lifeguards during the summer months only, from around late September to late April.** ⊠ *Henderson Parade, New Castle, New South Wales* ▨ *Free.*

Newcastle Museum. In the former headquarters of the Great Northern Railway, right on Newcastle Harbour, this museum tells the story of the city's coal mining and steel production. Visitors can don a hard hat to witness the Fire and Earth exhibition, which re-creates life in a steel mill complete with furnaces, theatrical drama, and interactive displays that shed light on the workers' challenging lives. Newcastle's other faces are captured with exhibits on Aboriginal history, the gorgeous beaches, and the earthquake that struck the city in 1989. A popular draw for kids, the Supernova Hands-on Science Centre explains how a heavy car is lifted, a tornado occurs, and magnetic fields work. ⊠ *Workshop Way, New Castle, New South Wales* ☎ *2/4974–1400* ⊕ *www.newcastlemuseum. com.au* ▨ *Free* ⊘ *Tues.–Sun. 10–5.*

WHERE TO EAT

$$$

MODERN
AUSTRALIAN

✕ **Scratchleys on the Wharf.** This swank establishment is as close as Newcastle comes to having an iconic restaurant. Enclosed on three sides by glass and perched over the harbor on the busy esplanade, Scratchleys opened not long after the Honeysuckle precinct transformed Newcastle into a hip and happening place more than a decade ago. The restaurant offers one of the best views in Newcastle and an extensive menu to please all-comers. Starters include seafood chowder, oysters, and prawn salad, while several dishes—king prawn linguine, and prawn satay with spicy peanut sauce—are available in either starter or main sizes. Non-seafood fans have steaks, lamb cutlets, and corn-fed chicken breast dishes to consider, and a range of vegetarian options and Hunter Valley cheeses to sustain them. $ *Average main: A$38* ⊠ *200 Wharf Rd., New Castle, New South Wales* ☎ *2/4929–1111* ⊕ *www.scratchleys.com.au.*

$$$
MODERN
AUSTRALIAN
✕ **Subo Newcastle.** A bright, intimate star in Newcastle's dining scene, Subo has quickly become the hot spot in town. A stylish bistro in the central business district, Subo regulars favor the A$85 five-course tasting plate, which might feature prawn carpaccio and foie gras, confit of chicken wings with blackened corn, Wagyu beef with smoked leeks, and chocolate-orange mousse with rum–and–orange syrup cake. $ *Average main: A$28* ⊠ *551D Hunter St., New Castle, New South Wales* ☎ *2/4023–4048* ⊕ *www.subo.com.au* ⊙ *Closed Mon. and Tues. No lunch Wed.–Sat.*

WHERE TO STAY

$$
HOTEL
🛏 **Chifley Executive Suites Newcastle.** On Scott Street, one block from the harbor, Chifley Executive Suites Newcastle has 17 two-bedroom apartments and 13 one-bedroom suites. **Pros:** great location. **Cons:** expensive on-site parking; central location can be noisy on weekends. $ *Rooms from: A$205* ⊠ *111 Scott St., New Castle, New South Wales* ☎ *02/4040–1200* ⊕ *www.chifleyhotels.com.au/newcastle* ⟿ *40 suites* ⦿ *No meals.*

$$$
HOTEL
🛏 **Crowne Plaza Newcastle.** Newcastle's most upscale hotel, the Crowne Plaza, is in the trendy Honeysuckle Precinct and has the best location of any hotel in town. **Pros:** great location. **Cons:** parking is expensive (but there is free on-street parking nearby). $ *Rooms from: A$330* ⊠ *Merewether and Wharf Sts., New Castle, New South Wales* ☎ *2/4907–5000* ⊕ *www.ichotelsgroup.com* ⟿ *175 rooms* ⦿ *No meals.*

$
HOTEL
🛏 **Ibis Newcastle.** Set about a kilometer (½ mile) from Newcastle's downtown, the Ibis is a moderately priced chain hotel with parking and a restaurant. **Pros:** excellent location; good price. **Cons:** not on beach or waterfront; expensive in-room Wi-Fi. $ *Rooms from: A$139* ⊠ *700 Hunter St., New Castle, New South Wales* ☎ *2/4925–2266* ⊕ *www.ibis.com* ⟿ *97 rooms* ⦿ *No meals.*

PORT MACQUARIE

390 km (243 miles) northeast of Sydney.

Port Macquarie was founded as a convict settlement in 1821 and is the third-oldest settlement in Australia. Set at the mouth of the Hastings River, the town was chosen for its isolation to serve as an open jail for prisoners convicted of second offenses in New South Wales. By the 1830s the pace of settlement was so brisk that the town was no longer isolated, and its usefulness as a jail had ended.

Today's Port Macquarie has few reminders of its convict past and is flourishing as a vacation area. With its pristine rivers and lakes and 13 regional beaches, including beautiful Town Beach and Shelley Beach, which both have sheltered swimming, it's a great place to get into water sports, catch a fish for dinner, and watch migrating humpback whales in season, usually May to August and September to November.

GETTING HERE AND AROUND

It's a 5½-hour drive from Sydney heading north on the Pacific Highway. Greyhound and Premier Motor Service run coaches from Sydney Central Station. NSW TrainLink trains operate three services daily between Sydney and the North Coast, though there is no direct train to Port Macquarie. Passengers depart at Wauchope station and then take a bus to Port Macquarie (a seven-hour journey). Busway Buses travel from Port Macquarie to nearby towns and also to Coffs Harbour and Grafton. Timetables are available at the Greater Port Macquarie Visitor Centre or online. Qantas and Virgin Australia have flights from Sydney.

ESSENTIALS

Visitor Information Visitor Information Centre ⊠ *The Glasshouse, Clarence and Hay Sts., Port Macquarie* ☎ *1300/303155, 02/6581–8000* ⊕ *www. portmacquarieinfo.com.au.*

EXPLORING

FAMILY **Koala Hospital.** Operated by the Koala Preservation Society of New South Wales, the town's Koala Hospital is both a worthy cause and a popular attraction. The Port Macquarie region supports many of these extremely appealing marsupials, and the hospital cares for 250 to 300 sick and injured koalas each year. The staff is passionate about their furry patients, and will happily tell you about the care the animals receive. You can walk around the grounds to view the recuperating animals; you can even adopt one (but you can't take it home). Try to visit during feeding times—8 in the morning or 3 in the afternoon. There are guided tours daily at 3. ⊠ *Macquarie Nature Reserve, Lord St.* ☎ *02/6584–1522* ⊕ *www.koalahospital.org.au* 🎫 *Donation requested* ⊗ *Daily 8–4:30.*

Port Macquarie Historical Museum. Housed in a two-story shop dating from 1836, this eclectic museum displays period costumes, memorabilia from World Wars I and II, farm implements, antique clocks and watches, and relics from the town's convict days. ⊠ *22 Clarence St.* ☎ *02/6583–1108* ⊕ *www.port-macquarie-historical-museum.org.au* 🎫 *A$5* ⊗ *Mon.–Sat. 9:30–4:30.*

Fodor'sChoice **Sea Acres Rainforest Centre.** This interpretive center comprises 178 pris-
★   tine acres of coastal rain forest on the southern side of Port Macquarie. There are more than 170 plant species here, including 300-year-old cabbage-tree palms, as well as native mammals, reptiles, and prolific birdlife. An elevated boardwalk allows you to stroll through the lush environment without disturbing the vegetation. The center has informative guided tours, as well as a gift shop and a pleasant rain-forest café run by a new French chef so you can enjoy a croque-monsieur while listening to the birdsong. ⊠ *Pacific Dr. near Shelley Beach Rd.* ☎ *02/6582–3355* ⊕ *www.environment.nsw.gov.au* 🎫 *A$8* ⊗ *Daily 9–4:30.*

Orange fungi growing on the Rainforest Tree at Dorrigo National Park

St. Thomas Church. This 1828 church, the country's third-oldest house of worship, was built by convicts using local cedar and stone blocks cemented together with powdered seashells. ✉ *Hay and William Sts.* ☎ *02/6584–1033* ⊙ *Weekdays 10–noon and 2–4.*

Unsurprisingly, most of the outdoor activities in this area revolve around the town's crystal-clear waters.

FISHING

Ocean Star. Deep-sea anglers will enjoy the daylong trips on this 40-foot custom Randel charting boat. Typical catches include snapper, pearl perch, dolphin fish, and jewfish. If you have cooking facilities, the crew is happy to clean, ice, and pack your catch. ✉ *Town Wharf* ☎ *0416/240877* ⊕ *www.oceanstarfishing.com.*

HORSEBACK RIDING

Bellrowan Valley Horseriding. Thirty minutes' drive inland from Port Macquarie, Bellrowan welcomes experts and beginners, and offers short trail rides and overnight treks. The two-day Great Aussie Pub Ride ends the day's ride in some of the region's most interesting pubs and costs A$385 with all meals and accommodation. A two-hour trail ride is A$85. ✉ *Crows Rd., Beechwood* ☎ *02/6587–5227* ⊕ *www.bellrowanvalley. com.au.*

SURFING

Port Macquarie Surf School. Head back to school and learn to ride the waves from some very competent coaches, all of whom are fully accredited, licensed, and insured with Surfing Australia. There are daily group lessons at 9 am, 11 am, and 2 pm (A$40 for two hours), or you can opt for one-on-one tutoring (A$60 per hour). Surfboards, wet suits, rash vests, and sunscreen are provided. ⊠ *46 Pacific Dr.* ☎ *02/6584–7733* ⊕ *www.portmacquariesurfschool.com.au.*

WHALE-WATCHING

Port Macquarie Cruise Adventures. Majestic humpback whales migrate past Port Macquarie nonstop from May to the end of November and Cruise Adventures offers great-value cruises on their fast 12-seater boats (A$30) for 1½ hours and cruises on a larger boat the *Discovery* (A$35) for 2 hours. The company also has both long and short cruises to see local bottlenose dolphins, which can be spotted year-round; these start at A$15 for a two-hour trip. ⊠ *Short St. Wharf* ☎ *1300/555890* ⊕ *www.cruiseadventures.com.au.*

WHERE TO EAT AND STAY

$$ ✕ **Ca Marche.** This prix-fixe restaurant in the lovely Cassegrain winery,
AUSTRALIAN a 20-minute drive south of Port Macquarie, has always been popular at lunch as diners gaze out over the sun-drenched vines and formal gardens. You may want to go all French and start with the escargot (snails cooked in their shells with garlic, parsley butter, and Pernod), or try the local Camden Haven oysters instead. Starters include exceptional confit duck salad and steak tartare, while a hearty main is the local eye fillet of beef with brandy sauce. The vineyard produces a wide variety of wines including Chardonnay, Verdelho, and Rosé, and the cellar door offers daily tastings from 9 to 5. The restaurant will open for bookings of 20 or more. $ *Average main: A$25* ⊠ *764 Fernbank Creek Rd., Fernbank Creek* ☎ *02/6582–8320* ⊕ *www.cassegrain-restaurant.com. au* ⊗ *No dinner.*

$$ ✕ **The Corner.** This stylish, contemporary café packs in the crowds,
AUSTRALIAN thanks its fabulously tasty and inexpensive meals, though you may need to exercise a little patience, as service can be a bit slow at times. Try the Corner Breakfast (A$19), which has just about everything from eggs the way you like them to ham-hock-braised beans. Return for dinner to sample the Yamba jewfish, baby beetroot, corn puree, and jamón. As the name suggests, it sits on a corner; it's part of the Macquarie Waters Hotel & Apartments complex. $ *Average main: A$32* ⊠ *Clarence and Munster Sts.* ☎ *02/6583–3300* ⊕ *www.cornerrestaurant.com. au* ⊗ *No dinner Sun.*

$$ 🛏 **Beachcomber Resort.** Spacious family-friendly accommodation can
RESORT be tough to find in Port Macquarie, which is why this self-catering resort opposite Town Beach garners high praise for its service and price. **Pros:** well-maintained BBQ area; spotless accommodation. **Cons:** the lack of elevators can be a pain if you're lugging children upstairs; if you don't have kids, you might feel outnumbered. $ *Rooms from: A$155* ⊠ *54 William St.* ☎ *02/6584–1881, 1800/001320* ⊕ *www. beachcomberresort.com.au* ➦ *22 apartments* ⊙ *No meals.*

$$ 🛏 **Best Western Plus HW Boutique Hotel.** Although the building dates
HOTEL from the late 1960s—when its sawtooth shape was considered stylish—it's filled with up-to-the-minute amenities: designer furnishings, luxurious linens, marble bathrooms, and private balconies with ocean and river views. **Pros:** a good Continental breakfast is brought to your room; toasters in rooms; beautiful breakfast room on the top floor

with ocean views. **Cons:** some street noise; a few rooms overlook car park. $ *Rooms from: A$245* ✉ *1 Stewart St.* ☎ *02/6583–1200* ⊕ *www. hwboutique.com.au* ⤴ *45 rooms* ⦿ *Breakfast.*

$$ 🖵 **The Observatory.** The most stylish digs in Port Macquarie are just a

HOTEL short walk across leafy parkland to the city's main beach. **Pros:** close to beach; great restaurants. **Cons:** packed with families in summer. $ *Rooms from: A$169* ✉ *40 William St.* ☎ *02/6586–8000* ⊕ *www. observatory.net.au* ⤴ *81 rooms, 2 penthouses* ⦿ *No meals.*

EN
ROUTE

Trial Bay Gaol. A jail dating from the 1870s, Trial Bay Gaol occupies a dramatic position on the cliffs overlooking the seaside village of South West Rocks, 100 km (62 miles) north of Port Macquarie. The building, now partly in ruins, was used to teach useful skills to the prisoners who constructed it, but the project proved too expensive and was abandoned in 1903. During World War I the building served as an internment camp for some 500 Germans. The A$7.50 admission includes entry to a small museum. Discovery tours are run during the school holidays in December and January, April or May (usually around the Easter holiday), July, and October. Make sure you climb the tower for a stunning view of the coast. To get there, travel north through Kempsey and turn off to South West Rocks and follow the signs. ✉ *Arakoon National Park, Cardwell St., South West Rocks* ☎ *02/6566–6168* ⊕ *www.trialbaygaol.com.*

BELLINGEN

210 km (130 miles) north of Port Macquarie, 520 km (323 miles) from Sydney.

In a river valley a few miles off the Pacific Highway, artsy Bellingen is one of the prettiest towns along the coast. Many of Bellingen's buildings have been classified by the National Trust, and the museum, cafés, galleries, and crafts outlets are favorite hangouts for artists, craft workers, and writers. You'll find food, entertainment, and 250 stalls at the community markets that take place on the third Sunday of every month.

GETTING HERE AND AROUND

It's a seven-hour drive from Sydney along the Pacific Highway, but the town is just 30 minutes from Coffs Harbour and its airport. NSW TrainLink trains run from Sydney three times a day and from Brisbane twice daily, stopping at Urunga, 10 km (6 miles) away. Both Greyhound and Premier Motor Service also run buses between Sydney and Urunga. From Urunga, either catch a taxi or a local Busways bus to Bellingen— though the bus is quite infrequent. There is also a Busways bus service from Coffs Harbour to Bellingen.

ESSENTIALS

Visitor Information Waterfall Way Visitor Centre ✉ *29–31 Hyde St.* ☎ *02/6655–1522, 1800/70575* ⊕ *www.bellingermagic.com.*

EXPLORING

Dorrigo National Park. From Bellingen a meandering and spectacular road leads inland to Dorrigo and then travels back east eventually reaching the Pacific Highway, close to Coffs Harbour. This circular scenic route, beginning along the Bellinger River, climbs more than 1,000 feet up the heavily wooded escarpment to the Dorrigo Plateau. At the top of the plateau is Dorrigo National Park, a small but outstanding subtropical rain forest that is included on the World Heritage list. Signposts along the main road indicate walking trails. The Satinbird Stroll is a short rain-forest walk, and the 6-km (4-mile) Cedar Falls Walk leads to the most spectacular of the park's many waterfalls. The national park is approximately 31 km (19 miles) from Bellingen. ⊠ *Dorrigo Rainforest Centre, Dome Rd., Dorrigo* ☎ *02/6657–2309* ⊕ *www.nationalparks. nsw.gov.au.*

Dorrigo Rainforest Centre. The excellent Dorrigo Rainforest Centre, open daily 9–4:30, has information, educational displays, and a shop. From here you can walk out high over the forest canopy along the **Sky-walk** boardwalk. ☎ *02/6657–2309* ⊕ *www.dorrigo.com.*

SPORTS AND THE OUTDOORS

CANOEING

Bellingen Canoe Adventures. Hire a canoe or join an organized expedition on the Bellinger River, which meanders its way through some of the most spectacular and picturesque areas in the area. This company, which emphasizes safety above everything else, offers a wide range of options including one-hour sunset tours (A$25), a half-day tour on calm water with tea (A$48), or full-day tours that promise the thrill of rapids and provide lunch as well (A$90). ☎ *02/6655–9955* ⊕ *www. canoeadventures.com.au.*

HIKING

Gambaarri Tours. If you are interested in local Aboriginal culture, join one of these half-day tours led by local elder Wiruunngga. You'll learn about local history and look for bush tucker as you visit the Promised Land and the Never Never River. Morning or afternoon tea is provided. Wiruunngga also offers tours out of Coffs (A$45). ☎ *02/6655–5195* ⊕ *www.heartlanddidgeridoos.com.au.*

HORSEBACK RIDING

Valery Trails. This large equestrian center is 10 km (6 miles) from Bellingen on the edge of Bongil Bongil National Park. They have 60 horses, and offer a variety of treks through the local rain forests. Choose from the popular two-hour rides (A$65), breakfast and afternoon barbecue rides, and a two-day ride to Bellingen to stay in the Federal Hotel for (A$450). ⊠ *758 Valery Rd., Valery* ☎ *02/6653–4301* ⊕ *www. valerytrails.com.au.*

WHERE TO STAY

$$
B&B/INN

⛺ **Koompartoo Retreat.** These self-contained hardwood cottages on a hillside overlooking Bellingen are superb examples of local craftsmanship, particularly in their use of timbers from surrounding forests. **Pros:** from the chalet verandas you can see kookaburras and black cockatoos; each cottage has small library. **Cons:** no wheelchair access; heating is noisy. $ *Rooms from: A$175* ⊠ *Rawson and Dudley Sts.* ☎ *02/6655–2326* ⊕ *www.koompartoo.com.au* ⇄ *4 cottages* ⊙| *No meals.*

COFFS HARBOUR

35 km (22 miles) northeast of Bellingen via the Pacific Hwy., 103 km (64 miles) from Bellingen via the inland scenic route along the Dorrigo Plateau, 534 km (320 miles) from Sydney.

The area surrounding Coffs Harbour is the state's "banana belt," where long, neat rows of banana palms cover the hillsides. Set at the foot of steep green hills, the town has great beaches and a mild climate. This idyllic combination has made it one of the most popular vacation spots along the coast. Coffs is also a convenient halfway point on the 1,000-km (620-mile) journey between Sydney and Brisbane.

GETTING HERE AND AROUND

Coffs Harbour is a comfortable 7½-hour drive from Sydney and a 6-hour drive from Brisbane. Regular Greyhound and Premier Buses connect the town to Sydney. There is a train station with daily NSW TrainLink services to and from Sydney and Brisbane. And the local airport, 6 km (4 miles) from the central Ocean Parade, is served by Qantas, Virgin Australia, and Brindabella Airlines (the latter between Coffs Harbour and Brisbane only). For more information, contact the visitor center, which is open 9–5 daily.

ESSENTIALS

Airport Information Coffs Harbour Airport ✉ *Hogbin Dr.* ☎ *02/6648–4837.*

Visitor Information Coffs Coast Visitors Information Centre ✉ *Pacific Hwy. at McLean St.* ☎ *02/6648–4990, 1300/369070* ⊕ *www.coffscoast.com.au.*

EXPLORING

FAMILY **The Big Banana.** Just north of the city, impossible to miss, is the Big Banana—the symbol of Coffs Harbour. This monumental piece of kitsch has stood at the site since 1964. It welcomes visitors to the Big Banana complex, which takes a fascinating look at the past, present, and future of horticulture. There's a multimedia display called "World of Bananas" and a walkway that meanders through the banana plantations and banana packing shed. A lookout high on the plantation hill provides great views to the coast, and is a good whale-watching vantage point July–November. The park is fantastic for kids and has varied rides all with different prices, including toboggan rides (A$6), a waterslide (A$16 for 90 minutes), an ice-skating rink (A$14.50), and laser tag (A$9.90). There's a café on the premises, as well as the Banana Barn, which sells the park's own jams, pickles, and fresh tropical fruit. ✉ *351 Pacific Hwy.* ☎ *02/6652–4355* ⊕ *www.bigbanana.com* 🖃 *A$16 for movie and plantation tour and either 2 toboggan rides or 1 ice-skating experience* ☉ *Daily 9–4:30.*

Muttonbird Island. The town has a lively and attractive harbor in the shelter of Muttonbird Island, and a stroll out to this nature reserve is delightful in the evening. To get here, follow the signs to the Coffs Harbour Jetty, then park near the marina. A wide path leads out along the breakwater and up the slope of the island. The trail is steep, but the views from the top are worth the effort. The island is named after the muttonbirds (also known as shearwaters) that nest here between

September and April. Between June and September Muttonbird Island is also a good spot for viewing migrating humpback whales.

FAMILY **Pet Porpoise Pool.** Near the port in Coffs Harbour, the Pet Porpoise Pool aquarium includes colorful reef fish, turtles, seals, penguins, baby crocodiles, and dolphins. Shows take place daily at 10 and 1, and visitors are advised to arrive 30 minutes earlier to get a good seat and receive free "dolphin kisses" from the cute critters before each show. Children may help feed and "shake hands" with dolphins, as well as interact with the seals. You can swim, pat, and play ball with the dolphin and seals in special group encounters if you book in advance. These sessions vary in price depending on time of year—during peak holiday season, seal encounters cost A$250 per person and dolphin encounters run around A$400 per person. The company's official name is Dolphin Marine Magic, and while most signs still point the way to Pet Porpoise Pool, they're planning eventually to change to the new name. ✉ *65 Orlando St., beside Coffs Creek* ☎ *02/6659–1900* 🌐 *www.dolphinmarinemagic.com.au* 🎟 *A$34* 🕐 *Daily 9–4.*

SPORTS AND THE OUTDOORS

SCUBA DIVING

The warm seas around Coffs Harbour make this particular part of the coast, with its moray eels, manta rays, turtles, and gray nurse sharks, a scuba diver's favorite. Best are the Solitary Islands, 7–21 km (4½–13 miles) offshore.

Jetty Dive Centre. This outfitter rents gear, schedules scuba and snorkeling trips, and hosts certification classes. A double-dive trip costs A$120; a one-day learn-to-dive course is A$249. There are also whale- and dolphin-watching cruises from June to October from A$59. ✉ *398 Harbour Dr.* ☎ *02/6651–1611* 🌐 *www.jettydive.com.au.*

WHITE-WATER RAFTING

Wildwater Rafting. This highly regarded company conducts half-day, one-day, and two-day rafting trips down the Nymboida River. Trips begin from Bonville, 14 km (9 miles) south of Coffs Harbour on the Pacific Highway, but pickups from the Coffs Harbour and Bellingen region can be arranged. Half-day trips are A$80, one-day trips are A$185, and two day trips cost A$430 per person including snacks and meals. Overnight trips feature camping on the riverbank, breakfast, and dinner. ✉ *16 Prince St.* ☎ *02/6653–2067* 🌐 *www.coffscentral.com/wildwater.*

WHERE TO EAT AND STAY

$$ ECLECTIC 🍴 **Shearwater Restaurant.** This waterfront restaurant with views of Coffs Creek (which is spotlighted at night—look for stingrays swimming by) is open for breakfast, lunch, and dinner, and leaves no culinary stone unturned in its search for novel flavors. The menu in the open-air dining room includes lunch dishes like prawn and scallop red curry. If you want a table on the deck in summer, book ahead. Service is friendly and attentive. The restaurant operates on a limited wintertime basis (June–August); call to confirm hours. [$] *Average main: A$30* ✉ *The Promenade, 321 Harbour Dr.* ☎ *02/6651–6053* 🌐 *www.shearwaterrestaurant.com.au.*

$$ 🖼 **BreakFree Aanuka Beach Resort.** Teak furniture and antiques collected
RESORT from Indonesia and the South Pacific fill the accommodations at this
resort, which sits amid palms, frangipani, and hibiscus. **Pros:** brilliant
setting in a private beachfront cove; great value for families. **Cons:**
some rooms need updating; kid-phobes might not appreciate all the
families. 💲 *Rooms from: A$169* ✉ *11 Firman Dr.* ☎ *02/6652–7555*
⊕ *www.breakfreeaanukabeachresort.com.au* ↗ *27 studios, 39 suites,*
12 villas ⊙| *Breakfast.*

$$$$ 🖼 **Smugglers on the Beach.** Five minutes' drive north of Coffs Harbour's
RESORT busy city center is this small resort with just 16 self-contained one-
to three-bedroom apartments, some with hot tubs, spread out among
tropical gardens. **Pros:** resort has fishing equipment and a BBQ, so you
can catch your dinner; beautiful beachside location. **Cons:** two-night
minimum; check-out is at 9:30 am. 💲 *Rooms from: A$310* ✉ *36 Sandy*
Beach Rd. ☎ *02/6653–6166* ⊕ *www.smugglers.com.au* ↗ *16 apart-*
ments ⊙| *No meals.*

BYRON BAY

247 km (154 miles) north of Coffs Harbour, 772 km (480 miles) north
of Sydney.

Byron Bay is the easternmost point on the Australian mainland, and
perhaps earns Australia its nickname the "Lucky Country." Fabulous
beaches, storms that spin rainbows across the mountains behind the
town, and a sunny, relaxed style cast a spell over practically everyone
who visits. For many years Byron Bay lured surfers with abundant
sunshine, perfect waves on Watego's Beach, and tolerant locals who
allowed them to sleep on the sand. These days a more upscale crowd
frequents Byron Bay.

Byron Bay is also one of the must-sees on the backpacker circuit, and
the town has a youthful energy that fuels late-night partying. There are
many art galleries and crafts shops, a great food scene, and numerous
adventure tours. The town is at its liveliest on the first Sunday of each
month, when Butler Street becomes a bustling market.

GETTING HERE AND AROUND
Byron is the North Coast's most popular destination, and is well served
by buses and trains from Sydney and Coffs Harbour. If driving, the
journey takes 11 hours from Sydney and 3½ hours from Coffs Harbour.
The closest airports are at Ballina and Lismore, both a 30-minute drive
away. Virgin Australia, Jetstar, and REX fly to Ballina; REX also flies
from Sydney to Lismore. All the usual car companies are there, or you
can get a taxi into Byron or take a Ballina-Byron shuttle bus (operated
by Byron Easy Bus) for A$15 one-way.

ESSENTIALS
Airport Shuttle Byron Easy Bus ☎ *02/6685–7447* ⊕ *www.byronbayshuttle.*
com.au.

Visitor Information Byron Visitor Centre ✉ *Old Station Master's Cottage, 80*
Jonson St. ☎ *02/6680–8558* ⊕ *www.visitbyronbay.com.*

There's no shortage of activities in Byron Bay.

EXPLORING

Cape Byron Lighthouse. The most powerful beacon on the Australian coastline, Cape Byron Lighthouse dominates the southern end of the beach at Byron Bay and attracts huge numbers of visitors. You can tour the lighthouse (no children under five) daily from 10 am, with the last tour departing at 3 pm. The tours are led by volunteers, and while there's no entry charge, a donation is appreciated. Whale-watching is popular between June and September, when migrating humpback whales come close to shore. Dolphins swim in these waters year-round, and you can often see pods of them from the cape. You can stay in either of the two six-person assistant light-keeper's cottages for A$340 a night in low season; prices rise from mid-December to late January and a two-week period over Easter (book well in advance during this period). There's a three-night minimum stay. ⊠ *Lighthouse Rd.* ☎ *02/6620–9300* ⊕ *www.byronbaylighthouse.com* ✉ *Free, suggested donation for tours* ⊗ *Grounds daily 8:30–sunset (summer), 9–sunset (winter).*

Cape Byron Walking Track. This popular trail circumnavigates a 150-acre reserve, passes through grasslands and rain forest, and offers sensational seas views as you circle the peninsula and the lighthouse. From several vantage points along the track you may spot dolphins in the waters below. The track begins east of the town on Lighthouse Road. ⊠ *Off Lighthouse Rd.*

OFF THE BEATEN PATH

Byron Bay Hinterland. Inland from Byron Bay is some of the most picturesque country in Australia. Undulating green hills that once boasted a thriving dairy industry are dotted with villages with a New Age vibe. There are small organic farms growing avocados, coffee, fruits, and macadamia nuts, and cafés in most villages. The best way to discover this gorgeous part of the world—nicknamed the Rainbow Region—is to grab a map and drive. From Byron, take the road toward the regional town of Lismore for about 15 km (9 miles) to the pretty village of **Bangalow.** Walk along the lovely main street lined with 19th-century storefronts and native Bangalow palms. Carefully follow your map and wind your way northwest for about 20 km (13 miles) to **Federal.** Meander, via the cute towns of **Rosebank** and **Dunoon,** to **The Channon,** where on the second Sunday of every month you'll find a wonderful market with dozens of stalls and entertainment.

Eternity Springs Art Farm. You may want to relax for a few days at the town's Eternity Springs Art Farm, a groovy B&B that also offers art classes and yoga. Prices are a steal, from A$100 a night (for a cute cabin for two) with a breakfast made from fresh farm ingredients. ✉ *483 Tuntable Creek Rd.* ☎ *02/6688–6385* ⊕ *www.eternitysprings.com.*

BEACHES

Several superb beaches lie in the vicinity of Byron Bay. In front of the town, Main Beach provides safe swimming, and Clarks Beach, closer to the cape, has better surf. The most famous surfing beach, however, is Watego's, the only entirely north-facing beach in the state. To the south of the lighthouse Tallow Beach extends for 6 km (4 miles) to a rocky stretch of coastline around Broken Head, which has a number of small sandy coves. Beyond Broken Head is lonely Seven Mile Beach. Topless sunbathing is popular on many Byron Bay beaches.

Main Beach. As the name suggests, Main Beach is right in the heart of Byron Bay, across the road from the much-loved Beach Hotel (a popular pub that has good restaurants and accommodation). It stretches southward for some 3 km (2 miles) where its name changes to Clarke's Beach and then The Pass, the latter a legendary surfing spot. Always busy in the summer months, the beach is most easily reached on foot from the city center. There's a seawall and swimming pool at the northern end, and about 300 feet offshore lies the wreck of the *Tassie 2,* a small ammunition supply boat that sunk around the end of World War II. Swimmers should always swim beside the flags as rips and currents can make this beach hazardous at times—an average of about nine swimmers annually require rescue. There are barbecues and picnic tables in the leafy park flanking the beach. **Amenities:** food and drink; lifeguards (summer only); showers; toilets. **Best for:** snorkeling; swimming; walking. ✉ *Jonson and Bay Sts.*

Watego's Beach. Named for a farming family who grew bananas and vegetables in the hinterland (now a residential area) just behind the beach, Watego's is a lovely 2,000-foot strip of golden sand backed by pandanus palms. It's sheltered from the winds and popular with all comers. If you fancy a walk it, you can reach the beach from the city center via the 4-km (2½-mile) Cape Byron Track. Otherwise, drive here and look for parking in the lot or on the street (it can be challenging during busy times). Coin-operated barbecues and picnic tables make this a perfect spot for do-it-yourself lunching, all in the shadow of the majestic Cape Byron Lighthouse, which looms over the beach. The upscale boutique hotel, Rae's of Watego's, is nearby. **Amenities:** lifeguards (summer only); parking (fee); toilets. **Best for:** swimming; sunrise. ⊠ *Marine Parade, off Palm Valley Dr.*

SPORTS AND THE OUTDOORS

KAYAKING

Go Sea Kayak. Owned and operated by local surf lifesavers (volunteer lifeguards), this new company runs three-hour kayak tours in two-person kayaks that venture out into the open ocean in search of viewing bottlenose dolphins, sea turtles, and even whales in the season. Guides weave in local Aboriginal history and point out the sights. Snorkeling is also included—A$69 per person. ⊠ *Apex Park, opposite 56 Lawson St.* ☎ *02/6685–8880* ⊕ *www.goseakayakbyronbay.com.au.*

SCUBA DIVING

The best local diving is at Julian Rocks Marine Reserve, some 3 km (2 miles) offshore, where the confluence of warm and cold currents supports a profusion of marine life.

Byron Bay Dive Centre. This dive center offers snorkeling and scuba-diving trips for all levels of experience, plus gear rental and instruction. The five-hour introductory diving course costs A$160; a single dive with all equipment and guide and some 50 minutes of diving near Julian Rocks costs A$95. A 60-minute snorkel trip, complete with wet suit, is A$55. ⊠ *9 Marvel St.* ☎ *02/6685–8333, 1800/243483* ⊕ *www.byronbaydivecentre.com.au.*

Sundive. This PADI dive center has courses for all levels of divers, as well as boat dives and snorkel trips. The first dive, with all equipment, is A$95. ⊠ *8 Middleton St.* ☎ *02/6685–7755, 1800/008755* ⊕ *www.sundive.com.au.*

WHERE TO EAT AND STAY

$$
CAFÉ
✕ **Byron Bay Beach Café.** A Byron Bay legend, this open-air café is a perfect place to sit in the morning sun and watch the waves. Breakfast runs the gamut from wholesome (award-winning locally produced Brookfarm Macadamia muesli with yogurt and banana) to hearty (corned-beef hash, sautéed spinach, fried egg with béarnaise sauce). For lunch, try the steamed mussels in Thai broth or the mini Wagyu burgers. The café is open for cocktails and dinner during the summer months of December and January and has an attached takeaway section for those who want to have light meals on the run. Reservations are recommended during the summer. $ *Average main: A$30* ⊠ *Clarks Beach, near parking lot at end of Lawson St.* ☎ *02/6685–8400* ⊕ *www.byronbeachcafe.com.au* ⊗ *No dinner Feb.–Nov.*

$$
AUSTRALIAN
Fodor's Choice
★
✕ **Fig Tree Restaurant & Rooms.** In this century-old farmhouse with distant views of Byron Bay the draw is upmarket Mod Oz cuisine blending Asian and Mediterranean flavors. Produce fresh from the owners' farm is featured on the menu, along with locally produced Bangalow duck, Bangalow pork belly, and Binna Burra sirloin steak. À la carte choices also include field and forest mushroom risotto and slow-roasted shoulder of lamb. There are inexpensive set menus throughout the week, including the four-course farmer's market menu on Thursday (A$55 for four courses; A$75 for six courses). As the name suggests, the restaurant

also has accommodation: the Dairy and the House, two cottages that have wonderful views and can both sleep up to eight people; prices are from A$400 a night in the holiday season of Christmas, January, and Easter with a minimum of two nights. The restaurant and rooms are 5 km (3 miles) inland from Byron Bay at Ewingsdale. $ *Average main: A$30* ⊠ *4 Sunrise La., Ewingsdale* ☎ *02/6684–7273* ⊕ *www. figtreerestaurant.com.au* ⊙ *Closed Mon.–Wed. No dinner Sun., no lunch Thurs. and Fri.*

$$$$
B&B/INN
Byron Bay Beach Bure. Three luxury bures—the Fijian word for cabin—may be only 650 feet from the city center, but the lush, peaceful setting makes it feel like a private oasis. **Pros:** perfect accommodation for a romantic getaway; two elevated bures have beach views. **Cons:** little to complain about here, but it can book up early. $ *Rooms from: A$380* ⊠ *36 Lawson St.* ☎ *02/6680–8483* ⊕ *www.byronbaybeachbure.com. au* 🛏 *3 bures* ◯ *Breakfast.*

$$$
B&B/INN
Julian's Apartments. These studio apartments just opposite Clarks Beach are neat, spacious, and well equipped. **Pros:** perfect for families (cots and baby supplies can be rented); this is the quiet end of Byron Bay town. **Cons:** taxi, or hike into town, required; popular, so book early. $ *Rooms from: A$293* ⊠ *124 Lighthouse Rd.* ☎ *02/6680–9697* ⊕ *www.juliansbyronbay.com* 🛏 *11 apartments* ◯ *No meals.*

$$$$
B&B/INN
Rae's on Watego's. If a high-design boutique hotel is your cup of tea, you'd be hard-pressed to do better than this luxurious Mediterranean-style villa surrounded by a tropical garden. **Pros:** perfect for a romantic break; superb food and spa. **Cons:** looking a bit tired; breakfast prices too high; have to take a taxi to town. $ *Rooms from: A$600* ⊠ *Watego's Beach, 8 Marine Parade* ☎ *02/6685–5366* ⊕ *www.raes.com.au* 🛏 *7 suites* ◯ *No meals.*

NIGHTLIFE

For a small town, Byron rocks by night. Fire dancing—where bare-chested men dance with flaming torches—is a local specialty. Bars and clubs are generally open until about 2 am on weekends and midnight on weekdays.

Arts Factory Village. Head to this legendary complex—also known as the Piggery—to catch a movie at the Pighouse Flicks, grab a bite, have a beer brewed at the on-site Byron Bay Brewery, or see a live band at the Buddha Bar. A Nomads backpackers lodge is attached to the venue, so expect a lively crowd especially at the weekly talent show. ⊠ *1 Skinners Shoot Rd., at Gordon St.* ☎ *02/6685–5833* ⊕ *www.pighouseflicks. com.au.*

Beach Bar. This lounge in the iconic Beach Hotel often hosts live bands. ⊠ *Bay and Jonson Sts.* ☎ *02/6685–6402* ⊕ *www.beachhotel.com.au.*

Cocomangas. This lively bar-restaurant-nightclub is a favorite of carousing backpackers, often hosting themed dance parties. ⊠ *32 Jonson St.* ☎ *02/6685–8493* ⊕ *www.cocomangas.com.au.*

Hotel Great Northern. Bands perform most evenings at this old-school pub. ⊠ *Jonson and Byron Sts.* ☎ *02/6685–6454* ⊕ *www.thenorthern. com.au.*

Railway Friendly Bar. Live music rocks this pub, known locally as The Rails, every night; it's built on the old railway station site. ⊠ *Jonson St. Railway Station* ☎ *02/6685–7662*.

SHOPPING

Byron Bay is one of the state's arts-and-crafts centers, with many innovative and high-quality articles for sale, such as leather goods, offbeat designer clothing, essential oils, natural cosmetics, and ironware. The community market, held on the first Sunday of every month, fills the Butler Street reserve with more than 300 stalls selling art, crafts, and local produce.

Byron Bay Hat Co. This local shopping institution carries great hats and bags perfect for the beach. ⊠ *4 Jonson St.* ☎ *02/6685–8357*.

Colin Heaney. Colin Heaney, a prolific artist based in Byron Bay who for many years was involved in sculpture and glass design, is now producing a luxurious range of women's wear including silk kaftans, scarves, and bathing suits. His showroom also carries a number of glass goblets and sculpture pieces. The boutique is open from 10 am to 4 pm on weekdays, and by appointment at other times. The company is moving to a new space in Byron Bay in summer 2014; call or check website for the new address. ☎ *02/6685–7798* ⊕ *www.colinheaney.com*.

EN ROUTE Fifty-three km (33 miles) northwest of Byron Bay is the towering, conical **Mt. Warning**, a 3,800-foot extinct volcano that dominates the pleasant town of Murwillumbah. Its radical shape can be seen from miles away, including the beaches at Byron.

A well-marked **walking track** winds up Mt. Warning, which is a World Heritage national park, from the Breakfast Creek parking area at its base. The 4½-km (2½-mile) track climbs steadily through fern forest and buttressed trees where you can often see native brush turkeys and pademelons (small wallaby-like marsupials). The last 650 feet of the ascent is a strenuous scramble up a steep rock face using chain-link handrails. The local Aboriginal name for the mountain is Wollumbin, which means "cloud catcher," and the metal walkways on the summit are sometimes shrouded in clouds. On a clear day, however, there are fabulous 360-degree views of the massive caldera, one of the largest in the world: national parks crown the southern, western, and northern rims, and the Tweed River flows seaward through the eroded eastern wall. Many people undertake the Mt. Warning ascent before dawn, so they can catch the first rays of light falling on mainland Australia.

World Heritage Rainforest Visitors Information Centre. For information about the walk and Mt. Warning National Park, visit the World Heritage Rainforest Visitors Information Centre in Murwillumbah. From here it is a 16½-km (10-mile) drive to the start of the walking track. Fill your water bottles in Murwillumbah; there is no drinking water in the park or on the mountain. Allow at least four hours up and back, and don't start the walk after 2 pm in winter. ⊠ *Tweed Valley Way at Alma St.* ☎ *02/6672–1340* ⊕ *www.tweedtourism.com.au* ☉ *Mon.–Sat. 9–4:30, Sun. 9:30–4*.

LORD HOWE ISLAND

Fringed by the world's southernmost coral reef as well as gorgeous, sheltered beaches, dominated by two dramatic peaks, and inhabited by just around 400 permanent residents—Lord Howe Island is a secluded slice of paradise that lies about 600 km (370 miles) east of mainland Australia. As a UNESCO World Heritage island, it welcomes just 400 visitors at any time, so it never feels overcrowded. Most visitors hire bicycles and spend their time snorkeling in the lagoon, hand-feeding fish, hiking, and bird-watching, while hardy types climb the summit of 875-meter (2,870-foot) Mt. Gower for sensational views.

GETTING HERE AND AROUND

Qantas subsidiary Qantas Link flies to Lord Howe Island from Sydney, Brisbane, and Port Macquarie. The flight from Sydney is 1 hour and 50 minutes. Flights from the other destinations are 10 minutes or so shorter. As Qantas is the only carrier, and only 400 tourists can visit the island, fares can be quite high—typically more than A$500 one-way. The most economical way to travel to Lord Howe is with an air-and-hotel package deal.

Just 10 km (6 miles) long and with a width varying from 300 meters (1,000 feet) to 2 km (1 mile), crescent-shape Lord Howe Island is compact and easy to navigate. The lagoon hugs the western shore of the island. The town, known as Old Settlement, is midway along the lagoon, and most accommodations are within an easy cycle ride or walk from there. The airport is slightly south of the town, and the two volcanic peaks—Mt. Lidgbird and Mt. Gower—dominate the island's southeast extremity. Good beaches are spread along the lagoon shore and on the eastern coast just a kilometer or two from town.

BEACHES

FAMILY
Fodor's Choice
★
Ned's Beach. This beautiful beach on the northeast side of the island is a magnet for fish because fishing bans protect them here. Brightly colored tropical creatures, such as parrot fish and their less-spectacular mullet mates (which are occasionally chased by a harmless reef shark), swim up to shore and greet visitors at the daily 4 pm fish feed. However, visitors can also feed them at other times—you can buy fish food to toss to them from a beach kiosk. This feeding frenzy is fun to watch. Bring snorkel gear to explore the coral a little farther out, or bring a picnic and relax on this beach that's one of the cleanest in Australia. The beach is an easy drive, cycle, or walk from town and the northern hotels. **Amenities:** none. **Best for:** snorkeling; sunrise; swimming; walking. ⊠ *Ned's Beach Rd., Ned's Beach, Lord Howe Island, New South Wales* ⊕ *www.lordhoweisland.info.*

SPORTS AND THE OUTDOORS

DIVING AND SNORKELING

Fodor's Choice
★
Lord Howe Island Marine Park. UNESCO World Heritage lists Lord Howe Island's beautiful lagoon, which is sheltered by the world's southernmost coral reef, stretching for some 6 km (4 miles) along the western coast. Contained within Lord Howe Island Marine Park, the lagoon harbors some 500 species of fish and 90 species of coral. There are several ways to explore the lagoon and the coral-filled beaches of the

eastern coast, which are only about 3 km (2 miles)—by glass-bottom boat, snorkeling, or scuba diving. Ned's Beach, the site of the island's fish frenzy, is perfect for snorkelers. Another great spot is the wreck of the ship *The Favourite,* at North Bay, the lagoon's northernmost point. Divers have more than 50 sites to choose from, ranging from shallow resort dives near the beach, to spectacular trenches, caves, and volcanic drop-offs. Experienced divers love the waters around Ball's Pyramid, which abound with kingfish and Galapagos sharks up to 14 feet long. ■TIP→ If you don't bring your own snorkeling gear, you can rent it from local resorts. ⊠ *Lord Howe Island Visitor Center, Middle and Lagoon Rds., Lord Howe Island, New South Wales* ☎ *02/6563–2114* ⊕ *www. lordhoweisland.info.*

FISHING

Fishing at Balls Pyramid. Towering some 1,800 feet above the ocean, Balls Pyramid is a unique rock stack and one of the world's tallest monoliths in water. Located 23 km (14 miles) south of Lord Howe Island, it's part of the pristine Lord Howe Island Marine Park, in which commercial fishing is banned and huge species of fish abound, making it a top destination for sportfishing. The boat trip to Balls Pyramid takes 75 minutes and is a perfect way to soak up stunning views back toward the island before you start reeling in the catch. Several dedicated fishing charter operators, including Blue Billie (a fifth-generation family of fishermen), run tours to the pyramid, offering half- and full-day expeditions with rates starting from around A\$170 per person. ⊠ *Lord Howe Island Marine Park, Lord Howe Island, New South Wales* ⊕ *www. lordhoweisland.info.*

HIKING

Mt. Gower. The larger of the two volcanic peaks located at the southern end of Lord Howe Island, Mt. Gower rises 875 meters (2,870 feet) above sea level. The hike to the summit is arduous and should be undertaken with a guide. Covering a distance of about 14 km (9 miles) round-trip and taking about 8½ hours to complete, it's a wonderful experience and affords sensational views across the island, the reef, and out to Ball's Pyramid, 23 km (14 miles) away. Along the way, guides point out rare plants and birdlife. Fifth-generation islander Jack Shick, of Lord Howe Island Tours, is a highly experienced guide and takes tours twice a week (Monday and Thursday); the cost is about A\$60 per person. ⊠ *Lord Howe Island, New South Wales* ☎ *02/6563–2218 Jack Shick* ⊕ *www.lordhoweislandtours.net.*

WHERE TO EAT

\$\$

SEAFOOD

✕ **Greenback's Eatery.** Named after a Lord Howe Island fishing vessel, Greenback's Eatery naturally specializes in fresh fish. This casual spot, basically a veranda attached to boat owner Dave Gardiner's house, is open five nights a week—the menu goes something like this: Tuesday and Friday set menu of either two or three courses, which may include sashimi or carpaccio, tempura fish, and perhaps sticky-date pudding or rosewater panna cotta; Thursday and Saturday feature fish, chips, and salad; Sunday is a buffet where, apart from fish, steak is available. Patrons can bring their own wine or beer. Dave also runs cooking classes on Tuesday afternoons, when you can learn to cook a number of dishes and then enjoy a three-course meal, all for A$150 per person. $ *Average main: A$30* ✉ *Anderson Rd., Middle Beach, Lord Howe Island, New South Wales* ☎ *02/6563–2208* ⊕ *www.fishlordhowe.com.au* ⊟ *No credit cards* ⊘ *Closed Mon. and Wed. No lunch.*

$$ ✕ **Lord Howe Golf Club.** This is a fine place to socialize with the locals and tourists and enjoy some honest, unpretentious food. The menu includes a variety of roasts (such as roast chicken or lamb), steak with garlic butter, schnitzel, fish, and salads, plus pizza on Sunday nights. Be sure to make a booking for Monday's "pie night," when both savory and sweet dessert pies are available. Friday night is the "big night out" on the island, when almost everyone turns up for the sunset barbecue—try the barbecue kingfish and grab an ice-cold beer. Desserts include what appears to be the island staple—sticky-date pudding—and ice creams. It's best to come early to take in the view over the golf links and the lagoon beyond. $ *Average main: A$20* ✉ *Lord Howe Island, New South Wales* ☎ *02/6563–2171* ⊕ *www.lordhowegolf.com.au.*

AUSTRALIAN
Fodor's Choice
★

$$ ✕ **Pandanus.** This lovely indoor-outdoor restaurant is run by chef Stephen Sia, who specializes in both Italian and Malaysian fare, with an emphasis on seafood—there's always something to suit all palates. Start with the salt-and-pepper squid or the Asian spring rolls. A bit spicier is the Malaysia seafood curry, which brims with shrimp, squid, fish, potatoes, and rice. Succulent pork belly and Asian-style chicken and basil please those not keen on fish, while seafood lovers relish the fresh-caught kingfish, yellowfin tuna, deep-sea cod, and trevally. Note the many blackboard specials, too. Stephen sources excellent island produce from local growers, everything from silver beets to eggs to strawberries. Regulars rave about the coconut-custard pie with ice cream. $ *Average main: A$23* ✉ *Pandanus Lodge, Anderson Rd., Lord Howe Island, Australian Capital Territory* ☎ *02/6563–2400* ⊘ *No lunch Sun.–Wed.*

MALAYSIAN

WHERE TO STAY

$$$$ 🛏 **Capella Lodge.** Nestled in the shadow of Mt. Gower, Capella Lodge is Lord Howe Island's most posh lodging. **Pros:** great location; fantastic views; pure luxury. **Cons:** steep rates. $ *Rooms from: A$700* ✉ *Lagoon Rd., Lord Howe Island, New South Wales* ☎ *02/6563–2008* ⊕ *www.lordhowe.com* ⇨ *9 suites* ⦿ *Some meals.*

B&B/INN

$$$$ 🛏 **Pinetrees Lodge.** Right on Lagoon Beach and a short walk from the popular bowling club, the Pinetrees Lodge has a terrific location, and is the largest accommodation on Lord Howe Island—with motel rooms, suites, and garden cottages. **Pros:** great amenities; excellent location. **Cons:** can be noisy with families in peak times. $ *Rooms from: A$410* ✉ *Lagoon Rd., Lord Howe Island, New South Wales* ☎ *02/9262–6585* ⊕ *www.pinetrees.com.au* ⇨ *34 rooms, 4 suites* ⦿ *All-inclusive.*

HOTEL
ALL-INCLUSIVE

CANBERRA AND THE A.C.T.

As the nation's capital, Canberra is sometimes maligned by outsiders, who see the city as lacking the coolness of Melbourne or the glamour of Sydney. But Canberra certainly has charms of its own, with its world-class museums (the majority of which are free), leafy open spaces, and the huge Lake Burley Griffin.

When Australia federated in 1901, both Sydney and Melbourne vied to be the nation's capital. But in the spirit of compromise, it was decided that a new city would be built, and Canberra and the Australian Capital Territory (A.C.T) were created when New South Wales ceded land to build a federal zone, based on the model of America's District of Columbia.

From the beginning this was to be a totally planned city. Walter Burley Griffin, a Chicago architect and associate of Frank Lloyd Wright, won an international design competition. Griffin arrived in Canberra in 1913 to supervise construction, but progress was slowed by two world wars and the Great Depression. By 1947 Canberra, with only 15,000 inhabitants, was little more than a country town.

Development increased during the 1950s, and the current population of more than 367,000 makes Canberra by far the largest inland city in Australia. The wide, tree-lined avenues and spacious parklands of present-day Canberra have largely fulfilled Griffin's original plan. The major public buildings are arranged on low knolls on either side of Lake Burley Griffin, the focus of the city. Satellite communities—using the same radial design of crescents and cul-de-sacs employed in Canberra—house the city's growing population.

GETTING HERE AND AROUND

AIR TRAVEL

Canberra Airport is 7 km (4½ miles) southeast of the city center. Flights are about a half hour to Sydney, an hour to Melbourne, and two hours to Brisbane. Qantas, Tiger Airways, and Virgin Australia fly to and from the capital, but there are no direct international flights. A taxi into the city is about A$25. A shuttle bus operated by Airport Express runs regularly between the airport and the city for A$10 per person. The buses run approximately every 45 minutes.

BUS TRAVEL

Canberra is served by two major bus lines, Greyhound Australia and Murrays Australia. One-way fares to Sydney start from A$36, and the trip takes just over three hours. Cheap Web deals can bring the price down to A$23.

The ACTION bus network operates weekdays 6:30 am–11:30 pm, Saturday 7 am–11:30 pm, and Sunday 8–7. There's a flat fare of A$4.20 per ride. A one-day unlimited-travel ticket costs A$8.

Bus Contacts ACTION Buses ✉ *Canberra City, Canberra, Australian Capital Territory* ⊕ *www.action.act.gov.au.* **Greyhound Australia** ☎ *1300/473946* ⊕ *www.greyhound.com.au.* **Murrays Australia** ☎ *13–2251* ⊕ *www.murrays.com. au.*

CAR TRAVEL

Canberra is difficult to negotiate by car, given its radial roads, erratic signage, and often considerable distances between suburbs. Still, because sights are scattered about and not easily connected on foot or by public transportation, a car is a good way to see the city itself, as well as the sights in the Australian Capital Territory.

Taxi and Shuttle Contacts Canberra Cabs ☎ *13–2227* ⊕ *www.canberracabs. com.au.*

TRAIN TRAVEL

The Canberra railway station is about 6 km (4 miles) southeast of the city center. NSW TrainLink (aka CountryLink) trains make the four-hour trip between Canberra and Sydney twice daily. A daily bus-rail service by NSW TrainLink makes the nine-hour run between Canberra and Melbourne.

Train Contacts Canberra Railway Station ✉ *Wentworth Ave. at Bourke Crescent, Kingston, Canberra* ☎ *02/6208–9700.* **NSW TrainLink** ☎ *13–2232* ⊕ *www.nswtrainlink.info.*

TOURS

A convenient (and fun!) way to see the major sights of Canberra is with the Canberra Explorer Bus, operated by Canberra Day Tours, which makes a regular circuit around the major attractions. Tickets are A$35, and you can hop on and off all day. Canberra resident and crypto-naturalist (a student of strange and hidden phenomena) Tim the Yowie Man (the name he's legally chosen) runs ghost tours of the city and its environs. His Weird Canberra Ghost & History Tour costs A$89 including refreshments.

The impressive Canberra and Region Visitor Centre, open weekdays 9–5 and weekends 9–4, is a convenient stop for those entering Canberra by road from Sydney or the north. The staff can book hotel rooms for you in Canberra.

Visitor Information Canberra Day Tours ☎ *0418/455099* ⊕ *www. canberradaytours.com.au.* **Weird Canberra Ghost & History Tour** ✉ *Canberra, Australian Capital Territory* ☎ *0407/769980* ⊕ *www.yowieman.com.au/ ghost-tours.*

ESSENTIALS

Visitor Information Canberra and Region Visitor Centre ✉ *330 Northbourne Ave., Dickson, Canberra, Australian Capital Territory* ☎ *02/6205–0044* ⊕ *www. visitcanberra.com.au.*

EXPLORING

Canberra's most important public buildings stand within the Parliamentary Triangle. Lake Burley Griffin wraps around the northeast edge, while Commonwealth and Kings avenues radiate from Capital Hill, the city's political and geographical epicenter, to form the west and south boundaries. The triangle can be explored comfortably on foot, but a vehicle is required to see the rest of this area. The monuments and other attractions within the Parliamentary Triangle and around Lake Burley Griffin are not identified by street numbers, but all are clearly signposted.

CENTRAL CANBERRA

You can visit virtually all of central Canberra's major attractions by car, but in some places parking and walking may be more convenient. Around town you can use the local ACTION buses, which stop at most of the other sights, or join the hop-on, hop-off Canberra Day Tours bus.

TOP ATTRACTIONS

Fodor's Choice
★

Australian War Memorial. Both as a moving memorial to Australians who served their country in wartime and as a military museum, this is a shrine of great national importance and the most popular attraction in the capital. The museum explores Australian military involvement from the late 19th century through the 1970s and Vietnam up to Iraq and Afghanistan today. Displays include a Lancaster bomber, a Spitfire, tanks, landing barges, and sections of two of the Japanese midget submarines that infiltrated Sydney Harbour during World War II, as well as more interactive displays in the Anzac Hall. One of the most moving places is the domed Tomb of the Unknown Soldier that stands above the Pool of Reflection and the Roll of Honour, which are two walls of names honoring the thousands of Australians who have died in all military conflicts. There are free 45-minute and 90-meeting tours, led by volunteers. You can best appreciate the impressive facade of the War Memorial from the broad avenue of **Anzac Parade.** Anzac is an acronym for the Australian and New Zealand Army Corps, formed during World War I. The avenue is flanked by several memorials commemorating the Army, Navy, Air Force, and Nursing Corps, as well as some of the campaigns in which Australian troops have fought, including the Vietnam War. ■TIP→ At closing time a bugler or bagpiper plays the emotive Last Post outside the Tomb of the Unknown Soldier ⊠ *Treloar Crescent, off Anzac Parade, Campbell* ☎ *02/6243–4211* ⊕ *www.awm. gov.au* ⊠ *Free* ☉ *Daily 10–5.*

Museum of Australian Democracy at Old Parliament House. This museum is inside the Old Parliament House. Curators use stories of real people and events to trace the history of democracy both in Australia and abroad. The museum features five exhibits, as well as the opportunity to see the original chambers and prime minister's office. There are free 45-minute guided tours every day starting at 9:45 am, with the last at 3:45 pm. While you're in the area, take a stroll through the delightful **Rose Gardens** on both sides of the Old Parliament House building. Across the road from the entrance, visit the controversial **Aboriginal Tent Embassy,** established in 1972 to proclaim the Aboriginal people as Australia's "first people" and to promote recognition of their fight for land rights. ⊠ *18 King George Terr., Parkes* ☎ *02/6270–8221* ⊕ *www. moadoph.gov.au* ⊠ *A$2* ☉ *Daily 9–5.*

National Film & Sound Archive. Housed in one of Canberra's most beautiful art deco buildings, this museum displays Australia's audiovisual cultural history. Among the many exhibits are costumes from films including *Muriel's Wedding, The Adventures of Priscilla Queen of the Desert,* and *Ned Kelly,* along with vintage film, sound equipment, and a film still collection of more than 300,000 images. You can relax in the small theater (designed along early 20th-century theater lines) and watch some of the country's early news reels and short films (some

Australian
National
Botanic
Gardens **4**

Australian
War Memorial ...**1**

High Court
of Australia **7**

Museum of
Australian
Democracy at
Old Parliament
House **10**

National
Film & Sound
Archive **3**

National
Gallery of
Australia **8**

National
Library
of Australia **5**

National
Museum
of Australia **2**

National
Portrait
Gallery **9**

Parliament
House **11**

Questacon–
The National
Science and
Technology
Centre **6**

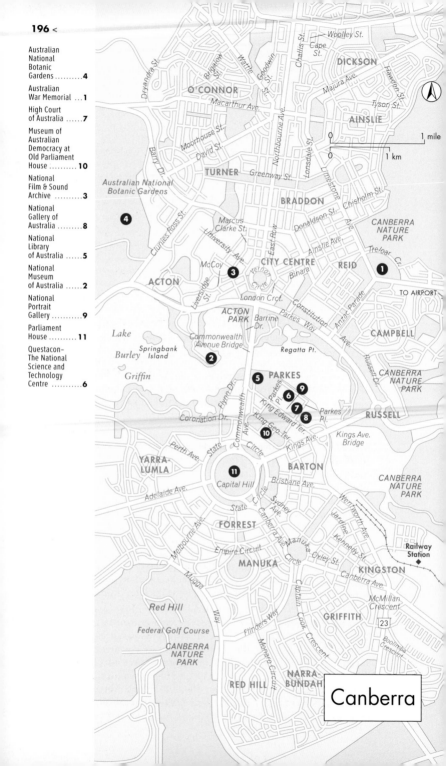

Canberra

are very funny). Watch arthouse movies (at an extra cost of around A$10–A$14) in the beautiful Arc cinema, which regularly screens classic movies and other nonmainstream cinematic gems. ⊠ *McCoy Circuit, Acton* ☎ *02/6248–2000* ⊕ *www.nfsa.gov.au* ⊠ *Free* ⊗ *Weekdays 9–5, weekends 10–5.*

Fodor'sChoice ★
National Gallery of Australia. The most comprehensive collection of Australian art in the country is on exhibit in the nation's premier art gallery, including superlative works of Aboriginal art and paintings by such famous native sons as Arthur Streeton, Sidney Nolan, and Arthur Boyd. The gallery also contains a sprinkling of works by European and American masters, including Rodin, Picasso, Pollock, and Warhol, as well as art and artifacts from closer to home, Southeast Asia. Free guided tours on a variety of topics with excellent guides begin in the foyer each day—check the website for details. A new wing, containing 13 galleries, is dedicated to indigenous art. The gallery extends outside into the Sculpture Garden, and the innovative Fog Sculpture takes place (outdoors) from 12:30 to 2 pm daily. ⊠ *Parkes Pl., Parkes* ☎ *02/6240–6502* ⊕ *www.nga.gov.au* ⊠ *Free* ⊗ *Daily 10–5.*

NEED A
BREAK?
Bookplate. A good spot to catch your breath amid the Parliamentary Triangle's mix of history, culture, and science is Bookplate, in the foyer of the National Library. It has lovely stained-glass windows and extends out onto a patio overlooking the lake. Sandwiches, salads, cakes, warming soup and curry in the winter, and tea and coffee are served weekdays 8:30–6 and weekends 11–3. ⊠ *Parkes Pl., Parkes* ☎ *02/6262–1154.*

National Library of Australia. Constructed loosely on the design of the Parthenon in Athens, this library houses more than 5 million books and 500,000 photographs, maps, drawings, and recordings of oral history. Don't miss the state-of-the-art Treasures Gallery, which features 80 of the library's prized pieces, such as Captain James Cook's journal of the *Endeavour* and Australia's only complete original convict uniform. A free Treasures Gallery tour takes place daily at 10:30 am, and a behind-the-scenes tour takes place on Thursday and Saturday at 2 pm. The café has a wonderful view, and the bookshop is a browser's and buyer's delight. ⊠ *Parkes Pl., Parkes* ☎ *02/6262–1111* ⊕ *www. nla.gov.au* ⊠ *Free* ⊗ *Mon.–Thurs. 9–9, Fri. and Sat. 9-5, Sun. 1:30–5.*

FAMILY
Fodor'sChoice ★
National Museum of Australia. This unstuffy museum is spectacularly set on Acton Peninsula, thrust out over the calm waters of Lake Burley Griffin. The museum highlights the stories of Australia and Australians by exploring the key people, events, and issues that shaped and influenced the nation. Memorabilia include a carcass of the extinct Tasmanian tiger, the old Bentley beloved by former Prime Minister Robert Menzies, and the black baby garments worn by dingo victim Azaria Chamberlain (whose story was made famous in the Meryl Streep film *A Cry in the Dark*). *Circa,* a 12-minute movie, gives a fascinating snapshot of Australian history and should be your first port of call. Children love the KSpace display, an exhibit where they can use computers and 3-D technology to design a space-age city of the future. The highlights and First Australians tours cost A$10 each, while a tour package that

includes a meal and a glass of wine in the restaurant is A$30. ✉ *Lennox Crossing, Acton Peninsula* ☎ *02/6208–5000, 1800/026132* ⊕ *www. nma.gov.au* ✆ *Free* ۞ *Daily 9–5.*

National Portrait Gallery. This terrific space is dedicated to portraits of people who have shaped Australia and who in some way reflect the national identity. Look out for famous faces like pop star Kylie Minogue and Olympic champion Cathy Freeman, as well as priceless portraits of Captain James Cook. The building on the south shore of Lake Burley Griffin caused some controversy, but most architecture fans like its simple, clean design. The gallery also has a good arts program offering talks and film screenings, and the café's outdoor terrace has lovely views. ✉ *King Edward Terr., Parkes* ☎ *02/6102–7000* ⊕ *www.portrait. gov.au* ✆ *Free* ۞ *Daily 10–5.*

Fodor's Choice **Parliament House.** Much of this vast futuristic structure is submerged,
★ covered by a domed glass roof that follows the contours of Capital Hill. You approach the building across a vast courtyard with a central mosaic titled *Meeting Place,* designed by Aboriginal artist Nelson Tjakamarra. Native timber has been used almost exclusively throughout the building, and the work of some of Australia's finest contemporary artists hangs on the walls.

Parliament generally sits Monday to Thursday mid-February to late June and mid-August to mid-December. Both chambers have public galleries, but the debates in the House of Representatives, where the prime minister sits, are livelier and more newsworthy than those in the Senate. Guided tours take place at 10, 1, and 3 daily. ✉ *Capital Hill* ☎ *02/6277–5399* ⊕ *www.aph.gov.au* ✆ *Free* ۞ *Daily 9–5, later when Parliament is sitting.*

Question Time. The best time to observe the House of Representatives is during Question Time, starting at 2, when the Government and the Opposition are most likely to be at each other's throats. To secure a ticket for Question Time, contact the sergeant-at-arms' office until 12:45 pm on the day you require a ticket. ☎ *02/6277–4889 sergeant-at-arms' office.*

WORTH NOTING

Australian National Botanic Gardens. Australian plants and trees have evolved in isolation from the rest of the world, and these delightful gardens on the lower slopes of Black Mountain display the continent's best collection of this unique flora. The rain forest, rock gardens, Tasmanian alpine garden, and eucalyptus lawn—with more than 600 species of eucalyptus—number among the 125-acre site's highlights. Two self-guided nature trails start from the rain-forest gully, and free guided tours depart from the visitor center daily at 11 and 2. Prebooked and more individualized guided tours cost A$5 per person. ✉ *Clunies Ross St., Acton* ☎ *02/6250–9540* ⊕ *www.anbg.gov.au* ✆ *Free* ۞ *Jan., weekdays 8:30–5, weekends 8:30–8; Feb.–Dec., daily 8:30–5. Visitor Center daily 9:30–4:30.*

High Court of Australia. As its name implies, this gleaming concrete-and-glass structure is the ultimate court of law in the nation's judicial system. The court of seven justices convenes only to determine constitutional

The Australian War Memorial, Canberra

matters or major principles of law. Inside the main entrance, the public hall contains a number of murals depicting constitutional and geographic themes. Each of the three courtrooms over which the justices preside has a public gallery, and you can observe the proceedings when the court is in session. ⊠ *Parkes Pl. off King Edward Terr., Parkes* ☎ *02/6270–6811* ⊕ *www.hcourt.gov.au* ⊠ *Free* ☉ *Weekdays 9:45– 4:30, Sun. noon–4.*

FAMILY
Fodor'sChoice
★

Questacon—The National Science and Technology Centre. This interactive science facility is the city's most entertaining museum, especially for kids. About 200 hands-on exhibits in seven galleries use high-tech computer gadgetry and everything from pendulums to feathers to illustrate principles of mathematics, physics, and human perception. There are daily stage shows (about such things as rockets and natural disasters), puppet shows, and talks. Staff members explain the scientific principles behind the exhibits. The free-fall slide (with a drop of 20 feet) and the 360-degree swing are huge hits with all ages. It's pricey, but kids (and their parents) love it. ⊠ *King Edward Terr. at Mall Rd. W, Parkes* ☎ *02/6270–2800, 1800/020603* ⊕ *www.questacon.edu.au* ⊠ *A$23* ☉ *Daily 9–5.*

AROUND CANBERRA AND THE A.C.T.
TOP ATTRACTIONS

FAMILY
Cockington Green Gardens. You'll feel like Gulliver walking through this miniature village and gardens 15 km (9 miles) northwest of the center of Canberra. Named after a small town in England, this site is a big hit with children who love wandering past the football stadium and hearing the roar of the crowd, and seeing classic structures such as Stonehenge,

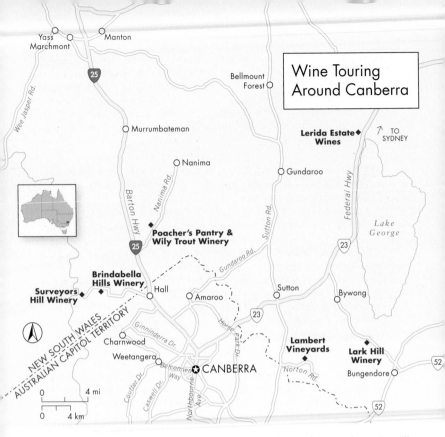

a miniature turf maze, windmills, and a cricket match on the village green. They'll also love taking a ride on the miniature train through the gardens. Cockington Green began as a miniature museum for all things English (country cottages, village church, etc.) more than 30 years ago; however, many international miniature buildings—such as the Tenoch-titian Temple in Mexico, the Chateau Bojnice in Slovakia, and India's Red Fort—have been added over the years. It is near Gold Creek Village shopping center; take the Barton Highway and head toward Yass. ⌂ *11 Gold Creek Rd., Nicholls* ☎ *02/6230–2273* ⊕ *www.cockingtongreen. com.au* ✉ *$18.50* ☉ *Daily 9:30–4:15.*

WINE TOURING AROUND CANBERRA

Wineries began popping up everywhere around Canberra in the late 1990s, once it was discovered that the cool climate was optimal for producing Chardonnays, Rieslings, Cabernets, Shirazes, Merlots, and Pinot Noirs. There are now about 140 vineyards, about 35 of which have cellar doors, set in the peaceful rural countryside surrounding the city—mostly small operations, where visiting the cellar door usually involves sampling the wines in the tasting room. There is no charge for tastings.

Most are a maximum of 30 minutes from the city and are concentrated in the villages of Hall and Murrumbateman and in the Lake George area and Bungendore. Many are open to visits on weekends only. If you want to explore the wineries on your own, pick up a copy of *The Canberra District Wineries Guide* from the Canberra and Region Visitor Centre, or check out the websites ⊕ *www.canberrawines.com.au* and ⊕ *www. yassvalley.com.au.*

WINERIES ALONG THE BARTON HIGHWAY

From Canberra take the Barton Highway (25) in the direction of Yass. After 20 km (12 miles) you'll pass the village of Hall and reach a handful of wineries, several of which are quite impressive.

Brindabella Hills Winery. It's worth heading to the cellar door at this winery (weekends only) to taste the Reserve Shiraz, one of the varieties that this family-run operation specializes in. The vineyard is ringed by the lovely Brindabella ranges, providing a gorgeous setting on a sunny day for a picnic or barbecue. Lunches, provided by local gourmet caterer Food for Friends, are served on weekends, often accompanied by a jazz band. The vineyard is 25 km (16 miles) north of Canberra. ⊠ *156 Woodgrove Close, Wallaroo, New South Wales* ☎ *02/6230–2583* ⊕ *www.brindabellahills.com.au* ☉ *Weekends 10–5.*

Poachers Pantry & Wily Trout Vineyard. This favorite among gourmands is 25 minutes from Canberra. Here you'll find a tasting room offering good examples of Pinot Noir and Shiraz, and fabulous food and smoked goods offered by Poachers Pantry and the award-winning Smokehouse Cafe. Stock up on picnic-style smoked meats, poultry, and vegetables at the Pantry, or visit the Cafe (Friday–Sunday only) for a memorable countryside dining experience in a historic cottage. Poachers Panty is one of the 25 operators who make up the Poacher's Way (⊕ *www.thepoachersway.com.au*), a collective of food emporiums, wineries, restaurants, galleries, and experiences that are loosely linked by a trail and that provide memorable regional experiences. ⊠ *431 Nanima Rd., Springrange, New South Wales* ☎ *02/6230–2487* ⊕ *www. poacherspantry.com.au* ☉ *Cellar door daily 10–5.*

Surveyors Hill Winery. Stop here to taste the Riesling, Chardonnay, Sauvignon Blanc, Rosé, and some dessert and sticky wines. In addition to the simple cellar door, the owners offer light meals to go with their wines. They make ample use of olives from their trees and other produce sourced from the property's gardens; seasonal produce is also sold. Guests can also stay overnight at the winery's B&B, which can accommodate up to 12 people in both the original family homestead and the new, more-modern apartments. ⊠ *215 Brooklands Rd., Wallaroo, New South Wales* ☎ *02/6230–2046* ⊕ *www.surhill.com.au* ☉ *Cellar door weekends 10–5.*

WINERIES ALONG THE FEDERAL HIGHWAY

From Canberra take the Federal Highway (23) for about 30 km (19 miles) north toward Sydney. There are a few wineries off the highway between Canberra and Lake George and a few not far from the lake.

Lambert Vineyards. You either like the style of this modern complex with cellar door or you don't—it provokes strong opinions on the Canberra

The Australian Federal Parliament, Canberra

wine trail. Its wines are generally popular, however. As it is more than 2,600 feet above sea level, it produces mostly red cool-climate varieties. After your tasting, don't miss the barrel room, which holds approximately 250 barrels of maturing wine. ⊠ *810 Norton Rd., Wamboin, New South Wales* ☎ *02/6238–3866* ⊕ *www.lambertvineyards.com.au* ⊙ *Weekends 10–4.*

Lark Hill Winery. This family-run enterprise overlooking (the usually bone-dry) Lake George specializes in biodynamic Riesling, Chardonnay, and Pinot Noir varieties. After your tasting, have lunch at the restaurant (weekends only) and sit out on the deck that looks out over the vines. ⊠ *Bungendore and Joe Rocks Rds., Bungendore, New South Wales* ☎ *02/6238–1393* ⊕ *www.larkhillwine.com.au* ⊙ *Wed.–Mon. 10–5.*

Lerida Estate Wines. About 45 km (28 miles) out of Canberra, this highly respected winery is as famous for its design by Pritzker Prize–winning architect Glenn Murcutt as it is for its mid-price bottles. Try the Proprietor's Selection if its available at the cellar door—the Chardonnay is excellent. The tasting room and adjoining café, which offers light seasonal meals, enjoy lovely views over the often dry Lake George. Visitors, in groups of six or more, who make an appointment in advance can take either a 40-minute or 60-minute tour of the winery followed by tutored wine tasting priced from A\$7.50 to A\$12.50 per person. ⊠ *Federal Hwy., Lake George, New South Wales* ☎ *02/6295–6640* ⊕ *www. leridaestate.com* ⊙ *Cellar door daily 10–5.*

SPORTS AND THE OUTDOORS

BICYCLING

Canberra has almost 160 km (100 miles) of cycle paths, and the city's relatively flat terrain and dry, mild climate make it a perfect place to explore on two wheels. One of the most popular cycle paths is the 40-km (25-mile) circuit around Lake Burley Griffin.

Mr. Spokes Bike Hire. This shop rents several different kinds of bikes as well as tandems and baby seats. Bikes cost A$20 for the first hour, including helmet rental, locks, and a map of cycle routes. Half-day hire (four hours) is A$30, and full-day costs A$40. ⌧ *Acton Ferry Terminal, Barrine Dr., Acton Park* ☎ *02/6257–1188* ⊕ *www.mrspokes.com.au.*

BOATING

Burley Griffin Boat Hire. You can rent paddleboats, kayaks, and canoes daily (except in winter—it's closed May–August) for use on Lake Burley Griffin from Burley Griffin Boat Hire. Hourly rates are A$15 for kayaks and A$25 for canoes; paddleboats are A$30. ⌧ *Acton Ferry Terminal, Barrine Dr., Acton Park* ☎ *02/6249–6861, 0417/623169* ⊕ *www.actboathire.com.*

Southern Cross Cruises. This tour company offers one-hour sailings (A$15) around Lake Burley Griffin on the MV *Southern Cross* on Sundays at 3 pm. On summer Thursdays there's a two-hour cruise that includes a tour of Government House gardens (A$23). Three-course Thursday dinner cruises and Sunday lunch cruises cost A$70. ⌧ *Southern Cross Club, Lotus Bay, 1 Mariner Pl. off Alexandrina Dr., Yarralumla* ☎ *02/6273–1784* ⊕ *www.cscc.com.au.*

HIKING

Namadgi National Park. Covering almost half the total area of the Australian Capital Territory's southwest, this national park has a well-maintained network of walking trails across mountain ranges, trout streams, and some of the most accessible subalpine forests in the country. Some parts of the park were severely burned in the January 2003 bushfires, but the recovery powers of the native bush have been truly remarkable. The park's boundaries are within 35 km (22 miles) of Canberra, and its former pastures, now empty of sheep and cattle, are grazed by hundreds of eastern gray kangaroos in the early morning and late afternoon. Car-based tent camping is permitted in three designated campgrounds: Orroral, Honeysuckle Creek and Mount Clear. Bookings are essential and can be made online (⊕ *www.bookings.act.gov.au*) or by phone. Snow covers the higher altitudes June–September. ■ TIP➜ Bushfires are a constant threat in summer time, so check ahead for conditions. ⌧ *Visitor center, Naas–Boboyan Rd., 3 km (2 miles) south of Tharwa, Tharwa* ☎ *02/6207–2900, 13–2281* ⊕ *www.tams.act.gov.au* ⌷ *Free* ☻ *Visitor center weekdays 9–4, weekends 9–4:30.*

Tidbinbilla Nature Reserve. The walking trails, wetlands, and animal exhibits within this reserve, many of which were badly damaged in the bushfires of 2003, have recovered impressively over the years. The park is 40 km (25 miles) southwest of Canberra. Tours, including "platypus pursuit" and boomerang throwing, are offered on weekends—some of these require a small fee. ✉ *Paddy's River Rd., Tidbinbilla* ☎ *02/6205–1233, 13–2281* 🌐 *www.tams.act.gov.au* 🎫 *A$10 per car per day (free for pedestrians and cyclists)* 🕒 *Visitor center weekdays 9–4:30, weekends 9–5. Reserve Grounds standard time weekdays 9–6, daylight saving time weekdays 9–5, weekends 8:30–6:30.*

WHERE TO EAT

The main restaurant precincts are around the city center and in the trendy suburbs of Manuka and Kingston. However, many fine eateries are tucked away in such suburban centers as Griffith, Ainslie, Belconnen, and Woden. In Dickson, Canberra's Chinatown, a line of inexpensive, casual eateries along Woolley Street includes many little spots serving Vietnamese, Malaysian, Chinese, Turkish, and Italian cuisine.

Use the coordinate (✣ B2) at the end of each listing to locate a site on the corresponding map.

CENTRAL CANBERRA AND NORTHERN SUBURBS

$$ ITALIAN

🍴 **Bicicletta.** Its name is Italian for bicycle and the motif is carried through his funky restaurant housed in the ultrahip Diamant Hotel, with two-wheeled images on the big umbrella-shape light fittings and pieces of memorabilia. The popular dining spot for lunch, dinner, and weekend breakfasts was once a student dormitory, and the interior's distressed look (featuring old bathroom tiles and shabby walls) has been left to add to the venue's funky feel. The menu features antipasti, pasta, a long list of pizzas, salads, and only a light smattering of meat and fish dishes. Start with the yummy large olives stuffed with savory mince, crumbed and lightly fried; or try the slow-cooked pork and veal meatballs. Thin-crust pizzas include the "fantasia": mozzarella, spinach, sausage, cherry tomatoes, and Gorgonzola. Pop in early for great pastries and good coffee and use the free Wi-Fi while you eat. [$] *Average main: A$24* ✉ *15 Edinburgh Ave., City Center* ☎ *02/6262–8683* 🌐 *www.bicicletta.com.au* ✣ *B3.*

$$ ECLECTIC

🍴 **The Chairman and Yip.** The menu at this longtime fusion favorite garners universal praise for its innovative mix of Asian and Western flavors against a backdrop of artifacts from Maoist China. Menu standouts include the sesame-crusted salmon with cinnamon-infused soy, and pork chops with red dates, ginseng, and honey. Finish with a delicious dessert, such as cinnamon–and–star anise crème brûlée. Watch for the special deals, such as the two-course lunch and two-course early-bird dinner, each for A$38.50, and lunch and dinner banquets from A$58 for seven courses. The service and wine list are outstanding, and you're welcome to bring your own bottle as well. [$] *Average main: A$30* ✉ *108 Bunda St., Canberra City* ☎ *02/6248–7109* 🌐 *thechairmanandyip.chairmangroup.com.au* ✍ *Reservations essential* 🕒 *Closed Sun. No lunch Sat.* ✣ *C2.*

$$$ AUSTRALIAN Fodor's Choice ★

🍴 **Courgette.** Creative food served in spacious, sedate surroundings is the specialty of this popular restaurant on the city's outer edge. The seasonal menu has such dreamy dishes as prosciutto-wrapped pan-seared scallops for starter, or, for a main, the crispy-skin snapper, fennel puree and Balmain-bug-filled zucchini (also known as courgette) flower. Leave room for the decadent warm Belgian chocolate fondant with raspberries and vanilla bean ice cream. The restaurant also offers a four-course menu for A$80 and an express lunch menu for A$60, which are bargains for a restaurant of this acclaim, and one with such an impressive wine list. $ *Average main: A$38* ⊠ *54 Marcus Clarke St., Canberra City* ☎ *02/6247–4042* ⊕ *www.courgette.com.au* ⊘ *Closed Sun. No lunch Sat.* ✛ *B2.*

$$ ✕ **Italian and Sons.** This lively restaurant calls itself a modern version
ITALIAN of the traditional Roman trattoria. It serves regional Italian cuisine using local produce, much of it from the owner's farm. Sit among the hanging salamis at tables covered in white paper and feast on antipasti such as chili and garlic prawns. Move on to one of the delicious pizzas (Sicilian anchovy, black olive, and baby caper are standouts), or one of the dishes of the day, like wood-roast suckling pig with apple and sage. Finish with Ligurian honey panna cotta, or one of the imported Italian cheeses. Bon appetito. $ *Average main: A$30* ⊠ *7 Lonsdale St.* ☎ *02/6162–4888* ⊕ *www.italianandsons.com.au* ⊘ *Closed Sun. No dinner Sat. or Mon.* ✛ *B2.*

$$ ✕ **Thirst Wine Bar & Eatery.** This busy Thai restaurant in the heart of
THAI Canberra draws its inspiration from the street-food stalls of Thailand. Waitstaff does an excellent job of suggesting just the right wines for your meal from an acclaimed, although small, wine list. The crispy-fish salad is a specialty, a mix of crisp fried-fish pieces with green mango, coriander, mint, roasted peanuts, and a chili dressing (have it with the Thirst Riesling). The main dish of green curry with ocean trout dumplings is not only intriguing but delicious. A tasting plate featuring such delights as corn fritters, Thai sausages, and popular Thai fish cakes is A$27.90 for two, while the "two-for-one" deals on Monday and Tuesday nights pulls in droves of locals—arrive early or expect a wait. $ *Average main: A$22* ⊠ *Melbourne Bldg., 20 West Row, Canberra City* ☎ *02/6257–0700* ⊕ *www.thirstwinebar.com.au* ⊘ *Closed Sun. No lunch Sat.–Tues.* ✛ *B3.*

SOUTHERN SUBURBS

$$ ✕ **Rubicon.** Everything about this cozy romantic restaurant speaks of
AUSTRALIAN attention to detail. Savor the melded flavors of prawns, clams, and crab chowder to start things off, then consider the duck confit and Toulouse sausage or pork belly cassoulet among the mains. Later you can linger over such delicious desserts as honey-rum panna cotta with baby figs and ginger ice cream. You can build your own degustation menu from the à la carte menu, choosing from four to seven courses. The four-course, for example, is A$60, or A$90 with paired wines. $ *Average main: A$34* ⊠ *6A Barker St., Griffith* ☎ *02/6295–9919* ⊕ *www.rubiconrestaurant.com.au* ⊘ *Closed Sun. No lunch Sat.* ✛ *C6.*

$$ ✕ **Silo Bakery.** It's not unusual to find a queue of hungry Canberrians
CAFÉ waiting to take away some of the delectable homemade pastries (try the black-currant and Cabernet tart) and breads. It's also possible to sit down for breakfast, brunch, or lunch at one of the few tables. The eggs with chili jam are popular, while the thin, crisp sourdough pizza topped with a mixture of mushrooms and hint of blue cheese is mouthwatering. Many people complain about the rude staff, but don't let it keep you

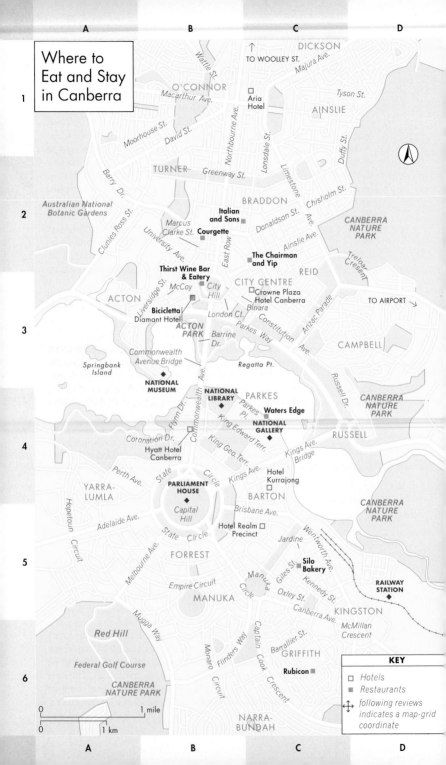

Where to Eat and Stay in Canberra

KEY

☐ Hotels
■ Restaurants
⊕ following reviews indicates a map-grid coordinate

A

O'CONNOR
Macarthur Ave.
Wattle St.
Moorhouse St.
David St.
Barry Dr.
TURNER
Greenway St.
Northbourne Ave.
Marcus Clarke St.
University Ave.
Clunies Ross St.
ACTON
McCoy
Liversidge St.
ACTON PARK
Commonwealth Avenue Bridge
Springbank Island
NATIONAL MUSEUM ◆
Flynn Dr.
Coronation Dr.
Hyatt Hotel Canberra ☐
Perth Ave.
YARRA-LUMLA
Hopetoun Circuit
Adelaide Ave.
Melbourne Ave.
Mugga Way
Red Hill
Federal Golf Course
CANBERRA NATURE PARK

B

Australian National Botanic Gardens
Italian and Sons ■
Courgette ■
Thirst Wine Bar & Eatery ■
Bicicletta ■
Diamant Hotel
East Row
City Hill
London Ct.
Barrine Dr.
Parkes Way
NATIONAL LIBRARY ◆
Commonwealth Ave.
Parkes Pl.
King Edward Terr.
King Geo. Terr.
King Ave.
PARLIAMENT HOUSE ◆
Capital Hill
State Circle
State Circle
Kings Ave.
Hotel Realm Precinct ☐
FORREST
Empire Circuit
Manuka Circle
MANUKA
Monaro Circuit
Flinders Way
Barrallier St.
Captain Cook Crescent
NARRA-BUNDAH

C

TO WOOLLEY ST. ↑
DICKSON
Majura Ave.
Aria Hotel ☐
Lonsdale St.
BRADDON
Donaldson St.
Ainslie Ave.
The Chairman and Yip ■
CITY CENTRE
REID
Crowne Plaza Hotel Canberra ☐
Binara
Constitution Ave.
Regatta Pt.
PARKES
Waters Edge ■
NATIONAL GALLERY ◆
Kings Ave. Bridge
Hotel Kurrajong ☐
BARTON
Brisbane Ave.
Jardine
Giles St.
Silo Bakery ■
Oxley St.
Kennedy St.
Canberra Ave.
Barrallier St.
GRIFFITH
Rubicon ■

D

Majura Ave.
Tyson St.
AINSLIE
Duffy St.
Limestone Ave.
Chisholm St.
CANBERRA NATURE PARK
Treloar Crescent
TO AIRPORT →
Anzac Parade
CAMPBELL
Russell Dr.
CANBERRA NATURE PARK
RUSSELL
Wentworth Ave.
RAILWAY STATION ◆
KINGSTON
McMillan Crescent

0 _____ 1 mile
0 _____ 1 km

from going—the food, especially those pastries, can make you forget the brusque service. Still, don't expect a place where you can linger for hours over brunch and the papers. [$] *Average main: A$22* ✉ *36 Giles St., Kingston* ☎ *02/6260–6060* 🌐 *www.silobakery.com.au* 🕒 *Closed Sun. and Mon. No dinner* ✥ *C5.*

$$$ ECLECTIC 🍴 **Waters Edge.** At this swanky eatery tables are set with fine linens and crystal, and huge windows look out over the sparkling waters of Lake Burley Griffin. The menu cleverly blends French and Mod Oz influences with dishes such as duck breast and pressed leg confit with potatoes and rosemary gratin and sautéed sweet cabbage, and a luscious dessert of passion-fruit soufflé and coconut–and–Kaffir lime sorbet. Those wishing to linger over lunch or dinner might opt for the three-course A$60 lunch or four-course A$88 dinner. An impressive wine list offers many by-the-glass vintages. [$] *Average main: A$38* ✉ *Commonwealth Pl. off Parkes Pl., Parkes* ☎ *02/6273–5066* 🌐 *www.courgette.com.au* 🕒 *No lunch Mon. and Tues.* ✥ *C4.*

3

WHERE TO STAY

For expanded hotel reviews, facilities, and current deals, visit Fodors.com.

CENTRAL CANBERRA AND NORTHERN SUBURBS

$$$ HOTEL 🏨 **Aria Hotel.** This contemporary, spick-and-span hotel is convenient for travelers with a car, as it's just over 2 km (1 mile) north of the city, but it's also accessible from central Canberra via the ACTION buses. **Pros:** quiet; good for long stays. **Cons:** a little out of the center of town. [$] *Rooms from: A$225* ✉ *45 Dooring St., Dickson* ☎ *02/6279–7000* 🌐 *www.ariahotel.com.au* 🛏 *128 rooms* 🍽 *No meals* ✥ *C1.*

$ HOTEL 🏨 **Crowne Plaza Hotel Canberra.** In a prime location between the city center and the National Convention Centre, this atrium-style hotel has a touch of luxury. **Pros:** excellent gym and pool; gambling fans will enjoy being next door to the casino. **Cons:** hotel bars can be noisy; expensive parking. [$] *Rooms from: A$148* ✉ *1 Binara St., Canberra City* ☎ *02/6247–8999, 1300/662218* 🌐 *www.crowneplaza.com.au* 🛏 *290 rooms, 6 suites* 🍽 *No meals* ✥ *C3.*

$$ HOTEL Fodor's Choice ★ 🏨 **Diamant Hotel.** In a city lacking in funk factor, the Diamant stands out thanks to its groovy blend of art deco chic exterior and quirky interior. **Pros:** a good array of restaurants and bars for a hotel of this size; beautifully landscaped modern gardens. **Cons:** bar and restaurants close early; cheaper rooms are on the small side. [$] *Rooms from: A$184* ✉ *15 Edinburgh Ave., City Center* ☎ *02/6175–2222* 🌐 *www.diamant.com.au* 🛏 *80 rooms* 🍽 *No meals* ✥ *B3.*

SOUTHERN SUBURBS

$$$ HOTEL 🏨 **Hotel Kurrajong.** Stay here for a chance to immerse yourself in Canberra's political history and be within walking distance of Parliament House and the National Gallery. **Pros:** great location; stylish; lots of history. **Cons:** doesn't offer as many facilities as larger hotels; restaurant not open on weekends [$] *Rooms from: A$260* ✉ *8 National Circuit, Barton* ☎ *02/6234–4444* 🌐 *www.hotelkurrajong.com.au* 🛏 *148 rooms* 🍽 *No meals* ✥ *C4.*

$$$ HOTEL [🏨] **Hotel Realm Precinct.** This modern hotel is set among a new development of residential apartments and trendy eateries, and is close to all the attractions of the Parliamentary Triangle. **Pros:** modern; good location; trendy dining options. **Cons:** can feel a bit geared to corporate travelers. [$] *Rooms from: A$240* ✉ *18 National Circuit, Barton* ☎ *02/6163–1888* 🌐 *www.hotelrealm.com.au* 🛏 *158 rooms* 🍴 *No meals* ✥ *C5.*

$$$$ HOTEL Fodor's Choice ★ [🏨] **Hyatt Hotel Canberra.** Occupying a National Heritage building dating from 1924, this elegant hotel has been restored to its original art deco splendor. **Pros:** friendly and unobtrusive service; superb location. **Cons:** expensive breakfasts; can be very busy. [$] *Rooms from: A$380* ✉ *Commonwealth Ave., Yarralumla* ☎ *13–1234, 02/6270–1234* 🌐 *www.canberra.hyatt.com* 🛏 *231 rooms, 18 suites* 🍴 *No meals* ✥ *B4.*

NIGHTLIFE AND THE ARTS

Canberra's nightlife has had an adrenalin injection in recent years, and there are great wine bars, pubs, and music venues. Most venues are clustered in the city center and the fashionable southern suburbs of Manuka and Kingston. Except on weekends, few places showcase live music.

The Thursday edition of the *Canberra Times* has a "What's On" section (in the *Times Out* supplement) listing performances around the city. The Saturday edition's Arts pages also list weekend happenings.

THE ARTS

MUSIC

Llewellyn Hall. The Australian National University's School of Music has classical recitals and modern-style concerts on-campus at Llewellyn Hall. The Australian Chamber Orchestral also performs here six times a year. ✉ *Childers St., Acton* ☎ *02/6125–2527* 🌐 *www.anu.edu.au.*

THEATER

Canberra Theatre Centre. The city's main live performance space has two different theaters that host productions by the Australian Ballet Company, touring theater companies, and overseas and local artists. ✉ *Civic Sq., Canberra City* ☎ *02/6275–2700* 🌐 *www.canberratheatrecentre.com.au.*

Erindale Theatre. Smaller stage and musical companies perform at neighborhood venues like this one. ✉ *McBryde Crescent, Wanniassa* ☎ *02/6207–2703* 🌐 *www.erindale.act.edu.au.*

The Street Theatre. This theater near the Australian National University campus showcases the best in local talent with excellent productions ranging from musicals to avant-garde plays. ✉ *15 Childers St., at University Ave., Canberra City* ☎ *02/6247–1223* 🌐 *www.thestreet.org.au.*

NIGHTLIFE

BARS AND CLUBS

The Academy Club. Canberra's liveliest nightspot draws hip crowd to its stylish, glitzy premises. The main room hosts DJs, live bands, and fun theme party nights. A roving photograper snaps partygoers and dancers. ✉ *50 Bunda St., Canberra City* ☎ *02/6253–2091* 🌐 *www.academyclub.com.au.*

Interior of the National Museum of Australia, Canberra

Tilley's Devine Café Gallery. This 1940s-style club was once just for women, but now anyone can sit at the wooden booths and enjoy a relaxing meeting with friends or a meal at this arty café that does a great breakfast; in fact the kitchen is open all day from 9 am to 10 pm (except Sunday). Established in 1984, the café stages a full range of cultural events from poetry readings to live music, particularly jazz and blues. Check the website for details. ⊠ *Wattle and Brigalow Sts., Lyneham* 🕾 *02/6247–7753* ⊕ *tilleys.com.au* ⊗ *Mon.–Sat. 9 am–10 pm, Sun. 9–6.*

CASINOS

Casino Canberra. The European-style gaming room beside the National Convention Centre forgoes slot machines in favor of more sociable games like roulette, blackjack, poker, and keno. There are 40 gaming tables here, and the complex includes a restaurant (which has live music) and two bars. The Galaxy Club Retro is open Saturday nights and stages vintage dance parties. ⊠ *Glebe Park, 21 Binara St., Canberra City* 🕾 *02/6257–7074* ⊕ *www.casinocanberra.com.au.*

SHOPPING

Canberra has quite a diverse range of shopping opportunities, including the large 300-store Canberra Centre on Bunda Street in the heart of the city, and the well-to-do inner suburbs of Manuka and Kingston, where designer clothes and home wares can be had. There are also a number of high-quality arts-and-crafts outlets where you are likely to come across some unusual gifts and souvenirs. The galleries and museums sell interesting and often innovative items designed and made in Australia.

CLOSE UP

Experiencing Aboriginal Culture

The Ngunnawal people were the first inhabitants of the area now known as Canberra and the A.C.T., and the name "Canberra" comes from the Ngunnawal word "Kambera." In NSW the Cammeraygal, Eora, Kamilaroi, Tharawal, Wiradjuri, and Wonnarua peoples were some of the original inhabitants, each grouping speaking a different language and practicing a culture that stretched back thousands of years.

Muru Mittigar Aboriginal Cultural Centre near Penrith, an hour's drive from Sydney, tells the story of the Darug people. You can try bush tucker and boomerang throwing, or learn about the native plants used for medicine and food. (⌧ 89–151 *Old Castlereagh Rd., Castlereagh, New South Wales* ☎ *02/4729-2377* ⊕ *www.murumittigar.com.au).*

Beaver Galleries. This space has four exhibition galleries and a sculpture garden, where works by contemporary Australian artists are showcased. There is also a café. ⌧ *81 Denison St., Deakin* ☎ *02/6282–5294* ⊕ *www.beavergalleries.com.au.*

Gold Creek Village. The charming streets of this shopping complex on the city's northern outskirts are lined with all sorts of fun little places to explore. Peek into art galleries and pottery shops, browse through clothing boutiques and gift stores, and nosh at several eateries. ⌧ *O'Hanlon Pl., Nicholls* ⊕ *www.goldcreekvillage.com.*

Old Bus Depot Markets. South of Lake Burley Griffin, this lively Sunday market is in the former Kingston bus depot. Handmade crafts are the staples here, and buskers and inexpensive exotic food enliven the shopping experience. The markets also run on Saturday throughout December leading up to Christmas. When you've had your fill, wander across the road to the Canberra Glassworks to watch artisans at work. ⌧ *Wentworth Ave., Kingston Foreshore, Kingston* ☎ *02/6295–3331* ⊕ *www.obdm.com.au.*

Solander Gallery. A range of paintings and sculpture by leading Australian artists are the bill of fare at this gallery open Friday–Sunday. ⌧ *10 Schlich St., Yarralumla* ☎ *02/6285–2218* ⊕ *www.solander.com.au.*

MELBOURNE

WELCOME TO MELBOURNE

TOP REASONS TO GO

★ **Fabulous Markets:** Melbourne has nearly a dozen major markets. The huge Queen Victoria Market (the Vic) has more than 1,000 stalls. Others include the "foodie heaven" Prahran Market, and St. Kilda's Sunday market, awash with pottery and all things arty.

★ **International Cuisine:** Melbourne's dining scene is a vast smorgasbord of cuisines: Chinese restaurants on Little Bourke Street are the equal of anything in Hong Kong. Richmond's Victoria Street convincingly incarnates Vietnam.

★ **Sizzling Nightlife:** Melbourne's nightlife centers on King Street and Flinders Lane, with dozens of retro-style bars and clubs. The city's famous live music scene can be viewed in historic pubs in Fitzroy, Collingwood, and Brunswick.

★ **Sports Galore:** Melburnians, like Aussies in general, do love a good match. The Melbourne Cup horse race in November brings the entire city to a standstill. The same is true of Australian Rules Football.

1 City Center. Why come? For arts, funky back alleys, shopping and Australia's best food. Explore the Southgate development, the arts district around the National Gallery of Victoria, and the King's Domain

2 Richmond. Heaven for foodies and fashionistas in need of retail therapy. Come here for a new wardrobe, a Vietnamese soup kitchen, a Korean barbecue, a Laotian banquet, or a Thai hole-in-the-wall.

3 East Melbourne. The harmonious streetscapes in this historic enclave of Victorian houses, which date from the boom following the gold rushes of the 1850s, are a great excuse for a stroll.

4 St. Kilda. Dozens of alfresco restaurants overflow into the streets and the cafés and bars are buzzing with young fashionistas.

5 Fitzroy. Come here if you're looking for an Afghan camel bag, a secondhand paperback, or live music and a beer in a backstreet beer garden.

GETTING ORIENTED

Melbourne, the capital of Victoria, is in the south of the state on Port Phillip Bay. With a population of almost 4 million people, it is the fastest-growing major city in Australia. The Yarra River cuts through the city center; the main business district is on the northern side, the southern side has arts, entertainment, and restaurant precincts. Several exclusive suburbs hug the southeastern shore of the bay. The Yarra Valley wineries and the Dandenongs Ranges are an hour's drive to the east, while the beaches and vineyards of the Mornington Peninsula are a 90-minute drive south of Melbourne. The Great Ocean Road begins at Torquay, southwest of Melbourne, and continues along the Southern Ocean coast to Portland, a distance of about 350 km (217 miles). The goldfields, spa country, and Grampians are between one and two hours northwest of Melbourne; the Murray River Region and its wineries are about a three-hour drive north to northeast of Melbourne.

4

Updated by
Chris Canty

Consistently rated among the "world's most livable cities" in quality-of-life surveys, Melbourne is built on a coastal plain at the top of the giant horseshoe of Port Phillip Bay. The city center is an orderly grid of streets where the state parliament, banks, multinational corporations, and splendid Victorian buildings that sprang up in the wake of the gold rush now stand. This is Melbourne's heart, which you can explore at a leisurely pace in a couple of days.

In Southbank, one of the newer precincts south of the city center, the Southgate development of bars, restaurants, and shops has refocused Melbourne's vision on the Yarra River. Once a blighted stretch of factories and run-down warehouses, the southern bank of the river is now a vibrant, exciting part of the city, and the river itself is finally taking its rightful place in Melbourne's psyche.

Just a hop away, Federation Square—with its host of galleries—has become a civic landmark for Melburnians. Stroll along the Esplanade in the suburb of St. Kilda, amble past the elegant houses of East Melbourne, enjoy the shops and cafés in Fitzroy or Carlton, rub shoulders with locals at the Victoria Market, nip into the Windsor for afternoon tea, or rent a canoe at Studley Park to paddle along one of the prettiest stretches of the Yarra—and you may discover Melbourne's soul as well as its heart.

PLANNING

WHEN TO GO

Melbourne and Victoria are at their most beautiful in autumn, from March to May. Days are crisp, and the foliage in parks and gardens is glorious. Melbourne winters can be gloomy, although the wild seas and leaden skies from June to August provide a suitable backdrop for the dramatic coastal scenery of the Great Ocean Road. By September the weather begins to clear, and the football finals are on. Book early to visit Melbourne during the Spring Racing Carnival and the Melbourne International Festival (late October/early November) and during mid-January when the Australian Open Tennis is staged.

GETTING HERE AND AROUND

Melbourne is most easily reached by plane, as it's hours by car from the nearest big city. International airlines flying into Melbourne include Air New Zealand, British Airways, United, Singapore Airlines, Emirates, Thai Airways, Malaysia Airlines, V Australia, and Qantas.

BY BUS AND TRAM

Melbourne is divided into two zones. Zone 1 is the urban core, where most travelers spend their time. For public transportation here, you'll need a ticket called a myki (a stored-money smartcard system). It can be purchased (A$6 for the card itself) at 7-11 stores, Melbourne Town Hall, and the Melbourne Visitors Centre at Federation Square. Each time you enter a train station, or hop on a tram or bus, you must touch one at the myki reader. It's valid for travel within a specific zone on any bus, tram, or train for two hours after purchase. For travelers, the most useful ticket is the Zone 1 day ticket, which costs A$7. Trams run until midnight, and can be hailed wherever you see a green-and-gold tram-stop sign.

BY CAR

Melbourne's regimented layout makes it easy to negotiate by car, but two unusual rules apply because of the tram traffic. Trams should be passed on the *left*, and when a tram stops to allow passengers to disembark, the cars behind it also must stop. Motorists using various tollways have 72 hours to pay the toll after using the highway. To pay by credit card, call ☎ *13–2629.* Alternatively, you can buy passes at the airport before using the tollways. A weekend pass is around A$15.

BY TRAIN

Southern Cross Railway Station is at Spencer and Little Collins streets. From here the countrywide V-Line has 11-hour trips to Sydney, as well as services to many regional centers in Victoria. V-Line buses connect with the trains to provide transport to coastal towns; take the train to Marshall (one stop beyond Geelong) to connect with a bus to Lorne, Apollo Bay, and Port Campbell, or travel by train to Warrnambool and take a bus to Port Fairy.

RESTAURANTS

Melbourne teems with top-quality restaurants, particularly in St. Kilda, South Yarra, Fitzroy, and the Waterfront City precinct. Lygon Street is still a favorite with those who love great coffee, aldente pasta, and Italian bakeries, while the city center also has many back alleys (known as laneways) with popular cafés. Reservations are generally advised, and although most places are licensed to sell alcohol, the few that aren't usually allow you to bring your own. Lunch is served noon–2:30, and dinner is usually 7–10:30. A 10% tip is customary for exemplary service, and there may be a corkage fee in BYO restaurants. *Prices in the restaurant reviews are the average cost of a main course at dinner or, if dinner isn't served, a lunch.*

HOTELS

Staying in the heart of Melbourne, on Collins or Flinders Streets and their nearby laneways, or at Southbank, is ideal for those who like dining and shopping. Another trendy area, a little out of town, is South Yarra, which also has excellent shopping. Wherever you stay, make sure you're near a tram, bus, or train line. *Prices in the hotel reviews are the lowest cost of a standard double room in high season. For expanded hotel reviews, visit Fodors.com.*

TOURS

A free City Circle tram run by Metropolitan Transit operates every 12 minutes 10–6 Sunday–Wednesday and 10–9 Thursday–Saturday on the fringe of the Central Business District, with stops on Flinders, Spencer, La Trobe, Victoria, and Spring streets. Look for the burgundy-and-cream trams. An orange tourist bus (the Melbourne City Tourist Shuttle, A$5 all day) does a loop around central and inner Melbourne suburbs daily, every 30 minutes between 9:30 and 4:30, stopping at 13 destinations including Federation Square, Docklands, South Yarra, and the Botanic Gardens. Metropolitan buses operate daily until around 9 pm to all suburbs, while the NightRider bus service runs between 1:30 am and 4:30 am on Saturday and 1:30 am and 5:30 am on Sunday.

Boat Tours. One of the best ways to see Melbourne is from the deck of a boat on the Yarra River. Melbourne River Cruises' fleet of modern, glass-enclosed boats operate 1- and 2½-hour Yarra River cruises daily (A$23 and A$29, respectively), traversing either west through the commercial heart of the city or east through the parks and gardens, or a combination of the two. Cruises run roughly every half hour from 10 to 4.

Bus Tours. Gray Line has guided tours of Melbourne and environs by bus and boat. The City Tour visits the city center's main attractions and some of the surrounding parks. The 3½-hour, A$60 tour departs daily at 8:20 am.

AAT Kings, Australian Pacific Tours, and Melbourne's Best Day Tours all have similar city highlight tours.

Food Tours. Foodies Dream Tours (2 hours, A$40) and cooking classes (2½ hours, A$90–A$110) are conducted at Queen Victoria Market.

Chocoholic Tours offers several Saturday tours for chocolate lovers: the Chocoholic Brunch Walk (10–noon) and the Chocoholic Indulgence Walk (noon–2), among others. Each offers a different combination of chocolate-fueled tastings and activities (A$39 each). Bookings are essential and departure points vary.

Vietnam on a Plate runs guided walking tours of the Asian food markets of Footscray and Springvale, visiting traditional herbalists, food stalls, and spice and herb specialists. The tours are designed for aspiring cooks and focus on sourcing and selecting the ingredients needed for authentic Asian cooking. A substantial Vietnamese lunch is included. Tours are usually given Saturday 9:30–2, and cost A$77. Reservations are essential.

Walking Tours. The Melbourne Greeter service, a Melbourne Information Centre program, provides free two- to four-hour tours by pairing you with a local volunteer who shares your interests. Melbourne's Golden Mile Heritage Trail runs guided walking tours of the city's architectural and historic sites. Tours, which cost A$29 and take two hours, depart daily at 10 am from Federation Square and finish at the Melbourne Town Hall weekdays and the Melbourne Museum on weekends.

Tour Operators AAT Kings ⊠ *Federation Sq. E, Flinders and Russell Sts., City Centre* ☎ *1300/228546* ⊕ *guidedtours.aatkings.com.* **Australian Pacific Touring (APT)** ⊠ *1230 Nepean Hwy., Level 4, Cheltenham* ☎ *03/9277–8555, 1300/336932* ⊕ *www.aptouring.com.au.* **Chocoholic Tours** ⊠ *145/28 Southgate Ave., Southbank* ☎ *03/9686–4655* ⊕ *www.chocoholictours.com.au.* **Foodies Dream Tours** ⊠ *Queen Victoria Market, Queen and Elizabeth Sts., City Center* ☎ *03/9320–5822* ⊕ *www.qvm.com.au.* **Golden Mile Heritage Trail** ☎ *03/9928–0000* ⊕ *www.melbournegoldenmile.com.au.* **Gray Line** ⊠ *Federation Sq. E, Flinders and Russell Sts., City Center* ☎ *1300/858687* ⊕ *www.grayline.com.au.* **Melbourne's Best Day Tours** ⊠ *Federation Sq., Flinders and Russell Sts., City Center* ☎ *1300/130550* ⊕ *www.melbournetours.com.au.* **Melbourne Greeters** ⊠ *Federation Sq., Flinders and Swanston Sts., City Center* ☎ *03/9658–9658 (weekdays), 03/9658–9942 (weekends)* ⊕ *www.melbourne.vic.gov.au/greeter.* **Melbourne River Cruises** ⊠ *Vault 11, Banana Alley, 367 Flinders St., City Center* ☎ *03/8610–2600* ⊕ *www.melbcruises.com.au.* **Vietnam on a Plate** ⊠ *Footscray Market, Hopkins and Leeds Sts., Footscray* ☎ *03/9332–6848* ⊕ *www.vietnamonaplate.com.au.*

VISITOR INFORMATION

The Melbourne Visitor Centre at Federation Square provides touring details in six languages. Large-screen videos and touch screens add to the experience, and permanent displays follow the city's history. Daily newspapers are available, and there's access to the Melbourne website (⊕ *www.visitmelbourne.com*). The center is open daily 9–6. The Best of Victoria Booking Service here can help if you're looking for accommodations. It also has cheap Internet access.

City Ambassadors—usually mature men and women easily spotted by their red uniforms—are volunteers for the City of Melbourne, and rove the central retail area providing directions and information for people needing their assistance (Monday–Saturday 10–4, Sunday noon–3).

A free bus route map is available from the Melbourne Visitor Centre.

Visitor Information Best of Victoria Booking Service ☎ *03/9928–0000, 1300/780045.* **City of Melbourne Ambassadors Program** ☎ *03/9658–9658.* **Melbourne Visitor Centre** ⊠ *Federation Sq., Flinders and Swanston Sts., City Center* ☎ *03/9658–9658* ⊕ *www.melbourne.vic.gov.au or www.thatsmelbourne.com.au.*

GREAT ITINERARIES

IF YOU HAVE 1 DAY

The free **City Circle Tram** is a hop-on and hop-off way to see many of the city's sights in a short time without exhausting yourself. The Parliament House tram stop gives access to the Princess Theatre, the grand Windsor Hotel, **Parliament House**, the "Paris End" of Collins Street, and St. Patrick's Cathedral. Get off at Flinders Street to take a peek at the infamous *Chloe* painting in **Young and Jackson's** pub, and then walk over the **Princes Bridge**. There you can stroll along the banks of the Yarra, looking back at Federation Square, and then wander along Southbank while checking out the restaurants and shops and the **Crown Casino**. A trip to the Eureka Skydeck, the southern hemisphere's highest viewing platform, will put the city into perspective, and up there you can decide whether to head

northeast to Fitzroy for an amble along groovy **Brunswick Street**, or north to **Carlton** to immerse yourself in Little Italy.

IF YOU HAVE 3 DAYS

You might squeeze in a bit more exploring on Day 1 with a stroll through Treasury Gardens and over to Fitzroy Gardens for a look at Captain Cook's Cottage, or see the sharks at the **Melbourne Aquarium** opposite Southbank. On your second day, stroll through the **Royal Botanic Gardens** and see the **Shrine of Remembrance**. Then take a tram along St. Kilda Road to the hip **Acland Street area**, in the suburb of **St. Kilda**, for dinner. On Day 3, tour Chapel Street's shops, restaurants, and bars; it's Melbourne's hippest district.

EXPLORING

CITY CENTER

The City Center (CBD) is designed in a grid formation, with myriad alleyways shooting off, often holding the city's jewels in (sometimes hidden) restaurants, galleries, and bars. The CBD is bounded by Spring Street in the east, Victoria Street to the north, Flinders Street to the South, and Spencer Street to the West. The Federation Square area, opposite the Flinders Street Station, is considered the CBD's heart and is an ideal starting point. The most popular shopping areas are the elegant eastern end of Collins Street and the busy pedestrian mall of Bourke Street. Spring Street holds many of the city's historic buildings from the mid-1800s.

GETTING HERE AND AROUND

Melbourne and its suburbs are well served by trams, trains, and buses. The free loop tram is perfect for sightseeing, but crowded on weekends. Trams run east–west and north–south across the city, and travel to the popular St. Kilda and Docklands. The Metro train network operates a City Loop service with stops at Flinders Street, Parliament, and Southern Cross Station, where you'll find connections with a network of trains to outer areas, including the Dandenong Ranges.

TOP ATTRACTIONS

Block Arcade. Melbourne's most elegant 19th-century shopping arcade dates from the 1880s, when "Marvelous Melbourne" was flush with the prosperity of the gold rushes. A century later, renovations scraped back the grime to reveal a magnificent mosaic floor. Tours (A$9) operate on Tuesday and Thursday at 1 pm. ⊠ *282 Collins St., City Center* ☎ *03/9654–5244.*

Federation Square. Encompassing a whole city block, the bold, abstract-style landmark was designed to be Melbourne's official meeting place, with a variety of attractions and restaurants within it. The square incorporates the second branch of the National Gallery of Victoria (Ian Potter Centre), which exhibits only Australian art, as well as the Australian Centre for the Moving Image; the Deakin Edge amphitheater, a contemporary music and theater performance venue; and the Melbourne Visitor Centre. ⊠ *Flinders St. between Swanston and Russell Sts., City Center* ☎ *03/9655–1900* ⊕ *www.fedsquare.com* ▣ *Free* ☉ *Daily 10–5; National Gallery of Victoria closed Mon.*

Fitzroy Gardens. This 65-acre expanse of European trees, manicured lawns, garden beds, statuary, and sweeping walks is Melbourne's most popular central park. Among its highlights is the **Avenue of Elms**, a majestic stand of 130-year-old trees that is one of the few in the world that has not been devastated by Dutch elm disease. ⊠ *Lansdowne St. at Wellington Parade, East Melbourne* ▣ *Free* ☉ *Daily sunrise–sunset.*

Flinders Street Station. Much more than just a train station, the term "meet under the clocks" is widely known and used, indicating the timepieces on the front of this grand Edwardian hub of Melbourne's suburban rail network as a favorite meeting place. When it was proposed to replace them with television screens, an uproar ensued. Today there are both clocks and screens. ⊠ *Flinders St. at St. Kilda Rd., City Center.*

The Hotel Windsor. Not just a grand hotel, the Windsor is home to one of Melbourne's proudest institutions—the ritual of afternoon tea (A$69 midweek), which is served daily noon–2 pm and 2:30–4:30. An even more indulgent dessert buffet (A$89), complete with chocolate fountain and other goodies, is added on weekends. Although the Grand Ball Room—a belle epoque extravaganza with a gilded ceiling and seven glass cupolas—is reserved for private functions, occasionally afternoon tea is served there, so it's best to call first to check. ⊠ *111 Spring St., City Center* ☎ *03/9633–6000* ⊕ *www.thewindsor.com.au.*

OFF THE
BEATEN
PATH

King's Domain Gardens. This expansive stretch of parkland includes Queen Victoria Gardens, Alexandra Gardens, the Shrine of Remembrance, the Pioneer Women's Garden, the Sidney Myer Music Bowl, and the Royal Botanic Gardens. The temple-style **Shrine of Remembrance** is designed so that a beam of sunlight passes over the Stone of Remembrance in the Inner Shrine at 11 am on Remembrance Day—the 11th day of the 11th month, when in 1918 the armistice marking the end of World War I was declared. ⊠ *Between St. Kilda and Domain Rds., Anderson St., and Yarra River, City Center.*

National Gallery of Victoria International. This massive, moat-encircled, bluestone-and-concrete edifice houses works from renowned

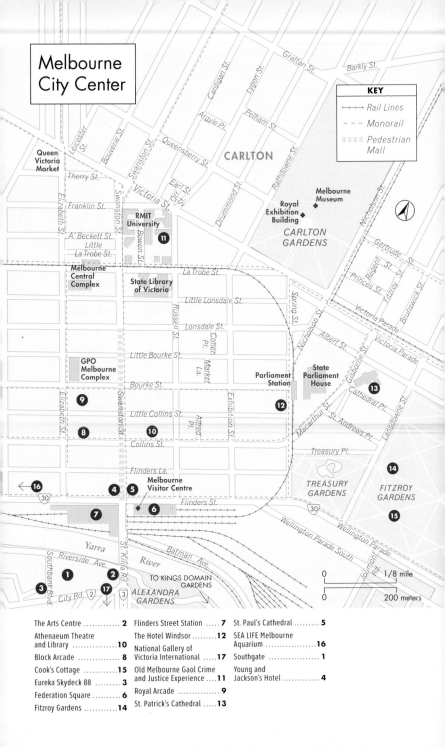

Melbourne City Center

Queen Victoria Market

Leicester St.

Bouverie St.

Queensberry St.

Argyle Pl.

Cardigan St.

Lygon St.

Grattan St.

Barkly St.

Pelham St.

CARLTON

Rathdowne St.

Therry St.

Swanston St.

Victoria St.

Earl St.

Drummond St.

Melbourne Museum

Nicholson St.

Elizabeth St.

Franklin St.

Swanston St.

RMIT University

Royal Exhibition Building

CARLTON GARDENS

Gertrude St.

A'Beckett St.

Little La Trobe St.

11

Bowen St.

La Trobe St.

Regent St.

Princes St.

Fitzroy St.

Brunswick St.

Melbourne Central Complex

State Library of Victoria

Little Lonsdale St.

Spring St.

Victoria Parade

Russell St.

Lonsdale St.

Cohen Pl.

Nicholson St.

Albert St.

Victoria Parade

GPO Melbourne Complex

Little Bourke St.

Market La.

Parliament Station

State Parliament House

Gisborne St.

Cathedral Pl.

13

Elizabeth St.

9

Swanston St.

Bourke St.

Exhibition St.

12

Macarthur St.

St. Andrews Pl.

Lansdowne St.

8

Little Collins St.

Alfred Pl.

10

Collins St.

Treasury Pl.

14

16

30

4 **5**

Flinders La.

Melbourne Visitor Centre

Flinders St.

6

TREASURY GARDENS

FITZROY GARDENS

15

7

Flinders St.

30

Wellington Parade

Yarra

River

Wellington Parade South

Jolimont Rd.

Riverside Ave.

St. Kilda Rd.

Batman Ave.

Southbank Blvd.

1

2

City Rd.

2

17

3

TO KINGS DOMAIN GARDENS

ALEXANDRA GARDENS

3

0   1/8 mile

0   200 meters

The Arts Centre **2**

Athenaeum Theatre and Library **10**

Block Arcade **8**

Cook's Cottage **15**

Eureka Skydeck 88 ...... **3**

Federation Square **6**

Fitzroy Gardens **14**

Flinders Street Station **7**

The Hotel Windsor **12**

National Gallery of Victoria International **17**

Old Melbourne Gaol Crime and Justice Experience **11**

Royal Arcade **9**

St. Patrick's Cathedral **13**

St. Paul's Cathedral **5**

SEA LIFE Melbourne Aquarium **16**

Southgate **1**

Young and Jackson's Hotel **4**

international painters, including Picasso, Renoir, and van Gogh. It also hosts international blockbuster exhibitions. An interactive Kids Space opened in 2011. A second branch of the National Gallery, in Federation Square in the city center, exhibits only Australian art. ☒ *180 St. Kilda Rd., South Melbourne* ☎ *03/8620–0222* ⊕ *www.ngv.vic. gov.au* 🖼 *Free* ⊙ *Wed.–Mon. 10–5; closed Tues. except public holidays (closed Christmas Day and Good Friday).*

Royal Arcade. Opened in 1870, this is the country's oldest shopping arcade, and despite alterations it retains an airy, graceful elegance that often transfixes passersby. Walk about 30 feet into the arcade to see the statues of Gog and Magog, the mythical monsters that toll the hour on either side of **Gaunt's Clock.** ☒ *335 Bourke St., City Center* ☎ *03/9670–7777* ⊕ *www.royalarcade.com.au.*

EXPLORING THE THEATERS

Melburnians love their theater, and major shows often open in Melbourne first. If you want to take in Broadway or West End–style theater in grand surroundings, check out what's playing at the Regent and the Princess. Both are owned by Marriner Theatres, which lovingly restored the Regent for its reopening in the mid-1990s. You can tread the boards (i.e., act on stage) with a theater-loving tour guide on the Historic Rambles tour. Contact Wilma Farrow (☎ *03/9820–0239*) for details. For performances, check out ⊕ *www.marrinertheatres. com.au.*

St. Patrick's Cathedral. Construction of the Gothic Revival building began in 1858 and took 82 years to finish. Ireland supplied Australia with many of its early immigrants, especially during the Irish potato famine in the mid-19th century. A statue of the Irish patriot Daniel O'Connell stands in the courtyard. ☒ *Cathedral Pl., East Melbourne* ☎ *03/9662–2233* ⊙ *Weekdays 7–5, Sat. 8–7, Sun. 8–7:30.*

St. Paul's Cathedral. This 1892 headquarters of Melbourne's Anglican faith is one of the most important works of William Butterfield, a leader of the Gothic Revival style in England. In 2006 the cathedral underwent a massive restoration. Outside is a statue of Matthew Flinders, the first seaman to circumnavigate Australia, between 1801 and 1803. ☒ *Flinders and Swanston Sts., City Center* ☎ *03/9653–4333* ⊙ *Weekdays 8–6, Sat. 9–4, Sun. 7:30–7:30.*

FAMILY **SEA LIFE Melbourne Aquarium.** Become part of the action as you stroll through a transparent tunnel surrounded by water and the denizens of the deep on the prowl. Or press your nose to the glass in the Antarctica exhibition and watch King and Gentoo penguins waddling around on ice and darting through water. You can also don snow gear and sit among the penguins. If you're feeling brave, do a shark dive—they're held daily, include scuba equipment, and are led by an instructor. The aquamarine building illuminates a previously dismal section of the Yarra riverbank, opposite Crown Casino. ☒ *Flinders and King Sts., City Center* ☎ *03/9620–0999* ⊕ *www.melbourneaquarium.com.au* 🖼 *A$35,* *shark dives from A$210, Penguin Passport A$199 weekdays, A$290 weekends ⊙ Daily 9:30–6 (last admission at 5).*

Southgate. On the river's edge next to the Arts Center, the development is a prime spot for lingering—designer shops, classy restaurants, bars, and casual eating places help locals and visitors while away the hours. The promenade links with the forecourt of Crown Casino and its hotels. ⊠ *Maffra St. at City Rd., Southbank* ☎ *03/9686–1000* ⊕ *www.celebratesouthgate.com.au.*

WORTH NOTING

The Arts Centre. Melbourne's most important cultural landmark is the venue for performances by the Australian Ballet, Opera Australia, Melbourne Theatre Company, and Melbourne Symphony Orchestra. It encompasses Hamer Hall, the Arts Complex, the original National Gallery of Victoria, and the outdoor Sidney Myer Music Bowl. Forty-five minute tours of the Gallery and State Theatre begin from the Smorgan Family Plaza at 11 am daily except Friday and Sunday. On Tuesday and Thursday, Hamer Hall tours are available at 5:30 pm. On Sunday a 90-minute backstage tour (no children under 12) begins at 11 am. At night, look for the center's spire, which creates a magical spectacle with brilliant fiber-optic cables. ⊠ *100 St. Kilda Rd., Melbourne* ☎ *03/9281–8000* ⊕ *www.theartscentre.com.au* ☎ *Tour A$20, backstage tour A$20, Hamer Hall tour A$30* ⊙ *Mon.–Sat. 9 am–11 pm, Sun. 10–5.*

Athenaeum Theatre and Library. The first talking picture show in Australia was screened in 1896 at this beautiful theater. Today is houses three venues—a membership library, a theater for live performances, and the Last Laugh Comedy Club *(see separate listing in Nightlife and the Arts).* ⊠ *188 Collins St., City Center* ☎ *03/9650–3100* ⊕ *www.melbourneathenaeum.org.au* ⊙ *Mon., Tues., Thurs., and Fri. 9:30–5; Wed. 11–8; Sat. 9:30–1.*

NEED A BREAK?

Journal. Next to the City Library, the café has leather couches, bookcases filled with magazines and newspapers, and communal tables where you can enjoy bruschetta, salads, antipasto platters, and selections from an excellent wine list from A$8 a glass. Journal Canteen, upstairs, offers a short lunch and dinner selection of delicious Sicilian courses. There is no obvious sign giving the café's name but you will hear the buzz as you near it. ⊠ *253 Flinders La., City Center* ☎ *03/9650–4399* ⊕ *journalcafe.com.au.*

Cook's Cottage. Once the on-leave residence of the Pacific navigator Captain James Cook, this modest two-story home, built in 1755 by Cook senior, was transported stone by stone from Great Ayton in Yorkshire, England, and rebuilt in the lush Fitzroy Gardens in 1934. It's believed that Cook lived in the cottage between his many voyages. The interior is simple, a suitable domestic realm for a man who spent much of his life in cramped quarters aboard sailing ships. ⊠ *Fitzroy Gardens near Lansdowne St. and Wellington Parade, East Melbourne* ☎ *03/9419–4677* ⊕ *www.cookscottage.com.au* ☎ *A$5* ⊙ *Daily 9–5.*

"What a wonderful city! I had fun shopping, visiting museums and eating out." —photo by Carly Miller, Fodors. com member

Eureka Skydeck 88. Named after the goldfields uprising of 1854, the Eureka Tower (which houses the 88th-level Eureka Skydeck 88) is the tallest residential building in the southern hemisphere. The funky-shape blue glass building, with an impressive gold cap, opened in May 2007. The Skydeck is the place to get a bird's-eye view of Melbourne and overcome your fear of heights. An enclosed all-glass cube, known as The Edge (A$12 additional charge), projects 3 meters (9.84 feet) out from the viewing platform—here you can stand, seemingly suspended, over the city on a clear glass floor. ⊠ *7 Riverside Quay, Southbank* ☎ *03/9693–8888* ⊕ *www.eurekaskydeck.com.au* ✉ *A$18.50* ⊙ *Daily 10–10.*

Old Melbourne Gaol Crime and Justice Experience. This bluestone building, the city's first jail, is now a museum that has three tiers of cells with catwalks around the upper levels and is rumored to be haunted. Its most famous inmate was the notorious bushranger Ned Kelly, who was hanged here in 1880. The Hangman's night tours (reservations essential) are a popular, if macabre, facet of Melbourne nightlife. Museum entry now includes "being arrested" next door at the City Watchhouse, where guides walk visitors through the experience of being incarcerated. It is run by the Victorian branch of the National Trust. ⊠ *Russell between LaTrobe and Victoria Sts., City Center* ☎ *03/8663–7228, 13–2849 (Ticketek, for night tours)* ⊕ *www.oldmelbournegaol.com. au* ✉ *A$22, night tours A$38* ⊙ *Daily 9:30–5; night tours: Wed., Fri., and Sat. at 7:30 pm.*

Young and Jackson's Hotel. Pubs are not generally known for their artwork, but climb the steps to the top-floor bar here to see *Chloe*, a painting

that has scandalized and titillated Melburnians for many decades. The larger-than-life nude, painted by George Lefebvre in Paris in 1875, has adorned the walls of Young and Jackson's Hotel (which now specializes in Australian microbrewed beers) since 1909. ⊠ *1 Swanston St.(opposite Flinders St. Station), City Center* ☎ *03/9650–3884* ⊕ *www. youngandjacksons.com.au.*

RICHMOND

Home of Victoria Street—Melbourne's "little Vietnam"—and the lively discount shopping stretch of Bridge Road, Richmond is 2 km (1 mile) east of the city center (take Tram 48 from Flinders Street). If you're looking for a new wardrobe, a Vietnamese soup kitchen, a Korean barbecue, a Laotian banquet, or a Thai hole-in-the-wall, this is the place to come.

GETTING HERE AND AROUND

Several tram lines connect central Melbourne with Richmond. Take Tram 70 from Flinders Street Station to Swan Street, Richmond; or take No. 109 from Bourke Street to Victoria Street. Tram 48 will take you from Flinders Street to Bridge Road, while Nos. 78 and 9 travel from Chapel Street (in South Yarra) to Richmond. Trains connect Flinders Street Station with Richmond Station. If driving, or even walking, proceed east along Flinders Street, which becomes Wellington Parade, past the Hilton and the Park Hotel to Hoddle Street.

EXPLORING

Bridge Road. Once a run-down area of Richmond, this street is now a bargain shopper's paradise. It's chockablock with clothing shops, cafés, and factory outlets selling leather goods, shoes, and gourmet foods. Take Tram 48 or 75 from the city. ⊠ *Bridge Rd., Richmond.*

Victoria Street. One of Melbourne's most popular "eat streets," this 2-km (1-mile) stretch has restaurants ranging from simple canteens (eat until you drop for A\$12) to tablecloth-and-candlelight dining spots. The street also features Vietnamese grocers, kitchenware stores, several art galleries, and several chichi drinking spots. Once a year at Tet, Vietnamese New Year (in January and February but the exact date varies from year to year), the street comes to life with a daylong Lunar Festival, with dragon dances, music and more food! ⊠ *Victoria St., Richmond.*

EAST MELBOURNE

The harmonious streetscapes in this historic enclave of Victorian houses, which date from the boom following the gold rushes of the 1850s, make East Melbourne a great neighborhood for a stroll.

GETTING HERE AND AROUND

East Melbourne's attractions are an easy walk from the city center. The Free City Circle tram travels along Spring Street, stopping at Parliament House and the City Museum at Old Treasury Melbourne. The free, orange-colored Melbourne City Tourist Shuttle bus also does a city loop and stops at the Sports and Entertainment Precinct, which is a short walk from the MCG and Fitzroy Gardens. Trams 48 and 74 travel along Flinders Street and Wellington Parade to East Melbourne sights: Fitzroy Gardens is on the north side of Wellington Parade, and the MCG is on the south side.

EXPLORING

Melbourne Cricket Ground (MCG). A tour of this complex is essential for an understanding of Melbourne's sporting obsession. You can get the stories behind it all at the new National Sports Museum. The site is a pleasant 10-minute walk from the city center or a tram ride (Nos. 48 and 75) to Jolimont Station. ⊠ *Jolimont Terr., East Melbourne* ☎ *03/9657–8888* ⊕ *www.mcg.org. au* ⊠ *A$20* ⊘ *Tours daily every half hr 10–3, except on event days. Museum 10–5 on non-event days.*

WALTZING MATILDA

Shopping mixes with history and a touch of patriotism at Melbourne Central shopping center. The main attraction, apart from the stores, is the historic brick shot tower, rising 165 feet above the center and encased in a glass cone. Built in 1890, the shot tower was used to make "shot" or bullets. Also suspended from the roof is a hot-air balloon and a huge fob-watch that entertains shoppers on the hour with a musical rendition of Australia's unofficial national anthem, "Waltzing Matilda." You'll find this huge shopping center on the corner of La Trobe and Swanston streets.

ST. KILDA

Most nights of the week dozens of alfresco restaurants overflow into the streets, and the cafés and bars buzz with young fashionistas. The holiday atmosphere continues on Sunday with open-air markets and people enjoying the beach. The seaside suburb still has a Victorian-era atmosphere—the tree-lined promenade and the classic pier extending out into Port Phillip Bay are perfect for strolling and people-watching. The quaintly named St. Kilda Sea Baths (now a modern swimming pool–spa complex) are housed in a turn-of-the-20th-century building. Although no one wanted to live there in the 1970s and '80s, it is now a very smart address, and many visitors choose to stay in St. Kilda and hop on the tram for a short scenic ride into the city.

GETTING HERE AND AROUND

Several trams travel to St. Kilda from central Melbourne. Trams 96 and 112 traverse the city center from its northern borders and go all the way south to St. Kilda. Tram 79 travels from North Richmond and No. 16 runs from Melbourne University along Swanston Street. A good place to get on a St. Kilda tram is at Flinders Street Station, or in Collins Street. It's a pleasant ride down St. Kilda Road, into Fitzroy Street and on to St. Kilda Beach.

EXPLORING

Acland Street. An alphabet soup of Chinese, French, Italian, and Lebanese eateries—along with a fantastic array of cake shops—lines the sidewalk of St. Kilda's ultrahip restaurant row. The street faces Luna Park. ⊠ *Acland St. between Barkly St. and Shakespeare Grove, St. Kilda.*

Luna Park. A much-photographed Melbourne landmark, the park's entrance is a huge, gaping mouth, swallowing visitors whole and delivering them into a world of ghost trains, pirate ships, and carousels. Built in 1912, the **Scenic Railway** is the park's most popular ride. It's said to be the oldest continually operating roller coaster in the world. The railway is less roller coaster and more a relaxed loop-the-loop, offering stunning views of Port Phillip Bay between each dip and turn. Several music festivals are held within the park's grounds each year. Luna Park is a five-minute stroll southeast of St. Kilda. ⊠ *Lower Esplanade, St. Kilda* ☎ *03/9525–5033, 1300/888272* ⊕ *www.lunapark.com. au* ✉ *Free entry, A$9.95 per ride, A$43.95 for unlimited rides* ☉ *Summer (late Oct.–Apr. 27): Fri. 7 pm–11 pm; Thurs. and Sat., school holidays, and public holidays 11–11; Sun.–Wed. 11–8. Winter (Apr. 28–late Oct.): daily (and public holidays) 11–6.*

FITZROY

Melbourne's bohemian quarter is 2 km (1 mile) northeast of the city center. If you're looking for an Afghan camel bag or a secondhand paperback, or perhaps to hear some tunes while sipping a pint in a backstreet beer garden, Fitzroy is the place. Take Tram 11 or 86 from the city.

GETTING HERE AND AROUND

Fitzroy is an easy place to access, both from the city and nearby suburbs. From the city, take the No. 112 from Collins Street (near Parliament House). It will take you all the way up Brunswick Street. In Bourke Street (also near Spring Street), hop on the No. 86 tram for a ride to Gertrude Street. Alternatively, you can take the South Morang train line from Flinders Street Station and alight at Clifton Hill. From there you can walk west to Fitzroy or board the No. 86 tram to Gertrude Street.

EXPLORING

Brunswick Street. Along with Lygon Street in nearby Carlton, Brunswick Street is one of Melbourne's favorite places to dine. You might want to step into a simple kebab shop serving tender meats for less than A$10, or opt for dinner at one of the stylish, highly regarded bar-restaurants. The street also has many galleries, bookstores, bars, arts-and-crafts shops, and clothes shops (vintage fashion is a feature). ⊠ *Brunswick St. between Alexandra and Victoria Parades, Fitzroy.*

BRUNSWICK

Just 4 km (2 miles) north of the city center, Brunswick is Melbourne's multicultural heart. Here Middle Eastern spice shops sit next to avant-garde galleries, Egyptian supermarkets, Turkish tile shops, Japanese yakitori eateries, Lebanese bakeries, Indian haberdasheries, and secondhand bookstores. Take Tram 19 from the city.

GETTING HERE AND AROUND

Tram 19 travels from Flinders Street Station in the city along Elizabeth Street all the way to Brunswick's main thoroughfare of Sydney Road. You can also catch a train to Brunswick; take the Upfield Railway Line from Flinders Street Station and alight at either Jewell or Brunswick stations—they're both in Brunswick.

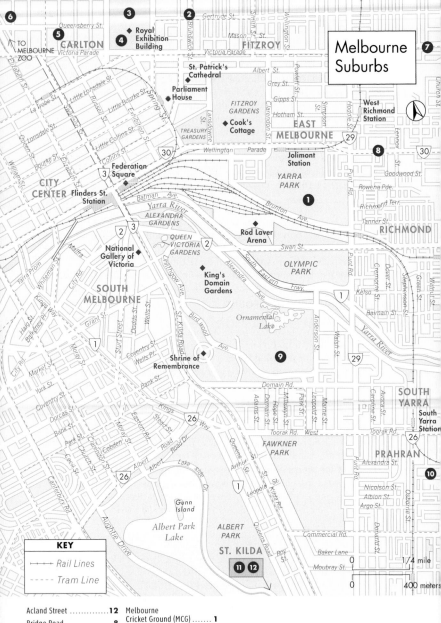

Melbourne Suburbs

6

Queensberry St.

3

Royal Exhibition Building

2

Gertrude St.

5 CARLTON

Victoria Parade

4

Brunswick St.

Mason St.

FITZROY

Victoria Parade

7

Church St.

TO MELBOURNE ZOO

Little Lonsdale St.

La Trobe St.

Lonsdale St.

Bourke St.

Little Bourke St.

Little Collins St.

Collins St.

Spring St.

Exhibition St.

St. Patrick's Cathedral

Parliament House

Albert St.

Grey St.

Gipps St.

Hotham St.

Powlett St.

Simpson St.

Hoddle St.

West Richmond Station

FITZROY GARDENS

Lansdowne St.

Clarendon St.

Cook's Cottage

EAST MELBOURNE

Lennox St.

29

30

Goodwood St.

CITY CENTER

Federation Square

3

Flinders St. Station

30

Wellington Parade

Jolimont Station

8

Rowena Pde.

Richmond Terr.

Tanner St.

RICHMOND

Batman Ave.

YARRA PARK

Brunton Ave.

1

Punt Rd.

Yarra River

ALEXANDRA GARDENS

2

3

QUEEN VICTORIA GARDENS

2

Rod Laver Arena

Swan St.

National Gallery of Victoria

King's Domain Gardens

OLYMPIC PARK

South Eastern Frwy.

Dover St.

Cremorne St.

Stephenson St.

Green St.

Walnut St.

SOUTH MELBOURNE

Maffra

City Rd.

Kings Way

Whiteman St.

Grant St.

Sturt Street

Dodds St.

Wells St.

St. Kilda Road

Birdwood Ave.

Alexandra Ave.

Ornamental Lake

Anderson St.

Walsh St.

1

29

Kelso St.

Bainaih St.

Yarra River

Haig St.

Bowen Pl.

Market St.

1

Coventry St.

Wells Pl.

Coventry St.

Shrine of Remembrance

9

Domain Rd.

SOUTH YARRA

York St.

Dorcas St.

Bank St.

Moray St.

Clarendon St.

Cobden St.

Park St.

Cecil St.

Church St.

26

Eastern Road

Moray St.

Kings Way

26

Domain St.

Adams St.

Hope St.

Millswyn St.

Park St.

Leopold St.

Marne St.

Toorak Rd. West

FAWKNER PARK

Caroline St.

Avoca St.

Toorak Rd.

South Yarra Station

26

PRAHRAN

Alexandra St.

10

Nicolson St.

Albion St.

Argo St.

Canterbury Rd.

Augustine Drive

Gunn Island

Albert Park Lake

Lake Side Dr.

Arthur St.

Queens St.

St. Kilda Rd.

Leopold St.

1

ALBERT PARK

Queens Road

Commercial Rd.

Punt Rd.

Osborne St.

Baker Lane

Mowbray St.

0   1/4 mile

0   400 meters

ST. KILDA

11 **12**

Roy St.

KEY

+−+ Rail Lines

--- Tram Line

Acland Street **12**

Bridge Road **8**

Brunswick Street **2**

Carlton Gardens **4**

Chapel Street **10**

Luna Park **11**

Lygon Street **5**

Melbourne Cricket Ground (MCG) **1**

Melbourne Museum **3**

Royal Botanic Gardens **9**

Sydney Road **6**

Victoria Street **7**

EXPLORING

Sydney Road. Cultures collide on Sydney Road as Arabic mingles with French, Hindi does battle with Bengali, and the muezzin's call to prayer argues with Lebanese pop music. Scents intoxicate and colors beguile. Cafés serving everything from pastries to *tagines* (Moroccan stews) to Turkish delight sit shoulder-to-shoulder along the roadside with quirky record shops, antiques auction houses, and Bollywood video stores. ⊠ *Sydney Rd. between Brunswick Rd. and Bell St., Brunswick.*

A DAY AT THE RACES

The usually serene atmosphere of Albert Park is turned into motor-head heaven every March, when Melbourne stages the Australian Grand Prix. It's the opening event of the Formula One season, with four full-throttle days of excitement on and off the track. Drivers scream around Albert Park Lake to the delight of fans and the horror of some nearby residents. Albert Park is 3 km (2 miles) south of the city center. ⊕ *www.grandprix.com.au.*

CARLTON

To see the best of Carlton's Victorian-era architecture, walk along Drummond Street, with its rows of gracious terrace houses (notably Rosaville at No. 46, Medley Hall at No. 48, and Lothian Terrace at No. 175), and Canning Street, which has a mix of workers' cottages and grander properties. Take Tram 1 or 8 from the city.

GETTING HERE AND AROUND

Carlton is served by the many of Melbourne's tram routes that run through and terminate at Melbourne University (located in Parkville, just north of Carlton). Tram routes 1 and 8 ride along Swanston Street in the city, and then turn into Lygon Street. Alternatively, you can take a train to Melbourne Central Station (on the City Loop line) and then walk north to Carlton, or catch a bus (Nos. 200, 201, 203, 207, 253) from that station to Carlton.

EXPLORING

Carlton Gardens. Forty acres of tree-lined paths, artificial lakes, and flower beds in this English-style 19th-century park are the backdrop for the outstanding Melbourne Museum, and the World Heritage–listed Royal Exhibition Building, erected in 1880. ⊠ *Victoria Parade at Nicholson, Carlton, and Rathdowne Sts., Carlton.*

Lygon Street. Known as Melbourne's Little Italy, Lygon Street is a perfect example of the city's multiculturalism: where once you'd have seen only Italian restaurants, there are now Thai, Malay, Caribbean, and Greek eateries. The city's famous café culture was also born here, with the arrival of Melbourne's first espresso machine at one of the street's Italian-owned cafés in the 1950s. ⊠ *Lygon St. between Victoria and Alexandra Parades, Carlton.*

FAMILY **Melbourne Museum.** A spectacular, postmodern building (in Carlton Gardens) houses displays of the varied cultures around Australia and the Pacific Islands. The Bunjilaka exhibit explores the traditions of the country's Aboriginal groups, while the Australia Gallery focuses on Victoria's heritage (and includes the preserved body of Australia's

The groovy cafés of St. Kilda

greatest racehorse, Phar Lap). There's plenty for kids, too, with the wooded Forest Gallery, Children's Gallery (housed in what looks like a giant Rubik's Cube), Mind and Body Gallery, and Science and Life Gallery. The museum regularly hosts touring blockbuster exhibitions (additional fee). ✉ *Carlton Gardens, 11 Nicholson St., Carlton* ☎ *13–1102, 03/8341–7777* ⊕ *www.museumvictoria.com.au/MelbourneMuseum* 🎫 *A$10, children free* ⏲ *Daily 10–5.*

SOUTH YARRA–PRAHRAN

One of the most chic and fashion-conscious areas to be on any given night is in South Yarra–Prahran. The area is chock-full of bars, eateries, and upscale boutiques.

GETTING HERE AND AROUND

Several trams, including Nos. 6, 8, 78, and 79, travel to either South Yarra or Prahran or both. No. 6 comes down St. Kilda Road from Flinders Street Station and turns into High Street, Prahran, while No. 8 turns into Domain Road (just south of the Royal Botanic Gardens) and then travels down Toorak Road. Trams 78 and 79 travel down Chapel Street from North Richmond. You can also catch a train to both South Yarra and Prahran; take the Sandringham Line from Flinders Street Station.

EXPLORING

Fodor'sChoice
★
Chapel Street. The heart of the trendy South Yarra–Prahran area, this long road is packed with pubs, bars, notable restaurants, and upscale boutiques—more than 1,000 shops can be found within the precinct.

Australian designers showcase their original designs at the fashion-conscious, upscale Toorak Road end of the street (nearest to the city). Walk south along Chapel Street to Greville Street and visit a small lane of hip bars, clothing boutiques, and record stores. Past Greville Street, at the south end of Chapel Street, it's grungier, with pawnshops and kitschy collectibles stores. ⊠ *Chapel St. between Toorak and Dandenong Rds., South Yarra–Prahran* ☎ *03/9529–6331* ⊕ *www.chapelstreet.com.au.*

FAMILY **Royal Botanic Gardens.** Within its 100 acres are 12,000 species of native and imported plants and trees, sweeping lawns, and ornamental lakes populated with ducks and swans that love to be fed. The Children's Garden is a fun and interactive place for kids to explore. Summer brings alfresco performances of classic plays, usually Shakespeare, and children's classics like *Wind in the Willows,* as well as the popular Moonlight Cinema series. The present design and layout were the brainchild of W.R. Guilfoyle, curator and director of the gardens from 1873 to 1910. ⊠ *Birdwood Ave., South Yarra* ☎ *03/9252–2300* ⊕ *www.rbg. vic.gov.au* ⊠ *Free* ☉ *Daily 7:30–sunset. Children's Garden: Wed.–Sun. 10–sunset (closed mid July–early Sept. for maintenance).*

OFF THE
BEATEN
PATH

Melbourne Zoo. Verdant gardens and open-environment animal enclosures are hallmarks of this world-renowned zoo, which is 4 km (2½ mi) north of the city center. A lion park, reptile house, and butterfly pavilion where more than 1,000 butterflies flutter through the rain-forest setting are on-site, as is a simulated African rain forest where a group of Western Lowland gorillas lives. The spectacular Trail of the Elephants, home of seven Asiatic elephants, has a village, tropical gardens, and a swimming pool. The orangutan sanctuary and baboon outlook are other highlights. It's possible to stay overnight with the Roar 'n' Snore package (A$195 per adult) and enjoy dinner, supper, breakfast, close encounters with animals, and a behind-the-scenes look at the zoo's operations. Twilight jazz bands serenade visitors on summer evenings. Children enter free. ⊠ *Elliott Ave., Parkville* ☎ *03/9285–9300* ⊕ *www. zoo.org.au* ⊠ *A$26.80, children free.* ☉ *Daily 9–5, select summer evenings to 9 or 9:30.*

BEACHES

Unlike Sydney, Melbourne is not known for its beaches. Nonetheless, there are several popular beaches on the shores of Port Phillip Bay. The best known are St. Kilda and Brighton Beach, the latter extremely picturesque, adorned with a colorful row of "bathing boxes" that runs along its shore. These vividly decorated little sheds are basically privately owned changing rooms, but can sell for as much as a house in some parts of the city, with many dating back to the 1940s.

The absence of waves fails to provide the conditions for surfing; however, the brisk winds that whip across Port Phillip Bay make most of these beaches ideal for windsurfing and kitesurfing.

Brighton Beach. Most commonly known for its 82 colorful and culturally significant bathing boxes, Brighton Beach is also ideal for families, since it's location in a cove means that it's protected from the wind. Perfect for those looking for a quieter spot to bathe than St. Kilda Beach, the Middle Brighton Baths is a nice place to view the boats and have a bite to eat. **Amenities:** toilets; parking (fee). **Best for:** solitude; swimming. ⊠ *Esplanade, Brighton.*

St. Kilda Beach. While there is no surf to speak of, this half-mile stretch of sand still remains one of the country's most lively beaches as it's close to bars, restaurants, and hotels. While most people like to hang out on the sand, windsurfing, sailing, rollerblading, and beach volleyball are other popular activities. Two iconic landmarks—St. Kilda Baths and St. Kilda Pier—are close by and give visitors something to do in those blistering hot summer afternoons. The Sunday foreshore market is just minutes away as well. **Amenities:** food and drink; toilets; parking (fee). **Best for:** partiers; swimming; windsurfing. ⊠ *Marine Parade, St. Kilda.*

SPORTS AND THE OUTDOORS

AUSTRALIAN RULES FOOTBALL

This fast, vigorous game, played between teams of 18, is one of four kinds of football Down Under. Aussies also play Rugby League, Rugby Union, and soccer, but Australian Rules, widely known as "footy," is the one to which Victoria, South Australia, the Top End, and Western Australia subscribe. It's the country's most popular spectator sport.

Despite its name, novice observers frequently ask the question: "What rules?" The ball can be kicked or punched in any direction, but never thrown. Players make spectacular leaps vying to catch a kicked ball before it touches the ground, for which they earn a free kick. The game is said to be at its finest in Melbourne.

Melbourne Cricket Ground. The Melbourne Cricket Ground is the prime venue for AFL games. ⊠ *Brunton Ave., Yarra Park* ☎ *03/9657–8867.*

Ticketmaster7. Tickets for Australian Rules Football are available through Ticketek (MCG games) or Ticketmaster (Etihad Stadium) or at the playing fields. ☎ *1300/136122 Ticketmaster, 13-2849 Ticketek* ⊕ *www.ticketmaster.com.au.*

BICYCLING

Melbourne and its environs contain more than 100 km (62 miles) of bike paths, including scenic routes along the Yarra River and Port Phillip Bay. The Beach Road Trail extends 19 km (12 miles) around Port Phillip Bay from Elwood Beach to Sandringham; the new Docklands area of Melbourne can be cycled around—start on the Southbank Promenade, travel west, and then cross over the new Webb Street to Docklands Park and Harbour Esplanade; you can join the Main Yarra Trail bicycle route at the mouth of the Yarra River, just north of the West Gate Bridge or at Southbank. You can then follow the Yarra River for 35 km (22 miles) until it meets up with the Mullum Mullum Creek Trail in Templestowe in Melbourne's eastern suburbs. Bicycle Victoria has all the details on biking trails.

Bikes can be rented for about A$25 per day from trailers alongside the bike paths.

Bicycle Victoria. This company can provide information about area bike paths. Its excellent website has trail maps and descriptions as well as directions. ✉ *4/246 Bourke St., City Center* ☎ *03/8636–8888* ⊕ *www. bv.com.au.*

Real Melbourne Bike Tours. The daily bike tours offered by this company promise to show the best of Melbourne. The four-hour rides (which depart at 10 am) include coffee and cakes in Little Italy and lunch. The company also rents bicycles from A$15 an hour (A$35 per day), and provides a map of five top rides, with suggestions of where to eat and drink. It's on the edge of the Yarra River just near Princes Bridge and Federation Square. ✉ *Vault 14, Federation Sq., City Centre* ☎ *0417/339203* ⊕ *www.rentabike.net.au* ✉ *A$110 per person.*

BOATING

Studley Park Boathouse. Studley Park Boathouse, which opened in 1864, rents canoes, kayaks, and rowboats for journeys on a peaceful stretch of the lower Yarra River, about 7 km (4½ miles) east of the city center. Rentals are A$36 per hour for a two-person canoe or rowboat and A$44 per hour for a four-person rowboat. The boathouse is open daily 9–5 and has a café (lunch and weekend breakfast) and restaurant (weekends) with lovely river views. ✉ *1 Boathouse Rd., Kew* ☎ *03/9853–1828* ⊕ *www.studleyparkboathouse.com.au.*

CAR RACING

Australian Formula 1 Grand Prix. Australian Formula 1 Grand Prix is a popular—but increasingly controversial—fixture on Melbourne's calendar of annual events. It's held every March in the suburb of Albert Park, a small neighborhood 4 km (2½ miles) south of the city that encompasses the area surrounding Albert Park Lake. ✉ *220 Albert Rd., South Melbourne* ☎ *03/9258–7100* ⊕ *www.grandprix.com.au.*

GOLF

Melbourne has the largest number of championship golf courses in Australia.

Albert Park Golf Course. Four kilometers (2½ miles) south of the city, Albert Park Golf Course is an 18-hole, par-72 course beside Albert Park Lake, where the Formula 1 Grand Prix is held in March. Greens fees are A$20 (9 holes, weekdays only) and A$30–A$33 (18 holes). ✉ *Queens Rd., Albert Park* ☎ *03/9510–5588* ⊕ *www.albertparkgolf.com.au.*

Brighton Public Golf Course. The 18-hole, par-67 Brighton Public Golf Course has lovely scenery, with trees and wetlands, but is quite busy on weekends and midweek mornings. Club rental is available. Greens fees are A$20 (9 holes), A$27 (18 holes). ✉ *230 Dendy St., Brighton* ☎ *03/9592–1388* ⊕ *www.brightongolfcourse.com.au.*

Sandringham Golf Links. Five minutes from the beach, Sandringham Golf Course is one of the better public courses, and one of several in Melbourne's renowned (coastal) Sand Belt. Sandringham is an 18-hole, par-72 course. Greens fees are A$30 (18 holes) and A$18.50 (9 holes). ⊠ *Cheltenham Rd., Sandringham* ☎ *03/9598–3590* ⊕ *www. sandringhamgolfcourse.com.au.*

Yarra Bend Golf Course. Despite being just 4 km (2½ miles) northeast from the city, this challenging course seems a world away, due to long length and surrounding parkland. Ten thousand bats have also made it their home on the back 9. A newly built golf range is ideal to practice your game before the round. Greens fees are A$31 (weekdays) and A$37 (weekends). ⊠ *Yarra Bend Rd., Fairfield* ☎ *03/9481–3729* ⊕ *www.yarrabendgolf.com.*

HORSE RACING

Melbourne is the only city in the world to declare a public holiday for a horse race—the Melbourne Cup—held on the first Tuesday in November since 1861. The Cup is also a fashion parade, and most of Melbourne society turns out in full regalia. The rest of the country comes to a standstill, with schools, shops, offices, and factories tuning in to the action.

The city has four top-class racetracks.

Caulfield Race Course. Ten kilometers (6 miles) from the city, Caulfield Race Course runs the Blue Diamond Stakes in February and the Caulfield Cup in October. ⊠ *Station St., Caulfield* ☎ *03/9257–7200* ⊕ *www. melbourneracingclub.net.au.*

Champions: Thoroughbred Racing Gallery. Champions: Thoroughbred Racing Gallery in the National Sports Museum is chock-full of horse-racing information, displays, and a mini-shrine to Australia's most famous racehorse, Phar Lap. ⊠ *Melbourne Cricket Ground, Brunton Ave., Yarra Park* ☎ *03/9657–8879* ⊕ *www.nsm.org.au* ⊟ *A$20* ☺ *10–5 on non-match days.*

Flemington Race Course. Three kilometers (2 miles) outside the city, Flemington Race Course is Australia's premier racecourse and home of the Melbourne Cup in November. ⊠ *448 Epsom Rd., Flemington* ☎ *03/9371–7171* ⊕ *www.vrc.net.au.*

Moonee Valley Race Course. Moonee Valley Race Course is 6 km (4 miles) from town and hosts the Cox Plate race in October. ⊠ *McPherson St., Moonee Ponds* ☎ *03/9373–2222* ⊕ *www.mvrc.net.au.*

Sportingbet Park. This park, 25 km (16 miles) from the city, hosts the Sandown Cup in November. ⊠ *Corrigan Rd. and Princes Hwy., Springvale* ☎ *03/9518–1300* ⊕ *www.sandown.net.au.*

TENNIS

Australian Open. Held in January, the Australian Open is one of the world's four Grand Slam tournaments. You can buy tickets at the event or from Ticketek. ⊠ *Batman Ave.* ⊕ *www.australianopen.com.*

Fawkner Park Tennis Centre. Fawkner Park Tennis Centre has six synthetic-grass outdoor courts. ✉ *Fawkner Park, Toorak Rd. W, South Yarra* ☎ *03/9820–0611* 🌐 *www.fawknerparktenniscentre.com.*

Melbourne Park Tennis Centre. Melbourne Park Tennis Centre has 26 outdoor and 12 hard indoor Rebound Ace courts, plus 8 Italian clay courts. Play is canceled during the Australian Open in January. ✉ *Batman Ave., City Center* ☎ *1300/836647* 🌐 *www.mopt.com.au.*

Powlett Reserve Tennis Centre. Powlett Reserve Tennis Centre has five synthetic-grass outdoor courts. ✉ *Powlett Reserve, Albert St., East Melbourne* ☎ *03/9417–6511* 🌐 *powlettreservetenniscentre.com.*

4

WHERE TO EAT

Melbourne has fabulous food, and is known in some circles as Australia's food capital. The restaurants themselves are often exceptionally stylish and elegant—or totally edgy and funky in their own individual way. Some are even deliberately grungy. The dining scene is a vast smorgasbord of cuisines and experiences that's constantly evolving. The swankiest (and most expensive) restaurants all have five- to eight-course degustation menus (with the opportunity to wine-match each course), but newer restaurants are opting for tapas-style or grazing plates. Flexibility is the new word in dining—restaurants are also funky bars and vice versa.

Prices in the reviews are the average cost of a main course at dinner or, if dinner is not served, at lunch. Use the coordinate (✣ B2) at the end of each listing to locate a site on the corresponding map.

CITY CENTER

$$ ITALIAN

🍴 **Becco.** Every city center needs a place like this, with a drop-in bar and lively dining room. At lunchtime no-time-to-dawdle business types tuck into gnocchi osso bucco with gremolata, while those with a sweet tooth will go weak at the knees over a decadently refreshing mixed gelato with almond praline. Things get a little moodier at night, when a Campari and soda at the bar is an almost compulsory precursor to dinner. [$] *Average main: A$35* ✉ *11–25 Crossley St., City Center* ☎ *03/9663–3000* 🌐 *www.becco.com.au* ✍ *Reservations essential* ⏲ *Closed Sun. and Mon.* ✣ *1:B4.*

$$$$ MODERN AUSTRALIAN

🍴 **ezard.** Chef Teage Ezard's adventurous—and often exhilarating—take on fusion pushes the boundaries between Eastern and Western flavors. Some combinations may appear unusual, like the panfried sesame-crusted John Dory with gnocchi, nettle, black rice paper, Jerusalem artichoke, and chestnut custard, but everything works deliciously at this spot in the funky Adelphi hotel. And as with all upscale restaurants these days, there's an eight-course tasting menu (A$160 per person), this one featuring mouthwatering steamed spanner crab dumplings with Yarra Valley salmon roe, chervil cress, and coconut *tom kha.* A three-course lunch express menu (includes glass of wine) is great value at A$55. The dessert menu by itself is a celebration of indulgence. [$] *Average main: A$53* ✉ *Adelphi Hotel, 187 Flinders La., City*

BEST BETS FOR
MELBOURNE DINING

Fodor's Choice ★	$$	By Cuisine
Anada, $$, p. 242	Anada, p. 242	MODERN AUSTRALIAN
Café di Stasio, $$$, p. 240	D.O.C., p. 239	ezard, $$$$, p. 235
Flower Drum, $$$, p. 236	HuTong Dumpling Bar, p. 237	Taxi Dining Room, $$$, p. 239
HuTong Dumpling Bar, $$, p. 237	The Commoner, p. 244	AUSTRALIAN
I Love Pho 264, $, p. 241	The Town Hall Hotel, p. 244	Charcoal Lane, $$, p. 244
Best by Price	$$$	Donovan's, $$$, p. 241
	Albert St Food and Wine, p. 245	ITALIAN
$	Café di Stasio, p. 240	Caffe e Cucina, $$, p. 241
Babka, p. 242	Flower Drum, p. 236	Grossi Florentino, $$$, p. 236
Brunetti, p. 239	Hanabishi, p. 236	
I Love Pho 264, p. 241	$$$$	MIDDLE EASTERN
MoVida Next Door, p. 237	ezard, p. 235	Abla's, $$, p. 239

Center 📞 *03/9639–6811* ⊕ *www.ezard.com.au* 🍴 *Reservations essential* 🕐 *Closed Sun. No lunch Sat.* ✛ *1:A5.*

$$$ ✕ **Flower Drum.** Superb Cantonese cuisine is the hallmark of one of Aus-
CANTONESE tralia's truly great Chinese restaurants, which is still receiving awards
Fodor's Choice after opening in 1975. The restrained elegance of the decor, deftness of
★ the service, and intelligence of the wine list puts most other restaurants
to shame. Those in the know don't order from the menu at all but sim-
ply ask the waiter to bring the specials, which often changes between
lunch and dinner with the arrival of produce fresh from suppliers; the
Cantonese roast duck is one of the highlights. A delicious finish to the
meal is the sweetened double-boiled almond soup. 💲 *Average main:
A$40* ⊠ *17 Market La., City Center* 📞 *03/9662–3655* ⊕ *www.flower-
drum.com* 🍴 *Reservations essential* 🕐 *No lunch Sun.* ✛ *1:B4.*

$$$ ✕ **Grossi Florentino.** Since 1928, dining at Florentino has meant expe-
ITALIAN riencing the pinnacle of Melbourne hospitality. After taking a seat in
the famous mural room, with its huge chandeliers, wooden panels,
and Florentine murals, you can sample dishes like venison loin with a
juniper crust and heirloom vegetables, and crab ravioli. The five-course
tasting menu, called the Gran Tour (A$140), is also a popular option.
Downstairs, the Grill has more business-like fare, while the Cellar Bar is
perfect for a glass of wine and pasta of the day. 💲 *Average main: A$56*
⊠ *80 Bourke St., City Center* 📞 *03/9662–1811* ⊕ *www.grossiflorentino.
com* 🍴 *Reservations essential* 🕐 *Closed Sun.* ✛ *1:B4.*

$$$ ✕ **Hanabishi.** Touted as the city's best Japanese restaurant, Hanabishi sits
JAPANESE in slightly seedy King Street, an area known for its bars, club venues,

and occasionally unsavory clientele. With wooden floors, blue walls, and traditional ceramic serving trays, Hanabishi is the playground of Osakan chef Akio Soga, whose seasonal menu includes such gems as oven-grilled Patagonian toothfish wrapped in aromatic cedar wood. There are long lists of hot and chilled sake and wines, ranging from reasonable to pricey. The bento boxes, which are culinary works of art, feature sought-after Wagyu beef and are a favorite with the lunchtime crowd. $ *Average main: A$39* ✉ *187 King St., City Center* ☎ *03/9670–1167* ⊕ *www.hanabishi.com.au* ⚞ *Reservations essential* ☉ *Closed weekends.* ✚ *1:A3.*

$$

CHINESE

Fodor's Choice

★

✕ **HuTong Dumpling Bar.** The name means "alleyway" and in a sea of dumpling houses in Melbourne, down this little alleyway, you'll find the best of them all. The boiled pork dumplings are the signature dish (A$13.20 for eight), though the panfried variations of pork, chicken, prawn, and chives hold up well, too. Wantons with Hot Chili Sauce (A$9.80) pack a punch and are great on a cold day. Staff are highly trained and if the space on the ground floor is too snug, ask to go upstairs where there's room to breathe. Bookings are essential, but if you're feeling lucky, arrive at 11:30 am on the dot to try for a table—there will probably already be a line of hopefuls. $ *Average main: A$25* ✉ *14-16 Market La., City Center* ☎ *03/9650–8128* ⊕ *www.hutong. com.au* ✚ *1:B4.*

$

SPANISH

✕ **MoVida Next Door.** As the name suggests, this popular Spanish tapas restaurant is next door to something—in this case the grown-up parent restaurant called MoVida. This is the casual little sister (or daughter) for those who don't want to linger too long over their dinner. Dishes range from tapas (from A$3.50 to A$9.50), like chorizo-filled Catalan potato bomb with spicy sauce, to *racion* (bigger plates ranging from A$12.50 to A$19), which might include pig's ear *a la plancha* (grilled) with guindillas. Finish the meal off with *churros con chocolate* (Spanish fried dough served with a hot, thick chocolate drink). If you're after a bigger meal, book table space at MoVida, next door. Both eateries are owned by Frank Camoora, who's made a big splash in the Melbourne dining scene since 2003. $ *Average main: A$18* ✉ *1 Hosier La., City Center* ☎ *03/9663–3038* ⊕ *www.movida.com.au* ☉ *Closed Mon. No lunch Tues.–Thurs.* ✚ *1:B5.*

$$

MODERN ASIAN

✕ **Seamstress Restaurant & Bar.** This bar-restaurant occupies a heritage-listed four-story building that has housed an undergarment manufacturer, a 1930s sweatshop, and even a brothel and a Buddhist temple (but not at the same time). Asian dishes, in small, medium, and large portions, are designed to be shared. Everything is served in an atmospheric brick-walled first-floor dining area decorated with swaths of fabric, and sewing machines; the wine selection is stored in battered metal luggage lockers. Small dishes include pods of snake bean and golden sweet kumara poached in wanton pastry, green pea, and coriander puree. Favorite medium dishes include the sublime crisp-fried fish of the day—perhaps hapuka—marinated in soybean and garlic paste, and served with a salad of dried guava and aromatic herbs. $ *Average main: A$26* ✉ *113 Lonsdale St., City Center* ☎ *03/9663–6363* ⊕ *www. seamstress.com.au* ☉ *Closed Sun. No lunch Sat.* ✚ *1:B4.*

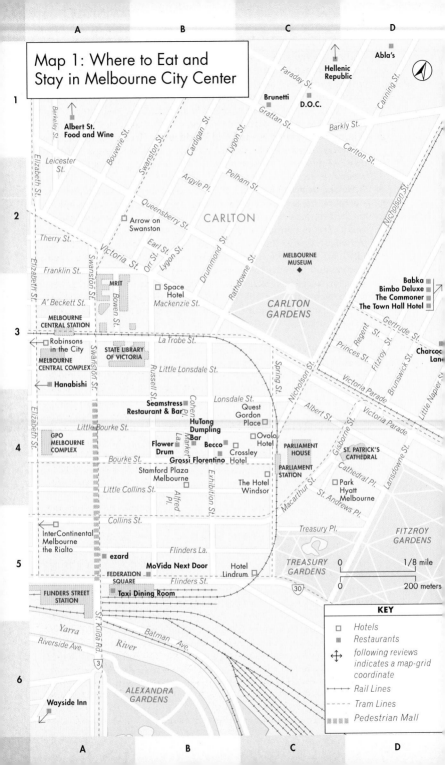

Map 1: Where to Eat and Stay in Melbourne City Center

A **B** **C** **D**

1

Berkeley St.

↑ Albert St. Food and Wine

Leicester St.

Bouverie St.

Swanston St.

Cardigan St.

Faraday St.

Grattan St.

Lygon St.

Brunetti

Hellenic Republic

Abla's

Canning St.

D.O.C.

Barkly St.

Carlton St.

Elizabeth St.

Therry St.

Argyle Pl.

Queensberry St.

Pelham St.

2

Arrow on Swanston

Earl St.

Lygon St.

Orr St.

Drummond St.

Rathdowne St.

CARLTON

MELBOURNE MUSEUM

Nicholson St.

Franklin St.

Victoria St.

Swanston St.

A'Beckett St.

MRIT

Bowen St.

Space Hotel

Mackenzie St.

CARLTON GARDENS

Babka
Bimbo Deluxe
The Commoner
The Town Hall Hotel

MELBOURNE CENTRAL STATION

3

Elizabeth St.

← ■ Robinsons in the City

MELBOURNE CENTRAL COMPLEX

← ■ Hanabishi

STATE LIBRARY OF VICTORIA

La Trobe St.

Little Lonsdale St.

Russell St.

Spring St.

Gertrude St.

Regent St.

Princes St.

Fitzroy St.

Brunswick St.

Charcoa Lane

Victoria Parade

4

GPO MELBOURNE COMPLEX

Swanston St.

Little Bourke St.

Seamstress Restaurant & Bar

Cohen Pl.

Lonsdale St.

Quest Gordon Place

Nicholson St.

Albert St.

Victoria Parade

Gisborne St.

Lansdowne St.

HuTong Dumpling Bar

La... Market...

Becco

Ovolo Hotel

PARLIAMENT HOUSE

ST. PATRICK'S CATHEDRAL

Flower Drum

Bourke St.

Grossi Florentino

Crossley Hotel

PARLIAMENT STATION

Cathedral Pl.

Stamford Plaza Melbourne

Exhibition St.

Little Collins St.

Alfred Pl.

The Hotel Windsor

Macarthur St.

St. Andrews Pl.

Park Hyatt Melbourne

5

Elizabeth St.

Collins St.

InterContinental Melbourne the Rialto

■ ezard

MoVida Next Door

FEDERATION SQUARE

Flinders La.

Flinders St.

Hotel Lindrum

Treasury Pl.

TREASURY GARDENS

FITZROY GARDENS

0   1/8 mile

0   200 meters

FLINDERS STREET STATION

■ Taxi Dining Room

Yarra

Riverside Ave.

River

Batman Ave.

30

6

↙ Wayside Inn

ALEXANDRA GARDENS

St. Kilda Rd.

3

KEY

- □ Hotels
- ■ Restaurants
- ⊕ following reviews indicates a map-grid coordinate
- ┼┼┼ Rail Lines
- - - - Tram Lines
- ▦▦▦ Pedestrian Mall

A **B** **C** **D**

$$$ MODERN AUSTRALIAN 🍴 **Taxi Dining Room.** Occupying an innovatively designed steel-and-glass space above Federation Square, Taxi boasts both extraordinary food and spectacular views over Melbourne. East meets West on a menu that combines Japanese flavors—soy tuna tataki, caramelized orange, and Sake Lee sauce—with such European-inspired fare as slowly braised lamb shoulder with a roasted lamb loin and saltbush jus. There is also an impressive list of new- and Old World wines. To taste some of Australia's best craft beers, have a premeal drink at the Transport Bar on the ground floor. [$] *Average main: A$42* ✉ *Level 1, Transport Hotel, Federation Sq., Flinders St. at St. Kilda Rd., City Center* ☎ *03/9654–8808* 🌐 *www.transporthotel.com.au* ✍ *Reservations essential* ✥ *1:A5.*

$$ STEAKHOUSE 🍴 **Wayside Inn.** Another addition to the city's new wave of gastropubs, this fully renovated historic building is a pleasant walk from bustling Southbank. The menu concentrates on high-quality aged cuts of steak from rural Victoria and Tasmania (which range A$32–$110), but the daily rotisserie, which features a different meat or poultry on the spit, is also popular (Friday's suckling pig is a winner).There's an impressive local craft beer list, knowledgeable staff, and a comfortable beer garden that round out the awesome experience. [$] *Average main: A$35* ✉ *446 City Rd., South Melbourne* ☎ *03/9682–9119* 🌐 *www.waysideinn.com.au* 🕒 *Closed Mon.* ✥ *1:A6.*

CARLTON

$$ LEBANESE 🍴 **Abla's.** Matriarch Abla Amad has been re-creating the much loved family recipes from her homeland of Lebanon since 1979. This intimate restaurant resembles a lounge room of a family house, which with Abla walking around talking to diners, adds to the feeling of being looked after. The signature dish, and one of the most well known in the city, is the exquisitely flavored rice pilaf with minced lamb, chicken, almonds, and pine nuts (A$27); it's also part of a 12-course banquet (A$60) for those hungry enough. Bookings are recommended and you can BYO wine. [$] *Average main: A$30* ✉ *109 Elgin St., Carlton* ☎ *03/9347–0006* 🌐 *www.ablas.com.au* 🕒 *No lunch Sat.–Wed.* ✥ *1:D1.*

$ CAFÉ 🍴 **Brunetti.** First opened in 1974, this iconic Romanesque bakery has moved around Carlton on several occasions, and the masses have followed with it—the latest move being in 2013 when they opened their biggest undertaking in the heart of Lygon Street. Despite its large size, the bakery is still filled with perfect biscotti, mouthwatering cakes, and great service. In addition to an expanded lunch menu, a wood-fire oven—specially imported from Italy—makes pizzas, and you can finish it all off with a perfect espresso—or European-style hot chocolate (thick)—and *cornetto con crema* (custard-filled croissant). You can enjoy all these tempting delights with the opening of branches in Flinders Lane and Myer department store in Bourke Street, while outlets in Fitzroy and Camberwell, a couple of miles east of Richmond, satisfy suburban sugar fiends and coffee cravers. [$] *Average main: A$13* ✉ *380 Lygon St., Carlton* ☎ *03/9347–2801* 🌐 *www.brunetti.com.au* ✥ *1:C1.*

$$ ITALIAN 🍴 **D.O.C.** A major player in Melbourne's pizza wars, D.O.C. has perfected the art of using fresh, simple ingredients to create something special. The real treats lie in their pizza of the day. One with scampi, salsa

Melbourne's restaurant scene is a global potpourri of ethnic influences.

verde, buffalo mozzarella, and mentuccia (a type of mint) might be on offer, or perhaps another with pork and venison sausage, wild mushroom and green chili (around A$25). Whatever is in season or comes in, they will use. A chocolate pizza is at the ready for the sweet tooths. They also have a delicatessen around the corner (✉ *330 Lygon St.*) which could be a good option for a packed lunch, and there's another location in the picturesque seaside town of Mornington. $ *Average main: A$25* ✉ *295 Drummond St., Carlton* ☎ *03/9347–2998* ⊕ *www. docgroup.net* ✛ *1:C1.*

ST. KILDA

$$$ ✕ **Café di Stasio.** This upscale bistro treads a fine line between mannered
ITALIAN elegance and decadence. A sleek marble bar and modishly ravaged walls
Fodor's Choice contribute to the sense that you've stepped into a scene from *La Dolce*
★ *Vita.* Happily, the restaurant is as serious about its food as its sense of style. Crisply roasted duck is now a local legend, and the pasta is always aldente. If the amazingly delicate crayfish omelet is on the menu, do yourself a favor and order it. A lunch special (two courses with wine and coffee) for A$35 is great value if you're nearby. For an informal drink before your meal, a new adjoining bar was built in 2013. $ *Average main: A$39* ✉ *31 Fitzroy St., St. Kilda* ☎ *03/9525–3999* ⊕ *distasio. com.au* ⚐ *Reservations essential* ✛ *2:A6.*

$$$ ✕ **Circa the Prince.** A complete makeover has transformed this previously intimate, silk- and organza-draped restaurant into a light-filled
AUSTRALIAN space featuring a central, glass-roofed courtyard. You could start with mountain-peppered wallaby with quandong caramel, then move on

to McIvor Farm Berkshire suckling pig with honey caramelized daikon with mustard greens. You can also join the sommelier in the see-through cellar to select a bottle from the exhaustive and tempting wine list. $ *Average main: A$39* ✉ *2 Acland St., St. Kilda* ☎ *03/9536–1122* ⊕ *www.circa.com.au/food* ⌕ *Reservations essential* ✣ *2:A6.*

$$
MEDITERRANEAN

✕ **Dog's Bar.** With its blazing fires, artfully smoky walls, and striking, art deco–ish wrought-iron ceiling lights, this two-decade-old restaurant has a lived-in, neighborly look and is an institution for the artistic crowd that frequents it. The food is good, wine is taken very seriously—there are more than 150 wines on the list—and the kitchen is open until late each night. A new art show opens every Sunday and there's live jazz each Sunday night. Throughout the year there are cabaret and comedy acts (admission from around A$15). If you're in St. Kilda, it's definitely a place to visit. $ *Average main: A$22* ✉ *54 Acland St., St. Kilda* ☎ *03/8534–3000* ⊕ *www.dogsbar.com.au* ✣ *2:A6.*

$$$
AUSTRALIAN

✕ **Donovan's.** Grab a window table at this popular bay-side restaurant (housed in the former 1920s bathing pavilion), and enjoy wide-open views of St. Kilda beach and its passing parade of in-line skaters, skateboarders, dog walkers, and ice-cream lickers. As you'd expect, seafood is the highlight, and it's expertly woven into wonderful pastas and risottos, as well as a scrumptious fish soup. A memorable dark chocolate fondant with nougat flavors and Sicilian pistachio ice cream will finish the meal off nicely. Owners Kevin and Gail Donovan are such natural hosts you may feel like bunking down on the plush cushions near the cozy fireplace. $ *Average main: A$44* ✉ *40 Jacka Blvd., St. Kilda* ☎ *03/9534–8221* ⊕ *www.donovanshouse.com.au* ⌕ *Reservations essential* ✣ *2:A6.*

SOUTH YARRA–PRAHRAN

$$
ITALIAN

✕ **Caffe e Cucina.** If you're looking for a quintessential Italian dining experience in a place where it's easy to imagine you're back in the old country, then this is it. Fashionable, look-at-me types flock here for coffee and pastry downstairs, or for more-leisurely meals upstairs in the warm, woody dining room. Try the melt-in-your-mouth gnocchi, or calamari Sant' Andrea (lightly floured and shallow fried). Save room for dessert—the tiramisu is even better looking than the crowd. $ *Average main: A$29* ✉ *581 Chapel St., South Yarra* ☎ *03/9827–4139* ⊕ *www.caffeecucina.com.au* ✣ *2:D5.*

RICHMOND

$
VIETNAMESE
Fodor'sChoice
★

✕ **I Love Pho 264.** Tucking into a steaming bowl of *phở* (traditional noodle soup) at this Victoria Street restaurant is like channeling the backstreets of Hanoi and Saigon. While they also serve crunchy, deep-fried spring rolls and flavor-packed rice-paper rolls, the mainstay of the menu (a blackboard on the wall) is various combinations of *bò* (beef) and *gà* (chicken) with noodles in aromatic stock. Each order comes with a piled plate of Vietnamese mint, bean shoots, and lemon wedges, and there are bottles of chili paste and fish sauce on every mock-marble plastic table. This restaurant is crowded with Vietnamese and other *phở* lovers on weekends, so you often have to queue on the footpath, But turnover is fast so it's never long before you are seated and eating some of Melbourne's best—and cheapest—food. [$] *Average main: A$10* ✉ *264 Victoria St., Richmond* ☎ *03/9427–7749* ✥ *2:C1.*

$$ CAFÉ 🍴 **Richmond Hill Café and Larder.** This bright and buzzy café–cum–produce store is popular with those seeking a late breakfast and brunch that extends well into the day. It's so popular you might have to wait briefly if you haven't booked a table. The bistro fare brims with wonderful flavors, from the pie of the day (perhaps a tartlet of silverbeet and taleggio cheese in a pumpkin and caraway crust) to the hand-cut pappardelle with belted Galloway short-rib ragu. Desserts are mouthwateringly simple and impossible to resist. After you've eaten, pick up some marvelous cheese and country-style bread from the adjoining cheese room and grocery. [$] *Average main: A$25* ✉ *48–50 Bridge Rd., Richmond* ☎ *03/9421–2808* 🌐 *www.rhcl.com.au* 🕒 *No dinner* ✥ *2:C2.*

FITZROY

$$ SPANISH Fodor's Choice ★ 🍴 **Anada.** A chalkboard on the exposed brick wall lists eight dry and six sweet sherries to start (or finish), and there are Spanish and Portuguese wines to accompany your selection of tapas and *raciones* (larger shared plates). Seated at a table or on a stool at the bar, you could begin with rabbit *empanadilla* (pastry pockets) and melt-in-your-mouth black pudding topped with a fried quail egg, and follow with vine-leaf-wrapped sardines with pistachio and orange blossom sauce. But leave room for dessert; the *churros* (Spanish donuts) and chocolate are sinful, while the Pedro Ximenez and muscatel ice cream could make an atheist believe in a culinary god. [$] *Average main: A$25* ✉ *197 Gertrude St., Fitzroy* ☎ *03/9415–6101* 🌐 *anada.com.au* 🕒 *No lunch weekdays* ✥ *2:B1.*

$ CAFÉ 🍴 **Babka.** Food lovers in the know are often found loitering at this tiny, bustling café. Try the excellent pastries, fresh-baked breads, or more-substantial offerings like the Russian borscht (beetroot and cabbage soup) or menemen—scrambled eggs with chili, mint, tomato, and a sprinkling of feta cheese. The corned beef sandwich is also a favorite. It's an all-day brunch-style café, and there are often lines, so be prepared to wait for a table. Some complain that the busy staff can be brusque. [$] *Average main: A$13* ✉ *358 Brunswick St., Fitzroy* ☎ *03/9416–0091* 🕒 *Closed Mon. No dinner* ✥ *1:D3.*

$ CAFÉ 🍴 **Bimbo Deluxe.** This bohemian bar, with deep comfy sofas and the feel of a local student hangout, has the cheapest and possibly the most delicious pizzas in town. On weekdays between noon and 4 pm, Saturday 7 to 9 pm and Monday–Thursday from 7 to 11 pm you can order a dinner-plate-size pizza (from 23 choices) for a mere A$4. The queues of students and hungry lunchers start to form outside around 11:55. If you miss the special, fear not: the same great pizzas are only A$7–A$9 at other times. Try the Agnello (tomato, mozzarella, spiced lamb, arugula, pine nuts, and sultanas). If you're hankering for a sugar rush, there are also sweet pizzas such as Belgian chocolate with mascarpone. A range of chilled infused vodkas—including watermelon and lychee—is available, as well as local craft beers. [$] *Average main: A$8* ✉ *376 Brunswick St., Fitzroy* ☎ *03/9419–8600* 🌐 *www.bimbodeluxe.com.au* ✥ *1:D3.*

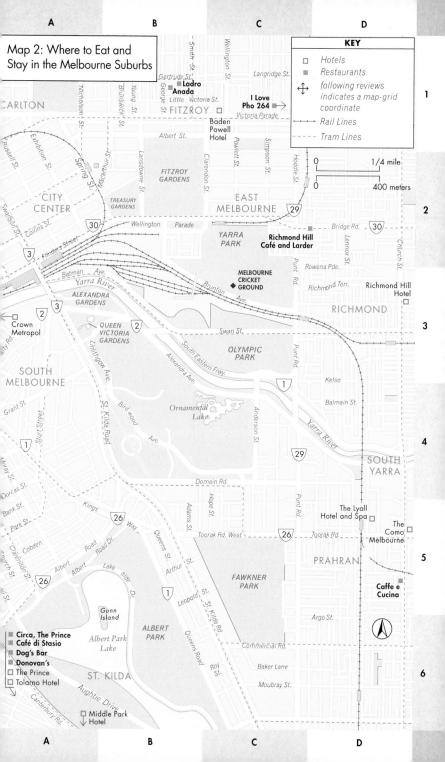

Map 2: Where to Eat and Stay in the Melbourne Suburbs

KEY

- □ Hotels
- ■ Restaurants
- ✛ following reviews indicates a map-grid coordinate
- Rail Lines
- Tram Lines

0 — 1/4 mile
0 — 400 meters

CARLTON

Ladro
Anada

FITZROY

Baden Powell Hotel

I Love Pho 264 →

EAST MELBOURNE

Richmond Hill Café and Larder

Richmond Hill Hotel

RICHMOND

CITY CENTER

MELBOURNE CRICKET GROUND

Crown Metropol

SOUTH MELBOURNE

OLYMPIC PARK

Ornamental Lake

SOUTH YARRA

The Lyall Hotel and Spa

The Como Melbourne

PRAHRAN

Caffe e Cucina

FAWKNER PARK

Gunn Island

Albert Park Lake

ALBERT PARK

- ■ Circa, The Prince
- ■ Café di Stasio
- ■ Dog's Bar
- ■ Donovan's
- □ The Prince
- □ Tolarno Hotel

ST. KILDA

□ Middle Park Hotel ↓

Street labels:
Smith St., Gertrude St., George St., Young St., Brunswick St., Nicholson St., Little Victoria St., Wellington St., Langridge St., Victoria Parade, Albert St., Powlett St., Clarendon St., Simpson St., Hoddie St., Bridge Rd., Lennox St., Church St., Rowena Pde., Richmond Terr., Punt Rd., Swan St., Kelso, Balmain St., Yarra River, Anderson St., South Eastern Frwy., Alexandra Ave., Birdwood Ave., St. Kilda Road, Linlithgow Ave., Queen Victoria Gardens, Alexandra Gardens, Batman Ave., Yarra River, Flinders Street, Collins St., Wellington Parade, Brunton Ave., Yarra Park, Treasury Gardens, Fitzroy Gardens, Lansdowne St., Macarthur St., Spring St., Swanston St., Russell St., Exhibition St., Domain Rd., Hope St., Adams St., Toorak Rd. West, Toorak Rd., Argo St., Commercial Rd., Baker Lane, Moubray St., Kings Way, Queens St., Arthur St., Leopold St., St. Kilda Rd., Lakeside Dr., Queens Road, Roy St., Aughtie Drive, Canterbury Rd., Grant St., Dorcas St., Bank St., Park St., Cobden St., Clarendon St., Church St., Albert Rd., Albert Rd. Dr., Sturt Street, Murray Rd.

$$ ✕**Charcoal Lane.** This young restaurant could be described as taking
AUSTRALIAN a leaf from celebrity chef Jamie Oliver's book, in that disadvantaged
people are given an opportunity to transform their lives by gaining a
traineeship in the restaurant business. Named after a song by acclaimed
Aboriginal singer/songwriter Archie Roach, Charcoal Lane is a joint
project between the charity Mission Australia and the Victorian Aborig-
inal Health Service. It is housed in the former health service community
center, dubbed Charcoal Lane by the many Aboriginal people who
for decades would drop in and swap stories and wisdom. The menu
includes many Australian bushland ingredients, and the dishes have an
Aboriginal influence. They might include starters of roasted marron
(freshwater crayfish) fondue with angel hair, lemon myrtle, and baby
basil, and hearty main courses such as kangaroo with broccoli puree,
black trumpette (mushrooms), truffle gnocchi, and bitter chocolate.
$ *Average main: A$35* ✉ *136 Gertrude St., Fitzroy* ☎ *03/9418–3400*
⊕ *www.charcoallane.com.au* ⊙ *Closed Sun. and Mon.* ✛ *1:D3.*

$$ ✕**The Commoner.** The street-facing dining room here is packed with
MODERN BRITISH young couples enjoying some of the town's best and most eclectic U.K.-
inspired food. The menu features "small food" taste sensations like
char-grilled octopus, blood orange, green peppers, and squid ink, and
more substantial offerings such as rolled pork belly, black pudding,
rutabaga, and grains. There's a roast every Sunday lunch, and regular set-price theme nights, such as "A Duck's Tale." The wine list has
depth in both Aussie and international selections. The space itself is
cozy, featuring original art, and there's an enclosed garden out back.
$ *Average main: A$32* ✉ *122 Johnston St., Fitzroy* ☎ *03/9415–6876*
⊕ *www.thecommoner.com.au* ⊙ *Closed Mon. and Tues. No lunch Wed.
and Thurs.* ✛ *1:D3.*

$$ ✕**Ladro.** A local favorite, this stellar Italian bistro emphasizes flavor
ITALIAN over starchy linen and stuffy attitude. Here eggplant is molded into
gentle round polpettes (meatball-like mounds), lamb rump is scented
with garlic and parsley and slow-roasted to impossible tenderness, and
the service is as upbeat as the wine list. Delicious wood-fired pizzas, that
some insist are the best in the city, are yet another reason to visit this
suburban gem (thankfully, it's only a short walk from the city). $ *Aver-
age main: A$26* ✉ *224 Gertrude St., Fitzroy* ☎ *03/9415–7575* ⊕ *ladro.
com.au* ⌂ *Reservations essential* ⊙ *No lunch Mon.–Sat.* ✛ *2:B1.*

$$ ✕**The Town Hall Hotel.** Considered one of the city's best gastropubs, the
MODERN ITALIAN husband-and-wife team of Michelle and Harry Lilai offer a refined taste
of Italy within a friendly and casual setting. In the bistro area you'll
find seasonal produce layered with Italian touches. Seared beef carpaccio with truffled beef tartare and Reggiano shavings is a good starter,
followed by roasted pheasant breast with cabbage and leg sausage in
vermouth and raisin jus. A casual bar area offers more-standard pub
fare but follows the same high standards in the kitchen. A great value
lunch menu (two courses with wine, A$35) is also available; be sure to
take a look at their selection of local craft beer. $ *Average main: A$35*
✉ *166 Johnston St., Fitzroy* ☎ *03/9416–5055* ⊕ *townhallhotel.net.au*
⊙ *Closed Mon.* ✛ *1:D3.*

BRUNSWICK

$$$ MEDITERRANEAN 🍴 **Albert St Food and Wine.** Many diners will be tempted to head straight to the dessert menu here, as Executive Chef Philippa Sibley is regarded as one of the country's finest dessert and pastry chefs. Her take on the humble Snickers bar has become a well-known indulgence, though it would be naive to ignore the rest of the Mediterranean-inspired menu. Housed in a former bank, the big airy room has a lively yet elegant feel. Dishes are seasonal and change regularly based on the availability of local organic produce. The pressed rabbit terrine is a nice beginning followed by their choucroute (French for dressed sauerkraut), which is rare on menus around town. An impressive wine list is at the ready, too. [$] *Average main: A$36* ✉ *382 Sydney Rd., Brunswick* 🌐 *www.albertst.com.au* 🕓 *Closed Mon.* ✥ *1:A1.*

$$ MODERN GREEK 🍴 **Hellenic Republic.** Owned by well-known TV chef George Calombaris, Hellenic Republic pays homage to Calombaris's Greek heritage, creating a lively taverna type setting with a focus on communal food. We suggest the Travezi Menu (A$58), which consists of 14 courses including meat from the omnipresent spit, whose mouthwatering scent envelopes the room upon entering. Scallops with skordalia crust are also excellent and straight off the boat. Naturally, the friendly staff will try to entice you into having a sip of ouzo, and since everyone else seems to be doing it, we suggest you do, too. [$] *Average main: A$30* ✉ *34 Lygon St., Brunswick East* ☎ *03/9381–1222* 🌐 *hellenicrepublic.com.au* 🕓 *No lunch Mon.–Thurs.* ✥ *1:C1.*

WHERE TO STAY

For expanded hotel reviews, visit Fodors.com.

CITY CENTER

$$$ HOTEL 🏨 **Crossley Hotel.** There's an unexpected sense of space and lots of light in this compact boutique hotel half a block from Chinatown. **Pros:** great location; good restaurant; reasonable price; **Cons:** redecorations planned over the next year. [$] *Rooms from: A$180* ✉ *51 Little Bourke St., City Center* ☎ *03/9639–1639* 🛏 *84 rooms, 4 apartments* 🍽 *Breakfast* ✥ *1:B4.*

$$$ HOTEL 🏨 **Crown Metropol.** Crown Casino's newest hotel may be huge (it has 665 rooms, making it one of the country's biggest), but it still retains an elegant boutique-type feel. **Pros:** casino area might not appeal to all. **Cons:** professional service; great spa center. [$] *Rooms from: A$255* ✉ *8 Whiteman St., Southbank* ☎ *03/9292–6211* 🌐 *www.crownmetropolmelbourne.com.au* 🛏 *632 rooms, 33 apartments* 🍽 *Breakfast* ✥ *2:A3.*

$$$ HOTEL 🏨 **Hotel Lindrum.** Housed in the heritage-listed Lindrum family billiards center, a short walk from Federation Square, this is one of Melbourne's savviest boutique properties. **Pros:** warm feel; exceptional service; full in-room entertainment systems. **Cons:** on busy thoroughfare. [$] *Rooms from: A$235* ✉ *26 Flinders St., City Center* ☎ *03/9668–1111* 🌐 *www.hotellindrum.com.au* 🛏 *59 rooms* 🍽 *Breakfast* ✥ *1:C5.*

$$$$
HOTEL
Fodor'sChoice
★

The Hotel Windsor. Built in 1883, this aristocrat of Melbourne hotels combines Victorian-era character with modern comforts, and is a must for history lovers. **Pros:** elegant heritage feel; central location. **Cons:** heritage rooms are fittingly Old World in decor. $ *Rooms from: A$385* ⊠ *111 Spring St., City Center* ☎ *03/9633–6000* ⊕ *www.thehotelwindsor.com.au* ⤳ *160 rooms, 20 suites* ⦿ *Breakfast* ⊹ *1:C4.*

$$$$
HOTEL

InterContinental Melbourne The Rialto. Tucked away behind one of Melbourne's most iconic Gothic facades, The Rialto is a five-star luxury hotel designed by William Pitt, the architect behind many Melbourne landmarks. **Pros:** spectacular, historic facade; great bar and club lounge. **Cons:** slightly corporate feel; fee for in-room Wi-Fi. $ *Rooms from: A$315* ⊠ *495 Collins St., City Center* ☎ *03/8627–1400* ⊕ *www.melbourne.intercontinental.com* ⤳ *253 rooms* ⦿ *No meals* ⊹ *1:A5.*

$$
HOTEL

Middle Park Hotel. In the picturesque suburb of Middle Park, towards the lively St. Kilda area, this 25-room hotel has been stylishly designed by renowned local architects Six Degrees, giving the 125-year-old building new life. **Pros:** historic surroundings; warm service. **Cons:** might be too far from city for some. $ *Rooms from: A$180* ⊠ *102 Canterbury Rd., Middle Park* ☎ *03/9690–1958* ⊕ *middleparkhotel.com.au* ⤳ *25 rooms* ⦿ *Breakfast* ⊹ *2:A6.*

$$$
HOTEL

Ovolo Hotel. Opened in late 2012, much effort has gone into making this 43-room boutique hotel uniquely stylish and comfortable, including its laneway location, which is ideal for those who want to be in the heart of the action. **Pros:** latest entertainment technology in the rooms; central location. **Cons:** area can be noisy late at night. $ *Rooms from: A$240* ⊠ *19 Little Bourke St., City Center* ☎ *03/8692–0777* ⊕ *www.ovolohotels.com* ⤳ *40 rooms, 3 penthouse suites* ⦿ *Breakfast* ⊹ *1:C4.*

$$$$
HOTEL
Fodor'sChoice
★

Park Hyatt Melbourne. Set right next to Fitzroy Gardens and opposite St. Patrick's Cathedral, this is one of Melbourne's most elegant hotels. **Pros:** lavish appointments; world-class service. **Cons:** fee for in-room Wi-Fi. $ *Rooms from: A$305* ⊠ *1 Parliament Sq., East Melbourne* ☎ *03/9224–1234* ✎ *Melbourne@hyatt.com.au* ⊕ *www.Hyatt.com* ⤳ *216 rooms, 24 suites* ⦿ *Breakfast* ⊹ *1:C4.*

$$
HOTEL

Quest Gordon Place. This National Trust–listed 1884 lodging house is one of the most interesting and comfortable apartment hotels in the city. **Pros:** modern apartment-style furnishings; great location. **Cons:** homey feel. $ *Rooms from: A$179* ⊠ *24 Little Bourke St., City Center* ☎ *03/9663–2888* ⊕ *www.questgordonplace.com.au* ⤳ *64 apartments* ⦿ *No meals* ⊹ *1:C4.*

$$
B&B/INN

Robinsons in the City. Melbourne's tiniest and possibly quaintest hotel occupies a converted 1850s bakery and 1906 baker's house. **Pros:** CBD-fringe location; great breakfast included; close to free city circle tram and free shuttle bus. **Cons:** a bit of a walk from the city center. $ *Rooms from: A$190* ⊠ *405 Spencer St., at Batman St., West Melbourne* ☎ *03/9329–2552* ⊕ *www.ritc.com.au* ⤳ *6 rooms* ⦿ *Breakfast* ⊹ *1:A3.*

$
HOTEL

Space Hotel. Located just minutes from bustling Lygon Street, Carlton Gardens, and Queen Victoria Market, this family-run venue targets budget travelers who like a bit more comfort. **Pros:** central location; newly appointed rooms. **Cons:** can get noisy with lively patrons. $ *Rooms* *from: A$80* ✉ *380 Russell St., City Center* ☎ *03/9662–3888* 🌐 *www.spacehotel.com.au* 🛏 *128 rooms* 🍴 *No meals* ✥ *1:B3.*

$$$$ HOTEL **Stamford Plaza Melbourne.** Diamond-faceted glass elevators carry guests from the marble lobby of this "Paris-end," all-suite hotel to rooms decorated with plush, rich hued velvets and art deco–ish crystal lamps. **Pros:** lush decor; great restaurant; central location. **Cons:** might not appeal to lovers of minimalist contemporary decor. [$] *Rooms from: A$365* ✉ *111 Little Collins St., City Center* ☎ *03/9659–1000* 🌐 *www.stamford.com.au* 🛏 *283 rooms* 🍴 *Breakfast* ✥ *1:B4.*

CARLTON

$ HOTEL **Arrow on Swanston.** Location and great value make up for the limited space in this CBD-edge hotel. **Pros:** easy walk to eateries and CBD attractions; inexpensive. **Cons:** limited space. [$] *Rooms from: A$110* ✉ *488 Swanston St., Carlton* ☎ *03/9225–9000* 🌐 *www.arrowonswanston.com.au* 🛏 *47 rooms, 38 apartments* 🍴 *No meals* ✥ *1:A2.*

ST. KILDA

$$$ HOTEL **The Prince.** Cutting-edge design, contemporary artworks and sculptural furniture, and spare yet inviting luxury make this boutique hotel perfect for aficionados of unfussy elegance. **Pros:** super comfortable rooms; gallery feel; great location. **Cons:** the modern shapes and neutral hues might not appeal to some. [$] *Rooms from: A$210* ✉ *2 Acland St., St. Kilda* ☎ *03/9536–1111* 🌐 *www.theprince.com.au* 🛏 *40 rooms* 🍴 *Breakfast* ✥ *2:A6.*

$$ HOTEL **Tolarno Hotel.** Set in the heart of St. Kilda's café, bar, and club precinct, Tolarno Hotel was once owned by artists who ran a gallery out of the space, and it still has an idiosyncratic artistic bent. **Pros:** great restaurant; cool vibe; heart-of-breezy-St. Kilda location. **Cons:** area can have a dubious crowd; can be noisy late at night; no elevator. [$] *Rooms from: A$155* ✉ *42 Fitzroy St., St. Kilda* ☎ *03/9537–0200* 🌐 *www.hoteltolarno.com.au* 🛏 *36 rooms* 🍴 *No meals* ✥ *2:A6.*

SOUTH YARRA–PRAHRAN

$$$ HOTEL Fodor's Choice ★ **The Como Melbourne.** With its opulent and funky modern furnishings, this luxury hotel is as popular with business travelers as it is with visiting artists and musicians. **Pros:** lavishly appointed rooms; great shopping and restaurants nearby. **Cons:** outside the city center. [$] *Rooms from: A$232* ✉ *630 Chapel St., South Yarra* ☎ *03/9825–2222* 🌐 *www.accorhotels.com* 🛏 *107 suites* 🍴 *Breakfast* ✥ *2:D5.*

$$$$ HOTEL **The Lyall Hotel and Spa.** The spacious one- and two-bedroom suites at this exclusive hotel make an art form of understated elegance, and they come with all the luxuries: CD and DVD players, velour bathrobes and slippers, gourmet minibars, and a pillow "menu." **Pros:** an extravagant spa; 24-hour bistro; 24-hour gym. **Cons:** outside city center. [$] *Rooms from: A$306* ✉ *14 Murphy St., South Yarra* ☎ *03/9868–8222* 🌐 *www.thelyall.com* 🛏 *40 suites* 🍴 *Breakfast* ✥ *2:D5.*

RICHMOND

$ HOTEL **Richmond Hill Hotel.** Just a short ride from the city center (on the No. 70 tram), this inexpensive boutique hotel occupies a garden-fronted 1918 mansion.**Pros:** city-fringe location; friendly service. **Cons:** somewhat spartan digs; a bit maze-like; front rooms get peak-hour traffic noise. [$] *Rooms from: A$132* ✉ *353 Church St., Richmond* ☎ *03/9428–6501* 🌐 *www.richmondhillhotel.com.au* 🛏 *42 rooms* 🍴 *Breakfast* ✣ *2:D3.*

EAST MELBOURNE

$ HOTEL **Baden Powell Hotel.** One of the best ways to experience Melbourne's historic pubs is to stay inside one, and the well-appointed Baden Powell Hotel is an ideal fit. **Pros:** food location for sport and nightlife; good value. **Cons:** strict check-in times; can be noisy on weekends. [$] *Rooms from: A$110* ✉ *61 Victoria Parade, Collingwood* ☎ *03/9486–0811* 🌐 *www.badenpowellhotel.com.au* 🛏 *11 rooms* 🍴 *No meals* ✣ *2:C1.*

NIGHTLIFE AND THE ARTS

THE ARTS

Melbourne Events, available from tourist outlets, is a comprehensive monthly guide to what's happening in town. For a complete listing of performing-arts events, galleries, and films, consult the "EG" (Entertainment Guide) supplement in the Friday edition of *The Age* newspaper. Tourism Victoria hosts a fantastic website (🌐 *www.visitmelbourne.com*) detailing all of Melbourne's upcoming and current events. The free local music magazine *Beat* is available at cafés, stores, markets, and bars. *Brother Sister* is the local gay paper.

MUSIC AND DANCE

Australian Ballet. In the 2,000-seat State Theatre at the Arts Centre, the Australian Ballet stages five programs annually, and presents visiting celebrity dancers from around the world. ✉ *The Arts Centre, 100 St. Kilda Rd., Southbank* ☎ *03/9669–2700, 13–6100 Ticketmaster* 🌐 *www.australianballet.com.au.*

Hamer Hall. This is Melbourne's premier concert venue and home to Melbourne Symphony Orchestra. ✉ *The Arts Centre, 100 St. Kilda Rd., Southbank* ☎ *03/9281–8000.*

Melbourne Symphony Orchestra. The Melbourne Symphony Orchestra performs year-round in the 2,600-seat Hamer Hall. ✉ *The Arts Centre, 100 St. Kilda Rd., Southbank* ☎ *13–6100 Ticketmaster* 🌐 *www.mso.com.au.*

Sidney Myer Music Bowl. Open-air concerts take place December through March at the Sidney Myer Music Bowl. ✉ *King's Domain near Swan St. Bridge, Melbourne* ☎ *13–6100 Ticketmaster.*

THEATER

Comedy Theatre. Revues and plays are staged at the Comedy Theatre, which along with the Princess, Regent, and Forum theaters is owned by the Marriner Group and often uses the same telephone number. ⊠ *240 Exhibition St., City Center* ☎ *03/9299–9800, 1300/111011* ⊕ *www.marrinergroup.com.au.*

fortyfivedownstairs. Cutting-edge independent theater, cabaret acts, and exhibitions are featured at fortyfivedownstairs. ⊠ *45 Flinders La., City Center* ☎ *03/9662–9966* ⊕ *www.fortyfivedownstairs.com.*

Half-Tix. The Half-Tix ticket booth in the Melbourne Town Hall sells tickets to theater attractions at half price on performance days. It's open Monday 10–2, Tuesday–Thursday 11–6, Friday 11–6:30, and Saturday 10–4. Phone for information about shows on sale (recorded message). No phone transactions and sales are cash only. ⊠ *Melbourne Town Hall, Swanston and Collins Sts., City Center* ☎ *03/9650–9420* ⊕ *www.halftixmelbourne.com.*

Melbourne Theatre Company. Australia's oldest professional theater company stages up to 12 productions per year in various venues around the city including the Arts Centre in St. Kilda Road. ⊠ *140 Southbank Blvd., Southbank* ☎ *03/8688–0800 box office* ⊕ *www.mtc.com.au.*

Playbox at the CUB Malthouse Company. The city's second-largest company, the **Malthouse Theatre**, stages about 10 new or contemporary productions a year. The CUB Malthouse is a flexible theater space designed for drama, dance, and circus performances. ⊠ *113 Sturt St., Southbank* ☎ *03/9685–5111* ⊕ *www.malthousetheatre.com.au.*

Regent Theatre. An ornate 1920s building, the Regent originally opened to screen movies but nowadays presents mainstream theatrical productions. ⊠ *191 Collins St., City Center* ☎ *03/9299–9800, 1300/111011 box office* ⊕ *www.marrinergroup.com.au.*

Theatre Works. This theater concentrates on contemporary Australian plays. ⊠ *14 Acland St., St. Kilda* ☎ *03/9534–3388* ⊕ *www.theatreworks.org.au.*

NIGHTLIFE

Most of the central city's dance clubs are along the King Street strip or nestled in Little Collins Street. Clubs usually open at 9 or 10 weekends and some weeknights, and stay open until the early-morning hours. Expect to pay a small cover at most clubs—between A$10 and A$15.

CITY CENTER

BARS

The Atrium Bar on 35. This cocktail bar on the 35th floor of the Sofitel Melbourne on Collins has spectacular views. ⊠ *25 Collins St., City Center* ☎ *03/9653–0000.*

Cookie. Located in a lofty warehouse-style space with exposed ceiling pipes and a balcony, Cookie focuses on domestic and international craft beer and great Thai food. ⊠ *252 Swanston St., City Center* ☎ *03/9663–7660* ⊕ *cookie.net.au.*

Gin Palace. Reminiscent of Hollywood's golden era, Gin Palace has more than enough types of martinis to satisfy any taste. ✉ *10 Russell Pl.(off Bourke St.), City Center* ☎ *03/9654–0533* ⊕ *ginpalace.com.au.*

Melbourne Supper Club. Age-buffed leather sofas, cigars, and an exhaustive wine list characterize the classy Melbourne Supper Club. ✉ *161 Spring St., City Center* ☎ *03/9654–6300.*

Mitre Tavern. One of the oldest pubs in town, locals love the unpretentious vibe, and U.K.-like surrounding. It's especially popular with nine-to-fivers who like an after-work beer. ✉ *5 Bank Pl., City Center* ☎ *03/9670–5644* ⊕ *www.mitretavern.com.au.*

Section 8. Located in a car park, and housed in a shipping container, Section 8 is a reliably trendy bar, popular with the artsy student crowd. ✉ *27–29 Tattersalls La., City Center* ☎ *0430/291–588* ⊕ *www.section8. com.au.*

Silk Road. Silk Road is an exotic bar with lavish decor and a serious collection of chandeliers. It's themed Venetian Bar and Shahanshah Lounge are gorgeous places for a drink. ✉ *425 Collins St., City Center* ☎ *03/9614–4888* ⊕ *www.silkroadmelbourne.com.*

COMEDY CLUBS

Last Laugh Comedy Club. This is a popular place to see top-class Australian and international comedy acts. ✉ *Athenaeum Theatre, 188 Collins St., City Center* ☎ *03/9650–6668* ⊕ *www.thecomedyclub.com.au.*

MUSIC CLUBS

Bennetts Lane. Bennetts is one of Melbourne's jazz mainstays, with international acts and the occasional megastar (like Prince) popping in. ✉ *25 Bennetts La., City Center* ☎ *03/9663–2856* ⊕ *www.bennettslane.com.*

Cherry Bar. This small and intimate rock 'n' roll bar is located on AC/DC Lane. The address alone says it all. ✉ *AC/DC La., City Center* ☎ *03/9639–8122* ⊕ *www.cherrybar.com.au.*

Ding Dong Lounge. You can catch headline rock acts at the Ding Dong Lounge. ✉ *Level 1, 18 Market La., City Center* ☎ *03/9662–1020* ⊕ *www.dingdonglounge.com.au.*

The Hi-Fi. The Hi-Fi is a popular venue for live local and lesser-known international rock bands. ✉ *125 Swanston St., City Center* ☎ *1300/843443 tickets* ⊕ *www.thehifi.com.au.*

Kitten Club. Tony Starr's Kitten Club has a 1950s feel (Dean Martin songs are popular) and there's weekend jazz; the opulent ladies' powder room is a big hit with the girls. ✉ *267 Little Collins St., City Center* ☎ *03/9650–2448* ⊕ *www.kittenclub.com.au.*

RICHMOND
MUSIC CLUBS

Corner Hotel. The Corner Hotel has alternative, reggae, rock, blues, and jazz acts with an emphasis on homegrown bands. Tasty pub meals can be had on the rooftop for a pre-gig dinner. ✉ *57 Swan St., Richmond* ☎ *03/9427–7300 bar, 03/9427–9198 tickets* ⊕ *cornerhotel.com.*

ST. KILDA
BARS

Fodor's Choice ★

Esplanade Hotel. Not only is this hallowed live music venue a great place to see local bands, but the Esplanade, or "Espy," is a historic pub—built in 1878—listed with the National Trust. ✉ *11 Upper Esplanade, St. Kilda* ☎ *03/9534–0211* ⊕ *www.espy.com.au.*

CONCERT VENUE

Palais Theatre. This theater features film, music festival openings, and concerts by Australian and international acts such as the Soweto Gospel Choir and Joe Bonamassa. ✉ *Lower Esplanade, St. Kilda* ☎ *03/9525–3240, 13–6100 Ticketmaster* ⊕ *www.palaistheatre.net.au.*

> ### A FUNNY NIGHT OUT
>
> Melburnians love a laugh, and the annual comedy festival is the funniest place to be to catch top Australian and international performers. The monthlong event takes place in the Town Hall and venues across town, and there are free events in open spaces. The festival also seeks out new talent and culminates with the Raw Comedy award for the best new Australian stand-up performer. If you're in town in April, you won't be laughing if you miss it. ⊕ *www.comedyfestival.com.au.*

4

MUSIC CLUBS

Prince of Wales. For rock and roll, punk, and grunge, head to the Prince Bandroom at the Prince of Wales, which attracts a straight and gay crowd. ✉ *29 Fitzroy St., St. Kilda* ☎ *03/9536–1168.*

FITZROY
BARS

The Everleigh. Since opening in 2011, The Everleigh has become one of the city's best cocktail bars. The dark lighting and soft tunes makes this the perfect spot for couples. ✉ *150–156 Gertrude St., upstairs, Fitzroy* ☎ *03/9416–2229* ⊕ *www.theeverleigh.com.*

Polly. Mix with coloful and quirky clientele and enjoy a traditional or contemporary cocktail—there are 55 conconctions to choose from; Polly's decor is a blend of 1920s style red-velvet lounges, gilt mirrors, and chandeliers. ✉ *401 Brunswick St., Fitzroy* ☎ *03/9417–0880* ⊕ *www.pollybar.com.au.*

MUSIC CLUBS

Night Cat. The Night Cat hosts bands and DJ's playing AfroCuban to disco dance music Thursday to Saturday evenings and the Latin big band on Sunday nights is legendary. ✉ *141 Johnston St., Fitzroy* ☎ *03/9417–0090* ⊕ *www.thenightcat.com.au.*

The Rainbow. Most nights of the week, for the past few decades, this great pub, located down a backstreet, has been showcasing local acts. There's also a great range of craft beers available, which you can enjoy in the beer garden during the warmer months. ✉ *27 St. David St., Fitzroy* ☎ *03/9419–4193* ⊕ *therainbow.com.au.*

Melbourne is known for its top-notch live theater.

SOUTH YARRA–PRAHRAN

BARS

Revolver Upstairs. This bar caters predominantly to the young partygoers, with early-morning recovery sessions—a time for revelers around town to keep on partying—that are especially popular. ✉ *229 Chapel St., Prahran* ☎ *03/9521–5985* ⊕ *revolverupstairs.com.au.*

BRUNSWICK

BARS

Alehouse Project. Regarded as having one of the best beer lists in the city, this local favorite also has an excellent menu, matched especially to the beers on offer. Head to the beer garden out the back in the warmer months. ✉ *280 Sydney Rd., Brunswick East* ☎ *03/9380–4090* ⊕ *www.thealehouseproject.com.au.*

Retreat Hotel. This expansive pub has local bands performing most nights of the week. It also has one of the city's best beer gardens. ✉ *280 Sydney Rd., Brunswick* ☎ *03/9380–4090* ⊕ *www.retreathotelbrunswick.com.au.*

Union Hotel. This family-friendly pub showcases local music on weekends. The atmosphere is always friendly and welcoming. ✉ *109 Union St., Brunswick West* ☎ *03/9388–2235* ⊕ *unionhotelbrunswick.com.au.*

SOUTH MELBOURNE AND SOUTHBANK

CASINO

Crown Casino. Melbourne's first gambling center has blackjack, roulette, and poker machines. The casino is part of the Crown Entertainment Complex, which also has dozens of restaurants, including branches of the famed Japanese chef Nobu and renowned Sydney chef Neil Perry's

Rockpool, shops, bars, and two nightclubs open until late. The Palms at Crown hosts international and Australian headliners. The casino is on the south bank of the Yarra. ⊠ *8 Whiteman St., Southbank* ☎ *03/9292–8888* ⊕ *www.crowncasino.com.au* ☽ *Daily 24 hrs.*

SHOPPING

Melbourne has firmly established itself as the nation's fashion capital. Australian designer labels are available on High Street in Armadale, on Toorak Road and Chapel Street in South Yarra, and on Bridge Road in Richmond. High-quality vintage clothing abounds on Greville Street in Prahran. Discount hunters will love the huge DFO (Discount Factory Outlet) right next door to Southern Cross Station on Spencer Street, with its many stores. Most shops are open Monday–Thursday 9–5:30, Friday until 9, and Saturday until 5. Major city stores are open Sunday until 5.

CITY CENTER

CLOTHING

Jack London. This trendy shop has British and European styled Mod Rocker gear, specializing in winter coats for men. Various locations are dotted around town including Shop 1/258 Flinders Lane in City Center, 238 Brunswick Street, Fitzroy, and 246 Chapel Street, Prahran. ⊠ *301 Swanston St., City Center* ☎ *03/9639–2144* ⊕ *www.jacklondon. com.au.*

DEPARTMENT STORES AND SHOPPING CENTERS

Block Arcade. An elegant 19th-century shopping plaza with mosaic-tile floors, Block Arcade contains the venerable Hopetoun Tea Rooms, the French Jewel Box, Orrefors Kosta Boda, Dasel Dolls and Bears, and Australian By Design. ⊠ *282 Collins St., City Center* ☎ *03/9654–5244* ⊕ *www.theblockarcade.com.au.*

Bourke Street Mall. Once the busiest east–west thoroughfare in the city, Bourke Street Mall is a pedestrian-only zone—but watch out for those trams! Two of the city's biggest department stores are here; an essential part of growing up in Melbourne is being taken to Myer at Christmas to see the window displays. ⊠ *Bourke St., City Center.*

Myer. Myer is one of the country's largest department stores, carrying myriad casual and luxury brands for men and women. ⊠ *314–336 Bourke St., between Elizabeth and Swanston Sts., City Center* ☎ *03/9661–1111.*

David Jones. This big department store has a large array of luxury brands for both men and women. ⊠ *310 Bourke St., between Elizabeth and Swanston Sts., City Center* ☎ *03/9643–2222.*

Bridge Road. In Richmond at the end of Flinders Street, east of the city, Bridge Road is a popular shopping strip for women's retail fashion that caters to all budgets. ⊠ *Bridge Rd., Richmond.*

Flinders Lane. Dotted with chic boutiques, many of them selling merchandise by up-and-coming Australian designers, Flinders Lane will make fashionistas happy. Between Swanston and Elizabeth streets, look for shops such as the boudoir-like accessories outlet *Christine* and *Alice Euphemia* (in Cathedral Arcade), which stocks eclectic, sometimes whimsical, clothing by young designers. ⊠ *Flinders La., City Center.*

Little Collins Street. A precinct of stores frequented by shoppers with perhaps more money than sense, Little Collins Street is still worth a visit. In between frock shops you'll find musty stores selling classic film posters, antique and estate jewelry, and Australian opals. At the eastern end of **Collins Street,** beyond the cream-and-red Romanesque facade of St. Michael's Uniting Church, is the **Paris End,** a name coined by Melburnians to identify the elegance of its fashionable shops as well as its general hauteur. Here you find big-name international designer clothing, bags and jewelry. ⊠ *Little Collins St., City Center.*

Melbourne Central. Here you'll find a dizzying shopping complex huge enough to enclose an 1880s redbrick shot tower (used to make bullets) in its atrium. ⊠ *300 Lonsdale St., City Center* ☎ *03/9922–1100.*

Royal Arcade. Built in 1846, Royal Arcade is Melbourne's oldest shopping plaza. It remains a lovely place to browse, and it's home to the splendid Gaunt's Clock, which tolls away the hours. ⊠ *355 Bourke St., City Center.*

Southgate. Southgate has a spectacular riverside location. The shops and eateries here are a short walk from both the city center across Princes Bridge and the Arts Center. There's outdoor seating next to the Southbank promenade. ⊠ *4 Southbank Promenade, Southbank* ☎ *03/9699–4311.*

MARKETS

Queen Victoria Market. This market has buzzed with food and bargain shoppers since 1878. With more than 1,000 mostly open-air stalls, this sprawling, spirited bazaar is the city's prime produce outlet—many Melburnians come here to buy strawberries, fresh flowers, imported cheeses, meat, and eye-bright fresh fish. On Sunday there is less food and more great deals on jeans, T-shirts, and souvenirs. It's open Tuesday and Thursday 6–2, Friday 6–5, Saturday 6–3, and Sunday 9–4. Market tours take you deep inside the labyrinth, and cooking classes are conducted by well-known chefs. Wandering entertainers and aromatic hot food stalls add to the vibe at the Suzuki Night Market, open 5:30–10 pm on Wednesday from November to late-February; this market focuses on art, crafts, and gifts. ⊠ *Elizabeth and Victoria Sts., City Center* ☎ *03/9320–5822* ⊕ *www.qvm.com.au.*

SHOES AND LEATHER GOODS

Mlag. If you're looking for high-quality European leather products for men and women, head to Mlag. ⊠ *31–33 Bridge Rd., Richmond* ☎ *03/9078–5181* ⊕ *www.mlag.com.au.*

ST. KILDA

MARKETS

The Esplanade Market St. Kilda. Open since 1970, this market started as an outlet for local artists. Today, it has up to 200 stalls selling contemporary paintings, crafts, pottery, jewelry, and homemade gifts. It's open every Sunday 10–5. ✉ *Upper Esplanade, St. Kilda* ☎ *03/9209–6634* ⊕ *www.stkildamarket.com.*

FITZROY

ART AND CRAFT GALLERIES

Gallery Gabrielle Pizzi. The gallery shows and sells the work of established and new Aboriginal artists from the communities of Balgo Hills, Papunya, Maningrida, Turkey Creek (Warmun), the Tiwi Islands, and others in the Central Desert, Top End, and Kimberley regions. ✉ *51 Victoria St., Fitzroy* ☎ *03/9416–4170* ⊕ *www.gabriellepizzi.com.au* ⊙ *Wed.–Fri. 10:30–5:30, Sat. noon–6.*

BOOKS

Books for Cooks. A fantastic array of cookbooks stock the shelves of Books for Cooks, including many from chefs at nearby restaurants. ✉ *233 Gertrude St., Fitzroy* ☎ *03/8415–1415* ⊕ *www.booksforcooks. com.au.*

CLOTHING

The Social Studio. This nonprofit store provides work experience, employment, and passageways for refugee youth. Limited-edition women's fashion designs are made using only reclaimed materials sourced from the local fashion industry. ✉ *128 Smith St., Collingwood* ⊕ *www. thesocialstudio.org.*

DEPARTMENT STORES AND SHOPPING CENTERS

Brunswick Street. Northeast of the city in Fitzroy, Brunswick Street has hip and grungy restaurants, coffee shops, gift stores, and clothing outlets selling the latest look. ✉ *Brunswick St., Fitzroy.*

Smith Street. Perhaps Melbourne hippest street, this colorful strip is dotted with bars, restaurants, and many vintage-style clothing shops. Toward the northern end are clothing factory outlets. ✉ *Smith St., Fitzroy.*

SOUTH YARRA–PRAHRAN

CLOTHING

Collette Dinnigan. Collette Dinnigan is a household name in Australia, having dressed celebrities such as Nicole Kidman and Cate Blanchett. This is a great place to shop for limited-edition feminine dresses. ✉ *1015 High St., Armadale* ☎ *03/9822–4332* ⊕ *www.collettedinnigan.com.au.*

DEPARTMENT STORES AND SHOPPING CENTERS

Chapel Street. This street is where you can find some of the ritziest boutiques in Melbourne, as well as cafés, art galleries, bars, and restaurants. ⊠ *Chapel St. between Toorak and Dandenong Rds., South Yarra–Prahran.*

High Street. Located between the suburbs of Prahran and Armadale, to the east of Chapel Street, High Street has the best collection of antiques shops in Australia. ⊠ *High St. between Chapel and Orrong Sts., South Yarra–Prahran.*

Jam Factory. The Jam Factory is a historic redbrick brewery-then-factory complex that house cinemas, fashion, food, and gift shops. ⊠ *500 Chapel St., South Yarra* ☎ *03/9825–4699* ⊕ *www.thejamfactory.com.au.*

MARKETS

Camberwell Sunday Market. Camberwell Sunday Market, about 6 km (3¾ miles) northeast of Chapel Street, South Yarra, is a popular haunt for seekers of the old and odd. More than 300 stalls sell antiques, pre-loved clothing, books, and knickknacks. Food vans provide sustenance. ⊠ *Station St., Camberwell* ⊕ *sundaymarket.com.au.*

Chapel Street Bazaar. Open daily 10–6, Chapel Street Bazaar has wooden cubicles and glass-fronted counters selling everything from estate jewelry and stylish secondhand clothes to porcelain and curios. ⊠ *217–223 Chapel St., Prahran* ☎ *03/9529–1727.*

Prahran Market. This market sells nothing but food—a fantastic, mouthwatering array imported from all over the world. It's open Tuesday, Thursday, and Saturday 7 am–5 pm, Friday 7 am–6 pm, and Sunday 10–3. ⊠ *163 Commercial Rd., South Yarra* ☎ *03/8290–8220* ⊕ *www.prahranmarket.com.au.*

SOUTH MELBOURNE AND SOUTHBANK

MARKETS

South Melbourne Market. Established in 1867, South Melbourne Market is Melbourne's second-oldest market. You'll find a huge selection of fresh produce and foodstuffs (their dim sums are famous). It's open Wednesday and weekends 8–4 and Friday 8–5. ⊠ *Cecil and Coventry Sts., South Melbourne* ☎ *03/9209–6295* ⊕ *www.southmelbournemarket.com.au.*

VICTORIA

WELCOME TO VICTORIA

TOP REASONS TO GO

★ **The Amazing Outdoors:** Victoria has outstanding national parks. Bushwalking, canoeing, fishing, rafting, and horse riding are all on the menu. If you're pushed for time, there are organized day trips to Port Campbell and the outcrops of the Grampians National Park.

★ **Golden Country:** You can still pan for gold—and find it—in rivers about an hour northwest of Melbourne. But the gold rush era's most attractive remnants are beautiful 19th-century towns constructed from its riches. Walking trails outline the stories of lucky strikes and miners' fights for justice.

★ **Wonderful Wineries:** You'll find hundreds of wineries across the state, particularly in the Yarra Valley, Rutherglen, and on the Mornington Peninsula. Winery tours, departing from Melbourne, are a relaxing way to see four to five wineries in one day.

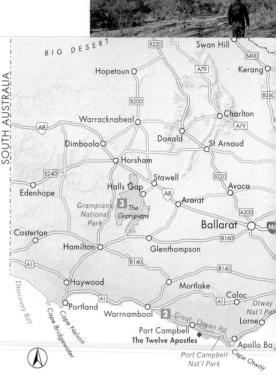

1 Side Trips from Melbourne. On the city's doorstep are dozens of wineries with fabulous restaurants, mist-swathed hills dotted with charming B&Bs and curio shops, forested walking trails noisy with multicolored parrots, gold-era towns flush with grand, boom-time buildings, and glorious beaches. It's a breeze to visit the Yarra Valley, Mornington Peninsula, the Goldfields, or the Dandenong Ranges on day trips.

2 Great Ocean Road. This is the ultimate road trip along the wave-lashed Southern Ocean. From Melbourne it's a 450-km (280-mile) coastal journey, with occasional detours into wooded hills dotted with fern gullies. Lighthouses, surfing beaches, and lively towns punctuate the road, but the headline attractions are the amazing shapes carved from the coastline, including the Twelve Apostles and the smaller rock stacks on show in this amazing sculpture park.

NEW SOUTH WALES

Murray River

Echuca

Shepparton

Wangaratta

Albury

Wodonga

Nagambie

Bendigo

Bright

Seymour

Kyneton

Yea

Mansfield

Sunbury

Eildon

GREAT DIVIDING RANGE

Alpine Nat'l Park

YARRA VALLEY

Healesville

MELBOURNE

DANDENONG RANGE

Werribee

Mornington Peninsula

Greelong

Traralgon

Sale

Queenscliff

Torquay

Sorrento

Leongatha

Gippsland Lakes Coastal Park

PHILLIP ISLAND

Cowes

Yarram

Bass Strait

Cape Liptrap

Corner Inlet

South Point

Wilsons Promontory

Wilsons Promontory

0   60 mi
0   60 km

GETTING ORIENTED

This compact state is a patchwork of spectacular landscapes just waiting to be explored. The Yarra Valley wineries and the Dandenong Ranges are an hour's drive east of Melbourne, while the beaches and vineyards of the Mornington Peninsula are a 90-minute drive south of the city. The Great Ocean Road begins at Torquay, southwest of Melbourne, and continues along the Southern Ocean coast to Portland, a distance of about 350 km (220 miles). The Goldfields and spa country are between one and two hours northwest of Melbourne. The Grampians and the Murray River region and its wineries are about a three-hour drive north to northeast of the city.

3 The Grampians. Encompassing a series of rugged sandstone ranges covered with native bushland, Grampians National Park is a wilderness area three hours from the heart of Melbourne. Spectacular rock formations including the Balconies, the Pinnacle, and the Fortress can be visited via walking trails. The Wonderland Range forms a wall behind the township of Halls Gap, which is a popular hangout for kangaroos.

4 Murray River Region. The mighty Murray River forms the border between Victoria and New South Wales, and is an aquatic playground. Houseboats, speedboats, and old paddle wheelers share the river, and golf courses, farms, historic towns, and stands of majestic eucalypt trees hug its banks. Wineries produce internationally acclaimed fortified wines and full-bodied reds.

Updated by
Tim Richards

Separated from New South Wales by the mighty Murray River and fronted by a beautiful coastline, Victoria boasts terrain as varied as any in Australia. Without venturing too far from the Melbourne city limits you can indulge in all sorts of pastimes—exploring the spectacular western coastline as far as the stunning Twelve Apostles; walking among the rocky outcrops, waterfalls, and fauna of the Grampians; visiting historic inland gold-mining communities; toasting the sunrise over the Yarra Valley vineyards from the basket of a hot-air balloon; or taking in a Murray River sunset from the deck of a paddle steamer.

Sweeping landscapes are quilted together in this compact state. Many of the state's best sights are within a day's drive of Melbourne. Go farther afield and you can experience the high-country solitude of Alpine National Park.

PLANNING

WHEN TO GO

Victoria is at its most beautiful in fall, March through May, when days are crisp, sunny, and clear and the foliage in parks and gardens is glorious. Winter, with its wild seas and leaden skies, stretches June through August in this region, providing a suitable backdrop for the dramatic coastal scenery. It's dry and sunny in the northeast, however, thanks to the cloud-blocking bulk of the Great Dividing Range. Northeast summers, December through February, are extremely hot, so it's best to travel here and through Gold Country in spring (September through November) and fall.

GREAT ITINERARIES

IF YOU HAVE 3 DAYS

On the first morning after leaving Melbourne, head for the town of Belgrave. Here you can ride the **Puffing Billy** train through the fern gullies and forests of the **Dandenongs**. In the afternoon, travel to **Phillip Island** for the endearing sunset penguin parade. Stay the night, and on the third morning meander along the coastal roads of the **Mornington Peninsula** through such stately towns as Sorrento and Portsea. Stop at a beach, or pick a Melbourne neighborhood or two to explore in the afternoon.

IF YOU HAVE 5 DAYS

Make your way west from Melbourne, stopping at Queenscliff on the Bellarine Peninsula, before setting off down the Great Ocean Road. (If you are starting from the Mornington Peninsula, you take the Sorrento-Queenscliff car and passenger ferry, which crosses Port Phillip Bay in 45 minutes.) The Great Ocean Road is one of the world's finest scenic drives, offering stops at some irresistible beaches. Overnight in **Lorne**, beneath the Otway Ranges, then drive west to **Port Campbell National Park**. Here you can view the Twelve Apostles rock formations and stroll along the beach. Continue to **Port Fairy** for the night, making sure that you check out the wonderful Bay of Islands and Bay of Martyrs rock stacks (in the sea) along the way. On Day 4 wander along the banks of Port Ferry's Moyne River and amble around Griffiths Island. You can then drive northeast to the Goldfields center of **Ballarat**. That evening you can explore the town's 19th-century streetscapes, then catch the sound-and-light show at Sovereign Hill. Spend the night here, and in the morning head to the wineries and spas around Daylesford before returning to Melbourne.

GETTING HERE AND AROUND

The best way to explore Victoria is by car. The state's road system is excellent, with clearly marked highways linking the Great Ocean Road to Wilson's Promontory, the Yarra Valley, the Murray River region, and the Mornington Peninsula. Distances are not as extreme as in other states. Many scenic places (Bendigo, Ballarat, Beechworth, and Echuca, for instance) are less than three hours from Melbourne; the vineyards of the Yarra Valley and the Mornington Peninsula are an easy 90-minute drive. Buses and trains, which cost less but take more time, also run between most regional centers.

RESTAURANTS

Chefs in Victoria take pride in their trendsetting preparations of fresh local produce. International flavors are found in both casual and upscale spots—and some of the best bargains can be found in local cafés. On Sunday be sure to join in the Victorian tradition of an all-day "brekky." *Prices in the reviews are the average cost of a main course at dinner or, if dinner is not served, at lunch.*

HOTELS

Accommodations in Victoria include grand country hotels, simple roadside motels, secluded bushland or seaside cabins, friendly bed-and-breakfasts, and backpacker hostels. Although you won't find many sprawling resorts in this state, most of the grand old mansions and country homes have air-conditioning, home-cooked meals, and free parking. Rates are usually reduced after school and national holidays. Melbourne Visitor Centre (⊕ *www.visitvictoria.com*) has a list of the state's accommodations to help you plan. *Prices in the reviews are the lowest cost of a standard double room in high season. For expanded hotel reviews, visit Fodors.com.*

SIDE TRIPS FROM MELBOURNE

Victoria's relatively compact size makes the state's principal attractions appealingly easy to reach, and the state's excellent road system makes driving the best option. There are a handful of enticing destinations within a 60- to 90-minute drive from Melbourne. Victoria is blessed with 21 distinct wine regions (and a total of 650 cellar doors, where you can try and buy the product). The Yarra Valley, 40 km (25 miles) east of Melbourne, is Victoria's oldest wine region and a pleasant place to spend a day on an organized tour. About 35 km (22 miles) south of the Yarra Valley is Olinda, a cute village at the heart of the Dandenong Ranges. This area of beautifully forested hills and valleys is a favorite weekend escape for Melburnians. The Mornington Peninsula is famous for its wineries and beaches. On the western shore of Port Phillip Bay, the Bellarine Peninsula also has a winery industry, but it's the grand 19th-century hotels of Queenscliff that most attract day-trippers.

YARRA VALLEY AND HEALESVILLE

65 km (40 miles) northeast of Melbourne

Fodor'sChoice The Yarra Valley spreads eastward from Melbourne's suburban fringe,
★ and is a popular area with both locals and international visitors. Because Melburnians often use the valley for weekend breaks, the best time to visit is on working weekdays when the crowds are thinner. The small, attractive towns are dotted with good cafés, restaurants, and shops; in the rolling countryside between them you'll find numerous fine wineries that have excellent restaurants with impressive food and views.

Healesville is a good base for travel to Yarra Valley wineries and the Dandenongs Region, as it's an easy drive from both. This pleasant town with a tree-shaded main street is also home to the Healesville Sanctuary, an open-plan zoo that showcases all manner of Australian native wildlife. Two popular areas within Yarra Ranges National Park—Badger Weir Walk and Maroondah Reservoir—are ideal for bushwalking and picnics.

GETTING HERE AND AROUND

Healesville, on the eastern side of the Yarra Valley, is 65 km (40 miles) from Melbourne. Take the Eastern Freeway from Melbourne to its junction with the Maroondah Highway and follow the signs to Lilydale and on to Healesville. Trains, operated by Metro, travel from central Melbourne to Lilydale, and McKenzie's buses connect Lilydale with Yarra Glen and Healesville via Route 685. It's advisable to have a car to explore the wineries, or take a half-day or full-day tour. Most tours will pick you up at your hotel.

TOURS

Several companies operate winery tours from Melbourne or the Yarra Valley itself. Tours generally include visits to four to five wineries and lunch. Wine Tours Victoria offers full-day tours departing from Melbourne and visiting four to five wineries and including lunch for A$147 per person. Minibuses are the most common form of transport for most tours, but daily from 11 to 4 for A$110 per person, Swans on Doongalla takes you out to four wineries along St. Huberts Road in a stretched horse-drawn carriage. A light lunch is served at Yering Farm winery. The meeting place is St. Huberts Winery. Rail enthusiasts can still enjoy the tracks even though regular passenger train services to Healesville ceased in 1980. You can travel along part of the track in railmotors (all-in-one motor and carriage) operated by the Yarra Valley Railway. The railmotors travel from Healesville through picturesque country, under bridges and through the historic TarraWarra brick tunnel and back again—a distance of about 8 km (5 miles) that takes about 45 minutes.

ESSENTIALS

Tour Operators Swans on Doongalla Horse Drawn Carriages ☎ 03/9762–1910 ⊕ www.swansondoongalla.com.au. **Wine Tours Victoria** ☎ 03/5428–8500 ⊕ www.winetours.com.au. **Yarra Valley Railway** ✉ Healesville-Kinglake Rd. ☎ 03/5962–2490 station ⊕ www.yarravalleyrailway.org.au 🎟 A$15 motor-rail rides ⊙ Sun. 10–4.**Yarra Valley Winery Tours** ☎ 03/5966–2372 ⊕ www.yarravalleywinerytours.com.au.

Transportation Contacts McKenzie's Tourist Services ☎ 03/5962–5088 ⊕ www.mckenzies.com.au.**Metro** ☎ 1800/800007 ⊕ www.metrotrains.com.au.

Visitor Information Yarra Valley Visitor Information Centre ✉ Old Courthouse, Harker St. ☎ 03/5962–2600 ⊕ www.visityarravalley.com.au.

EXPLORING

The Yarra Valley is also known for its wonderful produce—fruit, vegetables, herbs, bread, and cheeses—on sale at the monthly regional farmers' markets, including one at Yering Station *(see listing below)*.

De Bortoli. A family winery for three generations, De Bortoli was established (in New South Wales) in 1928, four years after the founder Vittorio De Bortoli and his wife Giuseppina migrated to Australia from northern Italy. Today, this Yarra Valley winery specializes in Chardonnay, Pinot Noir, and Riesling, along with a changing array of less-famous wines including Gamays, Pinot Blanc, and Sangiovese. Wine tastings cost A$5, which includes the famous Noble One, De Bortoli's most awarded wine since its release in 1982. The restaurant, which has stunning views of the surrounding vines, landscaped gardens, and mountains, serves delectable dishes using Yarra Valley produce; on weekends the fixed price two-course lunch is A$55 a head and the three-course option is A$68. You might like to start with an aperitif—perhaps

Side Trips From
Melbourne

the DB cocktail of sparkling wine, blood orange juice, and Campari (A$10). A popular feature is the cheese maturation and tasting room in the cellar-door area, where gourmet cheese-tasting plates are matched with wines (prices vary depending on produce chosen). A Mini Wine Adventure, which includes a wine tutorial, guided vineyard and winery tours, barrel tastings, hints on food and wine matching, and a three-course lunch, can be arranged by appointment at A$140 per head. ⊠ 58 Pinnacle La., Dixon's Creek ☎ 03/5965–2271 ⊕ www.debortoliyarra. com.au ☉ Daily 10–5; restaurant lunch Thurs.–Mon., dinner Sat. only.

Fodor'sChoice **Domaine Chandon.** This vineyard has one of the most spectacular set-
★ tings in the Yarra Valley; its Greenpoint tasting bar has enormous floor-to-ceiling windows providing fantastic views over the vineyards and the Yarra Ranges. Apart from sparkling wines—including Australia's only Pinot Noir–Shiraz blend—the winery produces Shiraz, Pinot Noir, Chardonnary, Sauvignon Blanc, and Rosé. Free guided tours, conducted daily at 11, 1, and 3, take visitors through the step-by-step production of sparkling wine, beginning among the vines and ending in the bottling area. Seasonal platters, tapas, and sharing plates (A$17–A$27) are served daily from 11 am in the Greenpoint brasserie, and each dish has a recommended accompanying wine (from A$10.50 a glass). Selections include a ground lamb brioche slider washed down with Chandon

Sparkling Pinot Noir Shiraz, or a duck leg, fennel, and mushroom pie, perhaps with a buttermilk-infused romaine and herb salad, and a glass of 2010 Chardonnay. ⊠ *727 Maroondah Hwy., Coldstream* ☎ *03/9738–9200* ⊕ *www.domainechandon.com.au* ⊙ *Daily 10:30–4:30.*

Grape Grazing Festival. Celebrate the Yarra Valley's locally produced wine, beer, cider, and food held in February, featuring wine tastings, music, and fine cuisine served under sunny summer skies. Events take place at numerous locations across the region, with most hosted by wineries. ⊠ *Yarra Glen* ☎ *03/9730–2447* ⊕ *www.grapegrazing.com.au.*

FAMILY **Healesville Sanctuary.** Come face-to-face with wedge-tailed eagles, grumpy wombats, nimble sugar gliders, and shy platypuses at Healesville Sanctuary, a lovely, leafy wildlife sanctuary housing native wildlife. Don't miss the twice-daily Spirits of the Sky show, during which raptors and parrots fly close overhead; and the daily Tales from Platypus Creek session, which features Australia's most unusual critter. You can pat a dingo or feed an emu on a Magic Moments experience (A$12 extra), and for A$195 you can join a platypus in the water via the Wade with the Platypus option. Another recently added highlight is the Land of Parrots aviary, wherein visitors can feed and interact with colorful birds. You can also book a behind-the-scenes tour of the animal hospital, where you may see wildlife recovering from injury or illness. Take a break and refuel at the Sanctuary Harvest café, which serves delicious snacks and meals. ⊠ *Badger Creek Rd.* ☎ *03/5957–2800, 1300/966784* ⊕ *www.zoo.org.au* ⊠ *A$26.80* ⊙ *Daily 9–5.*

Rochford Wines. This winery occupies a striking-looking property; its cellar door building crafted almost entirely of glass overlooks the vineyards and rolling green paddocks. The family-owned winery produces renowned Pinot Noir and Chardonnay, and has in recent years become the most happening place in the Yarra Valley—its huge amphitheater plays host to international and local performers during the annual Day on the Green concert series (recent acts have included INXS and Alicia Keys); in summer it screens movies under the stars. The wine-tasting bar is open daily 9–5. A stylish restaurant (offering two courses for A$55 and three courses for A$65 per person) and a casual café are both open seven days a week for breakfast and lunch; the café also serves all-day light meals. ⊠ *878 Maroondah Hwy., Coldstream* ☎ *03/5962–2119* ⊕ *www.rochfordwines.com* ⊙ *Daily 9–5.*

Yering Station. Victoria's first vineyard still has plenty of rustic charm, and it's a delightful place to eat, drink, and stay. An 1859 redbrick building is home to the cellar door, a wine-and-produce store, and the casual upstairs Matt's Bar ($$), where you can relax all day sipping wine and dining from a tasty menu beneath an arched timber ceiling. The property's architectural and gastronomical pièce de résistance is the winery building, which houses the Wine Bar Restaurant ($$$). It's a sweeping, hand-hewn stone building with floor-to-ceiling windows overlooking spectacular valley scenery. Those who would prefer just to wander and sip wines at the cellar door are free to take the self-guided winery tour through the sculpture gardens. A farmers' market takes place on the third Sunday of the month. ⊠ *38 Melba Hwy., Yarra Glen* ☎ *03/9730–0100* ⊕ *www.yering.com* ⊙ *Cellar door: 10–5 weekdays, 10–6 weekends; restaurant: lunch daily from noon (no dinner).*

SPORTS AND THE OUTDOORS
There are plenty of opportunities to get out in the fresh air in the Yarra Valley. Those with cash to spare can go ballooning; others may just like to walk or ride a bike along the trails or play golf at the three golf courses in the valley. Wine tasting is a given.

BALLOONING
Global Ballooning. This hot-air ballooning operation offers flights over the Yarra Valley. For A$290 per person you can take off at dawn and drift peacefully over the vineyards for an hour. For A$25 extra, enjoy a champagne breakfast after the flight at Rochford Wines. Check the website for accommodation packages. ☎ *1800/627661* ⊕ *www.globalballooning.com.au.*

BIKING
Yarra Valley Cycles. You can rent a bike (and compulsory helmet) from A$40 a day and Yarra Valley Cycles will point you in the right direction for the best cycling routes in the valley and nearby scenic regions. ⊠ *108 Main St., Lilydale* ✛ *Across the road from Lilydale Railway Station* ☎ *03/9735–1483* ⊕ *www.yarravalleycycles.com.*

BUSHWALKING
Yarra Ranges National Park. Stop at the Yarra Valley Visitor Information Centre in Healesville for the best advice on which areas to hike; a free Walks and Riding Trails map is available. You can also call Parks Victoria or visit their website for current conditions. ⊠ *Yarra Ranges National Park* ☎ *13–1963* ⊕ *www.parkweb.vic.gov.au.*

GOLFING
Warburton Golf Club. This gem of a course is hidden among the Yarra Ranges. For A$30 for 18 holes on weekends (A$24 weekdays) you can golf over meandering streams and bushland blooming with wildflowers. Although it's called a semiprivate club, visitors are very welcome to come and play 9 or 18 holes if they call and book in advance. Rental clubs are available if you didn't pack your own. The course is hilly and golf buggies can be hired for A$35. Warburton is 30 km (19 miles) southeast of Healesville. ⊠ *17 Dammans Rd., Warburton* ☎ *03/5966–2306* ⊕ *www.warburtongolf.com.au* ⛳ *18 holes. 5925 yds. Par 69.*

"Just a short drive from Melbourne is the captivating beauty of the Yarra Valley." —photo by lisargold, Fodors. com member

WHERE TO EAT AND STAY

For expanded hotel reviews, visit Fodors.com.

$$
PIZZA

✕ **Innocent Bystander.** Despite the lofty modern steel-and-glass interior, this spacious contemporary restaurant in the town of Healesville has a warm, welcoming feel, and serves excellent food. It also hosts a winery's cellar door, along with a gourmet food shop and bakery. Star of the menu is the pizza selection—try the Puttanesca pizza with Spanish white anchovies, capers, black olives, dill, and buffalo mozzarella (A$23), and wash it down with an in-house wine or a beer from the White Rabbit brewery next door. In the "not pizza" category are such gems as duck confit with honey-roasted pear, endive, and walnut salad (A$25). Don't overlook the house-made bread, it's spectacularly good. Weekdays the restaurant is open from 10 am to 10 pm; weekends it's open 8 am to 10 pm and serves breakfast in addition to the usual menu. $ *Average main: A$30* ✉ *336 Maroondah Hwy.* ☎ *03/5962–6111* ⊕ *www. innocentbystander.com.au.*

$$
MODERN
AUSTRALIAN

✕ **Stones of the Yarra Valley.** Housed in an old weather-beaten barn that has been beautifully restored, Stones of the Yarra Valley is set amid 50 acres of Cabernet vines and is surrounded by century-old oak trees, with views of the Yarra Ranges. This is a great place to have lunch, or just have a coffee or a wine at the casual Mezze Wine Bar. The weekend-only lunch menu might include lamb rump with sunchoke puree and baby vegetables, or fillet of blue-eye cod with butternut pumpkin and gnocchi (both A$32). Evening performances by well-known Australian artists, who have included jazz maestro James Morrison, take place throughout the year, and are excellent value at between A$100 to A$120 for a three-course meal (wine extra) and show. Sunday concerts featuring up-and-coming jazz and classical performers (A\$15–A\$30) are staged in the lovely hand-hewn stone chapel on the site on selected dates. $ *Average main: A\$33* ✉ *14 St. Huberts Rd., Coldstream* ☎ *03/9739–0900* ⊕ *www.stonesoftheyarravalley.com* 🍴 *Reservations essential* ⊗ *No lunch weekdays; no dinner Sun.–Thurs.*

$$$$ 🍴 **Balgownie Estate Vineyard Resort and Spa.** This resort has it all—stylish
HOTEL   suites and apartment-style accommodations with balconies overlooking the vineyards, plus a ton of other amenities. **Pros:** excellent facilities; on-site cellar door; great day spa. **Cons:** holds conferences, so may get busy at times. $ *Rooms from: A\$420* ✉ *Melba Hwy. and Gulf Rd., Yarra Glen* ☎ *03/9730–0700* ⊕ *www.balgownieestate.com.au* 🛏 *14 rooms, 55 suites* 🍴 *Breakfast.*

$$$$ 🍴 **Chateau Yering.** Once an 1860s homestead, whose grounds later
HOTEL   became the Yarra Valley's first vineyard, this luxury hotel features
Fodor'sChoice   opulent suites that have antique furniture and deep claw-foot bath-
★   tubs. **Pros:** grand living; delicious food. **Cons:** this lifestyle comes at a luxurious price. $ *Rooms from: A\$645* ✉ *42 Melba Hwy., Yarra Glen* ☎ *03/9237–3333, 1800/237333* ⊕ *www.chateauyering.com.au* 🛏 *32 suites* 🍴 *Some meals.*

$ 🍴 **Healesville Hotel.** Housed in a restored 1910 pub, this famous local
HOTEL   lodge has seven colorful, modern upstairs rooms (A\$130 a night in high season) with high ceilings, tall windows, and genteel touches such as handmade soaps. **Pros:** funky accommodation; great food, historic hotel. **Cons:** limited facilities; shared bathrooms within the main build-ing. $ *Rooms from: A\$130* ✉ *256 Maroondah Hwy.* ☎ *03/5962–4002* ⊕ *www.healesvillehotel.com.au* 🛏 *7 rooms, 2 cottages* 🍴 *Breakfast.*

SHOPPING

FAMILY   **Yarra Valley Chocolaterie.** Opened in 2012, this specialist chocolate and ice cream manufacturer has resident European chocolatiers that create a vast array of high-quality treats in all shapes and styles, including 38 types of handmade truffles. Many items include locally grown ingredi-ents such as rosemary and lavender, and there's a bush tucker range of chocolates incorporating native plant products such as lemon myrtle, jindilli nut, and wattle seed. ■ TIP→ The on-site café (\$) has a beauti-ful view over hilly green farmland and is a great place to eat chocolate and made-on-the-premises ice cream; it also serves light meals. We also suggest you buy a selection of chocolates to enjoy later. ✉ *35 Old Healesville Rd., Yarra Glen* ☎ *03/9730–2777* ⊕ *www.yvci.com.au.*

THE DANDENONG RANGES

Melburnians come to the beautiful Dandenong Ranges, also known simply as the Dandenongs, for a breath of fresh air, especially in fall when the deciduous trees turn golden and in spring when the public gardens explode into color with tulip, daffodil, azalea, and rhododen-dron blooms. At Mt. Dandenong, the highest point (2,077 feet), a scenic lookout known as SkyHigh Mt. Dandenong affords spectacular views over Melbourne and the bay beyond. Dandenong Ranges National

Park, which encompasses five smaller parks, including Sherbrooke Forest and Ferntree Gully, has dozens of walking trails.

The many villages (which include Olinda, Sassafras, Kalorama, Sherbrooke, and Kallista) have curio shops, art galleries, food emporiums, cafés, and restaurants, and are dotted with lovely B&Bs. Visitors should be aware that the Dandenong Ranges and the high point of Mt. Dandenong are completely different from Dandenong, an outer suburb of Melbourne (30 km [19 miles] southeast of the downtown and on the Pakenham railway line).

GETTING HERE AND AROUND

Motorists can either take the Yarra Valley route *(⇨ see above)*, turn off at Lilydale, and head south to Montrose and on to Olinda, or take the South Eastern Freeway or M1 (a toll applies) and exit at Ferntree Gully Road. From there, take the Mt. Dandenong Tourist Road and follow it to Olinda, arriving from the south. Trains travel from Flinders Street Station to Belgrave on the Belgrave line. This town is on the southern edge of the Dandenongs and is the home of the steam train called *Puffing Billy*. Other towns on the same railway line are Ferntree Gully and Upper Ferntree Gully.

Bus 688 runs from Upper Ferntree Gully Station through the trees to Sassafras and Olinda, then passes William Ricketts Sanctuary; while Bus 694 links Belgrave Station to the Mt. Dandenong Lookout, via the villages of Sherbrooke, Sassafras, and Olinda. Alternatively, take the train from Flinders Street Station to Croydon (on the Lilydale line), then take the 688 bus south to William Ricketts Sanctuary and Olinda.

TOURS

Half- and full-day trips from Melbourne are run by local tour operators, including Gray Line and Melbourne's Best Day Tours. Tours of the Dandenongs, including afternoon tea and a ride on the steam-powered train known as *Puffing Billy*, cost A$88–A$95 (half day) or A$189 (full day with one or more winery stops).

ESSENTIALS

Tour Operators Gray Line ⊠ *Federation Sq., Flinders and Russell Sts., City Center, Melbourne* ☎ *1300/858687* ⊕ *www.grayline.com.au.* **Melbourne's Best Day Tours** ⊠ *Federation Sq., Flinders and Russell Sts., City Center, Melbourne* ☎ *1300/130550, 03/9397–4911* ⊕ *www.melbournetours.com.au.*

Visitor Information Dandenong Ranges Information Centre ⊠ *1211 Burwood Hwy., Upper Ferntree Gully* ☎ *03/9758–7522, 1800/645505* ⊕ *www. experiencethedandenongs.com.au.*

EXPLORING

Cloudehill Gardens & Nursery. These glorious gardens are divided into 20 "garden rooms" that include the Rhododendron Woods, the Azalea Walk, and 80-year-old European beech trees. They were first established in the late 1890s as commercial and cut-flower gardens by the Woolrich family. A central terraced area with manicured hedges and a sculpture of a huge vase is stunning, as is the view across the mountain ranges from the garden café. The café serves breakfast, lunch, and afternoon tea daily; a popular dish is the "Chatter Platter" for two with a selection of cheeses, dips, prawns, and salad (A$50). ✉ *89 Olinda-Monbulk Rd., Olinda* ☎ *03/9751–1009* ⊕ *www.cloudehill.com.au* ✉ *A$10* ☉ *Gardens daily 10–5; café daily 9:30–5.*

George Tindale Memorial Garden. Azaleas, camellias, and hydrangeas spill down the hillsides in this 6-acre garden. While it is most colorful in spring, when the flowers are in bloom, and in autumn, when the introduced trees turn gold and yellow, it is also beautiful in winter if there is a touch of snow. It's located just 8 km (5 miles) north of Belgrave in the little forest settlement of Sherbrooke, where whipbird calls echo through the trees. ✉ *33 Sherbrooke Rd., Sherbrooke* ☎ *13–1963* ⊕ *parkweb.vic.gov.au* ☉ *Daily 10–5, last entry 4:30.*

Fodor'sChoice
★
National Rhododendron Gardens. The expansive gardens contain thousands of rhododendrons, azaleas, and camellias; in spring they put on a spectacular show of white, mauve, yellow, and pink blooms. Several kilometers of walking trails lead to vistas over the Yarra Valley, and the small Garden Explorer bus also provides transportation around the property in the springtime peak from mid-September to early November. The gardens are a short stroll from Olinda village. For a perfect afternoon, combine your visit with tea and scones in one of the little cafés around town. ✉ *The Georgian Rd., Olinda* ☎ *13–1963* ⊕ *parkweb.vic.gov.au* ✉ *Free* ☉ *Daily 10–5, last entry 4:30.*

FAMILY
Puffing Billy. This gleaming narrow-gauge steam train, based 40 km (25 miles) from Healesville in the town of Belgrave, runs on a line originally built in the early 1900s to open up the Dandenong Ranges to 20th-century pioneers. It's a great way to see the foothill landscapes. Daily trips between Belgrave and Emerald Lake pass through picturesque forests and over spectacular wooden trestle bridges. The 13-km (8-mile) trip takes an hour; it's another hour if you continue to the historic town of Gembrook. There are also lunch and dinner trips. ✉ *1 Old Monbulk Rd., Belgrave* ☎ *03/9757–0700* ⊕ *www.puffingbilly.com.au* ✉ *A$39; A$59 round-trip* ☉ *Daily; hrs vary.*

FAMILY
SkyHigh Mt. Dandenong. This lookout at the top of Mt. Dandenong has breathtaking views over Melbourne to the Mornington Peninsula and Port Phillip Bay. You can picnic or barbecue on the grounds, eat at the bistro (lunch and dinner), or stroll along the pleasant English Garden Walk while the kids get lost in the hedge maze. Other fun attractions include a Wishing Tree and the Giant's Chair. ✉ *26 Observatory Rd., Mt. Dandenong* ☎ *03/9751–0443* ⊕ *www.skyhighmtdandenong.com.au* ✉ *A$5 per car; maze A$6 adults, A$4 children* ☉ *Weekdays 9 am–10 pm, weekends 8 am–10 pm; bistro lunch and dinner daily, breakfast weekends.*

Fodor'sChoice
★
William Ricketts Sanctuary. Fern gardens, moss-covered rocks, waterfalls, towering mountain ash, and kiln-fired sculptures of Aborigines and Australian native animals fill this 4-acre property on Mt. Dandenong. William Ricketts, who established the sanctuary in the 1930s, meant it to stand as an embodiment of his philosophy: that people must act as custodians of the natural environment as Australia's Aborigines have for many millennia. ✉ *1402 Mt. Dandenong Tourist Rd., Mt. Dandenong* ☎ *13–1963 Parks Victoria* ⊕ *parkweb.vic.gov.au* ☉ *Daily 10–4:30.*

All aboard the *Puffing Billy* steam train

SPORTS AND THE OUTDOORS

HIKING

Dandenong Ranges National Park. Several reserves, including the Sherbrooke Forest—home to Sherbrooke Falls—make up this beautiful leafy and hilly national park. Trails include the Olinda Forest Trail (from Mt. Dandenong to Kallista), the Western Trail from the top of Mt. Dandenong to Ferntree Gully, the Sherbrooke Loop, and the Tourist Track from Sassafras to Emerald. Brochures and a trail map are available from the visitor information center at Upper Ferntree Gully and some cafés in the area. Trail maps can also be found on the park's website. ⊠ *Dandenong Ranges, Olinda* ☎ *13–1963* ⊕ *www.parkweb.vic.gov.au.*

Heidelberg School Artists' Trail. Stay fit and brush up on Australian art by following the trail that commemorates famous Melbourne artists of the late 19th century, including Arthur Streeton, Tom Roberts, and Frederick McCubbin. These artists all painted around the Heidelberg area east of Melbourne. The Dandenongs section of this 40-km (25-mile) trail (which begins in Templestowe, Melbourne) displays 9 of the route's 57 interpretive signs explaining the artists' work. ⊠ *Chalet Rd., Olinda* ☎ *13–1963.*

WHERE TO EAT AND STAY

For expanded hotel reviews, visit Fodors.com.

Olinda is the main village in the Dandenong Ranges region and a good base for exploring the area. It's actually two villages (Lower and Upper Olinda, though Lower Olinda is better known by the name of the peak it sits beneath, Mt. Dandenong). The two are connected by Monash Road, along which you'll find a lot of the town's B&Bs

and self-catering cottages. Olinda has a handful of good restaurants and cafés, and many specialty boutique stores selling curios and gifts. It's a short drive from here to the National Rhododendron Gardens, Olinda Falls picnic grounds, Cloudehill Gardens, and various hiking trails.

PERFECT PICNICS

The Dandenongs are heaven for fresh-air freaks and foodies. Pick up some goodies at Olinda's Saturday morning market and work up an appetite taking the 2-km (1½-mile) loop walk to Sherbrooke Falls from Donohue Picnic Grounds. Ask the tourist office about other great walks and picnic spots.

$$ ITALIAN 🍴 **The Ivy.** This excellent Italian-inspired restaurant sits on a prominent corner in Olinda Village, with a comfortable light-filled interior and a pleasant open-air terrace. Wood-fired pizzas are a highlight here, including such flavorsome examples as the Salsiccia (A$22.50), laden with Italian pork and fennel sausage. The stars of the dinner service are the wood-fired terra-cotta pots containing various slow-cooked dishes such as slow-roasted-garlic-and-rosemary lamb on Italian beans with goat's cheese, lemon-scented olive oil, and pesto (A$35). If you have room for dessert after that (which is doubtful), try the Dolci pizza topped with white chocolate raspberries, milk chocolate, and vanilla bean ice cream (A$15). [$] *Average main: A$27* ✉ *540 Mt. Dandenong Tourist Rd., Olinda* ☎ *03/9751–2388* 🌐 *www.theivyrestaurant.com.au* ⏲ *Closed Wed. No lunch Thurs.*

$ EUROPEAN 🍴 **Ranges.** This popular café-restaurant, right in the heart of Olinda, buzzes all day, and is the perfect place for a snack or meal after browsing the adjacent curio shops or gardens. It's open daily for breakfast, lunch, and morning and afternoon tea, and for dinner Tuesday to Saturday. Lunchtime fare includes an Asian-style salt-and-pepper calamari salad (A$19.90) or a daily homemade savory pie; at night you might want to begin with a cocktail while browsing the menu of hearty steaks and other tasty choices such as crispy Atlantic salmon with fennel salad, capers, and beetroot puree (A$35). [$] *Average main: A$30* ✉ *5 Olinda-Monbulk Rd., Olinda* ☎ *03/9751–2133* 🌐 *www.ranges.com.au* ⏲ *No dinner Sun. and Mon.*

$ AUSTRALIAN 🍴 **Ripe.** With crackling open fires in winter and a covered deck for summer grazing, this buzzy cottage café is the perfect place for a heart-warming casual lunch or afternoon tea. Savory offerings might include penne pasta tossed with prawns, red peppers, and spinach; or beef-and-vegetable pie with a side salad. And while the Dandenongs have a long tradition of Devonshire teas, this café is proudly scone-free; temptation here comes in the shape of mouthwatering cakes, all made with free-range eggs. You can also buy relishes, cheeses, and fresh Yarra Valley pasta to cook yourself—the smoked trout and goat cheese ravioli is delicious. [$] *Average main: A$22* ✉ *376 Mt. Dandenong Tourist Rd., Sassafras* ☎ *03/9755–2100* ✍ *Reservations not accepted* ⏲ *No dinner.*

$ EUROPEAN 🍴 **Wild Oak Restaurant and Bar.** Warm up the taste buds with items from the restaurant's popular small-dishes menu, which includes such treats as plum-and-five-spice meatballs (A$14.50) alongside the house-baked sourdough bread. A heartier main dish is the pan-seared kangaroo fillet with blue swimmer crab, stuffed tomatoes, and smoky tomato ragout (A$39). Chef and owner Ben Higgs also conducts hands-on cooking classes with different themes for groups (minimum four people). Jazz performers play on the last Friday night of every month. $\boxed{\$}$ *Average main: A$34* ✉ *232 Ridge Rd., Olinda* ☎ *03/9751–2033* ⊘ *Closed Mon. and Tues.*

$$$ 🏠 **Candlelight Cottage.** Curl up with a book in front of the open fire in this
RENTAL charming 1880s cottage, and you might be tempted not to do anything else in the Dandenongs. **Pros:** historic property; great breakfast. **Cons:** two-night minimum stay on weekends. $\boxed{\$}$ *Rooms from: A$295* ✉ *7 Monash Ave., Olinda* ☎ *03/9751–2464* ⊕ *www.candlelightcottages. com.au* ⤳ *4 cottages* ⦿ *Breakfast.*

MORNINGTON PENINSULA

The Mornington Peninsula circles the southeastern half of Port Phillip Bay. A much larger piece of land than it first appears, the peninsula is lapped by water on three sides and measures about 65 km (40 miles) by 35 km (22 miles). Along the bay's coast is a string of seaside villages stretching from the larger towns of Frankston and Mornington to the summer holiday towns of Mount Martha, Rosebud, Rye, Sorrento, and Portsea (which has one of the most dramatic—and hazardous—beaches in the region). On the Western Port Bay side the smaller settlements of Flinders, Somers, and Hastings have quieter beaches without the crowds.

Together with Main Ridge and Merricks, Red Hill is one of the state's premium producers of cool-climate wines, particularly Pinot Noir and Shiraz. The majority of the peninsula's 60 wineries are clustered around Red Hill and Red Hill South; however, there are another dozen or more dotted around areas farther north, including Moorooduc, Dromana, and Mount Martha. For an afternoon of fine wine, excellent seafood, and spectacular coastal views, plan a route that winds between vineyards. Red Hill has a busy produce-and-crafts market, which has been operating for decades and shows no signs of abating. It's held on the first Saturday morning of each month from September to May. A good website for getting all the lowdown on peninsular wineries is ⊕ *www. visitmorningtonvineyards.com.*

Sorrento is one of the region's prettiest beach towns and one of the most popular day-tripper spots on the peninsula. It's also the peninsula's oldest settlement, and thus is dotted with numerous historic buildings and National Trust sites (among them the Collins Settlement Historical Site, which marks the first settlement site at Sullivan Bay; and the Nepean Historical Society Museum, with its displays of Aboriginal artifacts and settlers' tools). In summer the town transforms from a sleepy seaside village into a hectic holiday hot spot. Sorrento Back Beach, with its rock pools and cliff-side trails, and Point King, with its piers and boathouses, are the two most popular hangouts.

Artist and sculptor William Ricketts (1898–1993) in front of his work, Mt. Dandenong

GETTING HERE AND AROUND

Renting a car in Melbourne and driving south along the Nepean Highway is the most practical way of seeing the Mornington Peninsula. At Frankston you can take the Frankston-Moorooduc Highway or stay on the Nepean Highway—eventually they both merge into the Mornington Peninsula Highway, which continues south to the various bayside towns. A train runs from Flinders Street Station to Frankston. At Frankston, connect with a diesel-train service to towns on the east of the peninsula including Hastings, Bittern, Point Crib, and Stony Point. Buses also run from Frankston to the bay-side towns; the No. 781 bus goes to Mornington and Mount Martha and the No. 782 and 783 buses travel to Hastings and Flinders on the Western Port side.

Inter Island Ferries runs a passenger service from Stony Point (on the eastern side of the peninsula) to Phillip Island, while the Queenscliff–Sorrento car and passenger ferry is the best way to travel between these two towns on opposite sides of the bay. The Frankston and Peninsula airport shuttle bus runs from Melbourne Airport's international terminal to Frankston and several other Mornington Peninsula towns.

WINERY TOURS

Amour of the Grape. Set winery tours for groups of two to seven passengers, and personal tours for those who want to devise their own itinerary, are offered by this company. The day's outing includes tastings at four or five preselected cellar doors, and a gourmet lunch and a glass of wine at a boutique winery café. Golf and spa tours are also available. ☎ 0414/5974-3286 ⊕ www.amourofthegrape.com.au ✉ A$175 *per person Mornington Peninsula pickup; central Melbourne pickup A$220 per person (for 4 to 7 people).*

Wine Tours Victoria. This Melbourne-based company operates tours of 2 to 10 people using minivans. They visit four to five wineries that may include Box Stallion and Willow Creek. Lunch with wine and coffee are also on the menu. ☎ *03/5428–8500, 1300/946386* ⊕ *www.winetours. com.au* 🖃 *A$150.*

ESSENTIALS

Transportation Frankston and Peninsula Airport Shuttle ☎ *03/9783– 1199* ⊕ *www.fapas.com.au.* **Inter Island Ferries** ☎ *03/9585–5730* ⊕ *www. interislandferries.com.au.* **Sorrento-Queenscliff Ferry** ☎ *03/5258–3244* ⊕ *www.searoad.com.au.*

Visitor Information Mornington Community Information and Support Centre ⊠ *320 Main St., Mornington* ☎ *03/5975–1644* ⊕ *www.morninfo.org.au.* **Mornington Peninsula Visitor Information Centre** ⊠ *359B Point Nepean Rd., Dromana* ☎ *03/5987–3078, 1800/804009* ⊕ *www.visitmorningtonpeninsula.org.*

EXPLORING

FAMILY **Arthurs Seat State Park.** Sweeping views of the surrounding countryside can be seen from this park, taking in Port Phillip Bay, Port Phillip Heads, and—on a clear day—the city skyline, the You Yangs, and Mt. Macedon. The mountain, which gives Arthurs Seat State Park its name, is the highest point on the Mornington Peninsula; it was named after Arthurs Seat in Edinburgh. A marked scenic drive snakes its way up to the summit, and walking tracks meander through the park's stands of eucalyptus. Seawinds, a public garden established by a local gardener in the 1940s, also forms part of the park and is a 10-minute walk or about 500 yards away. The road from Mornington is open at all times, so you can enjoy the spectacular mountaintop view by day or at night to see the lights. ⊠ *Arthurs Seat Rd., Arthur's Seat* ☎ *13–1963* ⊕ *www. parkweb.vic.gov.au* 🖃 *Free.*

EXPLORING THE WINERIES

A small bus tour that visits four to five wineries is the best way to explore the region. Tours leave from Melbourne and from peninsula towns. Most of the wineries listed here also have excellent restaurants on-site, and many of the restaurants we list are located in wineries, so there's no need to go hungry or thirsty!

Box Stallion. Housed in a rustic redbrick barn that was once home to the thoroughbred stallions of the illustrious Muranna Park racing stable, this award-winning winery and restaurant is set on 100 acres. Full of country charm, it's also said to be the peninsula's leading producer of varietal wine. The Shiraz is the stable's most awarded wine, while their Sauvignon Blanc and Pinot Noir have picked up a few medals as well. All wines are grown and made on the estate, and tours can be arranged for the technically savvy visitor with advanced notice. Meals, served either indoors in the barn cellar door (the former horse boxes have been retained as dining areas for small groups) or outside under big canvas umbrellas, will not break the bank. A grazing platter of many delicacies such as marinated vegetables, cheeses, olives, and dips suits

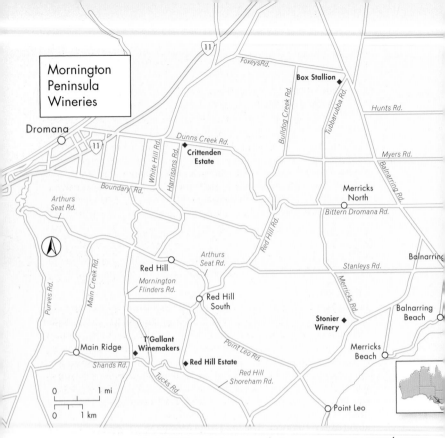

two people (A$35), and the soy-and-ginger prawns on roasted carrot puree with spinach and sesame salad is A$30. The starters are cheaper and often quite large. On Sunday there's live music from 1 to 4 pm. Wine tastings are free, but there are no group tastings on Sunday during the busy hours of 11–3. ⊠ *64 Tubbarubba Rd., Merricks North* ☎ *03/5989–7444* ⊕ *www.boxstallion.com.au* ⊙ *Daily 11–5.*

Crittenden Estate. One of the region's most picturesque wineries with a lovely lakeside setting, Crittenden Estate produces Chardonnay, Pinot Noir, Pinot Grigio, and some Spanish styles. The flagship Crittenden Estate Pinot Noir and Chardonnay are made from vines that are among the oldest on the peninsula. The cellar door is open for tastings daily, and winery tours can be arranged by appointment. The cellar door also contains a produce store selling olives, olive oil, dukkah, and other food that goes well with wine. The tasting room is wonderfully warm in winter, and while you sip you can admire the artworks that adorn the walls. The restaurant, Stillwater at Crittenden ($$$), is lovely year-round, and when the weather is fine diners sit out on a terrace under shady umbrellas while enjoying views over the lake. It is open daily for lunch and Friday and Saturday for dinner. ⊠ *25 Harrisons Rd., Dromana* ☎ *03/5981–8322 winery, 03/5981–9555 restaurant, 03/5987–3800* *cellar door* ⊕ *www.crittendenwines.com.au* ☉ *Cellar door daily 11–4; lunch daily noon–3, dinner Fri. and Sat. 6–11.*

Red Hill Estate. This winery, which has won numerous medals for its Chardonnay, Pinot Noir, and Shiraz, has an equally impressive view. Not only are there sweeping vistas over the 22-acre vineyards, but the magnificent waters of Western Port Bay are spread out in the distance. On clear days you can see as far as Phillip Island and Wilsons Promontory as you wander around the gardens. The award-winning cuisine and fabulous floor-to-ceiling windows make **Max's Restaurant** ($$$ ☎ *03/5931–0177* ☉ *No dinner Sun.–Thurs.*) the perfect place to while away at least half the day. You might start with Max's own tasting plate of all-local ingredients, which includes ocean trout, lamb, kangaroo, and a selection of local cheeses served with a glass of Red Hill Estate wine. For dessert, don't miss the rhubarb crumble with housemade apple-and-white-peppercorn ice cream. Although it may be a little chilly, winter is a good time to visit the winery, as several events are staged, including the Barrel Art Show, the Winter Winery Week in June, and a huge Tuscan feast in July. ⊠ *53 Shoreham Rd., Red Hill South* ☎ *03/5989–2838* ⊕ *www.redhillestate.com.au* ☉ *Daily 11–5.*

Stonier Winery. Established in 1978, Stonier Winery is considered a preeminent Mornington Peninsula producer of wines, which are made from the region's oldest vines. The establishment specializes in Chardonnay and Pinot Noir (produced from vines first planted in 1978 and 1982, respectively) and also produces a sparkling wine—the Stonier Pinot Noir Chardonnay. Although there's no restaurant, platters of local Red Hill cheeses accompany the daily tastings and, if time permits, visitors may be invited on an informal tour of the fermentation and barrel rooms. Several events take place during the year, such as the Pie and Pinot day in July (part of the regional Winter Wine Weekend), and a dedicated Sparkling day in December. ⊠ *2 Thompsons La., Merricks* ☎ *03/5989–8300* ⊕ *www.stoniers.com.au* ☉ *Daily 11–5.*

Fodor's Choice **T'Gallant Winemakers.** Home to the peninsula's first Pinot Grigio vines,
★ this popular Italian-themed winery also contains a restaurant. T'Gallant also produces excellent Pinot Noir, Chardonnay, and Muscat. If you're an art lover as well as a wine fan, you'll also admire the beautiful artwork on its bottle labels. The on-site restaurant La Baracca Trattoria ($$) and the alfresco Spuntino Bar ($) are always buzzing and the food is exceptional, with dishes made from local ingredients, including items from the house herb garden. Tuck into a crisp-based pizza or grilled sausages in the bar, or try the trattoria's slow-cooked lamb with broad beans, artichokes, baby potatoes, and garden herbs. The cellar door and restaurant/bar are open seven days a week, and there's live music every weekend at lunchtime and occasional cabaret nights. You can also sign up for the year-round Tre Gusti Cooking Classes. ⊠ *1385 Mornington–Flinders Rd., Main Ridge* ☎ *03/5989–6565* ⊕ *www.tgallant.com.au* ☉ *Daily 9–5.*

Continued on page 286

In recent decades Australia has emerged as an international wine powerhouse. The country's varied climate has proven favorable for growing high-quality grapes, and winemakers now produce some of the world's best Shiraz (Syrah) wines, as well as acclaimed Pinot Noirs and Rieslings. Wine sales currently contribute about $5.5 billion to the country's economy, and Australia is the third largest supplier to the United States behind France and Italy.

Touring wineries here is easy, as most properties have tasting rooms with regular hours. Whether you're sipping *in situ* at a winery or tasting wines at a shop in Sydney, here's how to get the most from your wine experience.

By Erica Watson

(top) Pinot noir grapes (right) Vineyard in One Tree Hill, South Australia

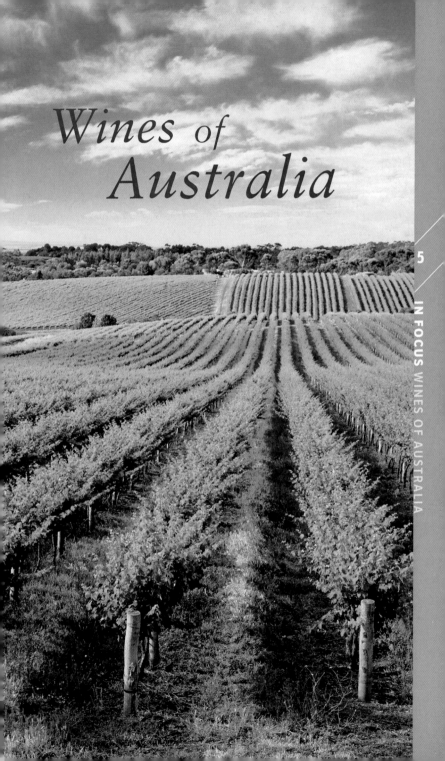

Wines of
Australia

WINE TRENDS: THEN AND NOW

(top left) Wine bottles await labels, (bottom left) Hunter Valley vista, (right) tasting in Barossa Valley

Although the first grapes in Australia arrived with British settlers in 1787, it really wasn't until the mid 1960s that a more refined tradition of wine making began to take hold. Prior to 1960, Australia's wine repertoire extended little beyond sherry and port, but after WWII, an influx of European immigrants, notably from Germany and Italy, opened the country's eyes to new tastes and production methods.

Australia now produces many classic varietals at prices from A$10 to A$40,000 (for a 1951 Penfolds Grange Hermitage, made by Australian pioneer Max Schubert). There are more than 60 wine regions dotted across the country and many of the smaller producers in lesser-known areas are beginning to flourish.

Although the industry has experienced rapid growth, it hasn't been without its problems. The health of the global economy, international competition, global warming, disease, drought, and bushfire have each presented challenges along the way.

These days, Australian vintners are known for combining old traditions with new ideas and technical innovations. While oak barrels are still widely used, stainless steel and plastic tanks are now recognized as suitable fermentation and storage methods. Screw caps, introduced more than a decade ago, are becoming more popular with winemakers and consumers.

The industry's lastest trends also include a growing interest in environmental sustainability, with organic and biodynamic wines appearing from numerous producers. The internet has revolutionized business, giving even the smallest vintners access to an international stage.

Like well-cellared wine, the palate of modern Australia is continually maturing. Whether your taste is for robust reds from Coonawarra and Barossa or the delicate and versatile whites of the Hunter Valley and Margaret River, Australia's winemakers are producing beautiful wines perfect to enjoy now or later.

AUSTRALIA'S DOMINANT VARIETALS

REDS

SHIRAZ

Australia's classic varietal. A full-bodied wine that, in hot areas, makes an earthy expression with softer acidity. Cooler regions produce a leaner, peppery style.

CABERNET SAUVIGNON

Dark red with black-currant and black cherry flavors, often with firm tannins and more acidity than Shiraz.

MERLOT

Intensely purple colored, full-bodied wine character-ized by moderate tannins, aromas of plum, and a velvety mouth-feel.

PINOT NOIR

Lighter-bodied with gentle tannins and fruity aromas of red berries.

WHITES

CHARDONNAY

Full-bodied wine that is often high in alcohol and low in acidity. Most Austra-lian versions are oaked.

RIESLING

Lighter-bodied wines with citrus and honey notes. Most are unoaked and dry or slightly off-dry.

SAUVIGNON BLANC

Makes crisp, dry wines with high acid and aromas of peach and lime.

SEMILLON

Light-bodied wines that have crisp acidity and complex flavors, including herbs, nuts, and honey.

WHITE BLENDS

Chardonnay-Semillon and Sauvignon Blanc-Semillon blends are popular. Semil-lon adds bright notes.

5

IN FOCUS WINES OF AUSTRALIA

WINE TOURING TIPS

Large vintners like Rosemount, McGuigan Wines, Jacobs Creek, Yalumba, and Wolf Blass are well equipped for visitors and many offer vineyard tours, as well as restaurants or cafes. Some require appointments.

Many boutique producers also have "cellar doors," a.k.a. tast-ing rooms, open seven days a week, but it is advisable to check their websites for de-tails. The average tastings cost around A$10 to A$15 for a flight of up to five different styles. Some include cheese, cracker, and fruit plates.

Winery in Clare Valley

AUSSIE WINE REGIONS

SOUTH AUSTRALIA

Barossa Valley

❶ BAROSSA VALLEY The country's best-known wine region, Barossa Valley has more than 550 grape growers, including some fifth- and sixth-generation families. Shiraz is highly celebrated, particularly the lauded Penfolds Grange. Cabernet Sauvignon, Grenache, Merlot, Riesling, Semillon, and Chardonnay are all well suited to Barossa's temperate climate, which is slightly cooler on its peaks and in neighboring Eden Valley. Big producers Jacobs Creek and Wolf Blass both have visitors centers with modern tasting rooms and restaurants. For a history lesson, take a tour at Langmeil Winery. An impressive property is Yalumba, with a stone winery and clock tower. So, too, is the well-established Peter Lehmann Estate on the banks of the North Para River.

❷ ADELAIDE HILLS For world-class Chardonnays, Sauvignon Blancs, Rieslings, and sparkling wines, look to the Adelaide Hills. Just 25 minutes from the center of Adelaide, this high-altitude region, amid Mount Lofty and down through the Piccadilly Valley, has nurtured elegantly refined white wines. The cooler climate also means that it's one of South Australia's leading producers of the temperamental Pinot Noir. There are about 25 cellars that offer tastings, including Petaluma Cellar, well known for its sparkling wines, Rieslings, and Chardonnays as well as its modern Bridgewater Mill restaurant. To try Italian varietals, head to Chain of Ponds. For excellent Sauvignon Blanc, stop into Shaw and Smith's 46-hectare estate.

Adelaide Hills

❸ MCLAREN VALE
Situated in the Fleurieu Peninsula region, McLaren Vale is an easy 40-minute trip south of Adelaide. Uniquely located by the coast, it's regarded as one of the more unpretentious regions thanks to laid-back beach lifestyle, passionate vintners, and family-owned wineries. This fusion of ideals, together with its warm climate, has most likely sparked its interest in experimenting with more exotic varieties such as Tempranillo, Zinfandel, and Mourvedre, as well as Viognier and Sangiovese. There are more than 60 cellar tasting rooms, ranging from the large producers such as Rosemount Estate and Tintara Winery to boutique producers such as Wirra Wirra, D'Arenberg, and Gemtree, each offering sales and wine flights that include the chance to sample local foods.

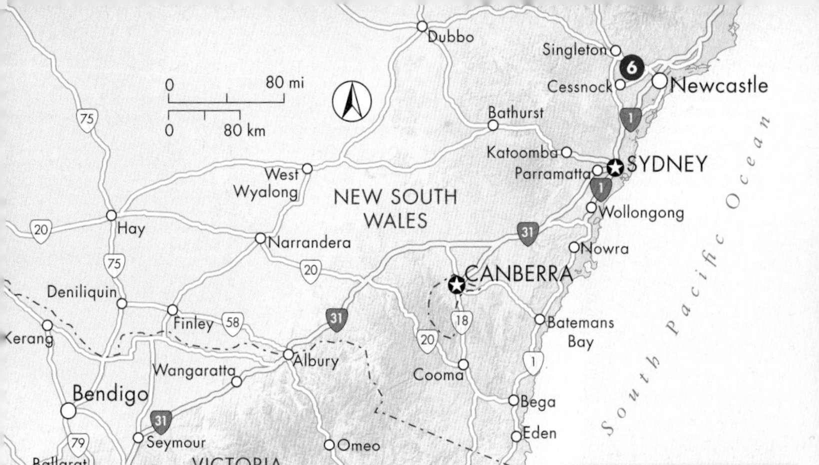

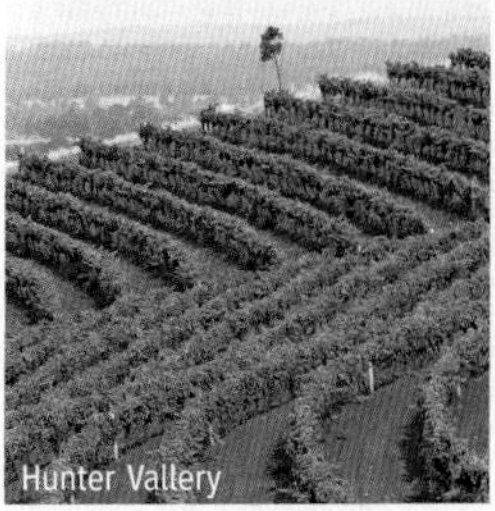
Hunter Valley

❹ LIMESTONE COAST

Coonawarra's long ripening season coupled with the region's "terra rossa" soil atop rich limestone beds is responsible for some of Australia's most famed wines, notably full-bodied reds. Often described as the Bordeaux of Australia, Coonawarra is a top spot for Cabernet Sauvignon, Cabernet blends, and spicy Shiraz. And they don't come any better than at places like Penley, Katnook Estate, Hollick, and Wynns Coonawarra Estate. Sixty kilometers to the north is Padthaway. While reds still prevail, the region's slightly warmer climate produces fruity Chardonnay and enjoyable Sauvignon Blanc, Verdelho, and Riesling. Built from limestone in 1882, the historic Padthaway Estate provides the perfect backdrop to sample some of the region's finest. Stonehaven and Henry's Drive are also worth a visit.

VICTORIA

❺ YARRA VALLEY

Close proximity to Melbourne makes the Yarra an easy choice if your touring time is limited. A cool climate and diverse mix of volcanic and clay soils have allowed Chardonnay and Pinot Noir to flourish. Other notable varieties here include Viognier, Gewürztraminer, Pinot Gris, and Sauvignon Blanc, as well as Malbec, Sangiovese, and Nebbiolo. Sparkling wine is also a winner and Domaine Chandon is a magnificent spot to enjoy some perfect bubbly. For a laidback experience, Lilydale is also a good choice. But upping the style stakes is the magnificent Yering Station with its modern Australian restaurant and gallery space. Elsewhere, De Bortoli sells delicious top-end wines.

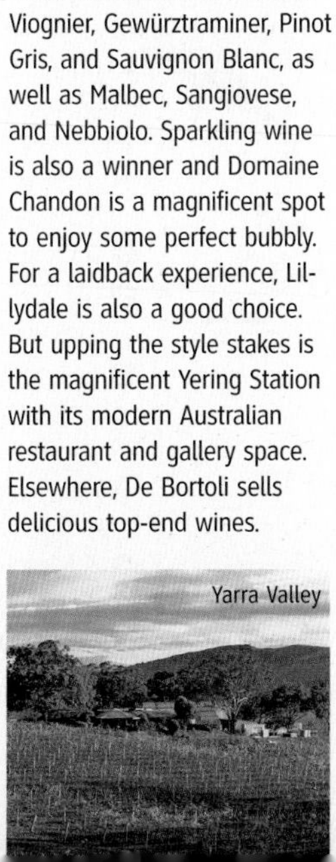
Yarra Valley

NEW SOUTH WALES

❻ HUNTER VALLEY

Despite being a producer of award-winning Chardonnay, Verdelho, and Shiraz, it's the honeyed Semillon, which can mature for up to two decades, that Hunter Valley does best. Split into upper and lower regions, it has more that 150 years of winemaking up its sleeve and 120 cellar doors. It's safe to say the Hunter knows how to entertain. From large-scale music concerts at Bimbadgen Estate and Tempus Two to the annual Jazz in the Vines event and other small food and wine festivals year-round, the region is constantly buzzing. Pokolbin, Broke, Wollombi, Lovedale, Rothbury and Mt View are the main areas to sample the regions best offerings. Autumn is an excellent time to visit.

AUSSIE WINE REGIONS

Margaret River

WESTERN AUSTRALIA

❼ MARGARET RIVER REGION With the first vines planted in 1967, Margaret River might be one of the country's younger wine areas but that hasn't stopped it from producing exceptionally high quality vintages. Cool breezes from the Indian Ocean and a steady, Mediterranean-style climate offer perfect conditions for developing complex styles of Chardonnay and minty-toned Cabernet Sauvignons. Shiraz, Merlot, Semillon, Sauvignon Blanc, and Chenin Blanc also thrive. Although the area produces about 20% of Australia's premium wines, it only accounts for about 3% of the nation's grapes. Try the West Australian Marron—or crayfish—with a crisp glass of Leeuwin Estate chardonnay. Cape Mentelle and Evans & Tate are also among the region's highlights, with many of their special releases sold only through their cellar doors.

Indian Ocean

Muchea
Sorrento
Scarborough
Fremantle ⊕ **PERTH** — 94 — Mundari
ROTTNEST ISLAND
Armadale — 40
GARDEN ISLAND Rockingham
Mandurah
Pinjarra
Waroona
Harvey — 20
Bunbury Collie
Geographe Bay
Dunsborough Busselton Balingup
Yallingup — 10
Margaret River ❼
Prevelly Karridale — 10 — Nannup Bridge Town
Kudardup Carlotta Manjim — 102
Augusta Pemberton
Nortcliffe — 1

0 _____ 40 mi
0 _____ 40 km

READING THE LABEL

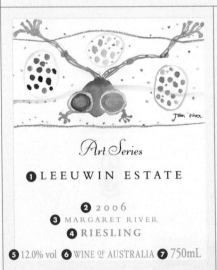

Art Series

❶ LEEUWIN ESTATE

❷ 2006
❸ MARGARET RIVER
❹ RIESLING
❺ 12.0% vol **❻** WINE OF AUSTRALIA **❼** 750mL

According to Australia's Label Integrity Program, when a wine label states region, grape variety, or vintage, then 85% of the wine contained in the bottle must come from that region, variety, or vintage.

❶ The producer of the wine.

❷ The vintage year, meaning the year the grapes were picked, crushed, and bottled.

❸ Australian GIs, or Geographic Indications, identify the region where the wine grapes were grown.

❹ The varietal, or type of grapes used to make the wine.

❺ The wine in this bottle contains 12% alcohol content by volume.

❻ The wine's country of origin.

❼ The volume of wine in the bottle.

MORE TASTING OPPORTUNITIES

Wine tasting at Mitchell Winery, Clare Valley

SIPPING IN SHOPS AND BARS

Even when you're not ensconced in the country's lush vineyards, high-quality wine isn't far away. The capital cities serve as a gateway for many of the wine country's top tastes.

In Sydney, try wine bars like the **Ivy's Ash Street Cellar**, **Glass Brasserie** wine bar at the Hilton Hotel and the **Gazebo Wine Garden** in Elizabeth Bay. **The Australian Wine Centre** in Circular Quay offers private tastings (with prior notice) and the **Ultimo Wine Centre** has free tastings each Saturday.

Heading south, visit Melbourne's **Prince Wine Store** at one of its three locations. Or soak up the atmosphere at **The Melbourne Supper Club** or **Melbourne Wine Room**. The bar of the award-winning **Press Club** restaurant also has an excellent Australian and international selection.

Apothecary 1878 on Adelaide's Hindley Street and **The Wine Underground**, just a few blocks away, both have a cosmopolitan ambience. Smaller vineyards are well represented at the city's **East End Cellars**.

In Perth, wine and dine alfresco at **Must Winebar** in Highgate. And **Amphoras Bar** in West Perth also has a long list of the country's best wines by the glass and bottle. No visit would be complete without heading to East Fremantle's **Wine Store**, for regular tastings and an extensive range of bottles. It also has an online store.

WINE FESTIVALS

Festivals offer chance to interact with the winemakers as well as sample local produce, especially cheese, fruit, and seafood. **The Barossa Vintage Festival** is one of the largest and longest running wine events in South Australia. Held in April each year it has everything from rare wine auctions to family friendly events. Other notables are **Adelaide's Tasting Australia** (April), **Coonawarra After Dark Weekend** (April), and **McLaren Vale Sea and Vines Festival** (June). In Western Australia, the **Margaret River Gourmet Escape** (April) celebrates culinary and winemaking talents.

RESEARCH & PLANNING

A little planning will allow you to make the perfect choices when it comes to deciding which regions to visit and where to taste. The websites of Australia's tourism commissions are filled with helpful planning informations. Not only do they offer winery information but also options for tours, accommodation and other sights to see while in the area. These include
⊕ *www.visitvictoria.com*,
⊕ *www.southaustralia.com*,
www.winecountry.com.au,
www.westernaustralia.com

Once on the ground, visitors centers such as the **Margaret River Wine Centre**, Adelaide's **National Wine Centre of Australia**, and **Hunter Valley Wine Country Tourism** can offer sound advice, especially on the best varietals and history of the regions.

Barossa Vintage Festival

5

IN FOCUS WINES OF AUSTRALIA

BE AMAZED

Victorians do love their mazes, and you'll find these quaint English-garden features dotted around the Mornington Peninsula. There are topiary and sculptured mazes, mystery lawn puzzles, and big garden chess sets.

Enchanted Maze Garden. Find your way through a traditional hedge maze or test your navigational skills in the indoor 3-D maze at this delightful attraction. The property also offers "tree surfing," in which participants make their way through an above-ground obstacle course. ⊠ *55 Purves Rd., Arthur's Seat* ☎ *03/5981-8449* ⊕ *www.enchantedmaze.com.au* ⊠ *A$29 gardens, A$59 tree surfing* ⊗ *Daily 10-6.*

Ashcombe Maze & Lavender Gardens. Check out the world's first circular rose maze, a Cypress-hedge maze, and a lavender labyrinth at this attraction, handily located near T'Gallant Winery. ⊠ *15 Shoreham Rd., Shoreham* ☎ *03/5989-8387* ⊕ *www.ashcombemaze.com.au* ⊠ *A$18.50* ⊗ *Daily 8-5.*

BEACHES

Rosebud Beach. Backing onto the suburb of Rosebud, this popular beach has been rated one of the safest in Victoria. The white sand flats extend a long way offshore and sand bars keep the area protected for swimming, while trees provide natural shade. The beach reserve includes a jetty (from which many locals fish), boat ramp, camping ground, and even a swimming pool. A picnic-and-barbecue area and playground in the adjacent Tom Salt Park make the beach a hit with families, and the adjacent Bay Trail walking and cycling track is popular. Nearby accommodation tends to be motels and cottages for rent. **Amenities:** food and drink; lifeguards; parking (free); showers; restrooms. **Best for:** swimming; walking. ⊠ *Point Nepean Rd. (end of Jetty Rd.), Rosebud.*

SPORTS AND THE OUTDOORS

DIVING AND SNORKELING

Bayplay Adventure Tours. This adventure tour company offers a variety of activities including diving, snorkeling, bike riding, and sea kayaking. You can explore colonies of weedy seadragons, swim through an octopus's garden, or feel the wash when dolphins leap over your kayak. Dives start from A$55, while a three-hour sea kayaking tour to a dolphin sanctuary costs A$99 per person. ⊠ *3755 Port Nepean Rd., Portsea* ☎ *03/5984-0888* ⊕ *www.bayplay.com.au.*

GOLF

Rosebud Park Public Golf Course. Situated on the steep slopes of Arthurs Seat overlooking Rosebud and Port Phillip Bay, this course provides spectacular views of greenery and water. The 18-hole course has some extremely challenging holes, a resident teaching professional, plenty of parking, and excellent picnic facilities. ⊠ *Elizabeth Dr., Rosebud* ☎ *03/5981-2833* ⊕ *www.rosebudpark.com.au* ⚐ *18 holes. 5800 yds. Par 70. Greens fee A$36* ⚲ *Facilities: putting green, golf carts, rental clubs, lessons.*

HIKING

The Mornington Peninsula is a memorable walking destination. There are walks for all levels of fitness and interest, from cliff-top strolls to the ultimate 26-km (16-mile) Two Bays Walking Track. Stop in at the visitor information centers at Dromana or Mornington to see what walking maps they have on hand, or contact Parks Victoria, the government body that manages the state's national parks.

Arthurs Seat State Park: There is a one-hour circuit walk to Kings Falls, and the relaxing Seawinds Gardens walk is less than a mile in length and takes only about half an hour.

Bushrangers Bay Walk: An exhilarating 6-km (4-mile) return walk along Western Port Bay begins at Cape Schanck Lighthouse and winds past basalt cliffs and Bushranger Bay, to finish at Main Creek.

Coppin's Track: A pleasant 3-km (2-mile) round-trip walk that stretches from Sorrento ocean beach (or Back Beach as it's known) to Jublilee point along the Bass Strait coastline.

Two Bays Walking Track: A hard-core 26-km (16-mile) walking track that links Dromana, on Port Phillip Bay, with Cape Schanck on Western Port Bay.

Mornington Peninsula Walking Tours. Take part in half- and full-day guided strolls, including one along Millionaires Walk with its lovely natural vistas and expensive mansions in Sorrento and Portsea. A two-day coast-to-coast walk costs A$80 per person per day including packed lunch, and is cheaper if more people join the walk; you can stay overnight in a cottage at Cape Schanck Lighthouse at your own expense (about A$180 including breakfast). ⊠ *29 Hughes Rd., Blairgowrie* ☎ *03/5984–4484, 0412/135142 mobile* ⊕ *www.mornpenwalks.com.au.*

Parks Victoria. This government agency manages all of Victoria's national parks. Its informative website includes information on safety considerations, special events, and park attractions. ☎ *13–1963* ⊕ *www. parkweb.vic.gov.au.*

HORSEBACK RIDING

Ace-Hi Beach Rides. In addition to its many horses, this company offers a 200-acre adventure park complete with a wildlife sanctuary and lots of activities for kids. Choose from pony rides, rock-wall climbs, or jaunts through the air on a zip line. Horse rides start from A$49 for an hour. ⊠ *810 Boneo Rd., Cape Schanck* ☎ *03/5988–6262* ⊕ *www. ace-hi.com.au.*

WHERE TO EAT AND STAY

For expanded hotel reviews, visit Fodors.com.

$ ✕ **Cellar & Pantry.** Busy produce store–cum–deli, this is the perfect place
DELI   to pick up the makings of a picnic lunch or a dinner in self-contained accommodation. It is packed full of crusty loaves, cured and fresh meats, fruits and vegetables, aromatic cheeses, olives, relishes and chutneys, and countless other goodies, most grown and/or made on the Mornington Peninsula. The veranda is a popular spot for a light breakfast or lunch, or coffee and cake; coffee beans and local wines are

also sold. $ *Average main: A$11* ✉ *141 Shoreham Rd., Red Hill South* ☎ *03/5989–2411* ⊕ *www.cellarandpantry.com.au.*

$$
FRENCH
Fodor's Choice
★

✕ **Montalto Vineyard & Olive Grove.** Overlooking an established vineyard with vistas of rolling green hills, this restaurant serves excellent French-inspired cuisine. Chef Barry Davis prepares such creative dishes as a snapper fillet with leek crust, red onion, tomato, and chervil vinaigrette (A$38); the dish is best matched with a Montalto Chardonnay. The menu changes regularly, based on available local produce. The wine list borrows from the best of the estate's vintages, as well as classic wines from other regions. The open-air Piazza Café (open weekends) dishes up pizza, warming winter soups, and summer salads. If it's a nice day, you can picnic on the grounds from baskets prepared by the restaurant. Take a moment to check out the herb garden and admire the sculptures on permanent display. If you're visiting from mid-February to late April you'll be able to see the entries in the Montalto Sculpture Prize and vote for your favorite. The expansive property also includes a natural wetlands and specially built boardwalks, so visitors have a chance of spotting more than 90 bird species. $ *Average main: A$36* ✉ *33 Shoreham Rd., Red Hill South* ☎ *03/5989–8412* ⊕ *www.montalto.com.au* ⊘ *Cellar door 11–5. No dinner Sun.–Thurs.*

$$
AUSTRALIAN
Fodor's Choice
★

✕ **Salix at Willow Creek.** Seasonal color changes along the vines make the Willow Creek Vineyard view through the restaurant's floor-to-ceiling windows spectacular year-round. This is one of the two dining options at this popular winery; the more casual Salix Bistro is off the stylish downstairs cellar door. The restaurant, owned by Bernard McCarthy, makes much of the property's own produce. Try the confit duck with Toulouse sausage, *cavalo nero*, and garlic crumble (A$36); the gnocchi crab with Coral Sea spanner crab and stinging nettle (A$32); or the small plate of house sugar-cured and smoked ocean trout (A$20). A star dessert is the Peninsula honey-and-amaretto cheesecake, with local figs, and honeycomb (A$17). The bistro, open noon–5 daily, provides a more casual ambience with the Salix Restaurant menu. The Willow Creek Vineyard opened in 1988 and concentrates on producing excellent Chardonnary and Pinot Noir from vines that have been tended by the same viticulturist since they were planted. In more recent times the owners have planted small quantities of Pinot Gris and Sauvignon Blanc. $ *Average main: A$37* ✉ *166 Balnarring Rd., Merricks North* ☎ *03/5989–7640* ⊕ *salixrestaurant.com.au* ⊘ *No dinner Sun.–Thurs.*

$$$
HOTEL

🛏 **Hotel Sorrento.** Built in 1871, this historic hotel offers attractive rooms that features exposed limestone, funky interiors, and water views. **Pros:** great location; impressive views from some rooms. **Cons:** limited facilities. $ *Rooms from: A$280* ✉ *15 Hotham Rd., Sorrento* ☎ *03/5984–8000* ⊕ *www.hotelsorrento.com.au* ⇌ *39 rooms* ¶○| *Breakfast.*

$$$
B&B/INN
Fodor's Choice
★

🛏 **Lakeside Villas at Crittenden Estate.** Wine and dine to your heart's content, then amble home to this accommodation perched next to a tranquil lake. **Pros:** fantastic position; stylish and snug. **Cons:** the nearby Stillwater Restaurant is open for dinner only on Friday and Saturday. $ *Rooms from: A$310* ✉ *25 Harrisons Rd., Dromana* ☎ *03/5987–3275* ⊕ *www.lakesidevillas.com.au* ⇌ *3 rooms* ¶○| *Breakfast.*

PHILLIP ISLAND

124 km (78 miles) southeast of Melbourne

South of Melbourne and just off the Mornington Peninsula, Phillip Island has long been a playground for Victorians. Both the coast and the interior are appealing, with beaches and native animals such as koalas among the attractions. The perennial highlight, however, is the famous Penguin Parade, in which the seabirds march ashore to the delight of onlookers.

At low tide you can walk across a basalt causeway to the Nobbies (rugged coastal rocks); a boardwalk here takes you around the wind-swept coastline to a blowhole. Thousands of shearwaters (also known as mutton birds) nest here from September to April, when they return north to the Bering Strait in the Arctic. Farther out, Seal Rocks host Australia's largest colony of fur seals; up to 20,000 creatures bask on the rocky platforms and cavort in the water here in midsummer. Boat tours cruise past these playful creatures in all but the coldest months.

GETTING HERE AND AROUND

To reach the island from Melbourne, take the Princes Freeway (M1) southeast to the South Gippsland Highway (M420), and follow this to the Bass Highway (A420). V/Line runs a combination train and bus service from Southern Cross Station to Cowes (with change at Dandenong railway station), a journey of 3½ hours. If you're on the Mornington Peninsula, there's a regular daily passenger ferry service from Stony Point (which can be reach aboard regular suburban commuter trains via Frankston) to Cowes.

TOURS

Day trips from Melbourne are run by local tour operators, including Gray Line. Tours of the Phillip Island Penguin Parade cost A$162 (penguins and koalas only) to A$186 (with an island tour and lunch). Wildlife Coast Cruises runs two-hour cruises from Cowes Jetty to the Nobbies and Seal Rocks, spending 20–30 minutes viewing the seal colony. Cruises run year-round with varying frequency, depending on the season. The company also runs half-day cruises to French Island October to April.

ESSENTIALS

Tour Operators Gray Line ☎ 1300/858687 ⊕ www.grayline.com. **Melbourne's Best Day Tours** ☎ 1300/130550 ⊕ www.melbournetours.com.au. **Wildlife Coast Cruises** ⊠ 13 The Esplanade, Cowes ☎ 1300/763739 ⊕ www.wildlifecoastcruises.com.au ☞ A$72.

Transportation Inter Island Ferries ☎ 03/9585–5730 24-hr info line ⊕ www.interislandferries.com.au. **V/Line** ☎ 1800/136196 ⊕ www.vline.com.au.

Visitor Information Phillip Island Visitor Information Centre ⊠ 895 Phillip Island Rd., Newhaven ☎ 03/5956–7447, 1300/366422 ⊕ www.visitphillipisland.com.

EXPLORING

Cowes. The seaside town of Cowes is the hub of Phillip Island; the pier is where you can board sightseeing cruises and the passenger ferry that travels across Western Port Bay to Stony Point on the Mornington Peninsula. It has a lively café scene and several quality gift shops interspersed with the traditionally cheaper tourist fare. Restaurant and hotel bookings are essential in the busy summer months. ⊠ *Cowes.*

FAMILY   **Koala Conservation Centre.** At this excellent wildlife center you can stroll along treetop-high boardwalks and view koalas in their natural habitat. At the visitor center you can learn some fascinating things about the cute furry creatures—such as how they sleep 21 hours a day. It is located just a short drive from the tourist information center at Newhaven; follow the signs along Phillip Island Tourist Road. ⊠ *1810 Phillip Island Tourist Rd., Cowes* ☎ *03/5951–2800* ⊕ *www.penguins. org.au/attractions/koala-conservation-centre* ⊠ *A$11.30* ⊗ *Daily 10–5.*

Fodor's Choice   **Penguin Parade.** Phillip Island's main draw is the nightly parade of Little
★   Penguins, also called Fairy Penguins, waddling from the sea to their burrows in nearby dunes. The parade of miniature penguins attracts onlookers year-round and crowds on summer weekends and holidays. There are several ways to view the Penguin Parade: general admission, with viewing from concrete bleachers; the Penguin Plus experience, which puts you on a smaller viewing platform that is closer to the action; the Guided Ranger Tour, which provides a spot on the sand with a ranger; and the VIP Tour, held in an elevated tower where up to 10 adults join the ranger who is narrating the action. The Ultimate Adventure Tour, for private groups, includes headphones and night-vision equipment and a secluded spot on a separate beach. The spectacle begins at around sunset each night; booking ahead is essential in summer and during public holidays. Wear closed shoes and warm clothing—even in summer—and rain protection gear. Make sure to arrive an hour before the tour begins. A good deal for visitors staying for a day is the 3 Park Pass, giving admission to the Penguin Parade, the Koala Conservation Centre, and Churchill Island. ⊠ *1019 Ventnor Rd., Summerlands* ☎ *03/5951–2800* ⊠ *General admission A$22.60; Penguin Plus viewing platform A$44; VIP Tour A$69; Guided Ranger Tour A$69; Ultimate Adventure Tour A$80; 3 Park Pass from A$38.40* ⊗ *Daily.*

BEACHES

Cape Woolamai Surf Beach. Phillip Island's only surf lifesaving club is based on this long, exposed stretch of prime surfing beach. The 4-km (2½-mile) beach can be hazardous, with strong undertows, so it's a spot for experienced surfers and swimmers only. All beachgoers are encouraged to swim between the safety flags that mark the patrolled area. Check with the club (☎ *03/5956–7311*) for patrol times. The Woolamai Beach Road runs off Phillip Island Road and is 14 km (9 miles) from Cowes. The nearest accommodation is generally cottage-style, with several places closer to the main road but none on the beach. Black Dolphin has a luxury penthouse and a cottage on the Cape, on Corona Road. **Amenities:** food and drink; lifeguards; parking (free); showers; restrooms. **Best for:** surfing; swimming. ⊠ *Woolamai Beach Rd., Cape Woolamai.*

Kitty Miller Bay. Regarded as one of Australia's best beaches, this south-facing beach provides excellent swimming and snorkeling, and a walking trail to view the remains of the wreck of the SS *Speke* at low tide. Sheltered by Watts Point and Kennon Head, the curved beach has low waves, with undertows only appearing when the waves whip up at high tide, which is the best time for surfing. There's not much shade and no kiosk, so bring water, food, and sunscreen with you. The beach is at the intersection with Watts Road. From Cowes, go either via Ventnor Road to Back Beach Road, or via Phillip Island Road and Back Beach Road, turning onto Kitty Miller Road. The beach is around 10 km (6 miles) from Cowes. The low-key nature of Phillip Island and the remote nature of the beach means that accommodation is usually B&B-style. Try the Kitty Miller Bay B&B on Watts Street. **Amenities:** parking (free). **Best for:** snorkeling; surfing; swimming; walking. ✉ *Kitty Miller Rd.*

SPORTS AND THE OUTDOORS

AUTO-RACING

Phillip Island Grand Prix Circuit. This racing circuit continues the island's long involvement with motor sports, dating back to 1928 when the Australian Grand Prix was run on local unpaved roads. The circuit was completely redeveloped in the 1980s, and in 1989 hosted the first Australian Motorcycle Grand Prix. The circuit holds regular races as well as big-ticket events, such as the MotoGP in October and Superbike World Championships in February. Speed freaks can buckle up for hot laps in a racing car (from A$330 for 30 minutes) driven by a professional driver year-round (dates and times vary, see website), or drive a go-kart (A$30 for 10 minutes) around a scale replica of the actual track. There are 60-minute guided walking tours of the track daily at 2 (subject to availability); a 45-meter slot car Grand Prix Circuit replica racing track; and a museum showcasing the island's motor racing history. ✉ *Back Beach Rd.* ☎ *03/5952–9400* 🌐 *www.phillipislandcircuit.com.au* 🎟 *A$19 tours, A$13.50 museum, A$8 slot cars* 🕒 *Daily 9–7; track tours at 2.*

WHERE TO EAT AND STAY

For expanded hotel reviews, visit Fodors.com.

$$ ECLECTIC 🍴 **Harry's on the Esplanade.** Spilling onto an upstairs terrace above the main Cowes beach, Harry's is a Phillip Island dining institution. Its menu, which changes regularly, draws heavily on seafood bought fresh from local trawlers, along with locally raised beef and lamb. Don't pass up the crayfish if it's on the menu. The wine list has an Australian emphasis and includes local wines. The bread is made on the premises, as are the pastries and ice cream. Harry's now offers breakfast on weekends starting at 10. [$] *Average main: A$32* ✉ *Upper level, 17 The Esplanade, Cowes* ☎ *03/5952–6226* 🌐 *www.harrysrestaurant.com.au* 🕒 *Closed Mon.*

$$ B&B/INN 🏨 **Glen Isla House.** A beautiful, safe swimming beach is right at the doorstep of this luxurious B&B, which contains six individually themed rooms. **Pros:** gorgeous furnishings; on a pristine beach; short drive to penguins. **Cons:** the heritage feel may not suit some. [$] *Rooms from:*

A$299 ✉ *230 Church St., Cowes* ☎ *03/5952–1882* ⊕ *www.glenisla. com* ↰ *1 king suite, 6 house rooms, 1 2-story gate cottage* ⦿ *Breakfast.*

QUEENSCLIFF

103 km (64 miles) southwest of Melbourne.

In the late 19th century Queenscliff was a favorite weekend destination for well-to-do Melburnians, who traveled on paddle steamers or by train to stay at the area's grand hotels, some of which are still in business today. Be sure to check out Fort Queenscliff, another landmark from bygone days. Good restaurants and quiet charm are also traits of Queenscliff. The playground of families during the day and dog walkers come dusk, Queenscliff is a restful alternative to the resort towns of Sorrento and Portsea on the other side of the bay. At the end of November the annual Queenscliff Music Festival (⊕ *www.qmf.net.au*) draws thousands of visitors to town.

GETTING HERE AND AROUND

The lovely coastal village of Queenscliff and nearby smaller sibling Point Lonsdale make for a worthy—and well-signposted—detour on the drive from Melbourne to the start of the Great Ocean Road.

It's about a 60- to 90-minute drive from Melbourne to Geelong via the Princes Freeway (M1), then to Queenscliff via the Bellarine Highway (B110). Trains run from Melbourne's Southern Cross Station to Geelong, where buses (Nos. 75 and 76) continue on to Queenscliff. The Queenscliff–Sorrento Ferry departs on the hour (in both directions) from 7 am to 6 pm and to 7 pm in the summer months. The journey takes 40 minutes and costs A$10 for pedestrians, A$69 for cars including two passengers in the high season.

It's easy to walk around Queenscliff's main attractions; ask at the visitor center in Hesse Street for maps. The Bellarine Railway, a narrow-gauge tourist train, runs between the towns of Queenscliff and Drysdale (a distance of 16 km [10 miles] several times a week, while on Saturday nights, and occasional Friday nights, between August and May the hugely popular Blues Train mixes dinner and live blues entertainment; tickets are A$95.20 per person.

ESSENTIALS

Transportation Bellarine Railway ✉ *Queenscliff Railway Station, 20 Symonds St.* ☎ *03/5258–2069* ⊕ *bellarinerailway.com.au.* **Queenscliff–Sorrento Ferry** ☎ *03/5258–3244* ⊕ *www.searoad.com.au.* **V/Line** ☎ *1800/800007* ⊕ *www.vline. com.au.*

Visitor Information Queenscliffe Visitor Information Centre ✉ *55 Hesse St.* ☎ *03/5258–4843, 1300/884843* ⊕ *www.queenscliffe.vic.gov.au.*

WHERE TO STAY

For expanded hotel reviews, visit Fodors.com.

$$$ ⬚ **Queenscliff Hotel.** If you're after period charm rather than sleek moder-
HOTEL   nity, this gloriously restored 19th-century beauty is for you, with its soaring, pressed-metal ceilings, stained-glass windows, and antique furnishings. **Pros:** grandly charming; good location; excellent on-site

restaurants. **Cons:** limited room facilities. $ *Rooms from: A$240* ✉ *16 Gellibrand St.* ☎ *03/5258-1066* ⊕ *www.queenscliffhotel.com.au* ✈ *15 rooms* ❐ *Breakfast.*

$$$
HOTEL
Fodor's Choice
★

☵ **Vue Grand Hotel.** Built in 1881, this stylish hotel blends Old World elegance with modern touches in its recently restored grand premises. **Pros:** grand experience; wonderful dining room. **Cons:** not on the seaside. $ *Rooms from: A$250* ✉ *46 Hesse St.* ☎ *03/5258-1544* ⊕ *www.vuegrand.com.au* ✈ *29 rooms, 3 suites* ❐ *Breakfast.*

■ EN
ROUTE

From Queenscliff, follow Great Ocean Road signs for 45 km (28 miles) to **Torquay,** Australia's premier surfing and windsurfing resort, and Bell's Beach, famous for its Easter surfing contests and its October international windsurfing competitions. The Great Ocean Road, a positively magnificent coastal drive, officially begins at Eastern View, 10 km (6 miles) east of Lorne. The seaside towns of Anglesea, Aireys Inlet, and Fairhaven are other good warm-weather swimming spots.

LIGHT UP YOUR TRIP

If you're into lighthouses, then this coast is a must-see. Here you can find seven historic lighthouses of varying shapes and sizes—from Point Lonsdale in the east to Portland in the west. Don't miss the tall red-capped white **Split Point lighthouse** at Aireys Inlet, while **Cape Otway lighthouse,** the oldest on mainland Australia, marks the point where the Southern Ocean and Bass Strait collide. Farther west at Portland is majestic **Cape Nelson Lighthouse,** high above ferocious seas. Guided tours are available.

5

GREAT OCEAN ROAD

The Great Ocean Road, which snakes along Victoria's rugged and windswept southwestern coast, is arguably Australia's most spectacular coastal drive. The road, built by returned soldiers after World War I along majestic cliffs, occasionally dips down to sea level. Here, in championship surfing country, some of the world's finest waves pound mile after mile of uninhabited, golden, sandy beaches and rocky headlands.

Although this region is actually on the southeast coast of the Australian mainland, it lies to the west of Melbourne, and so Melburnians refer to it as the "West Coast." From the city, you should allow two or more days for a West Coast sojourn.

Driving is the most convenient way to see the region, and the only way to really enjoy the Great Ocean Road. Although the route is officially deemed to be 243 km (152 miles), and runs between the towns of Torquay in the east and Allansford (near Warnambool) in the west, most people think of it as the much longer route that continues farther west to Port Fairy and Portland. Its many twists and turns and wonderful sights along the way take many hours to explore.

The going may be slow on the most scenic routes, especially during the summer holiday period. The winding road is notorious for its motor accidents (you'll notice roadside signs along the route reminding visitors

Sea kayaking in Apollo Bay

that Australia drives on the left), so take care on the bends and slow down.

TOURS

12 Apostles Helicopter rides are an exciting way to appreciate the awesome force of the Southern Ocean and this amazing natural sculpture park. Fifteen-minute flights take in the Twelve Apostles and Loch Ard Gorge; longer flights travel farther up the coast to the west and inland. Prices start at A$145 per person.

AAT Kings has a six-day tour from Melbourne to Adelaide that travels the length of the Great Ocean Road and also includes visits to Mt. Gambier and Kangaroo Island. The tour is A$1,995.

Adventure Tours Australia has two three-day tours that include both the Great Ocean Road and the Grampians National Park. Young backpackers are their target market, however anyone can join the tours, and a choice between dorm accommodation and singles or doubles is available. You can choose a one-day round-trip tour from Melbourne for A$128, or join one that continues on to Adelaide. On the Adelaide tour, members spend one night in Port Campbell (west of the Twelve Apostles) and another night in Halls Gap. It's A$390 for dorm accommodation and A$610 for a double or twin room, with two dinners and two breakfasts.

Auswalk. This tour company offers guided (seven-day) and self-guided (five- or eight-day) Great Ocean Walk tours. The self-guided walk takes you from Apollo Bay to the Twelve Apostles over eight days (seven nights), or the trip can be divided into two four-night segments. Walkers carry a day pack only; a support vehicle carries the luggage by car from hotel (or B&B) to hotel. Most tours include at least one night in the 19th-century Cape Otway Lighthouse cottages, and most meals are provided. Both guided and self-guided tours can be arranged year-round and require a minimum of two people. Auswalk also offers a set-date six-night group guided walk including pickup and drop-off from Melbourne Airport. The six-night group guided tour starts from A$2,495 per person (double) depending on the season. Self-guided tours are about A$1,000 less. Daily walks can range from five to seven hours, although the support vehicle can drive those who feel they have had enough walking for one day. ☎ *03/5356–4971* ⊕ *www.auswalk.com.au.*

Great Ocean Road Adventure Tours or GORATS as it's called, runs mountain-bike tours across the region. Many tours run to the town of Forrest, considered a mountain-bike mecca, with 15 trails showcasing the natural beauty of the Otway Ranges. GORATS specializes in school groups but can tailor-make trips for a minimum of two people. Prices start from A$85 per person for a two-hour trip, including bike, helmet, map, transport, and guide; pickups from local accommodations can be arranged. They also operate flat-water canoe tours on the Barwon, Anglesea, and Aire rivers.

Lighthouse Tours explore the majestic, and still operational, Split Point Lighthouse at Aireys Inlet, also known as the White Queen. You can see her for miles as you approach this section of the Great Ocean Road west of Anglesea—just look for the huge white tower with the red cap—and the views from the top are amazing. The 45-minute tours operate year-round, but bookings are required on weekdays. Tour cost is A$12.

Melbourne's Best Day Tours has a 4WD tour of the Great Ocean Road from Melbourne. Starting at 7:30 am, it includes breakfast and lunch, a lighthouse tour, rain-forest walks, the Otway Fly treetop walk, and sightseeing in Port Campbell National Park. The 12-hour tour takes a maximum of six people and costsA$326.

Mulloka Cruises give half-hour cruises around the Port Fairy Bay—a quick way to set your sea legs and see Port Fairy from a different angle. Boat owner Jane Grimshaw dispenses interesting information about the area. Cruises cost from A$10.

Port Campbell Boat Charters operates diving tours to the famous wreck sites as well as scenic cruises and fishing trips.

Southern Exposure Adventure Sports runs mountain-bike tours along the coast and in the nearby Great Otway National Park, kayaking tours, and surfing lessons. Surfing lessons are A$65 for two hours, and combined bike and kayaking tours can be arranged. Bookings are essential.

Spring Creek Horse Rides take you through the beautiful Otway National Park. It's a leisurely way to spend an hour or two. Located at Bellbrae, just a few miles inland from Torquay, rides are A$45 for one hour and A$65 for two.

ESSENTIALS

Tour Operators 12 Apostles Helicopters ⊠ *Twelve Apostles Information Centre, Great Ocean Rd. at Booringa Rd., Port Campbell* ☎ *03/5598–8283* ⊕ *www.12apostleshelicopters.com.au.* **AAT Kings** ⊠ *Melbourne Day Tours,*

Federation Sq., Flinders and Russell Sts., City Center, Melbourne ☎ *1300/228546* ⊕ *www.aatkings.com.au.* **Adventure Tours Australia** ☎ *1300/654604, 03/8102–7800* ⊕ *www.adventuretours.com.au.* **Auswalk** ☎ *03/5356–4971* ⊕ *www.auswalk.com.au.* **Great Ocean Road Adventure Tours** ☎ *0417/576973* ⊕ *www.gorats.com.au.* **Lighthouse Tours** ✉ *Split Point lighthouse, Federal St., Aireys Inlet* ☎ *1800/174045* ⊕ *www.splitpointlighthouse.com.au* 💰 *A$12.* **Melbourne's Best Day Tours** ✉ *Federation Sq., Flinders and Russell Sts., City Center, Melbourne* ☎ *1300/130550* ⊕ *www.melbournetours.com.au.* **Mulloka Cruises** ✉ *Martins Point, end of wharf, Port Fairy* ☎ *0408/514382 mobile, 03/5568–1790* ✉ *janegrimshaw@bigpond.com.* **Port Campbell Boat Charters** ✉ *32 Lord St., Port Campbell* ☎ *03/5598–6366, 0428/986366 mobile* ⊕ *www.portcampbellboatcharters.com.au.* **Southern Exposure Adventure Sports** ✉ *38 Bell St., Torquay* ☎ *03/5261–9170, 0425/784643 mobile* ⊕ *www. southernexposure.com.au.* **Spring Creek Horse Rides** ✉ *245 Portreath Rd., Belbrae* ☎ *03/5266–1541, 0403/167590 mobile* ⊕ *www.springcreekhorserides. com.au.*

Visitor Information **Geelong and Great Ocean Road Visitor Information Centre** ✉ *Princes Hwy.(at the gas station, 20 km [12 miles] before Geelong), Little River, Geelong* ☎ *03/5283–1735, 1800/620888* ⊕ *www. visitgeelongbellarine.com.au* ⊗ *Daily 9–5.* **Torquay Visitor Information Centre** ✉ *Surf City Plaza, Beach Rd., Torquay* ☎ *1300/620888, 03/5261–4219* ⊕ *www. visittorquay.org* ⊗ *Daily 9–5.*

LORNE

148 km (92 miles) southwest of Melbourne, 95 km (59 miles) southwest of Queenscliff, 50 km (31 miles) southwest of Torquay.

Located between sweeping Loutit Bay and the Otway Mountain Range, Lorne is one of the main towns on the Great Ocean Road, with a definite surf-and-holiday feel. It's the site of both a wild celebration every New Year's Eve and the popular Pier-to-Pub Swim held on the first weekend in January. Some people make their reservations a year or more in advance. It's also the starting point for the Great Ocean Road International Marathon held each May (the footrace ends in Apollo Bay). The town has a lively café and pub scene, as well as several upscale restaurants, trendy boutiques, and a day spa.

GETTING HERE AND AROUND

You really need a car to get to Lorne and other Great Ocean Road towns; the next best option is to take an organized tour. Public transport is available, but it's a long process: take the V/Line train to Geelong, then transfer to a bus to Apollo Bay, which stops at Lorne (about five hours). If driving, take the Princes Highway west from Melbourne across the Westgate Bridge to Geelong. From there, follow signs along the Surf Coast Highway to Torquay, where you'll connect with the Great Ocean Road.

ESSENTIALS

Visitor Information **Lorne Visitor Information Centre** ✉ *15 Mountjoy Parade* ☎ *03/5289–1152, 1800/620888* ⊕ *www.visitlorne.org.*

BEACHES

Lorne Beach. This stretch of the Victorian coast is also called The Shipwreck Coast, with reputedly up to 700 ships at rest offshore. Lorne itself has a shipwreck plaque walk along the foreshore, giving the history of local disasters and near-misses dating from 1854. The Lorne Surf Life Saving Club patrols the southern end of popular Lorne Beach, which runs south from the Erskine River for 1 km (½ mile). Although it's a fairly safe beach, especially in summer, care must be taken when the waves are high as the undertow can be dangerous. The beach has parking for 250 cars, a lookout, shade trees and shelters, barbecue and play areas, and a cycle track. The Lorne Beach Pavilion has a swimming pool and skate park as well. A camping ground and caravan park are also near the beach. Parking is available at the junction of Bay Street, Mountjoy Parade, and the Great Ocean Road or along the Great Ocean Road itself. Other entrances to the beach are via **Grove Street** or **William Street**. The Mantra Lorne resort, with 12 acres of gardens and a range of rooms and apartments, is directly on the beach. **Amenities:** food and drink;, lifeguards;, parking (free); showers; restrooms. **Best for:** surfing; swimming; walking. ✉ *Great Ocean Rd. at Bay St.*

SPORTS AND THE OUTDOORS

HIKING

The Great Ocean Road and the "Surf Coast" section of it around Torquay, Lorne, and Airleys Inlet have fantastic walks providing great cliff-top views, while inland a little way there are waterfalls and picnic grounds to explore.

The 30-km (19-mile) Surf Coast Walk, which begins near Jan Juc car park (1 mile west of Torquay) and ends around Moggs Creek Picnic Area at Aireys, can be done in short segments.

Inland from the towns of Fairweather and Eastern View is the vast Great Otway National Park, which has many picturesque walks, including the 12-km (7½-mile) walk from Aireys Inlet to Distillery Creek, which can be quite strenuous. There are also shorter and easier walks to Erskine Falls and Sheoak Falls just inland from Lorne. The Torquay and Lorne visitor centers have trail maps.

WHERE TO EAT AND STAY

For expanded hotel reviews, visit Fodors.com.

$$ SEAFOOD 🍴 **Marks.** Fresh seafood—from fried calamari to roasted flathead—is the draw at this Lorne institution, which has been going strong since 1989. The decor is "funky seaside," with bright walls, blue chairs, and a smattering of local art and sculpture for sale. The menu changes daily depending on what the fishermen have caught and what's growing in the restaurant's garden, but you'll always find oysters and steak on the menu, along with Atlantic salmon, and perhaps Sicilian seafood soup. For dessert there's nothing more delicious than the house-churned ice cream or the chocolate mousse served between vanilla biscuits with kahlua cream. Opening hours are extended during the summer months. [$] *Average main: A$32* ✉ *124 Mountjoy Parade* ☎ *03/5289–2787* 🌐 *www.marksrestaurant.com.au* 🕒 *Closed Sun. and Mon. and from Easter–mid Aug. No lunch Tues,–Fri.*

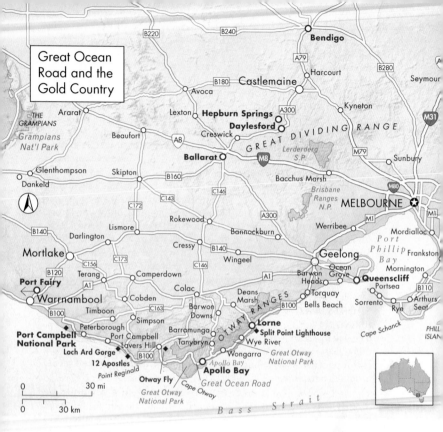

Great Ocean Road and the Gold Country

$$$
RESORT

Mantra Erskine Beach Resort. You can fall asleep listening to waves rolling ashore at this huge complex on 12 acres near the water's edge in Lorne. **Pros:** close to the beach; lots of facilities. **Cons:** fee for Internet. **$** *Rooms from: A$299* ⊠ *Mountjoy Parade* ☎ *03/5228–9777* ⊕ *www.mantraerskinebeachresort.com.au* ↝ *142 rooms, 135 apartments* ⊚ *Breakfast.*

EN ROUTE

Otway Fly. A spectacular 1,969-foot-long elevated treetop walk allows you to stroll a steel walkway above the rain-forest canopy. One section is springboard-cantilevered, and gently bounces as you pass over Young's Creek. The entrance is about an hour's drive and 70 km (43 miles) from Lorne. To get there, follow the Great Ocean Road until it joins Skenes Creek Road, then take Forrest Apollo Bay Road to Beech Forest Road, then Colac Lavers Hill Road until you reach the signed turnoff to Phillips Track. From the Fly you'll see the tops of giant myrtle beech, blackwood, and mountain ash trees, as well as spectacular views of the surrounding region. It's open daily 9–5 (last entry 4); tickets are A$25. ⊠ *360 Phillips Track* ☎ *03/5235–9200, 1800/300477* ⊕ *www.otwayfly.com.*

APOLLO BAY

45 km (28 miles) west of Lorne

A small attractive town on a wide curving bay, Apollo Bay is a quieter alternative to busy Great Ocean Road towns like Lorne. There's enough diversity to entertain visitors, with several places to eat and plenty of opportunities for aquatic activities. It's most popular as a jumping-off point for the famous rock formations of the Twelve Apostles Marine National Park, and the greenery of Great Otway National Park.

GETTING HERE AND AROUND

Driving is the most convenient way to get here. Otherwise take the combined V/Line train-bus option, which involves riding a train from Melbourne's Southern Cross Station to Geelong and then a bus along the Great Ocean Road to Apollo Bay, via Lorne and other Surf Coast towns.

BEACHES

Apollo Bay Beach. At the far reaches of the Great Ocean Road, 195 km (121 miles) from Melbourne, you'll find one of Victoria's most popular holiday beaches. Protected by seawalls and Point Bunbury, Apollo Bay has low waves at the south end with a shallow sandbar, although care must be taken with an undertow that gets stronger as you go north. The local surf lifesaving club patrols between flags at the southern end. The 3-km (almost 2-mile) beach runs parallel to the Great Ocean Road and Collingwood Street, and at the latter end there is a reserve with shade trees and a picnic area. Behind the street is a row of shops and cafés, and on most Saturdays, the Apollo Bay market sees stall holders lining the foreshore path to sell local produce and crafts. Behind the town, the green hills of the Otways provide a change of scenery. A lookout up a mountain pathway gives a view of a sunken steamship when the weather is clear. If you want to get closer to the sea, Apollo Bay Surf and Kayak offers kayaking tours to see the local seal colony, as well as providing surfing and paddleboarding lessons. The Seaview Motel and Apartments are near the beach, and some rooms have balconies looking over the view. **Amenities:** food and drink; lifeguards; parking (free); showers; restrooms. **Best for:** surfing; swimming; walking. ⊠ *Collingwood St.*

SPORTS AND THE OUTDOORS

DIVING

The Twelve Apostles Marine National Park and the nearby Arches Marine Sanctuary both provide fantastic diving opportunities. Local wrecks that can be explored with experienced guides include the *Napier* at Port Campbell, the famous *Loch Ard* (off Muttonbird Island), the *Schomberg* at Peterborough, and the *Fiji* near Moonlight Head. All wrecks are protected by federal law, and are not to be disturbed in any way. (⇨ *See Port Campbell boat charters in Tours, above.*)

HIKING

The Port Campbell National Park area, which is home to the Twelve Apostles, Loch Ard George, and other amazing landforms, has many good walks. Most are along wooden boardwalks; some also include steep stairs down to the beach. The Visitor Centre at Port Campbell has all the details.

Inland from Port Campbell is the Camperdown-Timboon Rail Trail (also known as the Coast to Crater Rail Trail). It passes by lakes and streams and open volcanic plains. It is suitable for walkers and mountain bikers. The 36-km (22-mile) trail has good signage. Ask at the tourist offices for details.

WHERE TO STAY

For expanded hotel reviews, visit Fodors.com.

$ HOTEL **Beachfront Motel.** You couldn't hope for better placement at this seaside town accommodation, which is located near beaches and shops. **Pros:** convenient location for a reasonable price. **Cons:** there may be some noise from the adjacent main road. [$] *Rooms from: A$135* ✉ *163 Great Ocean Rd.* ☎ *03/5237–6666* 🌐 *www.beachfrontmotel.com.au* 🛏 *10 rooms* 🍴 *No meals.*

$$$$ HOTEL Fodor's Choice ★ **Chris's Beacon Point Restaurant and Villas.** Set high in the Otway Ranges overlooking the Great Ocean Road and the sea, this is a wonderful place to dine or bed down for the night. **Pros:** sensational views. **Cons:** pricey; steep walk to rooms. [$] *Rooms from: A$320* ✉ *280 Skenes Creek Rd.* ☎ *03/5237–6411* 🌐 *www.chriss.com.au* 🛏 *4 villas, 5 studios* 🍴 *Breakfast.*

PORT CAMPBELL NATIONAL PARK

283 km (75 miles) southwest of Melbourne via the Great Ocean Rd., 90 km (56 miles) west of Apollo Bay, 135 km (83 miles) west of Lorne.

It is possible to visit Port Campbell National Park on an organized day trip from Melbourne, but a better alternative is to stay overnight at one of the nearby towns and explore the region over a half or full day. Port Campbell township is the logical place to base yourself, providing a range of accommodation and dining options. The 30-km (19-mile) coastal drive is crammed with amazing sea sculptures, and you'll be stopping in the car parks along the way to get out and walk along the boardwalks to viewing platforms and steps that lead down to the coast.

GETTING HERE AND AROUND

The scenic route to Port Campbell National Park (which is actually a few miles east of the town of Port Campbell) is via the Great Ocean Road from Torquay, via Lorne and Apollo Bay. A car is the best way to go. A shorter drive is via the Princes Highway (M1) from Melbourne to Warrnambool, then the Great Ocean Road east to Port Campbell. A V/Line train operates to Warrnambool, and then a bus can be taken to Port Campbell. The journey takes about five hours.

ESSENTIALS

Transportation V/Line ☎ *1800/800007* 🌐 *www.vline.com.au.*

EXPLORING

Fodor's Choice ★ **Port Campbell National Park.** Stretching some 30 km (19 miles) along Victoria's southern coastline, Port Campbell National Park is the site of some of the most famous and most beautiful geological formations in

Australia. The ferocious Southern Ocean has gnawed at the limestone cliffs along this coast for aeons, creating a sort of badlands-by-the-sea, where strangely shaped formations stand offshore amid the surf. The most famous of these formations is the Twelve Apostles, as much a symbol for Victoria as the Sydney Opera House is for New South Wales (The name has always been a misnomer, as there were originally only nine of these stone columns—or sea stacks as they are correctly termed. Collapses in 2005 and 2009 mean that seven remain). If you happen to be visiting the Twelve Apostles just after sunset, you're likely to see bands of Little Penguins returning to their burrows on the beach. There's a population of around 3,000 of these cute creatures in the area.

Loch Ard Gorge, named after the iron-hulled clipper that wrecked on the shores of nearby Mutton Bird Island in 1878, is another spectacular place to walk. Four of the *Loch Ard*'s victims are buried in a nearby cemetery, while a sign by the gorge tells the story of the ship and its crew. This stretch of coast is often called the Shipwreck Coast for the hundreds of vessels that have met untimely ends in the treacherous waters. The Historic Shipwreck Trail, with landmarks describing 25 of the disasters, stretches from Moonlight Head to Port Fairy.

5

The best time to visit the park is late September to April, when you can also witness the boisterous birdlife on nearby Mutton Bird Island. Toward nightfall, hundreds of hawks and kites circle the island in search of baby mutton birds emerging from their protective burrows. The birds of prey beat a hasty retreat at the sight of thousands of adult shearwaters approaching with food for their chicks as the last light fades from the sky. Other amazing sea stacks and stone formations farther west along the Great Ocean Road are also not to be missed. These include the Grotto, London Bridge (now an arch after an earlier collapse), and the spectacular Bay of Islands and Bay of Martyrs.

The Twelve Apostles Information Centre is open daily 9 to 5. A self-guided, 1½-hour Discovery Walk begins near Port Campbell Beach, where it's safe to swim. The pounding surf and undertow are treacherous at other nearby beaches. ✉ *Port Campbell National Park.*

WHERE TO EAT AND STAY

For expanded hotel reviews, visit Fodors.com.

$$ AUSTRALIAN 🍴 **Waves.** A relaxed main-street eatery with a spacious sundeck and friendly staff, Waves serves enormous breakfasts and fireside seafood dinners. Daily fish and curry specials are offered, and the regular menu provides such dishes as a half chicken cooked in a master stock and served with Asian vegetables, or char-grilled barramundi. Meat eaters can tuck into Angus scotch fillet and pork loin with caramelized apple. [$] *Average main: A$28* ✉ *29 Lord St., Port Campbell* ☎ *03/5598–6111* 🌐 *www.wavesportcampbell.com.au.*

$$ RENTAL 🏨 **Daysy Hill Country Cottages.** Set in manicured gardens with lavender-lined walkways, these five attractive sandstone-and-cedar cottages look over the Newfield Valley. **Pros:** good price; good location. **Cons:** limited facilities; minimum stay required. [$] *Rooms from: A$195* ✉ *2585 Cobden-Port Campbell Rd., Port Campbell* ☎ *03/5598–6226* 🌐 *www.daysyhillcottages.com.au* 🛏 *5 cottages, 4 suites, 3 cabins* 🍽 *No meals.*

Loch Ard Gorge in Port Campbell National Park, Great Ocean Road

$$ RENTAL 🏠 **Southern Ocean Villas.** Ideally situated on the edge of Port Campbell National Park, within short walking distance of the town center and beach, these villas are stylishly furnished and fitted with polished wood floors, picture windows, and high ceilings. **Pros:** good location near Twelve Apostles. **Cons:** located in sleepy town; difficult to find. [$] *Rooms from: A$280* ✉ *2 McCue St., Port Campbell* ☎ *03/5598–4200* 🌐 *www.southernoceanvillas.com* 🛏 *20 villas* 🍴 *No meals.*

EN ROUTE **Warrnambool.** About 66 km (41 miles) west of Port Campbell, Warrnambool is Victoria's southern right whale nursery. Platforms at Logan's Beach, about 3 km (2 miles) east of the city, provide views of an amazing marine show from June to September. Whales return to this beach every year to calve, with the females and young staying close to the shore and the males playing about 150 yards out to sea. ✉ *Warrnambool.*

PORT FAIRY

377 km (215 miles) southwest of Melbourne via the Great Ocean Rd.; it is shorter if you take the Princes Hwy. (M1)

Port Fairy is widely considered to be the state's prettiest village. The second-oldest town in Victoria, it was originally known as Belfast, and there are indeed echoes of Ireland in the landscape and architecture. More than 50 of the cottages and sturdy bluestone buildings that line the banks of the River Moyne have been classified as landmarks by the National Trust, and few towns repay a leisurely stroll so richly. Huge Norfolk Island pines line many of the streets, particularly Gipps Street, and the town is dotted with good cafés, pubs, and art galleries.

The town still thrives as the base for a fishing fleet, and as host to the Port Fairy Folk Festival, one of Australia's most famous musical events, held every March. The town has a large colony of short-tailed shearwaters that nest on Griffiths Island. Amazingly, these birds travel here from the Aleutian Islands near Alaska, always arriving within three days of September 22. You can take a 45-minute walk around the island on marked trails to the historic lighthouse.

GETTING HERE AND AROUND

The most convenient form of transport is by car; the 377-km (234-mile) trip along the Great Ocean Road from Melbourne takes about 6½ hours, and it's advisable to break the journey, as there's so much to see along the way. It's a shorter trip if you take the Princes Highway (M1). V/Line trains travel from Melbourne's Southern Cross Station to Warrnambool (three hours), and V/Line buses then make the short distance (29 km/18 miles) to Port Fairy.

ESSENTIALS

Transportation V/Line ☎ *1800/800007* ⊕ *www.vline.com.au.*

Visitor Information Port Fairy Visitor Information Centre ⊠ *Railway Pl., Bank St.* ☎ *03/5568–2682* ⊕ *www.port-fairy.com/vic.*

EXPLORING

Mott's Cottage. National Trust–listed Mott's Cottage is a restored limestone-and-timber cottage built by Sam Mott, a member of the 1830s whaling crew from the cutter *Fairy* who founded the town. ⊠ *5 Sackville St.* ☎ *03/5568–2682, 03/5568–2632* ▨ *A$2 donation* ☉ *Wed. and Sat. 2–4, or by appointment June–Aug.*

Port Fairy Historical Society. The historical society's museum contains relics from the 19th-century whaling days, when Port Fairy was a whaling station with one of the largest ports in Victoria. It also highlights the stories of the many ships that have come to grief along this dangerous coast. ⊠ *Old Courthouse, 30 Gipps St.* ☎ *03/5568–2263* ⊕ *www. historicalsociety.port-fairy.com* ▨ *A$4* ☉ *Sept.–June, Wed., Sat., and public holidays 2–5, Sun. 10:30–12:30; mid-July–Aug., Sat. 2–4.*

Tower Hill State Game Reserve. This reserve, packed with native Australian animals in their natural state, is co-managed by Parks Victoria and the Worn Gundidj Aboriginal Co-Operative, an organization that conducts cultural interpretative walks. Take its one-hour personalized bush and nature walk to learn about indigenous lifestyles, bush food, and medicine, and hear about the local inhabitants, which include emus, sugar gliders, koalas, kangaroos, birds, and reptiles. The standard tour is A$37; also ask about the availability of other occasional specialist tours, including night-time visits. Parks Victoria's website also has a map of the reserve and self-guided walking trails. ⊠ *Tower Hill State Game Reserve, Princes Hwy. between Port Fairy and Warrnambool, Tower Hill* ☎ *0428/318876 mobile* ⊕ *www.parkweb.vic.gov.au.*

SPORTS AND THE OUTDOORS

HIKING

There are several walks around Port Fairy that highlight the town's historical aspects and the area's great beauty. Pick up a Historic Walks map from the visitor center and follow a trail past some 30 beautiful buildings; it takes about an hour. The Port Fairy Maritime & Shipwreck Heritage Walk is a 2-km (1-mile) trail that passes the sites of several shipwrecks: the bark *Socrates,* which was battered by huge seas in 1843; the bark *Lydia,* which was wrecked off the coast in 1847; the schooner *Thistle,* which went down in 1837; and the brigantine *Essington,* which sank while moored at Port Fairy in 1852. Other historic attractions en route include the town port, the lifeboat station, riverside warehouses, cannons and gun emplacements at Battery Hill, and Griffiths Island Lighthouse. The walk is well marked.

Ten minutes or 14 km (9 miles) east of Port Fairy is Tower Hill State Game Reserve, nested in an extinct volcano. There are several walking trails and plenty of chances to see emus and kangaroos. About 40 minutes northeast is Mount Eccles National Park, another extinct volcano. Here there are four walks, including one to the crater rim and lava caves.

WHERE TO EAT AND STAY

For expanded hotel reviews, visit Fodors.com.

$$$ CAFÉ 🍴 **Time & Tide.** "High Tea by the High Sea" is the menu highlight of this luscious café, which—fortunately—has an appetite-stimulating Southern Ocean view. Take a seat on a high-backed chair and indulge in three tiers of savory tarts, finger sandwiches, brownies, filled meringues, and more. The Grand High Tea (A$49 per person) and Mini Grand (two tiers, A$35) include tea or coffee and a glass of sparkling Rosé. Also available are three share plates (A$29 each); all food on the Regional Taste Plate, which features cheeses, dips, and olives, comes from within 45 km (28 miles) of the café. [$] *Average main: A$49* ✉ *21 Thistle Pl.* ☎ *03/5568–2134* 🌐 *www.timeandtidehightea.com* 🕒 *Closed weekdays. No dinner.*

$ B&B/INN 🏨 **Merrijig Inn.** One of Victoria's oldest inns, this beautifully restored 1841 Georgian-style building overlooks Port Fairy's working wharf from King George Square. **Pros:** cute and cozy; great food. **Cons:** upstairs rooms have character, but they're small. [$] *Rooms from: A$150* ✉ *1 Campbell St.* ☎ *03/5568–2324* 🌐 *www.merrijiginn.com* 🛏 *4 rooms, 4 suites* 🍽 *Breakfast.*

$$$ B&B/INN Fodor's Choice ★ 🏨 **Oscars Waterfront Boutique Hotel.** Overlooking the waterfront and a marina of yachts, this hotel gives French provincial style an Australian edge. **Pros:** fantastic location; great breakfasts. **Cons:** town is dead in the off-season. [$] *Rooms from: A$325* ✉ *41B Gipps St.* ☎ *03/5568–3022* 🌐 *www.oscarswaterfront.com* 🛏 *6 rooms, 1 suite* 🍽 *Breakfast.*

THE GOLD COUNTRY

Victoria was changed forever in the early 1850s by the discovery of gold in the center of the state. News of fantastic gold deposits caused immigrants from every corner of the world to pour into Victoria to seek their fortunes as "diggers"—a name that has become synonymous with Australians ever since. Few miners became wealthy from their searches, however. The real money was made by those supplying goods and services to the thousands who had succumbed to gold fever.

Gold towns like Ballarat, Castlemaine, Maldon, and Bendigo sprang up like mushrooms to accommodate these fortune seekers, and prospered until the gold rush receded. Afterward, they became ghost towns or turned to agriculture to survive. However, many beautiful buildings were constructed from the spoils of gold, and these gracious old public buildings and grand hotels survive today and make a visit to Bendigo and Ballarat a pleasure for those who love classic architecture. Victoria's gold is again being mined in limited quantities, while these historic old towns remain interesting relics of Australia's past.

Although Victoria was not the first Australian state to experience a gold rush, when gold was discovered here in 1851 it became a veritable El Dorado. During the boom years of the 19th century, 90% of the gold mined in Australia came from the then British colony. The biggest finds were at Ballarat and then Bendigo, and the Ballarat diggings proved to be among the richest alluvial goldfields in the world.

For leisurely exploration of the Gold Country, a car is essential. Public transportation adequately serves the main centers, but access to smaller towns is less assured and even in the bigger towns attractions are spread out.

TOURS

Gray Line, Australian Pacific Tours, and AAT Kings cover the Gold Country; all three depart from the New Day Tour Centre in Federation Square at the corner of Flinders and Russell streets, Melbourne.

Contacts AAT Kings ☎ *1300/228546* ⊕ *www.aatkings.com.au.* **Australian Pacific Touring** ☎ *1300/336932* ⊕ *www.aptouring.com.au.* **Gray Line** ✉ *Federation Sq. E, Flinders and Russell Sts., City Center, Melbourne* ☎ *1300/858687* ⊕ *www.grayline.com.au.*

BALLARAT

106 km (66 miles) northwest of Melbourne.

In the local Aboriginal language, the name Ballarat means "resting place." In pre-gold-rush days, nearby Lake Wendouree provided the area with a plentiful supply of food. Once the gold boom hit, however, the town became much less restful; in 1854 Ballarat was the scene of the Battle of the Eureka Stockade, a skirmish that took place between miners and authorities over gold license fees that miners were forced to pay, though they had no vote. More than 20 men died in the battle. Today their flag—the Southern Cross—is a symbol of Australia's egalitarian spirit and can be viewed in the new Museum of Australian Democracy at Eureka (MADE).

Despite the harsh times, fortunes made from the mines (and from the miners) resulted in the grand Victorian architecture on Sturt and Lydiard streets—note the post office, the town hall, Craig's Royal Hotel, and Her Majesty's Theatre. The Old Colonists' Hall and the Mining Exchange (at 20 and 26 Lydiard Street, respectively) now house shops and cafés. The visitor center has a self-guided heritage walk.

GETTING HERE AND AROUND
It's an easy 80-minute drive to Ballarat along the Western Highway (M8) from Melbourne. The road, however, is the main artery between Melbourne and Adelaide, and many huge trucks also use the road. Take care and drive within the speed limit. From Ballarat you can easily drive north to the spa-country towns of Daylesford–Hepburn Springs and Bendigo on the Midland Highway. The city itself is well signposted. The city center is built around a well-planned grid and has ample parking. Local bus services run from Sturt Street, the main thoroughfare, to most of Ballarat's attractions.

V/Line operates trains to Ballarat and Bendigo from Melbourne.

ESSENTIALS
Transportation V/Line ☎ *1800/136196* ⊕ *www.vline.com.au.*

Visitor Information Ballarat Visitor Information Centre ✉ *43 Lydiard St. N* ☎ *1800/446633* ⊕ *www.visitballarat.com.au.*

EXPLORING
Art Gallery of Ballarat. This impressive art museum has a large collection of Australian art, from 19th-century works to contemporary pieces. Keep an eye out for its paintings by landscape artist Eugene von Guerard, who captured Ballarat as it appeared in the raucous early gold rush days. ✉ *40 Lydiard St.* ☎ *03/5320–5858* ⊕ *www.artgalleryofballarat. com.au* ☉ *Daily 10–5.*

Ballarat Botanical Gardens. On the shores of Lake Wendouree, the Ballarat Botanical Gardens are identifiable by the brilliant blooms and classical statuary. At the rear of the gardens, the Conservatory hosts events during the town's Begonia Festival held each March, with other events taking place near the lake. ✉ *Gillies St. N at Lake Gardens Ave.* ☎ *03/5320–5135* ⊕ *www.ballarat.com/botanicgardens/* ⊞ *Free* ☉ *Daily 7:30–6, conservatory 9–5.*

FAMILY **Ballarat Wildlife Park.** All sorts of native animals, including kangaroos and emus (which roam free), saltwater crocodiles, snakes, Tasmanian devils, wombats, and echidnas can be found at this wildlife sanctuary. Daily tours of the park are led at 11, with a koala show at 2, a wombat show at 2:30, and a crocodile feeding at 3. The park also has a café and picnic areas. ✉ *Fussel and York Sts., East Ballarat* ☎ *03/5333–5933* ⊕ *www.wildlifepark.com.au* ⊞ *A$25* ☉ *Daily 9–5:30.*

MADE. The Museum of Australian Democracy at Eureka (MADE) opened in 2013 on the site of the 1854 Eureka Stockade revolt, in which gold miners staged an armed rebellion against police corruption and for the establishment of democracy in Victoria. The museum brings

Typical architecture from the gold rush era on a main street in Ballarat

history to life via impressive interactive technology. Visitors learn about democracy around the world, and can admire the tattered but beautiful remains of the original Eureka Flag, which flew above the site of the battle. ⊠ *102 Stawell St. S* ☎ *1800/287113* ⊕ *www.made.org* 💷 *A$12* ⊗ *Daily 10–5.*

FAMILY **Sovereign Hill.** Built on the site of the former Sovereign Hill Quartz Mining Company's mines, this replica town provides an authentic look at life, work, and play during Ballarat's gold rush era. The main street features a hotel, blacksmith's shop, bakery, and post office—all perfectly preserved relics of their time. You can have your photo taken in period costumes, take a mineshaft tour, pan for gold (and find some), ride in a stagecoach, or head to the "lolly shop" to taste old-fashioned candy. Return at night for "Blood on the Southern Cross," a 90-minute sound-and-light spectacular that tells the story of the Eureka uprising. Your entry ticket also gets you into the **Gold Museum,** across Bradshaw Street, which displays an extensive collection of nuggets from the Ballarat diggings. ⊠ *Bradshaw St.* ☎ *03/5337–1100* ⊕ *www.sovereignhill. com.au* 💷 *A$48.50; A$107.50 (entry and Blood on the Southern Cross show)* ⊗ *Daily 10–5; 2 show sessions, times vary.*

WHERE TO EAT AND STAY
For expanded hotel reviews, visit Fodors.com.

$$ ✕ **The Forge.** This former industrial building now houses a pizzeria that
PIZZA serves top-notch wood-fired pizzas in a big dining room with long timber tables, wooden beams, and exposed brick walls. The pizzas are excellent, with light crusts and tasty toppings; try the Volcano (hot salami, chili pepper, Gorgonzola, feta, olives, and anchovies) for an entrée with

a zing. An unusual appetizer is the Oliver Twist, a stack of baked pizza strips bearing olives, chili pepper, and Victorian goat's cheese. $ *Average main: A$19* ⊠ *14 Armstrong St. North* ☎ *03/5337–6635* ⊕ *www. theforgepizzeria.com.au.*

$ ✕ **L'Espresso.** Meals at this low-
MEDITERRANEAN lighted local institution taste like they're from your grandmother's kitchen. It's open for breakfast and lunch daily and dinner (more expensive) on Friday, with specials like rolled and roasted pork belly with an orange, fennel and parsley salad, or slippery jack and pine mushroom bruschetta with goats cheese, chorizo, and aged balsamic. The zucchini and corn fritters with bacon, roasted tomatoes, and tomato jam are a great way to start the day. This was a popular record shop back in the 1970s, and decades later you can still buy blues, jazz, and interesting contemporary music CDs here. $ *Average main: A$18* ⊠ *417 Sturt St.* ☎ *03/5333–1789.*

$$ 🏨 **The Ansonia.** Built in the 1870s as professional offices, this building
HOTEL now houses an excellent boutique hotel. **Pros:** cozy; arty; free parking. **Cons:** rooms opening onto the atrium lack privacy. $ *Rooms from: A$199* ⊠ *32 Lydiard St.* ☎ *03/5332–4678* ⊕ *www.theansoniaonlydiard. com.au* ⌂ *16 rooms, 3 apartments* ⦿ *Breakfast.*

DAYLESFORD AND HEPBURN SPRINGS

109 km (68 miles) northwest of Melbourne, 45 km (28 miles) northeast of Ballarat.

Nestled in the slopes of the Great Dividing Range, Daylesford and its nearby twin, Hepburn Springs, are a spa lover's paradise. The water table here is naturally aerated with carbon dioxide and rich in soluble mineral salts, making it ideal for indulging in mineral baths and other rejuvenating treatments. The natural springs were first noted during the gold rush, and Swiss-Italian immigrants established a spa at Hepburn Springs in 1875. There are now about 70 natural springs in the area. The best time to visit the area is autumn, when the deciduous trees turn bronze and you can finish up a relaxing day next to an open fire with a glass of local red.

GETTING HERE AND AROUND

The twin towns of Daylesford and Hepburn Springs are easily reached by car from Melbourne. Take the Western Highway (M8) to Ballarat, then take the Midland Highway for another 40 km (25 miles) to Daylesford (via Creswick). Hepburn Springs is a mile or two from Daylesford.

LIQUID GOLD

The promise of gold "in them thar hills" drew mobs of prospectors in the 1850s, but today's visitors aren't looking to quench their thirst for riches. The "Great Grape Touring Route" (⊕ *www. greatgraperoute.com.au*) and the "Vine to Vintage Trail" (⊕ *www. bendigotourism.com*) are wonderful itineraries for those who love fine wine and food. Ballarat's climate produces great Pinot Noir and Chardonnay, while the Grampians is the birthplace of Great Western, Australia's first and best-known sparkling wine. The Pyrenees region is known for its classic Shiraz.

V/Line operates trains from Southern Cross Station, Melbourne, to Ballarat or Woodend (near Mount Macedon), and V/Line buses connect with the trains to take passengers to Daylesford.

ESSENTIALS

Transportation **V/Line** ☎ 1800/800007 ⊕ www.vline.com.au.

Visitor Information **Daylesford Regional Visitor Information Centre** ✉ 98 Vincent St. ☎ 03/5321–6123 ⊕ www.visitdaylesford.com.

EXPLORING

Convent Gallery. Perched on a hillside overlooking Daylesford, this gallery occupies a former nunnery that has been restored to its lovely Victorian state. It houses three levels of fine art and a nun-related museum. At the front of the gallery is Bad Habits, a sunny café that serves light lunches and snacks. Altar Bar is a hip place for a drink. The second-story penthouse suite is the ultimate in decadence, with its own hydrotherapy bath and a boudoir-style bedroom ($$$). ✉ 7 Daly St. ☎ 03/5348–3211 ⊕ www.theconvent.com.au ☜ A$5 ⊙ Daily 10–4.

Mineral Springs Reserve. Above the Hepburn Bathhouse and Spa, a path winds past a series of mineral springs in this 74-acre reserve. Each spring has a slightly different chemical composition—and a significantly different taste. You can bring empty bottles, if you like, and fill them for free with the mineral water of your choice. ✉ Mineral Springs Reserve, Hepburn Springs.

WHERE TO STAY

For expanded hotel reviews, visit Fodors.com.

$$
B&B/INN

The Dudley Boutique Hotel. This fine example of timber Federation-style architecture sits behind a neat hedge and picket gate on the main street of Hepburn Springs. **Pros:** tranquil garden setting; great heritage character. **Cons:** limited number of rooms may limit available booking dates. $ Rooms from: A$240 ✉ 101 Main Rd., Hepburn Springs ☎ 03/5348–3033 ⊕ www.thedudley.com.au ☜ 4 rooms ⦿ Breakfast.

$$$$
RENTAL
Fodor'sChoice
★

Lake House. Featuring one of Victoria's best restaurants, this rambling lakeside hotel adds a distinct glamour to spa country. **Pros:** renowned food; tranquil garden setting. **Cons:** two-night minimum stay at weekends. $ Rooms from: A$361 ✉ King St. ☎ 03/5348–3329 ⊕ www.lakehouse.com.au ☜ 21 rooms, 12 suites ⦿ Breakfast.

SHOPPING

SPAS

Fodor'sChoice
★

Hepburn Bathhouse & Spa. A destination for relaxation and wellness since the 19th century, this facility is the centerpiece of Australia's premier spa destination, and one of the largest and most spectacular spas in the country. The complex encompasses the original Edwardian Bathhouse (circa 1895), which houses private mineral baths and more than 30 wet-and-dry treatment rooms, and a stunning, contemporary building, where you find the public Bathhouse and the private Sanctuary area. Patrons can buy two-hour passes for the Bathhouse or the Sanctuary. The Bathhouse includes a relaxation mineral pool and a spa pool (A$26, Tuesday–Thursday and A$39 Friday–Monday), while the Sanctuary has underwater spa couches (for the ultimate in hydrotherapy), an aroma steam room, and a salt therapy pool (A$58 Tuesday–Thursday and A$83 Friday–Monday). There is also the day spa area, where you can choose from a long list of therapies, including body wraps and polishes, facials, and other treatments using the mineral waters. Products used in the spa include LaGaia, Eminence, and Thalgo, as well as a Hepburn Collection range specifically designed for Hepburn Bathhouse & Spa. ✉ *1 Mineral Springs Crescent, Hepburn Springs* ☎ *03/5321–6000* ⊕ *www.hepburnbathhouse.com* ☽ *Daily 9–6:30.*

BENDIGO

150 km (93 miles) northwest of Melbourne, 92 km (57 miles) south of Echuca.

Gold was discovered in the Bendigo district in 1851, and its boom lasted well into the 1880s. The city's magnificent public buildings bear witness to the richness of its mines. Today Bendigo is a bustling, enterprising small city, with distinguished buildings lining both sides of Pall Mall in the city center. These include the Shamrock Hotel, the General Post Office, and the Law Courts, all majestic examples of late-Victorian architecture. Although these glorious relics of a golden age dominate the landscape, the city is far from old-fashioned. You'll also find a lively café and restaurant scene, 30 boutique wineries, some of which can be visited on organized winery tours, and one of the best regional art galleries in Australia.

GETTING HERE AND AROUND

To reach Bendigo, take the Calder Highway northwest from Melbourne; the trip takes about 1 hour and 40 minutes. V/Line operates trains to Bendigo from Melbourne's Southern Cross Station, a journey of about two hours.

TOURS

Bendigo Gold. This company, based in the grounds of Ironbark Riding Centre, runs personalized gold-prospecting tours, as well as do-it-yourself gold-panning. A three-hour training session costs A$280 per person, including the rental of a detector that can be used for the rest of the day. It's A$380 per person for a full-day tour (which includes a the use of a detector). If you like the idea of striking it rich, you can also buy your own metal detector at the company's shop. ✉ *109 Watson St., White Hills* ☎ *03/5448–4140* ⊕ *www.bendigogold.com.au* 🏷 *A$280 training session; A$380 full day tour* ☽ *Mon.–Sat. 8:30–5, Sun. by appointment.*

Vintage Talking Tram. A good introduction to Bendigo is a tour aboard this hop-on, hop-off streetcar tour, which includes a taped commentary on the town's history. The half-hourly tram runs on an 8-km (5-mile) circuit between the Central Deborah Gold Mine and the Tram Museum, making six stops at historic sites. ☎ *03/5442–2821* ⊕ *www.bendigotramways.com* 🏷 *A$16* ☽ *Daily 10–4:20.*

ESSENTIALS

Transportation V/Line ☎ *1800/800007* ⊕ *www.vline.com.au.*

Visitor Information Bendigo Visitor Centre ✉ *51 Pall Mall* ☎ *03/5434–6060, 1800/813153* ⊕ *www.bendigotourism.com.au.*

EXPLORING

Fodor's Choice
★
Bendigo Art Gallery. A notable collection of contemporary Australian painting can be found in this beautiful gallery, including the work of Rupert Bunny, Emily Kame Kngwarreye, and Arthur Boyd. The gallery also has some significant 19th-century French realist and impressionist works, bequeathed by a local surgeon. International exhibitions are regularly hosted, such as 2013's "The Body Beautiful in Ancient Greece," featuring works from the British Museum's Greek and Roman collection. There's a free guided tour every day at 2 pm. ⊠ *42 View St.* ☎ *03/5434–6088* ⊕ *www.bendigoartgallery.com.au* ⊠ *Entry to permanent exhibition by donation; touring exhibitions A$20* ☾ *Daily 10–5.*

Bendigo Pottery. Australia's oldest working pottery turns out distinctive brown-and-cream style pieces that many Australians have in their kitchens. Founded in 1858, the historic workshop offers demonstrations. You can even get your hands dirty creating your own clay piece during a wheel-throwing lesson (bookings essential during school holidays); there's also a clay play area for small children. Impressive beehive brick kilns, which you can step inside, are star exhibits in the museum. It's 6½ km (4 miles) northeast of Bendigo on the way to Echuca. ⊠ *146 Midland Hwy., Epsom* ☎ *03/5448–4404* ⊕ *www.bendigopottery.com. au* ⊠ *Free, museum A$8, wheel-throwing lessons A$15 per half hr* ☾ *Daily 9–5.*

FAMILY **Central Deborah Gold Mine.** This historic mine, with a 1,665-foot shaft, yielded almost a ton of gold before it closed in 1954. Above ground you can pan for gold, see the old stamper battery, and climb up the poppet head, but the thrill of mining is felt below ground. Three underground tours explore different mine levels; on the Mine Experience you descend 200 feet to widened tunnels, while the Underground Adventure puts you another 78 feet deeper. Nine Levels of Darkness is the ultimate adventure here; over 4½ hours you sign on as a "new chum" and ride a tiny cage lift 748 feet down to dripping original tunnels, where you work a drill, "set" explosives, and climb ladders. ⊠ *76 Violet St.* ☎ *03/5443–8322* ⊕ *www.central-deborah.com* ⊠ *A$14 (above-ground area only); tours (including entry): Mine Experience A$28.50, Underground Adventure A$75, Nine Levels of Darkness A$199* ☾ *Daily 9–5 (last tour at 3:30).*

Golden Dragon Museum. The Chinese community's important role in Bendigo life, past and present, is explored within this museum. Its centerpieces are the century-old Loong imperial ceremonial dragon and the Sun Loong dragon, which, at more than 106 yards in length, is said to be the world's longest. When carried in procession, the body alone requires 52 carriers and 52 relievers, and more to carry the head, neck, and tail; the head alone weighs 64 pounds. Also on display are other ceremonial objects, costumes, and historic artifacts. The lovely Yi Yuan Gardens, opposite, with ponds and bridges, are part of the museum and close at 4:30. ⊠ *5–11 Bridge St.* ☎ *03/5441–5044* ⊕ *www. goldendragonmuseum.org* ⊠ *A$11* ☾ *Daily 9:30–5.*

Joss House. An active place of worship on the outskirts of the city, this small Chinese temple was built during the gold rush days by Chinese miners. At the height of the boom in the 1850s and 1860s, about a quarter of Bendigo's miners were Chinese. These men were usually dispatched from villages on the Chinese mainland, and they were expected to work hard and return as quickly as possible with their fortunes. Sadly, tensions with white miners were a feature of that era, along with anti-Chinese riots. Luckily this attractive element of their presence has endured from those turbulent times. ⊠ *3 Finn St.* ☎ *03/5442–1685* ⊕ *www.bendigojosshouse.com* ⊡ *A$5.50* ⊙ *Daily 11–4.*

WHERE TO EAT AND STAY
For expanded hotel reviews, visit Fodors.com.

$$ ✕ **Whirrakee Restaurant.** One of Bendigo's most decorative old buildings
FRENCH   is the perfect setting for this restaurant's fine French-accented food, starched white tablecloths, and exemplary, yet friendly, service. The menu reflects the best of local produce, and you might start with ravioli of Crystal Bay prawns with leeks, peas, and a sorrel emulsion; the Gorgonzola soufflé; or the spiced kangaroo salad. For the main course, try the butternut pumpkin fondant served with a pearl barley fritter, goats curd, pickled walnuts, and a grain mustard dressing, or the free-range chicken breast with preserved lemon, cauliflower, almonds, and tarragon. Make sure you leave room for the passion-fruit parfait or a chocolate treat. The wine list showcases local wineries. Ⓢ *Average main: A$32* ⊠ *17 View Point* ☎ *03/5441–5557* ⊕ *www.whirrakeerestaurant. com.au* ⊙ *No lunch Mon. and Tues.*

$$ ⌂ **Hotel Shamrock.** The lodgings at this landmark Victorian hotel in
B&B/INN   the city center range from traditional guest rooms to spacious suites. **Pros:** historic gold-era building; central location. **Cons:** limited facilities. Ⓢ *Rooms from: A$140* ⊠ *Pall Mall at Williamson St.* ☎ *03/5443–0333* ⊕ *www.hotelshamrock.com.au* ↜ *24 rooms, 4 suites* ⏍ *Breakfast.*

$$ ⌂ **Langley Hall.** Once an Edwardian mansion, this beautifully restored
HOTEL   bed-and-breakfast originally served as a residence for the Anglican archbishop of Bendigo. **Pros:** lovely garden; good price; 19th-century furnishings. **Cons:** few amenities; not walking distance from town. Ⓢ *Rooms from: A$195* ⊠ *484 Napier St., White Hills* ☎ *03/5443–3693* ⊕ *www.langleyhall.com.au* ↜ *6 rooms* ⏍ *Breakfast.*

THE GRAMPIANS

About 93 km (79 miles) north of Port Fairy are the Grampians, sometimes referred to by their Aboriginal name Gariwerd. This 415,000-acre region combines stunning mountain scenery, abundant native wildlife, and invigorating outdoor activities. The sharp sandstone peaks here were long ago forced up from an ancient seabed, and sculpted by aeons of wind and rain.

Today the park has more than 160 km (100 miles) of walking trails, as well as some 900 wildflower species, 200 species of birds, and 35 species of native mammals. The best time to visit is October–December, when wildflowers carpet the landscape, the weather is mild, and summer crowds have yet to arrive. There are several wineries in the region, including the historic Seppelt vineyard and winery at Great Western

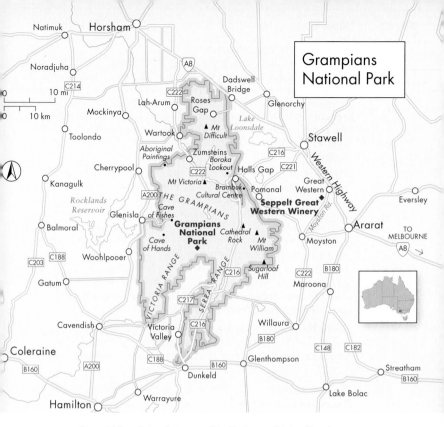

about 38 km (24 miles) east of Halls Gap, which offers fascinating tours of its underground wine cellars.

GRAMPIANS NATIONAL PARK

260 km (162 miles) west of Melbourne, 100 km (62 miles) north of Hamilton.

Bushwalking is by far the most popular activity in the national park. Some of the best walks include Mackenzie Falls, the walk to Mt. Abrupt (or Mt. Murdadjoog in the Aboriginal language), the Hollow Mountain walk, and another to Silverband Falls. Even if you're not a big walker you can still see many of the best-known rock formations. Elephant Hide, the Balconies, the Pinnacle, and the Fortress are only a short walk from a car park. Canoeing is another great way to get away from the crowds and experience the lakes and rivers of the Grampians.

The most popular attractions of the central Grampians region can be visited in one day. However, if you want to visit the fascinating Brambuk Aboriginal Cultural Centre and take in a few wineries, allow yourself another day or two. From the town of Halls Gap it's a 15-km (9-mile) drive (plus a 100-yard walk from the car park) to the spectacular Boroka Lookout.

GETTING HERE AND AROUND

Halls Gap (the base town for the Grampians National Park) is reached via Ballarat and Ararat on the Western Highway (Highway 8). The town is 260 km (162 miles) northwest of Melbourne, 97 km (60 miles) northeast of Hamilton, and 140 km (87 miles) west of Ballarat. V/Line operates trains to Ballarat from Melbourne. V/Line buses connect with the trains to take passengers to Halls Gap. For timetables and fares, contact V/Line.

TOURS

For those who love experiencing the great outdoors from different angles, Hangin' Out runs rock climbing and abseiling tours to suit beginners and more experienced climbers; they also have an all-day guided adventure walk (A$135) from Mt. Stapylton to Hollow Mountain in the north of the Grampians. A four-hour taste of real rock climbing and rappeling costs A$75 (minimum two people); a full-day introduction to the rope sports is A$130. Private guided single- and multi-pitch climbs can be arranged.

ESSENTIALS

Tour Operators Hangin' Out ☏ *0407/684831* ⊕ *www.hanginout.com.au.* **V/Line** ☏ *1800/800007* ⊕ *www.vline.com.au.*

Visitor Information Halls Gap Visitor Information Centre ⊠ *115 Grampians Rd., Halls Gap* ☏ *1800/065599* ⊕ *www.visithallsgap.com.au.* **Stawell and Grampians Visitor Information Centre** ⊠ *50 Western Hwy., Stawell* ☏ *03/5358–2314, 1800/330080* ⊕ *www.visitgrampians.com.au.*

EXPLORING

Fodor'sChoice ★ **Grampians National Park.** Comprising four mountain ranges—Mt. Difficult, Mt. William, Serra, and Victoria—the impressive Grampians National Park spills over 412,000 acres. Its rugged peaks, towering trees, waterfalls, creeks, and a plethora of wildlife attract bushwalkers, rock climbers, and nature lovers. Spectacular wildflowers carpet the region in spring, while a number of significant Aboriginal rock art sites make it an ideal place to learn about Victoria's indigenous history. The township of Halls Creek (population 600) sits within the national park, and with its 10,000 tourist beds it becomes quite a busy place in summer and at Easter. If you're staying in a self-catering accommodation, it's wise to stock up on groceries and wine in the big towns of Ballarat, Ararat, Hamilton, or Horsham, since prices at the Halls Gap general store are inflated. One of the most picturesque drives in the park is the 60-km (37-mile) stretch from Halls Gap to Dunkeld. Some areas in the park can be affected by fire and flood from year to year, so check with Parks Victoria for current road and camping conditions. ⊠ *Grampians National Park, Halls Gap* ☏ *13–1963* ⊕ *parkweb.vic.gov.au.*

Brambuk National Park & Cultural Centre. Owned and operated by Aboriginal people, this park and center provide a unique living history of indigenous culture in this part of Victoria. Displays of artwork, weapons, clothes, and tools give a glimpse into the life of Koori people (Aboriginal people of southeastern Australia). A film screened in the Dreaming Theatre describes the Creation legends of the Grampians mountains. Educational programs, including boomerang throwing, painting, and didgeridoo workshops, are presented daily and there is a bush tucker discovery walk and tasting most days. Ceremonial music and dances are performed weekly. Visitors can learn the significance of paintings at nearby Bunjil's Shelter on the Bunjil Creation tour, conducted on weekdays at 9:30 am. ⊠ *277 Grampians Tourist Rd., Halls Gap* ☎ *03/5361–4000* ⊕ *www.brambuk.com.au* ✉ *Free; films and activities A$5, bush-tucker walks A$11, Bunjil Creation tour A$50* ⊙ *Daily 9–5.*

OFF THE BEATEN PATH

Seppelt Great Western Winery. This old winery is also one of Australia's most famous, the name Great Western being associated with a long-lived sparkling wine. The winery makes the Salinger and Fleur de Lys ranges as well as a Sparkling Shiraz and various table wines. Beneath the winery is an underground labyrinth of tunnels, known as the Drives, dating back to 1868 and originally built by gold miners. This is where the best sparkling wines are kept. You can take a day tour of these tunnels and the nearby shaft house and taste 20 Seppelt wines, or enjoy a barbecue and evening tour. Packages to tour and dine in the Drives, including cheese platters, two or three courses, and wine tastings, are also available from A$120 per person. ⊠ *36 Cemetery Rd., Great Western* ☎ *03/5361–2239* ⊕ *www.seppelt.com.au* ✉ *Cellar door free (premium wine tasting A$5); tours A$16, night tour and barbecue A$70* ⊙ *Tastings daily 10–5; tunnel tours daily at 11 and 2.*

SPORTS AND THE OUTDOORS

CANOEING

Absolute Outdoors. If you want to experience the Grampians wilderness via its serene lakes, a half-day canoeing trip with this company may be the answer. It offers outings on Lake Bellfield, a little to the southeast of the township. They also offer rock climbing, abseiling, and mountain bike adventures within the park. They operate from a shop that sells outdoor equipment in Halls Gap. ⊠ *105 Main Rd. (a.k.a. Grampians Rd.), Halls Gap* ☎ *03/5356–4556* ⊕ *www.absoluteoutdoors.com.au* ✉ *Canoeing tours A$60 half day.*

HIKING

Auswalk. This long-established walking tour specialist operates guided and self-guided five-night inn-to-inn hikes. Luggage is transported between accommodation stops, a mix of B&Bs and motels. Maps and other information are provided for self-guided walkers, and only two participants are needed for a tour to take place. The terrain is graded "moderate" for 55% of the walk, with about 25% rated strenuous. Wildlife, particularly kangaroos and wallabies, is abundant in many areas transited, and wildflowers festoon the park from August to November. Trips usually run year-round, with the exception of July. Self-guided walks start at A$1,495 per person, and guided walks from A$2,795. ☎ *03/5356–4971* ⊕ *www.auswalk.com.au.*

WHERE TO EAT AND STAY

For expanded hotel reviews, visit Fodors.com.

$$

AUSTRALIAN

✕ **Kookaburra Bar & Bistro.** In the heart of Halls Gap, this is one of the town's best dining options and serves an imaginative range of dishes. You can graze on a crispy squid salad and spinach crepe, or tuck into a

Sitting on edge of Boroka Lookout in the Grampians National Park

risotto of duck slow-roasted with star anise. The mains range from sea to paddock, with blackened barramundi, kangaroo fillet, and sizzling steaks. Kookaburra's own ice cream, made daily with pure ingredients, is a great way to finish a meal. $ *Average main: A$29* ✉ *125 Grampian Rd., Halls Gap* ☎ *03/5356–4222* ⊕ *kookaburrabarbistro.com.au* ⊗ *Closed Mon. No lunch Tues.–Sat.*

$$
MODERN
AUSTRALIAN
Fodor'sChoice
★

✕ **Royal Mail Hotel.** Expansive views of the southern Grampians peaks are almost an unwelcome distraction from the extraordinary food plated up at the only hotel in the tiny town of Dunkeld, 64 km (40 miles) south of Halls Gap. The menu changes daily depending on the harvest from the kitchen gardens, specializing in organic and heirloom vegetables. Other produce comes from local beehives, free-range laying hens, nearby orchards, and an olive grove. Chef Robin Wickens continues the tradition of culinary innovation to create tasting and degustation dinner menus from A$100. There is also an à la carte bistro ($$$), and an excellent bar menu ($). With fine accommodation on-site, too, after dinner you can stroll to a spacious Mountain View or Garden View room, or apartment, all fitted with every modern convenience, or drive the 3 km (2 miles) to the hotel's historic Mt. Sturgeon farm, and sleep in a luxurious, period-furnished homestead bedroom or cozy stone cottage. $ *Average main: A$150* ✉ *98 Parker St., Dunkeld* ☎ *03/5577–2241* ⊕ *www.royalmail.com.au* ⌕ *Reservations essential* ⊗ *Restaurant and bar closed Mon. and Tues.*

$$$$
HOTEL
Fodor'sChoice
★

▦ **Boroka Downs.** On 300 acres of bush, scrub, and grassland, bordering the Grampians National Park, Boroka's six villas are nothing short of spectacular. **Pros:** luxurious; eco-friendly. **Cons:** all of this beauty comes at a high price. $ *Rooms from: A$495* ✉ *51 Birdswing Rd.,*

Halls Gap ☎ *03/5356–6243* ⊕ *www.borokadowns.com.au* ⤴ *6 villas* ⑩ *Breakfast.*

MURRAY RIVER REGION

From its birthplace in the folds of the Great Dividing Range in southern New South Wales, the Mighty Murray winds 2,574 km (1,596 miles) northwest and then south before it empties into Lake Alexandrina, south of Adelaide. But it is not as mighty as it once was. Recent droughts and overreliance on—and exploitation of—the Murray and its tributaries by irrigators, river towns, and the city of Adelaide have threatened the river's health and the livelihoods of the people who rely on it.

Water—its supply, collection, and use—is a subject on almost everyone's lips. A revamped but still controversial water-trading and buy-out system based on water access entitlements, which promises to reallocate precious Murray-Darling water, is one of a range of measures being implemented by Australia's federal and state governments to reduce the impact of climate change and improve and supplement existing water sources. Making the right decisions for the river and those dependent on it is a challenging balancing act.

Victoria exports more than A$200 million worth of wine annually, and Murray River Muscats and Ports are legendary. The Rutherglen area, in particular, produces the country's finest fortified wine (dessert wine or "stickies").

Steeped in history and natural beauty, the eastern Murray River valley and High Country region is a gourmet foodies' heaven known for its fruit, olives, honey, and cheeses, as well as a renowned wine region. The lovely town of Beechworth is an ideal place to break the drive between Sydney and Melbourne.

GETTING HERE AND AROUND

The wide-open spaces of the region surrounding the Murray River make driving the most sensible and feasible means of exploration. Rutherglen is 274 km (170 miles) north of Melbourne, about a 3½- to 4-hour drive up the Hume Freeway; Echuca is 204 km (127 miles) northwest of Melbourne, about a 2½-hour drive. These two Murray River towns are 194 km (121 miles) apart. V/Line trains (☎ *13–6196* ⊕ *www.vline.com.au*) run to most of the major towns in the region, including Echuca, Wangaratta, and Albury-Wodonga, with bus connections to Beechworth and Rutherglen; this access is useful if you do not have a car or want to avoid the long-distance drives. As with most country Victorian areas, direct train access from Melbourne to the main centers is reasonable, but getting between towns isn't as easy.

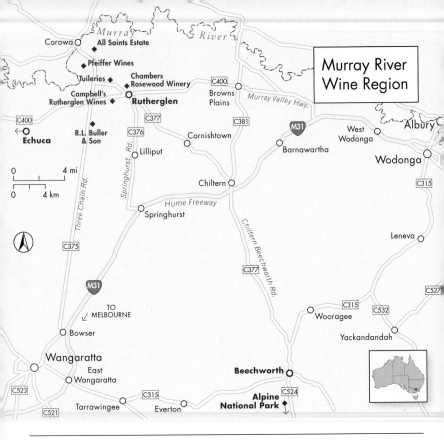

BEECHWORTH

271 km (168 miles) northeast of Melbourne, 96 km (60 miles) north-west of Alpine National Park, 44 km (26 miles) south of Rutherglen.

One of the prettiest towns in Victoria, Beechworth flourished during the gold rush. When gold ran out, the town of 30,000 was left with all the trappings of prosperity—fine banks, imposing public buildings, breweries, parks, and hotels wrapped in wrought iron—but with scarcely two nuggets to rub together. However, poverty protected the town from such modern improvements as aluminum window frames, and many historic treasures that might have been destroyed in the name of progress have been retained.

GETTING HERE AND AROUND

Beechworth and Rutherglen are on opposite sides of the Hume Freeway, the main Sydney–Melbourne artery. The 44-km (26-mile) Rutherglen-Beechworth Road (C377) connects both towns. Beechworth is about a three-hour drive from Melbourne, twice that from Sydney. Beechworth can also be reached by taking a train from Melbourne's Southern Cross Station to Wangaratta, then changing to a bus service to the town; it's about a 3½-hour journey.

CLOSE UP

Ned Kelly

The English have Robin Hood, the Americans Jesse James. Australians have Ned Kelly, an Irish-descended working-class youth whose struggles against police injustice and governmental indifference made him a legend (though whether he was a hero or villain can still be a hot topic of conversation). The best way to learn about this local legend is to visit the town of Beechworth, where a Ned Kelly Guided Walking Tour (A$10) departs from the visitor information center every day at 1:15 pm. You'll see the courthouse where he was tried and the jail where he was imprisoned during his many scrapes with the law. The Burke Museum displays one of his death masks, made shortly after he was hanged at Melbourne Gaol. If you long to hear more, visit Glenrowan (40 km [25 miles], southwest of Beechworth), the scene of his famous "last stand." It was here that Kelly, dressed in his legendary iron armor, walked alone down the main street fending off police bullets. He was finally shot in the leg and arrested. A huge statue, and a sound-and-light show that has received rather mixed reviews and is said to be "quite loud," commemorate Australia's most infamous outlaw.

5

ESSENTIALS

Visitor Information Beechworth Tourist Information Centre ✉ *Old Town Hall, 103 Ford St.* ☎ *03/5728–8065, 1300/366321* ⊕ *www.beechworthonline. com.au.*

EXPLORING

Burke Museum. This 150-year-old museum takes its name from Robert O'Hara Burke who, with William Wills, became one of the first white explorers to cross Australia from south to north in 1861. Burke served as superintendent of police in Beechworth from 1856 to 1859. Not surprisingly, the small area dedicated to Burke is overshadowed by the Ned Kelly collection: his death mask, replicas of the Kelly Gang's armor, and some memorabilia that give insight into the man and his misdeeds. The museum also displays a reconstructed streetscape of Beechworth in the 1880s. ✉ *Loch St.* ☎ *03/5728–8067* ⊕ *www.burkemuseum.com. au* 🖼 *A$8* ⊙ *Daily 10–5.*

Ford Street. A stroll along Ford Street is the best way to absorb the historic character and charm of Beechworth. Among the distinguished buildings are **Tanswell's Commercial Hotel,** the **Town Hall,** and the **Courthouse.** It was in the latter that the committal hearing for the famous bushranger Ned Kelly took place in August 1880. His feisty mother, Ellen Kelly, was also sentenced to three years in jail at this court. ✉ *Ford St.* ⊕ *www.beechworthonline.com.au.*

Murray Breweries. The 1920s temperance movement helped to turn this brewery's focus to the brewing of nonalcoholic cordials. The cordials are produced using old-time recipes and seasonal flavors, such as Sicilian blood orange, using the area's natural spring water. You'll find a display of antique brewing equipment, worldwide beer labels, and rare bottles. On the same site is the Beechworth Carriage Museum, a collection of 20 horse-drawn vehicles and Australian Light Horse

Infantry memorabilia from World War I. Tastings are free. ✉ *29 Last St.* ☎ *03/5728–1304, 1800/990098* ⊕ *www.murraybreweries.com.au* 🎫 *Free* ⊘ *Weekdays 10–4.*

SPORTS AND THE OUTDOORS

BICYCLING

The area from the Murray River to the mountains of northeast Victoria is ideal for mountain bike enthusiasts.

Beechworth Cycle & Saws. Rent a bicycle at this outlet on Beechworth's main street for A$25 for half a day and A$35 for a full day. ✉ *17 Camp St.* ☎ *03/5728–1402* ⊘ *Weekdays 9–5:30, Sat. 9–1, open Sun only during school holidays.*

Murray to Mountains Rail Trail. A 98-km (61-mile) paved trail stretches from Wangaratta to Bright, with a branch line to Beechworth and recent extensions to Milawa and Wandiligong. Bicycle rentals are available at Wangaratta, Beechworth, Bright, and Myrtleford. A trail map is available from the visitor centers at each of these towns, and can also be downloaded from the trail website. ✉ *Albert Rd.* ☎ *1800/801065* ⊕ *www.murraytomountains.com.au.*

HIKING

There are several national parks within easy reach of Beechworth: Chiltern-Mt. Pilot National Park, Beechworth Historic Park, Mount Buffalo National Park, Mount Granya State Park, and Warby Range State Park. The Beechworth visitor center and Parks Victoria have information on bushwalks. The town of Beechworth is the perfect place to get out and about and stretch your legs while admiring late 19th-century architecture. You can pick up a copy of "Echoes of History," a self-guided walking tour of the town from the visitor information center.

Parks Victoria. This government organization has information on Victoria's National Parks and walking trails. ☎ *13–1963* ⊕ *www.parkweb. vic.gov.au.*

WHERE TO STAY

For expanded hotel reviews, visit Fodors.com.

$$$ 🏠 **Country Charm Cottages.** Landscaped gardens overlooking Beech-
RENTAL worth Gorge surround these charming pine and cedar cottages. **Pros:** tranquil setting; great views. **Cons:** minimum two-night stay on weekends. 🛏 *Rooms from: A$220* ✉ *24 Malakoff Rd.* ☎ *03/5728–2435, 0488/440–101* ⊕ *www.countrycharmcottages.com.au* ⤳ *4 cottages* 🍴 *Breakfast.*

RUTHERGLEN

274 km (170 miles) northeast of Melbourne, 40 km (25 miles) northwest of Beechworth.

The surrounding red-loam soil signifies the beginning of the Rutherglen wine district, the source of Australia's finest fortified wines. If the term conjures up visions of cloying Ports, you're in for a surprise. In his authoritative *Australian Wine Compendium*, James Halliday says,

The mighty Murray River is the lifeblood of the region.

"Like Narcissus drowning in his own reflection, one can lose oneself in the aroma of a great old muscat."

The main event in the region is Tastes of Rutherglen, held over two consecutive weekends in March. The festival is a celebration of food, wine, and music—in particular jazz, folk, and country. Events are held in town and at all surrounding wineries. Another popular day in the vineyards is the Rutherglen Winery Walkabout held in June, when wine, food, and music are again on the menu.

GETTING HERE AND AROUND
See Beechworth above. Rutherglen is 274 km (170 miles) north of Melbourne, about a 3½- to 4-hour drive along the Hume Freeway. A V/Line train and bus service operates daily from Melbourne's Southern Cross Station via Seymour and Wangaratta, a journey of about 3 hours and 15 minutes.

TOURS
Rutherglen Bus and Tour offers winery tours for a minimum of four people, with visits to five to six wineries on half-day tours and eight to nine estates on day tours. Half-day tours cost A$40 per person, and day tours cost from A$55 per person (with pickup from Rutherglen accommodation only, though pickups from other towns can be arranged for A$10 per person).

ESSENTIALS
Transportation V/Line ☎ *1800/800007* ⊕ *www.vline.com.au.*

Visitor Information **Rutherglen Bus and Tour** ☎ *02/6032–8774* ⊕ *www.rutherglenbusandtour.com.* **Rutherglen Wine Experience and Visitor Information Centre** ⊠ *57 Main St.* ☎ *1800/622871* ⊕ *www.rutherglenvic.com.*

EXPLORING THE WINERIES

All Saints Estate. In business since 1864, this winery has a splendid, turreted castle that was built in the 1880s with capacious storage areas for its product. The old bottling hall and cellar have been revamped as a cheese tasting room, and a corrugated iron former Chinese dormitory is the property's third heritage-listed building. A guided tour of the winery can be arranged on request. The winery produces Muscat and Tokay made from 50-year-old vines, and a range of crisp whites and full-bodied reds. The on-site Indigo Food Company sells regional cheeses and condiments. The menu at the Terrace restaurant changes seasonally, but might include starters like seared scallops with curried cauliflower puree, and mains such as char-grilled, pasture-fed hanger steak from Cape Grim served with braised ox cheek, celeriac, and smoked bone marrow. Desserts are excellent, especially when combined with a formidable northeast fortified wine. The cellar door and cheese room are open daily; the restaurant is open for lunch from Wednesday to Sunday and for dinner on Saturday only. ⊠ *All Saints Rd., Wahgunyah* ✥ *9 km (5½ miles) southeast of Rutherglen* ☎ *02/6035–2222, 1800/021621* ⊕ *www.allsaintswine.com.au* 🖾 *Free* ☉ *Cellar door: Mon.–Sat. 9–5:30, Sun. 10–5:30; cheese room: daily 11–4.*

Campbell's Rutherglen Wines. Wines have been made here by five generations of the Campbell family, dating back to 1870. Brothers Colin and Malcolm Campbell, the winemaker and viticulturist respectively, have been at the helm for the past 40 years. Famed for its award-winning Bobbie Burns Shiraz and Merchant Prince Rare Rutherglen Muscat, the property covers a picturesque 160 acres. You can wander freely through the winery on a self-guided tour and taste wines at the cellar door, including rare and aged vintages. Vintage Reserve wines are available only at the cellar door. The winery does not have a restaurant, but takes part in the annual Tastes of Rutherglen wine festival, when food and music are on the agenda. It's 3 km (2 miles) from Rutherglen. ⊠ *4603 Murray Valley Hwy.* ☎ *02/6033–6000, 1800/359458* ⊕ *www.campbellswines.com.au* 🖾 *Free* ☉ *Mon.–Sat. 9–5, Sun. 10–5.*

Chambers Rosewood Winery. Established in the 1850s, this is one of Australia's heavyweight producers of fortified wines. Stephen Chambers's Muscats are legendary, with blending stocks that go back more than a century. Stephen runs a very relaxed winery, which is genuinely rustic, being just a few corrugated iron sheds in an off-the-beaten-track road. The cellar door is renowned for offering great value and plenty of tastings; you can take home reasonably priced red and white wine, Sherry, Port, Muscat, and Tokay—from the clean-skin variety (no-label stock) to big 2-liter flagons. There's no restaurant, just a cellar door, which also sells homemade jams and condiments. ⊠ *Barkley St. off Corowa Rd.* ☎ *02/6032–8641* 🖾 *Free* ☉ *Mon.–Sat. 9–5, Sun. 10–5.*

Pfeiffer Wines. Since its first vines were planted in 1895, this winery has made exceptional fortified wines and varietal wines, including

Chardonnay. It also has one of the few Australian plantings of Gamay, the classic French grape used to make Beaujolais. At this small rustic winery you can preorder (with at least 24 hours' notice) spring/summer picnic baskets stuffed with crusty bread, smoked trout, marinated lamb fillets, chicken breast slices, kipfler potato salad, cheese, cake, and a bottle of table wine; or autumn/winter hampers with treats such as soup, curry, and other tasty items for A$80 for two including plates and cutlery. Vegetarian baskets for two are A$80, and children's are A$12.50 per child. Cheese platters are available any time. Winemaker Jen Pfeiffer makes an aperitif called Pfeiffer Seriously Pink, along with a Chardonnay Marsanne, Shiraz, Merlot, and fortifieds such as Muscat, Muscadelle, and Topaque. ✉ *167 Distillery Rd., Wahgunyah* ✥ *9 km (5½ miles) southeast of Rutherglen* ☎ *02/6033–2805* 🌐 *www.pfeifferwinesrutherglen.com.au* 🎟 *Free* 🕒 *Mon.–Sat. 9–5, Sun. 10–5.*

R.L. Buller & Son. Established by Reginald Langdon Buller in 1921, this winery in Rutherglen produces delicious fortified wines and gutsy, full-bodied reds, the flagship being its Shiraz. As the old Shiraz vines are not irrigated, the annual yields are low, but the fruit produced has intense flavor, which winemaker Andrew Buller crafts into wines of great depth and elegance. There are also small plantings of rarer varieties such as Mondeuse. There are tastings and sales at the cellar door, but no restaurant. Also on the winery's grounds is **Buller Bird Park,** an aviary of native Australian birds. Group guided tours of both the winery and the bird park are possible by appointment. ✉ *2084 Federation Way* ☎ *02/6032–9660* 🌐 *www.bullerwines.com.au* 🎟 *Free* 🕒 *Mon.–Sat. 9–5, Sun. 10–5.*

WHERE TO STAY

For expanded hotel reviews, visit Fodors.com.

$$ HOTEL **Tuileries.** Incorporating a vineyard, olive groves, and a renowned restaurant, this accommodation feels like an exclusive retreat. **Pros:** beautifully appointed suites; tranquil country setting. **Cons:** next-to-no nightlife in Rutherglen. [$] *Rooms from: A$199* ✉ *13 Drummond St.* ☎ *02/6032–9033* 🌐 *www.tuileriesrutherglen.com.au* 🛏 *16 suites* 🍴 *Breakfast.*

ALPINE NATIONAL PARK

323 km (200 miles) northeast of Melbourne, 40–50 km (25–31 miles) south to southeast of Mt. Buffalo.

GETTING HERE AND AROUND

Bus services to Alpine National Park operate from Albury on the New South Wales border in the north. In ski season the Falls Creek Coach Service departs from Melbourne for Falls Creek via Mt. Beauty. V/Line's combined train and bus operates from Melbourne's Southern Cross Station to Wangaratta, with a connection on to Bright.

ESSENTIALS

Transportation Falls Creek Coach Service ☎ *03/5754–4024* 🌐 *www.fallscreekcoachservice.com.au.* **V/Line** ☎ *1800/800007* 🌐 *www.vline.com.au.*

Visitor Information Parks Victoria. For information on walks and parks in the area, contact this government organization. ☎ *13–1963* 🌐 *www.parkweb.vic.gov.au.*

EXPLORING

Alpine National Park. This national park covers three loosely connected areas in eastern Victoria, which follow the peaks of the Great Dividing Range. One of these areas, formerly Bogong National Park, contains some of the highest mountains on the continent. As such, it is a wintertime destination for skiers who flock to the resorts at Falls Creek, Mt. Buller, and Mt. Hotham.

The land around here is rich in history. *Bogong* is an Aboriginal word for "big moth," and it was to Mt. Bogong that Aborigines came each year after the winter thaw in search of bogong moths, considered a delicacy. Aborigines were eventually displaced by cattle ranchers who brought their cattle here to graze. The main townships in the area are Bright and Mount Beauty, both of which have visitor information centers. ✉ *Alpine National Park* ☎ *13–1963* 🌐 *parkweb.vic.gov.au.*

SPORTS AND THE OUTDOORS

The Alpine National Park really has two seasons—winter (from June to September) and the rest of the year. In winter the main activities are skiing, snowboarding, and tobogganing at Falls Creek, Mt. Buller, Mt. Hotham, and Dinner Plain. In spring, summer, and autumn these areas are perfect for bushwalking, cycling, horseback riding, and kayaking. The visitor centers and Parks Victoria have walking and cycling trail maps.

WHERE TO EAT

For expanded hotel reviews, visit Fodors.com.

$$$ ITALIAN ✕ **Simone's of Bright.** Awarded the title of Melbourne Food and Wine Festival Legend in 2009, Patrizia Simone heads the family team behind this renowned restaurant in a 19th-century cottage in the middle of town. The menu shows off Patrizia's passion for cooking rustic Italian food and using seasonal local produce: you might try stuffed zucchini flowers, roasted goat, or locally sourced venison. Simone's also offers a eight-course degustation menu (A$95). Herbs and some seasonal vegetables come from the kitchen garden and rhubarb comes fresh from the nearby Joe's Garden. Tables and chairs spill out onto the front patio during the summer. [$] *Average main: A$38* ✉ *98 Gavan St., Bright* ☎ *03/5755–2266* 🌐 *www.simonesbright.com.au* ✍ *Reservations essential* ⏲ *Closed Sun. and Mon.*

ECHUCA

206 km (128 miles) north of Melbourne, 194 km (120 miles) west of Rutherglen, 92 km (57 miles) north of Bendigo.

The name Echuca comes from a local Aboriginal word meaning "meeting of the waters," a reference to the town's location at the confluence of the Murray, Campaspe, and Goulburn rivers. In the second half of the 19th century Echuca was Australia's largest inland port. Many reminders of Echuca's colorful heyday remain in the restored paddle

Snow Gum trees on the Bogong High Plains in Alpine National Park

steamers, barges, and historic hotels, and in the Red Gum Works, the town's sawmill, now a working museum.

GETTING HERE AND AROUND

Echuca is a three-hour drive from Melbourne, reached most directly by the Northern Highway (Highway 75). V/Line trains take 3½ hours to reach Echuca from Melbourne's Southern Cross Station once or twice a day; at other times trains connect at Bendigo or Murchison East with bus services to Echuca.

ESSENTIALS

Visitor Information Echuca Moama Visitor Information Centre ⊠ *Old Pump Station, 2 Heygarth St.* ☎ *1800/804446* ⊕ *www.echucamoama.com.*

EXPLORING

Historic River Precinct. This zone's historic journey begins at the Port of Echuca office on Murray Esplanade, where you can purchase a ticket that gets you into several historic buildings. The **Bridge Hotel** was built by Henry Hopwood, ex-convict father of Echuca, who had the foresight to establish a punt, and then to build a bridge at this commercially strategic point on the river. The **Star Hotel**, built in the 1860s, has an underground bar and escape tunnel, which was used by after-hours drinkers in the 19th century to evade the police. The **Historic Wharf** displays the heavy-duty side of the river trade, including a warehouse, old railroad tracks, and riverboats. Among the vessels docked at the wharf is the PS *Adelaide* (built in 1866), the world's oldest operating wooden-hulled paddle steamer.

One-hour river excursions aboard the historic *Pevensey,* and the *Alexander Arbuthnot* (Echuca Paddlesteamers), and the *Canberra* and *Emmylou,* a 19th-century-style boat built in 1980–82 for a television series (Murray River Paddlesteamers), are a refreshing treat at the end of a hot summer's day. The paddle wheelers depart regularly from 10:15 am to 2:30 pm, with a 3:45 pm cruise sailing on weekends and public holidays; tickets are available from the post office or Bond Store on Murray Esplanade; a one-hour cruise on the PS *Emmylou* costs A$27. ✉ *52 Murray Esplanade* 🌐 *www.echucapaddlesteamers.net.au, www.emmylou.com.au.*

SPORTS AND THE OUTDOORS

BOATING

Murray River Houseboats. A popular pursuit on the Murray is to rent a houseboat and drift slowly down the river, and this operator's vessels are five-star floating experiences with Jacuzzis, state-of-the-art kitchens, and the latest appliances. They can sleep from 2 to 12 people and can be rented from three days to a week and longer. There are six boats for rent. Prices start from A$1,490 for three nights in the peak late-December/January period, for two to six people. ✉ *Riverboat Dock* ☎ *03/5480–2343* 🌐 *www.murrayriverhouseboats.com.au.*

CANOEING

River Country Adventours. If you want to canoe up a lazy river—the Goulburn, which is a tributary of the Murray—then you can for a half or full day with this tour company. Tours start from A$55 per person. ✉ *43 Edis St., Kyabram* ☎ *03/5852–2736, 0428/585227 mobile* 🌐 *www.adventours.com.au.*

WHERE TO EAT AND STAY

For expanded hotel reviews, visit Fodors.com.

$$ ECLECTIC Fodor's Choice ★ 🍴 **Oscar W's Wharfside.** Named after the last paddle steamer ever built in Echuca, Oscar W's is one of the port's finest restaurants. With a beautiful, tree-fringed view of the Murray River, it's a comfortable, relaxed establishment. The Redgum Grill and Deck Bar serves such treats as panfried Murray cod with fennel cream and candied chili, and kangaroo with bacon, garlic crostini, and onion marmalade. Pavlova and lamingtons (Australia's famous small chocolate-and-coconut-dipped sponge cakes) are stars of the dessert menu. Have a drink and watch the paddle steamers cruise by. [$] *Average main: A$39* ✉ *101 Murray Esplanade* ☎ *03/5482–5133* 🌐 *www.oscarws.com.au.*

$$$ B&B/INN 🏨 **PS Emmylou.** Departing from Echuca around sunset, this paddle steamer chugs downriver, fueled by red-gum logs, taking passengers on one-, two-, or three-night cruises. **Pros:** fabulous sense of history; lots of birdlife; lovely scenery. **Cons:** limited facilities. [$] *Rooms from: A$300* ✉ *57 Murray Esplanade* ☎ *03/5480–2237* 🌐 *www.emmylou.com.au* 🔑 *9 rooms without bath* 🕒 *Closed June–Aug.* 🍽 *Some meals.*

$$ HOTEL 🏨 **River Gallery Inn.** A 19th-century building just a stone's throw from the Port of Echuca houses this boutique couples-only hotel. **Pros:** historic atmosphere; room themes; great location. **Cons:** Wi-Fi patchy in some rooms. [$] *Rooms from: A$220* ✉ *578 High St.* ☎ *03/5480–6902* 🌐 *www.rivergalleryinn.com.au* 🔑 *8 rooms* 🍽 *Breakfast.*

TASMANIA

WELCOME TO TASMANIA

TOP REASONS TO GO

★ **Beautiful Walks:**
Tasmania has some of Australia's best walking terrain. The stunning mountains and coastlines of Mt. Field, South West, and Franklin-Gordon Wild Rivers national parks are a mecca for serious trekkers. Less strenuous but equally stunning walks can be taken around Cradle Mountain or on Freycinet Peninsula.

★ **Colonial Homes and Cottages:** Many of the Georgian mansions and charming cottages built during Tasmania's early days as a colony have been turned into unusual and hospitable accommodation options.

★ **Tassie Tastes:** While Tasmania's unspoiled surrounds make it hiking heaven, foodies are also well served, thanks to its beautiful produce and excellent wine.

1 Hobart. Perhaps Australia's most beautiful state capital, the compact city offers history and beautifully preserved colonial architecture in genteel surrounds.

2 Port Arthur and the Tasman Peninsula. The horrors of Tasmania's convict past are there to discover in the notorious penal settlement, which has been sensitively converted into an absorbing museum.

3 Freycinet National Park and East Coast Resorts. Deserted white-sand beaches, including the legendary Wineglass Bay, as well as some superb wineries, make the east coast a must-visit.

GETTING ORIENTED

About the size of West Virginia, and with a population of just over a half million, the island of Tasmania offers geographical diversity in stunning, easily navigable scenery. Surrounded by sea, the climate is of course maritime, with the west coast the wettest thanks to the roaring forties winds. On the other hand, the island's capital of Hobart, a proud port city that is Australia's second-oldest settlement, is Australia's second-driest city. The beautiful east coast is nearly always warmer and milder than the rest of the isle. This diversity has contributed to an amazing variety of vegetation, from eucalypt forest and alpine heathlands to large areas of cool temperate rain forests and moorlands.

4 Launceston. Tasmania's second-biggest city is a pleasant place to while away time thanks to its attractive parks and historic colonial mansions.

5 The Northwest. A nearly deserted rugged coastline and the dramatic landscapes of Cradle Mountain National Park make this area a must-visit for walkers.

Updated by
Russell Ward

Wild and dramatic landscapes, empty white beaches, heavenly food and wine—Tasmania's charms have been overlooked for too long by international travelers. Hikers have always known about the island's wilderness trails, which lead you through deserted forests and national parks, but now gourmands are discovering Tassie's superb local produce, making it a world-class gourmet destination, too.

Tasmania's attractions encompass the historic, the healthy, and the hedonistic. Although Tasmania now is an unspoiled reminder of a simpler, slower lifestyle away from the rat race, its bloody history is never far from the surface. Today, walking through the lovely grounds in Port Arthur, the notorious penal colony, or the unhurried streets of Australia's smallest capital city, Hobart, with its profusion of Georgian buildings, it's difficult to picture Tasmania as a land of turmoil and tragedy. But the destruction of the Aboriginal population, who are thought to have crossed into Tasmania approximately 36,000 years ago, is a dark stain on the island's memory.

In many ways Tasmania is still untamed, making it a hiker's delight. Twenty-eight percent of the land is preserved in national parks, where impenetrable rain forests and deep river gorges cut through the massive mountain valleys. The coastlines are scalloped with endless desolate beaches—some pristine white, fronting serene turquoise bays, and some rugged and rocky, facing churning, choppy seas.

These beautiful surrounds have led to Tasmania's newest claim to fame as a gourmet haven. Thanks to the island's many microclimates, you can grow or harvest virtually anything from superb dairy produce to wonderful meat, and its clear seas abound in wonderful seafood. Oenophiles have also discovered the island's wines, and the island's wine routes are well worth a slow meander.

PLANNING

WHEN TO GO

Cold weather–phobes beware: Tasmanian winters can draw freezing blasts from the Antarctic, so this is not the season to explore the highlands or wilderness areas. It's better in the colder months to enjoy the cozy interiors of colonial cottages and the open fireplaces of welcoming pubs.

Summer can be surprisingly hot—bushfires are common—but temperatures are generally lower than on the Australian mainland.

The best times to visit are autumn and spring; early autumn is beautiful, with deciduous trees in full color. Spring, with its splashes of pastel wildflowers and mild weather, is equally lovely.

Tasmania is a relaxing island with few crowds, except during the mid-December to mid-February school holiday period and at the end of the annual Sydney-to-Hobart yacht race just after Christmas. Most attractions and sights are open year-round.

GETTING HERE AND AROUND

Tasmania is compact—the drive from southern Hobart to northern Launceston takes little more than two hours. The easiest way to see the state is by car, as you can plan a somewhat circular route around the island. Begin in Hobart or Launceston, where car rentals are available from the airport and city agencies, or in Devonport if you arrive on the ferry from Melbourne. Allow plenty of time for stops along the way, as there are some fabulous views to be seen. Bring a sturdy pair of shoes for impromptu mountain and seaside walks; you'll most often have huge patches of forest and long expanses of white beaches all to yourself.

In some cases the street addresses for attractions may not include building numbers (in other words, only the name of the street will be given). Don't worry—this just means either that the street is short and the attractions are clearly visible or that signposts will clearly lead you there.

If you are exploring several national parks in the space of a few weeks or months it is recommended to buy a Holiday Park Pass that is valid for two months for A$60 per vehicle in the National Parks of Tasmania.

AIR TRAVEL

Hobart International Airport is 22 km (14 miles) east of Hobart, one hour by air from Melbourne or two hours from Sydney. Although most interstate flights connect through Melbourne, Qantas, Jetstar, and Virgin Australia also run direct flights to other mainland cities. Launceston airport is at Western Junction, 16 km (10 miles) south of central Launceston. It's served by Jetstar, Tiger Airways, and Virgin Australia.

On the island, King Island Airlines can get you to the northwest and King Island. Tickets can be booked through the airlines or through the Tasmanian Travel and Information Centre. Tasmanian Redline Coaches has an airport shuttle service for A$17 per person between the airport and its downtown depot. Metered taxis are available at the stand in front of the terminal. The fare to downtown Hobart is approximately A$40.

GREAT ITINERARIES

IF YOU HAVE 3 DAYS

Spend your first morning in **Hobart**, where you can stroll around the docks, Salamanca Place, and Battery Point, and have some caught-that-morning fish-and-chips from the harbor's floating chippies. After lunch, drive to **Richmond** and explore its 19th-century streetscape, then stay in a local B&B. On the second day head for **Port Arthur**, and spend the morning exploring the town's historic park, the site of the island's former penal colony. Take the afternoon to drive through the dramatic scenery of the Tasman Peninsula, noting the tessellated pavement and Tasman Arch blowhole near Eaglehawk Neck. Return to Hobart for the night, then on the third morning take a leisurely drive around the scenic **Huon Valley**. On return to Hobart, finish your tour with a trip to the summit of Mt. Wellington.

IF YOU HAVE 5 DAYS

Explore **Hobart** on foot the first morning, stopping for lunch at one of the waterfront restaurants at Elizabeth Street Pier, and then wander through historic **Richmond**. Spend the night in Hobart, then on the second day drive through the scenic **Huon Valley**. Return to Hobart for the night, and on the Day 3 drive to **Port Arthur**, taking in the beauty of the Tasman Peninsula on the way. Spend the night in Port Arthur, then drive early on the fourth day to **Freycinet National Park**. Climb the steep path to the outlook over Wineglass Bay, then descend to the sands for a picnic and swim. Stay the night in the park, then on Day 5 meander back through the east-coast wine regions. Return to the capital, topping off the day with city views from Mt. Wellington.

CAR TRAVEL

Port Arthur is an easy 90-minute drive from Hobart via the Arthur Highway. A private vehicle is essential if you want to explore parts of the Tasman Peninsula beyond the historic settlement. A vehicle is absolutely essential on the west coast. The road from Hobart travels through the Derwent Valley and past lovely historic towns before rising to the plateau of central Tasmania. Many of the northwest roads are twisty and even unpaved in the more remote areas, but two-wheel drive is sufficient for most touring. Be prepared for sudden weather changes: snow in the summertime is not uncommon in the highest areas. Lake St. Clair is 173 km (107 miles) northwest of Hobart, and can be reached via the Lyell Highway, or from Launceston via Deloraine or Poatina. Cradle Mountain is 85 km (53 miles) south of Devonport, and can be reached by car via Claude Road from Sheffield or via Wilmot. Both lead 30 km (19 miles) along Route C132 to Cradle Valley.

DISCOUNTS AND DEALS

If you're planning to explore all of the island, the See Tasmania Smartvisit Card (☎ *1300/661771* ⊕ *www.seetasmaniacard.com*) provides unbeatable convenience and value. Three-, 7-, and 10-day cards give you free (or greatly reduced) admission at more than 45 of Tasmania's most popular attractions.

RESTAURANTS

Although there are elegant dining options in the larger towns—especially Hobart—most eateries serve meals in a casual setting. Fiercely proud of their local produce, Tasmania's restaurateurs have packed their menus with home-grown seafood, beef, and cheeses, washed down with their famous cold-climate wines. Tasmanian wine is nearly unknown in the rest of the world, but that's not a comment on its quality; it's because Tasmanians tend to drink the vast majority of it themselves, leaving next to nothing to export. *Prices in the reviews are the average cost of a main course at dinner or, if dinner is not served, at lunch.*

HOTELS

The hospitality industry is thriving in Tasmania, so in popular areas you'll find a wide range of accommodation options, from inexpensive motels to genteel B&Bs, rustic lodges to luxury hotels. Most hotels will have air-conditioning, but bed-and-breakfast lodgings often do not. Apart from a few hotels right in the main city center, most Hobart accommodations have free parking. In many smaller places, especially the colonial-style cottages, no smoking is allowed inside. *Prices in the reviews are the lowest cost of a standard double room in high season. For expanded hotel reviews, visit Fodors.com.*

HOBART

Straddling the Derwent River at the foot of Mt. Wellington's forested slopes, Hobart was founded as a penal settlement in 1803. It's the second-oldest city in the country after Sydney, and it certainly rivals its mainland counterpart as Australia's most beautiful state capital. Close-set colonial brick-and-sandstone shops and homes line the narrow, quiet streets, creating a genteel setting for this historic city of 215,000. Life revolves around the broad Derwent River port, one of the deepest harbors in the world. Here warehouses that once stored Hobart's major exports of fruit, wool, and corn and products from the city's former whaling fleet still stand alongside the wharf today.

Hobart sparkles between Christmas and New Year's—summer Down Under—during the annual Sydney-to-Hobart yacht race. The event dominates conversations among Hobart's citizens, who descend on Constitution Dock to welcome the yachts and join in the boisterous festivities of the crews. The New Year also coincides with the Tastes of Tasmania Festival, when the dockside area comes alive with the best of Tasmanian food and wine on offer in numerous cafés, bars, and waterfront stalls. Otherwise, Hobart is a placid city whose nightlife is largely confined to excellent restaurants, jazz clubs, and the action at the Wrest Point Casino in Sandy Bay.

GETTING HERE AND AROUND

Hobart, being teeny-tiny, is eminently walkable; once you're in the city center, no attraction is more than 15 minutes' walk away, apart from the Cascade Brewery and the Museum of Old and New Art (MONA). Because of the many one-way streets, it's best to park a car and leave it for the day as you explore. If you prefer two wheels to two legs, you

Arthur
Circus **1**

Bonorong Wildlife
Sanctuary **7**

Brooke Street
Pier **3**

Cascade
Brewery **10**

Constitution
Dock **4**

Museum of Old
and New Art
(MONA) **9**

Penitentiary
Chapel Historic
Sight **6**

Royal
Tasmanian
Botanical
Gardens **8**

Salamanca
Place **2**

Tasmanian
Museum and
Art Gallery **5**

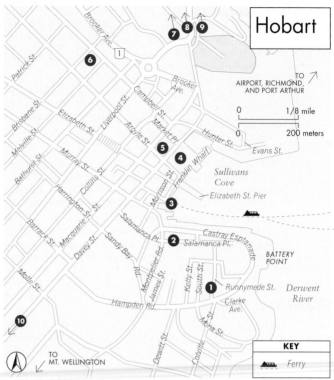

can hire trendy electric bicycles from the Henry Jones Art Hotel on Hunter Street for A$24 for five hours.

ESSENTIALS

Visitor Information Tasmanian Travel and Information Centre ✉ *20 Davey St., at Elizabeth St., Hobart City* ☎ *1800/990440, 03/6238–4222* ⊕ *www. hobarttravelcentre.com.au.*

EXPLORING

TOP ATTRACTIONS

Cascade Brewery. This is Australia's oldest and most picturesque brewery, producing fine Tasmanian beers since 1824. You can see its inner workings on the 90-minute tours, which require lots of walking and climbing, but you're rewarded with three free drinks at the end. Note that appropriate attire (long pants and closed-toe shoes only) is required, and tour reservations are essential. It's a 30-minute walk from the city center, or buses leave from Franklin Square every 35 minutes from 9:15 am. ✉ *140 Cascade Rd., South Hobart* ☎ *03/6224–1117* ⊕ *www. cascadebreweryco.com.au* 🖅 *A$25* ☉ *Tours daily at 11 and 1.*

Constitution Dock. Yachts competing in the annual Sydney-to-Hobart race moor at this colorful marina dock from the end of December through the first week of January. Buildings fronting the dock are century-old reminders of Hobart's trading history. Nearby Hunter Street is the original spot where British ships anchored. ⊠ *Argyle and Davey Sts., Hobart City* ⊠ *Free* ⊙ *Daily 24 hrs.*

Fodor's Choice ★ **Museum of Old and New Art (MONA).** Opened in 2011, Australia's largest privately funded museum is home to a diverse array of exhibits from Tasmanian millionaire David Walsh's private collection. The unusual collection of more than 400 often provocative pieces, including Sidney Nolan's *Snake*—an impressive mural made of more than 1,500 individual paintings—and Wim Delovoye's *Cloaca Professional*, an interesting contraption that transforms food into excrement. Each year, the museum also hosts the MOFO festival, Tasmania's largest contemporary musical festival. Sometimes compared with Bilbao's Guggenheim Museum, MONA offers an eclectic mix of antiquities and contemporary art. The unusual building itself is set into cliffs on the Berriedale Peninsula, and visitors to the museum use touch-screen devices to learn about the exhibits as they wander around through. To reach MONA, it's a 15-minute drive, or you can take the MONA-ROMA minibus from Hobart. There is also the MONA fast catamaran from the Hobart waterfront. ⊠ *651–655 Main Rd., Berriedale* ☎ *03/6277–9900* ⊕ *www.mona.net.au* ⊠ *A$20* ⊙ *Oct.–Dec. and Feb.–early May, Wed.–Mon. 10–6; Jan., daily 10–6; mid-May–Sept., Wed.–Mon. 10–5* ⊙ *Closed Tues. and Christmas Day.*

Fodor's Choice ★ **Salamanca Place.** Many of the warehouses once used by whalers from ships docking at Salamanca Place have been converted into delightful crafts shops, art galleries, and restaurants. At the boisterous Saturday market, which attracts all elements of Tasmanian society from hippies to the well-heeled, dealers in Tasmanian arts and crafts, antiques, old records, and books—and a fair bit of appalling junk—display their wares between 8:30 and 3. Keep an eye open for items made from beautiful Tasmanian timber, particularly Huon pine. ⊠ *Salamanca Pl., Hobart Waterfront* ⊕ *www.salamanca.com.au.*

WORTH NOTING

Arthur Circus. Hobart's best-preserved street is a charming collection of tiny houses and cottages in a circle around a village green on Runnymede Street, in the heart of historic Battery Point. Most of these private houses, which were built in the 1840s and 1850s, have been nicely restored. ⊠ *Arthur Circus, Battery Point.*

Brooke Street Pier. The busy waterfront at Brooke Street Pier is the city's key departure point for harbor cruises. Nearby **Elizabeth Street Pier** has trendy restaurants and bars. ⊠ *Franklin Wharf, Hobart City.*

OFF THE BEATEN PATH

Bonorong Wildlife Sanctuary. About 25 km (16 miles) north of Hobart on the highway toward Launceston, this sanctuary hosts a diverse selection of Australian species—many of which have been rescued—including koalas, wombats, quolls, and the adorable Tasmanian devil. Free feeding tours take place daily at 11:30 and 2. The private dusk tours are highly recommended, and provide a rare opportunity to experience Tassie's beautiful nocturnal animals at their most active. ⊠ *593 Briggs Rd., Brighton* ☎ *03/6268–1811* ⊕ *www.bonorong.com. au* 🎫 *A$25, dusk tours A$179 (2-person minimum)* ⊙ *Daily 9–5.*

BELLERIVE VILLAGE

Take the ferry across the River Derwent to Bellerive, a lovely little village-like suburb that will make you feel as if you've stepped back in history. There are great restaurants, and the view back to the city with Mt. Wellington looming in the background is impressive.

Penitentiary Chapel Historic Sight. Built and used during the early convict days, these buildings vividly portray Tasmania's penal, judicial, and religious heritage in their courtrooms, old cells, and underground tunnels. If you want to get spooked, come for the nighttime ghost tour (reservations necessary). ⊠ *Brisbane and Campbell Sts., Hobart City* ☎ *03/6231–0911, 0417/361392* ⊕ *www.penitentiarychapel.com* 🎫 *A$12, ghost tour A$15* ⊙ *Tours weekdays at 10, 11:30, 1, and 2:30, Sat. at 1 and 2:30; ghost tours Mon. and Fri. at 8:30 pm.*

FAMILY **Royal Tasmanian Botanical Gardens.** The largest area of open land in Hobart, these well-tended gardens are rarely crowded and provide a welcome relief from the city. Plants from all over the world are here—more than 6,000 exotic and native species in all. The collection of Tasmania's unique native flora is especially impressive. ⊠ *Lower Domain Rd., Queen's Domain* ☎ *03/6236–3075* ⊕ *www.rtbg.tas.gov.au* 🎫 *Free* ⊙ *Apr. and Sept., daily 8–5:30; May–Aug., daily 8–5; Oct.–Mar., daily 8–6:30.*

Tasmanian Museum and Art Gallery. In a building overlooking Constitution Dock, this art gallery is a good starting point for uncovering Tasmania's rich history. It's a great place in Hobart to learn about the island's Aboriginal culture and unique wildlife. There are free guided tours Wednesday to Sunday at 2:30 pm. ⊠ *5 Argyle St., Hobart City* ☎ *03/6211–4177* ⊕ *www.tmag.tas.gov.au* 🎫 *Free* ⊙ *Daily 10–5.*

BEACHES

Hobart, which is surrounded by water, has a number of spectacular sandy beaches, most of them close to the city center or Derwent estuary.

Cornelian Bay Beach. Just five minutes' drive from Hobart's city center, this safe and quiet beach lies immediately north of the Queen's Domain urban parkland. Assorted sailing boats sit offshore in Cornelian Bay, while a popular trail, the Queen's Walk, runs directly behind the beach. The Cornelian Bay trail is popular among the locals. Charming heritage-listed boathouses, picnic sites, and barbecues line the shore. The waterfront-facing Cornelian Bay Boathouse Restaurant is known for creative locally caught seafood and fresh Tasmanian produce. **Amenities:** food

Continued on page 342

FOLLOWING THE
CONVICT TRAIL

For many, Tasmania conjures up grim images of chain-ganged prisoners: British convicts banished from the motherland to languish on a distant island in a faraway colony.

Its humble (and brutal) beginning as a penal colony is a point of pride for many Australians. It's no small feat that a colony comprised of, among others, poor Irish, Scottish, and Welsh convicts—many imprisoned for crimes as petty as stealing a loaf of bread—were able to build what is now Australia. It epitomizes a toughness of character that Australians prize. Many here can accurately trace their lineage back to the incarcerated. Kevin Rudd, the country's former Prime Minister, is himself descended from six convicts, including Mary Wade, the youngest female prisoner transported to Australia at the age of 11.

Tasmania has a number of remarkably well-preserved convict sites, most of which are set on the isolated Tasman Peninsula, some 75 km (47 mi) southeast of Hobart. Here, the region's beautifully rugged landscape belies the horrors of the past. Exploring Tasmania's convict heritage and the dramatic beauty of the island are two sides of the same coin. The region's isolation, impenetrable rain forests, and sheer cliffs falling into the sea made it a perfect island prison. By following signs on what's called the Convict Trail, you'll go home with provocative insight into what life was like for the almost 75,000 souls sent to Tasmania between 1803 and 1853.

by Helena Iveson

The rugged and beautiful Tasmanian Coast.

TASMANIA'S CONVICT PAST

Port Arthur Historic Site

"It is impossible to convey, in words, any idea of the hideous phantasmagoria of shifting limbs and faces which moved through the evil-smelling twilight of this terrible prison-house. Callot might have drawn it, Dante might have suggested it, but a minute attempt to describe its horrors would but disgust. There are depths in humanity which one cannot explore, as there are mephitic caverns into which one dare not penetrate."

—Marcus Clarke's description of Port Arthur's Separate Prison in his famous novel *For the Term of his Natural Life.*

They came in chains to this hostile island, where the seasons were all the wrong way around and the sights and smells were unfamiliar. In the 50 years following the establishment of the first settlement in Tasmania (Van Diemen's Land) in 1803, 57,909 male and 13,392 female prisoners were sent to the island. From 1830 on, many ended up at the newly built penal settlement at Port Arthur, where the slightest infraction would be punished by 100 lashes or weeks of solitary confinement

on a diet of bread and water. Life was spent in chains, breaking up rocks or doing other menial tasks—all meant to keep criminal tendencies at bay.

The location of the settlement on the Tasman Peninsula was ideal for a prison. Joined to the rest of the island by a narrow neck of land with steep cliffs pounded by surging surf, it was easy to isolate and guard with half-starved dogs on the infamous dogline. Even though convicts were sentenced for a specific number of years, conditions were so brutal that even a few years could become a life sentence. With no chance of escape, some prisoners saw suicide as the only way out.

As the number of prisoners increased, more buildings went up. In time, the penal colony became a self-sufficient industrial center where prisoners sawed timber, built ships, laid bricks, cut stone, and made tiles, shoes, iron castings, and clothing.

A sculpture representing the infamous dogline at Eaglehawk Neck, Tasman Peninsula

HOW TO EXPLORE

GETTING HERE

To fully experience the trail, you'll need a car. It's possible to get to Port Arthur via operators such as Tassielink, but you can't access the whole trail by public transportation.

From Hobart head north to the well-preserved village of Richmond before continuing southeast on the Arthur Highway (A9) to the small town of Sorell. Not far from here is the infamous Eaglehawk neck, marking the start of the Tasman Peninsula. The Convict Trail runs in a circle around the peninsula, with signs clearly marking the many sites along the way.

TIMING

Port Arthur is 120 km (75 mi) or an hour and a half away from Hobart, but will take longer if you intend on making stops at Richmond and Sorell (which you should).

This trip can be done in one long day, but if you want to thoroughly explore the Tasman Peninsula, allow for two or three days. The Convict Trail booklet is available from visitor information centers across Tasmania and details the key sites and attractions along the route.

Isle of the Dead

Richmond Bridge and Church

EXPLORING

It's easy to forget that Port Arthur wasn't an isolated settlement. The whole of the Tasman Peninsula was part of a larger penal colony, so, for the full experience, don't overlook the smaller sights. There are plenty of cafés and accommodations along the way, so take your time.

STUNNING VIEWS

Don't miss the vistas at the Tasman National Park Lookout. The walk along dramatic sea cliffs, which are among the highest and most spectacular in Australia, is easy and rewarding. The views of Pirates Bay, Cape Hauy, and the two islands just off the coast called The Lanterns are spectacular.

EN ROUTE

Take a break at the famous Sorell Fruit Farm where from November to May it's pick-you-own-berry season (✉ *174 Pawleena Road, Sorell* ☎ *03/6265–2744* ⊕ *www.sorellfruitfarm.com* ⊙ *Oct., Mar., Apr., and May 10–4; Nov., Dec., Jan., and Feb. 8:30–5*).

TOURING THE CONVICT TRAIL

It's hard to absorb this disturbing story of human suffering. Around 73,000 convicts were transported here, and about 1 in 5 served time in Port Arthur, on Tasmania's southernmost tip.

Stone bridge at Richmond

❶ RICHMOND BRIDGE.
Australia's oldest bridge was built by convict labor in 1825 and is a lasting symbol of the island's convict heritage. Don't miss the village's gaol, which predates Port Arthur by five years.

❷ SORELL. This early settlement is where bloody bushranger battles were fought in the colony's formative years. Bushrangers were actually

Sorell Berry Farm

outlaws who lived in the bush. A walk around the town reveals some interesting heritage buildings; there are also plenty of antiques shops and cafes to keep you occupied.

❸ THE DOGLINE. Statues of snarling hounds represent the dogs that prevented the convicts from escaping and mark the infamous dogline along the narrow strip of land linking the Tasman Peninsula with the rest of Tasmania.

Old wooden jetty in Norfolk Bay

❹ NORFOLK BAY. This is the site of a human-powered tramway. Goods were unloaded from ships at the Convict Station and then transported to Port Arthur by a tram dragged by convicts across the peninsula. This saved the ship a dangerous journey across the peninsula's stormy bays.

❺ PORT ARTHUR. Walking among the peaceful ruins and quiet gardens, it's difficult to imagine that this place was hell-on-earth for the convicts. When the settlement closed in 1877, the area was renamed Carnarvon in an attempt to disconnect the land from the horrors associated with its former name. However, in 1927 it was reinstated as Port Arthur and opened to a public keen to embrace this aspect of the Australian story.

TRAIL MARKERS

The Convict Trail is marked with a broad arrow symbol that was stamped on convict-made goods. It's framed in yellow to reference the color of convict clothing.

Sandstone church at Port Arthur

❼ ISLE OF THE DEAD CONVICT CEMETERY. A small island in the harbor near Port Arthur is the final resting place for about a thousand people, most of them convicts and ex-convict paupers who were buried mostly in unmarked graves.

❽ NUBEENA was established as an outstation of Port Arthur and for many years was an important convict farming community. It was also the sight of a semaphore station, used to raise the alarm if a convict made a bid for freedom.

❾ SALTWATER RIVER. Exploring the abandoned mines reveals the terrible conditions in which the convicts suffered: restored tiny underground cells, totally without light and filled with fetid air give horrifying insight.

❿ KOONYA. The probation station here was once an important convict outpost known as the Cascades. It operated between 1843 and 1846 and you'll find a few isolated houses and a well-restored penitentiary that once held 400 men, at least a quarter of them in chains.

❻ POINT PUER BOYS PRISON. More than 3,000 boys, some as young as age nine, passed through here from 1834 to 1849. Located just across the harbor from the main Port Arthur settlement, this was the first jail in the British Empire built exclusively for juvenile male convicts. But just because they were young doesn't mean they were spared from hard labor like stone-cutting and construction. The prison was also infamous for its stern discipline—solitary

The Penitentiary Block

confinement, days at a time on a tread wheel, and whipping were standard punishments for even a trivial breach of the rules.

and drink; parking (free). **Best for:** solitude; walking. ⊠ *Cornelian Bay, Queen's Domain, Hobart* ☎ *03/6230–8233.*

Seven Mile Beach. One of Tassie's favorite beaches, this long, sandy stretch of sand is less than a 20-minute drive outside Hobart, close to the airport. It is both isolated and stunning to look at, although it can be noisy with planes taking off and landing nearby. Considered a great family beach, it's rarely crowded and is ideal for long walks along sand that's peppered with many unusual shells. The small surrounding community includes a playgrounds, golf courses, and restaurants. Seven Mile Beach Cabin and Caravan Park is set within a beautiful park alongside the beach. There are numerous day-use areas—No. 1 has unsheltered tables and a lawn area suitable for picnicking. **Amenities:** food and drink; parking (free); showers; toilets. **Best for:** solitude; walking; swimming. ⊠ *Seven Mile Beach, Hobart.*

SPORTS AND THE OUTDOORS

Hobartians are an outdoorsy lot who make the most of the city's waterfront location by fishing, cruising, and sailing or heading inland to Mt. Wellington to explore the many trails that start there.

BICYCLING

Although most of Hobart and its surrounding areas are too hilly to make for easy cycling, some old railway lines along the western bank of the Derwent River (which are quite flat) have been transformed into bicycle paths. These offer a relaxing way to explore parts of the city. Electric bikes can be rented from the Henry Jones Art Hotel on Hunter Street.

Derwent Bike Hire. This is a reliable outfitter for renting bikes, which provide a fun way to get around the city, particularly via the old railway lines along the western bank of the Derwent River. ⊠ *Regatta Grounds, Queen's Domain* ☎ *0428/899169, 03/6260–4426* 💲 *A$25 daily, A$140 weekly.*

BOAT TOURS

Captain Fell's Historic Ferries. Travelers love the old-fashioned ferries that take you on a leisurely cruise around the harbor as friendly tour guides point out the sights. ⊠ *Franklin Wharf Pier, Hobart Waterfront* ☎ *03/6223–5893* ⊕ *www.captainfellshistoricferries.com.au* 💲 *A$28* ⏱ *Daily 10:30 and 2:30.*

Peppermint Bay Cruises. This catamaran races through the majestic waterways of the Derwent River and the D'Entrecasteaux Channel to Peppermint Bay at Woodbridge and provides a fantastic way to spy some of Tasmania's epic wildlife. And it is abundant, from sea eagles and falcons soaring above the weathered cliffs to pods of dolphins swimming alongside the boat. Underwater cameras explore kelp forests and salmon in the floating fish farms. ⊠ *Peppermint Bay, 3435 Channel Hwy., Woodbridge* ☎ *03/6267–4088* ⊕ *www.peppermintbay.com.au* 💲 *A$98* ⏱ *Daily 10:30.*

FISHING

Tasmania's well-stocked lakes and streams are among the world's best for trout fishing. The season runs from August through May, and licensed trips can be arranged through the Tasmanian Travel and Information Centre.

Several professional fishing guides are based on the island. For information on these guides, as well as related tours, accommodations, and sea charters, check out ⊕ *www.troutguidestasmania.com.au* or inquire at the Tasmanian Travel and Information Centre for a professional guide in the area you are visiting.

Mr Flathead. If you fancy taking to the ocean to explore local fishing hot spots, check with this company that offers half- and full-day tours on which you'll find scores of flathead, whiting, and salmon. All rods, reels, and equipment are supplied. ⊠ *Dodges Ferry boat ramp, Tiger Head Rd., Dodges Ferry* ☎ *0439/617200* ⊕ *www.mrflathead.com.au.*

Rod & Fly Tasmania. Tasmania offers some world-class fishing, and if you'd like to catch some local trout in the region's wonderfully clear rivers, the friendly operator is a good choice for setting up an outing, with more than 30 years of experience. ⊠ *35 Misty Hill Rd., Mountain River* ☎ *03/6266–4480* ⊕ *www.rodandfly.com.au.*

HIKING

Pick up a Mt. Wellington Walk Map from the tourist office on Elizabeth Street in Hobart to make the most out of the park that towers over Hobart. Although shops around town stock outdoor equipment, you should bring your own gear if you're planning any serious bushwalking. Sneakers are adequate for walking around Mt. Wellington and along beaches. A car is necessary to access several of the trails around the peak.

Adventure Seekers. Go hiking with this guide company—you can choose from a range of breathtaking hikes around Tasmania. A nine-day South Coast trek starts in Hobart and explores the wild southern shoreline, but they conduct much shorter trips, too. ☎ *0400/882742* ⊕ *www. adventureseekers.com.au.*

WALKING TOURS

Hobart Historic Tours. This tour company offers guided walks through old Hobart, around the waterfront and maritime precinct, and a historic pub tour. A minimum of two people is required for all walks, which are available from late December through late April. ⊠ *20 Davey St., Hobart City* ☎ *03/6278–3338* ⊕ *www.hobarthistorictours.com.au* ⊠ *A$29.50.*

WHERE TO EAT

Constitution Dock is the perfect place for yacht-watching, as well as for gobbling fresh fish-and-chips from one of the punts (floating fish-and-chips shops) moored on the water. Ask for the daily specials, such as local blue grenadier or trevally, which cost A$7–A$12, or go for some freshly shucked oysters. The city's main restaurant areas include the docks and the streets around Salamanca Place.

$ INDIAN
🍴 **Annapurna.** In the bustling restaurant strip of North Hobart, this local favorite has maintained an enviable reputation for many years thanks to its consistently good-value Indian food. Tandoori, curries (take care, they can be searingly hot), and a wide selection of other Indian delicacies keep people coming back. Inexpensive lunch boxes are available. There is a second location in Salamanca Place. [$] *Average main: A$16* ✉ *305 Elizabeth St., North Hobart* ☎ *03/6236–9500* 🌐 *www.annapurnaindiancuisine.com* 🕘 *No lunch weekends.*

$$$ MODERN AUSTRALIAN Fodor's Choice ★
🍴 **Ethos Eat Drink.** Operated by one of Hobart's most trusted restaurateurs, the dishes at this lively spot feature a daily-changing list of seasonal ingredients available as six-course (A$70) or eight-course (A$90) set menus. Housed in an historic building (it was formerly a stable) in the heart of the city, the dining rooms exude charm. Typical tantalizing dishes include slow-cooked duck egg with pancetta, potatoes, and bread crumbs; and roasted goat served alongside eggplant, turnips, radishes, and leeks. There's also an excellent wine list and stellar desserts, including house-made chocolates. [$] *Average main: A$66* ✉ *100 Elizabeth St., Hobart City* ☎ *03/6231–1165* 🌐 *www.ethoseatdrink.com* ✍ *Reservations essential* 🕘 *Closed Sun. and Mon.*

$$$ MODERN AUSTRALIAN Fodor's Choice ★
🍴 **Garagistes.** One of the most exciting places to eat in Tasmania, Garagistes is leading the charge of cool new restaurants in Hobart serving up Mod Oz cuisine that utilizes the very best local producers. The three- and five-course set menus reflect the changing Tasmanian seasons—try the cacioricotta of ewe's milk, kohlrabi, broad beans, and lovage; or wild snapper with poached rhubarb, soured cream, and dried sea lettuce. Exquisite textures and flavors combine with a hip atmosphere to ensure a memorable dining experience. [$] *Average main: A$75* ✉ *103 Murray St., City Center* ☎ *03/6231–0558* 🌐 *www.garagistes.com.au* 🕘 *Closed Sun.–Tues. No lunch.*

$$$ ECLECTIC
🍴 **Henry's Restaurant.** Part of the Henry Jones Art Hotel, this small restaurant offers some of Hobart's best fine dining in arty surrounds. The food isn't overshadowed by the contemporary art on the walls thanks to the focus on seasonal produce in hearty dishes like slow-cooked pork belly with braised red cabbage, pickled apple, and daikon. The wine list features selections from only the finest Tasmanian, mainland Australian, and overseas wineries. [$] *Average main: A$40* ✉ *25 Hunter St., Hobart City* ☎ *03/6210–7700* 🌐 *www.thehenryjones.com* 🕘 *No lunch.*

$$$ AUSTRALIAN
🍴 **Lebrina.** Elegant surroundings in an 1840 brick colonial home inspire classic Tasmanian cooking in Hobart's most formal dining room. The best of the island's fresh produce is well utilized in such dishes as the twice-cooked Gruyère soufflé appetizer, or the seared loin of venison with fresh horseradish, served with red cabbage salad. Leave room for the superb Tasmanian cheese plate. The wine list includes many fine Tasmanian vintages. [$] *Average main: A$45* ✉ *155 New Town Rd., New Town* ☎ *03/6228–7775* ✍ *Reservations essential* 🕘 *Closed Sun. and Mon. No lunch.*

$$ CHINESE
🍴 **Me Wah.** Featuring a superb range of wines from around the world, this sumptuously decorated Sandy Bay eatery rivals many of the better Chinese restaurants in Sydney and Melbourne. There is a broad menu, ranging from the spendy long-cooked dish of braised abalone cooked

The extremely popular Saturday Salamanca Market

with Chinese mushrooms to traditional favorites, such as Me Wah's delicious steamed dumplings. The *yum cha* (traditional Cantonese tea service) available on weekends at lunchtime is well worth the short journey from the city center. $ *Average main: A$30* ⊠ *16 Magnet Ct., Sandy Bay* ☎ *03/6223–3688* ⊕ *www.mewah.com.au* ⊗ *Closed Mon.*

$$$
SEAFOOD
✕ **Mures Fish Centre.** On the top floor of this complex at Franklin wharf, the Upper Deck section has superb indoor and alfresco views of the harbor. Try the panfried kingfish with carrot puree, confit fennel, olive, almond cream, wild arugula, star anise, and vanilla butter if it's on the seasonal menu. Downstairs, Mures Lower Deck is a bistro-style alternative, where you can order, take a number, pick up your food, and eat at tables outside. Also in the complex is Mures Sushi Bar, where you can find fresh-out-of-water sushi and sashimi. $ *Average main: A$36* ⊠ *Victoria Dock, Hobart City* ☎ *03/6231–1999 Upper Deck, 03/6231–2009 Lower Deck, 03/6231–1790 Sushi Bar* ⊕ *www.murestasmania.com.au.*

$$$$
MODERN
AUSTRALIAN
✕ **The Point.** This revolving restaurant atop one of Hobart's tallest buildings (it's also home to the city's casino) offers breathtaking views, and the food is equally rewarding. The savory smoked Tasmanian salmon appetizer is a wonderful starter; for a main course, try the braised Robbins Island Wagyu beef brisket in an eggplant puree with black sesame, white carrots, and a licorice reduction. Meals here aren't cheap, so you might want to give the tables a try before heading up here. $ *Average main: A$50* ⊠ *Wrest Point Hotel, 410 Sandy Bay Rd., Sandy Bay* ☎ *03/6225–0112* ⊕ *www.pointrevolving.com.au* ⊗ *Reservations essential* ⊗ *No lunch Sat. and Tues.–Thurs.*

$$
BISTRO
✕ **Remi de Provence.** At Tasmania's leading classic French bistro you can sample authentic classic and contemporary Provençal fare accompanied

by superb wines. Add to that the elegant dining room aglow with mirrors and a lovely mural. This nicely valued bistro also has a terrific wine bar along with *cave à manger* where an extensive selection of cheeses, pâtés, and terrines are available. Be sure to try one of Remi's braised dishes, such as *coq au vin*, which are particularly popular—the twice-cooked lamb with zucchini puree and mint oil is quite good, too. $ *Average main: A$30* ⊠ *252 Macquarie St., City Center* ☎ *03/6223–3933* ⊕ *www.remideprovence.com.au* ⊗ *Closed Sun. and Mon.*

$$ ╳ **The Quarry Bar and Restaurant.** Set on the waterfront, this buzzy place
ECLECTIC offers imaginative food alfresco or indoors; it's a lovely place to linger inside in winter thanks to the roaring fire, but it can get busy in the evening and at the height of summer. When it comes to food, local produce is jazzed up—think pickled octopus with orange, fennel, and saffron salad for starters. Happily, there's also an extensive wine list, including more than 30 local drops by the glass. $ *Average main: A$25* ⊠ *27 Salamanca Pl., City Center* ☎ *03/6223–6552* ⊕ *www.thequarry.com.au.*

WHERE TO STAY

For expanded hotel reviews, visit Fodors.com.

Hobart has some lovely lodgings in old, historic houses and cottages, most of which have been beautifully restored. If you're seeking more modern conveniences, there are plenty of newer hotels, too.

$$ ⛫ **Corinda's Cottages.** This complex comprises a charming residence
B&B/INN built in the 1880s for Alfred Crisp, a wealthy timber merchant who later became Lord Mayor of Hobart, as well as three lovingly restored outbuildings in which each of the accommodations are located—these include a gardener's residence, servants' quarters, and coach house. **Pros:** wonderfully restored historic accommodation; generous buffet breakfast. **Cons:** no leisure facilities. $ *Rooms from: A$220* ⊠ *17 Glebe St., Glebe* ☎ *03/6234–1590* ⊕ *www.corindascottages.com.au* ⛫ *3 cottages* ⏐⊙⏐ *Breakfast.*

$$$ ⛫ **Henry Jones Art Hotel.** Arguably one of Australia's best hotels, right
HOTEL on the Hobart waterfront, this row of historic warehouses and a for-
Fodor'sChoice mer jam factory have been transformed into a sensational, art-theme
★ hotel, where the work of Tasmania's finest visual and performing artists is displayed. **Pros:** unstuffy and friendly staff despite the arty surrounds; stunning rooms worth lingering in. **Cons:** bathrooms could do with more soundproofing; your bill might be higher than you planned if you're tempted to buy the art on the walls. $ *Rooms from: A$250* ⊠ *25 Hunter St., City Center* ☎ *03/6210–7700, 1300/665581* ⊕ *www.thehenryjones.com* ⛫ *50 suites* ⏐⊙⏐ *No meals.*

$$$ ⛫ **Hotel Grand Chancellor.** Across the street from the old wharves and
HOTEL steps from some of the most exciting restaurants in Hobart, this imposing glass-and-stone building offers sumptuous accommodation in one of the city's best locations. **Pros:** steps away from the city's museums; offers familiar chain comforts. **Cons:** some traffic noise; stark lobby; fee for parking. $ *Rooms from: A$245* ⊠ *1 Davey St., Hobart City* ☎ *03/6235–4535, 1800/753379* ⊕ *www.ghihotels.com* ⛫ *240 rooms, 12 suites* ⏐⊙⏐ *No meals.*

$$$$
HOTEL
Fodor'sChoice
★
Islington Hotel. Built in 1847, this elegant Regency mansion was converted to a five-star luxury boutique hotel, and is now one of the finest lodgings in Australia. **Pros:** fully tailored hospitality experience; sophisticated service from staff. **Cons:** 20-minute walk to city center; not great for families. *$ Rooms from: A$350* ⊠ *321 Davey St., South Hobart* ☎ *03/6220–2123* ⊕ *www.islingtonhotel.com* ⤴ *11 suites* ○| *Breakfast.*

$$
HOTEL
Lodge on Elizabeth. This opulent grand manor, convict-built in 1829 and home over the years to many Hobart notables, is within walking distance of the city center, but far enough removed to feel like a sanctuary. **Pros:** bargain-priced Internet; convenient option for groups. **Cons:** a few bedrooms are on the small side; some street noise. *$ Rooms from: A$150* ⊠ *249 Elizabeth St., Hobart City* ☎ *03/6231–3830* ⊕ *www.thelodge.com.au* ⤴ *14 rooms* ○| *Breakfast.*

$$$$
HOTEL
Fodor'sChoice
★
MONA Pavilions. These eight high-style pavilions are easily Tasmania's most cutting-edge accommodations—the property is near Tasmania's new world-class experimental art museum, the Museum of Old and New Art (MONA). **Pros:** access to the breathtaking indoor infinity pool with views of the Derwent. **Cons:** lots of high-tech features that can be confusing to operate. *$ Rooms from: A$450* ⊠ *655 Main Rd., Berridale* ☎ *03/6277–9900* ⊕ *www.mona.net.au* ⤴ *8 chalets* ○| *No meals.*

$$
HOTEL
Old Woolstore Apartment Hotel. Offering a mix of standard rooms as well as studios and one- and two-bedroom apartments, this property just a block from Hobart's iconic waterfront occupies one of the city's oldest and most historic buildings, the Roberts Limited Woolstore. **Pros:** central location; complimentary parking; historic ambience. **Cons:** small balconies; confusing drive-in entrance; busy neighborhood. *$ Rooms from: A$250* ⊠ *1 Macquarie St., City Center* ☎ *800/814676, 03/6235–5355* ⊕ *www.oldwoolstore.com.au* ⤴ *242 units* ○| *Breakfast.*

$$$
RENTAL
Sullivans Cove Apartments. This is an impressive collection of 17 handsome, self-catered apartments spread across five waterfront precincts in Hobart. **Pros:** close to Salamanca Place shops and waterfront; stunning interiors. **Cons:** need to book early to reserve; some noise from adjoining businesses in waterfront precincts. *$ Rooms from: A$320* ⊠ *City Center* ☎ *03/6234–5063* ⊕ *www.sullivanscoveapartments.com.au* ⤴ *17 apartments* ○| *No meals.*

$$$
HOTEL
Villa Howden. Just a 15-minute drive from Hobart and along the edge of the renowned Huon Valley tourist route, this new and swanky 10-room boutique hotel has a distinctly Provençal feel. **Pros:** intimate setting; heated indoor pool; lots of fancy in-room amenities. **Cons:** short drive away from the city; a bit pricey. *$ Rooms from: A$375* ⊠ *77 Howden Rd., Howden* ☎ *03/6267–1161* ⊕ *www.villahowden.com.au* ⤴ *10 suites* ○| *Breakfast.*

NIGHTLIFE AND THE ARTS

Although Hobart has the only true nightlife scene in Tasmania, it's extremely tame compared to what's in Melbourne and Sydney. There are few dance clubs, and evenings out tend to revolve around a bottle of excellent local wine. Consult the Friday or Saturday editions of the *Mercury* newspaper before heading out. *This Week in Tasmania,* available at most hotels, is a comprehensive guide to current stage performances and contemporary music concerts.

BARS AND DANCE CLUBS

The waterfront area is lined with bars that cater to the after-work crowds.

Atrium Bar. Hotel Grand Chancellor's piano bar is a relaxing spot by the harbor where local professionals mingle alongside hotel guests. Adjoining the hotel lobby, the bar comfy chairs with waterfront views—an ideal setting for enjoying the fine cocktails, cold beers on tap, and enticing Tasmanian wines. ⊠ *1 Davey St., Hobart City* ☎ *03/6235–4535* ⊕ *www.grandchancellorhotels.com.*

Cargo Bar Pizza Lounge. This beautifully furnished, relatively new bar has inviting booth-style seats toward the back, a peaceful refuge during the busy dinner hour. Note the generous wine selection, with plenty of notable beers and spirits, too, and the tasty pizzas. In winter, sit outside under a heater and catch one of the occasional live acoustic performances. ⊠ *47–51 Salamanca Pl., Battery Point* ☎ *03/6223–7788.*

Grape Bar & Tapas. This popular wine-and-tapas bar has a wonderful shop where you can browse among 300 types of Tasmanian wines and pick up a cheese platter for an impromptu picnic. Choose to sit outside and watch the world go by or enjoy the intimate, laid-back indoor space. Wines are served in trendy Reidel O tumblers. There's live music in the evening toward the end of the week. ⊠ *55 Salamanca Pl., Battery Point* ☎ *03/6224–0611.*

Republic Bar and Cafe. The cool kids head to this raucous, art deco pub warmed by roaring log fires to watch nightly live music, including plenty of top Tasmanian bands. ⊠ *299 Elizabeth St., North Hobart* ☎ *03/6234–6954* ⊕ *www.republicbar.com.*

Round Midnight. Set in a former brothel that dates back more than a century, this spacious nightclub hosts top local and international DJs as well as live bands, with music ranging from blues to rock to dance. ⊠ *39 Salamanca Pl., Battery Point* ☎ *03/6223–2491.*

Sidecar. Owned by the team responsible for the similarly hip Garagistes restaurant, which is just around the corner, Sidecar is a quirky little bar with a groovy ambience to match. Serving food and drink from Wednesday to Sunday, this small but perfectly formed establishment has a modern and minimalist interior. A boutique drink list offers excellent gin and tonics. ⊠ *129 Bathurst St., City Center* ☎ *03/6231–1338* ⊕ *www.garagistes.com.au/sidecar.*

T42. Officially called Tavern 42 Degrees South, this lively waterfront spot is popular for both dining and drinking—it's something of a Hobart institution. Patrons have the choice of sitting inside or out, noshing on tapas, sipping wine, and looking out over the harbor. Service can be slow, but the location more than makes up for it. ⊠ *Elizabeth St. Pier, Hobart City* ☎ *03/6224–7742* ⊕ *www.tav42.com.au.*

SHOPPING

Tasmanian artisans and craftspeople work with diverse materials to fashion unusual pottery, metalwork, and wool garments. Items made from regional timber, including myrtle, sassafras, and Huon pine, are popular. The wonderful scenery around the island is an inspiration for numerous artists.

Along the Hobart waterfront at Salamanca Place are a large number of shops that sell arts and crafts. On Saturday (between 8 and 3) the area turns into a giant market, where still more local artists join produce growers, bric-a-brac sellers, and itinerant musicians to sell their wares.

SIDE TRIPS FROM HOBART

Hobart is a perfect base for short trips to some of Tasmania's most historic and scenic places. Although you can visit them in a day, if you can, stay a night or two and experience their delights at a leisurely pace.

THE HUON VALLEY

40 km (25 miles) south of Hobart.

Fodor's Choice ★ En route to the vast wilderness of South West National Park is the tranquil Huon Valley. Sheltered coasts and sandy beaches are pocketed with thick forests and small farms. William Bligh planted the first apple tree here, founding one of the region's major industries. Salmon and trout caught fresh from churning blue rivers are also delicious regional delicacies.

The valley is also famous for the Huon pine, much of which has been logged over the decades. The trees that remain are strictly protected, so other local timbers are used by the region's craftspeople.

EXPLORING

Hastings Caves and Thermal Springs. Spectacular cave formations and thermal pools amid a fern glade await at the Hastings Caves and Thermal Springs. The caves are about 125 km (78 miles) south of Hobart, past Huonville and Dover. You can take a tour of the chambers, or just relax at the well-equipped picnic areas and make use of the thermal pool. The route to the site is well marked from the town of Dover. Hours vary seasonally, so check ahead, but cave tours and springs access are generally daily from mid-morning to mid-afternoon. ⊠ *754 Hastings Caves Rd., Hastings* ☎ *03/6298–3209* ⊕ *www.parks.tas.gov.au* ⊠ *A$24* ☉ *Daily.*

Huon Valley Apple & Heritage Museum. En route to Huonville, this museum inside a former apple-packing shed is a remarkable time capsule, depicting the lives of the early Huon Valley settlers. The museum displays farming artifacts, picking and processing equipment, and early settler memorabilia from the area's orchards. There's also an art gallery. ⊠ *2064 Huon Hwy., Grove* ☎ *03/6266–4345* ⊕ *www.applemuseum. huonvalley.biz* ⊠ *A$5.50* ☉ *Sept.–May, daily 9–5; June–Aug., daily 10–4.*

6

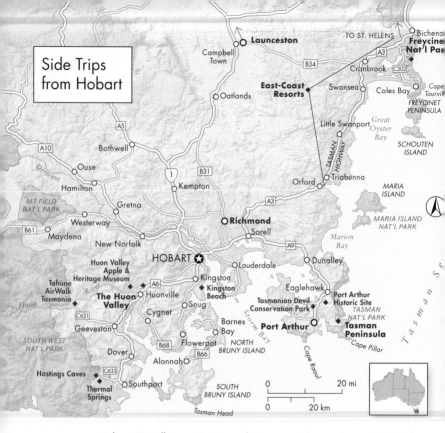

Side Trips
from Hobart

Tahune AirWalk Tasmania. Beyond Geeveston, the cantilevered, 1,880-foot-long Tahune AirWalk rises to 150 feet above the forest floor, providing a stunning panorama of the Huon and Picton rivers and the Hartz Mountains. The best views are from the platform at the end of the walkway, and if you have time, follow one of the trails that lead from the center through the surrounding forests. ⊠ *Tahune AirWalk and Visitor Centre, Tahune Forest Reserve, Arve Rd., Geeveston* ☎ *1300/6297–0068* ⊕ *tahuneairwalk.com.au* 🖱 *A$26* ⊙ *Summer, daily 9–5; winter, daily 10–4.*

BEACHES

Carlton Beach. Situated in the southeast of Tasmania in Frederick Henry Bay, this is a lovely beach well-regarded by surfers—almost 3 km (2 miles) in length and offers easy access from Carlton Beach Road. A 50-foot-high dune backs the beach, and residential properties line the beach road behind it. You'll find plenty of walking trails, and the Carlton Park Surf Life Saving Club lies at the eastern end, with lifeguards on duty in summer. **Amenities:** lifeguards; parking (free); showers; toilets. **Best for:** walking; surfing; swimming. ⊠ *1 Raprinner St., Carlton Beach.*

Kingston Beach. This is the first main swimming beach southwest of Hobart—it's less than 30 minutes' drive from the Huon Valley. The beach sits in front of the fairly developed town of Kingston, on the Derwent River at the mouth of Browns Rivulet. Shopping and housing sit behind and to the south of the beach, and a narrow reserve, picnic area, and playground back the sand. Kingston Beach is patrolled by the local Surf Life Saving Club; however, you should still keep clear of any boating activity in the south corner; the waters are quite deep directly off the beach. **Amenities:** food and drink; lifeguards; showers; toilets; parking (free). **Best for:** walking; surfing; swimming. ⊠ *Beach Rd. at Osbourne Esplanade, Kingston Beach.*

WHERE TO EAT AND STAY
For expanded hotel reviews, visit Fodors.com.

$$
AUSTRALIAN

✕ **Home Hill Winery Restaurant.** Large plate-glass windows open to the Home Hill winery's endless hillside vineyards at this boutique vineyard, cellar door, and restaurant—a true Tasmanian country retreat. The seasonal menu includes such delicacies as pan-seared Huon Atlantic salmon served on potato croquettes and garnished with spinach and poached egg. After dinner, you can head down to the cellar to enjoy a complimentary sampling of the winery's excellent cool-climate wines—try the Home Hill Chardonnay or a Late Harvest Sticky Wine. $ *Average main: A$30* ⊠ *38 Nairn St., Ranelagh* ☎ *03/6264–1200* ⊕ *homehillwines.com.au* ☾ *No dinner Sun.–Thurs.*

$
B&B/INN

🛏 **Heron's Rise Vineyard Cottages.** Mornings in any of the vineyard's three self-contained cottages are bucolic and gorgeous; you'll wake to glorious water views out over the flower gardens, where you might see rabbits nibbling while you soak up the tranquillity of this peaceful environment. **Pros:** peaceful surrounds; owners pride themselves on their eco-friendly accommodation. **Cons:** no leisure facilities; smoke from fireplaces might be a problem for the asthmatic. $ *Rooms from: A$175* ⊠ *Saddle Rd., Kettering* ☎ *03/6267–4339* ⊕ *www.heronsrise. com.au* ⇆ *3 cottages* ⏸ *Breakfast.*

RICHMOND

24 km (15 miles) northeast of Hobart.

Fodor's Choice
★

Twenty minutes' drive from Hobart and a century behind the big city, this colonial village in the Coal River valley is a major tourist magnet. Visitors stroll and browse through the craft shops, antiques stores, and cafés along the main street. Richmond is also home to a number of vineyards, all of which produce excellent cool-climate wines.

WHERE TO EAT AND STAY
For expanded hotel reviews, visit Fodors.com.

$
CAFÉ

✕ **Ashmore on Bridge Street.** Once you've perused all of Richmond's cute shops and historic sights, be sure to recharge in this surprisingly trendy café with an open roaring fire and a friendly owner. The creamy scrambled eggs on sourdough toast with Tasmanian cold smoked salmon and house relish is delicious for breakfast, and in the afternoon the huge and delectable Devonshire teas will have you sighing with pleasure. Dinner with a changing menu is offered Tuesday and Wednesday from 6. $ *Average main: A$15* ⊠ *34 Bridge St., Richmond* ☎ *03/6260–2238* ⊕ *www.ashmoreonbridge.com.au.*

6

$$ ╳**Frogmore Creek.** Wine tasting and two art galleries complement this
AUSTRALIAN unpretentious but upscale restaurant with floor-to-ceiling windows lead-
ing out to views over the vineyards of Frogmore Creek and the waters
of Barilla Bay. The à la carte menu emphasizes food and wine pairings.
Try the seared haunch of Doo Town venison with spiced beetroot and
pinot jus, and make sure to save room for the white chocolate–and–
sage mousse with sage-flower ice cream. $ *Average main: A$35* ✉ *699
Richmond Rd., Cambridge* ☎ *03/6248–4484* ⊕ *www.frogmorecreek.
com.au* ⋩ *Reservations essential* ☽ *No dinner.*

$ 🏠 **Mrs Currie's House B&B.** This gracious Georgian house, built between
B&B/INN 1820 and 1860, is set in a peaceful garden with lovely views over the vil-
lage of Richmond and the surrounding countryside. **Pros:** quaint accom-
modation and friendly owners. **Cons:** not particularly child-friendly;
showers are on the old-fashioned side. $ *Rooms from: A$150* ✉ *4
Franklin St.* ☎ *03/6260–2766* ⊕ *www.mrscurrieshouse.com.au* ⇴ *4
rooms* ⎮◎⎮ *Breakfast.*

PORT ARTHUR AND THE TASMAN PENINSULA

102 km (63 miles) southeast of Hobart.

When Governor George Arthur, lieutenant-governor of Van Diemen's
Land (now Tasmania), was looking for a site to dump his worst convict
offenders in 1830, the Tasman Peninsula was a natural choice. Joined to
the rest of Tasmania only by the narrow Eaglehawk Neck, the spit was
easy to isolate and guard. Between 1830 and 1877, more than 12,000
convicts served sentences at Port Arthur in Britain's equivalent of Devil's
Island. Dogs patrolled the narrow causeway, and guards spread rumors
that sharks infested the waters. Reminders of those dark days remain
in some of the area names—Dauntless Point, Stinking Point, Isle of
the Dead.

EXPLORING

Fodor'sChoice **Port Arthur Historic Site.** This property, formerly the grounds of the Port
★ Arthur Penal Settlement, is now a lovely—and quite large—historical
park with a fascinating convict past central to Tasmania's history. Be
prepared to do some walking between widely scattered sites. Begin at
the excellent visitor center, which introduces you to the experience by
"sentencing, transporting, and assigning" you before you set foot in
the colony. Most of the original buildings were damaged by bushfires
in 1895 and 1897, shortly after the settlement was abandoned, but you
can still see the beautiful church, round guardhouse, commandant's
residence, model prison, hospital, and government cottages.

The old **lunatic asylum** is now an excellent museum, with a scale model
of the Port Arthur settlement, a video history, and a collection of tools,
leg irons, and chains. Along with a walking tour of the grounds and
entrance to the museum, admission includes a harbor cruise, of which
there are eight scheduled daily in summer. There's a separate twice-daily
cruise to and tour of the **Isle of the Dead,** which sits in the middle of the
bay. It's estimated that 1,769 convicts and 180 others are buried here,
mostly in communal pits. Ghost tours (reservations are essential) leave
the visitor center at dusk and last about 90 minutes. ✉ *Arthur Hwy.*

Historic buildings from Tasmania's convict past can be seen in Port Arthur.

☎ *03/6251–2300, 1800/659101* ⊕ *www.portarthur.org.au* ✉ *A$35; Isle of the Dead Tour only A$15; Ghost Tour A$25; After Dark pass A$69 (which also includes a 2-course dinner).* ⊘ *Daily 8:30–dusk.*

Tasmanian Devil Conservation Park. This park is one of the best places to come face to face with real live Tasmanian devils. Spot these burrowing carnivorous marsupials (about the size of a small dog), as well as quolls, boobooks (small, spotted brown owls), masked owls, eagles, and other native fauna. The devils are fed six times throughout the day; call the office for exact hour. ✉ *5990 Port Arthur Hwy., Taranna* ✛ *11 km (7 miles) north of Port Arthur* ☎ *03/6250–3230* ⊕ *www. tasmaniandevilpark.com* ✉ *A$30* ⊘ *Daily 9–5.*

BEACHES

White Beach. It's less than a 10-minute drive from the historic former penal colony of Port Arthur to the pristine white sands of beautiful White Beach, a wild, unspoiled, crescent-shaped beach often named one of the most beautiful beaches in Australia. The breathtaking views from the beach are the most beautiful in all of Tasmania, stretching as far as the eye can see across Wedge Bay to Storm Bay and then beyond to the Hartz. The local trails are worth exploring, not far from the usually deserted 3-km (2-mile) beach, although world-class diving is also available at Eaglehawk Neck and decent surfing at Roaring Beach. White Beach Tourist Park fronts directly onto the beach, and the general area has a number of cafés and restaurants offering excellent local Tasmanian cuisine. **Amenities:** food and drink; toilets; parking (free). **Best for:** swimming; walking; solitude; sunrise; sunset; surfing; snorkeling. ✉ *White Beach Rd.*

WHERE TO EAT AND STAY

For expanded hotel reviews, visit Fodors.com.

$$ AUSTRALIAN 🍴 **Felons Bistro.** Feast on wonderfully fresh Tasmanian seafood and game in the heart of the Port Arthur Historic Site at this small but lovely restaurant. Standout appetizers include the area's local oysters. At teatime (dinner), pop in for one of the rich desserts. If you've built up an appetite during the day's visit, you'll relish the two-course meal prior to your spooky encounters on the Ghost Tour. There is also an inexpensive café in the visitor center. [$] *Average main: A$30* ✉ *Port Arthur Historic Site* ☎ *03/6251–2314, 1800/659101* 🌐 *www.portarthur.org.au.*

$$ B&B/INN 🏨 **Cascades Colonial Accommodation.** Part of a onetime convict outstation dating back to 1841, the original buildings here have been entirely restored and now contain antique colonial furnishings. **Pros:** beautifully modernized rustic chic; private beach is stunning. **Cons:** kitchens aren't big enough to whip up a gourmet feast; in peak seasons there is a minimum stay. [$] *Rooms from: A$200* ✉ *533 Main Rd., Koonya* ✣ *20 km (12 miles) north of Port Arthur* ☎ *03/6250–3873* 🌐 *www.cascadescolonial.com.au* 🛏 *4 cottages* 🍽 *Breakfast.*

FREYCINET NATIONAL PARK AND EAST-COAST RESORTS

The east coast enjoys Tasmania's mildest climate, pristine beaches, and excellent fishing spots. The stretches of white sand here are often so deserted that you can pretend you're Robinson Crusoe. The towns in this region are quiet but historically interesting; in Louisville, for example, you can catch a ferry to the Maria Island National Park, which was a whaling station and penal settlement in the mid-19th century. Farther north, the town of Swansea has numerous stone colonial buildings that have been restored as hotels and restaurants, as well as the unusual Spiky Bridge (so named because of its vertically placed sandstone "spikes") and the convict-built Three Arch Bridge, both of which date from 1845.

The jewel of the eastern coast is Freycinet National Park, renowned among adventure seekers and those who appreciate stunning scenery. The spectacular granite peaks of the Hazards and the idyllic protected beach at Wineglass Bay have been dazzling visitors to this peninsula since it became a park in 1916.

EAST-COAST RESORTS

Fodor's Choice ★ From Hobart, the east-coast Tasman Highway travels cross country to Orford, then passes through beautiful coastal scenery with spectacular white-sand beaches, usually completely deserted, before reaching Swansea. Bicheno, just north of Freycinet National Park, and St. Helens, which is farther north, are both fishing and holiday towns with quiet, sheltered harbors.

EXPLORING

Bay of Fires Lodge Walk. Taking the four-day guided Bay of Fires Walk along the coast north of St. Helens is a wonderful way to enjoy the rugged beauty and tranquillity of the coast. The walk, which is about 27 km (18 miles) long, winds along the edge of Mt. William National Park and allows you to visit stunning beaches, heathlands, Aboriginal sites, and peppermint forests, where a profusion of plant and animal life flourishes. During part of the relatively easy walk you'll stay at an ecologically sound campsite, which is as luxurious as it can get, with timber floors and kitchen facilities, and two nights at the dramatic, remote, and ecologically sustainable **Bay of Fires Lodge.** All meals are provided. For details and prices, check out ⊕ *www.bayoffires.com.au.* ⊠ *Bay of Fires* ☎ *03/6392–2211* ⊕ *www.bayoffires.com.au.*

BEACHES

Bicheno Beach. Extending 650 feet along the southern shore of Waubs Bay, this gentle beach is in the heart of pretty Bicheno. A secondary north-facing beach sits on the western side of the bay. Rounded granite rocks border and separate the two beaches. There is a car park and toilet facilities at the middle of the beach where Beach Street meets the sand, while the town itself sits on the slopes at the south end. A popular shoreline walking track follows the rocky coast around the headland. **Amenities:** toilets; food and drink; parking (free). **Best for:** walking; surfing; swimming. ⊠ *Bicheno.*

Friendly Beaches. Contained within the boundaries of the Freycinet National Park, this long, sweeping, beautiful beach is accessed from Coles Bay Road, 9 km (6 miles) south of the turnoff on the Tasman Highway. Enjoy going barefoot as the sand is extremely soft, fine, and bright as a result of its high silicon content. The waves are excellent for surfers, but there are strong rips and tidal currents, so exercise care. Start at the small parking area, take the short stroll to the beach, and bring water and sunscreen, as there are no nearby facilities. **Amenities:** parking (free). **Best for:** walking; surfing; swimming; solitude. ⊠ *Coles Bay Rd., Coles Bay*

SPORTS AND THE OUTDOORS

DIVING

Bicheno Dive Centre. The spectacular coastline and clear, cool-temperate waters make this a great destination for diving, and this well-established company offers a range of spectacular boat dives. Operating twice daily at 9 and 1, they also offer fishing charters targeting flathead, morwong, the elusive Tasmanian striped trumpeter, and tuna when in season. ⊠ *2 Scuba Ct., Bicheno* ☎ *03/6375–1138* ⊕ *www.bichenodive.com.au.*

HIKING

Wineglass to Wineglass. This exceptional tour run by the Freycinet Lodge is a 8-km (5-mile) guided walk to Wineglass Bay and then on through pristine forests. The guide is not only informative about the area's history and local animals, he also whips up a mean cup of coffee and brings out morning cakes and biscuits. At the end of the walk you're led to a clearing, where a table beautifully laid out with a white tablecloth is laden with local crayfish and oysters as well as some fine local

Pinot Noir and Chardonnay. You're then whisked back to the start on a boat, ending the trip in style. ✉ *Freycinet National Park, Coles Bay* ☎ *03/6225–7016* 🌐 *www.puretasmania.com.au* 🎟 *A$380.*

KAYAKING

Frecyinet is Tasmania's premier sea-kayaking destination, and it's possible to do guided tours or hire your own kayak and cruise around at your own pace.

Freycinet Adventures. Offering a memorable way to explore the spectacular coastline at a leisurely pace, this family-run company offers half-day kayaking tours around the peninsula. Guides point out local marine life, such as sea eagles. The company offers a good mix of packages aimed at all skill levels. ✉ *2 Freycinet Dr., Coles Bay* ☎ *03/6257–0500* 🌐 *www.freycinetadventures.com.au* 🎟 *A$95.*

WILDLIFE WATCHING

Bicheno Penguin Tours. At Bicheno, a very popular tour is the nightly hour-long vigil to see the penguins emerge from the water and clamber up to their nesting area. The daily tours begin at dusk, and penguin numbers often exceed 50. It's a magical opportunity to view these creatures up-close. ✉ *Tasman Hwy., Bicheno* ☎ *03/6375–1333* 🌐 *www.bichenopenguintours.com.au* 🎟 *A$25.*

WHERE TO STAY

For expanded hotel reviews, visit Fodors.com.

$$$$ RENTAL Fodor's Choice ★ 🏨 **Avalon Coastal Retreat.** This gorgeous three-bedroom house is the ultimate in exclusivity: it sits entirely alone on Tasmania's east coast, with just the occasional passing white-bellied sea eagle for company. **Pros:** unadulterated privacy; gorgeous views; fully stocked. **Cons:** there's only one house, and it books up quickly. [$] *Rooms from: A$900* ✉ *11922 Tasman Hwy., Rocky Hills* ☎ *1300/361136* 🌐 *www.avalonretreats.com.au/coastal* 🛏 *1 3-bedroom house* 🍴 *No meals.*

$$$ RESORT 🏨 **Diamond Island Resort.** Direct access to a deserted beach, island walks, and penguin viewing platforms are among the draws of this peaceful hideaway 1½ km (1 mile) north of Bicheno and overlooking the Tasman Sea. **Pros:** minutes from a superb beach; kitchenettes in all units; excellent restaurant on-site. **Cons:** rooms could use some refreshing. [$] *Rooms from: A$275* ✉ *69 Tasman Hwy., Bicheno* ☎ *03/6375–0100, 1800/030299* 🌐 *www.diamondisland.com.au* 🛏 *27 rooms* 🍴 *Breakfast.*

$$ RESORT 🏨 **Eastcoast Central Watersedge Resort.** This seaside complex in the town of Louisville is a great jumping-off point for exploring Maria Island National Park; the resort's catamaran, the *Eastcoaster Express,* makes three or four trips a day to the island. **Pros:** family-friendly resort; inexpensive and unpretentious. **Cons:** somewhat dated decor. [$] *Rooms from: A$180* ✉ *1 Louisville Rd., Louisville* ☎ *03/6257–1172* 🌐 *eastcoastcentral.com.au* 🛏 *48 rooms, 8 cabins, 30 caravan sites* 🍴 *No meals.*

$$ B&B/INN 🏨 **Meredith House.** Exquisite red-cedar furnishings and antiques decorate this grand 1853 refurbished residence in the center of Swansea. **Pros:** excellent service from affable hosts; superb freshly cooked breakfasts. **Cons:** gets lots of repeat visitors, so often books up well in advance; the mews rooms are not as charming as those in the main house. [$] *Rooms*

"We had driven from Friendly Beach further into the Park when we came across this beautiful area." —photo by Gary Ott, Fodors.com member

from: A$180 ⊠ *15 Noyes St., Swansea* ☎ *03/6257–8119* ⊕ *www. meredith-house.com.au* ⊸ *11 rooms* ¦O¦ *Breakfast.*

FREYCINET NATIONAL PARK

238 km (149 miles) north of Port Arthur, 214 km (133 miles) southwest of Launceston, 206 km (128 miles) northeast of Hobart.

The road onto the Freycinet Peninsula ends just past the township of Coles Bay; from that point the Freycinet National Park begins and covers 24,700 acres.

ESSENTIALS

Contact Freycinet National Park ⊠ *Park Office, Coles Bay Rd.* ☎ *03/6256–7000* ⊕ *www.parks.tas.gov.au.*

EXPLORING

Fodor's Choice ★ **Freycinet National Park.** Highlights of the dramatic scenery here include the mountain-size granite formations known as the **Hazards.** On the ocean side of the peninsula there are also sheer cliffs that drop into the deep-blue ocean; views from the lighthouse at Cape Tourville (reached by a narrow dirt road) are unforgettable. A series of tiny coves called the Honeymoon Bays provide a quieter perspective on the Great Oyster Bay side. **Wineglass Bay,** a perfect crescent of dazzling white sand, is best viewed from the lookout platform, about a 30-minute walk up a gentle hill from the parking lot; if you're feeling energetic, though, the view from the top of Mt. Amos, one of the Hazards, is worth the effort. A round-trip walk from the parking lot to Wineglass Bay takes about 2½ hours. The park's many trails are well signposted. Daily entry to the park costs A$12 per person and A$24 per vehicle. ✉ *Coles Bay Rd.* 🌐 *www.parks.tas.gov.au.*

BEACHES

Nine Mile Beach. A stone's throw from the historic town of Swansea, this long, sweeping beach is a favorite for swimming, fishing, and simply soaking up the views and peaceful surroundings—visitors enjoy uninterrupted views across Great Oyster Bay to Schouten Island, The Hazards, and the Freycinet Peninsula. Dangerous rips can be a concern here—take care, especially near the sand bar. The western end of the beach has a variety of lodgings and holiday rentals. Great Swanport lagoon and wetlands form the back side of the beach. There's parking for about 100 cars in the lot. **Amenities:** parking (free). **Best for:** walking; solitude; surfing; swimming. ✉ *Dolphin Sands Rd., Swansea.*

WHERE TO STAY

For expanded hotel reviews, visit Fodors.com.

$$$ RENTAL
🏨 **Edge of the Bay.** The outstanding views from these modern, minimalist-style water-view suites and cottages set along 27 acres of untouched wilderness stretch for miles across Great Oyster Bay to the Hazards. **Pros:** animals wander freely around the resort; idyllic setting. **Cons:** two-night minimum; restaurant menu is limited; no breakfast is served. [$] *Rooms from: A$260* ✉ *2308 Main Rd.* ☎ *03/6257–0102* 🌐 *www.edgeofthebay.com.au* 🛏 *14 suites, 7 cottages* 🍴 *No meals.*

$$$ RENTAL Fodor's Choice ★
🏨 **Freycinet Lodge.** Offering cabin-style accommodation scattered through the densely wooded forest overlooking Great Oyster Bay, this cushy eco-lodge has a remote setting that allows for an intimate connection with the surrounding scenic environment. **Pros:** superb food in fine-dining restaurant; perfect for getting away from it all. **Cons:** utilitarian furniture for the price; rooms can be on the cold side; no TVs, phones, or cell reception. [$] *Rooms from: A$275* ✉ *Freycinet National Park, Coles Bay Rd.* ☎ *03/6225–7000, 1800/420155* 🌐 *www.freycinetlodge.com.au* 🛏 *60 cabins* 🍴 *Multiple meal plans.*

$$$$ RESORT Fodor's Choice ★
🏨 **Saffire Freycinet.** Blame it on jaw-dropping views of Wineglass Bay and the Hazards Mountains that frame the resort, or the eco-friendly space-age architecture fit for the likes of James Bond—a far-flung luxe getaway doesn't get much better than this. **Pros:** views from every inch of the property; comfy, modern suites; great excursions; all-inclusive rates. **Cons:** extremely remote (transfers are not included); one restaurant; very pricey. [$] *Rooms from: A$1,800* ✉ *Coles Bay Rd., Freycinet Peninsula, Coles Bay* ☎ *03/6256–7888* 🌐 *www.saffire-freycinet.com.au* 🛏 *20 rooms* 🍴 *Multiple meal plans.*

LAUNCESTON

200 km (124 miles) north of Hobart.

Nestled in a fertile agricultural basin where the South Esk and North Esk rivers join to form the Tamar, the city of Launceston (pronounced *Lon*-sess-tun), or Lonie to locals, is the commercial center of Tasmania's northern region. Many unusual markets and shops are concentrated downtown (unlike Hobart, which has most of its stores in the historic center, set apart from the commercial district).

Launceston is far from bustling, and has a notable number of pleasant parks, late-19th-century homes, historic mansions, and private gardens. The sumptuous countryside that surrounds the city—rolling farmland and the rich loam of English-looking landscapes—set off by the South Esk River meandering through towering gorges, is also appealing.

EXPLORING

Cataract Gorge. Almost in the heart of the city, the South Esk River flows through the stunningly beautiful Cataract Gorge on its way toward the Tamar River. A 1-km (½-mile) path leads along the face of the precipices to the **Cliff Gardens Reserve,** where there are picnic tables, a pool, and a restaurant. Take the chairlift in the first basin for a thrilling aerial view of the gorge—at just over 900 feet, it's the longest single span in the world. Self-guided nature trails wind through the park, and it's a great place for a picnic. ⊠ *Basin Rd.* ☎ *03/6331–5915* ⊕ *www.launcestoncataractgorge.com.au* ⊠ *Gorge free, chairlift A$15* ☾ *Daily 9–4:30 (until 6 in summer).*

Franklin House. Built in 1838 by noted local businessman and brewer who had once been a convict, this fine late-Georgian house is notable for its beautiful cedar architecture and its collection of period English furniture, clocks, and fine china. Morning and afternoon teas are served in the tearoom. ⊠ *413 Hobart Rd., Franklin Village* ☎ *03/6344–7824* ⊕ *www.discovertasmania.com/attraction/franklinhouse* ⊠ *A$10* ☾ *Summer, daily 9–5; winter, daily 9–4.*

Queen Victoria Museum and Art Gallery. Opened in 1891, the gallery offers fascinating insights into the city's history, including the rich Aboriginal and colonial past. There's also a large natural-history collection of stuffed birds and animals (including the now-extinct thylacine, or Tasmanian tiger). ⊠ *2 Invermay Rd.* ☎ *03/6323–3777* ⊕ *www.qvmag.tas.gov.au* ⊠ *Free* ☾ *Daily 10–4.*

Fodor's Choice ★ **Tamar Valley Wine Route.** Along both sides of the Tamar River north of Launceston, the soil and cool weather are perfect for grape growing. Here in the Tamar Valley wine region, some of outstanding varieties grown include Pinot Noir, Riesling, and Chardonnay; the sparkling wines produced here are world-leading. A map of the route, available for download at their website, will help you to plan your visit. Noteworthy stops along the route are Moores Hill, Hollyman wines at Stoney Rise, Clovery Hill, and Jansz. To help pace yourself, pop into Strathlynn Restaurant at Ninth Island for an unbelievable rustic lunch inspired by the microculture of the Tamar. ⊕ *www.tamarvalleywineroute.com.au.*

SPORTS AND THE OUTDOORS

There are plenty of opportunities to spot wildlife, fish, or birds in the lovely countryside surrounding Launceston and the Tamar Valley.

BIRD-WATCHING

Tamar Island Wetlands. This bird sanctuary on the banks of the Tamar River just outside Launceston is the ideal place to see purple swamp hens and black swans from boardwalks over the wetlands while scanning the sky for white-breasted sea eagles or forest ravens. ⊠ *West Tamar Hwy., Riverside* ☎ *03/6327–3964* ⊕ *www.parks.tas.gov.au* ⊠ *A$5* ☉ *Daily dawn–dusk.*

RIVER CRUISES

Tamar River Cruises. This company conducts relaxing trips on the Tamar, past many wineries and into Cataract Gorge. ⊠ *Home Point Cruise Terminal, Home Point Parade* ☎ *03/6334–9900* ⊕ *www.tamarrivercruises. com.au* ⊠ *A$125.*

WALKING

Launceston Historic Walks. This professional outfit conducts a leisurely one-hour sightseeing stroll through the historic heart of the city. The guided walks leave from the 1842 Gallery and present an engaging look at Launceston's charming architecture and the city's colorful past. ⊠ *St. John St.* ☎ *03/6331–2213* ⊕ *www.1842.com.au* ⊠ *A$15* ☉ *Tues.–Sat. at 10, Mon. at 4.*

WILDLIFE-WATCHING

Pepperbush Adventures. This husband-and-wife team runs tours out of Launceston covering Tasmania's northeast and looking at local wildlife in its natural habitat. The full-day Quoll Patrol takes you to view the "bandit of the Bush," as well as wallabies, platypuses, and, if you're lucky, some devils. ⊠ *Elizabeth St.* ⊕ *www.pepperbush.com.au.*

ZIP LINING

FAMILY
Fodor'sChoice
★

Hollybank Treetops Adventure. Just 15 minutes' drive northeast of Launceston, this popular attraction that's especially appealing to kids offers three-hour zip-lining tours through a verdant forest canopy high above the Pipers River. ⊠ *66 Hollybank Rd., Underwood* ☎ *03/6395–1390* ⊕ *www.treetopsadventure.com.au* ⊠ *A$120* ☉ *Daily 9–7:30 (times vary depending on the season).*

WHERE TO EAT AND STAY

For expanded hotel reviews, visit Fodors.com.

$$
STEAKHOUSE

✕ **Jailhouse Grill.** If you have to go to jail, this is the place to do it—in a 130-year-old historic building where you'll dine on succulent grass-fed beef, typically of the Angus or Hereford breed. Despite being furnished with chains and bars, it was never actually a place for incarceration, so relax and feast on prime beef cuts (or fish and chicken), and an all-you-can-eat salad bar. The wine list is comprehensive. $ *Average main: A$30* ⊠ *32 Wellington St.* ☎ *03/6331–0466* ⊕ *www.jailhousegrill. com.au* ☉ *No lunch Mon.–Wed.*

$$$
AUSTRALIAN
Fodor'sChoice
★

✕ **Stillwater.** Part of Ritchie's Mill—a beautifully restored 1830s flour mill beside the Tamar River—this much-lauded restaurant serves wonderfully creative seafood dishes, usually with an Asian twist, such as the confit of Macquarie Harbour ocean trout with wasabi mash, trout crackle, and citrus-and-flying-fish-roe emulsion. The seven-course tasting menu includes wine pairings from the great selection of Tasmanian wines. A produce shop, café, wine bar, and art gallery are part of the same complex. $ *Average main: A$40* ⊠ *2 Paterson St.* ☎ *03/6331–4153* ⊕ *www.stillwater.net.au.*

$
B&B/INN

🏠 **Alice's Cottages.** Constructed from the remains of three 1840s buildings, this delightful B&B is full of whimsical touches. **Pros:** perfect for a romantic getaway, especially the "boudoir"-themed room; spa bathrooms are luxurious and decadent. **Cons:** not child-friendly. $ *Rooms from: A$160* ✉ *129 Balfour St.* ☎ *03/6334–2231* ⊕ *www.alicescottages. com.au* ⤳ *8 rooms* ❖ *Breakfast.*

$

B&B/INN

⊞ **Old Bakery Inn.** History comes alive at this colonial complex made up of a converted stable, the former baker's cottage, and the old bakery. **Pros:** quaint and sensitively restored rooms; great value. **Cons:** some noise from busy road; breakfast ends at 9 am sharp. $ *Rooms from: A$80* ✉ *York St.* ☎ *03/6331–7900, 1800/641264* ⊕ *www.oldbakeryinn. com.au* ⤳ *24 rooms* ❖ *Breakfast.*

$$$

HOTEL

⊞ **Peppers Seaport Hotel.** Superbly situated on the Tamar riverfront, this popular urban-chic hotel is part of the Seaport Dock area and is designed in the shape of a ship. **Pros:** lovely waterfront views from some rooms; immaculate lobby and service. **Cons:** reception isn't manned 24 hours; the waterfront scene isn't very lively. $ *Rooms from: A$230* ✉ *28 Seaport Blvd.* ☎ *03/6345–3333* ⊕ *www.peppers.com.au* ⤳ *24 rooms, 36 suites* ❖ *Breakfast.*

$

B&B/INN

⊞ **Waratah on York.** Built in 1862, this grand Italianate mansion has been superbly restored with spacious modern rooms tastefully decorated to reflect the era in which the building was constructed; six rooms have hot tubs. **Pros:** complimentary port in guest sitting rooms is a nice touch; helpful staff. **Cons:** a lot of stairs to climb; rooms are on the dark side. $ *Rooms from: A$130* ✉ *12 York St.* ☎ *03/6331–2081* ⊕ *www. waratahonyork.com.au* ⤳ *9 rooms* ❖ *Breakfast.*

THE NORTHWEST

Tasmania's northwestern region is one of the most beautiful and least explored areas of the state. For its sheer range of landscapes, from jagged mountain contours to ancient rain forests and alpine heathlands in the Cradle Mountain area alone, the northwest can't be matched. The region's beauty saw it designated the Tasmanian Wilderness World Heritage Area, protecting one of the last true wilderness regions on Earth.

These regions are a major draw for hikers and sightseers. The western side of the northwest tip of Tasmania bears the full force of the roaring forties winds coming across the Indian Ocean, and this part of Tasmania contains some of the island's most dramatic scenery. Mining was a major industry a century ago, and although some mines still operate, the townships have a rather forlorn look.

GETTING HERE AND AROUND

This region is not the easiest to get to (the nearest airport is as much as two hours away at Launceston) but the destination is certainly rewarding enough to make the journey worthwhile. Driving to Cradle Mountain from Launceston takes 2 hours, and 1½ hours from Devonport. It is possible to take public transport through coach operator Tassie Link, which connects the major transportation hubs with Cradle Mountain and Strahan, but for convenience, nothing beats renting your own car. It should be noted that the northern part of the Cradle Mountain–Lake St. Clair National Park (that is, Cradle Mountain itself) is accessed by roads inland from Devonport and the nearby town of Sheffield. The

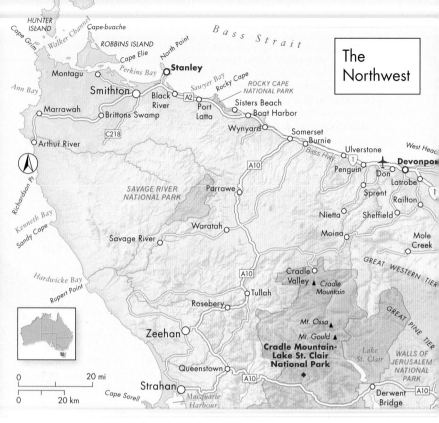

The Northwest

southerly Lake St. Clair end of the park, though, is reached by the Lyell Highway between Hobart and Queenstown at Derwent Bridge.

STANLEY

140 km (87 miles) northwest of Devonport, 400 km (248 miles) northwest of Hobart.

Stanley is one of the prettiest villages in Tasmania, and a must for anyone traveling in the northwest. A gathering of historic cottages at the foot of the Nut, Tasmania's version of Uluru (Ayers Rock), it's filled with friendly tearooms, interesting shops, and old country inns.

EXPLORING

Highfield Historic Site. At this atmospheric site you can explore the town's history at the fully restored Regency house and grounds where Van Diemen's Land Company, who settled the estate in 1824, once stood. Guides in period costumes are on hand to answer any questions. ⊠ *Green Hills Rd.* ☎ *03/6458–1100* ⊕ *www.historic-highfield. com.au* ✉ *A$10* ☉ *Sept.–mid-June, daily 9:30–4:30; late June–Aug., weekdays 10–4.*

The Nut. This sheer volcanic plug that's some 12.5 million years old rears up right behind the village—it's almost totally surrounded by the sea. You can ride a chairlift to the top of the 500-foot-high headland, where the views are breathtaking; or, you can make the 20-minute trek on a footpath leading to the summit, where walking trails lead in all directions. ⊠ *Browns Rd.* ☎ *03/6458–1286 Nut chairlifts* ⊠ *Chairlift A$9* ⊙ *Chairlift daily 9:30–5.*

BEACHES

Godfreys Beach. Just north of the Nut is Stanley's curving Godfreys Beach, at which you can detect elements of the region have been formed by volcanic activity—note the basalt rock formations. The 1-km (½-mile) beach is largely protected from the region's strong westerly winds, which can lead to waves of 3 feet or higher. This is a lovely stretch of sand for strolling, but it's a bit chilly for swimming. You can park at the lot near town, at the south end of the sand, where you'll also find a playground. **Amenities:** toilets; showers; parking (free). **Best for:** walking; solitude. ⊠ *Green Hill Rd.*

SPORTS AND THE OUTDOORS

FISHING

Murray's Day Out. The exuberant owner of this tour service takes guests out on a full day's fishing expedition, providing everything necessary, including lunch and refreshments, and imparting his fantastic knowledge of Tasmania. Some of his recommended common fishing spots include Stanley Wharf, Beauty Point, and Garden Island. Murray also offers personalized shopping and scenic day tours, overnight trips, and other customized excursions. ☎ *03/6424–5250* ⊕ *www.murraysdayout. com.au.*

WILDLIFE WATCHING

Stanley Seal Cruises. Twice a day (except in winter), the motor cruiser *Sylvia C* leads passengers on 75-minute journeys from Stanley's dock to Bull Rock, where they view delightful Australian fur seals basking on the Bass Strait rocks. Southern right whales are also sometimes spotted in the waters near the Nut. ⊠ *Dockside* ☎ *0419/550–134* ⊕ *www. stanleysealcruises.com.au* ⊠ *A$49* ⊙ *Sept.–mid-June.*

FAMILY **Wing's Wildlife Park.** This park, a 50-minute drive from Devonport, has one of the larger collections of Tasmanian wildlife in Australia, which as well as all the usual suspects includes an aquatic section where you can view albino rainbow trout and Atlantic salmon. Excellent guided tours can be tailored to your interests. ⊠ *137 Winduss Rd., Gunns Plains* ⊕ *www.wingswildlife.com.au* ⊠ *A$20* ⊙ *Daily 10–4.*

WHERE TO EAT AND STAY

For expanded hotel reviews, visit Fodors.com.

$$ ✕ **Stanley's on the Bay.** Set on the waterfront in the fully restored old
AUSTRALIAN Bond Store, this unpretentious restaurant specializes in succulent steaks and freshly cooked seafood. Try the eye fillet of beef—Australian terminology for the top-quality beef cut—topped with prawns, scallops, and fish fillets, served in a creamy white-wine sauce. ⓢ *Average main: A$25* ⊠ *15 Wharf Rd.* ☎ *03/6458–1404* ⊕ *www.stanleyvillage.com.au* ⊙ *Closed Sun and Aug. No lunch.*

Looking out across Cradle Mountain–Lake St. Clair National Park

$$ B&B/INN **Beachside Retreat West Inlet.** These modern, environmentally friendly cabins are located directly on waterfront sand dunes overlooking the sea with kilometers of absolutely private beach frontage. **Pros:** guests with special needs are well catered to; breathtaking views from cabins. **Cons:** two-night minimum; limited food availability on-site. [$] *Rooms from: A$200* ✉ *253 Stanley Hwy.* ☎ *03/6458–1350* 🌐 *www.beachsideretreat.com* 🛏 *5 cabins* 🍴 *Breakfast.*

$$ RENTAL **Touchwood Cottages.** Built in 1840 right near the Nut, this is one of Stanley's oldest homes, furnished with plenty of period pieces and known for its doorways of different sizes and an oddly shaped living room. **Pros:** relaxing and romantic play to stay. **Cons:** no baths in two of the cottages; no leisure facilities. [$] *Rooms from: A$180* ✉ *31 Church St.* ☎ *03/6458–1348* 🌐 *www.touchwoodstanley.com.au* 🛏 *3 rooms* 🍴 *Breakfast.*

CRADLE MOUNTAIN–LAKE ST. CLAIR NATIONAL PARK

173 km (107 miles) northwest of Hobart to Lake St. Clair at the southern end of the park, 85 km (53 miles) southwest of Devonport, 181 km (113 miles) from Launceston, 155 km (97 miles) northeast from Strahan to Cradle Mountain at the northern end of the park.

ESSENTIALS

Contacts **Cradle Mountain Visitor Centre** ✉ *4057 Cradle Mountain Rd., Cradle Mountain* ☎ *03/6492–1110* 🌐 *www.parks.tas.gov.au.* **Lake St. Clair Visitor Centre** ✉ *Lake St. Clair National Park, Derwent Bridge* ☎ *03/6289–1172* 🌐 *www.parks.tas.gov.au.*

EXPLORING

Cradle Mountain–Lake St. Clair National Park. This expansive, remote park contains some of the most spectacular alpine scenery and mountain trails in Australia. Popular with hikers of all abilities, the park has several high peaks, including Mt. Ossa, the highest in Tasmania (more than 5,300 feet). The Cradle Mountain section of the park lies in the north. The southern section of the park, centered on Lake St. Clair, is popular for boating and hiking. Many walking trails lead from the settlement at the southern end of the lake, which is surrounded by low hills and dense forest. Visitors are advised to park their cars in the free lot and then make use of the shuttle bus that runs from the Cradle Mountain Visitor Centre and makes stops at all the trails. In summer the bus runs every 15 minutes, in winter every 30 minutes. The entrance fee is A$16.50 per person.

One of the most famous trails in Australia, the **Overland Track** traverses 85 km (53 miles) between the park's northern and southern boundaries. The walk usually takes five to seven days, depending on the weather, and on clear days the mountain scenery seems to stretch forever. Hikers are charged A$200 to do the Overland during peak walking season (November to April), and Tasmania's Parks and Wildlife Service has provided several basic sleeping huts that are available on a first-come, first-served basis. Because space in the huts is limited, hikers are advised to bring their own tents. If you prefer to do the walk in comfort, you can use well-equipped, heated private structures managed by Cradle Mountain Huts. ⊠ *Cradle Mountain–Lake St. Clair National Park* ☎ *03/6492–1110* ⊕ *www.cradlehuts.com.au.*

SPORTS AND THE OUTDOORS

As well as the self-guided day and multiday walks you can do in Cradle Mountain, there are plenty of opportunities to see the sights from a horse, the air, or even a quad bike.

AIR TOURS

Cradle Mountain Helicopters. The views are magnificent on this company's scenic helicopter flights from Cradle Mountain village to the country's deepest gorge, Fury Gorge, and then on to picture-postcard Dove Lake, set against epic Cradle Mountain itself. Flights are relatively expensive at A$245 per person, but the panoramas over the rugged Tasmanian landscape are breathtaking. ⊠ *Cradle Mountain* ⊕ *www. cradlemountainhelicopters.com.au.*

HIKING

Cradle Mountain Coaches. This Devonport-based company offers afternoon guided walks to Cradle's glacial lakes and alpine forests with stunning views of Mt. Roland. ⊠ *283 Port Sorell Rd., Wesley Vale* ☎ *03/6427–7626* ⊕ *www.cradlemountaincoaches.com.au* ⌦ *A$149.*

HORSEBACK RIDING

Cradle Country Adventures. Choose from half-day, full-day, and multiday horse rides through stunning natural vistas—available packages are suitable for both novices and experienced riders. All equipment, guides, and transfers are included. ⊠ *Cradle Mountain* ☎ *1300/656069* ⊕ *www.cradleadventures.com.au.*

QUAD BIKING

Cradle Mountain Quad Bikes. Year-round you can hire a Suzuki Ozark 250 quad bike and ride it on a special track that winds up through ancient myrtle forests and alpine eucalypt forest. Four-wheel-drives are also available. Rates are from A$129 for two hours, including morning tea. ✉ *Cradle Mountain* ☎ *1300/656069* 🌐 *www.cradlemountainquadbikes.com.au.*

WHERE TO STAY

For expanded hotel reviews, visit Fodors.com.

$$ RESORT 🏨 **Cradle Mountain Chateau.** Five minutes' drive from the entrance to the national park is this corporate-style place—don't be misled by the word chateau—think upmarket lodge complete with rustic-style split-level rooms that face the woods and have perching posts that local birds flock to. **Pros:** the excellent spotlight animal tour at dusk is unmissable; the fine-dining restaurant offers delicious meals. **Cons:** can be packed with corporate events. [$] *Rooms from: A$200* ✉ *Cradle Mountain Rd., Cradle Mountain* ☎ *1800/420155, 03/6492–1404* 🌐 *www.cradlemountainchateau.com.au* 🛏 *60 rooms* 🍴 *No meals.*

$$$ RESORT 🏨 **Peppers Cradle Mountain Lodge.** This charming lodge with its collection of wood cabins dotted around the wilderness of Cradle Mountain Valley is a firm favorite with park visitors. **Pros:** good range of food options, including a restaurant, bistro, and bar; fireplaces are a hit in winter. **Cons:** some might rue the lack of home comforts—no room service, TV, or Internet (except in the lobby). [$] *Rooms from: A$250* ✉ *4038 Cradle Mountain Rd., Cradle Mountain* ☎ *03/8296–8010* 🌐 *www.cradlemountainlodge.com.au* 🛏 *96 rooms* 🍴 *Breakfast.*

BRISBANE AND
ITS BEACHES

WELCOME TO
BRISBANE AND ITS BEACHES

TOP REASONS
TO GO

★ **Enjoying the Outdoors:**
Choose from rain forests
and reefs, unspoiled
beaches and islands,
rushing rivers, dramatic
gorges, distinctive wildlife,
hiking, and water sports.

★ **Experiencing the Laid-
Back Vibe:** Queensland is
renowned for its relaxed
and welcoming feel, even
at the upmarket hotels and
fine-dining restaurants of
Brisbane and resort areas.

★ **Releasing Your Inner
Child:** Queensland's
Gold Coast is abuzz
with world-class theme
parks—from thrill rides and
water parks to Outback-
inspired extravaganzas.

★ **Seeing Wildlife:** Head
out to the southern end
of the Reef for millions of
fish, rays, turtles, and ceta-
ceans; or, on the mainland,
watch for rare birds and
mammals, endangered
frogs, dingoes, and koalas.

1 Brisbane. Affection-
ately dubbed Brisvegas,
Queensland's capital city is
a breezily cheerful, increasingly sophisticated city with
a thriving casino, cultural
attractions, and some
terrific eateries, galleries,
nightspots, and markets all
centered around the city's
sprawling river.

2 The Gold Coast. An
hour's drive south of
Brisbane, Queensland's first
coastal resort has expanded
into a busy strip of high-
rise hotels, action-packed
theme parks, casinos, bars,
eateries, and nightclubs. If
you need a break from the
bustle, walk down to the
beach and curl your toes in
the sand; alternatively, drive
west and spend a day (or
several) exploring the lush,
mountainous hinterland.

3 The Sunshine Coast.
This stretch of coast-
line about an hour north
of Brisbane is known
for its glorious beaches,
stunning national parks,
and mountain hinterland
dotted with charming,
heritage-style townships. In
recent years, new roads and
infrastructure have spurred
a boom in accommodation,
eateries, markets and other
attractions.

**4 Mackay-Capricorn
Islands.** This smattering of
coral cays along the southern end of the Great Barrier
Reef—including Heron,
Wilson, Lady Musgrave, and
Lady Elliot islands—is home
to a host of marine wildlife,
including seabirds, turtles,
rays, sharks, and millions of
dazzling tropical fish.

5 Fraser Island. A gigantic
sand island off Hervey Bay,
Fraser Island is paradise
for the active visitor. What
it lacks in luxe ameni-
ties it makes up for in
scenery: miles of white-sand
beaches, deep-blue lakes,
and bushland bristling with
wildlife—including some of
the world's most purebred
dingoes.

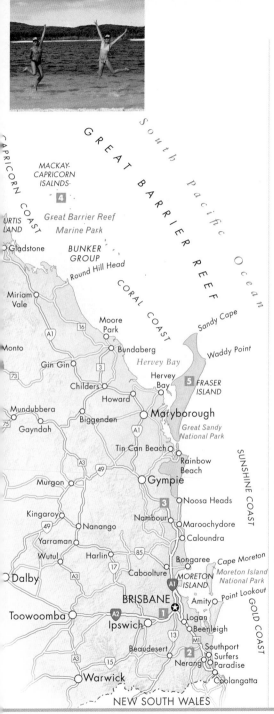

GETTING ORIENTED

At 1,727,999 square km (667,180 square miles) and more than four times the size of California, Queensland has enormous geographic variety. Its eastern seaboard stretches 5,200 km (3,224 miles) from the subtropical Gold Coast to the wild and steamy rain forests of the far north. Away from the coastal sugar and banana plantations, west of the Great Dividing Range, Queensland looks as arid and dust-blown as any other part of Australia's interior. Not surprisingly, most of the state's 4.6 million or so inhabitants reside on the coast. Brisbane and the beach resorts toward the south of the coast have experienced dramatic expansion over the past decade. The region's main attractions (apart from the kitschy "Big Things" that dot its highways) are its glorious coastline, the fertile hinterland surrounds, and the reefs and islands that lie offshore.

SUNSHINE COAST'S TOP BEACHES

Queensland's Sunshine Coast stretches from Caloundra in the south to Noosa Heads in the north. Along it you'll find everything from family-friendly beaches to thundering surf breaks to pretty sheltered coves ideal for snorkeling.

The Sunshine Coast has been developed more slowly and sensitively than its southern counterpart, the Gold Coast. Although it has its share of shops, cafés, and resorts, there are still dozens of clean, uncrowded beaches where you can sunbathe, stroll, cast a line, or jump in the unspoiled waters to swim, snorkel, and surf.

Some beaches are perfect for water sports such as sailing, windsurfing, kayaking, or wakeboarding. Others are known for their reliable surf breaks. You'll find secluded rocky coves where you can "fossick" (Australian for beachcomb) among rock pools, or don a mask and snorkel to come face-to-face with colorful fish, rays, sea stars, and squid. There are also safe, lifeguard-patrolled swimming beaches with playgrounds, skate parks, kiosks, changing rooms, and picnic facilities ideal for families.

WHEN TO GO

The Sunshine Coast is renowned for sunny skies and year-round balmy temperatures, but you can still optimize your experience with some good timing. Beaches can get crowded at peak season, and prices are higher. The most ideal time to visit is November and early December or March and April (except Easter week, which usually includes Queensland's weeklong fall school break), when crowds are fewer but the weather is still summery. Note that many beaches are only patrolled during peak times. January and February bring the most rain.

SUNSHINE BEACH

Lovely Sunshine Beach, the last easterly facing beach before Noosa, is patrolled year-round. Beach breaks, reliable swell, a rocky headland sheltering it from winds, and clear, glassy water make Sunshine popular with surfers. When northeasterlies blow, surf the northern pocket. Fish off the beach year-round for dart, bream, and flathead, or cast a long line into deep water to hook numerous seasonal species. Use covered picnic areas, barbecues, toilets, and parking.

MOOLOOLABA BEACH

This super-safe, family-friendly swimming beach is patrolled year-round, and has just enough swell to make it fun. Surfers might want to check out the left-hand break that sometimes forms off the rocks at the northern end. There are shady picnic areas with barbecues, playgrounds, showers, toilets, public phones, exercise areas, and parking—as well as the local meeting point, the Loo with a View. Stroll south along the coastal path to the river mouth and rock wall (off which you can fish, year-round, for bream); north to Alexandra Headland for views of the bay; or along Mooloolaba Esplanade, lined with casual eateries and boutiques.

COOLUM BEACH

Coolum Beach is a popular choice for families, boasting a surf club, skate park, playgrounds, changing rooms, toilets, kiosk, shorefront parks, and picnic areas. A long, white-sand beach, Coolum is patrolled year-round, and offers a nice beach break and some decent waves off the headland. Fish from the beach in the evening for jewfish, tailor, bream, and dart; catch bream around the headland, especially in winter. Walk south along the boardwalk to the headland park for magnificent coastal views, or north to quieter Peregian Beach with its patrolled surf, playground, and adjacent Environmental Park.

SAFETY

Most popular Sunshine Coast beaches are patrolled by lifeguards in school holiday and peak periods and on weekends throughout the warmer months. On some Sunshine Coast beaches, sandbanks, strong currents, and riptides make surf conditions challenging. Even on patrolled beaches, swimming unaccompanied is not recommended. Swim between the red-and-yellow flags, and follow lifeguards' directives. Locals are often the best sources of advice on where and when to dive in.

Sharks are rarely a problem; however, lifeguards keep watch and issue warnings if they're sighted. A more constant hazard is the harsh Queensland sun: apply SPF30-plus sunscreen at regular intervals. Get information on local beaches at ⊕ *coastalwatch.com*, and surf reports on Surf Life Saving Queensland's website, ⊕ *www.lifesaving.com.au*. Contact SLSQ Lifesaving on ☎ *07/3846–8000*.

COASTAL AND WILDERNESS WALKS

Southeast Queensland lays claim to some of the world's most superb wilderness areas, and the best way to explore them is on foot. Behind the Gold and Sunshine coasts are national parks, forests, and nature reserves dense with trails and walkways. Several also trace scenic sections of the coastline.

Coastal trails wind along the beachfront, trace rainforest-clad headlands, and meander through waterfront reserves from the Gold Coast to the national parkland north of Noosa.

A string of national parks and wilderness areas connects the Gold and Sunshine Coast hinterlands, with trails of varying lengths and degrees of difficulty. Walkers are rewarded with memorable sights: dramatic waterfalls and pristine pools, tracts of ancient rain forest, and glowworm caves; wildflowers, wildlife, and exceptional views, some stretching as far as the coast.

SAFETY

For bushwalking you'll need sturdy shoes with grip, a hat, sunscreen, insect repellent, wet- and cold-weather gear, drinking water, food, camping equipment and permits (if overnighting), and a map and compass. Leech-proof yourself by wearing long socks over your pant legs and carrying a lighter to burn off any hitchhikers. Let others know your planned route and timing, even for day hikes.

Over summer's wetter months trails may be muddy or closed. From January to March, conditions can be hot and humid. Watch for snakes. The NPRSR (⊕ www.nprsr.qld.gov.au) provides trail maps and up-to-date information.

QUEENSLAND'S GREAT WALKS

If your schedule allows it, tackle one of Queensland's Great Walks. A\$10-million state government initiative, the Great Walks aim to allow visitors of all ages and of average fitness to explore significant wilderness areas in a safe, eco-sensitive way.

A standout is the 54-km (34-mile) Gold Coast Hinterland Great Walk, linking the species-rich, Gondwana Rainforests of Australia World Heritage Area of Lamington and Spring-brook plateaus via the glorious Numinbah Valley. En route, you'll traverse ancient volcanic terrain and pristine rain forest, passing torrential streams and waterfalls and 3,000-year-old hoop pines. Allow three days for the full walk, camping at designated sites en route, or trek just one section.

The Sunshine Coast Hinterland Great Walk, a 58-km (36-mile) hike traversing the Blackall Range northwest of Brisbane, includes sections of Kondalilla and Mapleton Falls national parks, Maleny Forest Reserve, and Delicia Road Conserva-tion Park. The four- to six-day hike takes you past waterfalls and through open eucalypt and lush subtropical rain forest teeming with native birds, reptiles, and frogs.

The Cooloola Great Walk meanders through Great Sandy National Park north of Noosa. A 90-km (55-mile) network of graded walking tracks passes the spectacular multihued sand dunes of Rainbow Beach, and includes walks of varying distances and difficulty across a range of conditions.

Fraser Island Great Walk rewards hikers with exceptional scenery—wide, white-sand beaches, pristine deep-blue lakes, rain-forest tracts, and plenty of birds, reptiles, wallabies, and dingoes.

For downloadable trail maps and detailed information, visit ⊕ *www.nprsr.qld.gov.au.* For camping information and permits, go to ⊕ *www.qld.gov.au/camping* or phone ☎ *13–7468.*

SHORTER OPTIONS

Coastal Trails. Compact Burleigh Head National Park, midway between Surfer's Paradise and Coolangatta, includes coastal rain forest and heath that's home to wallabies, koalas, lizards, snakes, and brush turkeys. Trek the 2.8-km (1.75-mile) Rainforest Circuit for excel-lent views, or the shadier, shorter, 1.2-km (0.75-mile) Oceanview Walk

Hinterland Trails. Mt. Tamborine, Springwood, Witches Falls-Joalah, and Lamington national parks in the Gold Coast hinterland are all ideal for exploring on foot. Several wilderness retreats in the region offer guided bushwalks as part of the package.

West of the Sunshine Coast, short scenic walking trails in Kondal-lilla National Park near Montville take you past waterfalls, boulder-strewn streams, and lush rain forest abuzz with local wildlife. Or stroll along easy trails through Mary Cairncross Scenic Reserve, near Montville.

Updated by
Tess Curran

A fusion of Florida, Las Vegas, and the Caribbean, southern Queensland attracts crowd-lovers and escapists alike. Whether you want to surf or soak in the Pacific Ocean, stroll from cabana to casino with your favorite cocktail, hike through subtropical rain forests, or join seabirds and turtles on a pristine coral isle—it's all here.

Local license plates deem Queensland "The Sunshine State"—a laid-back stretch of beaches and sun where many Australians head for their vacations. The state has actively promoted tourism, and areas such as the Gold Coast, an hour south of Brisbane, and the Sunshine Coast, a roughly equivalent distance north of the capital, have expanded exponentially in recent years, with high-rise hotels, nightclubs, trendy bars and cafés, shopping precincts and beachfront amusements popping up on nearly every block. These thriving coastal strips are the major attraction of southern Queensland for Australians and foreign tourists alike—along with a scattering of islands, notably Fraser Island, off Hervey Bay, and the Mackay-Capricorn islands lying on the southern end of the Great Barrier Reef.

Queensland was thrust into the spotlight when Brisbane hosted the Commonwealth Games in 1982. The World Expo '88 and the 2001 Goodwill Games have ensured that it's remained there. Such big-name competitions exposed Brisbane to the wider world and helped to bring the city, along with other provincial capitals, to social and cultural maturity. Queensland is now a vibrant and cosmopolitan place to visit, and Sunshine Staters are far more likely to be city slickers than the "bushie" stereotype of decades past. Still, as with many regions blessed with abundant sunshine, the lifestyle here is relaxed.

PLANNING

WHEN TO GO

Temperatures average 15.6°C (60°F) between May and September with chillier nights, and 20°C (68°F) to 29°C (80°F) December to February. From December through March, expect periods of heavy rain. Temperatures run slightly cooler inland. Sea- and reef-side Queensland tends to fill up from mid-December through January, and can also be heavily booked in July, September, and throughout Easter. There's no daylight saving time in the state.

GETTING HERE AND AROUND

AIR TRAVEL

Qantas (⊕ *www.qantas.com.au*), Virgin Australia (⊕ *www.virginaustralia.com*), and a number of other carriers fly direct from U.S. cities to Australian capitals and regional tourist hubs. Qantas, Virgin Australia, and Jetstar (⊕ *www.jetstar.com.au*) link several regional centers throughout Queensland. Budget carrier TigerAir (⊕ *www.tigerair.com.au*) also covers most major centers, including the Sunshine Coast, Cairns, and Rockhampton.

BOAT TRAVEL

Ferries and charter boats ply the waters between the southeast Queensland mainland and its various islands and offshore resorts. Most make daily or more frequent return trips; some carry vehicles as well as passengers.

BUS TRAVEL

Buses service most major towns and tourist areas around southeast Queensland, and are reliable and affordable—though on many routes it's as cheap, and faster, to fly. During holiday periods on popular routes buses are often heavily booked; buy tickets in advance, and don't expect to stretch out, even on overnight services. Tourist offices can advise which companies go where.

CAR TRAVEL

Traveling outside of cities is often simplest and most comfortable by car. Roads are generally good, but signage varies in clarity; study maps and work out highway exits in advance (although most hire cars will have GPS systems installed). Be prepared for heavy traffic between Brisbane and the Gold and Sunshine coasts in peak periods. Expect temporary road closures and detours after heavy rains. Roads are narrow and winding in some parts of the hinterlands. You'll need a 4x4 to get around Fraser Island, the sand islands of Moreton Bay, and some national park roads and Outback tracks. You can rent a small runabout from about A$35 per day; a decent touring car from about A$45 a day, and a 4x4 from about A$80 per day. Gas costs vary, and tend to be pricier away from major towns and highways.

TRAIN TRAVEL

Frequent trains service routes between the capital and the Gold and Sunshine coasts. The Queensland Rail network links regional towns and tourist centers, and is a scenic way to travel (though on longer routes it's often cheaper to fly). The *Sunlander* and high-speed *Tilt Train* ply the coast between Brisbane and Rockhampton or Cairns, servicing towns that act as launching pads for island resorts.

RESTAURANTS

Once largely unfamiliar with the concept of specialized cuisine, Queensland is coming into its own as a new foodie hub. Cosmopolitan Brisbane boasts its share of modern Australian, Mediterranean, and Asian-influenced menus capitalizing on fresh regional produce, and the cuisine at many of Queensland's high-end resorts now rivals the standards of big-city fine-dining. Coastal tourist towns are full of casual open-air restaurants that take advantage of the tropical climate—an increasing number of them helmed by city-class chefs. Away from tourist hubs, steak, seafood, and the occasional Asian restaurant still tend to dominate. If you're on the road, an old-fashioned pub meal is more than satiating and a great way to get to know the locals. *Prices in the reviews are the average cost of a main course at dinner or, if dinner is not served, at lunch.*

HOTELS

Accommodations in this state run the gamut from rain-forest lodges, Outback pubs, backpacker hostels, and colonial "Queenslander" bed-and-breakfasts—beautiful timber houses built high on stilts, with wraparound verandas and character windows—to deluxe beachside resorts and big-city hotels. The luxury resorts are clustered around the major tourist areas of the Gold and Sunshine coasts and nearby islands such as Heron and Wilson. In smaller coastal towns, accommodation is mostly in motels, apartments, and B&Bs. There is also an increasing number of eco-friendly accommodation options which utilize green technologies such as renewable energy and water conservation systems to minimize their impact on the environs. Many of Queensland's island resorts fall into this category. *Prices in the reviews are the lowest cost of a standard double room in high season. For expanded reviews, facilities, and current deals, visit Fodors.com.*

TOURS

Guided day tours are a simple way to see Brisbane if your schedule is tight. View the city's many attractions from the comfort of a chauffeured coach, with a driver offering insider information. Buses are also great for covering the relatively short distances between Brisbane and nearly all of the mainland attractions covered in the chapter. Within an hour or two you can be taste-testing your way through the Tambourine or Scenic Rim wineries, or practicing your poker face at a Gold Coast casino.

Most day tours include admission to sights, refreshments, and on full-day tours, lunch, as well as commentary en route and time to explore. Australian Day Tours/JPT conducts half- and full-day tours of Brisbane and nearby Moreton Island; one- and two-day trips to and around the Gold Coast, Noosa Heads, and the Sunshine Coast, from A$35 to A$540; and a two-day Fraser Island tour for A$499 per person.

Contacts Australian Day Tours/JPT ✉ *Shop 18, 2 Elkhorn Ave., Surfers Paradise* ☎ *1300/363436, 07/5512–6444* ⊕ *www.daytours.com.au.*

GREAT ITINERARIES

IF YOU HAVE 3 DAYS
If you're after a Miami Beach–style holiday, fly into Brisbane and head straight for the glitzy Gold Coast, overnighting in Surfers Paradise. You could end the spree with a final night and morning in Lamington National Park renowned for its subtropical wilderness and birdlife.

IF YOU HAVE 5 DAYS
Do three days on shore and two days on the reef. Stay a night in Brisbane, then head to the Sunshine Coast for a hike in the Glasshouse Mountains on the way to Noosa Heads. Apart from beaches and surf, take in the Sunshine Coast's monument to kitsch, the Big Pineapple, and indulge in one of their famous sundaes. Then make your way north to Bundaberg or Gladstone for a flight to Lady Elliot, Heron, or Wilson islands to wildlife-watch, dive, and snorkel; or a ferry to Fraser Island, off Hervey Bay, where you can swim in pristine lakes, 4WD along beaches stretching 80 km (50 miles), and see wild dingoes.

BRISBANE

Founded in 1824 on the banks of the wide, meandering Brisbane River, the former penal colony of Brisbane was for many years regarded as just a big country town. Many beautiful timber Queenslander homes, built in the 1800s, still dot the riverbanks and inner suburbs, and in spring the city's numerous parks erupt in a riot of colorful jacaranda, poinciana, and bougainvillea blossoms. Today the Queensland capital is one of Australia's most up-and-coming cities: glittering high-rises mark its polished business center, slick fashion boutiques and restaurants abound, and numerous outdoor attractions beckon. In summer, temperatures here are broilingly hot and days are often humid, a reminder that this city is part of a subtropical region. Wear SPF 30-plus sunscreen and a broad-brimmed hat outdoors, even on overcast days.

Brisbane's inner suburbs, a 5- to 10-minute drive or 15- to 20-minute walk from the city center, have a mix of intriguing eateries and quiet accommodations. Fortitude Valley combines Chinatown with a cosmopolitan mix of clubs, cafés, and boutiques. Spring Hill has several high-quality hotels, and Paddington, New Farm, Petrie Terrace, West End, and Woolloongabba are full of an eclectic mix of restaurants and bars. Brisbane is also a convenient base for trips to the Sunshine and Gold coasts, the mountainous hinterlands, and the Moreton Bay islands.

GETTING HERE AND AROUND

AIR TRAVEL

Brisbane is Queensland's major transit hub. Qantas and Virgin Australia fly to all Australian capital cities and regional hubs around Queensland. Jetstar links Brisbane with the Fraser, Gold, and Sunshine coasts and regional cities farther north.

Brisbane International Airport is 9 km (5½ miles) from the city center. Coachtrans operates a bus service to meet all flights and drops

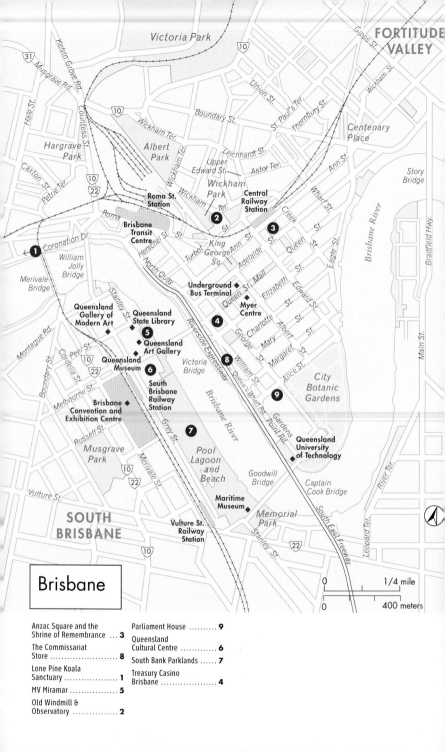

Brisbane

Anzac Square and the
Shrine of Remembrance ... **3**

The Commissariat
Store **8**

Lone Pine Koala
Sanctuary **1**

MV Miramar **5**

Old Windmill &
Observatory **2**

Parliament House **9**

Queensland
Cultural Centre **6**

South Bank Parklands **7**

Treasury Casino
Brisbane **4**

passengers door to door at major hotels throughout Brisbane and the Gold Coast. The one-way fare is A$20 to Brisbane, A$49 to Gold Coast hotels, with cheaper deals available for families.

Airtrain has rail services to stations throughout Brisbane and the Gold Coast. The one-way fare is A$16 per person, or A$30 for a round-trip from the airport to the city. Trains depart up to four times an hour, taking 20 minutes to reach the city center. Kids (5–14 years) travel free. Taxis to downtown Brisbane cost A$40 to A$50, depending on time of day.

BOAT AND FERRY TRAVEL

Speedy CityCat boats and City Ferries dock at 24 points along the Brisbane River from Hamilton to St Lucia, running every 12 or 13 minutes for most of the day (the last service is at 11:45 pm). The ferries are terrific for a quick survey of the Brisbane waterfront, from the city skyline to luxury homes and beautiful parkland. If you're staying within the CBD and South Bank, try the free CityHopper ferry which runs every 30 minutes between 6 am and midnight every day of the week.

BUS TRAVEL

Greyhound Australia, the country's only nationwide bus line, travels to around 1,100 destinations. Bus stops are well signposted, and vehicles usually run on schedule. It's 1,716 km (1,064 miles), a 30-hour journey, between Brisbane and Cairns. Book in person at Greyhound's Roma Street office, by phone, or online. Purchase point-to-point tickets or flexible passes that allow multiple stops. Some buses are also equipped with free Wi-Fi.

Crisps Coaches operates a daily service from Brisbane to the Southern Downs and towns to the city's south and west. TransLink's help line and website can help you find bus lines that run to your destination.

RENTAL CAR TRAVEL

Most major car rental companies have offices in Brisbane, including Avis, Thrifty, Budget, and Hertz. Four-wheel-drive vehicles, motor homes, and camper vans (sleeping two to six people) are available from Britz, Maui Rentals, and KEA Campers. If you're heading north along the coast or northwest into the bush, you can rent in Brisbane and drop off in Cairns or other towns. One-way rental fees usually apply.

Brisbane is 1,002 km (621 miles) from Sydney, a 12-hour drive along the Pacific Highway (Highway 1). Another route follows Highway 1 to Newcastle, then heads inland on the New England Highway (Highway 15). Either drive can be made in a long day, although two days or more are recommended for ample time to rest and sightsee.

TAXI TRAVEL

Taxis are metered and relatively inexpensive. They are usually available at designated taxi stands outside hotels, downtown, and at Brisbane Transit and Roma Street stations, although it is often best to phone for one.

TRAIN TRAVEL

CountryLink trains make the 14-hour journey between Sydney and Brisbane. Rail services from Brisbane city and airport to the Gold Coast run regularly from 5:30 am until midnight. The *Sunlander* plies Queensland's coast from Brisbane to Cairns three times weekly, taking 32 hours. All trains include the option of luxurious *Queenslander*-class carriages with twin-berth sleeping cabins and fine food and wine. The speedy, state-of-the-art *Tilt Train* runs from Brisbane to Cairns and Brisbane to Rockhampton twice a week, stopping at Mackay, Proserpine, Townsville, and other northern centers along the way.

Other long-distance passenger trains from Brisbane include the *Westlander,* to and from Charleville (twice weekly); and the *Spirit of the Outback,* to and from Longreach, via Rockhampton (twice weekly). Trains depart from Roma Street Station.

TOURS

Australian Day Tours/JPT conducts half- and full-day tours of Brisbane and nearby Moreton Island. CitySights, run by the Brisbane City Council, operates air-conditioned hop-on, hop-off tour buses that make circuits of city landmarks and other points of interest, including South Bank and Chinatown. They leave from Post Office Square every 45 minutes, starting at 9 am; last departure is 5 pm. You can buy tickets on the bus and get on or off at any of the 19 stops all day for A$35. At the Brisbane City Council office, pick up a self-guided BrisbaneCityWalk map (also available from tourist information offices and online), as well as brochures and maps detailing other designated Brisbane walking trails.

Kookaburra River Queens are paddle wheelers that run lunch, dinner, tea, and jazz cruises on the Brisbane River. Lunch cruises include scenic and historic commentary; live entertainment and dancing are highlights of dinner cruises. The weekend buffet dinner cruise is especially popular. Tours run A$20–A$89 per person.

Energetic visitors might want to scale Brisbane's Story Bridge for a 360-degree city overview; a climbing tour with Story Bridge Adventure Climb takes 2½ hours and costs A$99 per person, extra for twilight climbs.

ESSENTIALS

Airport Information and Transfers Airtrain ☎ *07/3216–3308, 1800/119091* ⊕ *www.airtrain.com.au.* **Brisbane International Airport** ✉ *Airport Dr., Brisbane Airport* ☎ *07/3406–3000* ⊕ *www.bne.com.au.* **Coachtrans Australia** ☎ *07/3358–9700, 1300/266–9466* ⊕ *www.coachtransonline.com.au.*

Boat and Ferry Information CityCat ferries ☎ *13–1230* ⊕ *www.translink.com. au.*

Bus Information Crisps Coaches ✉ *78 Grafton St., Warwick* ☎ *07/4661–8333* ⊕ *www.crisps.com.au.* **Greyhound Australia** ✉ *Level 3, Brisbane Transit Centre, Roma St., City Center* ☎ *1300/473946, 07/3236–3035* ⊕ *www.greyhound.com. au.* **TransLink** ☎ *13–1230* ⊕ *www.translink.com.au.*

Rental Cars Britz Australia Campervan Hire and Car Rentals ✉ *21 Industry Ct., Eagle Farm* ☎ *07/3868–1248, 1800/331454* ⊕ *www.britz.com.au.* **KEA Campers** ✉ *21 Industry Ct., Eagle Farm* ☎ *1800/705174* ⊕ *www.keacampers.*

com. **Maui Australia Motorhome Rentals and Car Hire** ⊠ *21 Industry Ct., Eagle Farm* ☎ *07/3630–1153* ⊕ *www.maui.com.au.*

Taxis Black and White Cabs ☎ *13–3222* ⊕ *www.blackandwhitecabs.com.au.* **Yellow Cab Co** ☎ *13–1924* ⊕ *www.yellowcab.com.au.*

Tour Operators Australian Day Tours/JPT ⊠ *Shop 18, 2 Elkhorn Ave., Surfers Paradise* ☎ *07/3489–6444, 1300/781362* ⊕ *www.daytours.com.au.* **Kookaburra River Queens** ⊠ *Eagle Street Pier, 45 Eagle St., City Center* ☎ *07/3221–1300* ⊕ *www.kookaburrariverqueens.com.* **Story Bridge Adventure Climb** ☎ *1300/254627* ⊕ *www.storybridgeadventureclimb.com.au.*

Trains Queensland Rail (QR) Travel Centre Traveltrain Holidays ⊠ *Central Railway Station Concourse, 305 Edward St., City Centre* ☎ *13/3235–1323, 07/131722* ⊕ *www.queenslandrail.com.au.*

Visitor Information Brisbane City Council ⊠ *266 George St., City Center* ☎ *07/3403–8888, 13/0013–4199* ⊕ *www.brisbane.qld.gov.au.*

EXPLORING

Brisbane's city-center landmarks—a mix of Victorian, Edwardian, and slick contemporary architecture—are best explored on foot. Most lie within the triangle formed by Ann Street and the bends of the Brisbane River. ■ TIP➔ Streets running toward the river are named after female British royalty; those parallel to the river after male royalty. The well-tended South Bank precinct has riverfront parklands and cultural centers, alfresco cafés, and weekend markets. Upriver, the quiet, leafy suburb of Fig Tree Pocket is home to Australia's best-known koala sanctuary.

TOP ATTRACTIONS

FAMILY **Lone Pine Koala Sanctuary.** Founded in 1927, Queensland's most famous
Fodor's Choice fauna park is recognized by the *Guinness Book of World Records* as the
★ world's first and largest koala sanctuary. The attractions for most people are the koalas themselves (130 in all!), although emus, wombats, crocs, bats, platypuses, and lorikeets also reside here. You can hand-feed baby kangaroos in the free-range 'roo and wallaby enclosure, have a snake wrapped around you, or cuddle a koala and have your photo taken with one (for A$16, until 4:30). There's also a thrice-daily sheepdog show and regular barn animal and bird feedings. ⊠ *708 Jesmond Rd., Fig Tree Pocket* ☎ *07/3378–1366, 1300/729742 Mirimar River Boat* ⊕ *www.koala.net* ⊠ *A$33* ☉ *Daily 9–5.*

MV Mirimar. A historic 1930s ferry, the MV *Mirimar* travels daily to Lone Pine Koala Sanctuary from the Cultural Centre pontoon beside Victoria Bridge, leaving at 10 sharp (board from 9:30 am) then departing Lone Pine at 1:45 and returning to the city at 3 pm (A$68 round-trip, including entrance to the sanctuary). Bus 430 from Platform B4, Queen Street Bus Station, and Bus 445 from Stop 40 on Adelaide Street also stop at the sanctuary. Taxis cost about A$40 from the city center, from which it's around 11 km (6½ miles) to the sanctuary. ⊠ *Near Victoria Bridge* ☎ *1300/3221–0300 Mirimar Cruises, 13/749426 TransLink.*

Lone Pine Koala Sanctuary, Brisbane

Fodor's Choice
★ **Queensland Cultural Centre.** This sunny riverside hub is literally the cultural center of Brisbane, with a variety of world-class facilities nestled together among landscaped lawns and cafés. The world famous Gallery of Modern Art (GoMA) with its ever-changing exhibitions and events is a must-visit, while a short stroll away the equally impressive Queensland Art Gallery, Queensland Museum, and Sciencentre offer attractions for both young and old. Meanwhile, you can't miss the green walls of the architecturally renowned State Library of Queensland (the giant scrabble board on Level 1 is always worth a visit), and across the road, the Queensland Performing Arts Centre (QPAC) bustles with concerts and stage shows. There's also a host of restaurants, cafés, shops selling quality gifts, art posters, books and cards, a ticketing agent (within QPAC), public-access computer terminals, and various interesting public spaces. Green Cabs (modern rickshaws) are a fun and unique way to get around and sightsee. From the Cultural Centre forecourt, they'll ferry passengers anywhere between West End and Fortitude Valley. ✉ *Melbourne and Grey Sts., South Bank, South Brisbane* ☎ *07/3840–7303 (galleries), 07/3840–7555 (museum), 07/3840–7810 (library), 07/3840–7482 (performing arts center)* ⊕ *www.qagoma.qld. gov.au* 🎟 *Free (excluding Sciencentre and certain GoMA exhibitions)* ☉ *Galleries weekdays 10–5, weekends 9–5; museum and Sciencentre daily 9:30–5; library Mon.–Thurs. 10–8, Fri.–Sun. 10–5.*

FAMILY **Roma Street Parkland.** The world's largest subtropical garden within a city is a gentle mix of forest paths and structured plantings surrounding a fish-stocked lake. Highlights include the Lilly Pilly Garden, with native evergreen rain-forest plants, interesting children's play areas, and the friendly resident birds and lizards. A range of public art pieces are also dotted throughout the park. Pack a picnic, take advantage of the free grills, or stop for lunch at on-site café Melange. Free hour-long guided garden tours begin daily at 10 and 2, or on weekends hop on the Parkland Explorer, a trackless train that gives guests a full tour of the gardens for a gold coin donation. There are also specialist art, heritage, curator's, or sensory tours (prebook these) and brochures for self-guided walks available online or from Colin Campbell Place. ⊠ *1 Parkland Blvd., City Center* ☎ *07/3006–4545* ⊕ *www.romastreetparkland.com* ⊠ *Free* ⊙ *Daily 24 hrs.*

FAMILY
Fodor's Choice
★

South Bank Parklands. One of the most appealing urban parks in Australia, this massive complex includes parklands, shops, a maritime museum, walking and cycling paths, a sprawling man-made beach and luxurious lagoons, a carved-wood pagoda, and excellent city views. The weekend Collective Markets (running until 9 pm on Saturday evenings) bristle with handmade goods, live entertainers, buskers, artists, and emerging designers, and almost every week you'll find a new festival or event coloring the Cultural Forecourt. Nearby Grey Street is lined with trendy shops and cafés, as well as contemporary international restaurants, bars, and an on-site cinema. The Wheel of Brisbane, a giant Ferris wheel at the northern entrance of South Bank, is also a must for travelers wanting a spectacular view of the city for A$15 per person. South Bank Parklands stretches along the riverbank south of Queensland Cultural Centre. ⊠ *Grey St. south of Melbourne St.* ☎ *07/3867–2051 (parklands), 07/3844–3464 (Wheel of Brisbane)* ⊕ *www.visitsouthbank.com.au* ⊠ *Parklands free, museum A$12* ⊙ *Parklands daily 5 am–midnight; info center daily 9–5; museum daily 9:30–4:30 (last entry 3:30); markets Sat. 10–9, Sun. 10–5.*

WORTH NOTING

Anzac Square and the Shrine of Remembrance. Paths stretch across manicured lawns toward the Doric Greek Revival shrine made of Queensland sandstone. An eternal flame burns here for Australian soldiers who died in World War I. In the Shrine of Remembrance, a subsurface crypt stores soil samples from key battlefields. On April 25, Anzac Day, a moving dawn service is held here in remembrance of Australia's fallen soldiers. ⊠ *Adelaide St. between Edward and Creek Sts., City Center* ⊠ *Free* ⊙ *Shrine weekdays 9–2.*

The Commissariat Store. Convict-built in 1829 on the site of the city's original timber wharf, this was Brisbane's first stone building. It has served variously as a customs house, storehouse, and immigrants' shelter, and is currently the headquarters of the Royal Historical Society of Queensland. The RGSQ library and museum, open to visitors, hold exhibitions, historical documents, manuscripts, and artifacts dating back to Brisbane's early colonial days. Group tours of the museum are welcome. ⊠ *115 William St., City Center* ☎ *07/3221–4198* ⊕ *www. queenslandhistory.org.au* ⊠ *A$6* ⊙ *Tues.–Fri. 10–4.*

Old Windmill & Observatory. This 1824 construction is the oldest remaining convict-built structure in Brisbane, dubbed the "Tower of Torture" by convicts forced to power a treadmill to crush the colony's grain on

Modern sculpture at the Queensland Cultural Centre, South Bank, Brisbane

windless days. When fire razed part of the city in 1864 the windmill survived, later repurposed as an observatory. Stripped of its blades, the tower now resembles a lighthouse. ✉ *Wickham Park, Wickham Terr., City Center* ☎ *07/3403–5048.*

Parliament House. Opened in 1868, this splendid, stone-clad, French Renaissance building with a Mount Isa copper roof earned its colonial designer a meager 200-guinea (A$440) fee. A legislative annex was added in the late 1970s. The interior is fitted with polished timber, brass, and frosted and engraved glass. There are free half-hour tours on weekday afternoons, depending on demand. High Tea is offered in the elegant Strangers' Dining Room from 10:30 am to noon the first Friday of every month (A$41 per person). The adjacent, kid-friendly City Botanic Gardens have native and exotic plants and theme areas, including the Bamboo Grove and Weeping Fig Avenue, along with sculptures, ponds, and an on-site café. ✉ *George and Alice Sts., City Center* ☎ *07/3406–7562* ⊕ *www.parliament.qld.gov.au* 🎫 *Free* ⊗ *Parliament House weekdays 9–5 (last tour 4 pm), gardens daily 24 hrs.*

Treasury Casino Brisbane. This Edwardian baroque edifice overlooking the river stands on the site of military barracks from the original penal settlement, flanked by bronze statuary. Constructed between 1885 and 1889, the former treasury reopened as a **hotel, casino, and entertainment complex.** In addition to three floors of gaming, the casino houses six eateries, five bars, and lavish accommodation suites. ✉ *Queen St. Mall, William and Elizabeth Sts., City Center* ☎ *07/3306–8888, 506–888* ⊕ *www.treasurybrisbane.com.au* 🎫 *Free* ⊗ *Daily 24 hrs.*

SPORTS AND THE OUTDOORS

BICYCLING

An extensive network of bicycle paths crisscrosses Brisbane. One of the best paths follows the level, recently upgraded Bicentennial Bikeway southeast along the Brisbane River, across the Goodwill Bridge, then along to South Bank Parklands or Kangaroo Point cliffs. The new Kuripla Bridge and Go Between Bridge are also both cyclist-friendly ways to cross the river between the city and South Brisbane.

Brisbane City Council. The Brisbane City Council website includes downloadable maps and lets you search for bikeways. Visitors can pick up Council-operated CityCycle bikes from 150 designated points around the inner city, returning them when they're done. ⊕ *www.brisbane. qld.gov.au.*

CLIMBING

Kangaroo Point cliffs, near the city center, are ideal for climbing and abseiling. You can kayak or paddleboard on the Brisbane River, and numerous scenic bushwalking, climbing, and rappelling sites lie less than 90 minutes by car from Brisbane. Government-run Outdoors Queensland (⊕ *www.qorf.org.au*) gives regional information and lists businesses offering adventure activities from hiking to horse riding.

Adventures Around Brisbane. Adventures Around Brisbane runs daily rock-climbing and abseiling sessions off Kangaroo Point cliffs, as well as bushwalks and adventure day trips to the scenic Glass House Mountains and Mt. Maroon. ⊠ *River Terr., Kangaroo Point* ☎ *1800/689453* ⊕ *www.adventuresaroundbrisbane.com.au* ✎ *A$79 2-hr rock-climbing session, A$79 2-hr sunset abseil, A$135–A$500 day tours.*

GOLF

St. Lucia Golf Links and Golf World. One of Brisbane's oldest golf courses, St. Lucia Golf Links and Golf World is an 18-hole, par-70 course open to visitors; greens fees are A$32 for 18 holes on weekdays, A$38 weekends, and half price on Monday. Dine on-site at the Hillstone clubhouse's recently refurbished Hundred Acre Bar overlooking the 18th green. ⊠ *Indooroopilly Rd. at Carawa St., St. Lucia* ☎ *07/3403–2556* ⊕ *www.hillstonestlucia.com.au.*

MULTISPORT OUTFITTERS

Riverlife Adventure Centre. Riverlife Adventure Centre runs guided rock-climbing and abseiling sessions off Kangaroo Point cliffs, cycling tours around Brisbane attractions, day and night kayaking, and stand-up paddleboarding trips on the Brisbane River (followed by prawns and drinks or a barbecue), bicycle and rollerblade hire, Segway tours, and indigenous culture experiences. A highlight is the Mirrabooka Aboriginal Cultural Experience, which includes a traditional performance by the Yuggera Aboriginal Dancers and hands-on instruction in fire-starting, instrument playing, boomerang throwing, and painting. ⊠ *Naval Stores, Lower River Terr., Kangaroo Point* ☎ *07/3891–5766* ⊕ *www. riverlife.com.au* ✎ *A$45–A$85.*

TENNIS

Tennis Queensland. With 23 international standard courts, the newly constructed, state-of-the-art **Queensland Tennis Centre** offers court rentals, coaching and tours, as well as a Pro Shop and café. It also regularly hosts large tournaments. ✉ *190 King Arthur Terr., Tennyson* ☎ *07/3120–7900* ⊕ *www.queenslandtenniscentre.com.au.*

WATER SPORTS

Moreton Bay. A half-hour's drive east of Brisbane city brings you to Moreton Bay, stretching 125 km (78 miles) from the Gold Coast to the Sunshine Coast. A number of operators based in Brisbane's bay-side suburbs—Manly, Redcliffe, Sandgate—run sailing, diving, sightseeing, and whale- and dolphin-watching trips around the bay, and trips to its various islands. Some cruises include tours of St. Helena Island's historic prison ruins; others visit Moreton Island, where you can toboggan down massive white-sand dunes. ✉ *Moreton Bay.*

Moreton Bay Escapes. Moreton Bay Escapes runs tours and charters around Moreton Island National Park that includes 4WD-driving, snorkeling, and sand-boarding. They'll also tailor excursions to incorporate hiking, sea-kayaking, bird-watching, and swimming with dolphins. ✉ *Moreton Bay* ☎ *1300/559355* ⊕ *www.moretonbayescapes.com.au.*

WHERE TO EAT

In the past decade Brisbane has transformed from a culinary backwater into a city full of inventive dining options. Top chefs have decamped to Brisbane's best eateries, and are busy putting put a fresh subtropical spin on Modern Australian, pan-Asian, and Mediterranean cuisine.

Imaginative dishes capitalize on abundant regional produce: fine fresh seafood—notably the local delicacy, the Moreton Bay bug (a sweet-fleshed crustacean)—premium steak, Darling Downs lamb, cheeses, macadamia nuts, avocadoes, olives, and fruit, matched with fine regional wines.

Most of the city's hip cafés and smart fine dining establishments are clustered in West End, Fortitude Valley, New Farm, Teneriffe, and Petrie Terrace; you'll also find some excellent eateries in the city center and the riverfront South Bank precinct, and a smattering around the suburbs, particularly Rosalie, Paddington, Milton, and Ascot. For terrific fresh seafood, head for Brisbane's bay-side suburbs, such as Manly, Redcliffe, and Sandgate.

Typically, dining ambience is relaxed, seating is alfresco, and well-mannered children are welcomed.

Use the coordinate (✛ B2) at the end of each listing to locate a site on the corresponding map.

$$ ✕ **Alfred & Constance.** A café by day, restaurant and bar by night, this hip
CAFÉ   Fortitude Valley establishment is as much worth a visit for its trendy decor and upbeat vibe as it is for its hearty, locally sourced fare. Stylish young waiters slide between the various quirkily designed seating "houses," where your steak, burger, or salad may appear from beneath giant elephant wall art or collections of suspended lanterns. Chefs work

enthusiastically in open view of patrons, using only the finest ingredients and premium free-range and organic meats. As the sun sets, the extensive cocktail menu comes out to play, with fresh, tropical flavors like Plantation Punch and Tiki Mai Tai making the perfect nightcap (or beginning!). $ *Average main: A$24* ⊠ *Alfred and Constance Sts., Fortitude Valley* ☎ *07/3251–6500* ⊕ *www.alfredandconstance.com.au* ✛ *C1.*

$$ ✕ **Archive Beer Boutique.** This boutique beer bar and bistro in cosmopolitan West End is the perfect place to start or end your evening. An extensive menu of finely crafted and specialty Australian beers is complemented by simple and inexpensive Mod Oz cuisine including eggplant Parmesan, twice-cooked lamb ribs, and classic calamari. Always bustling with an eclectic local crowd, Archive adds a trendy twist to traditional pub games with its bingo and trivia nights, pool competitions, and Sunday-afternoon live music. On weekends, set yourself up on the large timber deck with a bowl of thick, beer-battered chips and one of Archive's top brews while you watch the sun set over the bohemian village strip below. $ *Average main: A$19* ⊠ *100 Boundary St., West End* ☎ *07/3844–3419* ⊕ *www.archivebeerboutique.com.au* ✛ *A3.*

AUSTRALIAN

$$ ✕ **Breakfast Creek Hotel.** Perched on the wharf at Breakfast Creek, this iconic, heritage-listed hotel is as renowned for its lush tropical beer garden as its superb trademark steaks. Non-steak eaters also have plenty of options, including vegetarian dishes and fresh seafood. The hotel also boasts a new on-site coffee cart and café, and live entertainment on the weekends. $ *Average main: A$35* ⊠ *2 Kingsford Smith Dr., Albion* ☎ *07/3262–5988* ⊕ *www.breakfastcreekhotel.com* ✛ *C1.*

AUSTRALIAN

$ ✕ **Caxton Thai.** This unassuming restaurant on bustling Caxton Street is popular with locals and tourists alike for its fresh, flavorsome, and generously portioned cuisine. The most requested dish is the pork chop stir-fried with chili and basil; or dig into one of the restaurant's excellent laksas. Other than these, it's mostly traditional curries, soups, plenty of vegetarian options, and many noodle dishes, including a warm Thai salad (a mix of chicken, prawns, glass noodles, and seasonal vegetables). Finish off with fresh Thai fruit with ice cream. $ *Average main: A$15* ⊠ *47B Caxton St., Petrie Terrace* ☎ *07/3367–0300* ⊕ *www.caxtonthai. com.au* ☾ *No lunch* ✛ *A1.*

THAI

$$$ ✕ **e'cco.** Consistently ranked among the best restaurants in town, this petite eatery serves innovative food to a loyal following. The white-columned entry leads into a warm-toned dining room with an elegant open kitchen and bar. Seasonally changing Mediterranean and Asian-inspired dishes incorporate premium local produce. Patrons might start with grilled quail or duck terrine, and follow it with seared ocean trout or Wagyu rump steak. Each seasonal dessert selection is equally delectable: blueberry and panettone pudding, strawberry ripple parfait, and banana tarte tatin are just some of the indulgences you may encounter. Meanwhile, award-winning resident sommelier Alan Hunter will help you find your evening's perfect pairing. $ *Average main: A$42* ⊠ *100 Boundary St., City Center* ☎ *07/3831–8344* ⊕ *www.eccobistro.com* ⌲ *Reservations essential* ☾ *Closed Sun. and Mon. No lunch Sat.* ✛ *D1.*

MEDITERRANEAN

Fodor's Choice ★

7

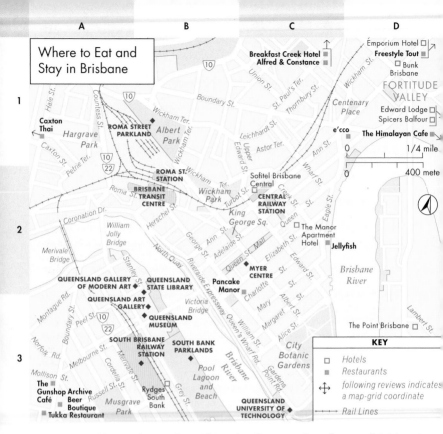

Where to Eat and Stay in Brisbane

Breakfast Creek Hotel
Alfred & Constance

Emporium Hotel
Freestyle Tout
Bunk Brisbane

FORTITUDE VALLEY

Centenary Place

Edward Lodge
Spicers Balfour

e'cco

The Himalayan Cafe

Caxton Thai

Hargrave Park

ROMA STREET PARKLAND

Albert Park

Leichhardt St.

Astor Ter.

Sofitel Brisbane Central

ROMA ST. STATION

BRISBANE TRANSIT CENTRE

Wickham Park

CENTRAL RAILWAY STATION

King George Sq.

William Jolly Bridge

Merivale Bridge

Queen St. Mall

The Manor Apartment Hotel

Jellyfish

QUEENSLAND GALLERY OF MODERN ART

QUEENSLAND STATE LIBRARY

Pancake Manor

MYER CENTRE

Brisbane River

QUEENSLAND ART GALLERY

QUEENSLAND MUSEUM

Victoria Bridge

SOUTH BRISBANE RAILWAY STATION

SOUTH BANK PARKLANDS

The Point Brisbane

Mollison St.

The Gunshop Café

Archive Beer Boutique

Tukka Restaurant

Rydges South Bank

Pool Lagoon and Beach

City Botanic Gardens

QUEENSLAND UNIVERSITY OF TECHNOLOGY

0 _____ 1/4 mile

0 _____ 400 mete

KEY

☐   *Hotels*
■   *Restaurants*
↔   *following reviews indicate*
     a map-grid coordinate
→→   *Rail Lines*

$
AUSTRALIAN
FAMILY

✕ **Freestyle Tout.** Set within a bustling complex of some of Brisbane's most popular restaurants, this gallery-café is famous for its beautiful, all-day desserts—including artfully designed sundaes, fruity tarts, sticky tortes, and a memorable white-chocolate raspberry brioche. The savory dining menu now includes interesting Mod Oz options served on tapas-inspired share plate stacks, as well as café-style fare. You can also take high tea here. The local Australian artwork displayed is refreshed every month and often for sale. $ *Average main: A$18* ⊠ *Shop 50, 1000 Ann St., Fortitude Valley* ☎ *07/3252–0214* ⊕ *www.freestyletout. com.au* ↔ *D1.*

$$
CAFÉ

✕ **The Gunshop Café.** Named after its previous life as an actual gun shop, this trendy West End café is the place to go for brunch on weekends (the potato-feta hash cakes with spinach, house-dried tomato, and herbed sour cream are locally famous). Unfinished brick walls where guns once hung lend a rustic ambience. Dine around wooden tables near the open kitchen or request a seat out on the sidewalk. A select but eclectic Mod Oz menu fuses Mediterranean and Asian flavors in dishes featuring premium Margaret River lamb, Angus beef, duck, and seafood; they also do vegetarian dishes and exciting salads, with produce sourced from local markets. Foodies flock here for lunch, dinner, or even just a coffee and dessert; the flourless orange-and-almond cake is particularly unforgettable. $ *Average main: A$32* ⊠ *53 Mollison St.,*

West End ☎ *07/3844–2241* 🌐 *www.thegunshopcafe.com* ⏲ *No dinner Sun. and Mon.* ✥ *A3.*

$ NEPALESE Fodor's Choice ★ 🍴 **The Himilayan Cafe.** Clusters of pendant lanterns and colorful Buddhist prayer flags welcome you to the Himalayan Cafe, one of Brisbane's most popular inner-city eats. At this Tibetan/Nepalese sanctuary, the homemade appetizer breads are perhaps as famous as the restaurant itself—divinely moist and fluffy, each is served with a minted yogurt dipping sauce in the traditional Himalayan style. When it comes to mains, there's something for everyone, from vegans and vegetarians to the most unswayable meat lovers: spicy noodle soups, tofu and vegetable curries, and succulent, tender lamb, beef, chicken and goat dishes in a range of flavors and intensities. For an extra treat, ask for a seat out back in one of the traditional Himalayan raised restaurant rooms. [$] *Average main: A$19* ✉ *640 Brunswick St., New Farm* ☎ *07/3358–4015* ✥ *D1.*

$$$ SEAFOOD 🍴 **Jellyfish.** At this upmarket riverside eatery, you can sit indoors on smart black-and-white chairs under low-slung, jellyfish-shaped lights, or outside on the breezy terrace, and choose from a Modern Australian menu that changes daily but always features 8–14 different species of fish—panfried or oven-roasted, steamed, seared, or with your choice of six available batters. Try the signature tempura soft-shell mud crab with green chili, shallots, and wasabi mayo; or the kingfish delicately flavored with watermelon and mint. The fresh, interesting menu also includes eye fillet steak, pork shoulder, and vegetarian options, as well as desserts such as Valrhona chocolate fondant and strawberry-and-basil-seed compote. The attached bar offers several wines by the glass. [$] *Average main: A$40* ✉ *Boardwalk, Riverside Centre, 123 Eagle St., Brisbane* ☎ *07/3220–2202* 🌐 *www.jellyfishrestaurant.com.au* ✍ *Reservations essential* ⏲ *No lunch weekends* ✥ *C2.*

$ CAFÉ FAMILY 🍴 **Pancake Manor.** Housed inside the historic, heritage-listed St Luke's Cathedral, this elegant 24-hour pancake parlor is a Brisbane institution. Guests can take a seat in one of the Manor's converted church pew booths and chow down on a tempting menu of snacks, salads, steaks, and sweets beneath the building's grand redbrick arches. For breakfast try the simple eggs Benedict or the hearty Aussie Sunrise, while dinner patrons will find a range of savory crepes and pancake dishes to please the palette. But it's desserts that Pancake Manor is really famous for: grilled bananas drizzled in creamy butterscotch sauce, set upon a fluffy short stack of pancakes with rich vanilla ice cream will surely hit the note. The bar downstairs has an all-day drinks menu of local and imported beers and wines; with its swift, attentive service, this is the place to venture when jet lag kicks in. [$] *Average main: A$16* ✉ *18 Charlotte St., City Center* ☎ *07/3221–6433* 🌐 *www.pancakemanor.com.au* ✥ *C2.*

$$ MODERN AUSTRALIAN 🍴 **Tukka Restaurant.** Earth-tone walls lined with Aboriginal artworks are a fitting backdrop for chef-owner Bryant Wells's native-inspired Modern Australian cuisine, featuring a range of lean local meats (seared wallaby, kangaroo, emu, croc tail, and possum) and seasonal produce, deliciously fused with native Australian herbs and spices. One excellent option is the appetizer platter of cured meats and flavorful indigenous berries and flowers, all served on a rustic wooden camphor platter.

7

The wine list showcases top vintages from boutique wineries around Australia. You can also buy Tukka's own line of spices, cured meats, glazed fruits, and sorbets, or ask for a "taste and smell" tour of the restaurants on-site back garden. [$] *Average main: A$32* ✉ *145 Boundary St., West End* ☎ *07/3846–6333* 🌐 *www.tukkarestaurant.com.au* ⏲ *No lunch weekdays* ✣ *A3.*

WHERE TO STAY

Twenty years ago Brisbane's accommodation options consisted of a few big hotels and some welcoming but nondescript motels and B&Bs. These days the inner-city area bristles with luxury hotels and smart serviced-apartment complexes. There are also a few excellent boutique hotels, some cut-above B&Bs, and modern backpacker hotels giving pricier digs a run for their money. Many have good-value packages and seasonal and last-minute specials. Jump online for the best deals.

Use the coordinate (✣ B2) at the end of each listing to locate a site on the corresponding map. For expanded hotel reviews, facilities, and current deals, visit Fodors.com.

$ B&B/INN 🏨 **Edward Lodge.** This charming, inner-suburban, art deco B&B is set among Asian-style tropical gardens and is close to cafés and restaurants, New Farm Park, Brisbane Powerhouse, and the CityCat ferry. **Pros:** free Wi-Fi; guest kitchen and laundry; vibrant area; free Continental breakfast. **Cons:** 15 minutes from the city; no room service. [$] *Rooms from: A$139* ✉ *75 Sydney St., New Farm* ☎ *07/3358–2680, 07/3358–3583* 🌐 *www.edwardlodge.com.au* 🛏 *9 suites, 1 apartment* 🍴 *Breakfast* ✣ *D1.*

$$$ HOTEL Fodor's Choice ★ 🏨 **Emporium Hotel.** Billing itself as a luxury boutique hotel, this contemporary, vibrantly designed establishment in lively Fortitude Valley boasts a rooftop swimming pool, exquisite cocktail bar, and easy access to some of the city's best restaurants. **Pros:** superb decor; terrific facilities; close to nightlife; wheelchair-accessible suite. **Cons:** outside the city center; expensive parking and Wi-Fi packages; can be noisy—ask for a room away from street. [$] *Rooms from: A$219* ✉ *1000 Ann St., Fortitude Valley* ☎ *07/3253–6999, 1300/883611* 🌐 *www.emporiumhotel.com.au* 🛏 *102 suites* 🍴 *No meals* ✣ *D1.*

$$ HOTEL 🏨 **The Manor Apartment Hotel.** Good old-fashioned service and charm are the hallmarks of Brisbane city's heritage-listed Manor Apartment Hotel. **Pros:** central location; free Continental breakfast; spacious rooms including handy kitchenettes. **Cons:** must book several weeks ahead; limited on-site parking; Wi-Fi extra. [$] *Rooms from: A$175* ✉ *289 Queen St., City Center* ☎ *07/3319–4700* 🌐 *www.manorapartments.com.au* 🛏 *45 studios, suites, and apartments* 🍴 *Breakfast* ✣ *C2.*

$$ HOTEL 🏨 **The Point Brisbane.** Across the river from the central business district, this modern hotel on picturesque Kangaroo Point has great city skyline and river views from each balcony. **Pros:** terrific on-site facilities; free Wi-Fi and parking; wheelchair-accessible rooms. **Cons:** a commute from the city; no meal plans. [$] *Rooms from: A$147* ✉ *21 Lambert St., Kangaroo Point* ☎ *07/3240–0888, 1800/088388* 🌐 *www.thepointbrisbane.com.au* 🛏 *137 rooms, 64 suites* 🍴 *No meals* ✣ *D3.*

$$$ HOTEL FAMILY **Rydges South Bank.** Surrounded by Brisbane's famous South Bank Parklands and Cultural Precinct, within walking distance of numerous attractions, this hotel is an excellent choice if location's your focus. **Pros:** lively location; good buffet breakfast; business center with free Internet and conference facilities. **Cons:** steep fees for Wi-Fi and parking; decor slightly dated; not all rooms have balconies so be sure to request one in advance. [$] *Rooms from: A$189* ✉ *9 Glenelg St., at Grey St., South Brisbane* ☎ *07/3364–0800* 🌐 *www.rydges.com/southbank* 🛏 *240 rooms, 64 suites* 🍴 *Multiple meal plans* ✣ *B3.*

$$$ HOTEL **Sofitel Brisbane Central.** Despite its position above the city's main rail station, this decadent, French-flavored hotel is a quiet and classy choice when it comes to city-center accommodation. **Pros:** prompt, pleasant service; excellent on-site facilities; superb buffet breakfast. **Cons:** pricey meals and minibar; charge for Wi-Fi and parking; compact bathrooms. [$] *Rooms from: A$275* ✉ *249 Turbot St., City Center* ☎ *07/3835–4444* 🌐 *www.sofitelbrisbane.com.au* 🛏 *409 rooms, 21 suites* 🍴 *Multiple meal plans* ✣ *C2.*

$$$ HOTEL Fodor's Choice ★ **Spicers Balfour.** With service, style, and hospitality above and beyond the call of duty, Spicers Balfour is a distinctly local, disarmingly welcoming experience, perfect for weary travelers looking for a home away from home. **Pros:** attentive and personalized service; close to public transport and ferry; free Wi-Fi and parking. **Cons:** outside the city center; compact rooms. [$] *Rooms from: A$299* ✉ *37 Balfour St., New Farm* ☎ *07/3358–8888* 🌐 *www.spicersgroup.com.au* 🛏 *9 suites* 🍴 *Breakfast* ✣ *D1.*

7

NIGHTLIFE AND THE ARTS

The Saturday edition of the *Courier–Mail* newspaper (🌐 *www.couriermail.com.au*) lists live gigs and concerts, ballet, opera, theater, jazz, and other events in its Life section, while Friday's *CM2* insert offers a comprehensive entertainment guide for the weekend ahead. *The Weekend Edition* (🌐 *www.theweekendedition.com.au*) has suburb-by-suburb listings of Brisbane's best cafés, restaurants, shopping, and nightlife spots, as well as weekly updates on new events and establishments around the city.

THE ARTS

ARTS CENTERS

Brisbane Powerhouse. Housed in a former coal power station, the heritage-listed Brisbane Powerhouse hosts frequent, often-free art exhibits and live performances in its flexible 200- and 400-seat theaters. Cafés, restaurants, bikeways, boardwalks, and picnic areas complement the spacious, contemporary art space, which also adjoins beautiful New Farm Park. A recent renovation added a new café-bar, a roof terrace, and enlarged theater spaces. ✉ *119 Lamington St., New Farm* ☎ *07/3358–8600 box office, 07/3358–8622 reception* 🌐 *www.brisbanepowerhouse.org.*

NIGHTLIFE
BARS

Cloudland. Designed as an "urban oasis" with fanciful decor, a retractable glass roof, and street-front waterfall flowing over its contemporary architectural facade, Cloudland restaurant and nightclub woos well-heeled locals and tourists alike with an extensive drinks menu, cut-above food, and an exciting, expensive ambience. ⊠ *641 Ann St., Fortitude Valley* ☎ *07/3872–6600* ⊕ *www.cloudland.tv.*

Cru Bar + Cellar. Sleek and sophisticated, Cru Bar + Cellar has leather ottomans, a long onyx bar, a French chandelier circa 1800, and a fine-wine-loving clientele. Cru's huge cellar houses hundreds of top Australian vintages, to drink on-site or later. Cheese tasting plates are available all day. ⊠ *James St. Market, 22 James St., Fortitude Valley* ☎ *07/3252–2400* ⊕ *www.crubar.com.*

> ### EARTH'S FASTEST MOVING ISLAND
>
> **Moreton Island** lies just 35 km (20 miles) offshore. This 38-km-long (23-mile-long) mass is shifting at an estimated 3¼ feet a year toward the Queensland coast. Attractions include tobogganing down sand dunes, bird-watching, dolphin spotting, water sports, and cetacean- and dugong-watching. Camping within Moreton Island National Park is possible (A\$5.60 per person permit; information available at ⊕ *www.nprsr.qld. gov.au*).

CASINOS

Treasury Casino Brisbane. With a "neat and tidy" dress code geared to securing an upscale clientele, The Treasury is a European-style casino with three levels of gaming beneath a stunning four-story atrium. Beneath a seduction of light and color, the facility comes alive at night with more than 80 gaming tables with 60 games and more than 1,300 machines, as well as six restaurants and six bars. It's open 24 hours. ⊠ *130 William St., City Center* ☎ *07/3306–8888* ⊕ *www. treasurybrisbane.com.au.*

SHOPPING

For more information on shopping in Brisbane, visit ⊕ *www.our-brisbane.com/shopping.*

ANTIQUES

Paddington Antique Centre. Located in a converted theater, the Paddington Antique Centre is filled with antiques and bric-a-brac, including colorful vintage clothing. Around 50 dealers operate within the center, alongside an elegant on-site café. It's open daily from 10–5. ⊠ *167 Latrobe Terr., Paddington* ☎ *07/3369–8088* ⊕ *www.paddingtonantiquecentre. com.au.*

AUSTRALIAN PRODUCTS

Woolloongabba Antique Centre. This vibrant, retro-themed warehouse includes 60-plus stalls, an on-site vintage café, and enough antiques and treats to excite the nostalgia in all of us. From fine china, collectibles, and the kitschiest of curiosities, to clothing, records, prints, paintings,

State library, Queensland Cultural Centre

home wares, games, and a vast collection of Australiana, it's the perfect place to pick up something unique. It's open every day, 9 am–5 pm. ⊠ *22 Wellington Rd., Woolloongabba* ☎ *07/3392–1114* ⊕ *www.woolloongabbaantiquecentre.com.*

MALLS AND ARCADES

MacArthur Central. Historic MacArthur Central, the WWII headquarters of U.S. General Douglas MacArthur, houses boutiques and specialty shops, a food court, and a museum. Located at the bottom of the Queen Street Mall, the streets surrounding the center also feature a range of high-end fashion boutiques that include Louis Vutton, Hermes, and Tiffany & Co. The MacArthur Museum is open to the public Tuesday, Thursday, and Sunday 10 am–3 pm. ⊠ *201 Edward St., City Center* ☎ *07/3211–7052 museum* ⊕ *www.mmb.org.au.*

Queen Street Mall. Fun and lively Queen Street Mall, considered the best downtown shopping area, attracts around 26 million visitors a year. Nearly a third of a mile long, the mall incorporates five major shopping centers, including the Myer Centre, Wintergarden, and Queens-Plaza, as well as two large department stores, Myer and David Jones, and four arcades: historic Tattersall's Arcade and MacArthur Central, heritage-listed Brisbane Arcade, and Broadway on the Mall, all housing designer boutiques and a range of specialty stores. On weekends, free entertainment and performances can often be found on the mall's two open stages. ⊠ *Queen St., City Center* ☎ *07/3229–5918* ⊕ *www.bnecity.com.au.*

MARKETS

Brisbane Powerhouse. The Brisbane Powerhouse hosts a local produce farmers' market from 6 am to noon on the second and fourth Saturday of the month. Enjoy a fresh, leisurely breakfast on the lawn by the river, and afterwards, stroll through nearby New Farm Park. ⊠ *119 Lamington St., New Farm* ☎ *07/3358–8600* ⊕ *www.brisbanepowerhouse.org.*

Riverside Markets. An eclectic arts-and-crafts bazaar meandering along the Brisbane River, the Riverside Markets offer everything from pressed flowers to hand-painted didgeridoos and homemade treats. It's open Sunday 7–3. ⊠ *Riverside Centre, 123 Eagle St., City Center* ☎ *07/3780–2807* ⊕ *www.brisbane-markets.com.au.*

OUTDOOR GEAR OUTFITTERS

Paddy Pallin. With stores throughout Australia, Paddy Pallin sells quality outdoor and travel gear, including hats, footwear, clothing, backpacks, and equipment. On staff are dedicated bushwalkers, rock climbers, and travelers. The store is open weekdays 9 am–5:30 pm, Saturday 9–5, and Sunday 10–4. ⊠ *108 Wickham St., Fortitude Valley* ☎ *07/3839–3811* ⊕ *www.paddypallin.com.au.*

WINERY TOURS FROM BRISBANE: SOUTHERN DOWNS

From Brisbane, the Granite Belt is 225 km (140 miles) west, Mt. Tamborine is 62 km (39 miles) southwest, and Scenic Rim wineries are around 135 km (85 miles) southwest.

If the Brisbane cityscape has given you a thirst for pastoral rolling hills—and fabulous wine—you're in luck, because some of Queensland's best viticultural regions lie within a two-hour drive of the city.

Drive two hours west on the Cunningham Highway and you'll reach the Southern Downs, where spring brings the scent of peach and apple blossoms and fall finds the region's 50-plus vineyards, concentrated around Stanthorpe, ripe for harvest. Winter is ideal for wine-country excursions, with clear days and tastings by fireplace by night. This area, extending from Cunninghams Gap in the east to Goondiwindi in the west, Allora in the north to Wallangarra in the south, is known as the Granite Belt.

The local Italian community pioneered viticulture here, planting the first Shiraz grapes in 1965. Today the Granite Belt is the state's largest wine region, with nearly 2,000 acres under vines and more than 50 cellar doors, most attached to family-run and boutique wineries. Thanks to its altitude (2,500–4,000 feet above sea level) and decomposed-granite soils, the region enjoys unique growing and ripening conditions, enabling the production of outstanding, full-bodied reds and extra-crisp whites.

Just over an hour's drive southwest of Brisbane, inland from the Gold Coast, you'll find the world's largest caldera and one of the state's most exciting emerging wine regions: the Scenic Rim. The region's rich volcanic soils, first planted with vines in the late 19th century, now produce fine red and white varieties. On the region's easterly edge, you'll find a dozen wineries and a distillery within a compact area around Mt, Tamborine.

GETTING HERE AND AROUND

Driving yourself is an option but may not be the best idea if you plan to skip the spit bucket on your tasting stops. However, for the self-guiders out there, the Granite Belt and Scenic Rim tourism boards provide downloadable maps. Find Granite Belt winery and walking trails at ⊕ *www.granitebeltwinecountry.com.au*, and Scenic Rim winery and trail maps at ⊕ *www.visitscenicrim.com.au*.

Arguably, the safest way to sample the offerings of the region's wineries is via guided tour. More than half a dozen companies run tours of wineries in the Scenic Rim and Mt. Tamborine areas, but most require groups of at least six people. Family-run Cork 'n Fork Winery Tours is an exception, running daily and overnight viticultural tours for couples and small groups to Mt. Tamborine and the Scenic Rim. Their popular full-day tour (A$140 per person) includes hotel pickups from the Gold Coast or Brisbane, lunch, and five winery visits with guided tastings.

Local operators Granite Highlands Maxi Tours runs half-day, full-day, weekend, and customized tours of Granite Belt wineries.

ESSENTIALS

Guided Tours Cork 'n Fork Winery Tours. Personalized mini-bus tours of the vineyards of Mt. Tamborine and the Scenic Rim. ☎ *07/5543–6584* ⊕ *www.corknfork.com.au*. **Granite Highlands Maxi Tours** ✉ *19 Amosfield Rd., Stanthorpe* ☎ *07/4681–3969* ⊕ *www.maxitours.com.au*.

EXPLORING

FAMILY **Girraween National Park.** One of the most popular parks in southeast Queensland, Girraween National Park—meaning "Place of Flowers"—sits at the end of the New England Tableland, a stepped plateau area with elevations ranging from 1,968 to 4,921 feet. The 17 km (11 miles) of walking tracks, most starting near the information center and picnic area, wind past granite outcrops, giant boulders, eucalyptus forests, and spectacular wildflowers in spring. Along the way you might encounter kangaroos, echidnas, brush-tailed possums, and turquoise parrots. To camp, you'll need a permit from NPRSR (⊕ *www.qld.gov.au/camping*). ✉ *Ballandean ✛ 11 km (7 miles) north of Wallangarra or 26 km (16 miles) south of Stanthorpe, off the New England Hwy.* ☎ *13/131304* ⊕ *parks.nprsr.qld.gov.au*.

EXPLORING THE WINERIES

Ballandean Estate Wines. Just south of Glen Aplin is the town of Ballandean, home to award-winning Ballandean Estate Wines, the oldest family-owned and -operated vineyard and winery in Queensland. The first grapes were grown on the Granite Belt site in 1931, and the tasting room is the original brick shed built in 1950. The Barrel Room Cafe behind it—with massive, 125-year-old wooden barrels lining one wall—serves modern Italian light lunches and coffee. There are 45-minute tours of the facility daily at 11 am. ✉ *354 Sundown Rd., Ballandean* ☎ *07/4684–1226* 🌐 *www.ballandeanestate.com* 🎟 *Free* ⏲ *Daily 9–5.*

Felsberg Winery. In the tiny town of Glen Aplin, 235 km (146 miles) southwest of Brisbane, is Felsberg Winery. Known for red and white wines (including an award-winning Merlot) made from hand-picked grapes grown at 850 meters, this Granite Belt winery has a tasting room and café inside a German-inspired château, with hilltop views over the Severn River valley and Granite Belt area. ✉ *116 Townsends Rd., Glen Aplin* ☎ *07/4683–4332* 🌐 *www.felsberg.com.au* 🎟 *Free* ⏲ *Daily 9:30–4:30.*

Normanby Wines. This is a friendly, family-run winery-vineyard established a decade ago. All its wines—including many medal winners—are made from grapes grown on the property. There are 14 from which to choose, including Verdelho, Shiraz, Durif, Chaumbourcin, Grenache, Veraz, Merlot, Viognier, and traditional fortified varieties. Taste and buy them at the cellar door, then wander through the vineyard and native gardens or enjoy a barbecue under the trees. Guided vineyard tours are available for a small extra charge, if staff are available. ✉ *178 Dunns Ave., Harrisville* ☎ *07/5467–1214* 🌐 *www.normanbywines.com.au* 🎟 *Free; A$3 tasting fee* ⏲ *Daily 10–5.*

Fodor's Choice ★ **Sirromet Wines at Mount Cotton.** Queensland's largest winery sits midway between Brisbane and the Gold Coast. Sirromet's much-lauded wines—distinctive reds, crisp whites, and some terrific blended varieties—can be sampled at their impressive cellar door. Award-winning on-site restaurant Lurleens, open for breakfast, lunch, and dinner on weekends (and selectively throughout the week), has an alfresco dining area with superb views to Moreton Bay. Live jazz livens things up on weekend afternoons. ✉ *850–938 Mount Cotton Rd., Mount Cotton* ☎ *07/3206–2999* 🌐 *www.sirromet.com* 🎟 *Tastings (up to 8 wines) A$5; guided tours from A$20* ⏲ *Cellar door daily 9–4:30.*

WHERE TO STAY

For expanded hotel reviews, facilities, and current deals, visit Fodors.com.

$$$$ RESORT ALL-INCLUSIVE **Spicers Peak Lodge.** If you're looking for an exclusive, all-inclusive mountain retreat with an entire mountaintop to itself and the views to match, look no further. **Pros:** world-class restaurant with terrific wine list; thoughtful, impeccable service; new bed-and-breakfast option almost cuts rates in half. **Cons:** all-inclusive package pricey, albeit worth it; no public transport to lodge. [$] *Rooms from: A$999* ✉ *Wilkinsons Rd., Maryvale* ☎ *1300/198386, 07/4666–1083* 🌐 *www.spicersgroup.com.au* 🛏 *10 suites, 2 lodges* 🍴 *All-inclusive.*

$$ RENTAL Fodor's Choice ★ **Vineyard Cottages and Café.** Built around a turn-of-the-20th-century church that's now the Vineyard Café, this property boasts seven period-style cottages set amid 2 acres of gardens, only two blocks from Ballandean village. **Pros:** good food and wine; warm ambience; comfortable; friendly service; disabled access. **Cons:** far from city attractions. [$] *Rooms from: A$230* ✉ *New England Hwy. near Bents Rd.,*

Ballandean ☎ *07/4684–1270* ⊕ *www.vineyardcottages.com.au* ⇥ *7
cottages* ⵀ⧉ *Multiple meal plans.*

THE GOLD COAST

Resorts, theme parks, and 300 days of sunshine a year ensure the Gold Coast, the most developed tourist destination and one of the fastest-growing regions in Australia, remains a popular destination year-round. Easter weekend and December through the last week of January and Australian school holidays are peak seasons. Around 80 km (50 miles)—an hour's drive—south of Brisbane, the Gold Coast stretches some 70 km (43 miles) from Labrador in the north to Coolangatta-Tweed Heads in the south, and has now sprawled as far inland as Nerang. Boasting an average daily temperature of 24°C (75°F), it has around three dozen patrolled beaches and 446 km (277 miles) of canals and tidal rivers: nine times the length of the canals of Venice.

GETTING HERE AND AROUND

Gold Coast Airport, also known as Coolangatta Airport, is the region's main transit point.

Access Hope Island via bridges from the west (Oxenford and Coomera) or from the eastern, coastal side (via Paradise Point, Hollywell, and Runaway Bay). Route 4, the Oxenford–Southport Road, begins in Oxenford at the Pacific Motorway's (M1's) Exit 57 and travels through Hope Island on its way to Hope Harbour, on the coast.

Driving distances and times from the Gold Coast via the Pacific Highway are 859 km (533 miles) and 12–13 hours to Sydney; 65 km (40 miles) and less than an hour to Brisbane's outskirts; and 1,815 km (1,125 miles) and 22 hours to Cairns.

The Gold Coast begins 65 km (40 miles) south of Brisbane. The Pacific Motorway, or M1, bypasses Gold Coast towns, but well-marked exits guide you to your destination. If you're coming from Brisbane International Airport by car, take the toll road over Gateway Bridge to avoid traversing Brisbane, then follow the signs to the Gold Coast.

Queensland Rail service connects Brisbane to Coomera, Helensvale, Nerang, Robina, and Varsity Lakes stations on the Gold Coast from 5:30 am until midnight. Alight at Coomera or Helensvale for the theme parks and northern suburbs; Nerang for Surfer's Paradise; and Robina or Varsity Lakes for Main Beach and all suburbs south of it. From rail stations, cabs and shuttle buses ferry visitors to nearby beaches, tourist centers, theme parks, and the airport. From any of these stations, it's a short (A$20–A$30) cab ride to the nearest Gold Coast town.

The Gold Coast's own light-rail tram service, G:Link, is currently being completed, with services ferrying passengers between Southport, Surfer's Paradise, and Broadbeach commencing operation mid-2014. For information, prices, and route options, visit ⊕ *www.goldlinq.com.au*.

Long-distance buses traveling between Sydney and Brisbane stop at Coolangatta and Surfers Paradise. Surfside Buslines' Gold Coast Tourist Shuttle runs around the clock between Gold Coast attractions, theme parks, and the airport, along the strip between Tweed Heads and South-port. Services run at five-minute intervals during the day and at least half-hourly after dark. Buy single tickets or a 3-, 5-, 7-, or 10-day Gold Pass (A$56–A$120) or Freedom Pass (A$71–A$135), which give you unlimited shuttle travel and theme park transfers; the Freedom Pass also includes a return Gold Coast airport transfer.

Approximate taxi fare from Gold Coast Airport to Currumbin is A$32; to Burleigh Heads, A$40; to Broadbeach, A$55; to Surfers Paradise, A$60; to Main Beach, A$65; and to the northern suburbs, more than A$95. Shuttle buses can be cheaper than cabs at A$5–A$35, depending on your destination. Before boarding, confirm that the bus stops near your accommodation.

Rental cars are a cost-effective option if you plan to tour the area. Most major car rental agencies have offices in Brisbane, Surfers Paradise, and at Gold Coast Airport. Companies operating on the Gold Coast include Avis, Budget, and Thrifty. Four-wheel-drive vehicles are available. It's strongly recommended that you prebook.

ESSENTIALS

Airport Gold Coast Airport (*Coolangatta Airport*). ⊠ *1 Eastern Ave., Bilinga* ☎ *07/5589–1100.*

Car Rental Avis ⊠ *Cypress Ave., Surfers Paradise* ☎ *07/5539–9388, 13/136333 reservations* ⊕ *www.avis.com.au.* **Budget** ⊠ *1 Ferny Ave., Surfers Paradise* ☎ *07/5538–1344, 1300/362848 reservations* ⊕ *www.budget.com.au.* **Thrifty** ⊠ *1006 Surfers Paradise Blvd., Surfers Paradise* ☎ *07/5570–9999, 1300/139009 reservations* ⊕ *www.thrifty.com.au.*

Ferry Zane's Water Taxi ⊠ *Runaway Bay Marina, 247 Bayview St., Runaway Bay* ☎ *0404/905970* ⊕ *www.inzanewatertaxis.com.au.*

Public Bus and Train Con-x-ion ☎ *07/5556–9888* ⊕ *www.con-x-ion.com.* **Gold Coast Tourist Shuttle** ☎ *07/5574–5111, 1300/655655* ⊕ *gcshuttle.com. au.* **Greyhound Australia** ⊠ *Surfers Paradise Transit Centre, 10 Beach Rd., Surfers Paradise* ☎ *1300/473946, 07/5531–6677* ⊕ *www.greyhound.com.au.* **Queensland Rail** ☎ *13–1617* ⊕ *www.qr.com.au.* **Surfside Buslines** ⊠ *1–10 Mercantile Ct., Ernest* ☎ *07/5539–9388, 13–1230 TransLink* ⊕ *www.surfside.com. au.* **TransLink** ☎ *13–1230* ⊕ *www.translink.com.au.*

Taxi Gold Coast Cabs ☎ *13–1008* ⊕ *www.gccabs.com.au.*

Visitor Information Gold Coast Tourism Information & Booking Centres. There's another location in the Domestic Terminal of the Gold Coast Airport. ⊠ *2 Cavill Ave., Surfers Paradise* ☎ *1300/309400, 07/5569–3830* ⊕ *www. visitgoldcoast.com.*

COOMERA AND OXENFORD

48–51 km (30–32 miles) south of Brisbane.

The biggest draws of these two northern Gold Coast suburbs are their family-oriented theme parks—Dreamworld, Warner Bros. Movie World, Wet 'n' Wild Water World, Paradise Country, the Australian

Outback Spectacular, and WhiteWater World. The sprawling complexes have many attractions: each takes about a day for a leisurely visit.

EXPLORING

FAMILY **Australian Outback Spectacular.** The Australian Outback Spectacular, one of six Village Roadshow theme parks in the area, lets visitors experience "the heart and soul of the Australian Outback." The exciting evening show features state-of-the-art visual effects and performances from top local stunt riders, interactive team racing, and live country music. Guests get a three-course "Aussie barbecue" dinner and complimentary drinks during the 90-minute, A$23 million extravaganza, plus a souvenir stockman's hat. Doors open at 6:15 pm; showtime is at 7:30 pm. A special Sunday matinee show takes place at 12:30 pm once a month, more frequently in high season. Return transfers from Gold Coast hotels cost A$20; on-site parking is free. This park (and neighboring theme parks Paradise Country, Warner Bros Movie World, and Wet 'n' Wild Water World) is a short taxi ride from Helensvale station. If driving, take Exit 60 at Oxenford off the M1 Pacific Motorway. ✉ *Pacific Motorway, Oxenford* ☎ *13/133386, 07/5519–6200 bookings* ⊕ *outbackspectacular.com.au* 🎟 *Tues., Wed., and Fri. A$99.99, Sat. A$110.* ⊙ *Closed Mon., Thurs., and Sun. (except monthly matinee).*

FAMILY

Fodor's Choice

★

Dreamworld. At Coomera's Dreamworld, the big draws are the "big eight": high-tech thrill rides including the aptly named Giant Drop, a 120-meter vertical plummet akin to skydiving; the nine-story, 360-degree pendulum swing of Claw; the turbulent Wipeout and screamingly fast, scarily high Tower of Terror; and new Pandamonium, a swinging rickshaw adventure. But it's certainly not all thrills and spills. Take a leisurely walk through Tiger Island where Bengal tigers and their gorgeous cubs swim, play, and even let you pet (and feed!) them; or get your picture taken with a cuddly koala in Koala Country. See more than 800 other native animals at conservation-focused on-site Wildlife Sanctuary, cool off in the artificial lagoon, or cruise the park's waterways on a paddle wheeler. Book ahead and you can also try the Flowrider (A$7), an amalgam of surfing and skateboarding. At the end of the day, a guided, two-hour Sunset Safari (A$25) promises close-up encounters with tigers and native wildlife (from 4:45 pm, in season). Beat the queues by buying an Earlybird Pass (A$10 extra, book well ahead) and take advantage of Q4U virtual queuing devices. The park is 45 minutes outside Brisbane and 20 to 25 minutes from Surfers Paradise along the M1 Pacific Motorway: take Exit 54 at Coomera. ✉ *1 Dreamworld Pkwy., Coomera* ☎ *07/5588–1111, 1800/073300* ⊕ *dreamworld.com.au* 🖃 *A$84.99 single entry (online); A$89.99 1-day World Pass (entry to DreamWorld and WhiteWater World); A$99.99 Holiday World Pass (unlimited entry to Dreamworld and WhiteWater World over 21 days)* ☉ *Daily 10–5.*

FAMILY

Paradise Country. Billed as "an authentic Australian farm experience," the park appeals to families with half-day farm tours beginning at 9:30 am, 11:45 am, and 1:45 pm (arrive half an hour prior to tour kick-off). You'll see displays of horsemanship, sheep shearing, boomerang throwing, and whip cracking, while kids will enjoy koala cuddling and kangaroo feeding. An optional barbecue lunch is also available. The park is directly behind the Australian Outback Spectacular. Car parking spaces are limited. ✉ *Pacific Motorway, Oxenford* ☎ *13/133386, 07/5519–6200* ⊕ *paradisecountry.com.au* 🖃 *A$19.99; A$39.99 (tour and lunch)* ☉ *Daily 9:30–5.*

FAMILY

Warner Bros. Movie World. One of the few movie theme parks outside the United States, Warner Bros. Movie World mixes an old Hollywood feel with live character shows, interactive adventures, and thrill rides for young and old. Get airborne on the Batwing Spaceshot, accelerate to 100 km (62 miles) an hour in two seconds on the awesome Superman Escape, or fight alien invasion in the new Justice League 3D. You can also check out vehicles, props, and costumes from the Batman blockbuster *Dark Knight*; enter a custom-built "immersive" movie set to watch precision driving and action-film-style stunts in the new *Hollywood Stunt Driver* show; and rocket through the air on the new Green Lantern coaster or Wild West Falls. Little kids will want to see the daily Main Street Star Parade, visit Bugs Bunny and friends in the WB Fun Zone and Looney Tunes River Ride, and catch the live show *What's Up Rock?* (daily at 11:30 am). With a large portion of its area now covered by a 4,000-square-meter (43,055-square-foot) roof, this park is a smart choice in bad weather. It's adjacent to Australian

Outback Spectacular. ✉ *Pacific Motorway, Oxenford* ☎ *13/5573–8495, 07/5573–3999* ⊕ *www.movieworld.com.au* 🎫 *A$84.99 (online); VIP pass A$109.99 (unlimited entry into Sea World, Movie World, and Wet'n'Wild for 12 months)* ◷ *Daily 10–5.*

FAMILY **Wet 'n' Wild Water World.** Oxenford's Wet 'n' Wild Water World boasts magnificent, adrenaline-pumping waterslides; a wave pool with 3-foot-high surf; tandem, entwined-tube and family-friendly slides; and the new Surfrider that simulates the sensation of surfing the world's biggest waves, plummeting you 30 meters (over 100 feet) while you spin on a giant board. In the Extreme H20 zone, you can plunge down pitch-black spirals of water in the Black Hole, hang on through the churning Tornado, race your friends on the Mach 5, or survive the scary Kamikaze: a giant, U-shaped, friction-free slide with a near-vertical 11-meter (36-foot) drop. Enough aquatic thrills? Take it easy on Calypso Beach, a "tropical island" fringed with white-sand beaches, or relax in the rolling surf of the 3-million-liter Giant Wave Pool. Meanwhile, kids will love Buccaneer Bay: a pirate-themed aquatic playground with multiple levels. Select pools and slides are heated May through September, when days are often still sunny and warm. The park is ½ km (¼ mile) down the Pacific Highway from Warner Bros. Movie World. ✉ *Pacific Hwy., Oxenford* ☎ *13–/3386, 07/5556–1660* ⊕ *www.wetnwild.com.au* 🎫 *A$59.99 (online); VIP Pass A$109.99 (unlimited entry to Sea World, Movie World, and Wet'n'Wild for 12 months).* ◷ *Oct.–Apr. 10–5, May.–Sept. 10–3:30.*

FAMILY
Fodor's Choice
★
WhiteWater World. Directly adjacent to Dreamworld, and under the same management, is the Gold Coast's latest thrill-seeker's theme park, WhiteWater World. Here you'll find state-of-the-art water rides including the Blue Ringed Octopus (BRO), a convoluted eight-lane racer slide; The Rip, Australia's biggest corkscrew-cored whirlpool; the dual-bowl Little Rippers ride; the Temple of Huey inner-tube "aquacoaster"; and the mat-free "drop and loop" of The Wedgie. Small kids will enjoy Pipeline Plunge, an enormous aquatic tree fort, while under-fivess are taken care of at shady, fully supervised Wiggle Bay. Relax and let the current take you away in the Cave of Waves, or learn to surf before or after public park hours by booking into Get Wet Surf School (A$75, including photos, transfers, and a guaranteed board stand up). Beat the queues with a prebooked Q4U device and early-bird entry. The park is close to Coomera railway station; from there, catch a Surfside bus to the park.

HOPE ISLAND

This isn't your average island. Like several Gold Coast islands, it is actually a mile or two inland, and is circled by the Coomera River and a series of canals. The resort has a marina full of luxury launches and yachts, two golf courses, a swanky hotel, beautiful condos, and upscale restaurants, nightclubs, and shops. Stop by if you're passing through for a glimpse into jet-set culture, Queensland style.

Hope Island is accessed via bridges from the west or east. Route 4, also known as the Oxenford–Southport Road, passes straight through.

7

✉ Dreamworld Pkwy., Coomera ☎ 07/5588–1111, 1800/438938 Get Wet Surf School 🌐 www.whitewaterworld.com.au 🎟 A$49.99 single entry (online); A$89.99 1-day World Pass (Dreamworld and WhiteWater World); A$99.99 Holiday Pass (unlimited entry to Dreamworld and WhiteWater World for 21 days). ⏲ Weekdays 10–3, weekends 10–4. Hrs extended during summer and school holidays.

WHERE TO STAY

For expanded hotel reviews, visit Fodors.com.

$$$$ RESORT 🏨 **Peppers Ruffles Lodge & Spa.** Set high on a hill in manicured gardens, six private villas, three tree houses, and an executive lodge suite with an expansive separate living room have views to the Gold Coast beaches and high-rises as well as the surrounding bushland. **Pros:** architecturally superb; feels luxurious; terrific food; breakfast included. **Cons:** must book well ahead; off the beaten track. *$ Rooms from: A$479 ✉ 423 Ruffles Rd., Willow Vale ☎ 07/5546–7411 🌐 www.ruffleslodge.com.au 🛏 10 villas (including 3 tree houses and 1 suite) 🍴 Breakfast.*

SOUTHPORT AND MAIN BEACH

16 km (10 miles) southeast of Oxenford.

South of Southport, look for the turnoff to the Spit, a natural peninsula that stretches 4 km (2½ miles) north, almost to the tip of South Stradbroke Island. Seaworld Drive runs the full length of the Spit, from Mariner's Cove (a popular covered area with affordable restaurants and fast-food outlets) to a nature reserve. This narrow peninsula is bordered by the Pacific Ocean to the east and the calm waters of the Broadwater (a long lagoon) to the west. Two of the Gold Coast's best hotels face each other across Seaworld Drive and are connected to Marina Mirage, arguably the most elegant shopping precinct on the Gold Coast. Farther up the road is Sea World itself.

EXPLORING

FAMILY **Sea World.** Australia's largest marine theme park, Sea World lets visitors get up close and personal with its resident dolphins, fur seals, sea lions, Fairy penguins, and polar bears (including new cub, Henry!). Hand-feed the 100-plus eagle, manta, and sting rays at Ray Reef, or take a walk through Shark Bay, the world's largest artificial lagoon system for sharks, where a state-of-the-art dual enclosure system keeps dangerous tiger sharks in one section and harmless reef sharks, rays, and fish in another. Patrons can dive in the latter, and get close-up views of the former through the massive windows that separate the lagoons. If you're after even more of a thrill, jump onboard The Sea Viper, Jet Rescue, or new Storm roller coasters, or make a splash at the park's various waterslides and interactive pool areas. Take a break and take in the view from the Sky High cable cars, or speed around the park on Sea World Monorail. Whatever you do, don't miss the daily Jet Stunt Extreme show, featuring the gravity-defying talents of the world's top Jet Ski stunt performers. Accommodation packages are offered at the adjacent Sea World Resort. *✉ Seaworld Dr., ocean-side end of this long street, The Spit, Main Beach ☎ 13/133386, 07/5588–2205 🌐 www.seaworld.*

Main beach in Byron Bay, Queensland's Gold Coast

com.au ✉ *A\$84.99 (online); VIP Pass A\$109.99 (unlimited entry to Sea World, Movie World, and Wet'n'Wild for 12 months)* ⊙ *Daily 10–5.*

SPORTS AND THE OUTDOORS

SURFING

Get Wet Surf School. The Gold Coast, renowned for long, white, sandy beaches and reliable breaks, is a terrific place to surf. Of the patrolled beaches, Main Beach, Surfer's Paradise, Broadbeach, Mermaid, Miami, and Nobby are the most popular; Kirra Beach, in the south, is arguably the area's best surf beach. Though the challenging break at Kirra is perhaps best left to the pros, most Gold Coast beaches are suitable for grommets (beginners). There are plenty of local surf schools happy to teach you, and board and wet suit hire outlets flank popular beaches. Local surfers and lifeguards are good sources of information about surf conditions and hazards—just remember to stay between the red and yellow flags!

Get Wet Surf School holds twice-daily group lessons (up to six students per coach) at a sheltered, crowd-free beach off the Spit, just north of Surfer's Paradise, as well as lessons outside park hours in the controlled environment of WhiteWater World's large wave pool (heated in winter). They also host private lessons and multiday surf tours. ⊠ *Seaworld Dr., Main Beach, Surfers Paradise* ☎ *1800/438938, 07/5532–9907 international* ⊕ *www.getwetsurf.com* ✉ *A\$55 (beach); A\$110 (private); A\$75 (wave pool)* ⊙ *Daily 10 am and 1 pm (beach); wave pool according to demand.*

WHERE TO EAT AND STAY

For expanded hotel reviews, visit Fodors.com.

$$
SEAFOOD

✕**Omeros Bros Seafood Restaurant.** The Omeros brothers, who arrived from Greece in 1953, have run seafood restaurants in Australia for more than 40 years. This one on the waterfront at the lovely Marina Mirage center offers dishes spanning the seafood spectrum—from bouillabaisse and classic surf-and-turf, to local barramundi, lobster, oysters, mud crab, and Moreton Bay bugs. There are also meat, vegetarian, and pasta dishes, and an extensive dessert menu. $ *Average main: A$35* ⊠ *Marina Mirage, Seaworld Dr., Shop 55/74* ☎ *07/5591–7222* ⊕ *www. omerosbros.com.*

$$$
MEDITERRANEAN

✕**Saks.** Located alongside Broadwater, only a short boardwalk removed from Palazzo Versace, is this hip restaurant and bar with wood floors, floor-to-ceiling windows, and indoor and outdoor areas. Relax on faux-suede lounge seats and ottomans while nibbling tapas, or nab a waterside table with views over the marina. Savor a steak or seafood dish, share a platter or pizza, or go for broke with one of Saks set menu options ranging A$39.90–A$80. Live music and DJs on Friday and Saturday nights and Sunday afternoons attract a crowd, as do the sensational cocktails. $ *Average main: A$55* ⊠ *Marina Mirage, 74 Seaworld Dr., Main Beach* ☎ *07/5591–2755* ⊕ *www.saksrestaurantandbar. com.au.*

$$$$
HOTEL
Fodor's Choice
★

Palazzo Versace. The famous Italian fashion house lent its flair to this stunning, decidedly opulent hotel, the first of its kind in the world. **Pros:** five-star service and dining; free self parking; refurbished in 2013. **Cons:** pricey; in-room Wi-Fi extra. $ *Rooms from: A$485* ⊠ *94 Seaworld Dr., adjoining Marina Mirage, Main Beach* ☎ *07/5509–8000* ⊕ *www. palazzoversace.com* ⤶ *146 rooms, 54 suites* ⊚| *Breakfast.*

SHOPPING

Marina Mirage Gold Coast. The sleek Marina Mirage Gold Coast is perhaps the most beautiful shopping and dining complex on the Gold Coast. Among its 80-plus stores are high-end gift and home wares; jewelry and designer fashion boutiques, including Hermès, Christiansen Copenhagen, and Calvin Klein, along with famous Australian brands; fine waterfront restaurants; beauty salons and day spas; and marina facilities. On Saturday morning (7–11 am), buy fresh gourmet produce at the Marina Mirage Gourmet Farmers' Markets. Surfside Buses 750 and 715 stop at the door. ⊠ *74 Seaworld Dr., Main Beach* ☎ *07/5555– 6400, 07/3103–2325 market* ⊕ *www.marinamirage.com.au.*

BROADBEACH

8 km (5 miles) south of Southport.

With clean beaches, great cafés, and trendy nightspots, Broadbeach is one of the most popular areas on the Gold Coast, especially with locals. It's also home to mega-shopping mall Pacific Fair, and is a good base for visiting the wildlife parks south of town.

SURFERS PARADISE

Before the Gold Coast existed as a tourism entity, there was Surfers Paradise: a stunning 3-km (2-mile) stretch of beach with great surf, 5 km (3 miles) south of Southport. Now overrun with high-rises, it's still a vibrant beachside town. Nightlife is the main draw: head to Orchid, Elkhorn, and Cavill avenues. Or, for stunning 360-degree views of the entire coast and hinterland, venture up to the SkyPoint observation deck located on the 77th floor of Surfers' famous Q1 Tower, the tallest building in the southern hemisphere.

Surfers Paradise Beachfront Markets. Thrice weekly, crowds flock to haggle for handmade crafts and gifts at the busy Surfers Paradise Beachfront Markets. ⊠ *The Esplanade between Hanlan St. and Elkhorn Ave.* 🖾 *Free* ☉ *Wed., Fri., and Sun. 5–10 pm.*

EXPLORING

FAMILY

Fodor's Choice

★

Currumbin Wildlife Sanctuary. A Gold Coast institution and perhaps the most ecologicallyminded wildlife facility in the region, Currumbin Wildlife Sanctuary is a 70-acre, not-for-profit National Trust Reserve featuring more than 60 koalas and an on-site wildlife hospital. Established in 1947 as a lorikeet sanctuary, it now shelters a wide variety of Australian species, including kangaroos, crocodiles, wombats, dingoes, Tasmanian devils, echidnas, emus, and rare birds. Ride the on-site mini train between the park's different precincts, or take in one of the more than 10 daily animal feedings, shows and performances. Currumbin's friendly 'roos (often with joeys in their pouches!) love to be petted and hand-fed, and the fleet of young koalas make for perfect cuddle and photo opportunities. Come at 8 am or 4 pm when the lorikeets are fed, or book a Segway Safari tour (A$45 for 50 minutes). You can also take a treetops ropes course, as well as visit nearby Superbee Honey World and Surf World Gold Coast, for an extra A$10 with a More Fun 4-in-1 Pass (A$59). ■TIP➔ Tickets are much cheaper if bought online in advance, especially in low season. The park also offers return transfers to and from the Gold Coast (book at ☎ *07/5534-0879*). All revenue goes towards Currumbin's work protecting, treating and rehabilitating local wildlife. ⊠ *28 Tomewin St., off Gold Coast Hwy., 14 km (8½ miles) south of Broadbeach, Currumbin* ☎ *07/5534–1266, 1300/886511* ⊕ *www.cws.org.au* 🖾 *General admission A$49; More Fun 4-in-1 Pass A$59; Experience Pass A$54* ☉ *Daily 8–5.*

FAMILY

David Fleay Wildlife Park. Located in the town of Burleigh Heads—7 km (4½ miles) south of Broadbeach—and named for an Australian wildlife naturalist, the park features a boardwalk trail through pristine wetlands and rain forests. Koalas, kangaroos, dingoes, platypuses, and crocodiles, grouped together in separate zones according to their natural habitat, are just some of the creatures you might see. A state-of-the-art nocturnal house displays threatened species and the elusive platypus. ■TIP➔ Daily presentations are free; the platypus feeding at 2:45 pm is a must-see. There's also a café and a gift shop. Family passes offer a significant admission discount. ⊠ *Tallebudgera Creek Rd. near W.*

Burleigh Rd., Burleigh Heads ☎ *07/5576–2411* ⊕ *www.fleayswildlife. com.au* ⊠ *A$19.45* ⊗ *Daily 9–5.*

WHERE TO STAY

For expanded hotel reviews, visit Fodors.com.

$$$
HOTEL

⬚ **Jupiters Hotel & Casino.** This massive, glitzy resort in central Broadbeach is always bustling. **Pros:** modern furnishings and facilities; great on-site entertainment options; close to shopping centers; free parking for guests. **Cons:** in-room Wi-Fi extra; can be noisy on weekends. $ *Rooms from: A$254* ⊠ *Broadbeach Island, Casino Dr. off Gold Coast Hwy.* ☎ *07/5592–8100, 1800/074344* ⊕ *www.jupitersgoldcoast. com.au* ⇆ *561 rooms, 29 suites, 2 penthouses* ⦿ *Breakfast.*

$$
HOTEL
Fodor's Choice
★

⬚ **QT Gold Coast.** One of Queensland's most popular destination hotels, the impeccably kept, retro-meets-modern QT Gold Coast boasts 360-degree views of the beach and hinterland, on-site restaurants and bars, and enough quirk and energy to make it stand brightly apart in a glut of beachside high-rises. **Pros:** lively atmosphere and vibrant design; excellent on-site food options; close to beach. **Cons:** pricey Wi-Fi; parking extra; area can be noisy at night (ask for a room on a higher level). $ *Rooms from: A$230* ⊠ *7 Staghorn Ave., Surfers Paradise* ☎ *07/5584–1200* ⊕ *www.qtgoldcoast.com.au* ⇆ *282 rooms, 15 suites* ⦿ *Multiple meal plans.*

NIGHTLIFE

Howl at the Moon. Howl at the Moon is fun if you like sing-alongs and know the words to hits from the '80s, '90s, and today. Every night pianists with vocal skills belt out a medley of tunes (some requested by patrons) on baby grands to an appreciative crowd of thirty- and fortysomethings. On weekends, grab a Cosmopolitan and hit the dance floor. ⊠ *Level 1, Neicon Plaza, 19/21 Victoria Mall* ☎ *07/5538–9911* ⊕ *www.howlatthemoon.com.au.*

Jupiters Casino. This casino provides flamboyant, round-the-clock entertainment. There are 70-plus blackjack, baccarat, craps, sic bo, Texas Hold'em poker, and keno tables, and more than 1,400 gaming machines on one level. There are also several private gaming and members' club rooms. Since the casino's A$53 million expansion over 2006–2008 there are even more dining, drinking, and entertainment options, including seven restaurants and eight bars. The elaborate new 2,300-seat showroom, completed in 2012, hosts glitzy stage shows, touring acts, and a range of concert productions. ⊠ *Casino Dr. off Gold Coast Hwy.* ☎ *07/5592–8100* ⊕ *www.jupitersgoldcoast.com.au.*

SHOPPING

Fodor's Choice
★

Pacific Fair. A sprawling indoor/outdoor shopping center, Pacific Fair is Queensland's largest mall, featuring a Myer department store, major retailers, and more than 300 specialty stores and services (including travel agencies, fashion outlets, and sports and outdoor gear). For a breather, head to the landscaped grounds with three small lakes, a children's park, and village green, or take in a movie at the 12-screen cinema complex. Pacific Fair is open Monday–Wednesday, Friday, and Saturday until 5:30 pm, Sunday until 4:30 pm; and Thursday until

9. ✉ *Hooker Blvd. at Gold Coast Hwy., opposite Jupiters Casino* ☎ *07/5581–5100* ⊕ *www.pacificfair.com.au.*

GOLD COAST HINTERLAND

No visit to the Gold Coast would be complete without an excursion to the region's verdant Hinterland. The natural grandeur of the area lies in dramatic contrast to the human-made excesses of the coastal strip. The Gold Coast Hinterland's superb national parks and nature reserves protect magnificent waterfalls, natural rock pools, mountain lookouts with expansive views of the surrounding terrain and coast, and an array of wildlife. Walking trails traverse rain forest dense with ancient trees. Among the parks lie boutique wineries and quaint villages where a high-rise is anything over one story. The parks form part of a unique, ancient geological region known as the Scenic Rim: a chain of mountains running parallel to the coast through southeast Queensland and northern New South Wales. Because it rises to 3,000 feet above sea level, some parts of the hinterland are 4°C–6°C (7°F–11°F) cooler than the coast.

GETTING HERE AND AROUND

The Hinterland's main areas—Tamborine Mountain, Lamington National Park, and Springbrook—can be reached from the Pacific Highway or via Beaudesert from Brisbane, and are a 30- to 40-minute drive inland from the Gold Coast. To reach Tamborine, around 80 km (50 miles) south of Brisbane and 36 km (24 miles) from Southport, take Exit 57 off the Pacific Motorway to the Oxenford–Tamborine Road; or take Exit 71 off the Pacific Motorway, the Nerang–Beaudesert Road, to Canungra. From Canungra, follow the signs to Tamborine, 4 km (2½ miles) along Tamborine Mountain Road. The Gold Coast Hinterland is ideal for touring by car: rent a vehicle, arm yourself with local maps, fill the tank, and take to the hills.

TOURS

From the Gold Coast, Mountain Coach Company buses pick passengers up from the major bus depots, most of the major hotels, and from Gold Coast Airport for O'Reilly's Rainforest Retreat in the Gold Coast Hinterland (A$84 round-trip day tour or individual transfer, departing at 8 am. Includes morning tea and wine tasting).

Australian Day Tours/JPT picks up passengers from Gold Coast hotels and The Brisbane Transit Centre daily at 8:45 am, and travels via Tamborine Mountain to the Hinterland. Day tours stop at O'Reilly's Rainforest Retreat, returning to the Gold Coast at 5:30, Brisbane at 6 pm. The cost—A$102 round-trip—is for a full-day tour, but Retreat guests can use it for transfers. Two-day Hinterland tours, with accommodation, dinner, and breakfast at O'Reilly's included, start at A$399. The company also runs nightly tours and guided night walks through local Hinterland caves which, when the sun is down, light up spectacularly with populations of glowworms. Departing from the Gold Coast at 5:30 pm, the tours run for four hours for A$99, with the option to include dinner.

Luke's Bluff Lookout on O'Reilly's Plateau, Lamington National Park

Hinterland accommodations, including O'Reilly's, Binna Burra Mountain Retreat, and Spicers Peak Lodge, shuttle guests to and from the coast. Various smaller coach tour companies, including winery tour operator Cork 'n Fork *(see Winery Tours)*, also visit Hinterland destinations.

ESSENTIALS

Coach Tours and Transfers Australian Day Tours/JPT ⊠ *Shop 18, 2 Elkhorn Ave., Surfers Paradise* ☎ *1300/5512–6444* ⊕ *www.daytours.com.au.*

Tours Mountain Coach Company ☎ *1300/762665* ⊕ *www.mountaincoach. com.au.*

EXPLORING

Lamington National Park. Part of the Gondwana Rainforests of Australia World Heritage Area, beautiful Lamington National Park is a lush, subtropical-temperate zone which shelters abundant and highly diverse plant and animal life. Forming part of the largest subtropical rain forest in the world, its 50,600-acre expanse comprises two sections: Binna Burra and Green Mountains. Find Antarctic beech trees dating back more than 3,000 years, as well as waterfalls, mountain pools, breathtaking views, bright wildflowers, and more than 160 native bird species. The Park is laced with 160 km (100 miles) of bushwalking tracks, ranging from 1.2 km (¾ mile) to 54 km (34 miles), with campsites along the way. All park camping areas require nightly permits (A$5.60), obtained in advance. ⊠ *Binna Burra* ☎ *13/137468* ⊕ *www.nprsr.qld. gov.au* 🖺 *Free* 🕙 *Daily 24 hrs.*

Springbrook National Park. The peaks of Springbrook National Park rise to around 3,000 feet, dominating the skyline west of the Gold Coast. The World Heritage–listed park has four regions: scenic Springbrook plateau, Mt. Cougal, Natural Bridge, and Numinbah. Waterfalls and cascades, Jurassic-age hoop pines, ancient rain forest, and native wildlife are highlights. Thanks to steep, winding roads and longish distances between sections, it takes at least a full day to explore this large park. It's about 30 km (19 miles) from the tiny hamlet of Springbrook to Natural Bridge—a waterfall that cascades through a cavern roof into an icy pool (reach it via a half-mile circuit track, an hour's round-trip). This cavern is home to Australia's largest glowworm colony, which at night illuminates the rock walls to stunning effect. Several waterfalls, including the area's largest, Purling Brook Falls, can be reached via a steepish 4-km (2½-mile) path (allow 15 minutes for each half mile). The 54-km (34-mile) Gold Coast Hinterland Great Walk extends from the Settlement campground to Green Mountains campsite in Tamborine National Park. For those short on time or energy, the lookout near the parking lot has beautiful waterfall views. Camping is permitted only in designated private campgrounds. ⊠ *Springbrook* ☎ *13–7468* ⊕ *www. springbrooktourism.com.au* ⊠ *Free* ☉ *Daily dawn–dusk.*

Fodor's Choice ★ **Tamborine National Park.** More than 20 million years ago, volcanic eruptions created rugged landscapes, while fertile volcanic soils produced the luxuriant tracts of rain forest that make up enchanting Tamborine National Park. This is the most developed region of the Gold Coast Hinterland, and it's worth spending at least a day or two here. Apart from the natural environment, there are wineries, lodges, restaurants, and the famed Gallery Walk, a 1-km-long (½-mile-long) street lined with art galleries. Some of the simplest (under two hours) and best trails here are the Cedar Creek Falls Track, with waterfall views; Palm Grove Rainforest Circuit; and Macdonald Rainforest Circuit, a quieter walk popular with bird-watchers. Start your visit with a stop at Tamborine Mountain Visitor Information Centre, open 10 am to 3 pm daily, and don't forget to stop by the local Botanic Gardens for a rest and a picnic. Several fragmented parks make up Tamborine National Park, including Cedar Creek, Palm Grove, Joalah, The Knoll, Witches Falls, and MacDonald. To the east of Witches Falls is **Joalah National Park,** where a 1½-km (1-mile) circuit takes you to a rocky pool at the base of Curtis Falls. ⊠ *Main Western Rd., Mt. Tamborine* ☎ *07/5545–3200 information center* ⊕ *www.tamborinemtncc.org.au.*

Witches Falls. Queensland's first national park, Witches Falls has excellent picnic facilities and a 3-km (2-mile) walk that snakes downhill through open rain forest and past lagoons. ⊠ *Tamborine National Park, Main Western Rd., North Tamborine.*

SPORTS AND THE OUTDOORS

HIKING
Bushwalking is a popular pastime in the national parks and nature reserves of the Gold Coast Hinterland, where an extensive network of well-maintained scenic trails caters to recreational walkers, serious hikers, campers, and wildlife lovers. The region's many protected wilderness tracts, including World Heritage–listed Gondwana Rainforests

of Australia (within Springbook National Park), contain hundreds of well-marked trails that vary from easy half-hour strolls to steep half-day hikes and multiday treks. Most Hinterland walks offer spectacular views and sights.

However, conditions can be challenging and changeable, so before setting out on longer hikes, get suitably equipped. Download local trail maps and detailed park info from NPRSR's website or regional visitor information offices, and follow NPRSR guidelines.

When walking, wear sturdy shoes, sunscreen, and protective gear; carry maps and a compass; and pack drinking water, emergency food supplies, and a well-charged mobile phone. If possible, walk in a group, especially on long hikes. Check local weather conditions with the Bureau of Meteorology and trail conditions on NPRSR's website before you go.

If exploring the national parks by car, check road conditions with the RACQ's website and be sure you have local maps, good tires, sound brakes, water, and a full tank of gas before setting out.

Contacts Department of National Parks, Recreation, Sport and Racing (NPRSR) ☎ *13/137468 camping permits and information* 🌐 *www.nprsr.qld.gov.au.* **RACQ** ☎ *1300/131905 road and travel information* 🌐 *www.racq.com.au.*

WHERE TO STAY

For expanded hotel reviews, visit Fodors.com.

$$ HOTEL FAMILY **Binna Burra Mountain Lodge & Campsite.** At the doorstep of Lamington National Park, this historic, eco-certified mountain lodge and campground is a bird-watcher's paradise, with sweeping views across heritage-listed rain forest and more than 160 km (99 miles) of walking trails. **Pros:** beautiful setting and wildlife; easy, interesting drive up mountain; old-fashioned, communal atmosphere. **Cons:** very basic meals for the price; limited organized activities. [$] *Rooms from: A$190* ✉ *Binna Burra Rd., Lamington National Park, via Beechmont* ☎ *07/5533–3622, 1300/246622* 🌐 *www.binnaburralodge.com.au* 🛏 *35 cabins (9 with shared bath), 3 studios, 5 apartments* 🍴 *Multiple meal plans.*

$$ RESORT FAMILY Fodor's Choice ★ **O'Reilly's Rainforest Retreat, Mountain Villas & Lost World Spa.** One thousand meters (3,280 feet) above sea level and immersed in the subtropical rain forests of World Heritage–listed Lamington National Park, the iconic, eco-certified O'Reilly's Rainforest Retreat offers atmosphere and adventure in equal doses. **Pros:** magical location; plenty of activities; excellent facilities. **Cons:** long drive up mountain—use a coach or transfer service if you're not confident on Australian roads. [$] *Rooms from: A$238* ✉ *Lamington National Park Rd., Canungra* ☎ *07/5502–4911, 1800/688722* 🌐 *www.oreillys.com.au* 🛏 *67 rooms, 5 suites, 48 villas* 🍴 *Multiple meal plans.*

$$$ RESORT **Pethers Rainforest Retreat.** On 12 acres of privately owned rain forest, this couples-only resort comprises 10 spacious tree houses with timber floors, French doors opening onto verandas, fireplaces, hot tubs, and open-plan interiors furnished with Asian antiques. **Pros:** luxurious appointments; glorious environs; no kids. **Cons:** no on-site dinner Sunday to Wednesday; limited mobile phone coverage. [$] *Rooms from: A$380* ✉ *28B Geissmann St., North Tamborine* ☎ *07/5545–4577*

retreat@pethers.com.au ⊕ www.pethers.com.au ☞ 10 tree houses
Breakfast.

THE SUNSHINE COAST

60 km (37 miles) north of Brisbane.

The Sunshine Coast is a 60-km (37-mile) stretch of white-sand beaches, inlets, lakes, and mountains that begins at the Glass House Mountains, an hour's drive north of Brisbane, and extends to Rainbow Beach in the north. Kenilworth is its inland extreme, 40 km (25 miles) from the ocean. For the most part, the Sunshine Coast has avoided the high-rise glitz of its southern cousin, the Gold Coast. Although there are plenty of stylish restaurants and luxurious hotels, this coast is best loved for its national parks, secluded coves, and relaxed beachside towns.

GETTING HERE AND AROUND

From Brisbane, drive 60 km (35 miles) north on the Bruce Highway, taking the Caloundra Road exit to get to the Sunshine Coast's southernmost beach town, Caloundra. Another 5 km (3 miles) along the highway, there's a well-marked exit to the Sunshine Motorway, which funnels you through to Sunshine Coast towns farther north via a series of large roundabouts (stay tuned for the appropriate exit). Follow the motorway north for 9½ km (6 miles) to get to the Brisbane Road–Mooloolaba exit; 15 km (9 miles) to reach the turn-off to Maroochydore; 29 km (18 miles) to the Yandina-Coolum Road exit for Coolum Beach; and 34 km (21 miles) to reach the Noosa turnoff.

Sunshine Coast Regional Council, Maroochy Tourist Information Centre has branches at the Sunshine Coast airport, Maroochydore, Mooloolaba, Coolum, and Montville.

AIR TRAVEL

Sunshine Coast Airport is the main airport for the area, servicing several flights a day by Jetstar, Qantas, and Virgin Australia from Sydney and Melbourne. By air from Maroochydore it's 2 hours 25 minutes to Melbourne, 2 hours 15 minutes to Adelaide, and 1 hour 35 minutes to Sydney. Park at the airport for around A$14 a day, A$65 a week.

BUS TRAVEL

SunAir Bus Service runs daily buses from Brisbane Airport and the Roma Street Transit Centre in Brisbane to all the main Sunshine Coast towns. Distances between towns are short (10 to 30 minutes' drive). SunAir also runs hourly services from Brisbane International Airport to Sunshine Coast and Hinterland towns (A$54–A$57), meeting every flight into and out of Sunshine Coast Airport and shuttling prebooked, prepaid passengers to and from Sunshine Coast towns south of the airport, including Maroochydore, Mooloolaba, and Caloundra (A$15–A$39 one-way).

Henry's Transport Group meets all flights, running buses from Maroochy Airport to the northern Sunshine Coast (A$25 to Noosa) and, on market days, to Eumundi.

CAR TRAVEL

A car is a virtual necessity on the Sunshine Coast. The traditional route to the coast from Brisbane is along the Bruce Highway (Highway 1) to the Glass House Mountains, with a turnoff at Cooroy. Taking the Sunshine Motorway may be faster, however: after 65 km (40 miles), turn off the Bruce Highway at Tanawha (toward Mooloolaba) and follow the signs. On either route, allow 1½ hours to get to the central coastal town of Coolum, a further half hour to reach Noosa, on the northern Sunshine Coast. The most scenic route is to turn off the Bruce Highway at the exit to Caloundra, then follow the coast to Noosa Heads.

TRAIN TRAVEL

Trains leave regularly from Roma Street Transit Centre in Brisbane en route to Nambour, the business hub of the Sunshine Coast. They continue on to Yandina, Eumundi, and other non-coastal towns. Once in Nambour, however, a car is a necessity unless you're a keen cyclist, so it may make more sense to drive from Brisbane.

ESSENTIALS

Airport Contacts Sunshine Coast Airport ⊠ *10 Electra La., Marcoola* ☎ *07/5453–1500* ⊕ *www.sunshinecoastairport.com.au.*

Bus Contacts Henry's Transport Group ☎ *07/5474–0199* ⊕ *www.henrys.com. au.* **SunAir Bus Service** ☎ *07/5477–0888, 1800/804340* ⊕ *www.sunair.com.au.*

Train Contacts Queensland Rail ☎ *13/131617* ⊕ *www.queenslandrail.com.au.*

Visitor Information Sunshine Coast Tourist Information Centre ☎ *1800/330142* ⊕ *www.sunshinecoastinformation.com.au.* **Tourism Noosa** ⊠ *61 Hastings St., Noosa Heads* ☎ *07/5430–5000, 1800/002624* ⊕ *www. visitnoosa.com.au.***Tourism Sunshine Coast** ⊠ *Airport House, 10 Electra La., Marcoola* ☎ *07/5459–9050* ⊕ *www.visitsunshinecoast.com.au.*

NOOSA

39 km (24 miles) northeast of Nambour, 17 km (11 miles) north of Coolum, 140 km (87 miles) north of Brisbane.

Set along the calm waters of Laguna Bay at the northern tip of the Sunshine Coast, Noosa is one of Australia's most stylish resort areas. Until the mid-1980s the town consisted of little more than a few shacks—then surfers discovered the spectacular waves that curl around the sheltering headland of Noosa National Park. Today Noosa is an enticing mix of surf, sand, and sophistication, with a serious reputation for distinctive, always-evolving cuisine. Views along the trail from Laguna Lookout to the top of the headland north of Main Street take in miles of magnificent beaches, ocean, and dense vegetation.

EXPLORING

Teewah Coloured Sands. About 3 km (2 miles) northeast of Noosa Heads you'll find the Teewah Coloured Sands, an area of multicolored dunes created in the Ice Age by natural chemicals in the soil. Teewah's sands stretch inland from the beach to a distance of about 17 km (11 miles); some of the 72 distinctly hued sands even form cliffs rising to 600 feet. A four-wheel-drive vehicle is essential for exploring this area and interesting sites to the north, such as Cooloola National Park—home to 1,300-plus species of plants, 700 native animals, and 44% of Australia's bird species—and Great Sandy National Park. Access is by ferry across the Noosa River at Tewantin.

Tour operators run day trips via cruise boat and four-wheel drive that take in these sights; some include visits to Fraser Island, north of Rainbow Beach. You can also explore the area on foot. One of Queensland's latest Great Walks winds through Cooloola National Park.

BEACHES

FAMILY **Noosa Main Beach.** With gentle waves and year-round lifeguard patrol, Noosa's Main Beach is a perfect swimming spot, ideal for families or those who aren't confident in the bigger swells. One of only a handful of beaches along Australia's coastline that faces north, Main Beach also hosts surfing lessons for beginners with Go Ride A Wave surf school (A$130, two-hour lesson). The beach backs onto leafy Hastings Street with its bustle of upmarket cafés, bars, restaurants, and shopping spots. For a quieter scene, adventure around the corner to **Noosa Spit**, a popular picnic spot and off-leash dog beach. **Amenities:** food and drink; lifeguards; parking; toilets; showers. **Best for:** swimming; walking; sunrise; sunset. ⊠ *Hastings St.* ⊕ *www.visitsunshinecoast.com.au.*

Sunshine Beach. Lovely Sunshine Beach, incorporating 16 km (10 miles) of beachfront that stretches north to Noosa national park, is patrolled year-round. Beach breaks, reliable swell, a rocky headland sheltering it from winds, and clear, glassy water make Sunshine popular with surfers. When northeasterlies blow, surf the northern pocket. Fish off the beach year-round for dart, bream, and flathead, or cast a long line into deep water to hook numerous seasonal species. From here, hike past nudist-friendly Alexandria Bay to Noosa, or end a long day of swimming with a beer or a meal at The Sunshine Beach Surf Club. **Amenities:** food and drink; lifeguards; parking; toilets; showers. **Best for:** surfing; swimming; walking; sunrise; sunset. ⊠ *Belmore Terr., Sunshine Beach.*

SPORTS AND THE OUTDOORS

RIVER CRUISING

Noosa Everglades Discovery. Eco-accredited Noosa Everglades Discovery runs half- and full-day river cruises and guided canoe trips through the glassy waters of the Noosa Everglades. ⊠ *Noosa Everglades, 186 Gympie Terr., Noosaville* ☎ *07/5449–0393* ⊕ *www.noosaevergladesdiscovery. com.au* ⊠ *Afternoon Tea Cruise A$79 ; Barbeque Lunch Cruise A$105; Bar-B-Canoe Day Tour A$125; 3-day Canoe & Camp A$155.*

SURFING

Go Ride a Wave. Go Ride a Wave offers equipment rentals and surfing lessons for beginners in the sheltered warmth of Noosa Heads Beach. Book in advance to secure two-hour beginner, group, or private lessons, with surfboard, wet suit, and all other equipment included in the fee (from A$65 per adult, A$55 per child). Make the most of your holiday with a Go All Day pass (from A$100), or a five-lesson Go Carve It Up pack from A$220. ■TIP→ Book online in advance to save. ⊠ *On the beach, Hastings St. near Haul St.* ☎ *1300/132441* ⊕ *www.gorideawave. com.au.*

WHERE TO EAT AND STAY

For expanded hotel reviews, visit Fodors.com.

$$ ✕**Berardo's Bistro on the Beach.** Expatriate New Yorker Jim Berardo
AUSTRALIAN came to Noosa to retire, but he ended up with two restaurants and
a kiosk. Berardo's Bistro, the more casual of the restaurants, has a
prime location right on Noosa's beach, and attracts a constant stream
of customers. Quirky fish sculptures line the walls; handblown char-
treuse carafes are on every table. The menu lists fresh juices, cocktails,
Berardo's Wagyu Burger (at lunch), and light meals that focus on sea-
food: have the fish of the day with a garnish of your choice; or linguine
with prawns, scallops, mussels, chili, parsley, and garlic. There's also
a gourmet deli bar with takeout options. $ *Average main: A$32* ⊠ *49
Hastings St., beachfront* ☎ *07/5448–0888* ⊕ *www.berardos.com.au.*

$$ ✕**Bistro C.** Spectacular views of the bay from the open dining area make
MODERN a stunning backdrop for this restaurant's Mod Oz cuisine. The fresh,
AUSTRALIAN tropical menu highlights seafood, though landlubbers can partake of
several meat and vegetarian dishes. Try the signature fresh medley
of local seafood, served in the pan, or seafood antipasto. Coffin Bay
oysters are also a delicious way to indulge, or try the local favorite:
beer-battered flathead with lemon and tartar sauce. Book ahead for
Thursday-night's "seafood platter": for A$85 you get cold then hot
platters for two, brimming with Moreton Bay bugs, prawns, squid,
mussels, salmon, and more (except in peak season). There's also a kids'
menu. $ *Average main: A$33* ⊠ *49 Hastings St., on the Beach Complex*
☎ *07/5447–2855* ⊕ *www.bistroc.com.au.*

$$$ ✕**Ricky's River Bar + Restaurant.** A dining room overlooking the Noosa
MODERN River makes this restaurant perfect for a relaxed lunch or a romantic
AUSTRALIAN dinner. The menu features "modern Noosa cuisine," in which Medi-
terranean flavors mingle with Australian ingredients. Sip a mojito or a
mango daiquiri and polish off a plate of tapas before moving on to a
main course of fresh reef fish, char-grilled eye-fillet, or confit of duck.
There's also a kids' menu. The adjacent River Bar serves a lighter menu,
including cheese plates, and has an extensive wine list. $ *Average main:
A$35* ⊠ *Noosa Wharf, Quamby Pl.* ☎ *07/5447–2455* ⊕ *www.rickys.
com.au.*

$$$ ⌂**Sheraton Noosa Resort & Spa.** Facing fashionable Hastings Street on
RESORT one side, the river on the other, you can't miss this elaborate, six-story,
horseshoe-shaped complex as you drive into Noosa Heads; it was
recently repainted a simple, chic white to highlight the sparkling azure
of the central pool. **Pros:** close to beach; beautiful pool area. **Cons:**
pricey; A$20 a day parking fee; slow Wi-Fi. $ *Rooms from: A$345*
⊠ *14–16 Hastings St.* ☎ *07/5449–4888* ⊕ *www.sheratonnoosaresort.
com* ⇆ *140 rooms, 29 suites, 7 spa studios* ⍾ *Multiple meal plans.*

PEREGIAN AND COOLUM

*Peregian is 11 km (7 miles) south of Noosa, with Coolum 17 km (11
miles) south of Noosa and 25 km (16 miles) northeast of Nambour.*

At the center of the Sunshine Coast, Coolum makes an ideal base for
exploring the countryside. It has one of the finest beaches in the region,

"We were walking along the beach in Noosa at sunset when we came across this guy building the sand castle. He was amazing!" —photo by jenwhitby, Fodors.com member

a growing reputation for good food and quality accommodation, and all the services you might need: banks with ATMs, medical centers, gas stations, pharmacies, supermarkets, gyms, beauty salons, and day spas—even a beachfront playground, kiosk, and skate park. Ten minutes north of Coolum is Peregian, a quaint little seaside town with numerous shops, eateries, and facilities, a string of stunning beaches, and a local produce and crafts market on the second and forth Sunday of the month.

BEACHES

FAMILY **Coolum Beach.** A popular choice for families, beautiful Coolum Beach boasts a surf club, skate park, playgrounds, changing rooms, toilets, kiosk, shorefront parks, and well-maintained picnic areas. A long, white-sand beach, Coolum is patrolled year-round, and offers a nice beach break and some decent, uncrowded waves off the headland. Fish from the beach in the evening for jewfish, tailor, bream, and dart; catch bream around the headland, especially in winter. Walk south along the boardwalk to the headland park for magnificent coastal views, or north to quieter Peregian Beach with its patrolled surf, playground, and adjacent Environmental Park. For a break from the sun, head down David Low Way for shops, cafés, and restaurants. **Amenities:** food and drink; lifeguards; parking; toilets; showers. **Best for:** surfing; swimming; walking; sunset. ⊠ *David Low Way, Coolum Beach* ⊕ *www. visitsunshinecoast.com.au.*

SPORTS AND THE OUTDOORS

SURFING

Coolum Surf School. Run by an expert surfer and local lifeguard, Coolum Surf School offers two-hour group and 90-minute private lessons, as well as board and gear hire. It's the only surf school in the area: find it 50 meters north of Coolum Surf Lifesaving Club, next to the skate park. ✉ *Coolum Boardriders Clubhouse, Tickle Park, David Low Way, Coolum Beach* ☎ *07/5446–5279* ⊕ *www.coolumsurfschool.com.au* 🏄 *A$110 single private lesson, A$55 beginner class (prices include gear)* ⊗ *Daily dawn–dusk; lessons by appointment.*

WHERE TO EAT AND STAY

For expanded hotel reviews, visit Fodors.com.

$$
MODERN
AUSTRALIAN
Fodor'sChoice
★

✕ **Pitchfork.** Positioned within the café and shopping strip along Peregian Beach, this restaurant entices crowds with its imaginative, seasonally changing Mod Oz cuisine. But Pitchfork's rustic furnishings, indoor and outdoor dining, and change-by-the-season menu aren't its only draws. The service is also superb, and staff are happy to cater specifically to gluten-free and vegetarian diners. Top dishes include the lightly fried stuffed zucchini flowers or seared Hervey Bay scallops to start, and the wild-mushroom-and-truffle-oil risotto for main. However, keep an eye out for their specials board—their duck pie is one to request. Booking in advance is highly recommended. $ *Average main: A$31* ✉ *5/4 Kingfisher Dr., Peregian Beach* ☎ *07/5471–3697* 🍽 *Reservations essential* ⊗ *Closed Mon.*

$$
RENTAL

🏨 **Coolum Seaside Holiday Apartments.** These sleek and spacious studios and one- to four-bedroom apartments are just around the corner from Coolum's restaurants, shops, and beach. **Pros:** good on-site facilities; free Wi-Fi; close to beach. **Cons:** dated decor and technology in some units. $ *Rooms from: A$275* ✉ *23 Beach Rd.* ☎ *1800/5255–7200, 07/5455–7200* ⊕ *www.coolumseaside.com* 🛏 *44 apartments* 🍽 *No meals.*

MAROOCHYDORE

18 km (11 miles) south of Coolum, 18 km (11 miles) east of Nambour.

Maroochydore, at the mouth of the Maroochy River, has been a popular beach resort town for years, and has its fair share of high-rise towers. Its draw is excellent surfing and swimming beaches.

BEACHES

FAMILY **Alexandra Headland.** South of Maroochydoore's main beach and just north of Mooloolaba, Alexandra Headland offers a reliable surf break in moderate to high swell. The beach is patrolled year-round, but swimmers need to take care to avoid the headland rocks at the southern end of the beach where there is often a strong rip. A shady park, barbecue and picnic area, kiosk, playground, skatepark, and walking and cycling tracks color the foreshore, with many alfresco cafés and restaurants also nearby. Cast a line at the river mouth or off the headland for bream, dart, whiting, and flathead, or take advantage of rip holes for beach fishing. **Amenities:** food and drink; lifeguards; parking; toilets;

showers. **Best for:** surfing; swimming; walking; sunset. ⊠ *Alexandra Parade, Alexandra Headland* ⊕ *www.visitsunshinecoast.com.au.*

Maroochydore Beach. Averaging waves around 3 feet, this long, picturesque white-sand beach is a great option for swimmers and amateur surfers alike. Patrolled year-round by one of Queensland's oldest surf life-saving clubs, rips are common along this strip, so stay in the central area between the red-and-yellow flags. A busy walking and cycling track runs adjacent to the beachfront, connecting visitors to both Cotton Tree and Alexandra Headland. A few minutes north is Maroochy River, a popular fishing spot and water-sports activities hub. As with almost all Sunshine Coast beaches, an array of shops, cafés, and eateries line the esplanade. **Amenities:** food and drink; lifeguards; parking; toilets; showers; water sports. **Best for:** swimming; walking; surfing; sunset. ⊠ *Alexandra Parade* ⊕ *www.visitsunshinecoast.com.au.*

WHERE TO EAT AND STAY
For expanded hotel reviews, visit Fodors.com.

$$$
AUSTRALIAN

✕ **ebb Waterfront.** Faux-suede sofas and ottomans in varying shades of cool blue set the mood at this riverside restaurant specializing in top-quality regional produce, particularly sustainably farmed local seafood. Floor-to-ceiling windows line one side of the long, open dining room, while the large, breezy outdoor area offers stunning views across the water. Chef Zarko Baru changes the award-winning Mod Oz menu seasonally. Try the Octopus Carpaccio or stuffed zucchini flowers before moving on to duck, lamb, or locally farmed barramundi. Complement your meal with a choice of wines from Australia's finest producers, and make sure to leave room for the excellent cheese plates and desserts. Ⓢ *Average main: A$38* ⊠ *6 Wharf St.* ☎ *07/5452–7771* ⊕ *www.ebbwaterfront.com* ◷ *No dinner Sun.–Wed.*

$
CAFÉ

✕ **Raw Energy.** Keep your fuel up for long days of swimming and surfing with a stop at Raw Energy, where freshly made smoothies and juices, hearty burgers and wraps, and fair-trade coffee will give you just the boost you need. Popular with locals and tourists alike, the light-and-healthy fare includes protein- and superfood-packed smoothies; seasonal, locally flavored fruit, veggie, and green juices; and an array of burgers stacked sky-high with fresh ingredients. For breakfast, try the famous Poached Eggs, delicious Potato Fritter Stack, or Acai Breakfast Bowl; or grab a homemade organic muffin and takeaway coffee and meander down to the seaside to watch the waves roll in. Ⓢ *Average main: A$12* ⊠ *20 Memorial Ave.* ☎ *07/5443–1777* ⊕ *www.rawenergy.com.au* ◷ *No dinner.*

$$
RENTAL
FAMILY

▦ **The Sebel Maroochydore.** Each spacious one- or two-bedroom apartment in this stylish, 15-level hotel has a curved feature wall and full kitchen bristling with modern European appliances. **Pros:** 25-meter (82-foot) pool and separate kids pool; good service; free parking. **Cons:** noise from pool area and traffic at night; beach is across a four-lane road; broadband Internet extra. Ⓢ *Rooms from: A$269* ⊠ *20 Aerodrome Rd.* ☎ *07/5479–8000* ⇆ *47 apartments, 6 penthouses* ⦿ *No meals.*

$ HOTEL **Twin Waters Resort.** About 9 km (5½ miles) north of Maroochydore, this hotel was built around a 15-acre saltwater lagoon bordering Maroochy River and Mudjimba Beach. **Pros:** great lawns and lagoon; free use of water-sports equipment; terrific kids' programs. **Cons:** housekeeping standards vary; buffet dinners pricey; lackluster spa. [$] *Rooms from: A$195* ✉ *Ocean Dr., Twin Waters* ☎ *07/5448–8000, 1800/072277* 🌐 *www.twinwatersresort.com.au* 🛏 *234 rooms, 126 suites* 🍴 *Breakfast.*

MOOLOOLABA

5 km (3 miles) south of Maroochydore.

Mooloolaba stretches along a lovely beach and riverbank, both an easy walk from town. The Esplanade has many casual cafés, upscale restaurants, and fashionable shops. Head to the town outskirts for picnic spots and prime coastal views.

EXPLORING

FAMILY **UnderWater World SEA LIFE Mooloolaba.** This multi-award-winning, all-weather sea life sanctuary features back-to-back marine presentations, including stingray feedings, guided shark tours, and seal and otter shows, all accompanied by informative talks. It features 16 zones over three levels, including Australia's largest and most interactive jellyfish display, and its famous underwater tunnel which lets you get face-to-face with the majestic creatures of the deep. Roll up your sleeves and tickle a sea star or a sea cucumber in the touch pool; or swim with seals (A$90), snorkel the reef (A$65) or scuba dive with resident sharks (A$255 for beginners, A$195 for certified divers). The twice-daily behind-the-scenes tour is also well worth it at only A$10 (prebooking is a must). A souvenir shop and a café are also on-site. The aquarium is part of Mooloolaba's Wharf Complex, which features a marina, restaurants, and a tavern. **TIP→ Don't forget to get your hand stamped so you can re-enter the park.** ✉ *10 Parkyn Parade, The Wharf* ☎ *07/5458–6280* 🌐 *www.underwaterworld.com.au* 🎟 *A$38* 🕒 *Daily 9–5.*

BEACHES

FAMILY **Mooloolaba Beach.** A safe, family-friendly swimming strand, Mooloolaba Beach is patrolled year-round, and has just enough swell to make it fun. Surfers might want to check out the left-hand break that sometimes forms off the rocks at the northern end. There are shady picnic areas with barbecues, playgrounds, and exercise areas—as well as the local meeting point, the Loo with a View. Stroll south along the coastal path to the river mouth and rock wall (off which you can fish, year-round, for bream); north to Alexandra Headland for views of the bay; or along Mooloolaba Esplanade, lined with casual eateries and boutiques. **Amenities:** food and drink; lifeguards; parking; toilets; showers. **Best for:** swimming; walking; sunrise; sunset. ✉ *Beach Terr.* 🌐 *www.visitsunshinecoast.com.au.*

WHERE TO EAT AND STAY

For expanded hotel reviews, visit Fodors.com.

$$ ITALIAN 🍴 **Bella Venezia Italian Restaurant & Bar.** A large mural of Venice, simple wooden tables, and terra-cotta floor tiles decorate this popular restaurant in an arcade off the Esplanade. You can eat in or take out traditional and modern Italian cuisine, such as the *Pesce del giorno* (fish of the day served with garlic chat potatoes and seasoned greens); *Saltimbocca alla Romana* (prime cut veal topped with prosciutto and sage); or fresh Coffin Bay oysters with lime mint and chili dressing. There's an extensive selection of pizza, pasta, and risotto, as well as wine and cocktails. Open daily from noon to late, they'll also deliver to local hotels. [$] *Average main: A$35* ✉ *95 The Esplanade* ☎ *07/5444–5844* 🌐 *www.bellav.com.au.*

$$ RENTAL 🏨 **Mantra Sirocco.** The futuristic curves of this popular apartment complex loom above Mooloolaba's main drag. **Pros:** fantastic views from big balconies; in-room Jacuzzis; friendly staff; free parking. **Cons:** minimum two-night stay; Wi-Fi extra. [$] *Rooms from: A$325* ✉ *59–75 The Esplanade* ☎ *07/5444–1400, 1800/811454 reservations* 🌐 *www.mantrasirocco.com.au* 🛏 *41 apartments, 2 penthouses* 🍽 *No meals.*

CALOUNDRA

29 km (18 miles) south of Maroochydore, 63 km (39 miles) south of Noosa, 91 km (56 miles) north of Brisbane.

This unassuming southern seaside town has nine beaches of its own, which include everything from placid wading beaches (King's Beach and Bulcock Beach are best for families) to bays with thundering surf, such as Dicky, Buddina, and Wurtulla beaches.

BEACHES

Bulcock Beach. Flanked by a timber boardwalk with stunning views across the coastline, Bulcock Beach is one of Caloundra's most popular surfing spots. Children will enjoy the small paddling pools that form across the sand at low tide, while nearby Happy Valley parkland creates the perfect canvas for games of Frisbee and traditional "Aussie" beachside cricket. Surf the break off Deepwater Point, or enjoy boogieboarding or bodysurfing in the swell closer to shore. Rips can form through the channel, so stay between the flags and only swim when the beach is patrolled (September–May). When you've had too much sun, head across the road for cafés, restaurants, shops, and a place to cool off. **Amenities:** lifeguards; parking; toilets. **Best for:** surfing; walking; sunrise; sunset. ✉ *The Esplanade.*

FAMILY Fodor's Choice ★ **King's Beach.** With rock pools, water fountains, an oceanfront saltwater swimming pool, and gentle, patrolled swimming areas, it's no surprise that festive King's Beach is one of the Sunshine Coast's most popular choices for families. The region's closest beach to Brisbane, it is also attracts plenty of surfers chasing the breaks toward the beach edges. King's foreshore is well landscaped, with seating and shade areas, as well as a bustling boardwalk. A grassy reserve, fronted by a seawall, runs alongside the beach, peppered with children's playgrounds, picnic spots, and barbecue areas. A range of beachside cafés and eateries surround. Deep rip holes run off the rocks for fishing. **Amenities:** food and drink; lifeguards; parking; toilets; showers. **Best for:** surfing; swimming; walking; sunset. ⊠ *Ormond Terr.*

WHERE TO EAT AND STAY
For expanded hotel reviews, visit Fodors.com.

$$ ╳ **mooo char + bar.** Owned by legendary (and now retired) Queensland
AUSTRALIAN   Rugby League footballer Allan "Alfie" Langer, this steak-centric restaurant has an ideal setting right on Bulcock Beach, overlooking the sheltered inlet known as Pumicestone Passage. The decor and design are light and bright, and there's both indoor and outdoor dining. Try the restaurant's deservedly popular steak, baked barramundi, or local king prawns, or take advantage of the popular A$15 lunch menu. The restaurant is open daily noon–late. $ *Average main: A$36* ⊠ *The Esplanade at Otranto Ave.* ☎ *07/5492–0800* ⊕ *www.alfies.net.au* ⌂ *Reservations essential.*

$$ 🛏 **Rolling Surf Resort.** The stunning white sands of Kings Beach front
RESORT   this resort enveloped in tropical gardens. **Pros:** huge pool; good on-site
Fodor's Choice   food options; right on the beach. **Cons:** two-night minimum stay in high
★   season; in-room Wi-Fi extra. $ *Rooms from: A$230* ⊠ *10 Levuka Ave., Kings Beach* ☎ *07/5491–9777, 1800/775559* ⊕ *www.rollingsurfresort.com.au* ➭ *74 apartments* ⦿ *Multiple meal plans.*

SUNSHINE COAST HINTERLAND

The Sunshine Coast Hinterland, extending from the Glass House Mountains just northwest of Brisbane to Eumundi and Yandina, west of the northern Sunshine Coast town of Noosa, is ideal terrain for daytrippers. Tracts of subtropical rain forest and mountainous areas linked by scenic drives and walking trails are interspersed with charming hillside villages, their main streets lined with cafés, galleries, gift shops, and guesthouses. Here you'll also find thriving markets; renowned restaurants and cooking schools; ginger, nut, and pineapple farms; theme and wildlife parks; and luxury B&Bs.

The Hinterland's southerly extent is the nine distinctive conical outcrops of the Glass House Mountains—the eroded remnants of ancient volcanoes—rising dramatically from a flattish landscape 45 km (27 miles) northwest of Brisbane. Get a great view of the mountains from Glass House Mountains Lookout, also the starting point for a scenic, 25-minute walk. Several longer trails begin from nearby vantage points, such as Mt. Beerburrum and Wild Horse Mountain Lookout. Nearby, you'll find Aussie World amusement park, the Ettamogah Pub, and the late Steve Irwin's famous Australia Zoo.

Meander north through the mountains to reach the arty village of Maleny, quaint, European-style Montville, and food-friendly Mapleton. Nearby, you'll find tranquil Baroon Lake and easy walking trails in Kondalilla National Park and Mary Cairncross Scenic Reserve.

Continue north to Yandina, where you'll find much-lauded restaurant Spirit House and the Ginger Factory, and Eumundi, known for

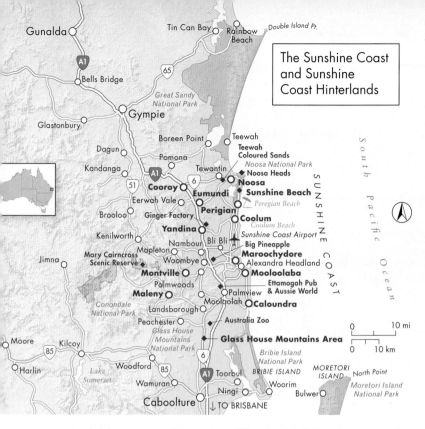

The Sunshine Coast and Sunshine Coast Hinterlands

its thriving twice-weekly markets. Hinterland hub Nambour, east of Mapleton, has shops, banks, and local attractions.

GETTING HERE AND AROUND

To get to the Sunshine Coast Hinterland from Brisbane, follow the Bruce Highway north for around 35 km (22 miles), taking the Glass House Mountains Road exit. A 10-km (6-mile) drive along Glass House Mountains Road brings you to the quaint Glass House Mountains Village. Access Glass House Mountains Lookout, 10 km (6 miles) from the village, via Glass House Mountains Tourist Route. Drive 10 km (6 miles) north along Glass House Mountains Road from the village to reach Maleny.

From Maleny, take the Landsborough-Maleny Road for 10 km (6 miles), turning right at Maleny–Montville Road, to get to Montville. From Montville it's a five-minute drive west on Western Avenue to Kondalilla National Park. A further 10 km (6 miles) drive northwest brings you to Mapleton, from which it's a 12-km (7-mile), 15-minute drive east to Nambour, en route to the Sunshine Coast.

From Nambour, a 20-minute drive east along Petrie Creek Road and David Low Way brings you to the mid-Sunshine Coast town of Maroochydore. Or drive 20 minutes north along the Bruce Highway to reach Eumundi, 20 km (12 miles) away. From here it's a half-hour,

Fishing at Bulcock Beach, Caloundra, Sunshine Coast

20-km (12-mile) drive east along the Eumundi–Noosa Road to Noosa, the northernmost town on the Sunshine Coast.

From Nambour it's an 8-km (5-mile) drive north along the Nambour Connection Road, then Old Bruce Highway, to reach Yandina. From Brisbane, it's an hour's drive north along the Bruce Highway: take the Coolum/Yandina exit.

It's around 60 km (35 miles) to Glass House Mountains Village; just under 100 km (60 miles) to Montville; and nearly 110 km (65 miles) to Maleny from Brisbane. Driving time is 60 minutes to the Glasshouse Mountains; around 1½ hours to Maleny and Montville, and a further 15-minute drive to Nambour and another 12-minute drive to Yandina. From the Sunshine Coast most parts of the Hinterland are less than an hour's drive inland.

You'll find few banks and money exchanges around the Sunshine Coast Hinterland: ■ TIP➔ Get cash in advance from ATMs in larger coastal towns such as Noosa. Alternatively, several are available at service stations along the Bruce Highway, or at stores and pubs in the Hinterland.

ESSENTIALS

Visitor Information Maleny Hinterland Visitor Information Centre ⊠ *Shop 2, 23 Maple St., Maleny* ☎ *07/5499–9788* ⊕ *www.malenycommunitycentre. org.* **Montville Visitors Information Centre** ⊠ *198 Main St., Montville* ☎ *07/5459–9050.*

GLASS HOUSE MOUNTAINS AREA

35 km (22 miles) north of Brisbane on Bruce Highway to the Glass House Mountains Road exit; 4 km (2.5 miles) south of Beerwah.

More than 20 million years old, the Glass House Mountains consist of nine conical outcrops—the eroded remnants of volcanoes—that rise dramatically from a flattish landscape northwest of Brisbane. Get a great view of the mountains from Glass House Mountains Lookout. Access is 10 km (6 miles) from the village via Glass House Mountains Tourist Route. The lookout is also the starting point for a scenic 25-minute walk. Several longer walks begin from nearby vantage points, such as Mt. Beerburrum and Wild Horse Mountain Lookout.

EXPLORING

FAMILY **Aussie World.** The colorful Aussie World amusement park, adjacent to the Ettamogah Pub, features several games rooms, a hall for "Funnybone Flicks," and a bustling fairground with 30-plus rides, including dodgem cars, a retro merry-go-round, Ferris wheel, roller coaster, log ride, minigolf—even a sideshow alley. Admission is cheap, the "old school" carnival vibe is fun and friendly, and the park is far less crowded than its Gold Coast equivalents. An eclectic range of specialty stores are also housed within the complex. ⊠ *73 Frizzo Rd., Palmview* ☎ *07/5494–5444* ⊕ *www.aussieworld.com.au* ⌨ *A$29 unlimited rides, minigolf, and flicks* ☉ *Daily 9–5.*

FAMILY **Australia Zoo.** Made famous by the late Steve Irwin, Australia Zoo features all manner of Australian animals: koalas, kangaroos, wallabies, dingoes, Tasmanian devils, snakes, and lizards—and, naturally, crocodiles. There are also otters, lemurs, tigers, red pandas, and a giant rainforest aviary. Daily shows feature crocs, birds of prey, koalas, and more. There are also plenty of extras on offer that let you get up close and personal with the residents, including petting and hand-feeding red pandas (A$80), or getting cozy with cheetahs ($150) and rhinos ($80). Get around the park on foot or try the free, hop-on, hop-off mini-trains. Private guided tours are also available. A courtesy bus shuttles visitors to and from Beerwah station and the Sunshine Coast. ⊠ *1638 Steve Irwin Way, 5 km (3 miles) north of Glass House Mountains, Beerwah* ☎ *07/5436–2000* ⊕ *www.australiazoo.com.au* ⌨ *A$59* ☉ *Daily 9–5 (last entry 4:30).*

Fodor's Choice ★

Ettamogah Pub. This pub, whose name (allegedly, Aboriginal for "place of good drink") and quirky design are based on the fictitious pub made famous by Aussie cartoonist Ken Maynard, looms 18 meters (55 feet) over the Bruce Highway just north of Palmview (21 km [13 miles] north of Glass House Mountains). The much-photographed watering hole is open daily from 9 am–late, and features an upstairs bistro, a beer garden, and a bar, the former priding itself on traditional Aussie pub meals. Kitsch Australiana and Maynard's cartoons adorn the pub walls, and almost all furniture is constructed from wood logged on site. Make sure to pack your camera for this one! ⊠ *73 Frizzo Rd., Palmview* ☎ *07/5494–5444.*

7

MONTVILLE

16 km (10 miles) northwest of Forest Glen.

This charming mountain village, settled in 1887, is known as the creative heart of the Sunshine Coast, as many artists live here. There are panoramic views of the coast from the main street, a charming mix of Tudor, Irish, and English cottages constructed of log or stone; Bavarian and Swiss houses; quaint B&Bs; and old Queenslander homes. Shops are a browser's delight, full of curiosities and locally made crafts, while galleries showcase more serious pieces by local artists. A new 1½-km (1-mile) zip line over the treetop canopies of Kondalilla National Park is also under construction, slated for completion in 2015. Note that the nearest major banks are in Nambour.

EXPLORING

FAMILY **Kondalilla National Park.** With its swimming hole, 295-foot waterfall, picnic grounds, and walking trails, Kondalilla National Park is a popular local attraction. Three bushwalks begin near the grassy picnic area: Picnic Creek Circuit, Rock Pools Walk, and the Kondalilla Falls Circuit. They're all rated easy to moderate and range from 2 km (1 mile) to 5 km (3 miles) in length. The **Sunshine Coast Hinterland Great Walk** (58 km [34 miles]) is accessible from the Falls Loop track, and links with parks farther north. Download maps from the Department of National Parks, Recreation, Sport and Racing website. Camping is not permitted within the park. ✉ *Kondalilla Falls Rd., off Montville–Mapleton Rd. near Flaxton* ☎ *13/5494–3983* 🌐 *www.nprsr.qld.gov.au* 🎟 *Free.*

WHERE TO EAT AND STAY

For expanded hotel reviews, visit Fodors.com.

$$ AUSTRALIAN 🍴 **Montville Café Bar Grill.** Twinkling with fairy lights by night and window-box blooms by day, this simple, "ye olde English"–style family pub on Montville's main street offers a free courtesy bus pick up to and from local accommodations. Start with the salt-and-pepper calamari, and work your way up to a generous 300-gram Black Angus rib fillet sourced from Queensland's own Channel Country, with a quality range of Australian wines to accompany. Live entertainment adds to the wholesome country feel on Friday and Saturday evenings, and Sunday afternoons starting at noon. [$] *Average main: A$28* ✉ *Main St.* ☎ *07/5278–5535* 🌐 *www.montvillepub.com.au.*

$$ CAFÉ 🍴 **Poets Cafe.** At this picturesque Montville institution, photographs of famous poets adorn the walls, and French doors open onto a balcony shaded by tall rain-forest trees. An eclectic menu includes gourmet open sandwiches, seafood risotto, barramundi, eye fillet steak, pasta dishes, and delectable cakes and desserts (save room for the caramel macadamia tart). The Main Street Gallery below sells contemporary Australian artwork, including glassware. [$] *Average main: A$30* ✉ *167 Main St.* ☎ *07/5478–5479 café, 07/5478–5050 gallery* 🌐 *www.weddingsatpoets.com.au* 🕒 *No dinner Sun.–Thurs.*

$$$ B&B/INN Fodor's Choice ★ 🏨 **Narrows Escape Rainforest Retreat.** In the midst of a verdant valley overlooking beautiful Lake Baroon, this tranquil retreat features six self-contained, luxuriously appointed cottages nestled deep in the rain forest. **Pros:** beautiful setting; spacious and secluded cottages; excellent

service and facilities. **Cons:** a little way out of town. [$] *Rooms from: A$360* ✉ *78 Narrows Rd.* ☎ *07/5478–5000* 🌐 *www.narrowsescape.com.au* 🛏 *6 cottages* 🍴 *Multiple meal plans.*

$$ B&B/INN FAMILY 🏨 **The Spotted Chook & Amelie's Petite Maison.** This Queenslander inn features a delightful French provincial ambience in a relaxing countryside setting. **Pros:** warm and welcoming service; delicious French-style country breakfasts included in rate; bicycles available for exploring the beautiful area; wheelchair-friendly cottage, ramps, and walkways. **Cons:** two-night minimum stay on weekends; no in-room Internet. [$] *Rooms from: A$275* ✉ *176 Western Ave.* ☎ *07/5442–9242* 🌐 *www.spottedchook.com.au* 🛏 *4 suites, 1 cottage* 🕒 *Closed Christmas Day, Boxing Day* 🍴 *Breakfast.*

$$$ B&B/INN 🏨 **Treetops Montville.** These cutting-edge-design tree houses perched on an escarpment are the ideal location for a romantic escape. **Pros:** stunning views; quiet; close to town. **Cons:** minimum two-night stay on weekends; no Wi-Fi. [$] *Rooms from: A$270* ✉ *4 Cynthia Hunt Dr., off Kondalilla Falls Rd., Flaxton* ☎ *07/5478–6618, 1800/087330* 🌐 *www.treetopsmontville.com.au* 🛏 *4 tree houses, 4 cabins* 🍴 *Multiple meal plans.*

MALENY

14 km (8½ miles) west of Montville.

The Hinterland village of Maleny is a lively mix of rural life, the arts, wineries, cafés, and cooperative ventures. First settled around 1880, eclectic Maleny is now a popular tourist center with a strong community spirit, as well as a working dairy town.

EXPLORING

Mary Cairncross Scenic Reserve. One of the area's most popular picnic spots, Mary Cairncross Scenic Reserve is 5 km (3 miles) southeast of Maleny at the intersection of the Landsborough–Maleny Road and Mountain View Road. The 130 acres of subtropical rain forest shelter an array of wildlife that includes bandicoots, goannas, echidnas, wallabies—and even pythons. There's an excellent information center and two easy walks. Eat in the café (serving fair-trade coffee and homemade cakes) or at picnic tables for magnificent views of the Glass House Mountains. ✉ *148 Mountain View Rd.* ☎ *07/5429–6122* 🌐 *www.marycairncross.com.au.*

WHERE TO EAT AND STAY

For expanded hotel reviews, visit Fodors.com.

$ CAFÉ 🍴 **Maple 3 Café.** Renowned for its great coffee and hearty breakfasts, this local favorite changes its menu daily, but there are always fresh salads, focaccias, pastas, and plenty of dessert options, including terrific cheesecake. Come in for breakfast or brunch, grab a sandwich and a huge slice of homemade cake, and head down to Lake Baroon for a picnic. Or just sit out front on the deck and watch affable Maleny townsfolk go about their day. [$] *Average main: A$18* ✉ *3 Maple St.* ☎ *07/5499–9177.*

$$$ B&B/INN 🏨 **Maleny Tropical Retreat.** At the end of a steep driveway lies a misty rainforest valley and this lovely B&B retreat. **Pros:** beautiful location; warm

and welcoming; large DVD library; good breakfasts; no kids. **Cons:** can be pricey on weekends. [$] *Rooms from: A$325* ✉ *540 Maleny–Montville Rd.* ☎ *07/5435–2113* 🌐 *www.malenytropicalretreat.com* 🛏 *3 rooms, 4 villas, 1 cabin* 🍴 *Breakfast.*

YANDINA, EUMUNDI, AND COOROY

Yandina is 110 km (68 miles) north of Brisbane on the Bruce Hwy.; Eumundi is 12 km (7½ miles) north of Yandina.

Yandina and Eumundi, just 12 km (7½ miles) apart, are home to some of the most iconic attractions in the area. Don't miss the Ginger Factory in Yandina, where you can learn—and eat—lots while enjoying the mini-amusement park-like attractions; or stop in at the tranquil Spirit House for a meal or cooking class. The Eumundi Markets (on Wednesday and Saturday) are also a must.

EXPLORING

Big Pineapple. Sunshine Plantation in Nambour, just over 100 km (63 miles) north of Brisbane, is home to the impossible-to-miss Big Pineapple. You'll pass it on your way wast if you head inland to Eumundi, Maleny, or Montvale. The 50-foot fiberglass monster towers over the highway. The original plantation train and farm tours still operate, although the property is in the process of renovation to return it to its former glory. Nonetheless, if you're interested in Australia's "Big" things (a series of large fiberglass roadside attractions that dot the country's road system) and are passing through anyway, it's worth a quick stop for a photo and a sundae. ✉ *76 Nambour Connection Rd., Woombye* ☎ *07/5442–1333* 🌐 *www.bigpineapple.com.au* 🎟 *Free; train tour package A$15* ⏲ *Daily 9–4.*

Fodor's Choice ★ **Eumundi Market.** The big attraction of this area is the twice-weekly Eumundi Market—the best street market on the Sunshine Coast. More than 300 stall-holders gather along Memorial Drive in the picturesque town of Eumundi to sell arts, crafts, clothing, accessories, and fresh and gourmet produce, from 7 am to 2 pm on Saturday and 8 am to 1:30 pm on Wednesday. Buses run to Eumundi from Noosa on market days, when the town swells to near-cosmopolitan proportions. Live musicians, poets, and masseurs keep the crowd relaxed. ✉ *80 Memorial Dr., Eumundi* ☎ *07/5442–7106* 🌐 *www.eumundimarkets.com.au.*

FAMILY **The Ginger Factory.** A legendary Queensland establishment, The Ginger Factory goes far beyond its original factory-door sale of ginger. You can still take a 40-minute guided tour of the world's only publically accessible ginger processing plant. A café and shop sell ginger in all forms—incorporated into jams, cookies, chocolates, ice cream, wine, and herbal products. There's also a train trip and a boat ride, a miniature rain forest for kids, a live beehive tour that includes a honey tasting, and plenty of shops to browse. Just up the road, you'll find the beautiful Yandina Historic House. ✉ *50 Pioneer Rd., Yandina* ☎ *07/5446–7100, 1800/067686* 🌐 *www.gingerfactory.com.au* 🎟 *Free entry; A$14.50–A$35 tours, demos, and rides* ⏲ *Daily 9–5.*

Eumundi Market, Eumundi, Sunshine Coast

WHERE TO EAT

$
BISTRO

✕ **Maison de Provence.** Run by French couple Eric and Francoise Pernoud, Maison de Provence is one part patisserie/café, one part French homewares shop, with all food made on-site. Find light meals like quiches and baguettes or the most delectable tarte aux fruits, eclairs, and other cakes and pastries. They also make their own tempting range of chocolates and macarons. At the back of a large corner balcony, this little café is a great spot to soak up some sun and fresh Hinterland air while treating yourself to a little bit of French delight. $ *Average main: A$17* ✉ *9/13 Garnet St., Cooroy* ☎ *07/5472–0077* ✉ *maisondeprovence@bigpond.com* ☉ *Closed Sun.*

$$
MODERN ASIAN
Fodor's Choice
★

✕ **Spirit House.** Mention that you're looking for a place to eat in Yandina, and even Brisbane foodies say "Spirit House." The restaurant's trio of credentialed chefs, who travel annually to Asia to get inspiration and skills, do a remarkable job re-creating contemporary Asian cuisine on Queensland soil. The menu, designed around plates to share, changes seasonally, with most ingredients sourced locally; a worthy signature dish is the whole crispy reef fish with tamarind-chili sauce. Save room for delectable desserts, best sampled in the tasting plate for two. The lush garden setting has a lagoon and Buddhist shrines. A hydroponic farm and cooking school are also on-site. $ *Average main: A$36* ✉ *20 Ninderry Rd., Yandina* ☎ *07/5446–8994* ⊕ *www.spirithouse.com.au* ✍ *Reservations essential* ☉ *No dinner Sun.–Tues.*

MACKAY–CAPRICORN ISLANDS

Despite its name, this group of islands lying offshore between Bundaberg and Rockhampton is closer to the southern half of Queensland than it is to the city of Mackay. The Mackay–Capricorn Islands comprise the section of the Great Barrier Reef known as Capricorn Marine Park, which stretches for 140 km (87 miles) and cuts through the Tropic of Capricorn, Heron Island being the closest point. This is a great area for wildlife: turtles use several of the islands as breeding grounds; seabirds nest here; and humpback whales pass through on their migration to Antarctica each spring—generally between July and October.

LADY ELLIOT ISLAND

Fodor's Choice
★

Positioned 80 km (50 miles) off the Queensland coast, Lady Elliot Island is a 104-acre coral cay on the southern tip of the Great Barrier Reef, within easy reach of Bundaberg and Hervey Bay. One of just six island resorts actually on the reef, it's a high-level Marine National Park Zone. Wildlife here easily outnumbers the guests (a maximum of 100 can visit at any one time)—and that reality is underscored by the ammoniacal odor of hundreds of nesting seabirds and, in season, the sounds and sights of them courting, mating, and nesting.

Divers will enjoy the easy access to the reef and the variety of diving sites around Lady Elliot. Fringed on all sides by coral reefs and blessed with a stunning white-sand, coral-strewn shore and bright azure waters, this oval isle seems to have been made for diving. There's a busy dive shop and a reef education center with marine-theme exhibits (plus an educational video library—great for rainy days). Inclement weather and choppy waves can lead to canceled dives and washed-out underwater visibility. When the waters are calm, you'll see turtles, morays, sharks, rays, and millions of tropical fish. Many divers visit Lady Elliot specifically to encounter the resident population of manta rays that feed off the coral.

From October to April, Lady Elliot becomes a busy breeding ground for crested and bridled terns, silver gulls, lesser frigate birds, and the rare red-tailed tropic bird. Between November and March, green and loggerhead turtles emerge from the water to lay their eggs; hatching takes place after January. During the hatchling season, staff biologists host guided turtle-watching night hikes. From about July through October, pods of humpback whales are visible from the beachfront restaurant.

Lady Elliot is one of the few islands in the area where camping—albeit modified—is part of the resort, and a back-to-basics, eco-friendly philosophy dominates the accommodations. ⊕ *www.ladyelliot.com.au.*

GETTING HERE AND AROUND

Lady Elliot is the only coral cay with its own airstrip. Small aircraft generally make the flight from Hervey Bay (40 minutes) or Bundaberg (30 minutes), though pickups can be arranged from as far south in Queensland as Coolangatta, on the Gold Coast (two hours). You can day-trip to Lady Elliot with Seair Pacific, too. The cost includes scenic

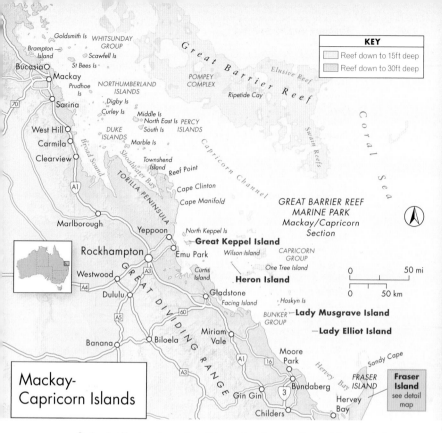

flight, buffet lunch, reef walking, glass-bottom boat ride, snorkeling, and island tour.

Tours require a minimum of 2 passengers and use planes that can carry up to 12. Strict luggage limits for both hand and checked baggage allow 10 kilograms (22 pounds) per person (for a small charge, divers can take an extra 10 kilograms in dive gear). If you exceed this limit, you can repack at the ticket-counter scale or wave good-bye to the plane.

ESSENTIALS

Airlines Seair Pacific ☎ 07/5599–4509 ⊕ www.seairpacific.com.au.

SPORTS AND THE OUTDOORS

At the resort dive shop you can rent equipment and arrange dive courses to more than a dozen excellent sites, including Lighthouse Bommie, home to a 40-strong manta ray colony, and the Blow Hole and Hiro's Cave. Refresher pool dives, a shore snorkeling trip, and guided reef, nature, and historical walks are free for resort guests. Off-boat snorkeling and glass-bottom boat rides are A$30. Boat dives and night dives start at A$65, but all guests are entitled to one complimentary combined tour during their stay. Open-water certification courses cost A$550; "Discover Scuba Diving" short courses are A$165; and referral courses, available to those who've completed the classroom and pool portions of a certification course prior to arrival, are A$450.

Diving here is weather-dependent, so plan accordingly if you intend doing a dive course over multiple days. Four-night packages, including buffet breakfast and dinner, a glass-bottomed boat tour, snorkeling tours, and reef tax, start at A$652 per person. Flights (from Hervey Bay, Fraser coast, Bundaberg, the Gold and Sunshine coasts, or Brisbane) are extra. Several other special deals and packages are available. There is a one-time A$15 environmental management charge for all nonpackage guests.

WHERE TO STAY

For expanded hotel reviews, visit Fodors.com.

$$$
RESORT
☂ **Lady Elliot Island Eco Resort.** On this pristine reef island you're more like a marine biologist at an island field camp than a tourist enjoying a luxury resort. **Pros:** eco-friendly; proximity to nature; friendly, knowledgable staff. **Cons:** few in-room modern conveniences; limited leisure options for rainy, non-diving days; minimum three-night stay during peak times. $ *Rooms from: A$492* 🕾 *07/5536–3644 (head office), 07/4156–4444 (resort)* ⊕ *www.ladyelliot.com.au* ⇨ *15 reef rooms, 6 garden units, 5 suites, 12 tents* ⎢⎔⎢ *Multiple meal plans.*

LADY MUSGRAVE ISLAND

This island sits at the southern end of the Great Barrier Reef Marine Park, about 40 km (25 nautical miles) north of Lady Elliot Island and 96 km (53 nautical miles) north east of Bundaberg. The cay has a 2,945-acre surrounding reef, about one-third of which is a massive yet calm lagoon, a true coral cay of 39.5 acres. Here day-trippers, yachties, divers, and campers converge, and the island has some of the best diving and snorkeling in Queensland. Campers have a chance to view the myriad sea life surrounding this tiny speck of land in the Pacific.

From October through April the island is a bird and turtle rookery, with black noddies, wedge-tailed shearwaters, bridled terns, more timid black-naped and roseate terns, and green and loggerhead turtles. There's also an abundance of flora, including casuarina and pisonia trees. ⊕ *www.ladymusgraveisland.com.*

GETTING HERE AND AROUND

Lady Musgrave Barrier Reef Cruises is the only carrier servicing Lady Musgrave Island. It primarily operates as a day-cruise service, but also ferries campers to the island. Boats depart daily at 8:30 am from the Town of 1770 marina on Captain Cook Drive, arriving around 75 minutes later (board from 8 am). Baggage is limited to about a cubic foot per person, as space on board is tight. You'll be expected to load most of your gear the evening prior to sailing; on the island, use wheelbarrows to haul it to the campground from the island drop-off point, 250 meters (275 yards) away. If you're carrying a dinghy for getting around the island, it costs an extra A$120 round-trip (hire dinghies from Burnett Boat Hire (🕾 *0414/721883*). Campers must have a NPRSR permit at time of boarding (A$5.60 per person, per night). If you're camping, you get substantial discounts on boat transfers April through June.

ESSENTIALS

Cruise Lady Musgrave Barrier Reef Cruises ☎ *07/4974–9077* ⊕ *www. lmcruises.com.au.*

SPORTS AND THE OUTDOORS

WATER SPORTS

Lady Musgrave Barrier Reef Cruises. This company operates a pontoon in the vast deep-water coral lagoon off Lady Musgrave Island, with an underwater observatory, snorkeling deck, changing rooms, and sheltered seating. Their Lady Musgrave day cruises get you out to the reef in 75 minutes. Day Cruise passengers can enjoy more than five hours on the reef, including a buffet lunch and a 90-minute stopover on the Outer Reef, at a pontoon within a sheltered lagoon where you can snorkel, view 350 varieties of colorful live coral and 1,300 species of tropical fish year-round from a submersible or glass-bottom boat, take a guided island walk, see migrating whales in season, or do some scuba diving or reef fishing before the boat cruises back to the mainland in the afternoon. Reef fishing and scuba diving are extra (for novice and certified divers, with or without gear). There's a per-person reef tax of A$10. Cruises depart daily from the Town of 1770 and include a tropical buffet lunch, morning and afternoon tea, activities on the reef, and most gear. The day trip, including most extras, is A$175 per person; visitors staying on-island pay A$350 return—but get to take the cruise twice. ☒ *Town of 1770 marina, Captain Cook Dr., Town of 1770* ☎ *07/4974–9077* ⊕ *www.lmcruises.com.au* ☒ *A$175 day cruise; A$20 reef fishing; A$70 or A$90 for 1 or 2 dives, certified diver (A$80 or A$120 including gear); A$95 introductory lesson and 1 dive with gear.*

HERON ISLAND

Fodor's Choice ★ Most resort islands lie well inside the shelter of the distant reef, but Heron Island, some 72 km (45 miles) northeast of the mainland port of Gladstone, is actually part of the reef. The waters off this 18-hectare (20-acre) island are spectacular, teeming with fish and coral, and ideal for snorkeling and scuba diving. The water is generally clearest in June and July and cloudiest during the rainy season, January and February. Heron Island operates on "island time"—an hour ahead of Eastern Standard Time—and at its own leisurely pace. You won't find much in the way of nightlife, as the island's single accommodation accepts a cozy maximum of 250 people—and there are no day-trippers. But these might be reasons why you decide to come here.

GETTING HERE AND AROUND

Once in Gladstone, passengers can board the high-speed, 34-meter Heron Islander from the city's marina. The launch makes the two-hour run to Heron Island from Gladstone, on the Queensland coast, for A$100 one-way, departing at 11 am daily and arriving at 2 pm in time for a late lunch. The return boat departs from Heron Island for the mainland at 2 pm island time (1:30 EST). This can be a rough journey: take ginger or anti-nausea medicine ½ hour before departure. A courtesy shuttle bus transfers guests from Gladstone Airport, leaving at 10:15 am daily, and meets all afternoon boats. (Fly to Gladstone from

Coral and Lighthouse, Lady Elliot Island

Brisbane, Mackay, Rockhampton, Townsville, and Cairns with Qantas or Virgin Australia.) You can also arrange transfers to and from Gladstone Station; get here on Queensland Rail's fast *Tilt Train* or *Sunlander* from the north or south (⊕ *www.queenslandrail.com.au*).

HeliReef makes 30-minute helicopter flights to Heron Island from Gladstone for A$395 one-way, with more service October through April. The baggage restriction is 15 kilograms (33 pounds) per person. Lockup facilities for excess baggage are free (or get it brought over on the daily launch for free). You can charter a helicopter to the island from Gladstone for A$2,450 (maximum five adults, one infant).

ESSENTIALS
Air Travel HeliReef ☎ 07/4946–9102 ⊕ www.helireef.com.au.

EXPLORING

Wilson Island. Only guests of the Heron Island Resort can visit uninhabited Wilson Island, a coral cay 15 km (9 miles) north of (and a 45-minute launch trip from) Heron Island. In January and February Wilson Island becomes the breeding ground for roseate terns and green and loggerhead turtles. The island also has its own exclusive, six-suite, premium tented resort, catering to a maximum of 12 guests (and no children under 13), with all meals and transfers included in the rate—from A$448 per person, per night (more nights mean lower rates). Combination packages allow for nights at both Heron and Wilson islands, including meals. Guest accommodation is only available certain months to guests not wishing to "book the whole island." ⊠ *Wilson Island* ☎ 1300/863248 ⊕ *www.wilsonisland.com*.

SPORTS AND THE OUTDOORS

You can book snorkeling, scuba diving, and fishing excursions as well as turtle-watching tours and sunset cruises through Heron Island Marine Centre & Dive Shop. Snorkeling lessons and refresher dive courses are free. Snorkeling trips are A$50.

DIVING

Various diving options include a resort diving course for beginners, including training and one guided dive, for A$190 (subsequent dives, A$139). For certified divers it's A$70 per dive, and just A$50 per dive upward of five dives. Night dives, including light stick and flashlight, are A$99. Three-, five-, and seven-night dive packages include multiple dives throughout Heron and Wistari reefs, as well as accommodation, breakfast, buffet lunch, dinner, and all tanks and weights, starting from A$270 per person per night. Half- and full-day dive boat charters are also available.

For all dives, prebooking is essential, and gear costs you extra. Children under 7 aren't permitted on snorkeling trips, under-10s can't go diving, and under-14s must be accompanied by an adult (and if diving, must be certified).

FISHING

Heron Island Marine Centre & Dive Shop. In addition to diving, snorkeling, and semisubmersible trips, Heron Island Marine Centre & Dive Shop runs three-hour fishing trips and half- and full-day guided reef-fishing charters for up to 10 passengers, with gear, tackle, and optional stops for snorkeling. Toast the sunset on an hour-long wine-and-cheese cruise or book a charter cruise for up to eight people. ☎ *07/4972–9055* 🌐 *www.heronisland.com* 🎟 *A$50 semisubmersible tour, A$50 90-min snorkeling trip, A$70–A$695 per-person scuba diving packages, A$115 3-hr fishing trip, A$75 sunset cruise. Half- and full-day group reef-fishing cruises and charter cruises can be booked upon request.* 🕒 *Daily 8–5:30.*

7

SNORKELING AND SEMISUBMERSIBLE

Nondivers wanting to explore their underwater environs can take a half-day snorkeling tour of Heron and Wistari reefs, or an hour-long, naturalist-guided semisubmersible tour. Guided reef and birdlife walks, movies under the stars, and visits to the island's Marine Research Station are free.

WHERE TO STAY

For expanded hotel reviews, visit Fodors.com.

$$$ RESORT 🏨 **Heron Island Resort.** Set among palm trees and connected by sand paths, this secluded, eco-certified resort offers six accommodation types, from the deluxe Beach House with private outdoor shower and beach boardwalk to the comparatively compact, garden-level Turtle Rooms. **Pros:** lots of activities; eco-friendly; under-12s stay and eat free (most packages). **Cons:** no mobile phone coverage; limited Wi-Fi; no TVs in rooms (though these could be pluses, too). [$] *Rooms from: A$419* ☎ *1300/863248, 07/4972–9055* 🌐 *www.heronisland.com* 🛏 *32 rooms, 76 suites, 1 house* 🍴 *Multiple meal plans.*

Scuba diving off Heron Island

GREAT KEPPEL ISLAND

Although Great Keppel is large, at 8 km (5 miles) by 11 km (7 miles), it lies 40 km (25 miles) from the Great Barrier Reef, which makes for a long trip from the mainland. There's lots to do, with walking trails, 17 stunning safe swimming beaches, excellent coral gardens in many sheltered coves, plenty of friendly local wildlife, and dozens of beach and water-sports activities available. A refurbished underwater observatory at nearby Middle Island lets you stay dry while viewing the local marine life from 6 meters below the ocean surface, including a confiscated Taiwanese fishing boat which has been deliberately sunk alongside the observatory to shelter tropical fish. An abundance of bushwalking tracks allows visitors to explore the island's interior and access secluded beaches. Several major resorts have closed down on Great Keppel in recent years, but there are plans in progress for their redevelopment.

GETTING HERE AND AROUND

AIR TRAVEL

Low-cost carrier Virgin Australia flies to Rockhampton from Brisbane, with connections to all major Australian cities. Qantas has direct flights to Rockhampton from Brisbane, Townsville, and Mackay, connecting to other capitals.

BOAT AND FERRY TRAVEL

Freedom Fast Cats ferries transfer guests to the island from Pier 1 at Rosslyn Bay Harbour, near Yeppoon (across the bay from the marina). Departures are mid-morning (check schedules) daily, with an additional departure Friday afternoon. Return trips back to the mainland are

Tuesday to Sunday early- to mid-afternoon, and an additional departure Friday morning. The cost is A$52 per person, round-trip. Depending on the time of your flight arrival, you may need to stay overnight in Rockhampton or Yeppoon before and after your island stay.

Keppel Bay Marina also runs day cruises to secluded coves and beaches: choose a glass-bottom-boat coral-viewing and fish-feeding cruise for A$73, or two full-day cruises: one includes a 1½-hour sail and optional snorkeling, kayaking, fishing, and coral-viewing, on Grace, plus refreshments and a buffet lunch, for A$115 per person, including reef tax and gear; a similar cruise with boom-netting is A$130.

ESSENTIALS

Airlines Peace Aviation ☎ *07/4927–4355, 0429/616758* 🌐 *www.peaceaviation.com.au.* **Virgin Australia** ☎ *13–6789* 🌐 *www.virginaustralia.com.* **Qantas** ☎ *13–1313* 🌐 *www.qantas.com.au.*

Ferries Freedom Fast Cats ☎ *07/4933–6888* 🌐 *www.freedomfastcats.com.* **Keppel Bay Marina** ☎ *07/4933–6244* 🌐 *www.keppelbaymarina.com.au.*

SPORTS AND THE OUTDOORS

WATER SPORTS

The Watersports Activities Hut. The Watersports Activities Hut at Great Keppel Island Holiday Village offers guided kayak and motorized canoe trips, and water taxi drop-offs to and pickups from surrounding beaches and islands. They also hire out water-sports equipment, including kayaks and catamarans, and offer banana and tube rides. ✉ *Fisherman's Beach, Great Keppel Island* 🌐 *www.gkiholidayvillage.com.au* 🎫 *From A$35* 🕒 *Daily.*

WHERE TO STAY

For expanded hotel reviews, visit Fodors.com.

$ RENTAL FAMILY 🏨 **Great Keppel Island Holiday Village.** Surrounded by stunning beaches and bush, this is a modest, quiet alternative for travelers looking to get back to basics without a party scene. **Pros:** beautiful and peaceful location; good value; friendly, helpful staff. **Cons:** patchy mobile phone coverage (Telstra and Optus okay); no Wi-Fi or TV; meals not provided. [$] *Rooms from: A$100* ☎ *07/4939–8655, 1800/537735* 🌐 *www.gkiholidayvillage.com.au* 🛏 *4 rooms, 2 houses, 2 cabins, 9 tents* 🍴 *No meals.*

FRASER ISLAND

Some 200 km (125 miles) north of Brisbane, Fraser Island, at 1,014 square km (391 square miles), is the largest of Queensland's islands and the most unusual. Fraser is the world's largest sand island—instead of coral reefs and coconut palms, it has wildflower-dotted meadows; 100-plus freshwater lakes; dense, tall stands of rain forest; towering dunes; sculpted, multicolor sand cliffs; up to 40,000 migratory shorebirds; and rare and endangered species including dugongs, turtles, Illidge's ant-blue butterfly, and eastern curlews—a lineup that won the island a place on UNESCO's World Heritage list.

The surf fishing is legendary, and humpback whales and their calves winter in Hervey Bay between May and September. The island also has Aboriginal sites dating back more than a millennium.

Hervey Bay is the name given to the expanse of water between Fraser Island and the Queensland coast, and to four nearby coastal towns—Urangan, Pialba, Scarness, and Torquay—that have merged into a single settlement. Hervey Bay and Rainbow Beach are the main jumping-off points for offshore excursions. (Maps and road signs usually refer to individual town names.)

> **GETTING HELP**
>
> Fraser Island does not have a resident doctor. Emergency medical assistance can be obtained at the ranger stations in Eurong, Waddy Point, and Dundubara, but these have variable hours—if no answer, phone the base station at Nambour on the mainland. Kingfisher Bay Resort has first-aid facilities and resident nursing staff.

GETTING HERE AND AROUND

AIR TRAVEL

Several direct air services on Jetstar, Qantas, and Virgin Australia connect Sydney and Fraser Coast (Hervey Bay) Airport. Wide Bay Shuttle buses link the airport to Urangan, meeting all flights.

BOAT AND FERRY TRAVEL

Numerous vehicular ferries service Fraser Island from Rainbow Beach and Hervey Bay. The *Rainbow Venture* and *Fraser Explorer* ferries run continuously 6 am–5:30 pm between Inskip Point, near Rainbow Beach, and Hook Point at the island's southern end.

The *Fraser Venture* barge makes the half-hour trip between River Heads, 20 minutes' drive south of Hervey Bay, and Wanggoolba Creek, opposite Eurong Bay Resort on the island's west coast, four times a day. The *Fraser Dawn* ferry departs from Urangan Boat Harbour for the 55-minute journey to Fraser Island's Moon Point twice a day. The thrice-daily Kingfisher vehicle barge connects River Heads with Kingfisher Bay Resort in 45 minutes. Fares for these services are interchangeable; tickets must be prebooked.

Kingfisher Bay also runs passenger catamarans from Urangan marina to Kingfisher Bay Resort on Fraser Island four times daily. The trip takes 45 minutes.

Manta Ray's two barges go between Inskip Point and Hook Point, making up to 40 round-trips daily, on demand, from 6 am to 5:30 pm. It's a short trip, so if you miss one barge the next will be along soon. Buy tickets online (recommended) or as you board.

CAR AND BUGGY TRAVEL

Fraser's east coast favors two Australian passions: beaches and vehicles. Unrestricted access has made this coast a giant sandbox for four-wheel-drive vehicles, busiest in school-holiday periods.

The southernmost tip of Fraser Island is just more than 200 km (125 miles) north of Brisbane. The simplest access is via barge from Rainbow Beach or Hervey Bay, 90 km (56 miles) farther north. For Rainbow

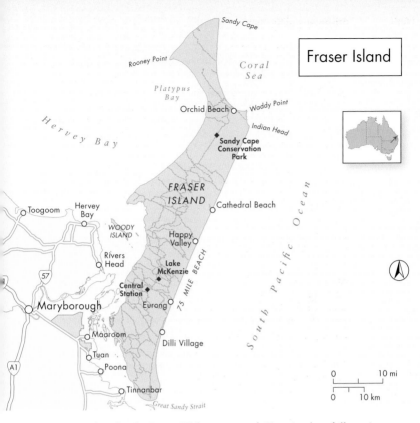

Fraser Island

Beach, take the Bruce Highway toward Gympie, then follow signs to Rainbow Beach. For Hervey Bay, head to Maryborough, then follow signs to Urangan.

Every vehicle entering the island by barge from the mainland must have a one-month Vehicle Access Permit (A$43.60). To obtain these and island camping permits (A$5.60 per person, per night), contact NPRSR.

You can rent four-wheel-drive vehicles at Kingfisher Bay Resort and Village for upward of A$280 a day, or from Budget car rentals at Urangan on the mainland for considerably less.

Four-wheel-drive rentals may be cheaper on the mainland, but factoring in the ferry ticket makes rental on-island a viable option. Most commodities, including gas, are pricier on-island.

Wet weather and sandy surfaces can make island driving challenging and hazardous. Consult NPRSR's website for detailed information on safe driving and local hazards. Basic mechanical assistance and tow-truck services are available from Eurong. Orchid Beach has emergency towing only. If you can't get the mechanical assistance you need, phone Eurong Police.

ESSENTIALS

Airport Contact Fraser Coast (Hervey Bay) Airport ✉ *Don Adams Dr., Hervey Bay* ☎ *07/4194–8100* ⊕ *www.frasercoastairport.com.au.*

Boat and Ferry Contacts Fraser Island Barges ☎ *07/4194–9300, 1800/227437* ⊕ *www.fraserislandferry.com.au.* Kingfisher Bay Ferry ☎ *1800/072555, 07/4194–9300* ⊕ *www.fraserislandferry.com.au.* Manta Ray Fraser Island Barges ☎ *07/5486–3935, 0418/872599* ⊕ *www.mantarayfraserislandbarge.com.au.*

Car Rental Budget Car Rental ✉ *Hervey Bay Airport, Airport Terminal, Hervey Bay* ☎ *07/4124–4064* ⊕ *www.budget.com.au.* Fraser Explorer Tours ☎ *1800/249122, 07/4194–9222* ⊕ *www.fraserexplorertours.com.au.* Kingfisher Bay Resort and Village ☎ *07/4194–9300, 1800/072555* ⊕ *www.kingfisherbay. com.*

Shuttle Bundaberg and Wide Bay Shuttle Service ☎ *0421/413446* ⊕ *www.bundabergshuttleservice.com.au.*

Tours Air Fraser Island ☎ *07/4125–3600* ⊕ *www.airfraserisland.com.au.* Kingfisher Bay Resort ☎ *1800/072555, 07/4194–9300* ⊕ *www.kingfisherbay. com.*

Vehicle Permits Department of National Parks, Recreation, Sport and Racing ☎ *13/137468 for info and permits* ⊕ *www.nprsr.qld.gov.au.*

Visitor Information Hervey Bay Visitor Information Centre ✉ *Hervey Bay Rd., Hervey Bay* ☎ *1800/4124–4050* ⊕ *www.visitfrasercoast.com.*

EXPLORING

Highlights of a drive along the east coast, which is known as Seventy-Five Mile Beach for its sheer distance, include **Eli Creek,** a great freshwater swimming hole. North of this popular spot lies the rusting hulk of the *Maheno,* half buried in the sand, a roost for seagulls and a prime hunting ground for anglers when the tailor are running. Once a luxury passenger steamship that operated between Australia and New Zealand (and served as a hospital ship during World War I), it was wrecked during a cyclone in 1935 as it was being towed to Japan to be sold for scrap metal. North of the wreck are the **Pinnacles**—dramatic, deep-red cliff formations. About 20 km (12 miles) south of Eli Creek, and surrounded by massive sand-blow (or dune), is **Lake Wabby,** the deepest of the island's lakes.

Note that swimming in the ocean off the island is not recommended because of the rough conditions and sharks that hunt close to shore. Stick to the inland lakes.

Fraser Island, Sandy Cape Conservation Park. This park covers the top third of Fraser Island. Beaches around Indian Head are known for their shell middens—shell heaps that were left behind after Aboriginal feasting. The head's name is another kind of relic: Captain James Cook saw Aborigines standing on the headland as he sailed past, and he therefore named the area after inhabitants he believed to be "Indians." Farther north, past Waddy Point, is one of Fraser Island's most

Camping on Fraser Island

CLOSE UP

The Queensland Parks and Wildlife Service manages the island and maintains ranger bases at Dundubara and Eurong. You can pitch a tent anywhere you don't see a "no camping" sign; there are four main public campgrounds—Central Station, Dundubara, and two at Waddy Point—though all sites on the Island require you to book your permit in advance. These campgrounds have fenced sites (advised if you have kids under 14), toilet blocks, drinking water, hot showers (some coin-operated), gas grills, phones, and other amenities. There are also smaller designated camping areas along Fraser Island's Great Walk, and a number of established beach campsites, all run by The Queensland Parks and Wildlife Service. They have toilet blocks, picnic tables, and walking trails. Most lack drinking water, so bring plenty with you. Because the entire island is a World Heritage site, permits for camping (A$5.60 per person, per night) are required.

magnificent variations on sand: wind and time have created enormous dunes. Nearby at Orchid Beach are a series of bubbling craters known as the Champagne Pools. ☎ *1300/130372* ⊕ *www.derm.qld.gov.au/ fraser.*

Wanggoolba Creek. A boardwalk heads south from Central Station to Wanggoolba Creek, a favorite spot for photographers. The little stream snakes through a green palm forest, trickling over a bed of white sand between clumps of rare angiopteris fern. The 1-km (½-mile) circuit takes 30 minutes to an hour.

SPORTS AND THE OUTDOORS
FISHING
Hervey Bay Fishing Charters. Contact Hervey Bay Fishing Charters to set up a fishing trip off Fraser Island. ✉ *51 Tristania Cr., Urangan* ☎ *07/4125–3958* ⊕ *www.herveybayfishingcharters.com.au.*

Offshore, Fraser Island. All freshwater fish are protected on Fraser Island, so you can't fish in lakes or streams, but just offshore is one of Australia's richest, most diverse fishing areas, with whiting, flathead, trevally, red emperor, snapper, sea perch, coronation trout, cod, and, in summer, mackerel, cobia, amberjack, and more. This is partly due to the diversity of habitat; choose between estuary, surf beach, reef, sport, and game fishing. On reef-fishing trips dolphins are commonly sighted, as are whales in season.

When angling off Fraser Island beaches and jetties, follow NPRSR guidelines. To discourage dingoes and other undesirable visitors, clean fish away from campsites and dispose of scraps carefully (bury fish scraps at least 30 centimeters, about a foot, below the tide line). Bag and size limits apply to some species: for details, go to ⊕ *www.nprsr. qld.gov.au.*

HIKING

Central Station. The island's excellent network of walking trails converges at Central Station, a former logging camp at the center of the island. Services here are limited to a map board, parking lot, and campground. It's a promising place for spotting dingoes. Comparative isolation has meant that Fraser Island's dingoes are the most purebred in Australia. They're also wild animals, so remember: don't feed them, watch from a distance, don't walk alone after dark, and keep a close eye on children, especially between late afternoon and early morning. Dingo alerts are in force around Eurong and Happy Valley.

Most of the island's well-marked trails are sandy tracks. Guides advise wearing sturdy shoes, wearing sunscreen, and carrying first-aid supplies and drinking water on all walks. ⊠ *Central Station.*

Pile Valley. One trail from Central Station leads through rain forest—growing, incredibly enough, straight out of the sand—to Pile Valley, which has a stand of giant satinay trees. Allow two hours to walk the full 4½-km (2¼-mile) circuit.

SWIMMING

Lake McKenzie. The center of Fraser Island is a quiet, natural garden of paperbark swamps, giant satinay and brush box forests, wildflower heaths, and 40 freshwater lakes. The spectacularly clear Lake McKenzie, ringed by a beach of incandescent white sand, is arguably the most stunning of the lakes and is the perfect place for a refreshing swim, day or night. ⊠ *Lake McKenzie.*

WHERE TO STAY

For expanded hotel reviews, visit Fodors.com.

$ 🏨 **Eurong Beach Resort.** This east-coast resort has the best of Fraser Island
RESORT at its doorstep. **Pros:** on-site general store; great location and facilities; magnificent pool. **Cons:** spotty mobile phone reception; slow, pricey Internet; decor is dated. Ⓢ *Rooms from: A$168* ⊠ *75 Mile Beach Rd.* ☎ *07/4127–9122, 1800/111808* ⊕ *www.eurong.com.au* ⤳ *124 rooms, including 16 apartments* ¶⊙¶ *Multiple meal plans.*

$$$ 🏨 **Kingfisher Bay Resort and Village.** This stylish, high-tech marriage of
RESORT glass, stainless steel, dark timber, and corrugated iron nestles in tree-cov-
FAMILY ered dunes on the island's west coast. **Pros:** terrific facilities and activities;
Fodor'sChoice eco-friendly; food is a cut above. **Cons:** west-coast beaches unsuitable
★ for 4WD vehicles; can be short-staffed during busy periods. Ⓢ *Rooms from: A$288* ⊠ *North White Cliffs, 75 Mile Beach* ☎ *07/4194–9300, 1800/072555* ⊕ *www.kingfisherbay.com* ⤳ *152 rooms, 109 villas, 184 beds in lodges (for 18–35s)* ¶⊙¶ *Multiple meal plans.*

8

THE GREAT BARRIER REEF

Including Cairns and the North Coast

WELCOME TO GREAT BARRIER REEF

TOP REASONS TO GO

★ **Reef Explorations:** There are thousands of spectacular dive sites scattered along the coral spine of the Great Barrier Reef. Some draw hundreds of divers and snorkelers a day with clouds of fish and coral formations.

★ **Wildlife Watching:** Flora and fauna on the islands themselves can be fascinating: rain forests, hills and rocky areas, and postcard-perfect beaches provide diverse habitat for everything from turtles, birds, and lizards to echidnas and bandicoots. On the mainland, Daintree National Park is home to the endangered southern cassowary.

★ **Cultural Immersion:** The Kuku Yalanji people have lived in the area between Port Douglas and Cookdown for millennia. A highlight of visiting the region is experiencing this unique landscape from the perspective of its traditional owners. Several day and multiday tours allow you to experience Kuku Yalanji culture and visit some of the area's spiritually significant sites.

1 Cairns. A laid-back tropical tourist hub built around a busy marina and swimming lagoon, Cairns bristles with hotels, tour agencies, dive-cruise boats, and travelers en route to the rain forest and reef. It has some fine retail stores and markets, plus a waterfront entertainment precinct.

2 North of Cairns. The pristine coastline north of Cairns is punctuated by charming villages and tourist towns, including Palm Cove, with its European Riviera ambience, and bustling Port Douglas, with its busy marina, sprawling resorts, and hip café scene. North of the Daintree River, World Heritage–listed wilderness extends to Cape Tribulation and beyond; here you'll find few services but some terrific, eco-friendly rain-forest retreats.

3 Whitsundays/Airlie Beach. The glorious Whitsunday Islands, just off the mid-north-Queensland coast, lure holidaymakers with world-class water sports, sheltered yacht anchorages, and resorts catering to every taste. Airlie Beach, the closest mainland town, buzzes with backpackers, who flock to its man-made lagoon, markets, bars, and budget digs. Well-heeled travelers might prefer the boutique retreats and resorts that hug the hillsides above the main drag.

4 North Coast islands. The upscale, eco-conscious boutique resort on Orpheus and Bedarra island, off Ingham and Mission Beach, is tailored to foodies and honeymooners, reclusive VIPs, and nature-loving travelers. Lizard and Fitzroy islands, off Cairns, offer ready access to world-class dive and game-fishing sites.

5 Townsville and Magnetic Island. Regional city Townsville has gracious heritage buildings, excellent museums and marine centers, and a well-maintained waterfront with a man-made swimming lagoon. Offshore, Magnetic Island is a popular holiday spot, with high-end and budget accommodation and an array of aquatic activities, including sea kayaking and scuba diving.

GETTING ORIENTED

A map linking all of northern Queensland's coastal ports and off-shore resorts from the Whitsundays north to Lizard Island would look like a lace-up boot 1,600 km (1,000 miles) long. However, you'd only see less than half the reef, which extends south to Lady Elliot Island and as far north as the near-roadless wilderness of Cape York and the shores of Papua New Guinea. If you're visiting the reef only briefly, it's simplest and most economical to day-trip from the mainland. Some reef-island resorts are accessible by boat; others can be reached only by plane, and both airfare and lodging rates can be expensive. Day trips depart from major coastal cities including Cairns, Port Douglas, Townsville, and Airlie Beach. Some island resorts, such as Hamilton, let you visit and use their facilities for the day—then return you to the mainland.

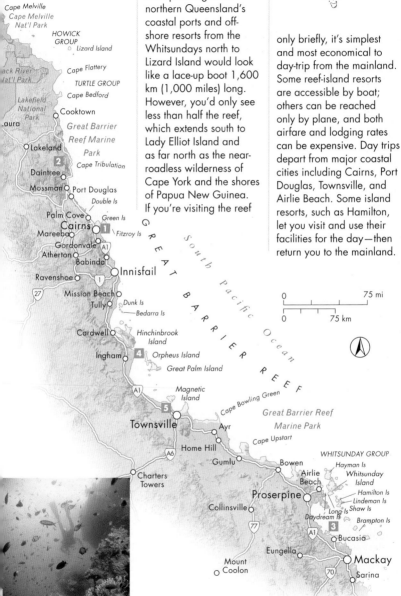

8

0   75 mi

0   75 km

SAILING THE WHITSUNDAY ISLANDS

The Whitsundays, 74 islands and dozens of islets scattered along Queensland's central coast off Airlie Beach, are favorite destinations among yachties and beach-lovers—and with good reason.

The Whitsunday islands, protected from Coral Sea swells by sheltering reefs and cooled by trade winds, offer hundreds of yacht anchorages in close proximity, making this ideal cruising territory. The aquamarine waters shimmer and sparkle—a light-scattering effect that results when fine sediment run-off from river systems is stirred up by the 3- to 5-meter tides that sweep the coast.

Island resorts offer safe moorings for passing yachts, and an array of water sports and facilities. Farther out, on the Barrier Reef, you'll find fine snorkeling, diving, and fishing sites. Most Whitsunday Islands are unspoiled national parks; just a few—Hayman, Hamilton, Daydream, South Molle, and South Long—have resorts.

WHEN TO GO

With a climate moderated by cooling trade winds, the Whitsundays are typically balmy year-round, though summer days can sometimes exceed 100 degrees Fahrenheit. Over winter (June–August) it's warm, clear, and sunny by day and cool—even chilly—at night. Steer clear of Australia's summer holidays to avoid hordes of local families who, despite often wet and stormy weather, flock here December to February. Spring and fall weather can be perfect, and these seasons are often the quietest, if you avoid school and Easter holidays. Migrating southern right and humpback whales traverse these waters between July and September.

WHERE CAN I FIND...

Underwater adventure? Most Whitsundays resorts have dedicated dive shops offering scuba and snorkeling lessons and gear hire; all either run or can organize day trips to dive and snorkeling spots nearby. Highlights include Heart Reef and vast Knuckle Reef Lagoon, where a purpose-built pontoon floats in sheltered waters teeming with tropical fish, turtles, and rays. Not keen to get wet? Take a semisubmersible coral-viewing tour, guided reef walk, or scenic heli-flight.

Luxury? At Qualia, Hamilton Island's most lavish accommodation, sleek suites have infinity pools and alfresco areas, artfully lighted after dark, and fine food and wine brought in from Hamilton's best restaurants. Bedarra, Orpheus, and Lizard Island resorts serve up gourmet meals and exclusive accommodations, while Paradise Bay Island Resort pampers its select group of guests with top-quality, all-natural furnishings and fabrics, Molton Brown toiletries, and cruises on the resort's own sailing cat. Recently revamped Hayman Resort, a magnificent sprawl of public areas and opulent suites, is solid enough to withstand a Category 5 cyclone and luxurious enough to satisfy the fussiest visitor. Here your needs are more than met: they're often spookily anticipated.

Family-friendliness? BreakFree Long Island Resort's jam-packed sports and activities program offers dozens of aquatic and land-based sports, most included in the rates. Daydream and Hamilton islands have dedicated kids' clubs, playgrounds, and myriad kid-at-heart features and activities. At Fitzroy Island Resort, children's activity programs mean parents can relax or join in the fun, while nature-based activities on Lizard and Hayman islands are great for older kids.

TOP REASONS TO GO

Aquatic playground
This is a snorkelers' and divers' paradise and one of the world's top sailing and cruising areas. It's also great for kayaking, windsurfing, and paragliding—and most resorts include nonmotorized water sports in their rates.

Tropical paradise
Enjoy a mild climate and warm, clear waters whatever the season, plus beautiful fine-white-sand beaches.

Gourmet destination
Several Whitsunday and Barrier Reef island resorts offer cuisine to rival that of high-end city establishments. Island-resort food runs the gamut from four-star gourmet fare to regional cuisine presented with site-specific twists.

Resort variety
You can easily divide your time between luxurious, leisurely resorts (such as Hayman, Lizard Island Resort, or Paradise Bay Island Resort on South Long Island) and a gregarious, activity-oriented isle (such as Hamilton or Daydream).

8

OUTDOOR ADVENTURES IN DAINTREE

Cape Tribulation, Daintree National Park is an ecological wonderland. Here you can see several of the world's most ancient plants and some of Australia's rarest creatures, protected by the Daintree's traditional owners, the Eastern Kuku Yalanji, for thousands of years.

The park extends over approximately 22,000 acres, although the entire Wet Tropics region—which stretches from Townsville to Cooktown and covers 1,200 square km (463 square miles)—was declared a UNESCO World Heritage site in 1988. Within it, experts have identified several species of angiosperms, the most primitive flowering plants in existence, many of which are found nowhere else on the planet.

WHEN TO GO

Clear, sunny days, comfortably cool nights, no stingers in the ocean and mud-free rain forest and mangrove trails: "the Dry" season is the most pleasant time to visit.

"The Wet"—roughly November through April—can be wonderful, too: foliage is lush and green; buds turn to hothouse blooms. Drawbacks include occasional flash flooding and road closures, high humidity, slippery tracks, and leeches and mosquitoes.

Spring and late fall can be a good compromise: the weather—and the water—are typically warm and clear, and activities are less heavily booked than during the dry season.

A SACRED SITE

With diverse plant and animal life, abundant fresh water, and tracts of fertile coastal lowland, the Daintree rain forest is rich terrain for the resourceful. Its traditional custodians are the Eastern Kuku Yalanji, a peaceable people who've been coexisting with and subsisting on the forest's abundant flora and fauna for tens of thousands of years. Their tribal lands stretch north almost as far as Cooktown, south as far as Mossman and west to the Palmer River, with the Kuku Yalanji traveling seasonally throughout the region.

Designating five rather than four seasons in a year, the Eastern Kuku Yalanji used changes in weather and growth cycles to guide hunting and foraging expeditions into the rain forest: when the *jun jun* (blue ginger) came into fruit, they'd catch *diwan* (Australian brush-turkey); when *jilngan* (mat grass) flowered, they'd collect *jarruka* (orange-footed scrubfowl) eggs; and year-round, they'd track tree-dwelling animals—*yawa* (possum), *kambi* (flying fox), and *murral* (tree kangaroo). Even today, members of the Kuku Yalanji can tell you which local plants can be eaten, used as medicines, and made into utensils, weapons, and shelter.

The Daintree's indigenous inhabitants believe many of the area's natural sites have spiritual significance, attributing particular power to Wundu (Thornton Peak), Manjal Dimbi (Mt. Demi), Wurrmbu (The Bluff), and Kulki (Cape Tribulation). Dozens of spots in the rain forest—waterfalls, crags, peaks, and creeks—are deemed by the Kuku Yalanji to have spiritual, healing, or regenerative powers. Take a walk with one of the area's traditional custodians to get an intimate, intriguing perspective on this extraordinary terrain.

Various indigenous-guided tours and experiences in the Daintree area focus on bush tucker and medicines, wildlife and hunting techniques, culture, history, and ritual. A waterhole just behind Daintree Eco Lodge & Spa is deemed a site of special significance for women: a dip in its healing waters is a female-only ritual.

TOP REASONS TO GO

Animals. Watch for the rare Bennett's tree kangaroo, believed to have evolved from possums; the endangered, spotted-tailed quoll, a marsupial carnivore; a giant white-tailed rat (prone to raiding campsites); and the Daintree River ringtail possum, found only around Thornton Peak and the upper reaches of the Daintree and Mossman rivers.

Birds. Daintree National Park shelters hundreds of bird species: azure kingfishers swoop on crabs in the creeks, white-rumped swiftlets dart above the canopy. The pied imperial pigeon flies south from Papua New Guinea to breed here—as does the glorious buff-breasted paradise kingfisher, distinguished by its orange underbelly, blue wings, and long white tail. Year-round, you'll see orange-footed scrubfowl foraging or building gigantic leaf-litter nest-mounds. If you're very lucky, you might even spot the 6-foot-tall, flightless southern cassowary.

8

Updated by
Merran White

A maze of 3,000 individual reefs and 900 islands stretching for 2,600 km (1,616 miles), the Great Barrier Reef is among the world's most spectacular natural attractions. Known as Australia's "Blue Outback," the reef is a haven for thousands of species of marine creatures as well as turtles and birds. Most visitors explore this section of Australia from one of the dozen-plus resorts strung along the coasts of islands in the southern half of the marine park, most of them in or north of the Whitsunday Islands group. Although most Barrier Reef islands are closer to the mainland than they are to the spectacular outer reef, all island resorts offer (or can organize) boat excursions to various outer-reef sites.

The reef was established as a marine park in 1975, and the United Nations designated the Great Barrier Reef a World Heritage site in 1981. Strict legislation was enacted in 2004, prohibiting fishing along most of the reef—a further attempt to protect the underwater treasures of this vast, delicate ecosystem. Any visitor over the age of four must pay an A$3.50 per day Environmental Management Charge ("reef tax") to support ongoing efforts to preserve the reef.

The Great Barrier Reef system began to form approximately 6,000–7,000 years ago, say marine scientists. It's comprised of individual reefs and islands, which lie to the east of the Coral Sea and extend south into the Pacific Ocean. Most of the reef is about 65 km (40 miles) off the Queensland coast, although some parts extend as far as 300 km (186 miles) offshore. Altogether, it covers an area bigger than Great Britain, forming the largest living feature on Earth and the only one visible from space.

PLANNING

WHEN TO GO

The bulk of the Great Barrier Reef islands lie north of the tropic of Capricorn in a monsoonal climate zone. In the hot, wet season (roughly December–April), expect tropical downpours that can limit outdoor activities and mar underwater visibility.

The warm days, clear skies, and pleasantly cool nights of the dry season, especially June–August, are ideal for traveling around and above Cairns. In the Whitsundays, some winter days may be too cool for swimming and nights can be chilly (pack a sweater and long pants).

The islands are warm, even in winter; during the summer months, temperatures regularly top 35 degrees Celsius (95 degrees Fahrenheit), and the farther north you go, the hotter it gets. The water temperature is mild to cool year-round; however, in jellyfish season (typically, November through May), you'll need to wear a full-body stinger suit to swim anywhere but within patrolled, netted areas.

GETTING HERE AND AROUND

AIR TRAVEL

Jetstar, Virgin Australia, and Qantas have daily direct flights linking capital cities around Australia to Cairns Airport (which also handles international flights). These airlines also have flights to Townsville, Whitsundays Coast (Proserpine), Hamilton Island, and Mackay airports, linking with east-coast capitals and major regional cities throughout Queensland. From these hubs, regular boat and charter air services are available to most of the Great Barrier Reef resorts. Generally, island charter flights are timed to connect with domestic flights, but double-check. ⇨ *For information about reaching the islands, see Getting Here and Around under each island's heading.*

BOAT TRAVEL

Usually, island launches are timed to connect with charter flights from island or mainland airports, but do ask. Crossings can be choppy; take ginger tablets for motion sickness ahead of time. If you're based on the mainland or in a hurry, many operators run day trips out to the reef and resort islands.

Several operators provide skipper-yourself (bareboat) and crewed charters to explore the Whitsundays. Almost all have five-day minimum charter periods; most offer discounts for multiday hire and optional extras such as catering. Packages start from around A$120 per person, per night, but can be several times that on crewed or luxury vessels.

BUS TRAVEL

Long-distance buses are an economical but often cramped way to travel along the North Queensland coast; don't expect to get much sleep on board. Shuttle buses transfer visitors from regional airports, Cairns, and beaches and towns to as far north as Cape Tribulation. They link airports, railway stations, and local towns to island ferry services departing from Mission Beach, Airlie Beach, and Shute Harbour. Hotel pickups are usually available; call ahead to confirm.

8

CAR TRAVEL

If you're visiting several North Queensland destinations, it may be simplest to drive. Most popular North Queensland routes are paved, though roads may be flooded in the wet season. A 4WD vehicle is advised. Leave extra time if you're crossing the Daintree River or driving between Port Douglas and Cairns—peak-season traffic and roadwork may create congestion. If you're heading farther north, fill up with gas at or before Wonga Beach, and carry water, tools, and supplies. Past this point, services are infrequent, and gas and goods can be pricey.

RESTAURANTS

Typically, restaurants on Barrier Reef islands are part of each island's main resort, so many resorts' rates include some or all meals. Some larger resorts have a range of restaurants, with formal dining rooms, outdoor barbecues, and seafood buffets; some have premium dining options for which you pay extra. Dress is generally "island casual." Some upscale restaurants—such as those on Hayman Island—require men to wear jackets for dinner and frown on flip-flop sandals. On the mainland you'll find plenty of casual, open-air restaurants, serving mainly Modern Australian–style meals that showcase seafood and regional produce. With a few notable exceptions, Cairns, Palm Cove, and Port Douglas are your best bets for upscale dining. *Prices in the reviews are the average cost of a main course at dinner or, if dinner is not served, at lunch.*

HOTELS

Most inhabited islands have just one main resort, typically offering a range of lodging types and prices. Choose island destinations based on your budget and the kind of vacation you want—active or relaxed, sociable or quiet, or a mix. Offerings range from luxurious enclaves with upscale facilities (Lizard, Orpheus, Bedarra, Hayman islands) to small, eco-focused retreats (Long Island) to activity-packed, family-friendly resorts (Long, South Molle, Daydream, and Fitzroy islands). The more rustic, remote resorts may lack modern conveniences such as, telephones, televisions, and Internet access. Even on some Barrier Reef resorts, Internet connections can be slow and mobile phone coverage limited or nonexistent, and critters may infiltrate your room. *Prices in the reviews are the lowest cost of a standard double room in high season. For expanded reviews, facilities, and current deals, visit Fodors.com.*

HEALTH AND SAFETY

You'll find large, well-equipped hospitals in Cairns, Townsville, and Mackay; doctors in Port Douglas and Airlie Beach, and nearby towns. Emergency services are scarce between the Daintree River and Cooktown. Island resort front-desk staff typically handle emergencies and can summon doctors and aerial ambulance services. Remote islands have "flying doctor" kits; Hamilton Island has its own doctors and Hayman has an on-site medical center. Contact Cairns Health Online (⊕ *www.cairnshealthonline.com*) for a list of GPs, hospitals, and pharmacies in the region.

GREAT ITINERARIES

Most visitors to the Great Barrier Reef combine stays on one or more islands with time in Queensland's coastal towns and national parks. With a week or more, you could stay at two very different Barrier Reef island resorts: perhaps at an activities-packed Whitsundays resort and one of the more remote northerly islands, allowing a day or two to travel between them. If you want to resort-hop, opt for the Whitsundays, where island resorts lie in relatively close proximity and are well serviced by water and air transport.

IF YOU HAVE 1 DAY
Take a boat from Cairns or Port Douglas to a pontoon on the outer reef for a day on the water.

A helicopter flight back to the mainland will give you an exhilarating aerial view of the reef and its islands. Alternatively, catch an early boat from Cairns to **Fitzroy Island** or from Shute Harbour to **Daydream Island**. Spend a couple of hours snorkeling, take a walk around, then relax on a quiet beach or in the resort bar.

IF YOU HAVE 3 DAYS
Pick one island that offers a variety of aquatic and land-based activities and attractions—flora and fauna, beaches and dive sites, sports and relaxation facilities, resort-style nightlife—and give yourself a taste of everything.

Avoid midday rays, even in winter, and wear a hat and SPF15+ sunscreen to prevent sunburn. Rehydrate often and take it easy in the heat.

Avoid touching coral: it is easily damaged, and can cut and sting. Clean cuts thoroughly, scrubbing with a brush and flushing the affected area with saline solution. Toxic and stinging jellyfish frequent waters off the mainland and some Barrier Reef islands over the warmer months. Avoid the ocean at these times, unless you're wearing a stinger suit. If in doubt, ask a local.

Mosquitoes, midges, and leeches can be a problem in wet summer months. Wear insect repellent to avoid being bitten; check extremities, especially between your toes, after walking in damp, forested areas, and remove leeches by applying a flame or salt.

Estuarine crocodiles live in rivers and coastal waters along the North Queensland coast and on some Barrier Reef islands. Don't swim where crocs live (ask a local), especially in breeding season, September to April—and never dangle your limbs over the sides of boats.

CAIRNS

Tourism is the lifeblood of Cairns (pronounced *Caans*). The city makes a good base for exploring the wild top half of Queensland, and tens of thousands of international travelers use it as a jumping-off point for activities such as scuba diving and snorkeling trips to the Barrier Reef, as well as boating, fishing, parasailing, scenic flights, and rainforest treks.

It's a tough environment, with intense heat and fierce wildlife. Along with wallabies and grey kangaroos in the savannah and tree kangaroos in the rain forest, you'll find stealthy saltwater crocodiles, venomous snakes, and jellyfish so deadly they put the region's stunning beaches off-limits to swimmers for nearly half the year. Yet despite this formidable setting, Cairns and tropical North Queensland are far from intimidating places. The people are warm and friendly, the sights spectacular, and—at the right time of year—the beachside lounging is world-class.

> ### ATM LOGISTICS
>
> Resorts on the following islands have money-changing facilities: Daydream, Fitzroy, Hamilton, Hayman, Lizard, Long, and Orpheus. It's better to change money before arriving on any resort island, however, as rates are generally more favorable on the mainland.

GETTING HERE AND AROUND

AIR TRAVEL

Cairns Airport is a major international gateway, and a connection point for flights to other parts of Queensland, including Townsville, Mackay, Rockhampton, Hamilton Island, and the Northern Territory, as well as all Australia's capital cities.

Airport Connections runs coaches between Cairns International Airport and town—an 8-km (5-mile) trip that takes about 10 minutes and costs A$14. The company also services Cairns's northern beaches, Palm Cove, Port Douglas, Silky Oaks Lodge (near Mossman), and Cape Tribulation (A$22 to upward of A$54), as well as Mission Beach to the south. Port Douglas–based Exemplar Express Chauffeured Coaches and Limousines provides bus services direct from the airport to Palm Cove and Port Douglas, just over an hour's drive north of Cairns by coach or limousine. Private taxis make these trips as well (A$23–A$27, airport to Cairns).

CAR TRAVEL

Between Brisbane and Cairns, the Bruce Highway rarely touches the coast. Unless you're planning to stop off en route or explore the Great Green Way, fly or take the fast Tilt Train or *Spirit of Queenslander* (⊕ *www.queenslandrailtravel.com.au*)train to Cairns, renting a vehicle on arrival. Avis, Budget, Hertz, and Europcar all have rental cars and four-wheel-drive vehicles available. An economical, reliable alternative is Cairns Leisure Wheels, just off Captain Cook Highway; it offers free delivery and pickup.

TOURS

BOAT TOURS

Fodor's Choice ★ Long-established Ocean Spirit Cruises runs full-day tours to glorious Michaelmas Cay, a remote Great Barrier Reef sand isle encircled by fish- and turtle-filled coral gardens. Cruise out to the cay on *Ocean Spirit*, a 105-foot luxury sailing catamaran, for four hours of guided snorkeling, semisubmersible coral-viewing tours, and marine biologist presentations, with a full buffet lunch, morning and afternoon tea, snorkeling gear, and reef tax included in the A$182 per person cost. *Ocean Spirit* departs daily from Cairns Reef Fleet Terminal. Transfers from Cairns and the Northern Beaches are available (A$19–A$26).

Coral Princess Cruise's comfortable expedition-style ships take no more than 50 passengers on three- (from A$1,347), four- (from A$1,685), and seven-day (from A$2,577) live-aboard trips, departing Cairns daily. Exclusive outer Barrier Reef moorings mean you see more of the marine life. Stops at Lizard, Dunk, and Fitzroy islands as well as CPC's own idyllic isle, Pelorus, allow you ample time to relax and explore. Friendly all-Aussie crew, dive guides, and an onboard marine biologist ensure scuba novices are up to speed and snorkelers are catered for. The per-person fare includes a glass-bottom coral-viewing tour, scuba skills sessions, snorkeling gear, twin-berth accommodation, all meals, and most activities.

NATURE TOURS

BTS Tours runs various trips out of Cairns and Port Douglas (and shuttle services between the two). From Cairns or Port Douglas, the popular full-day Daintree tour includes a croc-spotting river cruise, canoeing, swimming in rain-forest pools, guided walks, and a barbecue lunch (A$160–A$165). You could also take a half-day Mossman Gorge tour, which includes a 90-minute Kuku Yalanji–guided rain-forest walk, bush tea, and free time to swim, sightsee, and explore the Gorge (A$72).

Advanced eco–certified Wilderness Challenge runs 12-day Outback Queensland & Dinosaur Trail tours departing Cairns or the Gold Coast (A$4,995 per person, twin-share, or A$5,845 sole use), and 5- to 12-day fly/drive trips to Cape York Peninsula during the dry season, May through early October. Two popular five-day, fly/drive rock-art and rain-forest camping safaris between Cairns and Cape York cost A$1,895 and A$2,295 twin-share, or A$1,995/A$2,445 sole use; seven-day accommodated Cape York tours are A$3,295 twin-share, A$3,915 sole use. Most tours visit the world-renowned Quinkan Aboriginal rock-art site near Laura and stay in bush cabins and/or safari tents. All tours have a maximum of 12 guests and two senior guides.

Eco-certified Down Under Tours makes various half- and full-day trips and four-wheel-drive excursions, as well as reef trips, river cruises, white-water rafting, bungee jumping, and hot-air ballooning adventures, most departing from Cairns. Popular guided half- and full-day excursions take in the attractions of Kuranda (A$195–A$204), Hartley's Crocodile Adventures (A$89), and Mossman Gorge, the Daintree, and Cape Tribulation (A$189).

Blazing Saddles Adventures organizes two-hour horse rides (A$120) and all-terrain vehicle tours (A$130). A full-day horse-riding and ATV touring is A$195, and includes transfers, morning tea, gear, and a barbecue lunch. Each rider pays insurance of A$15.

CULTURAL TOURS

The Eastern Kuku Yalanji people have called the Daintree area home for tens of thousands of years, and have an intimate understanding of the terrain. Today the Kubirri Warra brothers pass on a little of that boundless ancestral wisdom on two-hour beach, mudflat, and mangrove walks (daily, 9:30 am and 1:30 pm, A$75) with Adventure North's

Kuku Yalanji Cultural Habitat Tours. Learn techniques for throwing spears, tracking coastal food sources, and much more from your knowledgeable, skillful guides. The company also offers two-hour night spearfishing walks (daily from 7:30 pm, A$150), as well as tour combinations and themed options, including multiday packages. Transfers between the Port Douglas area and Cooya Beach, a 25-minute drive north, are A$30. On Adventure North's Daintree Dreaming Tours, you can explore Cooya Beach and coastal mangroves, World Heritage–listed Daintree rain-forest trails, and Mossman Gorge with the area's traditional owners (A$209).

ESSENTIALS

Airport and Transfers Airport Connections ☎ 07/4098–2800 ⊕ www.tnqshuttle.com. **Cairns Airport** ⊠ Mick Borzi Dr. off Airport Ave., Aeroglen ☎ 07/4080–6703 ⊕ www.cairnsairport.com.

Boat Information Coral Princess Cruises ⊠ Head office, 24 Redden St., Portsmith ☎ 07/4040–9999, 1800/079545 ⊕ www.coralprincess.com.au. **Ocean Spirit Cruises** ⊠ Office 3–Level 1, Shangri-La Marina, 1 Spence St., CBD ☎ 07/4031–2920 ⊕ www.oceanspirit.com.au.

Car Rental Cairns Leisure Wheels ⊠ 314 Sheridan St., CBD ☎ 07/4051–8988 ⊕ www.leisurewheels.com.au.

Tour Operators Adventure North Australia: Daintree Dreaming Tour ⊠ 36 Aplin St. ☎ 07/4028–3376 ⊕ www.adventurenorthaustralia.com. **Blazing Saddles Adventures** ⊠ 154 Yorkeys Knob Rd., Kuranda ☎ 07/4085–0197 ⊕ www.blazingsaddles.com.au. **BTS Tours** ⊠ 49 Macrossan St., Port Douglas ☎ 07/4099–5665 ⊕ www.btstours.com.au. **Down Under Tours** ⊠ 26 Redden St., CBD ☎ 07/4035–5566 ⊕ www.downundertours.com. **Kuku Yalanji Cultural Habitat Tours** ☎ 07/4098–3437 ⊕ www.bamaway.com.au/KukuYalanji. **Wilderness Challenge 4WD Adventure Safaris** ☎ 07/4035–4488, 1800/354486 ⊕ www.wilderness-challenge.com.au.

Visitor Information The Cairns & Tropical North Visitor Information Centre (TTNQ) ⊠ 51 The Esplanade, between Spence and Shield Sts., CBD ☎ 07/4051–3588, 1800/093300 ⊕ www.cairnsgreatbarrierreef.org.au.

EXPLORING

Cosmopolitan Cairns, the unofficial capital of Far North Queensland, is Australia's 15th-largest city, with a burgeoning population pushing 135,000—more than 283,000 when you include the thriving hinterland). Once a sleepy tropical town sprawled around Trinity Bay and Inlet, the city has expanded hugely in recent decades, and now extends north to Holloway's Beach, west to the Atherton Tablelands, and south along the Great Green Way as far as Edmonton.

TOP ATTRACTIONS

FAMILY **Australian Butterfly Sanctuary.** More than 1,500 tropical butterflies—including dozens of the electric-blue Ulysses species and Australia's largest butterfly, the green-and-gold Cairns Birdwing—flutter within a compact rain-forest aviary, alighting on foliage, interpretative signage, and feeding stations. About 24,000 pupae are released into the

Australian
Butterfly
Sanctuary **9**

Birdworld
Kuranda **12**

Cairns Marlin
Marina **5**

Cairns Regional
Gallery **4**

The Esplanade **1**

Kuranda Koala
Gardens **11**

Kuranda Scenic
Railway **2**

Reef Teach **3**

Skyrail Rainforest
Cableway **8**

Tanka Arts
Centre **7**

Tjapukai
Aboriginal
Culture Park ...**10**

Undara Volcanic
National Park **6**

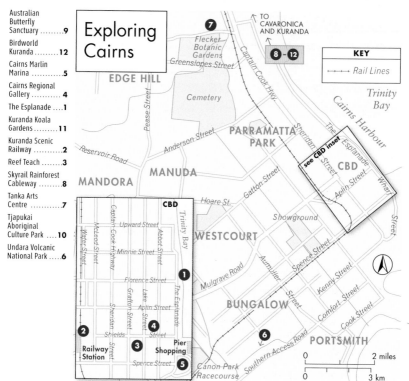

aviary each year, ensuring the colorful spectacle continues. Free half-hour guided tours of the aviary and caterpillar breeding area are full of fascinating tidbits. ⊠ *8 Rob Veivers Dr., Kuranda* ☎ *07/4093–7575* ⊕ *www.australianbutterflies.com* ☛ *A$19 entry and guided tour; A$56 2-park package (Australian Butterfly Sanctuary and Rainforestation); A$80 4-park package (Australian Butterfly Sanctuary, Rainforestation, Cairns Dome Zoo, and Wildlife Habitat in Port Douglas)* ⊗ *Daily 9:45–4, tours 10:15–3:15.*

FAMILY **Cairns Regional Gallery.** Occupying the impressive former Public Office Building constructed in the 1930s, Cairns Regional Gallery houses a hodgepodge of local, national, international, and indigenous artworks, including a fine collection of Australian photography, in its wood-paneled rooms. The shop stocks high-quality Australian giftware, toys, jewelry, prints, books, and cards. Prebook an hour-long guided tour; there are also kids' programs, classes, talks, and workshops. ⊠ *City Place, Shields and Abbott Sts., CBD* ☎ *07/4046–4800* ⊕ *www. cairnsregionalgallery.com.au* ☛ *A$5 (free, 1st Sat. of the month and for under-16s)* ⊗ *Weekdays 9–5, Sat. 10–5, Sun. 10–2.*

FAMILY **The Esplanade.** Fronting Cairns Harbour, this boardwalk is the focal
Fodor's Choice point of life in Cairns. Along the walk you'll encounter shady trees and
★ public art, picnic and barbecue facilities, a large saltwater swimming

SCENIC DRIVE: THE GREAT GREEN WAY

Great Green Way. A scenic section of the Bruce Highway locals call the Great Green Way links Cairns with Townsville, taking you through sugarcane, papaya, and banana plantations, past white-sand beaches and an island-dotted ocean. The 348-km (216-mile) drive takes about 4½ hours. ⊠ *Bruce Hwy. between Cairns and Townsville.*

Babinda Boulders. This is a popular swimming hole—and a sacred Aboriginal site. It's 7 km (5 miles) inland on The Boulders Road from the town of Babinda, accessible via the Bruce Highway about 60 km (37 miles) south of Cairns. You can also hike to the boulders, taking the 19-km (12-mile) **Goldfield Track (Wooroonooran National Park)** that starts in Goldsborough Valley, southwest of Cairns, and ends in Babinda Boulders car park. ⊠ *Babinda Information Centre, 1 Munro St., Babinda* ☎ *07/4067–1008 info center, 07/4067–6304 park ranger, 13–7468 camping* ⊕ *www. babindainfocentre.com.au* ⊙ *Information center daily 9–4.*

Paronella Park. A sprawling Spanish-style castle and gardens grace this offbeat National Trust site in the Mena Creek Falls rain forest. Explore the park on a self-guided botanical walk or 45-minute guided tour, enjoy Devonshire tea on the café's deck, buy local arts and crafts, and cool off under a 40-foot waterfall. On hour-long torch-lighted evening tours, you might spot eels, water dragons, fireflies, and glowworms. Allow at least three hours to explore. It's around 1½ hours' (about 60 miles) drive south of Cairns via the Bruce Highway. ⊠ *1671 Japoonvale Rd. (Old Bruce Hwy.), Mena Creek* ☎ *07/4065–0000* ⊕ *www.paronellapark.com.au* ⊒ *A$40* ⊙ *Daily 9–7:30.*

Tully Gorge National Park. In the wettest zone of the Wet Tropics World Heritage area, the mighty Tully River is a magnet for white-water rafters. Access Tully Gorge National Park via the town of Tully, 141 km (88 miles) or about two hours' drive south of Cairns, then continue for 54 km (34 miles)—approximately 40 minutes—along Jarra Creek and Cardstone roads to Kareeya Hydroelectric Station parking lot and viewing platform. Other excellent vantage points are the Tully Falls lookout, 24 km (15 miles) south of Ravenshoe, and the Flip Wilson and Frank Roberts lookouts. September to February, the short, wheelchair-accessible Rainforest Butterfly walk is filled with brilliant creatures. ⊠ *Tully Falls Rd., Koombooloomba* ☎ *07/4068–2288 ParksQ ranger, 13–7468 camping permits and general enquiries* ⊕ *www.nprsr.qld. gov.au/parks.*

Wooroonooran National Park. Extending south of Gordonvale to the Palmerston Highway near Innisfail, this is one of the most densely vegetated areas in Australia. Rain forest rules, from the lowland tropical variety to the stunted growth on Mt. Bartle Frere—at 5,287 feet, the highest point in Queensland. Tracks range from the easy 30-minute treks to challenging two-day trails. Josephine Falls is 75 km (47 miles) south of Cairns off the Bruce Highway, near Miriwinni. ⊠ *Josephine Falls Rd., Bartle Frere* ☎ *07/4067–1008 Babinda Information Centre* ⊕ *www.nprsr.qld.gov.au/ parks.*

lagoon, volleyball courts, an imaginative kids' playground, state-of-the-art skate plaza, and areas for fitness, markets, and live entertainment. A shallow, 4,800-square-meter (51,667-square-foot) saltwater lagoon swimming pool with a sandy shore, decking, and shelters, patrolled by lifeguards year-round, provides free, convenient relief from the often sticky air. Along the street opposite, you'll find shops, galleries, and eateries. ⊠ *The Esplanade, between Spence and Upward Sts., CBD* ☎ *07/4044-3715* ⊕ *www.cairnsesplanade.com.au* ⊠ *Free* ⊙ *Pool: daily 6 am–9 pm, closed Wed. 6 am–noon; Muddy's playground: daily 9 am–7 pm; volleyball courts: daily 9 am–9:30 pm, closed Wed. until 4; Esplanade Market: Sat. 8–4.*

FAMILY **Kuranda Scenic Railway.** The historic Kuranda Scenic Railway makes a 115-minute ascent through rain forest and 15 hand-hewn tunnels to pretty Kuranda village, gateway to the Atherton Tableland. Opt for a simple Heritage Class seat or splurge on a Gold Class ticket with fine local food and wine, table service, swanky decor, and a souvenir pack. Several tour packages are available, from full-day rain-forest safaris and visits to local Aboriginal centers and wildlife parks to simple round-trips combining rail and cable-car journeys. ⊠ *Cairns Railway Station, Bunda St., CBD* ☎ *07/4036–9333, 1800/079033* ⊕ *www.ksr.com. au* ⊠ *1-way ticket A$49–$A97, round-trip A$74–A$170; combined railway/cable-car/wildlife/aboriginal culture packages A$142–A$160* ⊙ *Departs from Cairns daily 8:30 am and 9:30 am, Kuranda at 2 and 3:30; Gold Class only on 9:30 and 3:30 services.*

FAMILY
Fodor's Choice
★
Reef Teach. Knowledgeable marine biologists and conservationists give entertaining talks and multimedia presentations, usually to packed houses about everything Great Barrier Reef–related, from sea turtles' sleep cycles to coral-killing starfish. Expect to learn more than you thought possible about the reef's evolution and the diverse inhabitants of this delicate marine ecosystem. The attached Marine Shop sells an array of reef-themed merchandise: T-shirts, DVDs, books, field guides, and souvenirs. Sign up for a Reef Teach seat by midday. ⊠ *Mainstreet Arcade, 81–85 Lake St., Level 2, CBD* ☎ *07/4031–7794* ⊕ *www. reefteach.com.au* ⊠ *A$18* ⊙ *Shows Tues.–Sat. 6:30–8:30.*

FAMILY
Fodor's Choice
★
Skyrail Rainforest Cableway. From the Skyrail terminal just north of Cairns, take a six-person cable car on a breathtaking 7½-km (5-mile) journey across pristine, World Heritage–listed rain-forest canopy to the highland village of Kuranda, where you can visit local wildlife parks and shop for local craft and Aboriginal art. At two stations along the way, you can hop off and explore (the Skyrail ticket price includes a short ranger-guided rain-forest tour at Red Peak, and there's an info center and lookout at Barron Falls). The cableway base station is 15 km (9 miles) north of Cairns. Many visitors take the Scenic Railway to Kuranda, the cableway on the return trip. ⊠ *Captain Cook Hwy. at Cairns Western Arterial Rd., Smithfield* ☎ *07/4038–1555* ⊕ *www. skyrail.com.au* ⊠ *1-way A$47, round-trip A$71 (self-drive); A$74–A$119 (with transfers); cable car with scenic railway/cultural/rain forest/wildlife experiences A$91–A$169* ⊙ *Daily 9–5:15 at 15-min intervals, last round-trip boards at 2:45; last one-way trip at 3:30.*

8

Tanks Arts Centre. This arts center is housed in a trio of repurposed World War II–era oil storage tanks in Cairns's lush Flecker Botanic Gardens, 4 km (2 miles) north of the Cairns city center. It has become a vital creative hub for the region, showcasing everything from dance and theater troupes to local folk, blues, jazz, and indigenous artists. The Centre hosts a colorful arts and food market, with live music and free kids' activities, on the last Sunday of the month from April to November. ✉ *46 Collins Ave., Edge Hill* ☎ *07/4032–6600* ⊕ *www.tanksartscentre. com* 🎫 *Galleries free, venue ticket prices vary.*

FAMILY **Tjapukai Aboriginal Cultural Park.** Located at the base of the Skyrail Rainforest Cableway, this park offers many opportunities to learn about indigenous Djabugay people through exhilarating dance performances, hands-on workshops in traditional fire-making, spear and boomerang throwing, didgeridoo lessons, and talks on bush tucker and natural medicines. You can buy Aboriginal artworks, artifacts, and instruments (including didgeridoos) on-site; buffet lunches and four-course dinners are also available. One of Australia's most informative cultural attractions, it's also one of the few that returns profits to the indigenous community. Ticket options include Tjapukai by Day and Tjapukai by Night, the latter a nightly four-course buffet dinner/performance package. ✉ *Cairns Western Arterial Rd. (next to Skyrail terminal), Cavaronica* ✛ *15 km (9 miles) north of Cairns* ☎ *07/4042–9900* ⊕ *www.tjapukai.com.au* 🎫 *Tjapukai by Day: A$36 self-drive, A$58 with Cairns transfers, A$60 with Northern Beaches transfers, A$27.50 buffet lunch; Tjapukai by Night: A$99 self-drive, A$121–A$123 with transfers* ⊙ *Daily 9–5, night show 7–9:30 pm.*

WORTH NOTING

FAMILY **Birdworld Kuranda.** One of your best chances to see the endangered Southern cassowary, a prehistoric emu-like bird, is at Birdworld Kuranda. It's also home to 350-plus birds from nearly 80 species, more than 25 of them native to vanishing rain-forest areas—flying freely in a gigantic aviary, many of them tame enough to perch on your shoulders. ■TIP→ **Wear a hat and sleeved shirt: birds' claws are scratchy.** ✉ *Kuranda Heritage Village, Rob Vievers Dr., Kuranda* ☎ *07/4093–9188* ⊕ *www. birdworldkuranda.com.au* 🎫 *A$17, Birdworld/Koala Gardens (self-drive) A$29, Birdworld/Koala Gardens/Butterfly Sanctuary (self-drive) A$46* ⊙ *Daily 9–4.*

Cairns Marlin Marina. This floating marina's 261 berths bristle with charter fishing, diving, and private vessels, including superyachts up to 60 meters (197 feet) long. At the Reef Fleet Terminal off Marlin Wharf, you'll find tour offices, shops, cafés, and Wi-Fi connectivity. Big-game fishing is a big business here; fish weighing more than 1,000 pounds have been caught in the waters off the reef. Most of the dive boats and catamarans that ply the Great Barrier Reef dock here or at nearby Trinity Wharf. ✉ *1 Spence St., CBD* ☎ *07/4052–3866* ⊕ *www.portsnorth. com.au.*

FAMILY **Kuranda Koala Gardens.** All kinds of Australian wildlife are housed here, but the namesake marsupials are star attractions. A half-hour stroll through the compact park also puts you eye-to-eye with wombats,

The Skyrail Rainforest Cableway outside Cairns

wallabies, freshwater crocs, lizards, and snakes in open walk-through enclosures. For an extra fee, have your photo taken with a tame koala. ☒ *Kuranda Heritage Village, Rob Vievers Dr., Kuranda* ☎ *07/4093–9953* ⊕ *www.koalagardens.com* ☒ *A$17; Koala Gardens/Birdworld pass: A$29; Koala Gardens/Birdworld/Buttefly Sanctuary pass A$46* ☉ *Daily 9–4.*

Undara Volcanic National Park. The lava tubes here are a fascinating geological oddity in the Outback. A volcanic outpouring 190,000 years ago created the hollow basalt, tubelike tunnels, many of which you can trek through on tours led by trained guides. Undara is the Aboriginal word for "a long way," and it's apt: one of the original lava tubes extended for 161 km (100 miles) in total, and several sections of it can be explored on guided tours. The lava tubes extend over an area of 580-odd square miles; some are 62 feet high and half a mile long. ☒ *Off the Gulf Developmenatal Rd. (Savannah Way), Mt. Surprise* ✢ *Take the Gulf Developmental Rd. (Savannah Way) past the turnoff to Undara Experience, 17 km (10½ miles) from the turn-off. Six km (3½ miles) farther, take a right-hand fork and drive another 9 km (5½ miles), then turn left at the fork and drive 6 km (3½ miles) on an all-weather gravel road to reach the Kalkani day-use area* ☎ *07/4097–1485 NPRSR parks, 07/4097–7700 Ravenshoe Visitor Information* ⊕ *www.nprsr.qld.gov.au* ☒ *Free* ☉ *Daily 24 hrs.*

OFF THE
BEATEN
PATH

SPORTS AND THE OUTDOORS

It's no surprise that lots of tours out of Cairns focus on the Great Barrier Reef. Half-day snorkeling, diving, and fishing trips out of Cairns, most departing from the Reef Fleet Terminal, start from around A$125; full-day trips start from about A$190. Scuba dives and gear generally cost extra. Typically you'll pay an additional A$6 in admin fees (which includes the A$3.50 per person reef tax), and you may also be hit with a Port Authority charge of around A$15 per person, per day.

Ask a few pertinent questions before booking diving tours: dive trips vary in size, and some cater specifically to, say, sightseers; others to experienced divers. If you're a beginner or Open Water diver, ensure that you book excursions that visit suitable dive sites, with certified staff on hand to assist you.

Cairns is also a great base for adventure activities and horse riding on the Atherton Tableland, ballooning over the Mareeba Valley, and day tours to the UNESCO World Heritage–listed Daintree rain forest. The offices of adventure-tour companies, tourist offices and booking agents are concentrated around the Esplanade.

MULTISPORT OPERATORS

Fodor's Choice ★ **Raging Thunder.** This operator has various adventure packages: dive and snorkel on the Barrier Reef; glide over the Mareeba Valley in a hot-air balloon; horseback ride or white-water raft through the hinterland's rugged gorges; hike and bungee-jump on the Atherton Tablelands; or sea kayak around Fitzroy Island. Some tours can be combined with a visit to Tjapukai Aboriginal Cultural Park or Cairns Wildlife Safari Reserve. Pricing varies vastly by activity, season, and other factors. ⊠ *52–54 Fearnley St., Portsmith* ☎ *07/4030–7990* ⊕ *www.ragingthunder.com.au.*

RnR White Water Rafting. This operator runs white-water rafting expeditions for adults on the Barron, North Johnstone, and Tully rivers, as well as reef and rain-forest trips, horse rides, ATV tours, balloon rides, and more. Prices start at A$133 for a half-day's Barron River rafting tour, and there's an additional A$25 rafting charge on white-water excursions. All gear and safety equipment is provided. ⊠ *CBD* ☎ *07/4041–9444* ⊕ *www.raft.com.au.*

SNORKELING AND DIVING

Deep Sea Divers Den. Long-established, PADI-5-star-rated Deep Sea Divers Den has a roaming permit that allows its guides to visit any part of the Great Barrier Reef, including 17 exclusive moorings on the reef's outer edge. Day trips include up to three dives or snorkeling opportunities; gear and lunch is included in the price, but reef tax (A$20) and photos cost extra. Expect to pay A$205 for a day trip with two certified dives, A$225 with three, or A$205 with one. It's A$140 for guided snorkeling tours. ⊠ *319 Draper St., CBD* ☎ *07/4046–7333* ⊕ *www.diversden.com.au.*

Fodor's Choice ★ **Mike Ball Dive Expeditions.** Mike Ball, an enthusiastic American who's been diving the Great Barrier Reef since 1969, runs multiday, multi-dive trips along the Queensland coastline on which experienced divers get to set their own bottom times and dive their own plans—or be expertly guided. Custom-built, twin-hulled live-aboard boats loaded with top-end gear, serious divers, and qualified chefs depart twice weekly to visit renowned dive sites and spot minke whales and sharks. Prices start at A$1,687 for a budget dorm berth. Allow for standard gear hire fees (A$44 per day) and nitrox (A$75–A$150), personal guides (A$150 per day), and reef tax (A$18 per day). Dive courses cost extra but there are several available, and the quality of instruction's high. ⊠ *143 Lake St., CBD* ☎ *07/4053–0500* ⊕ *www.mikeball.com.*

> ### KURANDA WILDLIFE PASS
>
> Tropical Kuranda offers several nature-oriented attractions, including the Australian Butterfly Sanctuary, Birdworld Kuranda, and Kuranda Koala Gardens. See these sites individually, visit on a Kuranda Wildlife Experience pass (A$46), which gives entry to all three, or buy a return Skyrail & Kuranda Wildlife Experience package that includes return Skyrail tickets (from A$117).

FAMILY **Ocean Spirit Cruises.** This operator offers daily trips (A$176) on its sleek sailing catamaran that include four hours at Michaelmas Cay on the Great Barrier Reef, a marine biologist presentation, guided snorkeling, a fish-feeding demonstration, a semisubmersible tour, morning and afternoon tea, and a buffet lunch. Reef and port charges are an extra A$6. If you're a beginner, have mobility issues, or aren't a strong swimmer, this might be the best operator for you. ⊠ *Reef Fleet Terminal, 1 Spence St., CBD* ☎ *07/4031–2920* ⊕ *www.oceanspirit.com.au.*

Pro Dive Cairns. This Advanced Ecotourism–certified operator runs multiday, live-aboard trips on three custom-built dive boats, and offers PADI-5-star-accredited courses at their state-of-the-art training facility in Cairns. Three-, four- and seven-day trips take a maximum of 28 divers and snorkelers to outer Barrier Reef, Cod Hole, Ribbon Reefs, and Coral Sea sites, where they can dive ecologically diverse sites with optimal visibility. Trips include accommodation in serviced quad-share, twin, or double cabins, TVs, and private en-suites. You also get chef-prepared meals, top-end gear, and guided dives. ⊠ *Pro Dive Cairns Training Centre, 116 Spence St., CBD* ☎ *07/4031–5255* ⊕ *www.prodivecairns.com.*

FAMILY **Tusa Dive.** Among Cairns's best dive boats are the custom-built fast cats
Fodor's Choice run by Tusa Dive, a PADI-, SSI-, and Advanced Ecotourism–accred-
★ ited outfit that whisks up to 64 passengers out to 2 of 16 sites on the Great Barrier Reef. Get dive briefs and info en route, along with continual refreshments including a big lunch. In the water, people of all ages and experience levels can dive (A$250–A$290 for beginners; A$225–A$245 for certified divers) or snorkel (A$180) under the watchful gaze of guides. Every passenger pays a A$10 reef tax. Three- and seven-day, multi-dive trips to Cod Hole and the Coral Sea start from A$510. ⊠ *Shield St. at The Esplanade, CBD* ☎ *07/4047–9100* ⊕ *www.tusadive.com.*

"This was taken at Steve's Bommie. This fish struck me as really angry that fate had made him tough-looking, yet pink." —Photo by Rowanne, Fodors.com member

WHERE TO EAT

Use the coordinate (✥ B2) at the end of each listing to locate a site on the corresponding map.

$$ INDONESIAN Fodor's Choice ★ 🍴 **Bayleaf Balinese Restaurant.** Dining in the open-sided restaurant or alfresco under the light of tiki torches, you can enjoy some of the most delicious, innovative cuisine in North Queensland. Choose from an expansive menu that combines traditional Balinese spices and recipes with native Australian ingredients—try the crocodile satay. The *be celeng base manis* (pork in sweet soy sauce) sounds simple, but is mouthwatering. The traditional rijsttafel feast for two includes rice with lots of curries, salads, fish dishes, stews, pickle sides, and, if you can squeeze them in, desserts. If you're here on a Friday or Saturday night, try the latest Bayleaf specialty: a whole "pig in a box," baked in hot coals. **TIP→ Don't eat lunch if you're planning to order the rijstaffel at dinner—it's huge.** [$] *Average main: A$26* ✉ *Bay Village Tropical Retreat, 227 Lake St., at Gatton St., CBD* ☎ *07/4047–7955* 🌐 *www.bayvillage.com.au/bayleaf* ✍ *Reservations essential* ⏰ *No lunch weekends* ✥ *A1.*

$ FAST FOOD FAMILY 🍴 **Cairns Night Markets Food Court.** The 13-outlet food court in these lively, night owl–friendly markets offers something for every palate, from spicy Malaysian *laksa* (coconut-milk soup) to sushi, kebabs, sweet-and-sour chicken, crepes, coffee, and ice cream. Officially, it's open daily with the markets, 5 to 11 pm, but many outlets start serving much earlier. [$] *Average main: A$13* ✉ *71–75 The Esplanade, between Shield and Spence Sts., CBD* ☎ *07/4051–7666* 🌐 *www.nightmarkets.com.au*

Reservations not accepted ☰ *No credit cards* ✚ *B3.*

$$$
ASIAN FUSION
Fodor's Choice
★

✕ **Hanuman Cairns.** A flavorful addition to Cairns's dining scene, this restaurant in the Hilton Cairns does wonders with tropical produce and Southeast Asian flavors. Moody violet lighting, Asian artifacts, and floor-to-ceiling windows fronting Trinity Inlet set the stage for vibrant tasting plates, and aromatic curries and wok-fried dishes. Order the entrée tasting plate for two (A$34) for a whistle-stop tour of Thai, Tamil, and Nonya cuisines. Dishes are well priced, but you'll probably want to order several. ■TIP→ **The lunchtime bento box special for A$15 makes a terrific picnic.** $ *Average main: A$31* ✉ *Hilton Cairns Hotel, 34 The Esplanade, CBD* ☎ *07/4052–6786* ⊕ *www.hanuman.com.au* ◷ *No lunch weekends* ✚ *B3.*

> ## BEACHES
>
> Since Cairns lacks city beaches, most people head out to the reef to swim and snorkel. North of the airport, neighboring areas including **Machans Beach, Holloways Beach, Yorkey's Knob, Trinity Beach,** and **Clifton Beach** are perfect for swimming from June through September and sometimes even October; check local weather reports. Avoid the ocean at other times, however, when deadly box jellyfish (marine stingers) and invisible-to-the-eye Irukandji jellyfish float in the waters along the coast.

$$$
AUSTRALIAN
Fodor's Choice
★

✕ **Ochre Restaurant.** Local seafood and native ingredients take top billing at this upscale yet relaxed Cairns institution that specializes in bush dining. Try the popular Australian antipasto platter: 'roo terrine, emu pâté, and crocodile wontons, with fine antipodean wines to match. Most dishes employ native foods and seasonal ingredients: sample wild-caught barramundi or emu fillet with bush tomato, or order a vegetarian, Australian game, or seafood platter to share (A$30, A$50, and A$69 per person, respectively). Ochre also offers an array of tasty Pacific Rim dishes on separate Japanese, Chinese, and Korean menus. The signature dessert, wattle-seed pavlova with Davidson plum sorbet and macadamia biscotti, makes a fine finish. $ *Average main: A$33* ✉ *43 Shields St., at Sheridan St., CBD* ☎ *07/4051–0100* ⊕ *www. ochrerestaurant.com.au* *Reservations essential* ◷ *No lunch weekends* ✚ *A3.*

$$
MODERN
AUSTRALIAN
FAMILY

✕ **Perrotta's at the Gallery.** This outdoor café with an attached wine bar at the Cairns Regional Gallery serves sumptuous breakfasts and brunches, including French toast with vanilla poached pear, King Island yogurt and raspberry caramel, baked eggs, frittata, and pulled pork on corn bread with eggs Benedict. Lunch fare includes warm chicken salads, pasta dishes, and various sandwiches. Tuck into Italian and modern Australian mains—perhaps slow-cooked lamb shoulder or roast pepper, tomato, and basil soup with red-claw yabbies (crayfish)—and desserts, such as vanilla-bean panna cotta with seasonal fruits. $ *Average main: A$25* ✉ *Gallery Deck, Cairns Regional Gallery, 38 Abbott St., at Shield St., CBD* ☎ *07/4031–5899* ⊕ *www.cairnsregionalgallery.com.au* ✚ *B3.*

$$$
MODERN FRENCH

✕ **Restaurant M Yogo.** Occupying a prime pier-front position, Restaurant M Yogo could be Cairns's best-placed restaurant. Here chef Masa puts a deft, modern-Japanese spin on classic French dishes. Enjoy his

8

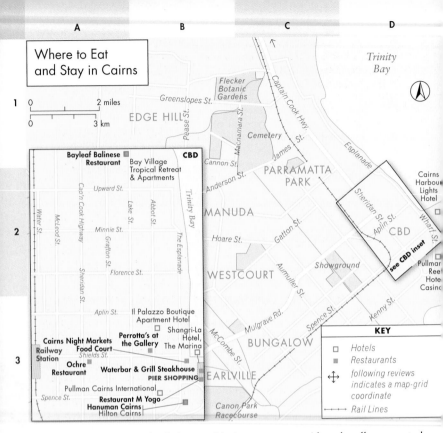

Where to Eat
and Stay in Cairns

creamy seafood risotto with tiger prawns, squid, and scallops; roasted duck breast in port-wine sauce; pan-seared wild barramundi or Tasmanian salmon; and premium grain-fed Wagyu tenderloin. The food is as inspiring as the marina, inlet, and mountain views. Waitstaff can help you select the perfect match from a well-chosen antipodean wine list. If you have room, desserts are equally pared back and delectable: Grand Marnier ice cream, mango mousse or sorbet, green tea "opera" cake, or a fluffy cream-cheese soufflé cake with Chantilly cream and seasonal fruits. The four-course set menu featuring a lobster main is good value at A$99. This is refined dining in relaxed environs, perfect for special occasions. $ *Average main: A$37* ⊠ *Shop G9, Pier Shopping, Pierpoint Rd.* ☎ *07/4051–0522* ⊕ *www.matureyogo.com* ⌕ *Reservations essential* ⊕ *B3.*

$$$
SEAFOOD
✕ **Waterbar & Grill Steakhouse.** At this busy waterfront eatery, you can gaze at Cairns's bustling marina while chowing down on a locally sourced, char-grilled steak. The steaks come in all cuts and sizes, with thick fries on the side, and there's also a nice selection of barbecued pork and lamb ribs, burgers, and straight-up seafood. Lunches offer lighter fare: pita wraps, salads, and pasta dishes. There's a hearty kids' menu and a long wine, beer, and cocktail list. Even though Waterbar is often packed, the airy open-plan design makes it seem less crowded. $ *Average main: A$35* ⊠ *Pier Shopping Centre, Pier Point Rd., Shop G1A,*

CBD ☎ *07/4031–1199* ⊕ *www.waterbarandgrill.com.au* ⊲ *Reservations essential* ✛ *B3.*

WHERE TO STAY

For expanded hotel reviews, visit Fodors.com.

$
RENTAL
FAMILY

Bay Village Tropical Retreat & Apartments. Resident manager Lyn Ullrich has translated years of expertise in high-end Sydney hospitality into this family-friendly accommodation complex. **Pros:** disabled-friendly room and public areas; handy guest laundry; sociable atmosphere; free Wi-Fi in public areas. **Cons:** pool area and ground-floor rooms can be noisy; standard rooms lack all but simple amenities. $ *Rooms from: A$150* ⊠ *227 Lake St., at Gatton St., CBD* ☎ *07/4051–4622* ⊕ *www.bayvillage.com.au* ⇲ *62 suites, 28 apartments* †◎† *No meals* ✛ *A1.*

$$
HOTEL

Cairns Harbour Lights Hotel. The modern apartments and studios at this hotel right on the Cairns waterfront are a two-minute stroll to Reef Fleet Terminal, making them ideal for early-morning reef trips. **Pros:** terrific central location; good dining options on-site; clean, comfortable, stylish rooms. **Cons:** daily fees for Internet access and parking; pool small, and can be chilly in cooler months; apartments lack laundry facilities. $ *Rooms from: A$279* ⊠ *1 Marlin Parade, Cairns* ☎ *07/4057–0800* ⊕ *www.accor.com* ⇲ *94 studios and apartments* †◎† *No meals* ✛ *D2.*

$$
HOTEL
Fodor's Choice
★

Hilton Cairns. This attractive hotel has an enviable location near the waterfront, a flotilla of services, and classy on-site drinking and dining options. **Pros:** modern, renovated rooms; expansive breakfast buffet; excellent on-site eateries. **Cons:** pricey Internet access; fee for parking; large tour groups can create extra traffic in public areas. $ *Rooms from: A$299* ⊠ *34 Esplanade, Cairns* ☎ *07/4050–2000* ⊕ *www3.hilton.com* ⇲ *264 rooms* †◎† *Multiple meal plans* ✛ *B3.*

$$
HOTEL

Il Palazzo Boutique Apartment Hotel. Cairns is a long way from Europe but you can imagine yourself on the Riviera at this intimate, centrally located continental-style hotel. **Pros:** free Austar cable channels and movies; helpful staff; clean, quiet rooms. **Cons:** dated decor; slow in-room Internet; free Wi-Fi only in public areas (bring a laptop). $ *Rooms from: A$250* ⊠ *62 Abbott St., CBD* ☎ *07/4041–2155, 1800/813222* ⊕ *www.ilpalazzo.com.au* ⇲ *38 suites* ✛ *B3.*

$$$
HOTEL

Pullmann Cairns International. Formerly a Sebel-branded property, this apartment-hotel near Cairns's waterfront has an impressive three-story lobby, smartly outfitted guest rooms, and a luxurious day spa. **Pros:** central location; good on-site services and facilities including tour desk and guest laundry. **Cons:** thin walls; old-style TVs; steep fees for Internet access and parking; main pool is chilly. $ *Rooms from: A$339* ⊠ *17 Abbot St., at Spence St., CBD* ☎ *07/4031–1300, 1800/079100* ⊕ *www.pullmancairnsinternational.com.au* ⇲ *321 rooms/suites* †◎† *No meals* ✛ *B3.*

$$$$
HOTEL
Fodor's Choice
★

Pullmann Reef Hotel Casino. Part of a lively entertainment complex in the heart of Cairns, this high-end hotel has spacious rooms and suites— as well as gaming tables, several restaurants and bars, a nightclub, a casino, an outdoor swimming pool, and a small wildlife sanctuary in its rooftop dome. **Pros:** several on-site entertainment and dining options;

8

helpful, high-end service. **Cons:** chilly pool; soft furnishings showing wear. [$] *Rooms from: A$490* ✉ *35–41 Wharf St., CBD* ☎ *07/4030–8888* 🌐 *www.pullmannhotels.com* 🛏 *128 rooms and suites* 🍴 *No meals* ✥ *D2.*

$$$ HOTEL 🏨 **Shangri-La Hotel, The Marina.** With a minimalist lobby, golden-orb chandeliers, and suede chaise longues, this resort is among Cairns's hippest. **Pros:** great views; free Wi-Fi and Internet; free use of beach towels and umbrellas; proximity to the marina. **Cons:** service can be spotty; lower-floor rooms are shabbier and can be noisy. [$] *Rooms from: A$330* ✉ *Pierpoint Rd., CBD* ☎ *07/4031–1411, 1800/222448* 🌐 *www.shangri-la.com/cairns/shangrila* 🛏 *230 rooms, 25 suites* 🍴 *No meals* ✥ *B3.*

NIGHTLIFE

Cairns's Esplanade and the CBD streets leading off it come alive at night, with most restaurants serving until late, and wine or a cold beer is a staple with evening meals. Several rowdy pubs catering to backpackers and younger travelers line the central section of City Place; a few bars and hotel venues manage to be upscale while remaining true to the city's easygoing spirit. Unless noted, bars are open nightly and there's no cover charge.

Lilo Bar & Restaurant. Cairns's only rooftop bar, atop the Rydges Plaza Hotel, is a relaxed, convivial watering-hole with lounge areas, pool decks, and private cabanas overlooking the city. It's perfect for sharing generously sized seasonal cocktails. There's plenty of space for patrons to mingle and enjoy the Miami-like ambience of this lofty oasis. ✉ *Rydges Plaza Cairns, Spence St., at Grafton St., Level 3, CBD* ☎ *07/4046–0300* 🌐 *www.lilowetbar.com.au.*

PJ O'Brien's Irish Pub. Part of a nationwide chain of traditional Irish pubs, PJ O'Brien's buzzes with backpackers swapping travel tales over pints and generally enjoying the *craic* (Gaelic for "good time"). It has good-value lunch and dinner deals (A$13), ladies' nights on Tuesday, and live party bands on weekends. ✉ *87 Lake St., CBD* ☎ *07/4031–5333* 🌐 *www.pjobriens.com.au.*

Vertigo Cocktail Bar & Lounge. This sleek bar-lounge off the main foyer of Pullman Reef Hotel Casino has live bands (including big-name acts) Thursday through Saturday, karaoke on Sunday, and big production shows two or three nights a week, followed by DJs and dancing. ✉ *Ground-floor foyer, Pullmann Reef Hotel Casino, 35–41 Wharf St., CBD* ☎ *07/4030–8888* 🌐 *www.reefcasino.com.au/vertigo.*

SHOPPING

MALLS

Cairns Central. Adjacent to Cairns Railway Station, Cairns Central houses 180-plus specialty stores, Myer and Target department stores, a food court, several coffee shops, and a six-screen cinema complex. Those who represent the property claim it's the largest shopping center in Far North Queensland, and that might just be the case. Stroller hire is available. ⊠ *McLeod and Spence Sts., CBD* ☎ *07/4041–4111* ⊕ *www. cairnscentral.com.au.*

The Pier at the Marina. Overlooking Trinity Bay and Marlin Marina, this low-rise waterfront complex houses the outlets of top Australian and international designers as well as a newsagent, bookstore, Internet café, galleries, salons, fitness facilities, and a visitor information center. There's also an interactive wildlife discovery center, Zoo To You, with daily wildlife shows. Many of The Pier's bars and restaurants open onto waterfront verandas and the marina boardwalk. ⊠ *Pier Point Rd., CBD* ☎ *07/4051–7244* ⊕ *www.thepier.com.au.*

MARKETS

Cairns Night Markets. If you're looking for bargain beachwear, local jewelery, arts and crafts, a massage, a meal, a coffee, or souvenirs, the Cairns Night Markets, open 5–11 pm weekdays, are the place to go. Bring cash—many of the 70-plus merchants charge additional fees for credit cards. ⊠ *71–75 The Esplanade, at Aplin St., CBD* ☎ *01/4051–7666* ⊕ *www.nightmarkets.com.au.*

Rusty's Markets. Cairns's iconic "street" market, Rusty's attracts 180-plus stallholders, who peddle everything from fresh tropical produce to art and crafts, jewelry, clothing, natural health and skin-care products, and massages, as well as all sorts of food. The market is covered, offering a pleasant respite from the sun. It's open Friday 5 am–6 pm, Saturday 6–3, and Sunday 6–2. ⊠ *57–89 Grafton St., CBD* ☎ *07/4051–5100, 0438/753–460* ⊕ *www.rustysmarkets.com.au.*

SPORTING GOODS

Tusa Dive Shop. This store stocks a wide range of big-name dive gear as well as stinger and wet suits, swimwear, kids' gear, and accessories such as snorkels and sunscreen. ⊠ *The Esplanade at Shields St., CBD* ☎ *07/4047–9120* ⊕ *www.tusadive.com* ⊙ *Daily 7:30 am–9 pm.*

NORTH OF CAIRNS

The Captain Cook Highway runs from Cairns to Mossman, a relatively civilized stretch known mostly for the resort towns of Palm Cove and Port Douglas. Past the Daintree River, wildlife parks and sunny coastal villages fade into sensationally wild terrain. If you came to Australia seeking high-octane sun, pristine coral cays, steamy jungles filled with exotic birdcalls and riotous vegetation, and a languid beachcomber lifestyle, head for the coast between Daintree and Cooktown.

The southern half of this coastline lies within Cape Tribulation, Daintree National Park, part of the Greater Daintree Wilderness Area, a region named to UNESCO's World Heritage list because of its unique ecology. To experience the area's natural splendor, there's no need to go past Cape Tribulation. However, the Bloomfield Track continues on to Cooktown, a frontier destination that tacks two days onto your itinerary. This rugged country breeds some maverick personalities offering fresh perspectives on Far North Queensland.

Prime time for visiting is May through September, when daily maximum temperatures average around 27°C (80°F) and the water is comfortably warm. During the wet season, November through April, expect rain, humidity, and lots of bugs. Highly poisonous box and Irukandji jellyfish make the coastline unsafe for swimming from October through May, but "jellies" hardly ever drift out as far as the reefs, so you're safe to get wet there.

PALM COVE

23 km (14 miles) north of Cairns.

Fodor'sChoice ★ A 35-minute drive north of Cairns, Palm Cove is one of Queensland's jewels: an idyllic, albeit expensive base from which to explore the far north. It's a quiet place, sought out by those in the know for its magnificent trees, calm waters, exceptionally clean beach, and excellent restaurants.

GETTING HERE AND AROUND

Getting here from Cairns is a cinch: by car, follow the signs from the city center to Captain Cook Highway, then head north, taking the Palm Cove turnoff after about 25 km (16 miles). Regular shuttle buses service Palm Cove from the airport and Cairns. Around this compact beach area, though, most people walk or cycle.

EXPLORING

A charming beachside village that sprawls back toward the highway, Palm Cove is easily navigated on foot. Many of the best accommodations, bars, and eateries are strung along the oceanfront strip of Williams Esplanade, fronting what has been dubbed Australia's cleanest beach. At its far north end, a five-minute stroll from the "village," there's a jetty and small marina.

TOP ATTRACTIONS

FAMILY **Cairns Tropical Zoo.** At this 10-acre zoo visitors can hand-feed tame kangaroos, cuddle with koalas, enjoy breakfast with the wildlife, and attend daily snake, crocodile, and bird shows. You'll also be able to see wombats, dingoes, endangered southern cassowaries, and the zoo's star resident—Sarge, a 17-foot, 660-pound centenarian croc. Have your photo taken with a koala, boa, or baby croc for A$18, or all three for A$36. Breakfast at the zoo (from A$53) runs daily until 9 am and includes park entry, full breakfast, and a wildlife presentation. ⊠ *Captain Cook Hwy.* ☎ *07/4055–3669* ⊕ *www.cairnstropicalzoo.com.au* ✉ *Entry A$33; 2-park pass to Cairns Tropical Zoo and Hartley's Crocodile Adventure A$61.20* ☉ *Daily 8:30–4.*

Hartley's Crocodile Adventures. Hartley's houses thousands of crocodiles as well as koalas, wallabies, snakes, lizards, southern cassowaries, and tropical birds in natural environs, accessible via boardwalks and boats. A lagoon cruise, on which keepers feed big crocs at close range, is included in your entry price. There are daily cassowary and koala feedings, and croc and snake shows. Most thrilling is the Big Croc Experience, which is held daily at 10:30 and 1 (book 24 hours ahead). It's your chance to handle squirming baby crocs and pole-feed gigantic

Palm Cove is one of many pristine beaches along the tropical Queensland coast.

ones, and includes a guided tour and commemorative photo. Lilies Restaurant showcases local delicacies, including crocodile, of course. If you don't feel like driving, **Down Under Tours** (☎ 07/4035–5577), **Tropical Horizon Tours** (☎ 07/4035–6445), and several other operators include Hartley's on their day-tour itineraries. ⊠ *Captain Cook Hwy., Wangetti Beach* ☎ 07/4055–3576 ⊕ *www.crocodileadventures. com* ⊠ *Entry A$35; Croc Encounter A$125, self-drive; 2-park pass to Hartley's and Cairns Tropical Zoo A$61.20* ⊗ *Daily 8:30–5.*

Fodor'sChoice
★
Mareeba Tropical Savanna and Wetlands Reserve. If you drive 70 km (44 miles) west of Palm Cove you'll encounter another world: giant termite mounds dot savanna scrub, and vast reclaimed wetlands give refuge to hundreds of bird species, including Australia's only stork, the Jabiru. Knowledgeable, enthusiastic staff run numerous nature-based excursions on and around the vast, lily-littered lagoons and savanna. A 2½-hour Sunset Reserve Safari combines a bird-watching cruise, a ranger-guided savanna drive on which you'll spot wallabies and kangaroos, a "billy" tea and bird-hide stop, and fine Aussie wine and cheese. Consider signing up for the Wetlands' fantastic four-day package for A$820; it includes rain-forest, reef, and Outback trips, along with deluxe safari-tent accommodation and some meals. Daily transfers to and from Cairns are available for around A$50 one-way. All proceeds feed back into the Wetlands' environmental work. ⊠ *Clancy's Lagoon Visitor Centre, 142 Pickford Rd., Biboohra* ☎ 07/4093–2514, 1800/788755 ⊕ *www.mareebawetlands.org and www.jabirusafarilodge.com.*

SPORTS AND THE OUTDOORS

Palm Cove makes a great base for rain-forest and reef activities—hiking, biking, horseback riding, rafting, ballooning, and ATV adventures on the Atherton Tableland; snorkeling, diving, and sailing around the Low Isles and Barrier Reef; sea kayaking just offshore; and scenic flights over just about anywhere a small plane can get on a tank of gas. Though few cruise or tour companies are based in this beachside enclave, many Cairns and Port Douglas–based operators offer Palm Cove transfers.

KAYAKING

FAMILY Fodor's Choice ★ **Palm Cove Watersports.** Paddling around history-rich Double Island, off Palm Cove Jetty, is a tranquil, eco-friendly way to get close to the local marine life: you'll often spot dolphins, stingrays, turtles, and colorful fish on this local operator's terrific sunrise tours and half-day snorkeling excursions. Helpful guides impart safety briefings and labor-saving tips on technique before you set out, and there are frequent stops for refreshments, snorkeling (May–November), and wildlife-watching en route. Even if you've never paddled before you're unlikely to capsize; the single and double kayaks are super-stable. Half-day trips circumnavigate Double Island, stopping off on the fringing reef about 1 km (½ mile) from shore and on a secluded beach. Transfers from Cairns (A$25 per person) and Port Douglas (A$30 per person) are available; bookings are essential. **TIP→ Safety and snorkeling gear is provided, but bring sunglasses, a hat, and sunscreen.** ✉ *79 Williams Esplanade, 100 meters south of Palm Cove Jetty* ☎ *0402/861011* 🌐 *www.palmcovewatersports.com* 🎟 *A$55 sunrise tour; A$110 half-day snorkel and kayak tour; A$8 reef tax/insurance.*

WHERE TO EAT

$$$ SEAFOOD 🍴 **Beach Almond Beach House.** This low-key eatery's simple beach-shack setting on Palm Cove's seafront underplays the freshness and flavor of its Modern Asian food. Seafood's the specialty here, and signature dishes include whole Singaporean chili mud crab and a two-person seafood platter (A$169). The small but satisfying menu is full of fresh spins on favorite dishes from around Southeast Asia, including green papaya salad, banana leaf–wrapped barramundi, and "tropical" lobster with turmeric, coconut, and mild chili. Beach Almond also serves leisurely lunches and coffee, and stays open later than many of its Palm Cove competitors at night. [$] *Average main: A$35* ✉ *145 Williams Esplanade* ☎ *07/4059–1908, 0488/145147* 🌐 *www.beachalmond.com.*

$$$ INTERNATIONAL 🍴 **Lime & Pepper Restaurant and Bar.** European flair meets great local produce at this upscale beachfront restaurant and bar. Lime & Pepper mixes fresh seafood, tropical fruits, and bush-tucker ingredients, such as native finger limes and Davidson plums, in innovative dishes, with a worthy wine list and tropical cocktails. Lunch, dinner, and the five-course degustation (A$159 per person, with matched wines) menus change seasonally. Stand-out entrées might include grilled Gulf of Carpentaria tiger prawns with a coffee-lime dressing, or lemon-myrtle-marinated Grimaud duck breast on orange risotto, with asparagus and vanilla foam. Desserts are suitably elegant as well. The cuisine might be sophisticated, but kids are catered to with their own menu. Service, with the odd exception in peak periods, is attentive and knowledgeable.

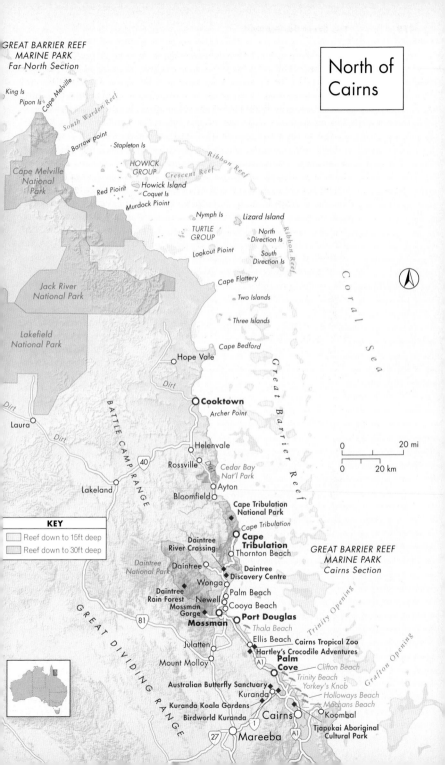

GREAT BARRIER REEF
MARINE PARK
Far North Section

North of Cairns

King Is
Pipon Is
Cape Melville
South Warden Reef
Barrow point
Stapleton Is
HOWICK GROUP
Crescent Reef
Ribbon Reef
Red Pioint
Howick Island
Coquet Is
Murdock Pioint

Cape Melville
National
Park

Nymph Is
TURTLE GROUP
Lizard Island
North Direction Is
South Direction Is
Ribbon Reef
Lookout Pioint

Jack River
National Park

Cape Flattery
Two Islands
Three Islands

C o r a l

Lakefield
National Park

Cape Bedford

S e a

Hope Vale

Dirt

Cooktown

Dirt

Archer Point

Great

Laura

Helenvale

Dirt

Rossville

Cedar Bay Nat'l Park

40

Lakeland

Ayton

Bloomfield

Barrier

Cape Tribulation
National Park

Cape Tribulation

Cape Tribulation

Daintree
River Crossing

Thornton Beach

Reef

*GREAT BARRIER REEF
MARINE PARK
Cairns Section*

Daintree National Park

Daintree

Daintree
Discovery Centre

Wonga

Daintree
Rain Forest

Newell

Palm Beach

Cooya Beach

Mossman
Gorge

Port Douglas

81

Mossman

Thala Beach

Trinity Opening

Julatten

Ellis Beach

Cairns Tropical Zoo

Hartley's Crocodile Adventures

GREAT

Mount Molloy

**Palm
Cove**

Clifton Beach
Trinity Beach
Yorkey's Knob

Grafton Opening

DIVIDING

Australian Butterfly Sanctuary

Kuranda

Holloways Beach
Machans Beach

Kuranda Koala Gardens

Koombal

Birdworld Kuranda

Cairns

RANGE

27

A1

Mareeba

**Tjapukai Aboriginal
Cultural Park**

KEY

	Reef down to 15ft deep
	Reef down to 30ft deep

0		20 mi
0		20 km

$ *Average main: A\$36* ⊠ *Peppers Beach Club & Spa, 123 Williams Esplanade* ☎ *07/4059–9200* ⊕ *www.peppers.com.au* ⚓ *Reservations essential.*

$$$
MODERN
AUSTRALIAN

✕ **NuNu Restaurant.** Sexy suede lounges, intimate banquettes, and unbroken views of the Coral Sea make lingering easy at this Palm Cove eatery. The menu teems with pared-back, innovative Mod Oz dishes that do justice to the region's produce. Start with a vanilla-ginger mojito or lime-coconut daiquiri, then select seveal tapas-style tasting plates, such as smoked red emperor served on a single betel leaf with peanut-papaya relish and salmon roe. Those with large appetites can choose from the "bold and robust" menu: a fragrant lamb pastilla, or barbecued Angus T-bone. Desserts are deceptively simple: passion-fruit soufflé, honeycomb dipped in Valrhona chocolate, or coconut snow eggs with black rice, banana ice-cream, and hibiscus. $ *Average main: A\$34* ⊠ *123 Williams Esplanade* ☎ *07/4059–1880* ⊕ *www.nunu.com.au* ☾ *Closed Tues. and Wed.*

$$$
MODERN ASIAN

✕ **Temple of Tastes.** Knowledgeable staff, an impressive wine and cocktail list, and a torch-lighted waterfront terrace are among the many reasons to dine at this excellent resort restaurant. You can expect generous servings of fresh Modern Australian food infused with Asian and South Pacific flavors. The lunch menu features chili squid and lamb burgers, while dinner includes local barramundi with Asian vegetables and tamarind sauce. If you're feeling indulgent, save room for a sinful Bartletts chocolate fondant or deconstructed lemon meringue pie. Temple's varied menu includes several gluten-free and vegetarian options, and there's a small kids' menu. $ *Average main: A\$36* ⊠ *Hotel Pullmann Palm Cove Sea Temple Resort and Spa, 5 Triton St.* ☎ *07/4059–9600* ⊕ *www. pullmanhotels.com* ⚓ *Reservations essential.*

$$$
MODERN
AUSTRALIAN
FAMILY
Fodor'sChoice
★

✕ **Vivo Bar and Grill.** Diners at this classy beachside eatery enjoy Coral Sea views framed by palms and melaleucas to go along with tropical cocktails and Mod Oz–meets–Mediterranean dishes. House muesli and freshly baked breads make this a favorite breakfast spot; panini, pasta, salads, and calamari pack in the crowds at lunch. At dinner, head chef Russell Molina transforms fresh seasonal produce, especially seafood, into inventive contemporary food in Vivo's gleaming open kitchen. Try his popular crispy-skin barramundi sautéed in wild mushrooms with Mareeba bush tomatoes and Shiraz jus, then indulge in a caramelized lemon tartlet with berry compote. The two- to three-course prix-fixe menu comes with a glass of Cape Mentelle wine (A\$39/A\$49 per person). A chic sunken bar forms the hub of this sociable haunt; between meals, Vivo's a popular spot for city-strong coffee, tapas, and cocktails. $ *Average main: A\$38* ⊠ *49 Williams Esplanade* ☎ *07/4059–0944* ⊕ *www.vivo.com.au.*

WHERE TO STAY

For expanded hotel reviews, visit Fodors.com.

$$$$
RESORT
Fodor'sChoice
★

▦ **Angsana Resort & Spa.** Fine landscaping, pools, barbecues, and sunny areas for relaxation enhance this classy colonial-style vacation complex fronting a palm-shaded white-sand beach. **Pros:** helpful staff; terrific location; upscale restaurant. **Cons:** no elevators; pools on the chilly side.

$ *Rooms from: A$510* ✉ *1 Veivers Rd.* ☎ *07/4055–3000, 1800/050019* ⊕ *www.angsana.com* ↴ *67 apartments* ⦿ *Breakfast.*

$$$ 🛏 **Kewarra Beach Resort & Spa.** This true-beachfront property just south
RESORT   of Palm Cove has its priorities right: Kewarra's sensitively designed,
FAMILY   sleekly appointed bungalows and restored pioneer's cottage overlook
Fodor's Choice   rain forests teeming with wildlife, free-form pools, or a private white-
★   sand beach. **Pros:** award-winning cuisine; high-end facilities and service;
eco-friendly ethos; spectacular grounds; free Wi-Fi (even on the beach).
Cons: a drive from Palm Cove's cafés; no on-site gym; rain-forest envi-
rons can mean the odd critter gets into your room. $ *Rooms from:*
A$299 ✉ *80 Kewarra St., Kewarra Beach* ☎ *07/4058–4000* ⊕ *www.*
kewarra.com ↴ *44 rooms* ⦿ *Multiple meal plans.*

$$ 🛏 **Peppers Beach Club & Spa.** Its beachfront location, excellent on-site din-
RESORT   ing, and sleek suites make this laid-back resort popular with city dwell-
FAMILY   ers seeking upscale relaxation. **Pros:** terrific dining options; laptops for
hire; free underground parking. **Cons:** gym equipment basic; main pool
area can be noisy; fee for Internet use. $ *Rooms from: A$351* ✉ *123*
Williams Esplanade ☎ *07/4059–9200 direct line, 1300/737444 toll-*
free in Australia, 07/5665–4426 Australia-wide reservations ⊕ *www.*
peppers.com.au/beach-club-spa ↴ *140 rooms and suites* ⦿ *Multiple*
meal plans.

$$$$ 🛏 **Reef House Resort & Spa.** This centrally located small resort, which was
RESORT   once a private residence, feels positively quaint, and that's a good thing
when you're looking for a low-key escape in this low-key resort area.
Pros: large rooms; complimentary sunset punch; free in-room Wi-Fi.
Cons: pools can be cold; breakfast is expensive; grounds relatively
small. $ *Rooms from: A$490* ✉ *99 Williams Esplanade* ☎ *07/4055–*
3633 ⊕ *www.reefhouse.com.au* ↴ *69 rooms* ⦿ *Multiple meal plans.*

8

PORT DOUGLAS

67½ km (42 miles) northwest of Cairns.

Known simply as "Port" to locals, Port Douglas offers almost as broad
a range of outdoor adventures as Cairns, but in a more compact, laid-
back setting. In this burgeoning tourist town there's a palpable buzz,
despite tropical haze and humidity. Travelers from all over the world
base themselves here, making excursions to the north's wild rain forests,
the savanna and wetlands west of Mareeba, and the Great Barrier Reef.
Varied lodgings, restaurants, and bars center on and around Port's main
strip, Macrossan Street.

Like much of North Queensland, Port Douglas was settled after gold
was discovered nearby. When local ore deposits dwindled in the 1880s,
it became a port for sugar milled in nearby Mossman until the 1950s.
The town's many old "Queenslander" buildings give it the feel of a
simple seaside settlement, despite its modern resorts and overbuilt landscape. The rain forests and beaches that envelop the town are, for the
most part, World Heritage sites—so while Port continues to grow in
popularity, the extraordinary environs that draw people here are protected from development.

GETTING HERE AND AROUND

By car, it's a scenic, 75-minute drive north to Port Douglas from Cairns: take Sheridan Street to the Captain Cook Highway, following it for around 60 km (35 miles) to the Port Douglas turnoff. North of Palm Cove, along the 30-km (19-mile) Marlin Coast, the road plays hide-and-seek with an idyllic stretch of shoreline, ducking inland through tunnels of tropical coastal forest and curving back to the surf to reach Port Douglas.

Around town, most people drive, walk, or cycle. It's about 5½ km (3½ miles), or an hour's level walk from the highway to the main street. Regular shuttle buses call in at major hotels and resorts day and night, ferrying travelers to and from Cairns, the airport, and nearby towns and attractions.

EXPLORING

Port Douglas is actually an isthmus, bounded by Four Mile Beach on one side, Dickson Inlet on the other, with the town's main retail, café, and restaurant strip, Macrossan Street, running up the center. The town sprawls as far as the highway, 5½ km (3½ miles) to the west, along Port Douglas Road, which is lined with upmarket resorts and holiday apartment complexes. At the far end of Macrossan Street, on Wharf Street, there's a busy marina.

FAMILY

Fodor's Choice

★

Wildlife Habitat. This world-class wildlife sanctuary just off the Captain Cook Highway is divided into "immersion" wetland, rain-forest, grass-land, and savanna habitats, enabling close creature encounters with everything from koalas to cassowaries and crocs. The park shelters more than 180 species of native wildlife in its 8-acre expanse, including Technicolor parrots, echidnas, emus, kangaroos, and crocodiles. The "tropical" buffet breakfast with the birds, served daily 8–10:30 (A$47, including sanctuary entry and a guided tour) is accompanied by avian residents so tame they'll perch on your shoulders—and may steal your food if you're distracted. You can also lunch with the lorikeets from noon to 2 daily (A$47), or join one of the sanctuary's free expert-guided tours, held several times daily (or book a VIP behind-the-scenes version). ⊠ *Port Douglas Rd. at Agincourt St.* ☎ *07/4099–3235* ⊕ *www.wildlifehabitat.com.au* ⊠ *A$32* ⊙ *Daily 8–5, last admission at 4.*

SPORTS AND THE OUTDOORS

Port Douglas is a great base for activities on the mainland and reef. Several tour companies conduct day trips into the rain forest and beyond in four-wheel-drive buses and vans; most include river cruises for crocodile-spotting and stops at local attractions. Various reef operators either base vessels at or pick up from Port Douglas Marina (formerly Marina Mirage). You can also horseback ride, bungee jump, raft, go off-roading, hike, mountain-bike, and balloon on and around the Atherton Tablelands, or go Outback for excellent bird- and wildlife-watching west of Mareeba, less than two hour's drive from Port.

FISHING

Norseman. Long-established MV *Norseman* is one of the best game-fishing boats on the Great Barrier Reef for novice and experienced anglers alike. Head out to the best spots on the reef's edge on a 60-foot, purpose-designed, high-tech vessel to fish for large pelagic species including Spanish mackerel, tuna, wahoo, and the elusive giant trevally. Closer in, find sea perch, mangrove jack, red and spangled emperor, and coral trout. It's A$215 for a full day (bait, equipment, instruction, refreshments, fuel levy, and reef taxes included; rod and reel hire is A$45 per day). Port Douglas accommodation transfers are free; it's A$45 for transfers from Cairns or the northern beaches. ⊠ *Closehaven Marina, Port St.* ☎ *07/4099–6668* ⊕ *www.mvnorseman.com.au.*

RIVER CRUISES

FAMILY **Crocodile Express.** Bird-watchers and photographers flock to Crocodile Express's flat-bottom boats to cruise the Daintree River on crocodile-spotting excursions; you may also see rare birds and outsized butterflies, flying foxes, snakes, and lizards en route. Sixty-minute cruises leave the Daintree Gateway, near the ferry crossing, at regular intervals from 8:30 am to 2:30 pm (A$25 per person); or you can board at Daintree Village Jetty and cruise the Upper Daintree regularly between 10 and 3:30 (A$25 pp). Extra cruises from both access points are scheduled in peak periods. ⊠ *5 Stewart St., end of Mossman–Daintree Rd., Daintree Village* ☎ *07/4098–6120* ⊕ *www.crocodileexpress.com.*

RAIN FOREST AND REEF TOURS

FAMILY
Fodor's Choice
★
Back Country Bliss Adventures. This company is based in Port Douglas but ranges much farther afield; its customized, culturally and eco-sensitive small-group day and multiday trips take you to nature and adventure hot spots in the Atherton Tablelands and Mareeba Wetlands to Cape Trib and Cooktown. They'll take you sea kayaking, wakeboarding, kite-surfing, rafting, mountain biking, drift-snorkeling in rain-forest streams, or "jungle surfing" over the canopy. Well-chosen wilderness locations, quality equipment, excellent staff including indigenous guides, and Wet Tropic World Heritage Tour Operator accreditation give the Bliss team the edge. ☎ *07/4099–3677* ⊕ *www.backcountrybliss.com.au.*

Daintree Tours by Deluxe Safaris. This operator conducts daylong, well-guided trips in top-of-the-line 4WD vehicles and custom-built trucks. Visit the Atherton Tablelands, Mossman Gorge, and Cape Tribulation (A$185) or take the rugged track to Bloomfield Falls (POA). All safaris stop for guided walks, swims, and croc-spotting cruises, and visit the Daintree Ice Cream Factory if time permits. You can also arrange a daylong private wildlife-spotting charter to the Outback, west of Mareeba. Ample lunch and refreshments, included in all excursions, ensure you keep your strength up. Port Douglas pickups and drop-offs make the early-morning starts simple. ⊠ *Shop 3A, 23 Warner St.* ☎ *07/4099–6406, 1800/005966* ⊕ *www.deluxesafaris.com.au.*

FAMILY **Reef and Rainforest Connections.** This long-established, eco-friendly operator offers day trips to Kuranda's attractions, including the historic Scenic Railway, the Skyrail Rainforest Cableway, and the Tjapukai Aboriginal Cultural Park or Rainforestation (A$155–A$205); excursions to Cape Tribulation, the Daintree rain forest, and Mossman Gorge; and Great Barrier Reef cruises with Quicksilver. The company also runs excursions to Cape Tribulation, the Daintree, and Mossman Gorge, and Great Barrier Reef cruises with Quicksilver Connections. ⊠ *40 Macrossan St.*

8

☎ *1300/780455 reservations, 07/4035–5566 administration* ⊕ *www. reefandrainforest.com.au.*

FAMILY

Fodor's Choice

★

Tony's Tropical Tours. This company gives entertaining small-group day tours in luxe land cruisers that take in rain-forest sights and attractions as far as Cape Tribulation (A$180) or, if you're prepared to get up earlier, the renowned and ruggedly beautiful Bloomfield Track (A$205). Well-informed, witty commentary from Tony and other local experts, and non-rushed, well-chosen stops and activities—from interpretative ancient-rain-forest walks and Daintree River wildlife (croc) cruises, to handmade ice-cream and tropical-fruit tasting—make these trips crowd-pleasers. Refreshments, included in the cost, are a cut above the norm: think plunger (French press) coffee, rain-forest tea, and a satisfying BBQ lunch with damper (traditional Aussie bushmen's bread). There's also a terrific charter tour to the crater lakes, Atherton Tablelands, and Mareeba Wetlands (A$1,020 for four people), on which you might see kangaroos, birdlife, and the famed Curtain Fig tree. ☎ *07/4099–3230* ⊕ *www.tropicaltours.com.au.*

SNORKELING AND DIVING

Eye to Eye Marine Encounters. On these all-inclusive dive/snorkel live-aboard trips, you can visit world-renowned northern Great Barrier Reef and Coral Sea sites, including 2,000-foot drop-offs and pristine coral gardens, top shark-spotting sites, and turtle-nesting grounds. John Rumney, who pioneered swim-with-whales in Queensland, brings 30 years of experience on the Reef and extensive ecological knowledge and nautical expertise to the expeditions, working with highly skilled divers, scientists, and skippers to ensure each trip is as exciting as it is eco-friendly. ✉ *10 Captain Cook Hwy.* ☎ *07/4098–5417, 0417/726622* ⊕ *www.marineencounters.com.au.*

FAMILY

Fodor's Choice

★

Poseidon. This advanced eco-certified operator conducts guided snorkeling and PADI-style diving trips to sites at three separate parts of the Agincourt Ribbon Reef on a small, usually uncrowded boat, and longer cruises to outer Great Barrier Reef sites, with excellent pre-dive briefings by a marine naturalist, high safety standards, and a wider-than-average choice of dive sites. A day's cruise to three Agincourt sites is A$220 for snorkelers, and includes morning and afternoon tea and a buffet lunch (Lycra suits, masks, snorkels, flotation devices, and wet suits are A$5 per day). The cruise with introductory diving, including dive gear and up to three underwater forays, is A$280 with one dive; subsequent dives are A$40 each. For certified divers, a full day in the water is A$240–A$275 (gear is an extra A$20 per day). Everyone pays a reef charge of A$6 on board. Port Douglas transfers are free; from Cairns or the Northern Beaches, it's A$30. ✉ *Grant and Macrossan Sts.* ☎ *1800/085674, 07/4099–4772* ⊕ *www.poseidon-cruises.com.au* 🚢 *From A$220 (cruise and snorkeling); from A$240 (with diving); A$6 reef/admin tax* ⊙ *Daily 8:30–4:30.*

FAMILY

Quicksilver Connections. This company runs fast, modern catamarans that speed you from Port Douglas' marina to a large commercial activity platform at Agincourt Reef on the outer Barrier Reef, where options include marine-biologist-guided snorkeling tours (A$54–A$72), introductory or certified scuba dives (extra A$110–A$155), 10-minute scenic heli-tours (A$159), and "Ocean Walker" seabed explorations (A$155). There's also a semisubmersible underwater observatory, included in the A$215 rate. A quieter sailing excursion to a Low Isles coral cay, closer to shore (A$167), includes a biologist-guided glass-bottom-boat trip and snorkeling. Everyone pays a A$6 reef tax. The staff is patient, efficient, and knowledgeable. The trip includes a varied lunch buffet and dive/snorkel gear. Transfers are available from Port Douglas accommodations, Palm Cove, the Northern Beaches, and Cairns (A$10–A$26). ⊠ *Port Douglas Marina, 1 Wharf St.* ☎ *07/4087–2100* ⊕ *www.quicksilver-cruises.com.*

The Silver Series: Silversonic. High-end catamaran Silversonic whisks visitors to three pristine dive-snorkel sites on Agincourt Reef, known for its high-visibility waters. There, you can spend five hours amid spectacular corals on the edge of the Coral Sea trench, with turtles, rays, tropical fish, large pelagic species, and, in season, the odd minke whale. Cruises run daily, weather permitting; the tariff includes a "tropical smorgasbord" lunch, morning and afternoon tea, free Wi-Fi, snorkeling, and gear; guided scuba dives cost extra. Coach transfers from local accommodations are included in the cruise fare; transfers to and from Palm Cove, the Northern Beaches, and Cairns are available for a surcharge. ⊠ *Port Douglas Marina, 1 Wharf St.* ☎ *07/4044–9944* ⊕ *www. silverseries.com.au* ➦ *Full-day snorkeling cruise, A$208; scuba diving A$35–A$65 (1 dive), A$55–A$120 (2 dives), A$75–A$80 (3 dives), A$6 reef tax/admin.*

WHERE TO EAT

$$$

FRENCH FUSION

Fodor's Choice

★

✕ **Harrisons Restaurant & Bar.** A classic "Queenslander" with a lovely outdoor cocktails area shaded by century-old mango trees and fine-dining inside, Harrisons impresses with deftly executed French–meets–Modern Australian dishes that showcase fresh seafood and premium regional produce. You might start with Moreton Bay bugs or yellowfin tuna sashimi; mains on offer include roasted barramundi or tender Chateaubriand of Victorian Black Angus steak (A$98 for two). Desserts run the gamut from light-as-air lemon meringue pie to a decadent Valrhona white chocolate and amaretto zabaglione with honeycomb. There's a six-course "menu gourmande" at A$100 per person, A$150 with matched wines. On the wine list, you'll find plenty of good mid-priced antipodean drops and a smattering of French ones. $ *Average main: A$40* ⊠ *22 Wharf St.* ☎ *07/4099–4011* ⊕ *www.harrisonsrestaurant. com.au* ➹ *Reservations essential.*

$$$

SEAFOOD

FAMILY

Fodor's Choice

★

✕ **On The Inlet Seafood Restaurant.** Choose your own live mud crab from holding tanks at this much-lauded seafood restaurant fronting Dickson Inlet. Watch yachts dock as you sit on the deck and down the sunset special: a generous bucket of prawns and a choice of beer, wine, or bubbly for A$18; arrive around 5 and you can watch resident giant 250-kilogram (550-pound) grouper, George, get fed. Modern Australian dishes put the focus on fine, fresh North Queensland produce, especially seafood, which is delivered direct from local fishing boats to the restaurant's pontoon. You can start with freshly shucked oysters or chili-salt calamari, then move on to beer-battered Spanish mackerel or a prosciutto-wrapped barramundi fillet. There's also an appealing kids'

8

menu (A$15, two courses) and a terrific wine and cocktail list. If you're planning to come during peak dinner hours, a reservation is highly recommended. $ *Average main: A$34* ⊠ *3 Inlet St.* ☎ *07/4099–5255* ⊕ *www.portdouglasseafood.com.*

$$$ ✕ **Salsa Bar & Grill.** Rub shoulders with local foodies and visitors-in-the-

MODERN
AUSTRALIAN
FAMILY
Fodor's Choice
★

know on the deck of this lively waterside institution. The large wooden deck overlooking Dickson Inlet becomes an intimate dining area after sunset. The tropical Modern Australia dinner menu features kangaroo loin, smoked duck breast, herb-crusted barramundi, yellowfin tuna, a house jambalaya loaded with yabbies (local crayfish), tiger prawns, squid, and crocodile sausage. There's an extensive antipodean wine list, and happy hour comes daily between 3 and 5, just right for a tropical daiquiri or two. Prebooking's strongly advised. $ *Average main: A$33* ⊠ *26 Wharf St.* ☎ *07/4099–4922* ⊕ *www.salsaportdouglas.com. au* ⌕ *Reservations essential.*

$$$ ✕ **Watergate Restaurant & Lounge Bar.** Atmospheric indoor-outdoor din-

MODERN
AUSTRALIAN

ing, attentive service, and a well-stocked bar are nice, but the primary draw at this relaxed restaurant is the food, which highlights the freshest local ingredients: reef fish and prawns straight off Port Douglas's fishing boats, and seasonal fruit, vegetables, and herbs from the Atherton Tableland. The seasonal menu might include dukkah-crusted kangaroo loin with beetroot-goat's cheese tart; prawn-scallop ravioli in a creamy chardonnay-leek sauce; apple-infused Tableland pork; or eye fillet with a smoked-crocodile croquette and Daintree coffee jus. Book ahead for dinner, especially in peak periods. $ *Average main: A$34* ⊠ *5/31 Macrossan St.* ☎ *07/4099–5544* ⊕ *www.watergateportdouglas. com.au* ☾ *No lunch.*

WHERE TO STAY

For expanded hotel reviews, visit Fodors.com.

$ ⛫ **Best Western Lazy Lizard Motor Inn.** The spacious, self-contained studio

HOTEL
FAMILY
Fodor's Choice
★

at this small motel provide the perfect escape from Port Douglas's tourist crush. **Pros:** friendly hosts; great rates; free cable TV channels and Wi-Fi; easy parking outside your door. **Cons:** reception closes at 7 pm; no on-site bar or restaurant. $ *Rooms from: A$195* ⊠ *121 Davidson St.* ☎ *07/4099–5900* ⊕ *www.bestwestern.com.au* ⮑ *22 studios* ☾ *Reception closed 7 pm–8 am* ❙◉❙ *Breakfast.*

$$$$ ⛫ **Coconut Grove Port Douglas.** These luxe apartments and penthouses

RENTAL

perched above Port's main strip have state-of-the-art furnishings and appliances, deep free-standing spa baths, and large entertaining spaces including huge, furnished balconies or decks. **Pros:** immaculate, user-friendly living areas; central location; free undercover parking. **Cons:** extra fees for Wi-Fi use and room servicing; reception closes at 5; 10 am check-out. $ *Rooms from: A$455* ⊠ *56 Macrossan St.* ☎ *07/4099–0600* ⊕ *www.coconutgroveportdouglas.com.au* ⮑ *31 apartments, 2 penthouses* ☾ *Reception closes daily 5 pm–8 am* ❙◉❙ *No meals.*

$$$ ⛫ **Mandalay Luxury Beachfront Apartments.** With beautiful Four-Mile

RENTAL
FAMILY

Beach just outside and shops and eateries a brisk walk away, you can't find a better location than these comfortable, expansive, fully equipped apartments. **Pros:** reasonable rates, especially for two-bedroom units; plenty of space; close to the beach. **Cons:** street outside is poorly lighted at night; no reception in off-peak hours; fee for Wi-Fi access; closest restaurants are a 10-minute walk away. $ *Rooms from: A$365* ⊠ *Garrick and Beryl Sts.* ☎ *07/4099–0100* ⊕ *www.mandalay.com.au* ⊸ *41 apartments* ⊘ *Reception closed daily after business hrs* ⫧⊙⫧ *No meals.*

$

RESORT

⌐ **Pink Flamingo Resort.** This gay-friendly boutique resort, set amid tropical gardens around a large, heated lagoon pool, is a perfect mix of hip and affordable, gregarious and relaxed. **Pros:** terrific grounds, facilities, and hosts; free public-area Wi-Fi and parking; A$10 per night discount for "eco-stays" (no housekeeping) and two+-day stays. **Cons:** 15- to 20-minute walk to beaches and Port Douglas's main strip (local buses, 7–midnight, stop 200 meters from the door); no in-room Wi-Fi; reception hours limited. $ *Rooms from: A$145* ⊠ *115 Davidson St.* ☎ *07/4099–6622 9–5 daily, 0419/213228 after hrs* ⊕ *www. pinkflamingo.com.au* ⊸ *10 villas, 2 studios* ⊘ *Reception closed Mon.– Sat. 5 pm–8am, and Sun. after 1 pm* ⫧⊙⫧ *No meals.*

$$

RESORT

Fodor's Choice

★

⌐ **Thala Beach Lodge.** Set on 145 acres of private beach, coconut groves, and forest, this eco-certified nature lodge is about low-key luxury. **Pros:** eco-friendly ethos; multiday packages; interesting free activities. **Cons:** no in-room Internet acess; limited food available between meals; 20-minute drive to Port Douglas. $ *Rooms from: A$289* ⊠ *Private Beach Rd. (off Bruce Hwy., 38½ km [24 miles] north of Cairns), Oak Beach* ☎ *07/4098–5700, 866/998–4252 toll-free from U.S.* ⊕ *www. thalabeach.com.au* ⊸ *45 rooms* ⫧⊙⫧ *Multiple meal plans.*

SHOPPING

FAMILY

Fodor's Choice

★

Port Douglas Markets. At the waterfront Port Douglas Markets, local growers and artisans gather on Sunday mornings to sell fresh tropical produce and gourmet goodies, original art and crafts, handmade garments, jewelry, books, and souvenirs by the shore. You can also get reflexology massages and hair-braiding and -beading. The atmosphere's relaxed, the crowd's colorful, and there's plenty of variety. ⊠ *Anzac Park, Wharf St. end of Macrossan St.* ☎ *0408/006788.*

MOSSMAN

14 km (8½ miles) northwest of Port Douglas, 75 km (47 miles) north of Cairns.

This sleepy sugarcane town of just a couple of thousand residents has shops, a medical center, and gas stations, but most visitors merely pass through en route to Mossman Gorge, the Daintree, and rain-forest accommodations.

GETTING HERE AND AROUND

From Port Douglas, it's 20 km (12 miles) or about 20 minutes' drive northwest to Mossman. From Cairns it's a 75-km (47-mile) drive along the Captain Cook Highway. There's little here to explore, but it's a good place to stop for supplies and has a few fine eateries.

ESSENTIALS

Visitor Information Destination Daintree ☎ *07/4098–0070* ⊕ *www. daintreevillage.asn.au.*

EXPLORING

Daintree Village, a half-hour drive north along the Mossman-Daintree Road, has restaurants, cafés, galleries, and access to croc river cruises. Drive 20 minutes northeast of Mossman to reach Wonga Beach, where you can stroll along the sand or go walkabout with indigenous guides.

Fodor'sChoice ★ **Mossman Gorge.** Just 5 km (3 miles) outside Mossman are the spectacular waterfalls and river that tumble through sheer-walled Mossman Gorge. There are several boulder-studded, croc-free swimming holes, and a 2½-km (1½-mile) rain-forest walking track and suspension bridge. (Swimming in the river itself is hazardous, crocs or no, due to swift currents, slippery rocks, and flash flooding.) Keep your eyes peeled for tree and musky rat-kangaroos, Boyd's water dragons, scrub fowl, turtles, and big, bright butterflies—and try to avoid stinging vines (plants with serrated-edge, heart-shaped leaves, found at rain-forest edges). If you intend to hike beyond the river and rain-forest circuits, inform one of the appropriate authorities: Queensland Parks & Wildlife Service (⊕ *info@nprsr.qld.gov.au*), Cairns and Tropical North Visitor Information Centre (☎ *07/4051–3588* ⊕ *info@ttnq.org.au*) or the area's local guardians, the Kuku Yalanji, who run the new Mossman Gorge Centre, which has an info-desk, café/restaurant, gift shop, gallery, restrooms, showers, and parking. ⊠ *Mossman Gorge Centre, 212r Mossman Gorge Rd.* ☎ *07/4098–2595* ⊕ *www.mossmangorge.com.au*.

SPORTS AND THE OUTDOORS

The spectacular wilderness around Mossman is ideal terrain for adventure sports and outdoor activities. If you have a day—or even a few hours—to spare, you can explore beaches, rain forest, and bushland trails on horseback, mountain bike, or ATV; take a scenic trek through Mossman Gorge; or drift-snorkel in the Upper Mossman River. The region's indigenous guardians, the Kuku Yalanji, run guided tours of their coastal hunting grounds near Wonga Beach, in the World Heritage–listed Daintree rain forest.

ABORIGINAL TOURS

FAMILY Fodor'sChoice ★ **Kuku Yalanji Cultural Habitat Tours.** On these relaxed coastal walks (A$75), Kubirri Warra brothers Linc and Brandon Walker, members of the Kuku Yalanji *bama* (people), take turns guiding groups through three diverse ecosystems along Cooya Beach, north of Port Douglas, demonstrating traditional plant use, pointing out bush tucker ingredients, recounting Dreamtime legends, and sharing their knowledge of indigenous culture and the area. On a two-hour night-spearing trip over similar terrain (A$150), the brothers teach hunting and gathering skills passed down by the Kuku Yalanji over millennia: observing, tracking, spear-throwing, and foraging, with plenty of jokes thrown in. Wear wading shoes, a hat, insect repellent, and (on day tours) sunscreen. Return transfers to the Port Douglas area are A$30. ⊠ *Mossman Gorge Rd., Mossman* ☎ *07/4098–2595* ⊕ *www.bamaway.com.au/KukuYalanji.aspx*.

Walkabout Adventures. This operator takes small groups on half- and full-day rain-forest safari and coastal hunting trips (A$150–A$190 per person), and runs an hour-long Daintree rain-forest walk that's perfect for time-pressed travelers (A$45). These excursions visit the world's oldest rain-forest, Mossman Gorge, and coastal mudflats, mangroves, and beaches, with swims in rain-forest streams, foraging beach and mangrove walks, and lessons on spear-throwing. The one-hour walk, departing Daintree Eco-Lodge & Spa most days, is best booked through the Eco-Lodge. Transfers are available from Port Douglas, Palm Cove, the Northern Beaches for a surcharge. ⊠ *Daintree Eco Lodge & Spa, 20 Daintree Rd., Daintree* ☎ *0429/2947–8206, 07/4098–6100 Daintree Eco-Lodge & Spa* ⊕ *www.walkaboutadventures.com.au* ☉ *Daily, prebooking essential.*

HELICOPTER EXCURSIONS

FAMILY

Fodor'sChoice

★

Vertical Adventures. The half- and full-day helicopter tours from Vertical Adventures whisk you from Great Barrier Reef sites to Daintree National Park and Mossman Gorge for guided kayak, mountain-bike, walking, or river-snorkeling adventures. Options include a half-day helicopter-kayak tour (A$349 per person with one to three guests; A$333 per person with four), and a half-day helicopter-river-snorkeling option (A$389/A$375). The Daintree Adventure Day includes a helicopter flight into the Daintree Rainforest, zip-line opportunities, and a crocodile-spotting river cruise (A$599/A$589). Helicopters depart from the Sheraton Mirage Country Club heli-pad near GBR's Sunbird Centre. Rates include flights, refreshments, all safety gear and equipment, entry fees, insurance, and transfers from Port Douglas, Mossman, and Oak (Thala) Beach; from Palm Cove or the Northern Beaches, it's A$35/A$50 return. ⊠ *4 Davidson St.* ☎ *07/4099–6310* ⊕ *www. verticaladventures.com.au.*

HORSEBACK RIDING

FAMILY

Daintree Station. Impressive displays of horsemanship and "jackeroo" (cowboy) skills are the draw at Daintree Station, which offers a daily Stockmans Lunch Muster complete with whip-cracking, cattle-driving, a bull catcher, ATVs, cattle dogs, stunt horses, and various other animals. It's all delivered with dry Outback humor and followed by a barbecue lunch, live music, and bush tales. Daily shows are staged in a 19th-century-inspired "Outback station shed" arena in rain-forest environs 12½ km (8 miles) north of Mossman or a 35-minute drive north of Port Douglas. After lunch, you can test your rodeo skills on a mechanical bull, or amuse the kids at the farm-animal petting zoo. ⊠ *Kingston Rd., Whyanbeel Valley* ☎ *07/4098–1149* ⊕ *www.daintreestation.com* ⊠ *A$63, A$120 with transfers (Stockmans Lunch Muster); A$99 (trail horse ride). Extra A$15 insurance levy for ATV tours and horse rides.*

WHERE TO STAY

For expanded hotel reviews, visit Fodors.com.

$$$

RESORT

Daintree EcoLodge & Spa. At this 30-acre boutique eco-resort in the ancient Daintree rain forest, elevated boardwalks protect the fragile environs and link the day spa, heated pool, restaurant, and 15 free-standing tree houses. **Pros:** alfresco spa treatments; luxe, house-made bathroom amenities; eco-friendly; lower rates with longer stays. **Cons:** some rooms lack seclusion; few rooms have reliable Wi-Fi access; bathrooms are basic for the price; noise from public areas carries to proximate rooms and spa. $ *Rooms from: A$365* ⊠ *20 Daintree Rd.,*

8

Silky Oaks Lodge, near Daintree National Park

3 km (2 miles) past Daintree village, 110 km (68 miles) north of Cairns ☎ *1800/808010 toll-free in Australia, 07/4098–6100* 🌐 *www.daintree-ecolodge.com.au* 🛏 *15 rooms* 🕓 *Reception closed daily 5 pm–9 am* 🍴 *No meals.*

$$$ RESORT Fodor's Choice ★ 🏨 **Silky Oaks Lodge.** Cocooned in national parkland, this Advanced Eco-tourism–certified hotel has luxe tree houses and suites clustered around an expansive open-sided lodge, day spa, and lagoon pool. **Pros:** lovely spa; free Wi-Fi in public areas; top-notch food; French-press coffee at breakfast. **Cons:** no in-room Internet; steep paths to some rooms (though you can call for a buggy pickup); occasional critters; access road can flood after heavy rain. [$] *Rooms from: A$398* ✉ *Finlayvale Rd., Mossman Gorge* ☎ *07/4098–1666* 🌐 *www.silkyoakslodge.com.au* 🛏 *37 rooms, 13 suites* 🍴 *Breakfast.*

CAPE TRIBULATION

35 km (22 miles) north of the Daintree River crossing, 140 km (87 miles) north of Cairns.

Set dramatically at the base of Mount Sorrow, Cape Tribulation was named by Captain James Cook after a nearby reef snagged the HMS *Endeavour,* forcing him to seek refuge at the site of present-day Cooktown. Today, the tiny settlement, little more than a general store and a few lodges, is the activities and accommodations base for the surrounding national park.

GETTING HERE AND AROUND

Daintree River Ferry. The turnoff for the Daintree River crossing is just under 30 km (18 miles) north of Mossman on the Daintree–Mossman Road, which winds through sugarcane plantations and towering green hills to the Daintree River, a short waterway fed by monsoonal rains that make it a favorite inland haunt for saltwater crocodiles. On the northerly side of the river, a sign announces Cape Tribulation National Park. There's just one ferry, carrying a maximum 27 vehicles, so although the crossing takes five minutes, the wait can be 15, especially between 11 am and 1 pm and in holiday periods. There's no need to prebook your passage, but do bring cash: credit cards aren't accepted. ☎ *07/4098–7536, 07/4099–9444* ⊕ *www.cairns.qld.gov.au/facilities-and-recreation/daintree-ferry* ⌦ *Round-trip: A$23 per car, A$9.50 motorbike, A$2 walk-on passenger/bicycle, A$46 multiday car pass (5 return trips)* ⊗ *Daily 6 am–midnight.*

The 140-km (86-mile) drive from Cairns to Cape Tribulation takes just under three hours. If you're renting a car, it's simplest to do so in Cairns or Port Douglas. This can be tough driving territory. The "highway" is narrow with just two lanes; many minor roads are rough and unpaved; and even major thruways in this area may be closed in the wet season due to flooding.

Mason's Cape Tribulation Tourist Information Centre & Shop and PK's Jungle Village, a little farther north on the opposite side of Cape Tribulation Road, are the last stops for food, supplies, and fuel as you head north. At PK's there's a supermarket, an ATM, and a pharmacy.

ATMs are scarce beyond Mossman. Get cash and gas at the service station and convenience store at Wonga Beach, or at PK's. North of the Daintree River, mobile phone coverage is limited (except in and around Mossman and Daintree Village and around Thornton Beach Kiosk), and you'll be lucky to get any signal once you get as far as Cape Tribulation.

Public transport is limited throughout the region. Coral Reef Coaches runs daily services between Cairns, Port Douglas, and Mossman/Silky Oaks Lodge. Sun Palm Transport's daily services link Cairns airport with Cairns, Palm Cove, and Port Douglas. Charter services to Mossman, Daintree, Cow Bay, and Cape Trib can also be arranged. The journey from Cairns to Port Douglas takes around two hours, with stops at most resorts on request.

ESSENTIALS

Bus Contacts Coral Reef Coaches ☎ *07/4098–2800* ⊕ *www.coralreefcoaches. com.au.* **Sun Palm Transport Group** ☎ *07/4087–2900* ⊕ *www. sunpalmtransport.com.au.*

Tours and Visitor Information Mason's Cape Tribulation Tourist Information Centre, Shop, & Mason's Tours ⌧ *3781 Cape Tribulation Rd.* ☎ *07/4098–0070* ⊕ *www.masonstours.com.au.* **PK's Jungle Village** ⌧ *PMB 7, Cape Tribulation Rd.* ☎ *1800/232333, 07/4098–0040* ⊕ *www.pksjunglevillage.com.au.*

EXPLORING

Cape Tribulation Road winds through rain forest north of Cow Bay, veering east to join the coast at Thornton Beach, then skirting a string of near-deserted beaches en route to Cape Trib. Accommodations, attractions, and access points for beaches, croc cruise boats, and mangrove and rain-forest boardwalks are well signposted from the main road.

These rugged-looking yet fragile environs, Kuku Yalanji tribal lands, are best explored with experienced, culturally sensitive and eco-conscious guides. Excursions by 4WD and on horseback, bicycle, boat, and foot are offered by a few dozen local operators and resorts.

If exploring off-road on your own, arm yourself with detailed local maps, supplies, and up-to-date information. Let a reliable person know your intended route and return time, and don't underestimate the wildness of this terrain.

Fodor's Choice
★
Cape Tribulation, Daintree National Park. The world's oldest tropical rain forest is an ecological wonderland: 85 of the 120 rarest species on Earth are found here, and new ones are still being discovered. The 22,000-acre park, part of the UNESCO World Heritage–listed Wet Tropics region, stretches along the coast and west into the jungle from Cow Bay, 40 km (25 miles) or around an hour's drive northwest of Mossman. Traditional owners, the Eastern Kuku Yalanji, who live in well-honed harmony with their rain-forest environs, attribute powerful properties to many local sites—so tread sensitively. Prime hiking season here is May through September, and many local operators offer guided Daintree rain-forest walks, longer hikes, and nighttime wildlife-spotting excursions. Gather information and maps from local rangers or the Queensland Parks and Wildlife Service's **ParksQ** website before hiking unguided, and stay on marked trails and boardwalks to avoid damaging your fragile surroundings. Whatever season you go, bring insect repellent. ☎ *13–7468* ⊕ *www.nprsr.qld.gov.au/parks/daintree-cape-tribulation.*

Daintree Discovery Centre. This World Heritage–accredited Wet Tropics Visitor Centre's elevated boardwalks and a high viewing tower enable you to overlook an astoundingly diverse tract of ancient rain forest. You can acquire information en route from handheld audio-guides, expert talks, and the on-site interpretative center. Four audio-guided trails include a Bush Tucker Trail and a Cassowary Circuit, although it's unlikely that you'll spot these large but well-camouflaged birds. Take the Aerial Walkway across part of the bush, then the stairs to the top of the 76-foot-high Canopy Tower. Keen students of botany and ecology might want to prebook a guided group tour. The shop sells books, cards, souvenirs, and clothing. ⊠ *Tulip Oak Rd. off Cape Tribulation Rd., Cow Bay* ☎ *07/4098–9171* ⊕ *www.daintree-rec.com.au* 🖃 *A$32 (includes 48-page guidebook/return entry for 7 days)* ☉ *Daily 8:30–5.*

SPORTS AND THE OUTDOORS
CANOPY TOURS

FAMILY **Jungle Surfing Canopy Tours.** It's an exhilarating perspective on the rain forest and reef: suspended above the canopy on flying-fox zip lines, your speed controlled by guides, you whiz along (and if you like, flip upside-down) over lush rain forest and Mason's Creek, stopping at five tree platforms for killer bird's-eye views. Sessions last 1½ to 2 hours (A$90) and depart eight times a day starting at 7:45 am. Nightly guided Jungle Adventures Nightwalks (A$40) explore the critter-filled 45-acre grounds, departing PK's Jungle Village reception at 7:30 pm. Transfers from most local accommodations are free, or self-drive to the central departure point. Thrice-weekly day-tour packages from Port Douglas include lunch at Whet. Note that Jungle Surfing is unsuitable for anyone weighing more than 120 kilograms (260 pounds), and that children under 18 must bring a medical certificate and waiver before they'll be allowed to zip-line. ⊠ *From The Boardwalk Cafe (next to PK's), off Cape Tribulation Rd.* ☎ *07/4098–0043* ⊕ *www.junglesurfing.com.au.*

GREAT BARRIER REEF TOURS

Ocean Safari. Eco-certified Ocean Safari runs half-day small-group tours that include snorkeling two pristine sites on the Great Barrier Reef, just half an hour's thrilling motorboat ride off Cape Trib Beach. Well-chosen sites on magnificent Mackay and Undine reefs teem with "Nemos" (clown anemone fish), turtles, rays, barracuda, potato cod, giant clams, nudibranchs, and an astounding array of corals. A maximum of 25 passengers and a rigid inflatable boat (with covered seating area and bathroom facilities) help make everyone comfortable. Expert guidance, wet suits, snorkeling gear, and EMC (reef) tax are included in the price; you can buy soft drinks, chocolate, and underwater cameras on board. Transfers from Cow Bay are A$10; pickups from Cape Trib accommodations are free. ⊠ *From The Boardwalk Cafe, opposite PK's, Cape Tribulation Rd.* ☎ *07/4098–0666* ⊕ *www.oceansafari.com. au* ▱ *A$123* ⊙ *Daily 9–12:30 and 1–4:30, weather permitting.*

WHERE TO EAT

$$$
MEDITERRANEAN

✕ **On The Turps Bar & Restaurant.** At this open-air restaurant in the Daintree rain forest, wallabies, bandicoots, and musky rat kangaroos might join you at the table as you tuck into Mod Oz–meets–Mediterranean food that highlights local, seasonal ingredients including fresh seafood, and wines from the well-stocked bar. On The Turps also does "tropical Continental" breakfasts and varied, good-value lunches, as well as leisurely morning and afternoon Devonshire teas. Arrive early for a dip in the creek, a rain-forest stroll, or a spa treatment. $ *Average main: A$33* ⊠ *Daintree-Cape Tribulation Heritage Lodge & Spa, Lot 236, R36, Turpentine Rd., 15 km (10 miles) north of Daintree River crossing* ☎ *07/4098–9321* ⊕ *www.heritagelodge.net.au.*

$$
MODERN
AUSTRALIAN
FAMILY
Fodor's Choice
★

✕ **Whet Cafe, Bar and Restaurant.** Stylish and hip yet comfortable, Whet's draws visitors and locals with its outdoor deck, perfect for long lunches and sunset cocktails; Modern Australian food, wine, and service; and an on-site boutique cinema. Regional and seasonal ingredients, including plenty of local seafood, are deftly combined in fresh, simple dishes with Asian and Mediterranean influences. Gluten-free and vegetarian meals are available, as are healthy options for kids. Booking ahead is a good idea at peak visitor times. Whet Flicks, a laid-back licensed 24-seat cinema upstairs, runs daily sessions of pre-DVD-release movies. Relax in air-conditioned comfort on beanbags, recliners, or leather lounges and enjoy tapas-style snacks with the film. $ *Average main: A$27*

8

✉ *Lot 1, Cape Tribulation Rd.* ☏ *07/4098–0007, 0411/033340* ⊕ *www. whet.net.au* ✉ *Cinema sessions, A$10.*

WHERE TO STAY

For expanded hotel reviews, visit Fodors.com.

Privately run campgrounds and small resorts can be found along Daintree Road at Myall Creek and Cape Tribulation.

$$$
B&B/INN
📷 **Cockatoo Hill Retreat.** The elegant solar-powered tree houses at this impeccably run boutique retreat invite relaxation and romance. **Pros:** helpful, thoughtful host; eco-friendly; peace and quiet. **Cons:** phone/Internet access only if you have Telstra service; 4WD required during or after heavy rain; no on-site food apart from breakfasts. $ *Rooms from: A$395* ✉ *13 Cape Tribulation Rd., Daintree* ☏ *07/4098–9277* ⊕ *www.cockatoohillretreat.com.au* ⤳ *4* ⦿ *Breakfast.*

$
B&B/INN
📷 **Daintree Wild Zoo Bed and Breakfast.** At this simple but well-run B&B adjoining Daintree Zoo, wallabies, kangaroos, and cockatoos often join guests at breakfast in the open-sided dining area. **Pros:** free public Wi-Fi; friendly, knowledgeable hosts; half-price entry and 24-hour guest access to the zoo. **Cons:** budget rooms lack en-suite bathrooms and in-room Wi-Fi; few in-room appointments; no on-site meals after breakfast. $ *Rooms from: A$185* ✉ *2,054 Mossman-Daintree Rd., Wonga* ☏ *07/4098–7272* ⊕ *www.daintreewildbnb.com.au* ⤳ *6 motel rooms, 4 budget rooms with shared bath* ⦿ *Breakfast.*

$$$
RESORT
FAMILY
📷 **Heritage Lodge & Spa.** Nestled in World Heritage–listed rain forest beside Cooper Creek, this secluded spa resort is a great antidote to stress. **Pros:** friendly fauna; lots of on-site facilities; tranquil rain-forest environs. **Cons:** limited cell-phone coverage; drive or longish trek to beach; occasional critters. $ *Rooms from: A$330* ✉ *Lot 236, R96, Turpentine Rd., Diwan* ⊹ *15 km (10 miles) north of the Daintree River ferry crossing* ☏ *07/4098–9321* ⊕ *www.heritagelodge.net.au* ⤳ *20 cabins* ⦿ *Breakfast.*

COOKTOWN

103 km (64 miles), around 3½-hours' drive, north of Cape Tribulation; 324 km (203-mile) or 5½-hours' drive north of Cairns.

Traveling north, Cooktown is the last major settlement on the east coast of the continent, sitting at the edge of a difficult wilderness. Its wide main street consists mainly of two-story pubs with four-wheel-drive vehicles parked out front. Despite the frontier air, Cooktown has an impressive history. It was here in 1770 that Captain James Cook beached HMS *Endeavour* to repair her hull. Any tour of Cooktown should begin at the waterfront, where a statue of Cook gazes out to sea, overlooking the spot where he landed.

GETTING HERE AND AROUND

By car from Cairns, take the inland highway, Peninsula Developmental Road, a 200-odd-mile stretch of fully paved road that barrels you through Australia's Outback—watch for errant cattle and 'roos on the drive. From Cape Tribulation, head up the Cooktown Developmental Road, or take the 4WD-only Bloomfield Track, just 97 km (60 miles),

"Taking a walk of faith across a rope bridge in Daintree Rainforest" —poimuffin, Fodors.com member

but challenging and sometimes flooded in the Wet. The Bloomfield Track journey, which roughly traces a series of indigenous story-line trails known as the Bama (People's) Way, takes around three hours, longer in wet weather; the Developmental Road is smoother but less scenic. Getting around Cooktown, a compact town, is a comparative cinch: drive, walk, or cycle.

EXPLORING

Cooktown has some lovely old buildings and a cemetery dating from the 1870s gold rush. Stroll along botanic gardens trails and uncrowded beaches, check out the environment interpretative center and visitor info-hub Nature's Powerhouse, cool off in the public swimming pool, and scale Grassy Hill around sunset for stupendous views.

James Cook Museum. Cooktown, in its heyday, was a gold-mining port town, with 64 pubs lining the 3-km-long (2-mile-long) main street; a significant slice of this colorful history is preserved here at the National Trust–run James Cook Museum. The former convent houses relics of the Palmer gold-mining and pastoral eras, including a Chinese joss house, along with Aboriginal artifacts, canoes, and mementos of Cook's voyage—notably, the anchor and one of six cannons jettisoned when the HMS *Endeavour* ran aground. The surprisingly nice shop sells books and souvenirs. It's recommended that you allow at least an hour to pore over the exhibits. ⊠ *Helen St. at Furneaux St.* ☎ *07/4069–5386* ⊕ *www. nationaltrustqld.org* ✉ *A$10* ⊙ *Daily 9:30–4; may close Feb. and Mar.*

SPORTS AND THE OUTDOORS

There's plenty of outdoorsy fun to be had in and around Cooktown. Book a diving, snorkeling, or game-fishing cruise to the outer Barrier Reef or Lizard Island; take a guided rock-art or rain-forest walk; go Outback on a multiday 4WD Cape York excursion; or charter a scenic heli-flight over both World Heritage areas.

CULTURAL TOURS

FAMILY

Fodor's Choice

★

Guurrbi Tours. An hour's drive inland of Cooktown lie ancient Aboriginal rock-art sites of immense significance. Their exact locations are a closely guarded secret—so who better to guide you than Nugal-warra elder Willie Gordon, a designated storyteller? Willie guides guests around his ancestral rock-art sites, set high in the hills behind Hope Vale, on scheduled day tours that pick up from accommodations around Cooktown. The 5½-hour Rainbow Serpent tour takes in half a dozen sites including the renowned Rainbow Serpent Cave; the afternoon Great Emu tour covers rock sites and caves near the Hope Vale community. En route, Willie shares the Dreamtime stories and traditional lore behind this extraordinary cave art, some of which was painted by his own grandfather. If you're self-driving to the Guurrbi Meeting Point, near Hope Vale Aboriginal Community (about 45 minutes from town), you can collect a map and directions from **Cooktown Motel Pam's Place** on Boundary Street (☎ 07/4069–5166). Guurrbi also offers multiday drive-tour packages. ✉ *Tours depart from Pam's Place, 9 Boundary St.* ☎ *07/4069–6043* ⊕ *www.guurrbitours.com* 🖃 *Rainbow Serpent tour: A$85 (self-drive), A$120 (with transportation from Cooktown); min. 2 people (single supplement A$40)* ⊗ *Mon.–Sat. from 7:45 am (Rainbow Serpent tour); from 1:45 pm (Great Emu tour); self-drivers join group at 8:30 am at Guurrbi Meeting Point.*

FISHING

The closest town on the Queensland coast to the Great Barrier Reef, Cooktown offers fast, easy access to some of the reef's best fishing (and dive) sites. Boats bristling with game-fishing gear depart from the marina daily, bound for famed fishing grounds on the outer reef, and at Egret and Boulder, 10 miles offshore. The likely catch: Spanish mackerel, sailfish, coral trout, red and spangled emperor, and black marlin.

Cooktown Fishing Adventures. Bottom-fish with hand lines, troll for giant black marlin, or pop lures over the reef with Cooktown Fishing Adventures, an established local operator with a 56-foot, 900 hp, fully equipped boat and energetic, safety-conscious crew. The company runs guided game-fishing excursions to local sites and specializes in multiday, live-aboard trips for up to eight people to renowned fishing areas off Lizard Island, Cod Hole, and Princess Charlotte Bay, with fishing equipment and tackle, snorkeling gear, galley-cooked meals, and more supplied. You can also fish the estuaries or go crabbing on the mangrove flats. ☎ *07/4069–5500, 0409/696775* ⊕ *www.cooktownfishingcharters. com* 🖃 *Prices vary according to charter* ⊗ *Daily, prebooking essential.*

WHERE TO STAY

For expanded hotel reviews, visit Fodors.com.

$ ⊞ **Seaview Motel.** This clean, quiet seafront establishment has five catego-
HOTEL   ries of accommodation, some newer than others: standard rooms with
FAMILY   older TVs and no kitchenettes; semi-self-contained rooms with microwave
and sink; newer "deluxe" motel rooms with large flat-screen TVs and
lounge/dining areas; a self-contained family unit; and split-level townhouses that have two bedrooms, full kitchens with dishwashers, separate
lounge and dining areas, and large flat-screen TVs. **Pros:** helpful staff; take-
out drinks and breakfast packs/toasters (for a fee); scenic location. **Cons:**
no screens on sliding doors to motel-room balconies; small pool; breakfast
restaurant may close outside of peak periods. $ *Rooms from: A$110*
✉ *178 Charlotte St.* ☎ *07/4069–5377* ⊕ *www.cooktownseaviewmotel.*
com.au ⤳ *38 motel rooms, 1 family unit, 3 townhouses* ⊚*Breakfast.*

$ ⊞ **The Sovereign Resort Hotel.** This attractive, two-story colonial-style
HOTEL   hotel in the heart of town is the best bet in Cooktown. **Pros:** good-
FAMILY   value apartments; free in-room Wi-Fi; airport/wharf transfers; terrific
gardens, BBQ area, and pool. **Cons:** restaurant not open for dinner
in the wet season; Continental breakfast buffet low on selection and
expensive. $ *Rooms from: A$180* ✉ *128 Charlotte St., at Green St.*
☎ *07/4043–0500* ⊕ *www.sovereign-resort.com.au* ⤳ *31 rooms, 7*
apartments ⊘ *Café closed Sun. No dinner Nov.–Mar.* ⊚*No meals.*

THE WHITSUNDAY ISLANDS AND AIRLIE BEACH

8

The Whitsundays are a group of 74 islands situated within 161 km
(100 miles) of each other and around 50 km (31 miles) from Shute
Harbour, the principal mainland departure point, though some boats
depart from Airlie Beach marina nearby. Discovered in 1770 by Captain
James Cook of the HMS *Endeavour*—though in fact not on Whitsunday itself, thanks to a time-zone change oversight on Cook's part—the
Whitsundays are a favorite sailing destination and an easy-access base
from which to explore the midsection of the Great Barrier Reef. Some of
the islands' beaches—notably, famous Whitehaven Beach—are picture-
postcard gorgeous, though vegetation on the islands themselves looks
more scrubby than tropical. In fact, the entire region is subtropical,
making for moderate air and water temperatures year-round. Most of
the Whitsunday Islands are national parks, and, although you'll spot
few animals on them, birds are plentiful—more than 150 species make
their homes here. Only a few of the islands have resorts; others serve
as destinations for day trips, beach time, and bushwalks, or simply as
backdrop at scenic moorings.

Camping is popular on the myriad islands of the Whitsunday group. To
pitch a tent on islands lying within national parks you need a A$5.60
per-person, per-night permit from the ParksQ (Queensland Department
of National Parks, Recreation, Sport & Racing [NPRSR]). The Whitsunday Information Centre, on the Bruce Highway at Proserpine, is
open weekdays 9–5, Saturday 9–3, Sunday 10–3.

AIRLIE BEACH

1,119 km (695 miles) or 13½ hours' drive north of Brisbane; 623 km (387 miles) south of Cairns via the Bruce Highway.

Airlie Beach's balmy climate and its proximity to the Whitsunday Islands, a resort and water-sports playground, make it hugely popular with partying backpackers and holiday makers en route to the islands and reef.

GETTING HERE AND AROUND

The Whitsunday Coast Airport near Proserpine, 36 km (23 miles) south-east of Airlie Beach, has direct daily flights to and from Brisbane and less frequent services to Sydney, on Virgin Blue and Jetstar. **Whitsunday Transit** buses connect the airport and Proserpine Railway Station to Airlie Beach, Cannonvale, and Shute Harbour, with services timed to meet all flights and passenger trains (drive time 30–40 minutes). It's A$12.10, one way, to or from Proserpine railway station. **Greyhound Australia** and **Oz Experience** offer daily services into Airlie Beach from Sydney, Brisbane, and towns between, and from Cairns. **Queensland Rail** operates seven long-distance northbound and seven southbound trains weekly that stop at Proserpine Railway Station, about 25 km (15 miles) from Airlie Beach.

Koala Adventures is popular with the younger backpacker set, and runs three-day sailing trips around the Whitsundays on a stable luxury catamaran for A$379. It includes local charges, all meals, guided bushwalks, snorkeling tours, a Whitehaven Beach excursion, and two nights' dorm accommodation at South Molle Island Resort.

Whitsunday Sailing Adventures runs several sailing, scuba, and snorkeling trips around the islands and Great Barrier Reef on a dozen-plus owner-operated vessels, including modern sailing cats and tall ships. Choose from dive and snorkeling excursions (a two-night, three-day live-aboard outer reef trip starts at A$699 per person, with subsequent dives A$30–A$70), two-night performance sailing adventures (A$699 per person, maximum 12), eco-friendly excursions (A$175), and two- and three-day catamaran sailing cruises (A$735 and A$895 per person, maximum eight).

ESSENTIALS

Airport Whitsunday Coast Airport ✉ *Lascelles Ave., Sir Reginald Ansett Dr., Proserpine* ☎ *07/4945–0200* ⊕ *www.whitsunday.qld.gov.au/aerodromes.*

Boat Tour Contacts Cumberland Charter Yachts ✉ *Abel Point Marina, Shingley Dr.* ☎ *07/4946–7500, 1800/075101* ⊕ *www.ccy.com.au.* **Koala Adventures** ✉ *Abel Point Marina* ☎ *07/4946–9433, 1800/466444 toll-free in Australia* ⊕ *www.koalaadventures.com.* **Queensland Yacht Charters** ✉ *Abel Point Marina* ☎ *07/4946–7400, 1800/075013* ⊕ *www.yachtcharters.com.au.* **Whitsunday Rent A Yacht** ✉ *6 Bay Terr., Shute Harbour* ☎ *07/4946–9232, 1800/075000* ⊕ *www.rentayacht.com.au.* **Whitsunday Sailing Adventures** ✉ *Ground fl., 6 Airlie Esplanade* ☎ *07/4940–2000, 1300/653100* ⊕ *www. whitsundaysailingadventures.com.au.*

Bus Contacts Greyhound Australia ☎ *1300/473946 in Australia, 07/4690–9999* ⊕ *www.greyhound.com.au.* **Oz Experience** ☎ *07/8132–8233,*

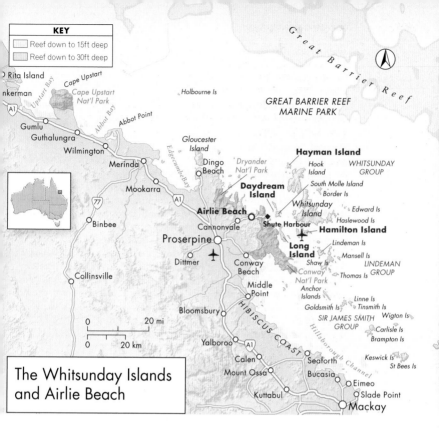

KEY
Reef down to 15ft deep
Reef down to 30ft deep

Great Barrier Reef

GREAT BARRIER REEF
MARINE PARK

Rita Island
nkerman
A1
Gumlu
Guthalungra
Wilmington
Merinda
Mookarra
A1
Binbee
Collinsville
Dittmer
Proserpine
Airlie Beach
Cannonvale
Conway Beach
Middle Point
Bloomsbury
Yalboroo
A1
Calen
Mount Ossa
Kuttabul
Seaforth
Bucasia
Eimeo
Slade Point
Mackay

Cape Upstart
Cape Upstart Nat'l Park
Upstart Bay
Abbot Bay
Abbot Point
Edgecumbe Bay
Holbourne Is
Gloucester Island
Dingo Beach
Dryander Nat'l Park
Daydream Island
Shute Harbour
Conway Nat'l Park
Hayman Island
Hook Island
WHITSUNDAY GROUP
South Molle Island
Border Is
Whitsunday Island
Edward Is
Haslewood Is
Hamilton Island
Long Island
Lindeman Is
Mansell Is
Shaw Is
Thomas Is
LINDEMAN GROUP
Anchor Islands
Goldsmith Is
Linne Is
Tinsmith Is
Wigton Is
SIR JAMES SMITH GROUP
Carlisle Is
Brampton Is
Keswick Is
St Bees Is
Hillsborough Channel
HIBISCUS COAST

0   20 mi
0   20 km

The Whitsunday Islands and Airlie Beach

1300/555287 in Aust. ⊕ www.ozexperience.com. **Whitsunday Transit**
☎ 07/4948–1515 ⊕ www.whitsundaytransit.com.au.

Train Contacts Proserpine Railway Station ⊠ Hinschen St., Proserpine
☎ 13/131617 in Australia, 07/4945–1013 ⊕ www.qr.com.au. **Queensland Rail**
☎ 1800/872467 ⊕ www.qr.com.au.

EXPLORING

Airlie's main street is packed with cafés, bars, tour agencies, and hotels, with homes and higher-end accommodations extending up the steep hills behind it. The waterfront Esplanade, with its boardwalk, landscaped gardens, swimming lagoon, and weekend markets, is generally lively.

FAMILY
Fodor's Choice
★

Airlie Beach Lagoon. This stinger-free swimming enclosure on Airlie's shorefront has dedicated lap-swimming lanes, real-sand "beaches," two adjoining children's pools, and sensor-activated lighting after dark. There are toilets, showers, and changing rooms nearby, and all pools are patrolled by trained lifeguards year-round. A tropical garden, crisscrossed with walkways and dotted with public art, picnic tables, and free electric BBQs, surround the lagoon, and there's a playground for the kids. Not surprisingly, it's hugely popular with locals and visitors, especially in stinger season. **Amenities:** food and drink;

lifeguards; toilets; showers. **Best for:** swimming. ✉ *The Esplanade at Broadwater Ave., parallel to Shute Harbour Rd.* ☎ *07/4945–0200* 🌐 *www.whitsunday.qld.gov.au* 🕐 *Patrolled daily, 8 am–9 pm (summer), 9–7 (winter).*

BEWARE

From October to May the ocean off beaches north of Rockhampton is rendered virtually unswimmable by toxic-tentacled box jellyfish.

FAMILY **Conway National Park.** Ten minutes' drive southeast of Airlie, Conway National Park is a 54,000-acre expanse of mangroves, woodlands, rocky cliffs, and tropical lowland rain forest that shelters the endangered Proserpine rock wallaby and other rare species, as well as plenty of sulphur-crested cockatoos, emerald doves, Australian brush-turkeys, and orange-footed scrubfowl. Most walking trails start at the park's picnic area off Shute Harbour Road, 6 km (3½ miles) from Airlie. Mount Rooper Walking Track, a 5.4-km (3-mile) circuit, meanders uphill through bushland to a lookout with breathtaking Whitsundays views. The 30-km (18½-mile), three-day Whitsunday Great Walk starts at the Brandy Creek car park and ends in Airlie Beach. Swamp Bay track follows the creek to a coral-strewn beach with a bush camping area. ✉ *Shute Harbour andMandalay Rds.* ☎ *07/4945–3711 (Whitsunday Visitor Information), 1800/801252, 13–7468 ParksQ hotline/camping permits* 🌐 *www.nprsr.qld.gov.au/parks/conway.*

Shute Harbour. Ten kilometers (6 miles) southeast of Airlie Beach along Shute Harbour Road, Shute Harbour is the main ferry terminal and gateway to the Whitsunday Islands and the reef. The large, sheltered inlet teems with boats—it's the second-busiest commuter port in Australia, after Sydney's Circular Quay. Though accommodation is available, the harbor is geared toward transferring visitors. For a great view over Shute Harbour and the Whitsunday Passage, drive to the top of Coral Point. ✉ *Shute Harbour Rd., Shute Harbour* 🌐 *www.shuteharbour.net.*

WHERE TO EAT

$$$ MODERN AUSTRALIAN FAMILY Fodor's Choice ★

🍴 **Déjà Vu Restaurant.** Alfresco tables and Balinese-style dining pavilions flank an infinity-edge pool at this classy Airlie eatery. The usual surf'n'turf options are replaced by inventive, seasonal Mod Oz–Mediterranean dishes. You can start with freshly shucked oysters or lemon-pepper calamari, followed by crispy-skinned Tasmanian salmon, kangaroo loin, or Moreton Bay bugs (crayfish) in season. Delectable desserts might include a passion-fruit semi-freddo with mango-lychee coulis, a gluten-free chocolate soufflé, or coconut panna cotta. Vegetarian and children's meals are available; the coffee's a cut above the norm, and the wine list is extensive. At lunch, tuck into simple seafood dishes, interesting salads, and gourmet panini for under A$28. Sunday's eight-course epicurean lunches with live entertainment are legendary (A$44.50 per person, beverages additional). [$] *Average main: A$36* ✉ *Water's Edge Resort, 4 Golden Orchid Dr.* ☎ *07/4948–4309* 🌐 *www.dejavurestaurant.com.au* 🕐 *Closed Mon. and Tues.*

$$ MODERN AUSTRALIAN

🍴 **Easy Cafe.** Tucked away in an arcade off the main strip, Easy Cafe is a terrific option for relaxed breakfasts, light lunches, and suppers, drawing a sociable mix of travelers and locals, who come for the reasonably priced, tasty food, and great coffee. In addition, there's good music, free Wi-Fi, board games, comfy sofas, and accommodating staff. Join the crowd that flocks here weekdays for the good-value Easy Breakfast; pop in during the day for terrific coffee and cake, a burger, or a cold beer. After five, they offer a small but varied menu of quality Modern Australian dishes; try the basil-cashew-nut-crusted rack of lamb with creamy mash. $ *Average main: A$28* ⊠ *Pavilion Arcade, 287 Shute Harbour Rd.* ☎ *07/4946–5559.*

WHERE TO STAY
For expanded hotel reviews, visit Fodors.com.

$ **Airlie Beach Hotel.** With the town's small beach at its doorstep, three
HOTEL eateries and bars downstairs, and the main street directly behind it,
FAMILY this hotel makes a convenient base. **Pros:** free Wi-Fi and undercover parking; on-site food and drink. **Cons:** no room service; rooms can be noisy. $ *Rooms from: A$189* ⊠ *16 The Esplanade, at Coconut Grove* ☎ *07/4964–1999, 1800/466233* ⊕ *www.airliebeachhotel.com.au* ⌑ *56 rooms, 4 suites.*

$$$ **Peppers Airlie Beach.** The expansive one- to three-bedroom apartments
RESORT at this high-end hillside resort are tailored for comfort, with spa baths the size of small cars, designer decor and appliances, high-end entertainment systems, free Wi-Fi, and big, furnished balconies with great views of the bay and yacht club. **Pros:** classy decor, food, and service; quiet location; buggies to ferry you up the resort's steep driveways. **Cons:** outdoor dining only; small pool area; 2% surcharge on credit-card payments; no in-room heating in winter. $ *Rooms from: A$299* ⊠ *Mt. Whitsunday Dr.* ☎ *07/4962–5100, 1300/737444* ⊕ *www.peppers.com. au* ⌑ *102 apartments* ⦿l *No meals.*

$ **Whitsunday Moorings B&B.** Overlooking Abel Point Marina, this metic-
B&B/INN ulously run B&B has everything you need: stupendous marina views,
Fodor'sChoice charming hosts, and terrific gourmet breakfasts, often accompanied by
★ colorful chirping parrots. **Pros:** charming, knowledgeable hosts; fab breakfasts; upmarket toiletries; free Wi-Fi. **Cons:** uphill walk from main street; open room plan best suited to couples. $ *Rooms from: A$195* ⊠ *37 Airlie Crescent* ☎ *07/4946–4692* ⊕ *www.whitsundaymooringsbb. com.au* ⌑ *3 rooms* ⦿l *Breakfast.*

NIGHTLIFE
Shute Harbour Road, the main strip, is where it all happens in Airlie Beach. Most main-street establishments cater to the backpacker crowd, with boisterous, college-style entertainment, live music, and a late-opening dance-club. Older and more sophisticated visitors gravitate to quieter establishments with pleasant outdoor areas, such as the bars and restaurants attached to some of the hillside resorts.

Beaches Bar & Bistro. The crowd is gregarious at Beaches Bar & Bistro, part of the hostel of the same name. Here, you can catch live bands most nights, eat hearty food cheaply from noon till 9, play pool, mingle in the big beer garden, and watch games on big-screen TVs. ⊠ *356 Shute Harbour Rd.* ☎ *07/4946–6244, 1800/636630* ⊕ *www.beaches.com.au.*

Beaches on the Whitsunday Islands group are among the state's best.

Mama Africa. When the main-street watering holes close around midnight, Airlie's party kicks on till late at hot, tribally-themed Mama Africa. ✉ *263 Shute Harbour Rd.* ☎ *07/4948–0438* 📧 *A$5.*

LONG ISLAND

This aptly named island lies south of Shute Harbour, 12 km (7 miles) west of Hamilton Island. Although it's 9 km (5½ miles) long and no more than 2 km (1 mile) wide—around 3,000 acres total—it has several walking trails through tracts of dense rain forest. Most of the island is national parkland, sheltering birds, butterflies, goannas, and wallabies. Some of its beaches are picturesque; others rocky and windblown. Though its waters are less clear than those off the outer reef islands, there are some excellent snorkeling spots on the island's fringing reef, where you'll share the balmy water with soft and hard corals, tropical fish, and turtles. You may also see dolphins and migrating humpback whales July through September.

GETTING HERE AND AROUND

You can reach Long Island several times a day between 9 am and 5:45 pm from Airlie Beach's Abel Point Marina with **Cruise Whitsundays**. The trip takes around 20 minutes and costs A$36, per person, one way. You can also reach Long Island via a fast, air-conditioned catamaran cruiser from Hamilton Island. Cruise Whitsundays Resort Connections services, scheduled to coincide with incoming and outgoing flights, depart Great Barrier Reef (Hamilton Island) Airport Jetty several times daily, picking up at Hamilton Island Marina en route (A$48 per person). You can also arrange coach-ferry transfers from Whitsunday Coast

(Proserpine) Airport and Proserpine Rail Station (A$55 per person); prebooking is essential.

Various regional operators, including Air Whitsunday and Hamilton Island Air, offer seaplane or helicopter transfers to Long Island resorts from regional airports including Great Barrier Reef (Hamilton Island), Whitsundays Airport near Airlie Beach, and Whitsundays Coast (Proserpine). Transfers are scheduled to coincide with incoming and outgoing flights. If your vacation time is limited, this is the fastest way to get here—but per-person costs can be steep. Trips require minimum passenger numbers, strict baggage limits apply, and prebooking is essential.

If you're keen to visit other resort isles from Hamilton Island, the on-island helicopter service, Hamilton Island Air, can transport you there. Helicopters take off on demand from Great Barrier Reef (Hamilton Island) Airport, flying to Long, Daydream, Hayman, and South Molle islands. Prebookings are essential for all charter flights; baggage is limited to 15 kg (33 pounds) per passenger, in soft-sided bags.

Virgin Australia and Jetstar have direct daily flights between Hamilton Island and Melbourne, Sydney, and Brisbane.

ESSENTIALS

Air Contacts **Air Whitsunday** ✉ *Air Whitsunday Airport, 12 Whitsunday Rd., off Shute Harbour Rd., Flametree, Airlie Beach* ☎ *07/4946–9111* 🌐 *www.airwhitsunday.com.au.* **Hamilton Island Air** ✉ *Great Barrier Reef (Hamilton Island) Airport, Palm Valley Way, Hamilton Island* ☎ *07/4969–9599* 🌐 *www.hamiltonair.com.au.*

SPORTS AND THE OUTDOORS

BOAT CRUISES

FAMILY Fodor's Choice ★ **Cruise Whitsundays.** This local outfit schedules single-, twin-, and three-island "Escapes," along with Great Barrier Reef diving and snorkeling excursions, on its fast, modern catamarans. Cruises run to Daydream Island (A$99–A$140), Daydream and Hamilton islands (A$140, or A$165 with breakfast on Daydream), and Daydream, Hamilton, and Whitsunday islands (A$195). All include lunch and gear. ✉ *Departs Palm Bay Jetty, South Long Island, Whitsunday Islands* ☎ *07/4946–4662* 🌐 *www.cruisewhitsundays.com.*

WHERE TO STAY

For expanded hotel reviews, visit Fodors.com.

$$ RESORT FAMILY 🏨 **BreakFree Long Island Resort.** A short walk over the hill from Palm Bay, this family-focused resort is big on outdoor activities, particularly water sports and group-oriented fun. **Pros:** numerous activities; good-value room-meal packages. **Cons:** can be noisy; groups of kids and teens run amok; heavy competition for equipment; fee for in-room safe and Internet; rooms not serviced daily. [$] *Rooms from: A$230* ✉ *Long Island, Whitsunday Passage, Whitsunday Islands* ☎ *07/4946–9400, 1800/075125* 🌐 *www.longislandresort.com.au* 🛏 *161 rooms, 31 lodges without bath* 🍴 *Multiple meal plans.*

$$$$ RESORT ALL-INCLUSIVE 🏨 **Paradise Bay Island Resort.** Talk about secluded—this exclusive, eco-friendly lodge on South Long Island's isolated southern tip consists of only 10 luxurious bungalows strung along a white-sand beach,

accessible only by helicopter. **Pros:** quality food; friendly wildlife; small carbon footprint. **Cons:** little variation in food; helicopter transfers to and from the island are A$798 per person, with a 15-kilogram (30-pound) baggage limit; no phone or Internet access; ban on electronic hair appliances. $ *Rooms from: A$1800* ⊠ *South Long Island, Whitsunday Islands* ☎ *07/4946–9777* ⊕ *www.paradisebay.com.au* ↘ *10 bungalows* ○ *All-inclusive.*

HAMILTON ISLAND

Though it's the most heavily populated and developed island in the Whitsunday group, more than 70% of Hamilton Island has been preserved in its natural state. The 1,482-acre island abounds in beautiful beaches (such as long, curving, palm-dotted Catseye Beach), bush trails, and spectacular lookouts. Yet for all its natural beauty, Hamilton's is more an action-packed, sociable holiday isle than a place to get away from it all.

Around 35 minutes by ferry from Shute Harbour, Hamilton buzzes with activity. Guests of the resort, and its various types of accommodation, including hotel-style and self-catering establishments, make up most of the itinerant population, but there are private residences here—as well as throngs of day-trippers from the mainland, other islands, and cruising yachts, who wander the island's bustling marina and village each day.

For a family-friendly, one-stop Whitsundays experience, Hamilton Island is a smart choice. Many of the resort accommodations allow kids under age 13 to stay free, provided they stay with parents and use existing beds (no roll-aways or cribs). Under-13s can even eat free at some island restaurants when staying at resort hotels, choosing from kids' menus.

The resort's set up like a small city, with its own school, post office and banking outlets, medical center, pharmacy, supermarket and DVD-hire store, plus shops, restaurants, bars, and a nightclub, all open to island guests and day-trippers. There's also an island beauty salon, and a day spa/relaxation center (open daily 10–6) that offers massage, aromatherapy treatments, and float-tank sessions. But little on Hamilton is free; prices—for food, activities, Internet use, even grocery items—can be steep. The ubiquitous golf carts that visitors hire to zip around the island are A$45 an hour, A$60 for three hours, and A$85 for 24 hours from Hamilton Island Buggy Rentals (7:30 am to 6 pm). Save a few bucks by using the free Island Shuttle service that runs around the island at regular intervals between 7 am and 11 pm.

GETTING HERE AND AROUND

Virgin Australia and Jetstar fly directly to Hamilton Island from Sydney, Melbourne, and Brisbane. You can take a Cruise Whitsundays ferry to the island from Abel Point Marina, Airlie Beach, or nearby Shute Harbour (A$56), or arrange a seaplane transfer from regional mainland airports at Proserpine or Mackay, or from Airlie Beach's Whitsunday Airport with Air Whitsunday. From Hamilton Island, the "hub" of the Whitsundays, you can catch a ferry to neighboring resort isles

Wind- and motor-powered water sports are popular on many Whitsunday Islands.

South Molle, Long, Daydream, and Hayman via fast ferry with Cruise Whitsundays Resort Connections, timed to coincide with incoming and outgoing flights from Hamilton's airport. You can get there faster by seaplane with Air Whitsunday (A$550) or helicopter with Hamilton Island Air.

Sunsail Australia. This operator has various yachts available for bareboat charter at Hamilton Island's marina. You can book a five-day-minimum charter yacht and sail around the Whitsundays' sheltered waters. Optional extras include professional skipper and cook, kayaks, and dinghy. Rates vary according to the number of days, number of passengers, vessel, and season. ⊠ *Front St.* ☎ *07/4948–9509, 1800/803988 toll-free in Australia, 888/350–3568 from U.S.* ⊕ *www.sunsail.com.au.*

ESSENTIALS

Buggy Rental Hamilton Island Buggy Rental ☎ *07/4946–8263, 13/7333* ⊕ *www.hamiltonisland.com.au/golf-buggy.*

Ferry Cruise Whitsundays ⊠ *Cruise Whitsundays Bldg., 2 Abel Point Marina, Airlie Beach* ☎ *07/4946–4662* ⊕ *www.cruisewhitsundays.com.*

Helicopter Hamilton Island Air ⊠ *Great Barrier Reef (Hamilton Island) Airport, Palm Valley Way, Hamilton Island* ☎ *07/4969–9599* ⊕ *www.hamiltonair.com.au.*

Seaplane Air Whitsunday ⊠ *Terminal 1, Whitsunday Airport, 12 Air Whitsunday Ave., Flametree, Ailrie Beach* ☎ *07/4946–9111* ⊕ *www.airwhitsunday.com.au.*

CASTAWAY CUISINE

On Hamilton, the Whitsundays' largest inhabited island, guests can eat and drink at a variety of restaurants and bars. Virtually all of them are managed by the Hamilton Island consortium, whose owners, the Oatley family, made their millions out of wine. The Oatleys are keen to further the island's reputation for quality wining and dining—recruiting big-city chefs, improving supply lines, scheduling epicurean events, and adding to the island's vast central cellar and produce store. Opportunities for young guns to work their way up through Hamilton's hierarchy, training under culinary heavyweights, bring a continuing stream of fresh talent to the island. The bad news? Staff don't always stay and as a result, food and service standards can be inconsistent—and as there's a virtual monopoly on dining options, prices tend to be steep.

EXPLORING

FAMILY **WILD LIFE Hamilton Island.** This charming wildlife sanctuary houses kangaroos, wallabies, wombats, birds, and reptiles, including a resident croc. There are daily breakfasts with the koalas (7–10). During school holiday periods, you can book a Sunset Spotlight tour that includes a 20-minute torch-lighted walk through the nocturnal animal enclosures at feeding time, and a light barbecue dinner. ⊠ *Resort Dr.* ☎ *07/4946–8305* ⊕ *www.wildlifehamiltonisland.com.au* ⊠ *A$20, unlimited entry for duration of HI stay; Breakfast with the Koalas, A$34; Sunset Spotlight tour A$35.*

SPORTS AND THE OUTDOORS

FISHING

Renegade Sports Fishing & Charters. The outer Great Barrier Reef offers world-class fishing for species including coral trout, mackerel, and tuna—and you have a better-than-average chance of landing one off the deck of a 38-foot flybridge game boat. Hamilton Island can arrange small-group sportfishing trips with Renegade Sports Fishing & Charters, with all equipment included. A full-day excursion is A$2,750 (private charter) or A$300 per person (shared); a half-day trip (8–noon or 1–5) costs A$1,750 (private charter) or A$190 per person (shared). Full-day tours also include morning and afternoon tea and a cheese/fruit platter at lunch. If time or your budget is tight, you can hire a dinghy for puttering about closer to shore. Organize it all through Hamilton Island's Tour Desk. ⊠ *D Arm, DWS berth, Hamilton Island Marina, Front St.* ☎ *07/4946–8305 tour desk* ⊕ *www.renegadecharters.com.au.*

GOLF

Fodor'sChoice **Dent Island Golf Course.** This Peter Thomson–designed championship
★ course has sweeping Whitsundays views from all 18 holes. You can hire clubs, take lessons, and practice your swing on the golf driving range at the Hamilton Island–run complex, which incorporates a swanky clubhouse, pro shop, restaurant, and bar. Clubs, shoes, caddy services, and lessons are also available. Ferries to Dent Island depart all day from 7:30 am from Hamilton Island Marina; allow five hours to play 18 holes and half that to play nine. Prices include GPS-fitted golf carts and ferry

transfers. ⊠ *Main St., Dent Island, Whitsunday Islands* ☏ *07/4949–9760* ⊕ *www.hamiltonislandgolfclub.com.au* 🖃 *A$180* ⚑ *18 holes, 6692 yards, par 71.*

GREAT BARRIER REEF TOURS

FAMILY
Fodor's Choice
★

Cruise Whitsundays Reefworld. On the outer edge of the Great Barrier Reef sits magnificent Hardy Reef Lagoon, and within it sits Reefworld, a state-of-the-art pontoon around which you can snorkel and dive along easy coral trails. There's a large underwater viewing chamber, a spacious sun deck, changing rooms and fresh-water showers, a kid-friendly snorkeling area, and a child-minding service. There's even a massage hut and accommodation for Reefsleep guests. There are many ways to explore the underwater environs: take a semisubmersible coral-viewing tour, guided snorkel safari (A$45), or an introductory (A$119) or certified dive (A$99) with gear included. A scenic heli-flight over famed Heart Reef starts from A$135 per person. ⊠ *Depart Hamilton Island Airport and Airport Jetty, Palm Valley Way* ☏ *07/4946–4662 Cruise Whitsundays, 07/4969–9599 Hamilton Island Air* ⊕ *www.cruisewhitsundays.com or www.helireef.com.au* 🖃 *A$225 Cruise Whitsundays Reefworld day trip; A$399 HI Air/Cruise Whitsundays fly-cruise.*

SCUBA DIVING

Hamilton Island Dive & Snorkel Tours. If you're keen on exploring the reef, Hamilton Island can organize everything from PADI-accredited courses to snorkeling trips to Whitehaven Beach and local reefs, and full-day cruises to outer Great Barrier Reef pontoon Reefworld. A catamaran excursion to the outer Great Barrier Reef (A$225) allows up to four hours on the Reefworld pontoon at Hardy Reef, which is ample time for one or two dives (minimum age 12). The fare includes a buffet lunch, morning and afternoon tea, snorkeling gear, wet suits, a semisubmersible tour, and use of Reefworld's underwater viewing chamber, waterslide, and facilities. The resort also organizes thrice-weekly, full-day circumnavigations of Whitsunday Island (A$165) by rigid inflatable speedboat (RIB); during the trip you can snorkel the fringing reef off Chalkie's Beach and local coral gardens, explore Whitehaven Beach, and anchor off Hill Inlet for a trek to the summit for stupendous Whitsundays views. ⊠ *Hamiton Island Marina, Front St. next to general store* ☏ *07/4946–9888 Dive Shop, 07/4946–8305 Tour Bookings Desk* ⊕ *www.hamiltonisland.com.au.*

WATER SPORTS

Hamilton Island Activities. Hamilton Island Resort has the widest selection of activities in the Whitsundays: game fishing, snorkeling, scuba diving, waterskiing, parasailing, jet skiing, wakeboarding, sea kayaking, speedboat adventure rides, and fish-feeding tours are all on the agenda. Everything can be booked through the island's central tour desk. The use of nonmotorized watercraft is free to resort guests through the Beach Hut (Hamilton Island Beach Sports) on Catseye Beach, with Beach Hut staff ready to give assistance, tips, and—for a fee—lessons. If the Coral Sea doesn't tempt you, there are well-marked walking trails, quad-bike and ATV tours, twilight 4WD "bush safaris," go-karts, a nine-pin bowling center, a target-shooting range, an aquatic driving range, public-access swimming pools, and an 18-hole golf course on nearby Dent Island.

8

The island's sports and fitness complex incorporates a state-of-the-art gym, a whirlpool spa and sauna, squash and floodlit tennis courts, and a mini-golf course. You can also sign up for various tours, cruises, and special events. ⊠ *Main Resort Complex, off Resort Dr., Hamilton Island, Whitsunday Islands* ☎ *07/4946–8305 tour desk, 13/7333 toll-free in Australia* ⊕ *www.hamiltonisland.com.au.*

Tour Booking Desk. Reserve Hamilton Island tours, cruises, and activities ahead of time through the island's central Tour Booking Desk. ☎ *07/4946–8305, 13–7333 toll-free, in Australia, 866/209–0891 toll-free, in U.S.* ⊕ *www.hamiltonisland.com.au.*

WHERE TO EAT

$$$$ ✕ **Bommie Restaurant.** With sail-shaped tables, chic Eames chairs, and
MODERN marina views, Bommie has a sophisticated, upmarket ambience and
AUSTRALIAN smart-casual dress code (collared shirts for men and no singlets, board-shorts or flip-flops). It proves the ideal setting for fine Modern Australian cuisine. Ravenous yachties might prefer to tuck into a tasty kangaroo fillet or a perfect seafood risotto. Leave space for tropically inspired desserts; standouts include blood-peach soufflé and house-made sorbets. A private dining room seats up to 14 (minimum 24 hours' notice required). ■TIP➔ Book well ahead to secure a table on the deck. $ *Average main: A$46* ⊠ *Hamilton Island Yacht Club, Front St., Hamilton Island, Whitsunday Islands* ☎ *07/4948–9433, 13/3777 toll-free in Australia* ⊕ *www.hamiltonisland.com.au/yachtclub/dining* ⊗ *Daily, dinner 6 pm till late (last bookings 9 pm)* ⊗ *Closed Sun. and Mon. No lunch.*

$$$ ✕ **coca chu.** Hamilton Island's only Asian eatery, coca chu appeals to all
ASIAN FUSION comers with its relaxed vibe, Catseye Beach views, busy Sunday yum chas, and a varied dinner menu that showcases regional produce and Southeast Asian flavors. The soft-shell crab with green papaya salad and *nahm jim* is a worthy signature dish. Families with young children should be aware there's only one "designated" kid's dish: simple soy chicken and rice. $ *Average main: A$34* ⊠ *Resort Complex, Catseye Beach* ☎ *07/4946–8580* ⊕ *www.hamiltonisland.com.au/coca-chu-restaurant* ⊗ *No lunch except on Sun. No dinnerSun.*

$$$$ ✕ **Denison Star Dinner Cruise.** The *Denison Star*, a magnificent 107-foot
MODERN motor cruiser hewn from Tasmanian Huon pine, glides out of Hamilton
AUSTRALIAN Island Marina most evenings for Cruise Indigo's small-group, starlit dinner cruise around the island's sheltered waters. As night falls, the skipper drops anchor in a scenic, secluded spot so that there's no rocking as you dine. You can start with sunset daiquiris and canapés, and then order from a four-course à la carte menu of Modern Australian dishes as your complimentary bottle of wine is uncorked. Stargaze from the upper deck as you cruise back to base. ■TIP➔ Leave your high heels at home and bring a jacket; it can get chilly on deck during the cooler months. $ *Average main: A$142* ⊠ *Cruise Indigo Jetty, Hamilton Island Marina, Front St.* ☎ *07/4946–8305, 13/7333 toll-free in Australia* ⊕ *www.hamiltonisland.com.au/dinner-cruise-denison-star* ⚍ *Reservations essential.*

$$ ECLECTIC FAMILY 🍴 **Manta Ray Café.** This could be the island's best all-rounder. Dine right by the marina on salads and pasta dishes, or join the queue for gourmet, wood-fired pizzas (also available as takeout or delivery). There's plenty on Manta Ray's menu to suit all tastes. Manta Ray's wine list is also a crowd-pleaser (though for a corkage charge of A$15, you can BYO special bottle). **TIP→ Kids under 12 staying at some HI resorts eat for free here till 7:30 pm.** [$] *Average main: A$29* ✉ *Front St.* ☎ *07/4946–8536 resort restaurant reservations, 07/4946–8213 takeout and delivery* 🌐 *www.hamiltonisland.com.au/manta-ray-cafe.*

$$$ SEAFOOD Fodor's Choice ★ 🍴 **Mariners Restaurant.** This breezy, upscale eatery turns the local catch into fresh contemporary dishes: artfully arranged sashimi, house-made tagliatelle marinara, Thai-style jumbo prawn curry, and a terrific hot-and-cold seafood platter (A$220 for two). You can also get vegetarian and non-seafood options, and wine from a bar stocked mainly with mid-priced antipodean vintages. Book a balcony table and watch yachts dock as you dine. [$] *Average main: A$44* ✉ *Marina Village, Front St.* ☎ *07/4946–8628* ✍ *Reservations essential* ⏲ *No lunch.*

$$$ ITALIAN 🍴 **Romanos Restaurant.** The full-frontal marina views from the broad balconies of this two-level waterfront eatery make it a favorite for family celebrations and romantic dining. The menu is loaded with traditional Italian fare such as osso buco as well as more inventive dishes, such as black linguine with Moreton Bay bug (crayfish) tails in a roasted-tomato-shellfish sauce. Dessert might be gelato, panna cotta, or tiramisu. There's a steep corkage charge (A$25) if you BYOB. [$] *Average main: A$37* ✉ *Marina Village, Front St., Harbourside* ☎ *07/4946–8212* 🌐 *www.hamiltonisland.com.au/romanos-restaurant* ✍ *Reservations essential* ⏲ *No lunch.*

WHERE TO STAY

For expanded hotel reviews, visit Fodors.com.

$$$$ RESORT 🏨 **Hamilton Island Beach Club.** The upscale amenities and no-kids policy mean this hotel swarms with couples, who can cool off in the infinity-edge pool, enjoy meals poolside, or admire the Catseye Beach and Coral Sea views from their balcony. **Pros:** beachfront location; free Wi-Fi; reasonably priced lunch menu. **Cons:** service standards vary. [$] *Rooms from: A$699* ✉ *9 Resort Dr., Hamilton Island, Whitsunday Islands* ☎ *02/9433–0444, 13/7333 toll-free in Australia* 🌐 *www.hamiltonisland.com.au* 🛏 *57 rooms* 🍽 *Multiple meal plans.*

$$$ RENTAL FAMILY 🏨 **Hamilton Island Holiday Homes.** Part of the Hamilton Island resort, Hamilton Island Holiday Homes manages more than 100 self-catered one- to five-bedroom vacation properties in prime locations around the island, including studio, split-level, and two-story designs. **Pros:** privacy; full kitchen and laundry facilities; complimentary use of many resort facilities; kids under 13 can eat free with their parents at selected HI restaurants. **Cons:** minimum four-day stays in holiday periods, two- or three-night minimum at other times; no in-house Wi-Fi; no housekeeping. [$] *Rooms from: A$360* ✉ *Bookings office, Front St.* ☎ *02/9433–0444, 13/7333 toll-free in Australia* 🌐 *www.hihh.com.au* 🍽 *No meals.*

$$$$ RESORT FAMILY 🏨 **Hamilton Island Palm Bungalows.** Spacious, self-contained, and with a relaxed island vibe, these steep-roofed, freestanding bungalows are great for families and self-sufficient travelers. **Pros:** free use of the

8

resort's gym/sports complex and nonmotorized watercraft; complimentary airport transfers; close to main pool, beach, and wildlife park. **Cons:** some bungalows can be musty; buggy hire not included; up a steepish hill; no Wi-Fi in rooms. $ *Rooms from: A$445* ⊠ *Hamilton Island, Whitsunday Islands, 3 Resort Dr.* ☎ *02/9433–0444, 13/7333 toll-free in Australia* ⊕ *www.hamiltonisland.com.au* ↷ *49 bungalows* ⊙ *Multiple meal plans.*

$$$$
HOTEL
FAMILY

⛰ **Hamilton Island Reef View Hotel.** Only rooms on higher floors of this hotel live up to the name—those on the fifth floor and above have unbroken Coral Sea vistas, while rooms on lower levels overlook a landscaped, tropical garden and pool. **Pros:** good breakfasts (included with stays of four-plus days); in higher-floor rooms, beds face the views; better-than-usual service. **Cons:** lower-level rooms can be noisy; pricey in-house food and drinks; fee for in-room Wi-Fi; cockatoos fly in open windows. $ *Rooms from: A$470* ⊠ *12 Resort Dr., Hamilton Island, Whitsunday Islands* ☎ *02/9433–0444, 13/7333 toll-free in Australia* ⊕ *www.hamiltonisland.com.au* ↷ *382 rooms and suites* ⊙ *Multiple meal plans.*

$$$$
RESORT
Fodor'sChoice
★

⛰ **Qualia.** With its private beach, infinity-edge pools, and complex of luxe freestanding pavilions, Hamilton Island's most exclusive resort has a tranquil, decadent ambience and impeccable service standards. **Pros:** glorious, tranquil location; fine food and wine; high-end everything. **Cons:** two-night minimum stay in peak periods; slow room service; pricey. $ *Rooms from: A$1150* ⊠ *Lot 10, 20 Whitsunday Blvd.* ☎ *02/9433–0444, 13/7777 toll-free in Australia* ⊕ *www.qualia.com.au* ↷ *60 suites* ⊙ *Breakfast.*

NIGHTLIFE

Hamilton Island has several resort bars and a nightclub, as well as a handful of independent ones: all except Qualia's are open to visitors. Find live music at the Reef Lounge and Sails, harborside tables at the Marina Tavern and Mariners, sundowner cocktails on the Bommie Deck at Hamilton Island Yacht Club or with panoramic island views at One Tree Hill, and post-sunset drinks at the Captains Club, above Bohemes Nightclub.

Bohemes Nightclub. At the new-look Bohemes, Hamilton Island's only dedicated late-night bar and dance-spot, you can drink and boogie till the wee hours to DJ-spun classic and contemporary music, and occasional live acts. It's usually open Thursday to Saturday until well after midnight, but opening hours, days, and entertainment line-ups vary with the season. ⊠ *Marina Village, Front St., Hamilton Island, Whitsunday Islands* ☎ *07/4946–9999* ⊕ *www.hamiltonisland.com.au.*

SHOPPING

Hamilton Island's Marina Village, along Front Street, houses shops selling resort and surf wear, children's clothes, souvenirs, and gifts. You'll also find an art gallery, design store, jeweler, florist, small supermarket, general store, pharmacy, newsstand, post office, pro golf shop, real-estate agent, bakery, bottle shop, and a hair salon on the island. In general, you'll pay more for goods and services here than for their equivalents on the mainland.

DAYDREAM ISLAND

The resort on this small, 42-acre island is especially welcoming to day-trippers. Around 30 minutes' boat ride from Shute Harbour, Abel Point Marina, or Hamilton Island, it's a perfect place to relax or pursue outdoor activities such as snorkeling and water sports—which are comparatively affordable here. The resort's lush gardens blend into a small tract of rain forest, frequented by tame wallabies and big-eyed, stilt-legged Stone curlews. The island is surrounded by clear blue water and coral reefs.

GETTING HERE AND AROUND

Cruise Whitsundays runs several daily services between Daydream Island and Great Barrier Reef (Hamilton Island) Airport Jetty, as well as from Whitsunday Coast (Proserpine) Airport and Proserpine Rail Station; and between the island and Abel Point Marina and (less frequently) Shute Harbour. Cruise Whitsunday Resort Connections offers direct island transfers from Hamilton Island Airport on modern, air-conditioned catamaran cruisers.

Although most people arrive by boat from Great Barrier Reef (Hamilton Island) Airport, an alternative is to fly to Whitsunday Coast (Proserpine) Airport on the mainland, catch a bus to Shute Harbour, then take a ferry to the island. Domestic airlines Virgin Australia and Jetstar have daily scheduled flights from Melbourne, Sydney, and Brisbane to both Great Barrier Reef (Hamilton Island) and Whitsunday Coast (Proserpine) airports; several long-distance rail services stop at Proserpine Rail Station, near Airlie Beach. Cruise Whitsundays ferry services are scheduled to coincide with incoming flight and trains, with coach transfers from Proserpine to the ferry port available. If you've prebooked an air transfer, a representative from Air Whitsunday will generally greet your incoming flight at the airport. Check with each carrier for weight and baggage restrictions.

SPORTS AND THE OUTDOORS

At Daydream Island Resort & Spa, many activities, such as water polo, beach volleyball, aquarobics, tennis and bocce, and the use of resort kayaks, paddleboards, and catamarans, are included in room rates. Guided fishing, snorkeling, and scuba-diving day trips, parasailing, jet skiing, waterskiing and wakeboarding sessions, guided sea kayak and ocean rafting excursions, glass-bottom boat tours, banana-boat tube rides, sunset sailing trips, and more can be arranged through the resort's Tour Desk for an additional charge. Non-guests can also book activities through the resort.

Daydream offers day trips to Whitehaven Beach on catamaran *Camira*, twilight sails on *Sundowner*; snorkel and dive cruises to Knuckle Reef Lagoon with classy local operator Cruise Whitsundays for A\$210; fishing trips with Sea Fever Sportfishing; and HeliReef scenic flights and excursions; as well as leisurely Ocean Rafting trips. To prebook on- or offshore activities prior to your arrival, phone ☎ *07/4948–8477* or email ✉ *discovery@daydreamisland.com*.

BOAT CRUISES

Sundowner Cruises. Two-hour twilight cruises on 59-foot catamaran *Sundowner* take up to four dozen guests on a tour of local islands, with sparkling wine, cheese, and tropical fruit platters included in the fare (A$49). Flat-topped and stable, the vessel has undercover and outdoor seating, and bathrooms. It departs two or three times weekly from Daydream Island. The bar is stocked with local and imported beers, Australian and New Zealand wines, and spirits. ⊠ *Daydream Island Jetty, Daydream Island, Whitsunday Islands* ☎ *07/4948–8477 Discovery Desk, Daydream Island* ⊕ *www.sundownercruises.com.au.*

FISHING

Sea Fever Sportfishing Whitsundays. The custom-built game-fishing boat *Sea Fever* picks up at Daydream Island's jetty at 6:20 am for a fast two-hour boat-ride to the outer Great Barrier Reef. There, you can cast poppers and jig for fiesty giant trevally, coral trout, shark, and red emperor; or sport-fish for large pelagics (Spanish and scaly mackerel, tuna, and barracuda), and, on the way back, troll with light tackle for sailfish and the elusive juvenile black marlin. The rate (A$420 per person, minimum four) includes expert guidance as well as bait, tackle, and lines. Lunch and nonalcoholic drinks and snacks are provided; BYO alcohol (limits apply) along with sunscreen, a brimmed hat, and sunglasses. ⊠ *Pickups from Daydream Island Jetty, Daydream Island, Whitsunday Islands* ☎ *07/4948–8477 Discovery Desk, Daydream Island, 07/4948–2798 Sea Fever, 0427/524975 Sea Fever (cell)* ⊕ *www.seafever.com.au.*

SNORKELING AND DIVING

Camira. The purple catamaran *Camira* offers day cruises to Whitehaven Beach that include a big barbecue lunch, time to swim and sunbathe, and a stop to snorkel off Hook Island on the way back. The fare (A$189 per person) includes lunch, snorkeling gear and tuition, and all beverages including alcoholic drinks. ⊠ *Pickups from Daydream Island Jetty, Daydream Island, Whitsunday Islands* ☎ *07/4948–8477 Discovery Desk, Daydream Island, 07/4946–4662 Cruise Whitsundays* ⊕ *www.daydreamisland.com or www.cruisewhitsundays.com.*

Fodor'sChoice ★ **Cruise Whitsundays.** This operator runs daylong snorkel and dive cruises to Knuckle Reef Lagoon along the balmy, translucent waters of the outer Great Barrier Reef (A$225). They include a big buffet lunch, snorkeling gear and guidance, and plenty of time to take advantage of the excellent facilities, from massages and reef talks to semisubmersible boat rides and Queensland's largest underwater viewing chamber. Keen to get your feet wet? Take a guided or self-guided snorkeling tour in the sheltered lagoon, or go scuba diving for an extra fee to see several marine species, including large pelagic fish (A$119 for the first scuba dive [beginner], A$99 [certified]; A$59 second dive, gear included). ⊠ *Pickups from Daydream Island Resort Jetty, Daydream Island, Whitsunday Islands* ☎ *07/4948–8477 Discovery Desk, Daydream Island, 07/4946–4662 Cruise Whitsundays* ⊕ *www.cruisewhitsundays.com or www.daydreamisland.com.*

Ocean Rafting. Long-established Ocean Rafting has access permits to visit protected areas in the Great Barrier Reef Marine Park, exclusive direct access to iconic Hill Inlet beach, and top snorkeling sites off uninhabited Hook and Border islands, where you can snorkel in spectacular subtropical environs. The "rafts"—11-meter-long former rescue crafts with undercover seating, powered by 500-horsepower engines, and crewed by a skipper and eco-guide—carry a maximum 28 people, so you're never snorkeling in a crowd. Choose from two tours: the Northern Exposure, with more time to snorkel, and the Southern Lights, with more beach time (A$151 per person). ⊠ *Daydream Island Jetty, Daydream Island, Whitsunday Islands* ☎ *07/4948–8477 Discovery Desk, Daydream Island, 07/4946–6848 Ocean Rafting* ⊕ *www.oceanrafting.com.au.*

WHERE TO STAY

For expanded hotel reviews, visit Fodors.com.

$$$$ ⛄ **Daydream Island Resort and Spa.** Colorfully decorated, with whimsical
RESORT touches—starfish-and-shell-embedded toilet seats, mermaid and dolphin statues, a giant chess set, and outsize marine mobiles and murals—this family-focused resort has youthful, cheerful staff; kids' facilities; and numerous public facilities, including a lovely day spa. **Pros:** classy spa; fun activities, notably the mini-golf and outdoor movie screenings; snorkeling off Lovers' Cove. **Cons:** teeming with kids; food lackluster; steep fees for kids' club, babysitting, and in-room Wi-Fi. $ *Rooms from: A$504* ⊠ *Lot 1, Daydream Island Rd., Daydream Island, Whitsunday Islands* ☎ *07/3259–2350, 1800/075040 toll-free in Australia* ⊕ *www.daydreamisland.com* ⤳ *280 rooms, 9 suites* ¶⊙¶ *Breakfast.*

HAYMAN ISLAND

Fodor's Choice
★
Hayman Island, in the northern Whitsunday Passage, is the closest of the Whitsunday resort isles to the outer Barrier Reef. The island, a 900-acre crescent with a series of hills along its spine, has just one resort, one of the oldest and most opulent in the region and popular with jet-setters who take their leisure seriously. The service—understated yet attentive—merits the price you pay for it; staff members even traverse the resort via tunnels so they're less of a "presence."

Reflecting pools, sandstone walkways, manicured tropical gardens, statuary, and waterfalls provide the feel of an exclusive club, while beautiful walking trails crisscross the island, leading to pristine coves and vantage points. The main beach sits right in front of the resort complex, but more secluded sands and fringing coral can be reached by boat or on foot.

GETTING HERE AND AROUND

Hayman has its own heliport, and can arrange helicopter or seaplane transfers from airports at Hamilton Island, Proserpine, Airlie Beach, and Mackay. From Hamilton Island, you can also transfer onto one of Hayman's luxury motor yachts. Tea, coffee, and Australian sparkling wine are served during the 60-minute trip to the island; on the return journey, you'll get full bar service, platters of food, tea, and espresso coffee. On board, you can complete your resort check-in and book tours, reef excursions, and island-based activities. Make sure you're ticketed all the way to Hayman Island, including the motor-yacht leg,

8

as purchasing the round-trip yacht journey from Hamilton Island to Hayman separately costs more.

Air Whitsunday provides seaplane connections from various regional airports: Airlie Beach, to Hamilton Island, and on request, Proserpine and Mackay. The resort can also arrange helicopter transfers for guests (minimum two). On all air transfers, baggage restrictions apply.

Flying by seaplane over Whitsunday and Hook islands, Langford Reef, and Hayman itself, is an exhilarating introduction to your Hayman Island vacation. Prebook through the resort or Air Whitsunday for a seamless charter seaplane connection from Great Barrier Reef (Hamilton Island) Airport; the cost is A$790, with up to four passengers, A$1,590 with up to six (though you can fit a few more people if everyone takes less baggage). Air Whitsunday can also arrange seaplane transfers to Hayman from mainland airports including Whitsunday (Airlie Beach), Whitsunday Coast (Proserpine), and Mackay. The flight takes approximately 15 minutes; baggage is strictly limited to 30 kilograms (66 pounds) per person, in soft-sided bags only; excess baggage can be safely stored at airports prior to departure if you've overpacked.

TOURS

Hayman Island Guest Services provides information on all guided tours around the island and excursions offshore.

ESSENTIALS

Tour Operators Hayman Island Guest Services ⊠ *One&Only Hayman Island, Great Barrier Reef* ☏ *07/4940–1838, 1800/122339 toll-free in Australia* ⊕ *www.hayman.com.au.*

SPORTS AND THE OUTDOORS

All nonmotorized water sports on Hayman Island—well-maintained catamarans, windsurfers, and paddleboards, lined up for guests' use on Hayman Beach—are included in the room rates. So is the use of Hayman's swimming pools, well-equipped indoor-outdoor gym, five floodlit tennis courts, squash and basketball facilities, and badminton, Ping-Pong, and croquet equipment. There's a complimentary golf driving range and 9-hole putting green; aqua-fitness, Zumba and "box fit" classes; and self-guided art and garden walks. You can also order a picnic hamper and arrange a beach drop-off—or take a hike along one of the island's well-maintained bush trails, which take you to lookouts, wildlife hotspots, and pristine beaches, coves, and coral gardens.

Some on-site activities cost extra: personal training sessions (A$85), Pilates and yoga classes (A$20); tennis lessons and clinics (A$20); inflatable-tube rides (from A$70); waterskiing and wakeboarding sessions; scuba training; and guided local tours. The five-star PADI-accredited Marine Centre at Hayman Marina has a training tank for diving lessons, and runs various dive courses, trips, and packages. It also hires and sells everything from snorkel and dive accessories to wet suits. All local aquatic tours and excursions, including guided local sea kayaking, snorkeling, and dive tours, can be booked through the Marine Centre at Hayman Marina. Arrange fitness sessions and off-site excursions— sailing, game-fishing, dive-snorkel outer reef excursions, scenic flights,

Parasailing off Hayman Island

and heli-golf tours to nearby Dent Island—through the resort or the individual operators (most pick up from Hayman on request).

DIVING AND SNORKELING

Cruise Whitsundays, Hayman Island. Hayman is the closest of the Whitsundays islands to the Great Barrier Reef—and it's a speedy ride on Cruise Whitsundays's wave-piercer craft to Knuckle Reef Lagoon pontoon on the outer reef. There, you can snorkel and dive over myriad corals, alongside rainbow-hued wrasse and clownfish, reef sharks, rays, and green sea turtles. Picking up from Hayman daily, the daylong dive-and-snorkel cruise includes paddleboards, snorkeling gear, a giant waterslide, and a vast underwater viewing chamber. You also get priority access to coral-viewing tours and various optional extras: guided snorkel safaris, scuba diving, scenic helicopter flights over Heart Reef, even massages. Cruise Whitsundays also runs shorter cruises around the Whitsundays and Whitehaven Beach. ⊠ *Hayman Island Jetty, Hayman Island, Great Barrier Reef* ☎ *07/4946–9102* ⊕ *www.cruisewhitsundays. com* ✉ *A$225 cruise, including buffet lunch; A$45 guided snorkeling safari, A$99 certified scuba dive, A$119 beginner dive, A$59 2nd dive.*

Fodor's Choice
★

Hayman Island Diving and Snorkeling. The only Whitsundays resort within the Great Barrier Reef Marine Park, Hayman offers fast access to some of the world's best underwater sites. Their guided scuba and snorkel excursions visit several inner-reef hot spots, including Hayman's own Bali Hai (a green sea turtle hangout) and beautiful Blue Pearl Bay, where you can swim among 1,500-odd species of fishes and 400 hard and soft corals. A guided dive tour of nearby inner Barrier Reef sites offers certified divers the chance to swim alongside green turtles, manta rays, and more (A$185). Hayman has expert dive instructors on-site and offers PADI scuba courses. Prices and times vary and are weather dependent; prebook through Hayman's Marine Centre (daily 8–4:30) at the marina. ✉ *Excursions depart from Hayman Island Jetty, Raintree Ave., Hayman Island, Great Barrier Reef* ☎ *07/4940–1838* ⊕ *www.hayman.com.au.*

Hayman Marine Centre. Handily located at Hayman's marina, a short stroll or buggy ride from the resort complex, this scuba training facility—also the place to enquire about and book local dive, snorkel, and sea kayaking tours and beach drop-offs—sells and rents out equipment, including dive and snorkel gear, accessories, and stinger suits. Non-motorized water-sports equipment—catamarans, kayaks, windsurfers, and the like—can be found lined up along Hayman Beach in front of the main resort pool. ✉ *Hayman Marina, off Raintree Ave., Hayman Island, Great Barrier Reef* ☎ *07/4940–1838* ⊕ *www.hayman.com.au.*

FISHING

Hayman Island Sportfishing. The outer edge of the Great Barrier Reef, with its abundant marine life, claims some of the best fishing grounds on the planet. This could be your chance to catch tuna, sailfish, wahoo, mahimahi, Spanish mackerel, giant trevally, or, if you're really lucky, black marlin. Hayman's Marine Centre runs game and bottom-fishing trips (A$280 per person) and private charters on the resort's game-fishing boat, its large deck perfect for landing the "big one." You can have your catch cleaned and cooked by Hayman's chefs that night. Note that species vary by season, and trips are dependent on numbers and weather. ■TIP➔ **If you're set on snagging a really big fish, visit September through February, when warmer waters attract larger species, including black marlin; March to August is prime time for tasty table fish.** ✉ *Excursions depart from Hayman Island Jetty, Raintree Ave., Hayman Island, Great Barrier Reef* ☎ *07/4940–1838* ⊕ *www. hayman.com.au.*

HELICOPTER TOURS

Fodor's Choice
★

Air Whitsunday, Hayman Island. This operator flies guests over Bait, Hardy, and Heart reefs en route to Reefworld, the largest pontoon on the outer Great Barrier Reef. A couple of hours gives you time to wander through its vast underwater viewing chamber, join a semi-submersible boat tour, snorkel with tropical fish and turtles, get a massage, or take a certified reef dive. A short seaplane flight over Hayman, Hook, and Whitsunday islands brings you to Whitehaven Beach, where you can swim and sunbathe. Air Whitsunday also runs island transfers, shorter scenic flights, and a half-day excursion to Hardy Reef pontoon. ✉ *Terminal 1, Whitsunday Airport, Air Whitsunday Rd., Flametree, Airlie Beach* ☎ *07/4946–9111 Air Whitsunday, 07/4940–1838 Hayman Guest Services* ⊕ *www.airwhitsunday.com.au.*

HeliReef Whitsunday. Local operator HeliReef runs an array of reef and island scenic flights, helicopter tours, and fly-cruise excursions, many of which include stop-offs on local islands, beaches, and Great Barrier Reef sites. An hour-long scenic helicopter flight over Whitehaven Beach and the Great Barrier Reef, including a flyover of renowned Heart Reef, is A$399 per person. A scenic six- to twelve-minute Whitsundays helicopter joy-flight gives you a bird's-eye glimpse of Hayman Island (A$99/A$145). A half-day excursion to Knuckle Reef pontoon is A$699 per person, while a full day's excursion to Reefworld on the outer Barrier Reef and Whitehaven Beach is A$999. A private picnic on Whitehaven Beach is A$399 per person, plus A$30 for a prepacked gourmet hamper, Champagne included. ✉ *Pickups from Hayman Island heliport, Raintree Ave., Hayman Island, Great Barrier Reef* ☎ *07/4946–9102* 🌐 *www.helireef.com.au.*

WILDLIFE WATCHING

Hayman Island Wildlife. Largely free of human traffic besides the odd hiker or snorkeler, Hayman Island gives sanctuary to numerous wild creatures, including the world's largest colony of endangered Proserpine rock wallabies. There are also lizards, butterflies, and many native birds, such as cockatoos, rainbow lorikeets, kookaburras, stone curlews, egrets, and sea eagles. The resort ponds and lagoons are home to barramundi, swans, and ducks; under the marina live tropical fish, rays, and turtles, especially evident at feeding time. The resort has regular fish feeds, bird-watching, wildlife-spotting walks, and guided excursions to local snorkeling and dive sites. ✉ *Hayman Island, Great Barrier Reef* ☎ *07/4940–1838* 🌐 *www.haymanisland.com.au.*

WHERE TO EAT

All restaurants are within the resort complex. Reservations are recommended and in some cases essential: they can be made with ease through the resort's concierge. Dress for all Hayman's evening restaurants is "smart resort wear"—no singlets, shorts, or flip-flops.

Restaurant opening times are staggered so you always have at least two dining options; guests can breakfast in their rooms or at Azure. During the day, eat at the Beach Pavilion, snack by the Pool Bar, or preorder a picnic hamper.

Hayman offers various epicurean events, including design-your-own dinners, with tables set up on Hayman Beach or in Rainforest Grove; and exclusive degustation dining experiences that include up to 12 courses, matched wines, culinary tips from your chef, and behind-scenes tours of Hayman's vast wine cellar.

$$$$ MODERN AUSTRALIAN 🍴 **Azure.** This glass-sided eatery right on the island's main beach affords glorious views. Dine indoors or alfresco; seating extends onto the sand. Truly splendid breakfasts include made-to-order eggs and a huge buffet spread: freshly baked breads and pastries, tropical fruits and juices, pancakes, cereals, meats, cheeses, and more. The nightly buffet and grill features seafood, sushi, and salad bars, an array of grilled and barbecued options, and pastries baked in Hayman's central kitchen for dessert. [$] *Average main: A$49* ✉ *Hayman Resort, Raintree Ave., Hayman Island, Great Barrier Reef* ☎ *07/4940–1838* 🌐 *www.hayman.com.au* 🕒 *No lunch. No dinner some nights, varying seasonally.*

$$$$ MODERN AUSTRALIAN Fodor's Choice ★ 🍴 **Fontaine.** Named for its central fountain, this elegant restaurant is the resort's culinary showpiece. Dishes here use premium ingredients, sourced locally and from around the world. Book early and you can reserve an outdoor dining platform over the Fontaine pool. A private dining room—with the option of designing your own menu, in

consultation with the resort's executive chef—is available year-round. $ *Average main: A$55* ⊠ *Hayman Resort, Raintree Ave., Hayman Island, Great Barrier Reef* ⊕ *www.hayman.com.au* ⚕ *Reservations essential* 🏛 *Jacket required* ⊘ *No lunch. Closed some nights, varying seasonally.*

$$$

ITALIAN

FAMILY

✕ **La Trattoria.** A classic Italian-style eatery with a crowd-pleasing menu of pasta, pizza, seafood, and traditional dishes, La Trattoria also offers a spectacular antipasto buffet and some excellent mid-priced reds. Seafood—Coffin Bay oysters, Yamba prawns, yellowfin tuna, and spanner crab—is well represented, as are heartier dishes such as roasted shoulder of lamb. Desserts run the gamut of Italian favorites, from tiramisu to gelato. Red-and-white checked tablecloths, hand-beaten pendant lamps, and rustic furnishings add to the sociable ambience, as does the live band, which starts up around 8 pm most evenings. $ *Average main: A$36* ⊠ *Raintree Ave., Hayman Island, Whitsunday Islands* ☎ *07/4940–1838* ⊕ *www.hayman.com.au* ⚕ *Reservations essential* ⊘ *No lunch. Closed some nights, varying seasonally.*

$$$

ASIAN

✕ **Oriental.** This lovely pan-Asian establishment, a Hayman staff favorite, overlooks a tranquil Japanese garden with rock pools and waterfalls, a teahouse, and dining platforms. Menu choices include Thai, Chinese, Japanese, and Indian dishes, and a separate vegetarian menu. $ *Average main: A$35* ⊠ *Hayman resort, Raintree Ave., Hayman Island, Great Barrier Reef* ☎ *07/4940–1838* ⊕ *www.hayman.com.au* ⚕ *Reservations essential* ⊘ *No lunch.*

WHERE TO STAY
For expanded hotel reviews, visit Fodors.com.

$$$$

RESORT

Fodor's Choice

★

🏨 **One&Only Hayman Island.** This magnificent resort is the grande dame of the Whitsundays, attracting worldly, high-flying guests seeking precious downtime. **Pros:** meticulous, attentive service; terrific food, wine, and activities; impeccable interiors; well-stocked boutiques. **Cons:** costly (albeit top-notch) food, drinks, and spa treatments; room-raiding cockatoos; a fair hike from some rooms to restaurants and public areas. $ *Rooms from: A$730* ⊠ *Raintree Ave., Hayman Island, Great Barrier Reef* ☎ *07/4940–1838, 1800/122339 toll-free in Australia* ⊕ *www. hayman.com.au* ⇲ *160 rooms, suites, penthouses, beach houses, and villas* ⟨◎⟩ *Breakfast.*

SHOPPING
Hayman has its own chichi shopping arcade next to the spa. Prices aren't cheap, but the merchandise is high-quality and well chosen. There are a couple of lovely boutiques stocked with designer clothes and accessories, swimwear, and resort wear for men, women, and kids, including enough stylish pieces to ensure you meet Hayman's "smart-resort-wear-for-dinner" dress code. There's a small high-end jeweler, a news agency that also sells photographic accessories and prints images, a medical center that fills pharmacy prescriptions, and a gift shop stocked with quality Australian-made and Hayman-branded merchandise, art, and crafts. If you're lucky, you'll visit during a sale: in the low season you might snare a bargain designer swimsuit, caftan, or beach bag. Stores are open daily until 5 or 6, depending on the season.

NORTH COAST ISLANDS

ORPHEUS ISLAND

Volcanic in origin, this narrow island—11 km (7 miles) long and 1 km (½ mile) wide, 3,500 acres total—uncoils like a snake in the waters between Halifax Bay and the Barrier Reef. It's part of the Palm Island Group, which consists of 10 islands, 8 of which are Aboriginal reservations. Orpheus is a national park, occupied only by a marine research station and the island's resort, refurbished in early 2012 under its new, eco-conscious owners, who added a large vegetable garden, a solar hot-water system, and a 21,134-gallon water tank, as well as an infinity-edge pool and several beachfront villas linked by a rear boardwalk.

Although there are patches of rain forest in the island's deeper gullies and around its sheltered bays, Orpheus is a true Barrier Reef island, ringed by seven unspoiled sandy beaches and superb coral reefs. Amazingly, 340 of the known 359 species of coral inhabit these waters, as do more than 1,100 types of tropical fish and the biggest giant clams in the southern hemisphere. The local marine life is easily accessed and extraordinary.

GETTING HERE AND AROUND

Orpheus Island lies 24 km (15 miles) offshore of Ingham, about 80 km (50 miles) northeast of Townsville, and 190 km (118 miles) south of Cairns. Nautilus Aviation helicopters depart daily at 2 pm from Townsville Airport's Domestic Gate Lounge 10, returning Orpheus guests to the mainland from 2:30 (A\$275 per person, one way); and from Cairns airport at 11 am daily, with return flights departing at noon (A\$550 per person, one way). You can also charter flights from other mainland ports and islands. Baggage should be soft-sided and is strictly limited to a maximum of 15 kilograms (33 pounds) per person. Excess baggage can be stored at Townsville Airport for free. Book flights with Orpheus Island Resort.

ESSENTIALS

Seaplane **Nautilus Aviation** ☎ *07/4725–6506* ⊕ *www.nautilusaviation.com.au.*

SPORTS AND THE OUTDOORS

Orpheus Island Resort is surrounded by walking trails, and there are spectacular snorkeling and diving sites right off the beaches, with manta rays the highlight. Resort guests get complimentary use of snorkeling and light fishing gear, as well as canoes, paddle-skis, catamarans, and motorized dinghies in which to buzz from cove to cove. The coral around Orpheus is some of the best in the area, and cruises to the outer reef can be arranged through the resort for an additional fee. Whereas most of the islands are more than 50 km (31 miles) from the reef, Orpheus is just 15 km (9 miles) away. Dive operators on the island provide scuba courses and various boat-diving options.

8

Continued on page 522

WHAT LIVES ON THE REEF?

Equivalent to the Amazon Rainforest
in its biodiversity, the Reef hosts the
earth's most abundant collection of
sea life. Resident species include (but
aren't limited to):

- More than 1,500 species of fish
- 5,000 species of mollusk
- 400 species of hard and soft coral
- 30 whale and dolphin species
- More than 500 species of sea plants
  and grasses
- 14 sea-snake species
- Six sea-turtle species
- 200 sea-bird species
- More than 150 species of shark

DIVING THE REEF

To astronauts who've seen it from space, the Great Barrier Reef resembles a vast, snaking wall—like a moat running parallel to Australia's entire northeastern coast. Almost unimaginably long at 1,430-odd miles, it's one of the few organic structures that can be seen from above the earth's atmosphere without a telescope.

(left) purple anthias; (above) pink coral

Up close, though, what looks (and from its name, sounds) like a barrier is in fact a labyrinthine complex with millions of points of entry. Mind-boggling in size and scope, encompassing more than 4,000 separate reefs, cays, and islands, the Reef could rightly be called its own subaqueous country.

An undersea enthusiast could spend a lifetime exploring this terrain—which ranges from dizzying chasms to sepulchral coral caves, and from lush underwater "gardens" to sandy sun-dappled shallows—without ever mapping all its resident wonders. Not only is the Reef system home to thousands upon thousands of sea-life species, the populations are changing all the time.

So how is a visitor—especially one with only a week to spend—supposed to plan a trip to this underwater Eden? How to choose among the seemingly endless spots for dropping anchor, donning fins and tanks, and plunging in?

With this many options, figuring out what you want to experience on the Reef is essential. If you've dreamed of floating among sea turtles, you'll likely need to head to a different location than if you want to swim with sharks; if you're an experienced deepwater diver with a taste for shipwrecks, you'll probably need to make separate arrangements from your friends who prefer to hover near the surface. There really is a spot for every kind of diver on the Reef; the trick is knowing where they are.

Luckily, many veteran divers agree about some of the Reef's most reliably excellent sites (and the best ways to access them). The selection compiled here should help you to—ahem—get your feet wet.

by Sarah Gold

8

IN FOCUS DIVING THE REEF

BEST DIVING EXPERIENCES

Potato Cod and diver at Cod Hole

BEST WRECK DIVE

The coral formations of the Reef, while dazzling for divers, have proven treacherous to ship captains for centuries. More than 1,500 shipwrecks have been found on the Reef thus far—and there are almost certainly more waiting to be discovered.

S.S. YONGALA

The hulk of this 360-foot steamship, which sank during a cyclone in 1911, is easily the most popular wreck dive on the Reef. Part of the appeal is its easy accessibility; the Yongala lies just a half-hour's boat ride off the coast of Townsville, and though some sections are fairly deep (around 90 feet), others are just 45 feet below the surface. The entire wreck is now encrusted with coral, and swarms with a profusion of species including giant grouper, sea snakes, green sea turtles, and spotted eagle rays.

Difficulty level: Intermediate. Divers should have some previous deep-water experience before visiting this site.

How to get there: Yongala Dive (www. yongaladive.com.au), based in Alva Beach (south of Townsville), runs trips to the wreck several times per week.

BEST SITE TO GET YOUR HEART RATE UP

For some thrill-seeking divers, the wonders of the Great Barrier Reef are even better when accompanied by an extra shot of adrenaline—and a few dozen sharks.

OSPREY REEF

More than 200 miles north of Cairns (and only accessible via a live-aboard dive trip), Osprey is peerless for divers hell-bent on a rendezvous with the ocean's most famous predators. The northernmost section of the reef, where two ocean currents converge (it's known as the North Horn), is an especially thronged feeding ground for white-tipped reef, gray reef, hammerhead, and tiger sharks.

Difficulty level: Intermediate. Though the North Horn's best shark-viewing areas are only at about 60 feet, even seasoned divers may feel understandably anxious.

How to get there: Mike Ball Dive Expeditions (www.mikeball.com) offers multi-day packages to Osprey Reef from Cairns and Port Douglas.

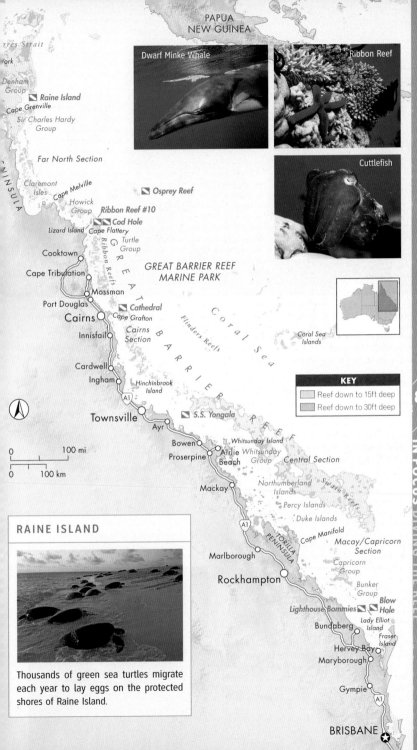

PAPUA
NEW GUINEA

Dwarf Minke Whale

Ribbon Reef

Cuttlefish

res Strait

ork

Denham
Group

Raine Island

Cape Grenville

Sir Charles Hardy
Group

Far North Section

Claremont
Isles

Cape Melville

Howick
Group

Osprey Reef

Ribbon Reef #10

Cod Hole

Lizard Island Cape Flattery

Turtle
Group

Cooktown

Cape Tribulation

Mossman

Port Douglas

Cairns

Cathedral

Cape Grafton

Innisfail

Cairns
Section

GREAT BARRIER REEF
MARINE PARK

Coral Sea

Flinders Reefs

Coral Sea
Islands

Cardwell

Ingham

A1

Hinchinbrook
Island

Townsville

Ayr

S.S. Yongala

KEY

Reef down to 15ft deep

Reef down to 30ft deep

8

IN FOCUS DIVING THE REEF

Bowen

Proserpine

Airlie
Beach

Whitsunday Island

Whitsunday
Group

Central Section

Mackay

Northumberland
Islands

Swath Reefs

Percy Islands

Duke Islands

Macay/Capricorn
Section

0   100 mi
0   100 km

RAINE ISLAND

Thousands of green sea turtles migrate
each year to lay eggs on the protected
shores of Raine Island.

Cape Manifold

Marlborough

Rockhampton

Capricorn
Group

Bunker
Group

Lighthouse Bommies

Blow
Hole

Lady Elliot
Island

Bundaberg

Hervey Bay

Fraser
Island

Maryborough

Gympie

A1

BRISBANE

Scuba isn't the only option; snorkelers have plenty of opportunities to get up close to coral, too.

BEST CORAL-FORMATION SITES

Whether they're hard formations that mimic the shapes of antlers, brains, and stacked plates, or soft feathery Gorgonians and anemones, the building blocks of Reef ecology are compelling in their own right.

BLOW HOLE

Set off the eastern coast of Lady Elliot Island, this cavern-like coral tube is almost 60 feet in length. Divers can enter from either end, and swim through an interior festooned with Technicolor hard and soft corals—and swarming with banded coral shrimp, crayon-bright nudibranchs (sea slugs), and fluttery lionfish.

Difficulty level: Easy. Unless you're claustrophobic. Divers need only be Open-Water certified to visit this site, which ranges in depth from about 40 to 65 feet.

How to get there: The dive center at Lady Elliot Island Resort (www.ladyelliot.com.au) runs dives to the Blow Hole several times daily.

Divers explore a swim-through coral formation.

CATHEDRAL

Part of Thetford Reef, which lies within day-tripping distance of coastal Cairns, Cathedral is a wonderland of coral spires and swim-through chasms. The towering coral heads include thick forests of blue staghorn, sea fans, and sea whips; in between are sandy-bottomed canyons where shafts of sunlight play over giant clam beds.

Difficulty level: Intermediate. Though many coral peaks lie just 15 to 20 feet below the surface, the deeper channels (which go down to 85 feet) can be disorienting.

How to get there: Silverseries (www.silverseries.com.au) runs day-long trips from Cairns that visit several Thetford sites.

BEST GUARANTEED CLOSE-ENCOUNTER SITES

While just about any dive site on the Reef will bring you face-to-face with fantastic marine creatures, a few particular spots maximize your chances.

RIBBON REEF NUMBER 10

The northernmost of the Ribbon Reefs (a group that extends off the Cairns coast all the way to the Torres Strait) is home to some famously curious sea creatures. At Cod Hole, divers have been hand-feeding the enormous, 70-pound resident potato cod for decades. Ribbon Reef Number 10 is also one of the only places on earth where visitors can have breathtakingly close contact with wild dwarf minke whales. These small, playful baleen whales stop here every June and July—and they often approach within a few feet of respectful divers.

Sea turtle and diver

Difficulty level: Easy. Divers need only be Open-Water certified to dive at the 50-foot Cod Hole; dwarf minke encounters are open to snorkelers.

How to get there: Several dive operators run live-aboard trips to the Ribbon Reefs, including Mike Ball Expeditions (www.mikeball.com), Pro Dive Cairns (www.prodivecairns.com), and Eye to Eye Marine Encounters (www.marine encounters.com.au).

LIGHTHOUSE BOMMIES

Part of the southerly Whitsunday group, Lady Elliot Island is surrounded by shallow, pristine waters that teem with life. In particular, the Lighthouse Bommies—freestanding coral formations set off the island's northwest coast—host a large population of manta rays, some of which have a wingspan twelve feet across.

Difficulty level: Easy. Divers need only be Open-Water certified to visit this site; the depth averages about 50 feet.

How to get there: The dive center at Lady Elliot Island Resort (www.ladyelliot.com.au) runs dives to the Bommies daily.

RAINE ISLAND

In the far north reaches of the Coral Sea off Cape York, this coral cay is one of the Reef's greatest—and most inaccessible—treasures. Its beaches comprise the world's largest nesting ground for endangered green sea turtles; during November and December more than 20,000 turtles per week mob the shores to lay their eggs. Because Raine is a strictly protected preserve, seeing this annual phenomenon is an exceedingly rare privilege. In fact, only one dive operator, Eye to Eye Marine Encounters, is sanctioned by the Marine Park Authority to visit the site—and only twice a year.

Difficulty level: Intermediate to Expert. The dive trips involve a heavy research component; participants not only dive among the turtles, but also collect data on them and fit them with satellite tags (some also tag tiger sharks, another rare endemic species).

How to get there: The 18 spots on these ten-day trips are in high demand; learn more at www.marineencounters.com.au.

SCUBA DIVING 101

(left) ProDive is one of several great dive companies on the Reef; (right) snorkelers receive instruction.

Visiting the Reef can be a snap even if you've never dived before; most local dive operators offer Open Water (entry-level) certification courses that can be completed in just three to five days. The course involves both classroom and pool training, followed by a written test and one or more open-water dives on the Reef. Once you're certified, you'll be able to dive to depths of up to 60 feet; you'll also be eligible to rent equipment and book dive trips all over the world.

TIGHT SCHEDULE?

If time is of the essence, ask about doing your Open Water class and in-pool training near home; some Reef operators may allow you to complete your certification (and get right to the good part—the actual ocean dives) once you arrive in Australia.

Though most serious divers insist that certification is necessary for scuba safety, if you're short on time you may find yourself tempted to take advantage of what are generally called "resort courses"—single-day instruction programs that allow you to dive at limited depths under strict supervision. As long as you choose a reputable operator (like Mike Ball Dive Expeditions, www.mikeball.com) and do exactly as your dive guides say, you'll likely be fine.

FLYING

No matter how you get yourself underwater, you'll need to make sure you don't schedule a flight and a dive in the same day. Flying too soon after diving can lead to "the bends"—an excruciating buildup of nitrogen bubbles in the bloodstream that requires a decompression chamber to alleviate. Since that's not anything you'd want to develop at the beginning of a transatlantic flight, be sure to wait 12 hours before flying after a single dive, 18 hours after multiple dives, and 24 hours if your dive(s) required decompression stops.

Regulators up! Reef visitors learn Scuba basics.

LOGISTICS

CERTIFYING ORGANIZATIONS
You'll find that all reliable dive operators—on the Reef and elsewhere—are affiliated with one of the three major international dive-training organizations: PADI (www.padi.com), NAUI (www.naui.org), or SSI (www.divessi.com). The certification requirements for all three are similar, and most dive shops and outfitters consider them interchangeable (i.e., they'll honor a certification from any of the three).

COSTS
The price for taking a full Open Water certification course (usually over four or five days of training) averages around A$500—but in many cases, rental equipment, wetsuits, and instruction manuals cost extra. Some dive shops have relationships with hotels, and offer dive/stay packages. One-day scuba resort courses usually cost around $200-$300, with all gear included.

EMERGENCIES
Before diving on the Reef, it's a good idea to purchase divers' insurance through the Divers Alert Network (DAN), an international organization that provides emergency medical assistance to divers. (Learn more about the different plans at www.diversalertnetwork. org). DAN also has a 24-hour emergency hotline staffed by doctors, emergency medical technicians, and nurses; for help with diving injuries or immediate medical advice, call (001) 919-684-4326 from Australia.

SNORKELING TIPS

Snorkelers explore Fitzroy Reef Lagoon.

■ If you're a beginner, avoid snorkeling in areas where there's chop or strong currents.

■ Every few minutes, look up and check what's floating ahead of you—you'll want to avoid boats, jellyfish, and other surface-swimmers.

■ Give corals, plants, and sea creatures a wide berth—for their protection and yours.

■ Coat every part of your back with high-SPF, waterproof sunscreen; the water's reflection greatly intensifies the sun's rays.

DIVING TIPS

■ Before heading off on a dive trip, have your doctor rule out any possible health complications.

■ Be sure your dive operator is affiliated with an internationally known training organization, such as PADI or NAUI.

■ Stick to dive trips and sites that are within your expertise level—the Reef is not the place to push safety limits.

■ Remember that in Australia, depths and weights use the metric system—so bring a conversion table if you need to.

■ Always dive with a partner, and always keep your partner in sight.

■ Never dive when you're feeling ill—especially if you're experiencing sinus congestion.

■ Never dive after consuming alcohol.

■ If you feel unwell or disoriented while diving, signal to your partner that you need to surface so she or he can accompany you.

8

IN FOCUS DIVING THE REEF

DANGERS OF THE REEF

(left) The Irukandji box jellyfish sting causes severe pain; (right) small sharks inhabit areas of the Reef.

Like any other wild natural habitat, the Reef is home to creatures that are capable of causing you harm—and possibly even killing you. But surprisingly, the most lethal Reef inhabitants aren't of the Shark Week variety. In fact, they're just about invisible.

THE DEADLIEST REEF DWELLER

Chironex fleckeri—better known as box jellyfish—are native to the same waters as the Reef. They also just happen to be the most poisonous sea creatures on the planet. Cube-shaped and transparent (which makes them almost impossible to see in the water), these jellies have tentacles whose stinging cells release an enormously potent venom on contact. A box-jelly sting causes excruciating pain, often followed very quickly (within three or four minutes) by death.

The good news about box jellies is that they're only rarely encountered on the outer Reef and islands (they're much more prevalent close to the mainland shore, especially in summer—which is why you may see beautiful North Queensland beaches completely empty on a hot December day). While the only sure way to prevent a box jellyfish sting is to stay out of the sea altogether, there are measures you can take to lessen the already minimal risks. First, consider wearing a full-length Lycra "sting suit" when you dive. Second, make sure your dive operator carries a supply of Chironex antivenom onboard your dive boat, just in case.

OTHER (LESS DEADLY) DANGERS

Although box jellyfish are by far the most dangerous creatures on the Reef, there are other "biteys" and "nasties" to be aware of. In particular, you should try to stay clear of a smaller box-jelly variety called Irukandji (whose sting causes delayed but often intense pain); Millepora, or stinging coral (which causes irritation and welts when it touches bare skin); sea snakes (who seldom bite humans, but whose poison can cause paralysis); and, yes, sharks (although you'll likely only see small ones on the Reef—the much more hyped Hammerheads, Tiger Sharks, and Great Whites prefer deeper and colder waters).

PROTECTING THE REEF

(left) Even the tiniest coral can serve as protective habitat; (right) divers explore a large coral formation.

Enormous though it may be, the Great Barrier Reef's ecosystem is one that requires a delicate balance. The interdependence of species here means that harming even a single food source—like a particular type of plankton—can have wide-ranging and even devastating effects.

The majority of the Reef is an official marine preserve that's managed and protected by the Great Barrier Reef Marine Park Authority. This government agency has developed a series of long-range programs to help protect the Reef—including population-monitoring of sealife species, water-temperature and salinity studies, and screening of all commercial fishing and tourism/recreational operations.

Since almost 2 million tourists visit the Reef each year, even day-trippers should be mindful of their impact on this fragile environment. Specifically, if you're planning to dive and snorkel here, you should:

■ Make sure your dive gear is secure, with no loose straps or dangling hoses that might snag on corals.

■ Swim slowly to avoid brushing against corals (and be especially mindful when wearing swim fins).

■ Avoid picking up or touching any corals, plants, or creatures (for your protection and theirs). No souvenirs, even empty shells or dead-looking coral.

■ Keep clear of all free-swimming sea creatures like sea turtles, dolphins, dugongs, or whales.

VOLUNTEERING ON THE REEF

If you'd like to do more to protect the Reef, the following organizations offer volunteer programs that allow you to help collect study data and monitor the health of reef species:

■ The Australian Marine Conservation Society: www.amcs.org.au

■ Reef Check Australia: www.reefcheckaustralia.org

■ UNESCO (United Nations Educational, Scientific, and Cultural Organization): whc.unesco.org

8

IN FOCUS DIVING THE REEF

BOAT CRUISES

Hinchinbrook and Palm Islands Tours. Orpheus Island resort guests can take helicopter flights over Hinchinbrook Island National Park, Australia's largest protected island wilderness; cruise the Hinchinbrook-Cardwell channel, seeking out saltwater crocs in island estuaries and anchoring in secluded coves for guided rain-forest treks to Zoe and Mulligan waterfalls; or take a leisurely cruise around the Palm Islands with stops to snorkel, explore significant sites, and take guided nature walks. ☎ *07/4777–7377* ⊕ *www.orpheus.com.au* ⊠ *Half-hr Hinchinbrook Island heli-flights A$375 per person; Hinchinbrook Island day cruise/tour charters: half-day A$500–A$650, full-day A$750–A$950 (1–14 passengers).*

FISHING

Orpheus Island Fishing. The tropical waters off Orpheus Island offer prized game and reef fish species. On group trips or solo dinghy excursions via motorized dinghy (free for guests' use, as is light tackle), tasty reef fish (red emperor and coral trout, sweetlip, and giant trevally) can be caught right off the island. On excursions to the outer reef, you'll get the chance to land large pelagics including black marlin, wahoo, Spanish mackerel, and dog-tooth tuna. Prebooking fishing charters is essential and all expeditions are subject to weather and tidal conditions. ⊠ *Orpheus Island Jetty* ☎ *07/4777–7377* ⊕ *www.orpheus.com.au.*

GREAT BARRIER REEF EXCURSIONS

Orpheus Island Diving & Snorkeling. Orpheus Island is encircled by fringing reef, with world-class dive and snorkeling sites an easy boat or dinghy ride away. Orpheus Island resort can arrange half-day dive and snorkeling trips around the neighboring Palm Islands, and full-day charter dive and snorkeling excursions to the outer Barrier Reef. Costs depend on passenger numbers and inclusions; booking ahead is essential. Resort guests can also preorder a gourmet picnic hamper and use one of the resort's motorized dinghies to visit secluded, boulder-strewn coves and snorkeling spots on the island's fringing reef. Often, you can snorkel directly off the beach into fish-filled coral gardens. ⊠ *Orpheus Island Resort Jetty* ☎ *07/4777–7377* ⊕ *www.orpheus.com.au.*

WHERE TO STAY

For expanded hotel reviews, visit Fodors.com.

$$$$
RESORT
Fodor's Choice
★

Orpheus Island. This unpretentious, eco-friendly resort epitomizes laid-back luxury, with sleekly appointed beachfront rooms, suites, and villas; romantic dining; boutique wines; and numerous outdoor activities included in the rate. **Pros:** idyllic environs; wonderful food and wine; free Wi-Fi in public areas; excellent underwater sites nearby. **Cons:** no in-room Internet; occasional geckos and insects indoors; two-night minimum stay. $ *Rooms from: A$1,800* ⊠ *Orpheus Island Resort* ☎ *07/4777–7377* ⊕ *www.orpheus.com.au* ⇥ *17 rooms and suites* ⦿ *Multiple meal plans.*

The North Coast islands are a hiker's paradise.

LIZARD ISLAND

The small, upscale resort on secluded Lizard Island, just under 150 miles off the North Queensland coast, is the farthest north of any Barrier Reef hideaway. At 2,500 acres, virtually all of it protected as a national park, it's larger than and quite different from other islands in the region. Composed mostly of granite, Lizard has a remarkable diversity of vegetation and terrain: grassy hills give way to rocky slabs interspersed with valleys of rain forest.

Ringed by two dozen white-sand beaches, the island has some of the best fringing coral in the region. Excellent walking trails lead to lookouts with spectacular views of the coast. The island's highest point, Cook's Look (1,180 feet), is the historic spot from which, in August 1770, Captain Cook finally spotted a safe passage through the reef that had held his vessel captive for a thousand miles. Large monitor lizards, after which the island is named, often bask in this area.

GETTING HERE AND AROUND

Lizard Island has its own small airstrip served by Hinterland Aviation. Hour-long flights to the island depart up to twice a day from Cairns, at 11 and 2, returning at 12:30 and 3:25; taking an hour and costing A$315 per person each way. Allow two hour's transit time for connecting international flights, one for domestic flight transits: check-in is 30 minutes prior to flight time at the Hinterland Aviation Terminal. You can also arrange charter flights to the island, with prices varying depending on the size of aircraft available (☎ *07/4043–1999 resort, 03/9426–7550 bookings*).

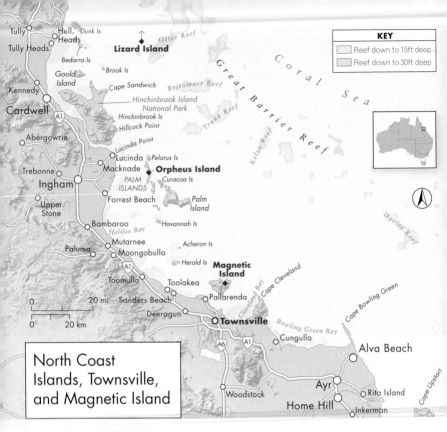

North Coast Islands, Townsville, and Magnetic Island

KEY

- Reef down to 15ft deep
- Reef down to 30ft deep

ESSENTIALS

Air Contacts Hinterland Aviation ☎ 07/4040–1333 ⊕ www.hinterlandaviation. com.au.

EXPLORING

Fodor's Choice **Cod Hole.** For divers and snorkelers, the usually crystal-clear waters off
★ Lizard Island are a dream. Cod Hole, 20 km (12 miles) from Lizard
Island, ranks among the best dive sites on Earth. Massive potato cod
swim up to divers like hungry puppies; it's an awesome experience,
considering that these fish can weigh 300 pounds and reach around 2
meters (6 feet) in length. The island lures big-game anglers from all over
the world from September to December, when black marlin are running.

SPORTS AND THE OUTDOORS

The lodge has catamarans, outboard dinghies, paddle-skis (including
glass-bottomed ones), fishing supplies, snorkeling gear, and lessons.
There is superb snorkeling around the island's fringing coral, or you
can cruise over it on a glass-bottomed paddle-ski tour. Self-guided bushwalking trails and nature slide shows get guests in touch with the local
flora and fauna. Arrange a picnic hamper with the kitchen staff and
take a dinghy out for an afternoon on your own private beach. All these
activities are included in your room rate.

Other activities cost extra: inner and outer reef dive/snorkel trips, night dives, scuba courses, and game- and bottom-fishing excursions (black marlin season runs September through December). For pricing, details, and to prebook activities, contact **Lizard Island Activities Desk** (☎ *1300/863248 or 07/9426–7550,* ⊕ *www.lizardisland.com.au*).

FISHING

Lizard Island is one of the big game-fishing centers in Australia, with several world records set here since the mid-1990s. Game fishing is generally best in spring and early summer, and giant black marlin weighing more than 1,000 pounds are no rarity. September through December, the folk from Lizard Island run full-day game-fishing trips to the outer reef; January through August, you can book half-day bottom-fishing excursions.

Lizard Island Sportfishing. Even though fishing is banned in the waters immediately off Lizard Island, world-renowned fishing grounds lie less than an hour away. From September to December, fishing enthusiasts arrive in droves to land tuna, sailfish, mahimahi, and, if they're lucky, the legendary "Grander" black marlin. From January to August, you might nab trevally, mackerel, or queenfish. Lizard Island Resort arranges small-group, high-adrenaline trips to the outer reef and half- and full-day inner reef excursions on its 51-foot Riviera Platinum Model Flybridge cruiser, *Fascination III.* An outer-reef game-fishing day trip, including heavy tackle, lunch, and light refreshments, costs around A$3,000 for up to four people; a half-day bottom-fishing excursion, with bait, light tackle, and refreshments, is about A$2,000; a full-day trip with lunch is around A$3,000. For all fishing trips, prebooking is essential. ✉ *Lizard Island Resort Jetty, Lizard Island, Great Barrier Reef* ☎ *03/9426–7550 bookings, 1300/863248 toll-free in Australia* ⊕ *www.lizardisland.net.*

HELICOPTER TOURS

Lizard Island Helicopter Tours. On these helicopter tours, you can get a bird's-eye view of Lizard Island's World Heritage–listed Barrier Reef and rain-forest environs. The tour traces the dramatic Cape York coastline, touches down on tropical isles, and swoops low to see turtles, dolphins, and crocodiles; in season, you might also spot manta rays and humpback whales. "Platinum Class" itineraries include a 30-minute "Lizard Island Discovery" flight, which passes over the famed Blue Lagoon (A$550); an hour-long Great Barrier Reef & Coastal Odyssey (A$990); a half-day, fully catered "Tropical Sands" champagne picnic with scenic heli-transfers to your own private sand strip (A$1,320); and 75- or 90-minute transfers between Lizard Island and sister resort Silky Oaks Lodge, near Mossman (A$1,600 each way). ✉ *Depart from Lizard Isand helipad, Lizard Island, Great Barrier Reef* ☎ *03/9426–7550 bookings, 1300/863248 toll-free in Australia* ⊕ *www.lizardisland.net.*

SCUBA DIVING

The reefs around Lizard Island have some of the best marine life and coral on the planet. The resort runs expertly guided scuba-diving and snorkeling trips on its custom-built dive boat to pristine sites on the Great Barrier Reef, including the Ribbon Reefs and globally renowned Cod Hole, as well as local dives, snorkeling excursions, and scuba courses.

Lizard Island Snorkeling & Diving. Lizard Island is a short boat ride from some of the richest, least spoiled sites on the Great Barrier Reef. Within an hour, you can dive the ribbon reefs or renowned Cod Hole, eyeballing giant potato cod, pelagic fish, turtles, rays and sharks. You can also take guided day or night dives to explore fish-filled coral gardens just offshore. Lizard Island Resort's 55-foot dive boat MV *Serranidae* makes reef excursions and morning dive-snorkel trips. It also offers privately guided dives to local fringing reefs and the Cobia Hole. Need scuba skills or gear? The resort has non-accredited Discover Scuba and PADI Referral courses, and a wide range of modern dive equipment for hire at its Beach Club. Use of snorkeling masks, snorkels, and fins is complimentary. ⊠ *Lizard Island Resort, Lizard Island, Great Barrier Reef* ☎ *03/9426–7550 bookings, 1300/863248 toll-free in Australia* ⊕ *www.lizardisland.net.*

WHERE TO STAY
For expanded hotel reviews, visit Fodors.com.

$$$$
RESORT
Fodor's Choice
★

Lizard Island Resort. Beloved by honeymooners, divers, and well-heeled travelers, this outer Great Barrier Reef resort ticks all the high-end tropical-island vacation boxes: luxurious beachfront accommodation, fine food and wine, and world-class diving and fishing. **Pros:** superb diving and fishing; quality food and wine; use of nonmotorized watercraft and dinghies. **Cons:** critters sometimes invade the rooms; lighting inadequate for reading; no cell-phone coverage. $ *Rooms from: A$1,628* ⊠ *Lizard Island, Great Barrier Reef* ☎ *03/9426–7550 bookings, 07/4043–1999 resort, 1300/863248 toll-free in Australia* ⊕ *www.lizardisland.com.au* ⤳ *39 villas, 1 pavilion* ♦ *Multiple meal plans.*

TOWNSVILLE AND MAGNETIC ISLAND

Townsville and adjacent twin city Thuringowa make up Australia's largest tropical city, with a combined population of around 200,000. It's the commercial capital of the north, and a major center for education, scientific research, and defense. Spread along the banks of Ross Creek and around the pink granite outcrop of Castle Hill, Townsville is a pleasant city of palm-fringed malls, historic colonial buildings, extensive parkland, and gardens. It's also the stepping-off point for Magnetic Island, one of the state's largest islands and a haven for wildlife.

GETTING HERE AND AROUND

Qantas flies frequently from Townsville Airport to Brisbane, Cairns, Cloncurry, Mount Isa, and Mackay, as well as to capital cities around Australia and overseas destinations. Jetstar has services to Brisbane, Sydney, and Melbourne; Virgin Australia connects Townsville with

Cairns, Brisbane, the Gold Coast, Rockhampton, Sydney, Melbourne, and Canberra. There are no air connections to Magnetic Island; you need to take a ferry from Townsville (one way, it's A$14.50 for a walk-on passenger; A$89 for a vehicle with up to six passengers). Townsville Taxis are available at the airport. The average cost of the ride to a city hotel is A$22, more after 7 pm.

Townsville is a flat, somewhat dull 1,358-km (844-mile), 16-hour drive from Brisbane. The 348-km (216-mile), 4½-hour journey from here to Cairns, with occasional Hinchinbrook Island views, is more scenic. Greyhound Australia coaches travel regularly to Cairns, Mount Isa, Rockhampton, Brisbane, and other destinations throughout Australia from the SeaLink Terminal on Townsville's Breakwater, also the departure point for Magnetic Island ferries, day cruises, and dive trips. Regular long-distance Queensland Rail services, most offering sleeper berths, connect Townsville with Brisbane, Cairns, Mount Isa, and dozens of towns en route.

Once in town, you can flag Townsville Taxis on the street, find one at taxi stands, hotels, and the island's ferry terminal, or book one online.

TOURS

The Tropicana Guided Adventure Company runs expertly guided, small-group expeditions to normally inaccessible bays and beaches around Magnetic Island in a stretch jeep.

The company's signature tour is its five-hour Wilderness Adventure, accessing remote, permit-only areas around Florence Bay and West Point. The excursion allows time to explore remote beaches, hike to lookouts, photograph wildlife, and watch the sun set over the sea from West Point. The tour leaves Nelly Bay Harbour daily at 2:30, returning in time for the 7:50 SeaLink ferry to Townsville (or dropping guests off at Magnetic Island accommodations).

Other day trips start from A$66 per person for a three-hour eco-orientation tour, departing daily at 11 from Nelly Bay near the taxi stand (catch the 10:30 SeaLink ferry from the mainland). An 8½-hour sightseeing tour of the island, including its wildlife hot spots and remote and tourist areas, leaves daily at 11 am from Magnetic Harbour (A$198, including lunch and refreshments).

ESSENTIALS

Ferry Contacts SeaLink Queensland ☎ *07/4726–0800* ⊕ *www.sealinkqld. com.au.*

Taxi Contacts Townsville Taxis ☎ *13–1008 local bookings, 07/4778–9555 interstate bookings* ⊕ *www.tsvtaxi.com.au.*

Tour Contacts ropicana Guided Adventure Company ☎ *07/4758–1800* ⊕ *www.tropicanatours.com.au.*

Visitor Information Flinders Square Visitor Information Centre ✉ *Flinders Mall near Stanley St., Townsville* ☎ *07/4721–3660, 1800/801902* ⊕ *www. townsvilleonline.com.au.*

TOWNSVILLE

This coastal city has little in the way of sandy beaches or surf, but it does have shady parks, charming colonial buildings, and a boardwalk-flanked waterfront Esplanade with a terrific man-made beach and picnic facilities. The historic town center has thrived recently, with an influx of lively eateries and bars. There are also some excellent museum and a world-class aquarium.

Queensland Parks and Wildlife Service has an office on Magnetic Island, but Townsville Enterprise's information kiosks in Flinders Square and the Museum of Tropical Queensland (MTQ), on the mainland, are the best sources of visitor info about the island.

EXPLORING

FAMILY **Billabong Sanctuary.** This 22-acre sanctuary shelters wombats, dingoes, wallabies, endangered bilbies, snakes, lizards, and numerous birds, such as cassowaries, emus, kookaburras, and cockatoos. There are 10 wildlife shows per day, including crocodile and cassowary feedings, venomous snake presentations, and turtle racing. Thrill-seekers can book a personal croc-feeding experience, with or without souvenir photo. ⊠ *Bruce Hwy., 17 km (11 miles) south of Townsville, Nome* ☎ *07/4778–8344* ⊕ *www.billabongsanctuary.com.au* ⊠ *A$32 entry; A$99 personal croc feed* ☉ *Daily 9–4.*

Castle Hill. The summit of pink-granite monolith Castle Hill, 1 km (½ miles) from the city center, provides great views of the city and Magnetic Island. While you're perched on top, think about the proud local resident who, with the aid of several scout troops, spent years in the 1970s piling rubble onto the peak to try to add the 23 feet that would make Castle Hill a mountain, officially speaking—which means a rise of at least 1,000 feet. These days, most people trek to the top along a steep walking track that doubles as one of Queensland's most scenic jogging routes. ⊠ *Castle Hill Lookout, Castle Hill Rd.* ☎ *1800/801902 Townsville Visitor Information.*

Flinders Street. A stroll along Flinders Street from the Strand to Stanley Street takes you past some of Townsville's most impressive turn-of-the-20th-century colonial structures. **Magnetic House** and several other historic buildings along the strip have been beautifully restored. The grand old **Queens Hotel** is a fine example of the early Victorian Classical Revival style, as is the **Perc Tucker Regional Gallery,** circa 1885, originally a bank. **Tattersalls Hotel,** circa 1865, is typical of its era, with wide verandas and fancy wrought-iron balustrades; today, it houses the rambunctious **Molly Malones** Irish pub. Once the town's post office, what's now **The Brewery** had an impressive masonry clock tower when it was erected in 1889. The tower was dismantled in 1942 so it wouldn't be a target during World War II air raids, and re-erected in 1964. **The Exchange**, Townsville's oldest pub, was built in 1869, burned down in 1881, and was rebuilt the following year. ⊠ *Flinders St.*

FAMILY **Museum of Tropical Queensland.** Centuries-old relics from the HMS *Pandora* (the ship sent by the British Admiralty to capture the mutinous *Bounty* crew) which sank in 1791 carrying 14 crew members of

Captain Bligh's infamous ship, are among the exhibits at this repository of the region's maritime, natural, and indigenous history. There's a fun introduction to North Queensland's culture and lifestyle, a shipwreck exhibit, and the ecology-focused Enchanted Rainforest. Displays of tropical wildlife, dinosaur fossils, local corals, and deep-sea creatures round out a diverse public collection. ⊠ *70–102 Flinders St. E* ☎ *07/4726–0600* ⊕ *www.mtq.qm.qld.gov.au* ⊠ *A$15* ⊙ *Daily 9:30–5.*

FAMILY **Queens Gardens.** Offering shade and serenity less than a mile from the CBD, Townsville's colonial-era botanic gardens occupies 10 verdant acres at the base of Castle Hill. Bordered by frangipani (plumeria) and towering Moreton Bay fig trees, whose unique dangling roots veil the entry to the grounds, the gardens are a wonderful place to picnic, stroll, or amuse the kids. There are play areas, a hedge maze, formal rose garden, fountains, and a lovely rain-forest walk. A compact aviary houses bright-plumed peacocks, lorikeets, and sulphur-crested cockatoos. ⊠ *Gregory and Paxton Sts.(enter off Gregory, Paxton, or Kennedy Sts.), North Ward* ☎ *07/4727–8330, 1300/878001 Townsville City Council, toll-free in Australia* ⊕ *www.townsville.qld.gov.au* ⊠ *Free.*

FAMILY
Fodor'sChoice
★
Reef HQ Aquarium. Come eye-to-eye with sharks, rays, giant trevally, and green sea turtles at the Reef HQ Aquarium. It houses a 200,000-gallon predator tank and a vast aquarium, open to the elements, populated with 120 species of hard and soft coral, as well as sea stars, spiky urchins, sponges, and more than 150 species of tropical fish. There's also a 20-meter (65-foot) Perspex underwater walkway, predator dive shows, twice-daily turtle talks (noon and 3), guided tours, and thrice-weekly shark feeds (2:30 on Tuesday, Thursday, and Sunday). ⊠ *2–68 Flinders St. E* ☎ *07/4750–0800* ⊕ *www.reefhq.com.au* ⊠ *A$26.50.*

FAMILY **Townsville Town Common Conservation Park.** Spot wallabies, echidnas, dingoes, goannas, and hundreds of bird species at this terrific wetlands conservation park. It's crisscrossed by walking and biking trails and dotted with bird blinds and a wildlife-viewing tower. You can take the easy, hour-long Forest Walk to see kingfishers and honey-eaters, or the Pallarenda to Tegoora Rock circuit for wetlands overviews. The 5-km (3-mile), two-plus-hour-long trail from Bald Rock to Mount Marlowl is worth the uphill trek for the regional panorama at the summit. Most trails start from Bald Rock parking lot, 7 km (4½ miles) from the park entrance on unpaved roads. ⊠ *Freshwater Lagoon Rd. off Cape Pallarenda Rd., near Rowes Bay Golf Club, Pallarenda* ☎ *07/4721–3660 Townsville Tourist Information, 07/4722–5244 QPWS Pallarenda, 13–7468 ParksQ infoline* ⊕ *www.nprsr.qld.gov.au/parks/townsville.*

BEACHES

Townsville is blessed with a golden, 2-km (1-mile) beach that stretches along the city's northern edge. The award-winning beach, with its associated pools, water park, and adjacent parklands, is hugely popular with the locals, especially over school holidays and summer.

FAMILY
Fodor'sChoice
★
The Strand. Dubbed Australia's Cleanest Beach, this palm-flanked stretch of sand—lined with jogging tracks and cycleways, picnic-friendly parklands, and hip beachfront bars—has swimming enclosures and a long pier perfect for fishing. The beach and its permanent swimming

enclosure, Strand Rock Pool, are fitted with temporary nets during box-jellyfish season, November–May. Free, kid-friendly Strand Water Park, open on weekends, is patrolled by lifeguards; the Rock Pool is closed every Tuesday and Wednesday for maintenance except in holiday periods. **Amenities:** food and drink; lifeguards; toilets. **Best for:** swimming. ⊠ *The Strand* ☎ *07/4727–9050.*

SPORTS AND THE OUTDOORS

KAYAKING

Magnetic Island Sea Kayaks. On these eco-friendly kayaking trips around Magnetic Island's quieter bays, you might spot turtles, dolphins, dugongs, sea eagles, ospreys, and, mid-July through mid-September, migrating whales and their calves. Two excursions are scheduled daily: a leisurely 4½-hour morning tour of beaches, coves, and bays; and a twilight paddle around Horseshoe Bay with a stop for sunset drinks. Rates include single or double kayaks, safety gear, expert instruction, commentary on the island's ecology, breakfast or sunset drinks, reef tax, and National Park entry fees. Experienced kayakers can also rent out single or double kayaks by the day, safety gear included. ⊠ *Horseshoe Bay boat ramp, Horseshoe Bay Rd., Magnetic Island* ☎ *07/4778–5424* ⊕ *www.seakayak.com.au* ✉ *A$85 double kayak, A$155 single kayak (morning tour); A$60 sunset tour; A$75 per day, single kayak hire, A$150 double kayak* ⊙ *Morning tour: daily from 8. Sunset tour: Wed., Fri., and Sat. from 2 hrs before sunset.*

SCUBA DIVING

Surrounded by tropical islands and warm waters, Townsville is a top-notch diving center. Diving courses, day trips, and multiday excursions tend to be less crowded than those in the hot spots of Cairns or the Whitsunday Islands.

About 16 km (10 miles) offshore, a 60-km (37-mile) boat ride southeast of Townsville, is the wreck of the mighty SS *Yongala*, a steamship that sank in 1911 and now lies 49 to 91 feet beneath the surface. It teems with marine life and is considered one of Australia's best dive sites. It can be explored on one- and two-day trips. All local dive operators conduct excursions to the wreck.

Adrenalin Dive. This local outfit runs day and live-aboard trips to popular sites on the Great Barrier Reef, including the wreck of the SS *Yongala*. The *Yongala* trip includes weight belt, tanks, two dives, and lunch; it's an extra A$40 for dive gear and A$10 for the introductory guided dive that's compulsory for novice divers. A two-night, live-aboard trip includes up to six dives, including one night dive. ⊠ *252 Walker St.* ☎ *07/4724–0600, 1300/664600 toll-free in Australia* ⊕ *www.adrenalindive.com.au* ✉ *1-day Yongala: A$226; 1-day GBR: A$196 snorkeler, A$226 diver, scuba gear extra A$40; 2-night live-aboard trip: from A$545 snorkeler, A$620 diver. Additional dives A$25–A$80; PADI Open Water Course, A$260.80; PADI Adventure Course A$180.*

WHERE TO EAT

$$$

MODERN
AUSTRALIAN

✕ **JAM Corner.** This restaurant sources terrific organic and tropical produce for its seasonal modern Australian menus. Even though the menu changes seasonally, it always features fresh seafood and premium

Australia meats: free-range chicken, Victorian spring lamb, Western Plains pork, Sunshine Coast crab, Coffin Bay oysters, and North Queensland seafood. For special occasions, there's a luxurious, chandelier-lighted private dining room; ask about occasional degustation lunches and dinners. ■TIP→ Reservations aren't essential, but it's a smart idea to book ahead. $ *Average main: A$34* ⊠ *1 Palmer St., South Townsville* ☎ *07/4721–4900* ⊕ *www.jamcorner.com.au* ☾ *Closed Mon. No dinner Sun.*

$$$
MODERN
AUSTRALIAN
Fodor's Choice
★

✕**A Touch of Salt.** This Modern Australian eatery ticks all the boxes: location, service, ambience, food, and wine. Mains are divided into "sea," "earth," and "land." The tempura soft-shell crab is a standout "sea" dish; a "land" selection might include confit duck leg with plum glaze; and an ever-changing "earth list" of vegetarian options might be pumpkin-almond ravioli. Small but artfully presented desserts taste as good as they look. There's also an excellent, largely Australian wine list. Prebooking is strongly recommended, especially if you want to sit outside on the spacious riverfront deck. $ *Average main: A$32* ⊠ *86 Ogden St.* ☎ *07/4724–4441* ⊕ *www.atouchofsalt.com.au.*

WHERE TO STAY

For expanded hotel reviews, visit Fodors.com.

$$$
HOTEL

▦**Oaks M on Palmer.** The smartly configured studios and suites at this hotel are a five-minute walk from Palmer Street's burgeoning dining precinct, and an easy stroll across the footbridge from Flinders Street and the ferry port. **Pros:** excellent in-room facilities; central location; 15% discount for two+-day stays. **Cons:** feels a tad clinical; service standards vary; fee for in-room Wi-Fi. $ *Rooms from: A$395* ⊠ *81 Palmer St.* ☎ *07/4753–2900 reception, 1300/559129 toll-free in Australia* ⊕ *www.theoaksgroup.com.au* ⌐⊃ *104 rooms* ¶◎¶ *No meals.*

$
RENTAL

▦**Yongala Lodge by The Strand.** Historic charm, courteous service, and excellent food and wine make up for the lack of modern conveniences at this classic Queenslander guest lodge. **Pros:** top-notch food and wine; courteous service; free cable TV. **Cons:** no in-room Wi-Fi; cheaper rooms are dated; guest-room walls a tad thin. $ *Rooms from: A$110* ⊠ *11 Fryer St., North Ward* ☎ *07/4772–4633* ⊕ *www.historicyongala.com.au* ⌐⊃ *10 rooms, 10 apartments* ¶◎¶ *No meals.*

NIGHTLIFE

Fodor's Choice
★

The Brewery. Townville's historic post office now houses this sociable brewpub, which serves light "tavern-style" meals and produces their own boutique beers on-site at the microbrewery. The owners have combined modern finishes to the building's original design, incorporating old post-office fittings, such as the main bar, once the stamp counter. The big Sunday brunches are deservedly popular. ⊠ *Flinders Mall, 252 Flinders St.* ☎ *07/4724–2999* ⊕ *www.townsvillebrewery.com.au.*

Monsoons Bar & Grill. Drink, dine, and mingle with the locals on the sun-drenched riverfront deck of this laid-back bar on Flinders Street's nightlife strip. There are billiard tables, arcade games, plasma TVs, Friday-night specials (including A$5 bar snacks), and live acoustic sessions on weekends. ⊠ *194 Flinders St. E* ☎ *07/4772–0900* ☾ *Closed Mon. and Wed.*

MAGNETIC ISLAND

More than half of Magnetic Island's 52 square km (20 square miles) is national parkland, laced with miles of walking trails and rising to 1,640 feet at the Mt. Cook summit. The terrain is littered with huge granite boulders and softened by tall hoop pines, eucalyptus forest, and rainforest gullies. A haven for wildlife, the island shelters rock wallabies, echidnas, frogs, possums, fruit bats, nonvenomous green tree snakes, and Northern Australia's largest population of wild koalas. Its beaches, mangroves, sea-grass beds, and fringing reefs support turtles nesting, fish hatching, and a significant dugong (manatee) population. You can take time out on 23 island beaches and dive nine offshore shipwrecks.

More than 2,500 people call "Maggie" home; most live on the island's eastern shore at Picnic Bay, Arcadia, Nelly Bay, and Horseshoe Bay. Many artists and craftspeople reside here, drawn by the serenity and scenic environs; you can see and buy their work at studios and galleries around the island.

GETTING HERE AND AROUND

The 40-minute Fantasea Cruising Magnetic ferry service has several scheduled services daily from the mainland to Maggie's Nelly Bay Ferry Terminal, 10 km (6 miles) offshore. The first ferry leaves Townsville at 5:20 am weekdays, 7:10 on weekends, with the last return service departing the island at 6:55 pm. One-way fares are A$89 for a vehicle with up to six people, A$14.50 for a person with no vehicle (bicycles free). SeaLink Queensland has a daily 25-minute catamaran service linking Townsville and Nelly Bay on Magnetic Island. Bus and island transfers meet the ferry during daylight hours. Up to 18 SeaLink ferries a day cruise out of Townsville between 5:30 am (6:30 Sunday) and 10:30 pm (11:30 pm Friday and Saturday), returning between 6:20 am (7:10 Sunday) and 11 pm (midnight Friday and Saturday); a one-way ticket costs A$16.

The tiny Mini Moke, a soft-top convertible version of the Mini-Minor car, is an ideal means by which to explore Magnetic Island. **MI Wheels**, next to the IGA supermarket near Nelly Bay Ferry Terminal, rents out Mokes, including fuel; driver's license required.

Motorbikes or scooters are a cheap and easy way to get around the island, though if you want to get off the main linking road and explore dirt roads and bush tracks, you'll have to rent a trail bike. **Road Runner Scooter Hire** rents trail bikes for A$65 per day, scooters from A$40, and dual-seat scooters from A$55 (9 am–5 pm). The cost includes helmets and unlimited mileage; you top up the gas yourself.

ESSENTIALS

Transportation **Fantasea Cruising Magnetic** ⊠ *22 Ross St., Townsville* ☎ *07/4796–9300* ⊕ *www.fantaseacruisingmagnetic.com.au.* **Magnetic Island Sunbus.** Get an overview of Magnetic Island riding the cheap, reliable local buses, which link Picnic Point, Nelly Bay, Arcadia, and Horseshoe Bay from dawn till late, and can be hailed from the roadside. Single-fare tickets or unlimited-travel day and weekly passes are available from the driver. The bus departs at regular intervals between 5:55 am and 9:45 pm (Sun.–Wed.), 10:25 (Thurs.), and midnight (Fri.–Sat.). Hail it between designated stops simply by standing at

MIGALOO THE ALBINO WHALE

Migaloo, the world's only documented white humpback whale, was first spotted in 1991 as he made his way up the Queensland coastline. A witty indigenous elder suggested the name Migaloo, an Aboriginal word for "white fella."

Every year thousands eagerly watch for a glimpse of Migaloo's distinctive pure-white dorsal fin, as the 14-meter (46-foot) whale makes his annual migration from the Antarctic to tropical waters in June and July. He's been spotted as far up Australia's east coast as Port Douglas, north of Cairns—usually from the decks of dive and cruise boats (which are forbidden by law from going within 500 meters of the rare cetacean). Sometimes Migaloo travels solo; on other journeys, he's accompanied by dolphins or fellow humpbacks.

Migaloo's not the only albino marine creature you might spot on your visit to Queensland: in early 2006, a tiny white sea turtle was found on Blacks Beach, Mackay, and shipped off to Reef HQ in nearby Townsville for rehab. Today he's doing well—and is a great deal larger.

Keen to know where Migaloo's heading? Go to the White Whale Research Centre's dedicated website, ⊕ www.migaloo.com.au, where whale-spotters document the migratory movements of this unique cetacean. To help to protect Migaloo and his mates, sign the online petition.

the roadside and raising your hand. ☎ 07/4778–5130 ⊕ www.sunbus.com.au ⛴ A$1.80–A3.60 single trip; A$A3.60–A$7.20 daily; A$14.40–A$28.80 weekly. **Magnetic Island Taxi Service** ☎ 13–1008 ⊕ www.131008.com. **MI Wheels** ⊠ 138 Sooning St., opposite the Ferry Terminal, Nelly Bay ☎ 07/4758–1111 ⊕ www.miwheels.com.au. **Road Runner Scooter Hire** ⊠ 3/64 Kelly St., Nelly Bay ☎ 07/4778–5222.

Visitor Information Queensland Parks and Wildlife Service, Magnetic Island ⊠ 22 Hurst St., Picnic Bay ☎ 07/4778–5378 ⊕ www.nprsr.qld.gov.au/parks/magnetic-island.

SPORTS AND THE OUTDOORS

The island has 24 km (15 miles) of hiking trails, most of which are relatively easy. The popular Forts Walk leads to World War II gun emplacements overlooking Horseshoe and Florence bays. At a leisurely pace, it takes 45 minutes each way from the Horseshoe–Radical Bay Road. Look up en route and you may spot a sleepy koala.

Some of the island's best views are on the 5-km (3-mile) Nelly Bay to Arcadia Walk. Look out for shell middens created over thousands of years by the island's Aboriginal owners, the Wulgurukaba, or "Canoe People."

Swimming and snorkeling are other popular activities, but from November to May, box jellyfish ("stingers") are a hazard: swim at Picnic and Horseshoe bays, which have stinger nets, and wear a protective suit. At other times, Alma Bay and Nelly Bay, as well as Picnic, Florence, Radical, Horseshoe, and Balding bays, are all suitable for swimming. Horseshoe has daily lifeguard patrols and a stinger-free swimming enclosure; Alma and Picnic bays are patrolled over weekends and school holiday periods, September to May.

Geoffrey Bay has a well-trafficked unofficial snorkel trail. Other good snorkeling spots include Nelly Bay, Alma Bay, and the northern ends of Florence and Arthur bays. Near the northeastern corner of the island, Radical Bay has a small, idyllic beach flanked by tree-covered rock outcrops. Horseshoe Bay, the island's largest beach, is lined with boat-rental outlets.

HORSEBACK RIDING

FAMILY
Fodor's Choice
★

Horseshoe Bay Ranch. Leaving only hoofprints on Magnetic Island's white-sand beaches, these eco-friendly horse rides offer the chance to go bareback swimming with your well-trained steed. Two- to three-hour rides (A$100) depart Horseshoe Bay Ranch daily at 9 and 3, wending their way along bush trails to a secluded beach, where you get to unsaddle and take the horses for a Coral Sea swim. Wear a bathing suit, shirt, long pants, socks, and closed shoes, and BYO drinking water and sunscreen. Safety helmets are provided, and a minimum of two guides accompanies each ride. ⊠ *38 Gifford St., Horseshoe Bay* ☎ *07/4778–5109* ⊕ *www.horseshoebayranch.com.au* ✉ *A$100 per person, guided ride; A$20 kid's pony ride.*

SNORKELING AND SCUBA DIVING

Pleasure Divers. The local guides at Pleasure divers run good-value dives to the SS *Yongala* shipwreck and pristine Lodestone Reef on the outer Barrier Reef. Trips includes two dives and buffet lunch; optional introductory dives, adventure diving, and guided dives (compulsory for those with fewer than 15 logged dives) cost extra. Reef dive and snorkel trips run Tuesday, Thursday, Friday, and Sunday; *Yongala* trips run Wednesday and Saturday from Nelly Bay Ferry Terminal and Townsville. Pleasure Divers run various PADI-accredited courses from the island, including refresher and three-day, four-dive Open Water courses. ⊠ *10 Marine Parade, Arcadia* ☎ *07/4778–5788, 1800/797797 toll-free in Australia* ⊕ *www.pleasuredivers.com.au* ✉ *A$50 local snorkel tour, A$95 guided local dive (A$33 subsequent dives); A$226 Yongala trip; A$196 for snorkelers, A$226 for divers, Lodestone Reef trip (A$40 scuba gear); A$125 scuba refresher course; A$349 PADI Open Water course, A$15 snorkel gear.*

TOAD RACES

Hotel Arcadia Toad Races. A Magnetic Island institution, the Arcadia's weekly toad races offer cut-price Aussie-style hilarity. After each race, the winners kiss their toads and collect the proceeds, with funds raised going to local charities. The Arcadia cane-toad races have been held every Wednesday night from 8 pm for nearly three decades. Even when the toads aren't racing, Hotel Arcadia's pumping, with three well-patronized bars, regular live bands, pool tables, and bistro meals. ⊠ *7 Marine Parade, Arcadia* ☎ *07/4778–5177, 1800/663666* ⊕ *www. hotelarcadia.com.au.*

8

WATER SPORTS

Adrenalin Jet Ski Tours. This operator offers tours through Magnetic Island's clear waters on SeaDoo 4-stroke Jet Skis. Choose between the three-hour island circumnavigation and the 90-minute "Top End" tour, with up to two people on each ski. All equipment and instruction are included in the rate; no license required. ✉ *9 Pacific Dr., Horseshoe Bay* ☎ *07/4778–5533, 0407/785533.*

Horseshoe Bay Watersports. This outfitter can take you tube-riding, wakeboarding, waterskiing, and sailing on a Hobi Cat in the translucent waters of Horseshoe Bay. All tube rides are for a minimum of two people, though an extra person can ride for free in the ski boat to take pictures. Horseshoe Bay Watersports also rents an array of water-sports gear and equipment. Find them beside the boat ramp at the center of Horseshoe Bay, weather permitting. ✉ *Boat ramp, Pacific Dr. at Horseshoe Bay Rd., Horseshoe Bay* ☎ *07/4758–1336* 🌐 *www.sailsonhorseshoe.com.au* 🎟 *From A$15 per person, tube rides; A$50 per hr, Hobi Cat hire.*

WHERE TO STAY

For expanded hotel reviews, visit Fodors.com.

Magnetic Island began "life" as a holiday-home getaway for Townsville residents; only recently has it attracted the kind of large-scale development that has transformed other islands near the Barrier Reef. Accommodations here are a mix of functional 1970s properties; small budget lodges; and newer, upmarket but relatively small apartment complexes and resorts. Luxurious Peppers Blue on Blue Resort is an exception to the rule.

$$ RESORT FAMILY 🏨 **Peppers Blue On Blue Resort.** The hotel and studio rooms, apartments, and penthouse suites at Blue on Blue are stylishly designed, with high-end entertainment systems, luxe amenities, and balconies overlooking the ferry port, pool or the island's private marina. **Pros:** top-notch food and wine; terrific pools; convenient launchpad for excursions. **Cons:** some suites lack full elevator access; lower-floor, ferry-side rooms are noisy; limited Wi-Fi access. [$] *Rooms from: A$273* ✉ *Adjacent to the ferry terminal, 123 Sooning St., Nelly Bay* ☎ *07/4758–2400, 1300/737444 reservations (toll-free in Australia)* 🌐 *www.peppers.com.au/blue-on-blue* 🛏 *60 twin rooms, 127 apartment suites and penthouses* 🍴 *Multiple meal plans.*

$$ HOTEL FAMILY 🏨 **Sails on Horseshoe.** This unassuming low-rise complex has a prime location on Horseshoe Bay, where visitors can stroll across the road to snorkel, hire kayaks, and take Jet Ski tours. **Pros:** terrific location; palm-shaded grounds; rainbow lorikeets on balcony railings in the mornings. **Cons:** dated furnishings; few on-site amenities; fee for Wi-Fi. [$] *Rooms from: A$230* ✉ *13–15 Pacific Dr., Horseshoe Bay* ☎ *07/4778–5117* 🌐 *www.sailsonhorseshoe.com.au* 🛏 *2 studios, 2 villas, 10 town-house apartments* 🍴 *No meals.*

ADELAIDE AND
SOUTH AUSTRALIA

WELCOME TO ADELAIDE AND SOUTH AUSTRALIA

TOP REASONS TO GO

★ **Arts and Music:** South Australia has fantastic events, from the renowned Adelaide Fringe Festival, to the internationally acclaimed Come Out festival, and the annual WOMADelaide celebration of world music.

★ **Bush Tucker:** The Australian palate has been reeducated in the pleasures of bush tucker—food that has been used for millennia by the Aboriginal people. Kangaroo, crocodile, emu, and other regional fare are now embraced by all.

★ **Historic Homes:** There are historic properties in both North Adelaide and in the Adelaide Hills, which have the best of both worlds: easy access to the city as well as to countryside vineyards and rustic villages.

★ **Wonderful Wines:** South Australia is considered Australia's premier wine state, and the top-notch wines of the Barossa Region, Clare Valley, McLaren Vale, Adelaide Hills, and Coonawarra are treasured by connoisseurs.

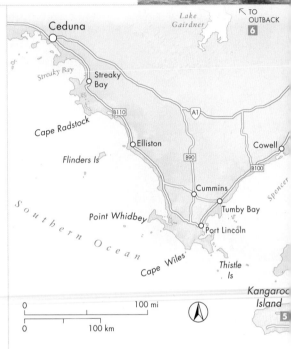

1 Adelaide. Heritage buildings line the small but perfectly formed center of South Australia's capital city. A diverse range of attractions, eateries, and bars makes the city a livelier option than its reputation would suggest.

2 The Barossa Wine Region. One of the country's best-known wine regions—expect rolling hills, delicious local produce, and some of the best Shiraz in the world.

3 The Clare Valley. Less visited than the Barossa. Riesling fans should meander through the valley, tasting as they go while enjoying some spectacular views of the Flinders Ranges.

4 Fleurieu Peninsula. Wine buffs on a short time frame shouldn't miss beautiful McLaren Vale and its amenable cellar doors, while beautiful beaches and dramatic cliff walks are only a short drive away.

GETTING ORIENTED

South Australia encompasses both the dry hot north of the Outback and the greener, more temperate south coast. The green belt includes Adelaide and its surrounding hills and orchards, the Barossa and Clare Valley vineyards, the beautiful Fleurieu Peninsula, and the cliffs and lagoons of the mighty Murray, Australia's longest river. Offshore, residents of Kangaroo Island live at a delightfully old-fashioned pace, savoring their domestic nature haven.

9

5 Kangaroo Island.
Remote, beautiful, and just verging on the right side of isolated, Australia's third-largest island is a paradise for animal lovers, and also offers some of the world's coolest accommodation.

6 The Outback. Heading north, a trip to South Australia's Outback gives visitors a glimpse into an arid and dramatic landscape that is unmistakably Australian.

Updated by
Tim Baker

Renowned for its celebrations of the arts, its multiple cultures, and its bountiful harvests from vines, land, and sea, South Australia is both diverse and divine. Here you can taste some of the country's finest wines, sample its best restaurants, and admire some of the world's most valuable gems. Or skip the state's sophisticated options and unwind on wildlife-rich Kangaroo Island, hike in the Flinders Ranges, or live underground like opal miners in the vast Outback.

Spread across a flat saucer of land between the Mt. Lofty ranges and the sea, the capital city of Adelaide is easy to explore. The wide streets of its 1½-square-km (½-square-mile) city center are organized in a simple grid that's ringed with parklands. The plan was laid out in 1836 by William Light, the colony's first surveyor-general, making Adelaide the only early-Australian capital not built by English convict labor. Today Light's plan is recognized as being far ahead of its time. This city of 1.1 million still moves at a leisurely pace, free of the typical urban menace of traffic jams thanks to Light's insistence that all roads be wide enough to turn a cannon.

Nearly 90% of South Australians live in the fertile south around Adelaide, because the region stands on the very doorstep of the harshest, driest land in the most arid of Earth's populated continents. Jagged hills and stony deserts fill the parched interior, which is virtually unchanged since the first settlers arrived. Desolate terrain and temperatures that top 48°C (118°F) have thwarted all but the most determined efforts to conquer the land. People who survive this region's challenges do so only through drastic measures, such as in the far-northern opal-mining town of Coober Pedy, where residents live underground.

Still, the deserts hold great surprises, and many clues to the country's history before European settlement. The ruggedly beautiful Flinders Ranges north of Adelaide hold Aboriginal cave paintings and fossil remains from when the area was an ancient seabed. Lake Eyre, a great salt lake, filled with water in the year 2000 for only the fourth time in its recorded history. The Nullarbor ("treeless") Plain stretches west across state lines in its tirelessly flat, ruthlessly arid march into Western Australia.

Yet South Australia is, perhaps ironically, gifted with the good life. It produces most of the nation's wine, and the sea ensures a plentiful supply of lobster and famed King George whiting. Cottages and guesthouses tucked away in the countryside around Adelaide are among the most charming and relaxing in Australia. Farther afield, unique experiences like watching seal pups cuddle with their mothers on Kangaroo Island would warm any heart. South Australia may not be grand in reputation, but its attractions are extraordinary, and after a visit you'll know you've indulged in one of Australia's best-kept secrets.

PLANNING

WHEN TO GO

Adelaide has the least rainfall of all Australian capital cities, and the midday summer heat is oppressive. The Outback in particular is too hot for comfortable touring during this time, but Outback winters are pleasantly warm. South Australia's national parks are open year-round. The best times to visit are in spring and autumn. In summer extreme fire danger may close walking tracks, and in winter heavy rain can make some roads impassable. Boating on the Murray River and Lake Alexandrina is best from October to March, when the long evenings are bathed in soft light. The ocean is warmest from December to March.

GETTING HERE AND AROUND

AIR TRAVEL

Adelaide Airport, 15 minutes from the city center, is a pleasant place to fly into and the state's main hub. The international and domestic terminals share a modern building complete with cafés, a tourist office, and free Wi-Fi.

International airlines serving Adelaide include Singapore Airlines, Malaysia Airlines, Cathay Pacific, Air New Zealand, Virgin Australia, and Emirates. Qantas also connects Adelaide with many international cities (usually via Melbourne or Sydney). Domestic airlines flying into Adelaide include Jetstar, REX/Regional Express, Tigerair, and Virgin Australia. You can also fly to Coober Pedy and Kangaroo Island from here.

BUS TRAVEL

Adelaide's Central Bus Station is the state's main hub for travel across the region as well as interstate services to Melbourne and Sydney. It's difficult and time-consuming to travel by bus to the wine regions, however; we recommend either renting a car or taking a tour.

CAR TRAVEL

The best way to experience this diverse state is by road. In general, driving conditions are excellent, although minor lanes are unpaved. It's two hours from Adelaide to the Barossa and Clare, the southern coast, and most other major sights, and less than an hour to McLaren Vale's wineries. The most direct route to the Flinders Ranges is via the

9

GREAT ITINERARIES

Many of the state's attractions are an easy drive from Adelaide. However, for a taste of the real South Australia a trip to a national park or to the Outback is definitely worth the extra travel time. Short flights between destinations make any journey possible within a day or overnight, but the more time you leave yourself to explore the virtues of this under-rated state, the better.

IF YOU HAVE 3 DAYS

Spend a leisurely day in **Adelaide** enjoying the museums and historic sights, as well as the bustling Central Market. Take a sunset stroll along the Torrens, then have dinner and drinks at one of the city's vibrant restaurants or wine bars. Spend the night, then on Day 2 tour the **Adelaide Hills**, strolling the streets of 19th-century villages and taking in the panorama from atop **Mt. Lofty**. Stay the night in a charming bed-and-breakfast in one of the region's small towns, or come back down to North Adelaide and rest among the beautiful sandstone homes. Save Day 3 for wine tasting in the **Barossa Region**.

IF YOU HAVE 5 DAYS

After exploring Adelaide for a day, expand your horizons beyond the city and take a tram-car ride to the beach at touristy Glenelg or its neighbors at laid back Brighton or posher Henley Beach, where you can laze on the white sands and dine at tasty outposts. Spend the night here or at a B&B on the **Fleurieu Peninsula,** then take Day 3 to explore the vineyards and catch the ferry to **Kangaroo Island.** After a night here, use Day 4 to explore and appreciate the island's wildlife and untamed beauty. Return to Adelaide in the afternoon on Day 5 and drive up to the **Adelaide Hills** for sunset at **Mt. Lofty.**

Princes Highway and Port Augusta, but a more interesting route takes you through the Clare Valley vineyards.

TRAIN TRAVEL

If you love train travel, you might find yourself stopping in Adelaide, as two classic train journeys also wind through this state: the *Ghan,* which runs north via Alice Springs to Darwin, and the *Indian Pacific,* which crosses the Nullarbor Plain to reach Perth. More prosaically, you can catch a train to Sydney or Melbourne, though often budget airlines are much cheaper.

RESTAURANTS

Foodies are spoiled for choice in South Australia; the region is famous throughout the country for its excellent produce. Make sure you try some of Adelaide's Mod Oz cuisine, with dishes showcasing oysters, crayfish, and King George whiting prepared with Asian and Mediterranean flavors. Bush foods are also available in some eateries; look for kangaroo, emu, and wattle seed.

Many restaurants close for a few days a week, so call ahead to check. Some upscale institutions require booking well in advance, and tables are tight during major city festivals and holidays. *Prices in the reviews are the average cost of a main course at dinner or, if dinner is not served, at lunch.*

HOTELS

As well as all the standard chains, South Australia is packed with delightful lodgings in contemporary studios, converted cottages, and grand mansions. Modern resorts sprawl along the coastal suburbs, the Barossa Valley, and other tourist centers, but intimate properties for 10 or fewer guests can easily be found

There is plenty of competition in Adelaide, so shop around for great deals. Outside the city, weekday nights are usually less expensive and two-night minimum bookings often apply. *Prices in the reviews are the lowest cost of a standard double room in high season. For expanded hotel reviews, visit Fodors.com.*

WINERIES

Oenophiles rejoice: in South Australia you've arrived in wine heaven. SA is the country's wine powerhouse, producing most of the nation's wine and boasting some of the oldest vineyards in the world. Thanks to its diverse geography and climate, the region produces a huge range of grape varieties—from cool-climate Rieslings in the Clare Valley to the big, full-bodied Shiraz wines of the world-famous Barossa. Less well known, McLaren Vale now punches above its weight with an exceptional variety of grapes, including Merlot, Chardonnay, and Cabernet Sauvignon, while just a 20-minute drive from Adelaide is Adelaide Hills, where temperatures are lower than the rest of the region, leading to great sparkling wines and Pinot Noir.

Although you can drive yourself to any of these regions, strict drunk driving laws mean that the unfortunate designated driver will be restricted to a few sips, if that. We highly recommend that you leave the driving to professionals. The most luxurious option is to go with Mary Anne Kennedy, the owner of A Taste of South Australia, who is one of the most knowledgeable regional food and wine guides. Her boutique tours of any region you choose (A$398; minimum two people, max five) are a taste treat.

A Taste of South Australia ☎ *08/8371–3553, 0419/861588* ⊕ *www.tastesa. com.au.*

ADELAIDE

Australians think of Adelaide as a city of churches, but Adelaide has outgrown its reputation as a sleepy country town dotted with cathedrals and spires. The Adelaide of this millennium is infinitely more complex, with a large, multiethnic population and thriving urban art and music scenes supported by a "space activation program" that encourages pop-up shops, markets, performances, street food, mini festivals, art exhibitions, and other "off-the-cuff" experiences in the cities underutilized streets and public spaces.

Bright and clean, leafy and beautiful Adelaide is a breeze to explore, with a grid pattern of streets encircled by parkland. The heart of the greenbelt is divided by the meandering River Torrens, which passes the Festival Centre in its prettiest stretch.

GETTING HERE AND AROUND

A car gives you the freedom to discover the country lanes and villages in the hills region outside the city, and Adelaide also has excellent road connections with other states. But South Australia is a big place, and we recommend flying if you're looking to save time. Adelaide has an excellent bus system, including the no-cost Adelaide FREE buses, which make about 30 downtown stops. Free guides to Adelaide's public bus lines are available from the Adelaide Metro Info Centre. The city's only surviving tram route now runs between the Entertainment Centre in Hindmarsh through the city to the beach at Glenelg. Ticketing is identical to that on city buses; travel between South Terrace and the Entertainment Centre on Port Road is free.

TOURS

Adelaide Sightseeing operates a morning city sights tour for A$64. The company also runs a daily afternoon bus tour of the Adelaide Hills and the German village of Hahndorf for A$64. For A$65, Gray Line Adelaide provides morning city tours that take in all the highlights. They depart from 85 Franklin Street at 9:30 am.

Tourabout Adelaide has private tours with tailored itineraries. Prices run from around A$30 for an Adelaide walking tour to A$280 for day-long excursions to the Barossa Valley. Jeff Easley, the owner and chief tour guide, can arrange almost anything.

ESSENTIALS

Taxi Suburban Taxis ☎ *13–1008* ⊕ *www.suburbantaxis.com.au.* **Yellow Cabs** ☎ *13–2227* ⊕ *www.yellowadelaide.com.au.*

Tour Operators Adelaide Sightseeing ✉ *85 Franklin St* ☎ *1300/769762* ⊕ *www.adelaidesightseeing.com.au.* **Gray Line Adelaide** ☎ *1300/858687* ⊕ *www.grayline.com.au.* **Tourabout Adelaide** ✉ *Wellington Business Centre, 2 Portrush Rd., Suite 24, Payneham* ☎ *08/8365–1115, 0408/809232* ⊕ *www. touraboutadelaide.com.au.*

Visitor Information South Australian Visitor Information Centre ✉ *108 North Terrace, ground fl., City Center* ☎ *1300/764227* ⊕ *www.southaustralia. com.*

EXPLORING

CITY CENTER

The tiny city center is where you'll find most of Adelaide's sights, shops, and grand stately buildings. Staying here means you're in the heart of what action there is in Adelaide. North of the Torrens River is North Adelaide, which is dominated by the spires of St. Peter's Cathedral. This genteel suburb is where the city's yuppies live, and it has some great neighborhood restaurants. For fun in the sun, head to touristy Glenelg and its cooler near neighbors, Henley Beach and Brighton. Greater Adelaide has great views over the city at Mt. Lofty and in Port Adelaide; seafaring fans will enjoy the South Australian Maritime Museum.

TOP ATTRACTIONS

FAMILY **Adelaide Zoo.** Australia's second-oldest zoo still retains much of its original architecture. Enter through the 1883 cast-iron gates to see such animals as the giant pandas, Sumatran tigers, Australian rain-forest birds, and chimpanzees housed in modern, natural settings. The zoo is world renowned for its captive breeding and release programs, and rare species including the red panda and South Australia's own yellow-footed rock wallaby are among its successes. In June 2008, the Australian government and Adelaide zoo signed a cooperative agreement to help secure the long-term survival of the giant panda, and in late 2009 Wang Wang and Funi arrived on loan from China to become the only giant pandas in the southern hemisphere, and the first to live permanently in Australia. Special VIP panda tours are now also available. Ask at the ticket office about tours and feeding times. ⊠ *Frome Rd., near War Memorial Dr, City Center* ☎ *08/8267–3255* ⊕ *www.zoossa.com.au* ☞ *A$31.50, kids under 14 A$18, families (2 adults, 2–3 kids) A$85* ⊙ *Daily 9:30–5.*

Art Gallery of South Australia. Many famous Australian painters, including Charles Conder, Margaret Preston, Clifford Possum Tjapaltjarri, Russell Drysdale, and Sidney Nolan, are represented in here. Extensive Renaissance and British artworks are on display, and the atrium houses Aboriginal pieces. There is usually a visiting exhibition, too. A café and bookshop are also on-site. ⊠ *North Terrace near Pulteney St., City Center* ☎ *08/8207–7000* ⊕ *www.artgallery.sa.gov.au* ☞ *Free* ⊙ *Daily 10–5.*

FAMILY **Botanic Gardens of Adelaide.** These magnificent formal gardens include
Fodor's Choice an international rose garden, giant water lilies, an avenue of Moreton
★ Bay fig trees, acres of green lawns, and duck ponds. The Bicentennial Conservatory—the largest single-span glass house in the southern hemisphere—provides an environment for lowland rain-forest species such as the cassowary palm and torch ginger. Daily free guided tours leave from the Schomburgk Pavilion at 10:30. On weekends there's often a wedding ceremony taking place somewhere on the grounds. In summer the Moonlight Cinema series (⊕ *www.moonlight.com.au*) screens new, classic, and cult films inside the garden at sunset; bring a picnic blanket and a bottle of wine. Tickets sell fast, so plan ahead. ⊠ *North Terrace, Botanic Park, City Center* ☎ *08/8222–9311* ⊕ *www.botanicgardens. sa.gov.au* ☞ *Gardens/Conservatory free* ⊙ *Gardens: weekdays 8 am, weekends 9 am, closing times vary seasonally. Bicentennial Conservatory: daily 10–4 (until 5 during daylight saving time).*

Migration Museum. Chronicled in this converted 19th-century Destitute Asylum, which later in the 19th century served as a school where Aboriginal children were forced to train as servants to the British, are the origins, hopes, and fates of some of the millions of immigrants who settled in Australia during the past two centuries. The museum is starkly realistic, and the bleak welcome that awaited many migrants is graphically illustrated. ⊠ *82 Kintore Ave., City Center* ☎ *08/8207–7580* ⊕ *www.history.sa.gov.au* ☞ *Free* ⊙ *Weekdays 10–5, weekends 1–5.*

Parliament House. Ten Corinthian columns are the most striking features of this classical parliament building. It was completed in two stages 50 years apart: the west wing in 1889 and the east wing in 1939. Alongside is **Old Parliament House,** which dates from 1843. There's a free guided

9

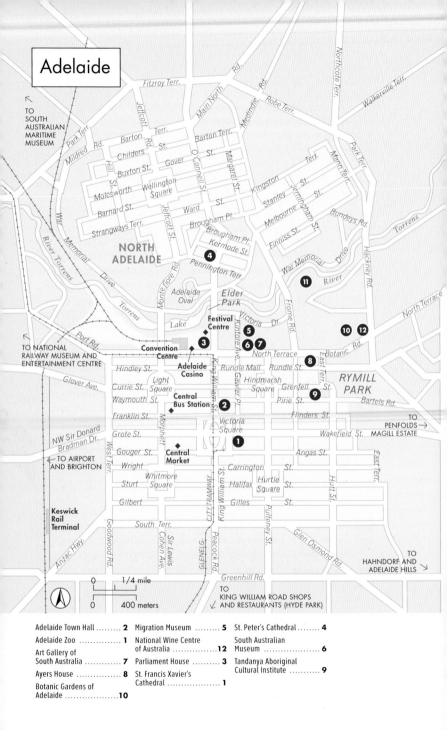

Adelaide

TO SOUTH AUSTRALIAN MARITIME MUSEUM

Fitzroy Terr.

NORTH ADELAIDE

TO NATIONAL RAILWAY MUSEUM AND ENTERTAINMENT CENTRE

Festival Centre

Convention Centre

Adelaide Casino

Central Bus Station

Central Market

Adelaide Oval

Elder Park

North Terrace

Rundle Mall

Rundle St.

Hindmarsh Square

RYMILL PARK

TO PENFOLDS
MAGILL ESTATE

NW Sir Donald Bradman Dr.

TO AIRPORT AND BRIGHTON

Keswick Rail Terminal

Victoria Square

Hurtle Square

Light Square

Whitmore Square

TO HAHNDORF AND ADELAIDE HILLS

CITY TRAMWAY

GLENELG

TO KING WILLIAM ROAD SHOPS AND RESTAURANTS (HYDE PARK)

0   1/4 mile
0   400 meters

Adelaide Town Hall 2

Adelaide Zoo 1

Art Gallery of
South Australia 7

Ayers House 8

Botanic Gardens of
Adelaide 10

Migration Museum 5

National Wine Centre
of Australia 12

Parliament House 3

St. Francis Xavier's
Cathedral 1

St. Peter's Cathedral 4

South Australian
Museum 6

Tandanya Aboriginal
Cultural Institute 9

tour of both houses weekdays at 10 and 2 during non-sitting days, and on Monday and Friday only when parliament is in session. The viewing gallery is open to the public when parliament is sitting. ⊠ *North Terrace at King William St., City Center* ☎ *08/8237–9100* ⊕ *www. parliament.sa.gov.au* 🖅 *Free.*

WHAT YOU'LL SEE

As soon as you pull into Adelaide you'll be greeted with the sight of tiny stone cottages aglow in morning sunshine, or august sandstone buildings gilded by nighttime floodlights. These are visual cues to the relaxed but vibrant arts and culture that emanate from here.

St. Peter's Cathedral. The spires and towers of this cathedral dramatically contrast with the nearby city skyline. St. Peter's is the epitome of Anglican architecture in Australia, and an important example of grand Gothic Revival. Free 45-minute guided tours are available Wednesday at 11 and Sunday at 12:30. ⊠ *1–19 King William St., North Adelaide* ☎ *08/8267–4551* ⊕ *www.stpeters-cathedral.org.au* 🖅 *Free* ☉ *Services daily.*

South Australian Museum. This museum's Australian Aboriginal Cultures Gallery—the world's largest—houses 3,000 items, including ceremonial dress and paintings from the Pacific Islands. Old black-and-white films show traditional dancing, and touch screens convey desert life. Also in the museum are an exhibit commemorating renowned Antarctic explorer Sir Douglas Mawson, after whom Australia's main Antarctic research station is named; a Fossil Gallery housing the fantastic opalized partial skeleton of a 19-foot-long plesiosaur; and a biodiversity gallery. There's also a café overlooking a grassy lawn. If you are traveling during local school holidays, there are fantastic interactive craft and education activities for children for a small fee. ⊠ *North Terrace near Gawler Pl., City Center* ☎ *08/8207–7500* ⊕ *www.samuseum.sa.gov. au* 🖅 *Free* ☉ *Daily 10–5; tours weekdays at 11, weekends at 2 and 3.*

Fodor'sChoice
★ **Tandanya Aboriginal Cultural Institute.** A must-see, Tandanya is the first major Aboriginal cultural facility of its kind in Australia. You'll find high-quality changing exhibitions of works by Aboriginal artists and a theater where you can watch didgeridoo performances (Tuesday to Friday at noon) and shows from Pacific Islanders at the same times at the weekend. There's a great gift shop, too, where you can buy CDs of local music. ⊠ *253 Grenfell St., City Center* ☎ *08/8224–3200* ⊕ *www. tandanya.com.au* 🖅 *Free* ☉ *Daily 10–5.*

WORTH NOTING

Adelaide Town Hall. An imposing building constructed in 1863 in Renaissance style, the Town Hall was modeled after buildings in Genoa and Florence. Tours visit the Colonel Light Room, where objects used to map and plan Adelaide are exhibited, and there are frequently traveling art exhibitions. The balcony of the Town Hall is famous for the appearance of the Beatles in 1964, which attracted the venue's largest crowd to date: approximately 300,000 screaming fans. If the guards aren't busy, they will show you around even when there isn't a tour scheduled. ⊠ *128 King William St., City Center* ☎ *08/8203–7203* ⊕ *www.*

Dusky leaf monkey langurs at the Adelaide Zoo

adelaidetownhall.com.au ⌧ *Free* ☉ *Weekdays 9–5; tours by appointment Mon. at 10 (excluding public holidays).*

Ayers House. Between 1855 and 1897 this sprawling colonial structure was the home of Sir Henry Ayers, South Australia's premier and the man for whom Uluru was originally named Ayers Rock. Most rooms—including the unusual Summer Sitting Room, in the cool of the basement—have been restored with period furnishings, and the state's best examples of 19th-century costumes are sometimes displayed in changing exhibitions. ■**TIP→ Admission includes a one-hour tour, but if you want to travel back to 1876, book the After Dark Tour (A$16) ahead of time.** ⌧ *288 North Terrace, City Center* ☏ *08/8223–1234* ⊕ *www.ayershousemuseum.org.au* ⌧ *A$10, kids under 16 A$5, kids under 12 free* ☉ *Tues.–Fri. 10–4, weekends 1–4.*

National Wine Centre of Australia. Timber, steel, and glass evoke the ribs of a huge wine barrel, and a soaring, open-plan concourse make this a spectacular showcase for Australian wines set in the Botanic Gardens. The Wine Discovery Journey takes you from neolithic pottery jars to a stainless-steel tank; you can even make your own virtual wine on a touch-screen computer. Some of the best vintages from more than 20 Australian wine-growing regions are also available for tasting at the Concourse Café (which offers a fantastic menu) from A$5. ⌧ *Hackney and Botanic Rds., City Center* ☏ *08/8303–3355* ⊕ *www.wineaustralia.com.au* ⌧ *Free* ☉ *Weekdays 8:30–5, weekends 9–5.*

St. Francis Xavier's Cathedral. This church faced a bitter battle over construction after the 1848 decision to build a Catholic cathedral. It's now a prominent, decorative church with a soaring nave, stone arches through to side aisles with dark-wood ceilings, and beautiful stained-glass windows. ⊠ *11 Wakefield St., at Victoria Sq., City Center* ☏ *08/8231–3551* ⊕ *www.adelcathparish.org* ✉ *Free* ☉ *Mass weekdays 8 am, 12:10, and 5:45 pm; Sat. 8 and 11:30 am; Sun. 7, 9, 11 am, and 6 pm.*

GREATER ADELAIDE

TOP ATTRACTIONS

Coopers Brewery. Founded by Thomas Cooper in 1862, this is Australia's only large-scale, independent, family-owned brewery. The Coopers beer story began when Thomas tried to create a tonic for his ailing wife, Ann, but instead created his first batch of beer. Customers grew in numbers as Thomas hand-delivered his all-natural ales and stout by horse and cart; the tradition lives on with guest appearances at special events by Clydesdales drawing the very same cart that Thomas once used. You can take guided tours (A$22) of the brew house and enjoy tastings of the award-winning signature Coopers ales, including Coopers Pale Ale, Coopers Sparkling Ale, and Coopers Stout, in the museum post tour. The museum features a display of the historic horse and cart, vintage Coopers delivery truck, and pictorials showcasing the history of the brewery. ⊠ *461 South Rd., Regency Park* ☏ *08/8440–1800* ⊕ *www. coopers.com.au* ✉ *Free; guided tours A$22* ☉ *Weekdays 8:30–7; guided tours Tues.–Fri. 1 pm (book in advance). Closed weekends.*

FAMILY **National Railway Museum.** Steam-train buffs will love this collection of locomotives and rolling stock in the former Port Adelaide railway yard. The largest of its kind in Australia, the collection includes enormous "mountain"-class engines and the "Tea and Sugar" train, once the lifeline for camps scattered across the deserts of South and Western Australia. Great for the family, train rides operate daily during local school holidays and on weekends. Train ride tickets are A$7 for adults, A$5 for children ages 3–15 or A$20 for families (two adults, two children). ⊠ *Lipson St. near St. Vincent's St., Port Adelaide* ☏ *08/8341–1690* ⊕ *www.natrailmuseum.org.au* ✉ *A$12, kids 5–16 A$6* ☉ *Daily 10–5.*

Fodor'sChoice **Penfolds Magill Estate.** Founded in 1844 by immigrant English doctor ★ Christopher Rawson Penfold, this is the birthplace of Australia's most famous wine, Penfolds Grange, and one of the world's only city wineries. Introduced in 1951, Grange is the flagship of a huge stable of wines priced from everyday to special-occasion (collectors pay thousands of dollars to complete sets of Grange). Hour-long winery tours (A$15) leave daily at 11 and 3. The Great Grange Tour is the ultimate Magill Estate experience; over 2½ hours you visit the original Penfold family cottage, tour the winery, and enjoy a tasting of premium wines, including Grange, and a selection of gourmet cheeses. This tour departs at 1 pm on the first and third Sunday of every month and costs A$150 per person (minimum of four); reservations are essential. ⊠ *78 Penfold Rd., Magill* ☏ *08/8301–5400* ⊕ *www.penfolds.com.au* ✉ *Free* ☉ *Daily 10–5.*

WORTH NOTING

FAMILY **The Beachouse.** This local entertainment complex, located on the Glenelg foreshore overlooking Holdfast Bay, is fun for children of all ages. There are waterslides, bumper cars, bumper boats, arcade games, minigolf, a miniature train (that children under 35 inches can ride), a modest

Ferris wheel, and a carousel serving visitors to Glenelg for more than 120 years. Admission is free but Fun Cards are used to purchase credits for use on the amusements. ⊠ *Colley Terrace, Glenelg* ☎ *08/8295–1511* ⊕ *www.thebeachouse.com.au* ✉ *Fun Cards A$2* ⊙ *Weekdays 10–5, weekends 9–7.*

FAMILY   **South Australian Maritime Museum.** Inside a restored stone warehouse, this museum brings maritime history vividly to life with ships' figureheads, shipwreck relics, and intricate scale models. In the basement you can lie in a bunk bed aboard an 1840s immigrant ship and hear passengers telling of life and death on their journeys to South Australia. In addition to the warehouse displays, the museum includes a lighthouse (worth climbing the 75 steps up to see the view), restored steam tug, and a WWII tender at the nearby wharf. ⊠ *126 Lipson St., Port Adelaide* ☎ *08/8207–6255* ⊕ *maritime.historysa.com.au* ✉ *A$10, A$5 for children (lighthouse entry included)* ⊙ *Daily 10–5; lighthouse closed Sat.*

BEACHES

Adelaide's beaches offer something for everyone. From North Haven in the north to Sellicks Beach in the south, most beaches are located less than 30 minutes from the city center. Glenelg Beach is the main tourist attraction framed by restaurants, bars, and attractions. Farther south the hills meet the sea as beaches jut out from cliff faces providing great swimming, fishing, and surfing spots.

FAMILY   **Glenelg Beach.** Located just 10 km (6 miles) from the Adelaide city cen-
Fodor'sChoice   ter, Glenelg is a charming beachside suburb known for its sandy beach,
★   historic jetty, serene marinas, bustling shops, hotels, restaurants, bars, and The Beachhouse entertainment complex. Trams lead the way to the beach carrying passengers along Jetty Road from the city while pedestrians weave in and out of the various retail outlets that line the strip. A day trip to Glenelg is a must, but this seaside resort setting offers plenty of options for backpackers to more discerning travelers to make this their Adelaide base. The beach is large, sandy, and the waters are calm. But expect to see large crowds on hotter days and depending on the season, seaweed can be a problem. **Amenities:** parking; toilets; lifeguards; showers; food and drink; water sports. **Best for:** swimming; sunrise; sunset; windsurfing; walking. ⊠ *Jetty Rd., Glenelg* ⊕ *glenelgsa.com.au.*

FAMILY   **Henley Beach.** The beach in this quiet coastal suburb offers white sand, gently lapping waves, summer entertainment, and a square known for popular dining spots. You'll find families spread out along the sand, and there are places on the grassy areas to enjoy picnics. The jetty is perfect for walking or fishing—drop a line in the water and try your luck. During summer, Henley Beach Square bordering the center of the beach itself comes alive with live music and festivals while eateries along Henley Beach Road bring the world to your plate—Asian, African, Mediterranean, and Indian mix with local cuisine. **Amenities:** food and drink; parking; toilets. **Best for:** swimming; sunrise; sunset; walking; windsurfing. ⊠ *Esplanade, Henley Beach.*

An exhibition at the Pacific Cultures Gallery, Adelaide

SPORTS AND THE OUTDOORS

Venue*Tix. Tickets for domestic and international one-day and test (five-day) cricket matches, other major sporting events, and concerts can be purchased through this ticket agency. ⊠ *Da Costa Arcade, Grenfell St. at Gawler Pl., City Center* ☎ *08/8225–8888* ⊕ *www.venuetix.com.au.*

AUSTRALIAN RULES FOOTBALL

Adelaide Oval. The stadium received a state-of-the-art upgrade in 2013 and is now the dual home for Australian Rules Football and cricket AFL—South Australia's most popular winter sport. The Aussie Rules season runs March to August and teams play on Thursday, Friday, Saturday, or Sunday; finals are in September. Cricket season is October–March and this is the main venue for interstate and international competition. ⊠ *War Memorial Dr., North Adelaide* ☎ *08/8211–1100* ⊕ *www.adelaideoval.com.au.*

BASKETBALL

Adelaide Arena. You'll find nothing but net at the home stadium for the Adelaide 36ers of the National Basketball League and the Adelaide Lightning of the Womens National Basketball League. Located in Findon, an inner western suburb of Adelaide, Adelaide Arena is a privately owned multipurpose indoor sports stadium. The NBL season runs from October to early March; playoffs are in late March, early April. The WNBL season runs from October to early February; playoffs are also in February. ⊠ *44A Crittenden Rd., Findon* ☎ *08/8444–6444* ⊕ *www. adelaide36ers.com.*

BICYCLING

Adelaide's parks, flat terrain, and uncluttered streets make it a perfect city for two-wheel exploring.

Linear Park Mountain Bike Hire. You can rent 21-speed mountain bikes by the hour or for A$30 per day and A$80–A$100 per week, including a helmet, lock, and maps. They're open daily 9–5 in winter, 9–6 in summer, or by appointment. You can also hire paddleboats to use on the Torrens River from here, and buy tickets to ride on the Popeye—Adelaide's famous 40-minute cruise along the river. ⊠ *Elder Park adjacent to Adelaide Festival Centre, City Center* ☎ *0400/596065.*

Tour Down Under. The first stop on the world cycling calendar, the Tour Down Under attracts riders from all over the world as part of the UCI Pro Tour. Outside of the Tour de France, the event attracts the biggest crowds in the world for eight days, taking in metropolitan and regional South Australia. ⊠ *Victoria Sq.* ☎ *08/8463–4701* ⊕ *www.tourdownunder.com.au.*

GOLF

City of Adelaide Golf Club. A 10-minute walk outside of the city, the City of Adelaide Golf Club—reputed to be one of the most picturesque golf settings in the country—runs one short (par 3) and two 18-hole courses. You can rent clubs and carts from the pro shop. Greens fees are from A$21 weekdays and A$24.50 weekends for the north course, A$25 weekdays and A$30 weekends for the south course. Playing hours are dawn to dusk daily. ⊠ *Entrance to par-3 course is off War Memorial Dr.; 18-hole courses are off Strangways Terrace, North Adelaide* ☎ *08/8267–2171* ⊕ *www.cityofadelaide.com.au.*

SOCCER

Coopers Stadium. Also known as Hindmarsh Stadium, this is a multipurpose venue and the first purpose-built soccer stadium in Australia. It's the home of the Australian A-League soccer team, Adelaide United. The national A-League season runs from October to March; finals are in April. ⊠ *Holden St., Hindmarsh* ☎ *08/8208–2222.*

WATER SPORTS

The Dolphin Boat. Youngsters—and the young at heart—will love a cruise on the Dolphin Boat, which allows you to swim with the cute and friendly animals. The dolphins and tour guides have developed a close relationship over the years, so you're guaranteed to get up close. In fact, if you don't get into the water to swim with the dolphins, they will refund the difference between the watch and the swim. ⊠ *Marina Pier, Holdfast Shores Marina, Glenelg* ☎ *0412/811838* ⊕ *www.dolphinboat.com.au* 🍴 *A$98 to swim, A$68 to watch.*

FAMILY **SA Aquatic & Leisure Centre.** Located next to Marion Shopping Centre, this new, state-of-the-art aquatic and recreation facility is designed to bring elite aquatic sport such as the 2012 Australian Olympic Swimming Trials to South Australia. However, the FINA-accredited pools, waterslides, and health club are open to visitors of all ages; there's even dedicated kiddie pools for the little ones. ⊠ *443 Morphett Rd., Oaklands Park* ☎ *08/8198–0198* ⊕ *www.saaquatic.ymca.org.au* 🍴 *Adults A$7.50, kids A$6, family passes A$21, waterslides A$2 per slide*

⏲ *Weekdays 5 am–10 pm, Sat. 5 am–8 pm, Sun. and holidays 7 am–8 pm; waterslides: weekends 1–5.*

WHERE TO EAT

Melbourne, Gouger, O'Connell, and Rundle streets, along with the Norwood Parade and Glenelg neighborhoods, are the main eating strips. In any of these areas it's fun to stroll around until a restaurant or café takes your fancy. Chinatown is also lively, and if you feel like an alfresco picnic, pick some delicious local produce from Central Market.

Use the coordinate (✥ B2) at the end of each listing to locate a site on the corresponding map.

CITY CENTER

$$ ITALIAN 🍴 **Amalfi Pizzeria Ristorante.** This place is rustic and noisy. If it weren't for the Australian accents here, you'd swear you were in a regional Italian eatery. The terrazzo-tile dining room is furnished with bare wooden tables, around which sit professionals and university students in enthusiastic conversation. The paper place-mat menu lists traditional pizza and pasta dishes in two sizes—appetizer and entrée—a must-order is the spaghetti marinara. As this is one of the most popular (read: packed) restaurants in the East End of Rundle Street, reservations are a good idea. Because the restaurant stays open late, it's also popular after a show or a movie. [$] *Average main: A$25* ✉ *29 Frome St., City Center* ☎ *08/8223–1948* 🌐 *www.amalfipizzaria.com.au* ⏲ *Closed Sun. No lunch Sat.* ✥ *C2.*

$ CAFÉ Fodor's Choice ★ 🍴 **Big Table.** Simply the best breakfast choice in Adelaide, Big Table has been at the Central Market for over 15 years, and regulars know to get there early for a chance at one of the few tables. Sitting up at the counter isn't too bad an option, however, especially when you have treats like fresh banana bread with rhubarb conserve and ricotta to look forward to. The enormous Big Brekkie lives up to its name, and offers quality as well as quantity with delicious thick-sliced local bacon and field mushrooms cooked with pesto and served on Turkish bread. [$] *Average main: A$11* ✉ *Adelaide Central Market, Southern Roadway, Stall 39/40, City Centre* ☎ *08/8212–3899* ▭ *No credit cards* ⏲ *Closed Sun. and Mon. No dinner* ✥ *B3.*

$$ AUSTRALIAN 🍴 **The Brasserie.** Chef Simon Bryant has become somewhat of a local celebrity, having appeared on a national weekly TV program. Although his restaurant has a lively and relaxed atmosphere, Bryant is renowned for his insistence on top-quality local produce. The menu from the open kitchen changes every season, but always makes use of local specialties from the Fleurieu Peninsula, Kangaroo Island, and the local Central Market around the corner. If Australia's national animal is on the menu, give it a try here. [$] *Average main: A$35* ✉ *Hilton Hotel, 233 Victoria Sq., City Center* ☎ *08/8237–0697* 🌐 *www.thebrasserie.com.au* ✍ *Reservations essential* ⏲ *No lunch weekends* ✥ *B3.*

$$$ ITALIAN 🍴 **Chianti Classico.** Family-run since 1985, Chianti Classico is all things to all people. Breakfast, lunch, or dinner. Big or small groups. Inside or outside dining. You can expect exquisite service and that host Maria Favaro will make every guest feel like the center of attention. Families

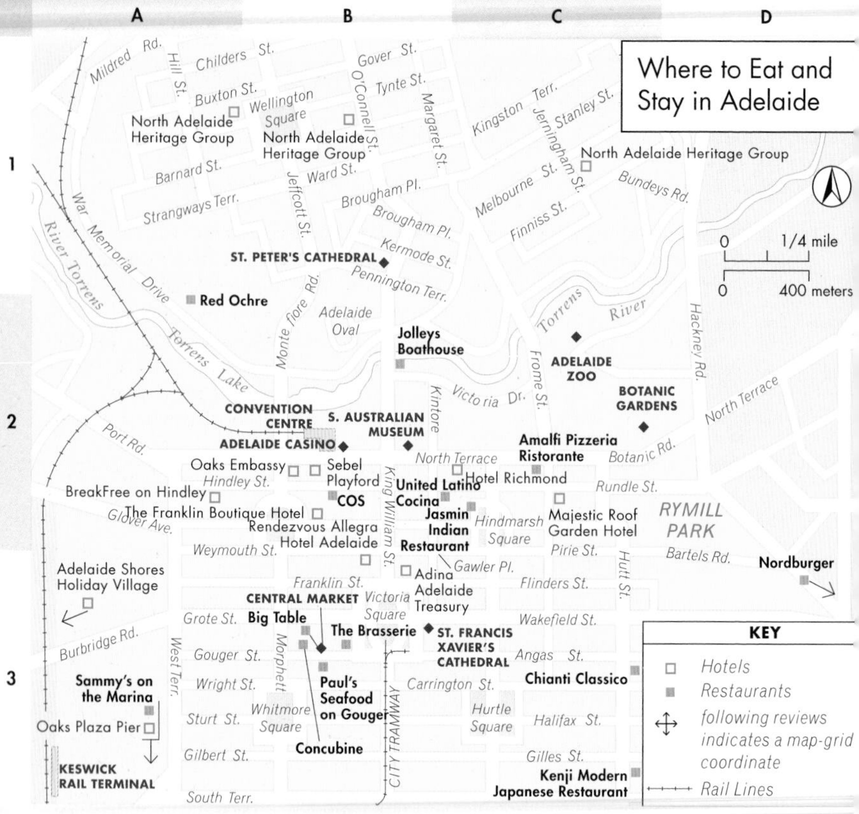

Where to Eat and Stay in Adelaide
A
B
C
D
1
2
3
Mildred Rd.
Childers St.
Hill St.
Buxton St.
Wellington Square
Gover St.
Tynte St.
O'Connell St.
Margaret St.
North Adelaide Heritage Group
North Adelaide Heritage Group
Barnard St.
Strangways Terr.
Jeffcott St.
Ward St.
Brougham Pl.
Brougham Pl.
Kingston Terr.
Jerningham St.
Stanley St.
North Adelaide Heritage Group
Melbourne St.
Bundeys Rd.
Finniss St.
0
1/4 mile
0
400 meters
War Memorial Drive
River Torrens
ST. PETER'S CATHEDRAL
Kermode St.
Pennington Terr.
Red Ochre
Monte fiore Rd.
Adelaide Oval
Jolleys Boathouse
Torrens River
Hackney Rd.
Torrens Lake
ADELAIDE ZOO
Frome St.
Kintore
Victoria Dr.
BOTANIC GARDENS
North Terrace
CONVENTION CENTRE
S. AUSTRALIAN MUSEUM
Port Rd.
ADELAIDE CASINO
Amalfi Pizzeria Ristorante
Botanic Rd.
Oaks Embassy
Sebel Playford
North Terrace
Hindley St.
Hotel Richmond
BreakFree on Hindley
COS
King William St.
United Latino Cocina
Rundle St.
The Franklin Boutique Hotel
Glover Ave.
Rendezvous Allegra Hotel Adelaide
Jasmin Indian Restaurant
Hindmarsh Square
Majestic Roof Garden Hotel
RYMILL PARK
Weymouth St.
Pirie St.
Bartels Rd.
Gawler Pl.
Adina Adelaide Treasury
Nordburger
Adelaide Shores Holiday Village
Franklin St.
Flinders St.
Hutt St.
CENTRAL MARKET
Victoria Square
Grote St.
Big Table
Wakefield St.
The Brasserie
ST. FRANCIS XAVIER'S CATHEDRAL
Burbridge Rd.
West Terr.
Gouger St.
Morphett
Angas St.
Sammy's on the Marina
Wright St.
Paul's Seafood on Gouger
Carrington St.
Chianti Classico
Oaks Plaza Pier
Sturt St.
Whitmore Square
CITY TRAMWAY
Hurtle Square
Halifax St.
Gilbert St.
Concubine
Gilles St.
KESWICK RAIL TERMINAL
Kenji Modern Japanese Restaurant
South Terr.
KEY
Hotels
Restaurants
following reviews indicates a map-grid coordinate
Rail Lines

mix with business people in the mornings for the award-winning breakfasts while the food connoisseurs show up in the evenings. The northern Italian cuisine is highlighted by the Genovese-style stuffed veal breast and the tagliolini with local blue swimmer crab and chili. But if it's a signature dish you're after, try the sumptuous slow-roasted rabbit with pancetta, port, and sage. [$] *Average main: A$30* ✉ *160 Hutt St., City Centre* ☎ *08/8232–7955* 🌐 *www.chianticlassico.com.au* ✥ *C3.*

$$ CHINESE FUSION 🍴 **Concubine.** This restaurant, located in Adelaide's premier Asian dining strip, features a fusion of modern Chinese dishes with traditional spices and fresh local produce. The food here is sensational; the wine and cocktail lists are intriguing; the service is flawless and friendly; and the ambience is second to none thanks to the funky decor and trendy vibe. The tangy tamarind duck keeps the customers coming back and the serving sizes on a full order of appetizers and entrées could be a challenge, albeit one to be relished, even without dessert. [$] *Average main: A$23* ✉ *132 Gouger St., City Centre* ☎ *08/8212–8288* 🌐 *www.concubine.com.au* 🕒 *Closed Mon.* ✥ *B3.*

$$$ MODERN AUSTRALIAN 🍴 **COS.** If you're in need of a fine steak, look no further. Located on trendy Leigh Street, COS is one of Adelaide's best spots for steak and seafood. The simplicity of these steaks—select from a 250-gram grain-fed yearling eye-fillet to a 500-gram rib-eye fillet—served with frites and side salad ensure even lunchers are not too gastronomically

challenged. An excellent selection of local and international boutique wines rounds out a complete meal. If seafood is your fancy, there are some excellent oyster options, not to mention signature dishes featuring king prawns, rock lobster, and King George whiting. $ *Average main: A$35* ✉ *18 Leigh St., City Centre* ☎ *08/8231–7611* ⊕ *www.justcos. com.au* ⊗ *Closed Sun.* ✛ *B2.*

$$$
INDIAN
Fodor's Choice
★

✕ **Jasmin Indian Restaurant.** Located in a basement off Hindmarsh Square, this elegant establishment is beautifully decorated with stylish timber furniture and local artwork. The dim lighting and relaxing background music really sets the mood for some quality Indian cuisine, which is what you'll get in spades—visiting Indian and English cricket teams dine here and you know those guys know a thing or two about good Indian food. You might want to try everything on the menu, and the Feed Me Menu allows for just that, but the Punjabi tandoori lamb and prawn sambal are considered perennial favorites. The staff are friendly and the service is exceptional. $ *Average main: A$23* ✉ *31 Hindmarsh Sq., City Centre* ☎ *08/8223–7837* ⊕ *www.jasmin.com.au* ⌦ *Reservations essential* ⊗ *Closed Sun. and Mon.* ✛ *C2.*

$$$
MODERN
AUSTRALIAN

✕ **Jolleys Boathouse.** Blue canvas directors' chairs and white-clothed wooden tables create a relaxed, nautical air here—which perfectly suits the location on the south bank of the River Torrens. Sliding glass doors open onto a full-width front balcony for alfresco dining. The imaginative Modern Australian menu changes seasonally, but might include a salad of grilled Kangaroo Island marron, green mango, basil and shallots, or sweet pork belly with red dates. Executives make up most lunch crowds, and warm evenings attract couples. There is a minimum of A$23 per person, however. $ *Average main: A$34* ✉ *1 Jolleys La., Victoria Dr. atKing William Rd., City Center* ☎ *08/8223–2891* ⊕ *www. jolleysboathouse.com* ⌦ *Reservations essential* ⊗ *No dinner Sun.* ✛ *B2.*

$$$
JAPANESE

✕ **Kenji Modern Japanese Restaurant.** Kenji, the chef and owner, is one of the few in Australia to hold a license to prepare fugu (pufferfish), so it goes without saying this should be first on your list—you'll experience a great amalgamation of taste, texture, and presentation. Other famous dishes include the extremely fresh sushi and sashimi boat (oysters, sushi, sashimi, pickled fish, etc.), which serves two or three people for a pricey A$65. The quality of the food is worth the price, though, and the ever-changing degustation menu is genius; plus, the miso-marinated olives are complimentary. $ *Average main: A$35* ✉ *242 Hutt St., City Centre* ☎ *08/8232–0944* ⊗ *Closed Sun. No lunch* ✛ *C3.*

$$
CAFÉ

✕ **Paul's Seafood on Gouger.** It may look like your run-of-the-mill chippie, but this Gouger Street veteran of more than 60 years is the place to get hooked on King George whiting. It's been hailed as one of Adelaide's best—and best-priced—seafood restaurants. The salt-and-pepper squid is another local favorite. For a great view of the bustle in the open kitchen, request a table upstairs on the ship's-deck-like mezzanine floor. $ *Average main: A$22* ✉ *79 Gouger St., City Center* ☎ *08/8231–9778* ✛ *B3.*

$$
MODERN
AUSTRALIAN

✕ **Red Ochre.** A sweeping view of Adelaide is the backdrop for contemporary workings of traditional bush meats, herbs, and fruits at this riverfront restaurant. The downstairs River Café, the restaurant's sister

9

venue, is more informal, and offers a modern Italian menu for lunch weekdays, while Red Ochre is only open for dinner. For a splurge, head upstairs; if you like your steaks, you'll love their Premium steaks served with onion puree and broccolini, bush tomato chimichurri, wattle-seeded mustard, pepper berry jam, and confit garlic. Don't miss the wattle-seed pavlova, Red Ochre's version of Australia's famous meringue dessert. $ *Average main: A$34* ⊠ *War Memorial Dr., North Adelaide* ☎ *08/8211–8555* ⊕ *www.redochre.com.au* ⌂ *Reservations essential* ⊗ *Closed Sun. No lunch.* ✛ *A2.*

$ ✕ **United Latino Cocina.** Long communal tables, funky artwork, and
MEXICAN Mexican tunes typify this tucked-away little restaurant along the side
FAMILY of the new Rundle Place development. Stylishly modern with Mexican slant, United Latino Cocina (known locally as ULC) is rapidly gaining momentum. The menu isn't long, but there is a nice variety that ranges from quesadillas and tacos to chicken wings and less traditional items such as loose-leaf green tea. Daily specials are always on offer and can be hard to look past, but the tostadas are well known, as are the fish taco and the ULC Dog—a chorizo sausage nestled in creamy jalapeño coleslaw, bean mash, cheese, and onion strings. $ *Average main: A$18* ⊠ *Francis St., City Center* ☎ *08/8232–0674* ⊕ *www.rundleplace.com. au* ⊗ *Closed Sun. No dinner Sat.–Thurs.* ✛ *B2.*

GREATER ADELAIDE

$ ✕ **Nordburger.** Good burgers are taking over Adelaide, but you won't
BURGER find too many better than those at Nordburger. Just a five-minute drive from the center of town, you'll find queues out the door—everyone's looking to catch a glimpse of Masterchef contestant and owner Michael Wheldon—of people waiting to sink their teeth into the signature American-style cheeseburgers and hot dogs. The staff is friendly, service is fast, and people sit at the counter or eat standing up by tall tables in the back, which combines for quick turnover. Be sure to try the PB&J Milkshake! $ *Average main: A$10* ⊠ *168 The Parade, Norwood* ☎ *08/8331–9923* ⊕ *www.nordburger.com* ⊗ *Closed Mon.* ✛ *D3.*

$$ ✕ **Sammy's on the Marina.** Enormous fishbowl windows frame views of
SEAFOOD million-dollar yachts at this restaurant—one of Adelaide's top seafood eateries—at the far end of Glenelg's glitzy Holdfast Marina. Watch the setting sun silhouette playing dolphins or a storm rolling across Gulf St. Vincent as you tuck into skewered scallops or crispy-skin Atlantic salmon wrapped in prosciutto and served over broccolini and baby carrots with salsa verde. The menu here charts South Australia's ocean bounty, and the hot seafood platter (for two people) would feed a school of sharks. $ *Average main: A$35* ⊠ *1–12 Holdfast Promenade, Glenelg* ☎ *08/8376–8211* ⊕ *www.sammys.net.au* ⌂ *Reservations essential* ✛ *A3.*

WHERE TO STAY

At first glance, large international, business-style hotels seem to dominate Adelaide—there's a Hilton, a Hyatt, a Sebel, and a Crowne Plaza—but there's actually a wide choice of places to rest your head. Adelaide's accommodations are a mix of traditional mid-rise hotels, backpacker hostels, an abundance of self-contained apartments, and charming bed-and-breakfasts, many in century-old sandstone buildings. With a car you'll be within easy reach of a Glenelg beach house or an Adelaide Hills B&B.

Use the coordinate (✛ 1:B2) at the end of each listing to locate a site on the corresponding map. For expanded hotel reviews, visit Fodors.com.

CITY CENTER

$$$
HOTEL
Adina Adelaide Treasury. Contemporary Italian furnishings in white, slate-gray, and ocher are juxtaposed with 19th-century Adelaide architecture in this stylish Victoria Square hotel. **Pros:** beautiful, classic building with light and airy reception rooms. **Cons:** no close parking; reception staff get overwhelmed at peak periods. $ *Rooms from: A$225* ⊠ *2 Flinders St., City Center* ☎ *08/8112–0000, 1300/633462* ⊕ *www.adinahotels.com.au* ⇆ *20 studio rooms, 59 apartments* ‖⊙‖ *Some meals* ✛ *B3.*

$$
HOTEL
BreakFree on Hindley. Step out your door at this three-story redbrick complex and you might think you're in the tropics; open-air walkways and palm trees suggest you're closer to the beach than the western-parkland end of Hindley Street. **Pros:** great value for money; kitchens are fully equipped for self-catering. **Cons:** basic furnishings; bathrooms could do with a face-lift. $ *Rooms from: A$109* ⊠ *255 Hindley St., City Center* ☎ *08/8217–2500* ⊕ *www.breakfree.com.au* ⇆ *48 studios, 94 2-bedroom apartments* ‖⊙‖ *Some meals* ✛ *A2.*

$$
B&B/INN
Fodor'sChoice
★
The Franklin Boutique Hotel. Situated above the Franklin Hotel—a pub known for its relaxed, but quirky atmosphere and good food and micro beers—this hotel is also a little bit different. **Pros:** free in-room snacks (including beer) and Wi-Fi; fun boutique experience; close to Central Market; Franklin Hotel pub is downstairs. **Cons:** limited capacity; potential for noise from the downstairs pub; open shower in bathroom allows for minor flooding. $ *Rooms from: A$200* ⊠ *92 Franklin St., City Center* ☎ *08/8410–0036* ⊕ *www.thefranklinhotel.com.au* ⇆ *7 rooms* ‖⊙‖ *Some meals* ✛ *B2.*

$$
HOTEL
Fodor'sChoice
★
Hotel Richmond. Situated in the center of Rundle Mall, the city's main shopping strip, the hotel is an original, 1920s art deco building and offers a boutique experience, trendy rooms, and luxurious suites. **Pros:** beautiful, classic building; trendy decor; Rundle Mall is right outside the door. **Cons:** foot traffic in Rundle Mall and the lively Lounge Bar can be noisy. $ *Rooms from: A$190* ⊠ *128 Rundle Mall, City Center* ☎ *08/8215–4444* ⊕ *www.hotelrichmond.com.au* ⇆ *30 rooms* ‖⊙‖ *All meals* ✛ *B2.*

$$$
HOTEL
FAMILY
Majestic Roof Garden Hotel. Modern and stylish, each room features modern bathrooms, king-size beds, and free Wi-Fi. **Pros:** 50 meters from the restaurants, bars, and shops of Rundle Street; the rooftop garden has uninterrupted views of the famous Adelaide Hills and East End. **Cons:** while very welcome, the bathrooms overshadow the sometimes very "standard" hotel rooms. $ *Rooms from: A$230* ⊠ *55 Frome St., City Center* ☎ *08/8100–4400* ⊕ *www.roofgardenhoteladelaide.com* ⇆ *120 suites* ‖⊙‖ *All meals* ✛ *C2.*

$$
HOTEL
Oaks Embassy. This hotel is ideally positioned to explore the River Torrens, visit the Adelaide Casino and Adelaide Convention Centre, or take in the many restaurants and nightlife spots along or surrounding

9

Hindley Street. **Pros:** good city views; well serviced by public transport; opposite Adelaide Casino and Adelaide Convention Centre; minutes from River Torrens, parklands, and Hindley Street entertainment precinct. **Cons:** cleanliness is good, but could be better. [$] *Rooms from: A$185* ✉ *96 North Terrace, Glenelg* ☎ *08/8124–9900* 🌐 *www.oakshotelsresorts.com* 🛏 *122 apartments* 🍴 *Some meals* ✥ *B2.*

$$$ HOTEL Fodor's Choice ★ 🏨 **Rendezvous Allegra Hotel Adelaide.** Black-tile-and-timber columns frame the Hollywood-glamorous marble lobby of this ultrasleek upscale hotel. **Pros:** five-star facilities; excellent wine list at the restaurant. **Cons:** tiny gym; more corporate than boutique in feel. [$] *Rooms from: A$210* ✉ *55 Waymouth St., City Center* ☎ *08/8115–8888* 🌐 *www.rendezvoushotels.com/adelaide* 🛏 *166 rooms, 35 suites* 🍴 *Some meals* ✥ *B2.*

$$$ HOTEL 🏨 **The Sebel Playford.** Showy chandeliers illuminate a movie-set-like celebration of art nouveau in the lobby of this luxury hotel. **Pros:** excellent breakfast spread; convivial bar. **Cons:** expensive Internet and parking. [$] *Rooms from: A$200* ✉ *120 North Terrace, City Center* ☎ *08/8213–8888* 🌐 *www.accorhotels.com* 🛏 *110 rooms, 72 suites* 🍴 *Some meals* ✥ *B2.*

GREATER ADELAIDE

$$ RESORT FAMILY 🏨 **Adelaide Shores Holiday Village.** The breeze is salty, the lawns are green, and white sand is only a few lazy steps from this summery resort on the city's coastal fringe. **Pros:** very family-friendly, with plenty of activities for kids and well-planned family rooms. **Cons:** bad choice for a romantic break; in peak season service levels drop. [$] *Rooms from: A$178* ✉ *Military Rd., West Beach* ☎ *08/8355–7360* 🌐 *www.adelaideshores.com.au* 🛏 *22 bungalows, 30 villas, 32 units* 🍴 *No meals* ✥ *A3.*

$$$ RENTAL Fodor's Choice ★ 🏨 **North Adelaide Heritage Group.** Tucked into the city's leafy, oldest section, these 18 lodgings are stunningly unique. **Pros:** historic properties in Adelaide's most upscale suburb; friendly owners give helpful tips on what to do. **Cons:** some properties can be on the dark side; not child-friendly. [$] *Rooms from: A$220* ✉ *82 Hill St., North Adelaide* ☎ *08/8267–2020* 🌐 *www.adelaideheritage.com* 🛏 *7 cottages, 3 suites, 8 apartments* 🍴 *Breakfast* ✥ *A1, B1, C1.*

$$$ RENTAL 🏨 **Oaks Plaza Pier.** Sea air wafts through open balcony doors in this all-apartment complex on Adelaide's favorite beach. **Pros:** steps from the beach; helpful reception staff who are full of advice. **Cons:** corporate feel to the lobby; the bars can get noisy and messy at peak times; expensive Internet. [$] *Rooms from: A$190* ✉ *16 Holdfast Promenade, Glenelg* ☎ *08/8350–6688, 1300/551111* 🌐 *www.theoaksgroup.com.au* 🛏 *121 1-bedroom apartments, 34 2-bedroom apartments* 🍴 *Some meals* ✥ *A3.*

NIGHTLIFE AND THE ARTS

THE ARTS

Adelaide truly is the festival state, and with the majority of the major events running at the end of summer in "Mad March," this is the best time to visit, as the city takes on an extra festive feel.

For a listing of performances and exhibitions, look to the entertainment pages of *The Advertiser*, Adelaide's daily newspaper. The *Adelaide*

Review, a free monthly arts paper, reviews exhibitions, galleries, and performances, and lists forthcoming events.

BASS Ticket Agency. This agency sells tickets for most live performances. ✉ *Adelaide Festival Centre, King William St., City Center* ☎ *13–1246* ⊕ *www.bass.net.au.*

ARTS CENTERS

Adelaide Entertainment Centre. Opened in 1991, most major concerts are held here but it also features a mix of everything from music, theater, and other performing arts to conventions and sporting events. ✉ *98 Port Rd., Hindmarsh* ☎ *08/8208–2222* ⊕ *www.theaec.net.*

Adelaide Festival Centre. This is the city's major venue for the performing arts. The State Opera, the State Theatre Company of South Australia, and the Adelaide Symphony Orchestra perform here regularly. Performances are in the Playhouse, the Festival and Space theaters, the outdoor amphitheater, and Her Majesty's Theatre at 58 Grote Street. The box office is open Monday–Saturday 9–6. ✉ *King William St., near North Terrac, City Center* ☎ *13–1246* ⊕ *www.adelaidefestivalcentre. com.au.*

FESTIVALS

Adelaide Festival of Arts. Australia's oldest arts festival takes place annually for three weeks in February and March. It's a cultural smorgasbord of outdoor opera, classical music, jazz, art exhibitions, film, a writer's festival, and cabaret presented by some of the world's top artists; it's held across the city at a variety of venues. ✉ *City Center* ⊕ *www. adelaidefestival.com.au.*

Adelaide Fringe Festival. The Fringe Festival, held over four weeks during February and March, is the second largest of its kind in the world. It's an open-access arts festival, which means it features cabaret, street performances, comedy, circus, music, visual art, theater, puppetry, dance, and design all over Adelaide and its surroundings. You'll find the carnival-like epicenter of the Fringe in The Garden of Unearthly Delights located in Rundle Park on the eastern side of the city. ✉ *City Center* ⊕ *www. adelaidefringe.com.au.*

WOMADelaide Festival. The annual four-day festival of world music, arts, and dance takes place in early March and attracts top musicians from all over the world to its stages in the picturesque Botanic Park. ✉ *Botanic Park, Hackney Rd.* ⊕ *www.womadelaide.com.au.*

NIGHTLIFE

There's something going on every evening in Adelaide, although clubs are especially packed on weekends. Cover charges vary according to the night and time of entry. Nightlife for the coming week is listed in "Adelaide (Scene)," a pull-out section of Thursday's edition of the *Advertiser. Rip It Up* is a free Thursday music-and-club publication aimed at the younger market. *Onion,* published fortnightly on Thursday, is Adelaide's top dance music magazine. *dB,* a twice-monthly free independent publication, covers music, arts, film, games, and dance.

Bars along Rundle Street, the west end of Hindley Street, and Gouger Street are trendy, while Hindley and Waymouth streets are lined with

9

The Art Gallery of South Australia

traditional pubs. North Adelaide's O'Connell Street buzzes every night, and the popular Sunday-evening beer-and-banter sessions really pack in the crowds. There are also a number of vibrant pubs on The Parade at Norwood and the Glenelg precinct, especially popular on a Sunday afternoon in the sun.

CITY CENTER

BARS AND CLUBS

Austral Hotel. The first bar in South Australia to put Coopers beer on tap, the Austral is a local favorite and a great place to drink outdoors. You can down shooters or sip cocktails from a long list while listening to a band play or a DJ spin groovy tunes. It's open daily 11 am–3 am. ⊠ *205 Rundle St., City Center* ☎ *08/8223–4660.*

Botanic Bar. This cool city lounge features cordovan banquettes that encircle the U-shaped, marble-top bar. Muddlers (crushed ice drinks) are the specialty, and bring in mostly young professionals, including off-duty medics from the nearby hospital. Celebrated Thai chef Nu Suandokmai recently returned home after years in Sydney to transform the restaurant menu, which now focuses on Thai street food. Botanic Bar is open until the wee hours Tuesday to Sunday. ⊠ *309 North Terrace, City Center* ☎ *08/8227–0799* ⊕ *www.botanicbar.com.au* ⊘ *Closed Mon.*

Casablabla. You'll find this multicultural tapas and lounge bar along trendy Leigh Street, the first of Adelaide's laneways (side alleys) to be rejuvenated. The atmosphere and live entertainment lineup is as unique as the contemporary fusion of Southeast Asian and Middle Eastern decor—Wednesday night is live Flamenco night! Head here for a mild-mannered restaurant by day or a pumping club by night.

✉ *12 Leigh St., City Center* ☎ *08/8231–3939* ⊕ *www.casablabla.com*
☼ *Closed Sun. and Mon.*

Clever Little Tailor. Adelaide has a newfound fascination with small bars and hole-in-the-wall-style venues, and the Clever Little Tailor was one of the city's first. Named after a German fairy tale, the warmth of this place is undeniable. The bar staff is welcoming and helpful and the venue is cozy and charming with its contemporary interior, exposed red bricks, and hanging ferns. The cocktails are delicious, too, and the boutique wine and beer list is impressive. Plus, the music is soft enough to chat to your heart's content. ✉ *19 Peel St., City Center* ⊕ *www. cleverlittletailor.com.au* ☼ *Closed Sun.*

The Curious Squire. In the yuppy end of town, the beer here is the great leveler. Here you can taste freshly brewed beer from the local Australian James Squire range, which is brewed on premise, or enroll in the one-hour Brewniversity courses that are held every Tuesday to get an insight into brewing process. There are a few curveballs thrown in when it comes to cocktails and the wine list is good albeit short—after all, this is a brewpub. The menu is full of pub snacks and bar food with the "curious" menu displayed above the bar on the huge cinema-style marquee. The "curious" dishes vary depending on the mood of the staff but the lasagna pizza seems a perennial favorite. ✉ *10 O'Connell St., City Center* ☎ *08/8267–6835* ⊕ *www.thecurioussquire.com.au* ☼ *Closed Mon.*

Grace Emily. You'll find bartenders spouting the mantra "No pokies, no TAB, no food"—pokies are the poker machines found in many pubs, and TAB, Australia's version of OTB, lets you place bets on horse races—at this multilevel music-lover's pub. Instead, there's live music nightly, and a pool table. The beer garden is one of the city's best, with secluded spots for those wanting a quiet tipple and big round tables for groups to drink en masse and alfresco. It's open daily 4 pm–late. ✉ *232 Waymouth St., City Center* ☎ *08/8231–5500.*

The Grace Establishment. This place is part bar, part restaurant, and part beer garden. At night things get lively and you'll see your fair share of hipsters, posh locals, and the manicured set. The food's good, too—they make their own salted caramel chocolate bar and DIY donuts allow diners to inject the jam inside the donuts using a syringe. ✉ *127 The Parade, City Center* ☎ *08/8333–1007* ⊕ *www.thegrace.net.au* ☼ *Closed Mon.*

Jack Ruby. Underground, convivial, and lively, this speakeasy meets Mississippi juke joint also has a hint of American diner thanks to the awesome Americana menu. This spot is named after the man who shot Lee Harvey Oswald. Co-owners Aaron Sandow, chef Sam Worrall-Thompson, and Gareth Lewis traveled the world to get the vibe just right, and it shows. Craft beer from the United States and Australia dominate the drinks menu, but if beer isn't your thing, try the spiked milk shakes or the various cocktails on offer. ✉ *89 King William St., basement, City Center* ☎ *08/8231–5795* ⊕ *www.jackruby.com.au.*

The Loft Oyster & Wine Bar. Perched above Gouger Street, The Loft is an eye-catching space that features a beautiful barrel vault ceiling and a stunning mix of dim lighting, heritage fixtures, and modern decor.

9

Oysters come in multiple styles, matched with an international wine list including some hard-to-find Australian gems. Cocktails here are inspired by recent trends in movies and TV and add to the feeling of being transported back to the 1920s. ✉ *128 Gouger St., Level 1, City Center* ☎ *08/8211–8887* ⊕ *www.loftbar.com.au.*

Rhino Room. Want to tickle your funny bone and grab a drink? This the home of Adelaide comedy, featuring live shows every Monday, Thursday, and Friday evenings. Some of Australia's best comedians as well as overseas acts grace the tiny stage; during the annual Fringe Festival you can catch a glimpse of some verified superstars. But it's also a funky little club in its own right, as art spills into the space from the attached Urban Cow Studio art gallery and live music and DJs fill the void when the laughs take a break on other nights. ✉ *13 Frome St., City Center* ☎ *08/8227–1611* ⊕ *www.rhinoroom.com.au* ✉ *A$13 from www. adelaidecomedy.com, A$15 at the door* ☽ *Closed Tues., Wed., and Sun.*

Supermild. The cavernous Supermild has a retro feel and is as unpretentious as they come, which fits in perfectly with the local nightlife scene. Grab a comfy sofa and chill out with a bunch of friends while listening to the local DJs doing their thing—either indie, retro, or funk, depending on the night. ✉ *182B Hindley St., City Center* ☎ *08/8212–8077* ☽ *Closed Sun.–Wed.*

Fodor'sChoice ★ **Udaberri.** One of the first of Adelaide's growing trend of "small bars," Udaberri is a cozy, intimate setting where some of the city's best wine and beer is served. The narrow space is reminiscent of a barn, but it's a very chic barn. DJs spin their groovy house beats but the music is never overpowering as interaction and conversation is encouraged. If you're lucky enough to beat the crowds to the loft, you can unwind on the sofas while enjoying the view and snacking on Basque-style tapas. ✉ *11–13 Leigh St., City Center* ☎ *08/8410–5733* ⊕ *www.udaberri.com. au* ☽ *Closed Sun. and Mon.*

CASINO **SkyCity.** Head to SkyCity for big-time casino gaming, including the highly animated Australian Two-up, in which you bet against the house on the fall of two coins. Five bars, including the stylish venue Loco, and three restaurants are also within the complex. It's one of a handful of places in Adelaide that keep pumping until dawn. ✉ *Station Rd., City Center* ☎ *08/8212–2811* ⊕ *www.skycityadelaide.com.au.*

GREATER ADELAIDE

BARS AND CLUBS **The Gov.** The favorite venue of a mixed crowd, young homeowners and long-term regulars come for Irish music sessions, all-weekend metal fests, and everything in between. Cabaret, comedy, Latin music—if you can name it, you can probably hear it here. There's good pub grub, too. It's open weekdays 11 am to late and Saturday noon to late. It's closed Sunday unless there is a show. ✉ *59 Port Rd., Hindmarsh* ☎ *08/8340–0744* ⊕ *www.thegov.com.au.*

Fodor'sChoice ★

Fodor'sChoice ★ **The Wheatsheaf Hotel.** South Australia is well known for its wine, but microbrewed, craft beer is rapidly forging its own reputation. At The Wheatsheaf you'll find the best of both worlds with a massive list of boutique wine and beer from all over the world. To top it off, whiskey is also given the rock star treatment. "The Wheaty" is also a live music venue that features an eclectic mix of acts from jazz-ska, nu-folk, alt-country, roots, rockabilly, and string quartets every night of the week. This is also a "Pokie Free" pub meaning you won't find a pokie machine (slot machine) in sight. Welcoming to all, the Wheaty is ultra-hip without being pretentious, leaving all labels—and egos—at the door. ⊠ *39 George St., Thebarton* ☎ *08/8443–4546* ⊕ *www.wheatsheafhotel.com.au.*

SHOPPING

If you are wondering where everyone in Adelaide is, you'll find them at Rundle Mall, the city's main shopping strip. Shops in the City Center are generally open Monday–Thursday 9–5:30, Friday 9–9, Saturday 9–5:30, and Sunday 11–5. Suburban shops are often open until 9 pm on Thursday night instead of Friday. As the center of the world's opal industry, Adelaide has many opal shops, which are around King William Street. Other good buys are South Australian regional wines, crafts, and Aboriginal artwork. The trendiest area to browse is King William Road in Hyde Park, a 20-minute walk south from Victoria Square. Outside of the city, the Marion Shopping Centre is packed with current trends, and Harbour Town next to Adelaide Airport is a great place to find a bargain.

CITY CENTER

ART AND CRAFT GALLERIES

Jam Factory. A contemporary craft-and-design center at the Lion's Arts Centre, Jam Factory exhibits and sells unique Australian glassware, ceramics, wood, and metal work. Its fantastic gift shop offers buyers a chance to purchase a handmade piece, including a description from the artist. ⊠ *19 Morphett St., City Center* ☎ *08/8231–0005* ⊕ *www. jamfactory.com.au* ⊙ *Mon.–Sat. 10–5, Sun. 1–5.*

Urban Cow Studio. For quirky locally made jewelry, pottery, glass, and sculptures, visit Urban Cow Studio. ⊠ *11 Frome St., City Center* ☎ *08/8232–6126* ⊕ *www.urbancow.com.au* ⊙ *Mon.–Thurs. 10–6, Fri. 10–9, Sat. 10–5, Sun. noon–5.*

DEPARTMENT STORES AND SHOPPING CENTERS

Fodor's Choice ★ **Rundle Mall.** Adelaide's main shopping area is Rundle Mall, a pedestrian plaza lined with boutiques, department stores—including Australia's two best known stores, Myer and David Jones—and arcades. Heritage-listed Adelaide Arcade is a Victorian-era jewel, with a decorative tiled floor, skylights, and dozens of shops behind huge timber-framed windows. As of this writing, the mall is receiving a major upgrade, but shoppers can still visit the vast array of retail outlets. Once complete, Rundle Mall will be a world-class shopping plaza and host to some of the world's biggest and most elite brands sprinkled amongst the local flavor. ⊠ *Rundle St. between King William and Pulteney Sts., City Center* ☎ *08/8203–7611* ⊕ *www.rundlemall.com.au.*

JEWELRY AND ACCESSORIES

Adelaide Exchange Jewellers. Located just off Rundle Mall, the exchange sells high-quality antique jewelry. They can also be found in Glenelg and Modbury. ⊠ *10 Stephens Pl., City Center* ☎ *08/8212–2496* ⊕ *www. adelaide-exchange.com.au.*

Australian Opal and Diamond Collection. One of Australia's leading opal merchants, wholesalers, exporters, and manufacturing jewelers, Australian Opal and Diamond Collection sells superb handcrafted one-of-a-kind opal jewelry. ⊠ *14 King William St., City Center* ☎ *08/8211–9995* ⊕ *www.aodc.net.au.*

MARKETS

Fodor's Choice
★

Central Market. One of the largest produce markets in the southern hemisphere, and Adelaide's pride and joy, the Central Market is chock-full of stellar local foods, including glistening-fresh fish, meat, crusty Vietnamese and Continental breads, German baked goods, cheeses of every shape and color, and old-fashioned lollies (candy). You can also buy souvenir T-shirts, CDs, books, cut flowers, and a great cup of coffee. The enthusiastic couple behind Adelaide's Top Food and Wine Tours (⊕ *www.topfoodandwinetours.com.au*) showcase Adelaide's food-and-wine lifestyle—as in the behind-the-scenes guided tour of the Central Market (A$80), which lets you meet stall holders, share their knowledge, and taste the wares. Tours are scheduled Tuesday and Thursday–Saturday at 9:30 am; reservations are essential. ⊠ *Gouger St., City Center* ☎ *08/8203–7494* ⊕ *www.adelaidecentralmarket.com. au* ☉ *Tues. 7–5:30, Wed. and Thurs. 9–5:30, Fri. 7 am–9 pm, Sat. 7 am–3 pm.*

WINE AND SPECIALTY FOOD

Fodor's Choice
★

Haigh's Chocolates. Australia's oldest chocolate manufacturer has tempted people with corner shop displays since 1915. The family-owned South Australian company produces exquisite truffles, pralines, and creams—as well as the chocolate bilby (an endangered Australian marsupial), Haigh's answer to the Easter bunny. ■TIP→ Free chocolate-making tours at the Haigh's Visitor Center at 154 Greenhill Road in Parkside run Monday–Saturday at 11, 1, and 2; bookings are essential. ⊠ *2 Rundle Mall, at King William St., City Center* ☎ *08/8231–2844* ⊕ *www. haighschocolates.com* ☉ *Mon.–Sat. 8:30–6, Sun. 10:30–5* ⊠ *Haigh's Visitors Centre, 154 Greenhill Rd., Parkside* ☎ *08/8372–7077.*

GREATER ADELAIDE

DEPARTMENT STORES AND SHOPPING CENTERS

Harbour Town Adelaide. For discount shopping, hop off the plane and head straight to nearby Harbour Town. You'll find Morrissey, JAG, Levi's, Esprit, Cue, Authentic Factory Outlet (Converse), and Woolworths among the 100 outlets. ⊠ *727 Tapleys Hill Rd., West Beach* ☎ *08/8355–1144* ⊕ *www.harbourtownadelaide.com.au* ☉ *Mon.–Wed. and Fri. 9–5:30, Thurs. 9–9, Sat. 9–5, Sun. 11–5.*

Marion Shopping Centre. Adelaide's largest shopping complex is easily accessible via public transport and contains more than 300 stores, including major department stores and boutiques, bars, restaurants, and the largest cinema complex in the state. ⊠ *297 Diagonal Rd., Marion* ☎ *08/8298–1188* ⊕ *www.westfield.com.au* ☉ *Mon.–Wed. and Fri. 9–5:30, Thurs. 9–9, Sat. 9–5, Sun. 11–5.*

SIDE TRIPS TO THE ADELAIDE HILLS

With their secluded green slopes and flowery gardens, the Adelaide Hills are a pastoral vision in this desert state. The patchwork quilt of vast orchards, neat vineyards, and avenues of tall conifers resembles the Bavarian countryside, a likeness fashioned by the many German immigrants who settled here in the 19th century. In summer the Hills are consistently cooler than the city, although the charming towns and wineries are pleasant to visit any time of year. To reach the region from Adelaide, head toward the M1 Princes Highway or drive down Pulteney Street, which becomes Unley Road and then Belair Road. From here signs point to Crafers and the freeway.

MT. LOFTY

16 km (10 miles) southeast of Adelaide.

There are splendid views of Adelaide from the lookout atop 2,300-foot Mt. Lofty, the coldest location in Adelaide, where snow is not uncommon in winter months. The energetic can follow some of the many trails that lead from the summit, or alternatively, have a cup of coffee in the café and enjoy the view in the warmth.

GETTING HERE AND AROUND

By car from Adelaide, take the Crafers exit off the South Eastern Freeway and follow Summit Road or from the eastern suburbs via Greenhill Road. You can get to the summit as well as the Mt. Lofty Botanic Gardens and Cleland Wildlife Park in about 40 minutes by catching Bus 842, 865, or 865F from Currie or Grenfell Street in the city center. Alight at bus stop 24A and connect to Bus 823.

A 3½-km (2-mile) round-trip walk from the Waterfall Gully parking lot in Cleland Conservation Park (15-minute drive from Adelaide) takes you along Waterfall Creek before climbing steeply to the white surveying tower on the summit; the track is closed on Total Fire Ban days.

ESSENTIALS

Transportation Adelaide Metro Info Centre ⊠ *Currie and King William Sts., City Center* ☎ *08/8210–1000* ⊕ *www.adelaidemetro.com.au.*

EXPLORING

FAMILY **Cleland Wildlife Park.** A short drive from Mt. Lofty Summit brings you to delightful Cleland Wildlife Park, where many animals roam free in three different forest habitats. Walking trails crisscross the park and its surroundings, and you're guaranteed to see emus and kangaroos in the grasslands and pelicans around the swampy billabongs. There are also enclosures for wombats and other less sociable animals. Koala cuddling is a highlight of koala close-up sessions (daily 11–noon, 2–4). Monthly two-hour night walks (A$32 for adult, A$19.50 for children 3–14) let you wander among nocturnal species such as potoroos and brush-tailed bettongs. Private guided tours can be arranged for A$103 per hour weekdays, A$155 per hour on the weekends. ▦TIP➔ **Reservations 48 hours prior are essential for tours.** The park is closed when there's a fire ban (usually between December and February). ⊠ *Summit Rd.* ☎ *08/8339–2444* ⊕ *www.cleland.sa.gov.au* ⊠ *A$20, A$10 children 3–14, A$50 family pass* ⊙ *Daily 9:30–5.*

Mt. Lofty Botanic Gardens. With its rhododendrons, magnolias, ferns, and exotic trees, these gardens are glorious in fall and spring; during these seasons, free guided walks leave the lower parking lot on Thursday at 10:30. ✉ *Picadilly entrance, 16 Lampert Rd.* ☎ *08/8370–8370* 🌐 *www.environment.sa.gov.au/botanicgardens* 🎟 *Free* 🕒 *Weekdays 8:30–4, weekends 10–5.*

NICE VIEWS

There is no better view of Adelaide—day or night—than the city-and-sea sweep from atop 2,300-foot Mt. Lofty. There's an appropriately named glass-front restaurant here called the Summit, though prices at both the café and restaurant are sky-high.

WHERE TO EAT AND STAY

For expanded hotel reviews, visit Fodors.com.

$$$ ECLECTIC 🍴 **The Summit.** If you suffer from vertigo, think twice about dining here; this glass-front building atop Mt. Lofty is all about dining with altitude. Café by morning and lunch, intimate candlelit restaurant by night, the menu here includes a local delicacy—kangaroo fillet with purple carrots, polenta, and kumquat. The wine list promotes Adelaide Hills vintages. While the food is good, you pay a premium for the view. [$] *Average main: A$35* ✉ *Mt. Lofty Lookout, Mt Lofty Summit Rd.* ☎ *08/8339–2600* 🌐 *www.mtloftysummit.com* ✍ *Reservations essential* 🕒 *No dinner Mon. and Tues.*

$$$ B&B/INN 🏨 **Mt. Lofty House.** From very English garden terraces below the summit of Mt. Lofty, this refined country house overlooks a patchwork of vineyards, farms, and bushland. **Pros:** peaceful location in stunning surroundings. **Cons:** dated furniture in rooms; restaurant is overpriced. [$] *Rooms from: A$289* ✉ *74 Summit Rd., Crafers* ☎ *08/8339–6777* 🌐 *www.mtloftyhouse.com.au* 🛏 *33 rooms* 🍽 *Breakfast.*

BRIDGEWATER

6 km (4 miles) north of Mylor, 22 km (14 miles) southeast of Adelaide.

Bridgewater came into existence in 1841 as a refreshment stop for bullock teams fording Cock's Creek. More English than German, with its flowing creek and flower-filled gardens, this leafy, tranquil village was officially planned in 1859 by the builder of the first Bridgewater flour mill.

GETTING HERE AND AROUND

From the city center, drive onto the Mount Barker Expressway until you see the Stirling exit. From there, travel through lush countryside following the signs to Bridgewater. The town itself is small and walkable. By public transport, catch Bus 864 or 864F from Currie Street in the city to stop 45.

EXPLORING

Petaluma's Bridgewater Mill. The handsome stone flour mill, built in 1860, stands at the western entrance to the town, where its waterwheel still churns away. These days the mill houses the first-class Bridgewater Mill Restaurant, where diners feast on fantastic local produce by the open fires in winter, or in the tree-covered beer garden in summer. The mill also serves as the shop front for Petaluma Wines, one of Australia's finest labels; try the Chardonnay and Viognier. The prestigious Croser champagne is matured on the building's lower level. ✉ *386 Mt. Barker Rd.* ☎ *08/8339–9222* ⊕ *www.petaluma.com.au* 🖃 *Free* ☉ *Daily 10–5.*

WHERE TO EAT AND STAY
For expanded hotel reviews, visit Fodors.com.

$$
ECLECTIC
FAMILY
✕ **Aldgate Pump Hotel.** You get a leisurely glimpse of local culture at this friendly two-story country pub. There is an extensive, eclectic selection of hearty pub fare such as Pump platters with everything from chicken wings to spring rolls to oysters. Warmed by log fires in winter, the dining room overlooks a shaded beer garden. The place is 2 km (1 mile) from Bridgewater, in the delightful village of Aldgate. $ *Average main: A$25* ✉ *1 Strathalbyn Rd., Aldgate* ☎ *08/8339–2015.*

$$$
AUSTRALIAN
Fodor'sChoice
★
✕ **Petaluma's Bridgewater Mill Restaurant.** A stylish and celebrated restaurant in a converted flour mill, this is one of the state's best dining spots. Using mostly local produce, chef Zac Ronayne creates an imaginative contemporary menu; dishes might include organic chicken, black bean butter, radish, broccolini, and XO sauce. In summer, book ahead to get a table on the deck beside the waterwheel. If you're feeling flush, ask to see the special wine list. On Sunday and public holidays, eating here means a three-course set price (A$90 per person) menu. The mill also serves as the cellar door for Petaluma Wines, one of Australia's finest labels; the prestigious Croser champagne is matured on the building's lower level. $ *Average main: A$39* ✉ *386 Mt. Barker Rd.* ☎ *08/8339–9200* ⊕ *www.petaluma.com.au* ⚘ *Reservations essential* ☉ *Closed Tues. and Wed. No dinner.*

$$$$
B&B/INN
🏠 **Thorngrove Manor Hotel.** This romantic Gothic folly of turrets and towers is *Lifestyles of the Rich and Famous* writ large. **Pros:** perfect for the archetypal romantic getaway. **Cons:** if you have to ask how expensive it is, you can't afford it. $ *Rooms from: A$790* ✉ *2 Glenside La., Crafers* ☎ *08/8339–6748* ⊕ *www.thorngrove.com.au* ⮡ *5 rooms* ⦿| *Breakfast.*

THE BAROSSA WINE REGION

Some of Australia's most famous vineyards are in the Barossa, just over an hour's drive northeast of Adelaide. More than 200 wineries across the two wide, shallow valleys that make up the region produce some of Australia's most celebrated wines, including aromatic Rhine Riesling, Seppeltsfield's unique, century-old Para Port—and Penfolds Grange, which sells for more than A$600.

Cultural roots set the Barossa apart. The area was settled by Silesian immigrants who left the German–Polish border region in the 1840s to escape religious persecution. These farmers brought traditions that you can't miss in the solid bluestone architecture, the tall slender spires of the Lutheran churches, and the *kuchen,* a cake as popular as the Devonshire tea introduced by British settlers. Together, these elements give the Barossa a charm that is unique among Australian wine-growing areas.

Most wineries in the Barossa operate sale rooms—called cellar doors—that usually have 6 to 12 varieties of wine available for tasting. You are not expected to sample the entire selection; to do so would overpower your taste buds. It's far better to give the tasting-room staff some idea of your personal preferences and let them suggest wine for you to sample. Some cellar doors charge a A$5 tasting fee, refundable against any purchase.

GETTING HERE AND AROUND

The most direct route from Adelaide to the Barossa is via the town of Gawler. From Adelaide, drive north on King William Street. About 1 km (½ mile) past the Torrens River Bridge, take the right fork onto Main North Road. After 6 km (4 miles) this road forks to the right—follow signs to the Sturt Highway and the town of Gawler. At Gawler leave the highway and follow the signs to Lyndoch on the Barossa's southern border. The 50-km (31-mile) journey should take just more than an hour. A more attractive, if circuitous, route to Lyndoch takes you through the Adelaide Hills' Chain of Ponds and Williamstown.

Because the Barossa wineries are relatively far apart, a car is by far the best way to get around. But keep in mind that there are stiff penalties for driving under the influence of alcohol—the legal blood-alcohol limit is 0.05g/100ml. Police in patrol cars can pull you over for a random breath test anywhere in the state, and roadside mobile breath-testing stations—locally known as "Booze Buses"—are particularly visible during special events, such as the biennial Barossa Vintage Festival, held over the Easter weekend in odd-numbered years. The best advice is to take a tour—**Barossa Epicurean Tours** (⊕ *www.barossatours.com.au*) are highly praised.

TOURS

Tracy and Tom Teichert have lived in the Barossa for 20 years and make excellent guides to the region's best wineries as well as where to buy some excellent local produce. They will make suggestions or they will take you wherever you fancy. They can pick you up from Adelaide (A$160) or more cheaply, from anywhere in the Barossa. Gray Line Adelaide's full-day tour of the Barossa Region (A$137) leaves from Adelaide Central Bus Station. It includes lunch at a winery. Enjoy Adelaide runs a full-day (A$95) Barossa tour that visits four vineyards and includes lunch. Groovy Grape Getaways offers full-day (A$90) Barossa tours with a visit to the Adelaide Hills and a barbecue lunch.

ESSENTIALS

Tour Operators Barossa EpicureanTours ☎ *0457/101487* ⊕ *www. barossatours.com.au.* **Enjoy Adelaide** ☎ *08/8332–1401* ⊕ *www.enjoyadelaide. com.au.* **Gray Line Adelaide** ☎ *1300/858687* ⊕ *www.grayline.com.au/adelaide.* **Groovy Grape Getaways** ☎ *08/8440–1640, 1800/661177* ⊕ *www.groovygrape. com.au.*

Visitor Information Barossa Visitors Centre ⊠ *66–68 Murray St., Tanunda* ☎ *08/8563–0600, 1300/852982* ⊕ *www.barossa.com* ⊙ *Weekdays 9–5, weekends 10–4.*

LYNDOCH

58 km (36 miles) northeast of Adelaide.

This pleasant little town surrounded by vineyards was established in 1840 and is the Barossa's oldest settlement site. It owes the spelling of

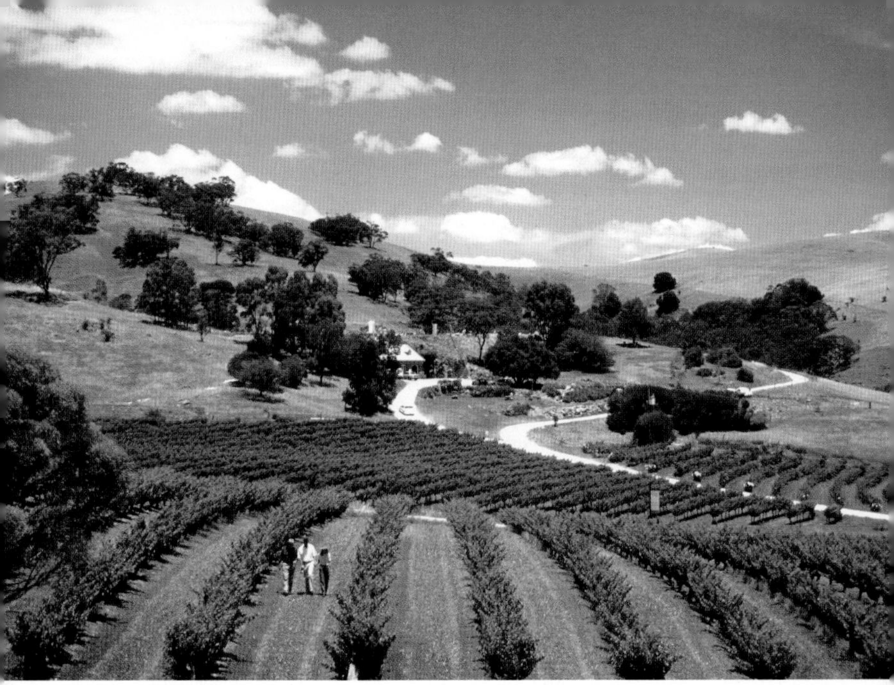

The vineyards of the Barossa Valley

its name to a draftsman's error—it was meant to be named after the British soldier Lord Lynedoch.

EXPLORING

Burge Family Winemakers. You can drink in a leafy vineyard view while tasting from the wine barrels in this understated cellar door. Winemaker Rick Burge's best include the powerful yet elegant Draycott Shiraz and Olive Hill Shiraz-Grenache-Mourvedre blend. There is also sometimes A Nice Red—read the label! ✉ *Barossa Valley Way near Hermann Thumm Dr.* ☎ *08/8524–4644* 🌐 *www.burgefamily.com.au* 🎟 *Free* 🕒 *Fri., Sat., and Mon. 10–5 (call ahead).*

Lyndoch Lavender Farm. A family-friendly tribute to the purple flower that adorns the hills, Lyndoch Lavender Farm grows more than 90 varieties on 6 lush acres high above Lyndoch. Light café meals are available, and the farm shop sells essential oils, creams, and other products, including wine from their adjacent vineyard. ✉ *Hoffnungsthal and Tweedies Gully Rds.* ☎ *08/8524–4538* 🌐 *www.lyndochlavenderfarm.com.au* 🎟 *A$2 during flowering season (Aug.–Jan.)* 🕒 *Feb.–July, weekends 10–4:30; Aug.–Jan., daily 10–4:30.*

WHERE TO STAY

For expanded hotel reviews, visit Fodors.com.

$$$$ B&B/INN Fodor's Choice ★ 🏨 **Abbotsford Country House.** Tranquillity reigns at this property on 50 acres of rolling beef farm with Barossa views. **Pros:** a serene and luxurious place to recover from all the wine tasting you will no doubt do; very welcoming hosts. **Cons:** dining in the restaurant is expensive; health nuts might rue the lack of gym and leisure facilities. [$] *Rooms*

9

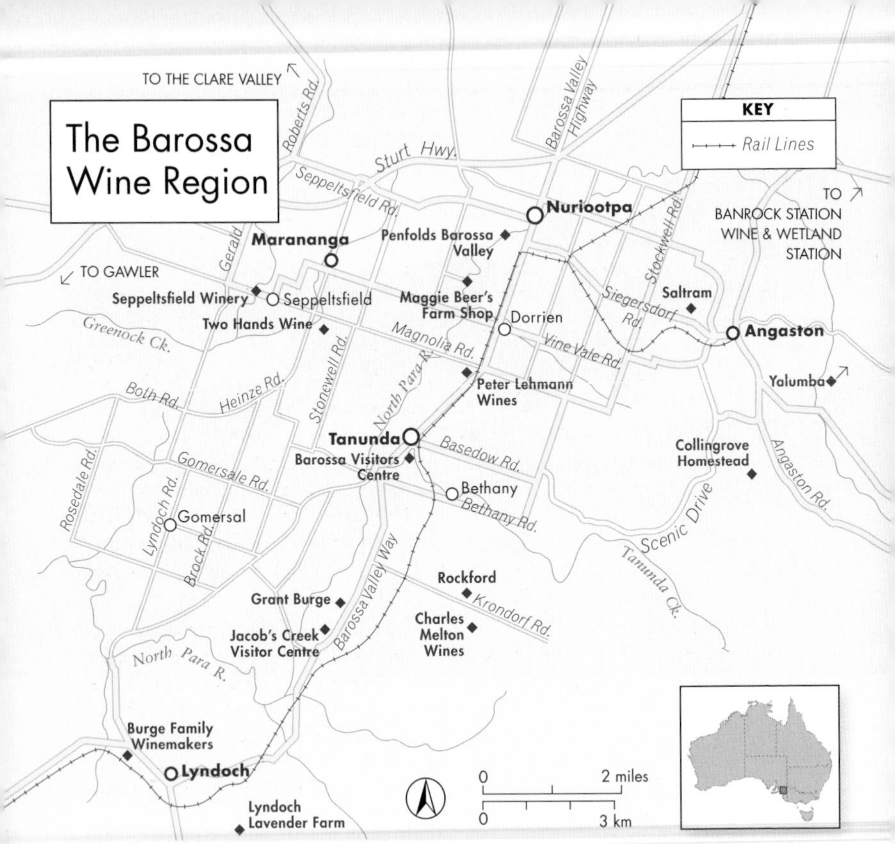

The Barossa Wine Region
KEY
Rail Lines
TO THE CLARE VALLEY
Roberts Rd.
Barossa Valley Highway
Sturt Hwy.
Seppeltsfield Rd.
Nuriootpa
TO BANROCK STATION WINE & WETLAND STATION
Gerald
Marananga
Penfolds Barossa Valley
Stockwell Rd.
TO GAWLER
Seppeltsfield Winery
Seppeltsfield
Maggie Beer's Farm Shop
Siegersdorf Rd.
Saltram
Greenock Ck.
Two Hands Wine
Dorrien
Angaston
Magnolia Rd.
Vine Vale Rd.
Stonewell Rd.
Yalumba
Both Rd.
Heinze Rd.
North Para R.
Peter Lehmann Wines
Tanunda
Collingrove Homestead
Basedow Rd.
Angaston Rd.
Rosedale Rd.
Gomersale Rd.
Barossa Visitors Centre
Bethany
Bethany Rd.
Scenic Drive
Lyndoch Rd.
Gomersal
Brock Rd.
Barossa Valley Way
Tanunda Ck.
Rockford
Grant Burge
Krondorf Rd.
Charles Melton Wines
Jacob's Creek Visitor Centre
North Para R.
Burge Family Winemakers
Lyndoch
Lyndoch Lavender Farm
0
2 miles
0
3 km

from: A$395 ✉ *Yaldara Dr. at Fuss Rd.* ☎ *08/8524–4662* 🌐 *www.abbotsfordhouse.com* 🛏 *8 rooms* 🍴 *Breakfast.*

$$ B&B/INN 🏨 **Belle Cottages.** Rose-filled gardens and sweeping rural acres surround these classic Australian accommodations. **Pros:** great discounts available for groups; comfortable and homely accommodation. **Cons:** not the place for an anonymous stay; some quirks to the plumbing. [$] *Rooms from: A$220* ✉ *8 King St.* ☎ *08/8524–4825, 0411/108800* 🌐 *www.bellescapes.com* 🛏 *11 cottages, 3 suites* 🍴 *Breakfast.*

$$$$ B&B/INN Fodor's Choice ★ 🏨 **Kingsford Homestead.** Set in a historic 1856 homestead on a 225-acre authentic sheep station, Kingsford Homestead offers one of the Barossa Valley's most exquisite experiences. **Pros:** personable hosts make you feel like family; gourmet farm-to-table seasonal menus; secluded feel yet easily accessible. **Cons:** two-night minimum; lunch not included. [$] *Rooms from: A$840* ✉ *Kingsford Rd., Kingsford* ☎ *08/8524–8120* 🌐 *www.kingsfordhomestead.com.au* 🛏 *6 suites, 1 cottage* 🍴 *Multiple meal plans.*

TANUNDA

13 km (8 miles) northeast of Lyndoch, 70 km (43 miles) northeast of Adelaide.

The cultural heart of the Barossa, Tanunda is its most German settlement. The four Lutheran churches in the town testify to its heritage, and dozens of shops selling German pastries, breads, and wursts (sausages)—not to mention wine—line the main street. Many of the valley's best wineries are close by.

EXPLORING

Charles Melton Wines. Tasting here is relaxed and casual in a brick-floor, timber-wall cellar door, which is warmed by a log fire in winter. After making sure the resident cats have vacated it first, settle into a director's chair at the long wooden table and let the staff pour. Nine Popes, a huge, decadent red blend, is the flagship wine, and the ruby-red Rosé of Virginia is arguably Australia's best rosé. You can enjoy a glass of either with a cheese platter or game pie on the veranda. ⊠ *Krondorf Rd. near Nitschke Rd.* ☎ *08/8563–3606* ⊕ *www.charlesmeltonwines. com.au* ⊡ *Free* ☺ *Daily 11–5.*

Grant Burge. This is one of the most successful of the Barossa's young, independent wine labels. Wines include impressive Chardonnays, crisp Rieslings, and powerful reds such as Meshach Shiraz. Don't miss the Holy Trinity—a highly acclaimed Rhône blend of Grenache, Shiraz, and Mourvedre. The cellar door is at Jacob's Creek, 5 km (3 miles) south of Tanunda. Don't come hungry, as there isn't any food available here. ⊠ *Barossa Valley Way near Koch Rd.* ☎ *08/8563–3700* ⊕ *www. grantburgewines.com.au* ⊡ *Free* ☺ *Daily 10–5.*

Jacob's Creek Visitor Centre. An impressive block of glass, steel, and recycled timber, Jacob's Creek Visitor Centre overlooks the creek whose name is familiar to wine drinkers around the world, as they export to more than 60 countries. The informative staff makes the place well worth a visit—it's certainly more than your run-of-the-mill visitor center. Inside the building, plasma screens and pictorial displays tell the history of the label. Cabernet Sauvignon, Merlot, Chardonnay, and the Shiraz-rosé, served chilled, can be tasted at a 60-foot-long counter. There is a lunch-only restaurant with broad glass doors opening onto a grassy lawn edged with towering eucalyptus trees, and there are workshops and tours you can join. ⊠ *Barossa Valley Way near Jacob's Creek* ☎ *08/8521–3000* ⊕ *www.jacobscreek.com* ⊡ *Free* ☺ *Daily 10–5.*

Peter Lehmann Wines. This winery is owned by a larger-than-life Barossa character whose wine consistently wins international awards. Art-hung stonework and a wood-burning fireplace make the tasting room one of the most pleasant in the valley. This is the only place to find Black Queen Sparkling Shiraz. Wooden tables on a shady lawn encourage picnicking on Barossa platters. Served daily, it's full of local produce and big enough for two. They also offer VIP tastings in a private room with food matchings. But you must book in advance. ⊠ *Para Rd. off Stelzer Rd.* ☎ *08/8563–2500* ⊕ *www.peterlehmannwines.com.au* ⊡ *Free* ☺ *Weekdays 9:30–5, Sat. 10:30–4:30, Sun. 9:30–4:30.*

9

Fodor's Choice ★ **Rockford.** Nestled in a lovely cobbled stable yard, Rockford is a small winery with a tasting room in an old stone barn. The specialties are heavy, rich wines made from some of the region's oldest vines. Several notable labels have appeared under the Rockford name—be sure to try the Cabernet Sauvignon and the Basket Press Shiraz (at cellar door from March until sold out), outstanding examples of these most traditional of Australian varieties. The owners pride themselves on their old-school methods. The same equipment (you can see in the yard) has been used for over a century. ✉ *Krondorf Rd. near Nitschke Rd.* ☎ *08/8563–2720* 🌐 *www.rockfordwines.com.au* 🎟 *Free* 🕒 *Daily 11–5.*

PACE YOURSELF

Home-smoked meats, organic farmhouse cheeses, and mouth-filling Shiraz—the Barossa is the ultimate picnic basket. Use this fact as an excuse for a long lunch, which will give you time to recover from all that wine tasting. Remember to pace yourself as you taste, and wherever possible, make use of those spit buckets you see at each winery. You'll be glad you did.

WHERE TO EAT AND STAY

For expanded hotel reviews, visit Fodors.com.

$$ AUSTRALIAN 🍴 **1918 Bistro & Grill.** This rustic and whimsical restaurant in a restored villa makes exemplary use of the Barossa's distinctive regional produce in a seasonal Oz menu flavored with tastes from Asia and the Middle East. Local olive oil and seasonal fruits and vegetables influence dishes like the delicious char-grilled octopus with cauliflower skordalia, pancetta, ruby grapefruit, and truffle oil. Meals are served beside a two-sided fireplace in winter and alfresco in the garden in summer. The mostly Barossa wine list includes rare classics and newcomers. [$] *Average main: A$31* ✉ *94 Murray St.* ☎ *08/8563–0405* 🌐 *www.1918.com.au* ✍ *Reservations essential.*

$ GERMAN 🍴 **Die Barossa Wurst Haus & Bakery.** For a hearty German lunch at a reasonable price, no place beats this small, friendly café and shop. The wurst is fresh from local butchers, the sauerkraut is direct from Germany, and the potato salad is made on-site from a secret recipe. [$] *Average main: A$9* ✉ *86A Murray St.* ☎ *08/8563–3598* 💳 *No credit cards* 🕒 *No dinner.*

$ B&B/INN 🏨 **Blickinstal Barossa Valley Retreat.** Its name means "view into the valley," which understates the breathtaking panoramas from this lovely B&B. **Pros:** great-value rooms with superb views across the valley; complimentary port in the evening. **Cons:** don't expect corporate-style facilities or an anonymous stay. [$] *Rooms from: A$180* ✉ *Rifle Range Rd.* ☎ *08/8563–2716, 0419/868921* 🌐 *www.users.bigpond.com/blickinstal* 🛏 *4 studios, 2 lodges* 🍽 *Breakfast.*

$$ B&B/INN 🏨 **Lawley Farm.** Amid 20 acres of grapes, in a courtyard shaded by gnarled peppercorn trees, these delightful stone cottage-style suites were assembled from the remains of barns dating from the Barossa's pioneering days. **Pros:** original buildings have been lovingly preserved; the breakfasts are legendary. **Cons:** no exercise facilities for working off all the local wine and produce. [$] *Rooms from: A$185* ✉ *Krondorf*

and Grocke Rds., Box 103 ☎ *08/8563–2141* ⊕ *www.lawleyfarm.com. au* ⤳ *4 suites* ❘⚭❘ *Breakfast.*

ANGASTON

16 km (10 miles) northeast of Tanunda via Menglers Hill Rd. Scenic Drive, 86 km (53 miles) northeast of Adelaide.

Named after George Fife Angas, the Englishman who founded the town and sponsored many of the German and British immigrants who came here, Angaston is full of jacaranda trees, and its main street is lined with stately stone buildings and tiny shops. Schulz Butchers has been making and selling wurst (German sausage) since 1939; 17 varieties hang above the counter. You can buy other delicious regional produce every Saturday morning at the Barossa Farmers Market, behind Vintners Bar & Grill.

EXPLORING

Collingrove Homestead. This was the ancestral home of the Angas family, the descendants of George Fife Angas, one of South Australia's founders. At the height of its fortunes, the family controlled more than 14 million acres from this house. Today the property is administered by the National Trust, and you can inspect the Angas family portraits and memorabilia, including Dresden china, a hand-painted Louis XV cabinet, and Chippendale chairs, on guided tours. You can also stay overnight at Collingrove in evocative Old World B&B luxury. ⊠ *450 Eden Valley Rd.* ☎ *08/8564–2061* ⊕ *www.collingrovehomestead.com. au* 🎫 *A$8* ☉ *Tours noon–3 weekdays, noon–4 weekends; booking advised, as hotel guests get priority.*

Saltram. Low-beamed ceilings and ivy-covered trellises give Saltram an urbanized sort of rustic charm. The vineyard's robust wine list includes the Pepperjack Barossa Grenache Rosé, a delightful vintage available only in summer. It's a delicious accompaniment to the Italian-influenced menu at the adjacent—and excellent—Salter's Kitchen restaurant. ⊠ *Murray St.* ☎ *08/8561–0200* ⊕ *www.saltramwines.com.au* 🎫 *Free* ☉ *Daily 10–5.*

Yalumba. Australia's oldest family-owned winery, Yalumba sits within a hugely impressive compound resembling an Italian monastery. The cellar door is decorated with mission-style furniture, antique wine-making materials, and mementos of the Hill Smith family, who first planted vines in the Barossa in 1849. The Octavius Shirazes are superb, and the "Y Series" Viognier is thoroughly enjoyable. ⊠ *Eden Valley Rd. just south of Valley Rd.* ☎ *08/8561–3200* ⊕ *www.yalumba.com* 🎫 *Free* ☉ *Daily 10–4:30.*

WHERE TO EAT

$$$

AUSTRALIAN

✕ **Vintners Bar & Grill.** The Barossa region is at its best in this sophisticated spot, where vivid contemporary artworks adorn the walls and wide windows look out on rows of vineyards. The short menu blends Australian, Mediterranean, and Asian flavors in such dishes as delicious truffled leek risotto with confit duck leg, roasted apple, and pinot jus. Scarlet and charcoal suede chairs and an upbeat jazz sound track make it easy to relax; top winemakers often come here to sample from the cellar's 160 wines. $ *Average main: A$36* ✉ *Stockwell Rd.* ☎ *08/8564–2488* ⊕ *www.vintners.com.au* ≼ *Reservations essential* ⊘ *No dinner Sun.*

NURIOOTPA

8 km (5 miles) northwest of Angaston, 74 km (46 miles) northeast of Adelaide.

Long before it was the Barossa's commercial center, Nuriootpa was used as a bartering place by local Aboriginal tribes, hence its name: Nuriootpa means "meeting place." Most locals call it Nurie.

EXPLORING

Fodor'sChoice ★ **Maggie Beer's Farm Shop.** Renowned cook and food writer Maggie Beer is an icon of Australian cuisine. Burned-fig jam, ice cream, *verjuice* (a golden liquid made from unfermented grape juice and used for flavoring), and her signature Pheasant Farm Pâté are some of the delights you can taste and buy at Maggie Beer's Farm Shop. Treat-filled picnic baskets are available all day to take out or dip into on the deck overlooking a tree-fringed pond full of turtles. Don't miss the daily cooking demonstrations at 2 pm. ✉ *50 Pheasant Farm Rd.* ☎ *08/8562–4477* ⊕ *www.maggiebeer.com.au* ✉ *Free, but bookings are required for cooking demonstrations for groups of 10 or more* ⊘ *Daily 10:30–5.*

Penfolds Barossa Valley. A very big brother to the 19th-century Magill Estate in Adelaide, this massive wine-making outfit in the center of Nuriootpa lets you taste Shiraz, Cabernet, Merlot, Chardonnay, and Riesling blends—but not the celebrated Grange—at the cellar door. To savor the flagship wine and other premium vintages, book a Taste of Grange Tour (A$150 per person, minimum of two). ✉ *30 Tanunda Rd.* ☎ *08/8568–9408* ⊕ *www.penfolds.com.au* ✉ *Free* ⊘ *Daily 10–5.*

OFF THE BEATEN PATH

Banrock Station Wine & Wetland Centre. The salt-scrub-patched Murray River floodplain 150 km (94 miles) east of Nuriootpa is an unlikely setting for a winery, but it is worth making the journey to this spot at Kingston-on-Murray. Within the stilted, mud-brick building perched above the vineyard and river lagoons you can select a wine to accompany an all-day grazing platter or lunch on the outdoor deck—try the pan-seared Murray Cod with corn puree, braised spring onions, and beetroot chips. Afterward, you can take an 8-km (5-mile) walk (A$5, bookings essential) to view the surrounding wetlands (which can be "drylands" during a drought), and learn about the ongoing wildlife habitat restoration and conservation work funded by Banrock Station wine sales. ✉ *Holmes Rd. just off Sturt Hwy., Kingston-on-Murray* ☎ *08/8583–0299* ⊕ *www.banrockstation.com.au* ✉ *Free* ⊘ *Daily 9–5.*

MARANANGA

6 km (4 miles) west of Nuriootpa, 68 km (42 miles) northeast of Adelaide.

The tiny hamlet of Marananga inhabits one of the prettiest corners of the Barossa. This area's original name was Gnadenfrei, which means

CLOSE UP

Fish Tales

With nearly 4,800 km (3,000 miles) of coastline and hundreds of miles of rivers, South Australia has almost as many opportunities for fishing as it has varieties of fish. You can join local anglers of all ages dangling hand lines from a jetty, casting into the surf from coastal rocks, hopping aboard charter boats, or spending a day sitting on a riverside log.

The Murray River is the place to head for callop (also called yellow belly or golden perch) and elusive Murray cod. In the river's backwaters you can also net a feed of yabbies, a type of freshwater crayfish, which make a wonderful appetizer before you tuck into the one that didn't get away. In the ocean King George whiting reigns supreme, but there is also excellent eating with mulloway, bream, snapper, snook, salmon, and sweep. The yellowtail kingfish, a great fighter usually found in deep water, prefers the shallower waters of Coffin Bay, off the Eyre Peninsula.

Baird Bay Ocean Eco Experience. This charter company runs fishing charters to Coffin Bay and other top spots. Children are welcome. ✉ *Baird Bay Rd., Baird Bay* ☎ *08/8626–5017* ⊕ *www.bairdbay.com* 💳 *A$140.*

Another popular destination is the Yorke Peninsula.

S.A. Fishing Adventures. This charter takes anglers to great spots around the Yorke Peninsula. ✉ *7 Gannet Crescent, Marion Bay* ☎ *08/8854– 4098* ⊕ *www.safishingadventures. com.au.*

Last, but certainly not least, is legendary Kangaroo Island.

Kangaroo Island Fishing Adventures. This tour operator has fast, clean boats and a live-aboard mother ship; the company takes groups in a 30-foot cruiser out in the Western River region (the island's north coast). ✉ *Western River Rd., Middle River* ☎ *08/8559–3232* ⊕ *www. kangarooislandadventures.com.au.*

"freed by the grace of God"—a reference to the religious persecution the German settlers suffered before they emigrated to Australia. Marananga, the Aboriginal name, was adopted in 1918, when a wave of anti-German sentiment spurred many name changes in the closing days of World War I.

EXPLORING

Seppeltsfield Winery. Joseph Seppelt was a Silesian farmer who purchased land in the Barossa after arriving in Australia in 1849. Under the control of his son, Benno, the wine-making business flourished, and today Seppeltsfield Winery and its splendid grounds are a tribute to the family's industry and enthusiasm. Fortified wine is a Seppeltsfield specialty; this is the only winery in the world that has ports for every year as far back as 1878. Most notable is the 100-year-old Para Liqueur Tawny. The Grenache, Chardonnay, Cabernet, and sparkling Shiraz are also worth tasting. Tours of the 19th-century distillery are run daily; you can also book 24 hours ahead for the Centenary Tour where you get to taste four of the six paramount wines as well as a 100-year-old wine and

Stomping the grapes at the Barossa Vintage Festival

one that was 100 years old in your birth year. There's a small snack bar that offers delicious cakes and afternoon teas. ✉ *Seppeltsfield Rd., 3 km (2 miles) west of Marananga, Seppeltsfield* 🕾 *08/8568–6217* ⊕ *www. seppeltsfield.com.au* ✆ *Free; Heritage Tour A$15, Taste Your Birth Year Tour A$50, Centenary Tour A$95* ☺ *Daily 10–5. Heritage Tours daily 11:30 and 3:30; Taste Your Birth Year Tour daily (by appointment) 1:30, Centenary Tour daily (by appointment) 2:30.*

Two Hands Wines. The interior of this 19th-century sandstone cottage is every bit as surprising as the wines produced here. Polished wood and glass surround the contemporary counter where the excellent staff leads you through the tasting of several "out of the box" red and white varietals and blends. The main event is Shiraz sourced from six wine regions. Compare and contrast Shiraz from Victoria and Padthaway (South Australia); and try the Barossa-grown Bad Impersonator. From Thursday to Sunday you can join a structured Masterclass Tasting (maximum eight people, bookings recommended) in the adjoining bake house, which has a glass floor over the original cellar. There are also fantastic tasting plates available in the adjoining dining area. ✉ *273 Neldner Rd.* 🕾 *08/8562–4566* ⊕ *www.twohandswines.com* ✆ *General tastings A$5 (refundable with purchase), Long Lunch Masterclass A$55* ☺ *Daily 10–5.*

WHERE TO STAY

For expanded hotel reviews, visit Fodors.com.

$$$$
B&B/INN
🖻 **The Lodge Country House.** Rambling and aristocratic, this bluestone homestead 3 km (2 miles) south of Marananga was built in 1903 for one of the 13 children of Joseph Seppelt, founder of the showpiece winery

across the road. **Pros:** beautiful gardens; informative hosts who delight in telling guests about the history of the place. **Cons:** not particularly suitable for kids. [$] *Rooms from: A$360* ✉ *120 Seppeltsfield Rd., Seppeltsfield* ☎ *08/8562–8277* 🌐 *www.thelodgecountryhouse.com.au* 🛏 *4 double rooms* 🍴 *Multiple meal plans.*

$$$$ RESORT **The Louise.** Prepare for pampering and privacy at this country estate on a quiet back road with glorious valley views. **Pros:** stunning rooms with beautiful private gardens. **Cons:** extras like Internet access are annoyingly expensive; pool and spa could use a face-lift. [$] *Rooms from: A$477* ✉ *Seppeltsfield and Stonewell Rds.* ☎ *08/8562–2722, 08/8562–4144 restaurant* 🌐 *www.thelouise.com.au, restaurant www.appellation.com.au* 🛏 *15 suites* 🍴 *Breakfast.*

THE CLARE VALLEY

Smaller and less well known than the Barossa, the Clare Valley nonetheless holds its own among Australia's wine-producing regions. Its robust reds and delicate whites are among the country's finest, and the Clare is generally regarded as the best area in Australia for fragrant, flavorsome Rieslings. On the fringe of the vast inland deserts, the Clare is a narrow sliver of fertile soil about 30 km (19 miles) long and 5 km (3 miles) wide, with a microclimate that makes it ideal for premium wine making.

The first vines were planted here as early as 1842, but it took a century and a half for the Clare Valley to take its deserved place on the national stage. The mix of small family wineries and large-scale producers, 150-year-old settlements and grand country houses, snug valleys and dense native forests, has rare charm.

GETTING HERE AND AROUND

The Clare Valley is about a 90-minute drive from Adelaide via Main North Road. From the center of Adelaide, head north on King William Street through the heart of North Adelaide. King William becomes O'Connell Street. After crossing Barton Terrace, look for Main North Road signs on the right. The road passes through the satellite town of Elizabeth, bypasses the center of Gawler, and then runs due north to Auburn, the first town of the Clare Valley when approaching from the capital. Main North Road continues down the middle of the valley to Clare.

As with the Barossa, a car is essential for exploring the Clare Valley in any depth. Taste wine in moderation if you're driving; as well as keeping yourself and others safe, you'll avoid paying the extremely high penalties for driving while intoxicated.

TOURS

Clare Valley Experiences combines wine and beer tasting with food, culture, and cycling on its tour of the region's major wineries and sites (A$215 for two people including lunch), departing from Clare. Barossa Epicurean Tours also offer a Clare option.

Contact **Barossa EpicureanTours** ☎ *0402/989647, 08/8564–2191* 🌐 *www.barossatours.com.au.* **Clare Valley Experiences** ✉ *29 Hope St., Clare Valley* ☎ *08/8842–1880* 🌐 *www.clarevalleyexperiences.com.*

ESSENTIALS

Visitor Information **Clare Valley Visitor Information Centre** ✉ *Main North and Spring Gully Rds., 6 km (4 miles) south of Clare, Clare* ☎ *1800/242131, 08/8842–2131* 🌐 *www.clarevalley.com.au* 🕒 *Weekdays 9–5, weekends and public holidays 10–4.*

SEVENHILL

126 km (78 miles) north of Adelaide.

Sevenhill is the Clare Valley's geographic center, and the location of the region's first winery, established by Jesuit priests in 1851 to produce altar wine. The area had been settled three years earlier by Austrian Jesuits who named their seminary after the seven hills of Rome.

The Riesling Trail, a walking and cycling track that follows an old Clare Valley railway line, runs through Sevenhill. The 35-km (22-mile) trail passes wineries and villages in gently rolling country between Auburn and Clare, and three loop trails take you to vineyards off the main track.

EXPLORING

Kilikanoon Wines. Now a bona fide star of the Clare Valley, Kilikanoon is renowned for multilayered reds, such as the dense, richly colored Oracle Shiraz (occasionally available for tasting); Prodigal Grenache is another beauty. ✉ *Penna La., 2 km (1 mile) off Main North Rd., Penwortham* ☎ *08/8843–4206* 🌐 *www.kilikanoon.com.au* 🎟 *Free* 🕒 *Thurs.–Mon. 11–5.*

Fodor's Choice ★ **Sevenhill Cellars.** The area's first winery, Sevenhill Cellars was created by the Jesuits, and they still run the show, with any profits going to education, mission work, and the needy within Australia. In the 1940s the winery branched out from sacramental wine to commercial production, and today 21 wine varieties, including Riesling (try the St. Aloysius label), Verdelho, Grenache, and fortified wines, account for 75% of its business. Book a guided tour with the charming Brother John May, Jesuit winemaker emeritus, who takes you to the cellars, the cemetery, and the church crypt where Jesuits have been interred since 1865. You can also rent bicycles here to explore the rolling hills and vineyards. ✉ *College Rd. just off Main North Rd.* ☎ *08/8843–4222* 🌐 *www.sevenhillcellars.com.au* 🎟 *Free; tours A$7.50* 🕒 *Weekdays 9–5, weekends 10–5; tours Tues. and Thurs. at 2.*

WHERE TO EAT

$$ AUSTRALIAN 🍴 **The Rising Sun Hotel.** People have watched the world go by from the veranda of this landmark hotel in Auburn, 16 km (10 miles) south of Sevenhill, since it was built in 1849. Pull up a chair overlooking the street and partake of the delicious Modern Australian food, perhaps kangaroo fillet with quandong (a native fruit) and sweet-potato mash, or butterfish in a batter of Coopers Pale Ale (Adelaide's own beer). The wine list shows off the Clare Valley's best. [$] *Average main: A$26* ✉ *19 Main North Rd., Auburn* ☎ *08/8849–2015* 🌐 *www.therisingsunhotel.com.au.*

$$ AUSTRALIAN 🍴 **Skillogalee Winery.** The dining area here spills from a 1850s cottage onto a beautiful veranda overlooking a flower-filled garden and rows of

grapevines. The menu changes seasonally, but you can't go wrong with the "vine pruner's lunch," chef Diana Palmer's spin on the British plowman's meal, a platter of rum-glazed local ham, cheddar cheese, chutney, and crusty bread. Entrées might include fish tagine with olives, apricots, and Skillogalee figs with saffron and lemon couscous or dukkah-crusted chicken breast. While most Clare restaurants have limited hours, Skillogalee is so popular it's open seven days a week. Gourmet picnic baskets can be ordered, and group dinners are available by prior arrangement. Skillogalee also has self-contained cottage accommodation. $ *Average main: A$22* ⊠ *Trevarrick Rd., Spring Gully* ☎ *08/8843–4311* ⊕ *www. skillogalee.com.au* ⌂ *Reservations essential* ⊙ *No dinner.*

CLARE

10 km (6 miles) north of Sevenhill, 136 km (84 miles) north of Adelaide.

The bustling town of Clare is the Clare Valley's commercial center. Unusual for ultra-English South Australia, many of its early settlers were Irish—hence the valley's name, after the Irish county Clare, and place-names such as Armagh and Donnybrook.

EXPLORING

Knappstein Enterprise Winery & Brewery. One of the most recognizable and popular wineries in the Clare Valley, Knappstein is located in the original 19th-century Enterprise Brewery, a heritage-listed building and a well-known landmark of a township that's oozing with history. Knappstein Hand Picked Riesling is consistently rated among Australia's finest, though the same could be said for any of the wines lovingly handcrafted here. There's also a microbrewery on-site that produces the award-winning Knappstein Reserve Lager, a premium Bavarian-style lager. ⊠ *2 Pioneer Ave.* ☎ *08/8841–2100* ⊕ *www.knappstein.com.au* ⊙ *Weekdays 9–5, Sat. 11–5, Sun. 11–4.*

Tim Adams Wines. The small, no-frills tasting room means there is nothing to distract you from discovering why Tim Adams Wines has a big reputation. The standout in an impressive collection of reds and whites, which includes a celebrated Riesling and delicious Pinot Gris, is the purple-red Aberfeldy Shiraz, made from hundred-year-old vines. You can buy wine by the glass and bottle to enjoy with a bring-your-own picnic on the veranda. ⊠ *Warenda Rd. just off Main North Rd., 5 km (3 miles) south of Clare* ☎ *1800/356326, 08/8842–2429* ⊕ *www. timadamswines.com.au* ⌂ *Free* ⊙ *Weekdays 10:30–5, weekends 11–5.*

WHERE TO STAY

For expanded hotel reviews, visit Fodors.com.

$
B&B/INN

Bungaree Station. Your journey back to colonial Australia begins at check-in at this family-owned farm; the reception area is in the original station store. **Pros:** fascinating insight into a working homestead; accommodation options for all budgets. **Cons:** city types might find it too rustic; food options are limited. $ *Rooms from: A$85* ⊠ *Main North Rd., 12 km (7 miles) north of Clare* ☎ *08/8842–2677* ⊕ *www. bungareestation.com.au* ⌖ *7 cottages, 3 rooms with shared bathrooms* ⊙| *Some meals.*

9

$$$$ RENTAL Fodor's Choice ★ 🏨 **North Bundaleer.** The spoils of wealthy pastoral life await you at this century-old sandstone homestead 61 km (38 miles) north of Clare, on the scenic route to the Flinders Ranges. **Pros:** relaxed and informal despite the grandeur; perfect for getting away from it all. **Cons:** city types might find it too secluded and intimate. [$] *Rooms from: A$400* ✉ *Spalding–Jamestown Rd., Jamestown* ☎ *08/8665–4024* 🌐 *www.northbundaleer.com.au* 🛏 *4 rooms* 🍴 *Multiple meal plans* ☞ *3 rooms, 1 suite.*

FLEURIEU PENINSULA

The Fleurieu has traditionally been seen as Adelaide's backyard. Generations of local families have vacationed in the string of beachside resorts between Victor Harbor and Goolwa, near the mouth of the Murray River. McLaren Vale wineries attract connoisseurs, and the beaches and bays bring in surfers, swimmers, and sun-seekers. The countryside, with its rolling hills and dramatic cliff scenery, is a joy to drive through.

Although the region is within easy reach of Adelaide, you should consider spending the night if you want to enjoy all it has to offer. You can also easily combine a visit here with one or more nights on Kangaroo Island. The ferry from Cape Jervis, at the end of the peninsula, takes less than an hour to reach Penneshaw on the island, and there are coach connections from Victor Harbor and Goolwa.

GETTING HERE AND AROUND

Renting a car in Adelaide and driving south is the best way to visit the Fleurieu Peninsula, especially if you wish to tour the wineries, which aren't served by public transportation.

The Fleurieu is an easy drive south from Adelaide. McLaren Vale itself is less than an hour away. Leave central Adelaide along South Terrace or West Terrace, linking with the Anzac Highway, which heads toward Glenelg. At the Gallipoli Underpass intersection with Main South Road, turn left. This road takes you almost to McLaren Vale. After a detour to visit the wineries, watch for signs for Victor Harbor Road. About 20 km (12 miles) south the highway splits. One road heads for Victor Harbor, the other for Goolwa. Those two places are connected by a major road that follows the coastline. Drivers heading to Cape Jervis and the Kangaroo Island ferries should stay on Main South Road.

ESSENTIALS

Visitor Information McLaren Vale and Fleurieu Visitor Centre ✉ *Main St., McLaren Vale* ☎ *08/8323–9944* 🌐 *www.mclarenvale.info* 🕒 *Weekdays 9–5, weekends and public holidays 10–4.* **Victor Harbor Visitor Information Centre** ✉ *The Causeway, Victor Harbor* ☎ *08/8557–0777, 1800/557094* 🌐 *www.tourismvictorharbor.com.au* 🕒 *Daily 9–5.*

MCLAREN VALE

39 km (24 miles) south of Adelaide.

The nearest wine region to Adelaide, this area has a distinctly modern, upscale look, even though many of the more than 80 wineries

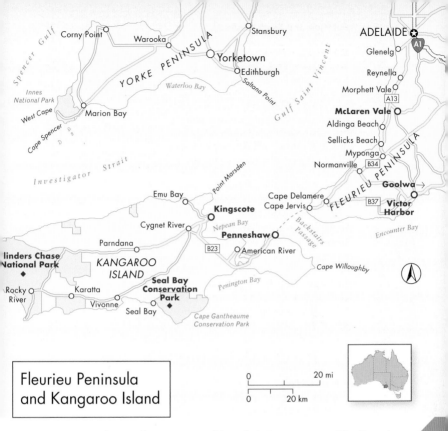

Fleurieu Peninsula
and Kangaroo Island

0		20 mi
0		20 km

in and around town are as old as their Barossa peers. The first vines were planted in 1838 at northern Reynella by Englishman John Reynell, who had collected them en route from the Cape of Good Hope. The McLaren Vale region has always been known for its big—and softer—reds, including Shiraz, as well as a few white varietals. Local microbrewed beer is also becoming an increasingly popular attraction in the region.

EXPLORING

Coriole Vineyards. The 1860s stone cellar door at Coriole Vineyards sits among nasturtiums and hollyhocks on a hill with stunning St. Vincent Gulf views. From the surrounding vines, winemakers Simon White and Mark Lloyd make some of Australia's best Italian varietal wines, such as Sangiovese and Nebbiolo. Coriole grows olives, too, and you can taste olive oils as well as wine. Enjoy a platter of estate-grown and local produce—cheese, smoked kangaroo, roasted vegetables, and chutney—in the flagstone courtyard (Friday to Monday). The hosted tastings led by Tim Nicholls are excellent and should be booked ahead. ⊠ *Chaffeys Rd. near Kays Rd.* ☎ *08/8323–8305* ⊕ *www.coriole.com* ⊠ *Free* ⊗ *Weekdays 10–5, weekends 11–5.*

d'Arenberg Wines. A fine restaurant complements excellent wine at d'Arenberg Wines, family-run since 1912. Winemaker Chester d'Arenberg Osborn is known for his quality whites, including the luscious Noble Riesling dessert wine, as well as powerful reds and fortified wines with equally compelling names. Reservations are essential for d'Arry's fine-dining Verandah restaurant, which overlooks the vineyards, the valley, and the sea. The tempting seasonal lunch-only menu uses local produce for its Mod Oz dishes. ✉ *Osborn Rd.* ☎ *08/882–335 cellar door, 08/8329–4848 restaurant* 🌐 *www.darenberg.com.au* 🎟 *Free* 🕒 *Daily 10–5.*

LIFE'S A PICNIC

Blessed Cheese. A progressive picnic matching South Australia's finest artisan cheese with wines from the region's best wineries. ✉ *150 Main Rd.* ☎ *08/8323–7958* 🌐 *www.blessedcheese.com.au* 🎟 *$30 per couple, Premium Trail A$75* 🕒 *No dinner.*

Pertaringa Wines. On a quiet, unpaved back road, boutique winery Pertaringa (meaning "belonging to the hills") makes limited quantities of mouth-filling reds and several whites. At the cellar door, facing the vines, you can sip Two Gentlemen's Grenache and Scarecrow Sauvignon Blanc, a great accompaniment to a bring-your-own picnic. It is worth buying some of the premium Over the Top Shiraz even without tasting—you won't be disappointed. ✉ *Hunt and Rifle Range Rd.* ☎ *08/8323–8125* 🌐 *www.pertaringa.com.au* 🎟 *Free* 🕒 *Daily 11–5.*

WHERE TO EAT AND STAY

For expanded hotel reviews, visit Fodors.com.

$ AUSTRALIAN 🍴 **Blessed Cheese.** It's hard to disappoint when cheese and chocolate are your specialties, particularly when they're adeptly paired with local wines. Blessed Cheese is a unique combination of cheese shop, licensed café, and provedore specializing in artisan cheeses, local and imported gourmet foods, and regional produce. You can pack a picnic for the day with platters for two available from A$60, dine in their licensed café with a regional breakfast or lunch, relax with cake and coffee, or sample their delicious range of cheeses. [$] *Average main: A$10* ✉ *150 Main Rd.* ☎ *08/8323–7958* 🌐 *www.blessedcheese.com.au* 🕒 *No dinner.*

$ AUSTRALIAN 🍴 **Bracegirdles at 190.** With its worn floorboards and pressed-metal ceilings, this café feels like a country corner store, but you'll also find a large alfresco area and undercover courtyard, perfect in spring. Come early for a cup of coffee, a piece of chocolate, and the best breakfast outside Adelaide. The menu shows off Fleurieu Peninsula produce: for a taste of McLaren Vale, order a tasting plate for two, and for something spicier, tuck into gluten-free salt-and-pepper squid (in season). **TIP→ Book ahead for weekends.** [$] *Average main: A$20* ✉ *190 Main Rd.* ☎ *08/8323–8558* 🌐 *www.bracegirdles.com.au/mclaren-vale.html.*

$$ AUSTRALIAN 🍴 **Star of Greece.** More for the linen-slacks-and-deck-shoes set than the board-shorts-and-sunscreen crowd, this extended weatherboard kiosk on the cliffs at Port Willunga, 10 km (6 miles) southwest of McLaren Vale, is beach-ball bright and extremely popular. Wooden chairs painted in mandarin, lime, and sky-blue stripes sit at paper-draped tables, and windows frame the aqua sea. (The offshore buoy marks where the three-masted *Star of Greece* foundered in 1888.) Reading the menu nets mostly seafood, and, depending upon the season, you might find

seared scallops wrapped in octopus bacon, or crispy skinned ocean trout on prawn salsa. [$] *Average main: A$30* ✉ *1 Esplanade, Port Willunga* ☎ *08/8557–7420* 🌐 *www.starofgreececafe.com.au* ✍ *Reservations essential* 🕒 *No dinner Sun.–Thurs, no lunch Mon. and Tues.*

$$$ B&B/INN 🏨 **Wine & Roses B&B.** It may look like a regular residential house from the outside, but this luxury B&B has an interior that's far from ordinary. **Pros:** perfect for a romantic getaway; the complimentary port is delicious. **Cons:** if all four suites are booked it's a little cramped; not child-friendly. [$] *Rooms from: A$230* ✉ *39 Caffrey St.* ☎ *08/8323–7654* 🌐 *www.wineandroses.com.au* 🛏 *4 suites* 🍴 *Breakfast.*

GOOLWA

44 km (27 miles) southeast of McLaren Vale, 83 km (51 miles) south of Adelaide.

Beautifully situated near the mouth of the mighty Murray River, which travels some 2,415 km (1,594 miles) from its source in New South Wales, Goolwa grew fat on the 19th-century river paddle-steamer trade. Today, with its enviable position close to the sea and the combined attractions of Lake Alexandrina and Coorong National Park, tourism has replaced river trade as the main source of income.

EXPLORING

FAMILY **Goolwa Wharf.** Set sail from here for daily tour cruises upon the *Spirit of the Coorong,* a fully equipped motorboat that offers a 4½-hour (A$84) or 6-hour cruise (A$98) to Coorong National Park. Both include guided walks, lunch, and afternoon tea. Visitors can also enjoy locally brewed craft beer at the Steam Exchange Brewery located in the old railway goods shed on the wharf or go shopping at the Goolwa Wharf Markets on the first and third Sunday of each month. ✉ *Goolwa Wharf* ☎ *08/8555–2203, 1800/442203 tour cruises* 🌐 *www.coorongcruises.com.au.*

FAMILY **Oscar W.** Goolwa is also the home port of paddle steamer *Oscar W.* Built in 1908, it's one of the few remaining wood-fired boiler ships. This boat holds the record for bringing the most bales of wool (2,500) along the Darling River, which flows into the Murray River. When not participating in commemorative cruises and paddleboat races, the boat is open for inspection and crusies. ✉ *Goolwa Wharf* ☎ *1300/466592* 🌐 *www.oscar-w.info* 🎟 *Donation requested to inspect boat; A$20 cruises.*

VICTOR HARBOR

18 km (11 miles) west of Goolwa, 83 km (51 miles) south of Adelaide.

As famous for its natural beauty and wildlife as for its resorts, Victor Harbor is South Australia's favorite seaside getaway. In 1802 English and French explorers Matthew Flinders and Nicolas Baudin met here at Encounter Bay, and by 1830 the harbor was a major whaling center. Pods of southern right whales came here to breed in winter, and they made for a profitable trade through the mid-1800s. By 1878 the whales were hunted nearly to extinction, but the return of these majestic

9

creatures to Victor Harbor in recent decades has established the city as a premier source of information on whales and whaling history.

EXPLORING

Bluff. Seven kilometers (4½ miles) west of Victor Harbor, the Bluff is where whalers once stood lookout for their prey. Today the granite outcrop, also known as Rosetta Head, serves the same purpose in very different circumstances. It's a steep, 1,400-foot climb to the top, on a formed trail, to enjoy the bluff views. ⊠ *The Bluff.*

FAMILY **Cockle Train.** Traveling the route of South Australia's first railway line—originally laid between Goolwa and Port Elliot, and extended to Victor Harbor in 1864— the line traces the lovely Southern Ocean beaches on its 16-km (10-mile), half-hour journey. The train runs by steam power, subject to availability and weather conditions, daily during summer school holidays (late December to late January), on Easter weekend, and on the third Sunday of each month from June to November. A diesel locomotive pulls the heritage passenger cars (or a diesel railcar operates) on other Sundays and public holidays, and days of Total Fire Ban. ⊠ *Railway Terrace near Coral St.* ☎ *08/8552–2782 on days the train is operating, 1300/655991* ⊕ *www.steamrangerheritagerailway. org* ☜ *Round-trip A$29.*

FAMILY **Granite Island.** This island is linked to the mainland by a 650-yard causeway, along which Clydesdales pull a double-decker tram. Within Granite Island Nature Park a self-guided walk leads around the island, and guided walking tours to view the colony of about 500 fairy penguins are run from the penguin interpretive center. There is also an excellent restaurant (lunch only) with deck dining overlooking the harbor entrance. Look out for seals in the shallows. ⊠ *Granite Island* ☎ *08/8552–7555* ⊕ *www.graniteisland.com.au* ☜ *Round-trip tram A$9, penguin tours A$12.50, penguin interpretive center A$6* ⊙ *Daily; penguin tours at dusk.*

FAMILY **South Australian Whale Centre.** The center tells the often graphic story of the whaling industry along South Australia's coast, particularly in Encounter Bay. Excellent interpretive displays spread over three floors focus on dolphins, seals, penguins, and whales—all of which can be seen in these waters. In whale-watching season the center has a 24-hour information hotline on sightings. There's a Discovery Trail and craft area for children. ⊠ *2 Railway Terrace* ☎ *08/8551–0750, 1900/942537 whale information* ⊕ *www.sawhalecentre.com* ☜ *A$9* ⊙ *Daily 10:30–5.*

OFF THE BEATEN PATH

Coorong National Park. A sliver of land stretching southeast of the Fleurieu Peninsula and completely separate from it, this park hugs the South Australian coast for more than 150 km (94 miles). Many Australians became aware of the Coorong's beauty from the 1970s film *Storm Boy*, which told the story of a boy's friendship with a pelican. These curious birds are one reason why the Coorong is a wetland area of world standing. There's an A$13 charge per vehicle. ⊠ *Accessible via Goolwa, Meningie, and Salt Creek off Hwy. 1, Coorong* ☎ *08/8575–1200* ⊕ *www.thecoorong.com.*

BEACHES

Boomer Beach. The surf here is very big thanks to the exposed reef break. Most waves are dumpers, hence the name Boomer, and can get up to 15 feet high. As a result, this is a beach for surfers and strong swimmers. Waves decrease toward Victor Harbor, providing lower surf and usually calm conditions. In summer the surf tends to be mostly flat, but you need to be vigilant of rocks, rips, and sharks year-round. There is an excellent view down the entire beach from the headland at Port Elliot; from here you can spot the southern right whale, which in winter claims this area as its territory. **Amenities:** lifeguards; parking; toilets. **Best for:** surfing; fishing; swimming. ✉ *Boomer Beach, Port Elliot.*

Horseshoe Bay, Port Elliot. This 2,300-foot-long beach faces east at the jetty and swings round to face south against Commodore Point. Thanks to the protection on either side, the waves are relatively low, making this a great swimming destination. However, the waves can be heavy during a high swell and surge up the steep beach. The safest swimming is at the western surf club end, where waves are always smallest. Fishing is popular around jetty and boundary rocks. **Amenities:** parking; toilets. **Best for:** swimming; walking. ✉ *Basham Parade, Port Elliot* ☎ *08/8554–2770.*

Middleton. One of South Australia's most popular surfing beaches is also one of its most hazardous due to the persistent high waves. The entire beach is composed of fine sand and waves averaging more than 2 meters breaking across a 500-meter-wide double bar surf zone. Numerous spilling breakers, substantial wave setup and set-down at the shoreline, and widely spaced rips during lower wave conditions are common characteristics here. Thanks to the wide surf zone, it is moderately safe to swim in the inner surf zone on the bar, but it is advised that swimmers do not venture beyond the first line of breakers as strong currents occupy the trough between the sand bars. **Amenities:** parking; toilets. **Best for:** surfing; walking. ✉ *Esplanade, Middleton.*

SPORTS AND THE OUTDOORS

BICYCLING

Encounter Bikeway. For cycling enthusiasts, there's Encounter Bikeway, a paved track that runs 30 km (19 miles) from the Bluff along a scenic coastal route to Laffin Point (east of Goolwa). Almost flat, the bikeway is suitable for riders of most ages and experience levels. **TIP→ When the Cockle Train is operating the Encounter Bikeway users can combine their trip with a journey on the train, traveling one way on the bike path and returning on the train.** ✉ *Encounter Bikeway* 🌐 *www.tourismvictorharbor.com.au.*

WHERE TO STAY

For expanded hotel reviews, visit Fodors.com.

$ HOTEL **The Bluff Resort Apartments.** The vibe is more tropical than maritime at Victor Harbor's upscale resort complex, with palm trees and spectacular surf as the backdrop for spacious, well-equipped rooms of varying configurations. **Pros:** stunning views of three islands; real "getaway" feel. **Cons:** expensive unless you get a last-minute deal; 15-minute drive from downtown. [$] *Rooms from: A$230* ✉ *123 Franklin Parade*

☎ *08/8552–4400* ⊕ *www.bluffresort.com.au* ⇆ *12 suites, 14 apart-ments, 12 upper studios, 4 poolside studios* ❑ *All meals.*

KANGAROO ISLAND

Kangaroo Island, Australia's third largest (after Tasmania and Melville), is barely 16 km (10 miles) from the Australian mainland. Yet the island belongs to another age—a folksy, friendly, less sophisticated time when you'd leave your car unlocked and knew everyone by name.

The island is most beautiful along the coastline, where the land is sculpted into a series of bays and inlets teeming with bird and marine life. The stark interior has its own charm, however, with pockets of red earth between stretches of bush and farmland. Wildlife is probably the island's greatest attraction; in a single day you can stroll along a beach crowded with sea lions and watch kangaroos, koalas, pelicans, and fairy penguins in their native environments.

Its towns and most of its accommodations are on the island's eastern third. The standout sights are on the southern coast, so if you've only one day—you could easily spend a week—it's best to tour the island in a clockwise direction, leaving the north-coast beaches for the afternoon. Before heading out, fill your gas tank and pack a picnic lunch. Shops are few and far between outside the towns, general stores being the main outlets for food and gas.

GETTING HERE AND AROUND

REX/Regional Express flies two times daily between Adelaide and King-scote, the island's main airport. Ask about holiday packages in conjunc-tion with SeaLink. Flights to the island take about 30 minutes.

SeaLink ferries allow access for cars through Penneshaw from Cape Jervis, at the tip of the Fleurieu Peninsula, a 90-minute drive from Adelaide. There are four daily sailings each way, with additional cross-ings at peak times. SeaLink operates the vehicular passenger ferry *Sea Lion 2000* and *Spirit of Kangaroo Island*, a designated freight boat with passenger facilities. These ferries make 45-minute crossings between Cape Jervis and Penneshaw. Ferries are the favored means of transpor-tation between the island and the mainland, and reservations are advis-able during the holidays. Adelaide Sightseeing operates coach tours of Kangaroo Island out of Adelaide in conjunction with the SeaLink ferry services from A$258 for a (very long) day trip.

Kangaroo Island's main attractions are widely scattered; you can see them best on a guided tour or by car. The main roads form a paved loop, which branches off to such major sites as Seal Bay and Admirals Arch and Remarkable Rocks in Flinders Chase National Park. Stretches of unpaved road lead to lighthouses at Cape Borda and Cape Willoughby, South Australia's oldest. Roads to the island's northern beaches, bays, and camping areas are also unpaved. These become very rutted in sum-mer, but they can be driven carefully in a conventional vehicle. Be alert for wildlife, especially at dawn, dusk, and after dark. Slow down and dip your lights so you don't blind the animals you see.

9

"Bryson on top of a Remarkable Rock at Flinders Chase National Park" —photo by Rich_B_Florida, Fodors.com member

TOURS

Exceptional Kangaroo Island has quality four-wheel-drive and bush-walking tours from A$385 per person per day. Tailor-made itineraries, including bird-watching and photography, and flight-accommodation packages can also be arranged. Kangaroo Island Odysseys operates luxury four-wheel-drive nature tours from one to three days priced from A$597 per person. Kangaroo Island Wilderness Tours has five personalized four-wheel-drive wilderness tours from one to four days and starting from A$430 per person (tour only); a range of accommodation packages is available.

SeaLink Kangaroo Island operates one-day (A$258) bus tours of the island, departing from Adelaide, in conjunction with the ferry service from Cape Jervis. They also can arrange fishing and self-drive tours and extended packages. Two-day/one-night tours are A$297 and up per person; two-day/one-night self-drive tours start at A$211 per person.

ESSENTIALS

Tour Operators Exceptional Kangaroo Island ☎ 08/8553–9119 ⊕ www. exceptionalkangarooisland.com. Kangaroo Island Odysseys ☎ 08/8553–0386 ⊕ www.kiodysseys.com.au. Kangaroo Island Wilderness Tours ☎ 08/8559–5033 ⊕ www.wildernesstours.com.au. SeaLink Kangaroo Island ✉ 440 King William St., Adelaide ☎ 13–1301 ⊕ www.sealink.com.au.

Transportation Adelaide Sightseeing ✉ 85 Franklin St., City Center, Adelaide ☎ 1300/769762 ⊕ www.adelaidesightseeing.com.au. REX/Regional Express ☎ 13–1713 ⊕ www.regionalexpress.com.au. SeaLink ☎ 13–1301 ⊕ www. sealink.com.au.

Visitor Information Department of Environment, Water and Natural Resources Office. The Kangaroo Island Pass (A$68, A$185 families) is available from any National Parks and Wildlife site, or from the Department of Environment, Water and Natural Resources Office or any Parks Pass outlet. The pass covers a selection of guided tours and park entry fees and is valid for a year. ⊠ *Natural Resources Centre Kangaroo Island, 37 Dauncey St., Kingscote* ☎ *08/8553–4444*

> ### HOW REMARKABLE
>
> Balanced precariously on the promontory of Kirkpatrick Point in Flinders Chase National Park, the Remarkable Rocks are aptly named. Sitting with your back against one of these fantastically shaped boulders is the best way to view sunset or sunrise on Kangaroo Island.

⊕ *www.environment.sa.gov.au/parks.* **Kangaroo Island Gateway Visitor Information Centre** ⊠ *Howard Dr., Pennesham* ☎ *1800/8553–1185* ⊕ *www.tourkangarooisland.com.au* ⊘ *Weekdays 9–5, weekends and public holidays 10–4.*

KINGSCOTE

121 km (75 miles) southwest of Adelaide.

Kangaroo Island's largest town, Kingscote is a good base for exploring. Reeves Point, at the town's northern end, is where South Australia's colonial history began. Settlers landed here in 1836 and established the first official town in the new colony. Little remains of the original settlement except Hope Cottage, now a small museum; several graves; and a huge, twisted mulberry tree that grew from a cutting the settlers brought from England—locals still use the fruit to make jam. Today American River, about halfway between Kingscote and Pennesham, the island's second-largest town, is another accommodation and restaurant hub.

EXPLORING

FAMILY **Pelican Feeding.** Make sure you catch the Pelican Feeding "show" at 5 pm daily on the rock wall beside Kingscote Jetty. A guide in fishing waders gives an informative and entertaining talk as he feeds handfuls of seafood to a comic mob of noisy pelicans. This is great fun. ⊠ *Kingscote Wharf* ☎ *08/8553–3112* ⊕ *www.kipenguincentre.com.au/pelican-feeding.php* ⊐ *A$5* ⊘ *Daily 5 pm.*

WHERE TO STAY

For expanded hotel reviews, visit Fodors.com.

$$$ ⊟ **Acacia Apartments.** A huge movie collection in the reception area
RENTAL confirms that the self-contained one- and two-bedroom units at this
FAMILY Reeve's Point complex are family-friendly. **Pros:** kid-friendly; very amenable owner. **Cons:** slightly overpriced; 10 am check-out time. ⓢ *Rooms from: A$265* ⊠ *3–5 Rawson St., Reeve's Point* ☎ *08/8553–0088, 1800/247007* ⊕ *www.acacia-apartments.com.au* ↰ *10 apartments* ⊺○⊺ *Breakfast.*

$$ ⊟ **Aurora Ozone Hotel.** The original Victorian facade on this two-story
HOTEL 1920s hotel, directly opposite the new section across the road, hides surprisingly modern and spacious rooms that overlook Nepean Bay. **Pros:**

across the street from the penguin colony; friendly staff. **Cons:** older rooms are old-fashioned, as is the breakfast. $ *Rooms from: A$156* ✉ *Commercial St.* ☎ *08/8553–2011, 1800/083133* ✎ *reservations@ ozone.auroraresorts.com.au* ⊕ *www.auroraresorts.com.au* ⤴ *75 rooms* ⵀⵀ *All meals.*

$$
RENTAL
FAMILY
▦ **Kangaroo Island Bayview Villas.** Located on a hillside overlooking Nepean Bay and the town of Kingscote, these bay-view villas are fully equipped, self-contained style accommodations with a private patio and barbecue facilities. **Pros:** panoramic views; self-contained; modern and spacious; good for groups and/or families. **Cons:** single-night surcharge is included for one-night stays. $ *Rooms from: A$199* ✉ *20 Reeves St.* ☎ *0488/178–867* ⊕ *www.bayview-villas.com.au* ⤴ *4 villas* ⵀⵀ *No meals.*

$
RESORT
▦ **Kangaroo Island Lodge.** Facing beautiful Eastern Cove at American River, the island's oldest resort has rooms that overlook open water or the saltwater pool; the most attractive are the "water-view" rooms, which have mud-brick walls, warm terra-cotta tones, and king-size beds. **Pros:** set in beautiful and peaceful surroundings; nearby trails lead to kangaroos and pelicans. **Cons:** dated rooms and distinctly ordinary breakfast. $ *Rooms from: A$108* ✉ *Scenic Dr., American River* ☎ *08/8553–7053, 1800/355581* ⊕ *www.kilodge.com.au* ⤴ *38 rooms* ⵀⵀ *Some meals.*

$$$
B&B/INN
▦ **Wanderers Rest.** Delightful local artworks dot the walls in this country inn's stylish units, all of which have king-size beds. **Pros:** simple, high-quality accommodation with stunning views. **Cons:** kids under 10 aren't allowed; tours and extras quickly add up. $ *Rooms from: A$253* ✉ *Bayview Rd., Lot 2, American River* ☎ *08/8553–7140* ⊕ *www. wanderersrest.com.au* ⤴ *8 suites* ⵀⵀ *Breakfast.*

PENNESHAW

62 km (39 miles) east of Kingscote.

This tiny ferry port has a huge population of penguins, which are visible on nocturnal tours. Gorgeous shoreline, views of spectacularly blue water, and rolling green hills are a few lovely surprises here.

EXPLORING

FAMILY **Penneshaw Penguin Centre.** Here there are two ways to view the delightful fairy penguins indigenous to Kangaroo Island. From the indoor interpretive center, where you can read about bird activity—including mating, nesting, and feeding—a boardwalk leads to a viewing platform above rocks and sand riddled with burrows. Because the penguins spend most of the day fishing at sea or inside their burrows, the best viewing is after sunset. You can take a self-guided walk or an informative guided tour, which starts with a talk and video at the center. You might see penguins waddling ashore, chicks emerging from their burrows to feed, or scruffy adults molting. ✉ *Middle and Bay Terraces* ☎ *08/8553–1103* 🖃 *Interpretive center free, guided tours A$10, self-guided walks A$8* ⊙ *Daily 6 pm–9:30 pm, tours at 7:30 pm and 8:30 pm in winter, 8:30 pm and 9:30 pm in summer* ⊙ *Closed Feb. 1–21.*

Sunset Winery. Sip smooth Chardonnay while overlooking Eastern Cove at this calm, cool, and pristine addition to Kangaroo Island's thriving wine industry. You can sample wines for free at the cellar door, and opt for the Savoury Platter: a selection of Kangaroo Island and regional cheeses, KI Source Relish, South Rock Salami, local olives, crackers, and more for A$25. Alternately, try a Dukkah Platter from the Fleurieu, served with local wild-olive oil and delicious local bread for A$15. ✉ *6284 Hog Bay Rd.* ☎ *08/8553–1378* 🌐 *www.sunset-wines.com.au* 🎫 *Free* 🕐 *Daily 11–5.*

OFF THE BEATEN PATH

Australia's oldest lighthouse stands on Kangaroo Island's easternmost point, Cape Willoughby, 27 km (17 miles) from Penneshaw, on a mostly unpaved road. You can explore the property around the towering, white lighthouse, but only guided tours (A$14.50 or KI Pass) can enter the 1852 building itself. Tours depart from the National Parks office in one of the three 1920s lighthouse keepers' cottages. The other two cottages have been converted into self-contained accommodations that let you experience Kangaroo Island at its most remote and wildest—it's always windy here!

BEACHES

Island Beach. Known locally as Millionaires' Row for its fabulous real estate, Island Beach is the quintessential beach holiday location. Framed by dense bushland, the sandy beach is secluded and stretches almost as far as the eye can see and provides very safe swimming. Walking along the coast toward American River yields plenty of bird-watching opportunities. **Amenities:** parking; food and drink. **Best for:** swimming; walking; solitude. ✉ *Off Island Beach Rd., Island Beach.*

WHERE TO EAT AND STAY

For expanded hotel reviews, visit Fodors.com.

$$ SEAFOOD — 🍴 **Fish of Penneshaw.** Belly up to the counter in this tiny shop for cheap local seafood, to take out or enjoy with a glass of wine in the seating area next door. Choose your fish—whiting, John Dory, garfish—from the blackboard menu and have it beer-battered, crumbed, or grilled. Or you might prefer a paper-wrapped parcel of scallops, prawns, lobster, and oysters (in season) shucked to order. The team behind the shop also runs 2 Birds & A Squid Catering, which prepares seafood packs and cooked meals for pickup or delivery to your accommodation anywhere on the island. [$] *Average main: A$25* ✉ *43 North Terrace* ☎ *08/8553–1177 Fish of Penneshaw, 08/8553–7406 2 Birds & A Squid* 🌐 *www.2birds1squid.com/fish-of-penneshaw* 💳 *No credit cards* 🕐 *Closed May–mid-Oct. No lunch.*

$$ HOTEL — 🏨 **Kangaroo Island Seafront Resort.** This hotel has an ideal position near the ferry terminal and overlooking Penneshaw Bay. **Pros:** steps away from ferry terminal and penguin viewing; spacious rooms. **Cons:** older parts of the hotel are showing their age; no air-conditioning in rooms. [$] *Rooms from: A$180* ✉ *49 North Terrace* ☎ *08/8553–1028, 1800/624624* 🌐 *www.seafront.com.au* 🛏 *25 rooms* 🍽 *Breakfast.*

$$ B&B/INN — 🏨 **Seaview Lodge.** Host Barbara Ewens welcomes you into her 1860s home at this elegant yet relaxing B&B. **Pros:** beautiful cottage-style gardens; stylishly furnished rooms. **Cons:** if full, the B&B can feel

claustrophobic; limited views of the ocean. [$] *Rooms from: A$220* ✉ *Lot 3, Willoughby Rd.* ☎ *08/8553–1132* 🌐 *www.seaviewlodge.com.au* 🛏 *5 rooms, 1 cottage* 🍴 *Breakfast.*

SEAL BAY CONSERVATION PARK

60 km (37 miles) southwest of Kingscote via South Coast Rd.

EXPLORING

FAMILY Fodor's Choice ★ **Seal Bay Conservation Park.** This top Kangaroo Island attraction gives you the chance to visit one of the state's largest Australian sea-lion colonies. About 300 animals usually lounge on the beach, except on stormy days, when they shelter in the dunes. You can only visit the beach, and get surprisingly close to females, pups, and bulls, on a tour with an interpretive officer; otherwise, you can follow the self-guided boardwalk to a lookout over the sand. **TIP→ Two-hour twilight tours are only available during South Australian daylight savings times and visitors must call ahead.** The park visitor center has fun and educational displays, and a touch table covered in sea-lion skins and bones. There is also a shop. ✉ *End of Seal Bay Rd., Seal Bay* ☎ *08/8559–4207* 🌐 *www.environment.sa.gov.au/sealbay/home* 🎟 *Group tour A$32 per person, twilight tour A$60, boardwalk A$15* ⏲ *Tours Dec. and Jan., daily 9–5, every 15–45 mins; Feb.–Nov., daily 9–5, every 45 mins.*

BEACHES

Fodor's Choice ★ **Vivonne Bay.** This is one of the most popular surfing beaches on the island's south coast; the 5-km (3-mile) white-sand beach is also one of the most pristine to swim. Safe swimming areas can be found near the jetty and boat ramp, or the sandy-bottomed Harriet River entering the bay. On the other side of the river, Point Ellen provides photographers with spectacular views of the Southern Ocean. Vivonne Bay is billed as the only safe harbor on the south coast of Kangaroo Island and is the base for crayfishing boats from November to May. You'll also find barbecue and picnic areas, toilets, and a camping area. The beach can be reached by taking the road just past the Vivonne Bay store. **Amenities:** parking; toilets; food and drink. **Best for:** swimming; surfing; solitude; walking. ✉ *Bayview Rd., Vivonne Bay.*

EN ROUTE **Island Beach-House.** Along South Coast Road, a red-earth side road leads to Vivonne Bay, a Mediterranean-looking fisherman's cove with electrifyingly blue-green waters and stark white sands. There's no better view of the bay than from Island Beach-House. With a glass-fronted semicircular lounge room facing the sea, this self-contained house has everything you need for a holiday, including a bread-making machine. You can order fresh-cooked lobster steaks from the owners, who operate professional lobster boats. ✉ *Lot 142, Crabb Rd., Vivonne Bay* ☎ *08/8346–8764* 🌐 *www.fergusonaustralia.com/kangarooisland.php.*

FLINDERS CHASE NATIONAL PARK

102 km (64 miles) west of Kingscote.

Some of Australia's most beautiful coastal scenery is in Flinders Chase National Park on Kangaroo Island.

"Naptime on the beach at Kangaroo Island" —photo by Istarr, Fodors.com member

EXPLORING

Flinders Chase National Park. The effects of seas crashing mercilessly onto Australia's southern coast are visible in the oddly shaped rocks on the island's shores. A limestone promontory was carved from beneath at Cape du Couedic on the southwestern coast, producing what is known as **Admiral's Arch.** From the boardwalk you can see the New Zealand fur seals that have colonized the area around the rock formation. About 4 km (2½ miles) farther east are the aptly named **Remarkable Rocks,** huge, fantastically shaped boulders balanced precariously on the promontory of Kirkpatrick Point. This is a great place to watch the sun set or rise.

Much of Kangaroo Island has been cultivated since settlement, but after being declared a national treasure in 1919, a huge area of original vegetation has been protected in Flinders Chase. In December 2007 a bushfire burned a large part of Flinders Chase, and its destructive power and the various stages of regeneration are now on show.

Flinders Chase has several 1½-km to 9-km (1-mile to 5½-mile) loop walking trails, which take one to three hours to complete. The trails meander along the rivers to the coast, passing mallee scrub and sugar gum forests, and explore the rugged shoreline. The 4-km (2½-mile) Snake Lagoon Hike follows Rocky River over and through a series of broad rocky terraces to the remote sandy beach where it meets the sea. The sign warning of freak waves is not just for show.

The park is on the island's western end, bounded by the Playford and West End highways. The state-of-the-art visitor center, open daily 9–5, is the largest National Parks and Wildlife office. Displays and touch

Lots of Remarkable Rocks, Flinders Chase National Park

screens explore the park's history and the different habitats and wildlife in Flinders Chase. The center provides park entry tickets and camping permits, and books stays at the heritage cabins. A shop sells souvenirs and provisions, and there is also a café. ⊠ *South Coast Rd., Flinders Chase* ⊕ *www.environment.sa.gov.au.*

SPORTS AND THE OUTDOORS
FISHING
Fishing is excellent on Kangaroo Island's beaches, bays, and rivers. The island's deep-sea fishing fleet holds several world records for tuna. No permit is required for recreational fishing, but minimum lengths and bag limits apply. You can pick up a fishing guide from the information center in Penneshaw.

Cooinda Fishing Charters. Cooinda runs fishing, diving, and combined fishing and diving charters from half a day to three days out of American River. ⊠ *American River Wharf, Muston* ☎ *0439/867713, 08/8553–1072* ⊕ *www.cooindafishingcharters.com.*

Hog Bay Corner Store & Cafe. You can rent fishing equipment from Hog Bay Corner Store & Cafe. ⊠ *3rd St. at North Terrace, Penneshaw* ☎ *08/8553–1151.*

The Kings Small Boat Fishing Charters. Fishing tours (maximum six passengers) and personalized charters are offered from half a day in American River waters. ⊠ *Bayview Rd., American River* ☎ *08/8553–7003* ⊡ *A$300 per boat (up to 3 people), A$100 per person 4–6 people.*

Turner Fuel. This spot sells fishing tackle and bait. ⊠ *26 Telegraph Rd., Kingscote* ☎ *08/8553–2725.*

SCUBA DIVING

Kangaroo Island waters offer arguably the best temperate-water diving in Australia. Divers can explore some of the more than 50 shipwrecks around the coast, and swim among corals, sponges, and fish. The beautiful leafy sea dragon is endemic to the island's north-coast waters.

Kangaroo Island Dive and Adventures. This company offers dives in unspoiled wilderness areas, shore-based dives in Kingscote, scuba lessons, tuna fishing adventures, and kayak rentals. ⊠ *15 Kingscote Terrace, Kingscote* ☎ *08/8553–3196* ⊕ *www.kangarooislanddiveandadventures. com.au.*

Kangaroo Island Diving Safaris. If you're interested in day trips, liveaboard tours, or dive training courses, Kangaroo Island Diving Safaris is a good place to start. They promise interactions with seals and dolphins on most trips. ⊠ *RSD 451, Kingscote* ☎ *08/8559–3225* ⊕ *www. kidivingsafaris.com.*

WHERE TO STAY

For expanded hotel reviews, visit Fodors.com.

$$
RESORT
Kangaroo Island Wilderness Retreat. With wallabies and possums treating the grounds as their own domain, this eco-friendly retreat is everything a wildlife-loving traveler could want. **Pros:** wonderful experience for animal lovers; free Internet access and DVD rental. **Cons:** only two time slots for dinner; basic rooms might disappoint city slickers. $ *Rooms from: A$190* ⊠ *1 South Coast Rd., Flinders Chase* ☎ *08/8559–7275* ⊕ *www.kiwr.com* ⤳ *18 courtyard rooms, 2 suites, 4 apartments, 7 lodge rooms* ⦙○⦙ *All meals.*

$$$$
HOTEL
ALL-INCLUSIVE
Fodor's Choice
★
Southern Ocean Lodge. This truly remarkable hotel might be the highlight of your trip—if money is no object. **Pros:** superb restaurant; simple but stunning decor exudes luxury and class. **Cons:** if you have to ask the price, you can't afford this place; sophisticated surroundings are not really suitable for children, though kids over six years are welcome. $ *Rooms from: A$990* ⊠ *Hanson Bay Rd., Kingscote* ☎ *08/8559–7347* ⊕ *www.southernoceanlodge.com.au* ⤳ *21 suites* ⦙○⦙ *All-inclusive.*

THE OUTBACK

South Australia is the country's driest state, and its Outback is an expanse of desert vegetation. But this land of scrubby salt bush and hardy eucalyptus trees is brightened after rain by wildflowers—including the state's floral emblem, the blood-red Sturt's desert pea, with its black, olive-like heart. The terrain is marked by geological uplifts, abrupt transitions between plateaus broken at the edges of ancient, long-inactive fault lines. Few roads track through this desert wilderness—the main highway is the Stuart, which runs all the way to Alice Springs in the Northern Territory.

The people of the Outback are as hardy as their surroundings. They are also often eccentric, colorful characters who happily bend your ear over a drink in the local pub. Remote, isolated communities attract loners, adventurers, fortune-seekers, and people simply on the run. In this unyielding country, you must be tough to survive.

COOBER PEDY

850 km (527 miles) northwest of Adelaide.

Known as much for the way most of its 3,500 inhabitants live—underground in dugouts gouged into the hills to escape the relentless heat—as for its opal riches, Coober Pedy is arguably Australia's most singular place. The town is ringed by mullock heaps, pyramids of rock and sand left over after mine shafts are dug.

Opals are Coober Pedy's reason for existence. Australia has 95% of the world's opal deposits, and Coober Pedy has the bulk of that wealth; this is the world's richest opal field.

Coober Pedy is a brick-and-corrugated-iron settlement propped unceremoniously on a scarred desert landscape. It's a town built for efficiency, not beauty. However, its ugliness has a kind of bizarre appeal. There's a feeling that you're in the last lawless outpost in the modern world, helped in no small part by the local film lore—*Priscilla Queen of the Desert, Pitch Black, Kangaroo Jack,* and *Mad Max 3* were filmed here. Once you go off the main street, you get an immediate sense of the apocalyptic.

GETTING HERE AND AROUND

REX/Regional Express Airlines flies direct to Coober Pedy from Adelaide Sunday–Friday. Because it's the only public carrier flying to Coober Pedy, prices are sometimes steep. However, anyone holding a valid ISIC, YHA, or VIP card is eligible for unlimited air travel throughout Australia on the Backpackers Pass for a flat rate of A$499 for one month, or A$949 for two months. The airport is open only when a flight is arriving or departing. At other times, contact the Desert Cave Hotel.

Greyhound Australia buses leave Adelaide's Central Bus Station for Coober Pedy daily. Tickets for the 12-hour ride can cost A$137–A$180 each way.

The main road to Coober Pedy is the Sturt Highway from Adelaide, 850 km (527 miles) to the south. Alice Springs is 700 km (434 miles) north of Coober Pedy. The drive from Adelaide to Coober Pedy takes about nine hours. From Alice Springs it's about seven hours.

A rental car enables you to see what lies beyond Hutchison Street, but an organized tour is a better way to do so. Budget is the only rental-car outlet in Coober Pedy. Although some roads are unpaved—those to the Breakaways and the Dog Fence, for example—surfaces are generally suitable for conventional vehicles. Check on road conditions with the police if there has been substantial rain.

The most interesting route to Flinders Ranges National Park from Adelaide takes you north through the Clare Valley vineyards and Burra's copper-mining villages. For a more direct journey to Wilpena Pound, follow the Princes Highway north to Port Augusta, and then head east toward Quorn and Hawker. A four-wheel-drive vehicle is highly recommended for traveling on the many gravel roads around the national park.

ESSENTIALS

Transportation Coober Pedy Airport ⊠ *Airport Rd., off Stuart Hwy., 2 km [1 mile] north of town* ☎ *08/8672–5688.* **Greyhound Australia** ⊠ *Hutchinson St.* ☎ *1800/801294, 1300/GREYHOUND* ⊕ *www.greyhound.com.au.* **REX/Regional Express** ☎ *13–1713* ⊕ *www.regionalexpress.com.au.*

Visitor Information Coober Pedy Tourist Information Centre ⊠ *Coober Pedy District Council Bldg., Hutchison St., LOT 773* ☎ *1800/637076* ⊕ *www. cooberpedy.sa.gov.au* ☯ *Weekdays 8:30–5, weekends 10–1.* **Wilpena Pound Visitor Centre** ⊠ *1 Wilpena Rd., Hawker* ☎ *08/8648–0048* ☯ *Daily 8–5.*

EXPLORING

Fossicking for opal gemstones—locally called noodling—requires no permit at the Jewellers Shop mining area at the edge of town. Take care in unmarked areas, and always watch your step, as the area is littered with abandoned opal mines down which you might fall. (Working mines are off-limits to visitors.)

Although most of Coober Pedy's devotions are decidedly material in nature, the town does have its share of spiritual houses of worship. In keeping with the town's layout, they, too, are underground. **St. Peter and St. Paul's Catholic Church** is a National Heritage–listed building, and the Anglican **Catacomb Church** is notable for its altar fashioned from a windlass (a winch) and lectern made from a log of mulga wood. The **Serbian Orthodox Church** is striking, with its scalloped ceiling, rock-carved icons, and brilliant stained-glass windows. The **Revival Fellowship Underground Church** has lively gospel services.

IN TOWN

Old Timers Mine. This is a genuine opal mine turned into a museum. Two underground houses, furnished in 1920s and 1980s styles, are part of the complex, where mining memorabilia is exhibited in an extensive network of hand-dug tunnels and shafts. You can also watch demonstrations of opal-mining machines. Tours are self-guided. ⊠ *Crowders Gully Rd. near Umoona Rd.* ☎ *08/8672–5555* ⊕ *www.oldtimersmine. com* ⊠ *A$15* ☯ *Daily 9–5.*

Umoona Opal Mine & Museum. This is an enormous underground complex with an original mine, a noteworthy video on the history of opal mining, an Aboriginal Interpretive Centre, and clean, underground bunk camping and cooking facilities. Guided tours of the mine are available. ⊠ *14 Hutchison St.* ☎ *08/8672–5288* ⊕ *www.umoonaopalmine.com.au* ⊠ *Museum free, tour A$10* ☯ *Daily 8–7; tours at 10, noon, 2, and 4.*

AROUND TOWN

Breakaways. A striking series of buttes and jagged hills centered on the Moon Plain is reminiscent of the American West. There are fossils and patches of petrified forest in this strange landscape, which has appealed to makers of apocalyptic films. *Mad Max 3—Beyond Thunderdome* was filmed here, as was *Ground Zero*. The scenery is especially evocative early in the morning. The Breakaways area is 30 km (19 miles) northeast of Coober Pedy. ■ TIP→ Permits to explore the area cost A$2.20 and can be collected from the Coober Pedy Tourist Information Centre in the District Council Office on Hutchinson Street.

✉ *Off Stuart Hwy., 33 km (20 miles) north of Coober Pedy* ⊕ *www.cooberpedy.sa.gov.au* ✉ *Permits A$2.20.*

Fodor's Choice ★

Mail Run Tour. This 12-hour, 600-km (372-mile) tour through the Outback (A$195) is one of the most unusual experiences anywhere, with stops at Outback cattle stations, bush pubs, and the world's longest man-made structure, the Dingo Fence. Tours depart Monday and Thursday at 8:45 am from Underground Books on Post Office Hill Road. ✉ *Lot 374, Post Office Hill Rd.* ☎ *08/8672–5226, 1800/069911* ⊕ *www.mailruntour.com.*

WHERE TO EAT AND STAY

For expanded hotel reviews, visit Fodors.com.

$

PIZZA

✕ **Stuart Range Caravan Park Pizzeria.** Locals swear that the pizzas at this popular Caravan Park are among Australia's best. The toppings combinations can be classic, creative, or gourmet, such as the Noon (with tomato, mushrooms, and onions) and the Garlic Prawn (with basil pesto and semi-dried tomatoes). $ *Average main: A$20* ✉ *Stuart Hwy. at Hutchison St.* ☎ *08/8672–5179, 1800/067787* ⊕ *www.stuartrangecaravanpark.com.au* ☽ *No lunch.*

$$

AUSTRALIAN

✕ **Umberto's.** Perched atop the monolithic Desert Cave Hotel, this eatery named after the hotel's founding developer is Coober Pedy's most urbane restaurant. The Mod Oz menu takes you from the Outback (oven-baked kangaroo loin with grilled figs) to the sea (lemon sole). $ *Average main: A$26* ✉ *Hutchison St.* ☎ *08/8672–5688* ⊕ *www.desertcave.com.au* ☽ *No lunch.*

$$$

HOTEL

▥ **Desert Cave Hotel.** What may be the world's only underground hotel presents a contemporary, blocky face to the desert town. **Pros:** unique place to stay; pool is welcome relief in the heat. **Cons:** not for the claustrophobic; overpriced for what you get. $ *Rooms from: A$250* ✉ *Lot 1, Hutchison St. at Post Office Hill Rd.* ☎ *08/8672–5688, 1800/088521* ⊕ *www.desertcave.com.au* ⇱ *50 suites incl. 19 underground* ⅋⊙ *Some meals.*

$

HOTEL

▥ **The Underground Motel.** The Breakaways sometimes seem close enough to touch at this hilltop motel, where you can lounge on a veranda watching the sun set on the rock formations 30 km (19 miles) across the desert. **Pros:** lovely patio to sit out on and watch the stars; very helpful owners. **Cons:** slightly out of town, which in the heat is a disadvantage. $ *Rooms from: A$110* ✉ *1185 Catacomb Rd.* ☎ *08/8672–5324* ⊕ *www.theundergroundmotel.com.au* ⇱ *6 rooms, 2 suites* ⅋⊙ *Breakfast.*

FLINDERS RANGES NATIONAL PARK

690 km (430 miles) southeast of Coober Pedy, 460 km (285 miles) northeast of Adelaide.

EXPLORING

Flinders Ranges National Park. Extending north from Spencer Gulf, the Flinders Ranges mountain chain includes one of Australia's most impressive Outback parks. These dry, folded, and cracked mountains, once the bed of an ancient sea, have been sculpted by millions of years of rain and sun. Cypress pine and casuarina cover this furrowed landscape

9

of deep valleys, which slope into creeks lined with river red gums. The area is utterly fascinating—both for geologists and for anyone else who revels in wild, raw scenery and exotic plant and animal life.

The numerous steep trails make the Flinders Ranges ideal for bushwalking, even though the park has few amenities. Water in this region is scarce, and should be carried at all times. The best time for walking is during the relatively cool months between April and October. This is also the wettest time of year, so you should be prepared for rain. Wildflowers, including the spectacular Sturt's desert pea, are abundant between September and late October.

The park's most spectacular walking trail leads to the summit of 3,840-foot **St. Mary's Peak,** the highest point on the Pound's rim and South Australia's second-tallest peak. The more scenic of the two routes to the top is the outside trail (15-km [9-mile] return); give yourself a full day to get up and back. The midsection of the ascent is steep and strenuous, but views from the summit—including the distant white glitter of the salt flats on Lake Frome—make the climb worthwhile. ✉ *End of Wilpena Rd., Hawker* ☎ *08/8648–6419* 🌐 *www.southaustralia.com/FlindersRangesOutback.aspx.*

WHERE TO STAY

For expanded hotel reviews, visit Fodors.com.

$$ RESORT 🏨 **Wilpena Pound Resort.** You couldn't ask for a more idyllic and civilized nature outpost than this popular resort at the entrance to Wilpena Pound. **Pros:** quiet and peaceful rooms; perfect for animal lovers. **Cons:** campsites can be overrun with school groups; permanent tents are overpriced. [$] *Rooms from: A$198* ✉ *1 Wilpena Rd., Hawker* ✣ *156 km (97 miles) off Princes Hwy. via the town of Hawker* ☎ *08/8648–0004* 🌐 *www.wilpenapound.com.au* 🛏 *34 rooms, 26 units* 🍴 *Some meals.*

THE OUTBACK

WELCOME TO THE OUTBACK

TOP REASONS TO GO

★ **National Parks:** With spectacular terrain and one-of-a-kind plant and animal species, rugged national parks tell the story of Australia's ancient landforms, especially across the Top End and Kimberley regions.

★ **Old Culture:** The Red Centre, Top End, and the Kimberley are the best places to experience one of the oldest cultures in the world, that of Australia's Aborigines.

★ **Red Heart:** Watching the sun rise and set at Uluru (Ayers Rock) is a once-in-a-lifetime experience you'll never forget.

★ **Old Culture:** The Kimberley, where a trail of ancient rock paintings can be traced across the land, reveals the history of the world's oldest continuous culture: that of Australia's Aborigines.

★ **Cable Beach:** It may be touristy, but riding a camel into the sunset on one of Australia's most beautiful beaches is hard to resist.

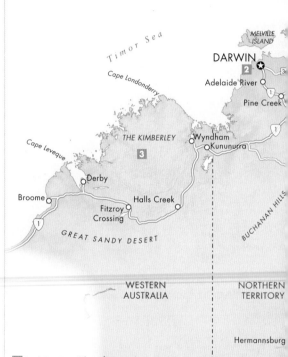

1 Red Centre. Uluru (Ayers Rock) is one of Australia's iconic images, and the main reason people visit the Red Centre. A striking sight, it is one of the world's largest monoliths, the last vestige of an ancient mountain range that looms 1,100 feet above the surrounding plain. But, there is more than just "the Rock" in the Red Centre—traditional Aboriginal "Dreamtime" stories overlie a region rich in geological wonders.

2 The Top End. The "Top End" of Australia packs in some of the world's great natural environments—and with few people to crowd the views. Add in modern and ancient Aboriginal art and locals with a definite individualistic attitude, and

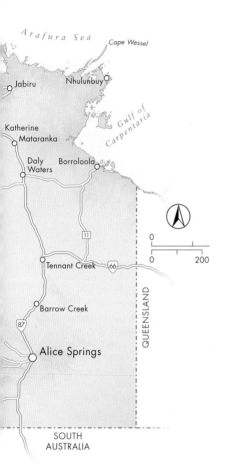

Arafura Sea

Cape Wessel

Jabiru Nhulunbuy

Gulf of Carpentaria

Katherine
Mataranka

Daly   Borroloola
Waters

11

0

0   200

Tennant Creek 66

QUEENSLAND

Barrow Creek

87

Alice Springs

SOUTH
AUSTRALIA

GETTING ORIENTED

Big, vast, expansive, huge—whichever way you cut it, the Northern Territory is daunting. This, in many respects, is the "real Australia" as you imagine it—remote, mostly uninhabited, the landscape ground down over millennia. Getting around by road will absorb days, if not weeks, but fortunately air services can cut the travel times between the gems of this vast area—the Red Centre, the Top End, and the Kimberley—to hours not days.

10

you have an Australia so different from Sydney and Melbourne that you'll think you're in another country entirely.

3 The Kimberley. Look no further than the Kimberley for a genuine Outback experience. This remote

area contains several of Australia's most spectacular national parks, and numerous tropical forests, croc-infested rivers, and soaring cliffs.

ABORIGINAL CULTURE

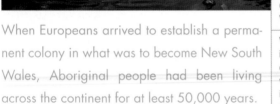

COMMUNITY VALUES

When Europeans arrived to establish a permanent colony in what was to become New South Wales, Aboriginal people had been living across the continent for at least 50,000 years.

Welcome to Country is an important ritual. Protocol dictates that people are welcomed when entering and learning about Country; for many this is simply good manners and respect. It's likely you will enjoy a Welcome to Country if you join any Aboriginal-guided tour.

Perhaps 600 different "clan groups" or "nations"—each with its own distinctive culture and beliefs—greeted the new settlers in a clash of civilizations that remains largely unresolved today. Despite the efforts of governments of all persuasions and society at large, Aboriginal people by all measures—economic, health, social, education—remain an underprivileged group.

But Aboriginal culture as expressed in oral tradition, art, and lifestyle and by sacred sites such as Uluru is of growing interest to travelers. Experiences range from organized tours to dance performances, shopping for traditional Aboriginal artifacts and art, and the opportunity to visit Aboriginal land to experience the daily lives of Aboriginal people. Tourism represents an important source of income ensuring that Aboriginal communities prosper and that their heritage is preserved.

In some cultures there were once strict rules about eye contact; you may find that some people follow this practice and won't make eye contact with you. This, or lowering the eyes, are two actions that are often a show of respect toward older people.

SACRED SITES

Uluru (Ayers Rock) is probably Australia's best-known natural site, but it also has significant cultural meaning for the traditional owners, the Anangu people. They believe they are direct descendants of the beings—which include a python, an emu, a blue-tongue lizard, and a poisonous snake—who formed the land and its physical features during the Tjukurpa (the "Dreamtime," or creation period). Rising more than 1,100 feet from the surrounding plain, Uluru is one of the world's largest monoliths, though such a classification belies the otherworldly, spiritual energy surrounding it.

Kakadu National Park contains some of the best ancient rock art accessible to visitors in Australia. The Anbangbang Gallery has a frieze of Aboriginal rock painting dating back thousands of years, while among the six galleries at Ubirr there is a 49-foot frieze of X-ray paintings depicting animals, birds, and fish. Warradjan Aboriginal Cultural Centre's large display, developed by the local Bininj/Mungguy people, provides detailed information about Aboriginal culture in Kakadu.

Purnululu National Park (the Bungle Bungles) is an amazing geological wonder and a site for Aboriginal culture. Although the Bungle Bungle Range was extensively used by Aboriginal people during the wet season, when plant and animal life was abundant, few Europeans knew of its existence until the mid-1980s. The area is rich in Aboriginal rock art, and there are also many burial sites, although these are not typically open to visitors.

Farther west in the **Kimberley Region** the pearling town of **Broome** is the starting point for many adventure tours into the remote Outback, and visiting Aboriginal communities such as Bardi Creek, Biridu Community, and One Arm Point Community with local Aboriginal guides. Geickie Gorge, Windjana Gorge, and Tunnel Creek combine wilderness scenery with indigenous rock art, lifestyles, and stories from the Dreamtime.

TOP SIGHTS

By far the best way to experience Aboriginal culture is on foot and with an experienced guide, though at some national parks, interpretive centers, signage and—occasionally—self-guided audio equipment mean you can visit on your own. On foot generally requires a level of fitness and surefootedness for trails and pathways; even the best locations are uneven and stony, and can include steep climbs. Boats provide an alternative, such as at Geikie Gorge and Kakadu, where guided tours along the waterways include information about Aboriginal culture.

From Broome, four-wheel-drive safaris can get you into remote Aboriginal communities where you can meet the locals and listen to campfire stories. If mobility is an issue, there are easily accessible interpretive centers at places like Uluru and Kakadu national parks that have extensive displays describing Aboriginal life.

10

Updated by
Lee Atkinson

Few visitors who explore Australia's remote Red Centre and wild Top End are left unmoved by the stark, expansive beauty of the landscape. The Outback's amazing World Heritage national parks, many on the ancestral homelands of the traditional indigenous owners, are home to some of Australia's most fascinating and iconic natural attractions, such as Ulruru (Ayers Rock), the magnificent Bungle Bungles, and the vast bird-filled wetlands and raging waterfalls of Kakadu. The Outback contains deeply carved rock canyons, deserts with unending horizons, and prolific wildlife. It is Australia at its wildest, rawest, and most sublime, and it's a landscape that will sear itself onto your memory forever.

The Top End of Australia is a geographic description—but it's also a state of mind. Isolated from the rest of Australia by thousands of miles of desert and lonely scrubland, Top Enders are different and proud of it, making the most of their isolation with a strongly independent and individualistic attitude. The region is a melting pot of cultures and traditions. Darwin and Broome—closer geographically to the cities of Southeast Asia than to any Australian counterparts—host the nation's most racially diverse populations: Aborigines, Anglos, and Asians share a tropical lifestyle.

In the west, the Kimberley offers some of the most dramatic landscapes in Australia. A land of rugged ranges and vast cattle stations, the Kimberley is still the frontier, a place even few Australians get to see. Like Top Enders, the people of the Kimberley region see themselves as living in a land apart from the rest of the nation, and it's easy to see why: climate extremes, inaccessibility of the landscape, and great distances combine to make the Kimberley one of the world's few uniquely unpeopled spaces.

For thousands of years this area of northern and central Australia has been home to Aboriginal communities that have undiminished ties to the land. Stunning examples of ancient Aboriginal rock art remain—on cliffs, in hidden valleys, and in city art galleries and cooperative art centers in remote communities. Aboriginal artwork has now moved into Australia's mainstream art movement, and some expensive canvases by Aboriginal artists decorate galleries, homes, and corporate boardrooms around the world. But there is more to Aboriginal culture than art, and there is no better place to try and understand it than here, on a guided tour of some of the country's most spiritually significant Aboriginal sites.

PLANNING

WHEN TO GO

May through September (Australia's winter) are the best months to visit the Red Centre and the Top End; nights are crisp and cold and days are pleasantly warm. Summer temperatures in the Centre—which can rise above 43°C (110°F)—are oppressive, while the wet season (December–April) means that Darwin and surroundings are hot, humid, and, well, wet. In the Kimberley May–November is the preferred season, with usually clear skies and balmy days and nights.

In the Top End the year is divided into the wet season (the Wet; December–April) and the dry season (the Dry; May–November). The Dry is a period of idyllic weather with warm days and cool nights, while the Wet brings monsoonal storms that dump an average of 52 inches of rain in a few months and result in widespread road closures. You can also catch spectacular electrical storms, particularly over the ocean. The "Build Up," in October, is the Top End's most oppressive weather period and should be avoided. The Kimberley has a similar wet season; however, the rainfall is less and generally comes in short, heavy storms. Cyclones also occur during this period and can disrupt travel arrangements.

GETTING HERE AND AROUND
AIR TRAVEL

10

Darwin is the main international arrival point. Qantas and Virgin Australia are Australia's main domestic airlines, and both operate an extensive network and regular services crisscrossing the country from all the major cities to regional centers like Alice Springs and Broome. Both airlines also have budget subsidiaries, Jetstar (Qantas) and Tigerair (Virgin Australia). Air North has an extensive network throughout the Top End and covers some Western Australia legs.

CAR AND BUS TRAVEL

Driving around the Northern Territory is relatively easy, with mostly good paved roads and light traffic outside Darwin. But distances can be daunting. For example, Adelaide to Alice Springs via the Stuart Highway is 1,000 miles, and can take 24 hours. From Darwin to Broome is 1,152 miles, a tiring two-day drive. Greyhound Australia operates an extensive network of long-distance coaches. Although major highways remain open, many regional roads are closed during the wet season due to flooding.

TRAIN TRAVEL

Great Southern Railways operates the *Ghan* from Adelaide north to Alice Springs, then on to Darwin twice a week; return services from Darwin to Adelaide are also twice a week.

RESTAURANTS

Restaurants and cafés in the Northern Territory are largely reflective of their location: in the Red Centre you'll find "bush tucker" menus with crocodile, kangaroo, camel, and native fruits, berries, and plants; in Darwin and Broome locally caught seafood are prepared with flavor influences from Asia. Many restaurants and cafés offer alfresco dining. Tips aren't expected, but an extra 10% for exceptional service is welcome. *Prices in the reviews are the average cost of a main course at dinner or, if dinner isn't served, at lunch.*

HOTELS

From five-star to basic, you'll find suitable accommodations throughout the region. The well-known international chains are largely in Darwin, but there are also sublime boutique accommodations set in wilderness or natural settings outside these centers, especially in the Kimberley. You can also experience Outback Australia at homesteads and working cattle stations, while owner-run bed-and-breakfasts provide comfort, charm, and a glimpse of local life. In the cities and the Outback there are plenty of less-than-memorable motels where you can at least get a clean bed for the night. Popular options—especially for families and small groups—are self-contained apartments, villas, and chalets. With two or three bedrooms, living areas, and kitchens, they allow you to save on dining costs by cooking your own meals; these are best if staying more than one night. *Prices in the reviews are the lowest cost of a standard double room in high season. For expanded reviews, facilities, and current deals, visit Fodors.com.*

HEALTH AND SAFETY

If you are self-driving—especially in remote areas—make sure you have enough fuel, water, and food and carry a first-aid kit. Let others know where you are going and for how long. If you go off bushwalking or hiking, bring adequate supplies and directions, and let others know your plan.

There are "critters" to avoid—snakes, crocodiles, and box jellyfish, for example. Mosquitoes are prevalent, so cover up and use a good insect repellent; the worst times for mosquitoes are dawn and dusk.

Respect the Australian sun, especially in summer. Sunburn is a real danger if you don't do what the Australians are urged to do: slip, slap, slop—that is, slip on a hat, slap on sunglasses, and slop on sunscreen. On popular beaches around major cities and towns, lifesavers (lifeguards) are usually on duty and put up flags to swim between, but generally most beaches are unguarded. Take extra care, especially where there are strong currents. Crocodiles are active in many of the Territory's waterways, so obey warning signs and check before swimming.

The emergency contact number for police, fire, and ambulance is ☎ *000*. From a GSM mobile (cell) phone the number is ☎ *112*.

GREAT ITINERARIES

The sheer size of the Northern Territory means it is impossible to cover it all on a short visit. You will need to be selective.

IF YOU HAVE 3 DAYS

Don't even think about trying to do more than one of the major spots or you'll be spending all your time in airports or on the road.

If you choose one of Australia's great icons—Uluru—you could fly directly to Ayers Rock Airport and spend two days there, taking a hike around the rock followed by a look at the **Uluru–Kata Tjuta Cultural Centre** near its base.

The next day take a sightseeing flight by helicopter or fixed-wing aircraft, then visit **Kata Tjuta** (the Olgas) to explore its extraordinary domes and end the day with sunset at the rock. A flight will get you to Alice Springs, where you can tour out to either the Eastern or Western MacDonnell Ranges to explore the gorges and take a dip in a waterhole.

If you make **Darwin** your starting point, head east early on the Arnhem Highway to Fogg Dam to view the birdlife. Continue into **Kakadu National Park** and picnic at the rock-art site at Ubirr. Take a scenic flight in the afternoon, then a trip to the Bowali Visitors Centre, and you can overnight in **Jabiru**.

On the second day, head to Nourlangie Rock; then continue to the Yellow Water Billabong cruise at **Cooinda** and stay there for the night. The next day, drive to **Litchfield National Park** and visit Florence, Tjaynera, or Wangi Falls.

The easiest way to see **Purnululu's** amazing "beehive" rock formations is from the air. To do this you'll need to fly to **Kununurra** from Darwin or **Broome**, then take a sightseeing flight.

TOURS

If you want to avoid the hassles of getting yourself around this vast region, then a tour group is certainly an option. Hundreds of tours and tour operators cover Western Australia and the Northern Territory, and can introduce you to the many experiences on offer here: four-wheel-drive treks, helicopter flights, bush-tucker-gathering expeditions, Aboriginal-guided walks, fishing safaris, and national park tours to name a few.

You can also take a day tour or shorter overnight tours up to, say, five days. Most of these operate from Darwin, Broome, Perth, and Alice Springs. The benefit is that all your transport, accommodation, meals, and sightseeing arrangements are preset, and you will get to see and do things you may otherwise miss if you try to organize them yourself.

Bill Peach Journeys. This agency runs Aircruising Australia, using private aircraft to fly you to the icon attractions of central Australia, staying overnight in best-available hotels and motels. Their 12-day Great Australian Aircruise departs from and returns to Sydney, and includes stops at Longreach (Queensland), Katherine, Kakadu, and Darwin in the Northern Territory; Kununurra and Broome in Western Australia; and

10

finally Uluru and Alice Springs in the Northern Territory. The inclusive cost starts at A$14,995. ☎ *02/9693–2233* ⊕ *www.billpeachjourneys. com.au.*

North Star Cruises. North Star Cruises operates the small luxury-expedition cruise ship *True North*, which takes just 36 passengers on 7-, 10- and 13-night cruises between Broome and Wyndham along the inaccessible Kimberley coastline. The cruises are adventure oriented, with daily activities including scenic walks, fishing, diving, snorkeling, and on-shore picnics. The ship has six expedition craft and its own helicopter for scenic flights. ⊠ *Shop 2, 25 Carnarvon St., Broome* ☎ *08/9192–1829* ⊕ *www.northstarcruises.com.au.*

RED CENTRE

The light in the Red Centre—named for the deep color of its desert soils—has a purity and vitality that photographs only begin to approach. For tens of thousands of years this vast desert territory in the south of the Northern Territory has been home to Australia's Aboriginal people. Uluru, also known as Ayers Rock, is a great symbol in Aboriginal traditions, as are many sacred sites among the Centre's mountain ranges, gorges, dry riverbeds, and spinifex plains.

The essence of this ancient land is epitomized in the paintings of the renowned Aboriginal landscape artist Albert Namatjira and his followers. Viewed away from the desert, their images of the MacDonnell Ranges may appear at first to be garish and unreal in their depiction of purple-and-red mountain ranges and stark-white ghost gum trees. Seeing the real thing makes it difficult to imagine executing the paintings in any other way.

Uluru (pronounced *oo-loo-roo*), that magnificent stone monolith rising from the plains, is but one focus in the Red Centre. Kata Tjuta (*ka*-ta *tchoo*-ta), also known as The Olgas, are another. Watarrka National Park and Kings Canyon, Mt. Conner, and the cliffs, gorges, and mountain chains of the MacDonnell Ranges are other worlds to explore.

The primary areas of interest are Alice Springs, which is flanked by the intriguing Eastern and Western MacDonnell Ranges; Kings Canyon; and Uluru–Kata Tjuta National Park, with neighboring Ayers Rock Resort. Unless you have more than three days, focus on only one of these areas.

ALICE SPRINGS

2,021 km (1,256 miles) northwest of Sydney, 1,319 km (820 miles) north of Adelaide, 1,976 km (1,228 miles) northeast of Perth

Once a ramshackle collection of buildings on dusty streets, Alice Springs—known colloquially as "the Alice" or just "Alice"—is today an incongruously suburban tourist center with a population of more than 30,000 (including about 2,000 Americans, many employed at Pine Gap, a joint Australian and U.S. satellite tracking station) in the middle of the desert. Alice derives most of its income from tourism, and more

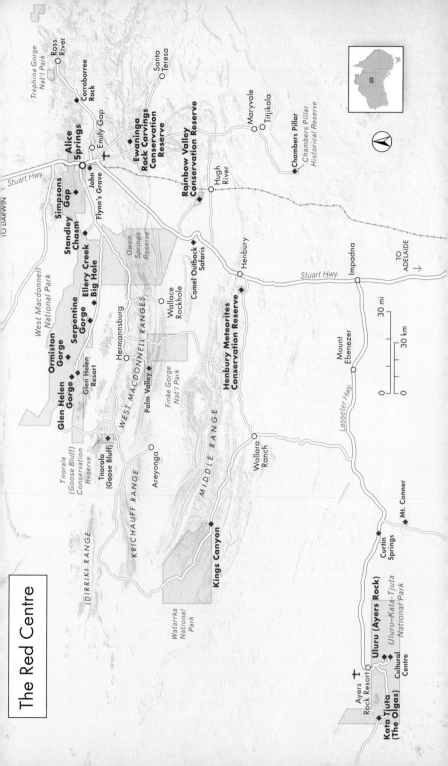

The Red Centre

Trephina Gorge Nat'l Park

Ross River

Corroborree Rock

Santa Teresa

Alice Springs

Emily Gap

Ewaninga Rock Carvings Conservation Reserve

Rainbow Valley Conservation Reserve

Maryvale

Titijikala

Chambers Pillar

Chambers Pillar Historical Reserve

Stuart Hwy.

TO DARWIN

Simpsons Gap

John

Flynn's Grave

Standley Chasm

Hugh River

Owen Springs Reserve

Ellery Creek Big Hole

Serpentine Gorge

Camel Ourback Safaris

Henbury

Stuart Hwy.

Impadna

TO ADELAIDE

West Macdonnell National Park

Ormiston Gorge

Wallace Rockhole

Henbury Meteorites Conservation Reserve

Glen Helen Gorge

Hermannsburg

Glen Helen Resort

WEST MACDONNELL RANGES

Palm Valley

Finke Gorge Nat'l Park

Mount Ebenezer

30 mi

30 km

Tnorala (Goose Bluff) Conservation Reserve

Tnorala (Goose Bluff)

Areyonga

MIDDLE RANGE

Lasseter Hwy.

IDIRRIKI RANGE

KRICHAUFF RANGE

Wallara Ranch

Kings Canyon

Watarrka National Park

Curtin Springs

Mt. Conner

Ayers Rock Resort

Uluru (Ayers Rock)

Uluru-Kata-Tjuta National Park

Cultural Centre

Kata Tjuta (The Olgas)

than 300,000 tourists visit annually. The town's ancient sites, a focus for the Arrernte Aboriginal people's ceremonial activities, lie cheek-by-jowl with air-conditioned shops and hotels. The MacDonnell Ranges dominate Alice Springs, changing color according to the time of day from brick red to purple.

GETTING HERE AND AROUND

Alice Springs Airport is 15 km (9 miles) southeast of town. Qantas flies in and out of Alice Springs daily with direct flights from Brisbane, Sydney, Melbourne, Adelaide, Perth, Darwin, and Cairns, as well as Ayers Rock. Tigerair flies direct from Melbourne and Sydney to Alice Springs on Tuesday, Wednesday, Thursday, and Saturday. It's three hours' flying time from Sydney, Melbourne, and Brisbane; two hours from Adelaide and Darwin; and about 40 minutes from Ayers Rock. Flights run less frequently in the "Wet" summer months.

Alice Springs Airport Shuttle Bus meets every flight. The ride to all hotels and residential addresses in town costs A$15 each way. On request, the bus will also pick you up at your hotel and take you back to the airport, though you must give four hours notice (☎ 08/8952–2111). From the airport, taxi fare to most parts of town is about A$35.

The *Ghan* train leaves Adelaide at 12:20 pm Sunday and Wednesday, arriving in Alice Springs at 1:45 pm Monday and Thursday. Return trains leave Alice Springs at 12:45 pm Thursday and 3:15 pm Sunday, arriving in Adelaide at 12:30 pm on Friday and Monday. On Monday and Thursday at 6 pm the *Ghan* continues to Darwin via Katherine, arriving at 5:30 pm Tuesday and 6:30 pm Friday. Trains from Darwin depart Wednesday at 10 am and Saturday at 9 am. The Alice Springs railway station is 2½ km (1½ miles) west of Todd Mall.

Ghan ✉ *Great Southern Railway* ☎ *08/132147 bookings* ⊕ *www.greatsouthernrail.com.au.*

The Stuart Highway, commonly called the Track, is the only road into Alice Springs. The town center lies east of the highway. The 1,693-km (1,000-mile) drive from Adelaide takes about 24 hours. The drive from Darwin is about 160 km (100 miles) shorter, and takes about 21 hours. Bus tours run between all Red Centre sites, as well as between Alice Springs and Ayers Rock Resort.

Traveling by car will give you the most flexible itinerary—although the trade-off is that you'll travel many long, lonely stretches of one-lane highway through the red-dust desert. Vehicles can be rented at Alice Springs and Ayers Rock Resort. The Central Australian Tourism Industry Association in Alice Springs books tours and rental cars, and provides motoring information.

SAFETY AND PRECAUTIONS

Please note that many Aborigines living in or around Alice Springs have been asked to leave their native villages by tribal elders because of their problems with alcohol. Crime and violence stemming from alcohol abuse can make Alice unsafe at night, and it's recommended you travel only by taxi after dark. Sections of the dry Todd riverbed function as makeshift campsites for some Aborigines, so caution is advised when traversing it.

TIMING

The best time to visit is between May and August, when the weather is mild during the day, although often freezing at night; the summer months can be blisteringly hot, and some tourism services are less frequent or stop altogether. Alice Springs is pleasant enough, but most of the Red Centre's attractions are outside the town. If visiting Uluru is the main reason for your visit to the Red Centre, you can skip Alice Springs and go directly to Uluru–Kata Tjuta National Park.

> **ART HUNT**
>
> If you're looking for Aboriginal art, galleries abound along Todd Mall (the main shopping street); they're filled with canvas and bark paintings, as well as handcrafted didgeridoos and other artifacts. You can also buy art directly from Aborigines on weekends outside Flynn Memorial Church in the mall.

TOURS

Tailormade Tours operate three-hour guided trips that include visits to the Royal Flying Doctor Service Base, School of the Air, Telegraph Station, and Anzac Hill scenic lookout.

ESSENTIALS

Taxi **Alice Springs Taxis** ☎ *08/8952–1877.*

Tour Operators **Tailormade Tours** ☎ *08/8952–1731, 1800/806641* ⊕ *www. tailormadetours.com.au.*

Visitor Information **Tourism Central Australia.** This company dispenses information, advice, and maps and will book tours and cars. ⊠ *Todd Mall at Parsons Street* ☎ *08/8952–5800, 1800/645199* ⊕ *www.discovercentralaustralia.com* ⊗ *Weekdays 8:30–5, weekends 9–4.*

EXPLORING

IN ALICE SPRINGS

FAMILY **Alice Springs Reptile Centre.** Thorny devils, frill-neck lizards, some of the world's deadliest snakes, and "Terry" the saltwater crocodile inhabit this park in the heart of town, opposite the Royal Flying Doctor Service. May to August (winter) the viewing is best from 11 to 3, when the reptiles are most active. There's also a gecko cave. Free talks are conducted daily at 11, 1, and 3:30, during which you can learn to pick up the pythons. ⊠ *9 Stuart Terr.* ☎ *08/8952–8900* ⊕ *www.reptilecentre. com.au* ⊡ *A$16* ⊗ *Daily 9:30–5.*

Royal Flying Doctor Service (RFDS). This much-visited tourist attraction in Alice Springs has a theater, interactive displays, and a full-scale replica of the fuselage of the service's current Pilatus PC12 aircraft. The site has long been the radio base for the Royal Flying Doctor Service, which directs doctors (using aircraft) on their house calls to remote settlements and homes hundreds of miles apart. The RFDS is a vital part of Outback life and fascinating to visitors. The center has historical displays and an audiovisual show. Tours run every half hour throughout the year, and there's a good café at the back. ⊠ *8–10 Stuart Terr.* ☎ *08/8958–8412* ⊕ *www.rfdsalicesprings.com.au* ⊡ *A$12* ⊗ *Mon.–Sat. 9–5, Sun. 1–5.*

10

The Outback just outside Alice Springs

FAMILY **School of the Air.** What do children who live hundreds of miles from the nearest school do for education? Find out at this informative visitor center, which harbors a working school within its walls. Uniquely Australian, discover how distance education has been delivered to the country's most remote parts since 1951; from pedal-operated radio systems to interactive online classes, it's come a long way. Best time to visit is before 3 pm on a school day so you can watch a live lesson; outside of school hours you can see a recorded lesson. ✉ *80 Head St.* ☎ *08/8951–6834* ⊕ *www.assoa.nt.edu.au* ✉ *$7.50* ⊙ *Mon.–Sat. 8:30–4:30, Sun. 1–4:30.*

OUTSIDE ALICE SPRINGS

FAMILY
Fodor'sChoice
★

Alice Springs Desert Park. Focusing on the desert, which makes up 70% of the Australian landmass, this 75-acre site contains 320 types of plants and 120 animal species in several Australian ecosystems—including the largest nocturnal-animal house in the southern hemisphere. An open-air habitat is also open at night, when animals are most active. Local Aboriginal guides share their native stories about the wildlife and the land. Don't miss the twice-daily birds of prey presentation. Allow about four hours to explore the park; it's 6½ km (4 miles) west of Alice Springs, and is on the Alice Wanderer and Tailormade bus itineraries. ✉ *Larapinta Dr.* ☎ *08/8951–8788* ⊕ *www.alicespringsdesertpark.com.au* ✉ *A$25* ⊙ *Daily 7:30–6.*

Araluen Cultural Precinct. The most distinctive building in this complex is the Museum of Central Australia, which charts the evolution of the land and its inhabitants—human and animal—around central Australia. Exhibits include a skeleton of the 10½-foot-tall *Dromornis stirtoni*, the largest bird to walk on Earth, which was found northeast of Alice. Also in the precinct are the (free) Aviation Museum, Territory Craft, and Araluen Centre, home to the Araluen Art Galleries and the Namatjira Gallery, a collection of renowned Aboriginal landscapes. The precinct is 2 km (1 mile) southwest of town, and is on most tourist bus itineraries. The entry pass is good for two days. ⊠ *61 Larapinta Dr.* ☎ *08/8951–1120* ⊕ *artsandmuseums.nt.gov.au/araluen-cultural-precinct* ▧ *A$15* ⊙ *Weekdays 10–4, weekends 11–4.*

OFF THE BEATEN PATH

Spectacular scenery and Aboriginal rock art in the MacDonnell Ranges east of the Alice are well worth a day or more of exploration. Emily Gap (a sacred Aboriginal site), Jessie Gap, and Corroboree Rock, once a setting for important men-only Aboriginal ceremonies, are within the first 44 km (27 miles) east of Alice Springs. Beyond these are Trephina Gorge, John Hayes Rockhole, and N'Dhala Gorge Nature Park (with numerous Aboriginal rock carvings).

Arltunga Historical Reserve, 110 km (69 miles) northeast of Alice, contains the ruins of a 19th-century gold-rush site. If you fancy fossicking (prospecting) for your own semiprecious stones, you can take your pick—and shovel—at Gemtree in the Harts Ranges, 140 km (87 miles) northeast of Alice. Ranger stations (☎ *08/8956–9765*) are at Trephina Gorge and John Hayes Rockhole.

SPORTS AND THE OUTDOORS

CAMEL RIDING

Pyndan Camel Tracks. Daily one-hour camel rides are offered by this company at noon, 2:30, and sunset (each A$50). They explore a valley of diverse habitat about 15 km (9 miles) from Alice Springs and surrounded by the ancient MacDonnell Ranges. Half-day morning rides at 9 am (A$110) allow you to spend more time with your camel, discovering the Ilparpa Valley and stopping for morning tea in a sandy river bed. ☎ *0416/170164* ⊕ *www.cameltracks.com.*

HIKING

The MacDonnell Ranges, the craggy desert mountains that frame Alice Springs, are rich with desert landscapes and Aboriginal significance. The **Emily and Jessie Gaps Nature Park,** located in the Eastern MacDonnells, just 10 km (6 miles) east of Alice Springs along the Ross Highway, contains registered sacred Aboriginal sites, including rock paintings depicting the caterpillar story of the Dreamtime—the Aboriginal stories of the world's creation.

The **Larapinta Trail** is a 223-km-long (145-mile-long) walking track that runs west from Alice Springs into the Western MacDonnell Ranges. It's a spectacular, though challenging, track that takes hikers through classically rugged and dry central Australian landscape. Hikers are encouraged to participate in the voluntary Overnight Walker Registration Scheme, designed to ensure that all trekkers on the trail can be tracked and accounted for in case of emergency. Contact the **Northern Territory Parks & Wildlife Service** (☎ *08/8951–8250*) for more information. **Tourism Central Australia** in Alice Springs (☎ *08/8952–5800*) can also advise you if you're interested in planning bushwalking itineraries.

10

Alice Springs
Desert Park **4**

Alice Springs
Reptile Centre ...**1**

Araluen Cultural
Precinct **3**

Royal Flying
Doctor Service
(RFDS) **2**

School of
the Air **5**

HOT-AIR BALLOONING

Outback Ballooning. At dawn on most mornings hot-air balloons float in the sky around Alice Springs. Outback Ballooning makes hotel pickups about an hour before dawn and returns between 9 am and 10 am. The A$290 fee covers 30 minutes of flying time, insurance, and a champagne breakfast. A 60-minute flight costs A$385. ■■**TIP→ Take warm clothes to beat the pre-dawn chill.** ⊠ *35 Kennett Ct., Ciccone* ☎ *1800/809790* ⊕ *www.outbackballooning.com.au.*

QUAD-BIKE RIDING

Outback Quad Adventures. Hop aboard a motorbike with four huge wheels and explore the Northern Territory's oldest working cattle station with Outback Quad Adventures. The company collects you from Alice Springs and takes you to the station, 17 km (10 miles) out of town on the edge of the MacDonnell Ranges. No special license is needed, and all tours are escorted by guides with two-way radios. Rides of 2½ hours (A$135) and 3½ hours (A$199) and overnight tours—which include barbecue dinner with wine, sleeping bags, and breakfast (A$399)—operate year-round. ⊠ *Undoolya Station, 1 Undoolya Rd.* ☎ *08/8953–0697.*

WHERE TO EAT

$$ AUSTRALIAN 🍴 **Barra on Todd.** As the name suggests, barramundi is the name of the game at this long-established and popular restaurant on the banks of the dry Todd River. You can try Thai-style barramundi spring rolls, saltbush dukkah-crusted barramundi, baked almond barramundi, and herb-and-macadamia-nut over-roasted barramundi, to name a few. The restaurant and bar, which are part of the Chifley Alice Springs Resort, are popular with locals, too. Other delicious dishes on offer include black-pepper crusted kangaroo fillet, wild clover lamb rack, and mango-glazed pork cutlet. And why not try the distinctly Australia dessert of banana Mars bar (yes, a Mars candy bar and a banana wrapped in pastry, deep fried, and served with macadamia nut ice cream and chocolate sauce). [$] *Average main: A$35* ✉ *34 Stott Terr.* ☎ *08/8952–3523.*

$$ AUSTRALIAN 🍴 **Bojangles Saloon and Restaurant.** Cowhide seats, tables made from old *Ghan* railway benches, and a life-size replica of bushranger Ned Kelly give this lively restaurant true Outback flavor. Food is classic Northern Territory tucker: barramundi, kangaroo, camel, emu, thick slabs of ribs, and huge steaks—although it receives mixed reviews. The beer, however, gets consistently high ratings. It's a very touristy watering hole but well worth dropping by for a drink or two and taking a few snaps of the Aussie decor. [$] *Average main: A$30* ✉ *80 Todd St.* ☎ *08/8952–2873.*

$$ ITALIAN 🍴 **Casa Nostra.** Red-and-white checkered tablecloths, Chianti bottles, and plastic grapes festoon this family-run Alice old-timer. Locals crowd in for traditional meat dishes, pizza, and pasta, including Al's Special, a dish of chicken parmigiana paired with pasta in a cream-and-black-pepper sauce that the chef took 15 years to perfect. Take a tip from the regulars and preorder a serving of vanilla slice for dessert, or you might miss out on this scrumptious cake of layered papery pastry and custard cream. BYO beer and wine. [$] *Average main: A$25* ✉ *Undoolya Rd. at Sturt Terr.* ☎ *08/8952–6749* ⏲ *Closed Sun. and late Dec.–mid-Jan.*

$$ ASIAN Fodor's Choice ★ 🍴 **Hanuman Thai.** With its Thai, Nonya (Malaysian), and Indian-flavored menu, this lovely spot is the only place in the desert to offer a range of big-city-quality southeast Asian food. The trumpet mushrooms topped with prawn and pork mince are popular, as is the barramundi poached in coconut sauce. Desserts include black-rice brûlée, and banana spring rolls with butterscotch sauce. This place is as popular with the locals as it is the tourists—which is always a good sign. [$] *Average main: A$25* ✉ *DoubleTree by Hilton Hotel Alice Springs, 82 Barrett Dr.* ☎ *08/8953–7188* 🌐 *www.hanuman.com.au* ✍ *Reservations essential* ⏲ *No lunch weekends.*

WHERE TO STAY

For expanded hotel reviews, visit Fodors.com.

$$$ HOTEL 🏨 **Chifley Alice Springs Resort.** This convenient spot might make you forget that you're surrounded by desert; the palm trees and broad, foliage-fringed lawns and pool area provide respite from the region's red dirt. **Pros:** short walk to shops; tour desk can book variety of tours; great beds; free Wi-Fi in rooms. **Cons:** convention facilities attract tour groups; no views. [$] *Rooms from: A$205* ✉ *34 Stott Terr.* ☎ *08/8951–4545* 🌐 *www.alicespringsresort.com.au* 🛏 *139 rooms* 🍽 *Some meals.*

$$ 🛏 **Desert Palms Resort.** A great place to escape the dust and the dry
RESORT   desert heat, you can dip your toes in the 24-hour island pool with a
waterfall and you might just stay put, lounging and gazing up at the
umbrella-like palm trees and red-and-pink bougainvillea. **Pros:** villas
are private, screened by foliage; palms trees and bougainvillea create
a tropical garden; golf course adjacent; licensed mini mart; free Wi-Fi
in all villas and by the pool. **Cons:** no restaurant; villas are adequate,
not fancy. $ *Rooms from: A$140* ✉ *74 Barrett Dr.* ☎ *08/8952–5977,
1800/678037 reservations* ⊕ *www.desertpalms.com.au* ↝ *80 cabins*
†◯ *Some meals.*

$ 🛏 **DoubleTree by Hilton Hotel Alice Springs.** Landscaped lawns with elegant
HOTEL   eucalyptus and palm trees greet you at this upscale international chain
about a mile outside town. **Pros:** excellent restaurant; many rooms
have views of MacDonnell Ranges; winner of environmental awards.
Cons: in suburban area; no shopping nearby; Internet A$27.50 per day.
$ *Rooms from: A$129* ✉ *82 Barrett Dr.* ☎ *08/8950–8000* ⊕ *double-
tree3.hilton.com* ↝ *229 rooms, 7 suites* †◯ *Some meals.*

$$ 🛏 **Lasseters Hotel Casino.** A popular place thanks to the great views of
HOTEL   the MacDonnell Ranges from guest rooms and the nightlife provided
by the adjacent casino, Lasseters is now the most luxurious resort in
Alice Springs following a A$35 million upgrade. **Pros:** mountain bikes
are complimentary; excellent views of MacDonnell Ranges; casino
and nightlife on-site; free in-room Wi-Fi. **Cons:** adjacent convention
center attracts big groups. $ *Rooms from: A$165* ✉ *93 Barrett Dr.*
☎ *08/8950–7777* ⊕ *www.lasseters.com.au* ↝ *205 rooms* †◯ *No meals.*

NIGHTLIFE AND THE ARTS

THE ARTS

Sounds of Starlight. This is the place to enjoy evocative Outback theater performances and didgeridoo music accompanied by a slide show
of Red Centre images. Ninety-minute concerts (A$30) are held at 8
pm Tuesday, Friday, and Saturday; 45-minute matinee shows (A$20),
April–November, Monday and Thursday 2 pm; call ahead to check
the schedule. Free didgeridoo classes (definitely good value) are held at
the venue during the day. ✉ *40 Todd Mall* ☎ *08/8953–0826* ⊕ *www.
soundsofstarlight.com.*

NIGHTLIFE

Lasseters Hotel Casino. Entry is free at Lasseters Hotel Casino, where the
action goes late into the night. More than 300 slot machines sit here,
plus blackjack, roulette, craps, and baccarat tables. The two bars have
entertainment most nights—the Juicy Rump is a favourite for its live
music. ✉ *93 Barrett Dr.* ☎ *08/8950–7777, 1800/808975.*

SHOPPING

Shopping in Alice Springs is all about Aboriginal art and artifacts.
Central Australian Aboriginal paintings are characterized by intricate
patterns of dots—and are commonly called sand paintings because they
were originally drawn on sand as ceremonial devices.

Papunya Tula Artists. Encouraged to paint a mural on a blank building
wall by a local schoolteacher in 1971, the Papunya Tula artists were
the founders of the modern western and central desert art movement.

This gallery showcases the work of some of the area's best artists. ✉ *63 Todd Mall* ☎ *08/8952–4731* ⊕ *www.papunyatula.com.au.*

Red Kangaroo Books. From bush poetry and traditional bush tucker recipes to anthropological texts on Aborigines and their culture, Red Kangaroo Books has an outstanding collection of literature pertaining to all things Australian. ✉ *79 Todd Mall* ☎ *08/8953–2137* ⊕ *www. redkangaroobooks.com.*

Todd Mall Markets. Held every other Sunday morning from 9 am until around 2 pm, March to December, the markets feature more than 100 stalls of local arts, crafts, and food. ■ **TIP➜ Search for the mango smoothie stall; they are possibly the best in the country.** ✉ *Todd St.* ☎ *0458/555–506* ⊕ *www.toddmallmarkets.com.au.*

WEST MACDONNELL RANGES

The West MacDonnell Ranges—stretching westward from just a few kilometers outside Alice Springs for around 200 km (125 miles)—are a spectacular series of red-rock mountains interspersed by canyons and narrow gorges. Each of the chasms and gorges has its own unique character, and in many there are waterholes where you can swim. Black-footed rock wallabies are among the wildlife to be spotted. The 223-km (139-mile) Larapinta Trail in the park is the showpiece of central Australian bushwalking. The trail is broken into 12 sections, each a one- to two-day walk.

GETTING HERE AND AROUND
To reach all the major sights, the Red Centre Way follows Larapinta Drive (the western continuation of Stott Terrace) from Alice Springs and Namatjira Drive westward to Glen Helen, about 130 km (81 miles) from Alice Springs. Roads leading off it access the highlights.

SAFETY AND PRECAUTIONS
Take care when bushwalking or hiking, as paths are usually rocky and uneven. Snakes inhabit most areas, so be cautious when walking through tall grass. You should always carry and drink plenty of water; at least one liter of water for every hour of walking in hot weather.

TOURS
Emu Run Tours. One-day tours are offered by air-conditioned bus to all the major sights in the park, including Simpsons Gap, Standley Chasm, the Ochre Pits, and Ormiston Gorge. The cost is from A$120. ✉ *72 Todd St., Alice Springs* ☎ *08/8953–7057* ⊕ *www.emurun.com.au.*

Trek Larapinta. Small-group guided bushwalks are available along the Larapinta Trail. Their 6-day tour costs from A$2,095; a longer tour completing the whole trail is 16 days (A$4,395). ☎ *1300/133278* ⊕ *www.treklarapinta.com.au.*

Wayoutback Desert Safaris. This company has a 2½-day, four-wheel-drive tour to the West MacDonnells, camping out overnight. The cost is from A$445. ✉ *30 Kidman St., Alice Springs* ☎ *08/8952–4324* ⊕ *www. wayoutback.com.au.*

10

ESSENTIALS

Visitor Information Simpsons Gap Visitor Information Centre (☎ 08/8951–8250) is 1 km (½ mile) from the turnoff into Simpsons Gap, 18 km (11 miles) from Alice Springs.

EXPLORING

These sights are organized by distance—from closest to farthest—from Alice Springs.

John Flynn's Grave. John Flynn, the Royal Flying Doctor Service founder, is memorialized at this spot. It's on a rise with the stark ranges behind, in a memorable setting 6 km (4 miles) west of Alice Springs. ⊠ *Larapinta Dr., Alice Springs* ⊕ *www.flynntrail.org.au* ⊠ *Free* ⊙ *Daily 24 hrs.*

Simpsons Gap. This is the closest gorge to Alice Springs. There is a bicycle track that winds from the city center to the Gap. Stark-white ghost gums, red rocks, and the purple-haze mountains provide a taste of the scenery to be seen farther into the ranges. The gap can be crowded in the morning and late afternoon, since these are the best times to see rock wallabies. ⊠ *Larapinta Dr., 18 km (11 miles) west of Alice Springs, then 6 km (4 miles) on side road, Alice Springs* ☎ *08/8951–8250* ⊠ *Free* ⊙ *Daily 5–8.*

Standley Chasm. This is one of the most impressive canyons in the MacDonnell Ranges. At midday, when the sun is directly overhead, the 10-yard-wide canyon glows red from the reflected light—this lasts for just 15 minutes. The walk from the parking lot takes about 20 minutes, and is rocky toward the end. There's a kiosk selling snacks and drinks at the park entrance. ⊠ *Larapinta Dr., 40 km (25 miles) west of Alice Springs, then 9 km (5½ miles) on Standley Chasm Rd., Alice Springs* ☎ *08/8956–7440* ⊕ *www.standleychasm.com.au* ⊠ *A$10* ⊙ *Daily 8–6.*

Ellery Creek Big Hole. This is one of the prettiest (and coldest) swimming holes in the Red Centre. It's also the deepest and most permanent water hole in the area, so you may glimpse wild creatures like wallabies or goannas (monitor lizards) quenching their thirst. Take the 3-km (2-mile) Dolomite Walk for a close-up look at this fascinating geological site. ⊠ *Namatjira Dr., Alice Springs* ⚑ *88 km (55 miles) west of Alice Springs* ☎ *08/8951–8250.*

Serpentine Gorge. This site is best experienced by taking a refreshing swim through the narrow, winding gorge. According to an Aboriginal myth a fierce serpent makes its home in the pool, hence the name. ⊠ *Namatjira Dr., 99 km (61 miles) west of Alice Springs, Alice Springs* ☎ *08/8951–8250.*

Glen Helen Gorge. The gorge slices through the MacDonnell Ranges, revealing dramatic rock layering and tilting. The gorge was cut by the sporadic Finke River, often described as the oldest river in the world. Here the river forms a broad, cold, permanent water hole that's perfect for a bracing swim. ⊠ *Namatjira Dr., 132 km (82 miles) west of Alice Springs, Alice Springs* ☎ *08/8951–8250.*

Ormiston Gorge. This gorge is breathtaking. A short climb takes you to Gum Tree Lookout, where you can see the spectacular 820-foot-high red gorge walls rising from the permanent pool below. There is a water

CLOSE UP

The Heartland

For most Australians the Red Centre is the mystical and legendary core of the continent, and Uluru is its beautiful focal point. Whether they have been there or not, locals believe its image symbolizes a steady pulse that radiates deep through the red earth, through the heartland, and all the way to the coasts.

Little more than a thumbprint within the vast Australian continent, the Red Centre is harsh and isolated. Its hard, relentless topography (and lack of conveniences) makes this one of the most difficult areas of the country to survive in, much less explore. But the early pioneers—some foolish, some hardy—managed to set up bases that thrived. They created cattle stations, introduced electricity, and implemented telegraph services, enabling them to maintain a lifestyle that, if not luxurious, was at least reasonably comfortable.

The people who now sparsely populate the Red Centre are a breed of their own. Many were born and grew up here, but many others were "blow-ins," immigrants from far-flung countries and folk from other Australian states who took up the challenge to make a life in the desert and stayed on as they succeeded. Either way, folks out here have a few common characteristics. They're laconic and down-to-earth, canny and astute, and likely to try to pull your leg when you least expect it.

No one could survive the isolation without a good sense of humor: Where else in the world would you hold a bottomless-boat race in a dry riverbed? The Henley-on-Todd, as it is known, is a sight to behold, with dozens of would-be skippers bumbling along within the bottomless-boat frames.

As the small towns grew and businesses quietly prospered in the mid-1800s, a rail link between Alice Springs and Adelaide was planned. However, the undercurrent of challenge and humor that touches all life here ran through this project as well. Construction began in 1877, but things went wrong from the start. No one had seen rain for ages, and no one expected it; hence, the track was laid right across a floodplain. It wasn't long before locals realized their mistake, when intermittent heavy floods regularly washed the tracks away. The railway is still in operation today, and all works well, but its history is one of many local jokes here.

The Red Centre is a special place where you will meet people whose generous and sincere hospitality may move you. The land and all its riches offer some of the most spectacular and unique sights on the planet, along with a sense of timelessness that will slow you down and fill your spirit. Take a moment to shade your eyes from the sun and pick up on the subtleties that nature has carefully protected and camouflaged here, and you will soon discover that the Red Centre is not the dead center.

10

Standley Chasm, West MacDonnell Ranges near Alice Springs

hole suitable for swimming. Trails include the 7-km (4½-mile) Ormiston Pound Walk. ⊠ *Namatjira Dr., Alice Springs* ✢ *135 km (84 miles) west of Alice Springs* ☎ *08/8956–7799.*

WHERE TO STAY

For expanded hotel reviews, visit Fodors.com.

$$ **Glen Helen Resort.** Better described as an Outback lodge, Glen Helen
RESORT Resort earns its charm from its traditional bush welcome and atmosphere. **Pros:** traditional Outback Australia atmosphere; easy access to Larapinta Walking Trail; plenty of opportunities to see local fauna. **Cons:** limited amenities in motel rooms; rooms 10–17 are next to the generator and very noisy. $ *Rooms from: A$175* ⊠ *1 Namatjira Dr., Alice Springs* ✢ *135 km (84 miles) west of Alice Springs* ☎ *08/8956–7489* ⊕ *www.glenhelen.com.au* ⤳ *25 motel rooms, 10 bunkhouse rooms, 105 unpowered sites, 38 powered sites* ❏ *Some meals.*

OFF THE BEATEN PATH

The 440-km (273-mile) drive to Uluru from Alice Springs along the Stuart and Lasseter highways takes about five hours—or longer if you veer off the track to see some other impressive geological sites.

Ewaninga Rock Carvings Conservation Reserve. More than 3,000 ancient Aboriginal rock engravings (petroglyphs) are etched into sandstone outcrops in Ewaninga Rock Carvings Conservation Reserve, 39 km (24 miles) south of Alice on the road to Chamber's Pillar. Early-morning and late-afternoon light are best for photographing the lines, circles, and animal tracks. A 2-km (1-mile) trail leads to several art sites. The reserve is open all day year-round and is accessible by regular (rather than four-wheel-drive) cars. ⊠ *Old South Rd., 39 km (24 miles) south of Alice Springs* ☎ *08/8951–8250* ❏ *Free.*

Henbury Meteorites Conservation Reserve. The Henbury Meteorites craters, 12 depressions between 6 feet and 600 feet across, are believed to have been formed by a meteorite shower about 5,000 years ago. One is 60 feet deep. To get here, you must travel 13 km (8 miles) off the highway on an unpaved road—conventional 2WD sedans will be fine. ⊠ *Ernest Giles Rd., 114 km (71 miles) south of Alice Springs and 13 km (8 miles) west of Stuart Hwy.* ☎ *08/8951–8250.*

Fodor'sChoice

★

Kings Canyon. In **Watarrka National Park,** Kings Canyon is one of the most spectacular sights in central Australia. Sprawling in scope, the canyon's sheer cliff walls shelter a world of ferns and woodlands, permanent springs, and rock pools. The main path is the 6-km (4-mile) Canyon Walk, which starts with a short but steep climb from the car park to the top of the escarpment; the view 886 feet down to the base of the canyon is amazing. An easier walk, called the Creek Walk, starts at the car park and winds through the base of the canyon and is just as worthwhile. Alternatively, see it all from above during the half-hour scenic helicopter flight over the canyon and range from Kings Canyon Resort (A$275 or A$145 for 15 minutes). ⊠ *Luritja Rd., 167 km (104 miles) from turnoff on Lasseter Hwy., Alice Springs.*

Rainbow Valley Conservation Reserve. Amazing formations in the sandstone cliffs of the James Range take on rainbow colors in the early-morning and late-afternoon light. The colors have been caused by water dissolving the red iron in the sandstone, and further erosion has created dramatic rock faces and squared towers. To reach the reserve, turn left off the Stuart Highway 75 km (46 miles) south of Alice. The next 22 km (13 miles) are on a dirt track, requiring a four-wheel-drive vehicle. ⊠ *Stuart Hwy., Alice Springs* ☎ *08/8951–8250* ⊕ *www.nt.gov.au/nreta/parks/find/rainbowvalley.html* ⊠ *Free.*

ULURU AND KATA TJUTA

It's easy to see why the Aborigines attach spiritual significance to Uluru (Ayers Rock). It rises magnificently above the plain and dramatically changes color throughout the day. At more than 1,100 feet, Uluru is one of the world's largest monoliths, though such a classification belies the otherworldly, spiritual energy surrounding it. The Anangu people are the traditional owners of the land around Uluru and Kata Tjuta. They believe they are direct descendants of the beings—which include a python, an emu, a blue-tongue lizard, and a poisonous snake—who formed the land and its physical features during the Tjukurpa (the "Dreamtime," or creation period).

Kata Tjuta (the Olgas), 53 km (33 miles) west of Uluru, is a series of 36 gigantic rock domes hiding a maze of fascinating gorges and crevasses. The names Ayers Rock and the Olgas are used out of familiarity alone; at the sites themselves, the Aboriginal Uluru and Kata Tjuta are the respective names of preference. The entire area is called Yulara, though the airport is still known as Ayers Rock.

Uluru and Kata Tjuta have very different compositions. Monolithic Uluru is a type of sandstone called arkose, while the rock domes at Kata Tjuta are composed of conglomerate. Both of these intriguing

10

sights lie within Uluru–Kata Tjuta National Park, which is protected as a World Heritage site. The whole experience is a bit like seeing the Grand Canyon turned inside out, and a visit here will be remembered for a lifetime.

In terms of where to eat and stay, Ayers Rock Resort, officially known as the township of Yulara, is a complex of lodgings, restaurants, and facilities, and is base camp for exploring Uluru and Kata Tjuta. The accommodations and services here are the only ones in the vicinity of the national park. Uluru is about a 20-minute drive from the resort area (there's a sunset-viewing area on the way); driving to Kata Tjuta will take another 30 minutes. The park entrance fee of A$25 is valid for three days.

The resort "village" includes a bank, newsstand, supermarket, several souvenir shops, Aboriginal art gallery, hair salon, and child-care center.

The accommodations at the resort, which range from luxury hotels to a campground, are all run by Voyages Indigenous Tourism Australia and share many of the same facilities. Indoor dining is limited to each hotel's restaurants and the less-expensive Geckos Cafe, all of which can be charged back to your room. All reservations can be made through Voyages Indigenous Tourism Australia (⊕ *www.voyages.com.au*)on-site, or their central reservations service in Sydney.

WATCH THE SKY

More stars and other astronomical sights, such as the fascinating Magellanic Clouds, are visible in the southern hemisphere than in the northern, and the desert night sky shows off their glory with diamond-like clarity. Look out for the Southern Cross, the constellation that navigators used for many centuries to find their way—most Australians will proudly point it out for you.

GETTING HERE AND AROUND

Qantas, along with its budget subsidiary, Jetstar, operates direct flights from Sydney and Cairns, and Virgin Australia flies direct from Sydney to Ayers Rock Airport, which is 5 km (3 miles) north of the resort complex. Passengers from other capital cities fly to Alice Springs to connect with flights to Ayers Rock Airport. Qantas flies daily 40-minute flights from Alice Springs to Ayers Rock.

AAT Kings runs a complimentary shuttle bus between the airport and Yulara, which meets every flight. If you have reservations at the resort, representatives wait outside the baggage-claim area of the airport to whisk you and other guests away on the 10-minute drive.

If you're driving from Alice Springs, it's a five-hour-plus, 440-km (273-mile) trip to Ayers Rock Resort. The road is paved, but lacks a shoulder, and is one lane in each direction for the duration, making it challenging and risky to overtake the four-trailer-long road trains. The route often induces fatigue; avoid driving at night as wildlife is prolific and you've a good chance of colliding with a kangaroo.

From the resort it's 19 km (12 miles) to Uluru or 53 km (33 miles) to Kata Tjuta. The road to Kata Tjuta is paved.

If you prefer to explore Uluru and Kata Tjuta on your own schedule, then renting your own car is a good idea; the only other ways to get to the national park are on group bus tours or by chauffeured taxi or coach. Avis, Hertz, and Thrifty all rent cars at Ayers Rock Resort. Arrange for your rental early, since cars are limited.

Transportation Contacts Automobile Association of N.T. ☏ *08/8956–2188, 13–1111 emergency road assistance* ⊕ *www.aant.com.au.***AAT Kings** ☏ *08/8956–2171, 1300/228546* ⊕ *www.aatkings.com.* **N.T. Road Report** ☏ *1800/246199* ⊕ *www.ntlis.nt.gov.au/roadreport/.*

SAFETY AND PRECAUTIONS

Water is vital in the Red Centre. It is easy to forget, but the dry atmosphere and the temperatures can make you prone to dehydration. If you are walking or climbing, you will need to consume additional water at regular intervals. You should carry at least 2 liters of water for every hour. Regardless of where you plan to travel, it is essential to carry plenty of water, 20 liters minimum.

TIMING

If seeing Uluru is your reason for visiting the Red Centre, there are tours that fly in and out, stopping just long enough to watch the rock at sunset. However, for a more leisurely visit, allow two days so you can also visit Kata Tjuta (The Olgas) nearby.

TOURS

AIR TOURS The best views of Uluru and Kata Tjuta are from the air. Light-plane tours, with courtesy hotel pickup from Ayers Rock Resort hotels, include 40-minute flights over Ayers Rock and The Olgas, and day tours to Kings Canyon and a huge meteorite crater known as Gosses Bluff. Prices run from A$105 to A$670 per person; for options, contact Ayers Rock Resort. Helicopter flights are A$140 per person for 15 minutes over Ayers Rock, or A$275 for 30 minutes over The Olgas and the rock.

Air Tour Contacts Ayers Rock Helicopters ☏ *08/8956–2077* ⊕ *www.helicoptergroup.com.* **Ayers Rock Scenic Flights** ☏ *08/8956–2345* ⊕ *www.ayersrockresort.com.au.***Professional Helicopter Services** ☏ *08/8956–2003* ⊕ *www.phs.com.au.*

ABORIGINAL TOURS Ayers Rock Resort organizes trips through the Uluru and Kata Tjuta region led by local Aboriginal people. Tours, which leave from the resort, include the guided bush tucker tours (A$85) and full-day 4WD trips to Cave Hill and into the desert of the Pitjantjatjara Lands of Central Australia (A$155) as well as sunrise tour at the base of Uluru (A$155 with breakfast). Guides are Aborigines who work with interpreters. Aboriginal art aficionados can attend dot-painting workshops (A$69).

CAMEL TOURS A great way to get out in the open and see the sights is from the back of one of the desert's creatures. Uluru Camel Tours has sunrise and sunset tours that last for 2½ hours for A$119; tours leave from the Ayers Rock Resort.

Uluru Camel Tours ☏ *08/8956–2444* ⊕ *ulurucameltours.com.au.*

ESSENTIALS

Banks and Currency Exchange ANZ bank has a branch and ATM at Yulara Village at Ayers Rock Resort.

Taxi Uluru Express ☎ 08/8956–2019 ⊕ www.uluruexpress.com.au.

Visitor Information The Uluru–Kata Tjuta Cultural Centre is on the park road just before you reach the rock. It also contains the park's ranger station. The Cultural Centre is open daily 7–6. The Ayers Rock Visitor Centre in the town Square at Yulara is open daily 9:30–4:30 and includes an interesting free museum.

Ayers Rock Visitor Centre ☎ 08/8957–7377. **Central Reservations Service** ✉ Ayers Rock Resort ☎ 1300/134044 ⊕ www.ayersrockresort.com.au. **Uluru–Kata Tjuta Cultural Centre** ☎ 08/8956–1128.

EXPLORING

Fodor's Choice
★

Kata Tjuta. Many visitors feel that Kata Tjuta is more satisfying to explore than Uluru. Uluru is one immense block, so you feel as if you're always on the outside looking in. Kata Tjuta, as its Aboriginal name ("many heads") suggests, is a collection of huge rocks hiding numerous gorges and chasms that you can enter and explore.

There are three main walks, the first from the parking lot into Walpa Gorge (formerly known as Olga Gorge), the deepest valley between the rocks. This is a 2-km (1-mile) walk, and the round-trip journey takes about one hour. The gorge is a desert refuge for plants and animals. The rocky track gently rises along a moisture-rich gully, passing inconspicuous rare plants and ending at a grove of flourishing spearwood.

More rewarding, but also more difficult, is the Valley of the Winds Walk. This 7½-km (4½-mile) walk is along a stony track to two spectacular lookouts—Karu and Karingana. Experienced walkers can complete this walk in about three hours. The Valley of the Winds walk is closed when temperatures rise above 36°C (97°F), which is after 11 am most days in summer.

The Kata Tjuta Viewing Area, 25 km (16 miles) along the Kata Tjuta Road, offers a magnificent vista, and is a relaxing place for a break. It's 600 meters from the car park, and interpretive panels explain the natural life around you. ✉ *Lasseter Hwy., 53 km (33 miles) west of Yulara.*

Fodor's Choice
★

Uluru. An inevitable sensation of excitement builds as you approach this great monolith. If you drive toward it in a rental car, you may find yourself gasping at the first glimpse through the windshield; if you're on a tour bus, you'll likely want to grab the person sitting next to you and point out the window as it looms larger and larger. Rising like an enormous red mountain in the middle of an otherwise completely flat desert, Uluru is a marvel to behold.

Uluru is circled by a road and walking trails. Two car parks—Mala and Kuniya—provide access for several of the walks, or you can choose to do the full circle of the Rock on the Base Walk.

As you work your way around Uluru, your perspective of the great rock changes significantly. You should allow four hours to walk the 10 km (6 miles) around the rock and explore the several deep crevices along the way. Some places are Aboriginal sacred sites and cannot be entered, nor can they be photographed. These are clearly signposted. Aboriginal art can be found in caves at the rock's base.

If you're looking for an easy walk that takes you just partway around the base, the **Mala Walk** is 2 km (1 mile) in length and almost all on flat land. The walk goes to the Kanju Gorge from the base of the climbing trail; park rangers provide free tours daily at 8 am from October to April and at 10 am from May to September.

The **Liru Walk** starts at the cultural center and takes you to the base of the Rock. Along the way are stands of mulga trees and—after rain—wildflowers. The track is wheelchair accessible, and the walk is an easy 1½ hours.

On the southern side of Uluru, the Kuniya Walk and Mutitjulu Waterhole trail starts at the Kuniya car park and is an easy 45-minute walk along a wheelchair-accessible trail to the water hole, home of Wanampi, an ancestral snake. A rock shelter used by Aborigines houses rock art.

Another popular way to experience Uluru is far less taxing but no less intense: watching the natural light reflect on it from one of the two sunset-viewing areas. As the last rays of daylight strike, the rock positively glows as if lighted from within. Just as quickly, the light is extinguished and the color changes to a somber mauve and finally to black. ✉ *Lasseter Hwy., Yulara.*

Uluru–Kata Tjuta Cultural Centre. The cultural center is the first thing you'll see after entering the park through a tollgate. The two buildings are built in a serpentine style, reflecting the Kuniya and Liru stories about two ancestral snakes who fought a long-ago battle on the southern side of Uluru. Inside, you can learn about Aboriginal history and the return of the park to Aboriginal ownership in 1983. There's also an excellent park ranger's station where you can get maps and hiking guides, as well as two art shops where you'll likely see indigenous artists at work. ✉ *Off Lasseter Hwy., Yulara* ☎ *08/8956–1128.*

WHERE TO EAT

$$ MEDITERRANEAN 🍴 **Geckos Cafe.** In the resort's main shopping center, this is the most casual dining option on-site, and relative to other eateries, it's quite reasonably priced. The all-day dining options include affordable appetizers, hamburgers, pastas, and pizzas. [$] *Average main: A$24* ✉ *Yulara Centre, Town Sq., Yulara* ☎ *08/8957–7722.*

$$$ AUSTRALIAN 🍴 **Mayu Restaurant.** This is by far, the resort's best food. The decor reflects local legends with a Kuniya Dreaming mural covering the rear wall. Appetizers and main courses are named after the Australian states. Specialties include barramundi and steak, prepared with a combination of traditional and Mod Oz flavors. [$] *Average main: A$37* ✉ *Sails in the Desert hotel, Yulara Dr., Yulara* ☎ *08/8957–7714* ✍ *Reservations essential* 🕒 *Closed Mon. and Tues. No lunch.*

$$ AUSTRALIAN 🍴 **Pioneer BBQ and Bar.** You'll see why Australians love cooking and dining outdoors at this eatery at the hostel-style Outback Pioneer Hotel & Lodge. You can order steak, prawn skewers, or a kangaroo kebab from the server, and then cook it to your liking on huge barbecues. [$] *Average*

10

The monumental Uluru as seen from the air

main: *A$30* ✉ *Outback Pioneer Hotel & Lodge, Yulara Dr., Yulara* ☎ *08/8957–7605* ⊘ *No lunch (bar is open).*

$

ECLECTIC

✕ **Pira Pool Bar.** A casual poolside bar at Sails in the Desert hotel, Pira offers an all-day menu, serving simple meals from 10 am to 7 pm; there's also a children's menu available. It's a nice spot for a late afternoon cocktail. $ *Average main: A$16* ✉ *Sails in the Desert Hotel, Yulara Dr., Yulara* ☎ *08/8957–7417.*

$$$$

AUSTRALIAN

Fodor's Choice

★

✕ **Sounds of Silence.** The most memorable group-dining experience in the region is the unique, but expensive (A$185 including transfers) Sounds of Silence, an elegant (although heavily attended) outdoor dinner served on a dune that provides sunset views of either Uluru or Kata Tjuta. Australian wines and Northern Territory specialty dishes—including bush salads and Australian game—are served at a lookout before you progress to a buffet meal on tables covered with crisp white linens, right in the desert. An astronomer takes you on a stargazing tour of the southern sky while you dine. A more intimate small-group *table d'hôte* four-course dinner (maximum 20 diners) is also available, called Tali Wiru, at a different vantage point where tables are set for two, four, or six (A$295). The dining tour includes transport to and from your hotel at Yulara. $ *Average main: A$185* ✉ *Yulara* ⊕ *www.ayersrockresort.com.au/sounds-of-silence* ⌂ *Reservations essential.*

WHERE TO STAY
For expanded hotel reviews, visit Fodors.com.

$$$$

HOTEL

🛏 **Desert Gardens Hotel.** This is the only hotel-style accommodation in the area that offer views of Uluru from (some) rooms. **Pros:** a relatively affordable view of Uluru *(compared to ⇨ Longitude 131, below);*

CLOSE UP

Climbing the Rock . . . or Not

There's only one trail that leads to the top of the rock. Though many people visit Uluru with the explicit intention of climbing it, there are a few things you should bear in mind before attempting this. First, Aboriginal people consider climbing the rock to be sacrilege—so if you believe in preserving the sanctity of sacred native sites, you should be content with admiring it from below. Your entry pass into the park even says, "It is requested that you respect the wishes of the Anangu by not climbing Uluru." The climb is not closed;

the Aboriginal people prefer that you choose to respect their law and culture by not climbing.

Second, if you do decide to make the climb, be aware that it's a strenuous hike, and not suitable for those who aren't physically fit. The ascent is about 1½ km (1 mile), and the round-trip climb takes about three hours. Sturdy hiking boots, a hat, sunscreen, and drinking water are absolute necessities. The climb is closed when temperatures rise above 36°C (97°F)—which means after 9 am most mornings in summertime.

central location for resort facilities; shady gardens among gum trees. **Cons:** busy resort entrance road passes hotel. $ *Rooms from: A$398* ⊠ *Yulara Dr., Yulara* ☎ *08/8957–7701* ⊕ *www.ayersrockresort.com.au/ desert/* ⮢ *218 rooms* ⊠ *Some meals.*

$$$$
RENTAL
⊞ **Emu Walk Apartments.** Self-catering one- and two-bedroom apartments with fully equipped kitchens, separate living rooms, and daily maid service are available at Emu Walk Apartments. **Pros:** extra beds ideal for families or traveling companions; kitchen allows for self-catering; adjacent to resort dining options and shops. **Cons:** room rates are pricey; rooms need refurbishment; limited amenities in rooms. $ *Rooms from: A$398* ⊠ *Yulara Dr., Yulara* ☎ *08/8957–7701* ⊕ *www.ayersrockresort. com.au/emu/* ⮢ *40 1-bedroom and 20 2-bedroom apartments* ⊠ *Some meals.*

$$$$
RESORT
ALL-INCLUSIVE
⊞ **Longitude 131°.** Set on its own in the desert 3 km (2 miles) from Ayers Rock Resort, a stay at Longitude 131° is the be-all and end-all of Outback luxury with 15 "tents" that pop out of the desert like a colony of perfect white domes. **Pros:** luxury tented accommodation, some convertible to twin share; dinner under the stars; touring included; attentive staff. **Cons:** the price is steep (though it is an all-inclusive experience); no bathtubs; minimum two-night stay. $ *Rooms from: A$2,200* ⊠ *Yulara* ☎ *08/8957–7131* ⊕ *www.longitude131.com.au* ⮢ *15 tents* ⊠ *Multiple meal plans.*

$$$
HOTEL
FAMILY
⊞ **Outback Pioneer Hotel & Lodge.** Outback Pioneer Hotel & Lodge is the most affordable hotel option at the resort and the most popular. **Pros:** lodge rooms are cheapest in the resort; swimming-pool area. **Cons:** resort shuttle bus to shops; hotel rooms are basic for the price. $ *Rooms from: A$260* ⊠ *Yulara Dr., Yulara* ☎ *08/8957–7606* ⊕ *www. ayersrockresort.com.au/outback/* ⮢ *125 hotel rooms, 42 budget rooms (30 with bathroom, 12 without bathroom); 168 lodge bunk beds* ⊠ *Some meals.*

10

"As we drove from Uluru (Ayers Rock), we approached Kata Tjuta. It consists of 36 domes and is as impressive and spiritual as Uluru." —Photo by Gary Ott, Fodors.com member

$$$$ RESORT **Sails in the Desert.** Architectural shade sails, ghost-gum-fringed lawns, Aboriginal art, and numerous facilities distinguish this upscale hotel option. **Pros:** Aboriginal artworks featured throughout; kids under 12 stay free. **Cons:** pricey. [$] *Rooms from: A$498* ✉ *Yulara Dr., Yulara* ☎ *08/8957–7417* 🌐 *www.ayersrockresort.com.au/sails* *214 rooms, 18 suites* 🍴 *Some meals.*

SHOPPING

Uluru–Kata Tjuta Cultural Centre. The cultural center not only has information about the Anangu people and their culture, it also houses beautiful art for purchase. The Ininti Cafe (☎ *08/8956–2214*) carries souvenirs and light food. The nearby Maruku Arts (☎ *08/8956–2558*) is owned by Aborigines and sells Aboriginal paintings and handicrafts. Canvases drape the walls at Walkatjara Art Centre (☎ *08/8956–2537*), where stories of Anangu culture and heritage are told. The cultural center itself is open daily 7–6 (information desk 8–5); Ininti Cafe is open daily 7–5; Maruku Arts is open daily 7:30–5:30; and Walkatjara art center is open daily 9–5. ✉ *Uluru–Kata Tjuta National Park* ☎ *08/8956–1128.*

THE TOP END

From Arnhem Land in the east—home to remote Aborigines—to the lush tropical city of Darwin and on to Broome in the west, the Top End is a region where individualistic people carve out their lives in what could be considered the real Australia. The region offers some of the most dramatic landscapes in Australia: a land of rugged ranges, tropical wetlands, and desert, of vast cattle stations and wonderful national

parks, including the bizarre, beautiful, red-and-black-stripe sandstone domes and towers of Purnululu National Park and Kakadu National Park, a wilderness area that is one of Australia's natural jewels and the reason many people come to the Top End.

DARWIN

3,146 km (1,955 miles) northwest of Sydney, 2,609 km (1,621 miles) north of Adelaide.

Darwin is Australia's most colorful, and exotic, capital city. Surrounded on three sides by the turquoise waters of the Timor Sea, the streets are lined with tropical flowers and trees. Warm and dry in winter, hot and steamy in summer, it's a relaxed and casual place, as well as a beguiling blend of tropical frontier outpost and Outback hardiness. Thanks to its close proximity to Southeast Asia and its multicultural population it also seems more like Asia than the rest of Australia.

Darwin is a city that has always had to fight for its survival. The seductiveness of contemporary Darwin lifestyles belies a history of failed attempts that date from 1824 when Europeans attempted to establish an enclave in this harsh, unyielding climate. The original 1869 settlement, called Palmerston, was built on a parcel of mangrove wetlands and scrub forest that had changed little in 15 million years. It was not until 1911, after it had already weathered the disastrous cyclones of 1878, 1882, and 1897, that the town was named after the scientist who had visited Australia's shores aboard the *Beagle* in 1839. During World War II it was bombed more than 60 times, as the harbor full of warships was a prime target for the Japanese war planes. Then, on the night of Christmas Eve 1974, the city was almost completely destroyed by Cyclone Tracy, Australia's greatest natural disaster.

It's a tribute to those who stayed and to those who have come to live here after Tracy that the rebuilt city now thrives as an administrative and commercial center for northern Australia. Old Darwin has been replaced by something of an edifice complex—such buildings as Parliament House and the Supreme Court all seem very grand for such a small city, especially one that prides itself on its casual, outdoor-centric lifestyle.

Today Darwin is the best place from which to explore Australia's Top End, with its wonders of Kakadu and the Kimberley region.

GETTING HERE AND AROUND

Darwin's International Airport is serviced from overseas by Qantas, Jetstar, Philippine Airlines, Air Asia, and Air North. Qantas flies from Darwin to Bali several times a week, SilkAir and Jetstar connect Darwin with Singapore, and Air North flies to East Timor.

Qantas, Air North, Virgin Australia, and Jetstar fly into Darwin regularly from other parts of Australia and operate regional flights within the Top End. Air North flies west to Kununurra and Broome, and east to Gove. The Darwin Airport Shuttle has regular service between the airport and the city's hotels. The cost is A$16 one-way, A$29 round-trip;

10

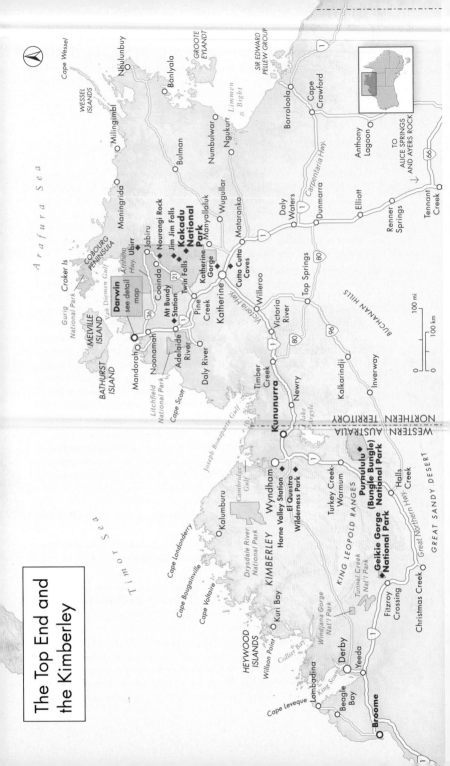

The Top End and the Kimberley

book a day in advance for hotel pickup. Taxis await at the airport's taxi rank. The journey downtown costs about A$25–A$30.

The *Ghan* train connects Darwin with Adelaide via Alice Springs on a two-night 2,979-km (1,861-mile) journey a couple of times a week.

Ghan ☎ *13–2147 bookings, 08/8213–4592* ⊕ *www.greatsouthernrail. com.au.*

The best way to get around Darwin is by car. The Stuart Highway is Darwin's land connection with the rest of Australia. By road Darwin is 15 hours from Alice Springs (1,491 km [926 miles]), 2½ days from Broome via the Great Northern Highway (1,875 km [1,165 miles]), 4–5 days from Brisbane (3,387 km [2,105 miles]), and 5–6 days from Perth (3,981 km [2,474 miles]).

For drivers headed outside the Northern Territory, one-way drop-off fees for rental vehicles are often twice as much as a weekly rental. If you don't feel like driving, the bus network in Darwin links the city with its far-flung suburbs, and a choice of minibus operators, including the 24-hour Metro minibuses, run all over town for fixed prices starting at A$4 per person. The main bus terminal (Darwin Bus) is on Harry Chan Avenue, near the Bennett Street end of Smith Street Mall. A minibus stand is also located at the front of Darwin's airport terminal.

SAFETY AND PRECAUTIONS
Swimming in the ocean is not recommended because of the box jellyfish, commonly known as "stingers." Salt and freshwater crocodiles are found in most Top End billabongs and rivers, and are occasionally seen even on Darwin beaches. The accessible rivers and billabongs are generally signposted if saltwater crocodiles are known to inhabit the area, but if you are not sure, don't swim.

Avoid driving outside towns after dark due to the dangers presented by buffalo, cattle, horses, donkeys, and kangaroos on the road. If your vehicle breaks down, stay with it; it is easier to find a missing vehicle than missing people. If you are going for a bushwalk, always tells someone your plan and when you expect to return.

TIMING
Although Darwin has some attractions, many people view the city as the entry point to the Top End's national parks, in particular Kakadu and Litchfield. Two days in the city will be enough to see the main attractions, after which you will want to head to Kakadu.

TOURS
Every day but Sunday, Darwin Day Tours conducts afternoon trips for A$69, and for A$144 (April–November) you can take the afternoon tour and finish with a harbor cruise. Tours include historic buildings, the main harbor, the Botanic Gardens, the Northern Territory Museum of Arts and Sciences, East Point Reserve, and Stokes Hill Wharf. Alternatively, for A$45 you can hop on and off the Tour Tub "City Sights" bus. It picks up at Knuckey Street, at the end of Smith Street Mall, and runs daily 9–4. Quirkier is the Duck About tour, using an amphibious vehicle to deliver you from land to water while seeing the sights, for (A$42). Daytime and sunset cruises explore a harbor five times the

Australian Aviation Heritage Centre **10**

Crocodylus Park and Zoo ... **9**

Crocosaurus Cove **4**

Defence of Darwin Experience **7**

George Brown Darwin Botanic Gardens **5**

Indo Pacific Marine **3**

Museum and Art Gallery of the Northern Territory **6**

Stokes Hill Wharf **1**

Territory Wildlife Park **8**

Victoria Hotel **2**

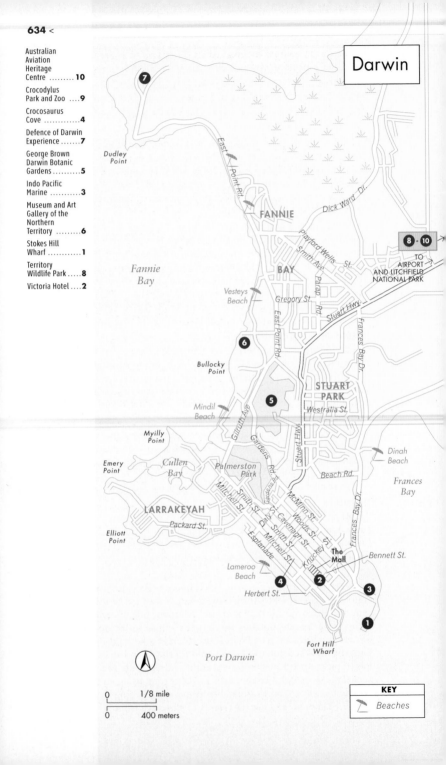

Darwin

Dudley Point

Fannie Bay

FANNIE

BAY

Vesteys Beach

Gregory St.

Bullocky Point

Mindil Beach

Myilly Point

Emery Point

Cullen Bay

Palmerston Park

LARRAKEYAH

Packard St.

Elliott Point

Lameroo Beach

Herbert St.

Port Darwin

STUART PARK

Westralia St.

Dinah Beach

Frances Bay

Beach Rd.

The Mall

Bennett St.

Fort Hill Wharf

East Point Rd.

Dick Ward Dr.

Playford Wells St.

Smith Ave.

Palap Rd.

Stuart Hwy.

Frances Bay Dr.

East Point Rd.

Gilruth Ave.

Gardens Rd.

Esplanade

McMinn St.

Woods St.

Cavenagh St.

Smith St.

Mitchell St.

Knuckey St.

Smith St.

Oaks St.

Daly St.

TO AIRPORT AND LITCHFIELD NATIONAL PARK

8 - 10

0   1/8 mile

0   400 meters

KEY	
	Beaches

size of Sydney's. A two-hour cruise on the *Spirit of Darwin* begins at A\$65. Trips depart daily from Cullen Bay Marina between April and October.

Tour Contacts Darwin Day Tours ☎ *1300/721365* ⊕ *www.darwindaytours.com.au.* **Duck About Tours** ☎ *1300/382522* ⊕ *www.duckabout.com.au.* **Spirit of Darwin** ☎ *0417/381977* ⊕ *spiritofdarwin.com.au.* **Tour Tub** ☎ *08/8985–6322* ⊕ *www.tourtub.com.au.*

ESSENTIALS

Taxis City Radio Taxis ☎ *08/8981–3777* ⊕ *www.radiotaxi.com.au.* **Darwin Radio Taxis** ☎ *13–1008 in local area, 08/8985–0777.*

Visitor Information Top End Tourism ✉ *6 Bennett St., City Center* ☎ *08/8980–6000, 1300/138886* ⊕ *www.tourismtopend.com.au.*

EXPLORING: CITY CENTER
TOP ATTRACTIONS

FAMILY **Crocosaurus Cove.** This is the place to go swimming with saltwater crocodiles and live to tell the tale. Although not as information-rich as Crocodylus Park (⇨ *below*), this more modern croc haven wins on the convenience front, positioned right in the heart of town. Feeding times and the Cage of Death, where visitors are lowered into croc-infested pools in a Perspex container (A\$160), are the highlights. Feeding happens at different times throughout the day in the four main sections: fish, big crocs, turtles, and nocturnal reptiles. ✉ *58 Mitchell St., Darwin City* ☎ *08/8981–7522* ⊕ *www.crocosauruscove.com* 🎫 *A\$32* ☉ *Daily 9–6.*

Stokes Hill Wharf. The best views of Darwin Harbour are from this working pier, which receives cargo ships, trawlers, defense vessels, and, occasionally, huge cruise liners. It's also a favorite spot for Darwinites to fish, and when the mackerel are running you can join scores of locals over a few beers. The cluster of cafés becomes crowded on weekends and when cruise ships arrive. On the city side, in the Waterfront Precinct, is the Wave Lagoon (entry A\$5 half day, A\$8 full day; open daily 10–6) and a free, stinger-free (safe from jellyfish) swimming lagoon. Both are understandably popular on hot days. ✉ *McMinn St., Darwin Harbour* ☎ *08/8981–4268.*

CROCS BITE!

The crocodile has long been a dominant predator in the wetland regions of Australia. Powerful and stealthy, the saltwater (estuarine) crocodile has little to fear—and that includes humans. More than 80,000 crocodiles are found in the coastal and tidal areas of rivers, as well as floodplains and freshwater reaches of rivers. In fact, they can be found in the larger rivers, lagoons, and billabongs right across northern Australia. Attacks on people are rare and deaths few (an average of one a year), but you should observe all no-swimming and warning signs, and treat crocs with respect.

10

WORTH NOTING

> **NEED A BREAK?**

Victoria Hotel. The balcony of the Victoria Hotel, overlooking the passing parade on Smith Street Mall, is a good place for a cool drink in the city center. A Darwin institution since its construction in 1890, the Vic has been hit by every cyclone and rebuilt afterward. ⊠ *27 Smith St. Mall, City Center* ☎ *08/8981–4011* ⊕ *www. thevichotel.com.*

Indo Pacific Marine. This marine interpretative center houses a large open tank with one of the few self-contained coral-reef ecosystems in the southern hemisphere—and it's been growing on its own for almost 20 years. Other exhibits include a static display of rare, deepwater coral skeletons and an exhibit explaining the effects of global warming on the planet. Night tours, which begin at 6:30 on Wednesday, Friday, and Sunday, take you by ultra-violet flashlight to view the biodiversity of the fluorescing reef and live venomous animals; the colors the coral produce are astounding. The tours include a four-course seafood dinner, followed by a nocturnal coral reef tour of the exhibitions. Bookings are essential. ⊠ *29 Stokes Hill Rd., Wharf Precinct* ☎ *08/8981–1294* ⊕ *www.indopacificmarine. com.au* ⊡ *A$24, night tours A$110* ☉ *Apr.–Oct., daily 10–4; Nov.– Mar. call for opening times.*

A TROPICAL SUMMER

Darwin's wet season—when the humidity rises and monsoonal rains dump around 52 inches—runs from December to April. The days offer a predictable mix of sunshine and afternoon showers, along with some spectacular thunder and lightning storms. There are fewer visitors at this time of the year, and Darwin slows to an even more relaxed pace. Across the Top End, waterfalls increase in size, floodplains rejuvenate to a lush green, and flowers bloom. Despite the rains, Darwinites still prefer the outdoors—eating, drinking, and shopping at the markets.

AROUND DARWIN

TOP ATTRACTIONS

FAMILY **Crocodylus Park and Zoo.** This research facility has an excellent air-conditioned crocodile museum and education center. There are more than 1,200 crocodiles here, from babies to giants up to 5 meters long. The saurian section of the zoo includes the croc-infested Bellairs Lagoon and pens for breeding and raising. The park also has enclosures with lions, tigers, cassowaries, primates, and turtles, and it holds one of the biggest snakes in Australia: a Burmese python weighing 140 kilograms (308 pounds). Tours and feedings are at 10, noon, 2, and 3:30. ⊠ *815 McMillans Rd., opposite Berrimah Police Centre, Berrimah* ☎ *08/8922–4500* ⊕ *www.crocodyluspark.com.au* ⊡ *A$40* ☉ *Daily 9–5.*

FAMILY **George Brown Darwin Botanic Gardens.** First planted in 1886 and largely destroyed by Cyclone Tracy, the 92-acre site today displays rain forest, mangroves, and open woodland environments. There are more than 450 species of palms growing in the gardens. A popular walk takes visitors on a self-guided tour of plants Aborigines used for medicinal purposes. The Children's Evolutionary Playground is an award-winning playground that traces the changes in plant groups through time, while the plant display house has tropical ferns, orchids, and other exotic plants. ⊠ *Gardens Rd. at Geranium St., Mindil Beach* ☎ *08/8981–1958* ⊕ *www.nt.gov.au/nreta/parks/botanic* ✉ *Free* ☉ *Geranium St. gates daily 7 am–7 pm, Gardens Rd. gates daily 7 am–7 pm; information center daily 8 am–4 pm.*

Fodor's Choice ★ **Museum and Art Gallery of the Northern Territory.** Collections at this excellent museum and art gallery encompass Aboriginal art and culture, maritime archaeology, Northern Territory history, and natural sciences. One gallery is devoted to Cyclone Tracy where you can listen to a terrifying recording of the howling winds, and you can see "Sweetheart," a 16-foot 10-inch stuffed saltwater crocodile that attacked fishing boats on the Finniss River in the 1970s. The Cornucopia Museum Café overlooks tropical gardens and Darwin Harbour and is open all day for meals. ⊠ *19 Conacher St., Bullocky Point, Fannie Bay* ☎ *08/8999–8264* ✉ *Free* ☉ *Weekdays 9–5, weekends and public holidays 10–5.*

FAMILY **Territory Wildlife Park.** In 1,000 acres of natural bushland, this impressive park is dedicated to the Northern Territory's native fauna and flora. In addition to saltwater crocodiles, water buffalo, dingoes, and waterbirds, it also has an underwater viewing area for observing freshwater fish and a nocturnal house kept dark for late night creatures. The treetop-level walkway through the huge aviary allows you to watch native birds from the swamps and forests at close range. Daily events include feeding at 9 am and a birds of prey display at 11 am and 2:30 pm. ⊠ *Cox Peninsula Rd., 47 km (29 miles) south of Darwin, Berry Springs* ☎ *08/8988–7200* ⊕ *www.territorywildlifepark.com.au* ✉ *A$26* ☉ *Daily 8:30–4; exit open until 6.*

WORTH NOTING

Australian Aviation Heritage Centre. Due to its isolation and sparse population, the Northern Territory played an important role in the expansion of aviation in Australia, and this impressive museum traces the history of flight Down Under. Planes on exhibition include a massive B-52 bomber on permanent loan from the United States, a recently retired RAAF F-111 fighter jet as well as a Japanese Zero shot down on the first day of bombing raids in 1942. ⊠ *557 Stuart Hwy., 8 km (5 miles) northeast of city center, Winnellie* ☎ *08/8947–2145* ⊕ *www. darwinsairwar.com.au* ✉ *A$14* ☉ *Daily 9–5.*

Defence of Darwin Experience. WWII came to Australia when 188 Japanese planes bombed Darwin on February 19, 1942, killing almost 1,000 people. This high-tech museum at East Point—opened in 2012 to commemorate the 70th anniversary of the attack—tells the story of the day and Darwin's role in the war. It's next door to the older Darwin Military Museum (included in entry fee), which has lots of guns and other military equipment on show. ⊠ *5434 Alec Fong Lim Dr., East Point* ☎ *08/8981–9702* ⊕ *www.defenceofdarwin.nt.gov.au* ✉ *A$14* ☉ *Daily 9:30–5.*

10

Enjoying an outdoor festival in Darwin

SPORTS AND THE OUTDOORS

FISHING

Barramundi, the best-known fish of the Top End, can weigh up to 110 pounds and are excellent fighting fish that taste great on the barbecue afterward.

Equinox Fishing Charters. Equinox Fishing Charters has half-day, day, and extended fishing trips using the 38-foot *Tsar,* which is licensed to carry 12 passengers and two crew, and *Equinox II,* which can carry 18–20 people. Full-day fishing charters with all meals and tackle provided are from A$260 per person. ⊠ *Shop 2, 64 Marina Blvd., Cullen Bay* ☎ *08/8942–2199* ⊕ *www.equinoxcharters.com.au.*

Northern Territory Fisheries Division's Recreational Fishing Office. The office has information on licenses and catch limits. ⊠ *Berrimah Research Farm, Makagon Rd., Berrimah* ☎ *08/8999–2144* ⊕ *www.nt.gov.au/ dpifm/Fisheries.*

OFF THE
BEATEN
PATH

Litchfield National Park. This beautiful park lies just 122 km (76 miles) south of Darwin off the Stuart Highway. Its 1,340 square km (515 square miles) are an untouched wilderness of monsoonal rain forests, rivers, and striking rock formations. The highlights are four separate, spectacular waterfalls—**Florence, Tjaynera, Wangi, and Tolmer Falls**— all of which have secluded plunge pools (⚠ The pools are suitable for swimming but occasionally there are crocs here, so observe any "no swimming" signs). There is also a dramatic group of large, freestanding sandstone pillars known as the **Lost City,** and the **Magnetic Termite Mounds,** which have an eerie resemblance to eroded grave markers, dot the black-soiled plains of the park's northern area. You'll need to camp if you want to stay in the park; campgrounds and RV sites are near several of the major sights (call the Parks and Wildlife Service of the Northern Territory at ☎ *08/8976–0282* for information). There are also a few restaurants and a modest hotel (the Batchelor Resort [☎ *08/8976–0123*], which has comfortable hotel rooms, as well as RV and camping facilities) in the nearby town of Batchelor. ✉ *Litchfield Park Rd., Litchfield Park.*

WHERE TO EAT

$$
AUSTRALIAN
✗ **Buzz Café.** Don't let the name fool you, it's more of a restaurant than a café and just one of several water-front eateries at Cullen Bay Marina. You can mingle at the bar with visiting boaties and locals relaxing by the water, then dine on fresh seafood presented in a contemporary Australian style. There's air-conditioned comfort in the glass-walled dining room, or you can head out to the umbrella-shaded decks overlooking yachts and cruisers moored in the marina. One of the more curious panoramas is from the men's glass-sheeted urinal, which has one-way views over the restaurant. ⓢ *Average main: A$30* ✉ *The Slipway, 48 Marina Blvd., Cullen Bay* ☎ *08/8941–1141* ☉ *Closed Sun. and Mon. and Christmas Eve–New Year's Day.*

$$
SEAFOOD
FAMILY
✗ **Crustaceans on the Wharf.** In a corrugated-iron storage shed at the end of a commercial pier, this is a good place to dine on local fish-and-chips on outdoor tables—this is more glorified take away than full-service restaurant. Seafood takes center stage here; standout choices include the Moreton Bay bugs (which are like small lobsters), calamari, and chili mud crabs, a specialty of the house. Kids under 10 eat free and they can feed the fish that gather in the water under the lights. ⓢ *Average main: A$35* ✉ *Stokes Hill Wharf, Wharf Precinct* ☎ *08/8981–8658* ⊕ *www.crustaceans.net.au.*

$$
THAI
Fodor'sChoice
★
✗ **Hanuman Darwin.** Excellent food and a wine list that includes the best from every grape-growing region in Australia are served against a backdrop of furnishings, tableware, and artworks from around the world in Hanuman's indoor and alfresco dining areas. By drawing on Thai, Nonya (Malaysian), and Indian tandoori culinary traditions, Hanuman's chefs turn local herbs, vegetables, and seafood into sumptuous and innovative dishes. Of special note are Hanuman oysters, lightly cooked in a spicy coriander-and-lemongrass sauce; Hanuman prawns; and any of the curries. ⓢ *Average main: A$30* ✉ *93 Mitchell St., City Center* ☎ *08/8941–3500* ⊕ *www.hanuman.com.au* ✍ *Reservations essential* ☉ *No lunch weekends.*

$$
ITALIAN
✗ **Il Lido.** This polished Italian restaurant is in Darwin's waterfront precinct and provides reflective views as you dine in the open air. The food is more modern Italian than traditional—recommended are the

---

GONE FISHING

Joining a local tour guide is the best way to hook a big one. They know the best spots and techniques, and their local knowledge can make an enjoyable experience even better. In the estuaries you can catch threadfin and blue salmon, cod, queenfish, golden snapper, and the Top End's most famous fighting fish, the barramundi—barra in the local parlance. You don't have to go far—Darwin's harbor teems with fish.

10

linguini with tiger prawns and the eight-hour roast lamb. It also has a nice cocktail bar and tapas lounge. [$] *Average main: A$30* ✉ *Wharf One, Kitchener Dr., Darwin Waterfront* ☎ *08/8941–0900* 🌐 *www.illidodarwin.com.au.*

> **WORD OF MOUTH**
>
> "We went on to Wangi Falls [in Litchfield National Park]. There were many people there. We ate our picnic and then went to the pool below the Falls. It was such a large pool that there was plenty of room to swim, and I had a good swim over to the Falls and back. We then walked along the boardwalk and through the monsoon forest and up to the Treetop Platform. It was shady and very pleasant." —Suelynne

$$ GREEK 🍴 **Manoli's Greek Taverna.** Darwin has a large Greek community and this unassuming family-run restaurant does a great souvlaki and other authentic Greek fare. Don't be put off by the outside appearance, which looks like a takeaway food store, or the basic decor, because the focus is all about the food. It gets lively on Friday and Saturday night with live traditional Greek music. [$] *Average main: A$24* ✉ *4/64 Smith St., Darwin City* ☎ *08/8981–9120* 🌐 *www.manolisgreektaverna.com.au* 🕓 *Closed Sun. No lunch Sat. and Mon.*

$$$ MODERN AUSTRALIAN 🍴 **Pee Wee's at the Point.** Uninterrupted views of Darwin Harbour at East Point Reserve make this restaurant a favorite with locals and visitors wanting a special night out. Dine inside with views of the harbor through large glass doors, or out on the tiered timber decks beneath the stars. The cooking is Modern Australian, and the carefully considered wine list has good values. Highlights include soft shell mud crabs, Thai fried gold band snapper, and pan-roasted wild saltwater barramundi. [$] *Average main: A$40* ✉ *Alec Fong Ling Dr., East Point Reserve, Fannie Bay* ☎ *08/8981–6868* 🌐 *www.peewees.com.au* ✍ *Reservations essential* 🕓 *No lunch.*

WHERE TO STAY

For expanded hotel reviews, visit Fodors.com.

$$$ HOTEL 🏨 **DoubleTree by Hilton Hotel Esplanade Darwin.** Most rooms have good views over Darwin Harbour from this hotel next door to the Darwin Entertainment Center. **Pros:** city-center location; large swimming pool; free parking. **Cons:** convention center attracts tour groups. [$] *Rooms from: A$249* ✉ *116 The Esplanade* ☎ *08/8980–0800, 800/007697* 🌐 *doubletree3.hilton.com* 🛏 *163 rooms, 34 suites* 🍽 *Some meals.*

$$$ HOTEL 🏨 **Novotel Atrium.** The hotel's bar and restaurant are set around a tiny artificial stream that flows through tropical plants in the middle of the lobby, which also features a central, vine-hung atrium. **Pros:** tropical garden in the atrium; some rooms have views over Darwin Harbour; close to shopping precinct. **Cons:** atrium can mean rooms are noisy; standard rooms are small, especially bathrooms. [$] *Rooms from: A$220* ✉ *100 Esplanade* ☎ *08/8941–0755* 🌐 *www.novotel.com* 🛏 *138 rooms, 2 suites* 🍽 *Some meals.*

$$$$ RESORT Fodor's Choice ★ 🏨 **Sky City Darwin.** The most luxurious place to stay in Darwin, the three-story hotel adjacent to the casino has beachfront accommodations set amid lush lawns and gardens and a huge lagoon-style swimming pool, complete with Darwin's only swim-up bar. **Pros:** close to Mindil

Tiwi islands sculptures at a gallery in Darwin

Beach Sunset Markets; excellent lagoon-style swimming pool; watch sunset while dining. **Cons:** casino operates 24 hours, so nights can be noisy; convention center attracts big groups. $ *Rooms from: A$435* ✉ *Gilruth Ave., Mindil Beach* ☎ *08/8943–8888, 1800/891118* ⊕ *www.skycitydarwin.com.au* ➳ *154 rooms* ❙❂❙ *Some meals.*

$$$ ⚏ **Vibe Hotel Darwin Waterfront.** This good-value hotel overlooks the
HOTEL wave pool and lagoon in the heart of the busy waterfront restaurant strip. **Pros:** great location. **Cons:** 10-minute walk to city center; no free parking. $ *Rooms from: A$269* ✉ *7 Kitchener Dr., Waterfront, Darwin City* ☎ *08/8982–9998* ⊕ *www.vibehotels.com.au* ➳ *120 rooms* ❙❂❙ *Some meals.*

NIGHTLIFE AND THE ARTS
THE ARTS
Darwin Entertainment Centre. The center has a large theater that stages concerts, dance, and drama. It also doubles as booking office for other big touring concerts in town—especially those at the Amphitheatre, one of Australia's best outdoor concert venues (entrance next to Botanic Gardens on Gardens Road). Check their website for current shows. ✉ *93 Mitchell St., City Center* ☎ *08/8980–3333 box office, 08/8980–3366 general inquiries* ⊕ *www.darwinentertainment.com.au.*

Fodor's Choice **Deckchair Cinema.** At this outdoor, 350-seat movie theater you can catch
★ a flick beneath the stars while relaxing on canvas deck chairs with a glass of wine. Australian, foreign, arthouse, or classic films are screened every night April–November. Gates open at 6:30 for the sunset, and picnic baskets (no BYO alcohol) are permitted, although there is a snack kiosk and a bar. The first movie screens at 7:30; second showing 9:30

pm. ✉ *Jervois Rd. off Kitchener Dr., Wharf Precinct* ☎ *08/8981–0700* ⊕ *www.deckchaircinema.com* 🎬 *A$15* ⊘ *Apr.–Nov.*

NIGHTLIFE

Bogarts Bar and Grill. Named after Humphrey, this small bar and restaurant is adorned with posters and memorabilia in a shabby chic kind of way, complete with couches and fantastic atmosphere. A favorite cocktail haunt for locals and a touch more sophisticated than the bars in the city center. ✉ *52 Gregory St., Parap* ☎ *08/8981–3561.*

Monsoons. This establishment has an 80-foot-long granite bar with 20 different beers on tap and wines from Australia and New Zealand and a party-all-night-every-night vibe. The kitchen serves up seafood, pastas, burgers, and steaks, and there is usually live music on Monday night. ✉ *46 Mitchell St., City Center* ☎ *08/8941–7171.*

Shenannigans Irish Pub. This pub has Guinness on tap, along with Kilkenny and Harp. Traditional Irish pub food is served, with meat roasts on Sunday. ✉ *69 Mitchell St., City Center* ☎ *08/8981–2100.*

Fodor's Choice **Ski Club.** This favorite "local secret" spot is "the" place to go for a sunset
★ beer in the tropics, and it's right next to the Museum and Art Gallery of the Northern Territory. Its plastic white chairs and tables add to the laid-back, "old Darwin" vibe. There's live music on weekends. ✉ *20 Conacher St., Fannie Bay* ☎ *08/8981–6630.*

SkyCity Darwin Casino. This casino is one of Darwin's most popular evening spots. The 700 gaming machines are open 24 hours, while gaming tables are open from noon until 4 am Thursday and Sunday and until 6 am Friday and Saturday. ✉ *Gilruth Ave., Mindil Beach* ☎ *08/8943–8888* ⊕ *www.skycitydarwin.com.au.*

Throb. Renowned for its floor shows and drag acts, Throb is Darwin's premier gay nightclub. Open Friday and Saturday only, the shows start around 1:30 am and the fun doesn't end until 4 am. Cover charge is A$10–A$15. ✉ *64 Smith St., City Center* ☎ *08/8942–3435* ⊕ *www.throbnightclub.com.au.*

Top End Hotel. For a beer and live music, visit the Top End Hotel, a Darwin landmark, which has the city's biggest, and shadiest, beer garden, a sports bar, a nightclub, and a band room. There's live music Thursday and Friday nights. ✉ *Daly and Mitchell Sts., Bicentennial Park* ☎ *08/8981–6511.*

THE INDIGENOUS ARTS SCENE

Start at the Museum and Art Gallery of the Northern Territory for a comprehensive understanding of indigenous art and artifacts. Then head to one of many art and craft outlets in and around Darwin to purchase an authentic and unique piece of art. In many indigenous communities throughout the tropical Outback—including Maningrida, Oenpelli, Tiwi islands, and Yirrikala—you can buy direct from the artist.

SHOPPING

MARKETS

Mindil Beach Sunset Market. This market is an extravaganza that takes place Thursday 5 pm–10 pm and Sunday 4 pm–9 pm from April to October; the Sunday market is smaller than Thursday's. Come in the late afternoon to snack at a choice of 60 stalls offering food from more than 25 different countries; shop at more than 200 artisans' booths; and enjoy singers, dancers, and musicians. Or join the other Darwinites with a bottle of wine to watch the sun plunge into the sea. ⊠ *Beach Rd., Mindil Beach* ☎ *08/8981–3454* ⊕ *www.mindil.com.au.*

Nightcliff Market. This market takes place Sunday 8 am–2 pm in Nightcliff Village, with craft and food stalls and entertainers; it's a great spot for breakfast. ⊠ *Pavonia Pl., Nightcliff* ☎ *0414/368773.*

Parap Markets. North of downtown, the Parap Markets are open Saturday 8 am–2 pm and have a terrific selection of ethnic Asian food, including some of the best laksa in the country. ⊠ *Parap Sq., Parap* ☎ *0438/882373, 08/8942–0805.*

Rapid Creek Markets. Open Sunday 8 am–1:30 pm, the Rapid Creek Markets are Darwin's oldest and have fresh food produce, as well as locally made handicrafts. ⊠ *Rapid Creek Shopping Centre, Trower Rd., Rapid Creek* ☎ *08/8948–4866.*

KAKADU NATIONAL PARK

Begins 117 km (73 miles) east of Darwin.

Fodor's Choice
★
This national park is a jewel among the Top End parks, and many visitors come to the region just to experience this tropical wilderness. Beginning east of Darwin, and covering some 19,800 square km (7,645 square miles), the park protects a large system of unspoiled rivers and creeks, as well as a rich Aboriginal heritage that extends back to the earliest days of humankind.

The superb gathering of Aboriginal rock art is one of Kakadu's major highlights. Two main types of Aboriginal artwork can be seen here. The Mimi style, which is the oldest, is believed to be up to 20,000 years old. Aborigines believe that Mimi spirits created the red-ocher stick figures to depict hunting scenes and other pictures of life at the time. The more recent artwork, known as X-ray painting, dates back fewer than 9,000 years and depicts freshwater animals—especially fish, turtles, and geese—living in floodplains created after the last ice age.

As the dry season progresses, billabongs (water holes) become increasingly important to the more than 280 species of birds that inhabit the park. Huge flocks often gather at Yellow Water, South Alligator River, and Magela Creek. Scenic flights over the wetlands and Arnhem Land escarpment provide unforgettable moments in the wet season. ⊠ *Jabiru* ⊕ *www.environment.gov.au/parks/kakadu.*

GETTING HERE AND AROUND

From Darwin it's a two- to three-hour drive along the Arnhem Highway east to the entrance to the park at Bowali Visitor Center. Although four-wheel-drive vehicles are not necessary to travel to the park, they

10

are required for many of the unpaved roads within, including the track to Jim Jim Falls. Entry is free, but you must buy a A$25 National Park permit, which is good for 14 days.

SAFETY AND PRECAUTIONS

If you are driving, watch out for road trains—large trucks up to 160 feet in length with up to four trailers behind a prime mover. They are common on Northern Territory roads, and you should give them plenty of room. Avoid driving after dark outside towns because of the high likelihood of straying animals—kangaroos and cattle in particular. It is a good idea to always tell someone of your plans if you intend traveling to remote places; the same applies when bushwalking. Always make sure you have adequate water and food.

TIMING

The best time to visit is between May and September during the Dry. The shortest time you should allow is a three-day, two-night itinerary from Darwin. This will provide opportunities to visit the major sights— a cruise on the East Alligator River; Ubirr, a major Aboriginal rock-art site; a flight-seeing flight from Jabiru Airport; Nourlangie Rock, another Aboriginal rock-art site; the Warradjan Aboriginal Cultural Centre, to learn about traditional Aboriginal people; and a sunset cruise on Yellow Water Billabong to see birds, crocodiles, and other wildlife. On the return to Darwin, you can visit Mamukala Wetlands for an abundance of birds and wildlife. A five-day itinerary will give you time to visit Jim Jim Falls and Twin Falls, a four-wheel-drive excursion.

TOURS

During the Dry, park rangers conduct free walks and tours at several popular locations. You can pick up a program at the entry station or at either of the visitor centers.

Far Out Adventures. Far Out Adventures runs customized tours of Kakadu, as well as other regions of the Top End, for small groups. ☎ 04/2715–2288 ⊕ www.farout.com.au.

Fodor's Choice ★ **Gagudju Dreaming.** The Gagudju Lodge Cooinda arranges magical boat tours of Yellow Water Billabong, the major water hole in Kakadu, where innumerable birds and crocodiles gather. There are six tours throughout the day as well as a night tour (no children under eight on the night tour); the sunrise and sunset cruises are best—both in terms of temperature and animal activity. Tours, which run most of the year, cost A$72 for 90 minutes and A$90 for two hours (6:45 am cruise A$99 but includes breakfast). ☎ 1800/8979–0145 ⊕ www.gagudju-dreaming.com.

Kakadu Air. This company makes scenic hour (A$240) and half-hour (A$140) flights out of Jabiru. In the Dry the flight encompasses the northern region, including Arnhem Land escarpment, Nourlangie and Mamakala Wetlands, East Alligator River, and Jabiru Township. During the Wet only, a similarly priced half-hour or one-hour flight takes in the Jim Jim and Twin falls, when they are most spectacular. Heli-tours are also available. ☎ 1800/089113, 08/8941–9611 ⊕ www.kakaduair.com.au.

ESSENTIALS

Visitor Information Kakadu National Park ☎ 08/8938–1120 ⊕ www.environment.gov.au/parks/kakadu/. **Tourism Top End** ⊠ 6 Bennett St., Darwin ☎ 08/8980–6000 ⊕ www.tourismtopend.com.au.

Bowali Visitor Centre. The visitor center has state-of-the-art audiovisual displays and traditional exhibits that give an introduction to the park's ecosystems and its bird population, the world's most diverse. ⊠ Arnhem and Kakadu Hwys. ☎ 08/8938–1120 ⊠ Free ☉ Daily 8–5.

Warradjan Cultural Centre. Named after the pig-nose turtle unique to the Top End, Warradjan Aboriginal Cultural Centre provides an excellent experience of local Bininj (pronounced *bin*-ing) tribal culture. Displays take you through the Aboriginal Creation period, following the path of the creation ancestor Rainbow Serpent through the ancient landscape of Kakadu. ⊠ 5 km (3 miles) off Kakadu Hwy. on road to Gagudju Lodge, Cooinda, Jim Jim ☎ 08/8979–0145 ⊠ Free ☉ Daily 9–5.

EXPLORING

Jim Jim Falls. The best way to gain a true appreciation of the natural beauty of Kakadu is to visit the waterfalls running off the escarpment. Some 39 km (24 miles) south of the park headquarters along the Kakadu Highway, a track leads off to the left toward Jim Jim Falls, 60 km (37 miles) away (about a two-hour drive). The track is unpaved, and you'll need a four-wheel-drive vehicle to navigate it. From the parking lot you have to walk 1 km (½ mile) over boulders to reach the falls and the plunge pools they have created at the base of the escarpment. After May, the water flow over the falls may cease, and the unpaved road is closed in the Wet. ▦ TIP→ The best way to see these falls at their best is on a scenic flight from Jabiru during the wet season. ⊠ Jim Jim Falls Track, Kakadu Hwy., Jim Jim.

Nourlangie Rock. Like the main Kakadu escarpment, Nourlangie Rock is a remnant of an ancient plateau that is slowly eroding, leaving sheer cliffs rising high above the floodplains. The main attraction is the **Anbangbang Gallery,** an excellent frieze of Aboriginal rock paintings. ⊠ 19 km (12 miles) from park headquarters on Kakadu Hwy.; turn left toward Nourlangie Rock, then follow paved road, accessible yr-round, 11 km (7 miles) to parking area ⊕ www.environment.gov.au/parks/kakadu ⊠ Free ☉ Daily 7 am–sunset.

Twin Falls. As you approach the Twin Falls, the ravine opens up dramatically to reveal a beautiful sandy beach scattered with palm trees, as well as the crystal waters of the falls spilling onto the end of the beach. This spot is a bit difficult to reach, but the trip is rewarding. Take the road to Jim Jim Falls, turn off just before the parking lot, and

10

Gunlom Falls in the Kakadu National Park

travel 10 km (6 miles) farther to the Twin Falls parking lot. A regular boat shuttle (A$15; buy your tickets before you go at Bowali Visitor Centre or Gagudju Lodge in Cooinda) operates a return service up the Twin Falls gorge, and then you need to walk over boulders, sand, and a boardwalk to the falls. Saltwater crocodiles may be in the water in the gorge, so visitors are urged not to enter the water. The round-trip, including the boat shuttle, takes around two hours. ⊠ *Off Jim Jim Rd.*

Ubirr. Ubirr has an impressive display of Aboriginal paintings scattered through six shelters in the rock. The main gallery contains a 49-foot frieze of X-ray paintings depicting animals, birds, and fish. A 1-km (½-mile) path around the rock leads to all the galleries. It's just a short clamber to the top for wonderful views over the surrounding wetlands, particularly at sunset. ■ TIP→ Take a torch to help you get down after sunset. Stop in at the Border Store and Cafe on your way in; they do lunch and a post-sunset Thai dinner and sell arts and crafts. Beware of wildlife on the roads if driving after dark. ⊠ *43 km (27 miles) north of park headquarters along paved road* ☎ *08/8979–2474 for the Border Store and Cafe* ⊕ *www.kakadu.com.au; www.environment.gov. au/parks/kakadu* ⊠ *Free* ⊙ *Apr.–Nov., daily 8:30–sunset; Dec.–Mar., daily 2–sunset.*

WHERE TO STAY
For expanded hotel reviews, visit Fodors.com.

There are several lodges in the park, and campgrounds at Merl, Muirella Park, Mardugal, and Gunlom have toilets, showers, and water. Sites are A$10 per night. Alcohol is not available in Jabiru, so stock up in Darwin.

$$ ⌂ **Aurora Kakadu.** This comfortable hotel has doubles and family rooms—which sleep up to five—spread through lush tropical gardens; the rooms and campgrounds are clean and provide good value for the money. **Pros:** fauna is abundant; tropical garden setting; free bottled water in rooms. **Cons:** some distance from park attractions; limited amenities in rooms; thin walls; own transport essential. [$] *Rooms from: A$169* ⊠ *Arnhem Hwy., 2½ km (1½ miles) before the highway crosses the South Alligator River* ☎ *08/8979–0166, 1800/818845* ⊕ *www.auroraresorts.com.au* ↬ *138 rooms, 36 powered sites, 250 tent sites* ❖❖*Some meals.*

HOTEL

> ## ANCIENT ART AND NATURE
>
> Almost the size of West Virginia, Kakadu National Park is an ancient landform, with wetlands, gorges, waterfalls, and rugged escarpments. It also has one of the highest concentrations of accessible Aboriginal rock-art sites in the world. Take a tour with an Aboriginal guide from one of the cultural centers near Jabiru or Cooinda. The art sites date back 20,000 years.

$$$ ⌂ **Gagudju Crocodile Holiday Inn.** Shaped like a crocodile, this unusual hotel with spacious, refurbished rooms is the best of the area's accommodation options. **Pros:** friendly, helpful staff; Aboriginal artwork on sale; Jabiru village within walking distance. **Cons:** pool area is small; ground-floor rooms can have "critters." [$] *Rooms from: A$255* ⊠ *1 Flinders St., Jabiru* ☎ *08/8979–9000, 1800/500401* ⊕ *www.gagudju-dreaming.com* ↬ *110 rooms* ❖❖ *Some meals.*

HOTEL

$$$$ ⌂ **Gagudju Lodge Cooinda.** Near Yellow Water Billabong, this facility has light, airy lodgings looking out over tropical gardens. **Pros:** center for Yellow Water Cruises; close to Aboriginal cultural center. **Cons:** 30 minutes from Jabiru shops; limited amenities in rooms; limited dining options. [$] *Rooms from: A$335* ⊠ *Kakadu Hwy., 2 km (1 mile) toward Yellow Water Wetlands, Cooinda* ☎ *08/8979–0145, 1800/500401* ⊕ *www.gagudju-dreaming.com* ↬ *48 rooms* ❖❖ *No meals.*

HOTEL

KATHERINE GORGE

30 km (18 miles) east of Katherine, 346 km (215 miles) southeast of Darwin, 543 km (337 miles) northeast of Kununurra.

Officially called Nitmiluk, the Aboriginal or Jawoyn name for the cicadas associated with the creation stories of the area, this stunning canyon formed by the Katherine River in Nitmiluk National Park is actually a series of 13 gorges, each separated by a jumble of boulders. The gorge is 12 km (7½ miles) long and in many places the red rocky walls are almost 230 feet high. During the wet season (November through to April), the gorge is full of raging water and saltwater crocodiles, but during the dry season you can hire canoes or take one of several cruises to explore the gorges. Rangers clear the river of dangerous crocodiles at the start of each season so you can also swim, if the harmless freshwater crocodiles don't bother you.

GETTING HERE AND AROUND

There are no commercial flight services that fly direct into Katherine: closest airport is Darwin, which is about a three-hour drive.

TOURS

Nitmiluk Tours. Although you can explore Katherine Gorge on foot on one of the many bushwalking trails, the best way to see the gorge is to hit the water. Jawoyn-owned Nitmiluk Tours offer a range of cruises, starting at A$75 for a two-hour trip that departs several times each day. Wear comfortable walking shoes as there is some walking involved between gorges. **TIP→ The best time to go is during the late afternoon, when you'll get the best photo opportunities as the walls of the gorge glow a deep red.** Canoe hire is A$51 for half a day, A$64 for a full day. Helicopter flights over the gorge start at A$101. ✉ *Nitmiluk National Park, Gorge Rd., Katherine* ☎ *08/8972–1253* 🌐 *www.nitmiluktours.com.au.*

WHERE TO STAY

For expanded hotel reviews, visit Fodors.com.

$$$$ RESORT **Cicada Lodge.** Enjoy sunsets over Katherine Gorge from the privacy of your room at the brand-new luxury Cicada Lodge. **Pros:** great location; excellent food and service; open during the wet season; free Wi-Fi; complimentary drink and snack each evening. **Cons:** expensive; tours and meals cost extra. [$] *Rooms from: A$323* ✉ *Nitmiluk National Park, Katherine* ☎ *08/8974–3100* 🌐 *cicadalodge.com.au* 🛏 *18 rooms* 🍴 *Breakfast.*

THE KIMBERLEY

Perched on the northwestern hump of the loneliest Australian state, only half as far from Indonesia as it is from Sydney, the Kimberley remains a frontier of sorts. The first European explorers, dubbed by one of their descendants as "cattle kings in grass castles," ventured into the heart of the region in 1879 to establish cattle stations. They subsequently became embroiled in one of the country's longest-lasting conflicts between white settlers and Aborigines, led by Jandamarra of the Bunuba people.

The Kimberley remains sparsely populated, with only 35,000 people living in an area of 351,200 square km (135,600 square miles). That's about 12 square km (4½ square miles) per person. The region is dotted with cattle stations and raked with craggy ocher ranges, croc-infested rivers, tropical forests, and towering cliffs. Several of the country's most spectacular national parks are here, including Purnululu (Bungle Bungle) National Park, a vast area of bizarrely shaped and colored rock formations that became widely known to white Australians only in 1983. Facilities in this remote region are few, but if you're looking for a genuine Outback experience, the Kimberley represents the opportunity of a lifetime.

KUNUNURRA

516 km (322 miles) west of Katherine, 840 km (525 miles) southwest of Darwin.

Kununurra is the eastern gateway to the Kimberley. With a population of 6,000, it's a modern, planned town developed in the 1960s for the nearby Lake Argyle and Ord River irrigation scheme. It's a convenient base from which to explore local attractions such as Mirima National Park (a mini–Bungle Bungle on the edge of town), Lake Argyle, and the River Ord. The town is also one starting point for adventure tours of the Kimberley; the other option is to start from Broome.

GETTING HERE AND AROUND

Distances in this part of the continent are colossal. Flying is the fastest and easiest way to get to the Kimberley. Both Virgin Australia and Air North have extensive air networks throughout the Top End, linking Kununurra to Broome, Perth, and Darwin.

From Darwin to Kununurra and the eastern extent of the Kimberley it's 827 km (513 miles). The route runs from Darwin to Katherine along the Stuart Highway, and then along the Victoria Highway to Kununurra. The entire road is paved but narrow in parts—especially so, it may seem, when a road train (an extremely long truck convoy) is coming the other way. Drive with care. Fuel and supplies can be bought at small settlements along the way, but you should always keep supplies in abundance and expect to pay a pretty penny.

SAFETY AND PRECAUTIONS

Driving long distances through the Kimberley can be an adventure, but also carries risks. For drivers not used to the conditions, and not taking adequate rest breaks, the combination of warm sun through the windshield, long sections of road, and lack of traffic can have a hypnotic effect. Take regular breaks every two hours to walk and have a stretch, and get plenty of sleep the night before. If you are feeling sleepy, stop immediately and take a break. Many vehicle crashes in this area are vehicle versus animal, often a kangaroo or straying cattle. Dusk and dawn are when animals are most active. If you see an animal on the road in front of you, brake firmly in a straight line and sound your horn. Do not swerve: it is safer to stay on the road.

10

TIMING

You should allow at least five days to see Kununurra and the East Kimberley, including your arrival and departure days. That will allow enough to visit the Ord River and cruise Lake Argyle, take a scenic flight to the Bungle Bungles and hike the area with a guide, and take a four-wheel-drive excursion to El Questro Wilderness Park. Winter—May to September—is the most popular time to visit, as days are warm and there is little rain. October to April is the wet season, and temperatures can be a lot higher—up to 45°C.

TOURS

APT Kimberley Wilderness Adventures. This agency conducts tours from Broome and Kununurra, which include excursions along Gibb River Road and into Purnululu National Park. A two-day tour from

Kununurra includes the Mitchell Plateau and Mitchell Falls, with an overnight in a wilderness camp. ☎ *08/9191–8200, 1800/889389* 🌐 *www.kimberleywilderness.com.au.*

East Kimberley Tours. This company's most popular day tour includes an eye-popping flight to Purnululu National Park, a four-wheel-drive tour to the famous "beehive domes" and Cathederal Gorge, lunch, and a return scenic flight over Argyle Diamond mine. The tour costs A$965. Overnight fly-in, fly-out tours to the park cost from A$1,480. ☎ *08/9168–2213* 🌐 *www.eastkimberleytours.com.au.*

Kingfisher Tours. This company operates scenic flights from Kununurra Airport. A two-hour scenic flight over the Bungle Bungles and other sights costs A$330. ☎ *08/9168–1333* 🌐 *kingfishertours.net.*

Lake Argyle Cruises. Excellent trips on Australia's largest expanse of freshwater, the man-made Lake Argyle, start with a bus trip, which run daily March to October. It's A$70 for the two-hour morning cruise, A$155 for the six-hour cruise, and A$90 for the sunset cruise (which starts around 2:45). ☎ *08/9168–7687* 🌐 *www.lakeargylecruises.com.*

Slingair Heliwork WA. This company conducts both fixed-wing and helicopter flights from Kununurra and Purnululu National Park. A 30-minute helicopter flight costs A$335 from their helipad in the Purnululu National Park. An alternative two-hour fixed-wing flight over the Bungle Bungle and Lake Argyle is A$335. There are loads of options for coasting over the region with a bird's-eye view, but a standout is the Kimberley Coastal five-hour scenic flight, covering the magnificent King George Falls, Berkeley River, an indigenous community and other local sites and including a ground tour of Aboriginal-owned Home Valley Station and some locations from the film *Australia*. The cost is A$769 and includes lunch and swimming. ☎ *08/9169–1300* 🌐 *www.slingair.com.au.*

ESSENTIALS

Taxis Taxi Services Kununurra ☎ *13–1008, 08/960675.* **Spud's Taxis** ☎ *08/9168–2553.*

Visitor Information Kununurra Visitor Centre ✉ *75 Coolibah Dr., Kununurra, Western Australia* ☎ *08/9168–1177, 1800/586868* 🌐 *www.visitkununurra.com.*

WHERE TO STAY

For expanded hotel reviews, visit Fodors.com.

$$ HOTEL 🏨 **Ibis Styles Kununurra Hotel.** Set in tropical gardens, the brightly furnished rooms provide a comfortable base from which to explore the eastern Kimberley. **Pros:** walking distance to downtown; colorful Aboriginal art theme in rooms; swimming pool in tropical gardens setting; breakfast included; 15 minutes free Internet. **Cons:** limited amenities in rooms; limited dining options. [$] *Rooms from: A$189* ✉ *Victoria Hwy. and Messmate Way, Kununurra, Western Australia* ☎ *08/9168–4000* 🌐 *www.accorhotels.com.au* 🛏 *60 rooms* 🍴 *Some meals.*

$$$ HOTEL 🏨 **Kununurra Country Club Resort.** In the center of town, this hotel is encircled by its own little rain forest of tropical gardens. **Pros:** complimentary airport shuttle; poolside dining and bars; easy walk to downtown. **Cons:** tour groups stay here; Wi-Fi is intermittent. [$] *Rooms from: A$257*

✉ *47 Coolibah Dr., Kununurra, Western Australia* ☎ *08/9168–1024* 🌐 *www.kununurracountryclub.com.au* 🛏 *90 rooms* 🍴 *Some meals.*

$$ RESORT 🏨 **Kununurra Lakeside Resort.** On the shores of Lake Kununurra sits this understated, tranquil resort, where you can see stunning sunsets over the water (especially toward the end of the Dry), and watch for fruit bats flying overhead. **Pros:** lakeside location; courtesy bus available; crocodile spotting at night. **Cons:** rooms are basic. [$] *Rooms from: A$205* ✉ *50 Casuarina Way, off Victoria Hwy., Kununurra, Western Australia* ☎ *08/9169–1092, 1800/786692* 🌐 *www.lakeside.com.au* 🛏 *42 rooms* 🍴 *No meals.*

OFF THE BEATEN PATH **El Questro Wilderness Park.** This 1-million-acre property features some of the most ruggedly beautiful country in the East Kimberley. El Questro has a full complement of such recreational activities as fishing, swimming, and horse and helicopter rides and offers individually tailored walking and four-wheel-drive tours. Four independent accommodation facilities are on-site, each different in style and budget: the luxury Homestead; the safari-style tented cabins at Emma Gorge Resort; and air-conditioned Riverside Bungalows and Riverside Campgrounds at the Station Township. Each has a restaurant, and rates (minimum two nights) at the Homestead include drinks and food, laundry, and activities. Round-trip transportation from Kununurra is available from A$240 per person. ✉ *1 Gibb River Rd., Kununurra, Western Australia* ✣ *100 km (60 miles) west of Kununurra, via Great Northern Hwy.; take Gibb River Rd. for 42 km (14 miles) from the hwy. exit* ☎ *03/9169–1777 Reservations, 08/9161–4388 Emma Gorge Resort, 1300/233432* 🌐 *www.elquestro.com.au* 🎟 *El Questro Wilderness Park permit (required) A$20 for 1- to 7-day pass with access to gorge walks, thermal springs, fishing holes, rivers, and use of the Emma Gorge Resort swimming pool* 🛏 *6 suites, 60 tented cabins, 12 bungalows, 28 campsites, 6 lodge cabins* 🕓 *Apr.–Oct., daily.*

Home Valley Station. If you've ever fancied being a cowboy (or cowgirl) this massive 3½-million-acre working cattle farm at the foot of the majestic Cockburn (pronounced *co-burn*) is the place to do it. Owned and operated by the traditional owners of the land, the Balanggarra people through the Indigenous Land Corporation, you can join a cattle muster or just take a half-day horse trek. Other activities include fishing and 4WD trips. If the landscapes look familiar it's because much of the Baz Luhrmann movie, *Australia*, starring Nicole Kidman and Hugh Jackman, was filmed here. There's a bar and restaurant on-site and a range of accommodations, from stylish bungalows complete with cowskin rugs, air-conditioning, fully stocked minibar, flat-screen cable TV, huge walk-in rain shower, and resident tree frogs. For those on a tighter budget there's the motel-style guesthouse rooms, eco-tents with a raised wooden floor and queen-sized bed, and remote bush camping beside the Pentecost River, 4 km (2½ miles) from the homestead. Transfers from Kununurra cost A$220; A$90 from neighboring ⇨ *El Questro.* ✉ *Home Valley Station, 120 km (75 miles) from Kununurra on the Gibb River Rd., Kununurra, Western Australia* ☎ *08/9161–4322, 02/8296–8010 reservations* 🌐 *www.hvstation.com.au* 🕓 *Closed Nov.–end of Apr.*

10

PURNULULU (BUNGLE BUNGLE) NATIONAL PARK

252 km (156 miles) southwest of Kununurra.

Fodor's Choice ★ This park covers nearly 3,120 square km (1,200 square miles) in the southeast corner of the Kimberley. Australians of European descent first "discovered" its great beehive-shaped domes—their English name is the Bungle Bungle—in 1983, proving how much of this vast continent remains outside of "white" experience. The local Kidja Aboriginal tribe, who knew about these scenic wonders long ago, called the area Purnululu, meaning sandstone.

The striking, black-and-orange-stripe mounds seem to bubble up from the landscape. Climbing on them is not permitted, because the sandstone layer beneath their thin crust of lichen and silica is fragile, and would quickly erode without protection. Walking tracks follow rocky, dry creek beds. One popular walk leads hikers along the **Piccaninny Creek** to **Piccaninny Gorge,** passing through gorges with towering 328-foot cliffs to which slender fan palms cling. ⊠ *Pum, Western Australia* ⊕ *parks.dpaw.wa.gov.au/park/purnululu* ☉ *Park closed Dec. 15–Apr. 1.*

GETTING HERE AND AROUND

The Bungle Bungle are 252 km (156 miles) south of Kununurra along the Great Northern Highway. A very rough, 55-km (34-mile) unpaved road, negotiable only in a four-wheel-drive vehicle, is the last stretch of road leading to the park from the turnoff near the Turkey Creek–Warmum Community. That part of the drive can take two to three hours, depending on the condition of the road. It's farther on to one of the three campgrounds, two public and one used by tour operators that is also available to self-drivers who prefer hot showers, flushing toilets, and regular beds. The most-visited section of the park is in the south, where there are rough walking trails to the main sights.

SAFETY AND PRECAUTIONS

The park is usually open from April to December (depending on whether the road is passable after the Wet); however, temperatures in April, October, November, and December can be blisteringly hot. If you travel in these months, make sure you have plenty of water and be sun-smart.

TIMING

Purnululu National Park can be visited in a day from Kununurra, but only with a flight and safari package. There are also tours available that include overnight camping, but the road trip from Kununurra takes the best part of a day. Driving yourself to the park is not recommended, as the last section is a very rough track suitable only for four-wheel-drive vehicles; it has been kept deliberately so to limit visitation. If you do decide to drive in yourself, be aware that there are few facilities in the park's public campgrounds; you need to take in all your own food and camping equipment.

ESSENTIALS

Visitor Information Kununurra Visitor Centre ☎ *08/9168–1177* ⊕ *www. visitkununurra.com.* **Purnululu Visitor Centre** ⊠ *Purnululu (Bungle Bungle) National Park, park entrance, Kununurra, Western Australia* ☎ *08/9168–7300*

parks.dpaw.wa.gov.au/park/purnululu
Daily 8–noon and 1–4:30.

EXPLORING

The most popular walking trails are in the south of the park, where the famous "beehives" are located. From Piccaninny Creek car park you can hike in to **Cathedral Gorge**; the walk takes about an hour. Take a 20-minute detour on the **Domes Walk** to see more of the famous sandstone "beehives." If you have more time, you can follow the **Piccaninny Creek** walk into **Piccaninny Gorge**, following an eroded river-bed and sandstone ledges. This will take all day, but you can return at

A FANTASY LANDSCAPE

For millions of years nature has savaged the rocks of Purnululu National Park with water and wind, creating one of the most unusual landscapes in the world. Traveling into the area is a remarkable experience—the timelessness of the ancient rocks draws you back across the millennia. All around, the conically weathered formations cluster together like a meeting of some metamorphic executives.

any time. In the north of the park there are walks to **Echidna Gorge** (about one hour), where dinosaur-era livistona palms cling to the cliffs and the gorge narrows to about 3 feet across, and **Mini Palms Gorge**, a rock-strewn gorge again filled with livistona palms. At the end there is a viewing platform overlooking the valley. Allow an hour for this walk.

WHERE TO STAY

Although there are two designated campsites in the area, neither has many facilities. Both the Bellburn Creek and Walardi campgrounds have simple chemical toilets; fresh drinking water is at both campgrounds. Kununurra Visitor Centre has information about the campsites. The two tour operators who fly clients in from Kununurra, Broome, and Halls Creek, and drive them around in four-wheel-drive vehicles, have comfortable bush camps that regular visitors can also pay to use and eat at. April through December, the most popular tours include an overnight stay. The mounds are closed from January through March.

10

GEIKIE GORGE NATIONAL PARK

Twenty kilometers (12½ miles) northeast of the township of Fitzroy Crossing, Geikie Gorge is part of a 350-million-year-old reef system formed from fossilized layers of algae—evolutionary precursors of coral reefs—when this area was still part of the Indian Ocean. The limestone walls you see today were cut and shaped by the mighty Fitzroy River; during the Wet, the normally placid waters roar through the region. The walls of the gorge are stained red from iron oxide, except where they have been leached of the mineral and turned white by the floods, which have washed as high as 52 feet from the bottom of the gorge.

When the Indian Ocean receded, it stranded a number of sea creatures, which managed to adapt to their altered conditions. Geikie is one of the few places in the world where freshwater barramundi, mussels, stingrays, and prawns swim. The park is also home to the freshwater

archerfish, which can spit water as far as a yard to knock insects out of the air. Aborigines call this place Kangu, meaning "big fishing hole."

Although there's a 5-km (3-mile) walking trail along the west side of the gorge, the opposite side is off-limits because it's a wildlife sanctuary. ⊠ *Great Northern Hwy., King Leopold Ranges, Western Australia.*

National Park Ranger Station. The best way to see the gorge is aboard one of the 90-minute boat tours led by a ranger from the National Park Ranger Station, departing at 8, 9:30, 11 and 3. The rangers are extremely knowledgeable, and helpful in pointing out the vegetation, strange limestone formations, and the many freshwater crocodiles along the way. You may also see part of the noisy fruit-bat colony that inhabits the region. The park is open for day visits daily from 6:30 am to 6:30 pm between April and November. Entry is restricted during the Wet, from December to March when the Fitzroy River floods. ⊠ *Great Northern Hwy., King Leopold Ranges, Western Australia* ☎ *08/9191–5121, 08/9191–5112* ⊕ *parks.dpaw.wa.gov.au/park/geikie-gorge.*

BROOME

1,032 km (640 miles) southwest of Kununurra via Halls Creek, 1,544 km (957 miles) southwest of Katherine, 1,859 km (1,152 miles) southwest of Darwin.

Broome is the holiday capital of the Kimberley. It's the only town in the region with sandy beaches, and is the base from which most strike out to see more of the region. In some ways, with its wooden sidewalks and charming Chinatown, it still retains the air of its past as a boisterous shantytown. However, with tourism increasing every year it is becoming noticeably upscale.

Long ago, Broome depended on pearling for its livelihood. By the early 20th century 300 to 400 sailing boats employing 3,000 men provided most of the world's mother-of-pearl shell. Many of the pearlers were Japanese, Malay, and Filipino, and the town is still a wonderful multicultural center today with the modern pearling industry very much at its heart. Each August during the famous Shinju Matsuri (Festival of the Pearl), Broome commemorates its early pearling years and heritage. The 10-day festival features many traditional Japanese ceremonies. Because of the popularity of the festival, advance bookings for accommodations are highly recommended. Several tour operators have multiday cruises out of Broome along the magnificent Kimberley coast. The myriad deserted islands and beaches, with 35-foot tides that create horizontal waterfalls and whirlpools, make it an adventurer's delight.

Broome marks the western extent of the Kimberley. From here it's another 2,250 km (1,395 miles) south to Perth, or 1,859 km (1,152 miles) back to Darwin.

GETTING HERE AND AROUND

Qantas and its subsidiaries fly to Broome from Brisbane, Sydney, Melbourne, and Adelaide via Perth. Direct flights from Sydney, Melbourne, and Brisbane are twice a week. Air North has an extensive air network throughout the Top End, linking Broome to Kununurra and Darwin.

Virgin Australia also services Broome from Perth, Kununurra, and Darwin. Broome's airport is right next to the center of town, on the northern side. Though it's called Broome International Airport, there are no scheduled overseas flights, but charter flights and private flights arrive there.

SAFETY AND PRECAUTIONS

From November to April there is a possibility of cyclones off the Kimberley coast. It is important that visitors are aware of the procedures to follow in the event of a cyclone alert. These procedures are provided in all accommodations and are also at the Broome Visitor Centre or the Shire of Broome office. Call ☎ *1300/659210* for cyclone watch and warning messages, or go online at ⊕ *www.bom.gov.au.*

November to April is also when mosquitoes are at their most prevalent. To avoid the discomfort of mosquito bites and any risk of infection, it is advisable to cover up at dawn and dusk and apply insect repellent, which is supplied in most hotels. Sand flies become more active in Broome on high tides; use the same prevention methods.

Tropical waters can contain various stingers. The two types of dangerous jellyfish are the chironex box jellyfish (a large but almost transparent jellyfish up to 12 inches across with ribbonlike tentacles from each of the four corners) and Irukandji (a tiny transparent jellyfish less than 1 inch across with four thin tentacles). Both are found during the summer months of November to May. Take care when swimming (wear protective clothing—a wet suit or lycra stinger suit to reduce exposure to potential stings) and obey signs displayed on the beaches at all times. Medical attention (pour vinegar onto the sting and call ☎ *000* for an ambulance) should be sought if someone is stung.

Saltwater crocodiles live in estuaries throughout the Kimberley, and freshwater Johnsons crocodiles hang out in freshwater gorges and lakes. Look for warning signs. Even if not signposted, advice from a reliable local authority should always be sought before swimming in rivers and waterholes.

TIMING

Ideally, you need at least five days in Broome and the West Kimberley, including your arrival and departure days. This will give you time to go swimming and sunbathing on Cable Beach, take a camel ride or go kayaking, then cruise on a restored pearl lugger. A scenic flight will show you the pristine Kimberley coastline and the horizontal waterfalls of Buccaneer Archipelago. A day tour will get you to Cape Leveque or Windjana Gorge. To go farther afield, join a four-wheel-drive safari; a two-day tour will show you the gorges of the area, including Geikie Gorge.

The most popular time to visit is from May to October, during the dry season.

TOURS

APT Kimberley Wilderness Adventures conducts tours from Broome, which include excursions along Gibb River Road and into Purnululu National Park. Their 15-day Kimberley Complete tour includes the gorges along the Gibb River Road, the Aboriginal culture of the

10

Mitchell Plateau, a scenic flight over the Mitchell Falls, Purnululu National Park, and an Aboriginal-guided tour through Geikie Gorge. The price is from A$8,795.

Broome Sightseeing Tours has a two-hour Broome town tour (A$55) that includes visits to Cable Beach, Gantheaume Point, Chinatown, Roebuck Bay, Sun Pictures, and the Japanese cemetery. It ends at Pearl Luggers in time for the attraction's next tour. A combination ticket must be pre-bought to access cheaper rates for both tours.

Pearl Sea Coastal Cruises has multiday Kimberley adventures along the region's magnificent coastline in their luxury *Kimberley Quest 11* cruiser. All meals and excursions (including fishing trips) are included in the cost of A$9,180 for 8 days to A$13,305 for 14 days. Cruising season runs from March to September.

Astro Tours organizes entertaining, informative night-sky tours of the Broome area. Two-hour shows (offered four nights a week) cost A$80, including transfers from your hotel, folding-stool seating, hot beverages, and cookies. The company also offers four-wheel-drive Outback stargazing adventures farther afield.

ESSENTIALS

Tour Operators APT Kimberley Wilderness Adventures ☎ *1300/278278* ⊕ *www.kimberleywilderness.com.au*. **Astro Tours** ☎ *0417/9193–5362* ⊕ *www. astrotours.net*. **Broome Sightseeing Tours** ☎ *08/9192–0000*. **Pearl Sea Coastal Cruises** ☎ *08/9193–6131* ⊕ *www.kimberleyquest.com.au*.

Visitor Information Broome Visitor Centre ⊠ *1 Hamersley St., Broome, Western Australia* ☎ *08/9195–2200* ⊕ *www.broomevisitorcentre.com.au*.

EXPLORING

Broome is a small, compact town that's easy to explore on foot—you can even walk to the airport on the edge of town. You will need transportation to get to and from Cable Beach, which is around 7 km (4½ miles) from the town center. Chinatown, with its historic buildings, pearl showrooms, and art galleries, is in the middle of the main street shopping strip, and Roebuck Bay is only a few blocks to the south.

TOP ATTRACTIONS

FAMILY

Fodor'sChoice

★

The Malcolm Douglas Wilderness Wildlife Park. Entering via the jaws of a giant crocodile, this huge park opens up to reveal the Kimberley's native species in a variety of habitats. From rare western quolls and bilbies to dingoes, flying foxes, barking owls, several types of kangaroo, and of course hundreds of crocodiles, the park will keep you entertained for hours. Don't miss the nocturnal sanctuary, which houses endangered species that are part of an important breeding program. Beware the replica croc at the entry—many people have been fooled and frightened by its lifelike appearance. Don't miss the famous croc feeding at 3 pm daily. ⊠ *Great Northern Hwy., Broome, Western Australia* ⊕ *Go 16 km (10 miles) out of Broome on the Great Northern Hwy. and see the sign pointing to the right.* ☎ *08/9193–6580* ⊕ *www.malcolmdouglas. com.au* ⊠ *A$35* ⊙ *Daily 2–5 pm.*

Pearl Luggers. This historical display sheds light on the difficulties and immense skill involved in pearl harvesting. It has two restored

CLOSE UP

Broome By Camelback

Though not native to Australia, camels played a large part in exploring and opening up the country's big, dry, and empty interior. In the 1800s, around 20,000 camels were imported from the Middle East to use for cross-country travel—along with handlers (many from Afghanistan) who cared for them.

When railways and roads became the prime methods of transport in the early 20th century, many camels were simply set free in the desert. A steady population of wild camels—some 1,000,000 of them—now roams across the Australian Outback.

Broome has for many years been a place where people enjoy camel rides—especially along the broad, desertlike sands of Cable Beach. Three tour companies in town now offer camel "adventures" on a daily basis; they're a great way to see the coast and get a taste of history.

Broome Camel Safaris. Open Monday–Saturday, Broome Camel Safaris offers 30-minute rides (A$35) or one-hour sunset rides (A$70). ⊠ Broome, Western Australia ☎ 0419/916101 ⊕ www. broomecamelsafaris.com.au.

Red Sun Camels. Morning and sunset rides are available every day on Cable Beach. The morning ride lasts for 40 minutes and costs A$55; the pre-sunset ride runs for 30 minutes and costs A$35; the sunset ride takes an hour and costs A$75. ⊠ Broome, Western Australia ☎ 08/9193-7423, 1800/184488 ⊕ www.redsuncamels. com.au.

Ships of the Desert. Ships of the Desert leads its camels in the morning and twice in the evening. Morning tours run for 40 minutes and cost A$50; half-hour afternoon strolls cost A$35 and the shadow-throwing sunset tour lasts an hour and costs A$70. ⊠ Broome, Western Australia ☎ 08/1995-4022 ⊕ www. shipsofthedesert.com.au.

10

luggers along with other such pearling equipment as diving suits and an A$100,000 pearl you can hold. Get an insight into the risky lives of pearl divers, who spent years aboard pearling luggers and diving for pearl shells, on the regular tours (allow 1 hour). This is a must-see for those interested in Broome's history. ⊠ *31 Dampier Terr., Broome, Western Australia* ☎ *08/9192-0000* ⊕ *www.pearlluggers.com.au* 🖃 *A$20* ⊙ *Daily 9–5; Apr.–Sept. tours run on the hour, Oct.–Mar. tours at 10 and 3.*

FAMILY **Sun Pictures.** Opened in 1916, Sun Pictures is the world's oldest operating outdoor movie theater. Here silent movies—accompanied by a pianist—were once shown to the public. These days current releases are shown in the very pleasant outdoors. Historical tours of the theater are also available weekdays at 10:30 am and 1 pm for A$5 per person. ⊠ *8 Carnarvon St., Broome, Western Australia* ☎ *08/9192-1077* ⊕ *www. broomemovies.com.au* 🖃 *A$16.50* ⊙ *Daily 6:30 pm–11 pm.*

Willie Creek Pearl Farm. You can watch demonstrations of the cultured pearling process—including the seeding of a live oyster and a boat ride to the marine farm—at Willie Creek Pearl Farm, 38 km (23½ miles) north of Broome. Drive out to the farm yourself (you must make reservations first and a 4WD is recommended), or join a four-hour tour bus leaving from town. There's also the option of taking a scenic helicopter ride while on the property. ⊠ *Willie Creek Rd., Broome, Western Australia ✛ Drive 9 km (5½ miles) east from Broome on Broome Hwy., turn left onto Cape Leveque Rd. for 15 km (9 miles), turn left onto Manari Rd. for 5 km (3 miles), turn left and follow signs for 2½ km (1½ mile). Allow about 1 hr* ☎ *08/9192–0000* ⊕ *www.williecreekpearls. com.au* ⊡ *A$55, bus tour A$95* ☉ *Guided tours daily every hr 9–3; less often in the wet season, Oct.–Mar.*

WORTH NOTING

Broome Bird Observatory. A nonprofit research, education, and accommodation facility, the Broome Bird Observatory provides the perfect opportunity to see many of the Kimberley's 310 bird species, some of which migrate annually from Siberia. On the shores of Roebuck Bay, 25 km (15 miles) east of Broome, the observatory has a prolific number of migratory waders. The observatory offers a variety of daily guided tours in the dry season (from May to around September) costing A$70 per person for a half-day tour departing from the observatory. Pickup from Broome can also be arranged. A full-day tour costs A$150 from the observatory and A$195 from Broome. Start times depend on the day of the week and the tides and season, but are typically from 8 am to 3 pm. ⊠ *Crab Creek Rd., 15 km (9 miles) from Broome Hwy., Broome, Western Australia* ☎ *08/9193–5600* ⊕ *www.broomebirdobservatory. com* ⊡ *A$5 recommended donation for day visitors* ☉ *Day visitors: 8–4; tour reservations essential.*

Cultured Pearling Monument. The life-size bronze statues of the Cultured Pearling Monument are near Chinatown. The monument depicts three pioneers of the cultured pearling industry that is so intertwined with the city's development and history. ⊠ *Carnarvon St., Broome, Western Australia.*

Japanese Cemetery. More than 900 pearl divers are buried in the Japanese Cemetery, on the road out to Broome's deepwater port. The graves testify to the contribution of the Japanese to the development of the industry in Broome, as well as to the perils of pearl gathering in the industry's early days. ⊠ *Port Dr., Broome, Western Australia.*

BEACHES

Fodor's Choice
★

Cable Beach. Watching the sun sink into the sea on Cable Beach is a nightly ritual for almost all visitors to Broome, who flock to the 22-km (14-mile) stretch of dazzling white sand lapped by turquoise water 7 km (4½ miles) from the center of town. The most popular way to watch the sunset is from the back of a swaying camel, but you can also unpack a picnic at the beachside park, drive a 4WD onto the sand, or sip a cocktail from the beachside bar at Cable Beach Resort. By day it's a lot less crowded, and north of the vehicle access ramp is a nude beach. It's good for swimming, but low tide can mean a long walk across sand to get to the water. Beware of marine stingers (box and Irukandji jellyfish) in the water from December through to April. **Amenities:** lifeguard;

Camel riding on Cable Beach, Broome

toilets; parking (free). **Best for:** swimming; walking; sunset. ⊠ *Cable Beach Rd. W, Broome, Western Australia.*

WHERE TO EAT

$$ ✕**Matso's Broome Brewery.** One of the most popular spots to eat and
AUSTRALIAN drink in Broome, this microbrewery in an old bank building overlooking Roebuck Bay serves bar snacks, burgers, steaks, and fish-and-chips. The fan-cooled bar is full of pearling memorabilia and historic photographs, although most people choose to sit on the breezy veranda or in the shady beer garden. The brewery produces eight craft beers and a very refreshing alcoholic ginger beer. $ *Average main: A$30* ⊠ *60 Hammersley St., Broome, Western Australia* ☎ *08/9193–5811* ⊕ *www. matsos.com.au.*

WHERE TO STAY

For expanded hotel reviews, visit Fodors.com.

$$$$ ⚏**Cable Beach Club Resort and Spa.** Broome's only accommodation that
RESORT faces the famous Cable Beach, this resort is the area's most luxurious place to stay. **Pros:** walk to Cable Beach; minigolf; reading room; peaceful, tropical atmosphere; distinctive architecture; separate swimming pool for adults. **Cons:** no shopping nearby; need transport to get into town. $ *Rooms from: A$395* ⊠ *Cable Beach Rd., Broome, Western Australia* ☎ *08/9192–0400* ⊕ *www.cablebeachclub.com* ⌐ *176 rooms, 45 bungalows, 7 villas, 3 suites* ❖| *Some meals.*

$$$$ ⚏**Eco Beach.** This wilderness retreat peers over a cliff edge and gazes
RESORT into the ocean, giving the impression it's incredibly remote while only being about an hour and a half drive—or a shorter helicopter flight—away. **Pros:** lots of activities; beautiful waterfront location; can

self-cater. **Cons:** no shopping nearby; isolated location; expensive dining. [$] *Rooms from: A$345* ✉ *Roebuck Bay, Broome, Western Australia* ☎ *08/9193–8015* 🌐 *www.ecobeach.com.au* 🛏 *29 eco tents; 24 villas (garden or ocean views), 2 beach houses* 🍴 *No meals.*

$$$$ B&B/INN 🏨 **McAlpine House.** Originally built for a pearling master, this luxury guesthouse in tropical gardens is full of exquisite Javanese teak furniture. **Pros:** restored pearling master's residence; luxurious suites; intimate, private spaces; complimentary airport transfers. **Cons:** limited leisure facilities; no children under 16. [$] *Rooms from: A$355* ✉ *55 Herbert St., Broome, Western Australia* ☎ *08/9192–0510* ✍ *reservations@mcalpinehouse.com* 🌐 *www.mcalpinehouse.com* 🛏 *8 rooms; one 5 bedroom villa, rented whole* 🍴 *Breakfast.*

$$$ RESORT 🏨 **Pintcada Cable Beach.** This glam resort seduces with its stunning pool, spa facilities, and chic bar that sit at the heart of the luxurious rooms and suites. **Pros:** great lap pool; great food; all rooms have private balcony or courtyard. **Cons:** 10-minute walk to beach; parking-lot-facing rooms are noisy. [$] *Rooms from: A$325* ✉ *Cable Beach, 10 Murray Rd., Broome, Western Australia* ☎ *08/9193–8340* 🌐 *www.pintcadacablebeach.com.au* 🛏 *72 rooms* 🍴 *Some meals.*

SHOPPING

Broome has an abundance of jewelry stores.

Kailis Australian Pearls. This shop specializes in high-quality, expensive pearls and jewelry. ✉ *Shop 3, 23 Dampier Terr., Broome, Western Australia* ☎ *08/9192–2061* 🌐 *www.kailisjewellery.com.au.*

Linneys. This store sells high-end jewelry. They also have an outlet at Cable Beach Club Resort and Spa. ✉ *25 Dampier Terr., Broome, Western Australia* ☎ *08/9192–2430* 🌐 *www.linneys.com.*

Paspaley Pearling. Family-owned Paspaley Pearling, in Chinatown, sells pearls and stylish local jewelry. ✉ *2 Short St., Broome, Western Australia* ☎ *08/9192–2203* 🌐 *www.paspaley.com.*

PERTH AND
WESTERN AUSTRALIA

WELCOME TO PERTH AND WESTERN AUSTRALIA

TOP REASONS TO GO

★ **Beach Heaven:** Some of Australia's finest beaches are in Western Australia. Hundreds of kilometers of virtually deserted sandy stretches and bays invite you to swim, surf, snorkel, or laze about.

★ **National Parks:** With spectacular terrain and one-of-a-kind plant and animal species, rugged national parks tell the story of Australia's age-old landforms, especially across the gorge-pocked Kimberley region.

★ **Slick Eats:** Perth's modern food revolution has made way for a smorgasbord of small bars and edgy restaurants excelling at local, seasonal fare.

★ **Wine Trails:** Follow the beautiful wine trails from Perth to the south coast to enjoy free tastings of internationally renowned drops at the cellar doors.

1 Perth.
A population boom has led to a significant urban revitalization in Western Australia's capital, with the inner city's beating heart now matching the wow-factor of its Caribbean-style coastline.

2 Fremantle. The port town has charm in spades, both for its curving, colonial streets and the quirky vibe of its residents.

3 Rottnest Island.
The ultimate escape, with no cars—bikes are the dominant mode of transport—no pretension, and no cares in the world. The promise of 63 beaches just 19 km (12 miles) from Perth has people flocking.

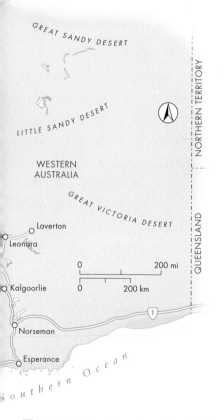

GREAT SANDY DESERT

LITTLE SANDY DESERT

WESTERN AUSTRALIA

GREAT VICTORIA DESERT

NORTHERN TERRITORY

QUEENSLAND

Laverton

Leonora

Kalgoorlie

Norseman

Esperance

Southern Ocean

0   200 mi
0   200 km

1

GETTING ORIENTED

Glance at a map of Australia and you'll see that the state of Western Australia (aka WA) encompasses one-third of the country. It's a massive slab, all 1 million square miles of it, so it may take longer than you expect to reach your destination. Such efforts will be rewarded, though, with fewer tourists to contend with and unadulterated nature. The state's glamour girl is undoubtedly the Margaret River wine region, as populated by native forests and rugged beaches as it is vineyards. But the capital city of Perth is going through a reinvention, transforming its sleepy core into a vibrant eating and drinking scene. Two of its gems, Fremantle and Rottnest Island, are mere day trips away. Journeying up the sparsely populated but beautiful northern coast is made easier with air travel— only tackle the roads if you have ample time.

4 The South West Wine Region. Towering native trees, epic surf, delightful winery-restaurants, and vineyards comb the coastal countryside. It's no wonder this area is regarded as one of the world's great wine regions.

Updated by
Fleur Bainger

Western Australia is a stunningly diverse place, with rugged interior deserts, endless, untrammeled white-sand beaches, a northern tropical wilderness, and a temperate forested south. The scenery here is magnificent; whether you travel through the rugged gorges and rock formations of the north; the green pastures, vineyards, and tall-tree forests of the south; or the coastline's vast, pristine beaches, you'll be struck by how much space there is here. If the crowds and crush of big-city life aren't your thing, this is the Australia you may never want to leave.

Perth, the capital city and home to nearly 70% of the state's 2.47 million residents, is a modern, pleasant metropolis with an easygoing, welcoming attitude. However, at 3,200 km (2,000 miles) from any other major city in the world, it has fondly been dubbed "the most isolated city on Earth." Its remoteness is part of what makes Western Australia so awe-inspiring.

It took more than 200 years after Dutch seafarer Dirk Hartog first landed on the coast of "New Holland" in 1616 in today's Shark Bay before British colonists arrived to establish the Swan River Colony (now Perth) in 1829. Progress was slow for half a century, but the discovery of gold around Kalgoorlie and Coolgardie in the 1890s brought people and wealth, especially to the fledgling city of Perth; much later, in the 1970s, the discovery of massive mineral deposits throughout the state began an economic upswing that still continues.

Western Australia produces much of Australia's mineral, energy, and agricultural wealth. More than 1,000 people move to WA each week, chasing the highs of its boom-and-bust cycle. Plenty is going on, too, with the airports being expanded, central train lines being sunk, linking the city's divided heart, as well as the long-term riverside development to be known as Elizabeth Quay (expect road delays). Fortunately for travelers, things are now starting to cool, leading to a more affordable experience in this land of inflated prices.

PLANNING

WHEN TO GO

You can visit Western Australia year-round, though the weather will influence your activities and sightseeing. Perth enjoys more sunny days than any other Australian capital city. Summer (December–February) in Perth is *hot* and temperatures can rise to 40°C (100°F), but the locals love it and flock to the beaches. Be aware major school and university holidays occur at this time. The Perth International Arts Festival (PIAF) in February is an excellent reason to visit. Weather-wise, March, April, November, and December are most pleasant, with sunny days and warm, comfortable temperatures. July and August are traditionally cool and wet.

GETTING HERE AND AROUND

AIR TRAVEL

Perth is the main international arrival point on this side of the country and is serviced by a dozen or more airlines. Qantas is Australia's main domestic airline, and with its budget subsidiary Jetstar operates an extensive network and regular services crisscrossing the country from all the major cities to regional centers like Exmouth and Broome. Virgin Australia competes with Qantas in major cities, and, after purchasing local carrier Skywest, now covers many regional centers such as Albany, Kununurra, Esperance, and Broome. Air North has an extensive network throughout the Top End and covers some WA legs in the north.

CAR AND BUS TRAVEL

Driving around Western Australia is relatively easy, with mostly good paved roads and light traffic outside Perth. While the distances in the Outback are daunting (Perth to Broome is 2,230 km [1,386 miles]), Perth to the Margaret River in the South West is less than four hours along good roads. Greyhound Australia and Integrity Coach Lines operate an extensive network of long-distance coaches. From Perth to Adelaide, expect to be on the road for 36 hours.

TRAIN TRAVEL

The *Indian Pacific*, operated by Great Southern Rail, links Sydney and Perth via Kalgoorlie and Adelaide, with once-weekly services each way (twice weekly in September and October). The trip takes around four days.

From Perth, TransWA operates train services to Bunbury twice daily and to Northam, Kalgoorlie, Geraldton, and Esperance, with coaches linking to other destinations.

Getting around Perth by train is quick and easy, with lines to Armadale, Clarkson, Midland, Joondalup, Fremantle, Mandurah, and Rockingham.

RESTAURANTS

A number of talented chefs have recently returned to Perth from overseas, bringing international trends, abilities, and standards with them. This influence, coupled with a healthy push for seasonal, local produce, has given the Perth dining scene an exciting shot in the arm. Waves of immigrants from Italy, the former Yugoslavia, and Asia also deliver cultural authenticity to the more traditional eateries. A British handover, fish-and-chips, remains one of the beach-going state's favorite picnic meals.

Expect to find Western Australian wines on the wine list when dining in most licensed restaurants in Perth and, of course, in the Margaret River wine region, where first-class food is matched with highly regarded vino.

Many restaurants and cafés offer alfresco dining. Tips aren't expected, but an extra 10% for exceptional service is welcome, particularly since Perth suffers from a sometimes justified reputation for offering below-par service. *Prices in the reviews are the average cost of a main course at dinner or, if dinner is not served, at lunch.*

HOTELS

From five-star to basic, you'll find suitable accommodations throughout the region. The well-known international chains are all in Perth but there are also sublime boutique accommodations. Perth has one of the highest occupancy rates in Australia, largely due to business travelers and this informs the room rates. Aim to book ahead, though last-minute bargains can be had, especially for weekends. Other popular options—especially for families and small groups—are self-contained apartments or villas. With two or three bedrooms, living areas, and kitchens, they allow you to save on dining costs by cooking your own meals; these are best if staying more than one night. *Prices in the reviews are the lowest cost of a standard double room in high season. For expanded reviews, facilities, and current deals, visit Fodors.com.*

HEALTH AND SAFETY

If you are self-driving—especially in remote areas—make sure you have enough fuel, water, and food and carry a first-aid kit. Let others know where you are going and for how long. Mosquitoes are prevalent, so cover up and use a good insect repellent; the worst times for mosquitoes are dawn and dusk.

Respect the Australian sun, especially in summer. Sunburn is a real danger if you don't follow the Australian mantra: slip, slap, slop—that is, slip on a hat, slap on sunglasses, and slop on sunscreen. On popular beaches around major cities and towns lifesavers (lifeguards) are usually on duty and put up flags to swim between, but generally most beaches are unguarded. Take extra care, especially where there are strong currents.

The emergency contact number for police, fire, and ambulance is ☎ *000.* From a GSM mobile (cell) phone the number is ☎ *112.*

PERTH

11

Buoyed by mineral wealth and foreign investment, Perth has high-rise buildings dotting the skyline, and an influx of immigrants gives the city a healthy diversity. Some of Australia's finest sandy beaches, sailing, and fishing are within 15 minute's drive of the city; the best seaside villages and postcard beaches lie just north of Fremantle. The main business thoroughfare is St. George's Terrace, an elegant street with a number of the city's most appealing sites. Perth's literal highlight is King's Park, 1,000 acres of greenery atop Mt. Eliza, which affords panoramic city views.

GETTING HERE

The main gateway to Western Australia is Perth's busy airport. It has three separate terminals—the original domestic terminal (about 11 km [7 miles] from Perth's central business district), and a secondary domestic terminal near the international hub (about 16 km [10 miles] away). A free shuttle bus connects the terminals 24 hours a day.

Taxis are at the airport around the clock. Trips to the city cost about A$40 and take around a half hour. Perth Airport Connect (☎ 08/9277–4666) operates frequent coach services from the terminals to Perth city hotels, and the East Perth train station. The cost to downtown Perth is A$15 from the domestic terminal; you must transfer there from the international terminal to take it.

Fewer people arrive by road or rail from the east. Crossing the Nullarbor Plain from the eastern states is one of the great rail journeys of the world. Great Southern Railways' *Indian Pacific* makes runs from Sydney and Adelaide, arriving at the East Perth Terminal. Greyhound Australia has long-distance coaches to Perth from eastern states capitals.

GETTING AROUND

Driving in Perth is relatively easy; just remember to stay on the left-hand side of the road, give way to traffic on your right, and avoid peak periods. All major car-rental companies have branches at the international and domestic airport terminals, while motor home and caravan hubs lie near airports.

Perth and its environs are well connected by Transperth buses. The main terminals are at the Esplanade Bus Port on Mounts Bay Road and at Wellington Street Bus Station. Buses run daily 6 am–11:30 pm, with reduced service on weekends and holidays. Rides within the city center are free. CAT (Central Area Transit) buses circle the city center, running frequently on weekdays 7–6 and Saturday 9–5. Routes and timetables are available from Transperth (☎ 13–6213 ⊕ *www.transperth. wa.gov.au*).

Transperth tickets are valid for two hours and can be used on Transperth trains and ferries. The ferries make daily runs from 6:50 am to 7:15 pm between Barrack Street Jetty in Perth to Mends Street, across the Swan River in South Perth. Reduced service runs on weekends and holidays.

Transperth trains also provide a quick way to get around the city. Most attractions are accessed via the Fremantle line, which traces the coast via Perth's most affluent suburbs. Other lines run east to Midland, north

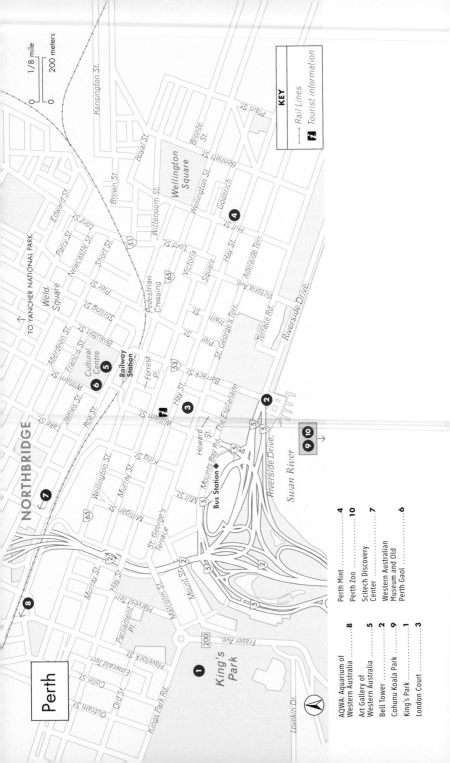

to Clarkson, southeast to Armadale, and south to Mandurah. Central-city train stations are in Wellington Street and Perth Underground at the corner of Williams and Murray streets. Tickets must be purchased at vending machines before boarding.

South West Coachlines. Daily services depart Perth Central Bus Station at the Esplanade Bus Port on Mounts Bay Road—as well as from Perth domestic and international airports—to South West towns, including Dunsborough and as far as Augusta. Services may vary according to season. ☎ *08/9261–7600 Perth office* ⊕ *www.southwestcoachlines. com.au.*

TIMING

Perth and surroundings can be visited in two to three days, if you're short on time and plan to explore farther afield. Spend the first day in central Perth, visiting Kings Park, the Perth Cultural Centre, the Hay Street and Murray Street shopping malls, great restaurants, and small bars, and, perhaps, the Swan Bells Tower. On the second day, head to Perth's most stunning piece of coastline, Cottesloe beach. Continue on to Fremantle, about 30 minutes from the city by train, where you can spend the rest of the day exploring this heritage port city. On the third day, take a day trip to Rottnest Island by ferry (30–60 minutes each way from the city center, Fremantle, or Hillarys). An upriver cruise to the Swan Valley that includes a visit to a winery and lunch also makes for a relaxing day.

TOURS

Australian Pinnacle Tours conduct day tours of Perth and its major attractions. You can also take a day tour of outer sights like Nambung National Park—with its weird limestone formation—Margaret River, or, with more time, Wave Rock near Hyden, and the Treetop Walk near Walpole (be aware that this is a long 14½-hour tour). Australian Pacific Touring has extended trips from Perth to Monkey Mia. City Sight Seeing has hop-on, hop-off trips around central Perth and to Kings Park on a double-decker, open-top bus. Tickets (A$25) are valid for two days and you can get on and off as you choose, or stay on for the full 90 minutes. Book online for discounts or pair your ticket with an experience with sister company, The Perth Tram Company, which runs sunset tours to Cottesloe and Fremantle in a wooden replica tram (A$60) on Tuesday and Thursday.

Rottnest Express runs excursions to Rottnest Island once daily from Perth and six to eight times daily from Fremantle, depending on the season. It also runs whale-watching tours in season, September and October, as does Rottnest Fast Ferries and Mills Charters.

Captain Cook Cruises has trips on the Swan River, traveling from Perth to the Indian Ocean at Fremantle with optional 1½-hour stopovers included. Cruises cost A$27 one way, A$37 return, or A$69 with lunch included. It also has tours upriver to the Swan Valley vineyards. Golden Sun Cruises has similar, cheaper offerings. Springtime in Western Australia (September–November) is synonymous with wildflowers, as 8,000 species blanket an area that stretches 645 km (400 miles) north and 403 km (250 miles) south of Perth. Tours of these areas are popular, and early reservations are essential. ■TIP➔ If you hire a car, check with local visitor centers to find out where the flowers are blooming.

Fodor'sChoice   **Two Feet and a Heartbeat.** These guys are award-winning for several rea-
★   sons: their walking tours are fun, informative, and wrap in elements
that reveal the personality of a city, such as street art, small bars, sculptures, and hidden relics. They offer a tour of the Perth Zoo, Bell Tower,
and Heritage Precinct with a ferry ride; a small bar and laneways (side
alleys) tour; and an off-the-tourist-track circuit of the city, plus various
tours in Fremantle. ■TIP➔ Book early for a "Tight arse Tuesday" tour,
which is half price (only A$20). ⊠ *Barrack and Hay Sts., CBD, Perth,
Western Australia* ☎ *1800/459388* ⊕ *www.twofeet.com.au.*

ESSENTIALS

Boat Tours Captain Cook Cruises ⊠ *Pier 3, Barrack Sq. Jetty, CBD, Perth,
Western Australia* ☎ *08/9325–3341* ⊕ *www.captaincookcruises.com.au.*
Catalina Adventures. This company offers heli-jet, harley-jet, and parasailing
options. ⊠ *Jetty 4, Barrack St. Jetty, CBD, Perth, Western Australia* ☎ *08/9225–
4166* ⊕ *www.catalinaadventures.com.au.***Golden Sun Cruises** ⊠ *Pier 4, Barrack
Sq. Jetty, CBD, Perth, Western Australia* ☎ *08/9325–9916 office, 0418/816166
bookings line* ⊕ *www.goldensuncruises.com.au.* **Rottnest Express** ⊠ *Pier
2, Barrack St. Jetty, CBD, Perth, Western Australia* ☎ *1300/467688* ⊕ *www.
rottnestexpress.com.au.*

Tour Contacts Australian Pacific Touring ☎ *1300/243137* ⊕ *www.
aptouring.com.au.* **Australian Pinnacle Tours** ⊠ *Shop 1, Barrack St. Jetty,
CBD, Perth, Western Australia* ☎ *08/8132–8288, 1300/551687* ⊕ *www.
australianpinnacletours.com.au.***Casey Australia Tours.** A range of extended
tours departing from Perth are available, including a 14-day four-wheel-drive
tour that traverses the iconic Gibb River Road and covers the Bungle Bungle
Range in Purnululu National Park, plus an optional flight over Mitchell Falls.
Some accommodation is in motels, but it's mostly camping—this is an outback
tour, after all! Prices start at A$4,050. ☎ *08/9339–4291, 1800/999677* ⊕ *www.
caseytours.com.au.* **Perth Tram Company** ☎ *08/9322–2006* ⊕ *www.perthtram.
com.au.*

Taxi Information Black & White ☎ *13–1008* ⊕ *www.bwtaxi.com.au.* **Swan
Taxis** ☎ *13–1330* ⊕ *www.swantaxis.com.au.*

Visitor Information Western Australia Visitor Centre ⊠ *55 William St., CBD,
Perth, Western Australia* ☎ *08/9483–1111, 1300/361351, 61/89483–1111 from
outside Australia* ⊕ *www.westernaustralia.com.*

EXPLORING

Because of its relative colonial youth, Perth has an advantage over most
other capital cities in that it was laid out with foresight. Streets were
planned so that pedestrian traffic could flow smoothly from one avenue
to the next, and this compact city remains easy to negotiate on foot.
Many points of interest are in the downtown area close to the banks
of the Swan River, while shopping arcades and pedestrian malls are a
short stroll away.

The city center (CBD, or Central Business District), a pleasant blend of old and new, runs along Perth's major business thoroughfare, St. George's Terrace, as well as on parallel Hay and Murray streets.

TOP ATTRACTIONS

FAMILY **AQWA: Aquarium of Western Australia.** Huge, colorful aquariums filled with some 400 different species of local sea creatures—including sharks that are 4 meters long—from along the 12,000 km (7,456 miles) of Western Australia's variable coastline are the fascinating draws of this boutique aquarium in northern Perth. Sharp-toothed sharks, stingrays, turtles, and thousands of fish swim overhead as you take the moving walkway beneath a transparent acrylic tunnel. You can even do a guided snorkel or scuba dive with the sharks for 30–45 minutes; bookings are essential. Perhaps most interesting is the change in habitats and species as you move from colder, southern waters to the tropics of Western Australia's north—AQWA boasts one of the largest living coral reef displays in the world. Check it out from above and then below in the underwater gallery. Other highlights include the rare seadragons and DANGERzone, featuring a deadly lineup of sea creatures. ⊠ *Hillarys Boat Harbour, 91 Southside Dr., Hillarys, Perth, Western Australia* ✣ *AQWA is a 20-min drive north of Perth's CBD via the Mitchell Freeway, turn left at Hepburn Ave. and continue to Hillarys Boat Harbour. Or, take the northern Joondalup train line. Alight at Warwick station and take Bus 423* ☎ *08/9447–7500* ⊕ *www.aqwa.com.au* ✉ *A$29; shark experience A$159, plus A$20 snorkel or A$40 scuba equipment rental* ☉ *Daily 10–5.*

Art Gallery of Western Australia. Founded in 1895, the Art Gallery of Western Australia is home to more than 17,000 treasures and numerous free exhibitions of indigenous and modern art—often lent by wealthy local collectors—which make it worth an afternoon's devotion. The collection of indigenous art is impressive, while other works include Australian and international paintings, sculpture, prints, crafts, and decorative arts. Free guided tours run regularly, though times vary; check the website for details. Generally, they're held at 1 pm Monday, Wednesday, Thursday, Saturday, and Sunday. Family-friendly tours are held on Sunday and during school holidays. There are also special tours for the vision impaired—phone or email ahead for bookings. Admission is free although donations are appreciated. An entry charge may apply to special exhibitions, many of which come direct from the Museum of Modern Art (MoMA) in New York City, thanks to a special collaboration between the two galleries that runs until March 2015. ▉TIP➔ There are also many seasonal, ticketed events, from intimate rock and pop concerts to late-night Friday viewings with a bar and comedians. ⊠ *Perth Cultural Centre, James St. at Beaufort and Roe Sts., CBD, Perth, Western Australia* ☎ *08/9492–6600* ⊕ *www.artgallery. wa.gov.au* ✉ *Free* ☉ *Wed.–Mon. 10–5 and until 9 pm Fri. during the MoMA Series.*

FAMILY

Fodor's Choice

★

King's Park. Locals boast that this is one of the few inner-city parks to dwarf New York City's Central Park; it covers 1,000-acres and grants eye-popping views of downtown Perth at sunrise, sunset, and all times in between. Once a gathering place for Aboriginal people and established as a public space in 1890, it's favored for picnics, parties, and weddings, as well as regular musical and theater presentations, plus the excellent summer Moonlight Cinema. In spring the gardens blaze with orchids, kangaroo paw, banksias, and other native wildflowers, making it ideal for a walk in the bushland. The steel-and-timber **Lotterywest Federation Walkway** takes you into the treetops and the 17-acre botanic garden of Australian flora. The **Synergy Parkland** details Western Australia's fossil and energy history. The **Lotterywest Family Area** has a playground for youngsters. Free walking tours, which depart from the Aspects Gift Shop on Fraser Avenue, take place daily at 10 am and 2 pm; November–June there's also a walk at noon. Details on seasonal and themed tours are available from the information kiosk near Fraser's Restaurant. ⊠ *Fraser Ave. at King's Park Rd., West Perth, Perth, Western Australia* ☎ *08/9480–3634* ⊕ *www.bgpa.wa.gov.au* 🖾 *Free* ⊙ *Daily 24 hrs.*

> ### THE VIEW FROM KING'S PARK
>
> The best spot is the manicured eastern edge of the park, past the border of tall, white-bark trees and overlooking Perth's Central Business District and the Swan River. While it's a jubilant place buzzing with friends and families picnicking, it also has a somber edge, home to the State War Memorial and its eternal flame, as well as the memorial to local victims of the 2002 terrorist bombing in Bali.

FAMILY **Yanchep National Park.** Sure, it's nice to cuddle a koala in an enclosure, but it's far more exciting to see them in the wild, just above your head. Take the 240-meter (787-foot) Koala Board Walk through native bush with your eyes raised skyward to see one of the state's largest populations of koalas. Watch for western gray kangaroos on the 2-km (1-mile) wetland walk trail around Loch McNess lake and then escape summer's heat by joining one of several daily underground tours of Crystal Cave (A$10.80 or A$27 for a family pass), where cooling caverns open up to impressive stalactite galleries and clear-water pools. Aboriginal Experience walks explaining the significance of native plants and animals to the Nyoongar people also make for a rewarding experience. ■ TIP→ Yanchep National Park is a 45-minute drive north of Perth and is open every day of the year; book tours and get walk trail information at McNess House Visitor Centre. National park entry is A$11 per vehicle. ⊠ *3499 Wanneroo Rd., Yanchep, Perth, Western Australia* ☎ *08/9303–7759 McNess House Visitor Centre* ⊕ *www.dpaw.wa.gov.au.*

WORTH NOTING
The Bell Tower. The spire-like Bell Tower is home to one of the world's largest musical instruments, the 12 antique Swan Bells, which have surprising historical links. Originally from St. Martin-in-the-Fields Church of London, England, these same bells were rung to celebrate the destruction of the Spanish Armada in 1588, the homecoming of Captain James Cook in 1771, and the coronation of every British monarch. The tower contains fascinating displays on the history of the bells and bell ringing, and provides stunning views of the Perth skyline and the nearby Swan River. ■ TIP→ Head to the lofty heights of the observation deck on

King's Park with downtown Perth in the distance

Level 6 for the Wow factor. Flat, closed shoes must be worn for access to the observation deck; stroller and wheelchair access are available via the elevator. ✉ *Barrack Sq., Barrack St. at Riverside Dr., CBD, Perth, Western Australia* ☎ *08/6210–0444* ⊕ *www.thebelltower.com. au* ✉ *A$14* ⊙ *Daily 10–4; bell-handling demonstrations (single bell) Wed. and Fri. 11:30 am–12:30 pm; full bell ringing Mon., Tues., Thurs., and weekends noon–1 pm.*

FAMILY **Cohunu Koala Park.** The main lure at this 30-acre property is the joy of cuddling a koala (for an additional A$25 fee). But the other native animals, such as emus, dingoes, wallabies, kangaroos, and wombats are worth visiting, too. Bear in mind that Cohunu (pronounced co-hu-na) is an attraction park, rather than a natural habitat, and some wildlife are caged. A miniature steam railway (A$4 per ride) operates mostly on weekends and school and public holidays. ✉ *Lot 802, Nettleton Rd., Byford, Perth, Western Australia* ✣ *Cohuna is a 40-min drive south of Perth's CBD. Take the South Western Hwy. to Byford, turn left at Nettleton Rd. for 500 meters* ☎ *08/9526–2966* ⊕ *www.cohunu.com. au* ✉ *A$15* ⊙ *Daily 10–5.*

London Court. Gold-mining entrepreneur Claude de Bernales built this quaint outdoor shopping arcade in 1937. Today it's a magnet for anyone with a camera wanting to recapture the atmosphere and architecture of Tudor England, and for those looking for Australian souvenirs. Along its length are statues of Sir Walter Raleigh and Dick Whittington, the legendary lord mayor of London. Above the arcade entry, costumed mechanical knights joust with one another when the clock strikes the quarter hour. ■TIP➔ Don't miss Pigeonhole; it's a great place to shop for souvenirs and gifts. ✉ *Between St. George's Terr. and Hay St., CBD, Perth, Western Australia.*

Perth Mint. All that glitters is gold at the Perth Mint, one of the oldest mints in the world still operating from its original premises, and a reminder of the great gold rush days at the turn of the 20th century. Established in 1899, it first refined gold from Western Australia's newly discovered goldfields, striking gold sovereigns for the British Empire. Today it still produces Australia's legal tender in pure gold, silver, and platinum bullion and commemorative coins for investors and collectors. Visitors can have a hands-on experience at the Mint—watch 200 ounces of molten gold being poured in time-honored fashion to form a gold bar; eye the biggest coin ever made, weighing 1 ton; get close to more than A$700,000 worth of gold bullion; see Australia's best collection of natural gold nuggets, including the 369-ounce Golden Beauty, one of the largest natural nuggets in the world; and discover your own weight in gold. ✉ *310 Hay St., CBD, Perth, Western Australia* ☎ *08/9421–7223* ⊕ *www.perthmint.com.au* ✆ *A$25* ⊗ *Daily 9–5 except on some public holidays; guided talks every half-hr 9:30–3:30; gold pour every hr 10–4* ⊗ *Closed Anzac Day, Good Friday, Christmas Day, and Boxing Day.*

FAMILY **Perth Zoo.** From kangaroos to crocodiles and venomous Aussie snakes to Asian sunbears and orangutans, this expansive, more than century-old zoo is an easy five-minute drive from Perth's CBD. Expect lush gardens—perfect for a BYO picnic—and different native habitats of various animals from around the world. Walk among Australian animals in an environment depicting the diversity of Australia's native landscape. Discover the Reptile Encounter, Rainforest Retreat, and the Australian Bushwalk. For something a little more exotic, there's the African Savannah, with rhinoceros, giraffe, lions, cheetahs, and baboons; and the Asian Rainforest, with elephants, red pandas, tigers, otters, apes, and monkeys. A number of special encounters are available, such as joining a keeper as they feed the lions, which is best booked and paid for in advance. Free guided walks depart daily at 11:30 am and 1:30 pm and there are more than a dozen free talks and presentations each day. A one-hour guided tour around the zoo on an electric Zebra Car, seating seven passengers and the driver, costs A$5 per person. ✉ *20 Labouchere Rd., South Perth, Perth, Western Australia* ⊹ *Catch the number 30 or 31 bus at Esplanade Busport or take a ferry ride across the Swan River from the bottom of Barrack St. and then a 10-min walk following the signs* ☎ *08/9474–0444, 08/9474–3551* ⊕ *www.perthzoo.wa.gov.au* ✆ *A$24.50* ⊗ *Daily 9–5.*

FAMILY **Scitech Discovery Centre.** Interactive science and technology displays educate and entertain visitors of all ages. There are more than 100 hands-on general science exhibits, as well as in-depth feature exhibitions. Daily science and puppet shows present science in an entertaining way, and the space shows in the newly refurbished planetarium should stretch your imagination as they take you to the far edges of the known universe. ■ TIP➔ Keep an eye out for the quirky facts that dot the space, including the fact that the heart of a giraffe is 2 feet long. ✉ *City West Centre, Sutherland St., West Perth, Perth, Western*

The Pinnacles of Nambung National Park, Western Australia

Australia 🕿 *08/9215–0700* 🌐 *www.scitech.org.au* ✉ *A\$17* 🕑 *Weekends, school holidays, and public holidays 10–5; weekdays 9:30–4.*

FAMILY **Western Australian Museum and Old Perth Gaol.** Whether you fancy getting close to a taxidermied wallaby, dinosaur fossils, meteorites, or hundreds of colorful butterflies, you'll find it all contained in the state's most comprehensive museum. The site also includes some of Perth's oldest structures, such as the Old Perth Gaol. Built of stone in 1856, this was Perth's first and only prison until 1888. After being decommissioned as a gaol (jail) it became Perth's first museum. Get a feeling for Perth's criminal past and have a coffee at the Muse Café in the leafy courtyard close to where executions once took place. Today it is part of a much larger museum where permanent exhibitions include "Diamonds to Dinosaurs," which uses fossils, rocks, and gemstones to take you back 3.5 billion years. "Katta Djinoong: First Peoples of Western Australia" has a fascinating collection of primitive tools and lifestyle artifacts used thousands of years ago by Australia's Aboriginals. International and national visiting exhibitions, though ticketed, are a highlight. ⊠ *Perth Cultural Centre, James and William Sts., CBD, Perth, Western Australia* 🕿 *08/9212–3700* 🌐 *www.museum.wa.gov.au* ✉ *Free; suggested donation A\$5* 🕑 *Daily 9:30–5.*

OFF THE BEATEN PATH

Batavia Coast. A drive along this part of the coast, which starts at Greenhead, 285 km (178 miles) north of Perth, and runs up to Kalbarri, takes you past white sands and emerald seas, and some lovely small towns. Among them are the fig-shaded, seaside village of **Dongara** and the more northerly **Central Greenough Historical Settlement,** whose restored colonial buildings—including a jail with original leg irons—date from

1858. A few miles north is **Geraldton,** whose skyline is dominated by the beautiful Byzantine St. Francis Xavier Cathedral. Its redeveloped foreshore playground is great for kids; also worth a visit is the haunting HMAS Sydney II Memorial, which is recognized as the only national War Memorial outside of Canberra, offering expansive views. The huge Batavia Coast Marina has a pedestrian plaza, shopping arcades, and the fascinating Western Australian Museum, which houses a collection of artifacts from the *Batavia,* a Dutch vessel shipwrecked in 1629. ⊠ *Batavia Coast, Western Australia.*

Nambung National Park. Imagine an eerie moonscape where pale yellow limestone formations loom as high as 15 feet: this is Nambung National Park and its most famous attraction, the **Pinnacles Desert.** Set on the Swan coastal plain 200 km (125 miles) north of Perth, it's now accessible in just under two hours along the scenic Indian Ocean Drive. Formed 200,000 years ago, the pinnacles are one of the world's most spectacular karst landscapes created by the dissolving action of water on exposed limestone beds that formed under windblown sand dunes. You can walk among them along a 1.2-km (0.7-mile) return walk that starts at the parking area. There's also a 4-km (2.5-mile) one-way Pinnacles Desert Loop scenic drive (not suitable for large RVs or buses). Stop in to the Pinnacles Desert Discovery Centre to see interpretative displays focused on the region's unique geology, flora, and fauna. August through October the heath blazes with wildflowers. ▉ TIP➔ Note the "No's:" No pinnacle climbing, no dogs, no bins, no drinking water, although water is available to purchase at the interpretative center and gift shop. Entrance fee is A$12 per car. ⊠ *Nambung National Park, Western Australia* ☎ *08/9652–7913, 08/9652–1911.*

BEACHES

FAMILY   **Cottesloe.** Perth's signature beach is as beguiling as it is relaxing, with
Fodor'sChoice   soft cream sand, transparent blue waters, and a strip of pubs and res-
★   taurants. Naturally, it's very popular, particularly on Sunday, when people of all ages picnic on grass beneath the row of Norfolk pines that also hosts masses of squawking birds. The water is fairly calm, though punchy waves can roll through, crashing mainly in shallow depths. "Sunday sessions"—afternoon beer drinking in two local pubs, the Ocean Beach Hotel and the Cottesloe Beach Hotel—are also held here. South of the Cottesloe groyne (jetty) is a reasonable surf break, but it's often crowded. ▉ TIP➔ Time your visit for the annual Sculptures by the Sea event, a shore-side exhibition of huge sculptures each March. **Amenities:** showers; toilets; food and drink; lifeguards; parking (free). **Best for:** swimming; walking; sunset. ⊠ *Marine Parade, Cottesloe, Perth, Western Australia* ⊕ *www.cottesloe.wa.gov.au.*

FAMILY   **North Cottesloe.** This is the quieter end of Cottesloe where local residents go to walk their dogs (a section by Grant Street is a designated dog beach), take an early morning dip, or share a sunset wine on the sand. The concrete walking path looks over the sandy beach and affords impressive views of the coastal mansions that look out to sea. Coastal reef fans out to the right of Grant Street and makes for good snorkeling, particularly as the water is calm and there are no rips or currents. ⚠ Beware of invisible jellyfish, known as stingers, which cause pain but pose little other threat. **Amenities:** showers; lifeguards. **Best for:** solitude; swimming; walking; snorkeling; sunset. ✉ *365 Marine Parade, North Cottesloe, Perth, Western Australia.*

Swanbourne. While lovely, Swanbourne tends to keep a lower profile within Perth's beach scene, largely due to its nudist-friendly stretch which is dominated by men. The southern end is popular thanks to the aptly named ocean-facing café, The Naked Fig, which serves breakfasts and light meals; there's a playground nearby. The sand is soft and the surf rises somewhat along this section, with parts favored by body boarders. It's just north of Cottesloe and is about 20 minutes from Perth's City Center. **Amenities:** toilets; showers; food and drink; parking (limited). **Best for:** nudists; sunset. ✉ *Marine Parade 278, Swanbourne, Western Australia.*

Trigg. Surfers and body boarders favor this beach, riding the transparent blue waves from Trigg Point and Trigg Island, sometimes crashing into the sandy bottom. Swimmers don masks and paddle to the snorkeling spot of Mettams Pool that is lovely on calm days but should be avoided when the swell is up. A hip coffee haunt, Yelo, is the best café in the area. Across the road away from the ocean, the Trigg Bushland Reserve makes for interesting, paved bushwalking—just follow the trail and its interpretive signage. ⚠ There is sometimes a strong undertow off this beach, and swimmers have struck trouble. **Amenities:** toilets; parking; food and drink; playground; lifeguards. **Best for:** snorkeling; surfing; sunset. ✉ *361 W. Coast Dr., Trigg, Perth, Western Australia.*

SPORTS AND THE OUTDOORS

BICYCLING

Perth's climate and its network of excellent trails make cycling a safe and enjoyable way to discover the city. But beware: summer temperatures can exceed 40°C (100°F) in the shade. A bicycle helmet is required by law, and carrying water is prudent. About Bike Hire, which rents bikes for A$10 an hour, A$36 a day, or A$80 a week, is open daily 9–5 with extended hours in high season. Free brochures detailing trails, including stops at historic spots, are available from the Western Australia Visitor Centre. Rentals are available at

About Bike Hire ✉ *Behind Causeway Car Park, 1-7 Riverside Dr., Perth, Western Australia* ☎ *08/9221–2665* ⊕ *www.aboutbikehire.com.au.*

SURFING

Western Australians take to the surf from a young age—and with world-famous surfing beaches right on the city's doorstep, it's no wonder. The most popular year-round beaches for body and board surfing are Scarborough and Trigg, where waves can reach 6–9 feet. There are also more than a dozen beaches heading north from Leighton (near Fremantle), including the Cables Artificial Reef (near Leighton) and Watermans (in the northern suburbs of Perth). Cottesloe Beach is favored by novice surfers and children; south of the groyne (a man-made breakwater or jetty) is popular with stand-up paddleboard riders.

If you venture outside the city, Rottnest Island's west end has good surf, and if you head south on the mainland coast, you'll find more than 20 surf locations from Cape Naturaliste to Cape Leeuwin. The Main Break at Margaret River is the best known, where waves often roll in at more than 12 feet, setting the scene for the annual Margaret River Pro, a World Championship Tour event on the Association of Surfing Professionals circuit, held in March at Surfers Point.

Wet suits are de rigueur for the colder months (May–September), when the surf is usually at its best.

Scarborough Beach Surf School. These surfer dudes have been pushing beginners out into the white water for more than 20 years. They specialize in adult lessons on Scarborough beach but will provide separate kiddy lessons, or family groups, too (11 years and up). If you want to get serious, there are several levels you can complete, and when you do, you'll be presented with a Surfing Australia Certificate. Single lessons are A$60 or a five-lesson course costs A$225. Courses run daily in summer (weekends in winter) 7:15–9:30 and 9:45–noon. ■ TIP→ **Courses sell out one week in advance so book ahead.** ✉ *The Esplanade, Scarborough, Western Australia* ☎ *08/9447–5637* ⊕ *www.surfschool.com.*

WATER SPORTS

FAMILY **Funcats Surfcat Hire.** If you want to enjoy the Swan River at a leisurely pace and possibly spot its resident dolphins, rent a 14-foot catamaran (A$40 per hour), kayak (A$20 per hour), or a stand-up paddleboard (A$20 per hour) from Funcats Surfcat Hire. Funcats operates from October to April and life jackets are included. ✉ *Coode St. Jetty, South Perth, Perth, Western Australia* ☎ *0408/926003.*

WA Surf. Perth has consistent winds, particularly in the afternoons, so it's one of the best places to learn to kite surf. WA Surf offers both kite surfing and stand-up paddleboard lessons year-round on the shores of Safety Bay, just south of Perth, where the water is flat and calm. As people improve, their kites increase in size, adding more power to their ride, so it can be as extreme or as mellow as you like. Safety systems are built in, so you can be detached from your kite in a couple of seconds if you get into trouble. Most people opt for a series of three two-hour lessons, but tricks can be taught to old hands, too. ✉ *Safety Bay Yacht Club, Safety Bay Rd. at Arcadia Dr., Safety Bay, Rockingham, Western Australia* ☎ *08/9592–1657* ⊕ *www.wasurf.com.au.*

WHERE TO EAT

Northbridge, northwest of the railway station, is *the* dining and nightclubbing center of Perth, and reasonably priced restaurants are everywhere. Elsewhere around Perth are seafood and international restaurants, some with stunning views over the Swan River, beachside, or city, and cantilevered windows that make for a seamless transition between indoor and alfresco dining.

For those on a budget, the noisy fun of a dim sum lunch at one of Perth's many traditional Asian teahouses (especially in Northbridge) is cheap and delicious. Along with a cup of green tea, you can enjoy steamed pork buns, fried chicken feet, and dumplings served at your table from a trolley. Food halls in Perth, Northbridge, and Fremantle are other budget options.

Use the coordinate (✣ B2) at the end of each listing to locate a site on the corresponding map.

$$ MODERN AUSTRALIAN Fodor's Choice ★

🍴 **Brookfield Place.** Like bees swarming a hive, once the clock hits 5 pm, punters flood Perth's CBD's main thoroughfare, St. Georges Terrace, and its strip of hip new venues. The best is at Brookfield Place, where the swanky Print Hall development hugs the huge new BHP tower. Print Hall is credited with dishing up some of the city's best Modern Australian fare, while Bob's Bar is a happening rooftop venue focusing on simple, tasty Asian eats. In between the two is Apple Daily, which focuses on Asian street food and more refined fare. At the toes of the BHP tower are some serious contenders in Bar Lafayette, a boho cocktail bar; The Trustee, a classy wine bar and restaurant; and Sushia, a Japanese restaurant with ocean-fresh food prepared in the huge open kitchen. During the day there's a bakery, café, burger bar, and food hall (hidden behind the BHP tower) offering plenty of lunch options. [$] *Average main: A$25* ✉ *123–137 St. Georges Terr., CBD, Perth, Western Australia* ☎ *08/9428–6400 general number* 🌐 *brookfieldplaceperth.com/eat-drink-shop* ✣ *C3.*

$$ MODERN AUSTRALIAN

🍴 **CBD Restaurant and Bar.** A popular place in Perth's West End, CBD buzzes loudest when the after-work crowd files in, favoring the alfresco tables that spill onto the sidewalk. The menu changes regularly, but could include a relish smothered steak sandwich; creamy chicken pappardelle; or barbecue pork belly. There's a pizza oven as well, with chorizo, garlic prawn, and mozzarella-topped pizzas from A$18.50. A big selection of table wine and "stickies" (dessert wines) are available by the glass. Late hours bring in the nightcap crowd after shows at the adjacent His Majesty's Theatre. [$] *Average main: A$35* ✉ *Hay and King Sts., CBD, Perth, Western Australia* ☎ *08/9263–1859* 🌐 *www.cbdrestaurant.com.au* ✣ *C3.*

$$$ AUSTRALIAN

🍴 **Coco's Riverside Bar and Restaurant.** Appealing to the glitzy, moneyed, cosmetically conscious crowd in Perth, you'll be lucky to get a table on Friday, when rollicking long lunches can extend well past sunset—unless you book in advance. The views are as good as the people-watching, and though the classic food is expensive, it's beautifully executed. The varied menu includes a seafood tasting plate perfect for sharing; Tasmanian aged-beef dishes; fresh fish of the day; and for dessert, baked bombe Alaska. It should ideally be washed down with a selection from the extensive wine list that includes many of the best labels from the Margaret River region. [$] *Average main: A$50* ✉ *Southshore Centre, 85 Esplanade, South Perth, Perth, Western Australia* ☎ *08/9474–3030* 🌐 *westvalley.com.au* ✍ *Reservations essential* ✥ *D4.*

$$ THAI 🍴 **Dusit Thai Restaurant.** Come here for authentic Thai food, lovingly prepared and served among traditional sculptures and artwork. Starters include *kra thong tong* (stir-fried diced prawns, minced chicken, and sweet corn in deep-fried cups); or *ma hor* (fruit slices topped with a mixture of minced chicken, shallots, peanuts, palm sugar, and coriander roots). Main-course specialties include *gang keo-wan* (green curry chicken) and *gang-ped* (hot and spicy red curry with green peas, bamboo strips, roast duck, and pineapple). Attentive service placing accent on detail—note the linen serviettes elaborately folded liked winged birds. Dusit Thai has been in Northbridge for more than 25 years. [$] *Average main: A$22* ✉ *249 James St., Northbridge, Perth, Western Australia* ☎ *08/9328–7647* 🌐 *www.dusitthai.com.au* 🕒 *Closed Mon. No lunch* ✥ *A3.*

$$$ MODERN AUSTRALIAN 🍴 **Fraser's Restaurant.** In fair weather the large outdoor area at this King's Park restaurant fills with people enjoying food and views of the city and Swan River. The ever-changing menu highlights fresh Western Australian produce. Look for zucchini and watercress soup; braised lamb shoulder with baby leek; or perhaps crisp fried flathead fillet, with fries and tartare. [$] *Average main: A$40* ✉ *King's Park, Fraser Ave., West Perth, Perth, Western Australia* ☎ *08/9481–7100* 🌐 *www.frasersrestaurant.com.au* ✍ *Reservations essential* ✥ *D1.*

$$ MODERN AUSTRALIAN Fodor's Choice ★ 🍴 **Il Lido Italian Canteen.** With a window seat onto iconic Cottesloe beach, this whitewashed canteen scores with simple, seasonal food delivered with finesse. Handmade pasta is a specialty—spaghetti ribboned around sweet Shark Bay crabmeat, flecked with baby capers and chili is a dish to die for. The house favorite, seared slices of pork and fennel seed sausage strewn on roasted cauliflower, is made from the owner's family recipe, as the knowledgeable staff attest. The wine list favors local producers and, pleasingly, offers quarts as well as bottles. Communal tables are de rigueur; the convivial alfresco area looks out to a coastal conga line of walkers, joggers, and cyclists. By night candles and '50s films projected silently on the wall deliver a romantic feel. [$] *Average main: A$28* ✉ *88 Marine Parade, Cottesloe, Perth, Western Australia* ☎ *08/9286–1111* 🌐 *www.illido.com.au* ✥ *B1.*

$$$ MODERN AUSTRALIAN 🍴 **Jackson's Restaurant.** A long list of awards over the past two decades has established Jackson's Restaurant as one of Perth's top dining establishments, but trends have led it to move away from its degustation menu to more casual, yet equally refined eats at fantastic prices. Chef Neal Jackson has launched a new lounge section, serving truffle popcorn; crab and mayo brioche buttie; and drunken chicken, tea egg, and wolfberries—all dishes range from A$7 to A$10. Pricier à la carte choices include roasted quail, foie gras, wood ear mushroom, and truffle ponzu or dry aged sirloin steak, potato crisps and Roquefort sauce. There are limited but excellent vegetarian choices as well, such as risotto of celery, apple, grapes, walnuts, and goat curd. [$] *Average main: A$42*

✉ *483 Beaufort St., Highgate, Perth, Western Australia* ☎ *08/9328–1177* 🌐 *www.jacksonsrestaurant.com.au* ⏲ *Closed Sun.* ✥ *A5.*

$ ITALIAN FAMILY 🍴 **Jamie's Italian.** The British celebrity chef and good food crusader Jamie Oliver has opened his biggest restaurant worldwide in Perth. Fun, fresh, and fabulous, Jamie's Italian serves up fantastic value with every dish. The queues may be a battle, but the polenta chips make up for it, chased with a side of crunchy apple slaw. Once your table is ready, settle in for the fennel sausage pappardelle pasta or the creamy blue swimmer crab risotto. Servings are generous enough to opt for the appetizer size (unless you're ravenous). **TIP→ Plan to dine during non-peak times.** [$] *Average main: A$18* ✉ *140 William St., CBD, Perth, Western Australia* ☎ *08/9363–8600* 🌐 *www.jamieoliver.com/italian/australia/perth* ✍ *Reservations essential* ✥ *B4.*

$$ ASIAN 🍴 **Joe's Oriental Diner.** On the street level of the Hyatt Regency Hotel, Joe's serves a wide range of dishes from Indonesia, Thailand, Malaysia, and Singapore, and makes for a convenient option if you're staying there. The rattan-and-bamboo interior is reminiscent of the many noodle houses throughout Southeast Asia, and meals are prepared in the spectacular open kitchen. Hearty soups and delicious noodle dishes, like *laksa* (rice noodles in a spicy coconut-milk broth with chicken, bean curd, fish cakes, fish balls, and prawns), are the standouts. Each dish carries a chili coding indicating its relative spiciness—so you won't breathe fire unless you want to. [$] *Average main: A$28* ✉ *Hyatt Regency, 99 Adelaide Terr., CBD, Perth, Western Australia* ☎ *08/9225–1239* 🌐 *www.perth.regency.hyatt.com/en/hotel/dining/JoesOrientalDiner* ⏲ *Closed Sun. No lunch Sat.* ✥ *D6.*

$$ MODERN AUSTRALIAN 🍴 **Lalla Rookh.** Anywhere that takes its name from a Kalgoorlie showgirl has got to have spunk, and Lalla Rookh has it in spades. The below-street-level venue on Perth's business strip is a real find, and combines a slick restaurant and tiny wine bar that introduces quaffers to local and "untampered-with-grape" varieties. The restaurant is headed up by chef Joel Valvasori, who describes his food as "Cucina Westraliana," combining modern Italian style with seasonal, local produce. Think cold smoked buffalo mozzarella with pickled green tomatoes; traditional, thin-crust pizza; and breaded free-range pork cutlet with fennel and orange. Consider going for the "chef's selection" of six dishes for A$55. The quality of the consumables is matched by the generous, informed, faultless service and you'll be reluctant to leave. [$] *Average main: A$30* ✉ *77 St. Georges Terr., CBD, Perth, Western Australia* ☎ *08/9325–7077* 🌐 *www.lallarookh.com.au* ✥ *C3.*

$$ MODERN AUSTRALIAN Fodor's Choice ★ 🍴 **The Old Crow.** The delectable slow-roasted beef, char-grilled brussels sprouts, and Cajun spiced fried chicken ensure that this delectable Northbridge venue is packed come sundown. Housed in an old-school cottage complete with bullnose veranda, it's heavy on charm—staff wear suspenders. Prices will please, too, with Southern American–influenced appetizers set at A$15.50 a pop, and nothing over A$35 in the mains department. The specialty is chimichanga, loaded with beans, corn, and pulled beef. While it's open for breakfast and lunch, dinner is when the atmosphere is best. [$] *Average main: A$30* ✉ *172 Newcastle*

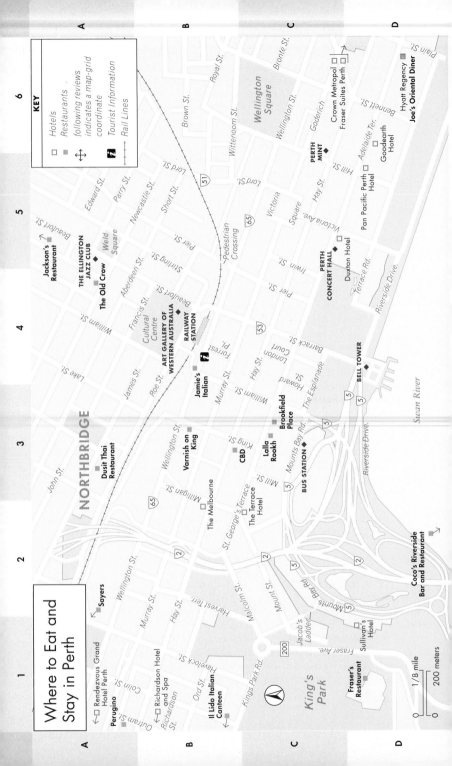

Where to Eat and Stay in Perth

KEY

- □ Hotels
- ▪ Restaurants
- following reviews indicates a map-grid coordinate
- 🛈 Tourist Information
- +++++ Rail Lines

NORTHBRIDGE

King's Park

Swan River

Wellington Square

Weld Square

Forrest Pl.

London Court

PERTH MINT

RAILWAY STATION

ART GALLERY OF WESTERN AUSTRALIA

Cultural Centre

THE ELLINGTON JAZZ CLUB

PERTH CONCERT HALL

BELL TOWER

BUS STATION

Brookfield Place

CBD

The Esplanade

Pedestrian Crossing

Jackson's Restaurant

The Old Crow

Dusit Thai Restaurant

Sayers

Perugino

Rendezvous Grand Hotel Perth

Richardson Hotel and Spa Richardson

Il Lido Italian Canteen

Fraser's Restaurant

Coco's Riverside Bar and Restaurant

Sullivan's Hotel

The Melbourne

The Terrace Hotel

Varnish on King

Jamie's Italian

Lalla Rookh

Duxton Hotel

Pan Pacific Perth Hotel

Crown Metropol

Fraser Suites Perth

Goodearth Hotel

Hyatt Regency

Joe's Oriental Diner

Jacob's Ladder

Swan River

1/8 mile

200 meters

Kings Park Rd.

Fraser Ave.

Mount St.

Malcolm St.

Mounts Bay Rd.

Mill St.

King St.

Milligan St.

Wellington St.

Murray St.

Hay St.

St. George's Terrace

Harvest Terr.

Havelock St.

Ord St.

Colin St.

Outram St.

Wellington St.

William St.

Lake St.

James St.

Roe St.

Francis St.

Aberdeen St.

Stirling St.

Pier St.

Beaufort St.

Short St.

Newcastle St.

Parry St.

Edward St.

Beaufort St.

John St.

Lord St.

Lord St.

Brown St.

Wittenoom St.

Royal St.

Bronte St.

Wellington St.

Goderich St.

Hill St.

Hay St.

Victoria Square

Victoria Ave.

Irwin St.

Pier St.

Barrack St.

Howard St.

Hay St.

Riverside Drive

Terrace Rd.

Adelaide Ter.

Bennett St.

Plain St.

Murray St.

William St.

St., Northbridge, Perth, Western Australia ☎ 08/9227–9995 🌐 theoldcrowperth.tumblr.com ⏲ Closed Tues. and Wed. ✣ A4.

$$ ITALIAN 🍴 **Perugino.** For nearly 30 years, chef Giuseppe Pagliaricci has taken an imaginative yet simple approach to the cuisine of his native Umbria, dishing up typical, homemade Italian fare to his loyal customers. Popular in old-school business and political circles, long lunch favorites include *scottadito di capretto* (char-grilled baby goat chops); or *paffutelli al salmone* (pasta pillows filled with local dhufish, shrimp, and scallops, in a smoked-salmon-and-cream sauce). The five-, six-, or seven-course degustation menu (booked in advance) highlights the best of the house. [$] *Average main: A$32 ✉ 77 Outram St., West Perth, Perth, Western Australia ☎ 08/9321–5420 🌐 www.perugino.com.au ✍ Reservations essential ⏲ Closed Sun. and Mon. No lunch Sat. ✣ A1.*

$ MODERN AUSTRALIAN 🍴 **Sayers.** When an overseas visitor asks, "Where should I go for breakfast?" the local response is often: "Sayers." The original Sayers in Leederville has long been Perth's go-to spot for flavor-rich breakfast dishes created with primo local/organic/seasonal ingredients. The simple chocolate and banana bread has achieved cult status, with the poached eggs and potato rosti, coriander-and-cumin spiked bean tagine, and Italian sausage with lemony wilted spinach not far behind. ⚠ **Expect queues and a possible wait for food.** Breakfast is served until 2 pm on Sunday. [$] *Average main: A$19 ✉ 224 Carr Pl., Leederville, Perth, Western Australia ☎ 08/9227–0429 🌐 www.sayersfood.com.au ⏲ No dinner ✣ A2.*

$$ MODERN AUSTRALIAN 🍴 **Varnish on King.** Since American whiskey is the specialty at this hard-to-find basement bar, you might expect the food to play second fiddle. But not with chef David Allison at the helm. Beef cheek and marrow is presented in a bone; prawn and lobster is blended into a hot-dog sausage; and sweet scampi is split in two and grilled to perfection. Artisan grunge may be the theme but foodie heaven could be another descriptor. The atmosphere is busy, so be prepared for close quarters. Oh, and the whiskey? You've got more than 150 varieties to choose from. **TIP→ The venue closes its doors at 10:30 pm (kitchen closes at 10 pm), but if you get in before then, you can stay till last call at midnight.** [$] *Average main: A$21 ✉ 75 King St., downstairs, Northbridge, Perth, Western Australia ☎ 08/9324–2237 🌐 varnishonking.com ⏲ Closed Sun. No lunch Sat. ✣ B3.*

WHERE TO STAY

Businesspeople from around the world are flocking to Western Australia, and consequently hotel rooms in Perth are at an unprecedented premium. Few new hotels have been built, so hotels are frequently at capacity, and prices are up. **TIP→ The wise will book early.**

Use the coordinate (✣B2) at the end of each listing to locate a site on the corresponding map. For expanded hotel reviews, visit Fodors.com.

$$$$ RESORT Fodor's Choice ★ 🏨 **Crown Metropol.** While across the river from the city center, Crown is like an island where everything is self-contained: myriad restaurants and bars, a theater, resort-style pool, 18-hole golf course, casino, nightclub and, of course, the pyramid-shaped hotel. **Pros:** impressive lobby

rises the full height of the building; Isika Spa adds luxury; some free parking. **Cons:** adjacent casino and nightclub attracts a boisterous crowd; atrium-style lobby creates noise in some rooms; Wi-Fi costs extra. $ *Rooms from: A$595* ✉ *Great Eastern Hwy. at Bolton Ave., Burswood, Perth, Western Australia* ☎ *08/9362–8888, 1800/999667* ⊕ *www.crownperth.com.au* ↪ *397 rooms, 19 suites* ⎮⊙⎮ *No meals* ✛ *C6.*

$$$$ 🏨 **Duxton Hotel.** Facing the Swan River and adjacent to the Perth Con-
HOTEL cert Hall, this elegant hotel sits at the eastern end of the business district, within easy walking distance of the city center. **Pros:** free Wi-Fi; minutes' walk to city-center shopping malls; popular restaurant with alfresco terrace; some rooms have river views; easy access to free bus. **Cons:** valet parking fee applies. $ *Rooms from: A$609* ✉ *1 St. George's Terr., CBD, Perth, Western Australia* ☎ *08/9261–8000, 1800/681118* ⊕ *www.duxtonhotels.com/perth* ↪ *291 rooms, 15 suites* ⎮⊙⎮ *No meals* ✛ *C5.*

$$$$ 🏨 **Fraser Suites Perth.** This flashy, executive-style hotel impresses guests
HOTEL with its good value, modern design, corporate standards, and the fact that every room is a self-containted suite. **Pros:** free Wi-Fi; free bikes; free city bus stop out front; excellent restaurant; fantastic views. **Cons:** far eastern end of the CBD; perfunctory reception. $ *Rooms from: A$325* ✉ *10 Adelaide Terr., East Perth, Perth, Western Australia* ☎ *08/9261–0000* ⊕ *perth.frasershospitality.com* ↪ *236 suites* ⎮⊙⎮ *No meals* ✛ *C6.*

$$$ 🏨 **Goodearth Hotel.** Tourist accommodation at a reasonable price can be
HOTEL hard to find close to Perth's CBD, which is why this business district, full-service apartment-style hotel is favored not only by regional Western Australians and their families, but also by dollar-conscious tourists. **Pros:** 24-hour lobby shop; free satellite TV; free Wi-Fi throughout hotel; Internet kiosk; complimentary bathroom facilities for early and late departures; on-site bar and restaurant. **Cons:** hair dryers only on request; small bathrooms; rooms near elevators can be noisy. $ *Rooms from: A$370* ✉ *195 Adelaide Terr., CBD, Perth, Western Australia* ☎ *08/9492–7777, 1800/098863* ⊕ *www.goodearthhotel.com.au* ↪ *180 rooms* ⎮⊙⎮ *Multiple meal plans* ✛ *D6.*

$$$ 🏨 **Hyatt Regency.** Big rooms, great river views, and an easy walk into
HOTEL Perth's central business district make this glamorous hotel a worthy choice, particularly if you score a weekend deal. **Pros:** 11 am check-out; river views from many rooms; evening nibbles and drinks in the executive lounge; café, bar, and restaurants in hotel. **Cons:** primarily a business market hotel with corporate decor; Wi-Fi for regular rooms and parking are additional costs; few dining options nearby. $ *Rooms from: A$220* ✉ *99 Adelaide Terr., CBD, Perth, Western Australia* ☎ *08/9225–1234* ⊕ *www.perth.hyatt.com* ↪ *367 rooms, 32 suites* ⎮⊙⎮ *No meals* ✛ *D6.*

$$ 🏨 **The Melbourne.** A restored 1890s building listed on the National Heri-
HOTEL tage Register houses this stylish boutique hotel that sits in the heart of the city, across from some excellent restaurants and fantastic shopping. **Pros:** city-center location; heritage decor throughout; minutes' walk to shopping malls; on-site bar, café, and restaurant. **Cons:** leisure facilities off-site; parking is off-site. $ *Rooms from: A$139* ✉ *Hay and Milligan*

Sts., CBD, Perth, Western Australia ☎ 08/9320–3333, 1800/685671 ⊕ www.melbournehotel.com.au ⤳ 34 rooms ⏏ No meals ⧾ B2.

$$$$ 🏨 **Pan Pacific Perth Hotel.** Sweeping views over the Swan River from
HOTEL many guest rooms are a feature of this 23-story, five-star hotel, a handy 10-minute walk from downtown. **Pros:** many rooms have river views; day spa and in-room spa services available; heated outdoor pool; 24-hour gym with steam rooms; Wi-Fi is complimentary in public areas. **Cons:** hotel is in an office area; parking and Internet access cost extra. ⑨ *Rooms from: A$400* ⊠ *207 Adelaide Terr., CBD, Perth, Western Australia* ☎ 08/9224–7777, 1877/324–4856 toll-free from U.S. ⊕ www. panpacific.com/perth ⤳ 436 rooms, 50 suites ⏏ No meals ⧾ D5.

$$$$ 🏨 **Rendezvous Grand Hotel Perth.** If all you want to do is swim and surf,
HOTEL and a 20-minute drive into the city doesn't bother you, then this newly refurbished, multistory beachfront hotel may be the ticket. **Pros:** great views of the Indian Ocean; walk straight on to Scarborough Beach; on-site bar; pool; tennis courts; shuttle to the city. **Cons:** few other attractions nearby; breakfast and parking cost extra; limited shopping facilities; dubious nightlife. ⑨ *Rooms from: A$500* ⊠ *The Esplanade, Scarborough Beach, Perth, Western Australia* ☎ 08/9245–1000, 1800/067680 ⊕ www.rendezvoushotels.com ⤳ 330 rooms, 6 suites ⏏ No meals ⧾ A1.

$$$$ 🏨 **The Richardson Hotel and Spa.** Tucked away in a quiet, tree-lined street
HOTEL in West Perth, The Richardson offers a discrete and indulgent stay without forgoing any of the amenities of the bigger downtown hotels—it's no surprise that this is where visiting celebrities stay. **Pros:** large rooms and suites; balconies, fridges, microwaves, Nespresso coffee machines, and evening turn-down service in all rooms; quiet; complimentary Wi-Fi; convenient frozen meal packs in modestly priced minibar. **Cons:** views mostly of surrounding buildings; Subiaco and shopping areas a 5- to 10-minute walk away. ⑨ *Rooms from: A$395* ⊠ *32 Richardson St., West Perth, Perth, Western Australia* ☎ 08/9217–8888 ⊕ www. therichardson.com.au ⤳ 54 rooms, 20 suites ⏏ No meals ⧾ B1.

$$ 🏨 **Sullivan's Hotel.** With the city's free CAT buses stopping right out
HOTEL front, this friendly, family-run hotel opposite waterfront parkland at the foot of King's Park manages to combine natural charms with city proximity. **Pros:** good-value beds for the area; close to King's Park; free public bus service at front; free Wi-Fi. **Cons:** no night service for free public bus; free parking subject to availability. ⑨ *Rooms from: A$199* ⊠ *166 Mounts Bay Rd., CBD, Perth, Western Australia* ☎ 08/9321–8022 ⊕ www.sullivans.com.au ⤳ 71 rooms ⏏ No meals ⧾ D1.

$$$ 🏨 **The Terrace Hotel.** Set in a fantastic location, this boutique hotel offers
HOTEL a glamorous, heritage-listed, luxury home away from home with an
Fodor's Choice on-site bar and restaurant. **Pros:** good online price specials; free Wi-Fi; ★ glamorous on-site restaurant and bar; leafy alfresco terrace; opulent surrounds; five-minute walk to city. **Cons:** valet parking costs extra. ⑨ *Rooms from: A$279* ⊠ *237 St. Georges Terr., CBD, Perth, Western Australia* ☎ 08/9214–4444 ⊕ www.terracehotelperth.com.au ⤳ 9 rooms, 6 suites ⏏ No meals ⧾ C2.

NIGHTLIFE AND THE ARTS

Details on cultural events in Perth are published in *Weekend West Australian* and *The Sunday Times*. A free weekly, *X-Press Magazine*, lists music, concerts, movies, entertainment reviews, and who's playing at pubs, clubs, and hotels. *SCOOP* magazine (⊕ *www.scooptraveller.com.au*), published quarterly, is an excellent guide to the essential Western Australian lifestyle.

THE ARTS

Ticketek. This is the main booking agent in Perth for the performing arts. It operates solely online, though there are several physical box offices at arts venues such as the Art Gallery of WA, the State Theatre, and His Majesty's Theatre in the CBD. ⊠ *Perth, Western Australia* ⊕ *www.bocsticketing.com.au*.

Perth International Arts Festival (PIAF). If you can, time your trip so you can attend this energetic, big-name summer festival that sees the city come alive with open-air music, fireworks spectaculars, indigenous performances, and world-famous artists. The PIAF is held February and March in venues throughout the city, and its more highbrow shows are tempered with the raucousness of the Perth Fringe World Festival, which runs in January and February. While most shows for both festivals are ticketed, there's also plenty of free outdoor performances. PIAF is Australia's oldest and biggest annual arts festival, running for more than 50 years. As part of the festival, the Lotterywest Festival Films screens films outdoors at the University of Western Australia's beautiful Somerville Auditorium, December–April. ⊠ *Perth, Western Australia* ☎ *08/6488–2000 for information and tickets* ⊕ *www.perthfestival.com.au*.

BALLET

West Australian Ballet Company. This world-class ballet company has a diverse repertoire that includes new, full-length story ballets, cutting-edge contemporary dance, and classic and neoclassic ballets. The company has earned an international reputation for excellence due to its overall innovation and creativity and performances are held throughout Perth, including His Majesty's Theatre, the Quarry Amphitheatre, and the State Theatre Centre. ⊠ *134 Whatley Crescent, Maylands, Perth, Western Australia* ☎ *08/9214–0707* ⊕ *www.waballet.com.au*.

CINEMA

Rooftop Movies. Perth's first—and only—rooftop cinema opened after a summer trial run sold out night after night. Crowning a seven-story car park, it shows cult films, old blockbusters, and cherished classics, with a few art-house and family-friendly selections thrown in. Colorful vintage caravans serve dude food on a carpet of faux grass and palm trees, while booze and pizzas can be delivered, but self-packed picnic baskets are equally welcome. Tickets are A$13. ■ **TIP→ Movies run each night, except Mondays, during the warmer months of October–April.** ⊠ *Roe St, car park, access off 129 James St., Northbridge, Perth, Western Australia* ✛ *Drive in at 68 Roe St., Northbridge; walk in off James St., opposite Northbridge Piazza, and take the elevator to the top* ☎ *08/9227–6288* ⊕ *rooftopmovies.com.au*.

CONCERTS

Perth Concert Hall. A starkly rectangular building overlooking the Swan River in the city center, the Perth Concert Hall stages regular recitals by the excellent West Australian Symphony Orchestra, as well as Australian and international performers. Adding to the appeal of the fine auditorium is the 3,000-pipe organ surrounded by a 160-person choir gallery. ■**TIP**➜ **The hall is said to have the best acoustics in Australia.** ⊠ *5 St. George's Terr., CBD, Perth, Western Australia* ☎ *08/9231–9900* ⊕ *www.perthconcerthall.com.au.*

OPERA

West Australian Opera Company. This company presents three seasons annually—in February, July, and November—at His Majesty's Theatre. They also perform the free Opera in the Park in Perth's Supreme Court Gardens each February. The company's repertoire includes classic opera, Gilbert and Sullivan operettas, and occasional musicals. ⊠ *His Majesty's Theatre, 825 Hay St., CBD, Perth, Western Australia* ☎ *08/9278–8999, 1300/795012 box office* ⊕ *www.waopera.asn.au.*

ROCKIN' IN PERTH

Thanks to pop, rock, and metal bands like Eskimo Joe, the John Butler Trio, the Waifs, Karnivool, Little Birdy, the Panda Band, and the Sleepy Jackson—who all started in Perth—the music scene here is thriving. Despite—or perhaps because of—their isolation from the rest of Australia, Western Australian musos are turning out some top-notch material. Music commentators claim there isn't a "Perth sound" as such, just a talented bunch of artists writing and performing original music. Check out ⊕ *www.xpressmag.com.au* for an up-to-date guide on live shows.

THEATER

Crown Theatre Perth. This venue has regular theatrical and musical productions from around Australia. Note that parking can be difficult on weekends. ⊠ *Great Eastern Hwy., Burswood, Perth, Western Australia* ☎ *13–2849 box office, 08/9362–7685* ⊕ *www.crownperth.com.au.*

His Majesty's Theatre. The opulent Edwardian His Majesty's Theatre, opened in 1904, is admired by those who step inside. His Maj, as it's locally known, is home to the West Australian Opera Company, hosts most theatrical productions in Perth; there's also a comedy lounge downstairs. Purchase tickets at the box office on-site, or via ⊕ *www.ticketek.com.au.* ⊠ *825 Hay St., CBD, Perth, Western Australia* ☎ *08/9265–0900* ⊕ *www.hismajestystheatre.com.au.*

Quarry Amphitheatre. For outdoor performances, the grass-terraced Quarry Amphitheatre is a unique and popular venue, particularly during the Perth International Arts Festival and warmer months. ⊠ *Waldron Dr. off Oceanic Dr., City Beach, Perth, Western Australia* ☎ *08/9385–7144* ⊕ *www.quarryamphitheatre.com.au.*

Regal Theatre. The 1930s-era Regal Theatre hosts local and visiting performances, ranging from comedy to musicals. ⊠ *474 Hay St., at Rokeby Rd., Subiaco, Perth, Western Australia* ☎ *08/9388–2066, 1300/795012 theater bookings* ⊕ *www.regaltheatre.com.au.*

The London Court shopping mall facade at Hay Walking Street, Perth

State Theatre Centre of Western Australia. The flashy, gilded State Theatre Centre of Western Australia features the 575-seat Heath Ledger Theatre and Studio Underground, a flexible performance space, while the Courtyard is a multipurpose outdoor events area. The State Theatre Centre presents contemporary performing arts, both theater and dance, and is the home of the Perth Theatre Company and Black Swan State Theatre Company. ✉ *174–176 William St., Northbridge, Perth, Western Australia* ☎ *08/9484–1133* ⊕ *www.statetheatrecentrewa.com.au.*

NIGHTLIFE

Perth's inner city has gone through a significant revitalization; it's now a hotbed of classy small bars that buzz until midnight and later. Twenty- and thirtysomethings also flock to Northbridge, Leederville, Mount Lawley, Subiaco, or Fremantle. Pubs generally close by midnight, which is when the crowds start arriving at the nightclubs; these tend to stay open until around 5 am.

BARS

Brass Monkey. This pub is in a huge, crimson-painted building with antique verandas and a lively, blokey vibe; it claims to be one of the oldest and most photographed pubs in WA. It has several areas with different moods, such as the beer garden, the new rooftop bar, the balcony couch zone, and the adjoining Grapeskin wine bar. Open-mike nights on Tuesday, burlesque shows on Wednesday, and karaoke on Friday may appeal to the fun-loving—though we suggest you avoid student night on Monday. ■ TIP→ There's no cover charge. ✉ *William and James Sts., Northbridge, Perth, Western Australia* ☎ *08/9227–9596* ⊕ *www.thebrassmonkey.com.au.*

Mechanics Institute. Perched above a gourmet burger bistro called Flip Side—yes, they deliver upstairs—this rooftop haunt is furnished with market umbrellas, upcycled bench tables, and retro couches, which make it both welcoming and hip. Unusually for Perth, access to the cocktail, wine, and craft beer bar is via a rear lane, adding to the intrigue. Owners of both top and bottom businesses—husband-and-wife team Hamish Fleming and Siobhan Blumann—say they wanted to create a neighborhood feel when they moved into the gritty urban suburb of Northbridge. ⊠ *Upstairs, accessed off James St., at rear of 222 William St., Northbridge, Perth, Western Australia* ☎ *08/9228–4189* ⊕ *mechanicsinstitutebar.com.au.*

Queen's Tavern. The Queen's, as it's known locally, has an excellent, thriving outdoor beer garden that features plenty of local and international craft brews. The upstairs bar has a relaxed lounge vibe, with DJs on Friday, Saturday, and Sunday. ⊠ *520 Beaufort St., Highgate, Perth, Western Australia* ☎ *08/9328–7267* ⊕ *www.thequeens.com.au.*

Subiaco Hotel. This hotel attracts a lively after-work crowd during the week—especially on Friday—and has an excellent, busy restaurant with a covered balcony perfect for people-watching. An extensive upgrade in 2013 has made it as smart and chic as its clientele. ■ TIP→ You'll get one of the best steaks in town here. ⊠ *465 Hay St., Subiaco, Perth, Western Australia* ☎ *08/9381–3069* ⊕ *www.subiacohotel.com.au.*

Universal Bar. This bar has live jazz and blues Wednesday–Sunday from late afternoon till late, and attracts an exuberant, middle-aged crowd who love to shake their booty. ⊠ *221 William St., Northbridge, Perth, Western Australia* ☎ *08/9227–6771* ⊕ *www.universalbar.com.au.*

JAZZ AND BLUES

The Ellington Jazz Club. Inspired by the New York jazz scene, the Ellington is *the* place for jazz in Perth. Catch live music seven nights a week in an intimate and sophisticated setting. A tapas and pizza menu is available. General entry is A\$15 weekdays or A\$20 weekends for a table or A\$10 at the bar. National and international acts attract a higher entry fee—check the website for details and book your spot online. ⊠ *191 Beaufort St., Northbridge, Perth, Western Australia* ☎ *08/9228–1088* ⊕ *www.ellingtonjazz.com.au* ⊗ *Mon.–Thurs. 7 pm–1 am, Fri. and Sat. 7 pm–3 am, Sun. 6 pm–midnight.*

The Laneway Lounge. This sexy little number is as sultry as the jazzy tunes that fill the discreet laneway space each night. A number of the cocktails use smoked ice cubes—not to be confused with tacky dry ice—giving the liquor a heavenly, charred dimension. Retire to the dining room for the dude-food inspired menu, with prawn popcorn, duck sliders, and barbecue wings on the starters list. Then head to the back lounge where jazz plays most nights. ■ TIP→ The bar is accessed down a laneway off Murray Street—look out for the "red carpet" painted on the tarmac. ⊠ *414A Murray St., Northbridge, Perth, Western Australia* ☎ *08/9321–2508* ⊕ *www.thelanewaylounge.com.au* ⊗ *Closed Sun. and Mon.*

NIGHTCLUBS

Connections Nightclub. This is Perth's number one gay-friendly nightclub, but it's far more dimensional than its drag queen shows, party beats, and mirror balls. The venue has just opened a classy, industrial-chic lounge bar within the club that opens two hours earlier, at 8 pm. It's like a small bar hidden in the busy core. The bar opens out to a fantastic open-air deck that has whistle-worthy views of the CBD. It's a great place to marvel at the skyline with a bespoke cocktail in hand. ■ TIP➜ The club and lounge bar stay open till 5 am on Friday and Saturday nights, making it one of the latest late-night venues in Perth. ⊠ *81 James St., Northbridge, Perth, Western Australia* ☎ *08/9328–5166* ⊕ *connectionsnightclub.com* ⊙ *Closed Sun.–Tues.*

Eve. Eve is a glitzy, two-story venue done up with stainless steel and retro fittings. Thursday through Sunday, the five bars, cozy lounge areas, stage, and dance floor with sound-and-light show reverberate to the sounds of renowned DJs spinning the latest dance tunes. Doors open at 9 pm. Free entry Friday through Sunday before 10 pm. ⊠ *Crown Perth, Great Eastern Hwy. at Bolton Ave., Burswood, Perth, Western Australia* ☎ *08/9362–7699* ⊕ *www.crownperth.com.au.*

Hip-e Club. The Hip-e Club, a Perth legend popular with young things in Leederville, plays one-hit-wonders from the '80s, the latest commercial hits, and favorite retro remixes. The famed student/backpacker night takes place on Tuesday; it's been running for more than 22 years. ⊠ *663 Newcastle St., Leederville, Perth, Western Australia* ☎ *08/9227–8899* ⊕ *www.hipeclub.com.au.*

Luxe Bar. Regarded as Perth's best cocktail bar, Luxe and its chocolate-toned interior appeals to a sophisticated, yet fun-loving, crowd. Get adventurous shaken or stirred libations until 2 am on Friday and Saturday, or midnight on Sunday. ⊠ *446 Beaufort St., Highgate, Perth, Western Australia* ☎ *08/9228–9680* ⊕ *www.luxebar.com.*

SHOPPING

Shopping in Perth, with its pedestrian-friendly central business district, vehicle-free malls, and many covered arcades, is a delight. Hay Street Mall and Murray Street Mall are the main city shopping areas with large department stores, linked by numerous arcades with small shops. In the suburbs, top retail strips include Napoleon Street in Cottesloe for classic, beachy clothing and homewares, Claremont Quarter in Claremont for fashion-forward garments, Oxford Street in Leederville for edgy threads and unique knickknacks, and Beaufort Street in Mount Lawley for idiosyncratic finds.

Australian souvenirs and iconic buys are on sale at small shops throughout the city and suburbs.

ART AND CRAFT GALLERIES

Creative Native. You can find authentic Aboriginal artifacts at Creative Native; their selection of Aboriginal art is extensive. Each piece of original artwork comes with a certificate of authenticity. ⊠ *Forrest Chase,*

Forrest Pl., Shop 58, CBD, Perth, Western Australia ☎ *08/9221–5800* ⊕ *www.creativenative.com.au.*

Indigenart–Mossenson Galleries. Get your fill of authentic Aboriginal art— far more than just dot paintings—by viewing one of the solo or group curated exhibitions by emerging and established artists and communities. Indigenart-Mossenson Galleries has been around since 1993 and is one of Australia's leading indigenous commercial galleries. ✉ *115 Hay St., Subiaco, Perth, Western Australia* ☎ *08/9388–2899* ⊕ *www. indigenart.com.au* ⊗ *Wed.–Sat. 11–4.*

Maalinup Aboriginal Gallery. Find true Aboriginal art as well as gifts and souvenirs, including soaps, bath, and beauty products featuring Australian native plants. Oils and clays are made on-site. Maalinup Aboriginal Gallery is owned and operated by local Aboriginal people. ✉ *10070 W. Swan Rd., Henley Brook, Western Australia* ☎ *08/9296–0711* ⊕ *www. maalinup.com.au* ⊗ *Closed Mon. and Tues.*

CLOTHING

R. M. Williams. This shop sells everything for the Australian bushman— and woman—including moleskin pants, hand-tooled leather boots, Akubra hats, and their characteristic cobalt blue shirts. ▐▐ TIP➔ **They have a discount store at Harbour Town shopping center on Wellington Street in West Perth.** ✉ *Hay St. Mall, Shop 38, CBD, Perth, Western Australia* ☎ *08/9321–7786* ⊕ *www.rmwilliams.com.au.*

DEPARTMENT STORES AND SHOPPING CENTERS

Claremont Quarter. For a mix of designer threads, high fashion, and comfy staples, head to this shiny enclosed shopping center. You'll find gorgeous Australian beauty products by Aesop and Jurlique; classic garments at Country Road; mature but glam women's wear at Carla Zampatti; cosmetics at Napoleon Perdis; and electrical goods and gadgets at Dick Smith—they're all Australian. For international brands, seek out Calvin Klein, French Connection, Karen Millen, and Mecca Cosmetica. There are half a dozen chic cafés, too—get a chocolate hit at Koko Black and great yum cha at Yamato Sushi. ✉ *9 Bayview Terr., Claremont, Western Australia* ☎ *08/286–5888* ⊕ *www.claremontquarter.com.au.*

Forrest Place. Flanked by the post office and the Forrest Chase Shopping Plaza, Forrest Place is the largest mall area in the city. It has a lovely fountain designed by artist Jeppe Hein, where children love to play on warm days. ▐▐ TIP➔ **There's a large cactus sculpture, opposite Perth Central Train Station, which makes for a good meeting spot.** ✉ *Forrest Pl., CBD, Perth, Western Australia.*

Harbour Town Perth. If you feel the need for retail therapy, here's a great spot to let loose, as every store—and there are a lot of them—sells discounted goods here. There are clothes for all ages and styles, shoes, sneakers, gifts, books, sporting gear, beauty products, and more. There are cafés on-site to refuel. ✉ *840 Wellington St., West Perth, Western Australia* ☎ *08/9321–2282 general number* ⊕ *www.harbourtownperth. com.au* ⊗ *Daily 24 hrs.*

Hay Street Mall. Running parallel to Murray Street and linked by numerous arcades, the Hay Street Mall is another extensive, mainstream shopping area. Make sure you wander through the arcades that connect Hay and Murray streets, such as **Carillion Arcade,** which have many more shops. ⊠ *Hay St., CBD, Perth, Western Australia.*

FREMANTLE

About 19 km (12 miles) southwest of Perth.

The port city of Fremantle is a jewel in Western Australia's crown, largely because of its colonial architectural heritage and hippy vibe. Freo (as the locals call it) is a city of largely friendly, interesting, and sometimes eccentric residents supportive of busking, street art, and alfresco dining. Like all great port cities, Freo is cosmopolitan, with mariners from all parts of the world strolling the streets—including thousands of U.S. Navy personnel on rest and recreation throughout the year. It's also a good jumping-off point for a day trip to Rottnest Island, where lovely beaches, rocky coves, and unique wallaby-like inhabitants called quokkas set the scene.

Modern Fremantle is a far cry from the barren, sandy plain that greeted the first wave of English settlers back in 1829 at the newly constituted Swan River Colony. Most were city dwellers, and after five months at sea in sailing ships they landed on salt-marsh flats that sorely tested their fortitude. Living in tents with packing cases for chairs, they found no edible crops, and the nearest freshwater was a distant 51 km (32 miles)—and a tortuous trip up the waters of the Swan. As a result they soon moved the settlement upriver to the vicinity of present-day Perth.

Fremantle remained the principal port, and many attractive limestone buildings were built to service the port traders. Australia's 1987 defense of the America's Cup—held in waters off Fremantle—triggered a major restoration of the colonial streetscapes. In the leafy suburbs nearly every other house is a restored 19th-century gem.

GETTING HERE AND AROUND

Bus information for service from Perth is available from Transperth (☎ *13–6213* ⊕ *www.transperth.wa.gov.au*). Their Central Area Bus Service (CAT) provides free transportation around Fremantle in orange buses. The route begins and ends outside the Fremantle Bus/Train Terminus, and stops include the Arts Centre, the cappuccino strip, and the Fremantle Market. CAT buses run every 10 minutes weekdays 7:30–6:30, and 10–6:30 on weekends and public holidays.

Trains bound for Fremantle depart from Perth approximately every 15–30 minutes from the Perth Central Station on Wellington Street. You can travel from Perth to Fremantle (or vice versa) in about 30 minutes. Tickets must be purchased at the ticket vending machines prior to travel.

If you are driving from downtown Perth, the most direct route is via Stirling Highway, from the foot of Kings Park; it will take about 35 minutes, depending on traffic.

Cab fare between 6 am and 6 pm weekdays is an initial A\$4.05 plus A\$1.66 every 1 km (½ mile). From 6 pm to 6 am and on weekends the rate rises to A\$5.90 plus A\$1.66 per 1 km (½ mile).

SAFETY AND PRECAUTIONS

Fremantle is a safe destination, and is popular with families, particularly on weekends and during the school holidays. It also has a lively night-life, and late-night crowds leaving pubs and clubs can—and do—cause problems. Taxis are in high demand late at night when other public transport stops operating.

TIMING

Fremantle can easily be visited in a day from Perth, though if you want to trip over to Rottnest Island you will have to add an extra day. Most of the sights are clustered in a relatively small area along Market Street and South Terrace, and close to the Fishing Boat Harbour, and you can take a walking tour or take a hop-on, hop-off tour tram.

TOURS

Dolphin Dive Fremantle. Got a budding diver in the family? Water babies will get a buzz from this beginner's experience, which departs Fremantle and heads to the subtropical waters of Rottnest Island. You get to swim through underwater archways flecked with electric-blue fish, inspect limestone caverns, and explore coral rimmed caves. If you're a newbie, opt for a "Discover Scuba" experience, which involves taking one person out with an instructor (A\$375) or a maximum of two (ask about the discounted price). Trips are also available for experienced divers—call the store for details. ⊠ *256 Hampton Rd., South Fremantle, Western Australia* ☎ *08/9335–9969* ⊕ *www.dolphindiveshop.com.*

Fremantle Tram Tours. This company runs hop-on-hop-off tours (A\$25) around the city daily from 9:45 am to approximately 3:30 pm, with six stops, all close to the major sights. A tour around Fremantle is a great way to get to know each area of the port city. A full-day tour is the Triple Tour, which includes a guided tour of Fremantle, a cruise on the Swan River to Perth, and a sightseeing tour in Perth. The tour finishes in Perth, but you can catch a train or bus back to Fremantle. The cost is A\$74, not including your return to Fremantle. On Friday nights, "ghostly tours" take in suspected haunted premises, with a dinner of fish-and-chips included. The cost is A\$70 per person. ⊠ *Perth, Western Australia* ☎ *08/9433–6674* ⊕ *www.fremantletrams.com.*

Two Feet and a Heartbeat. As you can guess from the name, this is a walking tour, but one with more fun than the usual historical yawn-fest. Enthusiastic, youthful guides will take you through Fremantle's historic streets pointing out things even locals don't know. The tour is a great way to get oriented as it passes a load of landmarks including the Fremantle Prison, the Roundhouse, and the Fishing Boat Harbour. You'll also stop in to see the modern art at Moore & Moore Gallery and the Kidogo Art House. The two-hour tour cost A\$40 and run Wednesday to Monday, departing at 10 am. Bookings are essential. ■ TIP➜ **The tour also includes 10% off lunch at Kailis Fish Market Café.** ⊠ *Fremantle Visitor Information Centre (meeting point), Kings Sq., High St., Fremantle, Western Australia* ☎ *1800/459388* ⊕ *www.twofeet.com.au.*

ESSENTIALS

Taxi Contacts Black & White ☎ *13–1008.* **Swan Taxis** ☎ *13–1330.*

Visitor Information **Fremantle Visitor Centre** ✉ *Kings Sq. at High St.,
Fremantle, Western Australia* 🕾 *08/9431–7878* ⊕ *www.fremantlewa.com.au*
⊙ *Weekdays 9–5, Sat. 9–4, Sun. 10–4.*

EXPLORING

An ideal place to start a leisurely stroll is South Terrace, known as the
Fremantle cappuccino strip. Wander alongside locals through sidewalk
cafés or browse in bookstores, art galleries, and souvenir shops until
you reach the Fremantle Markets. From South Terrace walk down to
the Fishing Boat Harbour where there's always activity—commercial
and pleasure craft bob about, and along the timber boardwalk is a
cluster of outdoor eateries and a microbrewery.

Between Phillimore Street and Marine Terrace in the West End is a
collection of some of the best-preserved heritage buildings in the state.
The Fremantle Railway Station on Elder Place is another good spot to
start a walk. Maps and details for 11 different self-guided walks are
available at the Fremantle Visitor Center; a popular heritage walk is
the Convict Trail, passing by 18 different sights and locations from
Fremantle's convict past.

TOP ATTRACTIONS

FAMILY **Fremantle Market.** The eclectic, artsy, and always bustling Fremantle Market has been housed in this huge Victorian building since 1897 and sells
everything from WA landscape photographs to incense, freshly roasted
coffee, toys, baby clothes, and fruit and vegetables out the back. You
can also get street food, such as Turkish gozlemes, German sausages,
corn on the cob, and fresh squeezed orange juice in the Yard. Around
150 stalls attract a colorful mix of locals and tourists. On weekends
and public holidays the market can get crowded, but the Market Bar is
a nice, if slightly shabby, place to take a break and watch the buskers.
Family-friendly events are also regularly held here. ✉ *South Terr. at
Henderson St., Fremantle, Western Australia* 🕾 *08/9335–2515* ⊕ *www.
fremantlemarkets.com.au* ⊙ *Hall: Fri. 9–8, weekends 9–6; Yard: Fri.
8–6, weekends 8–8.*

FAMILY **Fremantle Prison.** The former Fremantle Prison, built in the 1850s, is
where 44 inmates met their fate on the prison gallows between 1888
and 1964. Tours feature the classic-art cell, where a superb collection of
drawings by convict James Walsh decorates his quarters. Reservations
are required for the 90-minute Torchlight Tours (evening tours by flashlight). For the 2½-hour Tunnels Tour, visitors are provided with hard
hats, overalls, boots, and headlamps before descending 65 feet into the
labyrinthine tunnels that run beneath the prison; some of the tour is by
boat in underground waterways; reservations are also essential. Access
to the Prison gatehouse complex, for a simple wander, is free. ✉ *1
The Terrace, Fremantle, Western Australia* 🕾 *08/9336–9200* ⊕ *www.
fremantleprison.com.au* 🖾 *A$19, including a 75-min tour; Torchlight
Tour A$25, Tunnels Tour A$60* ⊙ *Daily 9–5 with tours every 30 mins
10 am–5 pm. Torchlight Tours Wed. and Fri., regularly from 6:30 pm;
last tour usually 9 pm. Tunnels Tour at 9:15, 9:45, 10:40, 12:20, 1:40,
2:40, 3:25* ⊙ *Closed Good Friday and Christmas Day.*

FAMILY   **Western Australian Maritime Museum.** Resembling an upside-down boat,
Fodor'sChoice   the Western Australian Maritime Museum sits at the edge of Fremantle
★   Harbour. It houses *Australia II,* winner of the 1983 America's Cup, and
has hands-on, rotating exhibits that are great fun for children. You can
also take one-hour guided tours of the adjacent submarine *Ovens,* a
former Royal Australian Navy World War II submarine. Tours depart
from the maritime museum every 30 minutes; reservations are recommended during school holidays. Another attraction is the Welcome
Walls, a record of all those who immigrated to Western Australia via
ship during the major postwar migration. A five-minute walk away on
Cliff Street in a separate, heritage building, the Shipwreck Galleries
house the recovered remains of Dutch wrecks, including the *Batavia*
(wrecked offshore in 1629), and the 1872 SS *Xantho* steamer. ✉ *West
end of Victoria Quay, Fremantle, Western Australia* ☎ *08/9431–8444
museum, 08/9431–8469 galleries* ⊕ *www.museum.wa.gov.au/maritime*
🖂 *Museum A$10 day pass, Ovens A$8, museum and Ovens A$15,
Shipwreck Gallery entry free, suggested donation A$5* ⊙ *Daily 9:30–5.*

WORTH NOTING

FAMILY   **Adventure World.** Not far from Fremantle, Adventure World is every
fun-loving kid's paradise—especially on a hot day, with water mountain
mat slides, rapids navigated in an inflatable tube, and bumper boats
with water cannons. The new 630-meter (2,066-foot) roller-coaster
ride called Abyss is guaranteed to thrill: it heads skyward for 10 stories, drops more than 30 meters (98 feet), and its loops deliver G-force
twists of up to 4.5. Inspired by ancient Druid guardians, its thrusts are
reportedly greater than those in a space shuttle launch. General entry
tickets allow you access to everything and are discounted after 2 pm.
✉ *179 Progress Dr., Bibra Lake, Western Australia* ☎ *08/9417–9666*
⊕ *adventureworld.net.au* 🖂 *A$52.40; family pass A$164.50* ⊙ *Thurs.–
Mon. 10–5* ⊙ *Closed Christmas Day and Good Friday and May–Sept.*

Fremantle Arts Centre. Like most of Fremantle, the fine, Gothic Revival
Fremantle Arts Centre (FAC) was built by convicts in the 19th century.
First used as a lunatic asylum, by 1900 it was overcrowded and nearly
shut down. It became a home for elderly women until 1942, when the
U.S. Navy turned it into its local submarine base in WWII. This time
has been captured in a new augmented reality iPad tour, accessed via
an app which digitally overlays historic content over the present-day
site. IPads can be borrowed for free or the app can also be downloaded
onto your own tablet.

As one of Australia's leading arts organizations, FAC offers an engaging cultural program year-round. Dynamic exhibitions, a gift shop, and
an expansive live music and special events program feature throughout
the year. In the warmer months, FAC also has free live music on Sunday at 2 pm, and people like to bring picnics and watch. ✉ *1 Finnerty
St., Fremantle, Western Australia* ☎ *08/9432–9555* ⊕ *www.fac.org.au*
🖂 *Free* ⊙ *Daily 10–5.*

Kings Square. Bounded by High, Queen, and William streets, Kings
Square is at the heart of the central business district. Shaded by
100-year-old Moreton Bay fig trees, it's a perfect place to watch the

world go by. Medieval-style benches complete the picture of European elegance. From October to April the square hosts a small market as well as bands and street performers. Bordering the square are **St. John's Anglican Church** and the **town hall.** ⊠ *Kings Sq. off William St., Fremantle, Western Australia* ⊕ *kingssquare.fremantle.wa.gov.au.*

Round House. An eye-catching landmark of early Fremantle atop an ocean-facing cliff, the Round House was built in 1831 by convicts to house other convicts. This curious, 12-sided building is the state's oldest surviving public structure. Its ramparts offer great vistas spanning from High Street to the Indian Ocean. Underneath, a tunnel was carved through the cliffs in the mid-1800s to give ships lying at anchor easy access from town. From the tunnel you can walk to the calm and quiet Bathers Beach where there used to be a whaling station, and listen for the firing of the cannon at 1 pm daily. Volunteer guides are on duty during opening hours. ⊠ *West end of High St., Fremantle, Western Australia* ☎ *08/9336–6897* ⊕ *www.fremantleroundhouse.com.au* 💲 *Donation suggested* ☉ *Daily 10:30–3:30.*

BEACHES

FAMILY   **Bathers Beach.** Sometimes, good things come in small packages. This flat, soft-sand beach sits hidden between the Fishing Boat Harbour and the Round House. It's an ideal spot to picnic with takeaway fish-and-chips. **Amenities:** food and drink. **Best for:** solitude; walking; swimming; sunset. ⊠ *Behind the Round House, accessed via Fleet St. or Mews Rd., Fremantle, Western Australia.*

FAMILY   **Leighton Beach.** Situated south of busy Cottesloe and about 30 minutes from central Perth, Leighton is a relatively quiet beach that's loved for its sugar-like sand and flat, calm water, which is perfect for those who like to paddle. It's equally loved by wind and kite surfers on windy days, who tear across the table-top surface. At the northern end of the beach, dogs are allowed to be off-leash, so expect to see lots of happy pooches running around. ■ TIP➔ It's close to the North Fremantle train station. **Amenities:** toilets; parking; lifeguards. **Best for:** swimming; walking; snorkeling; windsurfing; sunset. ⊠ *Leighton Beach Blvd., North Fremantle, Western Australia.*

FAMILY   **Port Beach.** A local favorite, wide Port Beach has small, gentle waves; water the color of Bombay Sapphire; and sugar-white sand. It butts up against Fremantle Harbour's North Quay wharf and stretches toward Leighton. Like most of the western-facing coast, the sunsets are epic and the views of Rottnest charming. **Amenities:** parking; lifeguards. **Best for:** swimming; walking; snorkeling; windsurfing; sunset. ⊠ *Port Beach Rd., North Fremantle, Western Australia.*

WHERE TO EAT

$ ✕ **Bread in Common.** We challenge you not to fall in love with Bread in
MODERN   Common. This industrial-chic bakery-cum-restaurant wins the gong
AUSTRALIAN   for hottest interior in town, with dozens of vintage-style globes stream-
Fodor's Choice   ing from the warehouse ceiling or looping in red electrical cord over
★

suspended beams. Their warm light illuminates long, wooden tables backed by distressed brick, all with views of the giant open kitchen. Herb boxes line the 1890s heritage facade, while out back is the wood-fired oven that pumps out three styles of crunchy organic bread. It's great value at A$2 per person, improved only by a serve of tangy olive oil or the creamy, crunchy pork, fennel, and pistachio whip. That said, it's worth leaving room for the smoky lamb ribs and the heirloom carrots squished into lashings of labneh (soft cheese made from yogurt), not to mention the crispy spuds roasted in duck fat. $ Average main: A$20 ☒ 43 Pakenham St., Fremantle, Western Australia ☎ 08/9336–1032 ⊕ www.breadincommon.com.au.

$$

ITALIAN

✕ **Capri Restaurant.** You may need to wait for a table (they take limited bookings), but the complimentary minestrone and crusty bread will tide you over at this Fremantle institution. You'll get a warm welcome from the Pizzale family, who have owned and run the restaurant for more than 50 years—the fourth generation is now in charge. Sit down to grilled calamari splashed with lemon; panfried scaloppine in white wine; rich spaghetti marinara; excellent steaks; and fresh salads. Simple white-linen tablecloths, carafes of chilled water—it's BYO—and the sounds of laughter and clinking glasses round out the experience. This is old-style Fremantle at its best. $ Average main: A$25 ☒ 21 South Terr., Fremantle, Western Australia ☎ 08/9335–1399 ⊕ www.caprirestaurantfremantle.com.

$$$

STEAKHOUSE

✕ **Char Char Bull.** Waterfront Fremantle is renowned for its seafood restaurants, so going to a harborside venue for steak seems almost irreverent—a bit like going to Italy for a curry—but meat lovers will revel in the juicy steak selection at Char Char Bull. This lively restaurant, with full table service, specializes in char-grilled prime beef selected from year-old, grass-fed Murray Grey cattle. Choose from tender filet mignon, tenderloin, sirloin, and rib eye cooked exactly how you like it, with all the trimmings. If you just can't go a day without fish, oysters, barramundi, garlic prawns, scallops, and wine-steamed mussels also feature on the menu, as does pizza. ▇ TIP➔ **Make reservations and ask for a table out on the deck.** $ Average main: A$40 ☒ Fishing Boat Harbour, 44 Mews Rd., Fremantle, Western Australia ☎ 08/9335–7666 ⊕ www.charcharbull.com.au.

$

SEAFOOD

FAMILY

✕ **Cicerello's.** No visit to Fremantle is complete without a stop at this locally famous fish-and-chippery, which was once featured on a postage stamp. Housed in a boathouse-style building fronting Fremantle's lovely Fishing Boat Harbour, this joint serves the real thing: fresh oysters, mussels, crabs, fish, lobsters, and chips, all wrapped up in butcher paper (no cardboard boxes or plastic plates here). While you eat, you can check out the huge aquarium and touch pool: the restaurant has more than 50 species of local marine life. Better still, on Tuesday kids eat for free. Cicerello's also has a restaurant in Mandurah. $ Average main: A$20 ☒ Fisherman's Wharf, 44 Mews Rd., Fremantle, Western Australia ☎ 08/9335–1911 ⊕ www.cicerellos.com.au.

$$

ITALIAN

✕ **Gino's Café.** The original owner, Gino, was so passionate about coffee that he closed his tailor shop to open this cappuccino-strip property with a busy alfresco terrace. Among the most popular drinks are the house coffee (Gino's Blend), and the Baby Chino—a froth of milk dusted with chocolate powder that young children love. The recently renovated Gino's opens at 6 am to serve coffee, then cooks an extensive choice of breakfasts from 7 am. The lunch menu focuses on focaccias and paninis while for dinner nearly two dozen different pasta dishes are available, including a superb penne alla vodka with chicken and spinach. $ *Average main: A$25* ⊠ *South Terr. at Collie St., Fremantle, Western Australia* ☎ *08/9336–1464* ⊕ *www.ginoscafe.com.au.*

> ### THE CUP
>
> In 1848, Britain's Queen Victoria authorized the creation of a solid silver cup for a yacht race that would be "open to all nations." In 1851, the New York Yacht Club challenged 16 English yachts and won with the boat *America*. The United States continued to win for 132 years straight until the upstart *Australia 11* won 4–3 in sensational style, and the Cup came to Fremantle. Australia was euphoric. Fremantle spruced up for the defense of the Cup in 1987, but the fairy tale ended in a 4–0 loss to the San Diego Yacht Club entrant. Today *Australia 11* is a centerpiece display at the WA Maritime Museum.

$$ ✕**Joe's Fish Shack.** Fremantle's
SEAFOOD quirkiest restaurant looks like everyone's vision of a run-down, weather-beaten Maine diner. With uninterrupted harbor views, authentic nautical bric-a-brac, and great food, you can't go wrong. Recommendations include the salt-and-pepper squid, stuffed tiger prawns, and chili mussels. An outdoor dining area provides restaurant food at take-out prices. $ *Average main: A$30* ⊠ *42 Mews Rd., Fremantle, Western Australia* ☎ *08/9336–7161* ⊕ *www.joesfishshack.com.au.*

$$ ✕**Moore & Moore.** You'll know this café-restaurant by the retro bikes
MODERN stacked out front next to the potted garden, eclectic-looking people,
AUSTRALIAN and live music that often streams from the doorway. There's an art gallery up the creaky stairs, but continue straight ahead past up-cycled furniture to the garden seating out the back. Their food is as tasty as the vibe is charming. Hugely popular for breakfast (even though they have a "no scrambled eggs" rule) it also makes for a great lunch option. Expect poached organic eggs with smoked salmon and asparagus; oven-baked tomato and chorizo egg pots; raw pizza; quinoa salads; and more eco-focused but super yummy dishes. It's feel-good all around. $ *Average main: A$25* ⊠ *46 Henry St., Fremantle, Western Australia* ☎ *08/9335–8825* ⊕ *www.mooreandmoorecafe.com.*

$$$ ✕**Ootong & Lincoln.** It says a lot about the café's style that they commis-
MODERN sioned a local street artist to paint a giant, multicolored zebra mural on
AUSTRALIAN an external wall. Inside, colorful communal tables are surrounded by
FAMILY dividers made from plumbing pipes while vintage tricycles line a shelf below the ceiling. Just as much love is put into the food. Everything is made from scratch—even the jams—and the eggs in the breakfast dishes are, naturally, free range. Go for the poached-egg-and-smoked-salmon dish that's pumped up with diced avocado and a corn-and-zucchini fritter, dolloped with hollandaise. $ *Average main: A$20* ⊠ *258 South*

Terr., South Fremantle, Western Australia ☎ *08/9335–6109* ⊕ *www.* *ootongandlincoln.com.au.*

$$ ✕ **Wild Poppy.** Sitting on the corner of bohemian Wray Avenue, Wild
SOUTH AFRICAN Poppy fits right in with its granny-chic patchwork upholstered lounges, crocheted cushions, mismatched crockery, and vintage paintings. Twists on the norm are what the South African owner-operators do best, blending their own culture with global flavors. The fried chili and masala eggs are a firm favorite, as is the black Thai rice pudding paired with a banana fritter. Sweet tooths will adore the Belgian waffle with salted caramel and ice cream while meat-lovers can opt for the Boerewors sausage. They also do standard options for those feeling less adventurous, but why be bland? Especially when everything is made from scratch in-house, using organic and free range ingredients, catering for gluten and dairy free diets. Even the cups and takeaway containers are fully compostable. $ *Average main: A$22* ⊠ *2 Wray Ave., Fremantle, Western Australia* ☎ *08/9430–8555.*

WHERE TO STAY

For expanded hotel reviews, visit Fodors.com.

$$$$ 🛏 **Esplanade Hotel Fremantle—By Rydges.** Part of a colonial-era hotel,
HOTEL this huge, well-located establishment has balconies facing either the park and nearby harbor, Essex Street, or the pool. **Pros:** central to Fremantle attractions; tropical garden setting around heated pool; three outdoor spas; ample dining and shopping options nearby. **Cons:** sea views are limited to some rooms; functions can make venues crowded; parking costs extra; rooms facing resort pool may encounter car park noise. $ *Rooms from: A$420* ⊠ *Marine Terr. at Essex St., Fremantle, Western Australia* ☎ *08/9432–4000, 1800/998201* ⊕ *www.* *esplanadehotelfremantle.com.au* ⤳ *293 rooms, 7 suites* ⦿ *No meals.*

$$ 🛏 **Fothergills of Fremantle.** Antiques, pottery, sculptures, bronzes, and
B&B/INN paintings adorn these three popular, two-story, 1892 limestone terrace houses opposite the old Fremantle prison. **Pros:** breakfast included; personalized service; good location; free Wi-Fi and parking. **Cons:** comfy shoes required for the walk to central Fremantle; limited facilities on-site. $ *Rooms from: A$195* ⊠ *18–22 Ord St., Fremantle, Western Australia* ☎ *08/9335–6784* ⊕ *www.fothergills.net.au* ⤳ *7 rooms* ⦿ *Breakfast.*

$$ 🛏 **Norfolk Hotel.** With an excellent location, leafy beer garden, and base-
HOTEL ment live music bar all part of its assets, this central accommodation has a lot going for it. **Pros:** free parking in central location; free Wi-Fi; light and airy; Fremantle Train Station a 10-minute walk away; free CAT bus nearby. **Cons:** shared facilities in some rooms; potential noise from pub. $ *Rooms from: A$180* ⊠ *47 South Terr., Fremantle, Western Australia* ☎ *08/9335–5405* ⊕ *www.norfolkhotel.com.au* ⤳ *9 rooms (4 en suite)* ⦿ *No meals.*

$$$ 🛏 **Port Mill Bed & Breakfast.** Discreetly concealed in a picture-postcard
B&B/INN courtyard reminiscent of Tuscany, this diminutive bed-and-breakfast contains four sunny, individually decorated suites, each with its own Juliette balcony; two overlooking the courtyard garden. **Pros:**

Kookaburra 12-meter yachts are tack-training for the Americas Cup.

heritage-listed accommodation; free Wi-Fi; discounts offered for longer stays; close to shopping, dining, and tourist attractions. **Cons:** parking nearby for a A$7/day fee; two-story building with winding stairs, no elevator. [$] *Rooms from: A$259* ✉ *3/17 Essex St., Fremantle, Western Australia* ☎ *08/9433–3832* 🌐 *www.portmillbb.com.au* 🛏 *4 suites* 🍴 *Breakfast.*

NIGHTLIFE

There's nothing more pleasant than relaxing in the evening at one of the sidewalk tables on the cappuccino strip. This area, along South Terrace, opens at 6 am and closes around 3 am.

Fly By Night Musicians Club. Don't be put off by the rather nondescript entry to this venue. Once an artillery drill hall and now a National Trust heritage property, it has a great tradition of music and dance, hosting excellent Australian and international artists, including Fremantle native John Butler, up to six nights a week. Many local bands and soloists owe their big breaks to Fly By Night Musicians Club, a smoke-free venue. Plenty of parking opposite the club. ✉ *1 Holdsworth St., at Parry St., Fremantle, Western Australia* ☎ *08/9430–5976* 🌐 *www.flybynight.org.*

Fodor's Choice ★ **Little Creatures.** Fancy a free tour of the brewery? How about borrowing a free, retro red bike for the day? Little Creatures has got a lot going for it—including its harborside location and fun-loving, artsy vibe—and it won't cost an arm and a leg. Sign up for the free tours that take you through every step on the beer-making process. Then, leave a photo copy of your credit card and driver's license or passport with the staff so you can borrow a bike. This is the best place in Fremantle to taste kangaroo—the skewers are excellent, as are the steamed mussels and thin base pizzas. Naturally, matching the food with beer is a must. Expect a pleasant surprise from the mid-strength Rogers beer. ✉ *40 Mews Rd., Fremantle, Western Australia* ☎ *08/9430–5555* ⊕ *www.littlecreatures.com.au.*

Metropolis Concert Club Fremantle. In the heart of Fremantle's cappuccino strip, Metropolis Concert Club Fremantle, a nonstop techno and funk dance venue, is a fun, if youth-dominated place to go on a Friday or Saturday night. ✉ *58 South Terr., Fremantle, Western Australia* ☎ *08/9336–1880* ⊕ *www.metropolisfremantle.com.au.*

Sail and Anchor Pub. Thanks to its selection of craft beers—40 on tap—and right-in-the-middle-of-it location, the heritage-listed Sail and Anchor Pub is a popular watering hole. Upstairs has comfy couches; you can watch buskers from the balcony; the front bar often has live music; and the bistro serves up no-nonsense pub grub. ✉ *64 South Terr., Fremantle, Western Australia* ☎ *08/9431–1666* ⊕ *www.sailandanchor.com.au.*

Who's Your Mumma. This city-style venue is on one of boho Fremantle's loveliest streets. Who's Your Mumma really comes alive at night. Its industrial globes put out warm light, and its wooden tables and chairs are packed with hip, fashionable, but friendly locals. ■ **TIP→ They also are open for breakfast at 8 am on weekends only, but they keep pumping out the goodness until 2 pm.** ✉ *142 South Terr., Fremantle, Western Australia* ⊕ *www.whosyourmumma.com.au.*

SHOPPING

Kakulas Sisters. A strong supporter of both WA and international produce, this unique Greek-owned provedore overflows with fragrances and sacks of goodies from across the globe. Delectable items such as Brazilian quince and guava pastries, goji berries, Tasmanian honey, Japanese teas, locally produced pestos and olives, roasted coffee beans, and European hard cheeses ensure that homesick, or simply nostalgic, visitors can enjoy a slice, sliver, or smell of home. ✉ *29–31 Market St., Fremantle, Western Australia* ☎ *08/9430–4445.*

FAMILY **Pickled Fairy & Other Myths.** A fairy theme pervades the Pickled Fairy & Other Myths, making it a delight for children and elves, with themed activities to entertain all involved. All staff are dressed as fairies and kids get sprinkled with magic dust and a wish. Fairy dresses, fairy books, and mystical magical knickknacks make this a treasure trove of potential presents for lucky little girls, or anyone with a numinous streak. ✉ *South Terrace Piazza, Shop 7B, Fremantle, Western Australia* ☎ *08/9430–5827* ⊕ *www.pickledfairy.com.au.*

ROTTNEST ISLAND

19 km (12 miles) west of Fremantle.

An easy 30-minute cruise from Fremantle, or about one hour down the Swan River from Perth, sunny, quirky Rottnest Island makes an ideal day trip. Known to locals as "Rotto," the former penal colony, boys' reformatory, and war base is as much a part of Western Australia as mine sites, colorful entrepreneurs, and untouched beaches. Its strange moniker—translated to mean rat's nest—can be attributed to 17th-century Dutch explorers who mistook the native marsupials called quokkas for cat-sized rats.

Much of the island's charm lies in the fact it's largely car free: rent a bike to make the most of it. The island has an interesting past, which is evident in its historic buildings. Though records of human occupation date back 6,500 years, when Aboriginal people inhabited the area, European settlement only dates back to 1829. Since then the island has been used for a variety of purposes, including attempts at agriculture, a boy's reformatory, a penal colony, and for military purposes in both the Great War and World War II. The Rottnest Museum is a great place to get the history of the place, further enhanced by the many free daily tours run by volunteers. You can also take a train trip and tour to Oliver Hill to see gun emplacements from World War II.

Of course most West Australians go to the island for the beaches, the swimming, and the laid-back atmosphere on Perth's doorstep. A warm ocean current passes by Rottnest, allowing it to host an unusual mix of tropical and temperate marine life. In fact, it's home to 135 species of tropical fish and 20 species of coral, and even air temperature is warmer than on the mainland.

GETTING HERE AND AROUND

A number of operators offer light plane and helicopter flights to Rottnest Island. Check the Rottnest Island Visitor Information Centre website for other options.

There are no taxis on Rottnest Island. Almost everyone rides bikes, which can either be rented when booking your ferry ticket, or once you arrive, at Rottnest Bike Hire.

Charter1 catamaran. Cuddle up onboard a 12½-meter (41-foot) island-circling catamaran that offers snorkeling and seal and dolphin spotting adventures to Rottnest Island's isolated bays by day, and gently rocking accommodation complete with stargazing by night. The day tours head to a small rocky island where Australian fur seals like to loll about, but once they see you splash into the ocean, they're keen to play and will swim around you in the water. From September to November, spot dolphins and humpback whales frolicking in the ocean. Snorkel tours (A\$68) run September–April, daily 11–1, and eco-adventure tours (A\$58) are at 1:15–3:15. Twilight sails (A\$48) make for another relaxing option. Bookings recommended. ■ TIP→ Snorkelling gear is provided. ⊠ *Rottnest Island, Western Australia* ☎ *0428/604794* ⊕ *www.charter1.com.au.*

Rottnest Air Taxi. This speedy air service to Rottnest Island flies from Perth's Jandakot airport. Round-trip fare is from around A$120 per person for a fully occupied aircraft (fewer passengers means prices rise; there's a four-seater and a six-seater aircraft). The service operates on demand, anytime during the day, weather permitting. Flight time is around 12 minutes. Telephone for flight times. ☎ *1800/500006 within Australia only, 0411/264547* ⊕ *www.rottnestairtaxi.com.au.*

Rottnest Express. Rottnest Express runs ferries to Rottnest Island from two locations in Fremantle, as well as from Perth. ☎ *1300/467688* ⊕ *www.rottnestexpress.com.au.*

Rottnest Fast Ferries. Rottnest Fast Ferries runs boats from Hillarys Boat Harbour. The ferries take approximately 45 minutes from Hillarys to Rottnest, with hotel pickups from Perth available. Round-trip prices, including entry to Rottnest are from A$84. Add bike rentals to the trip for a total fare of A$99; snorkel sets are A$15 extra. Whale-watching tours, which start from A$69 (early-September to early December), are also available. ☎ *08/9246–1039* ⊕ *rottnestfastferries.com.au* ☉ *Closed June, July (except school holidays), and Aug.*

SAFETY AND PRECAUTIONS

Be sun-smart, especially from October through April. Even on cloudy days people unused to being outdoors for any length of time can suffer severe sunburn. Wear a hat, long-sleeved shirt, and high-strength sunscreen. If you are a weak or novice swimmer, always swim with a friend; lifesavers (lifeguards) patrol certain beaches during peak holiday periods.

TIMING

Rottnest Island can be visited in a day. An early ferry gets you to the island with plenty of time to tour the main attractions or beaches, returning to Fremantle or Perth in the late afternoon. Staying an extra day or two gives you time to laze at a beach or go surfing or diving.

TOURS

The Rottnest Island Authority runs a narrated 90-minute coach tour of the island's highlights, including convict-built cottages, World War II gun emplacements, salt lakes, and the remote West End. Tours depart daily from Main Bus Stop. The Oliver Hill Railway made its debut in the mid-1990s, utilizing 6 km (4 miles) of reconstructed railway line to reach the island's World War II gun batteries. Information is available from the Rottnest Island Visitor Centre.

Bayseeker Bus. This company, which runs a continuous hop-on, hop-off island circuit, picks up and drops off passengers at the most beautiful bays and beaches. Day tickets are A$14 and can be purchased from the Rottnest Island Visitor Centre. Buses run 8:30–3:30, hourly in winter and half-hourly in summer until 4:30. Timetables are posted at all bus stops. ✉ *Thomson Bay, Henderson Ave., Rottnest Island, Western Australia* ☎ *08/9372–9732* ⊕ *www.rottnestisland.com.*

Discovery Tour. For those not keen on biking or hop-on, hop-off buses, the Rottnest Island Authority runs a popular Discovery Tour that gives an overview of the island's activities, history, environment, and wildlife over one hour and 45 minutes. Highlights of the tour are the

Wadjemup Lighthouse and the remote West End. Tours depart daily from the Main Bus Stop at 11:15, 1:40, and 1:50 (times subject to ferry services.) Tours cost A$35. Tickets available from the visitor center. ⊠ *Thompson Bay, Rottnest Island, Western Australia* ☎ *08/9372–9732.*

The Oliver Hill Train. Known as the *Captain Hussey,* the Oliver Hill Train is an ideal way to see the island. The route from the Main Settlement to Oliver Hill runs daily at 1:30, and connects with a guided tour of the historic Oliver Hill gun battery. The fare is A$26 and includes the guided tour. The train fare without the guided tours is A$18. Tickets are available at the visitor center. ⊠ *Thomson Bay, Rottnest Island, Western Australia* ☎ *08/9372–9732* ⊕ *www.rottnestisland.com.*

> **MARSUPIALS, NOT RATS**
>
> Quokkas were among the first Australian mammals ever seen by Europeans. In 1658, the Dutch Captain Willem De Vlamingh described them as rats, but in fact they are marsupials, carrying their young in a pouch. Once common around Perth, quokkas are now confined to isolated pockets on the mainland, but still thrive on their namesake Rottnest Island, where they are safe from predators, most of which have now been eradicated. Their cute, furry faces and small, round bodies make them very photogenic.

ESSENTIALS

Visitor Information Rottnest Island Visitor Centre ⊠ *Adjacent to Dome Café, Thomson Bay beachfront, Rottnest Island, Western Australia* ☎ *08/9372–9732* ⊕ *www.rottnestisland.com* ⊙ *Sat.–Thurs. 7:30– 5, Fri. 7:30–7:30.*

EXPLORING

The most convenient way to get around Rottnest is by bicycle, as private cars are not allowed on the island. A self-guided bicycle tour of the island covers 26 km (16 miles) and can take as little as three hours, although you really need an entire day to enjoy the beautiful surroundings.

Heading south from Thomson Bay, between Government House and Herschell Lakes, you'll find the Quokka Walk and a man-made causeway where you'll find a few quokka colonies. Continue south and to Oliver Hill and the Wadjemup Light House, where tours are run every half hour from 11 am until 2:30 pm. As you continue to Bickley Bay you can spot the wreckage of ships—the oldest dates from 1842—that came to rest on Rottnest's rocky coastline.

Follow the main road past Porpoise, Salmon, Strickland, and Wilson bays to West End, the windiest point on the island and another graveyard for unfortunate vessels. Heading back to Thomson Bay, the road passes a dozen rocky inlets and bays. Parakeet Bay, the prettiest, is at the northernmost tip of the island.

Rottnest Museum. At the Thomson Bay settlement, don't miss the Rottnest Museum, which includes mementos of the island's turbulent past. Staying true to local history, displays are housed in an old mill and hay store

Snorkeling at the Basin on Rottnest Island, Western Australia

built in 1857, showing local geology, natural and social history, and maritime lore with a bunch of surprising facts. It's open daily 10:45–3:30. **Wadjemup Lighthouse Tours**—find out what goes on within the confines of a working lighthouse and climb to the top of this heritage structure for fabulous 360-degree views. Tours depart daily, on demand, at 11 am and every half hour until 2:30 pm, and cost A$8. ⊠ *Thomson Bay, Digby Dr., Rottnest Island, Western Australia* ☏ *08/9372–9732* ⊕ *www.rottnestisland.com* ✉ *Donation suggested.*

BEACHES

There are some 63 beaches on Rottnest Island, suitable for swimming, surfing, snorkeling, and diving. The most popular include Geordie Bay, Little Parakeet, Parker Point, Little Salmon Bay, and the Basin.

Surfers and body-boarders will head for Stark Bay, Strickland Bay, and West End, while swimmers will love sandy white beaches at Pinkies Beach and the Basin. Beach spots for snorkeling and diving include Little Salmon Bay (it has underwater markers), and Parker Point.

FAMILY **The Basin.** This pool-like bay is one of Rottnest's most popular, both for its safe, shallow waters and for its proximity to the main settlement. Protected by an outer reef, the ocean is crystal clear, the waves are gentle and you'll sometimes see little fish darting about. **Amenities:** toilets; showers; lifeguards. **Best for:** swimming. ⊠ *Northwest of Thompson Bay, Rottnest Island, Western Australia* ⊕ *www.rottnestisland.com.*

Geordie Bay. Over the dunes is the whitest of white sand and the most azure waters of Geordie Bay. Photographed by many, its flat, motionless ocean makes for safe swimming. A confetti of yachts spreads across the bay in summer months (there are protected, boat-free swimming zones), and beachside accommodation mirrors the cove. Nearby, next to a minimart, find Geordie's Cafe (☎ *08/9292–5411*), one of the newest and best foodie options on the island. Open for breakfast, lunch, and dinner, it also offers plenty of gluten-free options. Expect to see furry quokkas looking for scraps. **Amenities:** toilets; showers. **Best for:** swimming. ✉ *Geordie Bay Rd., Rottnest Island, Western Australia.*

Little Salmon Bay. Make sure you pack your snorkeling gear for this one—due to Rottnest's warmer waters, created by the passing Leeuwin Current, there's a fascinating mix of tropical and temperate fish species in the clear waters. Aim to go at low tide and look out for bream, red-lipped morwong, zebrafish, and king wrasse, plus plenty of little colored fish. There are underwater plaques that guide you along a great snorkel trail and the waters are calm so you can enjoy flipping about. Coral reefs are about 100 meters (330 feet) out but worth checking out if you're a confident swimmer. **Amenities:** none. **Best for:** swimming; snorkeling. **■ TIP→ If it's overcrowded, head to the next, bigger beach, Salmon Bay.** ✉ *Little Salmon Bay, south west of Thompson Bay, off Parker Point Rd., Rottnest Island, Western Australia.*

SPORTS AND THE OUTDOORS

BIKING

Rottnest Bike Hire. You can rent bikes—the island's must-have item—from A$28 per day, with a returnable deposit of A$25 per bike. Tandem bikes and attachable buggies for little children can also be rented. Also for rent: snorkel sets, paddleboards, surfboards, bodyboards, wet suits, and beach cricket and soccer essentials. It's open daily 8:30–5:30, though hours vary according to the season (when there's no 6 pm ferry, it closes at 4 pm). Expect queues at ferry arrival times. ✉ *Thomson Bay, Rottnest Island, Western Australia* ☎ *08/9292–5105* 🌐 *www.rottnestisland.com.*

WHERE TO STAY

Accommodation on the island ranges from basic camping sites to self-contained holiday villas and hotels. Space is at a premium during the summer months, Easter, and school holidays. November can be busy because of the so-called "schoolies week," when high-school leavers celebrate the end of senior school. This time is best avoided. Outside these times, accommodation is easier to find. Check 🌐 *www.rottnestisland.com* for details.

For expanded hotel reviews, visit Fodors.com.

$$$ HOTEL 🏨 **Rottnest Lodge.** The largest hotel on Rottnest and the only one with a pool and spa facilities, its sturdy structure reveals an interesting past as a colonial barracks and a prison. **Pros:** centrally located; some rooms have lake views; some rooms ideal for families. **Cons:** not on beachfront; limited leisure facilities. [$] *Rooms from: A$220* ✉ *Kitson St., Rottnest Island, Western Australia* ☎ *08/9292–5161* 🌐 *www.rottnestlodge.com.au* 🛏 *80 rooms, including 15 premium rooms* 🍴 *Breakfast.*

THE SOUTH WEST WINE REGION

11

The South West—Western Australia's most popular destination, with more than 1.5 million visitors annually—should not be missed if you are coming to this state, a fact well known by Perth residents, who flock here year-round for the wines, beaches, surfing, marine wildlife, forests, locally produced crafts and artisan products, and the country vistas.

The region stretches from the port city of Bunbury—about two hours south of Perth by freeway and highway—through Busselton, Dunsborough, Margaret River (1½ hours farther south), and on to Augusta, at the tip of Cape Leeuwin.

Margaret River is best known for its fabulous wines—Chardonnay and Cabernet Sauvignon are the standout varieties—but the South West has wineries from well north of Bunbury to the south coast. Busselton, Dunsborough, Yallingup, Prevelly, and Margaret River are all suitable places to stay if you want to visit wineries; all but Margaret River are on the coast with easy beach access.

The best surfing beaches are on the coast between Cape Naturaliste and Cape Leeuwin.

All major South West towns have visitor centers that can arrange tours, book accommodations, and provide free information.

EN ROUTE Bunbury is a great stopover point where you can visit the Dolphin Discovery Centre to swim with wild dolphins (in season), or wade in shallow waters with them under the watchful eye of center volunteers and biologists. About 100 bottlenose dolphins make their permanent home in and around the waters of Koombana Bay off Bunbury, making your chances of seeing them in their natural habitat very high. You can also take a dolphin cruise with the Dolphin Discovery Centre, or an eco-conscious whale-watching excursion with Naturaliste Charters.

Bunbury Visitor Centre ⊠ *Old Railway Station, Carmody Pl., Bunbury, Western Australia* ☎ *08/9792–7205* ⊕ *www.visitbunbury.com.au* ⊗ *Weekdays 9–5, Sat. 9:30–4:30, Sun. and public holidays 10–2.*

Dolphin Discovery Centre. Get up close to wild dolphins at the Dolphin Discovery Centre. Two hundred dolphins have been identified in Koombana Bay—swim with them, book an eco-cruise, or stay on the beach and wade into the interaction zone. Enjoy the discovery center with its unique digital dolphinarium, interpretive panels and theater, dolphin skeleton, and café and gift shop. ▓TIP➜ Call first to book the weather-dependent swim and eco-cruises. Dolphin encounters are not guaranteed. ⊠ *830 Koombana Dr., Bunbury, Western Australia* ☎ *08/9791–3088* ⊕ *www.dolphindiscovery.com.au* ⊠ *Discovery Centre A$10; Swim On The Wild Side A$149; Eco-Cruise A$49* ⊗ *Oct.–May, daily 8–4; June–Sept., daily 9–2.*

Naturaliste Charters. This company runs eco-conscious whale-watching tours along the southwestern coastline, shifting from Augusta to Dunsborough as the whale migration shifts north from May to December. You can expect to see playful humpbacks and diving southern right whales, and if you're lucky, rare blue and minke whales. The local company also offers Eco Wilderness & Sunset Eco Tours from January

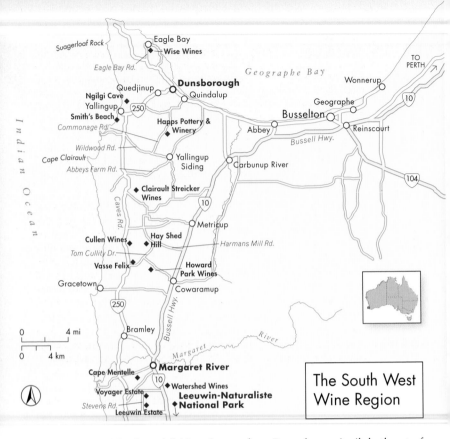

The South West Wine Region

to March, and fishing charters from December to April, both out of Dunsborough. ⊠ *Shop 1, Bayview Centro, Dunsborough, Western Australia* ☎ *08/9750–5500* ⊕ *www.whales-australia.com.*

DUNSBOROUGH

252 km (157 miles) south of Perth.

The attractive and fashionable seaside town of Dunsborough is perfect for a few days of swimming, sunning, and fishing—which is why it's become a popular holiday destination for many Perth families. Onshore attractions include Meelup Beach, a protected cove with calm swimming water, and the nearby wineries of Margaret River. Offshore, you can dive on the wreck of the HMAS *Swan*, the former Royal Australian Navy ship deliberately sunk in Geographe Bay at the end of its useful life, or take a cruise to see migrating humpback and southern right whales September–December.

GETTING HERE AND AROUND

From Perth, take the Kwinana Freeway south; it joins the Forrest Highway and then Highway 1 down the coast to Bunbury. Switch to Highway 10 through Busselton, then Caves Road to Dunsborough. If you drive from Perth, it will take around three hours. Alternatively, **South**

West Coachlines (☎ *08/9261–7600* ⊕ *southwestcoachlines.com.au*) has daily coach services from Perth Central Bus Station at the Esplanade Bus Port on Mounts Bay Road to South West towns, including Dunsborough. Once here, a rental car is recommended, as there is limited public transport, and some accommodations are in bushland or beach settings, away from the towns.

Dunsborough Car Rentals. Late-model vehicles are available at reasonable rates for touring the Margaret River region. ⊠ *201 Geographe Bay Rd., Quindalup, Dunsborough, Western Australia* ☎ *1800/449007* ⊕ *www. dunsboroughcarrentals.com.au.*

SAFETY AND PRECAUTIONS

The calm waters of Geographe Bay are home to a jellyfish with a nasty sting—colloquially named "stingers." They are not deadly but they are painful, and a sting occasionally requires hospitalization. They are hard to spot—the main body of the stinger is translucent and only about 2 inches across, and they trail hard-to-see black tentacles that are the cause for concern. They like warmer, very calm water, so still days in summer are when you are most likely to encounter them as they drift close to shore. Rubbing a sting is not recommended; try bathing in vinegar.

Mosquitoes are prevalent in summer, especially along the South West coast and in swamplands. To avoid being bitten by mosquitoes, cover up and use a repellent, especially around dawn and dusk, when mosquitoes are most active.

TIMING

Dunsborough (and the surrounding area) deserves at least two days, preferably three. Western Australian school holidays, especially the summer break over Christmas and New Year's Day, and Easter, are usually booked solid by Perth holiday makers with families. One week in November is also crowded for "schoolies week," when teenage students boisterously celebrate the end of their schooling life. The summer months (December–March) are best for swimming and beaches, while the heaviest surfing conditions are often best during the winter months (May–September) when wet suits are required.

TOURS

FAMILY

Fodor's Choice ★

Busselton Jetty and Underwater Observatory. At almost 2 km (1¼ miles) long, the 146-year-old Busselton Jetty is the longest timber jetty in the southern hemisphere. You can visit the Interpretive Center and Heritage Museum at the start of the jetty, then either catch the miniature train (45-minute ride) or walk to the fascinating Underwater Observatory—one of only seven in the world—where you'll spy all manner of soft, colorful coral as you descend the cylindrical, windowed observatory. Tours for up to 40 people run every hour, taking you 8 meters (26 feet) below the water. The warm Leeuwin Current and the sheltering effect of the jetty above have created a unique microclimate rich with colorful tropical and subtropical corals, sponges, fish, and invertebrates—there are 300 marine species in all. ■ TIP→ Booking is essential. ⊠ *Beachfront, Queen St., Busselton, Western Australia* ☎ *08/9754–0900* ⊕ *www. busseltonjetty.com.au* ✉ *1-hr Underwater Observatory Tour; return* *train ride and jetty day pass A$29.5; jetty only A$2.50; one-way train only A$11; Interpretive Centre & Heritage Museum free ⊙ Interpretive Center & Heritage Museum, May–Aug., daily 9–5; Sept.–Apr., daily 8:30–6. Underwater Observatory & Jetty Train Tour, May–Aug., on the hr 10–3; Sept.–Apr., on the hr 9–4.*

Cape Dive. This company has dive tours to the wreck of the HMAS *Swan*, a Royal Australian Navy River Class Destroyer Escort deliberately sunk in 30 meters of water off Dunsborough to become an artificial reef and dive wreck. Dives are tailored to novices and experienced divers alike. They also offer dives around the Busselton Jetty, where an abundance of corals and marine life have made their homes on the pylons. Cape Dive has recently added seasonal whale-watching to its suite of experiences. ⊠ *Shop 1, 222 Naturaliste Terr., Dunsborough, Western Australia* ☎ *08/9756–8778* ⊕ *www.capedive.com* ⊙ *Tues.– Sun. 9–5 (reduced hrs in colder months).*

Cellar d'Or Winery Tours. Cellar d'Or Winery Tours has daily tours of Margaret River region wineries from A$82 per person. The tours include pickup at your accommodation, wine tastings at five boutique wineries, platter lunch and beer tasting at a microbrewery, chocolate sampling, cheese and local produce tasting, and complimentary bottled water and wine glass. ☎ *0428/179729* ⊕ *www.cellardortours.com.au.*

ESSENTIALS

Mastercard and Visa are always taken at restaurants, lodgings, and shops; American Express and Diners Club are less acceptable, and the merchant may add a small surcharge.

Taxi Contacts Busselton Taxis ☎ *13–1008.* **Dunsborough Taxis** ☎ *08/9756–8688.*

Visitor Information Busselton Visitor Centre. Local experts man the phones to answer all questions, and tours are bookable via the Visitor Centre info line and website. ⊠ *Busselton beachfront, beach end of Queen St., Busselton, Western Australia* ☎ *08/9752–5800* ⊕ *www.geographebay.com* ⊙ *Weekdays 9–5, weekends 9–4:30* ⊙ *Closed Christmas Day.* **Dunsborough Visitor Centre** ⊠ *Dunsborough Park Shopping Centre, Seymour Blvd., Dunsborough, Western Australia* ☎ *08/9752–5800* ⊕ *www.geographebay.com* ⊙ *Weekdays 9:30–4:30, weekends and public holidays 10–3:30.*

EXPLORING THE WINERIES

Clairault Streicker Wines. This winery is known for its award-winning Chardonnay, Cabernet Sauvignon, and Cabernet Merlot, and loved for its natural bushland setting, about 18 km (11 miles) south of Dunsborough. The cellar door is modern in style with polished timber floors, natural stone, and walls of glass overlooking the scrub. The spacious café (open Thursday–Monday 11–4) has glass doors that open on to a large timber deck in warm weather—picnic blankets are available to borrow—while two huge stone fireplaces warm the tables in winter. The winery and restaurant are popular for weddings, especially during the spring and fall months. ⊠ *3277 Caves Rd., Wilyabrup, Western Australia* ☎ *08/9755–6225 cellar door café* ⊕ *www.clairault.com.au* ⊙ *Daily 10–5.*

Happs Pottery & Winery. Handmade mud bricks, recycled timbers, and stained-glass windows point to the origins of this family-owned and -built winery. A few kilometers from Dunsborough you'll find a friendly welcome, a huge range of wines to taste (33 at last reckoning), and—unique in this area—a pottery gallery in the same building. Erl Happ began his pottery business in 1970 then planted his first vines eight years later, going against local wisdom by planting Merlot. Later, a second vineyard was established near Karridale some 90 km (55 miles) to the south, with 31 varieties of grape, its wines produced under the Three Hills label. Free tastings allow you to try some wines only available at the cellar door, such as Fuchsia and preservative-free wines. His daughter-in-law Jacquie runs the pottery, his wife Roslyn has created a much-photographed garden courtyard, and son Myles works at the home studio, producing what is described as the biggest collection of pottery in the area. ⊠ *575 Commonage Rd., Dunsborough, Western Australia* ☎ *08/9755–3300* ⊕ *www.happs.com.au* ⊗ *Daily 10–5.*

Wise Wines. The view from the hilltop overlooking Geographe Bay is almost as good as the wines and food at this northernmost winery in the region, about a 15-minute drive from Dunsborough toward Cape Naturaliste. This family-owned boutique vineyard has a history of producing award-winning Chardonnay, though other wines have received accolades as well. Try the Sea Urchin or Bead Sparkling wines, or the single vineyard Eagle Bay. The adjacent Wise Vineyard restaurant is open for breakfast and lunch as well as dinner on Friday and Saturday nights. ■TIP➔ **If you can't bear to leave, a timber chalet called The Barn is available for a minimum stay of two nights.** ⊠ *80 Eagle Bay Rd., Dunsborough, Western Australia* ☎ *08/9750–3100 cellar door* ⊕ *www. wisewine.com.au* ⊗ *Daily 11–5.*

NEED A
BREAK?

Simmo's Ice Creamery and Fun Park. This is an institution for families and sweet tooths. Their menu includes up to 60 different flavors of ice cream and sorbet, including apple pie, mascarpone with fig, mango macadamia, and caramel choc fudge. Everything is made fresh daily, to devour in cones, waffles, and sundaes. There's coffee to go, and—for the kids—a great fun park with games including an 18 hole mini-golf course. You can have a picnic in the shady grounds and meet Edward, the ice cream–eating emu. ⊠ **161 Commonage Rd., Dunsborough, Western Australia** ☎ **08/9755–3745** ⊕ **www.simmos.com.au** ⊗ **Daily 10:30–5.**

BEACHES

FAMILY **Meelup Beach.** Sheltered from wind, this soft-sand haven makes for a gorgeous coastal escape. Its aquamarine blue waters attract many a visitor. Bring food with you because there are barbecue facilities and picnic tables. **Amenities:** toilets; showers. **Best for:** solitude; swimming; walking. ⊠ *Meelup Beach Rd., Dunsborough, Western Australia.*

WHERE TO EAT

$$
MODERN
AUSTRALIAN

✕ **Eagle Bay Brewery.** Fun is an essential ingredient in any restaurant, and the family-owned and -run Eagle Bay Brewery champions it. Grab a six-beer tasting tray so you can sample their many creations, then have a ball seeing which ones best complement the meals you choose. The food is pure gastro pub—the proper English gourmet sort—and the U.K.-born chef likes to dip into the organic kitchen garden for a fresh kick. The wood-fired pizzas are hard to pass up: our pick is the roast-pumpkin-and-zucchini concoction, topped with haloumi sumac and sunflower seeds. For heartier appetites, the scotch fillet lathered in green peppercorn sauce and served with a mushroom-and-bacon terrine is satisfying, but if you want to fit in dessert, opt for the lighter lentil and sesame fritters. $ *Average main: A$26* ⊠ *236 Eagle Bay Rd., Naturaliste, Western Australia* ☎ *08/9755–3554* ⊕ *eaglebaybrewing.com.au.*

$$$ ✕ **The Studio Bistro.** This is fancy pants food at its best. Ocean trout pastrami comes with quinoa and almond cream jelly; lamb cutlet is cooked
MODERN
AUSTRALIAN *sous-vide* then presented with potato galette and creamed spinach; quail is marinated in herbs then panfried, accompanied by whipped goat cheese and truffle oil powder. Salivating yet? Better still is the presentation, perhaps inspired by the art coating the restaurant walls; the bistro hosts regularly changing art exhibitions. Degustations, available daily (on request; A$120 with wine, A$90 without) are when the kitchen team really hits its stride, taking you to foodie nirvana with the six-course menu. $ *Average main: A$36* ⊠ *21/7 Marrinup Dr., Yallingup, Western Australia* ☎ *08/9756–6371* ⊕ *www.thestudiobistro.com.au* ⌂ *Reservations essential* ⊗ *Closed Tues. No lunch Fri.–Sat.*

$$$ ✕ **Wise Vineyard Restaurant.** Verdant bushland, manicured vineyards,
AUSTRALIAN and expansive views all the way down to Geographe Bay are showstopping features of this modern restaurant. Expect the unexpected and be pleasantly surprised by culinary creations that change with the turning of each season. In keeping, the accent is on the use of fresh, local produce. Look out for house-cured salmon, crunchy-edge pork belly with creamed truffle potatoes, or the Amelia Park lamb rack with polenta and pine nuts. The extensive dessert menu is just as appealing, so leave room for sweets. ∎**TIP**➜ On Friday night, pasta and risotto dishes are featured. $ *Average main: A$36* ⊠ *80 Eagle Bay Rd., Dunsborough, Western Australia* ☎ *08/9755–3331* ⊕ *www.wisefood.com* ⌂ *Reservations essential* ⊗ *No dinner Sun.–Thurs.*

WHERE TO STAY
For expanded hotel reviews, visit Fodors.com.

$$$ ⊡ **Broadwater Beach Resort Busselton.** Sunny public areas and extensive
HOTEL sports facilities make this one of the best accommodation choices on
FAMILY the Geographe Bay beach strip, especially for families with energetic children. **Pros:** walk straight onto beach; apartments ideal for families; numerous leisure facilities. **Cons:** own transport essential; limited dining options nearby; no shopping (except convenience) nearby. $ *Rooms from: A$290* ⊠ *Bussell Hwy at Holgate Rd., Busselton, Western Australia* ☎ *08/9754–1633* ⊕ *www.broadwaters.com.au* ⌁ *10 rooms, 15 apartments, 40 villas* ⦿| *No meals.*

$ ⊡ **Dunsborough Central Motel.** With a swimming pool, heated spa, and
HOTEL barbecue area, this motel for the dollar-conscious provides convenient, comfortable accommodations with en suites, and proximity to town and the beach. **Pros:** good-value beds for the area; guest laundry;

close to shops and dining options; Wi-Fi in all rooms (but there's a charge). **Cons:** not on the beachfront; no on-site restaurant. $ *Rooms from: A$140* ⊠ *50 Dunn Bay Rd., Dunsborough, Western Australia* ☎ *08/9756–7711* ⊕ *www.dunsboroughmotel.com.au* ⊅ *47 rooms* ⦁⦁ *No meals.*

$$$$ 🖼 **Pullman Resort Bunker Bay.** Sprawling down the hillside of the Cape
RESORT Naturaliste Ridge in bushland, this resort woos with its sexy infinity
Fodor's Choice pool, swanky rooms, and easy access to one of the area's best beaches.
★ **Pros:** large, luxurious rooms; quiet environment; walk straight onto the
beach; infinity pool with ocean views; on-site restaurant and bar. **Cons:**
limited sea views from rooms; own transport essential; no shopping
nearby. $ *Rooms from: A$415* ⊠ *Bunker Bay Rd. off Cape Naturaliste
Rd., Dunsborough, Western Australia* ☎ *1300/656565, 08/9756–9100*
⊕ *www.accorhotels.com* ⊅ *150 villas* ⦁⦁ *No meals.*

LEEUWIN–NATURALISTE NATIONAL PARK

*The northernmost part of the park is 266 km (165 miles) south of Perth,
25 km (16 miles) northwest of Dunsborough.*

GETTING HERE AND AROUND
From Perth take the Kwinana Freeway south; it joins the Forrest High-
way and then Highway 1 to Bunbury; switch to Highway 10 through
Busselton to Dunsborough. Because of its patchwork boundaries,
Leeuwin-Naturaliste National Park can be accessed at many points
along the coast. Caves Road, a secondary road from Dunsborough to
Augusta, provides the best access—all the side roads to the best coastal
spots come off this road. Only on a section through the Boranup Karri
Forest does Caves Road actually travel through the park for any distance. Marked trails are available from most of the coastal parking lots;
they vary from an easy 1-km (½-mile) trail from the car park at Cape
Naturaliste Lighthouse to a challenging 20-km (12-mile) full-day hike
between Cosy Corner and Skippy Rock, near Augusta.

SAFETY AND PRECAUTIONS
Although the temptation is to climb all over the rocky outcrops, such
as Canal Rocks, Sugarloaf Rock, and Skippy Rock, be aware of "king
waves" that rise up with little warning from the ocean. Take note of
the warning signs; at a few locations lifebuoys have been stationed for
just such incidents.

TIMING
Any time of the year is suitable for visiting the park. You can picnic, go
for a scenic drive, explore the caves, and go fishing, surfing, and bushwalking year-round. The summer months are best for swimming and
snorkeling, while whale-watching months are usually June-December,
starting in the south of the region and heading north as the season
progresses.

TOURS
Bushtucker Tours. This company has canoe, cave, and bush-tucker tours
daily from Margaret River. The tours give you an opportunity to see
inaccessible parts of the Margaret River, Aboriginal sites, and caves
while canoeing sections of the river down to the mouth at Surfers Point.

A short walk shows you the rich variety of "bush tucker" Aboriginals would have eaten, while lunch includes a selection of authentic bush-tucker foods. The tours (A$90) take about four hours. Winery and brewery tours are also available, departing from Bunbury, Busselton, Dunsborough, or Margaret River. ☎ 08/9757–9084, 0419/911971 ⊕ www.bushtuckertours.com.

EXPLORING

FAMILY

Fodor's Choice
★

Leeuwin-Naturaliste National Park. This national park clutches one of Western Australia's most spectacular coastlines, from Cape Naturaliste by Geographe Bay in the north, to Cape Leeuwin, close to Augusta in the south. The park is not a composite destination, rather a narrow patchwork of protected areas along the coast, intersected by beach access roads and small beachside villages, and traced by the Cape to Cape Trail.

The mostly unspoiled coastal vistas are as awe-inspiring as any in the world—on a calm day the view northwards from Yallingup past Sugarloaf Rock towards Cape Naturaliste is nature at its best and it's often sprinkled with surfing dolphins. Farther south, between Cowaramup Bay and Karridale, scenic lookouts allow you to access coastal cliffs and rocky shoreline that bear the brunt of giant ocean swells generated across thousands of miles of Indian Ocean.

In addition to the scenic attractions of the coast, the park sits over limestone ridges where numerous caves have formed over the millennia, leached out by dripping water. A number of these caves are open to the public, including Lake, Mammoth, Jewel, Moondyne Joe (June–December only), and Ngilgi. Boranup Karri Forest, near Karridale, creates a contrast to the coast—the distinctive, pale-bark hardwood giants reach 190 feet or more and dominate the hills and valleys of this area. This is the farthest west that karri trees grow in Western Australia, and, interestingly, Boranup is a regrowth forest; it was cut over by loggers more than 100 years ago, and 1961 wildfire destroyed many trees. The most breathtaking stretch lies about 20 minutes' drive south of Margaret River on Caves Road—you'll know it when you hit it because the beauty is unmistakable. ⊠ Off Caves Rd., Leeuwin-Naturaliste National Park, Western Australia ⊕ parks.dpaw.wa.gov.au/park/leeuwin-naturaliste.

Cape Naturaliste Lighthouse. At the northern end of Leeuwin-Naturaliste National Park stands Cape Naturaliste Lighthouse. A 1½-km-long (1-mile-long) trail leads from Cape Naturaliste to Canal Rocks, passing rugged cliffs, quiet bays, and curving beaches. You can opt for guided tours, on request (various routes and costs); the cape-to-cave trail wraps in Ngilgi Cave and a stunning stretch of coastline. Migrating whales are often spotted along this stretch, and from the lighthouse. This is also the start of the coast-hugging 138-km (86-mile) Cape-to-Cape Walk, for which there are also guided tours (Cape to Cape Tours are recommended for extended hikes; ☎ 0459/452–038 ⊕ capetocapetours.com.au). Four major cave systems are easily accessible within Leeuwin-Naturaliste National Park. ⇨ See individual cave listings for more information. ⊠ 1267 Cape Naturaliste Rd., Leeuwin-Naturaliste National

Park, Western Australia ☎ *08/9157–7411* ⊕ *www.geographebay.com/ tours/cape-naturaliste-lighthouse* ✉ *Guided tours of the lighthouse A$13* ۩ *Daily 9–4:30 (last entry at 4).*

CaveWorks. The CaveWorks display center at Lake Cave presents a good introduction to the whole cave system and how it was formed. There's a simulated cave tunnel called a cave crawl that allows kids to safely experience tight spaces. CaveWorks is open daily 9–5. ✉ *Caves Rd., Forest Grove, Margaret River, Western Australia* ☎ *08/9757–7411* ⊕ *www.margaretriver.com/caveworks-eco-centre-and-research.*

Jewel. The southernmost cave of the entire underground system, Jewel has one of the longest straw stalactites in any tourist cave in the world. There's also an interpretive center on site and a café nearby. ✉ *Caves Rd., Augusta, Western Australia* ☎ *08/9757–7411* ⊕ *www. margaretriver.com* ۩ *Daily 9:30–3:30, tours every hr on the half hr (more frequent during school vacation).*

Lake Cave. Centered around a tranquil, eerie-looking underground lake, Lake Cave is the deepest of all the open caves in the region, and there are tearooms on-site. Entry and tour cost at each of the caves is A$22 or you can buy a discounted pass for A$55 to visit Lake, Jewel, and Mammoth caves. There's also a discounted ticket that includes all three caves and Cape Leeuwin Lighthouse for A$70. ✉ *Caves Rd., Forest Grove, Margaret River, Western Australia* ☎ *08/9757–7411* ⊕ *www. margaretriver.com* ۩ *Daily 9:30–3:30, with tours every hr on the half hr.*

Mammoth Cave. Here you'll find ancient fossil remains of extinct animals. Self-guided tours are available, and you can add an audio experience. Wheelchair access is possible. ✉ *Caves Rd., Witchcliffe, Western Australia* ☎ *08/9757–7411* ⊕ *www.margaretriver.com* ✉ *Self-guided tours A$22* ۩ *Daily 9–5, with the last entry at 4.*

Ngilgi Cave. Near Yallingup, Ngilgi Cave is a main site for adventure caving. In between crawling through tight spots, sliding down smooth rock surfaces, and gazing at stalactites, you'll learn about the fascinating history of this special cave, explored by candlelight in the 1900s. Semi-guided cave tours take about one hour, cost A$21, and run every half hour from 9:30 to 4. Highly recommended adventure caving tours operate at 9:30 am weekdays. Prebooking at least 48 hours in advance is advised. Adventure tours cost from A$33 to A$152, and vary from 45 minutes to four hours in length, depending on the tour. ✉ *76 Yallingup Caves Rd., Yallingup, Western Australia* ☎ *08/9755–2152* ⊕ *www. geographebay.com/ngilgi-cave.*

Cape Leeuwin Lighthouse. The view from the top of the Cape Leeuwin Lighthouse, the tallest lighthouse on mainland Australia and only a 10-minute drive south of Augusta, allows you to witness the meeting of the Southern and the Indian oceans. In some places this alliance results in giant swells that crash against the rocks, in others, you'll spot whales surfacing (in season: May–September). While the ocean can be chilly, small coves are blessed with calm waters ideal for swimming. The lighthouse precinct is open daily 9–5 (last entry 4:45 pm; A$8). Guided tours to the top of the lighthouse (via a lengthy stairway) cost

Canal Rocks near Yallingup, Leeuwin-Naturaliste National Park, Western Australia

A\$20 and run daily every 40 minutes. The last tour is at 4:20 pm. ⊠ *Leeuwin Rd., Augusta, Western Australia* ☎ *08/9758–1920* ⊕ *www. margaretriver.com.*

Vasse Virgin. This surprising cottage industry smack dab in the middle of vineyards and olive trees is an aromatherapy feast. Inside a converted machinery shed, you'll find a chemical-free range of soaps and body care products hand blended with natural organic ingredients, as well as yummy olives, tapenades, duckahs, and pestos all without preservatives or artificial additives. A place for gastronomes and purists. Sniff, rub, scrub, pamper, and taste to your heart's content! ⊠ *135 Puzey Rd., Wilyabrup, Margaret River* ☎ *08/9755–6111* ⊕ *vassevirgin.com. au* ⊠ *Free* ☉ *Daily 10–5.*

BEACHES

Fodor's Choice ★ **Smiths Beach.** In a state of extraordinary beaches, this one rates high on the list. Bookended by rounded granite boulders, the caramel-hued sand sinks beneath your feet and the gentle, rolling waves beckon, daring you to cool off in the clean ocean. Edged by native bush, it's secluded and quiet but has plenty of accommodation options nearby, all hidden behind sand dunes. **Amenities:** toilets; food and drink; parking. **Best for:** solitude; swimming; walking; sunset. ⊠ *Smiths Beach Rd., Yallingup, Western Australia.*

FAMILY **Yallingup Beach.** Picture-perfect views, transparent water, clean, honey-colored sand, and a gentle pool of ocean that protects you from the waves beyond: what's not to love about this wide beach, out front of the hillside town of Yallingup? Parts of the ocean have soft seaweed growing thick on the bottom, making for interesting snorkeling. Surf breaks are near but elsewhere, at Smiths, Three Bears, Super Tubes, Injidup, and Rabbits. Ask the locals for directions as only some are signposted. There are limited food and drink options nearby, so come prepared. **Amenities:** showers; toilets; lifeguards; parking. **Best for:** snorkeling; swimming; walking; sunset. ✉ *Yallingup Beach Rd., Yallingup, Western Australia.*

WHERE TO EAT

$$$ AUSTRALIAN 🍴 **Lamont's Smiths Beach.** Just off Smiths Beach is the chic eatery–cum–delicatessen–cum–cellar door, Lamont's. It does a fantastic breakfast—think cured salmon with scrambled eggs—and is popular for "sundowners," which is the local description for a glass of wine by sunset, often with tapas. Café lunches are lovely and simple, but more refined options are available in the restaurant. From noon till late, dine on sage-and-prosciutto-wrapped chicken breast with whipped feta; confit duck leg drizzled with vino cotto jus; or grilled local snapper with a side of organic quinoa salad. Executive chef Kate Lamont is CEO and ambassador for Lamont's (check out her cookbooks). You're welcome to pop in for wine tasting at the cellar door without eating at the restaurant. [$] *Average main: A$25* ✉ *Smiths Beach Resort, Smiths Beach Rd., Yallingup, Western Australia* ☎ *08/9750–1299* 🌐 *www.lamonts.com.au* 🕒 *Wine store and deli Mon.–Sat. 8 am–7 pm, Sun. 8 am–6 pm; restaurant daily noon–9 pm.*

MARGARET RIVER

181 km (112 miles) south of Perth, 38 km (24 miles) south of Cape Naturaliste.

Fodor's Choice ★ The lovely town of Margaret River is considered the center of the South West's wine region, though vineyards and wineries stretch north and east of Bunbury to the south coast. Nevertheless, there are more than 140 wineries in the region of the same name (to confuse things further, there's also a river called Margaret River), offering tastings and sales of some of the world's best wines. The region is often compared to France's Bordeaux for its similar climate and soils; it's gaining huge national and international acclaim for its exceptional red and white vintages, the most notable labels touting Chardonnay, Sauvignon Blanc, Shiraz, and Cabernet-Merlot blends.

GETTING HERE AND AROUND

From Perth take Kwinana Freeway south; it joins Forrest Highway and then Highway 1 to Bunbury. Switch to Highway 10 through Busselton and on to Margaret River. Your best option is to rent a car in Perth. Public transport is nonexistent around the area, and using taxis will soon blow the budget. Most accommodations—farmstays, bushland chalets, and boutique hotels—as well as the wineries, the beaches, and other attractions, are outside the town, and you need your own transportation to reach them, though there are also good options in Margaret River itself.

SAFETY AND PRECAUTIONS

You are unlikely to have any personal safety concerns in the Margaret River area, except, perhaps, on the roads. Many of the roads leading to the wineries, the beaches, and your accommodation are narrow and winding, though traffic is usually light.

TIMING

Margaret River is a year-round destination, with each season bringing its pleasures. Summer is generally busier, especially December and January, as families from Perth arrive during the school holidays. Winter (June–September) brings rain and cooler temperatures, but the paddocks are green and there are not too many days when the rain doesn't ease to showers with lengthy fine breaks in between. If you are traveling from Perth, you can easily spend a week in the region; at the least, try to schedule several days to truly appreciate the area's attractions.

TOURS

Margaret River Visitor Centre is the best starting point if you want to do a tour. They will find the right tour for you, make the booking, and arrange pickup at your accommodation if necessary. Tour operators in the area offer tours as diverse as wineries and food tasting, horse-back riding, surfing, bushwalks, whale-watching, scenic flights, mountain biking, river cruises, rock climbing, and abseiling.

ESSENTIALS

Taxi Contacts **Margaret River Taxis** ☎ 08/9757–3444.

Visitor Information **Margaret River Visitor Centre.** Margaret River Visitor Centre has extensive information on the region. The friendly staff will answer all your questions, and can book accommodation, tours, and activities at no additional cost. ✉ *100 Bussell Hwy., Margaret River, Western Australia* ☎ *08/9780–5911* ⊕ *www.margaretriver.com* ⊙ *Daily 9–5.*

EXPLORING THE WINERIES

Cape Mentelle. One of the "founding five" wineries in the area, Cape Mentelle planted their first vines in 1970 on a 16-hectare block just outside Margaret River. Today it's still one of the most notable wineries. The adobe-style rammed-earth building and tasting rooms, so typical of the buildings in the Margaret River district, are as handsome and memorable as the wine. The winery produces Chardonnay, Sauvignon Blanc/Semillon, Botrytis Viognier (dessert wine), Cabernet/Merlot, Cabernet Sauvignon, Shiraz, and Zinfandel wines. They also offer a Behind the Scenes tour (A\$25), and a degustation tour and tasting (A\$80) Monday–Wednesday and Friday and Saturday at 11:30 am (less frequent May–October). In summer enjoy a balmy evening of food, wine, and film at the winery's outdoor movie nights. ✉ *331 Wallcliffe Rd., 4 km (2 miles) west of Margaret River, Margaret River, Western Australia* ☎ *08/9757–0888* ⊕ *www.capementelle.com.au* ⊙ *Daily 10–4:30.*

Cullen Wines. Biodynamic? Tick. Homegrown produce? Tick. Gorgeous vineyard setting? Tick. Stellar wines. Tick, tick, tick. Cullen isn't the flashiest winery in Margaret River, but its rustic, cottage feel is a strong part of the allure. Family owned since it began, it has long followed an ethos to care for the planet and exist sustainably, and it seems Mother

Nature is returning the favor. Fresh, flavorsome ingredients from the organic kitchen garden give considerable sparkle to the dishes. Think organic beef sirloin with pureed spinach and pumpkin and white bean salad, or seared scallops with pomegranate and octopus salad. Meanwhile, the cellar door serves crisp, clean, biodynamic wines with a pleasing flavor punch. Make a point of trying the exceptional Diana Madeline Cabernet Merlot. ■ TIP→ Enjoy lunch outside under the peppercorn trees in the sunshine. ⊠ *4323 Caves Rd., Wilyabrup, Margaret River, Western Australia* ☏ *08/9755–5277, 08/9755–5656* ⊕ *www. cullenwines.com.au* ☾ *Daily 10–4:30.*

Hay Shed Hill. Winemaker and owner Michael Kerrigan—once chief winemaker at neighboring Howard Park and Madfish Wines—is on a mission to produce "modern wines from old vines" under several different labels. His hands-on approach, using the best grapes from the 30-year-old plantings, has won show awards and five-star endorsements by wine writers. The tasting room breaks from the usual Margaret River architecture—no rammed earth, timber, and stone here, rather a lovely white-painted clapboard building, polished concrete floors, and pitched ceiling. As the name suggests, the building is the original hayshed on what was a dairy farm. A pleasant café (open 9–3:30) overlooking the vineyards serves casual breakfast and lunch—pizzas, salads, fish, and duck dishes plus well-selected cheese platters. ⊠ *511 Harmans Mill Rd., Wilyabrup, Margaret River, Western Australia* ☏ *08/9755–6046* ⊕ *hayshedhill.com.au* ☾ *Daily 9–5; cellar door daily 10–5.*

Howard Park Wines. One of the big pluses of stopping in at WA's largest boutique family-owned winery is that they have a number of labels you can taste, all fixed at different quality and price points. Beneath high ceilings and with views of vineyard rows, compare the Howard Park branded wines against the simpler MadFish and the elegant drops under their super premium offering, Marchand & Burch. Interestingly, feng shui principles were used to design the spacious tastings room. Floor-to-ceiling windows allow in plenty of light as well as giving views over the property, and even the door has specific measurements to allow good luck to flow through. Wines produced under the Howard Park label include Riesling, Chardonnay, Sauvignon Blanc, and Cabernet Sauvignon. ⊠ *Miamup Rd., Cowaramup, Margaret River, Western Australia* ☏ *08/9756–5200* ⊕ *www.burchfamilywines.com.au* ☾ *Daily 10–5.*

Leeuwin Estate. Their Art Series wines—especially the Chardonnay and Cabernet Sauvignon—have a deserved reputation as some of the best in the country, and feature on Australia's "most collected" list. Free tastings and guided tours (A\$15) are conducted on the property daily at 11 am, noon, and 3 pm, introducing you to the extensive art gallery in the cellar. Setting aside the entire afternoon is the way to go at Leeuwin's restaurant, open daily for lunch and for Saturday dinner. ■ TIP→ In February the estate holds its iconic Leeuwin Concerts; many international superstars—including Tom Jones, Diana Ross, Sting, and the late Ray Charles—have performed there against a backdrop of tall, floodlit karri trees. ⊠ *Stevens Rd. off Gnarawary Rd., Margaret River, Western Australia* ☏ *08/9759–0000* ⊕ *www.leeuwinestate.com.au* ☾ *Daily 10–5.*

Vasse Felix. Here you'll find a busy cellar door, excellent upstairs restaurant overlooking the vineyards, landscaped grounds, and an art gallery that houses regular exhibitions from the celebrated Holmes à Court Collection, featuring works from prominent Australian artists. In the winery, Virginia Willcock, who was awarded Australian Winemaker of the Year in 2012, is at the helm, perfecting the region's strong suits of Chardonnay and Cabernet Sauvignon, as well as developing clean, flavorsome Sauvignon Blanc, Semillon, and Shiraz. Grapes are plucked from vines planted as far back as 1967, when pioneer Dr. Tom Cullity established Vasse Felix as one of the first commercial wineries in the area. The award-winning, fine-dining restaurant has been headed by executive chef Aaron Carr since 1995 and is regarded as one of the region's best. With its feature floating fireplace it's welcoming in winter—book in advance for a table on the outside balcony during summertime. ⊠ *Tom Cullity Dr. at Caves Rd., Cowaramup, Western Australia* ☎ *08/9756–5000 cellar door, 08/9756–5050 restaurant* ⊕ *www.vassefelix.com.au* ⊘ *Daily 10–5.*

SPORTS AND THE OUTDOORS

HIKING

Marked trails through the Leeuwin-Naturaliste National Park provide many opportunities for hiking through the natural bushland and on coastal walks, with vistas along untouched rugged cliffs, rocky outcrops, and sandy bays. The **Cape-to-Cape Walk Track** runs 138 km (86 miles) from Cape Naturaliste to Cape Leeuwin, but can be broken into shorter sections. You will find the start points generally at beachside parking lots. A number of tour companies offer guided walks of varying duration, or drop-off and pickup services (as do some accommodations). **Canal Rocks to Wyadup** is a two-hour return walk from the car park on Canal Rocks Road; a one-hour walk via beach, rocks, and bushland begins at the Leeuwin Waterwheel, near Cape Leeuwin Lighthouse in Augusta; and a four-hour walk with expansive coastal views starts at the Hamelin Bay boat ramp and heads to Cosy Corner.

Away from the coast, a popular short walk is from the historic homestead of **Ellensbrook** (Ellensbrook Road off Caves Road, 13 km [8 miles] from Margaret River). The walk takes about 40 minutes to the **Meekadarabee Falls**, known to Aboriginal people as the "bathing place of the moon," and is best in winter and spring.

Brochures and maps on all walk trails in the region are available from the Margaret River Visitor Centre.

WHERE TO EAT

$$
MODERN
AUSTRALIAN
FAMILY

✕ **Arimia Estate.** The newest kid on the Margaret River block, boutique winery Arimia Estate has a charming, tree-surrounded cellar door and restaurant with a wraparound veranda perfect for lazy afternoons. Make a beeline for the deck and stay for a light lunch after sampling their award-winning wines. Savor the delicious pork shoulder terrine, before moving on to the pumpkin-and-nutmeg pappardelle sprinkled with toasted hazelnuts; the braised beef cheek with horseradish; or one of the wood-fired pizzas. Kids' meals are also available. Family-owned and -run since 1997 (the name Arimia is a combination of the owners' two daughter's names), the wines are described as "avant-garde" and aimed at the refined palette, categorized as Premium, Prestige, and Reserve. **TIP→ Don't be put off by the 2-km (1-mile) dirt road; it's well kept.** [$] *Average main: A$23* ✉ *242 Quininup Rd., Yallingup, Margaret River, Western Australia* ☎ *08/9755–2605* 🌐 *www.arimia.com.au* 🕒 *No dinner.*

$$$ MODERN AUSTRALIAN 🍴 **Flutes Restaurant.** The pastoral setting over the dammed waters of Wilyabrup Brook, encircled by olive groves in the midst of the Brookland Valley Vineyard, is almost as compelling as the cuisine. French bistro fare is mixed with tropical influences from the northern Australian town of Broome. Executive chef and restaurant owner François Morvan makes use of prime local produce, executing a variety of mouthwatering dishes including the ever-popular Chinese-style shredded duck with Rottnest scallops and candied chilies. You're unlikely to be disappointed by the "signature trio" of marron, salmon, and ocean-reared barramundi topped with goat cheese macadamia crumble, or the duck magret dotted with caper berries. The beef fillet also goes down well with a glass of one of Brookland Valley's award-winning wines. **TIP→ Reserve a seat by the window, or on the wooden deck that juts out over the picturesque dam.** [$] *Average main: A$42* ✉ *4070 Caves Rd., 5 km (3 miles) south of Metricup Rd., Wilyabrup, Margaret River, Western Australia* ☎ *08/9755–6250* 🌐 *www.flutes.com.au* ✍ *Reservations essential* 🕒 *No dinner.*

$$ BISTRO FAMILY 🍴 **Sea Gardens Cafe Restaurant.** Loved by locals for its laid-back breakfasts and sunset bistro-style dinners, Sea Gardens Café Restaurant is synonymous with the Margaret River scene. It's one of only a few restaurants south of Busselton with ocean views and definitely a place to see and be seen. At Seadies (as it's affectionately known) you can expect casual dining—gourmet pizzas made by chef Gilles England-Brassy, fresh local fish, thick scotch fillet steak, and delectably naughty cakes made by Rachel, his wife. People flock for the chicken burgers, chicken liver parfait, beer-battered fish-and-chips and crème brûlées. **TIP→ Go for the sunset, or early for the Bombie brekkie (named after the surf break opposite) and ask Gilles for his binoculars to check out the surfers or the whales. Get your dinner orders in before 8:30 pm to avoid disappointment.** [$] *Average main: A$26* ✉ *9 Mitchell Dr., Prevelly, Margaret River, Western Australia* ☎ *08/9757–3074* 🌐 *www.seagardens.com.au.*

$$ MODERN AUSTRALIAN FAMILY 🍴 **Settler's Tavern.** Sometimes you don't need to dab foams or wipe purees across a plate to impress. Sometimes you just have to serve up consistently good, hearty fare that fills the belly and doesn't burn a hole in the pocket. That's the reliable party trick at Settler's Tavern, in the heart of Margaret River township where finding a good value meal can otherwise be challenging. The crowds are testament to the fact that the pub's got the formula right, be it a thick scotch fillet cooked to perfection or a sweet and spicy Malaysian laksa jammed with prawns and herbs. The lack of pretension and warm vibe seal the deal. Expect a lively crowd and on really busy nights, a wait for food. Families are welcome. **TIP→ Free Wi-Fi is offered if you need to check emails over lunch.** ⚠ **The kitchen often closes at 8:30 pm, so get there earlier.**

$ *Average main: A$26* ✉ *114 Bussell Hwy., Margaret River, Western Australia* ☎ *08/9757–2398* ⊕ *www.settlerstavern.com.*

$$
CONTEMPORARY

✕ **Voyager Estate.** One of the appellation's grande dames, with its white-washed buildings and expansive, manicured gardens—featuring more than 1,000 roses—has opened a new Wine Room to deliver quaffing experience with a difference. While swilling their repertoire of wines, you'll also learn about the wine-making process in intimate surroundings. Opt for a seated tasting with tutelage from Voyager's team (A$10–A$30), or download their iPad app free from iTunes for a tour at your own pace. The tasting counter will take care of anyone looking for a more casual experience, with four wine tastingfs complimentary. The large restaurant with antique wooden furniture, brass chandeliers, and soaring cathedral ceilings is highly regarded. Dishes are inspired by the wine, naturally, and celebrate local, seasonal ingredients such as green asparagus, snow-white marron meat, ocean-fresh fish, and Margaret River–reared venison. High tea is also served starting at 3 pm daily. ▮TIP→ Book an estate tour in the safari-style bus with a private wine tasting (A$35), with lunch (A$75), or add on a six-course, wine-matched menu for A$175 total. Tours run Tuesday, Thursday, Saturday, and Sunday. $ *Average main: A$35* ✉ *Stevens Rd., Margaret River, Western Australia* ☎ *08/9757–6354* ⊕ *www.voyagerestate.com.au* ⊘ *No dinner.*

$$$
AUSTRALIAN
FAMILY

✕ **Watershed.** Families are welcomed at this large vineyard restaurant and café with its impressive modern architecture: big windows, and a wraparound deck offer uninterrupted views. The main restaurant menu changes each season; choices like the local marron, sweet corn puree, and roasted leek topped with mojito foam, or the lamb shoulder slow braised in red wine and served with confit garlic, smoked mash potato, and wild rice popcorn are show-stopping dishes. The adjacent café has an enclosed children's playground and caters to children with an appropriate, cheaper menu that still scores on the flavor scale in a casual setting. While the cellar door and restaurant are top-notch in terms of design and construction, it's the seriously award-winning wines that will hold your attention. ▮TIP→ Try the signature dish—the chef's Taste Plate consisting of all five entrée choices for A$56. You can be really decadent and do the same with the dessert dishes, for A$35. $ *Average main: A$38* ✉ *Bussell Hwy. at Darch Rd., Margaret River, Western Australia* ☎ *08/9758–8633* ⊕ *www.watershedwines.com.au* ⊘ *No dinner.*

$
CAFÉ
FAMILY

✕ **White Elephant Beach Café.** The umbrella-topped tables are hot property at this ocean-facing gem, particularly at breakfast time. Precede your bacon and eggs with a lovely beach stroll or strut along the walking track, which traces the coast from Prevelly to the White Elephant Beach Café. Lunch is equally impressive, with crispy baby calamari, Thai beef, or harissa spiced chickpea salad. Open for Margaret River's warmer months (September–May), it's a locals' favorite that provides excellent views of the region's main surf break, Surfers Point. $ *Average main: A$16* ✉ *Gnarabup Rd., Gnarabup, Margaret River, Western Australia* ☎ *08/9757–1990* ⊕ *www.whiteelephantcafe.com.au* ⊘ *No dinner.*

WHERE TO STAY

For expanded hotel reviews, visit Fodors.com.

$$$$ RESORT Fodor's Choice ★ **Cape Lodge.** Regarded as the grandest boutique property in Margaret River wine country, the lodge's five-bedroom residence and 22 luxury suites deliver in service, space, and views of an 8-acre vineyard that produces Sauvignon Blanc and Shiraz exclusively for guests. **Pros:** large, luxurious rooms, some with spas; highly regarded restaurant. **Cons:** no shopping nearby; limited evening dining options nearby; own transport essential. [$] *Rooms from: A$495* ✉ *3341 Caves Rd., Yallingup, Western Australia* ☎ *08/9755–6311* 🌐 *www.capelodge.com.au* *22 suites, 5-bedroom residence* 🍴 *Breakfast.*

$$$$ RENTAL Fodor's Choice ★ **Forest Rise Eco Retreat.** King size beds, fluffy robes, dreamy candlelit spas with overhead windows looking up to the forest canopy, and oh-so-private verandas make this eco-certified retreat a true sanctuary. **Pros:** totally self-contained; two mountain bikes per chalet; private chef and massage therapist on request; birds, possums, and kangaroos abound. **Cons:** robes cost extra; free Wi-Fi in office area only; minimum stays enforced; closest convenience store is 10-minute drive away, no shopping or dining nearby; not suitable for children. [$] *Rooms from: A$365* ✉ *231 Yelverton Rd., Yelverton, Margaret River, Western Australia* ☎ *08/9755–7110* 🌐 *www.forestrise.com.au* *10 chalets, 1 homestead* 🍴 *No meals.*

$$$ B&B/INN **Gilgara Retreat.** The romantic rooms in this replica 1870 station homestead have open fireplaces and access to a spacious, communal lounge, but if you need to spread out, choose the modern, split-level, self-catering garden suites with dreamy sunken spa baths, atriums, and private sitting areas that overlook the extensive woodland gardens. **Pros:** private lounge with log fire; free Wi-Fi; Continental breakfast included for Main House guests; lots of birds. **Cons:** standard main house rooms are small; no shopping nearby; minimum stays of two nights; no children allowed. [$] *Rooms from: A$230* ✉ *Caves and Carter Rds., Margaret River, Western Australia* ☎ *08/9757–2705* 🌐 *www.gilgara.com.au* *5 rooms, 8 suites* 🍴 *Breakfast.*

$$$ RESORT **Grand Mercure Basildene Manor.** Each of the rooms in this grand, circa-1912 house has been lovingly refurbished, though history still looms large in the main homestead, and due to its big-name chain ownership, there are loads of extras on offer. **Pros:** heritage rooms with new decor; lavish breakfast; quiet location; horse riding, tennis, bushwalking, and beach nearby. **Cons:** own transport essential; no lunch or dinner; dining options 1½ km (1 mile) away. [$] *Rooms from: A$279* ✉ *187 Wallcliffe Rd., Margaret River, Western Australia* ☎ *08/9757–3140* 🌐 *www.basildene.com.au* *17 rooms* 🍴 *Breakfast.*

$$$ HOTEL **Heritage Trail Lodge.** Nestled among the towering trees, this luxury retreat is only about ½ km (¼ mile) from Margaret River township and its spacious suites have hot tubs, king-size beds, and private balconies overlooking the forest. **Pros:** free Wi-Fi; walking trails nearby; 10-minute walk to shops and restaurants; bushland setting. **Cons:** no leisure facilities; children discouraged; two rooms face highway meaning traffic noise during day. [$] *Rooms from: A$210* ✉ *31 Bussell Hwy., Margaret*

River, Western Australia ☎ *08/9757–9595* 🌐 *www.heritage-trail-lodge.com.au* 🛏 *10 suites* 🍴 *Breakfast.*

$$ B&B/INN FAMILY **Riverglen Chalets.** In a magical woodland setting, Riverglen Chalets consists of modest, self-contained timber cabins interspersed among 7 acres of forest and gardens just a 10-minute stroll along the river into Margaret River township. **Pros:** secluded chalets; breakfast hampers supplied on request; some outdoor spas; communal games room; wildlife. **Cons:** some road noise during the day; bathroom amenities do not include shampoo. [$] *Rooms from: A$170* ✉ *Bussell Hwy. at Carters Rd., Margaret River, Western Australia* ☎ *08/9757–2101* 🌐 *www.riverglenchalets.com.au* 🛏 *14 chalets sleeping 2–8 persons* 🍴 *No meals.*

EN ROUTE **Nannup.** Rustic timber cottages and historic buildings characterize the small town of Nannup, 100 km (62 miles) east of Margaret River. Several scenic drives wind through the area, including the Blackwood River Tourist Drive, a 10-km (6-mile) ride along a section of river surrounded by hills with karri and jarrah forests. You can also canoe on the Blackwood River and wander through the Blythe Gardens. A map of the buildings used in the movie is also available from the Nannup Visitor Centre (open weekdays). At various times of the year look out for Nannup's popular festivals; music, flower and garden, art and photography, and the festival of country gardens that offers an artist's palette of WA's spring and autumn colors. ✉ *Nannup, Western Australia* 🌐 *www.nannupwa.com.*

Holberry House. If you'd like to spend the night, check out Holberry House, a charming colonial B&B with exposed beams and stone fireplaces, overlooking Blackwood Valley. The gardens are peppered with statues and sculptures set amongst a woodland of jarrrah trees through which Mount Folly Creek flows. For a small (courtesy) donation of A$4 at the main gate you can explore the extensive gardens without overnighting at the B & B. **TIP→ Ask about the facts and myths surrounding the legend of the Nannup Tiger.** ✉ *14 Grange Rd., Nannup, Western Australia* ☎ *08/9756–1276* 🌐 *www.holberryhouse.com.*

TRAVEL SMART
AUSTRALIA

GETTING HERE AND AROUND

Australia is divided into six states and two territories—Northern Territory (NT) and Australian Capital Territory (ACT)—similar to the District of Columbia. Tasmania, the smallest state, is an island off mainland Australia's southeast point.

▌ AIR TRAVEL

Sydney is Australia's main international hub, though it is also easy to get international flights to Melbourne, Brisbane, Cairns, and Perth. You can catch nonstop or one-stop flights to Australia from New York (21 hours via Los Angeles); Chicago (19 hours via Los Angeles); Los Angeles (14 hours nonstop); Vancouver (14 hours nonstop); Toronto (20 hours via Los Angeles or Vancouver); and London (20–24 hours via Hong Kong, Singapore, Kuala Lumpur, Dubai, or Bangkok).

Since Pacific-route flights from the United States to Australia cross the international date line, you lose a day, but regain it on the journey home.

Air Pass Information Aussie Airpass
☏ 800/227–4500 in U.S., 13–1313 in Australia ⊕ www.qantas.com.au. **Regional Express** ☏ 13–1713 ⊕ www.rex.com.au. **Visit Australia and New Zealand Pass** ⊕ www.oneworld.com.

Airline Security Issues Transportation Security Administration ☏ 866/289–9673 ⊕ www.tsa.gov.

AIRPORTS

Sydney Airport (SYD) is Australia's main air hub and the first port of call for more than half of the country's visitors. Terminal 1 is for all international flights, Qantas domestic flights operate out of Terminal 3, and Terminal 2 is for all other domestic flights (including Qantaslink, Virgin Australia, and Jetstar). A rail link connects the terminals underground, and frequent shuttle buses run between them aboveground. There is an excellent range of shops and restaurants in the international terminal.

Brisbane International Airport (BNE) is southern Queensland's main airport and rivals Sydney's in quality and services. There are separate domestic and international terminals. Cairns International Airport (CNS), in north Queensland, is the hub for northern Queensland and visits to the Great Barrier Reef.

Melbourne Airport (MEL) is sometimes known as "Tullamarine," after a neighboring suburb. International flights leave from Terminal 2; Qantas and Jetstar use Terminal 1 for their domestic operations. Virgin Blue makes up the bulk of the other domestic flights, which go from Terminal 3. Tiger Airways flies from Terminal 4.

South Australia's main airport is Adelaide International (ADL). Domestic flights and a few services to nearby Asian cities land at Darwin International Airport (DRW) in the Northern Territory. The hub for the Red Centre is Alice Springs Airport (ASP), which only receives domestic flights. Perth International Airport (PER) is the gateway to Western Australia. International flights operate from Terminal 1; Qantas domestic flights leave from Terminal 2; Terminal 3 is for Alliance Airlines, Ozjet, Skywest Airlines, and Virgin Australia.

Airport Information Adelaide Airport ☏ 08/8308–9211 ⊕ www.adelaideairport.com.au. **Alice Springs Airport** ☏ 08/8951–1211 ⊕ www.alicespringsairport.com.au. **Brisbane Airport** ☏ 07/3406–3000 ⊕ www.bne.com.au. **Cairns Airport** ☏ 07/4080–6703 ⊕ www.cairnsairport.com. **Darwin International Airport** ☏ 08/8920–1811 ⊕ www.darwinairport.com.au. **Melbourne Airport** ☏ 03/9297–1600 ⊕ www.melbourneairport.com.au. **Perth Airport** ☏ 08/9478–8888 ⊕ www.perthairport.com.au. **Sydney Airport** ☏ 02/9667–9111 ⊕ www.sydneyairport.au.

FLIGHTS
TO AUSTRALIA
Qantas is Australia's flagship carrier. It operates direct flights to Sydney from New York, San Francisco, and Los Angeles, and from Los Angeles to Melbourne and Brisbane. There are connecting Qantas flights to many other North American cities, and direct flights from various Australian airports to many Asian and European destinations. It's part of Oneworld Alliance, and has excellent standards of safety and comfort. Qantas flights aren't always the cheapest, but their Aussie Airpass includes three stops within Australia for the same price as your ticket from North America.

Jetstar is a low-cost local airline owned by Qantas, and has flights from Sydney, Melbourne, Brisbane, Cairns, Perth, Adelaide, and Darwin to Bali, Japan, New Zealand, Singapore, Thailand, Vietnam, and Honolulu. Other budget carriers, Virgin Australia and Virgin Samoa, fly to Tonga, Samoa, Fiji, Vanuatu, New Zealand, Indonesia, and the Cook Islands. Singapore Airlines–owned budget airline Tiger Airways flies from Perth to Singapore.

Airline Contacts Air New Zealand ☎ *1800/262–1234 in U.S., 13–2476 in Australia* ⊕ *www.airnewzealand.com. au*. **British Airways** ☎ *1800/247–9297 in U.S., 1300/767177 in Australia* ⊕ *www. britishairways.com*. **Cathay Pacific** ☎ *1800/233–2742 in U.S., 13–1747 in Australia* ⊕ *www.cathaypacific.com*. **Qantas** ☎ *1800/227–4500 in U.S., 13–1313 in Australia* ⊕ *www.qantas.com*. **United** ☎ *1800/538–2929 in U.S., 13–1777 in Australia* ⊕ *www. united.com*. **Virgin Australia** ☎ *855/444–0260 in U.S., 13–6789 in Australia* ⊕ *www. virginaustralia.com*.

WITHIN AUSTRALIA
Australia's large distances mean that flying is the locals' favorite way of getting from one city to another. In general, safety standards on domestic flights are high, flights are punctual, and there's plenty of timetable choice. On routes between popular destinations like Sydney, Melbourne, and Brisbane there are often several flights each hour.

Airline Contacts Airnorth ☎ *800/627474* ⊕ *www.airnorth.com.au*. **Jetstar** ☎ *13–1538* ⊕ *www.jetstar.com*. **Qantas** ☎ *13–1313* ⊕ *www.qantas.com.au*. **Regional Express** ☎ *13–1713* ⊕ *www.rex.com.au*. **Tiger Air** ☎ *02/9999–2888* ⊕ *www.tigerair.com*.

▌ BOAT TRAVEL

Organized boat tours from the Queensland mainland are the only way to visit the Great Barrier Reef. Cairns is the number-one point of departure, but boats also leave from Mackay, Airlie Beach, Townsville, and Port Douglas. Boats also run between the Whitsunday Islands. The Great Barrier Reef Marine Park Authority website has helpful advice on how to choose a tour operator, and lists which companies are ecotourism-certified.

The daily ferries *Spirit of Tasmania I* and *II* take 10 hours to connect Melbourne with Devonport on Tasmania's north coast. Make reservations as early as possible, particularly during the busy December and January school holidays.

Sealink Ferries transport passengers and vehicles between Cape Jervis on the South Australian coastline south of Adelaide, and Penneshaw on Kangaroo Island.

You can find out about ferry and cruise schedules for these and other scenic rides at most state tourism offices and on their websites. All operators accept major credit cards and cash.

Information Great Barrier Reef Marine Park Authority ☎ *07/4750–0700* ⊕ *www. gbrmpa.gov.au*. **Sealink Ferries** ☎ *13–1301* ⊕ *www.sealink.com.au*. **Spirit of Tasmania** ☎ *1800/634906* ⊕ *www.spiritoftasmania.com. au*.

▌ BUS TRAVEL

Bus travel in Australia is comfortable and well organized. Long-distance buses, also called "coaches," have air-conditioning, onboard toilets, reclining seats, and even attendants and videos on longer routes. By law, all are required to provide seat belts, and you are required to use them. Smoking is prohibited on all buses.

Australia's national bus network is run by Greyhound Australia (no connection to Greyhound in the United States), which serves far more destinations than any plane or train services. However, Australia is a vast continent, and bus travel here requires plenty of time. The journey from Sydney to Melbourne takes 15 hours, Adelaide to Perth takes 39 hours, and Brisbane to Cairns takes 30 hours. If you plan to visit specific regions, it could be worthwhile considering flying to a major hub, then using buses to explore the region when you get there.

Oz Experience is a private bus company aimed at budget travelers. They work in a similar way to Greyhound, and their routes take in both major cities and adventure destinations. They have a great selection of routes—you buy a pass, and then have unlimited stopovers along that route. You book onto each section by telephone as you travel. Oz Experience also has a hostel booking service, and will take you to the door of your hostel for no extra cost. For example, their Bruce Cobber Pass takes you along the coast between Sydney and Cairns and costs A$519.

You can book passes and individual tickets on Greyhound and Oz Experience buses online through their websites, over the telephone, or in person at their desks in bus terminals.

Bus Information Greyhound Australia
☎ *1300/473946* ⊕ *www.greyhound.com.au.*
Oz Experience ☎ *1300/555287* ⊕ *www. ozexperience.com.*

▌ CAR TRAVEL

Endless highways, fabulous scenery, bizarre little towns in the middle of nowhere: Australia is road-trip paradise. Even if you don't have time for major exploring, traveling by car can be a great way to explore a particular region at your own pace. Traffic in city centers can be terrible, so keep the car for the open road.

Driving is generally easy in Australia, once you adjust to traveling on the left side of the road. Road conditions on busy coastal highways usually pose few problems, though remote roads (even big highways) and routes through the desert are often a different story. When you're preparing a driving itinerary, it's vital to bear in mind the huge distances involved and calculate travel time and stopovers accordingly.

Most rental companies in Australia accept driving licenses from other countries, including the United States, provided that the information on the license is clear and in English. Otherwise, an International Driver's Permit is required (but they'll still want to see your regular license, too).

GASOLINE

Gas is known in Australia as "petrol." Self-service petrol stations are plentiful near major cities and in rural towns. In remote regions they can be few and far between, so fill up whenever you can. In really out-of-the-way places, carrying a spare petrol can is a good idea. Smaller petrol stations often close at night and on Sunday, though in major cities and on main highways there are plenty of stations open round the clock.

PARKING

On-street parking is usually plentiful in Australian cities, except in the traffic-heavy CBD (downtown area) of the big capitals. Electronic meters are the norm—you pay in advance, and there's usually a maximum stay, which you should respect, as Australian parking inspectors are very vigilant. Paid parking lots are also common, and are usually clearly signposted.

Outside the capitals, on-street parking is usually free, as are the lots outside malls and supermarkets.

RENTING A CAR

Australia's cities have good public transport, so there's not much point in renting a car if you're staying in an urban area, especially one popular with tourists. Step outside city limits, and a car is practically a necessity.

Rates for economy cars (a Hyundai Getz, Excel, or Accent or a Nissan Pulsar, for example) with unlimited mileage start at A$60 a day (plus fees).

Intercity highways are usually in good condition, but remoter roads—even those that look important on maps—are often unpaved or full of potholes. You can manage short distances on these in a car (for example, an access road to an attraction a few miles from the highway). For longer stretches and any Outback driving, a 4WD is necessary, as insurance generally doesn't cover damage to other types of cars traveling such roads. Only rent a 4WD if you're competent to drive one on tough surfaces like sand and bogs: rescue vehicles take a long time to get to the middle of nowhere.

Rental companies have varying policies and charges for unusual trips, such as lengthy cross-state expeditions around the Top End and Western Australia. Ask about additional mileage, fuel, and insurance charges if you're planning to cover a lot of ground.

Another popular way to see Australia is to rent a camper van (motor home). Nearly all have a toilet, shower, and cooking facilities; utensils and bed linen are usually included, too. Smaller vans for two can be rented for A$40–A$150 a day with unlimited mileage (there's usually a five-day minimum).

In Australia you must be 21 to rent a car, and rates may be higher if you're under 25. There is no upper age limit for rental so long as you have a valid international driver's license. Most companies charge

BUYING A CAR

For road trips longer than a couple of months, renting costs add up, so buying a car or van (and selling it at the end of your trip) might be more economical. Most camper-van agencies have a sales department; Kings Cross Car Market and Travellers Auto Barn are two reputable agencies that specialize in selling to and rebuying from visitors.

extra for each additional driver. It's compulsory for children to use car seats, so be sure to notify your agency when you book—most charge around A$9 per day for a baby or booster seat.

Your driver's license may not be recognized outside your home country. You may not be able to rent a car without an International Driving Permit (IDP), which can be used only in conjunction with a valid driver's license and which translates your license into 10 languages. Check the AAA website for more info as well as for IDPs ($15) themselves.

Car Rental Resources Australian Automobile Association ☎ 02/6247-7311 ⊕ www.aaa.asn.au. **American Automobile Association (AAA).** In the United States, the American Automobile Association is a good resource for rental options abroad. The most common way to contact the organization is through state and regional members. ☎ 315/797-5000 ⊕ www.aaa.com.

Local Rental Agencies Red Spot.Sixt Rentals ☎ 61/2/8303-2222 outside Australia, 1300/668810 in Australia ⊕ www.redspot.com.au. **Wicked Campers** ☎ 61/7/3217-0100 outside Australia, 1800/246869 in Australia ⊕ www.wickedcampers.com.au.

Major Agencies Alamo ☎ 888/222-9075 in U.S. ⊕ www.alamo.com. **Avis** ☎ 1800/331-1212 in U.S., 13-6333 in Australia ⊕ www.avis.com.au. **Budget** ☎ 800/472-3325 in U.S., 1300/362848 in Australia ⊕ www.budget.com. **Hertz** ☎ 800/654-3001 in U.S., 13-3039 in Australia ⊕ www.hertz.com. **National Car**

Rental ☎ 877/222-9058 ⊕ www.nationalcar. com. **Thrifty** ☎ 800/847-4389 in U.S., 1300/367227 in Australia ⊕ www.thrifty.com.

ROAD CONDITIONS

Except for some expressways in and around the major cities, most highways are two-lane roads with frequent passing lanes but no barrier separating the two directions of traffic. Main roads are usually paved and well maintained, though lanes are narrower than in the United States.

Outside big urban areas roundabouts are far more common than traffic lights—some towns have dozens of them. Remember that when driving on the left you go around a roundabout clockwise and give way to traffic entering from the left and already on the roundabout.

Potential road hazards multiply in rural areas. Driving standards, which are generally high in Australia, become more lax. Road surfaces deteriorate, becoming potholed or uneven. Fine sand sometimes fills the holes, making them hard to see. Windshield cracks caused by small stones are practically routine. Flash floods are also common during the summer months in northern Australia: when in doubt, turn back or seek advice from the police before crossing.

Animals—kangaroos and livestock, primarily—are common causes of road accidents, especially at night. If you see an animal near the edge of the road, slow down immediately, as they may just decide to step out in front of you. If they do, hitting the animal is generally preferable to swerving, as you can lose control of your car and roll. However, braking too suddenly into the animal can send it through your windshield. Ideally, you should report any livestock you kill to the nearest ranch, and should check dead kangaroos for joeys (babies carried in their pouches): if you find one, wrap it up and take it to the nearest vet.

"Road trains" are another Outback hazard: they're truck convoys made of several connected trailers, totaling up to 170 feet. They take a *long* time to brake, so keep your distance and overtake them only with extreme caution.

Outback driving can be exhausting and potentially dangerous. Avoid driving alone, and rest often. Carry plenty of water with you (4–5 liters per person per day)—high temperatures make dehydration a common problem on the road. Don't count on your cell phone working in the middle of nowhere, and if an emergency occurs never leave your vehicle: it's visible, and provides you shelter from the sun and cold. Stick by the side of the road: sooner or later, someone will come along.

ROADSIDE EMERGENCIES

000. If you have an emergency requiring an ambulance, the fire department, or the police, dial 000.

Many major highways now have telephones for breakdown assistance; you can also use your cell phone if you have one. Otherwise, flag down and ask a passing motorist to call the nearest motoring service organization for you. Most Australian drivers will be happy to assist, particularly in country areas.

Each state has its own motoring organization that provides assistance for vehicle breakdowns. When you rent a vehicle, check that you are entitled to assistance from the relevant motoring organization free of charge. A toll-free nationwide number is available for roadside assistance.

Emergency Services Emergency Services ☎ *000.* **Motoring Organization Hotline** ☎ *13-1111.*

RULES OF THE ROAD

Speed limits vary from state to state. As a rough guide, 50–60 kilometers per hour (kph) is the maximum in populated areas, reduced to 40 kph near schools. On open roads limits range from 100 to 130 kph—the equivalent of 62–80 mph. Limits are usually signposted clearly and regularly, and are enforced by police speed checks

FROM	TO	DISTANCE	MAIN HIGHWAY NAMES
Sydney	Melbourne	873 km (542 miles) /1,043 km (648 miles)	Hume/Princes
Sydney	Brisbane	982 km (610 miles)	Pacific
Brisbane	Cairns	1,699 km (1,056 miles)	Bruce
Melbourne	Adelaide	732 km (455 miles) /912 km (567 miles)	Dukes/Pacific
Adelaide	Perth	2,716 km (1,688 miles)	Eyre and Great Eastern
Adelaide	Alice Springs	1,544 km (959 miles)	Stuart
Alice Springs	Darwin	1,503 km (934 miles)	Stuart
Darwin	Cairns	2,885 km (1,793 miles)	Bruce, Flinders, Barkley, and Stuart

and—in state capitals—by automatic cameras.

Drunk driving, once a big problem in Australia, is controlled obsessively. The legal limit is 0.05% blood-alcohol level, and penalties are so high that many Aussies just don't drink if they're driving. Seat belts are mandatory nationwide. Children must be restrained in a seat appropriate to their size. Car-rental agencies can install these for about A$30 per week, with 24 hours' notice. It is illegal to use a mobile-phone handset when driving.

Traffic circles, called "roundabouts," are widely used at intersections; cars that have already entered the circle have the right-of-way. At designated intersections in Melbourne's central business district you must get into the left lane to make a right-hand turn—this is to facilitate crossing streetcar lines. Watch for the sign "right-hand turn from left lane only." Everywhere, watch for sudden changes in speed limits.

The Australian Automobile Association has a branch in each state, known as the National Roads and Motorists Association (NRMA) in New South Wales and Canberra, the Automobile Association in the Northern Territory (AANT), and the Royal Automobile Club (RAC) in all other states. It's affiliated with AAA worldwide, and offers reciprocal services to American members, including emergency road service, road maps, copies of each state and territory's Highway Code, and discounts on car rental and accommodations.

▌CRUISE SHIP TRAVEL

Coral Princess Cruises runs three- to seven-7 night cruises along the Great Barrier Reef; their Across the Top trip continues to Darwin. There's also a cruise between Darwin and Broome.

Pacific Dawn, Australia's biggest cruise liner, sails various one- and two-week Pacific and New Zealand cruises out of Brisbane. Their *Pacific Pearl* also cruises the Pacific from Sydney. It's owned by P&O, known in the rest of the world as Princess Cruises.

Princess Cruises' huge *Sapphire Princess* sails between New Zealand and Australia at the end of its 33-day cruise from Seattle, Washington. The smaller *Dawn Princess* visits Papua New Guinea, Vanuatu, and New Caledonia on its 18-day return cruise to Sydney.

Regent Seven Seas' *Seven Seas Mariner* docks at several points on Australia's south and east coast on cruises from Asia to Sydney and Auckland. Crystal Cruises' Kangaroos and Kiwis voyage—aboard *Crystal Serenity*—starts in Sydney and calls at Melbourne and Hobart before ending in Auckland. *Crystal Symphony* goes up past Brisbane, Cairns, the Barrier Reef, Darwin, and Indonesia to Singapore. Silversea's *Silver Whisper* has a similar route, and also runs between Australia and New Zealand.

Cunard's *Queen Elizabeth* sails from New York and San Francisco to Sydney, and calls at Australian ports on round-the-world cruises, too. So do its *Queen Mary 2* and *Queen Victoria*.

▌ TRAIN TRAVEL

Australia has a network of long-distance trains providing first- and economy-class service along the east and south coasts, across the south of the country from Sydney to Perth, and through the middle of the country between Adelaide and Darwin.

Most long-distance trains are operated by various state-government-owned enterprises. The luxurious exceptions to the rule are the *Ghan, Indian Pacific,* and *Overland,* all run by the private company Great Southern Rail. Rail Australia is the umbrella organization for all of these services outside the country.

The state-owned trains are usually punctual and comfortable. Economy class has reclining seats, and on longer routes there are sleeper classes. Second-class sleepers have shared bathrooms and sometimes you share your cabin with strangers, too. In first class you have the cabin to yourself and a small en suite bathroom. Meals are sometimes included. Comfort levels increase in Premium Red Service on the *Overland,* and Gold and Platinum Service on the *Ghan* and *Indian Pacific* and in the *Sunlander's* Queenslander class. The high-speed *Tilt Train* is aimed at business travelers, and has business-class-style reclining seats.

Information Great Southern Rail
☎ 1800/132147 in Australia, 618/213–4401 in U.S. ⊕ www.gsr.com.au.**NSW Train-Link** ☎ 13–2232 ⊕ www.nswtrainlink.info.
Queensland Rail ☎ 13–1617 ⊕ www.qr.com.au. **Rail Australia** ☎ 13–2147 in Australia, 618/213–4592 in U.S. ⊕ www.railaustralia.com.au.

ESSENTIALS

▌ ACCOMMODATIONS

Australia operates a rating system of one to five stars. Five-star hotels include on-site dining options, concierge and valet services, a business center, and, of course, very luxurious rooms. Four stars denote an exceptional property that just doesn't have all the extras they need for five. Three stars means quality fittings and service. Always ask about additional costs when pricing your hotel room.

APARTMENT AND HOUSE RENTALS

Judging from the huge number of short-term rental properties in Australia, many locals prefer doing their own thing to being in a hotel. It's easy for you to do likewise. Serviced apartments are the norm in big cities, and you can often rent one for only a night or two. Booking agency Move and Stay has an enormous range of properties, usually aimed at executives. Medina has top-end apartments and apart-hotels in all the big cities. Quest owns apartment complexes all around the country. Furnished Properties focuses on the Sydney area, and have reasonable rates.

In beach areas "units" are the thing: they're usually small detached houses or bungalows, often with a communal area with laundry facilities and a swimming pool. Maid service is usually optional here. In summer, units at popular beach resorts will often be booked months in advance, so make reservations in plenty of time. To find beach units online, you usually need to search for agencies dealing with a specific area rather than a nationwide company.

Contacts Adina Apartment Hotels ☎ 1300/9356–5061 ⊕ www.adinahotels.com. au. **Furnished Properties** ☎ 61/2/9518–8828 ⊕ www.furnishedproperties.com.au. **Move and Stay** ⊕ www.moveandstay.com. **Quest Serviced Apartments** ☎ 61/3/9645–8357,

1800/334033 ⊕ www.questapartments.com. au. **Villas & Apartments Abroad** ☎ 212/213–6435 ⊕ www.vaanyc.com. **Villas International** ☎ 415/499–9490, 800/221–2260 ⊕ www.villasintl.com.

BED-AND-BREAKFASTS

B&Bs are a big deal in Australia, and are popular in both urban and rural areas. The classic Aussie B&B is a family-run affair: expect clean, homey rooms, private bathrooms, and bountiful breakfasts. A room for two usually ranges from A$80 to A$200 a night. The word "boutique" in conjunction with a B&B implies a higher level of luxury—decorative, gastronomic, or both—and facilities, but all at a higher price.

OzBedandBreakfast.com has comprehensive listings that include boutique properties. Australian Bed and Breakfast has listings of B&Bs, farm stays, cottages, and more, all over the country.

Local tourist-information centers throughout Australia also have lists of B&Bs in their area.

Reservation Services The Australian Bed & Breakfast Book. This company publishes a yearly guide to Australian B&Bs and has online listings. ⊕ www.bbbook.com.au. **Bed & Breakfast.com** ☎ 512/322–2710, 800/462–2632 ⊕ www.bedandbreakfast.com. **Bed & Breakfast and Farmstay Association of NSW & ACT** ☎ 1300/888862, 02/4367–5505 ⊕ www.bedandbreakfast.org.au. **Bed & Breakfast Inns Online** ☎ 310/280–4363, 800/215–7365 ⊕ www.bbonline.com. **Hosted Accommodation Australia** ⊕ www.australianbedandbreakfast.com.au. **OzBedandBreakfast.com** ⊕ www.ozbedandbreakfast.com.

HOME AND FARM STAYS

Home and farm stays combine B&B-style accommodation with the chance to join in farm activities or explore the countryside. Some hosts run day trips, as well as horseback riding, hiking, and fishing trips. Accommodations vary from modest shearers' cabins to elegant homesteads; some include breakfast in the room price, others an evening meal. Families are usually welcomed. For two people the cost varies from A$100 to A$250 nightly. *Many of the B&B sites above also have farm-stay listings.*

Reservation Services Australian Farm Stays. This private company deals with luxury farm stays. ☎ 03/5824–3285 ⊕ www.australianfarmstay.com.au.

HOME EXCHANGES

With a direct home exchange you stay in someone else's home while they stay in yours. Some outfits also deal with vacation homes, so you're not actually staying in someone's full-time residence, just their vacant weekend place.

Although home exchanges aren't popular choice in Australia, there are still many options available, particularly on the east coast.

Exchange Clubs HomeExchange.com. This company charges $10.95 per month for a one-year online listing and use of the site. ☎ 800/877–8723 ⊕ www.homeexchange.com. **HomeLink International.** This company charges $89 for one-year full membership, and $25 for an additional listing for a second home. ☎ 800/638–3841 ⊕ www.homelink.org. **Intervac U.S.** For $99.99 you can have a Web-only membership at Intervac U.S. ☎ 800/756–4663 ⊕ us.intervac-homeexchange.com.

▌ COMMUNICATIONS

INTERNET

Internet access is widely available to travelers in Australia. Top-end hotels always have some sort of in-room access for laptop users—Wi-Fi is becoming the norm, otherwise there are data ports. Note that sometimes you are charged a hefty premium for using this service.

Australia's main telephone network, Telstra, has wireless hot spots all over the country. McDonalds and Starbucks (iiNet

customers only) have free Wi-Fi. Alternatively, you can pay using Telstra Phone-Away calling cards: there's no connection charge and online time costs A$0.20 per minute. Connections can be slow, however. You can buy a card at newsagents, Australia Post, convenience stores, or online. Telstra's website also has hot spot listings.

Contacts Cybercafes ⊕ www.cybercafes.com. **Telstra** ☎ 13–2200 ⊕ www.telstra.com.au.

PHONES

The country code for Australia is 61. To call Australia from the United States, dial the international access code (011), followed by the country code (61), the area or city code without the initial zero (e.g., 2), and the eight-digit phone number.

CALLING WITHIN AUSTRALIA

Australia's phone system is efficient and reliable. You can make local and long-distance calls from your hotel—usually with a surcharge—or from any public phone. There are public phones in shopping areas, on suburban streets, at train stations, and outside rural post offices—basically, they're everywhere. You can use coins or phone cards in most public phones; credit-card phones are common at airports.

All regular telephone numbers in Australia have eight digits. There are five area codes: 02 (for New South Wales and Australian Capital Territory), 03 (Victoria and Tasmania), 04 (for cell phones), 07 (for Queensland), and 08 (for Western Australia, South Australia, and Northern

Territory). Toll-free numbers begin with 1800, and numbers starting with 13 or 1300 are charged at local rates anywhere in the country.

Calls within the same area code are charged as local: A0.50¢ for an unlimited amount of time. Long-distance call rates vary by distance, and are timed. When you're calling long distance within Australia, remember to include the area code, even when you're calling from a number with the same area code. For example, when calling Canberra from Sydney, both of which have an 02 prefix, you still need to include the area code when you dial.

Directory Assistance Local Directory Assistance ☎ *1223.*

CALLING OUTSIDE AUSTRALIA

To call overseas from Australia, dial 0011, then the country code and the number. Kiosks and groceries in major cities sell international calling cards. You can also use credit cards on public phones.

The country code for the United States is 1.

You can use AT&T, Sprint, and MCI services from Australian phones, though some pay phones require you to put coins in to make the call. Using a prepaid calling card is generally cheaper.

Access Codes AT&T Direct ☎ *1800/881011 from Telstra phones, 1800/551155 from Optus phones.* MCI WorldPhone ☎ *1800/881100 from Telstra phones, 1800/551111 from Optus phones.* Skype ⊕ *www.skype.com.* Sprint International Access ☎ *1800/881877 from Telstra phones, 1800/551110 from Optus phones.*

Useful Numbers International Call Cost Information ☎ *1300–362–162.* International Directory Assistance ☎ *1225.*

CALLING CARDS

It's worth buying a phone card in Australia even if you plan to make just a few calls.

Telstra, Australia's main telephone company, has three different calling cards.

Their Phonecard is a prepaid card you can use for local, long-distance, or international calls from public pay phones. There are many other calling cards in Australia as well, often with better rates than Telstra's. Gotalk and onesuite.com are two popular examples, but there are many more. The best way to find one is to ask in a convenience store or newsagent's: they usually have a selection on hand, and you can compare rates to the country you're calling to. Note that many companies don't even print their access numbers on cards any more, but instead give you a slip of paper.

Contacts Gotalk ⊕ *www.gotalk.com.au.* Onesuite.com ☎ *866/417–8483* ⊕ *www. onesuite.com.* Telstra ☎ *13–2200* ⊕ *www. telstra.com.au.*

MOBILE PHONES

If you have a multiband phone (some countries use different frequencies from the ones used in the United States) and your service provider uses the world-standard GSM network (as do T-Mobile and Verizon), you can most likely use your phone abroad by contacting your provider to activate international roaming. This means that, while overseas, your mobile phone will use the network of a carrier in Australia with which your American carrier has a roaming agreement.

Roaming fees can be steep, however: 99¢ a minute is considered reasonable and calls can cost up to $7 a minute. In addition, overseas you normally pay the toll charges for incoming calls. It's almost always cheaper to send a text message than to make a call, since text messages have a low set fee, and receiving a text is often free; however, you should check with your provider on their overseas charges. The roaming expense to watch out for is the cost of data usage, which can be as much as $3 to look at one Web page on your smartphone. To avoid exorbitant charges, keep data roaming switched off on your phone while abroad and access local Wi-Fi spots when you want to send emails or access the Internet.

If you just want to make local calls, consider buying a new SIM card (note that your provider may have to unlock your phone for you to use a different SIM card) and a prepaid service plan in the destination. You'll then have a local number and can make local calls at local rates. If your trip is extensive, you could also simply buy or rent a cell phone in your destination, as the initial cost will be offset over time.

Nearly all Australian mobile phones use the GSM network. If you have an unlocked phone and intend to make calls to Australian numbers, it makes sense to buy a prepaid Australian SIM card on arrival—rates will be much better than using your U.S. network. Alternatively, you can rent a phone or a SIM card from companies like Vodafone. Rates start at A$5 per day for a handset and A$1 a day for a SIM. You can also buy a cheap, pay-as-you-go handset from Telstra, Virgin Mobile, or Optus. Cell-phone stores are abundant, and staff are used to assessing tourists' needs.

Contacts Cellular Abroad. This company rents and sells GMS phones, and sells SIM cards that work in many countries. ☎ 800/287–5072 ⊕ www.cellularabroad.com. **Mobal.** Mobal rents mobiles and sells GSM phones (starting at $49) that will operate in 140 countries. Per-call rates vary throughout the world. ☎ 888/888–9162 ⊕ www.mobal. com. **Optus** ⊕ www.optus.com.au. **Planet Fone.** This company rents cell phones, but the per-minute rates are expensive. ☎ 888/988–4777 ⊕ www.planetfone.com. **Virgin Mobile** ☎ 1300/555100 ⊕ www.virginmobile.com.au. **Vodafone** ☎ 1300/650410 ⊕ www.vodafone. com.au.

▊ CUSTOMS AND DUTIES

Australian customs regulations are unlike any other. As an island long isolated from the rest of the world, Australia is free from many pests and diseases endemic in other places, and it wants to stay that way. Customs procedures are very thorough, and it can take up to an hour to clear them.

All animals are subject to quarantine. Many foodstuffs and natural products are forbidden, including meat, dairy products, fresh fruit and vegetables, and all food served on aircraft. Most canned or preserved foods may be imported, but you have to declare them on your customs statement and have them inspected, along with wooden artifacts and seeds.

Airport sniffer dogs patrol arrivals areas, and even an innocent dried flower forgotten between the pages of a book could incur a serious fine. If in doubt, declare something—the worst-case scenario is that it will be taken from you, without a fine.

Otherwise, nonresidents over 18 may bring in 50 cigarettes (or 50 grams of cigars or tobacco) and 2¼ liters of alcohol. Adults can bring in other taxable goods (that is, luxury items like perfume) to the value of A$900.

Information Australian Customs and Border Protection Services. This organization is a good resource for information about duty-free allowances. ⊕ www.customs.gov. au. **Department of Agriculture, Fisheries and Forestry.** This department can tell you what you can and cannot bring into Australia. ☎ 1800/020504 ⊕ www.daff.gov.au/ biosecurity.

U.S. Information U.S. Customs and Border Protection ☎ 866/880–6582 ⊕ www.cbp.gov.

▊ EATING OUT

Fresh ingredients, friendly service, innovative flavor combinations, and great value for your money mean that eating out Down Under is usually a happy experience.

Australia's British heritage is evident in the hearty food served in pubs, roadhouses, and country hotels. It all seems to taste much better than food in Britain, though. Roast meat and potatoes; fish-and-chips;

pasties and pies swimming in gravy; flaky sausage rolls; sticky teacakes and fluffy scones—all these things are cheap and tasty counter staples. They give the big fast-food franchises a serious run for their money.

Some Australian restaurants serve prix-fixe dinners, but most are à la carte. The restaurants we list are the best in each price category.

MEALS AND MEALTIMES

Australians eat relatively early. Breakfast is typically between 7 and 10 am, and eating it out (usually at a café) is popular. Options range from toast or cereal through fruit and yogurt and muffins, pastries, and hotcakes to a full fry-up—eggs, bacon, sausages, baked beans, hash browns, tomatoes, and mushrooms. Morning coffee and afternoon tea are popular in-between meals.

For most locals lunch is usually lighter than dinner: a salad or a sandwich, say, usually between 11:30 am and 2:30 pm. Dinner is the main meal and begins around 6:30. In the cities, dining options are available outside these hours, but the choices are far more restricted in the countryside and smaller towns, where even takeaways close at 8:30 pm.

Unless otherwise noted, the restaurants listed in this guide are open daily for lunch and dinner.

PAYING

At most restaurants you ask for the bill at the end of the meal. At sandwich bars, burger joints, and takeaways you pay up front. Visa, MasterCard, and American Express are widely accepted in all but the simplest eateries.

RESERVATIONS AND DRESS

Regardless of where you are, it's a good idea to make a reservation if you can. In some places (Sydney, for example) it's expected. We only mention them specifically when reservations are essential (there's no other way you'll ever get a table) or when they are not accepted. For popular restaurants, book as far ahead as you can (often 30 days), and reconfirm as soon as you arrive. (Large parties should always call ahead to check the reservations policy.) We mention dress only when men are required to wear a jacket or a jacket and tie.

ELECTRICITY

The electrical current in Australia is 240 volts, 50 cycles alternating current (AC), so most American appliances can't be used without a transformer. Wall outlets take slanted three-prong plugs and plugs with two flat prongs set in a V.

Consider making a small investment in a universal adapter, which has several types of plugs in one lightweight, compact unit. Most laptops and mobile-phone chargers are dual voltage (i.e., they operate equally well on 110 and 220 volts), so require only an adapter. These days the same is true of small appliances such as hair dryers. Always check labels and manufacturer instructions to be sure. Don't use 110-volt outlets marked "for shavers only" for high-wattage appliances such as hair dryers.

HEALTH

The most common types of illnesses are caused by contaminated food and water. Mild cases of traveler's diarrhea may respond to Imodium (known generically as loperamide) or Pepto-Bismol. Be sure to drink plenty of fluids; if you can't keep fluids down, seek medical help immediately.

Infectious diseases can be airborne or passed via mosquitoes and ticks and through direct or indirect physical contact with animals or people. Some, including Norwalk-like viruses that affect your digestive tract, can be passed along through contaminated food. Speak with your physician and/or check the CDC or World Health Organization websites for health alerts, particularly if you're pregnant, traveling with children, or have a chronic illness.

OVER-THE-COUNTER REMEDIES

Familiar brands of nonprescription medications are available in pharmacies. Note that Tylenol is usually called paracetomol in Australia.

SHOTS AND MEDICATIONS

Unless you're arriving from an area that has been infected with yellow fever, typhoid, or cholera, you don't need to get any shots or carry medical certificates to enter Australia.

Australia is relatively free from diseases prevalent in many countries. In the far north there have been occasional localized outbreaks of dengue and Ross River fever—just take the usual precautions against mosquito bites (cover up your arms and legs and use ample repellent), and you should be fine.

SPECIFIC ISSUES IN AUSTRALIA

Australian health care is excellent, with highly trained medical professionals and well-equipped hospitals. Hygiene standards are also high and well monitored, so you can drink tap water and eat fresh produce without worrying. You may take a four weeks' supply of prescribed medication into Australia (more with a doctor's certificate)—if you run out, pharmacies require a prescription from an Australian doctor. The quickest way to find one is to ask your hotel or look under "M" (for Medical Practitioner) in the Yellow Pages.

Sunburn and sunstroke are the greatest health hazards when visiting Australia. Remember that there's a big hole in the ozone layer over Australia, so even on cloudy days the rays of light coming through are harmful. Stay out of the sun at midday and, regardless of whether you normally burn, follow the locals' example and slather on the sun cream. Protect your eyes with good-quality sunglasses, and try to cover up with a long-sleeve shirt, a hat, and pants or a beach wrap whenever possible. Keep in mind that you'll burn more easily at higher altitudes and in the water.

Dehydration is another concern, especially in the Outback. It's easy to avoid: carry plenty of water and drink it often.

No rural scene is complete without bush flies, a major annoyance. These tiny pests, found throughout Australia, are especially attracted to the eyes and mouth in search of the fluids that are secreted there. Some travelers resort to wearing a face net, which can be suspended from a hat with a drawstring device.

Some of the world's deadliest creatures call Australia home. The chances of running into one are low, but wherever you go, pay close heed to any warnings given by hotel staff, tour operators, lifeguards, or locals in general. The Outback has snakes and spiders, while on the coast there's everything from sharks to octopi, stonefish, and jellyfish. In northern Australia, rivers, lakes, billabongs, and even flooded streams are home to estuarine crocodiles. The best advice is to always be cautious, and double-check the situation at each stop with the appropriate authority.

Australian coastal waters are also home to strong currents known as "rips." Pay close attention to the flags raised on beaches, and only swim in areas patrolled by lifeguards. If you get caught in a rip, the standard advice is never to swim against it, as you rapidly become exhausted. Instead, try to relax and float parallel to the shore: eventually the current will subside and you will be able to swim back to the shore, albeit farther down the coast.

▮ HOLIDAYS

New Year's Day; Australia Day, January 26; **Good Friday; Easter Monday; Anzac Day,** April 25; **Christmas,** December 25; **Boxing Day,** December 26. There are also several state- and territory-specific public holidays.

▌ MAIL

All regular mail services are run by the efficient Australia Post, which has offices all over the country. Post offices are usually open only during business hours weekdays, but stamps are available from newsagents at other times. Postboxes for regular mail in Australia are usually bright red; express postboxes are yellow. Postage rates are A0.60¢ for domestic letters, A$2.60 per 50-gram (28.35 grams = 1 ounce) airmail letter, and A$1.70 for airmail postcards to North America—allow a week for letters and postcards to arrive.

Contact **Australia Post** ☎ 13-7678 ⊕ www. auspost.com.au.

▌ MONEY

The most expensive part of your trip to Australia will probably be getting there. Australian hotels are generally cheaper than similar establishments in North America, as is food.

Australians use debit cards wherever possible to pay for things—you can use your credit card, or pay cash, always in Australian dollars. ATMs are ubiquitous; it's very hard to change traveler's checks.

Prices for goods and services can be volatile at times. A 10% Goods and Services Tax (or GST—similar to V.A.T. in other countries) applies to most activities and goods, though some unprocessed foods are exempt.

Prices throughout this guide are given for adults. Substantially reduced fees are almost always available for children, students, and sometimes for senior citizens.

▌TIP→ Banks never have every foreign currency on hand, and it may take as long as a week to order. If you're planning to exchange funds before leaving home, don't wait until the last minute.

ATMS AND BANKS

Your own bank will probably charge a fee for using ATMs abroad; the foreign bank you use may also charge a fee. Nevertheless, you'll usually get a better rate of exchange at an ATM than you will at a currency-exchange office or even when changing money in a bank. And extracting funds as you need them is a safer option than carrying around a large amount of cash.

▌TIP→ PIN numbers with more than four digits are not recognized at ATMs in many countries. If yours has five or more, remember to change it before you leave.

For most travelers to Australia, ATMs are the easiest—and often cheapest—way to obtain Australia dollars. Australia's biggest banks are Westpac, ANZ, the Commonwealth Bank of Australia, and the National Australia Bank. Their ATMs all accept Cirrus and Plus cards. Smaller state-based banks are also common, but may not accept foreign cards. Major cities often have branches of international banks like Citibank or HSBC.

Before traveling, check if your bank has an agreement with any Australian banks for reduced ATM fees. For example, Bank of America customers can use Westpac ATMs to withdraw cash without incurring a fee.

CREDIT CARDS

It's a good idea to inform your credit-card company before you travel, especially if you're going abroad and don't travel internationally often. Otherwise, the credit-card company might put a hold on your card owing to unusual activity—not a good thing halfway through your trip. Record all your credit-card numbers—as well as the phone numbers to call if your cards are lost or stolen—in a safe place, so you're prepared should something go wrong. Both MasterCard and Visa have general numbers you can call (collect if you're abroad) if your card is lost, but you're better off calling the number of your issuing bank, since MasterCard and

Visa usually just transfer you to your bank; your bank's number is usually printed on your card.

If you plan to use your credit card for cash advances, you'll need to apply for a PIN at least two weeks before your trip. Although it's usually cheaper (and safer) to use a credit card abroad for large purchases (so you can cancel payments or be reimbursed if there's a problem), note that some credit-card companies *and* the banks that issue them add substantial percentages to all foreign transactions, whether they're in a foreign currency or not. Check on these fees before leaving home, so there won't be any surprises when you get the bill.

■ TIP→ Before you charge something, ask the merchant whether he or she plans to do a dynamic currency conversion (DCC). In such a transaction the credit-card *processor* (shop, restaurant, or hotel, not Visa or MasterCard) converts the currency and charges you in dollars. In most cases you'll pay the merchant a 3% fee for this service in addition to any credit-card company and issuing-bank foreign-transaction surcharges.

Dynamic currency conversion programs are becoming increasingly widespread. Merchants who participate in them are supposed to ask whether you want to be charged in dollars or the local currency, but they don't always do so. And even if they do offer you a choice, they may well avoid mentioning the additional surcharges. The good news is that you *do* have a choice. And if this practice really gets your goat, you can avoid it entirely thanks to American Express; with its cards, DCC simply isn't an option.

Most Australian establishments take credit cards: Visa and MasterCard are the most widely accepted, American Express and Diners Club aren't always accepted outside the cities. Just in case, bring enough cash to cover your expenses if you're visiting a national park or a remote area.

Reporting Lost Cards American Express ☎ 800/992–3404 in the U.S., 336/393–1111 collect from abroad, 1300/132639 in Australia ⊕ www.americanexpress.com. **Diners Club** ☎ 800/234–6377 in the U.S., 303/799–1504 collect from abroad, 1300/360060 in Australia ⊕ www.dinersclub.com. **MasterCard** ☎ 800/627–8372 in the U.S., 636/722–7111 collect from abroad, 1800/120113 in Australia ⊕ www.mastercard.com. **Visa** ☎ 800/847–2911 in the U.S., 410/581–9994 collect from abroad, 1800/125440 in Australia ⊕ www.visa.com.

CURRENCY AND EXCHANGE

Australia has its own dollar—assume all prices you see in Australia are quoted in Australian dollars. The currency operates on a decimal system, with the dollar (A$) as the basic unit and 100 cents (¢) equaling A$1. Bills, differentiated by color and size, come in A$100, A$50, A$20, A$10, and A$5 denominations, and are made of plastic rather than paper—you can even take them swimming with you. Coins are minted in A$2, A$1, A0.50¢, A0.20¢, A0.10¢, and A0.05¢ denominations.

At this writing, the exchange rate was about A$1.08 to the U.S. dollar.

■ TIP→ Even if a currency-exchange booth has a sign promising no commission, rest assured that there's some kind of huge, hidden fee. (Oh . . . that's right. The sign didn't say no *fee*.) And as for rates, you're almost always better off getting foreign currency at an ATM or exchanging money at a bank.

▌ PACKING

If Crocodile Dundee is your idea of an Aussie style icon, think again: Melburnians and Sydneysiders are as fashion-conscious as New Yorkers. In the big cities, slop around in shorts and you might as well wear an "I'm a tourist" badge. Instead, pack nicer jeans, Capri pants, skirts, or dress shorts for urban sightseeing. A jacket and tie or posh dress are only necessary if you plan on some seriously fine dining.

Things are a bit different out of town. No Aussie would be seen dead on the beach without their "thongs," as flip-flops are confusingly called here. Wherever you are, your accessories of choice are high-quality sunglasses and a hat with a brim—the sun is strong *and* dangerous. Carry insect repellent and avoid lotions or perfume in the tropics, as they attract mosquitoes and other insects.

A light sweater or jacket will keep you comfy in autumn, but winter in the southern states demands a heavier coat—ideally a raincoat with a zip-out wool lining. You should pack sturdy walking boots if you're planning any bushwalking, otherwise sneakers or flats are fine.

Australian pharmacies stock all the usual hygiene products (including tampons and condoms) and toiletries, plus a whole lot of fabulous local brands often not available overseas. There's also a mind-boggling range of sunscreens and insect repellents, so have no qualms about bringing everything in travel-size bottles and stocking up when you arrive. Oral contraceptive pills are usually prescription-only, though emergency contraceptive pills are available over the counter. Grocery stores and supermarkets frown on your using too many plastic bags—carry a foldable canvas tote and you'll blend in perfectly.

▍ PASSPORTS AND VISAS

To enter Australia for up to 90 days you need a valid passport and a visa (New Zealand nationals are the exception). These days, instead of a visa label or stamp in your passport, citizens of the United States (and many other countries) can get an Electronic Travel Authority (ETA). This is an electronically stored travel permit. It saves you time both when you apply—the process is all online—and when you arrive in Australia.

To obtain an ETA for Australia you must: 1) hold an ETA-eligible passport; 2) be visiting Australia for tourism, family, or business; 3) stay less than three months;

4) be in good health; and 5) have no criminal convictions. The Visitor ETA allows you as many visits of up to 90 days as you like within a 12-month period, but remember that no work in the country is allowed. If you're visiting Australia on business, a Short Validity Business ETA might be more appropriate. Technically, both are free of charge, but you need to pay a A$20 service charge by credit card. Children traveling on a parent's passport also need an ETA. You can apply for the ETA yourself or your travel agent can do it for you.

If you don't meet the ETA requirements or need a different kind of visa, you should contact your nearest Australian diplomatic office well in advance of your trip, as processing other visas takes time. Equally, if you plan to stay longer than three months you must obtain a paper visa (there's a A$130 fee). If you travel to Australia on an under-three-month ETA and later decide to extend your visit, then you must apply for a visa at the nearest Australian Immigration regional office (there's a A$250 fee).

At present, Australia doesn't require a notarized letter of permission if only one parent is traveling with a child, but it's always best to err on the side of caution and take along such a letter if you can.

▍ TAXES

Everyone leaving Australia pays an A$55 departure tax, euphemistically known as a Passenger Movement Charge. It's included in your airline ticket price. There's also a 10% V.A.T. equivalent known as Goods and Services Tax (GST), which is included in displayed prices. There is a G.S.T. refund for visitors on purchases totaling more than A$300 made in one store. You need to keep the receipts for these and present them at the Australian Customs Services booths that are after passport control in international airports. The tax is refunded to a credit card, even if you paid cash for the purchases. Allow an extra 30 minutes for this process.

▌ TIME

Without daylight saving time, Sydney is 14 hours ahead of New York and Toronto; 15 hours ahead of Chicago and Dallas; and 17 hours ahead of Los Angeles.

Australia has three major time zones. Eastern Standard Time (EST) applies in Tasmania, Victoria, New South Wales, and Queensland; Central Standard Time applies in South Australia and Northern Territory; and Western Standard Time applies in Western Australia. Central Standard Time is ½ hour behind EST, and Western Standard Time is 2 hours behind EST.

Within the EST zone, each state chooses a slightly different date on which to commence or end daylight saving—except for Queensland, where the powerful farm lobby has prevented the state from introducing daylight saving at all, since it would make the cows wake up an hour earlier. Western Australia and Northern Territory also decline to recognize daylight saving, which means that at certain times of the year Australia can have as many as six different time zones.

Time Zones Timeanddate.com. This website can help you figure out the correct time anywhere. ⊕ *www.timeanddate.com.*

▌ TOURS

ABORIGINAL ART

Aboriginal Travel. This agency has several Aboriginal art tours, including a five-day collectors tour and shorter rock-art tours. ☎ *61/8/8234–8324* ⊕ *www. aboriginaltravel.com.*

Adventure Tours Australia. This company runs a host of trips, many of which are Aboriginal-culture centric; the most art-focused is in Kakadu. ☎ *61/8132–8230* ⊕ *www.adventuretours.com.au.*

Kimberley Dreams. This agency runs a 12-day Aboriginal art tour through the Kimberley Region in northern Western Australia. ✉ *Northern Territory* ☎ *61/8/8942–0971, 1800/000521* ⊕ *www.kimberleys.com.au.*

Palya Art Tours. Pilot and art lover Helen Read flies you and guides you on Palya Art Tours' small-group tours. ⊕ *www.palya. com.au/palya-art-tours.*

BIKING

Backroads. You can enjoy biking, hiking, and water sports on the Great Barrier Reef in Backroads' multisport family Australian tour. ☎ *800/462–2848* ⊕ *www. backroads.com.*

BIRD-WATCHING

Follow That Bird. This Sydney-based company runs short birding tours in southeastern Australia. ✉ *3/59 Central Rd., Sydney, New South Wales* ☎ *61/2/9973–1865* ⊕ *www.followthatbird.com.au.*

Kimberley Birdwatching. There are around five small-group tours run in the Kimberley and Northern Australia every year by Kimberley Birdwatching: some are camping based, others involve farm stays. ✉ *Broome, Western Australia* ☎ *61/8/9192–1246* ⊕ *www.kimberleybirdwatching.com.au.*

Kirrama Wildlife Tours. This company runs several tours a year in northern and southwestern Australia. They range from 6 to 16 days ✉ *Queensland* ☎ *61/7/4065–5181* ⊕ *www.kirrama.com.au.*

CULTURE

Desert Tracks. Owned by the Aboriginal Pitjantjatjara people, Desert Tracks operates three- and five-day cultural tours in the Northern Territory and South Australia. ☎ *04/3950–0419* ⊕ *www.deserttracks. com.au.*

National Geographic Expeditions. Local experts lead National Geographic's Around the World trip, which takes in the Great Barrier Reef, but all that knowledge doesn't come cheap, nor does the private air transport they use. ☎ *888/966–8687* ⊕ *www. nationalgeographicexpeditions.com.*

Smithsonian Journeys. Learning is the focus of Smithsonian Journeys' small-group tours, which are led by university professors. Their 22-day Splendors of Australia and New Zealand tour covers a lot of Australia—and New Zealand, too. ☎ 855/338–8687 ⊕ *www. smithsonianjourneys.org.*

DIVING

Daintree Air Services. Local flight company Daintree Air Services' Ultimate Dive package includes 18 dives in nine days. The Great Barrier Reef, Coral Sea, and a wreck dive are included. ☎ *1800/246206 within Australia, 61/7/4034–9300* ⊕ *www. daintreeair.com.au.*

Dive Directory. This company runs multi-day live-aboard diving tours on the Great Barrier Reef. ☎ *61/7/4046–7303* ⊕ *www. divedirectory.com.au.*

Diversion Dive Travel. You can take diving tours of the Great Barrier Reef from Diversion Dive Travel. ✉ *Queensland* ☎ *1800/607913 within Australia, 617/4039–0200* ⊕ *www. diversiondivetravel.com.au.*

ECO-TOURS AND SAFARIS

Oz Tours Safaris. The certified eco-tour operators from Oz Tours Safaris run camping and accommodated safaris in northern Australia. ☎ *1800/079006 within Australia, 61/7/4055–9535* ⊕ *www.oztours. com.au.*

Sacred Earth Safaris. This tour company specializes in 4WD tours around Australia's Top End. ☎ *61/8/8981–8420* ⊕ *www. sacredearthsafaris.com.au.*

Wayoutback. This tour company employs certified eco-tour operators who run camping and accommodated safaris in northern Australia. ☎ *1300/551510 within Australia, 61/8/8952–4324* ⊕ *www.wayoutback. com.*

FLIGHTSEEING

Bill Peach Journeys. This company has 10 different air-cruising packages in Australia; the longest lasts 12 days and covers more than 10,000 km (6,200 miles). ☎ *61/2/9693–2233* ⊕ *www. billpeachjourneys.com.au.*

Daintree Air Services. This Queensland-based flight company offers several multiday packages. ☎ *1800/246206 within Australia, 61/7/4034–9300* ⊕ *www.daintreeair. com.au.*

FOOD AND WINE

Artisans of Leisure. This company's nine-day Food and Wine Australia tour divides time between vineyards, markets, and luxurious hotels. ☎ *800/214–8144* ⊕ *www. artisansofleisure.com.*

HIKING

Australian Walking Holidays. You can mix hiking with other adventure activities with one of Australian Walking Holidays' guided trips. ☎ *1300/8270–8400 in Australia* ⊕ *www.australianwalkingholidays. com.au.*

Auswalk. This company has a huge range of hiking expeditions all over Australia. There are group departures and customized self-guided tours. ☎ *61/3/5356–4971* ⊕ *www.auswalk.com.au.*

INDEX

A

A Touch of Salt ✕, *531*
A.C.T. (Australian Capital Territory). ⇨ *See* Canberra and the A.C.T.
Abbotsford Country House 🔲, *569–570*
Aboriginal art, *32–41.* ⇨ *See also* Museums and art galleries
Adelaide and South Australia, 545, 547
Brisbane, 382
Great Barrier Reef, 455, 458
Melbourne, 229–230
New South Wales, 195, 210
Outback, 604–605, 613, 615, 622, 627, 637, 642, 645, 646, 647
Perth and Western Australia, 673, 692–693
Sydney, 69, 82–83, 138
Tasmania, 336, 359
Victoria, 314–315
Aboriginal culture, *604–605*
Aboriginal Tent Embassy, *195*
Aboriginal tours, *744*
Great Barrier Reef, 480–481
Outback, 625
Sydney, 52, 53
Accommodations, *13, 735–736*
Acland Street, *226*
Adelaide and South Australia, *10, 538–600*
Adelaide Hills, *282, 565–567*
Adelaide Town Hall, *547–548*
Adelaide Zoo, *545*
Admiral's Arch, *573*
Admiralty House, *59*
Adventure trips and vacations
Brisbane, 385
Great Barrier Reef, 460, 475
New South Wales, 159
Tasmania, 360
Victoria, 294, 295
Adventure World, *697*
Air travel and tours, *728–729, 745*
Adelaide and South Australia, 541, 587, 596
Brisbane, 375, 377, 379, 397, 411, 428–429, 432, 434, 436
Great Barrier Reef, 449, 452, 470, 481, 505–506, 508–509, 523, 525
Melbourne, 215
New South Wales, 145, 169–170, 193
Outback, 607, 609–610, 612, 624, 625, 631, 633, 644, 649, 650, 656–657
Perth and Western Australia, 667, 669, 704, 705
Sydney, 49, 53
Tasmania, 331, 365
Victoria, 294
Air Whitsunday, Hayman Island, *508*
Airlie Beach, *490–494*
Airlie Beach Lagoon, *491–492*
Albert Park, *233*
Alice Springs, *610, 612–619*
Alice Springs Desert Park, *614*
Alice Springs Reptile Centre, *613*
All Saints Estate, *322*
Alpine National Park, *323–324*
Amusement parks, *399–403, 423, 697*
Anada ✕, *242*
Anbangbang Gallery, *645*
Andrew (Boy) **Charlton Pool,** *76, 102*
Angaston, *573–574*
Angsana Resort & Spa 🔲, *472–473*
Anzac Memorial, *83*
Anzac Parade, *195*
Anzac Square and the Shrine of Remembrance, *383*
Apartment and house rentals, *735*
Apollo Bay, *299*
AQWA: Aquarium of Western Australia, *673*
Araluen Cultural Precinct, *614–615*
Argyle Cut, *63*
Argyle Place, *64*
Argyle Stairs, *63*
ARQ (gay and lesbian club), *134*
Art galleries. ⇨ *See* Aboriginal art; Museums and art galleries
Art Gallery of Ballarat, *306*
Art Gallery of New South Wales, *69*
Art Gallery of South Australia, *545*
Art Gallery of Western Australia, *673*
Arthur's Circus, *335*
Arthurs Seat State Park, *275, 287*
Arts. ⇨ *See* Nightlife and the arts
Arts Centre, *222*
Aschombe Maze and Lavender Gardens, *286*
Athenaeum Theatre and Library, *222*
ATMs, *452, 741*
Aussie World, *423*
Australia Zoo, *423*
Australian Aviation Heritage Centre, *637*
Australian Butterfly Sanctuary, *454–455*
Australian Capital Territory. ⇨ *See* Canberra and the A.C.T.
Australian Museum, *82–83*
Australian National Botanic Gardens, *198*
Australian National Maritime Museum, *77–78*
Australian Outback Spectacular, *399*
Australian Rules Football, *20*
Adelaide and South Australia, 551
Melbourne, 232
Sydney, 99
Australian War Memorial, *195*
Avalon Coastal Retreat 🔲, *356*
Ayers House, *548*
Ayers Rock, *605*

B

Babinda Boulders, *456*
Back Country Bliss Adventures, *475*
Ballandean Estate Wines, *395–396*
Ballarat, *305–308*
Ballarat Botanical Gardens, *306*
Ballarat Wildlife Park, *306*
Ballooning
Great Barrier Reef, 460, 470
New South Wales, 170
Outback, 616
Victoria, 266
Balmoral Beach, *94*
Bangalow, *185*
Banks, *741*
Banrock Station Wine & Wetland Centre, *574*

Barossa Wine Region, *282,*
567–577
Barton Highway, *201*
Base Walk, *626*
Basketball, *551*
Batavia Coast, *677–678*
Bay of Fires Lodge Walk, *355*
Bayleaf Balinese Restaurant
✕ *, 462*
Beaches, *18, 23*
Adelaide and South Australia,
550, 586, 591, 592
Brisbane, 10, 370–371, 413,
415, 416–417, 418, 419–420
Great Barrier Reef, 463,
490–492, 529–530
Melbourne, 231–232
New South Wales, 185–186,
189
Outback, 660–661
Perth and Western Australia,
678–679, 698, 707–708, 713,
718–719
Sydney, 93–98
Tasmania, 336, 342, 350–351,
353, 355, 358, 363
Victoria, 286, 290–291, 297,
299
Beachhouse, The, *549–550*
Bed and breakfasts, *735*
Beechworth, *318–320*
Beer, *13, 167–168*
Bell Tower, *674–675*
Bellingen, *179–180*
Bendigo, *310–312*
Bendigo Art Gallery, *311*
Bendigo Pottery, *311*
Best Western Lazy Lizard Motor
Inn 🛏 *, 478*
Bicentennial Park, *93*
Bicycling
Adelaide and South Australia,
552, 586
Brisbane, 385
Great Barrier Reef, 470
Melbourne, 232–233
New South Wales, 169, 203
Perth and Western Australia,
679, 704, 708
Sydney, 52, 100
Tasmania, 342, 358
tours, 295, 744
Victoria, 266, 320
Big Banana, The, *181*
Big Pineapple, *426*
Big Table ✕ *, 553*
Billabong Sanctuary, *528*
bills ✕ *, 119*
Billy Wong ✕ *, 121*

Binnorie Dairy, *167*
Birdwatching, *19, 744*
Great Barrier Reef, 458,
468–469, 475
Outback, 637, 644, 658, 660
Tasmania, 359–360
Birdworld Kuranda, *458*
Bistro Molines ✕ *, 170–171*
Blackheath, *154, 162–163*
Block Arcade, *219*
Blue Mountains, *146–165*
Blue Mountains Walkabout,
161
Bluetongue Brewery Café,
167–168
Bluff, The, *585*
Boat travel, ferries, and tours,
729, 733–734
Adelaide and South Australia,
587
Brisbane, 375, 379, 381, 413,
430–431, 432, 434–435, 436
Great Barrier Reef, 449, 452–
453, 461, 475, 483, 485,
495, 497, 504, 522, 532
Melbourne, 216
Outback, 610, 633, 635, 644,
650, 656
Perth and Western Australia,
671–672, 704, 705
Sydney, 52, 53
Tasmania, 342, 360
Victoria, 275, 295, 326
Boating
Brisbane, 435
Great Barrier Reef, 461, 490,
495, 497, 504
Melbourne, 233
New South Wales, 203
Sydney, 100
Tasmania, 342, 360
Victoria, 326
Bondi Beach, *18, 96, 122–124,*
128
Bonorong Wildlife Conserva-
tion Centre, *336*
Boroka Downs 🛏 *, 316–317*
Botanic gardens
Adelaide and South Australia,
545, 566
Brisbane, 382–383
Great Barrier Reef, 529
Melbourne, 219, 229, 231
New South Wales, 148, 165,
168, 198
Outback, 636–637
Sydney, 55, 73–74, 79
Tasmania, 336
Victoria, 269–270, 286, 306

Botanic gardens of Adelaide,
545
Bowali Visitor Centre, *645*
Box Stallion (winery), *275–276*
Brambuk National Park and
Cultural Centre, *314–315*
Bread in Common ✕ *, 698–699*
Breakaways, *597, 599*
Brewery, The, *528, 531*
Briar Ridge Vineyard, *168*
Bridge Hotel, *325*
Bridge Road, *225*
BridgeClimb tour, *64*
Bridgewater, *566–567*
Bridgewater Mill Restaurant
✕ *, 567*
Brindabella Hills Winery, *201*
Brisbane, *10, 368–440*
Broadbeach, *404–407*
Bronte, *96*
Brooke Street Pier, *335*
Brookfield Place ✕ *, 681*
Broome, *605, 656–662*
Broome Bird Observatory, *660*
Brunswick, *227, 229, 245, 252*
Brunswick Street, *227*
Bunbury Visitor Centre, *709*
Bungle Bungle National Park,
17, 605, 652–653
Buon Ricordo ✕ *, 120*
Burge Family Winemakers, *569*
Burke Museum, *319*
Bus travel and tours, *730*
Adelaide and South Australia,
541
Brisbane, 375, 397–398,
407–408, 411
Great Barrier Reef, 449, 468
Melbourne, 215, 216
New South Wales, 159, 193
Outback, 607, 612, 619,
624–625
Perth and Western Australia,
667, 671, 694, 705, 711
Sydney, 49
Bushwalking
Brisbane, 408, 409–410
Outback, 615
Victoria, 266
Busselton Jetty and Underwa-
ter Observatory, *711–712*
Byron Bay, *183–188*
Byron Bay Hinterland, *184–185*

C

Cable Beach, *660–661*
Cableways
Great Barrier Reef, 457
New South Wales, 152

Café di Stasio ✕ , 240
Cairns, 451–467
Cairns Marlin Marina, 458
Cairns Regional Gallery, 455
Cairns Tropical Zoo, 468
Caloundra, 419–420
Camel trekking, 615, 625, 659
Camp Cove, 94
Campbell's Cove, 63
Campbell's Rutherglen Winery, 322
Camping
Brisbane, 408, 439
Outback, 638–639, 651, 653
Canberra and the A.C.T., 192–210
Canoeing
Brisbane, 413, 435
Melbourne, 233
New South Wales, 180
Perth and Western Australia, 715
Victoria, 315, 326
Canopy tours
Great Barrier Reef, 484–485
Tasmania, 360
Cape Byron Lighthouse, 184
Cape Byron Walking Track, 184
Cape Leeuwin Lighthouse, 717–718
Cape Lodge ☆ , 725
Cape Mentelle (winery), 720
Cape Naturaliste Lighthouse, 716–717
Cape Nelson Lighthouse, 293
Cape Otway Lighthouse, 293
Cape Tribulation, 482–486
Cape Tribulation, Daintree National Park, 484
Cape Willoughby, 591
Cape Woolamai Surf Beach, 290
Car racing, 229, 233, 291
Car travel and rentals, 730–733
Adelaide and South Australia, 541–542, 596
Brisbane, 375, 379, 395, 398, 407, 412, 421–422, 436–437
Great Barrier Reef, 450, 452, 468, 474
Melbourne, 215
New South Wales, 145, 193–194
Outback, 607, 633
Perth and Western Australia, 667, 669, 694, 711, 719
Sydney, 49
Tasmania, 332
Victoria, 261

Carlton, 229–230, 239–240, 247
Carlton Gardens, 229
Cascade Brewery, 334
Castle Hill, 528
Catacomb Church, 597
Cataract Gorge, 359
Cathedral Gorge, 653
CaveWorks, 717
Centennial Park, 87
Central Canberra, 195, 197–199, 204–205
Central Deborah Gold Mine, 311
Central Greeough Historical Settlement, 677–678
Central Market, 564
Chambers Rosewood Winery, 322
Channon, The, 185
Chapel Street, 230–231
Charles Melton Wines, 571
Chateau Yering ☆ , 268
Children, attractions for
Adelaide and South Australia, 545, 549–550, 552–553, 556, 557, 558, 565, 567, 583, 585, 589, 590, 592
Brisbane, 381, 382–383, 388, 389, 391, 395, 399, 400–401, 402–403, 405–406, 410, 413, 415, 416–417, 418, 419–420, 423, 424, 425, 426, 435, 440
Great Barrier Reef, 454–455, 457, 458–459, 461, 462–463, 468, 470, 472, 473, 474, 475–476, 477–478, 479, 480–481, 484–485, 486, 488, 489, 491–492, 495, 498, 499, 501–502, 510, 528, 529–530, 535, 536
Melbourne, 221–222, 229–230, 231
New South Wales, 160, 168, 176, 181, 182, 189, 197–198, 199–200
Outback, 613, 614, 635, 636–637, 639, 658, 659
Perth and Western Australia, 673–674, 675, 676–677, 678–679, 680, 683, 696, 697, 698, 699, 700–701, 703, 707, 711–712, 713, 714, 716, 718, 722–723, 724
Sydney, 57, 76, 77–78, 79, 80–81, 82–83, 88, 90, 92, 97, 122–123

Tasmania, 336, 360, 363
Victoria, 265, 268, 275, 290, 306, 307, 311
Chinatown, 79
Chinese Garden of Friendship, 79
Chris's Beacon Point Restaurant and Villas ☆ , 300
Churches
Adelaide and South Australia, 547, 548–549, 597
Melbourne, 221
New South Wales, 177
Sydney, 63–64, 71, 84–85
City Center (Adelaide), 544–545, 547–550, 561–562
City Center (Melbourne), 218, 223, 225, 235–237, 239, 245, 247
City Center (Sydney), 81–85, 109, 118, 126–127, 132–133, 136–138
Clairault Streicker Wines, 712
Clare, 579–580
Clare Valley, 577–580
Cleland Wildlife Park, 565
Clever Little Tailor (bar), 561
Cliff Gardens Reserve, 359
Climate, 42
Climbing
Brisbane, 385
Outback, 629
Cloudhill Gardens & Nursery, 269–270
Clovelly, 96–97
Cockington Green Gardens, 199–200
Cockle Bay Wharf, 79–80
Cockle Train, 585
Cod Hole, 524
Coffs Harbour, 181–183
Cohunu Koala Park, 675
Collingrove Homestead, 573
Commissariat Store, The, 383
Communications, 736–738
Como Melbourne, The ☆ , 247
Constitution Dock, 334–335
Convent Gallery, 309
Convict Trail, 337–341
Conway National Park, 492
Coober Pedy, 596–597, 599
Coober Pedy-Oodnadatta Mail Run Tour, 599
Coogee, 97
Cook's Cottage, 222
Cooktown, 486–489
Coolum, 414–416
Coolum Beach, 371, 415
Coomera, 398–402

Coopers Brewery, *549*
Coorong National Park, *585*
Cooroy, *426–427*
Coriole Vineyards, *581*
Cottesloe, *678*
Courgette ✕, *204–205*
Courthouse (Beechworth), *319*
Cowes, *290*
Cradle Mountain-Lake St. Clair National Park, *364–366*
Credit cards, *7, 741–742*
Cricket, *20*
Adelaide and South Australia, 551
Melbourne, 226, 232
Sydney, 99, 100
Crittenden Estate, *276–277*
Crocodile Express, *475*
Crocodiles, *468–469, 635, 658*
Crocodylus Park and Zoo, *636*
Crocosaurus Cave, *635*
Crown Metropol 🛏, *685–686*
Cruise Whitsundays, *494, 495, 499, 504*
Cruises. *⇨ See* Boat travel, ferries, and tours
Cuisine, *110–117, 498*
Cullen Wines, *720–721*
Cultural tours, *744–745*
Great Barrier Reef, 453–454, 488
Cultured Pearling Monument, *660*
Currency, *742*
Currumbin Wildlife Sanctuary, *405*
Customs and duties, *738*
Customs House, *64–65*

D

Daintree Discovery Centre, *484*
Daintree National Park, *446–447*
Daintree River Ferry, *483*
Dandenong Ranges, *268–273*
Dandenong Ranges National Park, *271*
d'Arenberg Wines, *581–582*
Darling Harbour, *77–81, 108–109, 126, 132, 136*
Darlinghurst, *119, 127*
Darwin, *631, 633, 635–643*
David Fleay Wildlife Park, *405–406*
Dawes Point Park, *63, 65*
Daydream Island, *503–505*
Daylesford, *308–310*
De Bortoli (winery), *263–264*
Deckchair Cinema, *641–642*

Dee Why-Long Reef, *98*
Defence of Darwin Experience, *637*
Déjà Vu Restaurant ✕, *492*
Dent Island Golf Course, *498–499*
Diamant Hotel 🛏, *207*
Dining. *⇨ See* Restaurants
Discounts and deals
Sydney, 50
Tasmania, 332
Diving, *19, 745*
Adelaide and South Australia, 595
Brisbane, 386, 429–430, 433
Great Barrier Reef, 458, 460–461, 470, 476, 488, 499, 504–505, 507–508, 511, 512–521, 522, 526, 530, 535
New South Wales, 182, 186, 189, 191
Sydney, 101–102
Tasmania, 355
tours, 745
Victoria, 286, 299
Dogline, The, *340*
Dolphin Discovery Center, *709*
Domain, *68–73*
Domaine Chandon (winery), *264–265*
Domes Walk, *653*
Dongara, *677*
Dorrigo National Park, *179–180*
Dorrigo Rainforest Centre, *180*
Dreamworld, *400*
Dunoon, *185*
Dunsborough, *710–715*
Duties and customs, *738*

E

East-Coast Resorts (Tasmania), *354–357*
East Melbourne, *225–226, 248*
Eastern suburbs, *85–88, 119–120, 127–128, 133–135, 138–140*
Eco tours, *476, 745*
e'cco ✕, *387*
Echidna Gorge, *653*
Echo Point, *154, 160*
Echuca, *324–326*
Economy, *22*
El Questro Wilderness Park, *651*
Electricity, *739*
Eli Creek, *438*
Elizabeth Bay, *86*
Elizabeth Bay House, *86–87*

Elizabeth Farm, *90*
Ellery Creek Big Hole, *620*
Emergencies, *12*
car travel and, 732
Emily and Jessie Gaps Nature Park, *615*
Emporium Hotel 🛏, *390*
Enchanted Maze Garden, *286*
Encounter Bikeway, *586*
Esplanade, The, *455, 457*
Eternity Springs Art Farm 🛏, *185*
Ethos Eat Drink ✕, *344*
Ettamogah Pub, *423*
Eumundi, *426–427*
Eumundi Market, *426*
Eureka Skydeck *88, 223*
Everglades Historic House and Gardens, *149*
Ewaninga Rock Carvings Conservation Reserve, *622*
Experiment Farm, *90*

F

Falls Reserve, *148*
Farm Cove, *55*
Farm stays, *735–736*
Featherdale Wildlife Park, *88, 90*
Federal Highway, *201–202*
Federation Square, *219*
Felsberg Winery, *396*
Festivals, seasonal events, and holidays, *740*
Adelaide and South Australia, 559
Melbourne, 251
New South Wales, 148
Sydney, 93
Victoria, 265, 285
Fig Tree Restaurant & Rooms ✕, *186–187*
Fishing
Adelaide and South Australia, 575, 594
Brisbane, 433, 439
Great Barrier Reef, 458, 474–475, 488, 498, 504, 508, 522, 525
New South Wales, 177, 191
Outback, 638, 639
Tasmania, 343, 363
Fitzroy, *227, 242, 244*
Fitzroy Gardens, *219*
Fleurieu Peninsula, *580–587*
Flinders Chase National Park, *592–595*
Flinders Ranges National Park, *599–600*

Flinders Street, *528*
Flinders Street Station, *219*
Florence Falls, *638*
Flower Drum ✕, *236*
Flynn, John, grave of, *620*
Fontaine ✕, *509–510*
Food tours, *745*
Melbourne, 216
Football. ⇨ See Australian
  Rules Football
Ford Street, *319*
Forest Rise Eco Resort 🏨,
  725
Fort Denison, *55–56*
Fort Scratchley, *174*
Four-wheel-drive tours
Brisbane, 436–437
Great Barrier Reef, 475
New South Wales, 160
Outback, 619, 652
Franklin Boutique Hotel 🏨,
  557
Franklin House, *359*
Fraser Island, *14–15, 435–440*
Fremantle, *694–703*
Fremantle Arts Centre, *697*
Fremantle Market, *696*
Fremantle Prison, *696*
Freycinet Lodge 🏨, *358*
Freycinet National Park, *354,
  357–358*

G

Gagudju Dreaming, *644*
Garagistes ✕, *344*
Garden Island, *59*
Garden Palace Gates, *71*
Gardens. ⇨ See Botanic
  gardens
Gaunt's Clock, *221*
Geikie Gorge National Park,
  653, 656
George Brown Darwin Botanic
  Gardens, *636–637*
George Tindale Memorial Gar-
  den, *270*
Geraldton, *678*
Ginger Factory, *426*
Girraween National Park, *395*
Glass House Mountains, *423*
Glen Helen Gorge, *620*
Glenbrook, *154, 158*
Glenelg Beach, *550*
Gold Coast, *397–411*
Gold Coast Hinterland,
  407–411
Gold Country, *305–312*
Gold Museum (Ballarat), *307*
Golden Dragon Museum, *311*

Golf
*Adelaide and South Australia,
  552*
Brisbane, 385
Great Barrier Reef, 498–499
Melbourne, 233–234
Victoria, 266, 286
Goolwa, *583*
Goolwa Wharf, *583*
Gov, The (nightclub), *562*
Government, *22*
Govett's Leap Lookout, *162*
Grampians, The, *312–317*
Grampians National Park,
  313–315
Granite Island, *585*
Grant Burge (winery), *571*
Great Barrier Reef, *10, 15–16,
  442–536*
Great Green Way, *456*
Great Keppel Island, *434–435*
Great Ocean Road, *293–304*
Greater Blue Mountain Area,
  15, 152
Greater Sydney, *88–93, 128,
  140*
Guurrbi Tours, *488*

H

Haigh's Chocolates (shop), *564*
Hamilton Island, *496–502*
Hanuman Cairns ✕, *463*
Hanuman Darwin ✕, *639*
Hanuman Thai ✕, *617*
Happs Winery, *713*
Harrisons Restaurant & Bar
  ✕, *477*
Harry's Café de Wheels ✕, *86*
Hartley's Crocodile Adven-
  tures, *468–469*
Hastings Caves and Thermal
  Springs, *349*
Hay Shed Hill (winery), *721*
Hayman Island, *505–510*
Hayman Island Diving and
  Snorkeling, *507–508*
Healesville, *262–268*
Healesville Sanctuary, *265*
Health concerns, *739–740*
Great Barrier Reef, 450–451
Outback, 608
*Perth and Western Australia,
  668*
Helicopter tours, *169–170,
  294, 365, 432, 481,
  505–506, 508–509, 525, 650,
  704, 745*
Henbury Meteorites Conserva-
  tion Reserve, *623*

Henry Jones Art Hotel 🏨, *346*
Hepburn Bathhouse & Spa,
  309–310
Hepburn Springs, *308–310*
Heron Island, *431–433*
High Court of Australia,
  198–199
Highfield Historic Site, *362*
Hiking
Brisbane, 409–410, 440
*Great Barrier Reef, 460, 470,
  534*
*New South Wales, 148,
  151–158, 162–163, 180, 191,
  203–204*
Outback, 615
*Perth and Western Australia,
  722*
Sydney, 100–101
Tasmania, 343, 355–356, 365
tours, 745
*Victoria, 271, 287, 297, 299–
  300, 304, 315, 320*
Hilton Cairns 🏨, *465*
Himalayan Café, The ✕, *389*
Historic River Precinct,
  325–326
Hobart and environs, *333–336,
  342–354*
Holberry House, *726*
Holidays. ⇨ See Festivals, sea-
  sonal events, and holidays
Hollybank Treetops Adven-
  ture, *360*
Holy Trinity Garrison Church,
  63–64
Home and farm stays, *735–736*
Home exchanges, *736*
Home Valley Station, *651*
Hope Island, *401*
Horse racing, *234*
Horseback riding
*Great Barrier Reef, 460, 470,
  481, 535*
*New South Wales, 163, 170,
  177, 180*
Tasmania, 365
Victoria, 287, 295
Horseshoe Bay Ranch, *535*
Hot-air ballooning, *170, 616*
Hotel Imperial, *164*
Hotel Richmond 🏨, *557*
Hotel Windsor, The 🏨, *219,
  246*
Hotels, *7, 735*
*prices, 52, 124, 146, 216, 262,
  333, 376, 450, 543, 608, 668*
House rentals, *735*
Howard Park Wines, *721*

Hunter Valley Gardens, *168*
Hunter Valley Wine Country Visitors Information Centre, *166*
Hunter Valley Wine Region, *166–172, 283*
Huon Valley, *349–351*
Huon Valley Apple Museum, *349*
HuTong Dumpling Bar ✕, *237*
Hyatt Hotel Canberra 📷, *208*
Hyde Park, *83*
Hyde Park Barracks, *70*

I

I Love Pho 264 ✕, *241–242*
Icebergs Dining Room and Bar ✕, *123*
Il Lido Italian Canteen ✕, *682*
Indo Pacific Marine, *636*
Internet, *736*
Island Beach-House, *592*
Isle of the Dead, *341, 352–353*
Islington Hotel 📷, *347*
Itineraries, *24–31*
Adelaide and South Australia, 542
Brisbane, 377
Great Barrier Reef, 451
Melbourne, 218
New South Wales, 146
Outback, 609
Sydney, 51
Tasmania, 332
Victoria, 261

J

Jacob's Creek Visitor Centre, *571*
James Cook Museum, *487*
Jaolah National Park, *409*
Japanese Cemetery, *660*
Jasmin Indian Restaurant ✕, *555*
Jenolan Caves, *164*
Jet skiing, *536*
Jewel Cave, *717*
Jim Jim Falls, *645*
John Flynn's Grave, *620*
Joss House, *311–312*
Jungle Surfing Canopy Tours, *484–485*

K

Kakadu National Park, *605, 643–647*
Kangaroo Island, *587–595*
Kata Tjuta, *623–630*
Katherine Gorge, *647–648*

Katoomba, *150, 159–162*
Kayaking
Brisbane, 435
Great Barrier Reef, 460, 470, 530
Melbourne, 233
New South Wales, 186
Tasmania, 356
Victoria, 295
Kelly, Ned, *319*
Kewarra Beach Resort & Spa 📷, *473*
Kilikanoon Wines, *578*
Kimberley, The, *648–662*
Kingfisher Bay Resort and Village ✕📷, *440*
King's Beach, *419–420*
Kings Canyon, *623*
Kings Cross, *119–120, 127*
King's Domain Gardens, *219*
King's Park, *673–674*
King's Square, *697–698*
Kingscote, *589–590*
Kingsford Homestead 📷, *570*
Kirribilli, *59*
Kirribilli House, *59*
Kitty Miller Bay, *291*
Knappstein Enterprise Winery & Brewery, *579*
Koala Conservation Centre, *290*
Koala Hospital, *176*
Koala Park Sanctuary, *92*
Kondalilla National Park, *424*
Koonya, *341*
Kuku Yalanji Cultural Habitat Tours, *480*
Kununurra, *649–651*
Kuranda Koala Gardens, *458–459*
Kuranda Scenic Railway, *457*
Kuranda Wildlife Pass, *461*
Ku-ring-gai Chase National Park, *92*

L

Lady Elliot Island, *428–430*
Lady Jane, *94, 96*
Lady Musgrave Island, *430–431*
Lake Cave, *717*
Lake House 📷, *309*
Lake Wabby, *438*
Lakeside Villas at Crittenden Estate 📷, *288*
Lambert Vineyards, *201–202*
Lamington National Park, *408*
Langham Sydney, The 📷, *125*
Language, *645*

Larapinta Trail, *615*
Lark Hill Winery, *202*
Launceston, *358–361*
Leeuwin Estate (winery), *721*
Leeuwin-Naturaliste National Park, *715–719*
Lerida Estate Wines, *202*
Leura, *149–150*
Leura Garden Festival, *148*
Leuralla, *149–150*
LG IMAX Theatre, *80*
Lighthouses
Adelaide and South Australia, 591
New South Wales, 184
Perth and Western Australia, 707, 716, 717–718
Sydney, 61
Victoria, 293, 295
Limestone Coast, *283*
Lindemans Winery Ben Ean, *168*
Liru Walk, *627*
Litchfield National Park *638–639*
Literature, *22*
Little Creatures (brewery), *702–703*
Lizard Island, *523–526*
Lizard Island Resort 📷, *526*
Lodging. ⇨ *See* Hotels
London Court, *675–676*
Lone Pine Koala Sanctuary, *381*
Long Island, *494–496*
Lord Howe Golf Club ✕, *192*
Lord Howe Island, *189, 191–192*
Lord Howe Island Marine Park, *189, 191*
Lorne, *296–298*
Lost City, *638*
Lower Fort Street, *65*
Luna Park, *226–227*
Lunatic asylum, *352*
Lurline House 📷, *162*
Lygon Street, *229*
Lyndoch, *568–570*
Lyndoch Lavendar Farm, *569*

M

Mackay-Capricorn Islands, *428–435*
Macquarie Lighthouse, *61*
Macquarie Street, *68–73*
Madame Tussauds Sydney, *78–79*
MADE (Museum of Australian Democracy at Eureka), *306–307*

Maggie Beer's Farm Shop, *574*
Magnetic House, *528*
Magnetic Island, *532, 534–536*
Magnetic Termite Mounds, *638*
Mail and shipping, *741*
Mail Run Tour, *599*
Main Beach, *402–404*
Mala Walk, *627*
Malcolm Douglas Wilderness Wildlife Park, *658*
Maleny, *425–426*
Mammmoth Cave, *717*
Manly Beach, *98, 128*
Marananga, *574–577*
Mareeba Tropical Savanna & Wetlands Reserve, *469*
Margan Family Winegrowers, *168–169*
Margaret River, *18, 719–726*
Margaret River region, *284*
Marina Mirage Gold Coast, *404*
Mariners Restaurant ✕ , *501*
Marlin Marina, *458*
Maroochydore, *416–418*
Martin Place, *84*
Mary Cairncross Scenic Reserve, *425*
Mazes, *286*
McLaren Vale, *282, 580–583*
McWilliams Mount Pleasant Estate, *169*
Meekadarabee Falls, *722*
Melba House 🖼 , *162*
Melbourne, *10, 212–256*
Melbourne, side trips, *262–277, 286–293*
Melbourne Aquarium, *221–222*
Melbourne Cricket Ground (MCG), *226*
Melbourne Museum, *229–230*
Melbourne Zoo, *231*
Merewether Baths, *174*
Middle Harbour, *59–60*
Middle Head, *60*
Migaloo, *534*
Migration Museum, *545*
Mike Ball Dive Expeditions, *460–461*
Mineral Springs Reserve, *309*
Mini Palms Gorge, *653*
Molly Malones, *528*
MONA Pavilions 🖼 , *347*
Money matters, *741–742*
Montalto Vineyard & Olive Grove ✕ , *288*
Montville, *424–425*
Mooloolaba, *418–419*
Mooloolaba Beach, *371*

Moreton Island, *392*
Mornington Peninsula, *273–277, 286–288*
Mossman, *479–482*
Mossman Gorge, *480*
Mott's Cottage, *303*
Mount Lofty, *566*
Mount Lofty Botanic Gardens, *566*
Mount Tomah Botanic Garden, *165*
Mount Victoria, *163–165*
Mount Warning, *188*
Mrs. Macquarie's Chair, *77*
Mrs. Macquarie's Point, *77*
Multisport outfitters, *385*
Murray Breweries Beechworth, *319–320*
Murray River region, *317–326*
Museum and Art Gallery of the Northern Territory, *637*
Museum of Australian Democracy at Eureka, *306–307*
Museum of Australian Democracy at Old Parliament House, *195*
Museum of Contemporary Art, *65*
Museum of Old and New Art (MONA), *335*
Museum of Sydney, *70–71*
Museum of Tropical Queensland, *528–529*
Museums and art galleries
Adelaide and South Australia, 545, 547, 549, 550, 563, 597
Brisbane, 382, 383
Great Barrier Reef, 455, 487, 528–529
Melbourne, 219, 221, 223, 229–230
New South Wales, 148, 149–150, 174, 176, 195, 197–198, 199, 210
Outback, 614–615, 637, 645
Perth and Western Australia, 673, 677, 697, 706–707
Sydney, 65, 69, 70–71, 77–79, 80, 82–83, 87
Tasmania, 335, 336, 349, 359
Victoria, 303, 306–307, 309, 311, 319
Muttonbird Island, *181–182*
MV Mirimar, *381*

N

Namadgi National Park, *203*
Nambung National Park, *678*
Nannup, *726*

Narrows Escape Rainforest Reyreat 🖼 , *424–425*
National Film and Sound Archive, *195, 197*
National Gallery of Australia, *197*
National Gallery of Victoria International, *219, 221*
National Library of Australia, *197*
National Museum of Australia, *197–198*
National Park Ranger Station, *656*
National parks
Adelaide and South Australia, 585, 592–595, 599–600
Brisbane, 395, 408–409, 424, 438
Great Barrier Reef, 446–447, 456, 459, 484, 492
New South Wales, 179–180, 203
Outback, 605, 623, 638–639, 643–647, 653–654, 656
Perth and Western Australia, 674, 678, 715–719
Sydney, 57, 91–92
Tasmania, 357–358, 364–366
Victoria, 263, 266, 270, 299, 300–302, 314–315, 323–324
National Portrait Gallery, *198*
National Railway Museum, *549*
National Rhododendron Gardens, *270*
National Wine Centre of Australia, *548*
Nature tours
Great Barrier Reef, 453
Tasmania, 355–356
New South Wales, *10, 142–210*
Newcastle, *172, 174–176*
Newcastle Museum, *174*
Ngilgi Cave, *717*
Nielsen Park, *96*
Nightlife and the arts
Adelaide and South Australia, 558–563
Brisbane, 406
Great Barrier Reef, 466, 493–494, 502, 531
Melbourne, 248–253
New South Wales, 187–188, 208–209
Outback, 618, 642
Perth and Western Australia, 688–692, 702–703
Sydney, 128–135
Tasmania, 347–348

Noosa, *412–414*
Norfolk Bay, *340*
Norman Lindsay Gallery and Museum, *148*
Normanby Wines, *396*
North Adelaide Heritage Group 🏨 , *558*
North Bundaleer 🏨 , *580*
North Coast (New South Wales), *172–192*
North Coast Islands (Great Barrier Reef), *511, 522–526*
North Cottesloe, *678–679*
North of Cairns, *467–489*
Northern Suburbs, *204–205*
Northwest, *361–366*
Nourlangie Rock, *645*
Nubeena, *341*
Nuriootpa, *574*
Nurses Walk, *63, 65*
Nut, The (volcanic plug), *363*

O
Observatory Hill, *65*
Ochre Restaurant ✕ , *463*
Old Crow, The ✕ , *683, 685*
Old Government House, *90–91*
Old Melbourne Gaol Crime and Justice Experience, *223*
Old Parliament House, *545, 547*
Old Timers Mine, *597*
Old Windmill & Observatory, *383–384*
On The Inlet Seafood Restaurant ✕ , *477–478*
One&Only Hayman Island 🏨 , *510*
O'Reilly's Rainforest Retreat Villas & Lost World Spa 🏨 , *410*
Ormiston Gorge, *620, 622*
Orpheus Island, *511, 522*
Orpheus Island 🏨 , *522*
Oscar W (paddle-steamer), *583*
Oscar Waterfront Botique Hotel ✕ , *304*
Oscar W's Wharfside ✕ , *326*
Otway Fly, *298*
Outback, The, *10, 602–662*
Adelaide and South Australia, 539, 595–600
Overland Track, *365*
Overseas Passenger Terminal, *65, 68*
Oxenford, *398–402*

P
Pacific Fair (shops), *406–407*
Packing, *525, 742–743*

Paddington, *87–88, 120, 127*
Paddington Markets, *140*
Palazzo Versace 🏨 , *404*
Palm Beach, *98*
Palm Cove, *468–470, 472–473*
Palm Cove Watersports, *470*
Paradise Country, *400*
Park Hyatt Melbourne 🏨 , *246*
Park Hyatt Sydney 🏨 , *125*
Parks. ⇨ *See* National parks
Parliament House (Adelaide), *545, 547*
Parliament House (Brisbane), *484*
Parliament House (Canberra), *198*
Paronella Park, *456*
Parramatta, *90*
Passports and visas, *743*
Pearl Luggers, *658–659*
Pelican Feeding, *589*
Penfolds Barossa Valley, *574*
Penfolds Magill Estate, *549*
Penguin Parade, *290*
Penguin tours, *356*
Penitentiary Chapel Historic Sight, *336*
Penneshaw, *590–592*
Penneshaw Penguin Centre, *590*
Perc Tucker Regional Gallery, *528*
Peregian, *413–416*
Pertaringa (winery), *582*
Perth and Western Australia, *10, 664–726*
Perth Mint, *676*
Perth Zoo, *676*
Pet Porpoise Pool, *182*
Petaluma's Bridgewater Mill, *566–567*
Petaluma's Bridgewater Mill Restaurant ✕ , *567*
Peter Lehmann Wines, *571*
Pfeiffer Wines, *322–323*
Phillip Island, *289–293*
Phillip Island Grand Prix Circuit, *291*
Piccaninny Creek and Gorge, *653*
Pinnacles, *438*
Pitchfork ✕ , *416*
Planes. ⇨ *See* Air travel and tours
Poachers Pantry & Wily Trout Winery, *201*
Pokolbin, *166–172*
Port Arthur and the Tasman Peninsula, *352–354*

Port Arthur Historic Site, *352–353*
Port Campbell National Park, *300–302*
Port Douglas, *473–479*
Port Douglas Markets, *479*
Port Fairy, *302–304*
Port Fairy Historical Society Museum, *303*
Port Macquarie, *175–179*
Port Macquarie Historical Museum, *176*
Poseidon (tour operator), *476*
Potts Point, *119–120, 127–128*
Powerhouse Museum, *80*
Prices, *7*
Adelaide and South Australia, 543
Brisbane, 376
dining, 50, 104, 145, 215, 261, 333, 376, 450, 543, 608, 668
Great Barrier Reef, 450
lodging, 52, 124, 146, 216, 262, 333, 376, 450, 543, 608, 668
Melbourne, 216, 216
New South Wales, 145, 146
Outback, 608
Perth and Western Australia, 668
Sydney, 104, 124
Tasmania, 333
Victoria, 261, 262
Puffing Billy, *270*
Pullman Reef Hotel Casino 🏨 , *465–466*
Pullman Resort Bunker Bay 🏨 , *715*
Purnululu (Bungle Bungle) National Park, *17, 605, 652–653*
Pyrmont Bridge, *80*

Q
QT Gold Coast 🏨 , *406*
Quad-bike riding, *366, 616*
Qualia 🏨 , *502*
Quarantine Station, *56–57*
Queen Victoria Building (QVB), *84*
Queen Victoria Museum and Art Gallery, *359*
Queen's Gardens, *529*
Queens Hotel, *528*
Queenscliff, *292–293*
Queensland, *16–17*
Queensland Cultural Centre, *382*

Questacon-The National Science and Technology Centre, 199
Question Time, 198
Quokkas, 796

R

R.L. Buller & Son Winery, 323
Rafting, 182, 460, 470
Raging Thunder (tour operator), 460
Rainbow Valley Conservation Reserve, 623
Red Centre, 610–630
Red Hill Estate (winery), 277
Red Lantern on Crown ✕, 122
Reef HQ Aquarium, 529
Reef Teach, 457
Religion, 22
Remarkable Rocks, 589, 593
Rendezvous Allegra Hotel Adelaide 🏨, 558
Restaurants, 7, 13, 738–739
  prices, 50, 104, 145, 215, 261, 333, 376, 450, 543, 608, 668
Revival Fellowship Underground Church, 597
Richmond (Melbourne), 225, 241–242, 248
Richmond (Tasmania), 351–352
Richmond Bridge, 340
Rochford Wines, 265
Rockford (winery), 572
Rockpool ✕, 118
Rocks, The, 61–65, 68, 105, 108, 124–126, 131–132, 136
Rolling Surf Resort 🏨, 420
Roma Street Parkland, 382–383
Rose Bay, 61
Rosebank, 185
Rottnest Island, 704–708
Rottnest Museum, 706–707
Round House, 698
Royal Arcade, 221
Royal Botanic Gardens (Melbourne), 231
Royal Botanic Gardens (Sydney), 55, 73–74
Royal Flying Doctor Service (RFDS), 613
Royal Mail Hotel 🏨, 316
Royal National Park, 91–92
Royal Tasmanian Botanical Gardens, 336
Rugby, 20, 101
Rundle Mall, 563
Rutherglen, 320–323

S

Safaris, 745
Safety, 12
  Brisbane, 371, 372
  Great Barrier Reef, 450–451, 492
  Outback, 608, 612, 619, 625, 633, 644, 649, 652, 657
  Perth and Western Australia, 668, 695, 705, 711, 715, 720
Saffire Freycinet 🏨, 358
Sailing, 19
  Brisbane, 386
  Great Barrier Reef, 444, 470, 490
  Sydney, 100
St. Andrew's Cathedral, 84–85
St. Francis Xavier Cathedral, 548–549
St. James Church, 71
St. Kilda, 226–227, 240–241, 247, 255
St. Mary's Cathedral (Sydney), 85
St. Mary's Peak, 600
St. Patrick's Cathedral, 221
St. Paul's Cathedral, 221
St. Peter and St. Paul's Catholic Church, 597
St. Peter's Cathedral, 547
St. Thomas Church, 177
Salamanca Place, 335
Salix at Willow Creek ✕, 288
Salsa Bar & Grill ✕, 478
Saltram, 573
Saltwater River, 341
Sandy Cape Conservation Park, 438–439
Scenic Railway, 152, 160, 227
Scenic Skyway, 152, 160
Scenic World, 160
School of the Air, 614
Scitech Discovery Centre, 676–677
Scuba diving. ⇨ See Diving
Sculpture by the Sea, 129
Sea Acres Rainforest Centre, 176
SEA LIFE Melbourne Aquarium, 221–222
SEA LIFE Sydney Aquarium, 79
Sea World, 402–403
Seal Bay Conservation Park, 592
Seal-watching
  Adelaide and South Australia, 592
  Tasmania, 363

Seasonal events. ⇨ See Festivals, seasonal events, and holidays
Semisubmersible tours, 433, 461
Seppelt Great Western Winery, 315
Seppeltfield Winery, 575–576
Serbian Orthodox Church, 597
Serpentine Gorge, 620
Sevenhill, 578–579
Sevenhill Cellars, 578
Shangri-La Hotel Sydney 🏨, 126
Shopping
  Adelaide and South Australia, 563–564
  Brisbane, 392–394, 404, 406–407
  Great Barrier Reef, 466–467, 479, 502, 510
  Melbourne, 221, 253–256
  New South Wales, 150, 164, 188, 209–210
  Outback, 618–619, 630, 643, 662
  Perth and Western Australia, 692–694, 703
  Sydney, 135–140
  Tasmania, 349
  Victoria, 268
Shrine of Remembrance (Brisbane), 383
Shrine of Remembrance (Melbourne), 219
Shute Harbour, 492
Silk's Brasserie ✕, 150
Silky Oaks Lodge 🏨, 482
Simpsons Gap, 620
Simpsons of Potts Point 🏨, 128
Sirromet Wines of Mount Cotton, 396
Ski Club, 642
Skiing
  Victoria, 324
Sky City Darwin 🏨, 640–641
Skyhigh Mount Dandenong, 270
Skyrail Rain Forest Cableway, 457
Smiths Beach, 718
Snorkeling
  Brisbane, 386, 429–430, 433
  Great Barrier Reef, 460–461, 470, 476, 499, 504–505, 511, 522, 535
  New South Wales, 189, 191
  Victoria, 286

Soccer, 552
Sorrell, 340
Sounds of Silence ✕, 628
South Australia. ⇨ See Adelaide and South Australia
South Australian Maritime Museum, 550
South Australian Museum, 547
South Australian Whale Centre, 585
South Bank Parklands, 383
South East Pylon, 64
South-West Wine Region, 709–726
South Yarra-Prahran, 230–231, 241, 247, 252, 255–256
Southern Cross, 624
Southern Ocean Lodge ☉, 595
Southern Suburbs, 205, 207
Southgate, 222
Southport, 402–404
Sovereign Hill, 307
Spicers Balfour ☉, 491
Spirit House ✕, 427
Split Point Lighthouse, 293
Sports and outdoor activities. ⇨ See under specific sport
Springbrook National Park, 409
Standley Chasm, 620
Stanley, 362–364
State Library of New South Wales, 71–72
State Parliament House, 72
Stillwater ✕, 360
Stokes Hill Wharf, 635
Stonier Winery, 277
Strand, The (beach), 529–530
Sublime Point Lookout, 150
Suez Canal, 68
Sun Pictures, 659
Sunset Winery, 591
Sunshine Beach, 371, 413
Sunshine Coast, 411–412
Sunshine Coast Hinterland, 420–427
Surf Lifesaving Clubs, 99
Surfing
Brisbane, 403, 405, 413, 416
New South Wales, 177–178
Perth and Western Australia, 679–680
Sydney, 102
Surry Hills, 121–122
Surveyors Hill Winery, 201
Swanbourne, 679
Swimming, 21
Adelaide and South Australia, 552
Brisbane, 440

Great Barrier Reef, 534–535
Newcastle, 174
Sydney, 76, 102–103
with dolphins, 182, 552, 709
Sydney, 10, 44–140
Sydney Aquarium, 79
Sydney City Center, 81–85, 109, 118, 126–127, 132–133, 136–138
Sydney Cove, 61
Sydney Dance Company, 129
Sydney Fish Market, 80
Sydney Harbour, 55–61, 104–105, 131
Sydney Harbour Bridge, 47, 64
Sydney Harbour National Park, 47, 57
Sydney Hospital, 72–73
Sydney Jewish Museum, 87
Sydney Observatory, 63, 68
Sydney Olympic Park, 92–93
Sydney Opera House, 15, 47, 75–76, 129
Sydney Road, 229
Sydney Tower, 83
Sydney Town Hall, 85
Sydney Visitor Centre at the Rocks, 63, 68
Sydney Wildlife World, 80–81
Symbols, 7

T

Tahune AirWalk Tasmania, 350
Tamar Island Wetlands, 359–360
Tamar Valley Wine Route, 359
Tamarama, 97
Tamborine National Park, 409
Tandanya Aboriginal Cultural Institute, 547
Tanks Arts Centre, 458
Tanswell's Commercial Hotel, 319
Tanunda, 571–573
Taronga Zoo, 47, 57
Tasman Peninsula, 352–354
Tasmania, 10, 14, 328–366
Tasmanian Devil Conservation Park, 353
Tasmanian Devils, 335
Tasmanian Museum and Art Gallery, 336
Tattersalls Hotel, 528
Taxes, 743–744
Taxis and limousines
Brisbane, 379, 398
Perth and Western Australia, 694
Sydney, 49–50

Teewah Coloured Sands, 412–413
Telephones, 736–738
Tempus Two (winery), 169
Tennis, 20
Brisbane, 386
Melbourne, 234–235
Sydney, 103
Terrace Hotel ☉, 687
Territory Wildlife Park, 637
Tetsuya's ✕, 118
T'Gallant Winemakers, 277
Thala Beach Lodge ☉, 479
Tidbinbilla Nature Reserve, 203–204
Tim Adams Wines, 579
Time, 744
Timing the visit, 42
Adelaide and South Australia, 541
Brisbane, 375
Great Barrier Reef, 444, 446, 449, 468
Melbourne, 214–215
New South Wales, 144–145
Outback, 607, 613, 625, 633, 644, 649, 652, 657
Perth and Western Australia, 667, 671, 695, 705, 711, 715, 720
Sydney, 48–49
Tasmania, 331
Victoria, 260
Tipping, 13
Tjapukai Aboriginal Cultural Park, 458
Tjaynera Falls, 638
Toad races, 535
Tolmer Falls, 638
Tony's Tropical Tours, 476
Top End, The, 630–631, 633, 635–648
Torquay, 293
Touch of Salt, A ✕, 531
Tourism, 22
Tours and packages, 744–745
Adelaide and South Australia, 544, 568, 577, 588, 599
Brisbane, 376, 380, 386, 394–396, 407–408
Great Barrier Reef, 452–454, 475–477, 480–481, 484–485, 488, 499, 506, 527
Melbourne, 216–217
New South Wales, 159, 160–161, 166, 168–169, 180, 186, 194, 200–202
Outback, 605, 609–610, 613, 619, 625, 633, 635, 636, 644, 648, 649–650, 657–658

Perth and Western Australia,
  671–672, 695, 705–706,
  711–712, 715–716, 720
Sydney, 51–54, 64, 76
Tasmania, 355–356, 359–360,
  363, 365–366
Victoria, 263, 269, 274–275,
  281, 287, 289, 294–295,
  303, 305, 310, 311, 314,
  321, 326
Tower Hill State Game Reserve,
  303
Town Hall (Adelaide), *547–548*
Town Hall (Beechworth), *319*
Townsville, *528–531*
Townsville Town Common Con-
  servation Park, *529*
Train travel and tours, *734*
Adelaide and South Australia,
  542, 585
Brisbane, 375–376, 380, 397,
  412
Great Barrier Reef, 457
Melbourne, 215
New South Wales, 145, 152,
  159, 194
Outback, 608, 612
Perth and Western Australia,
  667, 669, 671, 706
Sydney, 50
Victoria, 270
Trains, Planes and Automobiles
  (shop), *164*
Tram travel and tours
Melbourne, 215
Perth and Western Australia,
  695
Sydney, 50
Victoria, 310
Transportation, *728–734*
Treasury Casino Brisbane,
  384, 392
Treetop walks, *298*
Trial Bay Gaol, *179*
Trigg, *679*
Tully Gorge National Park, *456*
Tusa Dive, *461*
Twin Falls, *645–646*
Two Hands (winery), *576*
Tyrrell's Wines, *169*

U

Ubirr, *646*
Udaberri (bar), *562*
Uluru, *605, 623–630*
Uluru-Kata Tjuta Cultural Cen-
  tre, *627, 630*
Uluru-Kara Tjuta National
  Park, *16*

Umoona Opal Mine & Museum,
  587
Undara Volcanic National
  Park, *459*
UnderWater World, *418*
Upper George Street, *68*

V

Vasse Felix, *722*
Vaucluse, *58*
Vaucluse House, *58–59*
Vertical Adventures, *481*
Victor Harbor, *583, 585–587*
Victoria, *10, 258–326*
Victoria Barracks, *88*
Victoria Street, *225*
Vineyard Cottages and Café
  ✕🖪 , *396–397*
Visas and passports, *743*
Visitor information, *12*
Melbourne, 217
New South Wales, 146, 194
Perth and Western Australia,
  672
Sydney, 54
Victoria, 263, 269, 275, 303
Viva Bar and Grill ✕ , *472*
Vivonne Bay, *592*
Vue Grand Hotel 🖪 , *293*

W

Wadjemup Lighthouse Tours,
  707
Walkabout Adventures,
  480–481
Walking and walking tours
Brisbane, 372, 373
Great Barrier Reef, 511
Melbourne, 217
New South Wales, 160–161,
  184, 188
Outback, 626, 627, 653
Perth and Western Australia,
  672, 695
Sydney, 54, 63
Tasmania, 343, 355, 360
Victoria, 287, 294–295, 315,
  319
Walpa Gorge, *626*
Wanggoolba Creek, *439*
Wangi Falls, *638*
Warner Bros. Movie World,
  400–401
Warradjan Cultural Centre,
  645
Warrnambool, *302*
Watarrka National Park,
  623

Water sports, *18*
Adelaide and South Australia,
  552–553
Brisbane, 386, 435
Great Barrier Reef, 485, 488,
  495, 497, 498, 499–500,
  503–505, 506–508, 524–525,
  536
Perth and Western Australia,
  680
Waterfalls
Brisbane, 409
New South Wales, 148
Outback, 638, 645–646
Perth and Western Australia,
  722
Watsons Bay, *61*
Weather, *42, 636*
Wentworth Falls, *147–149*
West MacDonnell Ranges,
  619–620, 622–623
Western Australia, *10,*
  664–726
Western Australian Maritime
  Museum, *697*
Western Australian Museum
  and Old Perth Gaol, *677*
Wet 'n' Wild Water World, *401*
Whale-watching
Adelaide and South Australia,
  585
Brisbane, 386
Great Barrier Reef, 534
New South Wales, 178
Perth and Western Australia,
  709–710
Tasmania, 363
Victoria, 302
Wheatsheaf Hotel, The (club),
  562–563
Whet Cafe, Bar & Restaurant
  ✕, *485–486*
WhiteWater World, *401–402*
Whitsunday Islands, *444,*
  489–510
Whitsunday Moorings B&B
  🖪 , *493*
WILD LIFE Hamilton Island, *498*
WILD LIFE Sydney Zoo, *80–81*
Wildlife Habitat, *474*
Wildlife watching, *19*
Adelaide and South Australia,
  565, 589, 592
Brisbane, 381, 405–406, 425
Great Barrier Reef, 447, 454–
  455, 458–459, 461, 468–469,
  474, 498, 509, 528
Outback, 613, 614, 635, 636,
  637, 644, 658

Tasmania, *336, 353, 356, 359–360, 363*
Victoria, *265, 290, 303, 306*
William Ricketts Sanctuary, *270*
Willie Creek Pearl Farm, *659–660*
Wilson Island, *432*
Wily Trout Winery, *201*
Windsurfing, *103*
Wineglass Bay, *357*
Wineries and wine, *13, 18, 278–285*
Adelaide and South Australia, *543, 548, 549, 567–577, 581–582, 591*
Brisbane, *394–397*
New South Wales, *166–172, 200–202*
Perth and Western Australia, *712–713, 720–722*

Tasmania, *359*
tours, *263, 274–275, 281, 321, 321, 568, 577, 712, 745*
Victoria, *258, 263–266, 274–285, 308, 315, 321, 322–323, 315, 321, 322–323*
Wise Wines, *713*
Witches Falls, *409*
Woollahra, *120–121*
Woolloomooloo, *120, 128*
Wooroonooran National Park, *456*
World Heritage Rainforest Visitors Information Centre, *188*
World Heritage Sites, *14–17*

Y

Yalumba, *573*
Yanchep National Park, *674*
Yandina, *426–427*

Yarra Ranges National Park, *266*
Yarra Valley, *18, 262–268, 283*
Yering Station Winery, *266*
Young and Jackson's Hotel, *223, 225*

Z

Zip-lining, *360, 484–485*
Zoos
Adelaide and South Australia, *545, 565*
Brisbane, *423*
Great Barrier Reef, *468*
Melbourne, *231*
Outback, *636, 637*
Perth and Western Australia, *676*
Sydney, *47, 57, 80–81, 88, 90*
Victoria, *306*

PHOTO CREDITS

Ern Mainka/Alamy. Chapter 6: Tasmania: 327, Mago World Image/age fotostock. 329 (top), logical-dog, Fodors.com member. 329 (bottom left), Gary Ott, Fodors.com member. 329 (bottom right), Masha1, Fodors.com member. 330, Joe Shemesh /Tourism Tasmania. 337 (top), Tourism Tasmania. 337 (bottom), Rachael Bowes/Alamy. 338 (top), Tourism Tasmania. 338 (bottom), Lyndon Giffard/Alamy. 339 (top), Tourism Tasmania. 339 (bottom), Alistair Scott/Alamy. 340 (top), David Moore/Alamy. 340 (center), David Parker/Alamy. 340 (bottom), Nick Osborne/Tourism Tasmania. 341 (top), Alistair Scott/Alamy. 341 (bottom), David Parker/Alamy. 345, Christian Kober/age fotostock. 353, Chris Bell/Tourism Tasmania. 357, Gary Ott, Fodors.com member. 364, Gabi Mocatta/Tourism Tasmania. Chapter 7: Brisbane and its Beaches: 367, Alan Jensen/Tourism Queensland. 368, Scott Sherrin, Fodors.com member. 369, Allison Kleine, Fodors.com member. 370, Alan Jensen/Tourism Queensland. 371 (top), Ezra Patchett/Tourism Queensland. 371 (bottom), Peter Lik/Tourism Queensland. 372, Murray Waite & Assoc./Tourism Queensland. 373 (top), Alan Jensen/Tourism Queensland. 373 (bottom), Murray Waite & Assoc/Tourism Queensland. 374, ROSS EASON/Tourism Queensland. 382, Michael Schmid/Flickr. 384, Bjanka Kadic/Alamy. 393, Andrew Holt/Alamy. 403, Dattatreya/Alamy. 408, Murray Waite & Associates/Tourism Queensland. 415, jenwhitby, Fodors.com member. 422, ROSS EASON/Tourism Queensland. 427, Ezra Patchett/Tourism Queensland. 432, Darren Jew/Tourism Queensland. 434, Gary Bell/Tourism Queensland. Chapter 8: The Great Barrier Reef: 441, Lincoln J. Fowler/Tourism Australia Copyright. 442 (top), carla184, Fodors.com member. 442 (bottom), sgusky, Fodors.com member. 443, David Menkes, Fodors.com member. 444, Tourism Queensland. 445 (top), Daydream Island/Tourism Queensland. 445 (bottom), Murray Waite & Associates/Tourism Queensland. 446, Jess Moss. 447 (top and bottom), Daintree Eco Lodge & Spa. 448, Stuart Ireland/Spirit of Freedom. 459, Skyrail Rainforest Cableway, Cairns, Tropical North Queensland, Australia. 462, Rowanne, Fodors.com member. 469, Robert Francis/age fotostock. 482, Voyages Hotels & Resorts. 487, poimuffin, Fodors.com member. 494, Tourism Queensland. 497, Paul Ewart/ Tourism Queensland. 507, Arco Images GmbH/Alamy. 512, Pictor/age fotostock. 513, Tourism Queensland. 514, Ulla Lohmann/age fotostock. 515 (top left and bottom left), John Rumney/marineencounters.com.au. 515 (top right), Richard Ling/wikipedia.org. 515 (bottom right), JUNIORS BILDARCHIV/age fotostock. 516 (top), Tourism Queensland. 516 (bottom), Tourism Australia. 517, Reinhard Dirscherl/age fotostock. 518 (top left), Pro Dive Cairns. 518 (top right), Murray Waite & Associates/Tourism Queensland. 518 (bottom), Pro Dive Cairns. 519, Darren Jew/Tourism Queensland. 520 (left), Visual&Written SL/Alamy. 520 (right), Per-Andre Hoffmann/age fotostock. 521 (left), Gary Bell/age fotostock. 521 (right), JTB Photo/age fotostock. 523, Don Fuchs/age fotostock. 533, Reinhard Dirscherl/age fotostock. Chapter 9: Adelaide and South Australia: 537, Wayne Lynch/age fotostock. 538, cyndyq, Fodors.com member. 539 (top left), David Menkes. 539 (bottom left), Ira Starr, Fodors.com member. 539 (right), David Menkes, Fodors.com member. 540, Chris Kapa/Tourism Australia. 548, David Moore/Alamy. 551, Paul Kingsley/Alamy. 560, V H/age fotostock. 569, Tom Keating/Tourism Australia. 576, South Australian Tourism Commission. 584, Robert Francis/age fotostock. 588, Rich_B_Florida, Fodors.com member. 593, Ira Starr, Fodors.com member. 594, Matt Netthiem/SATC. 598, Craig Ingram/SATC. Chapter 10: The Outback: 601, Steve Strike/Tourism Australia. 602, Jane Horlings, Fodors.com member. 603, Reginaca, Fodors.com member. 604, David Silva/Tourism NT. 605 (top), Anson Smart/Tourism Australia. 605 (bottom), Andrew Frolows/Tourism Australia. 606, Rowanne, Fodors.com member. 614, Chris McLennan/Connections/Tourism Australia. 622, David Wall/age fotostock. 628, Corey Leopold/wikipedia.org. 630, Gary Ott, Fodors.com member. 638, Peter Eve/Tourism NT. 641, Sylvain Grandadam/age fotostock. 646, Jennifer Fry/age fotostock. 654-55, Gunter Lenz/age fotostock. 661, Darren Tieste/Tourism Australia. Chapter 11: Perth and Western Australia: 663, robertpaulyoung/Flickr. 664, Photobank/Shutterstock. 665 (top), Tupungato/Shutterstock. 665 (bottom), Juergen Hasenkopf/Alamy. 666, raydignity/Shutterstock. 675, Michael Willis/Alamy. 677, Martin Rugner/age fotostock. 690, Ingo Jezierski/age fotostock. 702, Kos Picture Source Ltd/Alamy. 707, Jon Arnold Images Ltd/Alamy. 718, Jochen Schlenker/age fotostock. Back cover (from left to right): Robert Wallace/Tourism Australia; kwest/Shutterstock; Stuart Ireland/Spirit of Freedom. Spine: Andras Deak/iStockphoto.

ABOUT OUR WRITERS

Lee Atkinson, freelance travel writer and author of eight books and two apps about traveling in and around Australia, has been writing about her adventures on and off the road for major Australian newspapers and travel magazines since 1991. For this edition she updated The Outback chapter. You can follow her on Twitter or Instagram at @OzyRoadTripper.

Perth-based journalist **Fleur Bainger** found her calling in freelance travel, food, and culture writing and podcasting. After many years reporting for ABC radio (Australia), she now crisscrosses Western Australia for *Australian Traveller, Australian Geographic,* and *The Sydney Morning Herald's Traveller.* She has commando-crawled remote sand dunes to watch turtles lay their eggs in Gnaraloo, scaled high trees in Pemberton, and surfed the white water at one of the world's best surf spots in Margaret River.

Tim Baker has spent several years as a freelance journalist writing for multiple Australian publications. He currently works in media and public relations and welcomes every opportunity to travel and create content online or in print. For this edition, he updated the Adelaide and South Australia chapter.

Chris Canty has been a travel journalist for more than 15 years. He has a master's degree in tourism, and has called Scotland, Estonia, Vietnam, England, and Argentina home. His passion is discovering craft beers throughout the world, and will happily cross a border or three just to sample something different. He lectures in journalism and writes about all things lifestyle in Melbourne.

Tess Curran is a journalist, editor, and aspiring photographer raised in the lazy sunshine of Australia's southeast. She harbors a secret dream to complete a caravan journey around the country while still in her twenties. The deputy editor of *Peppermint* magazine for five years, she is also passionate about new trends in travel inspired by a "leave things better"

philosophy: from sustainable and community-led tourism to peer-to-peer networks and the sharing economy.

A journalist for 25 years, **Caroline Gladstone** has traveled across Australia, around the world, and on the high seas. Caroline writes for newspapers and magazines in Australia, including the *Sunday Telegraph,* the *Sun Herald, The Sydney Morning Herald, The Australian, Luxury Travel, Cruise Passenger* magazine, and more. Cruising is her specialty and she's sailed on some 50 ships of all shapes and sizes. She also co-authored the Fodor's inaugural guide to Tahiti and French Polynesia.

Tim Richards fell into travel writing after living and teaching in Egypt and Poland. He contributes travel articles regularly to the *Sydney Morning Herald* and *The Age* newspapers, has authored apps and e-books, and writes about travel in his blog: www.aerohaveno.com. He lives in Melbourne's lively downtown with his wife, Narrelle, and their apartment-bound cat Petra. For this edition he updated the Victoria chapter.

Russell Ward is a long-time Sydney resident who calls the stunning Northern Beaches his home. He is responsible for the popular website In Search of a Life Less Ordinary. He writes on travel, expat, and finance topics for the *Telegraph* in the United Kingdom, among others. He is also founder of TheInternationalWriter.com, a content writing agency for businesses and brands. For this edition, Russell updated the Experience, Travel Smart, and Tasmania chapters.

Merran White, a former national travel editor for Australia's CitySearch, has worked with *Time Out* guides in London, concierge.com, Australia's *Vacations & Travel,* and various cruise and in-flight publications, including Virgin Australia's *Voyeur.* She's authored two books for solo women travelers, and spends her vacations beachcombing, scuba diving, and communing with wildlife.